Oxford Pocket School Dictionary

Chief Editor: Andrew Delahunty
Editor: Fred McDonald
Introduction and Supplement: John Mannion

Dylan

OXFORD
UNIVERSITY PRESS

OXFORD
UNIVERSITY PRESS

Great Clarendon Street, Oxford OX2 6DP

Oxford University Press is a department of the University of Oxford.
It furthers the University's objective of excellence in research, scholarship, and education by publishing worldwide in

Oxford New York
Auckland Cape Town Dar es Salaam Hong Kong Karachi
Kuala Lumpur Madrid Melbourne Mexico City Nairobi New Delhi
Shanghai Taipei Toronto

with offices in

Argentina Austria Brazil Chile Czech Republic France Greece
Guatemala Hungary Italy Japan Poland Portugal Singapore
South Korea Switzerland Thailand Turkey Ukraine Vietnam

First published 1990
Second edition 1996
Third edition 2003
Fourth edition with supplement 2005
This edition 2007

British Library cataloguing in Publication Data available

ISBN 978-0-19-911538-9

10 9 8 7 6 5 4

Typeset in OUP Argo and OUP Swift

Printed in **Italy by Rotolito Lombarda**

Contents

Preface

This dictionary has been specially written for secondary school students aged 11–16 years. It should serve as a working tool in the classroom and accustom its users to the style in which most adult dictionaries are written, but at the same time be easy to use because it avoids abbreviations and similar conventions.

This new edition has been updated with over 100 new up-to-date headwords and senses, many of them reflecting recent developments in the language of ICT such as *weblog*, *broadband*, *browser*, *hyperlink*, *hypertext*, and *text* as a verb. Other new entries include words such as *bling-bling*, *globalization*, *biodiversity*, and *ecosystem*. There are also world English words such as *brinjal*, *condominium*, *cookie*, *didgeridoo*, *haka*, *joey*, and *Kiwi*. These are words that are used by speakers of English in different parts of the world that users of this dictionary will encounter in their everyday life and schoolwork. Inflections of all verbs and plurals of nouns are spelt out in full, and comparatives and superlatives of many adjectives and adverbs are also given. Pronunciation of difficult words is given in a simple look-and-say system without special symbols. Definitions are clearly expressed, with careful explanations of difficult concepts and technical terms (e.g. *amplitude, hindsight, hormone, irony*), and many examples of words in use are provided. There are a number of notes on correct usage, grammatical points, and words that are easily confused (e.g. *alternate/alternative*). Direct opposites or parallel terms are sometimes indicated (e.g. *maximum/minimum, optimist/pessimist, libel/slander*). Prefixes and suffixes are entered at the appropriate place in the alphabetical sequence.

Etymologies are given for all words, with the exception of obvious derivatives and compounds. The etymologies are intended to introduce the idea that words have a history as well as a meaning, to demonstrate the connection between related words and help with recognition of word elements, and to show the variety of languages that have contributed to English. It is hoped that the etymologies will also arouse the curiosity of users so that they will be encouraged to look in a larger dictionary for more detailed information. A new feature is the inclusion of 35 word family boxes, which list words in the dictionary that share a common etymology.

The publisher and editors are indebted to all the people who were involved in planning, compiling and, for this new edition, updating this dictionary. Thanks go to John Mannion for compiling the Introduction and Supplement.

AD

Introduction

At first sight a dictionary seems like a simple book. It's just a list of words with their meanings arranged in alphabetical order. But when you stop to think about it, makers of dictionaries have some difficult problems to solve. First of all, what is a word? For example, is *child* a different word from *children*? Are *sing* and *sung* different words? Are *lead* ('heavy metal') and *lead* ('to shown the way') the same words? And what about *read* (pronounced 'red') and *read* (pronounced 'reed')? Secondly, what does a word mean? Words like *hat* may present few problems but when we say *phone* do we mean a telephone or do we mean to speak to someone on a telephone? Then there is the problem of what order to put words in. Do we start with the word's 'original' meaning, so that *nice* is defined as 'precise or exact'; or do we start with the way the word is used today, so that *nice* is defined as 'pleasant'?

Dictionaries have evolved over the years and have found ways of solving most of the problems mentioned above. To see that *child* and *children* are the same word we need to now that one is a singular form and the other is plural. We need to know about verb tenses to tell that *sing* and *sung* are the same and we need to know about parts of speech, or word classes, to spot the difference between *phone* as a noun and *phone* as a verb. A little knowledge of the history, or *etymology*, of a word will help us with the difference between the two sorts of *lead* and a system for showing pronunciation will help with *read* and *read*. Recent developments in computer databases have helped dictionary makers to decide which meaning of a word is the most common and therefore the order in which to place the meanings.

Of course some problems remain unsolved. Even in the biggest dictionaries you will not find out what *a* or *to* mean, though you will find descriptions of what they do. And dictionaries go out of date quickly because the language they describe is constantly changing. A few years ago, for instance, the very old word *text* was only ever listed as a noun but today one of its primary meanings is as a verb, as in *to text* someone a message.

How did dictionaries develop?

Until about the time of the English Civil War very few people worried about spelling at all and the earliest English dictionaries were just lists of 'hard words' compiled by individuals. These tended to get copied by the next dictionary maker and added to as time went on. During the Civil War the demand for printed materials was so high that printers began to adopt standardised spellings rather than having to stop and think about each word. Eventually the demand grew for a really thorough record of written English. The first great dictionary of the English language was the one compiled by Samuel Johnson and published in 1755. He attempted to define each word and give some idea of its origins and usage. Many of his decisions still affect the way we spell today. For instance, Johnson introduced a 'b' in debt because he thought it should reflect its Latin original *debitum*. He also, mistakenly added a 'd' to admiral because he thought the word came from the Latin 'admire' rather than the Arabic word for commander 'amir'.

Later, in the 19th century, James Murray was given the task of compiling a New English Dictionary on historical principals. This became the *Oxford English Dictionary* which is now the world's largest. Murray worked with teams of people who combed books and other printed matter in attempt to understand the meaning of each word and trace its historical development. This was a huge task and the first *OED* took years to compile. In America Noah Webster attempted to simplify spelling when he wrote his dictionary and Webster's influence gave rise to many of the differences between English and American spellings today, such as *color* - *colour* and *defense* - *defence*.

A great difference between older dictionaries and modern ones is that older dictionary writers attempted to influence and 'improve' the English language, whereas modern dictionaries work hardest at accurately recording language as it changes and develops. This does not entirely remove their influence, of course and many people think that a word is not really a word until it is recorded in a major dictionary.

How does a word get into a dictionary?

The simple answer to this question is that people use it. If enough people use a word it will eventually appear in print and dictionary compilers will spot it. Some words like 'blitz' or 'bikini' become instantly recognizable around the world because of news events but others like 'text' (as a verb) or 'blog' (short for 'weblog') gradually spread from a few enthusiasts. Thousands of new words are invented every year - think of all the names for scientific advances - but only a few become generally known and make their way into the permanent record of a dictionary. At the other end of the formality scale, thousands of slang terms are coined and discarded every year but if everybody learns them, as with 'bling' or 'chav', the dictionary will record them.

Dictionary Features

headwords in bold to find words more easily

plurals for nouns where they cause difficulty

cake *NOUN* **cakes 1** a baked food made from a mixture of flour, fat, eggs, sugar, etc. **2** a shaped or hardened mass • *a cake of soap; fish cakes.*
[from a Scandinavian language]

calligraphy (*say* kal-ig-raf-ee) *NOUN* the art of beautiful handwriting.
[from Greek *kalos* = beautiful, + *-graphy*]

regional labels

candy *NOUN* **candies** (*American*) sweets; a sweet.
[from Arabic *kand* = sugar]

canny *ADJECTIVE* **cannier**, **canniest** shrewd.
▷ **cannily** *adverb*
[from *can*[2]]

comparatives and superlatives of adjectives and adverbs

headwords are numbered when they have different meanings and/or origins

cape[1] *NOUN* **capes** a cloak.
[from Latin *cappa* = hood]

cape[2] *NOUN* **capes** a large piece of high land that sticks out into the sea.
[from Latin *caput* = head]

irregular or unusual spellings for verb forms

abbreviations

CD *ABBREVIATION* compact disc.

cede (*say* seed) *VERB* **cedes**, **ceding**, **ceded** give up your rights to something; surrender • *They had to cede some of their territory.*
[from Latin *cedere* = yield]
WORD FAMILY There are a number of English words that are related to *cede* because part of their original meaning comes from the Latin word *cedere* meaning 'to go or yield'. These include *accede*, *concede*, *intercede*, *precede*, *recede*, and *secede*.

word families show how groups of words are related to one another

trademark

Cellophane *NOUN* (*trademark*) a thin transparent wrapping material.
[from *cellulose* + *diaphane* = a transparent substance]

word origins are given to increase language knowledge

word class or part of speech to build grammatical skills

definitions are clear and accurate

cite (*say* sight) *VERB* **cites**, **citing**, **cited** quote as an example.
▷ **citation** *noun*
[from Latin *citare* = call]

usage notes are given for words that cause difficulty

complementary *ADJECTIVE* completing; forming a complement.
USAGE Do not confuse with **complimentary**.

subject labels point to specific

congruent *ADJECTIVE* (*in mathematics*) having exactly the same shape and size • *congruent triangles.*
▷ **congruence** *noun*
[from Latin]

words that are derived from headwords are given at the end of entries

different meanings of one word are numbered

crack *NOUN* **cracks 1** a line on the surface of something where it has broken but not come completely apart. **2** a narrow gap. **3** a sudden sharp noise. **4** a knock • *a crack on the head.* **5** (*informal*) a joke; a wisecrack. **6** a drug made from cocaine.

up-to-date examples show words used in context

crack *ADJECTIVE* (*informal*) first-class • *He is a crack shot.*

crack *VERB* **cracks**, **cracking**, **cracked** **1** make or get a crack; split. **2** make a sudden sharp noise. **3** break down • *He cracked under the strain.*

set phrases and idioms are defined

- **crack a joke** tell a joke.
- **crack down on** (*informal*) stop something that is illegal or against rules.
- **get cracking** (*informal*) get busy.

[from Old English]

pronunciation guides to help with words that cause difficulty

cross-references

czar (*say* zar) *NOUN* **czars** a different spelling of **tsar**.

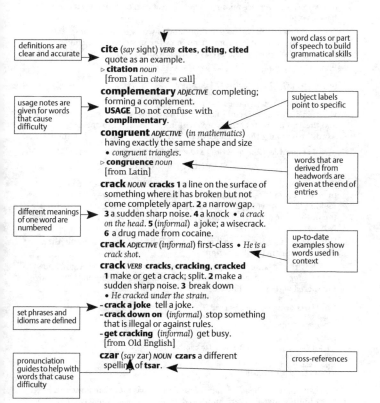

What do you use a dictionary for?

If your answer to this is 'To look up spellings' or even 'To check the meaning of a word', then you are missing out on a great deal that modern dictionaries have to offer.

Dictionaries can tell you how to pronounce a word, what part of speech it is, where in the world it has come from, how the meaning has changed over time and what other words are associated with the word you are interested in.

How do I find the words I want?

We do not read dictionaries in the same way that we read novels. Finding words in dictionaries is complicated by two things; the thickness of the book and the arrangement of the words within entries. You can speed up finding words by breaking the alphabet in to four *quartiles,* as in the diagram below.

1 st quartile	2nd quartile	3rd quartile	4th quartile
ABCDE	FGHIJKLM	NOPQRS	TUVWXYZ

Suppose you are looking for the word *nirvana.* This is in the third quartile (N to S) so you would open the dictionary just past the half- way mark and start looking there. As you get nearer to your word check the guide words at the top of the page (for instance nippy and nominee) to see if your word falls between them.

When you arrive at the correct place in the dictionary you will find the headword nirvana with a definition.

Words with the same spelling but with a different meaning or origin, known as *homographs,* are given separate entries with a space between them, and numbered with a raised figure

peer^{1} *VERB* **peers, peering, peered**
look at something closely or with difficulty.
[perhaps from *appear*]

peer^{2} *NOUN* **peers**
1 a noble. **2** someone who is equal to another in rank, merit, or age etc. • *She had no peer.*
▷ **peeress** *noun*
[from Latin *par* = equal]

You can see from the *peer*^{2} that *peer* as a noun has more than one meaning. The different meanings are numbered. Look up *round* if you wish to see how many meanings an apparently simple word can have. In this dictionary *round* has:

3 meanings as an adjective
4 main meanings as an adverb
4 meanings as a preposition
6 meanings as a noun
2 meanings as a verb

How does the dictionary help with pronunciation?

In this dictionary help is given when two words have the same spelling but are pronounced differently and when a word is difficult or unusual. The pronunciation is given in brackets with *say* or *rhymes* with, e.g.

chaos (*say* **kay**- oss) *NOUN*

toll [1] (rhymes with *hole*) *NOUN*

Words are broken up into small units (usually of one syllable), and the syllable that is spoken with most stress is shown in bold. The following letter combinations are always used:

oo	shows	the sound	as	in	soon	
uu	"	"	"	"	"	book
th	"	"	"	"	"	thin
th	"	"	"	"	"	this
zh	"	"	"	"	"	vision

What about grammar?

The part of speech for each word is printed italics (e.g., *adjective, noun, verb)* after the word and before its definition. Some words have different meanings according to which parts of speech they belong to. In this case, the different meanings are given with no spaces between the different entries e.g.

barricade *NOUN* **barricades**
a barrier, especially one put up hastily across a street or door.

barricade *VERB* **barricades, barricading, barricaded**
block a street or door with a barricade.

Many words change in use. Nouns have plurals, verbs change according to tense and adjectives and adverbs have comparative and superlative forms. These different forms are given after the word class (part of speech).

The first verb form given (ending in - *s*) is used for the present tense.

The second form given (ending in - *ing*) is the present participle.

When three verb forms are given, e.g.

the third form is both the past tense (as in 'he *admitted* it') and the past participle ('it was *admitted*')

admit *VERB* **admits, admitting, admitted**

When four forms are given, e.g.

come *VERB* **comes, coming, came, come**

freeze *VERB* **freezes, freezing, froze, frozen**

the third is the past tense (as in 'he *came*', 'it *froze*') and the fourth is the past participle ('he had *come*', 'it was *frozen*').

Finally, some words have different meanings in combination with others. These *phrases* are listed and defined under the relevant part of speech e.g.

jump *VERB* **jumps, jumping, jumped**
1 move up suddenly from the ground into the air. **2** go over something by jumping • *The horse jumped the fence.* **3** pass over something; miss out part of a book etc. **4** move suddenly in surprise. **5** pass quickly to a different place or level.
- **jump at** accept something eagerly.
- **jump on** start criticizing someone.
- **jump the gun** start before you should.
- **jump the queue** not wait your turn.

jump *NOUN* **jumps**
1 a jumping movement. **2** an obstacle to jump over. **3** a sudden rise or change.
[origin unknown]

Can the dictionary help with language in use?

Not all words can be used in every situation. Some words can be used among friends but not in an official document. Equally some words, such as *mass*, have different meanings according to whether you are in a Catholic church, in a physics lesson, or in everyday conversation. Other words, such as *nick*, have colloquial meanings as well as their everyday meaning. *Informal* or *slang* terms are therefore labelled, as are special subject meanings to help you choose the right word for the right occasion.

Examples of words in use are given in italics to help make a definition clearer, e.g.

beware *VERB*
be careful • *Beware of pickpockets.*

Where there are possibilities of confusion *usage notes* are provided. There are over 200 of these in the dictionary that provide help on correct usage, points of grammar and words that are easily confused, e.g.

less *ADJECTIVE & ADVERB*
smaller in amount; not so much • *Make less noise. It is less important.*
USAGE Do not use *less* when you mean *fewer*. You should use *fewer* when you are talking about a number of individual things, and *less* when you are talking about a quantity or mass of something: *The less batter you make, the fewer pancakes you'll get.*

What about the origins of words?

Information about the history (or etymology) of a word is given in square brackets at the end of its entry, e.g.

shirty ADJECTIVE (*informal*)
annoyed.
[perhaps from *Keep your shirt on!* = calm down, don't be angry]

The original meaning of a word often shows how English has changed over time and the way different words have been adapted to different purposes. For instance the old English word *scir* which meant 'shining, noble or pure' has given us the word *sheer* as in 'sheer drop'. This is clearly a specialisation of the 'pure' part of the original word.

The word *nice* on the other hand has travelled from the Latin word *nescius*, meaning 'ignorant or foolish', through 'precise and exact' to the modern meaning of 'pleasant or kind.' In this case the 'precise' meaning has become more generalised over time – although linguists are still uncertain about how the word went from 'foolish' to 'exact'.

Other words commemorate people or historical events. For example:

Sandwich	The Earl of Sandwich, a keen gambler, is said to have invented the sliced bread snack because he did not wish to leave the card table
Bikini	Bikini atoll was the scene of an atomic test in 1946. The two piece bathing suit was developed at about the same time.
Magenta	This colour takes its name from an Italian battle. A new artificial dye was given the name Magenta presumably because it was red like the blood spilled in the battle.

Every word has its story and a dictionary is a good place to start investigating them.

What about the development of English?

English began to develop in the 5th century but from the very beginning it was influenced by other languages. Christian missionaries used Latin, Viking settlers spoke Old Norse, and from 1066 onwards the ruling classes spoke French. English absorbed words from all these languages.

We can tell something about life in England after 1066 by looking at the words used for food and animals.

sheep – Old English	mutton Old French
cow – Old English	beef – Old French
swine (pig) – Old English	pork – Old French

Clearly English speakers looked after the animals in the field and French speakers ate the meat. Another indication of post- Norman conquest life is the large number of words from Old French that are connected with the military and the law.

Eventually even the English kings learned to speak English (the first was Richard II who died in 1400) and from the 16th century onwards explorers, traders, settlers, empire builders and missionaries took English to every corner of the globe. As English travelled it borrowed words from hundreds of other languages. For instance, *alligator* comes from Spanish, *algebra* from Arabic, *mammoth* from Russian, *bungalow* from Hindi, *shawl* from Persian or Urdu, and *skunk* from a Native American language.

Other examples include:

bread [from Old English]

cake [from a Scandinavian language]

cereal [from *Ceres*, the Roman goddess of farming]

cheese [from Old English, taken from Latin]

chocolate [via French or Spanish from Nahuatl (a Central American language)]

coffee [from Arabic *kahwa*]

cream [from old French]

liquorice [from Greek *glykys* = sweet + *rhiza* = root]

tea [via Dutch from Chinese]

Is it possible to trace the connections between words?

Words tend to build on each other; some become more specialised whilst others acquire more general meanings. In addition English allows the addition of suffixes and prefixes to root words so that one common root can have many different branches. This process is illustrated in this dictionary with 35 word family boxes. These show how groups of words that contain the same set of letters are related to each other e.g.

diction *NOUN*
1 a person's way of speaking words • *clear diction.* **2** a writer's choice of words.
[from Latin *dictio* = saying, word]
USAGE There are a number of English words that are related to *diction* because part of their original meaning comes from the Latin words *dicere* meaning 'to say or speak' or *dictio* meaning 'saying or word'. These include *benediction, contradict, dictate, dictator, dictionary, edict, interdict,* and *predict.*

Aa

a *ADJECTIVE* (called the *indefinite article* and changing to **an** before most vowel sounds) **1** one (but not any special one) • *Can you lend me a book?* **2** each; per • *We see it once a day* or *once an hour.*
[from Old English *an* = one]

a-[1] *PREFIX* **1** on; to; towards (as in *afoot*, *ashore*, *aside*). **2** in the process of (as in *a-hunting*).
[from the preposition *on*]

a-[2] *PREFIX* (**an-** is used before a vowel sound) not; without (as in *asymmetrical*, *anarchy*).
[from Greek *a-* = not]

ab- *PREFIX* (changing to **abs-** before *c* and *t*) away; from (as in *abduct*, *abnormal*, *abstract*).
[from Latin *ab* = away]

aback *ADVERB* – **taken aback** surprised.
[from Old English *on baec* = backwards]

abacus (*say* ab-a-kus) *NOUN* **abacuses** a frame used for counting with beads sliding on wires.
[from Greek]

abandon *VERB* **abandons**, **abandoning**, **abandoned** **1** give up • *We never abandoned hope.* **2** leave something without intending to return • *Abandon ship!*
▷ **abandonment** *noun*

abandon *NOUN* a careless and uncontrolled manner • *She danced with great abandon.*
[from old French]

abase *VERB* **abases**, **abasing**, **abased** make a person feel humble or humiliated.
[from old French]

abashed *ADJECTIVE* embarrassed.
[from old French *esbair* = astound]

abate *VERB* **abates**, **abating**, **abated** make or become less; die down • *The storm had abated.*
▷ **abatement** *noun*
[from Latin *battuere* = to beat]

abattoir (*say* ab-at-wahr) *NOUN* **abattoirs** a place where animals are killed for food; a slaughterhouse.
[French, from *abattre* = knock down, destroy]

abbey *NOUN* **abbeys** **1** a monastery or convent. **2** a church that was once part of a monastery • *Westminster Abbey.*
[same origin as *abbot*]

abbot *NOUN* **abbots** the head of an abbey.
[via Latin and Greek from Aramaic (a language once spoken in the Middle East), *abba* = father]

abbreviate *VERB* **abbreviates**, **abbreviating**, **abbreviated** shorten something.
[from Latin *brevis* = short, brief]

abbreviation *NOUN* **abbreviations** **1** a shortened form of a word or words, especially one using the initial letters, such as GCSE, St., USA. **2** abbreviating something.

abdicate *VERB* **abdicates**, **abdicating**, **abdicated** **1** resign from a throne. **2** give up an important responsibility.
▷ **abdication** *noun*
[from Latin]

abdomen (*say* ab-dom-en) *NOUN* **abdomens** **1** the lower front part of a person's or animal's body, containing the stomach, intestines, and other digestive organs. **2** the rear section of an insect's body.
▷ **abdominal** (*say* ab-**dom**-in-al) *adjective*
[Latin]

abduct *VERB* **abducts**, **abducting**, **abducted** take a person away illegally; kidnap.
▷ **abduction** *noun* **abductor** *noun*
[from *ab-* + Latin *ductum* = led]

abet *VERB* **abets**, **abetting**, **abetted** help or encourage someone to commit a crime.
[from old French *abeter* = urge]

abeyance (*say* ab-ay-ans) *NOUN*
– **in abeyance** not being used at the moment; suspended • *More serious punishments are being held in abeyance.*
[from old French]

abhor *VERB* **abhors**, **abhorring**, **abhorred** (*formal*) hate something very much.
▷ **abhorrent** *adjective* **abhorrence** *noun*
[from Latin *abhorrere* = shrink away in horror]

A

abide *VERB* **abides, abiding, abided** (*old use; past tense*) **abode** **1** remain or dwell somewhere. **2** bear or tolerate • *I can't abide wasps.*
- **abide by** keep a promise etc.
[from Old English]

abiding *ADJECTIVE* lasting or permanent.

ability *NOUN* **abilities** **1** being able to do something. **2** cleverness or talent.

abject (*say* ab-jekt) *ADJECTIVE* **1** wretched or miserable • *They were living in abject poverty.* **2** humble • *an abject apology.*
[from *ab-* + Latin *-jectum* = thrown]

ablaze *ADJECTIVE* blazing; on fire.

able *ADJECTIVE* **1** having the power or skill or opportunity to do something. **2** skilful or clever.
▷ **ably** *adverb*
[from old French]

-able *SUFFIX* (also **-ble, -ible**, and **-uble**) forms adjectives (e.g. *readable, legible*). The nouns formed from these end in **-bility** (e.g. *readability, legibility*).
[from Latin]

able-bodied *ADJECTIVE* fit and healthy; not disabled.

abnormal *ADJECTIVE* not normal; unusual.
▷ **abnormally** *adverb* **abnormality** *noun*
[from *ab-* + *normal*]

aboard *ADVERB* & *PREPOSITION* on or into a ship or aircraft or train.
[from *a-*[1] + *board*]

abode *NOUN* **abodes** (*formal*) the place where someone lives.
[from *abide*]

abolish *VERB* **abolishes, abolishing, abolished** put an end to a law or custom etc.
▷ **abolition** (*say* ab-ol-**ish**-on) *noun*
[from Latin *abolere* = destroy]

abominable *ADJECTIVE* very bad or unpleasant.
▷ **abominably** *adverb*

abominate *VERB* **abominates, abominating, abominated** hate something very much.
▷ **abomination** *noun*
[from Latin *abominari* = regard as a bad omen]

aborigine (*say* ab-er-ij-in-ee) *NOUN* **aborigines** one of the original inhabitants of a country.
▷ **aboriginal** *adjective* & *noun*
- **Aborigine** one of the original inhabitants of Australia who lived there before the Europeans arrived.
[from Latin *ab origine* = from the beginning]

abort *VERB* **aborts, aborting, aborted** put an end to something before it has been completed • *They aborted the space flight because of problems.*
[from Latin *aboriri* = miscarry]

abortion *NOUN* **abortions** an operation to remove an unborn child from the womb before it has developed enough to survive.

abortive *ADJECTIVE* unsuccessful • *an abortive attempt.*

abound *VERB* **abounds, abounding, abounded** **1** be plentiful or abundant • *Fish abound in the river.* **2** have something in great quantities • *The river abounds in fish.*
[from Latin *abundare* = overflow]

about *PREPOSITION* **1** near in amount or size or time etc. • *It costs about £5. Come about two o'clock.* **2** on the subject of; in connection with • *Tell me about your holiday.* **3** all round; in various parts of • *They ran about the playground.*

about *ADVERB* **1** in various directions • *They were running about.* **2** not far away • *He is somewhere about.*
- **be about to** be going to do something.
[from *a-*[1] + Old English *butan* = outside]

above *PREPOSITION* **1** higher than. **2** more than.

above *ADVERB* at or to a higher place.
[from Old English]

above board *ADJECTIVE* & *ADVERB* honest; without deception.
[from card-players cheating by changing their cards under the table]

abrade *VERB* **abrades, abrading, abraded** scrape or wear something away by rubbing it.
▷ **abrasion** *noun*
[from *ab-* + Latin *radere* = to scrape]

abrasive *ADJECTIVE* **1** that abrades things • *an abrasive wheel.* **2** harsh • *an abrasive manner.*

B C D E F G H I J K L M N O P Q R S T U V W X Y Z

abrasive *NOUN* **abrasives** a rough substance used for rubbing or polishing things.

abreast *ADVERB* **1** side by side. **2** keeping up with something.
[from *a-*[1] + *breast*]

abridge *VERB* **abridges, abridging, abridged** shorten a book etc. by using fewer words • *an abridged edition.*
▷ **abridgement** *noun*
[same origin as *abbreviate*]

abroad *ADVERB* in or to another country.
[from *a-*[1] + *broad*]

abrupt *ADJECTIVE* **1** sudden or hasty • *his abrupt departure.* **2** rather rude and unfriendly; curt • *She has quite an abrupt manner.*
▷ **abruptly** *adverb* **abruptness** *noun*
[from *ab-* + Latin *ruptum* = broken]

abs- *PREFIX* away; from. SEE **ab-**.

abscess (*say* ab-sis) *NOUN* **abscesses** an inflamed place where pus has formed in the body.
[from Latin]

abscond *VERB* **absconds, absconding, absconded** go away secretly • *The cashier had absconded with the money.*
[from Latin]

abseil *VERB* **abseils, abseiling, abseiled** lower yourself down a steep cliff or rock by sliding down a rope.
[from German *ab* = down + *Seil* = rope]

absent *ADJECTIVE* not here; not present • *absent from school.*
▷ **absence** *noun*

absent (*say* ab-sent) *VERB* **absents, absenting, absented**
- **absent yourself** stay away.
[from *abs-* + Latin *esse* = to be]

absentee *NOUN* **absentees** a person who is absent.
▷ **absenteeism** *noun*

absent-minded *ADJECTIVE* having your mind on other things; forgetful.

absolute *ADJECTIVE* complete; not restricted • *absolute power.*
[same origin as *absolve*]

absolutely *ADVERB* **1** completely. **2** (*informal*) yes, I agree.

absolute zero *NOUN* the lowest possible temperature, calculated as -273.15°C.

absolution *NOUN* a priest's formal statement that someone's sins are forgiven.

absolve *VERB* **absolves, absolving, absolved** **1** clear a person of blame or guilt. **2** release a person from a promise or obligation.
[from *ab-* + Latin *solvere* = set free]

absorb *VERB* **absorbs, absorbing, absorbed** **1** soak up a liquid or gas. **2** receive something and reduce its effects • *The buffers absorbed most of the shock.* **3** take up a person's attention or time.
▷ **absorption** *noun*
[from *ab-* + Latin *sorbere* = suck in]

absorbent *ADJECTIVE* able to soak up liquids easily • *absorbent paper.*

abstain *VERB* **abstains, abstaining, abstained** **1** keep yourself from doing something; refrain. **2** choose not to use your vote.
▷ **abstention** *noun*
[from *abs-* + Latin *tenere* = hold]

abstemious (*say* ab-steem-ee-us) *ADJECTIVE* eating or drinking only small amounts; not greedy.
▷ **abstemiously** *adverb* **abstemiousness** *noun*
[from *abs-* + Latin *temetum* = alcoholic drink]

abstinence *NOUN* abstaining, especially from alcohol.
▷ **abstinent** *adjective*
[same origin as *abstain*]

abstract (*say* ab-strakt) *ADJECTIVE* **1** concerned with ideas, not solid objects • *Truth, hope, danger are all abstract.* **2** (said about a painting or sculpture) showing the artist's ideas or feelings, not showing a recognizable person or thing.

abstract (*say* ab-strakt) *VERB* **abstracts, abstracting, abstracted** take out; remove • *He abstracted some cards from the pack.*
▷ **abstraction** *noun*

A

abstract (*say* ab-strakt) *NOUN* **abstracts** **1** a summary. **2** an abstract painting or sculpture.
[from *abs-* + Latin *trahere* = pull]

abstracted *ADJECTIVE* with your mind on other things; not paying attention.

abstruse (*say* ab-strooss) *ADJECTIVE* hard to understand; obscure.
[from Latin *abstrusus* = hidden]

absurd *ADJECTIVE* ridiculous or foolish.
▷ **absurdly** *adverb* **absurdity** *noun*
[from Latin *absurdus* = out of tune]

abundance *NOUN* a large amount, plenty.
[same origin as *abound*]

abundant *ADJECTIVE* plentiful.
▷ **abundantly** *adverb*

abuse (*say* ab-yooz) *VERB* **abuses, abusing, abused** **1** use something badly or wrongly; misuse. **2** hurt someone or treat them cruelly. **3** say unpleasant things about a person or thing.

abuse (*say* ab-yooss) *NOUN* **abuses** **1** a misuse • *the abuse of power.* **2** physical harm or cruelty done to someone. **3** words abusing a person or thing; insults.
[from *ab-* + *use*]

abusive *ADJECTIVE* rude and insulting • *abusive remarks.*

abut *VERB* **abuts, abutting, abutted** end against something • *Their shed abuts against ours.*
▷ **abutment** *noun*
[from old French]

abysmal (*say* ab-iz-mal) *ADJECTIVE* extremely bad • *abysmal ignorance.*
[from *abyss*]

abyss (*say* ab-iss) *NOUN* **abysses** an extremely deep pit.
[from Greek *abyssos* = bottomless]

AC *ABBREVIATION* alternating current.

ac- *PREFIX* to; towards. SEE **ad-**.

academic *ADJECTIVE* **1** to do with education or studying, especially at a school or college or university. **2** theoretical; having no practical use • *an academic point.*

academic *NOUN* **academics** a university or college teacher.

academy *NOUN* **academies** **1** a school or college, especially one for specialized training. **2** a society of scholars or artists • *The Royal Academy.*
[from *Akademeia*, the name of the garden where the Greek philosopher Plato taught his pupils]

accede (*say* ak-seed) *VERB* **accedes, acceding, acceded** **1** agree to what is asked or suggested • *accede to a request.* **2** take office; become king or queen • *She acceded to the throne.*
[from *ac-* + Latin *cedere* = go]

accelerate *VERB* **accelerates, accelerating, accelerated** make or become quicker; increase speed.
[from *ac-* + Latin *celer* = swift]

acceleration *NOUN* **accelerations** **1** the rate at which the speed of something increases. **2** the rate of change of velocity.

accelerator *NOUN* **accelerators** **1** the pedal that a driver presses to make a motor vehicle go faster. **2** a thing used to increase the speed of something.

accent (*say* ak-sent) *NOUN* **accents** **1** the way a person pronounces the words of a language • *She has a French accent.* **2** emphasis or stress • *In 'fairy', the accent is on 'fair-'.* **3** a mark placed over a letter to show how it is pronounced, e.g. in *résumé*.

accent (*say* ak-sent) *VERB* **accents, accenting, accented** pronounce part of a word more strongly than the other parts; emphasize.
[from *ac-* + Latin *cantus* = song]

accentuate (*say* ak-sent-yoo-ayt) *VERB* **accentuates, accentuating, accentuated** make something more obvious; emphasize.
▷ **accentuation** *noun*

accept *VERB* **accepts, accepting, accepted** **1** take a thing that is offered or presented. **2** say yes to an invitation, offer, etc.
▷ **acceptance** *noun*
[from *ac-* + Latin *capere* = take]
USAGE Do not confuse with **except**.

acceptable *ADJECTIVE* good enough to accept; pleasing.
▷ **acceptably** *adverb*

access (*say* ak-sess) *NOUN* **1** a way to enter or reach something. **2** the right to use or look at something.

access *VERB* **accesses, accessing, accessed** find information that has been stored in a computer.
[same origin as *accede*]

accessible *ADJECTIVE* able to be reached or understood easily.
▷ **accessibly** *adverb* **accessibility** *noun*

accession *NOUN* **accessions** **1** reaching a rank or position; becoming king or queen. **2** an addition • *recent accessions to our library.*
[from Latin *accessio* = coming to, something come to or added]

accessory (*say* ak-sess-er-ee) *NOUN* **accessories** **1** an extra thing that goes with something. **2** a person who helps another with a crime.
[from Latin *accessorius* = added]

accident *NOUN* **accidents** an unexpected happening, especially one causing injury or damage.
- **by accident** by chance; without its being arranged in advance.
[from Latin *accidere* = happen]

accidental *ADJECTIVE* happening or done by accident.
▷ **accidentally** *adverb*

acclaim *VERB* **acclaims, acclaiming, acclaimed** welcome or applaud.
▷ **acclaim** *noun* **acclamation** *noun*
[from *ac-* + Latin *clamare* = to shout]

acclimatize *VERB* **acclimatizes, acclimatizing, acclimatized** make or become used to a new climate or new surroundings.
▷ **acclimatization** *noun*
[from *ac-* + French *climat* = climate + *-ize*]

accolade (*say* ak-ol-ayd) *NOUN* **accolades** praise or a prize given to someone for something they have done.
[from *ac-* + Latin *collum* = neck (because in the past, when a man was knighted, the king embraced him round the neck)]

accommodate *VERB* **accommodates, accommodating, accommodated** **1** provide somebody with a place to live, work, or sleep overnight. **2** help by providing something • *We can accommodate you with skis.*
[from Latin *accommodare* = make suitable for]

accommodating *ADJECTIVE* willing to help or cooperate.

accommodation *NOUN* somewhere to live, work, or sleep overnight.

accompanist *NOUN* **accompanists** a pianist etc. who accompanies a singer or another musician.

accompany *VERB* **accompanies, accompanying, accompanied** **1** go somewhere with somebody. **2** be present with something • *Thunder accompanied the storm.* **3** play music, especially on a piano, that supports a singer or another player etc.
▷ **accompaniment** *noun*
[from old French]

accomplice (*say* a-kum-pliss) *NOUN* **accomplices** a person who helps another in a crime etc.
[from old French]

accomplish *VERB* **accomplishes, accomplishing, accomplished** do something successfully.
▷ **accomplishment** *noun*
[from *ac-* + Latin *complere* = to complete]

accomplished *ADJECTIVE* skilled.

accord *NOUN* agreement; consent.
- **of your own accord** without being asked or compelled.

accord *VERB* **accords, according, accorded** **1** be consistent with something. **2** (*formal*) give • *He was accorded this privilege.*
[from old French]

accordance *NOUN* - **in accordance with** in agreement with • *This is done in accordance with the rules.*

according *ADVERB* - **according to** **1** as stated by • *According to him, we are stupid.* **2** in relation to • *Price the apples according to their size.*

a b c d e f g h i j k l m n o p q r s t u v w x y z

A

accordingly *ADVERB* **1** in the way that is required • *I've given you your instructions and I expect you to act accordingly.* **2** therefore.

accordion *NOUN* **accordions** a portable musical instrument like a large concertina with a set of piano-type keys at one end, played by squeezing it in and out and pressing the keys.
[via German from Italian *accordare* = to tune an instrument]

accost *VERB* **accosts, accosting, accosted** approach and speak to a person.
[via French from Italian]

account *NOUN* **accounts** **1** a statement of money owed, spent, or received; a bill. **2** an arrangement to keep money in a bank etc. **3** a description or report.
- **on account of** because of.
- **on no account** under no circumstances; certainly not.
- **take something into account** consider or include it when making a decision or calculation.

account *VERB* **accounts, accounting, accounted**
- **account for** make it clear why something happens.
[from *ac-* + old French *counte* = story, sum]

accountable *ADJECTIVE* responsible; having to explain why you have done something.
▷ **accountability** *noun*

accountant *NOUN* **accountants** a person whose job is keeping or inspecting financial accounts.
▷ **accountancy** *noun*

accounting *NOUN* keeping financial accounts.

accoutrements (*say* a-koo-trim-ents) *PLURAL NOUN* equipment.
[French]

accredited *ADJECTIVE* officially recognized • *our accredited agent.*
[from French *accréditer* = vouch for]

accretion (*say* a-kree-shon) *NOUN* **accretions** a growth or increase in which things are added gradually.
[same origin as *accrue*]

accrue (*say* a-kroo) *VERB* **accrues, accruing, accrued** **1** gradually increase over a period of time. **2** accumulate.
▷ **accrual** *noun*
[from *ac-* + Latin *crescere* = grow]

accumulate *VERB* **accumulates, accumulating, accumulated** **1** collect; pile up. **2** increase in quantity.
▷ **accumulation** *noun*
[from *ac-* + Latin *cumulus* = heap]

accumulator *NOUN* **accumulators** a storage battery.

accurate *ADJECTIVE* correct or exact.
▷ **accurately** *adverb* **accuracy** *noun*
[from *ac-* + Latin *cura* = care]

accusation *NOUN* **accusations** accusing someone; a statement accusing a person of a fault or crime etc.

accuse *VERB* **accuses, accusing, accused** say that a person has committed a crime etc.; blame.
▷ **accuser** *noun*
[from *ac-* + Latin *causa* = cause]

accustom *VERB* **accustoms, accustoming, accustomed** make a person become used to something.
[from *ac-* + *custom*]

ace *NOUN* **aces** **1** a playing card with one spot. **2** a very skilful person or thing. **3** (in tennis) a serve that is too good for the other player to reach.
[from Latin *as* = unit]

acerbic (*say* a-serb-ik) *ADJECTIVE* having a sharp manner of speaking.
[from Latin *acerbus* = sour-tasting]

acetylene (*say* a-set-il-een) *NOUN* a gas that burns with a bright flame, used in cutting and welding metal.
[from Latin]

ache *NOUN* **aches** a dull continuous pain.

ache *VERB* **aches, aching, ached** have an ache.
[from Old English]

achieve *VERB* **achieves, achieving, achieved** succeed in doing or producing something.
▷ **achievable** *adjective* **achievement** *noun*
[from old French *a chief* = to a head]

acid *NOUN* **acids** a chemical substance that contains hydrogen and neutralizes alkalis. The hydrogen can be replaced by a metal to form a salt.
▷ **acidic** *adjective* **acidity** *noun*

acid *ADJECTIVE* **1** sharp-tasting; sour. **2** looking or sounding bitter • *an acid reply.*
▷ **acidly** *adverb*
[from Latin *acere* = to be sour]

acid rain *NOUN* rain made acid by mixing with waste gases from factories etc.

ackee (*say* ak-i) *NOUN* **1** a tropical tree from West Africa. **2** the fruit of this tree.

acknowledge *VERB* **acknowledges, acknowledging, acknowledged 1** admit that something is true. **2** state that you have received or noticed something • *They wrote back to acknowledge my application.* **3** express thanks or appreciation for something.
▷ **acknowledgement** *noun*
[from Old English *acknow* = confess, + *knowledge*]

acme (*say* ak-mee) *NOUN* the highest degree of something • *the acme of perfection.*
[from Greek *akme* = highest point]

acne (*say* ak-nee) *NOUN* inflamed red pimples on the face and neck.
[same origin as *acme*]

acorn *NOUN* **acorns** the seed of the oak tree.
[from Old English]

acoustic (*say* a-koo-stik) *ADJECTIVE* **1** to do with sound or hearing. **2** (said about a musical instrument) not electronic • *an acoustic guitar.*
▷ **acoustically** *adverb*
[from Greek *akouein* = hear]

acoustics (*say* a-koo-stiks) *PLURAL NOUN* **1** the qualities of a hall etc. that make it good or bad for carrying sound. **2** the properties of sound.

acquaint *VERB* **acquaints, acquainting, acquainted** tell somebody about something • *Acquaint him with the facts.*
- **be acquainted with** know slightly.
[from old French]

acquaintance *NOUN* **acquaintances 1** a person you know slightly. **2** being acquainted.

acquiesce (*say* ak-wee-ess) *VERB* **acquiesces, acquiescing, acquiesced** agree to something.
▷ **acquiescent** *adjective* **acquiescence** *noun*
[from *ac-* + Latin *quiescere* = to rest]

acquire *VERB* **acquires, acquiring, acquired** obtain.
[from *ac-* + Latin *quaerere* = seek]

acquisition *NOUN* **1** something you have acquired recently. **2** the process of acquiring something.

acquisitive (*say* a-kwiz-it-iv) *ADJECTIVE* eager to acquire things.

acquit *VERB* **acquits, acquitting, acquitted** decide that somebody is not guilty • *The jury acquitted her.*
▷ **acquittal** *noun*
- **acquit yourself well** perform or do something well.
[from *ac-* + Latin *quietus* = at rest]

acre (*say* ay-ker) *NOUN* **acres** an area of land measuring 4,840 square yards or 0.405 hectares.
▷ **acreage** *noun*
[from Old English *aecer* = field]

acrid *ADJECTIVE* bitter • *an acrid smell.*
[from Latin *acer* = sharp, pungent, bitter]

acrimonious (*say* ak-rim-**oh**-nee-us) *ADJECTIVE* (said about a person's manner or words) bitter and bad-tempered.
▷ **acrimony** (*say* **ak**-rim-on-ee) *noun*
[same origin as *acrid*]

acrobat *NOUN* **acrobats** a person who performs spectacular gymnastic stunts for entertainment.
▷ **acrobatic** *adjective* **acrobatics** *plural noun*
[from Greek *akrobatos* = walking on tiptoe]

acronym (*say* ak-ron-im) *NOUN* **acronyms** a word or name that is formed from the initial letters of other words and pronounced as a word in its own right • *Nato is an acronym of North Atlantic Treaty Organization.*
[from Greek *akros* = top + *onyma* = name]

across *PREPOSITION & ADVERB* **1** from one side to the other • *Swim across the river. Are you across yet?* **2** on the opposite side • *the house across the street.*
[from French *à croix* = crosswise]

A

acrostic *NOUN* **acrostics** a word puzzle or poem in which the first or last letters of each line form a word or words.
[from Greek *akros* = top + *stikhos* = a line of verse]

acrylic (*say* a-**kril**-ik) *NOUN* a kind of fibre, plastic, or resin made from an organic acid.
[from *acrolein*, the substance from which acrylic is made]

acrylics *PLURAL NOUN* a type of paint used by artists.

act *NOUN* **acts** **1** something someone does. **2** a pretence • *She is only putting on an act.* **3** one of the main divisions of a play or opera. **4** each of a series of short performances in a programme of entertainment • *a juggling act.* **5** a law passed by a parliament.

act *VERB* **acts, acting, acted** **1** do something; perform actions. **2** perform a part in a play or film etc. **3** function; have an effect.
[from Latin *actus* = doing, performing]

action *NOUN* **actions** **1** doing something. **2** something done. **3** a battle; fighting • *He was killed in action.* **4** a lawsuit.
- **out of action** not working or functioning.
- **take action** do something.

action replay *NOUN* **action replays** playing back a piece of sports action on television, especially in slow motion.

activate *VERB* **activates, activating, activated** start something working.
▷ **activation** *noun* **activator** *noun*

active *ADJECTIVE* **1** taking part in many activities; energetic. **2** functioning or working; in operation • *an active volcano.* **3** (said about a form of a verb) used when the subject of the verb is performing the action. In 'The shop *sells* videos' the verb is active; in 'Videos *are sold* by the shop' the verb is passive.
▷ **actively** *adverb* **activeness** *noun*

activist *NOUN* **activists** a person who is active and energetic, especially in politics.

activity *NOUN* **activities** **1** an action or occupation • *outdoor activities.* **2** being active or lively.

actor *NOUN* **actors** a person who acts a part in a play or film etc.

actress *NOUN* **actresses** a woman who acts a part in a play or film etc.

actual *ADJECTIVE* real.
▷ **actually** *adverb* **actuality** *noun*
[from Latin *actualis* = active, practical]

actuate *VERB* **actuates, actuating, actuated** (*formal*) start something working; activate.
▷ **actuation** *noun*

acumen (*say* **ak**-yoo-men) *NOUN* sharpness of mind.
[Latin, = a point]

acupuncture (*say* **ak**-yoo-punk-cher) *NOUN* pricking parts of the body with needles to relieve pain or cure disease.
▷ **acupuncturist** *noun*
[from Latin *acu* = with a needle, + *puncture*]

acute *ADJECTIVE* **1** sharp or strong • *acute pain.* **2** having a sharp mind.
▷ **acutely** *adverb* **acuteness** *noun*
[from Latin *acus* = needle]

acute accent *NOUN* **acute accents** a mark over a vowel, as over *é* in *résumé*.

acute angle *NOUN* **acute angles** an angle of less than 90°.

AD *ABBREVIATION* Anno Domini (Latin = in the year of Our Lord), used in dates counted from the birth of Jesus Christ.

ad- *PREFIX* (changing to **ac-**, **af-**, **ag-**, **al-**, **an-**, **ap-**, **ar-**, **as-**, **at-** before certain consonants) to; towards (as in *adapt*, *admit*).
[from Latin *ad* = to]

adamant (*say* **ad**-am-ant) *ADJECTIVE* firm and not giving way to requests.
[from Greek]

Adam's apple *NOUN* **Adam's apples** the lump at the front of a man's neck.
[from the story that when Adam (the first man, according to the Bible) ate an apple, which God had forbidden him to do, a piece of it stuck in his throat]

adapt *VERB* **adapts, adapting, adapted** **1** change something so that it is suitable for a new purpose. **2** to become used to a new situation.
▷ **adaptable** *adjective* **adaptation** *noun*
[from *ad-* + Latin *aptus* = suitable, apt]

adaptor *NOUN* **adaptors** a device to connect pieces of electrical or other equipment.

add *VERB* **adds, adding, added 1** put one thing with another. **2** make another remark.
- **add up 1** make or find a total. **2** (*informal*) make sense; seem reasonable.
[from Latin]

addenda *PLURAL NOUN* things added at the end of a book.
[Latin, = things to be added]

adder *NOUN* **adders** a small poisonous snake.
[from Old English; originally called *a nadder*, which became *an adder*]

addict *NOUN* **addicts** a person who does or uses something that he or she cannot give up.
▷ **addicted** *adjective* **addiction** *noun*
[from Latin]

addictive *ADJECTIVE* causing a habit that people cannot give up • *an addictive drug.*

addition *NOUN* **additions 1** the process of adding. **2** something added.
- **in addition** also; as an extra thing.
▷ **additional** *adjective* **additionally** *adverb*

additive *NOUN* **additives** a substance added to another in small amounts for a special purpose, e.g. as a flavouring.

addled *ADJECTIVE* **1** (said about eggs) rotted and producing no chick after being brooded. **2** confused.
[from Old English]

address *NOUN* **addresses 1** the details of the place where someone lives or of where letters etc. should be delivered to a person or firm. **2** (*in computing*) the part of an instruction that shows where a piece of information is stored in a computer's memory. **3** a speech to an audience.

address *VERB* **addresses, addressing, addressed 1** write an address on a parcel etc. **2** make a speech or remark etc. to somebody.
[from old French]

addressee *NOUN* **addressees** the person to whom a letter etc. is addressed.

adenoids *PLURAL NOUN* thick spongy flesh at the back of the nose and throat, which may hinder breathing.
[from Greek *aden* = gland]

adept (*say* a-**dept**) *ADJECTIVE* very skilful.
[from Latin]

adequate *ADJECTIVE* enough or good enough.
▷ **adequately** *adverb* **adequacy** *noun*
[from Latin]

adhere *VERB* **adheres, adhering, adhered** stick to something.
▷ **adhesion** *noun*
[from *ad-* + Latin *haerere* = to stick]

adherent (*say* ad-**heer**-ent) *NOUN* **adherents** a person who supports a certain group or theory etc.
▷ **adherence** *noun*

adhesive *ADJECTIVE* sticky; causing things to stick together.

adhesive *NOUN* **adhesives** a substance used to stick things together; glue.
[same origin as *adhere*]

ad hoc *ADJECTIVE & ADVERB* done or arranged only when necessary and not planned in advance • *We had to make a number of ad hoc decisions.*
[Latin, = for this]

adieu (*say* a-**dew**) *INTERJECTION* goodbye.
[from French *à* = to + *Dieu* = God]

ad infinitum (*say* in-fin-**I**-tum) *ADVERB* without limit; for ever.
[Latin, = to infinity]

adjacent *ADJECTIVE* near or next to • *I waited in an adjacent room.*
[from *ad-* + Latin *jacens* = lying]

adjective *NOUN* **adjectives** a word that describes a noun or adds to its meaning, e.g. *big, honest, strange, our.*
▷ **adjectival** *adjective*

adjoin *VERB* **adjoins, adjoining, adjoined** be next or nearest to something.
[same origin as *adjunct*]

adjourn (*say* a-**jern**) *VERB* **adjourns, adjourning, adjourned 1** break off a meeting etc. until a later time. **2** break off and go somewhere else • *They adjourned to the library.*
▷ **adjournment** *noun*
[from Latin, = to another day]

adjudge *VERB* **adjudges, adjudging, adjudged** judge; give a decision • *He was adjudged to be guilty.*
[same origin as *adjudicate*]

A

adjudicate (*say* a-joo-dik-ayt) VERB **adjudicates, adjudicating, adjudicated** act as judge in a competition etc.
▷ **adjudication** *noun* **adjudicator** *noun*
[from *ad-* + Latin *judex* = a judge]

adjunct (*say* aj-unkt) NOUN **adjuncts** something added that is useful but not essential.
[from *ad-* + Latin *junctum* = joined]

adjust VERB **adjusts, adjusting, adjusted** **1** put a thing into its proper position or order. **2** alter something so that it fits or is suitable.
▷ **adjustable** *adjective* **adjustment** *noun*
[from *ad-* + Latin *juxta* = close to]

ad lib ADVERB as you like; freely.
[from Latin *ad libitum* = according to pleasure]

ad-lib VERB **ad-libs, ad-libbing, ad-libbed** say or do something without any rehearsal or preparation.

administer VERB **administers, administering, administered** **1** give or provide something • *He administered medicine.* **2** manage business affairs; administrate.
[from *ad-* + Latin *ministrare* = serve]

administrate VERB **administrates, administrating, administrated** manage public or business affairs.
▷ **administrator** *noun* **administrative** *adjective*
[same origin as *administer*]

administration NOUN **administrations** **1** administering. **2** the management of public or business affairs. **3** the people who manage an organization etc.; the government.

admirable ADJECTIVE worth admiring; excellent.
▷ **admirably** *adverb*

admiral NOUN **admirals** a naval officer of high rank.
[from Arabic *amir* = commander]

admire VERB **admires, admiring, admired** **1** look at something and enjoy it. **2** think that someone or something is very good.
▷ **admiration** *noun* **admirer** *noun*
[from *ad-* + Latin *mirari* = wonder at]

admissible ADJECTIVE able to be admitted or allowed • *admissible evidence.*

admission NOUN **admissions** **1** admitting. **2** the charge for being allowed to go in. **3** a statement admitting something; a confession.

admit VERB **admits, admitting, admitted** **1** allow someone or something to come in. **2** state reluctantly that something is true; confess • *We admit that the task is difficult. He admitted his crime.*
[from *ad-* + Latin *mittere* = send]

admittance NOUN being allowed to go in, especially to a private place.

admittedly ADVERB as an agreed fact; without denying it.

admonish VERB **admonishes, admonishing, admonished** advise or warn someone firmly but mildly.
▷ **admonition** *noun*
[from *ad-* + Latin *monere* = advise]

ad nauseam (*say* naw-see-am) ADVERB until people are sick of it.
[Latin, = to sickness]

ado NOUN - **without more** or **further ado** without wasting any more time.
[originally in *much ado* = much to do]

adolescence (*say* ad-ol-ess-ens) NOUN the time between being a child and being an adult.
[from *ad-* + Latin *alescere* = grow up]

adolescent NOUN **adolescents** a young person at the age between being a child and being an adult.
▷ **adolescent** *adjective*

adopt VERB **adopts, adopting, adopted** **1** take someone into your family as your own child. **2** accept something; take something and use it • *They adopted new methods of working.*
▷ **adoption** *noun*
[from *ad-* + Latin *optare* = choose]

adore VERB **adores, adoring, adored** love a person or thing very much.
▷ **adorable** *adjective* **adoration** *noun*
[from *ad-* + Latin *orare* = pray]

adorn VERB **adorns, adorning, adorned** decorate.
▷ **adornment** *noun*
[from *ad-* + Latin *ornare* = furnish, decorate]

adrenalin (*say* a-**dren**-al-in) *NOUN* a hormone produced when you are afraid or excited. It stimulates the nervous system, making your heart beat faster and increasing your energy and your ability to move quickly.
[from *ad-* + *renal* (because adrenalin is made by the adrenal glands, above the kidneys)]

adrift *ADJECTIVE* & *ADVERB* drifting.
[from *a-*[1] + *drift*]

adroit (*say* a-**droit**) *ADJECTIVE* skilful.
[from French *à droit* = according to right]

adulation *NOUN* very great flattery.
[from old French]

adult (*say* **ad**-ult) *NOUN* **adults** a fully grown or mature person.
[from Latin *adultus* = grown up]

adulterate *VERB* **adulterates, adulterating, adulterated** make a thing impure or less good by adding something to it.
▷ **adulteration** *noun*
[from Latin]

adultery *NOUN* being unfaithful to your wife or husband by having sexual intercourse with someone else.
▷ **adulterer** *noun* **adulterous** *adjective*
[from Latin]

advance *NOUN* **advances 1** a forward movement; progress. **2** an increase. **3** a loan; payment made before it is due.
- **in advance** beforehand; ahead.

advance *ADJECTIVE* given or arranged beforehand • *advance warning.*

advance *VERB* **advances, advancing, advanced 1** move forward; make progress. **2** lend or pay money ahead of the proper time • *Can you advance me a month's salary?*
▷ **advancement** *noun*
[from old French]

advantage *NOUN* **advantages**
1 something useful or helpful. **2** (in tennis) the next point won after deuce.
- **take advantage of** use a person or thing profitably or unfairly.
- **to advantage** making a good effect • *The painting can be seen to its best advantage here.*
- **to your advantage** profitable or helpful to you.
[from French *avant* = before]

advantageous (*say* ad-van-**tay**-jus) *ADJECTIVE* giving an advantage; beneficial.

Advent *NOUN* the period just before Christmas, when Christians celebrate the coming of Christ.

advent *NOUN* the arrival of a new person or thing • *the advent of computers.*
[from *ad-* + Latin *venire* = come]
WORD FAMILY There are a number of English words that are related to *advent* because part of their original meaning comes from the Latin word *venire* meaning 'to come'. These include *adventure*, *contravene*, *convene*, *intervene*, *invent*, *prevent*, *supervene*, and *venture*.

adventure *NOUN* **adventures 1** an exciting or dangerous experience. **2** willingness to take risks.
▷ **adventurer** *noun*
[same origin as *advent*]

adventurous *ADJECTIVE* willing to take risks and do new things.

adverb *NOUN* **adverbs** a word that adds to the meaning of a verb or adjective or another adverb and tells how, when, or where something happens, e.g. *gently*, *soon*, and *upstairs*.
▷ **adverbial** *adjective* **adverbially** *adverb*
[from *ad-* + Latin *verbum* = word]

adversary (*say* **ad**-ver-ser-ee) *NOUN* **adversaries** an opponent or enemy.

adverse *ADJECTIVE* unfavourable or harmful • *adverse effects.*
▷ **adversely** *adverb*
[from Latin *adversus* = opposite, from *ad-* + *versus* = turned]
USAGE Do not confuse with **averse**.

adversity *NOUN* **adversities** trouble or misfortune.

advert *NOUN* **adverts** (*informal*) an advertisement.

advertise *VERB* **advertises, advertising, advertised 1** praise goods etc. in order to encourage people to buy or use them. **2** make something publicly known • *advertise a meeting.* **3** give information about someone you need for a job • *A local firm was advertising for a secretary.*
▷ **advertiser** *noun*
[from old French]

A

advertisement *NOUN* **advertisements** a public notice or announcement, especially one advertising goods or services in newspapers, on posters, or in broadcasts.

advice *NOUN* **1** telling a person what you think he or she should do. **2** a piece of information • *We received advice that the goods had been dispatched.*
[originally = opinion, point of view: from *ad-* + Latin *videre* = see]
USAGE Do not confuse with the verb **advise**.

advisable *ADJECTIVE* that is the wise thing to do.
▷ **advisability** *noun*

advise *VERB* **advises, advising, advised**
1 give somebody advice; recommend.
2 inform.
▷ **adviser** *noun* **advisory** *adjective*
[same origin as *advice*]

advocate (*say* ad-vok-ayt) *VERB* **advocates, advocating, advocated** speak in favour of something; recommend • *We advocate changing the law.*

advocate (*say* ad-vok-at) *NOUN* **advocates**
1 a person who advocates a policy etc. • *She is an advocate of women's rights.* **2** a lawyer presenting someone's case in a lawcourt.
[from *ad-* + Latin *vocare* = call, speak]

aegis (*say* ee-jiss) *NOUN* – **under the aegis of** under the protection or with the support of • *The scheme is under the aegis of the Scout Association.*
[from Greek *aigis* = magical shield of the god Zeus]

aerate (*say* air-ayt) *VERB* **aerates, aerating, aerated** **1** add air to something. **2** add carbon dioxide to a liquid • *aerated water.*
[same origin as *aero-*]

aerial *ADJECTIVE* **1** in or from the air. **2** to do with aircraft.

aerial *NOUN* **aerials** a wire or rod etc. for receiving or transmitting radio or television signals.
[same origin as *aero-*]

aero- *PREFIX* to do with air or aircraft (as in *aeronautics*).
[from Greek *aer* = air]

aerobatics *PLURAL NOUN* spectacular performances by flying aircraft.
▷ **aerobatic** *adjective*
[from *aero-* + *acrobatics*]

aerobics *PLURAL NOUN* exercises to stimulate breathing and strengthen the heart and lungs.
▷ **aerobic** *adjective*
[from *aero-* + Greek *bios* = life]

aerodrome *NOUN* **aerodromes** an airfield.
[from *aero-* + Greek *dromos* = running-track]

aerodynamic *ADJECTIVE* designed to move through the air quickly and easily.

aeronautics *NOUN* the study of aircraft and flying.
▷ **aeronautic** *adjective* **aeronautical** *adjective*
[from *aero-* + *nautical*]

aeroplane *NOUN* **aeroplanes** a flying machine with wings.
[from *aero-* + *plane*[1]]

aerosol *NOUN* **aerosols** a container that holds a liquid under pressure and can let it out in a fine spray.
[from *aero-* + *solution*]

aerospace *NOUN* the earth's atmosphere and space beyond it.
[from *aero-* + *space*]

aesthetic (*say* iss-thet-ik) *ADJECTIVE* to do with the appreciation of beautiful things.
[from Greek *aisthesthai* = perceive]

af- *PREFIX* to; towards. SEE **ad-**.

afar *ADVERB* far away • *The din was heard from afar.*
[from *a-*[1] + *far*]

affable *ADJECTIVE* polite and friendly.
▷ **affably** *adverb* **affability** *noun*
[from *af-* + Latin *fari* = speak]

affair *NOUN* **affairs** **1** an event or matter • *The party was a grand affair.* **2** a temporary sexual relationship between two people who are not married to each other.
[from French *à faire* = to do]

affairs *PLURAL NOUN* the business and activities that are part of private or public life • *Keep out of my affairs; current affairs.*

affect *VERB* **affects, affecting, affected**
1 have an effect on; influence. **2** pretend • *She affected ignorance.*
[from *af-* + Latin *facere* = do]
USAGE The word *affect* is a verb. Do not confuse it with the noun **effect**.

affectation *NOUN* **affectations** unnatural behaviour that is intended to impress other people.

affected *ADJECTIVE* pretended and unnatural.

affection *NOUN* **affections** a strong liking for a person.

affectionate *ADJECTIVE* showing affection; loving.
▷ **affectionately** *adverb*
[from Latin *affectionatus* = devoted]

affidavit (*say* af-id-ay-vit) *NOUN* **affidavits** a statement written down and sworn to be true, for use as legal evidence.
[Latin, = he or she has stated on oath]

affiliated *ADJECTIVE* officially connected with a larger organization.
[from Latin *affiliatum* = adopted, from *af-* + *filius* = son]

affinity *NOUN* **affinities** attraction, relationship, or similarity to each other • *There are many affinities between the two languages.*
[from French]

affirm *VERB* **affirms, affirming, affirmed** state something definitely or firmly.
▷ **affirmation** *noun*
[from *af-* + Latin *firmus* = firm]

affirmative *ADJECTIVE* that says 'yes' • *an affirmative reply.* (COMPARE **negative**)

affix (*say* a-fiks) *VERB* **affixes, affixing, affixed** attach; add in writing • *affix a stamp; affix your signature.*

affix (*say* aff-iks) *NOUN* **affixes** a prefix or suffix.
[from *af-* + Latin *fixare* = fix]

afflict *VERB* **afflicts, afflicting, afflicted** cause somebody to suffer • *He is afflicted with arthritis.*
▷ **affliction** *noun*
[from *af-* + Latin *flictum* = struck]

affluent (*say* af-loo-ent) *ADJECTIVE* rich.
▷ **affluence** *noun*
[from Latin *affluens* = overflowing, from *af-* + *fluens* = flowing]

afford *VERB* **affords, affording, afforded**
1 have enough money to pay for something. **2** have enough time or resources etc. to do something. **3** to be able to do something without a risk • *You can't afford to be critical.*
[from Old English]

afforestation *NOUN* the planting of trees to form a forest.
[from *af-* + Latin *foresta* = forest]

affray *NOUN* **affrays** fighting or rioting in public.
[from old French]

affront *VERB* **affronts, affronting, affronted** insult or offend someone.

affront *NOUN* **affronts** an insult.
[from Latin *ad frontem* = to the face]

afield *ADVERB* at or to a distance; away from home • *travelling far afield.*
[from *a-*[1] + *field*]

aflame *ADJECTIVE* & *ADVERB* in flames; glowing.
[from *a-*[1] + *flame*]

afloat *ADJECTIVE* & *ADVERB* floating; on the sea.
[from *a-*[1] + *float*]

afoot *ADJECTIVE* happening • *Great changes are afoot.*
[originally = on foot, moving: from *a-*[1] + *foot*]

aforesaid *ADJECTIVE* mentioned previously.
[from *afore* = before, + *said*]

afraid *ADJECTIVE* frightened or alarmed.
- **I'm afraid** I regret • *I'm afraid I won't be able to come.*
[past participle of an old word *affray* = attack, frighten]

afresh *ADVERB* again; in a new way • *We must start afresh.*
[from *a-*[1] + *fresh*]

African *ADJECTIVE* to do with Africa or its people.

African *NOUN* **Africans** an African person.

Afrikaans (*say* af-rik-**ahns**) *NOUN* a language developed from Dutch, used in South Africa.
[Dutch, = African]

A

Afrikaner (*say* af-rik-ah-ner) *NOUN* **Afrikaners** a White person in South Africa whose language is Afrikaans.

Afro- *PREFIX* African.

Afro-Caribbean *ADJECTIVE* to do with Caribbean (especially West Indian) people whose ancestors came from Africa.

aft *ADVERB* at or towards the back of a ship or aircraft.
[from Old English, related to *after*]

after *PREPOSITION* **1** later than • *Come after tea.* **2** behind in place or order • *Which letter comes after H?* **3** trying to catch; pursuing • *Run after him.* **4** in spite of • *We can come after all.* **5** in imitation or honour of • *She is named after her aunt.* **6** about or concerning • *He asked after you.*

after *ADVERB* **1** behind • *Jill came tumbling after.* **2** later • *It came a week after.*
[from Old English]

afterbirth *NOUN* the placenta and other membranes that come out of the mother's womb after she has given birth.

aftermath *NOUN* events or circumstances that come after something bad or unpleasant • *the aftermath of the earthquake.*
[from *after* + *math* = mowing (i.e. new grass that grows after a mowing)]

afternoon *NOUN* **afternoons** the time from noon or lunchtime to evening.

aftershave *NOUN* a pleasant-smelling lotion that men put on their skin after shaving.

afterthought *NOUN* **afterthoughts** something thought of or added later.

afterwards *ADVERB* at a later time.
[from *after* + *-wards*]

ag- *PREFIX* to; towards. SEE **ad-**.

again *ADVERB* **1** another time; once more • *try again.* **2** as before • *You will soon be well again.* **3** besides; moreover.
[from Old English *ongean* = in the opposite direction, back to the beginning]

against *PREPOSITION* **1** touching or hitting • *He leant against the wall.* **2** in opposition to; not in favour of • *They voted against the proposal.* **3** in preparation for • *Protect them against the cold.*
[from *again*]

age *NOUN* **ages** **1** the length of time a person has lived or a thing has existed. **2** a special period of history or geology • *the ice age.*
- **ages** *plural noun* (*informal*) a very long time • *We've been waiting for ages.*
- **come of age** reach the age at which you have an adult's legal rights and obligations (now at 18 years; formerly 21).

age *VERB* **ages, ageing, aged** make or become old.
[from old French]

aged *ADJECTIVE* **1** (*say* ayjd) having the age of • *a girl aged 9.* **2** (*say* ay-jid) very old • *an aged man.*

age group *NOUN* **age groups** people who are all of the same age.

agency *NOUN* **agencies** **1** the office or business of an agent • *a travel agency.* **2** the means by which something is done • *Flowers are pollinated by the agency of bees.*
[same origin as *agent*]

agenda (*say* a-jen-da) *NOUN* **agendas** a list of things to be done or discussed • *The agenda is rather long.*
[Latin, = things to be done]

agent *NOUN* **agents** **1** a person who organizes things for other people • *a travel agent.* **2** a spy • *a secret agent.*
[from Latin *agens* = doing things]

agglomeration *NOUN* **agglomerations** a mass of things collected together.
[from *ag-* + Latin *glomus* = mass]

aggravate *VERB* **aggravates, aggravating, aggravated** **1** make a thing worse or more serious. **2** (*informal*) annoy.
▷ **aggravation** *noun*
[from *ag-* + Latin *gravare* = load heavily]

aggregate (*say* ag-rig-at) *ADJECTIVE* combined or total • *the aggregate amount.*

aggregate *NOUN* **aggregates** a total amount or score.
[from *ag-* + Latin *gregatum* = herded together]

aggression *NOUN* starting an attack or war etc.; aggressive behaviour.
[from Latin *aggredi* = attack, from *ag-* = against + *gradi* = step, move]

aggressive *ADJECTIVE* likely to attack people; forceful.
▷ **aggressively** *adverb* **aggressiveness** *noun*

aggressor *NOUN* **aggressors** the person or nation that started an attack or war etc.

aggrieved (*say* a-**greevd**) *ADJECTIVE* resentful because of being treated unfairly. [same origin as *aggravate*]

aghast *ADJECTIVE* horrified. [from Old English]

agile *ADJECTIVE* moving quickly or easily.
▷ **agilely** *adverb* **agility** *noun*
[from Latin *agere* = do]

agitate *VERB* **agitates, agitating, agitated** **1** make someone feel upset or anxious. **2** stir up public interest or concern; campaign • *They agitated for a new bypass.* **3** shake something about.
▷ **agitation** *noun* **agitator** *noun*
[from Latin *agitare* = shake]

aglow *ADJECTIVE* glowing. [from *a-*^{1} + *glow*]

agnostic (*say* ag-**nost**-ik) *NOUN* **agnostics** a person who believes that it is impossible to know whether God exists.
▷ **agnosticism** *noun*
[from *a-*^{2} + Greek *gnostikos* = knowing]

ago *ADVERB* in the past • *long ago.* [from Middle English *agone* = gone by]

agog *ADJECTIVE* eager and excited. [from French *en gogues* = in a happy mood, ready for fun]

agony *NOUN* **agonies** extremely great pain or suffering.
▷ **agonizing** *adjective*
[from Greek *agon* = a struggle]

agoraphobia (*say* ag-er-a-**foh**-bee-a) *NOUN* abnormal fear of being in open spaces. [from Greek *agora* = market place, + *phobia*]

agrarian (*say* a-**grair**-ee-an) *ADJECTIVE* to do with farm land or its cultivation. [from Latin *ager* = field]

agree *VERB* **agrees, agreeing, agreed** **1** think or say the same as another person etc. **2** consent • *She agreed to come.* **3** suit a person's health or digestion • *Curry doesn't agree with me.* **4** correspond in grammatical number, gender, or person. In 'They were good teachers' *they* agrees with *teachers* (both are plural forms) and *were* agrees with *they*; *was* would be incorrect because it is singular.
[from old French]

agreeable *ADJECTIVE* **1** willing • *We shall go if you are agreeable.* **2** pleasant • *an agreeable place.*
▷ **agreeably** *adverb*

agreement *NOUN* **agreements** **1** agreeing. **2** an arrangement that people have agreed on.

agriculture *NOUN* cultivating land on a large scale and rearing livestock; farming.
▷ **agricultural** *adjective*
[from Latin *agri* = of a field, + *culture*]

aground *ADVERB* & *ADJECTIVE* stranded on the bottom in shallow water. [from *a-*^{1} + *ground*]

ah *INTERJECTION* an exclamation of surprise, pity, admiration, etc.

ahead *ADVERB* **1** further forward; in front. **2** forwards • *Full steam ahead!* [from *a-*^{1} + *head*]

ahoy *INTERJECTION* an exclamation used by seamen to call attention.

aid *NOUN* **aids** **1** help. **2** something that helps • *a hearing aid.* **3** money, food, etc. sent to another country to help it • *overseas aid.*
- **in aid of** for the purpose of; to help something.

aid *VERB* **aids, aiding, aided** help. [from old French]

aide *NOUN* **aides** an assistant. [French]

aide-de-camp (*say* ay-der-**kahm**) *NOUN* **aides-de-camp** a military officer who is the assistant to a senior officer. [French, = camp- helper]

Aids *NOUN* a disease caused by the HIV virus, which greatly weakens a person's ability to resist infections. [from the initial letters of 'acquired immune deficiency syndrome']

ail *VERB* **ails, ailing, ailed** (*old use*) be ill; make a person ill • *What ails you?* [from Old English]

ailing *ADJECTIVE* **1** ill; in poor health. **2** in difficulties; not successful • *the ailing ship industry.*

A

ailment *NOUN* **ailments** a slight illness.

aim *VERB* **aims, aiming, aimed** **1** point a gun etc. **2** throw or kick in a particular direction. **3** try or intend to do something.

aim *NOUN* **aims** **1** aiming a gun etc. **2** a purpose or intention.
[via old French *amer* from Latin *aestimare* = estimate]

aimless *ADJECTIVE* without a purpose.
▷ **aimlessly** *adverb*

air *NOUN* **airs** **1** the mixture of gases that surrounds the earth and which everyone breathes. **2** the open space above the earth. **3** a tune or melody. **4** an appearance or impression of something • *an air of mystery.* **5** an impressive or haughty manner • *He puts on airs.*
- **by air** in or by aircraft.
- **on the air** on radio or television.

air *VERB* **airs, airing, aired** **1** put clothes etc. in a warm place to finish drying. **2** ventilate a room. **3** express • *He aired his opinions.*
[from old French]

airborne *ADJECTIVE* **1** (said about an aircraft) in flight. **2** carried by the air or by aircraft.

air-conditioning *NOUN* a system for controlling the temperature, purity, etc. of the air in a room or building.
▷ **air-conditioned** *adjective*

aircraft *NOUN* **aircraft** an aeroplane, glider, or helicopter etc.

aircraft carrier *NOUN* **aircraft carriers** a large ship with a long deck where aircraft can take off and land.

airfield *NOUN* **airfields** an area equipped with runways etc. where aircraft can take off and land.

air force *NOUN* **air forces** the part of a country's armed forces that is equipped with aircraft.

airgun *NOUN* **airguns** a gun in which compressed air shoots a pellet or dart.

airline *NOUN* **airlines** a company that provides a regular service of transport by aircraft.

airliner *NOUN* **airliners** a large aircraft for carrying passengers.

airlock *NOUN* **airlocks** **1** a compartment with an airtight door at each end, through which people can go in and out of a pressurized chamber. **2** a bubble of air that stops liquid flowing through a pipe.

airmail *NOUN* mail carried by air.

airman *NOUN* **airmen** a man who is a member of an air force or of the crew of an aircraft.

airplane *NOUN* **airplanes** (*American*) an aeroplane.

airport *NOUN* **airports** a place where aircraft land and take off, with passenger terminals and other buildings.

air raid *NOUN* **air raids** an attack by aircraft.

airship *NOUN* **airships** a large balloon with engines, designed to carry passengers or goods.

airstrip *NOUN* **airstrips** a strip of ground prepared for aircraft to land and take off.

airtight *ADJECTIVE* not letting air in or out.

airworthy *ADJECTIVE* (said about an aircraft) fit to fly.
▷ **airworthiness** *noun*

airy *ADJECTIVE* **1** with plenty of fresh air. **2** light as air. **3** vague and insincere • *airy promises.*
▷ **airily** *adverb*

aisle (*say* I'll) *NOUN* **aisles** **1** a passage between or beside rows of seats or pews. **2** a side part of a church.
[from old French]

ajar *ADVERB & ADJECTIVE* slightly open • *Leave the door ajar.*
[literally = turned: from *a-*[1] + Old English *cerr* = a turn]

akimbo *ADVERB* - **arms akimbo** with hands on hips and elbows out.
[from Old Norse]

akin *ADJECTIVE* related or similar to • *a feeling akin to regret.*
[from Old English *a* = of, + *kin*]

al- *PREFIX* to; towards. SEE **ad-**.

alabaster (*say* al-a-bast-er) *NOUN* a kind of hard stone, usually white.
[from Greek]

à la carte *ADJECTIVE* & *ADVERB* ordered and paid for as separate items from a menu. (COMPARE **table d'hôte**)
[French, = from the menu]

alacrity *NOUN* speed and willingness • *She accepted with alacrity.*
[from Latin]

alarm *NOUN* **alarms** **1** a warning sound or signal; a piece of equipment for giving this. **2** a feeling of fear or worry. **3** an alarm clock.

alarm *VERB* **alarms, alarming, alarmed** make someone frightened or anxious.
▷ **alarming** *adjective*
[from Italian *all' arme!* = to arms!: compare this with *alert*]

alarm clock *NOUN* **alarm clocks** a clock that can be set to ring or bleep at a fixed time to wake a sleeping person.

alarmist *NOUN* **alarmists** a person who raises unnecessary alarm.

alas *INTERJECTION* an exclamation of sorrow.
[from Latin *lassus* = weary]

albatross *NOUN* **albatrosses** a large seabird with very long wings.
[from Arabic]

albino (*say* al-been-oh) *NOUN* **albinos** a person or animal with no colouring pigment in the skin and hair (which are white).
[from Latin *albus* = white]

album *NOUN* **albums** **1** a book with blank pages in which to keep a collection of photographs, stamps, autographs, etc. **2** a collection of songs on a CD, record, or tape.
[Latin, = white piece of stone etc. on which to write things]

albumen (*say* al-bew-min) *NOUN* the white of an egg.
[from Latin *albus* = white]

alchemy (*say* al-kim-ee) *NOUN* an early form of chemistry, the chief aim of which was to turn ordinary metals into gold.
▷ **alchemist** *noun*
[from Arabic *al-kimiya* = the art of changing metals]

alcohol *NOUN* **1** a colourless liquid made by fermenting sugar or starch. **2** drinks containing this liquid (e.g. wine, beer, whisky), that can make people drunk.
[from Arabic]

alcoholic *ADJECTIVE* containing alcohol.

alcoholic *NOUN* **alcoholics** a person who is seriously addicted to alcohol.
▷ **alcoholism** *noun*

alcove *NOUN* **alcoves** a section of a room etc. that is set back from the main part; a recess.
[from Arabic *al-kubba* = the arch]

alder *NOUN* **alders** a kind of tree, often growing in marshy places.
[from Old English]

alderman (*say* awl-der-man) *NOUN* **aldermen** a senior member of an English county or borough council.
[from Old English *aldor* = elder, chief, + *man*]

ale *NOUN* **ales** beer.
[from Old English]

alert *ADJECTIVE* watching for something; ready to act.
▷ **alertly** *adverb* **alertness** *noun*

alert *NOUN* **alerts** a warning or alarm.
- **on the alert** on the lookout; watchful.

alert *VERB* **alerts, alerting, alerted** warn someone of danger etc.; make someone aware of something.
[from Italian *all' erta!* = to the watchtower!: compare this with *alarm*]

A level *NOUN* **A levels** advanced level in GCSE.

alfresco *ADJECTIVE* & *ADVERB* in the open air • *an alfresco meal.*
[from Italian *al fresco* = in the fresh air]

algae (*say* al-jee) *PLURAL NOUN* plants that grow in water, with no true stems or leaves.
[Latin, = seaweed]

algebra (*say* al-jib-ra) *NOUN* mathematics in which letters and symbols are used to represent quantities.
▷ **algebraic** (*say* al-jib-ray-ik) *adjective*
[from Arabic *al-jabr* = putting together broken parts]

algorithm (*say* al-ger-ithum) *NOUN* **algorithms** a logical process used for solving a problem in a number of steps, often written out as a flow-chart in a computer program.
[via Latin from Arabic]

alias (*say* ay-lee-as) *NOUN* **aliases** a false or different name.

A

alias *ADVERB* also named • *Clark Kent, alias Superman.*
[Latin, = at another time, otherwise]

alibi (*say* al-ib-I) *NOUN* **alibis** evidence that a person accused of a crime was somewhere else when it was committed.
[Latin, = at another place]
USAGE This word is sometimes used as if it simply means 'an excuse'. Some people dislike this use, so it is probably best to avoid it.

alien (*say* ay-lee-en) *NOUN* **aliens** **1** a person who is not a citizen of the country where he or she is living; a foreigner. **2** a being from another world.

alien *ADJECTIVE* **1** foreign. **2** unnatural • *Cruelty is alien to her nature.*
[from Latin *alius* = other]

alienate (*say* ay-lee-en-ayt) *VERB* **alienates, alienating, alienated** make a person become unfriendly or not willing to help you.
▷ **alienation** *noun*

alight[1] *ADJECTIVE* **1** on fire. **2** lit up.
[from *a-*[1] + *light*[1]]

alight[2] *VERB* **alights, alighting, alighted** **1** get out of a vehicle or down from a horse etc. **2** fly down and settle • *The bird alighted on a branch.*
[from *a-*[1] + *light*[2]]

align (*say* al-I'n) *VERB* **aligns, aligning, aligned** **1** arrange things in a line. **2** join as an ally • *They aligned themselves with the Germans.*
▷ **alignment** *noun*
[from French *à ligne* = into line]

alike *ADJECTIVE & ADVERB* like one another; in the same way • *The twins are very alike. Treat them alike.*
[from Old English]

alimentary canal *NOUN* **alimentary canals** the tube along which food passes from the mouth to the anus while it is being digested and absorbed by the body.
[from Latin *alimentum* = food]

alimony *NOUN* (*American*) money paid by someone to his or her wife or husband after they are separated or divorced; maintenance.
[from Latin *alimonia* = nourishment]

alive *ADJECTIVE* **1** living. **2** alert or aware • *Be alive to the possible dangers.*
[from Old English *on life* = in life]

alkali (*say* alk-al-I) *NOUN* **alkalis** a chemical substance that neutralizes an acid to form a salt.
▷ **alkaline** *adjective*
[from Arabic *al-kali* = the ashes (because alkali was first obtained from the ashes of seaweed)]

all *ADJECTIVE* the whole number or amount of • *All my books are here; all day.*

all *NOUN* **1** everything • *That is all I know.* **2** everybody • *All are agreed.*

all *ADVERB* **1** completely • *She was dressed all in white.* **2** to each team or competitor • *The score is fifteen all.*
- **all in** (*informal*) exhausted • *I'm all in.*
- **all-in** *adjective* including or allowing everything • *an all-in price.*
- **all there** (*informal*) having an alert mind.
- **all the same** in spite of this; making no difference • *I like him, all the same.*
[from Old English]

Allah *NOUN* the Muslim name of God.

allay (*say* a-lay) *VERB* **allays, allaying, allayed** calm or relieve • *to allay their fears.*
[from Old English *alecgan* = lay down]

all-clear *NOUN* a signal that a danger has passed.

allegation (*say* al-ig-ay-shon) *NOUN* **allegations** a statement made without proof.

allege (*say* a-lej) *VERB* **alleges, alleging, alleged** say something without being able to prove it • *He alleged that I had cheated.*
▷ **allegedly** (*say* a-lej-id-lee) *adverb*
[from old French]

allegiance (*say* a-lee-jans) *NOUN* **allegiances** loyalty.
[from old French; related to *liege*]

allegory (*say* al-ig-er-ee) *NOUN* **allegories** a story in which the characters and events represent or symbolize a deeper meaning, e.g. to teach a moral lesson.
▷ **allegorical** (*say* al-ig-o-rik-al) *adjective*
[from Greek *allos* = other + *-agoria* = speaking]

alleluia *INTERJECTION* praise to God.
[from Hebrew]

allergic ADJECTIVE very sensitive to something that may make you ill • *He is allergic to pollen, which gives him hay fever.*
▷ **allergy** (*say* al-er-jee) *noun*
[via German from Greek *allos* = other, different]

alleviate (*say* a-lee-vee-ayt) VERB **alleviates, alleviating, alleviated** make a thing less severe • *to alleviate pain.*
▷ **alleviation** *noun*
[from Latin *alleviare* = lighten the weight of]

alley NOUN **alleys** **1** a narrow street or passage. **2** a place where you can play bowls or skittles.
[from French *aller* = go]

alliance (*say* a-leye-ans) NOUN **alliances** an association formed by countries or groups who wish to support each other.
[same origin as *ally*]

allied ADJECTIVE **1** joined as allies; on the same side. **2** of the same kind.

alligator NOUN **alligators** a large reptile of the crocodile family.
[from Spanish *el lagarto* = the lizard]

alliteration NOUN the repetition of the same letter or sound at the beginning of several words, e.g. in *whisper words of wisdom.*
[from *al-* + Latin *littera* = letter]

allocate VERB **allocates, allocating, allocated** allot; set something aside for a particular purpose.
▷ **allocation** *noun*
[from *al-* + Latin *locus* = a place]

allot VERB **allots, allotting, allotted** give portions, jobs, etc. to different people.
[from old French *aloter* = distribute by lot (sense 2)]

allotment NOUN **allotments** **1** a small rented piece of public land used for growing vegetables, fruit, or flowers. **2** allotting; the amount allotted.

allow VERB **allows, allowing, allowed** **1** permit • *Smoking is not allowed.* **2** permit someone to have something; provide with • *She was allowed £10 for books.* **3** agree • *I allow that you have been patient.*
▷ **allowable** *adjective*
[from old French]

allowance NOUN **allowances** an amount of money that is given regularly for a particular purpose.
- **make allowances** be considerate; excuse • *Make allowances for his age.*

alloy NOUN **alloys** a metal formed by mixing two or more metals etc.
[from old French; related to *ally*]

all right ADJECTIVE & ADVERB **1** satisfactory. **2** in good condition. **3** as desired. **4** yes, I consent.

all-round ADJECTIVE general; not specialist • *an all-round athlete.*
▷ **all-rounder** *noun*

allude VERB **alludes, alluding, alluded** mention something briefly or indirectly • *He alluded to his wealth.*
[from Latin]
USAGE Do not confuse with **elude**.

allure VERB **allures, alluring, allured** attract or fascinate someone.
▷ **allure** *noun* **alluring** *adjective*
[from old French; related to *lure*]

allusion NOUN **allusions** a reference made to something without actually naming it.
[same origin as *allude*]

alluvium (*say* a-loo-vee-um) NOUN sand and soil etc. deposited by a river or flood.
▷ **alluvial** *adjective*
[from *al-* + Latin *luere* = to wash]

ally (*say* al-eye) NOUN **allies** **1** a country in alliance with another. **2** a person who cooperates with another.

ally VERB **allies, allying, allied** form an alliance.
[from *al-* + Latin *ligare* = bind]

almanac NOUN **almanacs** an annual publication containing a calendar and other information.
[from Greek]

almighty ADJECTIVE **1** having complete power. **2** (*informal*) very great • *an almighty din.*
- **the Almighty** a name for God.

almond (*say* ah-mond) NOUN **almonds** an oval edible nut.
[from Greek]

almost ADVERB near to being something but not quite • *almost ready.*
[from Old English]

A

alms (*say* ahmz) PLURAL NOUN (*old use*) money and gifts given to the poor.
[from Old English]

almshouse NOUN **almshouses** a house founded by charity for poor people.

aloft ADVERB high up; up in the air.
[from Old Norse]

alone ADJECTIVE & ADVERB without any other people or things; without help.
[from *all one*]

along PREPOSITION following the length of something • *Walk along the path.*

along ADVERB **1** on or onwards • *Push it along.* **2** accompanying somebody • *I've brought my brother along.*
[from Old English]

alongside PREPOSITION & ADVERB next to something; beside.

aloof ADVERB apart; not taking part • *We stayed aloof from their quarrels.*

aloof ADJECTIVE distant and not friendly in manner • *She seemed aloof.*
[from old French]

aloud ADVERB in a voice that can be heard.
[from *a-*[1] + *loud*]

alpha NOUN the first letter of the Greek alphabet, equivalent to Roman *A, a.*

alphabet NOUN **alphabets** the letters used in a language, usually arranged in a set order.
▷ **alphabetical** *adjective*
alphabetically *adverb*
[from *alpha, beta*, the first two letters of the Greek alphabet]

alpine ADJECTIVE to do with high mountains • *alpine plants.*
[from the Alps, mountains in Switzerland]

already ADVERB by now; before now.
[from *all* + *ready*]

Alsatian (*say* al-say-shan) NOUN **Alsatians** a German shepherd dog.
[from *Alsace*, in north-eastern France: the name was adopted during the First World War, when British people disliked anything that was German]

also ADVERB in addition; besides.
[from Old English]

altar NOUN **altars** a table or similar structure used in religious ceremonies.
[via Old English from Latin *altus* = high]
USAGE Do not confuse with the verb **alter**.

alter VERB **alters, altering, altered** make or become different; change.
▷ **alteration** *noun*
[from Latin *alter* = other]
USAGE Do not confuse with the noun **altar**.

altercation (*say* ol-ter-kay-shon) NOUN **altercations** a noisy argument or quarrel.
[from Latin]

alter ego NOUN **alter egos** another, very different, side of someone's personality • *Superman's alter ego, Clark Kent.*
[Latin, = other self]

alternate (*say* ol-tern-at) ADJECTIVE **1** happening or coming one after the other • *alternate layers of sponge and cream.* **2** one in every two • *We meet up on alternate Fridays.*
▷ **alternately** *adverb*
USAGE See the note at **alternative**.

alternate (*say* ol-tern-ayt) VERB **alternates, alternating, alternated** use or come alternately.
▷ **alternation** *noun* **alternator** *noun*
[from Latin *alternus* = every other one, from *alter* = other]

alternating current NOUN **alternating currents** electric current that keeps reversing its direction at regular intervals.

alternative ADJECTIVE available instead of something else.
▷ **alternatively** *adverb*
USAGE Do not confuse **alternative** with **alternate**. If there are *alternative colours* it means that there is a choice of two or more colours, but *alternate colours* means that there is first one colour and then the other.

alternative NOUN **alternatives** one of two or more possibilities.
- **no alternative** no choice.

alternative medicine NOUN types of medical treatment that are not based on ordinary medicine. Acupuncture, homeopathy, and osteopathy are all forms of alternative medicine.

although CONJUNCTION though.
[from *all* + *though*]

altimeter *NOUN* **altimeters** an instrument used in aircraft etc. for showing the height above sea level.
[from Latin *altus* = high, + *meter*]

altitude *NOUN* **altitudes** the height of something, especially above sea level.
[from Latin *altus* = high]

alto *NOUN* **altos 1** an adult male singer with a very high voice. **2** a contralto.
[Italian, = high]

altogether *ADVERB* **1** with all included; in total • *The outfit costs £50 altogether.*
2 completely • *The stream dries up altogether in summer.* **3** on the whole • *Altogether, it was a good concert.*
[from *all* + *together*]
USAGE Do not confuse **altogether** and **all together**.

altruistic (*say* al-troo-**ist**-ik) *ADJECTIVE* unselfish; thinking of other people's welfare.
▷ **altruist** *noun* **altruism** *noun*
[from Italian *altrui* = somebody else]

aluminium *NOUN* a lightweight silver-coloured metal.
[from Latin]

always *ADVERB* **1** at all times. **2** often • *You are always crying.* **3** whatever happens • *You can always sleep on the floor.*
[from Old English]

Alzheimer's disease *NOUN* a serious disease of the brain which affects some old people and makes them confused and forgetful.
[named after a German scientist, A. *Alzheimer*]

a.m. *ABBREVIATION* before noon.
[short for Latin *ante meridiem* = before noon]

amalgam *NOUN* **amalgams 1** an alloy of mercury. **2** a mixture or combination.
[from Latin]

amalgamate *VERB* **amalgamates, amalgamating, amalgamated** mix or combine.
▷ **amalgamation** *noun*
[originally = make an amalgam]

amass *VERB* **amasses, amassing, amassed** heap up; collect.
[from *ad-* + *mass*[1]]

amateur (*say* am-at-er) *NOUN* **amateurs** a person who does something as a hobby, not as a professional.
[from Latin *amator* = lover]

amateurish *ADJECTIVE* not done or made very well; not skilful.

amaze *VERB* **amazes, amazing, amazed** surprise somebody greatly; fill with wonder.
▷ **amazement** *noun*
[from Old English]

amazing *ADJECTIVE* very surprising or remarkable.

ambassador *NOUN* **ambassadors** a person sent to a foreign country to represent his or her own government.
[from old French; related to *embassy*]

amber *NOUN* **1** a hard clear yellowish substance used for making ornaments. **2** a yellow traffic light shown as a signal for caution, placed between red for 'stop' and green for 'go'.
[from Arabic]

ambi- *PREFIX* both; on both sides (as in *ambidextrous*).
[from Latin *ambo* = both]

ambidextrous *ADJECTIVE* able to use either your left hand or your right hand equally well.
[from *ambi-* + *dextrous* = skilful (related to *dexterity*)]

ambient *ADJECTIVE* **1** in the immediately surrounding area • *the ambient temperature.* **2** (of music) quiet and relaxing.
[via French from Latin *ambire* = to go round]

ambiguous *ADJECTIVE* having more than one possible meaning; unclear.
▷ **ambiguously** *adverb* **ambiguity** *noun*
[from Latin *ambiguus* = doubtful, shifting, from *ambi-* + *agere* = drive, go]

ambition *NOUN* **ambitions 1** a strong desire to achieve something. **2** the thing desired.
[from Latin *ambire* = go around, especially to persuade people to vote for you]

ambitious *ADJECTIVE* full of ambition.

ambivalent (*say* am-**biv**-al-ent) *ADJECTIVE* having mixed feelings about something (e.g. both liking and disliking it).
▷ **ambivalence** *noun*
[from *ambi-* + Latin *valens* = strong]

amble *VERB* **ambles, ambling, ambled** walk at a slow easy pace.
[from Latin *ambulare* = walk]

ambrosia (*say* am-**broh**-zee-a) *NOUN* something delicious.
[in Greek mythology, ambrosia was the food of the gods]

ambulance *NOUN* **ambulances** a vehicle equipped to carry sick or injured people.
[from French *hôpital ambulant*, a mobile military hospital; from Latin *ambulare* = walk]

ambush *NOUN* **ambushes** a surprise attack from troops etc. who have concealed themselves.

ambush *VERB* **ambushes, ambushing, ambushed** attack someone after lying in wait for them.
[from old French]

ameliorate (*say* a-**mee**-lee-er-ayt) *VERB* **ameliorates, ameliorating, ameliorated** (*formal*) make or become better; improve.
▷ **amelioration** *noun*
[from *ad-* + Latin *melior* = better]

amen *INTERJECTION* a word used at the end of a prayer or hymn, meaning 'may it be so'.
[Hebrew, = certainly]

amenable (*say* a-**meen**-a-bul) *ADJECTIVE* willing to be guided or controlled by something • *He is not amenable to discipline.*
[from French *amener* = to lead]

amend *VERB* **amends, amending, amended** alter something in order to improve it.
- **make amends** make up for having done something wrong; atone.
▷ **amendment** *noun*
[same origin as *emend*]

amenity (*say* a-**men**-it-ee or a-**meen**-it-ee) *NOUN* **amenities** a pleasant or useful feature of a place • *The town has many amenities, such as a sports centre and a multiplex cinema.*
[from Latin *amoenus* = pleasant]

American *ADJECTIVE* **1** to do with the continent of America. **2** to do with the United States of America.
▷ **American** *noun*

amethyst *NOUN* **amethysts** a purple precious stone.
[from Greek *lithos amethystos* = stone against drunkenness (because people believed that they would not get drunk if there was an amethyst in their drink)]

amiable *ADJECTIVE* friendly and good-tempered.
▷ **amiably** *adverb*
[same origin as *amicable*]

amicable *ADJECTIVE* friendly.
▷ **amicably** *adverb*
[from Latin *amicus* = friend]

amid or **amidst** *PREPOSITION* in the middle of; among.
[from *a-*[1] + *mid*]

amino acid (*say* a-**meen**-oh) *NOUN* **amino acids** an acid found in proteins.
[from *ammonia*, because the amino acids contain the same group of atoms as ammonia]

amiss *ADJECTIVE* wrong or faulty • *She knew something was amiss.*

amiss *ADVERB* wrongly or faultily.
- **take amiss** be offended by • *Don't take what I'm about to say amiss.*
[from Old Norse]

ammonia *NOUN* a colourless gas or liquid with a strong smell.
[from Latin]

ammunition *NOUN* a supply of bullets, shells, grenades, etc. for use in fighting.
[from French *la munition*, wrongly taken as *l'ammunition*]

amnesia (*say* am-**nee**-zee-a) *NOUN* loss of memory.
[from Greek *a-* = without, + *-mnesis* = memory]

amnesty *NOUN* **amnesties** a general pardon for people who have committed a crime.
[from Greek *amnestia* = forgetfulness (because the crimes are legally 'forgotten')]

amoeba (*say* a-**mee**-ba) *NOUN* **amoebas** a microscopic creature consisting of a single cell which constantly changes shape and can split itself in two.
[from Greek *amoibe* = change]

amok *ADVERB* - **run amok** rush about wildly in a violent rage.
[from Malay (a language spoken in Malaysia), = fighting mad]

among or **amongst** *PREPOSITION*
1 surrounded by; in • *There were weeds among the flowers.* **2** between • *Divide the sweets among the children.*
[from Old English *ongemang* = in a crowd]

amoral (*say* ay-moral) *ADJECTIVE* not based on moral standards; neither moral nor immoral.
[from *a-*² + *moral*]

amorous *ADJECTIVE* showing or feeling sexual love • *amorous glances.*
[from Latin *amor* = love]

amorphous (*say* a-mor-fus) *ADJECTIVE* shapeless • *an amorphous mass.*
[from *a-*² + Greek *morphe* = form]

amount *NOUN* **amounts** **1** a quantity. **2** a total.

amount *VERB* **amounts, amounting, amounted**
- **amount to** **1** add up to. **2** be equivalent to • *Their reply amounts to a refusal.*
[from Latin *ad montem* = to the mountain, upwards]

amp *NOUN* **amps** **1** an ampere. **2** (*informal*) an amplifier.

ampere (*say* am-pair) *NOUN* **amperes** a unit for measuring electric current.
[named after the French scientist A. M. *Ampère*]

ampersand *NOUN* **ampersands** the symbol & (= and).
[from the phrase *and per se and* = '& by itself means and' (Latin *per se* = by itself). The symbol '&' was added to the end of the alphabet in children's school books, and when they came to it, pupils reciting the alphabet would say the phrase; they thought it was the name of the symbol]

amphetamine *NOUN* **amphetamines** a drug used as a stimulant.
[from the names of chemicals from which it is made]

amphi- *PREFIX* both; on both sides; in both places (as in *amphibian*).
[from Greek *amphi* = around]

amphibian *NOUN* **amphibians** **1** an animal able to live both on land and in water, such as a frog, toad, newt, and salamander. **2** a vehicle that can move on both land and water.
[from *amphi-* + Greek *bios* = life]

amphibious *ADJECTIVE* able to live or move both on land and in water.

amphitheatre *NOUN* **amphitheatres** an oval or circular unroofed building with tiers of seats round a central arena.
[from Greek *amphi* = all round, + *theatre*]
USAGE This word does not mean 'an ancient theatre'. Greek and Roman theatres were semicircular.

ample *ADJECTIVE* **1** quite enough • *ample provisions.* **2** large.
▷ **amply** *adverb*
[from Latin *amplus* = large, plentiful]

amplifier *NOUN* **amplifiers** a piece of equipment for making a sound or electrical signal louder or stronger.

amplify *VERB* **amplifies, amplifying, amplified** **1** make a sound or electrical signal louder or stronger. **2** give more details about something • *Could you amplify that point?*
▷ **amplification** *noun*
[from Latin *amplificare* = make larger]

amplitude *NOUN* **1** (*in science*) the greatest distance that a wave, especially a sound wave, vibrates. **2** largeness or abundance.
[same origin as *ample*]

amputate *VERB* **amputates, amputating, amputated** cut off an arm or leg by a surgical operation.
▷ **amputation** *noun*
[from Latin *amb-* = around + *putare* cut off, prune]

amuse *VERB* **amuses, amusing, amused** **1** make a person laugh or smile. **2** make time pass pleasantly for someone.
▷ **amusing** *adjective*
[from French *amuser* = distract; related to *muse*]

amusement *NOUN* **amusements** **1** being amused. **2** a way of passing time pleasantly.

amusement arcade *NOUN* **amusement arcades** an indoor area where people can play on automatic game machines.

amusement park *NOUN* **amusement parks** a large outdoor area with fairground rides and other amusements.

an *ADJECTIVE*, SEE **a**.

an-[1] *PREFIX* not; without. SEE **a-**[2].

an-[2] *PREFIX* to; towards. SEE **ad-**.

ana- *PREFIX* up; back (as in *analysis*). [Greek, = up]

anachronism (*say* an-ak-ron-izm) *NOUN* **anachronisms** something wrongly placed in a particular historical period, or regarded as out of date • *Bows and arrows would be an anachronism in modern warfare.* [from *ana-* + Greek *chronos* = time]

anaemia (*say* a-nee-mee-a) *NOUN* a poor condition of the blood that makes a person pale.
▷ **anaemic** *adjective*
[from *an-*[1] + Greek *haima* = blood]

anaesthetic (*say* an-iss-thet-ik) *NOUN* **anaesthetics** a substance or gas that makes you unable to feel pain.
▷ **anaesthesia** *noun*
[from *an-*[1] + Greek *aisthesis* = sensation]

anaesthetist (*say* an-ees-thet-ist) *NOUN* **anaesthetists** a person trained to give anaesthetics.
▷ **anaesthetize** *verb*

anagram *NOUN* **anagrams** a word or phrase made by rearranging the letters of another • *'Strap' is an anagram of 'parts'.* [from *ana-* + Greek *gramma* = letter]

anal (*say* ay-nal) *ADJECTIVE* to do with the anus.

analgesic (*say* an-al-jee-sik) *NOUN* **analgesics** a substance that relieves pain. [from *an-*[1] + Greek *algesis* = pain]

analogy (*say* a-nal-oj-ee) *NOUN* **analogies** a comparison or similarity between two things that are alike in some ways • *the analogy between the human heart and a pump.*
▷ **analogous** *adjective*
[from Greek]

analyse *VERB* **analyses, analysing, analysed** **1** examine and interpret something • *This book analyses the causes of the war.* **2** separate something into its parts.

analysis *NOUN* **analyses** **1** a detailed examination of something. **2** a separation of something into its parts.
▷ **analytic** *adjective* **analytical** *adjective*
[from Greek, = dissolving, loosening]

analyst *NOUN* **analysts** a person who analyses things.

anarchist (*say* an-er-kist) *NOUN* **anarchists** a person who believes that all forms of government are bad and should be abolished.

anarchy (*say* an-er-kee) *NOUN* **1** lack of government or control, resulting in lawlessness. **2** complete disorder. [from *an-*[1] + *-archy*]

anathema *NOUN* something you detest • *All blood sports are anathema to me.* [from Greek]

anatomy (*say* an-at-om-ee) *NOUN* **1** the study of the structure of the bodies of humans or animals. **2** the structure of an animal's body.
▷ **anatomical** *adjective* **anatomist** *noun*
[from *ana-* + Greek *tome* = cutting]

ancestor *NOUN* **ancestors** anyone from whom a person is descended.
▷ **ancestral** *adjective* **ancestry** *noun*
[from Latin, literally = one who goes before]

anchor *NOUN* **anchors** a heavy object joined to a ship by a chain or rope and dropped to the bottom of the sea to stop the ship from moving.

anchor *VERB* **anchors, anchoring, anchored** **1** fix or be fixed by an anchor. **2** fix something firmly. [from Latin]

anchorage *NOUN* **anchorages** a place where a ship can be anchored.

anchovy *NOUN* **anchovies** a small fish with a strong flavour. [from Spanish or Portuguese]

ancient *ADJECTIVE* **1** very old. **2** belonging to the distant past • *ancient history.* [from old French]

ancillary (*say* an-sil-er-ee) *ADJECTIVE* helping or supporting the people who do the main work • *ancillary staff.* [from Latin *ancilla* = servant]

and *CONJUNCTION* **1** together with; in addition to • *We had cakes and buns.* **2** so that; with this result • *Work hard and you will pass.* **3** to • *Go and buy a pen.*
[from Old English]

android *NOUN* **androids** (in science fiction) a robot that looks like a human being.
[from Greek *andros* = man]

anecdote *NOUN* **anecdotes** a short amusing or interesting story about a real person or thing.
[from Greek *anekdota* = things that have not been published]

anemone (*say* a-**nem**-on-ee) *NOUN* **anemones** a plant with cup-shaped red, purple, or white flowers.
[from Greek, = windflower (from the belief that the flower opens when it is windy)]

anew *ADVERB* again; in a new or different way • *We must begin anew.*
[from Old English *of* = from, + *new*]

angel *NOUN* **angels** **1** an attendant or messenger of God. **2** a very kind or beautiful person.
▷ **angelic** (*say* an-**jel**-ik) *adjective*
[from Greek *angelos* = messenger]

angelica *NOUN* a sweet-smelling plant whose crystallized stalks are used in cookery as a decoration.
[from Latin *herba angelica* = angelic plant (because it was believed to cure plague)]

anger *NOUN* a strong feeling that you want to quarrel or fight with someone.

anger *VERB* **angers, angering, angered** make a person angry.
[from Old Norse]

angle *NOUN* **angles** **1** the space between two lines or surfaces that meet; the amount by which a line or surface must be turned to make it lie along another. **2** a point of view.

angle *VERB* **angles, angling, angled** **1** put something in a slanting position. **2** present news etc. from one point of view.
[from Latin *angulus* = corner]

angler *NOUN* **anglers** a person who fishes with a fishing rod and line.
▷ **angling** *noun*
[from Old English *angul* = fishing- hook]

Anglican *ADJECTIVE* to do with the Church of England.
▷ **Anglican** *noun*

Anglo- *PREFIX* English or British • *an Anglo-French agreement.*
[from the *Angles*, a Germanic tribe who came to England in the 5th century and eventually gave their name to it]

Anglo-Saxon *NOUN* **Anglo-Saxons** **1** an English person, especially of the time before the Norman conquest in 1066. **2** the form of English spoken from about 700 to 1150; Old English.
[from Old English *Angulseaxe* = an English Saxon (contrasted with the Old Saxons on the Continent)]

angry *ADJECTIVE* **angrier, angriest** feeling anger.
▷ **angrily** *adverb*

anguish *NOUN* severe suffering or misery.
▷ **anguished** *adjective*
[same origin as *anxious*]

angular *ADJECTIVE* **1** having angles or sharp corners. **2** (said about a person) bony, not plump.

animal *NOUN* **animals** **1** a living thing that can feel and usually move about • *Horses, birds, fish, bees, and people are all animals.* **2** a cruel or uncivilized person.
[from Latin *animalis* = having breath]

animate *VERB* **animates, animating, animated** **1** make a thing lively. **2** produce something as an animated film.
▷ **animator** *noun*

animated *ADJECTIVE* **1** lively and excited. **2** (said about a film) made by photographing a series of still pictures and showing them rapidly one after another, so they appear to move.

animation *NOUN* **1** being lively or excited. **2** the technique of making a film by photographing a series of still pictures.

animosity (*say* an-im-**oss**-it-ee) *NOUN* **animosities** a feeling of hostility.
[originally = courage: from Latin *animus* = spirit]

aniseed *NOUN* a sweet-smelling seed used for flavouring things.
[from Greek *anison* + *seed*]

ankle *NOUN* **ankles** the part of the leg where it joins the foot.
[from Old English; distantly related to *angle*]

annals *PLURAL NOUN* a history of events, especially when written year by year.
[from Latin *annales* = yearly books]

annex *VERB* **annexes, annexing, annexed** **1** take possession of something and add it to what you have already. **2** add or join a thing to something else.
[from *an-*² + Latin *nexum* = tied]

annexe *NOUN* **annexes** a building added to a larger or more important building.
[same origin as *annex*]

annihilate (*say* an-I-il-ayt) *VERB* **annihilates, annihilating, annihilated** destroy something completely.
▷ **annihilation** *noun*
[from *an-*² + Latin *nihil* = nothing]

anniversary *NOUN* **anniversaries** a day when you remember something special that happened on the same day in a previous year.
[from Latin *annus* = year + *versum* = turned]

annotate (*say* an-oh-tayt) *VERB* **annotates, annotating, annotated** add notes of explanation to something written or printed.
▷ **annotation** *noun*
[from *an-*² + Latin *notare* = to note]

announce *VERB* **announces, announcing, announced** make something known, especially by saying it publicly or to an audience.
▷ **announcement** *noun*
[from *an-*² + Latin *nuntius* = messenger]

announcer *NOUN* **announcers** a person who announces items in a broadcast.

annoy *VERB* **annoys, annoying, annoyed** **1** make a person slightly angry. **2** be troublesome to someone.
▷ **annoyance** *noun*
[from Latin *in odio* = hateful]

annual *ADJECTIVE* **1** happening or done once a year • *her annual visit.* **2** calculated over one year • *our annual income.* **3** living for one year or one season • *an annual plant.*
▷ **annually** *adverb*

annual *NOUN* **annuals** **1** a book that comes out once a year. **2** an annual plant.
[from Latin *annus* = year]

annuity (*say* a-new-it-ee) *NOUN* **annuities** a fixed annual allowance of money, especially from a kind of investment.
[same origin as *annual*]

annul *VERB* **annuls, annulling, annulled** cancel a law or contract; end something legally • *Their marriage was annulled.*
▷ **annulment** *noun*
[from *an-*² + Latin *nullus* = none]

anode *NOUN* **anodes** the electrode by which electric current enters a device. (COMPARE **cathode**)
[from *ana-* = up + Greek *hodos* = way]

anoint *VERB* **anoints, anointing, anointed** put oil or ointment on something, especially in a religious ceremony.
[from Latin]

anomaly (*say* an-om-al-ee) *NOUN* **anomalies** something that does not follow the general rule or that is unlike the usual or normal kind.
[from *an-*¹ = not + Greek *homalos* = even]

anon *ADVERB* (*old use*) soon • *I will say more about this anon.*
[from Old English *on ane* = in one, at once]

anon. *ABBREVIATION* anonymous.

anonymous (*say* an-on-im-us) *ADJECTIVE* without the name of the person responsible being known or made public • *an anonymous donation.*
▷ **anonymously** *adverb* **anonymity** (*say* an-on-im-it-ee) *noun*
[from *an-*¹ + Greek *onyma* = name]

anorak *NOUN* **anoraks** a thick warm jacket with a hood.
[from an Inuit word]

anorexia (*say* an-er-eks-ee-a) *NOUN* an illness that makes a person so anxious to lose weight that he or she refuses to eat.
▷ **anorexic** *adjective*
[from *an-*¹ + Greek *orexis* = appetite]

another *ADJECTIVE* & *PRONOUN* a different or extra person or thing • *another day; choose another.*

answer *NOUN* **answers** **1** a reply. **2** the solution to a problem.

answer *VERB* **answers, answering, answered** **1** give or find an answer to; reply. **2** respond to a signal • *Answer the telephone.*
- **answer back** reply cheekily.
- **answer for** be responsible for.
- **answer to** correspond to • *This answers to the description of the stolen bag.*
[from Old English]

answerable *ADJECTIVE* **1** able to be answered. **2** having to be responsible for something.

answering machine *NOUN* **answering machines** a machine that records messages from people who telephone while you are out.

answerphone *NOUN* **answerphones** a telephone answering machine.

ant *NOUN* **ants** a very small insect that lives as one of an organized group.
[from Old English]

ant- *PREFIX* against; preventing. SEE **anti-**.

antagonism (*say* an-tag-on-izm) *NOUN* an unfriendly feeling; hostility.
▷ **antagonist** *noun* **antagonistic** *adjective*
[from *ant-* + Greek *agon* = struggle]

antagonize *VERB* **antagonizes, antagonizing, antagonized** make a person feel hostile or angry.

ante- *PREFIX* before (as in *ante-room*).
[from Latin]

anteater *NOUN* **anteaters** an animal that feeds on ants and termites.

antediluvian (*say* an-tee-dil-oo-vee-an) *ADJECTIVE* **1** belonging to the time before Noah's Flood in the Old Testament. **2** (*informal*) very old or out of date.
[from *ante-* + Latin *diluvium* = deluge]

antelope *NOUN* **antelope** or **antelopes** a fast-running animal like a deer, found in Africa and parts of Asia.
[from Greek]

antenatal (*say* an-tee-nay-tal) *ADJECTIVE* before birth; during pregnancy.

antenna *NOUN* **antennae** **1** a feeler on the head of an insect or crustacean. **antennas** **2** an aerial.
[Latin]

anterior *ADJECTIVE* **1** at or near the front. (The opposite is **posterior**.) **2** earlier.
[Latin, = further forward]

ante-room *NOUN* **ante-rooms** a room leading to a more important room.

anthem *NOUN* **anthems** a religious or patriotic song, usually sung by a choir or group of people.
[from Latin]

anther *NOUN* **anthers** the part of a flower's stamen that contains pollen.
[from Greek *anthos* = flower]

anthill *NOUN* **anthills** a mound over an ants' nest.

anthology *NOUN* **anthologies** a collection of poems, stories, songs, etc. in one book.
[from Greek *anthos* = flower + *-logia* = collection]

anthracite *NOUN* a kind of hard coal.
[from Greek *anthrax* = coal, carbuncle]

anthrax *NOUN* a disease of sheep and cattle that can also infect people.
[same origin as *anthracite* (because of the carbuncles that the disease causes)]

anthropoid *ADJECTIVE* like a human being • *Gorillas are anthropoid apes.*
[from Greek *anthropos* = human being]

anthropology *NOUN* the study of human beings and their customs.
▷ **anthropological** *adjective* **anthropologist** *noun*
[from Greek *anthropos* = human being, + *-logy*]

anti- *PREFIX* (changing to **ant-** before a vowel) against; preventing (as in *antifreeze*).
[from Greek *anti* = against]

anti-aircraft *ADJECTIVE* used against enemy aircraft.

antibiotic *NOUN* **antibiotics** a substance (e.g. penicillin) that destroys bacteria or prevents them from growing.
[from *anti-* + Greek *bios* = life]

antibody *NOUN* **antibodies** a protein that forms in the blood as a defence against certain substances which it then attacks and destroys.
[from *anti-* + *body* (sense 5)]

A

anticipate *VERB* **anticipates, anticipating, anticipated** **1** take action in advance about something you are aware of • *A good teacher learns to anticipate what students will ask.* **2** act before someone else does • *Others may have anticipated Columbus in discovering America.* **3** expect • *We anticipate that it will rain.*
▷ **anticipation** *noun* **anticipatory** *adjective*
[from *ante-* + Latin *capere* = take]
USAGE Many people regard use **3** as incorrect; it is better to avoid it and use 'expect'.

anticlimax *NOUN* **anticlimaxes** a disappointing ending or result where something exciting had been expected.

anticlockwise *ADVERB* & *ADJECTIVE* moving in the direction opposite to clockwise.

antics *PLURAL NOUN* funny or foolish actions.
[from *antic* = strange, grotesque, from Italian *antico* = ancient, antique]

anticyclone *NOUN* **anticyclones** an area where air pressure is high, usually producing fine settled weather.
[from *anti-* + *cyclone*, because the pressure at the centre of a cyclone is low]

antidote *NOUN* **antidotes** something that acts against the effects of a poison or disease.
[from *anti-* + Greek *dotos* = given]

antifreeze *NOUN* a liquid added to water to make it less likely to freeze.

antihistamine *NOUN* **antihistamines** a drug that protects people against unpleasant effects when they are allergic to something.
[from *anti-* + *histamine*, a substance in the body which is released when someone meets whatever they are allergic to, and which causes the unpleasant effects]

antimony *NOUN* a brittle silvery metal.
[from Latin]

antipathy (*say* an-**tip**-ath-ee) *NOUN* a strong dislike.
[from *anti-* + Greek *pathos* = feeling]

antipodes (*say* an-**tip**-od-eez) *PLURAL NOUN* places on opposite sides of the earth.
- **the Antipodes** Australia, New Zealand, and the areas near them, which are almost exactly opposite Europe.
▷ **antipodean** *adjective*
[from Greek, = having the feet opposite (*podes* = feet)]

antiquarian (*say* anti-**kwair**-ee-an) *ADJECTIVE* to do with the study of antiques.

antiquated *ADJECTIVE* old-fashioned.

antique (*say* an-**teek**) *ADJECTIVE* very old; belonging to the distant past.

antique *NOUN* **antiques** something that is valuable because it is very old.
[from Latin *antiquus* = ancient, from *ante* = before]

antiquities *PLURAL NOUN* objects that were made in ancient times.

antiquity (*say* an-**tik**-wit-ee) *NOUN* ancient times.

anti-Semitic (*say* anti-sim-**it**-ik) *ADJECTIVE* hostile or prejudiced towards Jews.
▷ **anti-Semitism** (*say* anti-**sem**-it-izm) *noun*

antiseptic *ADJECTIVE* **1** able to destroy bacteria, especially those that cause things to become septic or to decay. **2** thoroughly clean and free from germs.

antiseptic *NOUN* **antiseptics** a substance with an antiseptic effect.

antisocial *ADJECTIVE* unfriendly or inconsiderate towards other people.

antistatic *ADJECTIVE* counteracting the effects of static electricity.

antithesis (*say* an-**tith**-iss-iss) *NOUN* **antitheses** **1** the exact opposite of something • *Slavery is the antithesis of freedom.* **2** a contrast of ideas.
[from *anti-* + Greek *thesis* = placing]

antitoxin *NOUN* **antitoxins** a substance that neutralizes a toxin and prevents it from having a harmful effect.
▷ **antitoxic** *adjective*

antivivisectionist *NOUN* **antivivisectionists** a person who is opposed to making experiments on live animals.

antler *NOUN* **antlers** the branching horn of a deer.
[from old French]

antonym (*say* ant-on-im) *NOUN* **antonyms** a word that is opposite in meaning to another • *'Soft' is an antonym of 'hard'.*
[from *ant-* + Greek *onyma* = name]

anus (*say* ay-nus) *NOUN* **anuses** the opening at the lower end of the alimentary canal, through which solid waste matter is passed out of the body.
[Latin]

anvil *NOUN* **anvils** a large block of iron on which a blacksmith hammers metal into shape.
[from Old English *an* = on + *filt-* = beat]

anxious *ADJECTIVE* **1** worried. **2** eager • *She is anxious to please us.*
▷ **anxiously** *adverb* **anxiety** *noun*
[from Latin *angere* = choke, squeeze, oppress]

any *ADJECTIVE* & *PRONOUN* **1** one or some • *Have you any wool? There isn't any.* **2** no matter which • *Come any day you like.* **3** every • *Any fool knows that!*

any *ADVERB* at all; in some degree • *Is that any better?*
[from Old English]

anybody *NOUN* & *PRONOUN* any person.

anyhow *ADVERB* **1** anyway. **2** (*informal*) carelessly • *He does his work anyhow.*

anyone *NOUN* & *PRONOUN* anybody.

anything *NOUN* & *PRONOUN* any thing.

anyway *ADVERB* whatever happens; whatever the situation may be.

anywhere *ADVERB* in or to any place.

anywhere *PRONOUN* any place • *Anywhere will do.*

Anzac *NOUN* **Anzacs** a soldier in the Australian and New Zealand Army Corps.
[from the initial letters of the name of the Corps]

aorta (*say* ay-or-ta) *NOUN* **aortas** the main artery that carries blood away from the left side of the heart.
[from Greek]

ap-[1] *PREFIX* to; towards. SEE **ad-**.

ap-[2] *PREFIX* from; out or away. SEE **apo-**.

apace *ADVERB* quickly.
[from French *à pas* = step by step]

apart *ADVERB* **1** away from each other; separately • *Keep your desks apart.* **2** into pieces • *It fell apart.* **3** excluded • *Joking apart, what do you think of it?*
- **apart from** excluding, other than.
[from French *à* = to + *part* = side]

apartheid (*say* a-part-hayt) *NOUN* the political policy that used to be practised in South Africa, of keeping people of different races apart.
[Afrikaans, = being apart]

apartment *NOUN* **apartments** **1** a set of rooms. **2** (*American*) a flat.
[from Italian *appartare* = to separate]

apathy (*say* ap-ath-ee) *NOUN* not having much interest in or caring about something.
▷ **apathetic** (*say* ap-a-thet-ik) *adjective*
[from *a-*[2] + Greek *pathos* = feeling]

ape *NOUN* **apes** any of the four kinds of monkey (gorillas, chimpanzees, orang-utans, gibbons) that do not have a tail.

ape *VERB* **apes**, **aping**, **aped** imitate or mimic.
[from Old English]

aperitif (*say* a-perri-teef) *NOUN* **aperitifs** an alcoholic drink taken before a meal to stimulate the appetite.
[French]

aperture *NOUN* **apertures** an opening.
[from Latin *aperire* = to open]

apex (*say* ay-peks) *NOUN* **apexes** the tip or highest point.
[Latin]

aphid (*say* ay-fid) *NOUN* **aphids** a tiny insect (e.g. a greenfly) that sucks the juices from plants.
[from *aphis*]

aphis (*say* ay-fiss) *NOUN* **aphides** (*say* ay-fid-eez) an aphid.
[Latin]

aphorism (*say* af-er-izm) *NOUN* **aphorisms** a short witty saying.
[from Greek *aphorizein* = define, limit]

A B C D E F G H I J K L M N O P Q R S T U V W X Y Z

apiary (*say* ay-pee-er-ee) *NOUN* **apiaries** a place with a number of hives where bees are kept.
▷ **apiarist** *noun*
[from Latin *apis* = bee]

apiece *ADVERB* to, for, or by each • *They cost five pence apiece.*
[from *a piece*]

aplomb (*say* a-**plom**) *NOUN* dignity and confidence • *She handled the press conference with aplomb.*
[from French = straight as a plumb line]

apo- *PREFIX* (changing to **ap-** before a vowel or *h*) from; out or away (as in *Apostle*).
[from Greek *apo* = away from]

apocryphal (*say* a-**pok**-rif-al) *ADJECTIVE* not likely to be true; invented • *This account of his travels is apocryphal.*
[from the *Apocrypha*, books of the Old Testament that were not accepted by the Jews as part of the Hebrew Scriptures]

apologetic *ADJECTIVE* making an apology.
▷ **apologetically** *adverb*

apologize *VERB* **apologizes, apologizing, apologized** make an apology.

apology *NOUN* **apologies 1** a statement saying that you are sorry for having done something wrong or badly. **2** something very poor • *this feeble apology for a meal.*
[from Greek *apologia* = a speech in your own defence]

apoplexy (*say* **ap**-op-lek-see) *NOUN*
1 sudden loss of the ability to feel and move, caused by the blocking or breaking of a blood vessel in the brain. **2** (*informal*) rage or anger.
▷ **apoplectic** *adjective*
[from Greek, = a stroke]

Apostle *NOUN* **Apostles** any of the twelve men sent out by Christ to preach the Gospel.
[from Greek *apostellein* = send out]

apostrophe (*say* a-**poss**-trof-ee) *NOUN* **apostrophes** the punctuation mark ' used to show that letters have been missed out (as in *I can't* = I cannot) or to show possession (as in *the boy's book; the boys' books*).
[from *apo-* + Greek *strophe* = turning]

apothecary (*say* a-**poth**-ik-er-ee) *NOUN* **apothecaries** (*old use*) a chemist who prepares medicines.
[from Latin *apothecarius* = storekeeper]

appal *VERB* **appals, appalling, appalled** fill a person with horror; shock somebody very much.
[from Old French *apalir* = become pale]

appalling *ADJECTIVE* shocking; very unpleasant.

apparatus *NOUN* the equipment for a particular experiment or job etc.
[from Latin *apparare* = prepare, get ready]

apparel *NOUN* (*formal*) clothing.
[from old French]

apparent *ADJECTIVE* **1** clear or obvious • *His embarrassment was apparent to everyone.* **2** seeming; appearing to be true but not really so • *I could not understand her apparent indifference.*
▷ **apparently** *adverb*
[same origin as *appear*]

apparition *NOUN* **apparitions 1** a ghost. **2** something strange or surprising that appears.
[same origin as *appear*]

appeal *VERB* **appeals, appealing, appealed 1** ask for something that you badly need • *They appealed for funds.* **2** ask for a decision to be changed • *He appealed against the prison sentence.* **3** seem attractive or interesting • *Golf doesn't appeal to me.*

appeal *NOUN* **appeals 1** asking for something you badly need. **2** asking for a decision to be changed. **3** attraction or interest.
[from old French]

appear *VERB* **appears, appearing, appeared 1** come into sight; begin to exist. **2** seem. **3** take part in a play, film, or show etc.
[from *ap-*[1] + Latin *parere* = come into]

appearance *NOUN* **appearances**
1 appearing. **2** what somebody looks like; what something appears to be.

appease *VERB* **appeases, appeasing, appeased** calm or pacify someone, especially by giving in to demands.
▷ **appeasement** *noun*
[from French *à* = to + *paix* = peace]

append *VERB* **appends, appending, appended** add at the end; attach.
[from *ap-*[1] + Latin *pendere* = hang]

appendage *NOUN* **appendages** something added or attached; a thing that forms a natural part of something larger.

appendicitis *NOUN* inflammation of the appendix.

appendix *NOUN* **appendixes 1** a small tube leading off from the intestine. **appendices 2** a section added at the end of a book.
[same origin as *append*]

appetite *NOUN* **appetites 1** desire for food. **2** an enthusiasm for something • *an appetite for violent films.*
[from *ap-*[1] + Latin *petere* = seek]

appetizer *NOUN* **appetizers** a small amount of food eaten before the main meal.

appetizing *ADJECTIVE* (said about food) looking and smelling good to eat.

applaud *VERB* **applauds, applauding, applauded** show that you like something, especially by clapping your hands.
[from *ap-*[1] + Latin *plaudere* = clap hands]

applause *NOUN* clapping.

apple *NOUN* **apples** a round fruit with a red, yellow, or green skin.
- **the apple of your eye** a person or thing that you love and are proud of.
[from Old English]

appliance *NOUN* **appliances** a device or piece of equipment • *electrical appliances.*
[from *apply*]

applicable (*say* ap-lik-a-bul) *ADJECTIVE* able to be applied; suitable or relevant.

applicant *NOUN* **applicants** a person who applies for a job or position.

application *NOUN* **applications 1** the action of applying. **2** a formal request. **3** the ability to apply yourself. **4** (*in computing*) a program or piece of software designed for a particular purpose.

applied *ADJECTIVE* put to practical use • *applied maths.*

appliqué (*say* a-plee-kay) *NOUN* needlework in which cut-out pieces of material are sewn or fixed decoratively on another piece.
[French, = put on]

apply *VERB* **applies, applying, applied 1** put one thing on another. **2** start using something. **3** make a formal request • *apply for a job.* **4** concern; be relevant • *This rule does not apply to you.*
- **apply yourself** give all your attention to a job; work diligently.
[from *ap-*[1] + Latin *plicare* = to fold]

appoint *VERB* **appoints, appointing, appointed 1** choose a person for a job. **2** arrange something officially • *They appointed a time for the meeting.*
[from old French]

appointment *NOUN* **appointments 1** an arrangement to meet or visit somebody at a particular time. **2** choosing somebody for a job. **3** a job or position.

apportion *VERB* **apportions, apportioning, apportioned** divide something into shares; allot.
[from old French]

apposite (*say* ap-o-zit) *ADJECTIVE* (said about a remark) suitable or relevant.
[from Latin *appositus* = applied]

apposition *NOUN* placing things together, especially nouns and phrases in a grammatical relationship. In *the reign of Elizabeth, our Queen*, 'our Queen' is in apposition to 'Elizabeth'.
[from Latin]

appraise *VERB* **appraises, appraising, appraised** estimate the value or quality of a person or thing.
▷ **appraisal** *noun*
[from old French; related to *price*]

appreciable *ADJECTIVE* enough to be noticed or felt; perceptible.
▷ **appreciably** *adverb*

appreciate *VERB* **appreciates, appreciating, appreciated 1** enjoy or value something. **2** understand. **3** increase in value.
▷ **appreciation** *noun* **appreciative** *adjective*
[from *ap-*[1] + Latin *pretium* = price]

A

apprehend *VERB* **apprehends, apprehending, apprehended** 1 seize or arrest someone. 2 understand.
[from *ap-*[1] + Latin *prehendere* = to grasp]

apprehension *NOUN* 1 fear or worry. 2 understanding. 3 the arrest of a person.

apprehensive *ADJECTIVE* anxious or worried.

apprentice *NOUN* **apprentices** a person who is learning a trade or craft by a legal agreement with an employer.
▷ **apprenticeship** *noun*

apprentice *VERB* **apprentices, apprenticing, apprenticed** place a person as an apprentice.
[from French *apprendre* = learn]

approach *VERB* **approaches, approaching, approached** 1 come near. 2 go to someone with a request or offer • *They approached me for help.* 3 set about doing something or tackling a problem.

approach *NOUN* **approaches** 1 approaching. 2 a way or road.
[from old French]

approachable *ADJECTIVE* friendly and easy to talk to.

approbation *NOUN* approval.
[same origin as *approve*]

appropriate (*say* a-**proh**-pree-at) *ADJECTIVE* suitable.
▷ **appropriately** *adverb*

appropriate (*say* a-**proh**-pree-ayt) *VERB* **appropriates, appropriating, appropriated** take something and use it as your own.
▷ **appropriation** *noun*
[from Latin]

approval *NOUN* approving somebody or something.
- **on approval** received by a customer to examine before deciding to buy.

approve *VERB* **approves, approving, approved** 1 say or think that a person or thing is good or suitable. 2 agree formally to something • *The committee has approved the expenditure.*
[from *ap-*[1] + Latin *probus* = good]

approximate (*say* a-**proks**-im-at) *ADJECTIVE* almost exact or correct but not completely so.
▷ **approximately** *adverb*

approximate (*say* a-**proks**-im-ayt) *VERB* **approximates, approximating, approximated** make or be almost the same as something.
▷ **approximation** *noun*
[from *ap-*[1] + Latin *proximus* = very near]

apricot *NOUN* **apricots** a juicy orange-coloured fruit with a stone in it.
[from Spanish or Portuguese]

April *NOUN* the fourth month of the year.
[Latin *Aprilis*]

apron *NOUN* **aprons** 1 a piece of clothing worn over the front of the body, especially to protect other clothes. 2 a hard-surfaced area on an airfield where aircraft are loaded and unloaded.
[originally *a naperon*, from French *nappe* = tablecloth]

apron stage *NOUN* **apron stages** a part of a theatre stage in front of the curtain.

apropos (*say* ap-rop-**oh**) *ADVERB* concerning • *Apropos of money, where's that £10 you owe me?*
[from French *à propos* = to the purpose]

apse *NOUN* **apses** a domed semicircular part at the east end of a church.
[from Greek *apsis* = arch, vault, wheel]

apt *ADJECTIVE* 1 likely • *He is apt to be careless.* 2 suitable • *an apt quotation.*
▷ **aptly** *adverb* **aptness** *noun*
[from Latin *aptus* = fitted]

aptitude *NOUN* a talent or skill • *an aptitude for languages.*

aqualung *NOUN* **aqualungs** a diver's portable breathing apparatus, with cylinders of compressed air connected to a face mask.
[from Latin *aqua* = water, + *lung*]

aquamarine *NOUN* **aquamarines** a bluish-green precious stone.
[from Latin *aqua marina* = sea water]

aquarium *NOUN* **aquariums** a tank or building in which live fish and other water animals are displayed.
[from Latin *aquarius* = of water]

aquatic *ADJECTIVE* to do with water • *aquatic sports.*
[from Latin *aqua* = water]

aquatint *NOUN* **aquatints** an etching made on copper by using nitric acid.
[from Italian]

aqueduct *NOUN* **aqueducts** a bridge carrying a water channel across low ground or a valley.
[from Latin *aqua* = water + *ducere* = to lead]

aquiline (*say* ak-wil-I'n) *ADJECTIVE* hooked like an eagle's beak • *an aquiline nose.*
[from Latin *aquila* = eagle]

ar- *PREFIX* to; towards. SEE **ad-**.

Arab *NOUN* **Arabs** a member of a Semitic people living in parts of the Middle East and North Africa.
▷ **Arabian** *adjective*

arabesque (*say* a-rab-esk) *NOUN* **arabesques 1** (in dancing) a position with one leg stretched backwards in the air. **2** an ornamental design of leaves and branches.
[French, = Arabian (because the leaf and branch designs were first used in Arabic art)]

Arabic *ADJECTIVE* to do with the Arabs or their language.

Arabic *NOUN* the language of the Arabs.

arabic numerals *PLURAL NOUN* the figures 1, 2, 3, 4, etc. (COMPARE **Roman numerals**)

arable *ADJECTIVE* suitable for ploughing or growing crops on • *arable land.*
[from Latin *arare* = to plough]

arachnid (*say* a-rak-nid) *NOUN* **arachnids** a member of the group of animals that includes spiders and scorpions.
[from Greek *arachne* = spider]

arbiter *NOUN* **arbiters** a person who has the power to decide what shall be done or used etc.
[Latin, = judge, supreme ruler]

arbitrary (*say* ar-bit-rer-ee) *ADJECTIVE* chosen or done on an impulse, not according to a rule or law • *an arbitrary decision.*
▷ **arbitrarily** *adverb*
[originally = according to an arbiter's decision, not according to rules]

arbitration *NOUN* settling a dispute by calling in someone from outside to make a decision.
▷ **arbitrate** *verb* **arbitrator** *noun*
[from Latin *arbitrari* = to judge]

arboreal (*say* ar-bor-ee-al) *ADJECTIVE* to do with trees; living in trees.
[from Latin *arbor* = tree]

arboretum (*say* ar-ber-ee-tum) *NOUN* **arboretums** or **arboreta** a place where trees are grown for study and display.
[from Latin *arbor* = tree]

arbour (*say* ar-ber) *NOUN* **arbours** a shady place among trees.
[from Latin *arbor* = tree]

arc *NOUN* **arcs 1** a curve; part of the circumference of a circle. **2** a luminous electric current passing between two electrodes.
[from Latin *arcus* = a bow or curve]

arcade *NOUN* **arcades** a covered passage or area, especially for shopping.
[French or Italian, from Latin *arcus* = curve (because early arcades had curved roofs)]

arcane *ADJECTIVE* secret or mysterious.
[from Latin *arcere* = to shut up, from *arca* = box]

arch¹ *NOUN* **arches 1** a curved structure that helps to support a bridge or other building etc. **2** something shaped like this.

arch *VERB* **arches, arching, arched** form something into an arch; curve • *The cat arched its back and hissed.*
[same origin as *arc*]

arch² *ADJECTIVE* pretending to be playful; mischievous • *an arch smile.*
▷ **archly** *adverb*
[from Greek *archos* = a chief]

arch- *PREFIX* chief or principal (as in *arch-enemy*).

-arch or **-archy** *SUFFIXES* form nouns meaning 'ruler' or 'rule, ruling' (e.g. *monarch, monarchy*).
[from Greek *archein* = to rule]

A

archaeology (*say* ar-kee-**ol**-oj-ee) NOUN the study of ancient civilizations by digging for the remains of their buildings, tools, etc. and examining them.
▷ **archaeological** *adjective*
archaeologist *noun*
[from Greek *archaios* = old, + *-logy*]

archaic (*say* ar-**kay**-ik) ADJECTIVE belonging to former or ancient times.
[from Greek *arche* = beginning]

archangel NOUN **archangels** an angel of the highest rank.

archbishop NOUN **archbishops** the chief bishop of a region.

archdeacon NOUN **archdeacons** a senior priest ranking next below a bishop.

arch-enemy NOUN **arch-enemies** the chief enemy.

archer NOUN **archers** a person who shoots with a bow and arrows.
[from Latin *arcus* = a bow or curve]

archery NOUN the sport of shooting at a target with a bow and arrows.

archetype (*say* **ark**-i-typ) NOUN **archetypes** 1 the original form or model from which others are copied. 2 a typical example of something.
[from *arch-* + *type*]

archipelago (*say* ark-i-**pel**-ag-oh) NOUN **archipelagos** a large group of islands, or the sea containing these.
[from *arch-* + Greek *pelagos* = sea]

architect (*say* **ark**-i-tekt) NOUN **architects** a person who designs buildings.
[from *arch-* + Greek *tekton* = builder]

architecture NOUN 1 the process of designing buildings. 2 a particular style of building • *Elizabethan architecture.*
▷ **architectural** *adjective*

archive NOUN (*in computing*) copies of a computer's files that are put on disk or on tape in a compressed form for long-term storage
▷ **archive** *verb*

archives (*say* **ark**-I'vz) PLURAL NOUN the historical documents etc. of an organization or community.
[from Greek *archeia* = public records]

archivist (*say* **ar**-kiv-ist) NOUN **archivists** a person trained to deal with archives.

archway NOUN **archways** an arched passage or entrance.

-archy SUFFIX , SEE **-arch**.

arc lamp or **arc light** NOUN **arc lamps, arc lights** a light using an electric arc.

arctic ADJECTIVE very cold • *The weather was arctic.*
[from the Arctic, the area round the North Pole]

ardent ADJECTIVE enthusiastic or passionate.
▷ **ardently** *adverb*
[from Latin *ardens* = burning]

ardour (*say* **ar**-der) NOUN enthusiasm or passion.
[from old French; related to *ardent*]

arduous ADJECTIVE needing much effort; laborious.
▷ **arduously** *adverb*
[from Latin *arduus* = steep]

area NOUN **areas** 1 the extent or measurement of a surface; the amount of space a surface covers • *The area of the room is 20 square metres.* 2 a particular region or piece of land. 3 a subject or activity.
[Latin, = piece of ground]

arena (*say* a-**reen**-a) NOUN **arenas** the level area in the centre of an amphitheatre or sports stadium.
[Latin, = sand (because the floors of Roman arenas were covered with sand)]

aren't (*mainly spoken*) are not.
- **aren't I?** (*informal*) am I not?

arguable ADJECTIVE 1 able to be stated as a possibility. 2 open to doubt; not certain.
▷ **arguably** *adverb*

argue VERB **argues, arguing, argued** 1 say that you disagree; exchange angry comments. 2 state that something is true and give reasons.
[from Latin]

argument NOUN **arguments** 1 a disagreement or quarrel. 2 a reason or series of reasons put forward.

argumentative ADJECTIVE fond of arguing.

aria (*say* **ar**-ee-a) NOUN **arias** a solo in an opera or oratorio.
[Italian; related to *air*]

B C D E F G H I J K L M N O P Q R S T U V W X Y Z

-arian *SUFFIX* forms nouns and adjectives (e.g. *vegetarian*) showing members of a group.
[from Latin]

arid *ADJECTIVE* dry and barren.
[from Latin]

arise *VERB* **arises, arising, arose, arisen** **1** come into existence; come to people's notice • *Problems arose.* **2** (*old use*) rise; stand up • *Arise, Sir Francis.*
[from Old English]

aristocracy (*say* a-ris-**tok**-ra-see) *NOUN* people of the highest social rank; members of the nobility.
[from Greek *aristos* = best, + *-cracy*]

aristocrat (*say* a-ris-tok-rat) *NOUN* **aristocrats** a member of the aristocracy.
▷ **aristocratic** *adjective*

arithmetic *NOUN* the science or study of numbers; calculating with numbers.
▷ **arithmetical** *adjective*
[from Greek *arithmos* = number]

ark *NOUN* **arks** **1** (in the Bible) the ship in which Noah and his family escaped the Flood. **2** a wooden box in which the writings of the Jewish Law were kept.
[from Latin *arca* = box]

arm[1] *NOUN* **arms** **1** either of the two upper limbs of the body, between the shoulder and the hand. **2** a sleeve. **3** something shaped like an arm or jutting out from a main part. **4** the raised side part of a chair.
▷ **armful** *noun*
[Old English]

arm[2] *VERB* **arms, arming, armed** **1** supply someone with weapons. **2** prepare for war.
▷ **armed** *adjective*
[from Latin *arma* = weapons]

armada (*say* ar-**mah**-da) *NOUN* **armadas** a fleet of warships.
- **the Armada** or **Spanish Armada** the warships sent by Spain to invade England in 1588.
[Spanish, = navy, from Latin *armata* = armed]

armadillo *NOUN* **armadillos** a small burrowing South American animal whose body is covered with a shell of bony plates.
[Spanish, = little armed man]

armaments *PLURAL NOUN* the weapons of an army etc.
[from Latin *arma* = weapons]

armature *NOUN* **armatures** the current-carrying part of a dynamo or electric motor.
[from Latin]

armchair *NOUN* **armchairs** a chair with arms.

armed forces or **armed services** *PLURAL NOUN* a country's army, navy, and air force.

armistice *NOUN* **armistices** an agreement to stop fighting in a war or battle.
[from Latin *arma* = weapons + *sistere* = stop]

armour *NOUN* **1** a protective covering for the body, formerly worn in fighting. **2** a metal covering on a warship, tank, or car to protect it from missiles.
▷ **armoured** *adjective*
[same origin as *arm*[2]]

armoury *NOUN* **armouries** a place where weapons and ammunition are stored.

armpit *NOUN* **armpits** the hollow underneath the top of the arm, below the shoulder.

arms *PLURAL NOUN* **1** weapons. **2** a coat of arms.
- **up in arms** protesting vigorously.
[same origin as *arm*[2]]

arms race *NOUN* competition between nations in building up supplies of weapons, especially nuclear weapons.

army *NOUN* **armies** **1** a large number of people trained to fight on land. **2** a large group.
[via old French *armée* from Latin *armata* = armed]

aroma (*say* a-**roh**-ma) *NOUN* **aromas** a smell, especially a pleasant one.
▷ **aromatic** (*say* a-ro-**mat**-ik) *adjective*
[from Greek *aroma* = spice]

aromatherapy *NOUN* the use of aromatic oils obtained from plants to make you feel less pain or stress and become more relaxed.
[from Greek *aroma* = spice]

around *ADVERB* & *PREPOSITION* all round; about.
[from *a-*[1] + *round*]

A

arouse *VERB* **arouses, arousing, aroused** **1** stir up a feeling in someone • *You've aroused my curiosity.* **2** wake someone up.
[from *a-*[1] + *rouse*]

arpeggio (*say* ar-pej-ee-oh) *NOUN* **arpeggios** (*in music*) the notes of a chord played one after the other instead of together.
[from Italian *arpa* = harp]

arrange *VERB* **arranges, arranging, arranged** **1** put things into a certain order; adjust. **2** form plans for something • *We arranged to be there.* **3** prepare music for a particular purpose.
▷ **arrangement** *noun*
[from old French; related to *range*]

arrant *ADJECTIVE* thorough and obvious • *Arrant nonsense!*
[a different spelling of *errant*]

array *NOUN* **arrays** **1** a display. **2** an orderly arrangement.

array *VERB* **arrays, arraying, arrayed** **1** arrange in order. **2** dress or clothe.
[from *ar-* + old form of *ready*]

arrears *PLURAL NOUN* **1** money that is owing and ought to have been paid earlier. **2** a backlog of work etc.
- **in arrears** behind with payments.
[from *ar-* + Latin *retro* = backwards, behind]

arrest *VERB* **arrests, arresting, arrested** **1** seize a person by authority of the law. **2** stop or check a process or movement.

arrest *NOUN* **arrests** **1** arresting somebody • *The police made several arrests.* **2** stopping something.
[from old French]

arrive *VERB* **arrives, arriving, arrived** **1** reach the end of a journey or a point on it. **2** come to a decision or agreement. **3** come • *The great day arrived.*
▷ **arrival** *noun*
[from *ar-* + Latin *ripa* = shore]

arrogant *ADJECTIVE* behaving in an unpleasantly proud way because you think you are superior to other people.
▷ **arrogantly** *adverb* **arrogance** *noun*
[from Latin *arrogare* = claim, demand]

arrow *NOUN* **arrows** **1** a pointed stick to be shot from a bow. **2** a sign with an outward-pointing V at the end, used to show direction or position.
▷ **arrowhead** *noun*
[from Old Norse]

arsenal *NOUN* **arsenals** a place where weapons and ammunition are stored or manufactured.
[from Arabic *dar-sinaa* = workshop]

arsenic *NOUN* a very poisonous metallic substance.
[originally the name of arsenic sulphide, which is yellow; from Persian *zar* = gold]

arson *NOUN* the crime of deliberately setting fire to a house or building.
▷ **arsonist** *noun*
[from Latin *ardere* = burn]

art *NOUN* **arts** **1** producing something beautiful, especially by painting, drawing, or sculpture; things produced in this way. **2** a skill • *the art of sailing.*
[from Latin]

artefact *NOUN* **artefacts** an object made by humans, especially one from the past that is studied by archaeologists.
[from Latin *arte* = by art + *factum* = made]

artery *NOUN* **arteries** **1** one of the tubes that carry blood away from the heart to all parts of the body. (COMPARE **vein**) **2** an important road or route.
▷ **arterial** (*say* ar-teer-ee-al) *adjective*
[from Latin]

artesian well *NOUN* **artesian wells** a well that is bored straight down into a place where water will rise easily to the surface.
[French *artésien* = of Artois, a region of France where wells of this type were first made]

artful *ADJECTIVE* crafty.
▷ **artfully** *adverb*

arthritis (*say* arth-ry-tiss) *NOUN* a disease that makes joints in the body stiff and painful.
▷ **arthritic** (*say* arth-rit-ik) *adjective*
[from Greek *arthron* = joint]

arthropod *NOUN* **arthropods** an animal of the group that includes insects, spiders, crabs, and centipedes.
[from Greek *arthron* = joint + *podes* = feet (because arthropods have jointed limbs)]

artichoke *NOUN* **artichokes** a kind of plant with a flower head used as a vegetable.
[from Arabic]

article *NOUN* **articles** **1** a piece of writing published in a newspaper or magazine. **2** an object.
- **definite article** the word 'the'.
- **indefinite article** the word 'a' or 'an'.
[same origin as *articulate*]

articulate (*say* ar-tik-yoo-lat) *ADJECTIVE* able to express things clearly and fluently.

articulate (*say* ar-tik-yoo-layt) *VERB* **articulates, articulating, articulated**
1 say or speak clearly. **2** connect by a joint.
▷ **articulation** *noun*
[from Latin *artus* = joint]

articulated *ADJECTIVE* (said about a vehicle) in two sections that are connected by a flexible joint • *an articulated lorry.*

artifice *NOUN* **artifices** a piece of trickery; a clever device.
[same origin as *artificial*]

artificial *ADJECTIVE* not natural; made by human beings in imitation of a natural thing.
▷ **artificially** *adverb* **artificiality** *noun*
[from Latin *ars* = art + *facere* = make]

artificial intelligence *NOUN* the use of computers to perform tasks normally requiring human intelligence, e.g. decision-making.

artificial respiration *NOUN* helping somebody to start breathing again after their breathing has stopped.

artillery *NOUN* **1** large guns. **2** the part of the army that uses large guns.
[from old French]

artisan (*say* art-iz-an) *NOUN* **artisans** a skilled worker.
[from Italian; related to *art*]

artist *NOUN* **artists** **1** a person who produces works of art, especially a painter. **2** an entertainer.
▷ **artistry** *noun*

artistic *ADJECTIVE* **1** to do with art or artists. **2** having a talent for art.
▷ **artistically** *adverb*

artless *ADJECTIVE* simple and natural; not artful.
▷ **artlessly** *adverb*

arts *PLURAL NOUN* subjects (e.g. languages, literature, history) in which opinion and understanding are very important, as opposed to sciences where measurements and calculations are used.
- **the arts** painting, music, and writing etc., considered together.

-ary *SUFFIX* to do with; of that kind: forms adjectives (e.g. *contrary*, *primary*) or nouns (e.g. *dictionary*, *January*).
[from Latin]

as *ADVERB* equally or similarly • *This is just as easy.*

as *PREPOSITION* in the function or role of • *Use it as a handle.*

as *CONJUNCTION* **1** when or while • *She slipped as she got off the bus.* **2** because • *As he was late, we missed the train.* **3** in a way that • *Leave it as it is.*
- **as for** with regard to • *As for you, I despise you.*
- **as it were** in a way • *She became, as it were, her own enemy.*
- **as well** also.
[from Old English]

as- *PREFIX* to; towards. SEE **ad-**.

A/S *ABBREVIATION* advanced supplementary level in GCSE.

asbestos *NOUN* a fireproof material made up of fine soft fibres.
[from Greek, = unquenchable]

ascend *VERB* **ascends, ascending, ascended** go up.
- **ascend the throne** become king or queen.
[from Latin *ascendere* = climb up]

ascendancy *NOUN* being in control • *They gained ascendancy over others.*

ascendant *ADJECTIVE* rising.
- **in the ascendant** having greater power or influence.

ascension *NOUN* ascending.

ascent *NOUN* **ascents** **1** ascending. **2** a way up; an upward path or slope.

ascertain (*say* as-er-tayn) *VERB* **ascertains, ascertaining, ascertained** find something out by asking.
▷ **ascertainable** *adjective*
[from old French]

ascetic (*say* a-set-ik) *ADJECTIVE* not allowing yourself pleasure and luxuries.
▷ **asceticism** *noun*

ascetic *NOUN* **ascetics** a person who leads an ascetic life, often for religious reasons.
[from Greek *asketes* = hermit]

ascribe *VERB* **ascribes**, **ascribing**, **ascribed** regard something as belonging to or caused by; attribute • *She ascribes her success to good luck.*
[from *as-* + Latin *scribere* = write]

aseptic (*say* ay-**sep**-tik) *ADJECTIVE* clean and free from bacteria that cause things to become septic.
[from *a-*[2] = not + *septic*]

asexual *ADJECTIVE* (*in biology*) by other than sexual methods • *asexual reproduction.*
[from *a-*[2] = not + *sexual*]

ash[1] *NOUN* **ashes** the powder that is left after something has been burned.
▷ **ashy** *adjective*
[from Old English *aesce*]

ash[2] *NOUN* **ashes** a tree with silver-grey bark.
[from Old English *aesc*]

ashamed *ADJECTIVE* feeling shame.

ashen *ADJECTIVE* grey or pale • *his ashen face.*

ashore *ADVERB* to or on the shore.

ashtray *NOUN* **ashtrays** a small bowl for tobacco ash.

Asian *ADJECTIVE* to do with Asia or its people.

Asian *NOUN* **Asians** an Asian person.

Asiatic *ADJECTIVE* to do with Asia.

aside *ADVERB* **1** to or at one side • *pull it aside.* **2** away; in reserve.

aside *NOUN* **asides** words spoken so that only certain people will hear.

asinine (*say* ass-in-l'n) *ADJECTIVE* silly or stupid.
[same origin as *ass*]

ask *VERB* **asks**, **asking**, **asked** **1** speak so as to find out or get something. **2** invite • *Ask her to the party.*
[from Old English]

askance (*say* a-**skanss**) *ADVERB* – **look askance at** regard a person or situation with distrust or disapproval.
[origin unknown]

askew *ADVERB* & *ADJECTIVE* crooked; not straight or level.
[from *a-*[1] + *skew*]

asleep *ADVERB* & *ADJECTIVE* sleeping.

asp *NOUN* **asps** a small poisonous snake.
[from Greek]

asparagus *NOUN* a plant whose young shoots are eaten as a vegetable.
[from Greek]

aspect *NOUN* **aspects** **1** one part of a problem or situation • *Violence was the worst aspect of the crime.* **2** a person's or thing's appearance • *The forest had a sinister aspect.* **3** the direction a house etc. faces • *This room has a southern aspect.*
[from *as-* + Latin *specere* = to look]

aspen *NOUN* **aspens** a tree with leaves that move in the slightest wind.
[from Old English]

asperity *NOUN* harshness or severity.
[from Latin *asper* = rough]

aspersions *PLURAL NOUN* – **cast aspersions on somebody** attack his or her reputation or integrity.
[from *asperse* = spatter (with water or mud), from *as-* + Latin *spergere* = sprinkle]

asphalt (*say* **ass**-falt) *NOUN* a sticky black substance like tar, often mixed with gravel to surface roads, etc.
[from French]

asphyxia (*say* ass-**fiks**-ee-a) *NOUN* suffocation.
[Greek, = stopping of the pulse]

asphyxiate (*say* ass-**fiks**-ee-ayt) *VERB* **asphyxiates**, **asphyxiating**, **asphyxiated** suffocate.
▷ **asphyxiation** *noun*
[from *asphyxia*]

aspic *NOUN* a savoury jelly used for coating meats, eggs, etc.
[French]

aspidistra *NOUN* **aspidistras** a house plant with broad leaves.
[from Greek *aspis* = a shield]

aspirant (*say* **asp**-er-ant) *NOUN* **aspirants** a person who aspires to something.

aspirate (*say* **asp**-er-at) *NOUN* **aspirates** the sound of 'h'.
[same origin as *aspire*]

aspiration *NOUN* **aspirations** ambition; strong desire.

aspire *VERB* **aspires, aspiring, aspired** have an ambition to achieve something
• *He aspired to be world champion.*
[from *ad-* = to + Latin *spirare* = breathe]

aspirin *NOUN* **aspirins** a medicinal drug used to relieve pain or reduce fever.
[German]

ass *NOUN* **asses** **1** a donkey. **2** (*informal*) a stupid person.
[from Latin *asinus* = donkey]

assail *VERB* **assails, assailing, assailed** attack.
▷ **assailant** *noun*
[from Latin *assilire* = leap upon]

assassin *NOUN* **assassins** a person who assassinates somebody.
[from Arabic *hashishi* = hashish-takers, used as a name for a group of Muslims at the time of the Crusades, who were believed to take hashish before going out to kill Christian leaders]

assassinate *VERB* **assassinates, assassinating, assassinated** kill an important person deliberately and violently, especially for political reasons.
▷ **assassination** *noun*

assault *NOUN* **assaults** a violent or illegal attack.

assault *VERB* **assaults, assaulting, assaulted** make an assault on someone.
[same origin as *assail*]

assay (*say* a-say) *NOUN* **assays** a test made on metal or ore to discover its quality.
[from French *essai* = trial]

assegai (*say* ass-ig-I) *NOUN* **assegais** an iron-tipped spear used by South African peoples.
[from Arabic]

assemble *VERB* **assembles, assembling, assembled** **1** bring or come together. **2** fit or put together the parts of something.
▷ **assemblage** *noun*
[from *as-* + Latin *simul* = together]

assembly *NOUN* **assemblies** **1** assembling. **2** a regular meeting, such as when everybody in a school meets together. **3** people who regularly meet for a special purpose; a parliament.

assembly line *NOUN* **assembly lines** a series of workers and machines along which a product passes to be assembled part by part.

assent *VERB* **assents, assenting, assented** consent; say you agree.

assent *NOUN* consent or approval.
[from *as-* + Latin *sentire* = feel, think]

assert *VERB* **asserts, asserting, asserted** state something firmly.
▷ **assertion** *noun*
- **assert yourself** behave in a confident and forceful way.
[from Latin]

assertive *ADJECTIVE* acting forcefully and with confidence.

assess *VERB* **assesses, assessing, assessed** decide or estimate the value or quality of a person or thing.
▷ **assessment** *noun* **assessor** *noun*
[from Latin *assessor* = an assistant judge]

asset *NOUN* **assets** something useful or valuable to someone.
[from old French]

assets *PLURAL NOUN* a person's or company's property that could be sold to pay debts or raise money.

assiduous (*say* a-sid-yoo-us) *ADJECTIVE* working hard; persevering.
▷ **assiduously** *adverb* **assiduity** *noun*
[from Latin]

assign *VERB* **assigns, assigning, assigned** **1** give or allot. **2** appoint a person to perform a task.
[from *as-* + Latin *signare* = mark out]

assignation (*say* ass-ig-**nay**-shon) *NOUN* **assignations** **1** an arrangement to meet someone. **2** assigning something.

assignment *NOUN* **assignments** **1** assigning. **2** something assigned; a task given to someone.

assimilate *VERB* **assimilates, assimilating, assimilated** take in and absorb something, e.g. nourishment into the body or knowledge into the mind.
▷ **assimilation** *noun*
[from *as-* + Latin *similis* = similar]

A

assist *VERB* **assists, assisting, assisted** help.
▷ **assistance** *noun*
[from Latin *assistere* = stand by]

assistant *NOUN* **assistants** **1** a person who assists another; a helper. **2** a person who serves customers in a shop.

assistant *ADJECTIVE* helping a person and ranking next below him or her • *the assistant manager.*

associate (*say* a-**soh**-si-ayt) *VERB* **associates, associating, associated** **1** connect things in your mind • *I don't associate Ryan with fitness and healthy living.* **2** spend time or have dealings with a group of people.

associate (*say* a-**soh**-si-at) *NOUN* **associates** a colleague or companion; a partner.
▷ **associate** *adjective*
[from *as-* + Latin *socius* = an ally]

association *NOUN* **associations** **1** an organization of people; a society. **2** associating. **3** a connection or link in your mind.

Association Football *NOUN* a form of football using a round ball that may not be handled during play except by the goalkeeper.

assonance (*say* **ass**-on-ans) *NOUN* similarity of vowel sounds, e.g. in *vermin* and *furnish.*
[from *as-* + Latin *sonus* = sound]

assorted *ADJECTIVE* of various sorts put together; mixed • *assorted sweets.*

assortment *NOUN* **assortments** a mixed collection of things.

assuage (*say* a-**swayj**) *VERB* **assuages, assuaging, assuaged** soothe; make something less severe • *We drank to assuage our thirst.*
[from *as-* + Latin *suavis* = pleasant]

assume *VERB* **assumes, assuming, assumed** **1** accept without proof that something is true or sure to happen. **2** take on; undertake • *She assumed the extra responsibility.* **3** put on • *He assumed an innocent expression.*
- **assumed name** a false name.
▷ **assumption** *noun*
[from *as-* + Latin *sumere* = take]

assurance *NOUN* **assurances** **1** a promise or guarantee that something is true or will happen. **2** a kind of life insurance. **3** confidence in yourself.

assure *VERB* **assures, assuring, assured** **1** tell somebody confidently; promise. **2** make certain.
[from *as-* + Latin *securus* = secure]

aster *NOUN* **asters** a garden plant with daisy-like flowers in various colours.
[from Greek *aster* = star]

asterisk *NOUN* **asterisks** a star-shaped sign * used to draw attention to something.
[from Greek *asteriskos* = little star]

astern *ADVERB* **1** at the back of a ship or aircraft. **2** backwards • *Full speed astern!*

asteroid *NOUN* **asteroids** one of the small planets found mainly between the orbits of Mars and Jupiter.
[same origin as *aster*]

asthma (*say* **ass**-ma) *NOUN* a disease that makes breathing difficult.
▷ **asthmatic** *adjective* & *noun*
[Greek]

astigmatism (*say* a-**stig**-mat-izm) *NOUN* a defect that prevents an eye or lens from focusing properly.
▷ **astigmatic** *adjective*
[from *a*-[2] = not + Greek *stigma* = a point]

astonish *VERB* **astonishes, astonishing, astonished** surprise somebody greatly.
▷ **astonishment** *noun*
[same origin as *astound*]

astound *VERB* **astounds, astounding, astounded** astonish; shock somebody greatly.
[from old French; related to *stun*]

astral *ADJECTIVE* to do with the stars.
[from Greek *astron* = star]

astray *ADVERB* & *ADJECTIVE* away from the right path or place or course of action.
- **go astray** be lost or mislaid.
- **lead astray** make someone do something wrong.

astride *ADVERB* & *PREPOSITION* with one leg on each side of something.

astringent *ADJECTIVE* **1** causing skin or body tissue to contract. **2** harsh or severe • *astringent criticism.*
[from *as-* + Latin *stringere* = bind tightly]

astrology *NOUN* the study of how the stars and planets may influence people's lives.
▷ **astrologer** *noun* **astrological** *adjective*
[from Greek *astron* = star, + *-logy*]

astronaut *NOUN* **astronauts** a person who travels in a spacecraft.
[from Greek *astron* = star + *nautes* = sailor]

astronomical *ADJECTIVE* **1** to do with astronomy. **2** extremely large • *The restaurant's prices are astronomical.*

astronomy *NOUN* the study of the stars and planets and their movements.
▷ **astronomer** *noun*
[from Greek *astron* = star + *-nomia* = arrangement]

astute *ADJECTIVE* clever and good at understanding situations quickly; shrewd.
▷ **astutely** *adverb* **astuteness** *noun*
[from Latin *astus* = cleverness, cunning]

asunder *ADVERB* apart; into pieces.
[from Old English]

asylum *NOUN* **asylums** **1** refuge and safety offered by one country to political refugees from another. **2** (*old use*) an institution for the care of mentally ill people.
[from Greek *asylon* = refuge]

asymmetrical (*say* ay-sim-et-rik-al) *ADJECTIVE* not symmetrical.
▷ **asymmetrically** *adverb*

at *PREPOSITION* This word is used to show **1** position (*at the top*), **2** time (*at midnight*), **3** condition (*Stand at ease*), **4** direction towards something (*Aim at the target*), **5** level or price etc. (*Sell them at £1 each*), **6** cause (*We were annoyed at his failure*).
- **at all** in any way.
- **at it** doing or working at something.
- **at once** **1** immediately. **2** at the same time • *It all came out at once.*

[from Old English]

at- *PREFIX* to; towards. SEE **ad-**.

-ate *SUFFIX* forms **1** adjectives (e.g. *passionate*), **2** nouns showing status or function (e.g. *magistrate*) or (in scientific use) nouns meaning salts of certain acids (e.g. *nitrate*), (COMPARE **-ite**) **3** verbs (e.g. *create*, *fascinate*).
[from Latin]

atheist (*say* ayth-ee-ist) *NOUN* **atheists** a person who believes that there is no God.
▷ **atheism** *noun*
[from *a-*² + Greek *theos* = god]

athlete *NOUN* **athletes** a person who is good at sport, especially athletics.
[from Greek *athlein* = compete for a prize]

athletic *ADJECTIVE* **1** physically strong and active. **2** to do with athletes.
▷ **athletically** *adverb*

athletics *PLURAL NOUN* physical exercises and sports, e.g. running, jumping, and throwing.

-ation *SUFFIX* forms nouns, often from verbs (e.g. *creation*, *organization*, *starvation*).
[from Latin]

atlas *NOUN* **atlases** a book of maps.
[named after Atlas, a giant in Greek mythology, who was made to support the universe on his shoulders]

atmosphere *NOUN* **atmospheres** **1** the air around the earth. **2** a feeling or mood given by surroundings • *the happy atmosphere of the fairground.* **3** a unit of pressure, equal to the pressure of the atmosphere at sea level.
▷ **atmospheric** *adjective*
[from Greek *atmos* = vapour, + *sphere*]

atoll *NOUN* **atolls** a ring-shaped coral reef.
[from Maldivian (the language spoken in the Maldives)]

atom *NOUN* **atoms** the smallest particle of a chemical element.
[from Greek *atomos* = indivisible]

atom bomb or **atomic bomb** *NOUN* **atom bombs**, **atomic bombs** a bomb using atomic energy.

atomic *ADJECTIVE* **1** to do with an atom or atoms. **2** to do with atomic energy or atom bombs.

atomic energy *NOUN* energy created by splitting the nuclei of certain atoms.

atomic number *NOUN* **atomic numbers** (*in science*) the number of protons in the nucleus of the atom of a chemical element.

atomizer *NOUN* **atomizers** a device for making a liquid into a fine spray.

A B C D E F G H I J K L M N O P Q R S T U V W X Y Z

atone *VERB* **atones, atoning, atoned** make amends; make up for having done something wrong.
▷ **atonement** *noun*
[from *at one*]

atrocious (*say* a-troh-shus) *ADJECTIVE* extremely bad or wicked • *atrocious weather.*
▷ **atrociously** *adverb*
[from Latin *atrox* = cruel]

atrocity (*say* a-tross-it-ee) *NOUN* **atrocities** something extremely bad or wicked; wickedness.

attach *VERB* **attaches, attaching, attached** **1** fix or join to something else. **2** think of something as belonging to something else • *We attach great importance to fitness.*
▷ **attachment** *noun*
- **attached to** fond of.
[via old French from Germanic]

attaché (*say* a-tash-ay) *NOUN* **attachés** a special assistant to an ambassador • *our military attaché.*
[French, = attached]

attaché case *NOUN* **attaché cases** a small case in which documents etc. may be carried.

attack *NOUN* **attacks** **1** a violent attempt to hurt or overcome somebody. **2** a piece of strong criticism. **3** sudden illness or pain. **4** the players in a team whose job is to score goals; an attempt to score a goal.

attack *VERB* **attacks, attacking, attacked** make an attack.
▷ **attacker** *noun*
[from French; related to *attach*]

attain *VERB* **attains, attaining, attained** accomplish; succeed in doing or getting something.
▷ **attainable** *adjective* **attainment** *noun*
[from *at-* + Latin *tangere* = touch]

attempt *VERB* **attempts, attempting, attempted** make an effort to do something; try.

attempt *NOUN* **attempts** an effort to do something; a try.
[from *at-* + Latin *temptare* = try]

attend *VERB* **attends, attending, attended** **1** be present somewhere; go somewhere on a regular basis. **2** look after someone. **3** spend time dealing with something.
[via old French from *at-* + Latin *tendere* = stretch]

attendance *NOUN* **attendances** **1** the act of attending or being present. **2** the number of people present at an event • *an attendance of 5,000.*

attendant *NOUN* **attendants** a person who helps or accompanies someone.

attention *NOUN* **1** giving concentration and careful thought • *Pay attention to what I'm saying.* **2** a position in which a soldier etc. stands with feet together and arms straight downwards.

attentive *ADJECTIVE* giving attention to something.
▷ **attentively** *adverb* **attentiveness** *noun*

attenuate *VERB* **attenuates, attenuating, attenuated** make a thing thinner or weaker.
▷ **attenuation** *noun*
[from *at-* + Latin *tenuis* = thin]

attest *VERB* **attests, attesting, attested** declare or prove that something is true or genuine.
▷ **attestation** *noun*
[from *at-* + Latin *testari* = be a witness]

attic *NOUN* **attics** a room in the roof of a house.
[via French from Greek]

attire *NOUN* (*formal*) clothes.

attire *VERB* **attires, attiring, attired** (*formal*) dress.
[from old French *atirer* = equip]

attitude *NOUN* **attitudes** **1** a way of thinking or behaving. **2** the position of the body or its parts; posture.
[French]

attorney *NOUN* **attorneys** **1** a person who is appointed to act on behalf of another in business matters. **2** (*American*) a lawyer.
[from old French]

attract *VERB* **attracts, attracting, attracted** 1 get someone's attention or interest; seem pleasant to someone. 2 pull something by means of a physical force • *Magnets attract metal pins.*
[from *at-* + Latin *tractum* = pulled]

attraction *NOUN* **attractions** 1 the process of attracting, or the ability to attract. 2 something that attracts visitors • *a tourist attraction.*

attractive *ADJECTIVE* 1 pleasant or good-looking. 2 interesting or appealing • *an attractive plan.*
▷ **attractively** *adverb* **attractiveness** *noun*

attribute (*say* a-trib-yoot) *VERB* **attributes, attributing, attributed** regard something as belonging to or created by • *We attribute his success to hard work.*
▷ **attribution** *noun*

attribute (*say* at-rib-yoot) *NOUN* **attributes** a quality or characteristic • *Kindness is one of his attributes.*
[from *at-* + Latin *tribuere* = allot]

attributive (*say* a-trib-yoo-tiv) *ADJECTIVE* (*in grammar*) expressing an attribute and placed before the word it describes, e.g. *old* in *the old dog.* (COMPARE **predicative**)
▷ **attributively** *adverb*

attrition (*say* a-trish-on) *NOUN* gradually wearing down an enemy by repeatedly attacking them.
[from Latin]

attuned *ADJECTIVE* adjusted to something • *My eyes were now attuned to the darkness.*
[from *at-* + *tune*]

aubergine (*say* oh-ber-zheen) *NOUN* **aubergines** the deep-purple fruit of the eggplant.
[via French and Arabic from Sanskrit]

auburn *ADJECTIVE* (said about hair) reddish-brown.
[from old French]

auction *NOUN* **auctions** a public sale where things are sold to the person who offers the most money for them.

auction *VERB* **auctions, auctioning, auctioned** sell something by auction.
▷ **auctioneer** *noun*
[from Latin *auctum* = increased]

audacious (*say* aw-day-shus) *ADJECTIVE* bold or daring.
▷ **audaciously** *adverb* **audacity** *noun*
[from Latin *audax* = bold]

audible *ADJECTIVE* loud enough to be heard.
▷ **audibly** *adverb* **audibility** *noun*
[from Latin *audire* = hear]

audience *NOUN* **audiences** 1 people who have gathered to hear or watch something. 2 a formal interview with an important person.
[from Latin *audire* = hear]

audio *NOUN* reproduced sounds.

audio-visual *ADJECTIVE* using both sound and pictures to give information.

audit *NOUN* **audits** an official examination of financial accounts to see that they are correct.

audit *VERB* **audits, auditing, audited** make an audit of accounts.
▷ **auditor** *noun*
[from Latin *audire* = hear (because originally the accounts were read out)]

audition *NOUN* **auditions** a test to see if an actor or musician is suitable for a job.
▷ **audition** *verb*
[same origin as *audience*]

auditorium *NOUN* **auditoriums** the part of a theatre or hall where the audience sits.
[Latin, = place for hearing]

au fait (*say* oh fay) *ADJECTIVE* knowing a subject or procedure etc. well.
[French, = to the point]

augment *VERB* **augments, augmenting, augmented** increase or add to something.
▷ **augmentation** *noun*
[from Latin *augere* = increase]

au gratin (*say* oh grat-an) *ADJECTIVE* cooked with a crisp topping of breadcrumbs or grated cheese.
[French]

augur (*say* awg-er) *VERB* **augurs, auguring, augured** be a sign of what is to come • *These exam results augur well.*
[from Latin *augur* = prophet]

August *NOUN* the eighth month of the year.
[named after *Augustus* Caesar, the first Roman emperor]

A

august (*say* aw-gust) *ADJECTIVE* majestic or imposing.
[from Latin *augustus* = majestic]

auk *NOUN* **auks** a kind of seabird.
[from Old Norse]

aunt *NOUN* **aunts** the sister of your father or mother; your uncle's wife.
[from Latin]

auntie or **aunty** *NOUN* **aunties** (*informal*) aunt.

au pair (*say* oh pair) *NOUN* **au pairs** a person from abroad, usually a young woman, who works for a time in someone's home.
[French]

aura (*say* or-a) *NOUN* **auras** a general feeling surrounding a person or thing • *an aura of happiness.*
[Greek, = breeze]

aural (*say* or-al) *ADJECTIVE* to do with the ear or hearing.
▷ **aurally** *adverb*
[from Latin *auris* = ear]
USAGE Do not confuse with **oral**.

au revoir (*say* oh rev-wahr) *INTERJECTION* goodbye for the moment.
[French, literally = to be seeing again]

aurora (*say* aw-raw-ra) *NOUN* **auroras** bands of coloured light appearing in the sky at night, the **aurora borealis** (*say* bor-ee-ay-liss) in the northern hemisphere and the **aurora australis** (*say* aw-stray-liss) in the southern hemisphere.
[Latin: *aurora* = dawn; *borealis* = of the north; *australis* = of the south]

auspices (*say* aw-spiss-eez) *PLURAL NOUN* protection or support • *under the auspices of the Red Cross.*
[originally = omens; later = influence, protection; same origin as *auspicious*]

auspicious (*say* aw-spish-us) *ADJECTIVE* fortunate or favourable • *an auspicious start.*
[from Latin *auspicium* = telling the future from the behaviour of birds, from *avis* = bird]

austere (*say* aw-steer) *ADJECTIVE* very simple and plain; without luxuries.
▷ **austerely** *adverb* **austerity** *noun*
[from Greek *austeros* = severe]

aut- *PREFIX* self-; of or by yourself or itself. SEE **auto-**.

authentic *ADJECTIVE* genuine • *an authentic signature.*
▷ **authentically** *adverb* **authenticity** *noun*
[from Greek]

authenticate *VERB* **authenticates, authenticating, authenticated** confirm something as being authentic.
▷ **authentication** *noun*

author *NOUN* **authors** the writer of a book, play, poem, etc.
▷ **authorship** *noun*
[from Latin *auctor* = originator]

authoritarian *ADJECTIVE* believing that people should be completely obedient to those in authority.

authoritative *ADJECTIVE* having proper authority or expert knowledge; official.

authority *NOUN* **authorities** **1** the right or power to give orders to other people. **2** a person or organization with the right to give orders. **3** an expert; a book etc. that gives reliable information • *an authority on spiders.*
[same origin as *author*]

authorize *VERB* **authorizes, authorizing, authorized** give official permission for something.
▷ **authorization** *noun*

autistic (*say* aw-tist-ik) *ADJECTIVE* having a disability that makes someone unable to communicate with other people or respond to surroundings.
▷ **autism** *noun*
[from *auto-*]

auto *NOUN* **autos** (*informal esp. American*) a car • *the auto industry.*

auto- *PREFIX* (changing to **aut-** before a vowel) self-; of or by yourself or itself (as in *autograph, automatic*).
[from Greek *autos* = self]

autobiography *NOUN* **autobiographies** the story of a person's life written by himself or herself.
▷ **autobiographical** *adjective*

autocracy (*say* aw-tok-ra-see) *NOUN* **autocracies** rule by one person with unlimited power; despotism.
[from *auto-* + *-cracy*]

autocrat *NOUN* **autocrats** a ruler with unlimited power.
▷ **autocratic** *adjective* **autocratically** *adverb*

autocue *NOUN* **autocues** (*trademark*) a device that displays the script for a television presenter or newsreader to read.

autograph *NOUN* **autographs** the signature of a famous person.
▷ **autograph** *verb*
[from *auto-* + *-graph*]

automate *VERB* **automates**, **automating**, **automated** work something by automation.

automatic *ADJECTIVE* **1** working on its own without continuous attention or control by people. **2** done without thinking.
▷ **automatically** *adverb*
[from Greek *automatos* = self-operating]

automation *NOUN* making processes automatic; using machines instead of people to do jobs.

automaton (*say* aw-tom-at-on) *NOUN* **automatons** **1** a robot. **2** a person who seems to act mechanically without thinking.
[same origin as *automatic*]

automobile *NOUN* **automobiles** (*American*) a car.
[from *auto-* + *mobile*]

autonomy (*say* aw-ton-om-ee) *NOUN* **1** self-government. **2** the right to act independently without being told what to do.
▷ **autonomous** *adjective*
[from *auto-* + Greek *-nomia* = arrangement]

autopsy (*say* aw-top-see) *NOUN* **autopsies** a post-mortem.
[from Greek *autopsia* = seeing with your own eyes]

autumn *NOUN* **autumns** the season between summer and winter.
▷ **autumnal** *adjective*
[from old French]

auxiliary *ADJECTIVE* giving help and support • *auxiliary services.*

auxiliary *NOUN* **auxiliaries** a helper.
[from Latin *auxilium* = help]

auxiliary verb *NOUN* **auxiliary verbs** a verb such as *do*, *have*, and *will*, which is used to form parts of other verbs, e.g. *have* in *I have finished.*

avail *NOUN* - **to** or **of no avail** of no use; without success • *Their pleas for mercy were all to no avail.*

avail *VERB* **avails**, **availing**, **availed**
- **avail yourself of** make use of something • *Could I avail myself of your bicycle?*
[from Latin *valere* = be strong]

available *ADJECTIVE* ready or able to be used; obtainable.
▷ **availability** *noun*

avalanche *NOUN* **avalanches** a mass of snow or rock falling down the side of a mountain.
[French, from *avaler* = descend]

avant-garde (*say* av-ahn-gard) *NOUN* people who use a very modern style in art or literature etc.
[French, = vanguard]

avarice (*say* av-er-iss) *NOUN* greed for money or possessions.
▷ **avaricious** *adjective*
[from Latin *avarus* = greedy]

avenge *VERB* **avenges**, **avenging**, **avenged** take vengeance for something done to harm you.
▷ **avenger** *noun*
[from old French; related to *vindicate*]

avenue *NOUN* **avenues** **1** a wide street. **2** a road with trees along both sides.
[from French *avenir* = approach]

average *NOUN* **averages** **1** the value obtained by adding several quantities together and dividing by the number of quantities. **2** the usual or ordinary standard.

average *ADJECTIVE* **1** worked out as an average • *Their average age is ten.* **2** of the usual or ordinary standard.

average *VERB* **averages**, **averaging**, **averaged** work out, produce, or amount to as an average.
[from Arabic]

averse *ADJECTIVE* unwilling; feeling opposed to something • *I'm not averse to a bit of hard work.*
[same origin as *avert*]
USAGE Do not confuse with **adverse**.

aversion *NOUN* a strong dislike.

A B C D E F G H I J K L M N O P Q R S T U V W X Y Z

avert *VERB* **averts, averting, averted**
1 turn something away • *People averted their eyes from the accident.* **2** prevent • *We averted a disaster.*
[from *ab-* = away + Latin *vertere* = turn]

aviary *NOUN* **aviaries** a large cage or building for keeping birds.
[from Latin *avis* = bird]

aviation *NOUN* the flying of aircraft.
▷ **aviator** *noun*
[from Latin *avis* = bird]

avid (*say* av-id) *ADJECTIVE* eager • *an avid reader.*
▷ **avidly** *adverb* **avidity** *noun*
[from Latin *avere* = long for]

avocado (*say* av-ok-ah-doh) *NOUN* **avocados** a pear-shaped tropical fruit.
[via Spanish from Nahuatl (a Central American language)]

avoid *VERB* **avoids, avoiding, avoided**
1 keep yourself away from someone or something. **2** keep yourself from doing something; refrain from • *Avoid rash promises.*
▷ **avoidable** *adjective* **avoidance** *noun*
[from old French]

avoirdupois (*say* av-er-dew-**poiz**) *NOUN* a system of weights using the unit of 16 ounces = 1 pound.
[French, = goods of weight (goods sold by weight)]

avuncular *ADJECTIVE* kind and friendly towards someone younger, like an uncle.
[from Latin]

await *VERB* **awaits, awaiting, awaited** wait for.
[from old French]

awake *VERB* **awakes, awaking, awoke, awoken** wake up.

awake *ADJECTIVE* not asleep.
[from Old English]

awaken *VERB* **awakens, awakening, awakened** wake up.
▷ **awakening** *noun*
[from Old English]

award *VERB* **awards, awarding, awarded** give something officially as a prize, payment, or penalty.

award *NOUN* **awards** something awarded, such as a prize or a sum of money.
[from old French]

aware *ADJECTIVE* knowing or realizing something • *Were you aware of the danger?*
▷ **awareness** *noun*
[from Old English]

awash *ADJECTIVE* with waves or water flooding over it.
[from *a-*[1] + *wash*]

away *ADVERB* **1** to or at a distance; not at the usual place. **2** out of existence • *The water had boiled away.* **3** continuously or persistently • *We worked away at it.*

away *ADJECTIVE* played on an opponent's ground • *an away match.*
[from Old English]

awe *NOUN* fearful or deeply respectful wonder • *The mountains always fill me with awe.*
▷ **awed** *adjective* **awestricken** *adjective* **awestruck** *adjective*
[from Old English]

aweigh *ADVERB* hanging just clear of the sea bottom • *The anchor is aweigh.*
[from *a-*[1] + *weigh*]

awesome *ADJECTIVE* causing awe.
[from *awe* + *-some*]

awful *ADJECTIVE* **1** very bad • *an awful accident.* **2** (*informal*) very great • *That's an awful lot of money.*
▷ **awfully** *adverb*
[from *awe* + *-ful*]

awhile *ADVERB* for a short time.
[from *a* + *while*]

awkward *ADJECTIVE* **1** difficult to use or deal with; not convenient. **2** clumsy; not skilful.
▷ **awkwardly** *adverb* **awkwardness** *noun*
[from Old Norse *ofugr* = turned the wrong way]

awl *NOUN* **awls** a small pointed tool for making holes in leather, wood, etc.
[from Old English]

awning *NOUN* **awnings** a roof-like shelter made of canvas etc.
[origin unknown]

awry *ADVERB* & *ADJECTIVE* **1** twisted to one side; crooked. **2** wrong; not according to plan, • *Our plans have gone awry.*
[from *a-*[1] + *wry*]

axe *NOUN* **axes** **1** a tool for chopping things. **2** (*informal*) dismissal or redundancy • *A number of workers face the axe.*
- **have an axe to grind** have a personal interest in something and want to take care of it.

axe *VERB* **axes**, **axing**, **axed** **1** cancel or abolish something. **2** reduce something greatly.
[from Old English]

axiom *NOUN* **axioms** an established general truth or principle.
▷ **axiomatic** *adjective*
[from Greek]

axis *NOUN* **axes** **1** a line through the centre of a spinning object. **2** a line dividing a thing in half. **3** the horizontal or vertical line on a graph.
[Latin, = axle]

axle *NOUN* **axles** the rod through the centre of a wheel, on which the wheel turns.
[from Old Norse]

ayatollah (*say* I-a-**tol**-a) *NOUN* **ayatollahs** a Muslim religious leader in Iran.
[from Arabic *ayatu-llah* = sign from God]

aye (*say* I) *ADVERB* yes.
[origin unknown]

azalea (*say* a-**zay**-lee-a) *NOUN* **azaleas** a kind of flowering shrub.
[from Greek, = dry (because the plant grows well in dry soil)]

azure *ADJECTIVE* sky-blue.
[via old French from Persian]

Bb

baa *NOUN* **baas** the cry of a sheep or lamb.

babble *VERB* **babbles**, **babbling**, **babbled** **1** talk very quickly without making sense. **2** make a murmuring sound.
▷ **babble** *noun* **babbler** *noun*
[imitating the sound]

babe *NOUN* **babes** a baby.
[same as *baby*]

baboon *NOUN* **baboons** a kind of large monkey from Africa and Asia, with a long muzzle and short tail.
[from French]

baby *NOUN* **babies** a very young child or animal.
▷ **babyish** *adjective*
[probably from the sounds a baby makes when it first tries to speak]

babysitter *NOUN* **babysitters** someone who looks after a child while its parents are out.

bachelor *NOUN* **bachelors** a man who has not married.
- **Bachelor of Arts** or **Science** a person who has taken a first degree in arts or science.
[from French]

bacillus (*say* ba-**sil**-us) *NOUN* **bacilli** a rod-shaped bacterium.
[Latin, = little stick]

back *NOUN* **backs** **1** the part that is furthest from the front. **2** the back part of the body from the shoulders to the buttocks. **3** the part of a chair etc. that your back rests against. **4** a defending player near the goal in football, hockey, etc.

back *ADJECTIVE* **1** placed at or near the back. **2** to do with the back • *back pain.*

back *ADVERB* **1** to or towards the back. **2** to the place you have come from • *Go back home.* **3** to an earlier time or position • *Put the clocks back one hour.*

back *VERB* **backs**, **backing**, **backed** **1** move backwards. **2** give someone support or help. **3** bet on something. **4** cover the back of something • *Back the rug with canvas.*
▷ **backer** *noun*
- **back out** refuse to do what you agreed to do.
- **back up** **1** give support or help to a person or thing. **2** (*in computing*) make a spare copy of a file, disk, etc. to be stored in safety separately from the original.
back-up*noun*
[from Old English]

backbencher *NOUN* **backbenchers** a Member of Parliament who does not hold an important position.

backbiting *NOUN* saying unkind or nasty things about someone who is not there.

backbone *NOUN* **backbones** the column of small bones down the centre of the back; the spine.

backdrop *NOUN* **backdrops** a large, painted cloth that is hung across the back of a stage.

backfire *VERB* **backfires, backfiring, backfired** 1 if a car backfires, it makes a loud noise, caused by an explosion in the exhaust pipe. 2 if a plan backfires, it goes wrong.

backgammon *NOUN* a game played on a board with draughts and dice.
[from *back* (because sometimes pieces must go back to the start) + Old English *gamen* = game]

background *NOUN* 1 the back part of a picture, scene, or view etc. 2 the conditions influencing something. 3 a person's family, upbringing, and education.
- **in the background** not noticeable or obvious.

backhand *NOUN* **backhands** a stroke made in tennis etc. with the back of the hand turned outwards.
▷ **backhanded** *adjective*

backing *NOUN* 1 support. 2 material that is used to line the back of something. 3 musical accompaniment.

backlash *NOUN* **backlashes** a violent reaction to an event.

backlog *NOUN* **backlogs** an amount of work that should have been finished but is still waiting to be done.

backpack *NOUN* **backpacks** a rucksack.
▷ **backpacker** *noun*

backside *NOUN* **backsides** (*informal*) the buttocks.

backstroke *NOUN* a way of swimming lying on your back.

backward *ADJECTIVE* 1 going backwards. 2 slow at learning or developing.
▷ **backwardness** *noun*

backward *ADVERB* backwards.
USAGE The adverb *backward* is mainly used in American English.

backwards *ADVERB* 1 to or towards the back. 2 with the back end going first. 3 in reverse order • *Count backwards.*
- **backwards and forwards** in each direction alternately; to and fro.

backwater *NOUN* **backwaters** 1 a branch of a river that comes to a dead end with stagnant water. 2 a quiet place that is not affected by progress or new ideas.

backyard *NOUN* **backyards** 1 a yard at the back of a house 2 (*American*) a back garden.

bacon *NOUN* smoked or salted meat from the back or sides of a pig.
[via French from Germanic; related to *back*]

bacterium *NOUN* **bacteria** a microscopic organism that can cause disease.
▷ **bacterial** *adjective*
[from Greek *bakterion* = little cane]
USAGE Note that it is a mistake to use the plural form *bacteria* as if it were the singular. It is incorrect to say 'a bacteria' or 'this bacteria'; correct usage is *this bacterium* or *these bacteria*.

bad *ADJECTIVE* **worse, worst** 1 not having the right qualities; not good. 2 wicked or evil. 3 serious or severe • *a bad accident.* 4 ill or unhealthy. 5 harmful • *Sweets are bad for your teeth.* 6 decayed or rotten • *This meat has gone bad.*
- **not bad** quite good.
▷ **badness** *noun*
[*bad* is probably from Old English; *worse* and *worst* are from Old English *wyrsa*, related to *war*]

bade *old past tense* of **bid**².

badge *NOUN* **badges** a button or sign that you wear to show people who you are or what school or club etc. you belong to.
[origin unknown]

badger *NOUN* **badgers** a grey burrowing animal with a black and white head.

badger *VERB* **badgers, badgering, badgered** keep asking someone to do something; pester.
[perhaps from *badge* (because of the markings on a badger's head)]

badly *ADVERB* **worse, worst** 1 in a bad way; not well. 2 severely; causing much injury • *He was badly wounded.* 3 very much • *She badly wanted to win.*

badminton *NOUN* a game in which players use rackets to hit a light object called a shuttlecock across a high net.
[the name of a stately home in SW England where the game was first played]

baffle *VERB* **baffles, baffling, baffled** puzzle or confuse somebody.
▷ **bafflement** *noun*
[origin unknown]

bag *NOUN* **bags** a container made of a soft material, for holding or carrying things.
- **bags** (*informal*) plenty • *bags of room.*

bag *VERB* **bags, bagging, bagged**
1 (*informal*) catch or claim something. **2** put something into bags.
[from Old Norse]

bagatelle *NOUN* a game played on a board in which small balls are struck into holes.
[from Italian]

baggage *NOUN* luggage.
[from old French]

baggy *ADJECTIVE* (said about clothes) large and loose.

bagpipes *PLURAL NOUN* a musical instrument in which air is squeezed out of a bag into pipes. Bagpipes are played especially in Scotland.

bail[1] *NOUN* money that is paid or promised as a guarantee that a person who is accused of a crime will return for trial if he or she is released in the meantime.

bail *VERB* **bails, bailing, bailed** provide bail for a person.
[from old French *bail* = custody, jurisdiction; related to *bail*[2]]

bail[2] *NOUN* **bails** one of the two small pieces of wood placed on top of the stumps in cricket.
[from old French *bail* = palisade]

bail[3] *VERB* **bails, bailing, bailed** scoop out water that has got into a boat.
[from French *baille* = bucket]

bailey *NOUN* **baileys** the courtyard of a castle; the wall round this courtyard.
[same origin as *bail*[2]]

bailiff *NOUN* **bailiffs** **1** a law officer who helps a sheriff by serving writs and performing arrests. **2** an official who takes people's property when they owe money.
[from old French; related to *bail*[1]]

Bairam (*say* by-**rahm**) *NOUN* either of two Muslim festivals, one in the tenth month and one in the twelfth month of the Islamic year.
[from Turkish]

bairn *NOUN* **bairns** (*Scottish*) a child.
[from Old English]

Baisakhi *NOUN* a Sikh festival held in April.

bait *NOUN* **1** food that is put on a hook or in a trap to catch fish or animals. **2** something that is meant to tempt someone.

bait *VERB* **baits, baiting, baited** **1** put bait on a hook or in a trap. **2** try to make someone angry by teasing them.
[from Old Norse; related to *bite*]

baize *NOUN* the thick green cloth that is used for covering snooker tables.
[same origin as *bay*[5] (because the cloth was originally reddish- brown)]

bake *VERB* **bakes, baking, baked** **1** cook in an oven. **2** make or become very hot.
3 make a thing hard by heating it.
[from Old English]

baked beans *PLURAL NOUN* cooked white beans, usually tinned with tomato sauce.

baker *NOUN* **bakers** a person who bakes and sells bread or cakes.
▷ **bakery** *noun*

baking soda *NOUN* sodium bicarbonate.

bakkie *NOUN* **bakkies** (*S. African*)
1 a small pick-up truck with an open back.
2 a small bowl or basin.
[from Afrikaans]

balaclava or **balaclava helmet** *NOUN* **balaclavas, balaclava helmets** a hood covering the head and neck and part of the face.
[named after *Balaclava*, a village in the Crimea (because the helmets were worn by soldiers fighting near there during the Crimean War)]

balance *NOUN* **balances** **1** a steady position, with the weight or amount evenly distributed. **2** a person's feeling of being steady. **3** a device for weighing things, with two containers hanging from a bar. **4** the difference between money paid into an account and money taken out of it. **5** the amount of money that someone owes.

A B C D E F G H I J K L M N O P Q R S T U V W X Y Z

balance *VERB* **balances, balancing, balanced** make or be steady or equal. [from Latin]

balcony *NOUN* **balconies 1** a platform that sticks out from an outside wall of a building. **2** the upstairs part of a theatre or cinema. [from Italian]

bald *ADJECTIVE* **1** without hair on the top of the head. **2** with no details; blunt • *a bald statement.*
▷ **baldly** *adverb* **baldness** *noun*
[origin unknown]

bale[1] *NOUN* **bales** a large bundle of hay, straw, cotton, etc., usually tied up tightly. [probably from Dutch; related to *ball*[1]]

bale[2] *VERB* **bales, baling, baled**
- **bale out** jump out of an aircraft with a parachute.
[a different spelling of *bail*[3]]

baleful *ADJECTIVE* menacing or harmful • *a baleful frown.*
▷ **balefully** *adverb*
[from Old English *balu* = evil]

ball[1] *NOUN* **balls 1** a round object used in many games. **2** anything that has a round shape • *a ball of string.*
- **ball of the foot** the rounded part of the foot at the base of the big toe.
[from Old Norse]

ball[2] *NOUN* **balls** a formal party where people dance. [same origin as *ballet*]

ballad *NOUN* **ballads** a simple song or poem that tells a story. [from old French]

ballast (*say* bal-ast) *NOUN* heavy material that is carried in a ship to keep it steady. [probably from a Scandinavian language]

ball bearings *PLURAL NOUN* small steel balls rolling in a groove on which machine parts can move easily.

ballcock *NOUN* **ballcocks** a floating ball that controls the water level in a cistern. [from *ball*[1] + *cock* = tap]

ballerina (*say* bal-er-een-a) *NOUN* **ballerinas** a female ballet dancer. [Italian, = female dancing teacher]

ballet (*say* bal-ay) *NOUN* **ballets** a stage entertainment that tells a story with dancing, mime, and music. [via French from Italian]

ballistic (*say* bal-ist-ik) *ADJECTIVE* to do with objects that are fired through the air, especially bullets and missiles. [from Greek *ballein* = to throw]

ballistic missile *NOUN* **ballistic missiles** a missile that is initially powered and guided and then falls under gravity on its target.

balloon *NOUN* **balloons 1** a bag made of thin rubber that can be inflated and used as a toy or decoration. **2** a large round bag inflated with hot air or light gases to make it rise in the air, often carrying a basket in which passengers may ride. **3** an outline round spoken words in a strip cartoon. [from French or Italian; related to *ball*[1]]

ballot *NOUN* **ballots 1** a secret method of voting, usually by making a mark on a piece of paper. **2** a piece of paper on which a vote is made.

ballot *VERB* **ballots, balloting, balloted** invite people to vote for something by a ballot.
[from Italian *ballotta* = small ball (because one way of voting is by placing a ball in a box; the colour of the ball shows whether you are voting for something or against it)]

ballpoint pen *NOUN* **ballpoint pens** a pen with a tiny ball round which the ink flows.

ballroom *NOUN* **ballrooms** a large room where dances are held.

balm *NOUN* **1** a sweet-scented ointment. **2** something that soothes you. [same origin as *balsam*]

balmy *ADJECTIVE* **1** sweet-scented like balm. **2** soft and warm • *a balmy breeze.*

balsa *NOUN* a kind of very lightweight wood. [Spanish, = raft (because balsa was used for building rafts and small boats)]

balsam *NOUN* **balsams 1** a kind of sweet-smelling gum produced by certain trees. **2** a tree producing balsam. [from Latin *balsamum*]

balti *NOUN* **baltis** a type of Pakistani curry, cooked in a bowl-shaped pan. [perhaps from *Baltistan*, a region in the Himalayas]

balustrade *NOUN* **balustrades** a row of short posts or pillars that supports a rail or strip of stonework round a balcony or staircase.
[from Italian *balustra* = pomegranate flower (because the pillars of a balustrade were the same shape as the flower)]

bamboo *NOUN* **bamboos** **1** a tall plant with hard hollow stems. **2** a stem of the bamboo plant.
[via Dutch from Malay (a language spoken in Malaysia)]

bamboozle *VERB* **bamboozles, bamboozling, bamboozled** (*informal*) puzzle or trick someone.
[origin unknown]

ban *VERB* **bans, banning, banned** forbid something officially.

ban *NOUN* **bans** an order that bans something.
[from Old English]

banal (*say* ban-**ahl**) *ADJECTIVE* ordinary and uninteresting.
▷ **banality** *noun*
[from French]

banana *NOUN* **bananas** a long curved fruit with a yellow or green skin.
[via Spanish and Portuguese from Mande (a group of languages spoken in west Africa)]

band[1] *NOUN* **bands** **1** a strip or loop of something. **2** a range of values, wavelengths, etc.
[via French from Germanic; related to *bind*]

band[2] *NOUN* **bands** **1** an organized group of people doing something together • *a band of robbers.* **2** a group of people playing music together.

band *VERB* **bands, banding, banded** form an organized group.
[from French]

bandage *NOUN* **bandages** a strip of material for binding up a wound.
▷ **bandage** *verb*
[French; related to *band*[1]]

bandit *NOUN* **bandits** a member of a gang of robbers who attack travellers.
[from Latin *bannire* = banish]

bandstand *NOUN* **bandstands** a platform for a band playing music outdoors, usually in a park.

bandwagon *NOUN* – **jump on the bandwagon** join other people in something that is successful.

bandy[1] *ADJECTIVE* having legs that curve outwards at the knees.
[from *bandy* = a kind of hockey stick]

bandy[2] *VERB* **bandies, bandying, bandied** if a word or story is bandied about, it is mentioned or told by a lot of different people.
[probably from French]

bane *NOUN* a cause of trouble or worry etc.
• *Exams are the bane of our lives!*
[from Old English]

bang *NOUN* **bangs** **1** a sudden loud noise like that of an explosion. **2** a sharp blow or knock.

bang *VERB* **bangs, banging, banged** **1** hit or shut something noisily. **2** make a sudden loud noise.

bang *ADVERB* **1** with a bang; suddenly. **2** (*informal*) exactly • *bang in the middle.*
[imitating the sound]

banger *NOUN* **bangers** **1** a firework that explodes noisily. **2** (*slang*) a sausage. **3** (*slang*) a noisy old car.

bangle *NOUN* **bangles** a stiff bracelet.
[from Hindi]

banish *VERB* **banishes, banishing, banished** **1** punish a person by ordering them to leave a place. **2** drive away doubts or fears.
▷ **banishment** *noun*
[via French from Germanic; related to *ban*]

banisters *PLURAL NOUN* a handrail with upright supports beside a staircase.
[a different spelling of *baluster*, related to *balustrade*]

banjo *NOUN* **banjos** an instrument like a guitar with a round body.
[a Black American word]

bank[1] *NOUN* **banks** **1** a slope. **2** a long piled-up mass of sand, snow, cloud, etc. **3** a row of lights or switches.

bank *VERB* **banks, banking, banked** **1** build or form a bank. **2** tilt sideways while changing direction • *The plane banked as it prepared to land.*
[from Old Norse]

a b c d e f g h i j k l m n o p q r s t u v w x y z

A B C D E F G H I J K L M N O P Q R S T U V W X Y Z

bank[2] *NOUN* **banks** **1** a business that looks after people's money. **2** a reserve supply • *a blood bank.*

bank *VERB* **banks, banking, banked** put money in a bank.
- **bank on** rely on.
[from Italian]

banker *NOUN* **bankers** a person who runs a bank.

bank holiday *NOUN* **bank holidays** a public holiday, when banks are officially closed.

banknote *NOUN* **banknotes** a piece of paper money issued by a bank.

bankrupt *ADJECTIVE* unable to pay your debts.
▷ **bankruptcy** *noun*
[from *bank*[2] + Latin *ruptum* = broken]

banner *NOUN* **banners** **1** a flag. **2** a strip of cloth with a design or slogan on it, carried on a pole or two poles in a procession or demonstration.
[from Latin]

banns *PLURAL NOUN* an announcement in a church that the two people named are going to marry each other.
[plural of *ban* = proclamation]

banquet *NOUN* **banquets** a formal public meal.
▷ **banqueting** *noun*
[French, = little bench]

bantam *NOUN* **bantams** a kind of small hen.
[from *Bantam*, the name of a district of Java]

banter *NOUN* playful teasing or joking.
▷ **banter** *verb*
[origin unknown]

Bantu *NOUN* **Bantu** or **Bantus** **1** a member of a group of central and southern African peoples. **2** the group of languages spoken by these peoples.
[the Bantu word for *people*]

bap *NOUN* **baps** a soft flat bread roll.
[origin unknown]

baptism *NOUN* **baptisms** baptizing.

Baptist *NOUN* **Baptists** a member of a group of Christians who believe that a person should not be baptized until he or she is old enough to understand what baptism means.

baptize *VERB* **baptizes, baptizing, baptized** receive a person into the Christian Church in a ceremony in which he or she is sprinkled with or dipped in water, and usually given a name or names.
[from Greek *baptizein* = to dip]

bar *NOUN* **bars** **1** a long piece of something hard • *a gold bar.* **2** a counter or room where refreshments, especially alcoholic drinks, are served. **3** a barrier or obstruction. **4** one of the small equal sections into which music is divided • *three beats to the bar.*
- **the Bar** barristers.

bar *VERB* **bars, barring, barred** **1** fasten something with a bar or bars. **2** block or obstruct • *A man with a dog barred the way.* **3** forbid or ban.
[from French]

barb *NOUN* **barbs** the backward-pointing spike of a spear, arrow, or fish hook, which makes the point stay in.
[from Latin *barba* = beard]

barbarian *NOUN* **barbarians** an uncivilized or brutal person.
[from Greek *barbaros* = babbling, not speaking Greek]

barbaric or **barbarous** *ADJECTIVE* savage and cruel.
▷ **barbarity** *noun* **barbarism** *noun*

barbecue *NOUN* **barbecues** **1** a metal frame for grilling food over an open fire outdoors. **2** a party where food is cooked in this way.

barbecue *VERB* **barbecues, barbecuing, barbecued** cook food on a barbecue.
[via Spanish from Arawak (a South American language)]

barbed *ADJECTIVE* **1** having a barb or barbs. **2** a barbed comment or remark is deliberately hurtful.

barbed wire *NOUN* wire with small spikes in it, used to make fences.

barber *NOUN* **barbers** a men's hairdresser.
[from Latin *barba* = beard]

bar chart *NOUN* **bar charts** a diagram that shows amounts as bars of equal width but varying height.

bar code *NOUN* **bar codes** a set of black lines that are printed on goods, library books, etc., and can be read by a computer to give information about the goods, books, etc.

bard *NOUN* **bards** (*formal*) a poet or minstrel.
[a Celtic word]

bare *ADJECTIVE* **1** without clothing or covering. **2** empty • *The cupboard was bare.* **3** plain; without details • *the bare facts.* **4** only just enough • *the bare necessities of life.*
▷ **bareness** *noun*

bare *VERB* **bares, baring, bared** uncover or reveal • *The dog bared its teeth in a snarl.*
[from Old English]

bareback *ADJECTIVE* & *ADVERB* riding on a horse without a saddle.

barefaced *ADJECTIVE* shameless; bold and unconcealed • *He told a barefaced lie.*

barely *ADVERB* only just; with difficulty.

bargain *NOUN* **bargains** **1** an agreement about buying or selling or exchanging something. **2** something that you buy cheaply.

bargain *VERB* **bargains, bargaining, bargained** argue over the price to be paid or what you will do in return for something.
- **bargain for** be prepared for or expect • *He got more than he bargained for.*
[from French]

barge *NOUN* **barges** a long flat-bottomed boat used on canals.

barge *VERB* **barges, barging, barged** push or knock against roughly.
- **barge in** rush into a room rudely.
[from Latin *barca* = boat]

baritone *NOUN* **baritones** a male singer with a voice between a tenor and a bass.
[from Greek *barys* = heavy, + *tone*]

barium (*say* bair-ee-um) *NOUN* a soft silvery-white metal.
[from Greek]

bark[1] *NOUN* **barks** the short harsh sound made by a dog or fox.
▷ **bark** *verb*
[from Old English *beorc*, imitating the sound]

bark[2] *NOUN* the outer covering of a tree's branches or trunk.
[from Old Norse]

barley *NOUN* a cereal plant from which malt is made.
[from Old English]

barley sugar *NOUN* **barley sugars** a sweet made from boiled sugar.

bar mitzvah *NOUN* **bar mitzvahs** a religious ceremony for Jewish boys aged 13.
[Hebrew, = son of the commandment]

barmy *ADJECTIVE* (*slang*) crazy.
[literally full of *barm* = yeast, froth]

barn *NOUN* **barns** a farm building for storing hay or grain etc.
▷ **barnyard** *noun*
[from Old English]

barnacle *NOUN* **barnacles** a shellfish that attaches itself to rocks and the bottoms of ships.
[from Latin]

barn dance *NOUN* **barn dances** a kind of country dance; an informal gathering for dancing.

barometer (*say* ba-**rom**-it-er) *NOUN* **barometers** an instrument that measures air pressure, used in forecasting the weather.
[from Greek *baros* = weight, + *meter*]

baron *NOUN* **barons** **1** a member of the lowest rank of noblemen. **2** a powerful owner of an industry or business • *a newspaper baron.*
▷ **barony** *noun* **baronial** (*say* ba-**roh**-nee-al) *adjective*
[from Latin *baro* = man, warrior]

baroness *NOUN* **baronesses** a female baron or a baron's wife.

baronet *NOUN* **baronets** a nobleman ranking below a baron but above a knight.
▷ **baronetcy** *noun*
[same origin as *baron*]

baroque (*say* ba-**rok**) *NOUN* an elaborately decorated style of architecture used in the 17th and 18th centuries.
[from French]

barrack *VERB* **barracks, barracking, barracked** **1** shout loud insulting comments at a performer or speaker. **2** (*Australian*) support or encourage.

barracks *NOUN* a large building or group of buildings for soldiers to live in.
[via French from Spanish or Italian]

barrage (*say* ba-rah*zh*) *NOUN* **barrages** **1** a dam built across a river. **2** heavy gunfire. **3** a large amount of something • *a barrage of questions.*
[from French; related to *bar*]

barrel *NOUN* **barrels** **1** a large rounded container with flat ends. **2** the metal tube of a gun, through which the shot is fired.
[from Latin *barriculus* = a small cask]

barrel organ *NOUN* **barrel organs** a musical instrument which you play by turning a handle.

barren *ADJECTIVE* **1** (said about a woman) not able to have children. **2** (said about land) not fertile.
▷ **barrenness** *noun*
[from old French]

barricade *NOUN* **barricades** a barrier, especially one put up hastily across a street or door.

barricade *VERB* **barricades, barricading, barricaded** block a street or door with a barricade.
[French, from Spanish *barrica* = barrel (because barrels were sometimes used to build barricades)]

barrier *NOUN* **barriers** **1** a fence or wall that prevents people from getting past. **2** something that stops you doing something.
[from old French; related to *bar*]

barrier reef *NOUN* **barrier reefs** a coral reef close to the shore but separated from it by a channel of deep water.

barrister *NOUN* **barristers** a lawyer who represents people in the higher lawcourts.
[originally one who was allowed to pass the *bar*, a partition separating qualified lawyers from students]

barrow[1] *NOUN* **barrows** **1** a wheelbarrow. **2** a small cart that is pushed or pulled by hand.
[from Old English; related to *bear*[2]]

barrow[2] *NOUN* **barrows** a mound of earth over a prehistoric grave.
[from Old English; related to *burrow*]

barter *VERB* **barters, bartering, bartered** trade by exchanging goods for other goods, not for money.
USAGE This word does not mean 'to bargain'.

barter *NOUN* **barters** the system of bartering.
[probably from old French]

basalt (*say* bas-awlt) *NOUN* a kind of dark volcanic rock.
[from Greek]

base[1] *NOUN* **bases** **1** the lowest part of something; the part on which a thing stands. **2** a starting point or foundation; a basis. **3** a headquarters. **4** each of the four corners that must be reached by a runner in baseball. **5** a substance that can combine with an acid to form a salt. **6** (*in mathematics*) the number in terms of which other numbers can be expressed in a number system. 10 is the base of the decimal system and 2 is the base of the binary system.

base *VERB* **bases, basing, based** use something as a starting point or foundation • *The story is based on facts.*
[same origin as *basis*]

base[2] *ADJECTIVE* **1** dishonourable • *base motives.* **2** not of great value • *base metals.*
▷ **basely** *adverb* **baseness** *noun*
[from French *bas* = low]

baseball *NOUN* **baseballs** **1** an American game in which runs are scored by hitting a ball and running round a series of four bases. **2** the ball used in this game.

basement *NOUN* **basements** a room or rooms below ground level.
[probably via Dutch from Italian; related to *base*[1]]

bash *VERB* **bashes, bashing, bashed** hit hard.

bash *NOUN* **bashes** **1** a hard hit. **2** (*informal*) a try • *Have a bash at it.*
[imitating the sound]

bashful *ADJECTIVE* shy and self-conscious.
▷ **bashfully** *adverb*
[from *abash*]

basic *ADJECTIVE* forming the first or most important part • *Bread is a basic food.*
[from *base*[1]]

basically *ADVERB* at the simplest or most fundamental level.

basilica (*say* ba-zil-ik-a) *NOUN* **basilicas** a large oblong church with two rows of columns and an apse at one end.
[Latin, = royal palace]

basilisk (*say* baz-il-isk) *NOUN* **basilisks** a mythical reptile that was said to be able to kill people just by looking at them.
[from Greek *basilikos* = a kind of snake]

basin *NOUN* **basins** **1** a deep bowl. **2** a washbasin. **3** a sheltered area of water for mooring boats. **4** the area from which water drains into a river • *the Amazon basin.*
[from old French]

basis *NOUN* **bases** something to start from or add to; the main principle or ingredient.
[Greek, = step, stepping]

bask *VERB* **basks, basking, basked** sit or lie comfortably warming yourself in the sun.
[origin unknown]

basket *NOUN* **baskets** a container for holding or carrying things, made of strips of flexible material or wire woven together.
[probably from Latin]

basketball *NOUN* **basketballs** **1** a game in which goals are scored by putting a ball through high nets. **2** the ball used in this game.

bass[1] (*say* bayss) *ADJECTIVE* deep-sounding; the bass part of a piece of music is the lowest part.

bass *NOUN* **basses** **1** a male singer with a very deep voice. **2** a bass instrument or part.
[from *base*[2] = low]

bass[2] (*say* bas) *NOUN* **bass** a fish of the perch family.
[from Old English]

basset *NOUN* **bassets** a short-legged dog used for hunting hares.
[same origin as *base*[2]]

bassoon *NOUN* **bassoons** a bass woodwind instrument.
[from Italian *basso* = low]

bastard *NOUN* **bastards** **1** (*old use*) an illegitimate child. **2** (*slang*) an unpleasant or difficult person or thing.
[from old French]

baste *VERB* **bastes, basting, basted** moisten meat with fat while it is cooking.
[origin unknown]

bastion *NOUN* **bastions** **1** a projecting part of a fortified building. **2** something that protects a belief or way of life.
[from Italian *bastire* = to build]

bat[1] *NOUN* **bats** **1** a shaped piece of wood used to hit the ball in cricket, baseball, etc. **2** a batsman • *their opening bat.*
- **off your own bat** without help from other people.

bat *VERB* **bats, batting, batted** use a bat in cricket etc.
[from Old English]

bat[2] *NOUN* **bats** a flying animal that looks like a mouse with wings.
[from a Scandinavian language]

batch *NOUN* **batches** a set of things or people dealt with together.
[from Old English; related to *bake*]

bated *ADJECTIVE* - **with bated breath** anxiously; hardly daring to speak.
[from *abate*]

bath *NOUN* **baths** **1** washing your whole body while sitting in water. **2** a large container for water in which to wash your whole body; this water • *Your bath is getting cold.* **3** a liquid in which something is placed • *an acid bath.*

bath *VERB* **baths, bathing, bathed** wash in a bath.
[from Old English; related to *bathe*]

bathe *VERB* **bathes, bathing, bathed** **1** go swimming. **2** wash something gently.
▷ **bathe** *noun* **bather** *noun* **bathing suit** *noun*
[from Old English; related to *bath*]

bathos *NOUN* a sudden change from a serious subject or tone to a ridiculous or trivial one.
[Greek, = depth]

bathroom *NOUN* **bathrooms** **1** a room containing a bath. **2** (*American*) a room containing a toilet.

baths *PLURAL NOUN* **1** a building with rooms where people can bath. **2** a public swimming pool.

B

baton *NOUN* **batons** a short stick, e.g. one used to conduct an orchestra or in a relay race.
[from French]

batsman *NOUN* **batsmen** a player who uses a bat in cricket etc.

battalion *NOUN* **battalions** an army unit containing two or more companies.
[from Italian *battaglia* = battle]

batten *NOUN* **battens** a strip of wood or metal that holds something in place.

batten *VERB* **battens, battening, battened** fasten something down firmly.
[from old French]

batter *VERB* **batters, battering, battered** hit hard and often.

batter *NOUN* **batters 1** a beaten mixture of flour, eggs, and milk, used for making pancakes etc. **2** a player who is batting in baseball.
[from Latin *battuere* = to beat]

battering ram *NOUN* **battering rams** a heavy pole that is used to break down walls or gates.

battery *NOUN* **batteries 1** a device for storing and supplying electricity. **2** a set of similar pieces of equipment; a group of large guns. **3** a series of cages in which poultry or animals are kept close together • *battery farming.*
[same origin as *batter*]

battle *NOUN* **battles 1** a fight between two armies. **2** a struggle.
▷ **battlefield** *noun* **battleground** *noun*

battle *VERB* **battles, battling, battled** fight or struggle.
[same origin as *batter*]

battlements *PLURAL NOUN* the top of a castle wall, often with gaps from which the defenders could fire at the enemy.

battleship *NOUN* **battleships** a heavily armed warship.

batty *ADJECTIVE* (*slang*) crazy.
[from the phrase *bats in the belfry* = crazy]

bauble *NOUN* **baubles** a bright, showy, but valueless ornament.
[from old French *baubel* = toy]

baulk *VERB* **baulks, baulking, baulked** **1** stop and refuse to go on • *The horse baulked at the fence.* **2** frustrate; prevent from doing or getting something.
[from Old Norse]

bauxite *NOUN* the clay-like substance from which aluminium is obtained.
[from *Les Baux*, a place in France, where it was first found]

bawdy *ADJECTIVE* **bawdier, bawdiest** referring to sex in a humorous way.
▷ **bawdiness** *noun*
[from *bawd* = a brothel-keeper]

bawl *VERB* **bawls, bawling, bawled** **1** shout. **2** cry noisily.
[imitating the sound]

bay[1] *NOUN* **bays** a place where the shore curves inwards.
[from Spanish]

bay[2] *NOUN* **bays** an alcove or compartment.
[from Latin *batare* = gape]

bay[3] *NOUN* **bays** a kind of laurel tree with leaves that are used as a flavouring in cooking.
[originally = laurel berry, from Latin *bacca* = berry]

bay[4] *NOUN* **bays** the long deep cry of a hunting hound or other large dog.
- **at bay** cornered but defiantly facing attackers • *a stag at bay.*
- **keep at bay** prevent something from coming near or causing harm • *We need laws to keep poverty at bay.*
[from French]

bay[5] *ADJECTIVE* reddish-brown.
[from Latin *badius*]

bayonet *NOUN* **bayonets** a blade that can be fixed to the end of a rifle and used for stabbing.
[named after *Bayonne* in France, where it was first used]

bay window *NOUN* **bay windows** a window that sticks out from the main wall of a house.
[from *bay*[2]]

bazaar *NOUN* **bazaars** 1 a market place in an Eastern country. 2 a sale to raise money for a charity etc.
[from Persian *bazar* = market]

bazooka *NOUN* **bazookas** a portable weapon for firing anti-tank rockets.
[the word originally meant a musical instrument rather like a trombone]

BBC *ABBREVIATION* British Broadcasting Corporation.

BC *ABBREVIATION* before Christ (used with dates counting back from the birth of Jesus Christ).

be *VERB* **am, are, is; was, were; being, been** 1 exist; occupy a position • *The shop is on the corner.* 2 happen; take place • *The wedding is tomorrow.*
This verb is also used 1 to join subject and complement (*He is my teacher*), 2 to form parts of other verbs (*It is raining. He was killed*).
- **have been** have gone to or come to as a visitor etc. • *We have been to Rome.*
[from Old English]

be- *PREFIX* used to form verbs (as in *befriend, belittle*) or strengthen their meaning (as in *begrudge*).
[from Old English]

beach *NOUN* **beaches** the part of the seashore nearest to the water.
[probably from Old English]

beached *ADJECTIVE* (said about a whale) stranded on a beach.

beacon *NOUN* **beacons** a light or fire used as a signal or warning.
[from Old English; related to *beckon*]

bead *NOUN* **beads** 1 a small piece of a hard substance with a hole in it for threading with others on a string or wire, e.g. to make a necklace. 2 a drop of liquid • *a bead of sweat.*
[from Old English *gebed* = prayer (because people kept count of the prayers they said by moving the beads on a rosary)]

beadle *NOUN* **beadles** 1 an official with ceremonial duties in a church or college. 2 (*old use*) an official of a parish.
[from Old English]

beady *ADJECTIVE* (said about eyes) small and bright.

beagle *NOUN* **beagles** a small hound used for hunting hares.
▷ **beagling** *noun*
[from old French; related to *bay*[4]]

beak *NOUN* **beaks** the hard horny part of a bird's mouth.
[from Latin *beccus*, of Celtic origin]

beaker *NOUN* **beakers** 1 a tall drinking mug, often without a handle. 2 a glass container used for pouring liquids in a laboratory.
[from Old Norse]

beam *NOUN* **beams** 1 a long thick bar of wood or metal. 2 a ray or stream of light or other radiation. 3 a happy smile.

beam *VERB* **beams, beaming, beamed** 1 smile happily. 2 send out a beam of light or other radiation.
[from Old English]

bean *NOUN* **beans** 1 a kind of plant with seeds growing in pods. 2 its seed or pod eaten as food. 3 the seed of coffee.
[from Old English]

bean sprout *NOUN* **bean sprouts** a sprout of a bean seed that can be eaten either cooked or raw.

bear[1] *NOUN* **bears** a large heavy animal with thick fur and large teeth and claws.
[from Old English *bera*]

bear[2] *VERB* **bears, bearing, bore, borne** 1 carry or support. 2 have or show a mark etc. • *She still bears the scar.* 3 endure or stand • *I can't bear all this noise.* 4 produce or give birth to • *She bore him two sons.*
▷ **bearer** *noun*
- **bear in mind** remember something and take it into account.
- **bear out** support or confirm.
[from Old English *beran*]

bearable *ADJECTIVE* able to be endured; tolerable.

beard *NOUN* **beards** hair on a man's chin.
▷ **bearded** *adjective*

beard *VERB* **beards, bearding, bearded** come face to face with a person and challenge him or her boldly.
[from Old English; the verb originally = to grab someone's beard]

bearing *NOUN* **bearings** **1** the way a person stands, walks, behaves, etc. **2** relevance • *My friendship with Tom has no bearing on his selection for the team.* **3** the direction or position of one thing in relation to another. **4** a device for preventing friction in a machine • *ball bearings.*
- **get your bearings** work out where you are in relation to things.
[from *bear*[2]]

beast *NOUN* **beasts** **1** any large four-footed animal. **2** (*informal*) a cruel or vicious person.
▷ **beastly** *adjective*
[from Latin *bestia*]

beat *VERB* **beats, beating, beat, beaten** **1** hit often, especially with a stick. **2** defeat somebody or do better than them. **3** shape or flatten something by beating it. **4** stir vigorously. **5** make regular movements • *The heart beats.*
▷ **beater** *noun*
- **beat up** attack someone very violently.

beat *NOUN* **beats** **1** a regular rhythm or stroke • *the beat of your heart.* **2** emphasis in rhythm; the strong rhythm of pop music. **3** a policeman's regular route.
[from Old English]

beatific (*say* bee-a-**tif**-ik) *ADJECTIVE* showing great happiness • *a beatific smile.*
[from Latin *beatus* = blessed]

beautiful *ADJECTIVE* attractive to your senses or your mind.
▷ **beautifully** *adverb*

beautify *VERB* **beautifies, beautifying, beautified** make someone beautiful.
▷ **beautification** *noun*

beauty *NOUN* **beauties** **1** a quality that gives pleasure to your senses or your mind. **2** a person or thing that has beauty. **3** an excellent example of something.
[from old French]

beaver *NOUN* **beavers** an animal with soft brown fur and strong teeth; it builds its home in a deep pool which it makes by damming a stream.

beaver *VERB* **beavers, beavering, beavered** work hard • *He's beavering away on the computer.*
[from Old English]

becalmed *ADJECTIVE* (in sailing) unable to move because there is no wind.

because *CONJUNCTION* for the reason that.
- **because of** for the reason of • *He limped because of his bad leg.*
[from *by* + *cause*]

beck *NOUN* - **at someone's beck and call** always ready and waiting to do what he or she asks.
[from *beckon*]

beckon *VERB* **beckons, beckoning, beckoned** make a sign to a person asking him or her to come.
[from Old English; related to *beacon*]

become *VERB* **becomes, becoming, became, become** **1** come or grow to be; begin to be • *It became dark.* **2** be suitable for; make a person look attractive.
- **become of** happen to • *What became of it?*
[from Old English]

bed *NOUN* **beds** **1** a piece of furniture that you sleep or rest on, especially one with a mattress and coverings. **2** a piece of a garden where plants are grown. **3** the bottom of the sea or of a river. **4** a flat base; a foundation. **5** a layer of rock or soil.
[from Old English]

bedclothes *PLURAL NOUN* sheets, blankets, etc.

bedding *NOUN* mattresses and bedclothes.

bedlam *NOUN* uproar.
[from *Bedlam*, the popular name of the Hospital of St Mary of Bethlehem, a London mental hospital in the 14th century]

Bedouin (*say* **bed**-oo-in) *NOUN* **Bedouin** a member of an Arab people living in tents in the desert.
[from Arabic *badawi* = desert- dweller]

bedpan *NOUN* **bedpans** a container for use as a lavatory by a bedridden person.

bedraggled (*say* bid-**rag**-eld) *ADJECTIVE* very untidy; wet and dirty.
[from *be-* + *draggle* = make dirty]

bedridden *ADJECTIVE* too weak or ill to get out of bed.

bedrock *NOUN* **1** solid rock beneath soil. **2** the fundamental facts or principles on which an idea or belief is based.

bedroom *NOUN* **bedrooms** a room for sleeping in.

bedsitter *NOUN* **bedsitters** a room used for both living and sleeping in.

bedspread *NOUN* **bedspreads** a covering spread over a bed during the day.

bedstead *NOUN* **bedsteads** the framework of a bed.
[originally the place where a bed stood; from *bed* + *stead* = place]

bedtime *NOUN* **bedtimes** the time for going to bed.

bee *NOUN* **bees** a stinging insect with four wings that makes honey.
[from Old English]

beech *NOUN* **beeches** a tree with smooth bark and glossy leaves.
[from Old English]

beef *NOUN* meat from an ox, bull, or cow.
[from old French]

beefeater *NOUN* **beefeaters** a guard at the Tower of London, wearing Tudor dress as uniform.
[originally a scornful word for a fat, lazy servant]

beefy *ADJECTIVE* having a solid muscular body.
▷ **beefiness** *noun*

beehive *NOUN* **beehives** a box or other container for bees to live in.

beeline *NOUN* - **make a beeline for** go straight or quickly towards something.
[because a bee was believed to fly in a straight line back to its hive]

beer *NOUN* **beers** an alcoholic drink made from malt and hops.
▷ **beery** *adjective*
[from Old English]

beeswax *NOUN* a yellow substance produced by bees, used for polishing wood.

beet *NOUN* **beet** or **beets** a plant with a thick root used as a vegetable or for making sugar.
[from Old English]

beetle *NOUN* **beetles** an insect with hard shiny wing covers.
[from Old English; related to *bite*]

beetling *ADJECTIVE* prominent; overhanging • *beetling brows.*

beetroot *NOUN* **beetroot** the dark red root of beet used as a vegetable.

befall *VERB* **befalls, befalling, befell, befallen** (*formal*) happen to someone.
[from *be-* + *fall* = happen]

befitting *ADJECTIVE* suitable.

before *ADVERB* at an earlier time • *Have you been here before?*

before *PREPOSITION & CONJUNCTION* **1** earlier than • *I was here before you!* **2** in front of • *He came before the judge.*
[from Old English]

beforehand *ADVERB* earlier; in readiness.
[from *before* + *hand* (with the idea of your hand doing something before someone else's does)]

befriend *VERB* **befriends, befriending, befriended** make friends with someone.

beg *VERB* **begs, begging, begged** **1** ask to be given money, food, etc. **2** ask seriously or desperately.
- **beg the question** argue in an illogical way by relying on the result that you are trying to prove.
- **go begging** be available.
- **I beg your pardon** I apologize; I did not hear what you said.
[probably from Old English]

beget *VERB* **begets, begetting, begot, begotten** (*old use*) **1** be the father of someone. **2** produce • *War begets misery.*
[from Old English]

beggar *NOUN* **beggars** **1** a person who lives by begging. **2** (*informal*) a person • *You lucky beggar!*
▷ **beggary** *noun*

begin *VERB* **begins, beginning, began, begun** **1** do the earliest or first part of something; start speaking. **2** come into existence • *The problem began last year.* **3** have something as its first part • *The word begins with B.*
[from Old English]

beginner *NOUN* **beginners** a person who is just beginning to learn a subject.

beginning *NOUN* **beginnings** the start of something.

begone *VERB* (*old use*) go away immediately • *Begone dull care!*
[from *be* + *gone*]

begonia (*say* big-**oh**-nee-a) *NOUN* **begonias** a garden plant with brightly coloured flowers.
[named after Michel *Bégon*, a Frenchman who encouraged the study of plants]

begot *past tense* of **beget**.

begrudge *VERB* **begrudges, begrudging, begrudged** resent having to give or allow something; grudge.

beguile (*say* big-I'll) *VERB* **beguiles, beguiling, beguiled** **1** amuse or fascinate. **2** deceive.
[from *be-* + *guile*]

behalf *NOUN* - **on behalf of** for the benefit of someone else or as their representative • *We are collecting money on behalf of cancer research.*
- **on my behalf** for me.
[from an old phrase *bi halve him* = on his side]
USAGE Do not use *on behalf of* (= for someone else) when you mean *on the part of* (= by someone). For example, do not say *This was a serious mistake on behalf of the government* when you mean *on the part of the government*.

behave *VERB* **behaves, behaving, behaved** **1** act in a particular way • *They behaved badly.* **2** show good manners • *Behave yourself!*
▷ **behaviour** *noun* **behavioural** *adjective*
[from *be-* + *have*]

behead *VERB* **beheads, beheading, beheaded** cut the head off a person or thing; execute a person in this way.
[from Old English]

behest *NOUN* (*formal*)
- **at a person's behest** done because they have asked or commanded you to do it • *At Laura's behest we took the notice down from the window.*
[from Old English]

behind *ADVERB* **1** at or to the back; at a place people have left • *Don't leave it behind.* **2** not making good progress; late • *I'm behind with my rent.*

behind *PREPOSITION* **1** at or to the back of; on the further side of. **2** having made less progress than • *He is behind the others in French.* **3** supporting; causing • *What is behind all this trouble?*
- **behind a person's back** kept secret from him or her deceitfully.
- **behind the times** out of date.

behind *NOUN* **behinds** (*informal*) a person's bottom.
[from Old English]

behindhand *ADVERB* & *ADJECTIVE* **1** late. **2** out of date.
[from *behind* + *hand*, on the pattern of *beforehand*]

behold *VERB* **beholds, beholding, beheld** (*old use*) see.
▷ **beholder** *noun*
[from Old English]

behove *VERB* **behoves, behoving, behoved** be a person's duty • *It behoves you to be loyal.*
[from Old English]

beige (*say* bayzh) *NOUN* & *ADJECTIVE* a very light brown colour.
[French]

being *NOUN* **beings** **1** existence. **2** a creature.

belated *ADJECTIVE* coming very late or too late.
▷ **belatedly** *adverb*

belay *VERB* **belays, belaying, belayed** fasten a rope by winding it round a peg or spike.
[from Dutch]

belch *VERB* **belches, belching, belched** **1** send out wind from your stomach through your mouth noisily. **2** send out fire or smoke etc. from an opening.
▷ **belch** *noun*
[from Old English]

beleaguered (*say* bil-**eeg**-erd) *ADJECTIVE* **1** under siege. **2** experiencing a lot of difficulties or criticism.
[from Dutch *belegeren* = camp round]

belfry *NOUN* **belfries** a tower or part of a tower in which bells hang.
[from old French]

belief *NOUN* **beliefs** **1** believing. **2** something a person believes.
[from Old English]

believe *VERB* **believes, believing, believed** think that something is true or that someone is telling the truth.
▷ **believable** *adjective* **believer** *noun*
- **believe in** think that something exists or is good or can be relied on.
[from Old English]

belittle *VERB* **belittles, belittling, belittled** make something seem of little value • *Do not belittle their success.*
▷ **belittlement** *noun*

bell *NOUN* **bells** **1** a cup-shaped metal instrument that makes a ringing sound when struck by the clapper hanging inside it. **2** any device that makes a ringing or buzzing sound to attract attention. **3** a bell-shaped object.
[from Old English]

belle *NOUN* **belles** a beautiful woman.
[French]

bellicose (*say* bel-ik-ohs) *ADJECTIVE* eager to fight.
[from Latin *bellum* = war]

belligerent (*say* bil-ij-er-ent) *ADJECTIVE* **1** aggressive; eager to fight. **2** fighting; engaged in a war.
▷ **belligerently** *adverb* **belligerence** *noun*
[from Latin *bellum* = war + *gerens* = waging]

bellow *NOUN* **bellows** **1** the loud deep sound made by a bull or other large animal. **2** a deep shout.

bellow *VERB* **bellows, bellowing, bellowed** give a deep shout.
[origin unknown]

bellows *PLURAL NOUN* a device for pumping air into a fire, organ pipes, etc.
[from Old English]

belly *NOUN* **bellies** the abdomen; the stomach.
[from Old English]

belong *VERB* **belongs, belonging, belonged** have a proper place • *The pans belong in the kitchen.*
- **belong to** be the property of; be a member of • *We belong to the same club.*
[from *be-* + *long* = owing to, because of]

belongings *PLURAL NOUN* a person's possessions.

beloved *ADJECTIVE* dearly loved.

below *ADVERB* at or to a lower position; underneath • *There's fire down below.*

below *PREPOSITION* lower than; under • *The temperature was ten degrees below zero.*

belt *NOUN* **belts** **1** a strip of cloth or leather etc. worn round the waist. **2** a band of flexible material used in machinery. **3** a long narrow area • *a belt of rain.*

belt *VERB* **belts, belting, belted** **1** put a belt round something. **2** (*slang*) hit or beat. **3** (*slang*) rush along.
[via Old English from Latin]

bemused *ADJECTIVE* **1** puzzled or confused. **2** lost in thought.
[from *be-* + *muse*, in the sense 'wonder']

bench *NOUN* **benches** **1** a long seat. **2** a long table for working at. **3** the seat where judges or magistrates sit; the judges or magistrates hearing a lawsuit.
[from Old English]

benchmark *NOUN* **benchmarks** a standard by which something can be judged or measured • *Her CD sets the benchmark for everyone else to follow.*

bend *VERB* **bends, bending, bent** **1** change from being straight. **2** turn downwards; stoop • *She bent to pick it up.*

bend *NOUN* **bends** a place where something bends; a curve or turn • *a bend in the road.*
[from Old English]

bene- (*say* ben-ee) *PREFIX* well (as in *benefit*, *benevolent*).
[from Latin *bene* = well]

beneath *PREPOSITION* **1** under. **2** unworthy of • *Cheating is beneath you.*

beneath *ADVERB* underneath.
[from Old English]

benediction *NOUN* **benedictions** a blessing.
[from *bene-* + Latin *dicere* = to say]

benefactor *NOUN* **benefactors** a person who gives money or other help.
[from *bene-* + Latin *factor* = doer]

beneficial *ADJECTIVE* having a good or helpful effect; advantageous.
[from Latin *beneficium* = favour, support]

A B C D E F G H I J K L M N O P Q R S T U V W X Y Z

beneficiary (*say* ben-if-**ish**-er-ee) *NOUN* **beneficiaries** a person who receives benefits, especially from a will.
[same origin as *beneficial*]

benefit *NOUN* **benefits** **1** something that is helpful or profitable. **2** a payment to which a person is entitled from government funds or from an insurance policy.

benefit *VERB* **benefits**, **benefiting**, **benefited** **1** do good to a person or thing. **2** receive a benefit.
[from *bene-* + Latin *facere* = do]

benevolent *ADJECTIVE* **1** kind and helpful. **2** formed for charitable purposes • *a benevolent fund.*
▷ **benevolently** *adverb* **benevolence** *noun*
[from *bene-* + Latin *volens* = wishing]

benign (*say* bin-**I'n**) *ADJECTIVE* **1** kindly. **2** favourable. **3** (said about a disease) mild, not malignant.
▷ **benignly** *adverb*
[from Latin *benignus* = kind-hearted]

benison *NOUN* **benisons** (*old use*) a blessing.
[from French]

bent *ADJECTIVE* curved or crooked.
- **bent on** intending to do something.

bent *NOUN* a talent for something.

benzene *NOUN* a substance obtained from coal tar and used as a solvent, motor fuel, and in the manufacture of plastics.
[via French from Arabic *lubanjawi* = incense from Sumatra]

benzine *NOUN* a spirit obtained from petroleum and used in dry cleaning.
[same origin as *benzene*]

bequeath *VERB* **bequeaths**, **bequeathing**, **bequeathed** leave something to a person, especially in a will.
[from *be-* + Old English *cwethan* = say]

bequest *NOUN* **bequests** something left to a person, especially in a will.
[from *be-* + Old English *cwiss* = saying, a statement]

bereaved *ADJECTIVE* suffering from the recent death of a close relative.
▷ **bereavement** *noun*
[from *be-* + an old word *reave* = take forcibly]

bereft *ADJECTIVE* deprived of something • *They were bereft of hope.*
[old past participle of *bereave*]

beret (*say* **bair**-ay) *NOUN* **berets** a round flat cap.
[from French]

berg *NOUN* **bergs** (*S. African*) a mountain.
[via Afrikaans from Dutch *bergh* = mountain]

beriberi (*say* berry-berry) *NOUN* a tropical disease caused by a vitamin deficiency.
[from Sinhalese (a language spoken in Sri Lanka)]

berry *NOUN* **berries** any small round juicy fruit without a stone.
[from Old English]

berserk (*say* ber-serk) *ADJECTIVE* - **go berserk** become uncontrollably violent.
[from Icelandic *berserkr* = wild warrior, from *ber-* = bear + *serkr* = coat]

berth *NOUN* **berths** **1** a sleeping place on a ship or train. **2** a place where a ship can moor.
- **give a wide berth** keep at a safe distance from a person or thing.

berth *VERB* **berths**, **berthing**, **berthed** moor in a berth.
[from *bear*[2]]

beryl *NOUN* **beryls** a pale-green precious stone.
[from French]

beseech *VERB* **beseeches**, **beseeching**, **beseeched** or **besought** ask earnestly; implore.
[from *be-* + *seek*]

beset *VERB* **besets**, **besetting**, **beset** attack from all sides • *They are beset with problems.*
[from Old English]

beside *PREPOSITION* **1** by the side of; near. **2** compared with.
- **be beside himself** or **herself** etc. be very excited or upset.
[from Old English *be sidan* = by the side]

besides *PREPOSITION* & *ADVERB* in addition to; also • *Who came besides you?* • *And besides, it's the wrong colour.*
[same origin as *beside*]

besiege *VERB* **besieges, besieging, besieged** 1 surround a place in order to capture it. 2 crowd round • *Fans besieged the singer after the concert.*

besotted *ADJECTIVE* too fond of something; fond in a silly way.
[from *be-* + *sot* = make stupid]

besought *past tense* of **beseech**.

best *ADJECTIVE* of the most excellent kind; most able to do something.

best *ADVERB* 1 in the best way; most. 2 most usefully; most wisely • *We had best go.*
[from Old English]

bestial (*say* best-ee-al) *ADJECTIVE* to do with or like a beast.
▷ **bestiality** *noun*
[from Latin *bestia* = beast]

best man *NOUN* the bridegroom's chief attendant at a wedding.

bestow *VERB* **bestows, bestowing, bestowed** present to someone.
▷ **bestowal** *noun*
[from *be-* + *stow*]

best-seller *NOUN* **best-sellers** a book sold in large numbers.

bet *NOUN* **bets** 1 an agreement that you will receive money if you are correct in choosing the winner of a race, game, etc. or in saying something will happen, and will lose money if you are not correct. 2 the money you risk losing in a bet.

bet *VERB* **bets, betting, bet** or **betted** 1 make a bet. 2 (*informal*) think most likely; predict • *I bet he will forget.*
[origin unknown]

beta (*say* beet-a) *NOUN* the second letter of the Greek alphabet, equivalent to Roman *B, b.*

bête noire (*say* bayt nwahr) *NOUN* a person or thing you greatly dislike.
[French, = black beast]

betide *VERB* - **woe betide you** trouble will come to you.
[from *be-* + Old English *tidan* = happen]

betoken *VERB* **betokens, betokening, betokened** be a sign of.
[from Old English]

betray *VERB* **betrays, betraying, betrayed** 1 be disloyal to a person or country etc. 2 reveal something without meaning to.
▷ **betrayal** *noun* **betrayer** *noun*
[from *be-* + Latin *tradere* = deliver]

betrothed *ADJECTIVE* (*formal*) engaged to be married.
▷ **betroth** *verb* **betrothal** *noun*
[from *be-* + *troth*]

better *ADJECTIVE* 1 more excellent; more satisfactory. 2 recovered from illness.
- **get the better of** defeat or outwit.

better *ADVERB* 1 in a better way; more. 2 more usefully; more wisely • *We had better go.*
- **be better off** be more fortunate, e.g. by having more money.

better *VERB* **betters, bettering, bettered** 1 improve something. 2 do better than.
▷ **betterment** *noun*
[from Old English]

between *PREPOSITION* & *ADVERB* 1 within two or more given limits • *between the walls.* 2 connecting two or more people, places, or things • *The train runs between London and Glasgow.* 3 shared by • *Divide this money between you.* 4 separating; comparing • *Can you tell the difference between them?*
[from Old English]
USAGE The preposition *between* should be followed by the object form of the pronoun (*me, her, him, them,* or *us*). The expression 'between you and I' is incorrect; say *between you and me.*

betwixt *PREPOSITION* & *ADVERB* (*old use*) between.
[from Old English]

bevel *VERB* **bevels, bevelling, bevelled** give a sloping edge to something.
[from old French]

beverage *NOUN* **beverages** any kind of drink.
[from old French]

bevy *NOUN* **bevies** a large group • *a bevy of beauties.*
[origin unknown]

bewail *VERB* **bewails, bewailing, bewailed** mourn for something.

beware *VERB* be careful • *Beware of pickpockets.*
[from *be-* + *ware* = wary]

bewilder *VERB* **bewilders, bewildering, bewildered** puzzle someone hopelessly.
▷ **bewilderment** *noun*
[from *be-* + an old word *wilder* = lose your way]

bewitch *VERB* **bewitches, bewitching, bewitched** **1** put a magic spell on someone. **2** delight someone very much.
[from *be-* + *witch* = put under a spell]

beyond *PREPOSITION & ADVERB* **1** further than; further on • *Don't go beyond the fence.*
2 outside the range of; too difficult for • *The problem is beyond me.*
[from Old English]

Bhagavadgita *NOUN* the most famous book of the Hindu religion.
[Sanskrit, = Song of the Lord]

bhangra *NOUN* a style of music that combines traditional Punjabi music with rock music.
[from Punjabi (a language spoken in the Punjab)]

bi- *PREFIX* **1** two (as in *bicycle*). **2** twice (as in *biannual*).
[from Latin *bis* = twice]

biannual *ADJECTIVE* happening twice a year.
▷ **biannually** *adverb*
USAGE Do not confuse this word with **biennial**.

bias *NOUN* **biases** **1** a feeling or influence for or against someone or something; a prejudice. **2** a tendency to swerve. **3** a slanting direction.
[from old French]

biased *ADJECTIVE* prejudiced.

bib *NOUN* **bibs** **1** a cloth or covering put under a baby's chin during meals. **2** the part of an apron above the waist.
[probably from Latin *bibere* = to drink]

Bible *NOUN* **Bibles** the sacred book of the Jews (the Old Testament) and of the Christians (the Old and New Testament).
[from Greek *biblia* = books (originally = rolls of papyrus from Byblos, a port now in Lebanon)]

biblical *ADJECTIVE* to do with or in the Bible.

bibliography (*say* bib-lee-og-ra-fee) *NOUN* **bibliographies** **1** a list of books about a subject or by a particular author. **2** the study of books and their history.
▷ **bibliographical** *adjective*
[from Greek *biblion* = book, + *-graphy*]

bicarbonate *NOUN* a kind of carbonate.
[from *bi-* + *carbonate*]

bicentenary (*say* by-sen-**teen**-er-ee) *NOUN* **bicentenaries** a 200th anniversary.
▷ **bicentennial** (*say* by-sen-**ten**-ee-al) *adjective*
[from *bi-* + *centenary*]

biceps (*say* **by**-seps) *NOUN* **biceps** the large muscle at the front of the arm above the elbow.
[Latin, = two-headed (because its end is attached at two points)]

bicker *VERB* **bickers, bickering, bickered** quarrel over unimportant things; squabble.
[origin unknown]

bicuspid *NOUN* **bicuspids** a tooth with two points.
[from *bi-* + Latin *cuspis* = sharp point]

bicycle *NOUN* **bicycles** a two-wheeled vehicle driven by pedals.
▷ **bicyclist** *noun*
[from *bi-* + Greek *kyklos* = circle, wheel]

bid *NOUN* **bids** **1** the offer of an amount you are willing to pay for something, especially at an auction. **2** an attempt.

bid *VERB* **bids, bidding, bid** make a bid.
▷ **bidder** *noun*

bid *VERB* **bids, bidding, bid** (or (*old use*) **bade, bid** or **bidden**) **1** say as a greeting or farewell • *I bid you all good night.*
2 command • *Do as you are bid* or *bidden*.
[from two Old English words; *biddan* = to ask, and *beodan* = to announce or command]

bidding *NOUN* if you do someone's bidding, you do what they tell you to do.

bide *VERB* **bides, biding, bided**
- **bide your time** wait for the right time to do something.
[from Old English]

bidet (*say* bee-day) *NOUN* **bidets** a low washbasin to sit on for washing the lower part of the body.
[from French *bidet* = a pony (because you sit astride it)]

biennial (*say* by-**en**-ee-al) *ADJECTIVE* **1** lasting for two years. **2** happening once every two years.
▷ **biennially** *adverb*

biennial *NOUN* **biennials** a plant that lives for two years, flowering and dying in the second year.
[from Latin *biennis* = of two years]
USAGE Do not confuse this word with **biannual**.

bier (*say* beer) *NOUN* **biers** a movable stand on which a coffin or a dead body is placed before it is buried.
[from Old English]

bifocal (*say* by-**foh**-kal) *ADJECTIVE* (said about lenses for glasses) made in two sections, with the upper part for looking at distant objects and the lower part for reading.

bifocals *PLURAL NOUN* bifocal glasses.

big *ADJECTIVE* **bigger**, **biggest** **1** large. **2** important • *the big match.* **3** more grown-up; elder • *my big sister.*
[origin unknown]

bigamy (*say* **big**-a-mee) *NOUN* the crime of marrying a person when you are already married to someone else.
▷ **bigamous** *adjective* **bigamist** *noun*
[from *bi-* + Greek *-gamos* = married]

bight *NOUN* **bights** a long inward curve in a coast.
[from Old English]

bigot *NOUN* **bigots** a bigoted person.
[French]

bigoted *ADJECTIVE* narrow-minded and intolerant.
▷ **bigotry** *noun*

bike *NOUN* **bikes** (*informal*) a bicycle or motorcycle.
[abbreviation of *bicycle*]

bikini *NOUN* **bikinis** a woman's two-piece swimsuit.
[named after the island of *Bikini* in the Pacific Ocean, where an atomic bomb test was carried out in 1946, at about the time the bikini was first worn (both caused great excitement)]

bilateral *ADJECTIVE* **1** of or on two sides. **2** between two people or groups • *a bilateral agreement.*
[from *bi-* + *lateral*]

bilberry *NOUN* **bilberries** a small dark-blue edible berry.
[probably from Old Norse]

bile *NOUN* a bitter liquid produced by the liver, helping to digest fats.
[from Latin]

bilge *NOUN* **bilges** (**the bilges**) **1** the bottom of a ship; the water that collects there. **2** (*slang*) nonsense; worthless ideas.
[a different spelling of *bulge*]

bilingual (*say* by-**ling**-wal) *ADJECTIVE* **1** able to speak two languages well. **2** written in two languages.
[from *bi-* + Latin *lingua* = language]

bilious *ADJECTIVE* feeling sick; sickly.
▷ **biliousness** *noun*
[from *bile*]

-bility *SUFFIX*, SEE **-able**.

bill[1] *NOUN* **bills** **1** a written statement of charges for goods or services that have been supplied. **2** a poster. **3** a list; a programme of entertainment. **4** the draft of a proposed law to be discussed by parliament. **5** (*American*) a banknote.
- **bill of fare** a menu.
[same origin as *bull*[2]]

bill[2] *NOUN* **bills** a bird's beak.
[from Old English]

billabong *NOUN* **billabongs** (in Australia) a backwater.
[an Aboriginal word]

billboard *NOUN* a hoarding for advertisements.

billet *NOUN* **billets** a lodging for troops, especially in a private house.

billet *VERB* **billets**, **billeting**, **billeted** house someone in a billet.
[originally = an order to house troops: from Latin *bulla* = seal, sealed letter]

billiards *NOUN* a game in which three balls are struck with cues on a cloth-covered table (**billiard table**).
[from French *billard* = cue]

billion *NOUN* **billions** **1** a thousand million (1,000,000,000). **2** (*old use*) a million million (1,000,000,000,000).
▷ **billionth** *adjective* & *noun*
[French, from *bi-* + *million*]
USAGE Although the word originally meant a million million, nowadays it usually means a thousand million.

billow *NOUN* **billows** a huge wave.

billow *VERB* **billows, billowing, billowed** rise or roll like waves.
[from Old Norse]

billy *NOUN* **billies** a pot with a lid, used by campers etc. as a kettle or cooking pot.
▷ **billycan** *noun*
[from Australian Aboriginal *billa* = water]

billy goat *NOUN* **billy goats** a male goat. (COMPARE **nanny goat**)
[from the name *Billy*]

bin *NOUN* **bins** a large or deep container, especially one for rubbish or litter.
[via Old English from a Celtic word]

binary (*say* by-ner-ee) *ADJECTIVE* involving sets of two; consisting of two parts.
[from Latin]

binary digit *NOUN* **binary digits** either of the two digits (0 and 1) used in the binary system.

binary number *NOUN* **binary numbers** a number expressed in the binary system.

binary system or **binary notation** *NOUN* a system of expressing numbers by using the digits 0 and 1 only, used in computing.

bind *VERB* **binds, binding, bound** **1** fasten material round something. **2** fasten the pages of a book into a cover. **3** tie up or tie together. **4** make somebody agree to do something.
▷ **binder** *noun*
- **bind a person over** make him or her agree not to break the law.

bind *NOUN* (*slang*) a nuisance; a bore.
[from Old English]

binding *NOUN* **bindings** something that binds, especially the covers, glue, etc. of a book.

binding *ADJECTIVE* (said about an agreement or promise) that must be carried out or obeyed.

bine *NOUN* the flexible stem of the hop plant.
[a different spelling of *bind*]

binge *NOUN* **binges** (*slang*) a time spent eating a lot of food.
[origin unknown]

bingo *NOUN* a game using cards on which numbered squares are crossed out as the numbers are called out at random.
[origin unknown]

binoculars *PLURAL NOUN* a device with lenses for both eyes, making distant objects seem nearer.
[from Latin *bini* = two together + *oculus* = eye]

bio- *PREFIX* life (as in *biology*).
[from Greek *bios* = life]

biochemistry *NOUN* the study of the chemical composition and processes of living things.
▷ **biochemical** *adjective* **biochemist** *noun*

biodegradable *ADJECTIVE* able to be broken down by bacteria in the environment • *All our packaging is biodegradable.*

biodiversity *NOUN* the existence of a large number of different kinds of animals and plants in an area.

biography (*say* by-og-ra-fee) *NOUN* **biographies** the story of a person's life.
▷ **biographical** *adjective* **biographer** *noun*

biology *NOUN* the scientific study of the life and structure of living things.
▷ **biological** *adjective* **biologist** *noun*

bionic (*say* by-on-ik) *ADJECTIVE* (said about a person or parts of the body) operated by electronic devices.
[from *bio-* + *electronic*]

biopsy (*say* by-op-see) *NOUN* **biopsies** examination of tissue from a living body.
[from *bio-* + *autopsy*]

bipartite *ADJECTIVE* having two parts; involving two groups • *a bipartite agreement.*
[from *bi-* + Latin *partitum* = divided, parted]

biped (*say* by-ped) *NOUN* **bipeds** a two-footed animal.
[from *bi-* + Latin *pedes* = feet]

biplane *NOUN* **biplanes** an aeroplane with two sets of wings, one above the other.
[from *bi-* + *plane*[1]]

birch *NOUN* **birches** **1** a deciduous tree with slender branches. **2** a bundle of birch branches for flogging people.
[from Old English]

bird *NOUN* **birds** **1** an animal with feathers, two wings, and two legs. **2** (*slang*) a young woman.
[from Old English]

birdie *NOUN* **birdies** **1** (*informal*) a bird. **2** a score of one stroke under par for a hole at golf.

bird of prey *NOUN* **birds of prey** a bird that feeds on animal flesh, such as an eagle or hawk.

bird's-eye view *NOUN* a view of something from above.

Biro *NOUN* **Biros** (*trademark*) a kind of ballpoint pen.
[named after its Hungarian inventor, L. *Biró*]

birth *NOUN* **births** **1** the process by which a baby or young animal comes out from its mother's body. **2** origin; parentage • *He is of noble birth.*
[from Old Norse]

birth control *NOUN* ways of avoiding conceiving a baby.

birthday *NOUN* **birthdays** the anniversary of the day a person was born.

birthmark *NOUN* **birthmarks** a coloured mark that has been on a person's skin since birth.

birth rate *NOUN* **birth rates** the number of children born in one year for every 1,000 people.

birthright *NOUN* a right or privilege to which a person is entitled through being born into a particular family or country.

biscuit *NOUN* **biscuits** a small flat kind of cake that has been baked until it is crisp.
[from Latin *bis* = twice + *coctus* = cooked (because originally they were baked and then dried out in a cool oven to make them keep longer)]

bisect (*say* by-sekt) *VERB* **bisects, bisecting, bisected** divide something into two equal parts.
▷ **bisection** *noun* **bisector** *noun*
[from *bi-* + Latin *sectum* = cut]

bishop *NOUN* **bishops** **1** an important member of the clergy in charge of all the churches in a city or district. **2** a chess piece shaped like a bishop's mitre.
[via Old English from Latin *episcopus*]

bishopric *NOUN* **bishoprics** the position or diocese of a bishop.

bismuth *NOUN* **1** a greyish-white metal. **2** a compound of this used in medicine.
[Latin from German]

bison (*say* by-son) *NOUN* **bison** a wild ox found in North America and Europe, with a large shaggy head.
[Latin]

bistro *NOUN* **bistros** a small restaurant.
[French]

bit[1] *NOUN* **bits** **1** a small piece or amount of something. **2** the metal part of a horse's bridle that is put into its mouth. **3** the part of a tool that cuts or grips things when twisted.
- **a bit** **1** a short distance or time • *Wait a bit.* **2** slightly • *I'm a bit worried.*
- **bit by bit** gradually.
[from Old English; related to *bite*]

bit[2] *past tense* of **bite**.

bit[3] *NOUN* **bits** (*in computing*) the smallest unit of information in a computer, expressed as a choice between two possibilities.
[from *binary digit*]

bitch *NOUN* **bitches** **1** a female dog, fox, or wolf. **2** (*informal*) a spiteful woman.
▷ **bitchy** *adjective*
[from Old English]

bite *VERB* **bites, biting, bit, bitten** **1** cut or take something with your teeth. **2** penetrate; sting. **3** accept bait • *The fish are biting.*
- **bite the dust** die or be killed.

bite *NOUN* **bites** **1** an act of biting • *She took a bite.* **2** a wound or mark made by biting • *an insect bite.* **3** a snack.
[from Old English; related to *bit*[1]]

bitter *ADJECTIVE* **1** tasting sharp, not sweet. **2** feeling or causing mental pain or resentment • *a bitter disappointment.* **3** very cold.
▷ **bitterly** *adverb* **bitterness** *noun*
[from Old English; related to *bite*]

bittern *NOUN* **bitterns** a marsh bird, the male of which makes a booming cry.
[from old French]

bitumen (*say* bit-yoo-min) *NOUN* a black substance used for covering roads etc.
[Latin]

bivalve *NOUN* **bivalves** a shellfish, such as an oyster or mussel, that has a shell with two hinged parts.

bivouac (*say* biv-oo-ak) *NOUN* **bivouacs** a temporary camp without tents.

bivouac *VERB* **bivouacs, bivouacking, bivouacked** camp in a bivouac.
[French]

bizarre (*say* biz-ar) *ADJECTIVE* very odd in appearance or effect.
[from Italian *bizarro* = angry]

blab *VERB* **blabs, blabbing, blabbed** let out a secret.
[imitating the sound]

black *NOUN* **blacks** **1** the very darkest colour, like coal or soot. **2** a person with dark skin, especially a person with African or Australian Aboriginal ancestry.

black *ADJECTIVE* **1** of the colour black. **2** having dark skin. **3** dismal; not hopeful • *The outlook is black.* **4** hostile; disapproving • *He gave me a black look.* **5** very dirty. **6** (said about coffee or tea) without milk.
▷ **blackly** *adverb* **blackness** *noun*

black *VERB* **blacks, blacking, blacked** make a thing black.
- **black out** **1** faint, lose consciousness. **2** cover windows etc. so that no light can penetrate.
▷ **blackout** *noun*
[from Old English]

blackberry *NOUN* **blackberries** a sweet black berry.

blackbird *NOUN* **blackbirds** a European songbird, the male of which is black.

blackboard *NOUN* **blackboards** a dark board for writing on with chalk.

black box *NOUN* **black boxes** a flight recorder.

black economy *NOUN* employment in which payments are concealed to avoid tax.

blacken *VERB* **blackens, blackening, blackened** make or become black.

black eye *NOUN* **black eyes** an eye with a bruise round it.

blackguard (*say* blag-erd) *NOUN* **blackguards** (*old use*) a wicked person.
[originally the *black guard* = the servants who did the dirty jobs]

blackhead *NOUN* **blackheads** a small black spot in the skin.

black hole *NOUN* **black holes** a region in outer space with such a strong gravitational field that no matter or radiation can escape from it.

black ice *NOUN* thin transparent ice on roads.

blackleg *NOUN* **blacklegs** a person who works while their fellow workers are on strike.
[originally a disease affecting sheep]

blacklist *VERB* **blacklists, blacklisting, blacklisted** put someone on a list of those who are disapproved of.

black magic *NOUN* evil magic.

blackmail *VERB* **blackmails, blackmailing, blackmailed** demand money from someone by threatening to reveal something that they want to keep secret.
▷ **blackmail** *noun* **blackmailer** *noun*
[from *black* + *mail*²; literally = black armour or protection]

black market *NOUN* **black markets** illegal trading.

black sheep *NOUN* a member of a family or other group who is seen as a disgrace to it.

blacksmith *NOUN* **blacksmiths** a person who makes and repairs iron things, especially one who makes and fits horseshoes.
[because of the dark colour of iron]

black spot *NOUN* **black spots** a dangerous place.

bladder *NOUN* **bladders** **1** the bag-like part of the body in which urine collects. **2** the inflatable bag inside a football.
[from Old English]

blade *NOUN* **blades** **1** the flat cutting edge of a knife, sword, axe, etc. **2** the flat wide part of an oar, spade, propeller, etc. **3** a flat narrow leaf • *blades of grass.* **4** a broad flat bone • *shoulder blade.*
[from Old English]

blame *VERB* **blames, blaming, blamed** **1** say that somebody or something has caused what is wrong • *They blamed me.* **2** find fault with someone • *We can't blame them for wanting a holiday.*

blame *NOUN* **blames** responsibility for what is wrong.
[from old French]

blameless *ADJECTIVE* deserving no blame; innocent.

blanch *VERB* **blanches, blanching, blanched** make or become white or pale • *He blanched with fear.*
[from French *blanc* = white]

blancmange (*say* bla-**monj**) *NOUN* **blancmanges** a jelly-like pudding made with milk.
[from French *blanc* = white + *mange* = eat]

bland *ADJECTIVE* **1** having a mild flavour rather than a strong one. **2** gentle and casual; not irritating or stimulating • *a bland manner.*
▷ **blandly** *adverb* **blandness** *noun*
[from Latin *blandus* = soft, smooth]

blandishments *PLURAL NOUN* flattering or coaxing words.
[same origin as *bland*]

blank *ADJECTIVE* **1** not written or printed on; unmarked. **2** without interest or expression • *a blank look.* **3** empty of thoughts • *My mind's gone blank.*
▷ **blankly** *adverb* **blankness** *noun*

blank *NOUN* **blanks** **1** an empty space. **2** a blank cartridge.
[from French *blanc* = white]

blank cartridge *NOUN* **blank cartridges** a cartridge that makes a noise but does not fire a bullet.

blank cheque *NOUN* **blank cheques** a cheque with the amount not yet filled in.

blanket *NOUN* **blankets** **1** a warm cloth covering used on a bed etc. **2** any thick soft covering • *a blanket of snow.*

blanket *ADJECTIVE* covering all cases or instances • *a blanket ban.*
[originally = woollen cloth which had not been dyed; from French *blanc* = white]

blank verse *NOUN* verse written without rhyme, usually in lines of ten syllables.

blare *VERB* **blares, blaring, blared** make a loud harsh sound.
▷ **blare** *noun*
[imitating the sound]

blasé (*say* **blah**-zay) *ADJECTIVE* bored or unimpressed by things because you are used to them.
[French]

blaspheme (*say* blas-**feem**) *VERB* **blasphemes, blaspheming, blasphemed** talk or write irreverently about sacred things.
[from Greek *blasphemos* = evil- speaking]

blasphemy (*say* **blas**-fim-ee) *NOUN* **blasphemies** irreverent talk about sacred things.
▷ **blasphemous** *adjective*

blast *NOUN* **blasts** **1** a strong rush of wind or air. **2** a loud noise • *the blast of the trumpets.*

blast *VERB* **blasts, blasting, blasted** blow up with explosives.
- **blast off** launch by the firing of rockets.
▷ **blast-off** *noun*
[from Old English; related to *blow*[1]]

blast furnace *NOUN* **blast furnaces** a furnace for smelting ore, with hot air driven in.

blatant (*say* **blay**-tant) *ADJECTIVE* very obvious • *a blatant lie.*
▷ **blatantly** *adverb*
[from an old word meaning 'noisy']

blaze[1] *NOUN* **blazes** a very bright flame, fire, or light.

blaze *VERB* **blazes, blazing, blazed** **1** burn or shine brightly. **2** show great feeling • *He was blazing with anger.*
[from Old English]

blaze[2] *VERB* **blazes, blazing, blazed**
- **blaze a trail** show the way for others to follow.
[origin unknown]

A B C D E F G H I J K L M N O P Q R S T U V W X Y Z

blazer *NOUN* **blazers** a kind of jacket, often with a badge or in the colours of a school or team etc.
[from *blaze*[1] (because originally blazers were made in very bright colours and were thought of as shining or 'blazing')]

-ble *SUFFIX*, SEE **-able**.

bleach *VERB* **bleaches, bleaching, bleached** make or become white.

bleach *NOUN* **bleaches** a substance used to bleach things.
[from Old English; related to *bleak*]

bleak *ADJECTIVE* **1** bare and cold • *a bleak hillside.* **2** dreary or miserable • *a bleak future.*
▷ **bleakly** *adverb* **bleakness** *noun*
[from Old English; related to *bleach*]

bleary *ADJECTIVE* watery and not seeing clearly • *bleary eyes.*
▷ **blearily** *adverb*
[origin unknown]

bleat *NOUN* **bleats** the cry of a lamb, goat, or calf.

bleat *VERB* **bleats, bleating, bleated** make a bleat.
[imitating the sound]

bleed *VERB* **bleeds, bleeding, bled** **1** lose blood. **2** draw blood or fluid from.
[from Old English; related to *blood*]

bleep *NOUN* **bleeps** a short high sound used as a signal.
▷ **bleep** *verb*
[imitating the sound]

bleeper *NOUN* **bleepers** a small electronic device that bleeps when the wearer is contacted.

blemish *NOUN* **blemishes** a flaw; a mark that spoils a thing's appearance.
▷ **blemish** *verb*
[from old French]

blench *VERB* **blenches, blenching, blenched** flinch.
[from Old English]

blend *VERB* **blends, blending, blended** mix smoothly or easily.

blend *NOUN* **blends** a mixture.
[probably from a Scandinavian word]

blender *NOUN* **blenders** an electric machine used to mix food or turn it into liquid.

bless *VERB* **blesses, blessing, blessed** **1** make sacred or holy. **2** bring God's favour on a person or thing.
[from Old English]

blessing *NOUN* **blessings** **1** a prayer that blesses a person or thing; being blessed. **2** something that people are glad of.

blight *NOUN* **blights** **1** a disease that withers plants. **2** something that spoils or damages something • *Vandalism is a blight on our community.*

blight *VERB* **blights, blighting, blighted** **1** affect with blight. **2** spoil or damage something • *Knee injuries have blighted his career.*
[origin unknown]

blind *ADJECTIVE* **1** without the ability to see. **2** without any thought or understanding • *blind obedience.* **3** (said about a tube, passage, or road) closed at one end.
▷ **blindly** *adverb* **blindness** *noun*

blind *VERB* **blinds, blinding, blinded** make a person blind.

blind *NOUN* **blinds** **1** a screen for a window. **2** a deception; something used to hide the truth • *His journey was a blind.*
[from Old English]

blind date *NOUN* **blind dates** a date between people who have not met before.

blindfold *NOUN* **blindfolds** a strip of cloth tied round someone's eyes so that they cannot see.

blindfold *VERB* **blindfolds, blindfolding, blindfolded** cover someone's eyes with a blindfold.
[from Old English *blindfeld* = struck blind, from *blind* + *fell*[2]]

blind spot *NOUN* **blind spots** a subject that you do not understand or know much about.

bling-bling or **bling** *NOUN* (*informal*) showy and expensive jewellery and clothes.
[perhaps from the sound of pieces of jewellery clashing together]

blink *VERB* **blinks, blinking, blinked** shut and open your eyes rapidly.
▷ **blink** *noun*
[from *blench*, influenced by Dutch *blinken* = shine]

blinkers *PLURAL NOUN* leather pieces fixed on a bridle to prevent a horse from seeing sideways.
▷ **blinkered** *adjective*
[originally a person who was half-blind; from *blink*]

bliss *NOUN* perfect happiness.
▷ **blissful** *adjective* **blissfully** *adverb*
[from Old English; related to *blithe*]

blister *NOUN* **blisters** a swelling like a bubble, especially on skin.
▷ **blister** *verb*
[origin unknown]

blithe *ADJECTIVE* casual and carefree.
▷ **blithely** *adverb*
[from Old English; related to *bliss*]

blitz *NOUN* **blitzes** **1** a sudden violent attack. **2** the bombing of London in 1940.
[short for German *Blitzkrieg* (*Blitz* = lightning, *Krieg* = war)]

blizzard *NOUN* **blizzards** a severe snowstorm.
[origin unknown]

bloated *ADJECTIVE* swollen by fat, gas, or liquid.
[from Old Norse *blautr* = soft]

bloater *NOUN* **bloaters** a salted smoked herring.
[same origin as *bloated*]

blob *NOUN* **blobs** a small round mass of something • *blobs of paint.*
[because *blob* sounds squelchy, like liquid]

bloc *NOUN* **blocs** a group of parties or countries who have formed an alliance.
[French, = block]

block *NOUN* **blocks** **1** a solid piece of something. **2** an obstruction. **3** a large building divided into flats or offices. **4** a group of buildings.

block *VERB* **blocks, blocking, blocked** obstruct; prevent something from moving or being used.
▷ **blockage** *noun*
[via French from Dutch]

blockade *NOUN* **blockades** the blocking of a city or port etc. in order to prevent people and goods from going in or out.

blockade *VERB* **blockades, blockading, blockaded** set up a blockade of a place.
[from *block*]

block letters *PLURAL NOUN* plain capital letters.

blogger *NOUN* **bloggers** (*informal*) someone who keeps a weblog, a diary on the Internet, or who writes fiction and posts it on the Internet.
▷ **blog** *noun* **blogging** *noun*
[from *weblogger*]

bloke *NOUN* **blokes** (*informal*) a man.
[from an old language used by Irish and Welsh gypsies]

blond or **blonde** *ADJECTIVE* fair-haired; fair.
[from Latin *blondus* = yellow]

blonde *NOUN* **blondes** a fair-haired girl or woman.

blood *NOUN* **1** the red liquid that flows through veins and arteries. **2** family relationship; ancestry • *He is of royal blood.*
- **in cold blood** deliberately and cruelly.
[from Old English; related to *bleed*]

blood bank *NOUN* **blood banks** a place where supplies of blood and plasma for transfusions are stored.

bloodbath *NOUN* **bloodbaths** a massacre.

blood donor *NOUN* **blood donors** a person who gives blood for use in transfusions.

blood group *NOUN* **blood groups** any of the classes or types of human blood.

bloodhound *NOUN* **bloodhounds** a large dog that was used to track people by their scent.

bloodshed *NOUN* the killing or wounding of people.

bloodshot *ADJECTIVE* (said about eyes) streaked with red.

blood sport *NOUN* **blood sports** a sport that involves wounding or killing animals.

bloodstream *NOUN* the blood circulating in the body.

bloodthirsty *ADJECTIVE* eager for bloodshed.

B

blood vessel *NOUN* **blood vessels** a tube carrying blood in the body; an artery, vein, or capillary.

bloody *ADJECTIVE* **bloodier**, **bloodiest** **1** bloodstained. **2** with much bloodshed • *a bloody battle.*

bloody-minded *ADJECTIVE* deliberately awkward and not helpful.

bloom *NOUN* **blooms** **1** a flower. **2** the fine powder on fresh ripe grapes etc.

bloom *VERB* **blooms**, **blooming**, **bloomed** produce flowers.
[from Old Norse]

blossom *NOUN* **blossoms** a flower or mass of flowers, especially on a fruit tree.

blossom *VERB* **blossoms**, **blossoming**, **blossomed** **1** produce flowers. **2** develop into something • *She blossomed into a fine singer.*
[from Old English]

blot *NOUN* **blots** **1** a spot of ink. **2** a flaw or fault; something ugly • *a blot on the landscape.*

blot *VERB* **blots**, **blotting**, **blotted** **1** make a blot or blots on something. **2** dry with blotting paper.
- **blot out** **1** cross out thickly. **2** obscure • *Fog blotted out the view.*
[probably from a Scandinavian language]

blotch *NOUN* **blotches** an untidy patch of colour.
▷ **blotchy** *adjective*
[related to *blot*]

blotter *NOUN* **blotters** a pad of blotting paper; a holder for blotting paper.

blotting paper *NOUN* absorbent paper for soaking up ink from writing.

blouse *NOUN* **blouses** a loose piece of clothing like a shirt, worn by women.
[from French]

blow[1] *VERB* **blows**, **blowing**, **blew**, **blown** **1** send out a current of air. **2** move in or with a current of air • *His hat blew off.* **3** make or sound something by blowing • *blow bubbles*; • *blow the whistle.* **4** melt with too strong an electric current • *A fuse has blown.* **5** (*slang*) damn • *Blow you!*
- **blow up** **1** inflate. **2** explode. **3** shatter by an explosion.

blow *NOUN* **blows** the action of blowing.
[from Old English]

blow[2] *NOUN* **blows** **1** a hard knock or hit. **2** a shock; a disaster.
[origin unknown]

blowlamp or **blowtorch** *NOUN* **blowlamps, blowtorches** a portable device for directing a very hot flame at a surface.

blowpipe *NOUN* **blowpipes** a tube for sending out a dart or pellet by blowing.

blubber *NOUN* the fat of whales.
[originally = sea foam; probably related to *bubble*]

bludge *VERB* **bludges**, **bludging**, **bludged** (*Australian/NZ*)(*informal*) **1** live off someone else's earnings or on state benefits. **2** avoid work and responsibilities.
[from *bludger* = someone taking profit without work]

bludgeon (*say* bluj-on) *NOUN* **bludgeons** a short stick with a thickened end, used as a weapon.

bludgeon *VERB* **bludgeons**, **bludgeoning**, **bludgeoned** hit someone several times with a heavy stick or other object.
[origin unknown]

blue *NOUN* **blues** the colour of a cloudless sky.
- **out of the blue** unexpectedly.

blue *ADJECTIVE* **1** of the colour blue. **2** unhappy; depressed. **3** indecent; obscene • *blue films.*
▷ **blueness** *noun*
[via French from Germanic]

bluebell *NOUN* **bluebells** a plant with blue bell-shaped flowers.

blue blood *NOUN* aristocratic family.

bluebottle *NOUN* **bluebottles** a large bluish fly.
[origin unknown]

blueprint *NOUN* **blueprints** a detailed plan.
[because copies of plans were made on blue paper]

blues *NOUN* a slow sad jazz song or tune.
- **the blues** a very sad feeling; depression.
[short for *blue devils*, spiteful demons believed to cause depression]

bluff[1] *VERB* **bluffs, bluffing, bluffed** deceive someone, especially by pretending to be someone else or to be able to do something.

bluff *NOUN* **bluffs** bluffing; a threat that you make but do not intend to carry out.
[from Dutch *bluffen* = boast]

bluff[2] *ADJECTIVE* frank and hearty in manner.
▷ **bluffness** *noun*

bluff *NOUN* **bluffs** a cliff with a broad steep front.
[originally a sailor's word to describe a blunt ship's bow]

bluish *ADJECTIVE* rather blue.

blunder *NOUN* **blunders** a stupid mistake.

blunder *VERB* **blunders, blundering, blundered** **1** make a blunder. **2** move clumsily and uncertainly.
[probably from a Scandinavian language]

blunderbuss *NOUN* **blunderbusses** an old type of gun that fired many balls in one shot.
[from Dutch *donderbus* = thunder gun]

blunt *ADJECTIVE* **1** not sharp. **2** speaking in plain terms; straightforward • *a blunt refusal.*
▷ **bluntly** *adverb* **bluntness** *noun*

blunt *VERB* **blunts, blunting, blunted** make a thing blunt.
[probably from a Scandinavian language]

blur *VERB* **blurs, blurring, blurred** make or become indistinct or smeared.

blur *NOUN* **blurs** an indistinct appearance • *Without his glasses on, everything was a blur.*
[origin unknown]

blurt *VERB* **blurts, blurting, blurted** say something suddenly or tactlessly • *He blurted it out.*
[origin unknown]

blush *VERB* **blushes, blushing, blushed** become red in the face because you are ashamed or embarrassed.

blush *NOUN* **blushes** reddening in the face.
[from Old English]

bluster *VERB* **blusters, blustering, blustered** **1** blow in gusts; be windy. **2** talk loudly and aggressively.
▷ **blustery** *adjective*
[imitating the sound]

BMX *ABBREVIATION* a kind of bicycle for use in racing on a dirt track.
[short for *b*icycle *m*otocross (*x* standing for *cross*)]

boa (*say* boh-a) or **boa constrictor** *NOUN* **boas, boa constrictors** a large South American snake that squeezes its prey so that it suffocates it.
[Latin]

boar *NOUN* **boars** **1** a wild pig. **2** a male pig.
[from Old English]

board *NOUN* **boards** **1** a flat piece of wood. **2** a flat piece of stiff material, e.g. a chessboard. **3** daily meals supplied in return for payment or work • *board and lodging.* **4** a committee.
- **on board** on or in a ship, aircraft, etc.

board *VERB* **boards, boarding, boarded** **1** go on board a ship, etc. **2** give or get meals and accommodation.
- **board up** block with fixed boards.
[from Old English]

boarder *NOUN* **boarders** **1** a pupil who lives at a boarding school during the term. **2** a lodger who receives meals.

boarding house *NOUN* **boarding houses** a house where people obtain board and lodging for payment.

boarding school *NOUN* **boarding schools** a school where pupils live during the term.

boast *VERB* **boasts, boasting, boasted** **1** speak with great pride and try to impress people. **2** have something to be proud of • *The town boasts a fine park.*
▷ **boastful** *adjective* **boastfully** *adverb*

boast *NOUN* **boasts** a boastful statement.
[origin unknown]

boat *NOUN* **boats** a vehicle built to travel on water and carry people etc.
- **in the same boat** in the same situation; suffering the same difficulties.
[from Old English]

boater *NOUN* **boaters** a hard flat straw hat.
[originally worn by men *boating*]

boating *NOUN* going out in a boat (especially a rowing boat) for pleasure.

boatswain (*say* **boh**-sun) *NOUN* **boatswains** a ship's officer in charge of rigging, boats, anchors, etc.
[from *boat* + *swain* = servant]

bob *VERB* **bobs, bobbing, bobbed** move quickly up and down.
[origin unknown]

bobbin *NOUN* **bobbins** a small spool holding thread or wire in a machine.
[from French]

bobble *NOUN* **bobbles** a small round ornament, often made of wool.
[origin unknown]

bobsleigh or **bobsled** *NOUN* **bobsleighs, bobsleds** a sledge with two sets of runners.
[origin unknown]

bode *VERB* **bodes, boding, boded** be a sign or omen of what is to come • *It bodes well.*
[from Old English]

bodice *NOUN* **bodices** the upper part of a dress.
[from *body*]

bodily *ADJECTIVE* to do with your body.

bodily by taking hold of someone's body • *He was picked up bodily and bundled into the car.*

bodkin *NOUN* **bodkins** a thick blunt needle for drawing tape etc. through a hem.
[origin unknown]

body *NOUN* **bodies** **1** the structure consisting of bones and flesh etc. of a person or animal; the main part of this apart from the head and limbs. **2** a corpse. **3** the main part of something. **4** a group or quantity regarded as a unit • *the school's governing body.* **5** a distinct object or piece of matter • *Stars and planets are heavenly bodies.*
[from Old English]

bodyguard *NOUN* **bodyguards** a guard to protect a person's life.

Boer (*say* **boh**-er) *NOUN* **Boers** **1** an Afrikaner. **2** (*historical*) an early Dutch inhabitant of South Africa.
[Dutch, = farmer]

boffin *NOUN* **boffins** (*informal*) a person involved in scientific or technical research.
[origin unknown]

bog *NOUN* **bogs** an area of wet spongy ground.
▷ **boggy** *adjective*
- **bogged down** stuck and unable to make any progress.
[Scottish Gaelic, = soft]

boggle *VERB* **boggles, boggling, boggled** be amazed or puzzled • *The mind boggles at the idea.*
[from dialect *bogle* = bogy]

bogus *ADJECTIVE* not real; sham.
[an American word; origin unknown]

bogy *NOUN* **bogies** **1** an evil spirit. **2** something that frightens people.
▷ **bogyman** *noun*
[origin unknown]

boil[1] *VERB* **boils, boiling, boiled** **1** make or become hot enough to bubble and give off steam. **2** cook or wash something in boiling water. **3** be very hot.

boil *NOUN* boiling point • *Bring the milk to the boil.*
[from old French]

boil[2] *NOUN* **boils** an inflamed swelling under the skin.
[from Old English]

boiler *NOUN* **boilers** a container in which water is heated or clothes are boiled.

boiling point *NOUN* **boiling points** the temperature at which something boils.

boisterous *ADJECTIVE* noisy and lively.
[origin unknown]

bold *ADJECTIVE* **1** confident and courageous. **2** impudent. **3** (said about colours, designs, etc.) strong and vivid.
▷ **boldly** *adverb* **boldness** *noun*
[from Old English]

bole *NOUN* **boles** the trunk of a tree.
[from Old Norse]

bollard *NOUN* **bollards** **1** a short thick post to which a ship's mooring-rope may be tied. **2** a short post for directing traffic or keeping it off a pavement etc.
[probably the same origin as *bole*]

bolster *NOUN* **bolsters** a long pillow for placing across a bed under other pillows.

bolster *VERB* **bolsters, bolstering, bolstered** add extra support.
[from Old English]

bolt *NOUN* **bolts** **1** a sliding bar for fastening a door. **2** a thick metal pin for fastening things together. **3** a sliding bar that opens and closes the breech of a rifle. **4** a shaft of lightning. **5** an arrow shot from a crossbow. **6** the action of bolting.
- **a bolt from the blue** a surprise, usually an unpleasant one.
- **bolt upright** quite upright.

bolt *VERB* **bolts, bolting, bolted** **1** fasten with a bolt or bolts. **2** run away or escape. **3** swallow food quickly.
[from Old English]

bomb *NOUN* **bombs** an explosive device.
- **the bomb** the nuclear bomb.

bomb *VERB* **bombs, bombing, bombed** attack a place with bombs.
[probably from Greek *bombos* = booming]

bombard *VERB* **bombards, bombarding, bombarded** **1** attack with gunfire or many missiles. **2** direct a large number of questions or comments etc. at somebody.
▷ **bombardment** *noun*
[same origin as *bomb*]

bombastic (*say* bom-**bast**-ik) *ADJECTIVE* using pompous words.
[from *bombast* = material used for padding; later 'padded' language, with long or unnecessary words]

bomber *NOUN* **bombers** **1** someone who plants or sets off a bomb. **2** an aeroplane from which bombs are dropped.

bombshell *NOUN* **bombshells** a great shock.

bona fide (*say* **boh**-na **fy**-dee) *ADJECTIVE* genuine; without fraud • *Are they bona fide tourists or spies?*
[Latin, = in good faith]

bona fides (*say* **boh**-na **fy**-deez) *PLURAL NOUN* honest intention; sincerity • *We do not doubt his bona fides.*
[Latin, = good faith]

bonanza (*say* bon-**an**-za) *NOUN* **bonanzas** sudden great wealth or luck.
[originally an American word; from Spanish, = good weather, prosperity]

bond *NOUN* **bonds** **1** a close friendship or connection between two or more people. **2 bonds** ropes or chains used to tie someone up. **3** a document stating an agreement.

bond *VERB* **bonds, bonding, bonded** become closely linked or connected.
[a different spelling of *band*[1]]

bondage *NOUN* slavery; captivity.

bone *NOUN* **bones** **1** one of the hard whitish parts that make up the skeleton of a person's or animal's body. **2** the substance from which these parts are made.

bone *VERB* **bones, boning, boned** remove the bones from meat or fish.
[from Old English]

bone dry *ADJECTIVE* quite dry.

bonfire *NOUN* **bonfires** an outdoor fire to burn rubbish or celebrate something.
[originally *bone fire*, = a fire to dispose of people's or animals' bones]

bonnet *NOUN* **bonnets** **1** a hat with strings that tie under the chin. **2** a Scottish beret. **3** the hinged cover over a car engine.
[from Latin *abonnis* = hat]

bonny *ADJECTIVE* **bonnier, bonniest** **1** healthy-looking. **2** (*Scottish*) good-looking.
[from French *bon* = good]

bonus (*say* **boh**-nus) *NOUN* **bonuses** **1** an extra payment in addition to a person's normal wages. **2** an extra benefit.
[from Latin *bonus* = good]

bon voyage (*say* bawn vwah-**yah***zh*) *INTERJECTION* pleasant journey!
[French]

bony *ADJECTIVE* **1** with large bones; having bones with little flesh on them. **2** full of bones. **3** like bones.

boo *VERB* **boos, booing, booed** shout 'boo' in disapproval.
▷ **boo** *noun*

booby *NOUN* **boobies** a babyish or stupid person.
[from Spanish]

booby prize *NOUN* **booby prizes** a prize given as a joke to someone who comes last in a contest.

booby trap *NOUN* **booby traps** something designed to hit or injure someone unexpectedly.

B

book *NOUN* **books** a set of sheets of paper, usually with printing or writing on them, fastened together inside a cover.
▷ **bookseller** *noun* **bookshop** *noun* **bookstall** *noun*

book *VERB* **books, booking, booked** **1** reserve a place in a theatre, hotel, train, etc. **2** enter a person in a police record • *The police booked him for speeding.*
[from Old English]

bookcase *NOUN* **bookcases** a piece of furniture with shelves for books.

bookkeeping *NOUN* recording details of the money that is spent and received by a business.
▷ **bookkeeper** *noun*

booklet *NOUN* **booklets** a small thin book.

bookmaker *NOUN* **bookmakers** a person whose business is taking bets, especially bets made on horse races.
[because the bets used to be written down in a notebook]

bookmark *NOUN* **bookmarks** **1** something to mark a place in a book. **2** (*in computing*) a record of the address of a file, Internet page, etc. so that you can find it again quickly.

bookworm *NOUN* **bookworms** **1** a grub that eats holes in books. **2** a person who loves reading.

boom[1] *VERB* **booms, booming, boomed** **1** make a deep hollow sound. **2** be growing and prospering • *Business is booming.*

boom *NOUN* **booms** **1** a deep hollow sound. **2** prosperity; growth.
[imitating the sound]

boom[2] *NOUN* **booms** **1** a long pole at the bottom of a sail to keep it stretched. **2** a long pole carrying a microphone etc. **3** a chain or floating barrier that can be placed across a river or a harbour entrance.
[from Dutch, = beam, tree]

boomerang *NOUN* **boomerangs** a curved piece of wood that can be thrown so that it returns to the thrower, originally used by Australian Aborigines.
[an Australian Aboriginal word]

boon *NOUN* **boons** something that makes life easier.
[from Old Norse *bon* = prayer]

boon companion *NOUN* **boon companions** a friendly companion.
[from French *bon* = good]

boor *NOUN* **boors** an ill-mannered person.
▷ **boorish** *adjective*
[same origin as *Boer*]

boost *VERB* **boosts, boosting, boosted** **1** increase the strength, value, or reputation of a person or thing. **2** push something upwards.
▷ **booster** *noun*

boost *NOUN* **boosts** **1** an increase. **2** an upward push.
[origin unknown]

boot *NOUN* **boots** **1** a shoe that covers the foot and ankle or leg. **2** the compartment for luggage in a car.
▷ **booted** *adjective*

boot *VERB* **boots, booting, booted** **1** kick hard. **2** switch a computer on and get it ready to use.
[via Old Norse from French]

bootee *NOUN* **bootees** a baby's knitted boot.

booth *NOUN* **booths** a small enclosure.
[from Old Norse]

booty *NOUN* valuable goods taken away by soldiers after a battle.
[from old German *buite* = exchange, sharing out]

booze *VERB* **boozes, boozing, boozed** (*slang*) drink alcohol.

booze *NOUN* (*slang*) alcoholic drink.
[from old Dutch *busen* = drink too much alcohol]

borax *NOUN* a soluble white powder used in making glass, detergents, etc.
[via Latin and Arabic from Pahlavi (an old form of Persian)]

border *NOUN* **borders** **1** the boundary of a country; the part near this. **2** an edge. **3** something placed round an edge to strengthen or decorate it. **4** a strip of ground round a garden or part of it.

border *VERB* **borders, bordering, bordered** put or be a border to something.
[from old French]

borderline *NOUN* **borderlines** a boundary.

borderline *ADJECTIVE* only just belonging to a particular group or category • *You're a borderline pass.*

bore[1] *VERB* **bores, boring, bored 1** drill a hole. **2** get through by pushing.

bore *NOUN* **bores 1** the width of the inside of a gun barrel. **2** a hole made by boring. [from Old English]

bore[2] *VERB* **bores, boring, bored** make somebody feel uninterested by being dull.

bore *NOUN* **bores** a boring person or thing.
▷ **boredom** *noun*
[origin unknown]

bore[3] *NOUN* **bores** a tidal wave with a steep front that moves up some estuaries.
[from Old Norse *bara* = wave]

bore[4] *past tense* of **bear**[2].

bored *ADJECTIVE* weary and uninterested because something is so dull.

USAGE You can say that you are *bored with* something or *bored by* something: *I'm bored with this game.* It is not acceptable in standard English to say *bored of.*

boring *ADJECTIVE* tedious and uninteresting.

born *ADJECTIVE* **1** having come into existence by birth. (See the note on **borne**.) **2** having a certain natural quality or ability • *a born leader.*
[from Old English]

borne *past participle* of **bear**[2].

USAGE The word *borne* is used before *by* or after *have, has,* or *had,* e.g. *children borne by Eve; she had borne him a son.* The word *born* is used e.g. in *a son was born.*

borough (*say* burra) *NOUN* **boroughs** an important town or district.
[from Old English *burg* = fortress or fortified town]

borrow *VERB* **borrows, borrowing, borrowed 1** get something to use for a time, with the intention to give it back afterwards. **2** obtain money as a loan.
▷ **borrower** *noun*
[from Old English]

USAGE Do not confuse **borrow** with **lend**, which means just the opposite.

bosom *NOUN* **bosoms** a woman's breasts.
[from Old English]

boss[1] *NOUN* **bosses** (*informal*) a manager; a person whose job is to give orders to workers etc.

boss *VERB* **bosses, bossing, bossed** (*slang*) order someone about.
[from Dutch *baas* = master]

boss[2] *NOUN* **bosses** a round raised knob or stud.
[from old French]

bossy *ADJECTIVE* fond of ordering people about.
▷ **bossiness** *noun*

botany *NOUN* the study of plants.
▷ **botanical** *adjective* **botanist** *noun*
[from Greek *botane* = a plant]

botch *VERB* **botches, botching, botched** spoil something by poor or clumsy work.
[origin unknown]

both *ADJECTIVE & PRONOUN* the two; not only one • *Are both films good? Both are old.*

both *ADVERB* - **both ... and** not only ... but also • *The house is both small and ugly.*
[from Old Norse]

bother *VERB* **bothers, bothering, bothered 1** cause somebody trouble or worry; pester. **2** take trouble; feel concern • *Don't bother to reply.*

bother *NOUN* trouble or worry.
[probably from Irish *bodhraim* = deafen, annoy]

bottle *NOUN* **bottles 1** a narrow-necked container for liquids. **2** (*slang*) courage • *She showed a lot of bottle.*

bottle *VERB* **bottles, bottling, bottled** put or store something in bottles.
- **bottle up** if you bottle up your feelings, you keep them to yourself.
[same origin as *butt*[2]]

bottle bank *NOUN* **bottle banks** a large container in which used glass bottles are collected for recycling.

bottleneck *NOUN* **bottlenecks** a narrow place where something, especially traffic, cannot flow freely.

bottom *NOUN* **bottoms 1** the lowest part; the base. **2** the part furthest away • *the bottom of the garden.* **3** a person's buttocks.

bottom *ADJECTIVE* lowest • *the bottom shelf.*
[from Old English]

A B C D E F G H I J K L M N O P Q R S T U V W X Y Z

bottomless *ADJECTIVE* extremely deep.

boudoir (*say* boo-dwar) *NOUN* **boudoirs** a woman's private room.
[French, = place to sulk in]

bough *NOUN* **boughs** a large branch coming from the trunk of a tree.
[from Old English]

boulder *NOUN* **boulders** a very large smooth stone.
[from a Scandinavian word]

boulevard (*say* bool-ev-ard) *NOUN* **boulevards** a wide street, often with trees.
[French, related to *bulwark*]

bounce *VERB* **bounces, bouncing, bounced** **1** spring back when thrown against something. **2** make a ball etc. bounce. **3** (said about a cheque) be sent back by the bank because there is not enough money in the account. **4** jump suddenly; move in a lively manner.

bounce *NOUN* **bounces** **1** the action or power of bouncing. **2** a lively confident manner • *full of bounce.*
▷ **bouncy** *adjective*
[origin unknown]

bouncer *NOUN* **bouncers** **1** a person who stands at the door of a club etc. and stops unwanted people coming in or makes troublemakers leave. **2** a ball in cricket that bounces high.

bound[1] *VERB* **bounds, bounding, bounded** jump or spring; run with jumping movements.

bound *NOUN* **bounds** a bounding movement.
[from old French *bondir*]

bound[2] *past tense* of **bind**.

bound *ADJECTIVE* obstructed or hindered by something • *The airport is fog-bound.*
- **bound to** certain to • *He is bound to fail.*
- **bound up with** closely connected with • *Happiness is bound up with success.*

bound[3] *ADJECTIVE* going towards something • *We are bound for Spain.*
[from Old Norse]

bound[4] *VERB* **bounds, bounding, bounded** limit; be the boundary of • *Their land is bounded by the river.*
[from old French *bonde*]

boundary *NOUN* **boundaries** **1** a line that marks a limit. **2** a hit to the boundary of a cricket field.
[from *bound*[4]]

bounden *ADJECTIVE* obligatory • *your bounden duty.*
[from *bind*]

bounds *PLURAL NOUN* limits • *This was beyond the bounds of possibility.*
- **out of bounds** where you are not allowed to go.
[from *bound*[4]]

bountiful *ADJECTIVE* **1** plentiful; abundant • *bountiful harvest.* **2** giving generously.

bounty *NOUN* **bounties** **1** a generous gift. **2** generosity in giving things. **3** a reward for doing something.
[from Latin *bonitas* = goodness]

bouquet (*say* boh-kay) *NOUN* **bouquets** a bunch of flowers.
[French, = group of trees]

bout *NOUN* **bouts** **1** a boxing or wrestling contest. **2** a period of exercise or work or illness • *a bout of flu.*
[probably from old German]

boutique (*say* boo-teek) *NOUN* **boutiques** a small shop selling fashionable clothes.
[French]

bovine (*say* boh-vyn) *ADJECTIVE* **1** to do with or like cattle. **2** stupid.
[from Latin *bovis* = of an ox]

bow[1] (*rhymes with* **go**) *NOUN* **bows** **1** a strip of wood curved by a tight string joining its ends, used for shooting arrows. **2** a wooden rod with horsehair stretched between its ends, used for playing a violin etc. **3** a knot made with loops.
[from Old English *boga*]

bow[2] (*rhymes with* **cow**) *VERB* **bows, bowing, bowed** **1** bend your body forwards to show respect or as a greeting. **2** bend downwards • *bowed by the weight.*

bow *NOUN* **bows** bowing your body.
[from Old English *bugan*]

bow[3] (*rhymes with* **cow**) *NOUN* **bows** the front part of a ship.
[from old German or Dutch]

bowels *PLURAL NOUN* the intestines.
[from Latin *botellus* = little sausage]

bower *NOUN* **bowers** a leafy shelter.
[from Old English; related to *build*]

bowl[1] *NOUN* **bowls** **1** a rounded usually deep container for food or liquid. **2** the rounded part of a spoon or tobacco pipe etc.
[from Old English]

bowl[2] *NOUN* **bowls** a ball used in the game of
- **bowls** or in bowling, when heavy balls are rolled towards skittles.

bowl *VERB* **bowls, bowling, bowled** **1** send a ball to be played by a batsman. **2** get a batsman out by bowling. **3** send a ball etc. rolling.
[from old French]

bow-legged *ADJECTIVE* having legs that curve outwards at the knees; bandy.

bowler[1] *NOUN* **bowlers** a person who bowls.

bowler[2] or **bowler hat** *NOUN* **bowlers, bowler hats** a man's stiff felt hat with a rounded top.
[named after William *Bowler*, who designed it]

bowling *NOUN* **1** the game of bowls. **2** the game of knocking down skittles with a heavy ball.

bow tie *NOUN* **bow ties** a man's necktie tied into a bow.

bow window *NOUN* **bow windows** a curved window.

box[1] *NOUN* **boxes** **1** a container made of wood, cardboard, etc., usually with a top or lid. **2** a rectangular space to be filled in on a form, computer screen, etc. **3** a compartment in a theatre, lawcourt, etc. • *witness box.* **4** a hut or shelter • *sentry box.* **5** a small evergreen shrub.
- **the box** (*informal*) television.

box *VERB* **boxes, boxing, boxed** put something into a box.
[from Latin]

box[2] *VERB* **boxes, boxing, boxed** fight with the fists as a sport.
▷ **boxing** *noun*
[origin unknown]

boxer *NOUN* **boxers** **1** a person who boxes. **2** a dog that looks like a bulldog.

Boxing Day *NOUN* the first weekday after Christmas Day.
[from the old custom of giving presents (*Christmas boxes*) to tradesmen and servants on that day]

box number *NOUN* **box numbers** the number used as an address in replying to newspaper advertisements.

box office *NOUN* **box offices** an office for booking seats at a theatre or cinema etc.
[because boxes could be reserved there]

boy *NOUN* **boys** **1** a male child. **2** a young man.
▷ **boyhood** *noun* **boyish** *adjective*
[origin unknown]

boycott *VERB* **boycotts, boycotting, boycotted** refuse to use or have anything to do with • *They boycotted the buses when the fares went up.*
▷ **boycott** *noun*
[from the name of Captain *Boycott*, a harsh landlord in Ireland whose tenants in 1880 refused to deal with him]

boyfriend *NOUN* **boyfriends** a person's regular male friend or lover.

bra *NOUN* **bras** a piece of underwear worn by women to support their breasts.
[abbreviation of French *brassière*]

brace *NOUN* **braces** **1** a device for holding things in place. **2** a pair • *a brace of pheasants.*

brace *VERB* **braces, bracing, braced** support; make a thing firm against something.
[from Latin *bracchia* = arms]

bracelet *NOUN* **bracelets** an ornament worn round the wrist.
[same origin as *brace*]

braces *PLURAL NOUN* straps to hold trousers up, passing over the shoulders.

bracing *ADJECTIVE* making you feel refreshed and healthy • *the bracing sea breeze.*

bracken *NOUN* a type of large fern that grows in open country; a mass of these ferns.
[from Old Norse]

A B C D E F G H I J K L M N O P Q R S T U V W X Y Z

bracket *NOUN* **brackets** **1** a mark used in pairs to enclose words or figures. There are round brackets ( ) and square brackets [ ]. **2** a support attached to a wall etc. **3** a group or range between certain limits • *a high income bracket*.

bracket *VERB* **brackets, bracketing, bracketed** **1** enclose in brackets. **2** put things together because they are similar.
[from Latin *bracae* = breeches]

brackish *ADJECTIVE* (said about water) slightly salty.
[from German or Dutch *brac* = salt water]

brae (*say* bray) *NOUN* **braes** (*Scottish*) a hillside.
[from Old Norse]

brag *VERB* **brags, bragging, bragged** boast.
[origin unknown]

braggart *NOUN* **braggarts** a person who brags.

Brahmin *NOUN* **Brahmins** a member of the highest Hindu class, originally priests.
[from Sanskrit *brahman* = priest]

braid *NOUN* **braids** **1** a plait of hair. **2** a strip of cloth with a woven decorative pattern, used as trimming.

braid *VERB* **braids, braiding, braided** **1** plait. **2** trim with braid.
[from Old English]

Braille (*rhymes with* **mail**) *NOUN* a system of representing letters etc. by raised dots which blind people can read by touch.
[named after Louis *Braille*, a blind French teacher who invented it in about 1830]

brain *NOUN* **brains** **1** the organ inside the top of the head that controls the body. **2** the mind; intelligence.
[from Old English]

brainwash *VERB* **brainwashes, brainwashing, brainwashed** force a person to give up one set of ideas or beliefs and accept new ones; indoctrinate.

brainwave *NOUN* **brainwaves** a sudden bright idea.

brainy *ADJECTIVE* clever; intelligent.

braise *VERB* **braises, braising, braised** cook slowly in a little liquid in a closed container.
[same origin as *brazier*]

brake *NOUN* **brakes** a device for slowing or stopping something.

brake *VERB* **brakes, braking, braked** use a brake.
[origin unknown]

bramble *NOUN* **brambles** a blackberry bush or a prickly bush like it.
[from Old English; related to *broom*]

bran *NOUN* ground-up husks of corn.
[from old French]

branch *NOUN* **branches** **1** a woody arm-like part of a tree or shrub. **2** a part of a railway, road, or river etc. that leads off from the main part. **3** a shop or office etc. that belongs to a large organization.

branch *VERB* **branches, branching, branched** form a branch.
- **branch out** start something new.
[from Latin *branca* = a paw]

brand *NOUN* **brands** **1** a particular make of goods. **2** a mark made by branding. **3** a piece of burning wood.
▷ **brand name** *noun*

brand *VERB* **brands, branding, branded** **1** mark cattle or sheep etc. with a hot iron to identify them. **2** sell goods under a particular trade mark.
[from Old English]

brandish *VERB* **brandishes, brandishing, brandished** wave something about.
[via old French from Germanic; related to *brand*]

brand new *ADJECTIVE* completely new.

brandy *NOUN* **brandies** a strong alcoholic drink, usually made from wine.
[from Dutch *brandewijn* = burnt (distilled) wine]

brash *ADJECTIVE* **1** impudent. **2** reckless.
[origin unknown]

brass *NOUN* **brasses** **1** a metal that is an alloy of copper and zinc. **2** wind instruments made of brass, e.g. trumpets and trombones.
▷ **brass** *adjective* **brassy** *adjective*
[from Old English]

brass band *NOUN* **brass bands** a musical band made up of brass instruments.

brassière (*say* bras-ee-air) *NOUN* **brassières** a bra.
[French]

brat *NOUN* **brats** (*contemptuous*) a child.
[origin unknown]

bravado (*say* brav-**ah**-doh) *NOUN* a display of boldness.
[from Spanish]

brave *ADJECTIVE* having or showing courage.
▷ **bravely** *adverb* **bravery** *noun*

brave *NOUN* **braves** a Native American warrior.

brave *VERB* **braves, braving, braved** face and endure something bravely.
[from Latin *barbarus* = barbarous]

bravo (*say* brah-**voh**) *INTERJECTION* well done!
[Italian]

brawl *NOUN* **brawls** a noisy quarrel or fight.

brawl *VERB* **brawls, brawling, brawled** take part in a brawl.
[origin unknown]

brawn *NOUN* **1** muscular strength. **2** cold boiled pork or veal pressed in a mould.
[via old French from Germanic]

brawny *ADJECTIVE* strong and muscular.

bray *NOUN* **brays** the loud harsh cry of a donkey.
▷ **bray** *verb*
[from old French *braire* = to cry]

brazen *ADJECTIVE* **1** made of brass. **2** shameless • *brazen impudence.*

brazen *VERB* **brazens, brazening, brazened**
- **brazen it out** behave, after doing wrong, as if you have nothing to be ashamed of.
[from Old English]

brazier (*say* **bray**-zee-er) *NOUN* **braziers** a metal framework for holding burning coals.
[from French *braise* = coals, embers]

breach *NOUN* **breaches** **1** the breaking of an agreement or rule. **2** a broken place; a gap.

breach *VERB* **breaches, breaching, breached** break through; make a gap.
[via old French from Germanic; related to *break*]

bread *NOUN* **breads** a food made by baking flour and water, usually with yeast.
▷ **breadcrumbs** *plural noun*
[from Old English]

breadth *NOUN* width; broadness.
[from Old English]

breadwinner *NOUN* **breadwinners** the member of a family who earns money to support the others.

break *VERB* **breaks, breaking, broke, broken** **1** divide or fall into pieces by hitting or pressing. **2** damage; stop working properly. **3** fail to keep a promise or law etc. **4** stop for a time; end • *She broke her silence.* **5** change • *the weather broke.* **6** (said about a boy's voice) become suddenly deeper at puberty. **7** (said about waves) fall in foam. **8** go suddenly or with force • *They broke through.* **9** appear suddenly • *Dawn had broken.*
▷ **breakage** *noun*
- **break a record** do better than anyone else has done before.
- **break down** **1** stop working properly. **2** collapse.
- **break out** **1** begin suddenly. **2** escape.
- **break the news** make something known.
- **break up** **1** break into small parts. **2** separate at the end of a school term. **3** end your relationship with someone • *My brother and his girlfriend have broken up.*

break *NOUN* **breaks** **1** a broken place; a gap. **2** an escape; a sudden dash. **3** a short rest from work. **4** a number of points scored continuously in snooker etc. **5** (*informal*) a piece of luck; a fair chance • *Give me a break.*
- **break of day** dawn.
[from Old English]

breakable *ADJECTIVE* able to be broken.

breakdown *NOUN* **breakdowns** **1** breaking down; failure. **2** a period of mental illness caused by anxiety or depression. **3** an analysis of accounts or statistics. **4** a sudden failure to work, esp. by a car • *We had a breakdown on the motorway; the breakdown of law and order.*

breaker *NOUN* **breakers** a large wave breaking on the shore.

breakfast *NOUN* **breakfasts** the first meal of the day.
[from *break* + *fast*[2]]

breakneck *ADJECTIVE* dangerously fast • *He had to drive at breakneck speed to get there on time.*

breakthrough *NOUN* **breakthroughs** an important advance or achievement.

A B C D E F G H I J K L M N O P Q R S T U V W X Y Z

breakwater *NOUN* **breakwaters** a wall built out into the sea to protect a coast from heavy waves.

bream *NOUN* **bream** a kind of fish with an arched back.
[via old French from Germanic]

breast *NOUN* **breasts** **1** one of the two fleshy parts on the upper front of a woman's body that produce milk to feed a baby. **2** a person's or animal's chest.
[from Old English]

breastbone *NOUN* **breastbones** the flat bone down the centre of the chest or breast.

breastplate *NOUN* **breastplates** a piece of armour covering the chest.

breath (*say* breth) *NOUN* **breaths** **1** air drawn into the lungs and sent out again. **2** a gentle blowing • *a breath of wind.*
- **out of breath** panting.
- **take your breath away** surprise or delight you greatly.
- **under your breath** in a whisper.

[from Old English]

breathalyser *NOUN* **breathalysers** a device for measuring the amount of alcohol in a person's breath.
▷ **breathalyse** *verb*
[from *breath* + *analyse*]

breathe (*say* breeth) *VERB* **breathes, breathing, breathed** **1** take air into the body and send it out again. **2** speak or utter • *Don't breathe a word of this.*
[from *breath*]

breather (*say* bree-*th*er) *NOUN* **breathers** a pause for rest • *Let's take a breather.*

breathless *ADJECTIVE* out of breath.

breathtaking *ADJECTIVE* very surprising or delightful.

breech *NOUN* **breeches** the back part of a gun barrel, where the bullets are put in.
[from Old English *brec* = hindquarters]

breeches (*say* brich-iz) *PLURAL NOUN* trousers reaching to just below the knees.
[same origin as *breech*]

breed *VERB* **breeds, breeding, bred** **1** produce young creatures. **2** keep animals in order to produce young ones from them. **3** bring up or train. **4** create or produce • *Poverty breeds illness.*
▷ **breeder** *noun*

breed *NOUN* **breeds** a variety of animals with qualities inherited from their parents.
[from Old English; related to *brood*]

breeze *NOUN* **breezes** a wind.
▷ **breezy** *adjective*
[probably from Spanish]

breeze block *NOUN* **breeze blocks** a lightweight building block made of cinders and cement.
[same origin as *brazier*]

brethren *PLURAL NOUN* (*old use*) brothers.
[the old plural of *brother*]

breve (*say* breev) *NOUN* **breves** a note in music, lasting eight times as long as a crotchet.
[same origin as *brief*]

brevity *NOUN* shortness; briefness.
[same origin as *brief*]

brew *VERB* **brews, brewing, brewed** **1** make beer or tea. **2** develop • *Trouble is brewing.*

brew *NOUN* **brews** a brewed drink.
[from Old English]

brewer *NOUN* **brewers** a person who brews beer for sale.

brewery *NOUN* **breweries** a place where beer is brewed.

briar *NOUN* **briars** a different spelling of *brier*.

bribe *NOUN* **bribes** money or a gift offered to a person to influence him or her.

bribe *VERB* **bribes, bribing, bribed** give someone a bribe.
▷ **bribery** *noun*
[from Old French *briber* = beg]

brick *NOUN* **bricks** **1** a small hard block of baked clay etc. used to build walls. **2** a rectangular block of something.

brick *VERB* **bricks, bricking, bricked** close something with bricks • *We bricked up the gap in the wall.*
[from old German or Dutch]

bricklayer *NOUN* **bricklayers** a worker who builds with bricks.

bride *NOUN* **brides** a woman on her wedding day.
▷ **bridal** *adjective*
[from Old English]

bridegroom *NOUN* **bridegrooms** a man on his wedding day.
[from Old English *brydguma* = bride's man]

bridesmaid *NOUN* **bridesmaids** a girl or unmarried woman who attends the bride at a wedding.

bridge[1] *NOUN* **bridges** **1** a structure built over and across a river, railway, or road etc. to allow people to cross it. **2** a high platform above a ship's deck, for the officer in charge. **3** the bony upper part of the nose. **4** something that connects things.

bridge *VERB* **bridges, bridging, bridged** make or form a bridge over something.
[from Old English]

bridge[2] *NOUN* a card game rather like whist.
[origin unknown]

bridle *NOUN* **bridles** the part of a horse's harness that fits over its head.
[from Old English; related to *braid*]

bridleway or **bridle path** *NOUN* **bridleways, bridle paths** a road suitable for horses but not for vehicles.

brief *ADJECTIVE* short.
▷ **briefly** *adverb* **briefness** *noun*
- **in brief** in a few words.

brief *NOUN* **briefs** instructions and information given to someone, especially to a barrister.

brief *VERB* **briefs, briefing, briefed** **1** give a brief to a barrister. **2** instruct or inform someone concisely in advance.
[from Latin *brevis* = short]

briefcase *NOUN* **briefcases** a flat case for carrying documents etc.

briefing *NOUN* **briefings** a meeting to give someone concise instructions or information.

briefs *PLURAL NOUN* very short knickers or underpants.

brier *NOUN* **brier** a thorny bush, especially the wild rose.
[from Old English]

brigade *NOUN* **brigades** **1** a large unit of an army. **2** a group of people organized for a special purpose • *the fire brigade.*
[from Italian *brigata* = a troop]

brigadier *NOUN* **brigadiers** an army officer who commands a brigade, higher in rank than a colonel.

brigand *NOUN* **brigands** a member of a band of robbers.
[from Italian *brigante* = foot soldier]

bright *ADJECTIVE* **1** giving a strong light; shining. **2** clever. **3** cheerful.
▷ **brightly** *adverb* **brightness** *noun*
[from Old English]

brighten *VERB* **brightens, brightening, brightened** make or become brighter.

brilliant *ADJECTIVE* **1** very bright; sparkling. **2** very clever.
▷ **brilliantly** *adverb* **brilliance** *noun*
[from Italian *brillare* = shine]

brim *NOUN* **brims** **1** the edge of a cup, bowl, or other container. **2** the bottom part of a hat that sticks out.

brim *VERB* **brims, brimming, brimmed** be full to the brim.
- **brim over** overflow.
[origin unknown]

brimful *ADJECTIVE* full to the brim.

brimstone *NOUN* (*old use*) sulphur.
[from Old English *brynstan* = burning stone]

brine *NOUN* salt water.
▷ **briny** *adjective*
[from Old English]

bring *VERB* **brings, bringing, brought** cause a person or thing to come; lead; carry.
- **bring about** cause to happen.
- **bring off** achieve; do something successfully.
- **bring up** **1** look after and train growing children. **2** mention a subject. **3** vomit. **4** cause to stop suddenly.
[from Old English]

brinjal *NOUN* **brinjals** (*Indian & S. African*) an aubergine or eggplant.
[from Arabic]

brink *NOUN* **brinks** **1** the edge of a steep place or of a stretch of water. **2** the point beyond which something will happen • *We were on the brink of war.*
[from Old Norse *brekka* = hill, slope]

brisk *ADJECTIVE* quick and lively.
▷ **briskly** *adverb* **briskness** *noun*
[same origin as *brusque*]

A B C D E F G H I J K L M N O P Q R S T U V W X Y Z

bristle *NOUN* **bristles** **1** a short stiff hair. **2** one of the stiff pieces of hair, wire, or plastic etc. in a brush.
▷ **bristly** *adjective*

bristle *VERB* **bristles, bristling, bristled** **1** (said about an animal) raise its bristles in anger or fear. **2** show indignation.
- **bristle with** be full of • *The plan bristled with problems.*
[from Old English]

Britain *NOUN* the island made up of England, Scotland, and Wales, with the small adjacent islands; Great Britain.
USAGE Note the difference in use between the terms *Britain, Great Britain*, the *United Kingdom*, and the *British Isles*. Great Britain (or Britain) is used to refer to the island made up of England, Scotland, and Wales. The United Kingdom includes Great Britain and Northern Ireland. The British Isles refers to the whole of the island group which includes Great Britain, Ireland, and all the smaller nearby islands.

British Isles *PLURAL NOUN* the island group which includes Great Britain, Ireland, and all the smaller nearby islands.
USAGE See note at **Britain**.

brittle *ADJECTIVE* hard but easy to break or snap.
▷ **brittleness** *noun*
[from Old English]

broach *VERB* **broaches, broaching, broached** **1** start a discussion of something • *We were unwilling to broach the subject.* **2** make a hole in something and draw out liquid.
[from old French]

broad *ADJECTIVE* **1** large across; wide. **2** full and complete • *broad daylight.* **3** in general terms; not detailed • *We are in broad agreement.* **4** strong and unmistakable • *a broad hint;* • *a broad accent.*
▷ **broadly** *adverb* **broadness** *noun*
[from Old English]

broadband *NOUN* (*in computing*) a system for connecting computers to the Internet at very high speed.

broad bean *NOUN* **broad beans** a bean with large flat seeds.

broadcast *NOUN* **broadcasts** a programme sent out on the radio or on television.

broadcast *VERB* **broadcasts, broadcasting, broadcast** send out a programme on the radio or on television.
▷ **broadcaster** *noun*
[originally = to scatter widely: from *broad* + *cast*]

broaden *VERB* **broadens, broadening, broadened** make or become broader.

broad-minded *ADJECTIVE* tolerant; not easily shocked.

broadside *NOUN* **broadsides** **1** firing by all guns on one side of a ship. **2** a verbal attack.
- **broadside on** sideways on.
[originally = the side of a ship, above the waterline]

brocade *NOUN* material woven with raised patterns.
[from Italian]

broccoli *NOUN* **broccoli** a kind of cauliflower with greenish flowerheads.
[Italian, = cabbage- heads]

brochure (*say* **broh**-shoor) *NOUN* **brochures** a booklet or pamphlet containing information.
[from French, = stitching (because originally the pages were roughly stitched together)]

brogue[1] (*rhymes with* **rogue**) *NOUN* **brogues** a strong kind of shoe.
[via Scottish Gaelic and Irish from Old Norse]

brogue[2] *NOUN* **brogues** a strong accent • *He spoke with an Irish brogue.*
[origin unknown]

broil *VERB* **broils, broiling, broiled** **1** cook on a fire or gridiron. **2** make or be very hot.
[from French *brûler* = to burn]

broke *ADJECTIVE* (*informal*) having spent all your money.
[old past participle of *break*]

broken-hearted *ADJECTIVE* overwhelmed with grief.

broken home *NOUN* **broken homes** a family in which the parents are divorced or separated.

broker *NOUN* **brokers** a person who buys and sells things, especially shares, for other people.

brolly *NOUN* **brollies** (*informal*) an umbrella.

bromide *NOUN* a substance used in medicine to calm the nerves.
[from *bromine*, a chemical from which bromide is made]

bronchial (*say* **bronk-ee-al**) *ADJECTIVE* to do with the tubes that lead from the windpipe to the lungs.
[from Greek *bronchos* = windpipe]

bronchitis (*say* bronk-I-tiss) *NOUN* a disease with bronchial inflammation, which makes you cough a lot.
[from Greek *bronchos* = windpipe, + *-itis*]

bronze *NOUN* **bronzes** **1** a metal that is an alloy of copper and tin. **2** something made of bronze. **3** a bronze medal, awarded as third prize. **4** yellowish-brown.
▷ **bronze** *adjective*
[probably from Persian *birinj* = brass]

Bronze Age *NOUN* the time when tools and weapons were made of bronze.

brooch *NOUN* **brooches** an ornament with a hinged pin for fastening it on to clothes.
[a different spelling of *broach*]

brood *NOUN* **broods** young birds that were hatched together.

brood *VERB* **broods, brooding, brooded**
1 sit on eggs to hatch them. **2** keep thinking and worrying about something.
[from Old English]

broody *ADJECTIVE* **1** (said about a hen) wanting to sit on eggs. **2** thoughtful; brooding. **3** (said about a woman) longing to have children.

brook[1] *NOUN* **brooks** a small stream.
[from Old English *broc*]

brook[2] *VERB* **brooks, brooking, brooked**
tolerate • *She would brook no argument.*
[from Old English *brucan*]

broom *NOUN* **brooms** **1** a brush with a long handle, for sweeping. **2** a shrub with yellow, white, or pink flowers.
[from Old English *brom* = the plant (from which brushes used to be made)]

broomstick *NOUN* **broomsticks** a broom handle.

broth *NOUN* **broths** a kind of thin soup.
[from Old English]

brothel *NOUN* **brothels** a house in which women work as prostitutes.
[from Old English *breothan* = degenerate, get worse]

brother *NOUN* **brothers** **1** a son of the same parents as another person. **2** a man who is a fellow member of a Church, trade union, etc.
▷ **brotherly** *adjective*
[from Old English]

brotherhood *NOUN* **brotherhoods**
1 friendliness and companionship between men. **2** a society or association of men.

brother-in-law *NOUN* **brothers-in-law**
the brother of a married person's husband or wife; the husband of a person's sister.

brow *NOUN* **brows** **1** an eyebrow. **2** the forehead. **3** the ridge at the top of a hill; the edge of a cliff.
[from Old English]

brown *NOUN* **browns** a colour between orange and black, like the colour of dark wood.

brown *ADJECTIVE* **1** of the colour brown.
2 having a brown skin; suntanned.

brown *VERB* **browns, browning, browned** make or become brown.
[from Old English]

brownfield *ADJECTIVE* a brownfield site is a piece of land that had buildings on it in the past and that may now be cleared for new buildings to be built.

Brownie *NOUN* **Brownies** a member of a junior branch of the Guides.

browse *VERB* **browses, browsing, browsed** **1** read or look at something casually. **2** feed on grass or leaves.
[from old French]

browser *NOUN* **browsers** (*in computing*) a piece of computer software that enables a user to look at Web pages on the Internet.
[from *browse*]

bruise *NOUN* **bruises** a dark mark made on the skin by hitting it.

bruise *VERB* **bruises, bruising, bruised** give or get a bruise or bruises.
[from Old English]

brunch *NOUN* (*informal*) a late-morning meal combining breakfast and lunch.
[from *breakfast* and *lunch*]

brunette *NOUN* **brunettes** a woman with dark-brown hair.
[from French *brun* = brown, + *-ette*]

brunt *NOUN* the chief impact or strain
• *They bore the brunt of the attack.*
[origin unknown]

brush *NOUN* **brushes** **1** an implement used for cleaning or painting things or for smoothing the hair, usually with pieces of hair, wire, or plastic etc. set in a solid base. **2** a fox's bushy tail. **3** brushing • *Give it a good brush.* **4** a short fight • *They had a brush with the enemy.* **5** undergrowth, bushes, and shrubs that often grow under trees.

brush *VERB* **brushes, brushing, brushed** **1** use a brush on something. **2** touch gently in passing.
- **brush up** revise a subject.
[from old French]

brusque (*say* bruusk) *ADJECTIVE* curt and offhand in manner.
▷ **brusquely** *adverb*
[via French from Italian *brusco* = sour]

Brussels sprouts *PLURAL NOUN* the edible buds of a kind of cabbage.
[named after Brussels, the capital of Belgium]

brutal *ADJECTIVE* very cruel.
▷ **brutally** *adverb* **brutality** *noun*

brute *NOUN* **brutes** **1** a brutal person. **2** an animal.
▷ **brutish** *adjective*
[from Latin *brutus* = stupid]

B.Sc. *ABBREVIATION* Bachelor of Science.

BSE *ABBREVIATION* bovine spongiform encephalopathy; a fatal disease of cattle that affects the nervous system and makes the cow stagger about. BSE is sometimes known as 'mad cow disease'.

bubble *NOUN* **bubbles** **1** a thin transparent ball of liquid filled with air or gas. **2** a small ball of air in something.
▷ **bubbly** *adjective*

bubble *VERB* **bubbles, bubbling, bubbled** **1** send up bubbles; rise in bubbles. **2** show great liveliness.
[related to *burble*]

bubblegum *NOUN* chewing gum that can be blown into large bubbles.

buccaneer *NOUN* **buccaneers** a pirate.
[from French]

buck[1] *NOUN* **bucks** a male deer, rabbit, or hare.

buck *VERB* **bucks, bucking, bucked** (said about a horse) jump with its back arched.
- **buck up** (*informal*) **1** hurry. **2** cheer up.
[from Old English]

buck[2] *NOUN* - **pass the buck** (*slang*) pass the responsibility for something to another person.
▷ **buck-passing** *noun*
[origin unknown]

buck[3] *NOUN* (*American & Australian/NZ*) a dollar.

bucket *NOUN* **buckets** a container with a handle, for carrying liquids etc.
▷ **bucketful** *noun*
[from French]

buckle[1] *NOUN* **buckles** a device through which a belt or strap is threaded to fasten it.

buckle *VERB* **buckles, buckling, buckled** fasten something with a buckle.
[from Latin *buccula* = cheek- strap of a helmet]

buckle[2] *VERB* **buckles, buckling, buckled** bend or crumple.
- **buckle down to** start working hard at something.
[from French *boucler* = bulge]

buckler *NOUN* **bucklers** a small round shield.
[from old French]

bucolic (*say* bew-kol-ik) *ADJECTIVE* to do with country life.
[from Greek *boukolos* = herdsman]

bud *NOUN* **buds** a flower or leaf before it opens.
[origin unknown]

Buddhism (*say* **buud**-izm) *NOUN* a faith that started in Asia and follows the teachings of the Indian philosopher Gautama Buddha, who lived in the 5th century BC.
▷ **Buddhist** *noun*
[from Sanskrit *Buddha* = enlightened one]

budding *ADJECTIVE* beginning to develop • *a budding poet.*
[from *bud*]

buddy *NOUN* **buddies** (*informal*) a friend.
[probably from *brother*]

budge *VERB* **budges, budging, budged** if you cannot budge something, you cannot move it at all.
[from French]

budgerigar *NOUN* **budgerigars** an Australian bird often kept as a pet in a cage.
[from Australian Aboriginal *budgeri* = good + *gar* = cockatoo]

budget *NOUN* **budgets 1** a plan for spending money wisely. **2** an amount of money set aside for a purpose.
▷ **budgetary** *adjective*
- **the Budget** the Chancellor of the Exchequer's statement of plans to raise money (e.g. by taxes).

budget *VERB* **budgets, budgeting, budgeted** plan how much you are going to spend.
[from old French *bougette* = small leather bag, purse]

budgie *NOUN* **budgies** (*informal*) a budgerigar.

buff *NOUN* **buffs** (*informal*) a person who is very interested in a subject and knows a lot about it • *a computer buff.*
[from *buff* adjective originally describing people who went to watch fires, from the buff-coloured uniforms once worn by New York firemen]

buff *ADJECTIVE* of a dull yellow colour.

buff *VERB* **buffs, buffing, buffed** polish with soft material.
[from *buff leather* = leather of buffalo hide]

buffalo *NOUN* **buffalo** or **buffaloes** a large ox. Different kinds are found in Asia, Africa, and North America (where they are also called *bison*).
[from Portuguese]

buffer *NOUN* **buffers 1** something that softens a blow, especially a device on a railway engine or wagon or at the end of a track. **2** (*in computing*) a memory in which text or data can be stored temporarily.
[from an old word *buff* = a blow (as in *blind man's buff*): related to *buffet*[2]]

buffer state *NOUN* **buffer states** a small country between two powerful ones, thought to reduce the chance of these two attacking each other.

buffet[1] (*say* **buu**-fay) *NOUN* **buffets 1** a cafe at a station. **2** a meal where guests serve themselves.
[from French = stool]

buffet[2] (*say* **buf**-it) *NOUN* **buffets** a hit, especially with the hand.

buffet *VERB* **buffets, buffeting, buffeted** hit or knock • *Strong winds buffeted the aircraft.*
[from old French *buffe* = a blow]

buffoon *NOUN* **buffoons** a person who plays the fool.
▷ **buffoonery** *noun*
[from Latin *buffo* = clown]

bug *NOUN* **bugs 1** an insect. **2** an error in a computer program that prevents it working properly. **3** (*informal*) a germ or virus. **4** (*informal*) a secret hidden microphone.

bug *VERB* **bugs, bugging, bugged** (*slang*) **1** fit with a secret hidden microphone. **2** annoy.
[origin unknown]

bugbear *NOUN* **bugbears** something you fear or dislike.
[from an old word *bug* = bogy]

buggy *NOUN* **buggies 1** a kind of chair on wheels for pushing young children around. **2** a light, horse-drawn carriage.
[origin unknown]

bugle *NOUN* **bugles** a brass instrument like a small trumpet, used for sounding military signals.
▷ **bugler** *noun*
[origin unknown]

build *VERB* **builds, building, built** make something by putting parts together.
- **build in** include.

built-in *adjective*
- **build up** 1 establish gradually. 2 accumulate. 3 cover an area with buildings. 4 make stronger or more famous • *build up a reputation.*
built-up *adjective*

build *NOUN* **builds** the shape of someone's body • *of slender build.*
[from Old English]

builder *NOUN* **builders** someone who puts up buildings.

building *NOUN* **buildings** 1 the process of constructing houses and other structures. 2 a permanent built structure that people can go into.

building society *NOUN* **building societies** an organization that accepts deposits of money and lends to people who want to buy houses.

bulb *NOUN* **bulbs** 1 a thick rounded part of a plant from which a stem grows up and roots grow down. 2 a rounded part of something • *the bulb of a thermometer.* 3 a glass globe that produces electric light.
▷ **bulbous** *adjective*
[from Greek *bolbos* = onion]

bulge *NOUN* **bulges** a rounded swelling; an outward curve.
▷ **bulgy** *adjective*

bulge *VERB* **bulges, bulging, bulged** form or cause to form a bulge.
[from Latin *bulga* = bag]

bulimia (*say* bew-**lim**-ia) *NOUN* an illness that makes someone alternately overeat and fast, often making themselves vomit after eating.
▷ **bulimic** *adjective*
[Greek, = hunger of an ox]

bulk *NOUN* **bulks** 1 the size of something, especially when it is large. 2 the greater portion; the majority • *The bulk of the population voted for it.*
- **in bulk** in large amounts.

bulk *VERB* **bulks, bulking, bulked** increase the size or thickness of something • *bulk it out.*
[from Old English]

bulky *ADJECTIVE* **bulkier, bulkiest** taking up a lot of space.
▷ **bulkiness** *noun*

bull[1] *NOUN* **bulls** 1 the fully-grown male of cattle. 2 a male seal, whale, or elephant.
[from Old Norse]

bull[2] *NOUN* **bulls** an edict issued by the Pope.
[from Latin *bulla* = seal, sealed letter]

bulldog *NOUN* **bulldogs** a dog of a powerful courageous breed with a short thick neck.
[because it was used for attacking tethered bulls in the sport of 'bull- baiting']

bulldoze *VERB* **bulldozes, bulldozing, bulldozed** clear with a bulldozer.
[originally American; origin unknown]

bulldozer *NOUN* **bulldozers** a powerful tractor with a wide metal blade or scoop in front, used for shifting soil or clearing ground.

bullet *NOUN* **bullets** a small piece of shaped metal shot from a rifle or revolver.
[from French *boulet* = little ball]

bulletin *NOUN* **bulletins** 1 a short announcement of news on radio or television. 2 a regular newsletter or report.
[via French from Italian; related to *bull*[2]]

bulletin board *NOUN* **bulletin boards** 1 (*American*) a noticeboard. 2 (*in computing*) a site on a computer system where any user can read or write messages.

bulletproof *ADJECTIVE* able to keep out bullets.

bullfight *NOUN* **bullfights** in Spain, a public entertainment in which bulls are tormented and killed in an arena.
▷ **bullfighter** *noun*

bullfinch *NOUN* **bullfinches** a bird with a strong beak and a pink breast.

bullion *NOUN* bars of gold or silver.
[from old French *bouillon* = a mint]

bullock *NOUN* **bullocks** a young castrated bull.
[from Old English *bulloc* = young bull]

bull's-eye *NOUN* **bull's-eyes** 1 the centre of a target. 2 a hard shiny peppermint sweet.

bully *VERB* **bullies, bullying, bullied** 1 use strength or power to hurt or frighten a weaker person. 2 start play in hockey, when two opponents tap the ground and each other's stick • *bully off.*

bully *NOUN* **bullies** someone who bullies people.
[probably from Dutch]

bulrush *NOUN* **bulrushes** a tall rush with a thick velvety head.
[probably from *bull*[1], suggesting something large]

bulwark *NOUN* **bulwarks** a wall of earth built as a defence; a protection.
[from German or Dutch]

bulwarks *PLURAL NOUN* a ship's side above the level of the deck.

bum *NOUN* **bums** (*slang*) a person's bottom.
[origin unknown]

bumble *VERB* **bumbles, bumbling, bumbled** move or behave or speak clumsily.
[related to *boom*[1]]

bumble-bee *NOUN* **bumble-bees** a large bee with a loud hum.

bump *VERB* **bumps, bumping, bumped** 1 knock against something. 2 move along with jolts.
- **bump into** (*informal*) meet by chance.
- **bump off** (*slang*) kill.

bump *NOUN* **bumps** 1 the action or sound of bumping. 2 a swelling or lump.
▷ **bumpy** *adjective*
[imitating the sound]

bumper[1] *NOUN* **bumpers** a bar along the front or back of a motor vehicle to protect it in collisions.

bumper[2] *ADJECTIVE* unusually large or plentiful • *a bumper crop.*

bumpkin *NOUN* **bumpkins** a country person with awkward manners.
[from Dutch]

bumptious (*say* bump-shus) *ADJECTIVE* loud and conceited.
▷ **bumptiousness** *noun*
[from *bump*; made up as a joke]

bun *NOUN* **buns** 1 a small round sweet cake. 2 hair twisted into a round bunch at the back of the head.
[origin unknown]

bunch *NOUN* **bunches** a number of things joined or fastened together.
[origin unknown]

bundle *NOUN* **bundles** a number of things tied or wrapped together.

bundle *VERB* **bundles, bundling, bundled** 1 make a number of things into a bundle. 2 push hurriedly or carelessly • *They bundled him into a taxi.*
[probably from old German or old Dutch]

bung *NOUN* **bungs** a stopper for closing a hole in a barrel or jar.

bung *VERB* **bungs, bunging, bunged** (*slang*) throw • *Bung it here.*
- **bunged up** (*informal*) blocked.
[from old Dutch]

bungalow *NOUN* **bungalows** a house without any upstairs rooms.
[from Hindi *bangla* = of Bengal]

bungee jumping *NOUN* the sport of jumping from a height with a long piece of elastic (called a **bungee**) tied to your legs to stop you from hitting the ground.
[origin unknown]

bungle *VERB* **bungles, bungling, bungled** make a mess of doing something.
▷ **bungler** *noun*
[because *bungle* sounds clumsy]

bunion *NOUN* **bunions** a swelling at the side of the joint where the big toe joins the foot.
[origin unknown]

bunk[1] *NOUN* **bunks** a bed built like a shelf.
[origin unknown]

bunk[2] *NOUN* - **do a bunk** (*slang*) run away.
▷ **bunk** *verb*
[origin unknown]

bunker *NOUN* **bunkers** 1 a container for storing fuel. 2 a sandy hollow built as an obstacle on a golf course. 3 an underground shelter.
[origin unknown]

bunny *NOUN* **bunnies** (*informal*) a rabbit.
[from dialect *bun* = rabbit]

Bunsen burner *NOUN* **Bunsen burners** a small gas burner used in scientific work.
[named after a German scientist, R. W. *Bunsen*]

a b c d e f g h i j k l m n o p q r s t u v w x y z

A B C D E F G H I J K L M N O P Q R S T U V W X Y Z

bunting[1] *NOUN* **buntings** a kind of small bird.
[origin unknown]

bunting[2] *NOUN* strips of small flags hung up to decorate streets and buildings.
[origin unknown]

buoy (*say* boi) *NOUN* **buoys** a floating object anchored to mark a channel or underwater rocks etc.

buoy *VERB* **buoys, buoying, buoyed 1** keep something afloat. **2** hearten or cheer someone • *They were buoyed up with new hope.*
[probably from old Dutch]

buoyant (*say* **boi**-ant) *ADJECTIVE* **1** able to float. **2** light-hearted; cheerful.
▷ **buoyancy** *noun*
[from French or Spanish; related to *buoy*]

bur *NOUN* **burs** a different spelling of *burr* (seed case).
[from a Scandinavian language]

burble *VERB* **burbles, burbling, burbled** make a gentle murmuring sound.
▷ **burble** *noun*
[imitating the sound]

burden *NOUN* **burdens 1** a heavy load that you have to carry. **2** something troublesome that you have to put up with • *Exams are a burden.*
▷ **burdensome** *adjective*

burden *VERB* **burdens, burdening, burdened** put a burden on a person etc.
[from Old English]

bureau (*say* **bewr**-oh) *NOUN* **bureaux 1** a writing desk. **2** a business office • *They will tell you at the Information Bureau.*
[French, = desk]

bureaucracy (*say* bewr-**ok**-ra-see) *NOUN* the use of too many rules and forms by officials, especially in government departments.
▷ **bureaucratic** (*say* bewr-ok-**rat**-ik) *adjective*
[from *bureau* + *-cracy*]

bureaucrat (*say* **bewr**-ok-rat) *NOUN* **bureaucrats** a person who works in a government department.

burgeon (*say* **ber**-jon) *VERB* **burgeons, burgeoning, burgeoned** grow rapidly.
[from French]

burger *NOUN* **burgers** a hamburger.
[short for *hamburger* = from *Hamburg*, a city in Germany; the first syllable was dropped because people thought it referred to ham]

burglar *NOUN* **burglars** a person who breaks into a building in order to steal things.
▷ **burglary** *noun*
[from French]

burgle *VERB* **burgles, burgling, burgled** rob a place as a burglar.
[from *burglar*]

burgundy *NOUN* **burgundies** a rich red or white wine.
[originally made in Burgundy in France]

burial *NOUN* **burials** burying somebody.

burlesque (*say* ber-**lesk**) *NOUN* **burlesques** a comical imitation.
[via French from Italian *burla* = ridicule, joke]

burly *ADJECTIVE* **burlier, burliest** having a strong heavy body.
[from Old English]

burn[1] *VERB* **burns, burning, burned** or **burnt 1** blaze or glow with fire; produce heat or light by combustion. **2** damage or destroy something by fire, heat, or chemicals. **3** be damaged or destroyed by fire etc. **4** feel very hot.
USAGE The word *burnt* (not *burned*) is always used when an adjective is required, e.g. in *burnt wood*. As parts of the verb, either *burned* or *burnt* may be used, e.g. *the wood had burned* or *had burnt completely*.

burn *NOUN* **burns 1** a mark or injury made by burning. **2** the firing of a spacecraft's rockets.
[from Old English *birnan*]

burn[2] *NOUN* **burns** (*Scottish*) a brook.
[from Old English *burna*]

burner *NOUN* **burners** the part of a lamp or cooker that gives out the flame.

burning *ADJECTIVE* **1** intense • *a burning ambition.* **2** very important; hotly discussed • *a burning question.*

burnish *VERB* **burnishes, burnishing, burnished** polish by rubbing.
[from old French]

burr *NOUN* **burrs** **1** a plant's seed case or flower that clings to hair or clothes. **2** a whirring sound. **3** a soft country accent. [a different spelling of *bur*]

burrow *NOUN* **burrows** a hole or tunnel dug by a rabbit or fox etc. as a dwelling.

burrow *VERB* **burrows, burrowing, burrowed** **1** dig a burrow. **2** push your way through or into something; search deeply • *She burrowed in her handbag.* [a different spelling of *borough*]

bursar *NOUN* **bursars** a person who manages the finances and other business of a school or college. [from Latin *bursa* = a bag]

bursary *NOUN* **bursaries** a grant given to a student.

burst *VERB* **bursts, bursting, burst** **1** break or force apart. **2** come or start suddenly • *It burst into flames.* • *They burst out laughing.* **3** be very full • *bursting with energy.*

burst *NOUN* **bursts** **1** a split caused by something bursting. **2** something short and forceful • *a burst of gunfire.* [from Old English]

bury *VERB* **buries, burying, buried** **1** place a dead body in the earth, a tomb, or the sea. **2** put underground; cover up.
- **bury the hatchet** agree to stop quarrelling or fighting.
[from Old English]

bus *NOUN* **buses** a large vehicle for passengers to travel in. [short for *omnibus*]

busby *NOUN* **busbies** a tall fur cap worn by some regiments on ceremonial occasions. [origin unknown]

bush *NOUN* **bushes** **1** a shrub. **2** wild uncultivated land, especially in Africa and Australia.
▷ **bushy** *adjective*
[from old French or Old Norse]

bushel *NOUN* **bushels** a measure for grain and fruit (8 gallons or 4 pecks). [from old French]

bushman *NOUN* **bushmen** (*Australian/NZ*) a person who has a lot of experience of living or travelling in remote country areas.

busily *ADVERB* in a busy way.

business (*say* biz-niss) *NOUN* **businesses** **1** a person's concern or responsibilities • *Mind your own business.* **2** an affair or subject • *I'm tired of the whole business.* **3** a shop or firm. **4** buying and selling things; trade.
▷ **businessman** *noun* **businesswoman** *noun*
[from Old English *bisignis* = busyness]

businesslike *ADJECTIVE* practical; well-organized.

busker *NOUN* **buskers** a person who plays music in the street for money.
▷ **busking** *noun*
[from an old word *busk* = be a pedlar]

bust[1] *NOUN* **busts** **1** a sculpture of a person's head, shoulders, and chest. **2** the upper front part of a woman's body. [from Latin]

bust[2] *VERB* **busts, busting, bust** (*informal*) break something. [a different spelling of *burst*]

bustard *NOUN* **bustards** a large bird that can run very swiftly. [from old French]

bustle[1] *VERB* **bustles, bustling, bustled** hurry in a busy or excited way.

bustle *NOUN* hurried or excited activity. [probably from Old Norse]

bustle[2] *NOUN* **bustles** padding used to puff out the top of a long skirt at the back. [origin unknown]

busy *ADJECTIVE* **busier, busiest** **1** having much to do; occupied. **2** full of activity. **3** (said about a telephone line) engaged.
▷ **busily** *adverb* **busyness** *noun*

busy *VERB* **busies, busying, busied**
- **busy yourself** occupy yourself; keep busy.
[from Old English]

busybody *NOUN* **busybodies** a person who meddles or interferes.

but *CONJUNCTION* however; nevertheless • *I wanted to go, but I couldn't.*

but *PREPOSITION* except • *There is no one here but me.*

but *ADVERB* only; no more than • *We can but try.* [from Old English]

butcher *NOUN* **butchers** **1** a person who cuts up meat and sells it. **2** a person who kills cruelly or needlessly.
▷ **butchery** *noun*

butcher *VERB* **butchers, butchering, butchered** kill cruelly or needlessly.
[from old French]

butler *NOUN* **butlers** a male servant in charge of other servants in a large private house.
[from Old French *bouteillier* = bottler]

butt[1] *NOUN* **butts** **1** the thicker end of a weapon or tool. **2** a stub • *cigarette butts.*
[from Dutch *bot* = stumpy]

butt[2] *NOUN* **butts** a large cask or barrel.
[from Latin *buttis* = cask]

butt[3] *NOUN* **butts** a person or thing that is a target for ridicule or teasing • *He was the butt of their jokes.*
[from Old French *but* = goal]

butt[4] *VERB* **butts, butting, butted** **1** push or hit with the head as a ram or goat does. **2** place the edges of things together.
- **butt in** interrupt or meddle.
[from Old French *buter* = hit]

butter *NOUN* a soft fatty food made by churning cream.
▷ **buttery** *adjective*
[from Old English]

buttercup *NOUN* **buttercups** a wild plant with bright yellow cup-shaped flowers.

butter-fingers *NOUN* a clumsy person who often drops things.

butterfly *NOUN* **butterflies** **1** an insect with large white or coloured wings. **2** a swimming stroke in which both arms are lifted at the same time.

buttermilk *NOUN* the liquid that is left after butter has been made.

butterscotch *NOUN* a kind of hard toffee.

buttock *NOUN* **buttocks** either of the two fleshy rounded parts of your bottom.
[from Old English]

button *NOUN* **buttons** **1** a knob or disc sewn on clothes as a fastening or ornament. **2** a small knob pressed to work an electric device.

button *VERB* **buttons, buttoning, buttoned** fasten something with a button or buttons.
[from old French]

buttonhole *NOUN* **buttonholes** **1** a slit through which a button passes to fasten clothes. **2** a flower worn on a lapel.

buttonhole *VERB* **buttonholes, buttonholing, buttonholed** stop somebody so that you can talk to him or her.

buttress *NOUN* **buttresses** a support built against a wall.
[same origin as *butt*[4]]

buy *VERB* **buys, buying, bought** get something by paying for it.
▷ **buyer** *noun*

buy *NOUN* **buys** something that is bought.
[from Old English]

buzz *NOUN* **buzzes** a vibrating humming sound.
- **get a buzz from something** (*slang*) find something exciting.

buzz *VERB* **buzzes, buzzing, buzzed** **1** make a buzz. **2** threaten an aircraft by deliberately flying close to it.
[imitating the sound]

buzzard *NOUN* **buzzards** a kind of hawk.
[from Latin *buteo* = falcon]

buzzer *NOUN* **buzzers** a device that makes a buzzing sound as a signal.

by *PREPOSITION* This word is used to show **1** closeness (*Sit by me*), **2** direction or route (*We got here by a short cut*), **3** time (*They came by night*), **4** manner or method (*cooking by gas*), **5** amount (*You missed it by inches*).
- **by the way** incidentally.
- **by yourself** alone; without help.

by *ADVERB* **1** past • *I can't get by.* **2** in reserve; for future use • *Put it by.*
- **by and by** soon; later on.
- **by and large** on the whole.
[from Old English]

bye *NOUN* **byes** **1** a run scored in cricket when the ball goes past the batsman without being touched. **2** having no opponent for one round in a tournament and so going on to the next round as if you had won.
[from *by-* = at the side, extra]

bye-bye *INTERJECTION* goodbye.

by-election *NOUN* **by-elections** an election to replace a Member of Parliament who has died or resigned.
[from *by-* = extra (an 'extra' election between general elections)]

bygone *ADJECTIVE* belonging to the past.
- **let bygones be bygones** forgive and forget.

by-law *NOUN* **by-laws** a law that applies only to a particular town or district.
[from Old Norse *byjarlagu* = town law]

bypass *NOUN* **bypasses** **1** a road taking traffic round a city or congested area. **2** a channel that allows something to flow when the main route is blocked.

bypass *VERB* **bypasses, bypassing, bypassed** avoid something by means of a bypass.

by-product *NOUN* **by-products** something useful produced while something else is being made.
[from *by-* = at the side, besides]

byre *NOUN* **byres** a cowshed.
[from Old English]

byroad *NOUN* **byroads** a minor road.

bystander *NOUN* **bystanders** a person standing near but taking no part when something happens.

byte *NOUN* **bytes** (*in Computing*) a fixed number of bits (= binary digits) in a computer, often representing a single character.
[an invented word]

byway *NOUN* **byways** a byroad.

byword *NOUN* **bywords** a person or thing spoken of as a famous example • *Their firm became a byword for quality.*
[from Old English *biwyrde* = proverb]

Cc

cab *NOUN* **cabs** **1** a taxi. **2** a compartment for the driver of a lorry, train, bus, or crane.
[short for *cabriolet* = a light horsedrawn carriage]

cabaret (*say* kab-er-ay) *NOUN* **cabarets** an entertainment provided for the customers in a restaurant or nightclub.
[from old French]

cabbage *NOUN* **cabbages** a vegetable with green or purple leaves.
[from old French *caboche* = head]

caber *NOUN* **cabers** a tree trunk used in the sport of 'tossing the caber'.
[from Scottish Gaelic or Irish]

cabin *NOUN* **cabins** **1** a hut or shelter. **2** a room for sleeping on a ship. **3** the part of an aircraft in which passengers sit. **4** a driver's cab.
[from Latin]

Cabinet *NOUN* the group of chief ministers, chosen by the Prime Minister, who meet to decide government policy.

cabinet *NOUN* **cabinets** a cupboard or container with drawers or shelves.
[from *cabin*]

cable *NOUN* **cables** **1** a thick rope of fibre or wire; a thick chain. **2** a covered group of wires laid underground for transmitting electrical signals. **3** a telegram sent overseas.
[from Latin *capulum* = halter]

cable car *NOUN* **cable cars** a small cabin suspended on a moving cable, used for carrying people up and down a mountainside.

cable television *NOUN* a broadcasting service with signals transmitted by cable to the sets of people who have paid to receive it.

cacao (*say* ka-kay-oh) *NOUN* **cacaos** a tropical tree with a seed from which cocoa and chocolate are made.
[via Spanish from Nahuatl (a Central American language)]

cache (*say* kash) *NOUN* **caches** a hidden store of things, especially valuable things.
[French, from *cacher* = to hide]

cackle *NOUN* **cackles** **1** a loud silly laugh. **2** noisy chatter. **3** the loud clucking noise a hen makes.
▷ **cackle** *verb*
[from old German or Dutch *kake* = jaw]

cacophony (*say* kak-off-on-ee) *NOUN* **cacophonies** a loud harsh unpleasant sound.
▷ **cacophonous** *adjective*
[from Greek *kakophonia* = bad sound]

cactus *NOUN* **cacti** a fleshy plant, usually with prickles, from a hot dry climate.
[from Greek]

cad *NOUN* **cads** a dishonourable person.
[short for *caddie* or *cadet*]

cadaverous (*say* kad-av-er-us) *ADJECTIVE* pale and gaunt.
[from Latin *cadaver* = corpse]

caddie *NOUN* **caddies** a person who carries a golfer's clubs during a game.
[from *cadet*]

caddy *NOUN* **caddies** a small box for holding tea.
[from Malay (a language spoken in Malaysia) or Javanese (a language spoken in Indonesia)]

cadence (*say* kay-denss) *NOUN* **cadences** **1** rhythm; the rise and fall of the voice in speaking. **2** the final notes of a musical phrase.
[via French from Latin *cadere* = fall]

cadenza (*say* ka-den-za) *NOUN* **cadenzas** an elaborate passage for a solo instrument or singer, to show the performer's skill.
[via Italian from Latin *cadere* = fall]

cadet *NOUN* **cadets** a young person being trained for the armed forces or the police.
[French, = younger son]

cadge *VERB* **cadges, cadging, cadged** get something by begging for it.
[origin unknown]

cadmium *NOUN* a metal that looks like tin.
[from Latin]

Caesarean or **Caesarean section** (*say* siz-air-ee-an) *NOUN* **Caesareans, Caesarean sections** a surgical operation for taking a baby out of the mother's womb.
[so called because Julius Caesar is said to have been born in this way]

caesura (*say* siz-yoor-a) *NOUN* a short pause in a line of verse.
[from Latin *caedere* = cut]

cafe (*say* kaf-ay) *NOUN* **cafes** a small restaurant.
[French, = coffee, coffee house]

cafeteria (*say* kaf-it-eer-ee-a) *NOUN* **cafeterias** a self-service cafe.
[American Spanish, from *café*]

caffeine (*say* kaf-een) *NOUN* a stimulant substance found in tea and coffee.
[French, from *café* = coffee]

caftan *NOUN* **caftans** a long loose coat or dress.
[from Persian]

cage *NOUN* **cages** **1** a container with bars or wires, in which birds or animals are kept. **2** the enclosed platform of a lift.
[from French]

cagoule (*say* kag-ool) *NOUN* **cagoules** a waterproof jacket.
[French, = cowl]

cairn *NOUN* **cairns** a pile of loose stones set up as a landmark or monument.
[from Scottish Gaelic]

cajole *VERB* **cajoles, cajoling, cajoled** persuade someone to do something by flattering them; coax.
[from French]

cake *NOUN* **cakes** **1** a baked food made from a mixture of flour, fat, eggs, sugar, etc. **2** a shaped or hardened mass • *a cake of soap; fish cakes.*
[from a Scandinavian language]

caked *ADJECTIVE* covered with dried mud etc.

calamine *NOUN* a pink powder used to make a soothing lotion for the skin.
[from Latin]

calamity *NOUN* **calamities** a disaster.
▷ **calamitous** *adjective*
[from Latin]

calcium *NOUN* a chemical substance found in teeth, bones, and lime.
[from Latin *calx* = *lime*[1]]

calculate *VERB* **calculates, calculating, calculated** **1** work something out by using mathematics. **2** plan something deliberately; intend • *Her remarks were calculated to hurt me.*
▷ **calculable** *adjective* **calculation** *noun*
[same origin as *calculus*]

calculating *ADJECTIVE* planning things carefully so that you get what you want.

calculator *NOUN* **calculators** a small electronic device for making calculations.

calculus *NOUN* mathematics for working out problems about rates of change.
[from Latin *calculus* = small stone (used on an abacus)]

calendar *NOUN* **calendars** a chart or set of pages showing the dates of the month or year.
[from Latin *kalendae* = the first day of the month]

calf[1] *NOUN* **calves** a young cow, whale, seal, etc.
[from Old English]

calf[2] *NOUN* **calves** the fleshy back part of the leg below the knee.
[from Old Norse]

calibrate (*say* kal-i-brayt) *VERB* **calibrates, calibrating, calibrated** mark a gauge or instrument with a scale of measurements.
▷ **calibration** *noun*
[from *calibre*]

calibre (*say* kal-ib-er) *NOUN* **calibres 1** the diameter of a tube or gun barrel, or of a bullet etc. **2** ability or importance • *someone of your calibre.*
[French]

calico *NOUN* a kind of cotton cloth.
[from Calicut, a town in India, from which the cloth was sent overseas]

caliph (*say* kal-if or kay-lif) *NOUN* **caliphs** the former title of the ruler in certain Muslim countries.
[from Arabic *khalifa* = successor of Muhammad]

call *NOUN* **calls 1** a shout or cry. **2** a visit. **3** telephoning somebody. **4** a summons.

call *VERB* **calls, calling, called 1** shout or speak loudly, e.g. to attract someone's attention. **2** telephone somebody. **3** name a person or thing • *They've decided to call the baby Alexander.* **4** tell somebody to come to you; summon. **5** make a short visit.
▷ **caller** *noun*
- **call a person's bluff** challenge a person to do what was threatened, and expose the fact that it was a bluff.
- **call for 1** come and collect. **2** require • *The scandal calls for investigation.*
- **call off** cancel or postpone.
- **call up** summon to join the armed forces.

[from Old Norse]

call box *NOUN* **call boxes** a telephone box.

calligraphy (*say* kal-**ig**-raf-ee) *NOUN* the art of beautiful handwriting.
[from Greek *kalos* = beautiful, + *-graphy*]

calling *NOUN* **callings** an occupation; a profession or trade.
[from the idea that God had called you to that occupation]

calliper *NOUN* **callipers** a support for a weak or injured leg.
[a different spelling of *calibre*]

callipers *PLURAL NOUN* compasses for measuring the width of tubes or of round objects.
[from *calliper*]

callous (*say* **kal**-us) *ADJECTIVE* hard-hearted; unsympathetic.
▷ **callously** *adverb* **callousness** *noun*
[same origin as *callus*]

callow *ADJECTIVE* immature and inexperienced.
▷ **callowly** *adverb* **callowness** *noun*
[from Old English]

callus *NOUN* **calluses** a small patch of skin that has become thick and hard through being continually pressed or rubbed.
[from Latin *callum* = hard skin]

calm *ADJECTIVE* **1** quiet and still; not windy. **2** not excited or agitated.
▷ **calmly** *adverb* **calmness** *noun*

calm *VERB* **calms, calming, calmed** make or become calm.
[from Greek *kauma* = hot time of the day (when people rested)]

calorie *NOUN* **calories** a unit for measuring an amount of heat or the energy produced by food.
▷ **calorific** *adjective*
[from Latin *calor* = heat]

calumny (*say* **kal**-um-nee) *NOUN* **calumnies** an untrue statement that damages a person's reputation; slander.
[from Latin]

calve *VERB* **calves, calving, calved** give birth to a calf.

calypso *NOUN* **calypsos** a West Indian song about current happenings, made up as the singer goes along.
[origin unknown]

calyx (*say* kay-liks) *NOUN* **calyces** a ring of leaves (*sepals*) forming the outer case of a bud.
[from Greek]

camaraderie (*say* kam-er-**ah**-der-ee) *NOUN* comradeship.
[French, from *camarade* = comrade]

camber *NOUN* **cambers** a slight upward curve or arch, e.g. on a road to allow drainage.
[from Latin *camurus* = curved inwards]

cambric *NOUN* thin linen or cotton cloth.
[from *Cambrai*, a town in France, where it was first made]

camcorder *NOUN* **camcorders** a combined video camera and sound recorder.
[from *camera* + *recorder*]

camel *NOUN* **camels** a large animal with a long neck and either one or two humps on its back, used in desert countries for riding and for carrying goods.
[from Greek]

camellia *NOUN* **camellias** a kind of evergreen flowering shrub.
[Latin, named after Joseph *Camellus*, a botanist]

cameo (*say* **kam**-ee-oh) *NOUN* **cameos** **1** a small hard piece of stone carved with a raised design in its upper layer. **2** a short part in a play or film, usually one played by a well-known actor.
[from old French]

camera *NOUN* **cameras** a device for taking photographs, films, or television pictures.
▷ **cameraman** *noun*
- **in camera** in a judge's private room; in private.
[Latin, = vault, chamber]

camomile *NOUN* **camomiles** a plant with sweet-smelling daisy-like flowers.
[from Greek *khamaimelon* = earth apple (because of the smell of the flowers)]

camouflage (*say* **kam**-off-lahzh) *NOUN* a way of hiding things by making them look like part of their surroundings.

camouflage *VERB* **camouflages**, **camouflaging**, **camouflaged** hide by camouflage.
[from French *camoufler* = disguise]

camp *NOUN* **camps** a place where people live in tents or huts for a short time.
▷ **campsite** *noun*

camp *VERB* **camps**, **camping**, **camped** **1** put up a tent or tents. **2** have a holiday in a tent.
▷ **camper** *noun*
[same origin as *campus*]

campaign *NOUN* **campaigns** **1** a series of battles in one area or with one purpose. **2** a planned series of actions, usually to arouse interest in something • *an advertising campaign.*

campaign *VERB* **campaigns**, **campaigning**, **campaigned** take part in a campaign • *They are campaigning to save the rainforests.*
▷ **campaigner** *noun*
[from Latin *campania* = a piece of open ground]

camphor *NOUN* a strong-smelling white substance used in medicine and mothballs and in making plastics.
[via French, Latin, Arabic, and Malay (a language spoken in Malaysia), from Sanskrit]

campion *NOUN* **campions** a wild plant with pink or white flowers.
[origin unknown]

campus *NOUN* **campuses** the grounds of a university or college.
[Latin, = field]

can[1] *NOUN* **cans** **1** a sealed tin in which food or drink is preserved. **2** a metal or plastic container for liquids.

can *VERB* **cans**, **canning**, **canned** preserve in a sealed can.
▷ **canner** *noun*
[from Old English *canne* = container for liquids]

can[2] *AUXILIARY VERB* *past tense* **could** **1** be able to • *He can play the violin.* **2** have permission to • *You can go.*
[from Old English *cunnan* = know, know how to do]
USAGE Some people object to *can* being used with the meaning 'have permission to' and insist that you should only use *may* for this meaning. *Can* is widely used in this meaning, however, and in most situations there is little reason to prefer *may*. *May* is appropriate, though, in formal or official writing.

canal *NOUN* **canals** **1** an artificial river cut through land so that boats can sail along it or so that it can drain or irrigate an area. **2** a tube through which food or air passes in a plant or animal body • *the alimentary canal.*
[same origin as *channel*]

canary *NOUN* **canaries** a small yellow bird that sings.
[because it came from the Canary Islands]

cancan *NOUN* **cancans** a lively dance in which the legs are kicked very high.
[French]

cancel *VERB* **cancels, cancelling, cancelled** **1** say that something planned will not be done or will not take place. **2** stop an order or instruction for something. **3** mark a stamp or ticket etc. so that it cannot be used again.
▷ **cancellation** *noun*
- **cancel out** stop each other's effect • *The good and harm cancel each other out.*
[from Latin *cancellare* = cross out]

cancer *NOUN* **cancers** **1** a disease in which harmful growths form in the body. **2** a tumour, especially a harmful one.
▷ **cancerous** *adjective*
[Latin, = crab, creeping ulcer]

candelabrum (*say* kan-dil-**ab**-rum) *NOUN* **candelabra** a candlestick with several branches for holding candles.
[from Latin *candela* = candle]

candid *ADJECTIVE* frank and honest.
▷ **candidly** *adverb*
[from Latin *candidus* = white]

candidate *NOUN* **candidates** **1** a person who wants to be elected or chosen for a particular job or position etc. **2** a person taking an examination.
▷ **candidacy** *noun* **candidature** *noun*
[from Latin *candidus* = white (because Roman candidates for office had to wear a pure white toga)]

candied *ADJECTIVE* coated or preserved in sugar.
[from *candy*]

candle *NOUN* **candles** a stick of wax with a wick through it, giving light when burning.
▷ **candlelight** *noun*
[Old English from Latin, from *candere* = be white, shine]

candlestick *NOUN* **candlesticks** a holder for a candle or candles.

candour (*say* **kan**-der) *NOUN* being candid; frankness.

candy *NOUN* **candies** (*American*) sweets; a sweet.
[from Arabic *kand* = sugar]

candyfloss *NOUN* **candyflosses** a fluffy mass of very thin strands of spun sugar.

cane *NOUN* **canes** **1** the stem of a reed or tall grass etc. **2** a thin stick.

cane *VERB* **canes, caning, caned** beat someone with a cane.
[from Greek]

canine (*say* **kayn**-I'n) *ADJECTIVE* to do with dogs.

canine *NOUN* **canines** **1** a dog. **2** a pointed tooth at the front of the mouth.
[from Latin *canis* = dog]

canister *NOUN* **canisters** a metal container.
[from Greek *kanastron* = wicker basket; related to *cane*]

canker *NOUN* a disease that rots the wood of trees and plants or causes ulcers and sores on animals.
[same origin as *cancer*]

cannabis *NOUN* hemp, especially when smoked as a drug.
[from *Cannabis*, the Latin name of the hemp plant]

cannibal *NOUN* **cannibals** **1** a person who eats human flesh. **2** an animal that eats animals of its own kind.
▷ **cannibalism** *noun*
[from Spanish *Canibales*, the name given to the original inhabitants of the Caribbean islands, who the Spanish thought ate people]

cannibalize *VERB* **cannibalizes, cannibalizing, cannibalized** take a machine or vehicle apart to provide spare parts for others.
▷ **cannibalization** *noun*

cannon *NOUN* **cannon** **1** a large heavy gun. **cannons** **2** the hitting of two balls in billiards by the third ball.

A B **C** D E F G H I J K L M N O P Q R S T U V W X Y Z

cannon *VERB* **cannons, cannoning, cannoned** bump into something heavily.
[via French from Italian *cannone* = large tube]
USAGE Do not confuse with **canon**.

cannon ball *NOUN* **cannon balls** a large solid ball fired from a cannon.

cannot can not.

canny *ADJECTIVE* **cannier, canniest** shrewd.
▷ **cannily** *adverb*
[from *can*²]

canoe *NOUN* **canoes** a narrow lightweight boat, moved forwards with paddles.

canoe *VERB* **canoes, canoeing, canoed** travel in a canoe.
▷ **canoeist** *noun*
[via Spanish from Carib (the language of the original inhabitants of the Caribbean)]

canon *NOUN* **canons** **1** a general principle; a rule. **2** a clergyman of a cathedral.
[from Greek *kanon* = rule]
USAGE Do not confuse with **cannon**.

canonize *VERB* **canonizes, canonizing, canonized** declare officially that someone is a saint.
▷ **canonization** *noun*
[from *canon*, in the sense 'list of those accepted as saints by the church']

canopy *NOUN* **canopies** **1** a hanging cover forming a shelter above a throne, bed, or person etc. **2** the part of a parachute that spreads in the air.
[from Greek *konopeion* = bed with a mosquito net]

cant¹ *VERB* slope or tilt.
[from a Dutch word meaning 'edge']

cant² *NOUN* **1** insincere talk. **2** jargon.
[from Latin *cantare* = sing]

can't (*mainly spoken*) cannot.

cantaloup *NOUN* **cantaloups** a small round orange-coloured melon.
[from *Cantaluppi*, a place near Rome, where it was first grown in Europe]

cantankerous *ADJECTIVE* bad-tempered.
[origin unknown]

cantata (*say* kant-ah-ta) *NOUN* **cantatas** a musical composition for singers, like an oratorio but shorter.
[from Italian *cantare* = sing]

canteen *NOUN* **canteens** **1** a restaurant for workers in a factory or office. **2** a case or box containing a set of cutlery. **3** a soldier's or camper's water flask.
[via French from Italian]

canter *NOUN* a gentle gallop.

canter *VERB* **canters, cantering, cantered** go or ride at a canter.
[short for 'Canterbury gallop', the gentle pace at which pilgrims were said to travel to Canterbury in the Middle Ages]

canticle *NOUN* **canticles** a song or chant with words taken from the Bible.
[from Latin *canticulum* = little song]

cantilever *NOUN* **cantilevers** a beam or girder fixed at one end only and used to support a bridge etc.
[origin unknown]

canton *NOUN* **cantons** each of the districts into which Switzerland is divided.
[from French]

canvas *NOUN* **canvases** **1** a kind of strong coarse cloth. **2** a piece of canvas for painting on; a painting.
[from Latin *cannabis* = hemp, from whose fibres cloth was made]

canvass *VERB* **canvasses, canvassing, canvassed** visit people to ask them for their support, especially in an election.
▷ **canvasser** *noun*
[originally = to catch in a net or bag: from *canvas*]

canyon *NOUN* **canyons** a deep valley, usually with a river running through it.
[from Spanish *cañón* = tube]

cap *NOUN* **caps** **1** a soft hat without a brim but often with a peak. **2** a special headdress, e.g. that worn by a nurse. **3** a cap showing membership of a sports team. **4** a cap-like cover or top. **5** something that makes a bang when fired in a toy pistol.

cap *VERB* **caps, capping, capped** **1** put a cap or cover on something; cover. **2** award a sports cap to someone chosen to be in a team. **3** do better than something • *Can you cap that joke?*
[same origin as *cape*¹]

capable *ADJECTIVE* able to do something.
▷ **capably** *adverb* **capability** *noun*
[from Latin; related to *capacity*]

capacious (*say* ka-pay-shus) *ADJECTIVE* roomy; able to hold a large amount.
[same origin as *capacity*]

capacity *NOUN* **capacities** **1** the amount that something can hold. **2** ability or capability. **3** the position that someone occupies • *In my capacity as your guardian I am responsible for you.*
[from Latin *capere* = take, hold]

cape[1] *NOUN* **capes** a cloak.
[from Latin *cappa* = hood]

cape[2] *NOUN* **capes** a large piece of high land that sticks out into the sea.
[from Latin *caput* = head]

caper[1] *VERB* **capers, capering, capered** jump about playfully.

caper *NOUN* **capers** **1** jumping about playfully. **2** (*slang*) an activity or adventure.
[from Latin *caper* = goat]

caper[2] *NOUN* **capers** a bud of a prickly shrub, pickled for use in sauces etc.
[from Greek]

capillary (*say* ka-pil-er-ee) *NOUN* **capillaries** any of the very fine blood vessels that connect veins and arteries.

capillary *ADJECTIVE* to do with or occurring in a very narrow tube; to do with a capillary.
[from Latin *capillus* = hair]

capital *NOUN* **capitals** **1** a capital city. **2** a capital letter. **3** the top part of a pillar. **4** money or property that can be used to produce more wealth.

capital *ADJECTIVE* **1** important. **2** (*informal*) excellent.
[from Latin *caput* = head]

capital city *NOUN* **capital cities** the most important city in a country.

capitalism (*say* kap-it-al-izm) *NOUN* an economic system in which trade and industry are controlled by private owners for profit, and not by the state. (COMPARE **Communism**)

capitalist (*say* kap-it-al-ist) *NOUN* **capitalists** **1** a person who has a lot of wealth invested; a rich person. **2** a person who is in favour of capitalism.

capitalize (*say* kap-it-al-I'z) *VERB* **capitalizes, capitalizing, capitalized** **1** write or print as a capital letter. **2** change something into capital (= money or property); provide with capital.
▷ **capitalization** *noun*
- **capitalize on** profit by something; use it to your own advantage • *You could capitalize on your skill at drawing.*

capital letter *NOUN* **capital letters** a large letter of the kind used at the start of a name or sentence.

capital punishment *NOUN* punishing criminals by putting them to death.

capitulate *VERB* **capitulates, capitulating, capitulated** admit that you are defeated and surrender.
▷ **capitulation** *noun*
[from Latin]

cappuccino *NOUN* **cappuccinos** milky coffee made frothy with pressurized steam.
[Italian: named after the Capuchin monks who wore coffee-coloured habits]

caprice (*say* ka-preess) *NOUN* **caprices** a capricious action or impulse; a whim.
[via French from Italian]

capricious (*say* ka-prish-us) *ADJECTIVE* deciding or changing your mind in an impulsive way.
▷ **capriciously** *adverb* **capriciousness** *noun*

capsize *VERB* **capsizes, capsizing, capsized** overturn • *The boat capsized.*
[origin unknown]

capstan *NOUN* **capstans** a thick post that can be turned to pull in a rope or cable etc. that winds round it as it turns.
[from Latin *capere* = seize]

capsule *NOUN* **capsules** **1** a hollow pill containing medicine. **2** a plant's seed case that splits open when ripe. **3** a compartment of a spacecraft that can be separated from the main part.
[same origin as *case*[1]]

captain *NOUN* **captains** **1** a person in command of a ship or aircraft. **2** the leader in a sports team. **3** an army officer ranking next below a major; a naval officer ranking next below a commodore.
▷ **captaincy** *noun*

A B **C** D E F G H I J K L M N O P Q R S T U V W X Y Z

captain *VERB* **captains, captaining, captained** be the captain of a sports team etc.
[from Latin *capitanus* = chief]

caption *NOUN* **captions** **1** the words printed with a picture to describe it. **2** a short title or heading in a newspaper or magazine.
[from Latin]

captious (*say* kap-shus) *ADJECTIVE* pointing out small mistakes or faults.
[same origin as *captive*]

captivate *VERB* **captivates, captivating, captivated** charm or delight someone.
▷ **captivation** *noun*
[same origin as *captive*]

captive *NOUN* **captives** someone taken prisoner.

captive *ADJECTIVE* taken prisoner; unable to escape.
▷ **captivity** *noun*
[from Latin *capere* = take, seize]

captor *NOUN* **captors** someone who has captured a person or animal.

capture *VERB* **captures, capturing, captured** **1** take someone prisoner. **2** take or obtain by force, trickery, skill, or attraction • *He captured her heart.* **3** (*in computing*) put data in a form that can be stored in a computer.

capture *NOUN* capturing someone or something.
[same origin as *captive*]

car *NOUN* **cars** **1** a motor car. **2** a carriage • *dining car.*
[from old French]

carafe (*say* ka-raf) *NOUN* **carafes** a glass bottle holding wine or water for pouring out at the table.
[via French from Italian]

caramel *NOUN* **caramels** **1** a kind of toffee tasting like burnt sugar. **2** burnt sugar used for colouring and flavouring food.
[via French from Spanish]

carapace (*say* ka-ra-payss) *NOUN* **carapaces** the shell on the back of a tortoise or crustacean.
[via French from Spanish]

carat *NOUN* **carats** **1** a measure of weight for precious stones. **2** a measure of the purity of gold • *Pure gold is 24 carats.*
[via French and Italian from Arabic]

caravan *NOUN* **caravans** **1** a vehicle towed by a car and used for living in. **2** a group of people travelling together across desert country.
▷ **caravanning** *noun*
[via French from Persian]

caraway *NOUN* a plant with spicy seeds that are used for flavouring food.
[from Greek *karon* = cumin]

carbohydrate *NOUN* **carbohydrates** a compound of carbon, oxygen, and hydrogen (e.g. sugar or starch).
[from *carbon* + *-hydrate* = combined with water]

carbolic *NOUN* a kind of disinfectant.
[from *carbon* (from which it is made)]

carbon *NOUN* **carbons** **1** an element that is present in all living things and that occurs in its pure form as diamond and graphite. **2** carbon paper. **3** a carbon copy.
[from Latin *carbo* = coal]

carbonate *NOUN* **carbonates** a compound that gives off carbon dioxide when mixed with acid.

carbonated *ADJECTIVE* with carbon dioxide added • *Carbonated drinks are fizzy.*

carbon copy *NOUN* **carbon copies** **1** a copy made with carbon paper. **2** an exact copy.

carbon dioxide *NOUN* a gas formed when things burn, or breathed out by humans and animals.

carboniferous *ADJECTIVE* producing coal.
[from *carbon* + Latin *ferre* = to bear]

carbon paper *NOUN* thin paper with a coloured coating, placed between sheets of paper to make copies of what is written or typed on the top sheet.

carbuncle *NOUN* **carbuncles** **1** a bad abscess in the skin. **2** a bright-red gem.
[from Latin *carbunculus* = small coal]

carburettor *NOUN* **carburettors** a device for mixing fuel and air in an engine.
[from *carbon* (which the fuel contains)]

carcass *NOUN* **carcasses** **1** the dead body of an animal. **2** the bony part of a bird's body after the meat has been eaten.
[from French]

carcinogen *NOUN* **carcinogens** any substance that produces cancer.
[from Greek *karkinoma* = tumour]

card *NOUN* **cards** **1** thick stiff paper or thin cardboard. **2** a small piece of stiff paper for writing or printing on, especially to send messages or greetings or to record information. **3** a small, oblong piece of plastic issued to a customer by a bank or building society, giving details of their account. **4** a playing card.
- **cards** *plural noun* a game using playing cards.
- **on the cards** likely; possible.
[from Latin *charta* = papyrus leaf, paper]

cardboard *NOUN* a kind of thin board made of layers of paper or wood fibre.

cardiac (*say* kard-ee-ak) *ADJECTIVE* to do with the heart.
[from Greek *kardia* = heart]

cardigan *NOUN* **cardigans** a knitted jacket.
[named after the Earl of *Cardigan*, a commander in the Crimean War; cardigans were first worn by the troops in that war]

cardinal *NOUN* **cardinals** a senior priest in the Roman Catholic Church.

cardinal *ADJECTIVE* **1** chief; most important • *the cardinal features of our plan.* **2** deep scarlet, like a cardinal's cassock.
[from old French]

cardinal number *NOUN* **cardinal numbers** a number for counting things, e.g. one, two, three, etc. (COMPARE **ordinal number**)

cardinal point *NOUN* **cardinal points** each of the four main points of the compass (North, South, East, West).

cardiology *NOUN* the study of the structure and diseases of the heart.
▷ **cardiological** *adjective* **cardiologist** *noun*
[from Greek *kardia* = heart, + *-logy*]

care *NOUN* **cares** **1** serious attention and thought • *Plan your holiday with care.* **2** caution to avoid damage or loss • *Glass- handle with care.* **3** protection or supervision • *Leave the child in my care.* **4** worry or anxiety • *She was free from care.*
- **take care** be especially careful.
- **take care of** look after.

care *VERB* **cares, caring, cared** **1** feel interested or concerned. **2** feel affection.
- **care for** **1** have in your care. **2** be fond of.
[from Old English]

career *NOUN* **careers** the series of jobs that someone has as they make progress in their occupation.

career *VERB* **careers, careering, careered** rush along wildly.
[from Latin; related to *car*]

carefree *ADJECTIVE* without worries or responsibilities.

careful *ADJECTIVE* **1** giving serious thought and attention to something. **2** avoiding damage or danger etc.; cautious.
▷ **carefully** *adverb* **carefulness** *noun*

careless *ADJECTIVE* not careful.
▷ **carelessly** *adverb* **carelessness** *noun*

caress *NOUN* **caresses** a gentle loving touch.

caress *VERB* **caresses, caressing, caressed** touch lovingly.
[from Latin *carus* = dear]

caret *NOUN* **carets** a mark (^) showing where something is to be inserted in writing or printing.
[Latin, = it is lacking]

caretaker *NOUN* **caretakers** a person employed to look after a school, block of flats, etc.

cargo *NOUN* **cargoes** goods carried in a ship or aircraft.
[from Spanish]

Caribbean *ADJECTIVE* to do with or from the Caribbean Sea, a part of the Atlantic Ocean east of Central America.

caribou (*say* ka-rib-oo) *NOUN* **caribou** a North American reindeer.
[from a Native American word meaning 'snow- shoveller' (because the caribou scrapes away the snow to feed on the grass underneath)]

A B **C** D E F G H I J K L M N O P Q R S T U V W X Y Z

caricature *NOUN* **caricatures** an amusing or exaggerated picture of someone.
[from Italian *caricare* = exaggerate]

caries (*say* **kair**-eez) *NOUN* decay in teeth or bones.
[Latin]

carmine *ADJECTIVE* & *NOUN* deep red.
[via old French from Arabic; related to *crimson*]

carnage *NOUN* the killing of many people.
[same origin as *carnal*]

carnal *ADJECTIVE* to do with the body as opposed to the spirit; not spiritual.
[from Latin *carnis* = of flesh]

carnation *NOUN* **carnations** a garden flower with a sweet smell.
[via Arabic from Greek]

carnival *NOUN* **carnivals** a festival, often with a procession of people in fancy dress.
[from Latin *carnis* = of flesh (because originally this meant the festivities before Lent, when meat was given up until Easter)]

carnivorous (*say* kar-**niv**-er-us) *ADJECTIVE* meat-eating. (COMPARE **herbivorous**)
▷ **carnivore** *noun*
[from Latin *carnis* = of flesh + *vorare* = devour]

carol *NOUN* **carols** a Christmas hymn.
▷ **caroller** *noun* **carolling** *noun*
[from old French]

carouse *VERB* **carouses, carousing, caroused** drink alcohol and enjoy yourself with other people.
[from German *gar aus trinken* = drink to the bottom of the glass]

carousel (*say* ka-roo-**sel**) *NOUN* **carousels** **1** (*American*) a roundabout at a fair. **2** a conveyor belt that goes round in a circle, e.g. for baggage at an airport.
[via French from Italian]

carp[1] *NOUN* **carp** an edible freshwater fish.
[from Latin *carpa*]

carp[2] *VERB* **carps, carping, carped** keep finding fault.
[from Latin *carpere* = slander]

car park *NOUN* **car parks** an area where cars may be parked.

carpenter *NOUN* **carpenters** a person who makes things out of wood.
▷ **carpentry** *noun*
[from a Latin word meaning 'carriage-maker']

carpet *NOUN* **carpets** a thick soft covering for a floor.
▷ **carpeted** *adjective* **carpeting** *noun*
[from old French]

carport *NOUN* **carports** a shelter for a car.

carriage *NOUN* **carriages** **1** one of the separate parts of a train, where passengers sit. **2** a passenger vehicle pulled by horses. **3** carrying goods from one place to another; the cost of carrying goods • *Carriage is extra.* **4** a moving part carrying or holding something in a machine.
[same origin as *carry*]

carriageway *NOUN* **carriageways** the part of a road on which vehicles travel.

carrier *NOUN* **carriers** a person or thing that carries something.

carrier bag *NOUN* **carrier bags** a plastic or paper bag with handles.

carrier pigeon *NOUN* **carrier pigeons** a pigeon used to carry messages.

carrion *NOUN* dead and decaying flesh.
[from Latin *caro* = flesh]

carrot *NOUN* **carrots** a plant with a thick orange-coloured root used as a vegetable.
[from Greek]

carry *VERB* **carries, carrying, carried** **1** take something from one place to another. **2** support the weight of something. **3** take an amount into the next column when adding figures. **4** be heard a long way away • *Sound carries in the mountains.* **5** if a motion is carried, it is approved by most people at the meeting • *The motion was carried by ten votes to six.*
- **be carried away** be very excited.
- **carry on** **1** continue. **2** (*informal*) behave excitedly. **3** (*informal*) complain.
- **carry out** put into practice.

[from old French *carier*; related to *car*]

cart *NOUN* **carts** an open vehicle for carrying loads.

cart *VERB* **carts, carting, carted** **1** carry in a cart. **2** (*informal*) carry something heavy or tiring • *I've carted these books all round the school.*
[from Old Norse]

carte blanche (*say* kart **blahnsh**) *NOUN* freedom to act as you think best.
[French, = blank paper]

carthorse *NOUN* **carthorses** a large strong horse used for pulling heavy loads.

cartilage *NOUN* tough white flexible tissue attached to a bone.
[from Latin]

cartography *NOUN* drawing maps.
▷ **cartographer** *noun* **cartographic** *adjective*
[from French *carte* = map, + *-graphy*]

carton *NOUN* **cartons** a cardboard or plastic container.
[French; related to *card*]

cartoon *NOUN* **cartoons** **1** an amusing drawing. **2** a series of drawings that tell a story. **3** an animated film.
▷ **cartoonist** *noun*
[originally = a drawing on stiff paper; from Italian, related to *card*]

cartridge *NOUN* **cartridges** **1** a case containing the explosive for a bullet or shell. **2** a container holding film for a camera, ink for a printer, ink for a pen, etc. **3** the device that holds the stylus of a record player.
[from French *cartouche*]

cartwheel *NOUN* **cartwheels** **1** the wheel of a cart. **2** a handstand balancing on each hand in turn with arms and legs spread like spokes of a wheel.

carve *VERB* **carves, carving, carved** **1** make something by cutting wood or stone etc. **2** cut cooked meat into slices.
▷ **carver** *noun*
[from Old English]

cascade *NOUN* **cascades** a waterfall.

cascade *VERB* **cascades, cascading, cascaded** fall like a cascade.
[same origin as *case*²]

case¹ *NOUN* **cases** **1** a container. **2** a suitcase.
[from Latin *capsa* = box]

case² *NOUN* **cases** **1** an example of something existing or occurring; a situation • *In every case we found that someone had cheated.* **2** something investigated by police etc. or by a lawcourt • *a murder case.* **3** a set of facts or arguments to support something • *She put forward a good case for equality.* **4** the form of a word that shows how it is related to other words. *Fred's* is the possessive case of *Fred*; *him* is the objective case of *he*.
- **in any case** anyway.
- **in case** because something may happen.
[from Latin *casus* = a fall, an occasion]

casement *NOUN* **casements** a window that opens on hinges at its side.
[same origin as *case*¹]

cash *NOUN* **1** money in coin or notes. **2** immediate payment for goods.

cash *VERB* **cashes, cashing, cashed** change a cheque etc. for cash.
[originally = a cash box; from Latin *capsa* = box]

cash card *NOUN* **cash cards** a plastic card used to draw money from a cash dispenser.

cash dispenser *NOUN* **cash dispensers** a machine, usually outside a bank or building society, from which people can draw out cash by using a cash card.

cashew *NOUN* **cashews** a kind of small nut.
[via Portuguese from Tupi (a South American language)]

cashier *NOUN* **cashiers** a person who takes in and pays out money in a bank or takes payments in a shop.

cashmere *NOUN* very fine soft wool.
[from *Kashmir* in Asia, where it was first produced]

cashpoint *NOUN* **cashpoints** a cash dispenser.

cash register *NOUN* **cash registers** a machine that records and stores the money received in a shop.

casing *NOUN* **casings** a protective covering.
[from *case*¹]

casino *NOUN* **casinos** a public building or room for gambling.
[Italian, = little house]

cask *NOUN* **casks** a barrel.
[from French or Spanish]

A B C D E F G H I J K L M N O P Q R S T U V W X Y Z

casket *NOUN* **caskets** a small box for jewellery etc.
[origin unknown]

cassava *NOUN* a tropical plant with starchy roots that are an important source of food in tropical countries.
[from Taino (a South American language)]

casserole *NOUN* **casseroles** **1** a covered dish in which food is cooked and served. **2** food cooked in a casserole.
[from Greek]

cassette *NOUN* **cassettes** a small sealed case containing recording tape, film, etc.
▷ **cassette player** *noun*
[French, = little case]

cassock *NOUN* **cassocks** a long piece of clothing worn by clergy and members of a church choir.
[via French from Italian]

cast *VERB* **casts, casting, cast** **1** throw. **2** shed or throw off. **3** make a vote. **4** make something of metal or plaster in a mould. **5** choose performers for a play or film etc.

cast *NOUN* **casts** **1** a shape made by pouring liquid metal or plaster into a mould. **2** all the performers in a play or film.
[from Old Norse]

castanets *PLURAL NOUN* two pieces of wood, ivory, etc. held in one hand and clapped together to make a clicking sound, usually for dancing.
[from Spanish *castañetas* = little chestnuts]

castaway *NOUN* **castaways** a shipwrecked person.
[originally = an outcast; from *cast* + *away*]

caste *NOUN* **castes** (in India) one of the social classes into which Hindus are born.
[from Spanish or Portuguese *casta* = descent (from the same ancestors)]

castigate *VERB* **castigates, castigating, castigated** punish or rebuke someone severely.
▷ **castigation** *noun*
[from Latin *castigare* = punish]

casting vote *NOUN* **casting votes** the vote that decides which group wins when the votes on each side are equal.

cast iron *NOUN* a hard alloy of iron made by casting it in a mould.

castle *NOUN* **castles** **1** a large old fortified building. **2** a piece in chess, also called a *rook*.
- **castles in the air** daydreams.
[from Latin *castellum* = fort]

castor *NOUN* **castors** a small wheel on the leg of a table, chair, etc.
[from *cast*]

castor oil *NOUN* oil from the seeds of a tropical plant, used as a laxative.
[origin unknown]

castor sugar *NOUN* finely-ground white sugar.

castrate *VERB* **castrates, castrating, castrated** remove the testicles of a male animal; geld. (COMPARE **spay**)
▷ **castration** *noun*
[from Latin]

casual *ADJECTIVE* **1** happening by chance; not planned. **2** not careful; not methodical. **3** informal; suitable for informal occasions • *casual clothes.* **4** not permanent • *casual work.*
▷ **casually** *adverb* **casualness** *noun*
[same origin as *case*²]

casualty *NOUN* **casualties** a person who is killed or injured in war or in an accident.
[originally = chance; same origin as *case*²]

casualty department *NOUN* **casualty departments** the department of a hospital that deals with emergency patients.

cat *NOUN* **cats** **1** a small furry domestic animal. **2** a wild animal of the same family as a domestic cat, e.g. a lion, tiger, or leopard.
- **let the cat out of the bag** reveal a secret.
[from Old English]

cata- *PREFIX* (becoming **cat-** before a vowel; combining with an *h* to become **cath-**) **1** down (as in *catapult*). **2** thoroughly (as in *catalogue*).
[from Greek *kata* = down]

cataclysm (*say* kat-a-klizm) *NOUN* **cataclysms** a violent upheaval or disaster.
[from *cata-* + Greek *klyzein* = to wash]

catacombs (*say* kat-a-koomz) *PLURAL NOUN* underground passages with compartments for tombs.
[the name of a large catacomb in Rome]

catafalque (*say* kat-a-falk) *NOUN* **catafalques** a decorated platform for a person's coffin.
[via French from Italian]

catalogue *NOUN* **catalogues** **1** a list of things (e.g. of books in a library), usually arranged in order. **2** a book containing a list of things that can be bought • *our Christmas catalogue.*

catalogue *VERB* **catalogues, cataloguing, catalogued** enter something in a catalogue.
[from *cata-* + Greek *legein* = choose]

catalyst (*say* kat-a-list) *NOUN* **catalysts** **1** something that starts or speeds up a chemical reaction. **2** something that brings about a change.
[from *cata-* + Greek *lysis* = loosening]

catalytic converter *NOUN* **catalytic converters** a device fitted to a car's exhaust system, with a catalyst for converting pollutant gases into less harmful ones.

catamaran *NOUN* **catamarans** a boat with twin hulls.
[from Tamil *kattumaram* = tied wood]

catapult *NOUN* **catapults** **1** a device with elastic for shooting small stones. **2** an ancient military weapon for hurling stones etc.

catapult *VERB* **catapults, catapulting, catapulted** hurl or rush violently.
[from *cata-* + Greek *pellein* = throw]

cataract *NOUN* **cataracts** **1** a large waterfall or rush of water. **2** a cloudy area that forms in the eye and prevents a person from seeing clearly.
[from Greek]

catarrh (*say* ka-tar) *NOUN* inflammation in your nose that makes it drip a watery fluid.
[from Greek *katarrhein* = flow down]

catastrophe (*say* ka-tass-trof-ee) *NOUN* **catastrophes** a sudden great disaster.
▷ **catastrophic** (*say* kat-a-**strof**-ik) *adjective*, **catastrophically** *adverb*
[from *cata-* + Greek *strephein* = to turn]

catch *VERB* **catches, catching, caught** **1** take and hold something. **2** arrest or capture. **3** overtake. **4** be in time to get on a bus or train etc. **5** be infected with an illness. **6** hear • *I didn't catch what he said.* **7** discover someone doing something wrong • *She was caught smoking in the playground.* **8** make or become snagged or entangled • *I caught my dress on a nail.* **9** hit; strike • *The blow caught him on the nose.*
- **catch fire** start burning.
- **catch it** (*informal*) be scolded or punished.
- **catch on** (*informal*) **1** become popular. **2** understand.
- **catch out** discover someone in a mistake.

catch *NOUN* **catches** **1** catching something. **2** something caught or worth catching. **3** a hidden difficulty. **4** a device for fastening something.
[same origin as *chase*]

catching *ADJECTIVE* infectious.

catchment area *NOUN* **catchment areas** **1** the area from which a hospital takes patients or a school takes pupils. **2** the whole area from which water drains into a river or reservoir.

catchphrase *NOUN* **catchphrases** a popular phrase.

catchy *ADJECTIVE* (said about a tune) pleasant and easy to remember.

catechism (*say* kat-ik-izm) *NOUN* **catechisms** a set of questions and answers that give the basic beliefs of a religion.
[from Greek]

categorical (*say* kat-ig-o-rik-al) *ADJECTIVE* definite and absolute • *a categorical refusal.*
▷ **categorically** *adverb*
[same origin as *category*]

category *NOUN* **categories** a set of people or things classified as being similar to each other.
[from Greek *kategoria* = statement, accusation]

cater *VERB* **caters, catering, catered** **1** provide food, especially for a lot of people. **2** provide what is needed.
▷ **caterer** *noun*
[from old French *acateour* = a person who buys food etc.]

caterpillar *NOUN* **caterpillars** the creeping worm-like creature that turns into a butterfly or moth.
[from Old French *chatepelose* = hairy cat]

cath- *PREFIX*, SEE **cata-**.

cathedral *NOUN* **cathedrals** the most important church of a district, usually containing the bishop's throne.
[from Greek *kathedra* = seat]

Catherine wheel *NOUN* **Catherine wheels** a firework that spins round.
[named after St Catherine, who was martyred on a spiked wheel]

cathode *NOUN* **cathodes** the electrode by which electric current leaves a device. (COMPARE **anode**)
[from *cata-* = down + Greek *hodos* = way]

cathode ray tube *NOUN* **cathode ray tubes** a tube used in televisions and computers, in which a beam of electrons from a cathode produces an image on a fluorescent screen.

Catholic *ADJECTIVE* **1** belonging to the Roman Catholic Church. **2** of all Christians • *the Holy Catholic Church.*
▷ **Catholicism** *noun*

Catholic *NOUN* **Catholics** a Roman Catholic.

catholic *ADJECTIVE* including most things • *Her taste in literature is catholic.*
[from Greek *katholikos* = universal]

catkin *NOUN* a spike of small soft flowers on trees such as hazel and willow.
[from Dutch]

catnap *NOUN* **catnaps** a short sleep.

Catseye *NOUN* **Catseyes** (*trademark*) one of a line of reflecting studs marking the centre or edge of a road.

cattle *PLURAL NOUN* animals with horns and hoofs, kept by farmers for their milk and beef.
[same origin as *chattel*]

catty *ADJECTIVE* **cattier**, **cattiest** speaking or spoken spitefully.

catwalk *NOUN* **catwalks** a long platform that models walk along at a fashion show.

caucus *NOUN* **caucuses** a small group within a political party, influencing decisions and policy etc.
[from a Native American word = adviser]

cauldron *NOUN* **cauldrons** a large deep pot for boiling things in.
[from Latin *caldarium* = hot bath]

cauliflower *NOUN* **cauliflowers** a cabbage with a large head of white flowers.
[from French *chou fleuri* = flowered cabbage]

cause *NOUN* **causes** **1** a person or thing that makes something happen or produces an effect. **2** a reason • *There is no cause for worry.* **3** a purpose for which people work; an organization or charity.

cause *VERB* **causes**, **causing**, **caused** be the cause of; make something happen.
[from Latin]

causeway *NOUN* **causeways** a raised road across low or marshy ground.
[from an old word *causey* = embankment, + *way*]

caustic *ADJECTIVE* **1** able to burn or wear things away by chemical action. **2** sarcastic.
▷ **caustically** *adverb*
[from Greek *kaustikos* = capable of burning]

cauterize *VERB* **cauterizes**, **cauterizing**, **cauterized** burn the surface of flesh to destroy infection or stop bleeding.
▷ **cauterization** *noun*
[from Greek *kauterion* = branding-iron]

caution *NOUN* **cautions** **1** care taken in order to avoid danger etc. **2** a warning.

caution *VERB* **cautions**, **cautioning**, **cautioned** warn someone.
[from Latin *cavere* = beware]

cautionary *ADJECTIVE* giving a warning.

cautious *ADJECTIVE* showing caution.
▷ **cautiously** *adverb* **cautiousness** *noun*

cavalcade *NOUN* **cavalcades** a procession.
[from Italian *cavalcare* = ride]

Cavalier *NOUN* **Cavaliers** a supporter of King Charles I in the English Civil War (1642-9).
[from French *chevalier* = knight, from Latin *caballus* = horse]

cavalry *NOUN* soldiers who fight on horseback or in armoured vehicles. (COMPARE **infantry**)
[from Latin *caballus* = horse]

cave *NOUN* **caves** a large hollow place in the side of a hill or cliff, or underground.

cave *VERB* **caves, caving, caved**
- **cave in 1** fall inwards. **2** give way in an argument.
[from Latin *cavus* = hollow]

caveat (*say* kav-ee-at) *NOUN* **caveats** a warning.
[Latin, = let a person beware]

caveman *NOUN* **cavemen** a person living in a cave in prehistoric times.

cavern *NOUN* **caverns** a large cave.
▷ **cavernous** *adjective*
[same origin as *cave*]

caviare (*say* kav-ee-ar) *NOUN* the pickled roe of sturgeon or other large fish.
[from Italian or French, probably from Greek]

cavil *VERB* **cavils, cavilling, cavilled** raise petty objections.
[from Latin *cavilla* = mockery]

caving *NOUN* exploring caves.

cavity *NOUN* **cavities** a hollow or hole.
[same origin as *cave*]

cavort (*say* ka-vort) *VERB* **cavorts, cavorting, cavorted** jump or run about excitedly.
[originally American; origin unknown]

caw *NOUN* **caws** the harsh cry of a crow etc.

CB *ABBREVIATION* citizens' band.

cc *ABBREVIATION* cubic centimetre(s).

CD *ABBREVIATION* compact disc.

CD-ROM *ABBREVIATION* compact disc read-only memory; a compact disc on which large amounts of data can be stored and then displayed on a computer screen.

CDT *ABBREVIATION* craft, design, and technology.

cease *VERB* **ceases, ceasing, ceased** stop or end.
[from Latin; related to *cede*]

ceasefire *NOUN* **ceasefires** a signal to stop firing.

ceaseless *ADJECTIVE* not ceasing.

cedar *NOUN* **cedars** an evergreen tree with hard fragrant wood.
▷ **cedarwood** *noun*
[from Greek]

cede (*say* seed) *VERB* **cedes, ceding, ceded** give up your rights to something; surrender
• *They had to cede some of their territory.*
[from Latin *cedere* = yield]
WORD FAMILY There are a number of English words that are related to *cede* because part of their original meaning comes from the Latin word *cedere* meaning 'to go or yield'. These include *accede*, *concede*, *intercede*, *precede*, *recede*, and *secede*.

cedilla (*say* sid-il-a) *NOUN* **cedillas** a mark under *c* in certain languages to show that it is pronounced as *s*, e.g. in *façade*.
[from Spanish, = a little *z*]

ceilidh (*say* kay-lee) *NOUN* **ceilidhs** an informal gathering for music, singing, and dancing, originating from Scotland and Ireland.
[from old Irish]

ceiling *NOUN* **ceilings 1** the flat surface under the top of a room. **2** the highest limit that something can reach.
[origin unknown]

celandine *NOUN* **celandines** a small wild plant with yellow flowers.
[from Greek]

celebrate *VERB* **celebrates, celebrating, celebrated 1** do something special or enjoyable to show that a day or event is important. **2** perform a religious ceremony.
▷ **celebrant** *noun* **celebration** *noun*
[from Latin]

celebrated *ADJECTIVE* famous.

celebrity *NOUN* **celebrities 1** a famous person. **2** fame; being famous.

celery *NOUN* a vegetable with crisp white or green stems.
[from Greek]

celestial (*say* sil-est-ee-al) *ADJECTIVE* **1** to do with the sky. **2** to do with heaven; divine.
- **celestial bodies** stars etc.
[from Latin]

celibate (*say* sel-ib-at) *ADJECTIVE* remaining unmarried or not having sexual intercourse, especially for religious reasons.
▷ **celibacy** *noun*
[from Latin *caelebs* = unmarried]

cell *NOUN* **cells** **1** a small room where a prisoner is locked up. **2** a small room in a monastery. **3** a microscopic unit of living matter. **4** a compartment of a honeycomb. **5** a device for producing electric current chemically. **6** a small group or unit in an organization etc.
[from Latin *cella* = storeroom]

cellar *NOUN* **cellars** an underground room.
[same origin as *cell*]

cello (*say* chel-oh) *NOUN* **cellos** a musical instrument like a large violin, placed between the knees of a player.
▷ **cellist** *noun*
[from Italian *violoncello* = small double bass]

Cellophane *NOUN* (*trademark*) a thin transparent wrapping material.
[from *cellulose* + *diaphane* = a transparent substance]

cellular *ADJECTIVE* **1** to do with or containing cells. **2** with an open mesh • *cellular blankets.* **3** (said about a telephone) using a network of radio stations to allow messages to be sent over a wide area.

celluloid *NOUN* a kind of plastic.
[from *cellulose*, from which it is made]

cellulose *NOUN* tissue that forms the main part of all plants and trees.
[from Latin]

Celsius (*say* sel-see-us) *ADJECTIVE* measuring temperature on a scale using 100 degrees, where water freezes at 0° and boils at 100°.
[named after A. *Celsius*, a Swedish astronomer, who invented it]

Celtic (*say* kel-tik) *ADJECTIVE* to do with the languages or inhabitants of ancient Britain and France before the Romans came, or of their descendants, e.g. Irish, Welsh, Gaelic.

cement *NOUN* **1** a mixture of lime and clay used in building, to join bricks together, etc. **2** a strong glue.

cement *VERB* **cements, cementing, cemented** **1** put cement on something. **2** join firmly; strengthen.
[from Latin]

cemetery (*say* sem-et-ree) *NOUN* **cemeteries** a place where people are buried.
[from Greek *koimeterion* = dormitory]

cenotaph (*say* sen-o-taf) *NOUN* **cenotaphs** a monument, especially as a war memorial, to people who are buried elsewhere.
[from Greek *kenos* = empty + *taphos* = tomb]

censer *NOUN* **censers** a container in which incense is burnt.
[same origin as *incense*]

censor *NOUN* **censors** a person who examines films, books, letters, etc. and removes or bans anything that seems harmful.
▷ **censor** *verb* **censorship** *noun*
[Latin, = magistrate with power to ban unsuitable people from ceremonies; from *censere* = to judge]
USAGE Do not confuse with **censure**.

censorious (*say* sen-sor-ee-us) *ADJECTIVE* criticizing something strongly.
[from Latin *censorius* = like a censor]

censure (*say* sen-sher) *NOUN* strong criticism or disapproval of something.
▷ **censure** *verb*
[same origin as *census*]
USAGE Do not confuse with *censor*.

census *NOUN* **censuses** an official count or survey of the population of a country or area.
[from Latin *censere* = estimate, judge]

cent *NOUN* **cents** a coin worth one-hundredth of a dollar.
[from Latin *centum* = 100]

centaur (*say* sen-tor) *NOUN* **centaurs** (in Greek myths) a creature with the upper body, head, and arms of a man and the lower body of a horse.
[from Greek]

centenarian (*say* sent-in-air-ee-an) *NOUN* **centenarians** a person who is 100 years old or more.
[same origin as *centenary*]

centenary (*say* sen-teen-er-ee) *NOUN* **centenaries** a 100th anniversary.
▷ **centennial** (*say* sen-ten-ee-al) *adjective*
[from Latin *centenarius* = containing a hundred]

centi- *PREFIX* **1** one hundred (as in *centipede*). **2** one-hundredth (as in *centimetre*).
[from Latin *centum* = 100]

centigrade *ADJECTIVE* Celsius.
[from *centi-* + Latin *gradus* = step]

centimetre *NOUN* **centimetres** one-hundredth of a metre, about four-tenths of an inch.

centipede *NOUN* **centipedes** a small crawling creature with a long body and many legs.
[from *centi-* + Latin *pedes* = feet]

central *ADJECTIVE* **1** to do with or at the centre. **2** most important.
▷ **centrally** *adverb*

central heating *NOUN* a system of heating a building from one source by circulating hot water or hot air or steam in pipes or by linked radiators.

centralize *VERB* **centralizes, centralizing, centralized** bring under a central authority's control.
▷ **centralization** *noun*

centre *NOUN* **centres** **1** the middle point or part. **2** an important place. **3** a building or place for a special purpose • *shopping centre; sports centre.*

centre *VERB* **centres, centring, centred** place something at the centre.
- **centre on** or **centre around** **1** be concentrated in. **2** have as its main subject or concern.
[from Greek *kentron* = sharp point, point of a pair of compasses]

centre forward *NOUN* **centre forwards** the player in the middle of the forward line in football or hockey.

centre of gravity *NOUN* **centres of gravity** the point in an object around which its mass is perfectly balanced.

centrifugal *ADJECTIVE* moving away from the centre; using centrifugal force.
[from Latin *centrum* = centre + *fugere* = flee]

centrifugal force *NOUN* a force that makes a thing that is travelling round a central point fly outwards off its circular path.

centurion (*say* sent-yoor-ee-on) *NOUN* **centurions** an officer in the ancient Roman army, originally commanding a hundred men.
[from Latin *centum* = 100]

century *NOUN* **centuries** **1** a period of one hundred years. **2** a hundred runs scored by a batsman in an innings at cricket.
[from Latin *centum* = 100]

cephalopod (*say* sef-al-o-pod) *NOUN* **cephalopods** a mollusc (such as an octopus or squid) that has a head with a ring of tentacles round the mouth.
[from Greek *kephale* = head + *podos* = of a foot]

ceramic *ADJECTIVE* to do with or made of pottery.
[from Greek]

ceramics *PLURAL NOUN* pottery-making.

cereal *NOUN* **cereals** **1** a grass producing seeds which are used as food, e.g. wheat, barley, rice. **2** a breakfast food made from these seeds.
[from *Ceres*, the Roman goddess of farming]
USAGE Do not confuse with **serial**.

cerebral (*say* se-rib-ral) *ADJECTIVE* to do with the brain.
[from Latin *cerebrum* = brain]

cerebral palsy *NOUN* a condition caused by brain damage before birth that makes a person suffer from spasms of the muscles and jerky movements.

ceremonial *ADJECTIVE* to do with or used in a ceremony; formal.
▷ **ceremonially** *adverb*

ceremonious *ADJECTIVE* full of ceremony; elaborately performed.

ceremony *NOUN* **ceremonies** the formal actions carried out on an important occasion, e.g. at a wedding or a funeral.
[from Latin *caerimonia* = worship, ritual]

certain *ADJECTIVE* sure; without doubt.
- **a certain person** or **thing** a person or thing that is known but not named.
[from Latin *certus* = settled, sure]

certainly *ADVERB* **1** for certain. **2** yes.

certainty *NOUN* **certainties** **1** something that is sure to happen. **2** being sure.

A B **C** D E F G H I J K L M N O P Q R S T U V W X Y Z

certificate *NOUN* **certificates** an official written or printed statement giving information about a person etc. • *a birth certificate.*
[same origin as *certify*]

certify *VERB* **certifies, certifying, certified** declare formally that something is true.
▷ **certification** *noun*
[from Latin *certificare* = make something certain]

cervix *NOUN* **cervices** (*say* ser-vis-ees) the entrance to the womb.
▷ **cervical** *adjective*
[Latin, = neck]

cessation *NOUN* ceasing.

cesspit or **cesspool** *NOUN* **cesspits, cesspools** a covered pit where liquid waste or sewage is stored temporarily.
[origin unknown]

CFC *ABBREVIATION* chlorofluorocarbon; a gas containing chlorine and fluorine that is thought to be harmful to the ozone layer in the Earth's atmosphere.

chafe *VERB* **chafes, chafing, chafed** **1** make or become sore by rubbing. **2** become irritated or impatient • *We chafed at the delay.*
[from French *chauffer* = make warm]

chaff[1] *NOUN* husks of corn, separated from the seed.
[from Old English]

chaff[2] *VERB* tease someone.
[origin unknown]

chaffinch *NOUN* **chaffinches** a kind of finch.
[from *chaff*[1] (because it searched the chaff for seeds the threshers had missed)]

chagrin (*say* shag-rin) *NOUN* a feeling of being annoyed or disappointed.
[French]

chain *NOUN* **chains** **1** a row of metal rings fastened together. **2** a connected series of things • *a chain of mountains; a chain of events.* **3** a number of shops, hotels, or other businesses owned by the same company.

chain *VERB* **chains, chaining, chained** fasten something with a chain or chains.
[from old French]

chain letter *NOUN* **chain letters** a letter that you are asked to copy and send to several other people, who are supposed to do the same.

chain reaction *NOUN* **chain reactions** a series of happenings in which each causes the next.

chain store *NOUN* **chain stores** one of a number of similar shops owned by the same firm.

chair *NOUN* **chairs** **1** a movable seat, with a back, for one person. **2** the person in charge at a meeting.

chair *VERB* **chairs, chairing, chaired** be in charge of a meeting • *Who will chair this meeting?*
[from old French; related to *cathedral*]

chairman *NOUN* **chairmen** the person who is in charge of a meeting.
▷ **chairmanship** *noun*
USAGE The word *chairman* may be used of a man or of a woman; they are addressed formally as *Mr Chairman* and *Madam Chairman.*

chairperson *NOUN* **chairpersons** a chairman.

chalet (*say* shal-ay) *NOUN* **chalets** **1** a Swiss hut or cottage. **2** a hut in a holiday camp etc.
[Swiss French]

chalice *NOUN* **chalices** a large goblet for holding wine, especially one from which the Communion wine is drunk in Christian services.
[from Latin *calix* = cup]

chalk *NOUN* **chalks** **1** a soft white or coloured stick used for writing on blackboards or for drawing. **2** soft white limestone.
▷ **chalky** *adjective*
[from Old English]

challenge *NOUN* **challenges** **1** a task or activity that is new and exciting but also difficult. **2** a call to someone to take part in a contest or to show their ability or strength.

challenge *VERB* **challenges, challenging, challenged** **1** make a challenge to someone. **2** be a challenge to someone. **3** question whether something is true or correct.
▷ **challenger** *noun* **challenging** *adjective*
[from old French]

chamber *NOUN* **chambers** **1** (*old use*) a room. **2** a hall used for meetings of a parliament etc.; the members of the group using it. **3** a compartment in machinery etc.
[same origin as *camera*]

chamberlain *NOUN* **chamberlains** an official who manages the household of a sovereign or great noble.
[from old French]

chambermaid *NOUN* **chambermaids** a woman employed to clean bedrooms at a hotel etc.

chamber music *NOUN* classical music for a small group of players.

chamber pot *NOUN* **chamber pots** a receptacle for urine etc., used in a bedroom.

chameleon (*say* kam-ee-lee-on) *NOUN* **chameleons** a small lizard that can change its colour to that of its surroundings.
[from Greek *khamaileon*, literally = ground lion]

chamois *NOUN* **chamois** **1** (*say* **sham**-wa) **1** a small wild antelope living in the mountains. **2** (*say* **sham**-ee) a piece of soft yellow leather used for washing and polishing things.
[French]

champ *VERB* **champs, champing, champed** munch or bite something noisily.
[imitating the sound]

champagne (*say* sham-**payn**) *NOUN* a bubbly white wine from Champagne in France.

champion *NOUN* **champions** **1** a person or thing that has defeated all the others in a sport or competition etc. **2** someone who supports a cause by fighting, speaking, etc.
▷ **championship** *noun*

champion *VERB* **champions, championing, championed** support a cause by fighting or speaking for it.
[from old French]

chance *NOUN* **chances** **1** an opportunity or possibility • *Now is your chance to escape.* **2** the way things happen without being planned • *I met her by chance.*
- **take a chance** take a risk.

chance *VERB* **chances, chancing, chanced** **1** happen by chance • *I chanced to meet her.* **2** risk • *Let's chance it.*
[from old French]

chancel *NOUN* **chancels** the part of a church nearest to the altar.
[from Latin]

chancellor *NOUN* **chancellors** **1** an important government or legal official. **2** the chief minister of the government in some European countries.
[from Latin *cancellarius* = secretary]

Chancellor of the Exchequer *NOUN* the government minister in charge of a country's finances and taxes.

chancy *ADJECTIVE* risky.

chandelier (*say* shand-il-**eer**) *NOUN* **chandeliers** a support for several lights or candles that hangs from the ceiling.
[from French *chandelle* = candle]

change *VERB* **changes, changing, changed** **1** make or become different. **2** exchange. **3** put on different clothes. **4** go from one train or bus etc. to another. **5** to give smaller units of money, or money in another currency, for an amount of money • *Can you change £20?*

change *NOUN* **changes** **1** changing; a difference in doing something. **2** coins or notes of small values. **3** money given back to the payer when the price is less than the amount handed over. **4** a fresh set of clothes. **5** a variation in routine • *Let's walk home for a change.*
[from old French]

changeable *ADJECTIVE* likely to change; changing frequently • *changeable weather.*

changeling *NOUN* **changelings** a child who is believed to have been substituted secretly for another, especially by fairies.

channel *NOUN* **channels** **1** a stretch of water connecting two seas. **2** a broadcasting wavelength. **3** a way for water to flow along. **4** the part of a river or sea that is deep enough for ships.

channel *VERB* **channels, channelling, channelled** **1** make a channel in something. **2** direct something through a channel or other route.
[from Latin *canalis* = canal]

chant *NOUN* **chants** **1** a tune to which words with no regular rhythm are fitted, especially one used in church music. **2** a rhythmic call or shout.

chant *VERB* **chants, chanting, chanted** **1** sing a chant. **2** call out words in a rhythm. [from Latin *cantare* = sing]

chaos (*say* kay-oss) *NOUN* great disorder.
▷ **chaotic** *adjective* **chaotically** *adverb*
[Greek, = bottomless pit]

chap *NOUN* **chaps** (*informal*) a man. [short for *chapman*, an old word for a pedlar]

chapatti *NOUN* **chapattis** a flat cake of unleavened bread, used in Indian cookery. [Hindi, from *chapana* = flatten or roll out]

chapel *NOUN* **chapels** **1** a small building or room used for Christian worship. **2** a section of a large church, with its own altar. [from old French]

chaperone (*say* shap-er-ohn) *NOUN* **chaperones** an older woman in charge of a young one on social occasions.
▷ **chaperone** *verb*
[from old French]

chaplain *NOUN* **chaplains** a member of the clergy who regularly works in a college, hospital, prison, regiment, etc. [from old French]

chapped *ADJECTIVE* with skin split or cracked from cold etc. [origin unknown]

chapter *NOUN* **chapters** **1** a division of a book. **2** the clergy of a cathedral or members of a monastery. The room where they meet is called a **chapter house**. [from Latin]

char[1] *VERB* **chars, charring, charred** make or become black by burning. [from *charcoal*]

char[2] *NOUN* **chars** a charwoman.

character *NOUN* **characters** **1** a person in a story, film, or play. **2** all the qualities that make a person or thing what he, she, or it is. **3** a letter of the alphabet or other written symbol. [from Greek]

characteristic *NOUN* **characteristics** a quality that forms part of a person's or thing's character.

characteristic *ADJECTIVE* typical of a person or thing.
▷ **characteristically** *adverb*

characterize *VERB* **characterizes, characterizing, characterized** **1** be a characteristic of. **2** describe the character of.
▷ **characterization** *noun*

charade (*say* sha-rahd) *NOUN* **charades** **1** a scene in the game of *charades*, in which people try to guess a word from other people's acting. **2** a pretence. [French]

charcoal *NOUN* a black substance made by burning wood slowly. Charcoal can be used for drawing with. [origin unknown]

charge *NOUN* **charges** **1** the price asked for something. **2** a rushing attack. **3** the amount of explosive needed to fire a gun etc. **4** electricity in something. **5** an accusation that someone has committed a crime. **6** a person or thing in someone's care.
- **in charge** in control; deciding what will happen to a person or thing.

charge *VERB* **charges, charging, charged** **1** ask a particular price. **2** rush forward in an attack. **3** give an electric charge to something. **4** accuse someone of committing a crime. **5** entrust someone with a responsibility or task. [from Latin *carcare* = to load]

charger *NOUN* **chargers** (*old use*) a cavalry horse.

chariot *NOUN* **chariots** a horse-drawn vehicle with two wheels, used in ancient times for fighting, racing, etc.
▷ **charioteer** *noun*
[from old French; related to *car*]

charisma (*say* ka-riz-ma) *NOUN* the special quality that makes a person attractive or influential. [Greek, = divine favour]

charismatic (*say* ka-riz-mat-ik) *ADJECTIVE* having charisma.

charity *NOUN* **charities** **1** an organization set up to help people who are poor, ill, or disabled or have suffered a disaster. **2** giving money or help etc. to the needy. **3** kindness and sympathy towards others; being unwilling to think badly of people.
▷ **charitable** *adjective* **charitably** *adverb*
[from Latin *caritas* = love]

charlatan (*say* shar-la-tan) *NOUN* **charlatans** a person who falsely claims to be an expert.
[from Italian *ciarlatano* = babbler]

charm *NOUN* **charms** **1** the power to please or delight people; attractiveness. **2** a magic spell. **3** a small object believed to bring good luck. **4** an ornament worn on a bracelet etc.

charm *VERB* **charms, charming, charmed** **1** give pleasure or delight to people. **2** put a spell on someone; bewitch.
▷ **charmer** *noun*
[from Latin *carmen* = song or spell]

charnel house *NOUN* **charnel houses** a place in which the bodies or bones of the dead are kept.
[same origin as *carnal*]

chart *NOUN* **charts** **1** a map for people sailing ships or flying aircraft. **2** an outline map showing special information • *a weather chart.* **3** a diagram, list, or table giving information in an orderly way.
- **the charts** a list of the records that are most popular.

chart *VERB* **charts, charting, charted** make a chart of something; map.
[same origin as *card*]

charter *NOUN* **charters** **1** an official document giving somebody certain rights etc. **2** chartering an aircraft, ship, or vehicle.

charter *VERB* **charters, chartering, chartered** **1** hire an aircraft, ship, or vehicle. **2** give a charter to someone.
[same origin as *card*]

chartered accountant *NOUN* **chartered accountants** an accountant who is qualified according to the rules of a professional association that has a royal charter.

charwoman *NOUN* **charwomen** (*old use*) a woman employed as a cleaner.
[from Old English *cerr* = task]

chary (*say* chair-ee) *ADJECTIVE* cautious about doing or giving something.
[from Old English]

chase *VERB* **chases, chasing, chased** go quickly after a person or thing in order to capture or catch them up or drive them away.
▷ **chase** *noun*
[from Latin *captare* = capture]

chasm (*say* kazm) *NOUN* **chasms** a deep opening in the ground.
[from Greek *chasma* = gaping hollow]

chassis (*say* shas-ee) *NOUN* **chassis** the framework under a car etc., on which other parts are mounted.
[originally = window frame; related to *casement*]

chaste *ADJECTIVE* not having sexual intercourse at all, or only with the person you are married to.
[from Latin *castus* = pure]

chasten (*say* chay-sen) *VERB* **chastens, chastening, chastened** make someone realize that they have behaved badly or done something wrong.
[from Latin *castigare* = castigate]

chastise *VERB* **chastises, chastising, chastised** punish or scold someone severely.
▷ **chastisement** *noun*
[same origin as *chasten*]

chastity (*say* chas-ti-ti) *NOUN* being chaste, especially by not having sexual intercourse.

chat *NOUN* **chats** a friendly conversation.

chat *VERB* **chats, chatting, chatted** have a friendly conversation.
[from *chatter*]

château (*say* shat-oh) *NOUN* **châteaux** a castle or large country house in France.
[French; related to *castle*]

chattel *NOUN* **chattels** (*old use*) something you own that can be moved from place to place, as distinct from a house or land.
[from old French *chatel*; related to *capital*]

chatter *VERB* **chatters, chattering, chattered** **1** talk quickly about unimportant things; keep on talking. **2** (said about the teeth) make a rattling sound because you are cold or frightened.
▷ **chatterer** *noun*

chatter *NOUN* chattering talk or sound.
[imitating the sound]

chatterbox *NOUN* **chatterboxes** a talkative person.

chauffeur (*say* **shoh**-fer) *NOUN* **chauffeurs** a person employed to drive a car.
[French, = stoker]

chauvinism (*say* **shoh**-vin-izm) *NOUN* **1** prejudiced belief that your own country is superior to any other. **2** the belief of some men that men are superior to women.
▷ **chauvinist** *noun* **chauvinistic** *adjective*
[from the name of Nicolas *Chauvin*, a French soldier in Napoleon's army, noted for his extreme patriotism]

cheap *ADJECTIVE* **1** low in price; not expensive. **2** of poor quality; of low value.
▷ **cheaply** *adverb* **cheapness** *noun*
[from Old English *ceap* = a bargain]

cheapen *VERB* **cheapens, cheapening, cheapened** make cheap.

cheat *VERB* **cheats, cheating, cheated 1** try to do well in an examination or game by breaking the rules. **2** trick or deceive somebody so they lose something.

cheat *NOUN* **cheats** a person who cheats.
[from old French]

check[1] *VERB* **checks, checking, checked 1** make sure that something is correct or in good condition. **2** make something stop or go slower.

check *NOUN* **checks 1** checking something. **2** stopping or slowing; a pause. **3** a receipt; a bill in a restaurant. **4** the situation in chess when a king may be captured.
[from the saying of 'check' when playing chess, to show that your opponent's king is in danger: from Persian *shah* = king]

check[2] *NOUN* **checks** a pattern of squares.
▷ **checked** *adjective*
[from *chequered*]

checkmate *NOUN* the winning situation in chess.
▷ **checkmate** *verb*
[from Persian *shah mat* = the king is dead]

checkout *NOUN* **checkouts** a place where goods are paid for in a self-service shop.

check-up *NOUN* **check-ups** a routine medical or dental examination.

Cheddar *NOUN* a kind of cheese.
[named after Cheddar in Somerset]

cheek *NOUN* **cheeks 1** the side of the face below the eye. **2** rude or disrespectful behaviour; impudence.
[from Old English]

cheeky *ADJECTIVE* rude or disrespectful; impudent.
▷ **cheekily** *adverb* **cheekiness** *noun*

cheer *NOUN* **cheers 1** a shout of praise or pleasure or encouragement. **2** cheerfulness • *full of good cheer.*

cheer *VERB* **cheers, cheering, cheered 1** give a cheer. **2** gladden or encourage somebody.
- **cheer up** make or become cheerful.
[originally = a person's expression; from old French *chiere* = face]

cheerful *ADJECTIVE* **1** looking or sounding happy. **2** pleasantly bright or colourful.
▷ **cheerfully** *adverb* **cheerfulness** *noun*

cheerio *INTERJECTION* (*informal*) goodbye.

cheerless *ADJECTIVE* gloomy or dreary.

cheers *EXCLAMATION* (*informal*) **1** a word that people say to each other as they lift up their glasses to drink. **2** goodbye. **3** thank you.

cheery *ADJECTIVE* bright and cheerful.

cheese *NOUN* **cheeses** a solid food made from milk.
[from Old English, taken from Latin]

cheesecake *NOUN* **cheesecakes** a dessert made of a mixture of sweetened curds on a layer of biscuit.

cheetah *NOUN* **cheetahs** a large spotted animal of the cat family that can run extremely fast.
[from Hindi]

chef (*say* shef) *NOUN* **chefs** the cook in a hotel or restaurant.
[French, = chief]

chemical *ADJECTIVE* to do with or produced by chemistry.

chemical *NOUN* **chemicals** a substance obtained by or used in chemistry.
[from Latin *alchimia* = alchemy]

chemist *NOUN* **chemists** **1** a person who makes or sells medicines. **2** a shop selling medicines, cosmetics, etc. **3** an expert in chemistry.
[from Latin *alchimista* = alchemist]

chemistry *NOUN* **1** the way that substances combine and react with one another. **2** the study of substances and their reactions etc.
[from *chemist*]

chemotherapy *NOUN* the treatment of disease, especially cancer, by the use of chemical substances.

cheque *NOUN* **cheques** a printed form on which you write instructions to a bank to pay out money from your account.
[a different spelling of *check*[1]]

chequered *ADJECTIVE* marked with a pattern of squares.
[same origin as *exchequer*]

cherish *VERB* **cherishes, cherishing, cherished** **1** look after a person or thing lovingly. **2** be fond of.
[from French *cher* = dear]

cherry *NOUN* **cherries** a small soft round fruit with a stone.
[from old French]

cherub *NOUN* **cherubim** or **cherubs** an angel, often pictured as a chubby child with wings.
▷ **cherubic** (*say* che-**roo**-bik) *adjective*
[from Hebrew]

chess *NOUN* a game for two players with sixteen pieces each (called **chessmen**) on a board of 64 squares (a **chessboard**).
[from old French *esches* = checks]

chest *NOUN* **chests** **1** the front part of the body between the neck and the waist. **2** a large strong box for storing things in.
[from Old English]

chestnut *NOUN* **chestnuts** **1** a tree that produces hard brown nuts. **2** the nut of this tree. **3** an old joke or story.
[from Greek]

chest of drawers *NOUN* **chests of drawers** a piece of furniture with drawers for storing clothes etc.

chevron (*say* **shev**-ron) *NOUN* **chevrons** a V-shaped stripe.
[from old French]

chew *VERB* **chews, chewing, chewed** grind food between the teeth.
▷ **chewy** *adjective*
[from Old English]

chewing gum *NOUN* a sticky flavoured type of sweet for chewing.

chic (*say* sheek) *ADJECTIVE* stylish and elegant.
[French]

chicanery (*say* shik-**ayn**-er-ee) *NOUN* trickery.
[from French *chicaner* = quibble]

chick *NOUN* **chicks** a very young bird.
[shortened form of *chicken*]

chicken *NOUN* **chickens** **1** a young hen. **2** a hen's flesh used as food.

chicken *ADJECTIVE* (*slang*) afraid to do something; cowardly.

chicken *VERB* **chickens, chickening, chickened**
- **chicken out** (*slang*) not take part in something because you are afraid.
[from Old English]

chickenpox *NOUN* a disease that produces red spots on the skin.
[probably because the disease is mild]

chickpea *NOUN* **chickpeas** the yellow seed of a plant of the pea family, eaten as a vegetable.
[from French *chiche* = chickpea, + *pea*]

chicory *NOUN* a plant whose leaves are used as salad.
[from Greek]

chide *VERB* **chides, chiding, chided, chidden** scold.
[from Old English]

chief *NOUN* **chiefs** **1** a leader or ruler of a people, especially of a Native American tribe. **2** a person with the highest rank or authority.

chief *ADJECTIVE* most important; main.
▷ **chiefly** *adverb*
[from French]

chieftain *NOUN* **chieftains** the chief of a tribe or clan.

chiffon (*say* **shif**-on) *NOUN* a very thin almost transparent fabric.
[French]

chilblain *NOUN* **chilblains** a sore swollen place, usually on a hand or foot, caused by cold weather.
[from *chill* + *blain* = a sore]

child *NOUN* **children** **1** a young person; a boy or girl. **2** someone's son or daughter.
[from Old English]

childhood *NOUN* **childhoods** the time when a person is a child.

childish *ADJECTIVE* **1** like a child; unsuitable for a grown person. **2** silly and immature.
▷ **childishly** *adverb*

childless *ADJECTIVE* having no children.

childminder *NOUN* **childminders** a person who is paid to look after children while their parents are out at work.

chill *NOUN* **chills** **1** unpleasant coldness. **2** an illness that makes you shiver.

chill *VERB* **chills, chilling, chilled** **1** make a person or thing cold. **2** (*informal*) relax completely.
[from Old English]

chilli *NOUN* **chillies** the hot-tasting pod of a red pepper.
[via Spanish from Nahuatl (a Central American language)]

chilli con carne *NOUN* a stew of chilli-flavoured minced beef and beans.
[Spanish, = chilli with meat]

chilly *ADJECTIVE* **1** rather cold. **2** unfriendly • *We got a chilly reception.*
▷ **chilliness** *noun*

chime *NOUN* **chimes** a series of notes sounded by a set of bells each making a different musical sound.

chime *VERB* **chimes, chiming, chimed** make a chime.
[origin unknown]

chimney *NOUN* **chimneys** a tall pipe or structure that carries smoke away from a fire.
[from French]

chimney pot *NOUN* **chimney pots** a pipe fitted to the top of a chimney.

chimney sweep *NOUN* **chimney sweeps** a person who cleans soot from inside chimneys.

chimpanzee *NOUN* **chimpanzees** an intelligent African ape, smaller than a gorilla.
[via French from Kikongo (an African language)]

chin *NOUN* **chins** the lower part of the face below the mouth.
[from Old English]

china *NOUN* thin delicate pottery.
[from Persian *chini* = from China]

chink *NOUN* **chinks** **1** a narrow opening • *a chink in the curtains.* **2** a chinking sound.

chink *VERB* **chinks, chinking, chinked** make a sound like glasses or coins being struck together.
[origin unknown]

chintz *NOUN* a shiny cotton cloth used for making curtains etc.
[from Hindi]

chip *NOUN* **chips** **1** a thin piece cut or broken off something hard. **2** a fried oblong strip of potato. **3** a place where a small piece has been knocked off something. **4** a small counter used in games. **5** a microchip.
- **a chip off the old block** a child who is very like his or her father or mother.
- **have a chip on your shoulder** feel resentful or defensive about something.

chip *VERB* **chips, chipping, chipped** **1** knock small pieces off something. **2** cut a potato into chips.
[from Old English]

chipboard *NOUN* board made from chips of wood pressed and stuck together.

chipolata *NOUN* **chipolatas** a small spicy sausage.
[via French from Italian]

chiropody (*say* ki-rop-od-ee) *NOUN* medical treatment of the feet, e.g. corns.
▷ **chiropodist** *noun*
[from Greek *cheir* = hand + *podos* = of the foot (because chiropodists originally treated both hands and feet)]

chirp *VERB* **chirps, chirping, chirped** make short sharp sounds like a small bird.
▷ **chirp** *noun*
[imitating the sound]

chirpy *ADJECTIVE* lively and cheerful.

chisel *NOUN* **chisels** a tool with a sharp end for shaping wood, stone, etc.

chisel *VERB* **chisels, chiselling, chiselled** shape or cut something with a chisel.
[from old French]

chivalrous (*say* shiv-al-rus) *ADJECTIVE* being considerate and helpful towards people less strong than yourself.
▷ **chivalry** *noun*
[= like a perfect knight (same origin as *Cavalier*)]

chive *NOUN* **chives** a small herb with leaves that taste like onions.
[from Latin *cepa* = onion]

chivvy *VERB* **chivvies, chivvying, chivvied** try to make someone hurry.
[probably from *Chevy Chase*, the scene of a skirmish which was the subject of an old ballad]

chlorinate *VERB* **chlorinates, chlorinating, chlorinated** put chlorine into something.
▷ **chlorination** *noun*

chlorine (*say* klor-een) *NOUN* a greenish-yellow gas used to disinfect water etc.
[from Greek *chloros* = green]

chloroform (*say* klo-ro-form) *NOUN* a liquid that gives off a vapour that makes people unconscious.

chlorophyll (*say* klo-ro-fil) *NOUN* the substance that makes plants green.
[from Greek *chloros* = green + *phyllon* = leaf]

choc ice *NOUN* **choc ices** a bar of ice cream covered with chocolate.

chock *NOUN* **chocks** a block or wedge used to prevent something, especially an aeroplane, from moving.
[from old French]

chock-a-block *ADJECTIVE* crammed or crowded together.
[origin unknown]

chock-full *ADJECTIVE* crammed full.

chocolate *NOUN* **chocolates 1** a solid brown food or powder made from roasted cacao seeds. **2** a drink made with this powder. **3** a sweet made of or covered with chocolate.
[via French or Spanish from Nahuatl (a Central American language)]

choice *NOUN* **choices 1** choosing between things. **2** the range of things from which someone can choose • *There is a wide choice of holidays.* **3** a person or thing chosen • *This is my choice.*

choice *ADJECTIVE* of the best quality • *choice bananas.*
[via old French from Germanic]

choir *NOUN* **choirs** a group of people trained to sing together, especially in a church.
▷ **choirboy** *noun* **choirgirl** *noun*
[from Latin *chorus* = choir]

choke *VERB* **chokes, choking, choked 1** cause somebody to stop breathing properly. **2** be unable to breathe properly. **3** block up; clog.

choke *NOUN* **chokes** a device controlling the flow of air into the engine of a motor vehicle.
[from Old English]

cholera (*say* kol-er-a) *NOUN* an infectious disease that is often fatal.
[from Greek]

cholesterol (*say* kol-est-er-ol) *NOUN* a fatty substance that can clog the arteries.
[from Greek *chole* = bile + *stereos* = stiff]

choose *VERB* **chooses, choosing, chose, chosen** decide which you are going to take from among a number of people or things.
▷ **choosy** *adjective*
[from Old English]

chop *VERB* **chops, chopping, chopped** cut or hit something with a heavy blow.

chop *NOUN* **chops 1** a chopping blow. **2** a small thick slice of meat, usually on a rib.
[origin unknown]

chopper *NOUN* **choppers 1** a chopping tool; a small axe. **2** (*slang*) a helicopter.

choppy *ADJECTIVE* **choppier, choppiest** (said about the sea) not smooth; full of small waves.
▷ **choppiness** *noun*

chopsticks *PLURAL NOUN* a pair of thin sticks used for lifting Chinese and Japanese food to your mouth.
[from pidgin English, literally = quick sticks]

chop suey *NOUN* **chop sueys** a Chinese dish of meat fried with bean sprouts and vegetables served with rice.
[from Chinese *tsaap sui* = mixed bits]

choral *ADJECTIVE* to do with or sung by a choir or chorus.
[from Latin]

chorale (*say* kor-**ahl**) *NOUN* **chorales** a choral composition using the words of a hymn.
[via German from Latin]

chord[1] (*say* kord) *NOUN* **chords** a number of musical notes sounded together.
[from *accord*]

chord[2] (*say* kord) *NOUN* **chords** a straight line joining two points on a curve.
[a different spelling of *cord*]
USAGE Do not confuse with **cord**.

chore (*say* chor) *NOUN* **chores** a regular or dull task.
[a different spelling of *char*]

choreography (*say* ko-ree-og-ra-fee) *NOUN* the art of writing the steps for ballets or stage dances.
▷ **choreographer** *noun*
[from Greek *choreia* = dance, + *-graphy*]

chorister (*say* **ko**-rist-er) *NOUN* **choristers** a member of a choir.
[from old French]

chortle *NOUN* **chortles** a loud chuckle.
▷ **chortle** *verb*
[a mixture of *chuckle* and *snort*: invented by Lewis Carroll]

chorus *NOUN* **choruses** **1** the words repeated after each verse of a song or poem. **2** music sung by a group of people. **3** a group singing together.

chorus *VERB* **choruses**, **chorusing**, **chorused** sing or speak in chorus.
[Latin, from Greek *choros*]

chow mein *NOUN* a Chinese dish of fried noodles with shredded meat or shrimps etc. and vegetables.
[from Chinese *chao mian* = fried noodles]

christen *VERB* **christens**, **christening**, **christened** **1** baptize. **2** give a name or nickname to a person or thing.
▷ **christening** *noun*
[from Old English *cristnian* = make someone a Christian]

Christian *NOUN* **Christians** a person who believes in Jesus Christ and his teachings.

Christian *ADJECTIVE* to do with Christians or their beliefs.
▷ **Christianity** *noun*

Christian name *NOUN* **Christian names** a name given to a person at his or her christening; a person's first name.

Christmas *NOUN* **Christmases** the day (25 December) when Christians commemorate the birth of Jesus Christ; the days round it.
[from Old English *Cristes maesse* = the feast day of Christ]

Christmas pudding *NOUN* **Christmas puddings** a dark pudding containing dried fruit etc., eaten at Christmas.

Christmas tree *NOUN* **Christmas trees** an evergreen or artificial tree decorated at Christmas.

chromatic (*say* krom-**at**-ik) *ADJECTIVE* to do with colours.
[from Greek *chroma* = colour]

chromatic scale *NOUN* **chromatic scales** a musical scale going up or down in semitones.

chrome (*say* krohm) *NOUN* chromium.
[from Greek *chroma* = colour (because its compounds have brilliant colours)]

chromium (*say* **kroh**-mee-um) *NOUN* a shiny silvery metal.
[from *chrome*]

chromosome (*say* **kroh**-mos-ohm) *NOUN* **chromosomes** a tiny thread-like part of an animal cell or plant cell, carrying genes.
[from Greek *chroma* = colour + *soma* = body]

chronic *ADJECTIVE* lasting for a long time • *a chronic illness.*
▷ **chronically** *adverb*
[from Greek *chronikos* = to do with time]
WORD FAMILY There are a number of English words that are related to *chronic* because part of their original meaning comes from the Greek word *chronos* meaning 'time'. These include *anachronism*, *chronicle*, *chronological*, *chronology*, *chronometer*, and *synchronize*.

chronicle *NOUN* **chronicles** a record of events in the order that they happened.
[same origin as *chronic*]

chronological *ADJECTIVE* arranged in the order that things happened.
▷ **chronologically** *adverb*

chronology (*say* kron-**ol**-oj-ee) *NOUN* the arrangement of events in the order in which they happened, e.g. in history or geology.
[from Greek *chronos* = time, + *-logy*]

chronometer (*say* kron-**om**-it-er) *NOUN* **chronometers** a very exact device for measuring time.
[from Greek *chronos* = time, + *meter*]

chrysalis *NOUN* **chrysalises** the hard cover a caterpillar makes round itself before it changes into a butterfly or moth.
[from Greek *chrysos* = gold (because some are this colour)]

chrysanthemum *NOUN* **chrysanthemums** a garden flower that blooms in autumn.
[originally = a kind of marigold: from Greek *chrysos* = gold + *anthemon* = flower]

chubby *ADJECTIVE* **chubbier, chubbiest** plump.
▷ **chubbiness** *noun*
[origin unknown]

chuck[1] *VERB* **chucks, chucking, chucked** (*informal*) throw.
[origin unknown]

chuck[2] *NOUN* **chucks 1** the gripping part of a lathe. **2** the part of a drill that holds the bit.
[originally = lump or block: a different spelling of *chock*]

chuckle *NOUN* **chuckles** a quiet laugh.

chuckle *VERB* **chuckles, chuckling, chuckled** laugh quietly.
[origin unknown]

chug *VERB* **chugs, chugging, chugged** make the sound of an engine running slowly.
[imitating the sound]

chum *NOUN* **chums** (*informal*) a friend.
▷ **chummy** *adjective*
[short for *chamber-fellow* = a person you share a room with]

chunk *NOUN* **chunks** a thick piece of something.
▷ **chunky** *adjective*
[a different spelling of *chuck*[2]]

chupatty (*say* chup-**at**-ee) *NOUN* **chupatties** a different spelling of *chapatti*.

church *NOUN* **churches 1** a public building for Christian worship. **2** a religious service in a church • *I will see you after church.* **3** a particular Christian religion, e.g. the Church of England.
[via Old English from Greek *kyriakon* = Lord's house]

churchyard *NOUN* **churchyards** the ground round a church, often used as a graveyard.

churlish *ADJECTIVE* ill-mannered and unfriendly; surly.
[= like a *churl* = a peasant]

churn *NOUN* **churns 1** a large can in which milk is carried from a farm. **2** a machine in which milk is beaten to make butter.

churn *VERB* **churns, churning, churned 1** make butter in a churn. **2** stir or swirl vigorously.
- **churn out** produce something in large quantities.
[from Old English]

chute (*say* shoot) *NOUN* **chutes** a steep channel for people or things to slide down.
[French, = a fall]

chutney *NOUN* **chutneys** a strong-tasting mixture of fruit, peppers, etc., eaten with meat.
[from Hindi *chatni*]

CID *ABBREVIATION* Criminal Investigation Department.

-cide *SUFFIX* forms nouns meaning 'killing' or 'killer' (e.g. *homicide*).
[from Latin *caedere* = kill]

cider *NOUN* **ciders** an alcoholic drink made from apples.
[via French and Latin from Hebrew]

cigar *NOUN* **cigars** a roll of compressed tobacco leaves for smoking.
[from Spanish]

cigarette *NOUN* **cigarettes** a small roll of shredded tobacco in thin paper for smoking.
[French, = little cigar]

cinder *NOUN* **cinders** a small piece of partly burnt coal or wood.
[from Old English]

cine camera (*say* **sin**-ee) *NOUN* **cine cameras** a camera used for taking moving pictures.
[from Greek *kinema* = movement, + *camera*]

cinema *NOUN* **cinemas** **1** a place where films are shown. **2** the business or art of making films.
[from Greek *kinema* = movement]

cinnamon (*say* sin-a-mon) *NOUN* a yellowish-brown spice.
[from Greek]

cipher (*say* sy-fer) *NOUN* **ciphers** **1** a kind of code. **2** the symbol 0, representing nought or zero.
[from Arabic *sifr* = nought]

circle *NOUN* **circles** **1** a perfectly round flat shape or thing. **2** the balcony of a cinema or theatre. **3** a number of people with similar interests.

circle *VERB* **circles, circling, circled** move in a circle; go round something.
[from Latin *circus*]

circuit (*say* ser-kit) *NOUN* **circuits** **1** a circular line or journey. **2** a track for motor racing. **3** the path of an electric current.
[from Latin *circum* = round + *itum* = gone]

circuitous (*say* ser-kew-it-us) *ADJECTIVE* going a long way round, not direct.

circular *ADJECTIVE* **1** shaped like a circle; round. **2** moving round a circle.
▷ **circularity** *noun*

circular *NOUN* **circulars** a letter or advertisement sent to a number of people.

circulate *VERB* **circulates, circulating, circulated** **1** go round something continuously • *Blood circulates in the body.* **2** pass from place to place. **3** send something round to a number of people.

circulation *NOUN* **circulations** **1** the movement of blood around the body. **2** the number of copies of each issue of a newspaper or magazine that are sold or distributed.

circum- *PREFIX* around (as in *circumference*).
[from Latin *circum* = around]

circumcise *VERB* **circumcises, circumcising, circumcised** cut off the fold of skin at the tip of the penis.
▷ **circumcision** *noun*
[from *circum-* + Latin *caedere* = cut]

circumference *NOUN* **circumferences** the line or distance round something, especially round a circle.
[from *circum-* + Latin *ferens* = carrying]

circumflex accent *NOUN* **circumflex accents** a mark (^) over a vowel.
[from *circum-* + Latin *flectere* = bend]

circumlocution *NOUN* **circumlocutions** a roundabout expression, using many words where a few would do, e.g. 'at this moment in time' for 'now'.

circumnavigate *VERB* **circumnavigates, circumnavigating, circumnavigated** sail completely round something.
▷ **circumnavigation** *noun*
[from *circum-* + *navigate*]

circumscribe *VERB* **circumscribes, circumscribing, circumscribed** **1** draw a line round something. **2** limit or restrict something • *Her powers are circumscribed by many regulations.*
[from *circum-* + Latin *scribere* = write]

circumspect *ADJECTIVE* cautious and watchful.
▷ **circumspection** *noun*
[from *circum-* + Latin *specere* = to look]

circumstance *NOUN* **circumstances** a fact or condition connected with an event or person or action.
[from *circum-* + Latin *stans* = standing]

circumstantial (*say* ser-kum-stan-shal) *ADJECTIVE* consisting of facts that strongly suggest something but do not actually prove it • *circumstantial evidence.*

circumvent *VERB* **circumvents, circumventing, circumvented** find a way of avoiding something • *We managed to circumvent the rules.*
▷ **circumvention** *noun*
[from *circum-* + Latin *ventum* = come]

circus *NOUN* **circuses** a travelling show usually performed in a tent, with clowns, acrobats, and sometimes trained animals.
[Latin, = ring]

cirrus (*say* si-rus) *NOUN* **cirri** cloud made up of light wispy streaks.
[Latin, = curl]

cistern *NOUN* **cisterns** a tank for storing water.
[from Latin]

citadel *NOUN* **citadels** a fortress protecting a city.
[from Italian]

cite (*say* sight) *VERB* **cites, citing, cited** quote as an example.
▷ **citation** *noun*
[from Latin *citare* = call]

citizen *NOUN* **citizens** a person belonging to a particular city or country.
[same origin as *city*]

citizenry *NOUN* all the citizens.

citizens' band *NOUN* a range of special radio frequencies on which people can speak to one another over short distances.

citizenship *NOUN* the rights or duties of a citizen.

citrus fruit *NOUN* **citrus fruits** a lemon, orange, grapefruit, or other sharp-tasting fruit.
[Latin]

city *NOUN* **cities** a large important town, often having a cathedral.
- **the City** the oldest part of London, now a centre of commerce and finance.
[from Latin *civitas* = city]

civic *ADJECTIVE* **1** to do with a city or town. **2** to do with citizens.
[from Latin *civis* = citizen]

civics *NOUN* the study of the rights and duties of citizens.

civil *ADJECTIVE* **1** polite and courteous. **2** to do with citizens. **3** to do with civilians; not military • *civil aviation.*
▷ **civilly** *adverb*
[from Latin]

civil engineering *NOUN* the work of designing or maintaining roads, bridges, dams, etc.
▷ **civil engineer** *noun*

civilian *NOUN* **civilians** a person who is not serving in the armed forces.
[from *civil*]

civility *NOUN* **civilities** politeness.

civilization *NOUN* **civilizations** **1** a society or culture at a particular time in history • *ancient civilizations.* **2** a developed or organized way of life • *We were far from civilization.*

civilize *VERB* **civilizes, civilizing, civilized** **1** bring culture and education to a primitive community. **2** improve a person's behaviour and manners.
[from French]

civil rights *PLURAL NOUN* the rights of citizens, especially to have freedom, equality, and the right to vote.

Civil Service *NOUN* people employed by the government in various departments other than the armed forces.

civil war *NOUN* **civil wars** war between groups of people of the same country.

clack *NOUN* **clacks** a short sharp sound like that of plates struck together.
▷ **clack** *verb*
[imitating the sound]

clad *ADJECTIVE* clothed or covered.
[old past tense of *clothe*]

claim *VERB* **claims, claiming, claimed** **1** ask for something to which you believe you have a right. **2** declare; state something without being able to prove it.
▷ **claimant** *noun*

claim *NOUN* **claims** **1** claiming. **2** something claimed. **3** a piece of ground claimed or assigned to someone for mining etc.
[same origin as *clamour*]

clairvoyant *NOUN* **clairvoyants** a person who is said to be able to predict future events or know about things that are happening out of sight.
▷ **clairvoyance** *noun*
[from French *clair* = clear + *voyant* = seeing]

clam *NOUN* **clams** a large shellfish.
[from Old English *clam* = something that grips tightly; related to *clamp*]

clamber *VERB* **clambers, clambering, clambered** climb with difficulty.
[from *clamb*, the old past tense of *climb*]

clammy *ADJECTIVE* damp and slimy.
[from Old English *claeman* = smear, make sticky]

clamour *NOUN* **clamours** **1** a loud confused noise. **2** an outcry; a loud protest or demand.
▷ **clamorous** *adjective*

clamour *VERB* **clamours, clamouring, clamoured** make a loud protest or demand.
[from Latin *clamare* = call out]

clamp *NOUN* **clamps** a device for holding things tightly.

clamp *VERB* **clamps, clamping, clamped** **1** fix something with a clamp. **2** fix something firmly.
- **clamp down on** become stricter about something or put a stop to it.
[probably from old German; related to *clam*]

clan *NOUN* **clans** a group sharing the same ancestor, especially in Scotland.
[Scottish Gaelic]

clandestine (*say* klan-**dest**-in) *ADJECTIVE* done secretly; kept secret.
[from Latin]

clang *NOUN* **clangs** a loud ringing sound.
▷ **clang** *verb*
[imitating the sound]

clank *NOUN* **clanks** a sound like heavy pieces of metal banging together.
▷ **clank** *verb*
[imitating the sound]

clap *VERB* **claps, clapping, clapped** **1** strike the palms of the hands together loudly, especially as applause. **2** slap in a friendly way • *I clapped him on the shoulder.* **3** put quickly • *They clapped him into jail.*

clap *NOUN* **claps** **1** a sudden sharp noise • *a clap of thunder.* **2** a round of clapping • *Give the winners a clap.* **3** a friendly slap.
[from Old English]

clapper *NOUN* **clappers** the tongue or hanging piece inside a bell that strikes against the bell to make it sound.

claptrap *NOUN* insincere or foolish talk.
[originally = something done or said just to get applause]

claret *NOUN* **clarets** a kind of red wine.
[from old French *vin claret* = clear wine]

clarify *VERB* **clarifies, clarifying, clarified** make something clear or easier to understand.
▷ **clarification** *noun*
[from Latin *clarus* = clear]

clarinet *NOUN* **clarinets** a woodwind instrument.
▷ **clarinettist** *noun*
[from French]

clarion *NOUN* **clarions** an old type of trumpet.
[same origin as *clarify*]

clarity *NOUN* clearness.
[same origin as *clarify*]

clash *VERB* **clashes, clashing, clashed** **1** make a loud sound like that of cymbals banging together. **2** happen inconveniently at the same time. **3** have a fight or argument. **4** (said about colours) look unpleasant together.
▷ **clash** *noun*
[imitating the sound]

clasp *NOUN* **clasps** **1** a device for fastening things, with interlocking parts. **2** a tight grasp.

clasp *VERB* **clasps, clasping, clasped** **1** grasp or hold tightly. **2** fasten with a clasp.
[origin unknown]

class *NOUN* **classes** **1** a group of children, students, etc. who are taught together. **2** a group of similar people, animals, or things. **3** people of the same social or economic level. **4** level of quality • *first class.*

class *VERB* **classes, classing, classed** arrange things in classes or groups; classify.
[from Latin *classis* = a social division of the Roman people]

classic *ADJECTIVE* generally agreed to be excellent or important.

classic *NOUN* **classics** a classic book, film, writer, etc.
[from Latin *classicus* = of the highest class]

classical *ADJECTIVE* **1** to do with ancient Greek or Roman literature, art. **2** serious or conventional in style • *classical music.*

classics *NOUN* the study of ancient Greek and Latin languages and literature.
[because they were considered better than modern works]

classified *ADJECTIVE* **1** put into classes or groups. **2** (said about information) declared officially to be secret and available only to certain people.

classify *VERB* **classifies, classifying, classified** arrange things in classes or groups.
▷ **classification** *noun*
[from *classification*, from French]

classmate *NOUN* **classmates** someone in the same class at school.

classroom *NOUN* **classrooms** a room where a class of children or students is taught.

clatter *VERB* **clatters, clattering, clattered** make a sound like hard objects rattling together.

clatter *NOUN* a clattering noise.
[imitating the sound]

clause *NOUN* **clauses** **1** a single part of a treaty, law, or contract. **2** (*in grammar*) part of a sentence, with its own verb • *There are two clauses in 'We choose what we want'.*
[from Latin]

claustrophobia *NOUN* fear of being inside an enclosed space.
[from Latin *claustrum* = enclosed space, + *phobia*]

claw *NOUN* **claws** **1** a sharp nail on a bird's or animal's foot. **2** a claw-like part or device used for grasping things.

claw *VERB* **claws, clawing, clawed** grasp, pull, or scratch with a claw or hand.
[from Old English]

clay *NOUN* a kind of stiff sticky earth that becomes hard when baked, used for making bricks and pottery.
▷ **clayey** *adjective*
[from Old English]

-cle *SUFFIX*, SEE **-cule**.

clean *ADJECTIVE* **1** without any dirt or marks or stains. **2** fresh; not yet used. **3** honourable; not unfair • *a clean fight.* **4** not indecent. **5** a clean catch is one made skilfully with no fumbling.
▷ **cleanness** *noun*

clean *VERB* **cleans, cleaning, cleaned** make a thing clean.

clean *ADVERB* completely • *I clean forgot.*
[from Old English]

cleaner *NOUN* **cleaners** **1** a person who cleans things, especially rooms etc. **2** something used for cleaning things.

cleanliness (*say* **klen**-li-nis) *NOUN* being clean.

cleanly (*say* **kleen**-lee) *ADVERB* in a clean way.

cleanse (*say* klenz) *VERB* **cleanses, cleansing, cleansed** **1** clean. **2** make pure.
▷ **cleanser** *noun*
[from Old English]

clear *ADJECTIVE* **1** transparent; not muddy or cloudy. **2** easy to see or hear or understand; distinct. **3** free from obstacles or unwanted things; free from guilt • *a clear conscience.* **4** complete • *Give three clear days' notice.*
▷ **clearly** *adverb* **clearness** *noun*

clear *ADVERB* **1** distinctly; clearly • *We heard you loud and clear.* **2** completely • *He got clear away.* **3** apart; not in contact • *Stand clear of the doors.*

clear *VERB* **clears, clearing, cleared** **1** make or become clear. **2** show that someone is innocent or reliable. **3** jump over something without touching it. **4** get approval or authorization for something • *Clear this with the headmaster.*
- **clear away** remove used plates etc. after a meal.
- **clear off** or **out** (*informal*) go away.
- **clear up** **1** make things tidy. **2** become better or brighter. **3** solve • *clear up the mystery.*

[same origin as *clarify*]

clearance *NOUN* **clearances** **1** clearing something. **2** getting rid of unwanted goods. **3** the space between two things.

clearing *NOUN* **clearings** an open space in a forest.

cleavage *NOUN* the hollow between a woman's breasts.

cleave[1] *VERB* **cleaves, cleaving;** *past tense* **cleaved, clove** or **cleft;** *past participle* **cleft** or **cloven** **1** divide by chopping; split. **2** make a way through • *cleaving the waves.*
[from Old English *cleofan*]

cleave[2] *VERB* **cleaves, cleaving, cleaved** (*old use*) cling to something.
[from Old English *clifian*]

cleaver *NOUN* **cleavers** a butcher's chopping tool.

clef *NOUN* **clefs** a symbol on a stave in music, showing the pitch of the notes • *treble clef; bass clef.*
[French, = key]

cleft *past tense* of **cleave**[1].

cleft *NOUN* **clefts** a split in something.

clemency *NOUN* gentleness or mildness; mercy.
[from Latin]

clench *VERB* **clenches, clenching, clenched** close teeth or fingers tightly.
[from Old English]

clergy *NOUN* the people who have been ordained as priests or ministers of the Christian Church.
▷ **clergyman** *noun* **clergywoman** *noun*
[same origin as *clerical*]

clerical *ADJECTIVE* **1** to do with the routine work in an office, such as filing and writing letters. **2** to do with the clergy.
[via Latin from Greek *klerikos* = belonging to the Christian Church]

clerk (*say* klark) *NOUN* **clerks** a person employed to keep records or accounts, deal with papers in an office, etc.
[originally = a Christian minister: same origin as *clerical*]

clever *ADJECTIVE* **1** quick at learning and understanding things. **2** skilful.
▷ **cleverly** *adverb* **cleverness** *noun*
[origin unknown]

cliché (*say* klee-shay) *NOUN* **clichés** a phrase or idea that is used so often that it has little meaning.
[French, = stereotyped]

click *NOUN* **clicks** a short sharp sound.
▷ **click** *verb*
[imitating the sound]

client *NOUN* **clients** a person who gets help or advice from a professional person such as a lawyer, accountant, architect, etc.; a customer.
[from Latin *cliens* = one who listens]

clientele (*say* klee-on-tel) *NOUN* customers.
[from French]

cliff *NOUN* **cliffs** a steep rock face, especially on a coast.
[from Old English]

cliffhanger *NOUN* **cliffhangers** a tense and exciting ending to an episode of a story.

climate *NOUN* **climates** the regular weather conditions of an area.
▷ **climatic** (*say* kly-mat-ik) *adjective*
[from Greek *klima* = zone, region]

climax *NOUN* **climaxes** the most interesting or important point of a story, series of events, etc.
[from Greek *klimax* = ladder]

climb *VERB* **climbs, climbing, climbed** **1** go up or over or down something. **2** grow upwards. **3** go higher.
▷ **climb** *noun* **climber** *noun*
- **climb down** admit that you have been wrong.
[from Old English]

clinch *VERB* **clinches, clinching, clinched** **1** settle something definitely • *We hope to clinch the deal today.* **2** (in boxing) be clasping each other.
▷ **clinch** *noun*
[a different spelling of *clench*]

cling *VERB* **clings, clinging, clung** hold on tightly.
[from Old English]

cling film *NOUN* a thin clinging transparent film, used as a covering for food.

clinic *NOUN* **clinics** a place where people see doctors etc. for treatment or advice.
[from Greek *klinike* = teaching (of medicine) at the bedside]

clinical *ADJECTIVE* **1** to do with the medical treatment of patients. **2** cool and unemotional.
▷ **clinically** *adverb*

clink *NOUN* **clinks** a thin sharp sound like glasses being struck together.
▷ **clink** *verb*
[probably from old Dutch]

clip[1] *NOUN* **clips** a fastener for keeping things together, usually worked by a spring.

clip *VERB* **clips, clipping, clipped** fasten with a clip.
[from Old English *clyppan* = embrace, hug]

clip[2] *VERB* **clips, clipping, clipped** **1** cut with shears or scissors etc. **2** (*informal*) hit.

clip *NOUN* **clips** **1** a short piece of film shown on its own. **2** (*informal*) a hit on the head.
[from Old Norse]

clipper *NOUN* **clippers** an old type of fast sailing ship.
[from *clip*[2], in the sense = move quickly]

clippers *PLURAL NOUN* an instrument for cutting hair.

clique (*say* kleek) *NOUN* **cliques** a small group of people who stick together and keep others out.
[French]

clitoris *NOUN* **clitorises** the small sensitive lump of flesh near the opening of a woman's vagina.
[Latin, from Greek]

cloak *NOUN* **cloaks** a sleeveless piece of outdoor clothing that hangs loosely from the shoulders.

cloak *VERB* **cloaks, cloaking, cloaked** cover or conceal.
[from old French]

cloakroom *NOUN* **cloakrooms 1** a place where people can leave coats and bags while visiting a building. **2** a lavatory.

clobber *VERB* **clobbers, clobbering, clobbered** (*slang*) **1** hit hard again and again. **2** defeat completely.
[origin unknown]

cloche (*say* klosh) *NOUN* **cloches** a glass or plastic cover to protect outdoor plants.
[French, = bell (because of the shape)]

clock *NOUN* **clocks 1** a device that shows what the time is. **2** a measuring device with a dial or digital display.

clock *VERB* **clocks, clocking, clocked**
- **clock in** or **out** register the time you arrive at work or leave work.
- **clock up** reach a certain speed.

[from Latin *clocca* = bell]

clockwise *ADVERB* & *ADJECTIVE* moving round a circle in the same direction as a clock's hands.
[from *clock* + *-wise*]

clockwork *NOUN* a mechanism with a spring that has to be wound up.
- **like clockwork** very regularly.

clod *NOUN* **clods** a lump of earth or clay.
[a different spelling of *clot*]

clog *NOUN* **clogs** a shoe with a wooden sole.

clog *VERB* **clogs, clogging, clogged** block up.
[origin unknown]

cloister *NOUN* **cloisters** a covered path along the side of a church or monastery etc., round a courtyard.
[from Latin *claustrum* = enclosed place]

clone *NOUN* **clones** an animal or plant made from the cells of another animal or plant and therefore exactly like it.

clone *VERB* **clones, cloning, cloned** produce a clone of an animal or plant.
[from Greek *klon* = a cutting from a plant]

close[1] (*say* klohss) *ADJECTIVE* **1** near. **2** detailed or concentrated • *with close attention.* **3** tight; with little empty space • *a close fit.* **4** in which competitors are nearly equal • *a close contest.* **5** stuffy.
▷ **closely** *adverb* **closeness** *noun*

close *ADVERB* closely • *close behind.*

close *NOUN* **closes 1** a street that is closed at one end. **2** an enclosed area, especially round a cathedral.
[same origin as *close*[2]]

close[2] (*say* klohz) *VERB* **closes, closing, closed 1** shut. **2** end.
- **close in 1** get nearer. **2** if the days are closing in, they are getting shorter.

close *NOUN* end • *at the close of play.*
[via old French from Latin *claudere*]

closet *NOUN* **closets** (*American*) a cupboard or storeroom.

closet *VERB* **closets, closeting, closeted** shut yourself away in a private room.
[old French, = small enclosed space]

close-up *NOUN* **close-ups** a photograph or piece of film taken at close range.

closure *NOUN* **closures** closing.

clot *NOUN* **clots 1** a small mass of blood, cream, etc. that has become solid. **2** (*slang*) a stupid person.

clot *VERB* **clots, clotting, clotted** form clots.
[from Old English]

cloth *NOUN* **cloths 1** woven material or felt. **2** a piece of this material. **3** a tablecloth.
[from Old English]

clothe *VERB* **clothes, clothing, clothed** put clothes on someone.
[from *cloth*]

A B C D E F G H I J K L M N O P Q R S T U V W X Y Z

clothes *PLURAL NOUN* things worn to cover the body.
[from *cloth*]

clothing *NOUN* clothes.

clotted cream *NOUN* cream thickened by being scalded.

cloud *NOUN* **clouds 1** a mass of condensed water vapour floating in the sky. **2** a mass of smoke, dust, etc., in the air.

cloud *VERB* **clouds, clouding, clouded** become cloudy.
[from Old English]

cloudburst *NOUN* **cloudbursts** a sudden heavy rainstorm.

cloudless *ADJECTIVE* without clouds.

cloudy *ADJECTIVE* **cloudier, cloudiest 1** full of clouds. **2** not transparent • *The liquid became cloudy.*
▷ **cloudiness** *noun*

clout *VERB* **clouts, clouting, clouted** (*informal*) hit.
▷ **clout** *noun*
[from Old English]

clove[1] *NOUN* **cloves** the dried bud of a tropical tree, used as a spice.
[from old French]

clove[2] *NOUN* **cloves** one of the small bulbs in a compound bulb • *a clove of garlic.*
[from Old English]

clove[3] *past tense* of **cleave**[1].

cloven *past participle* of **cleave**[1]
- **cloven hoof** a hoof that is divided, like those of cows and sheep.

clover *NOUN* a small plant usually with three leaves on each stalk.
- **in clover** in ease and luxury.
[from Old English]

clown *NOUN* **clowns 1** a performer who does amusing tricks and actions, especially in a circus. **2** a person who does silly things.

clown *VERB* **clowns, clowning, clowned** do silly things, especially to amuse other people.
[origin unknown]

cloying *ADJECTIVE* sickeningly sweet.
[from an old word *accloy* = overfill, disgust]

club *NOUN* **clubs 1** a heavy stick used as a weapon. **2** a stick with a shaped head used to hit the ball in golf. **3** a group of people who meet because they are interested in the same thing; the building where they meet. **4** a playing card with black clover leaves on it.

club *VERB* **clubs, clubbing, clubbed** hit with a heavy stick.
- **club together** join with other people in order to pay for something • *club together to buy a boat.*
[from Old Norse]

cluck *VERB* **clucks, clucking, clucked** make a hen's throaty cry.
▷ **cluck** *noun*
[imitating the sound]

clue *NOUN* **clues** something that helps a person to solve a puzzle or a mystery.
- **not have a clue** (*informal*) be stupid or helpless.
[originally a ball of thread: in Greek legend, the warrior Theseus had to go into a maze (the Labyrinth); as he went in he unwound a ball of thread, and found his way out by winding it up again]

clump *NOUN* **clumps 1** a cluster or mass of things. **2** a clumping sound.

clump *VERB* **clumps, clumping, clumped** **1** form a cluster or mass. **2** walk with a heavy tread.
[from old German]

clumsy *ADJECTIVE* **clumsier, clumsiest** **1** heavy and ungraceful; likely to knock things over or drop things. **2** not skilful; not tactful • *a clumsy apology.*
▷ **clumsily** *adverb* **clumsiness** *noun*
[probably from a Scandinavian language]

cluster *NOUN* **clusters** a small close group.

cluster *VERB* **clusters, clustering, clustered** form a cluster.
[from Old English]

clutch[1] *VERB* **clutches, clutching, clutched** grasp tightly.

clutch *NOUN* **clutches 1** a tight grasp. **2** a device for connecting and disconnecting the engine of a motor vehicle from its gears.
[from Old English]

clutch[2] *NOUN* **clutches** a set of eggs for hatching.
[from Old Norse *klekja* = to hatch]

clutter *NOUN* things lying about untidily.

clutter *VERB* **clutters, cluttering, cluttered** fill with clutter • *Piles of books and papers cluttered her desk.*
[from an old word *clotter* = to clot]

Co. *ABBREVIATION* Company.

c/o *ABBREVIATION* care of.

co- *PREFIX* **1** together, jointly (as in *coexistence, cooperate*). **2** joint (as in *co-pilot*).
[same origin as *com-*]

coach *NOUN* **coaches 1** a bus used for long journeys. **2** a carriage of a railway train. **3** a large horse-drawn carriage with four wheels. **4** an instructor in sports. **5** a teacher giving private specialized tuition.

coach *VERB* **coaches, coaching, coached** instruct or train somebody, especially in sports.
[from Hungarian *kocsi szekér* = cart from *Kocs*, a town in Hungary]

coagulate *VERB* **coagulates, coagulating, coagulated** change from liquid to semi-solid; clot.
▷ **coagulation** *noun*
[from Latin]

coal *NOUN* a hard black mineral substance used for burning to supply heat; a piece of this.
▷ **coalfield** *noun*
[from Old English]

coalesce (*say* koh-a-less) *VERB* **coalesces, coalescing, coalesced** combine and form one whole thing.
▷ **coalescence** *noun*
[from *co-* + Latin *alescere* = grow up]

coalition *NOUN* **coalitions** a temporary alliance, especially of two or more political parties in order to form a government.
[same origin as *coalesce*]

coarse *ADJECTIVE* **1** not smooth, not delicate; rough. **2** composed of large particles; not fine. **3** not refined; vulgar.
▷ **coarsely** *adverb* **coarseness** *noun*
[origin unknown]

coarsen *VERB* **coarsens, coarsening, coarsened** make or become coarse.

coast *NOUN* **coasts** the seashore or the land close to it.
▷ **coastal** *adjective* **coastline** *noun*
- **the coast is clear** there is no chance of being seen or hindered.

coast *VERB* **coasts, coasting, coasted** ride downhill without using power.
[from Latin *costa* = rib, side]

coastguard *NOUN* **coastguards** a person whose job is to keep watch on the coast, detect or prevent smuggling, etc.

coat *NOUN* **coats 1** a piece of clothing with sleeves, worn over other clothes. **2** the hair or fur on an animal's body. **3** a coating • *a coat of paint.*

coat *VERB* **coats, coating, coated** cover something with a coating.
[from old French]

coating *NOUN* **coatings** a covering layer.

coat of arms *NOUN* **coats of arms** a design on a shield, used as an emblem by a family, city, etc.

coax *VERB* **coaxes, coaxing, coaxed** persuade someone gently or patiently.
[from an old word *cokes* = a stupid person]

cob *NOUN* **cobs 1** the central part of an ear of maize, on which the corn grows. **2** a sturdy horse for riding. **3** a male swan. (The female is a *pen.*)
[origin unknown]

cobalt *NOUN* a hard silvery-white metal.
[from German *Kobalt* = demon (because it was believed to harm the silver ore with which it was found)]

cobber *NOUN* **cobbers** (*informal*) (*Australian/NZ*) a friend or companion.
[possibly related to an English dialect word *cob* meaning 'take a liking to']

cobble[1] *NOUN* **cobbles** a rounded stone used for paving streets etc.
▷ **cobblestone** *noun* **cobbled** *adjective*
[from *cob*, in the sense = round, stout]

cobble[2] *VERB* **cobbles, cobbling, cobbled** make or mend roughly.
[from *cobbler*]

cobbler *NOUN* **cobblers** someone who mends shoes.
[origin unknown]

cobra (*say* koh-bra) *NOUN* **cobras** a poisonous snake that can rear up.
[from Portuguese *cobra de capello* = snake with a hood]

cobweb *NOUN* **cobwebs** the thin sticky net made by a spider to trap insects.
[from Old English *coppe* = spider, + *web*]

cocaine *NOUN* a drug made from the leaves of a tropical plant called *coca*.

cock *NOUN* **cocks** **1** a male chicken. **2** a male bird. **3** a stopcock. **4** a lever in a gun.

cock *VERB* **cocks, cocking, cocked** **1** make a gun ready to fire by raising the cock. **2** turn something upwards or in a particular direction • *The dog cocked its ears.*
[from Old English]

cockatoo *NOUN* **cockatoos** a crested parrot.
[via Dutch from Malay (a language spoken in Malaysia)]

cocked hat *NOUN* **cocked hats** a triangular hat worn with some uniforms.
[originally = a hat with the brim turned upwards]

cockerel *NOUN* **cockerels** a young male chicken.
[from *cock*]

cocker spaniel *NOUN* **cocker spaniels** a kind of small spaniel.
[because they were used to hunt woodcock]

cock-eyed *ADJECTIVE* (*slang*) **1** crooked; not straight. **2** absurd.
[from *cock* = turn]

cockle *NOUN* **cockles** an edible shellfish.
[from old French *coquille* = shell]

cockney *NOUN* **cockneys** **1** a person born in the East End of London. **2** the dialect or accent of cockneys.
[originally = a small, misshapen egg, believed to be a cock's egg (because country people believed townspeople were feeble)]

cockpit *NOUN* **cockpits** the compartment where the pilot of an aircraft sits.
[from the pits where cock fights took place]

cockroach *NOUN* **cockroaches** a dark brown beetle-like insect, often found in dirty houses.
[from Spanish]

cocksure *ADJECTIVE* very sure; too confident.
[from *cock* (used to avoid saying *God* in oaths)]

cocktail *NOUN* **cocktails** **1** a mixed alcoholic drink. **2** a food containing shellfish or fruit.
[originally = a racehorse that was not a thoroughbred (because carthorses had their tails cut so that they stood up like a cock's tail)]

cocky *ADJECTIVE* **cockier, cockiest** (*informal*) too self-confident.
▷ **cockiness** *noun*
[= proud as a cock]

cocoa *NOUN* **cocoas** **1** a hot drink made from a powder of crushed cacao seeds. **2** this powder.
[a different spelling of *cacao*]

coconut *NOUN* **coconuts** **1** a large round nut that grows on a kind of palm tree. **2** its white lining, used in sweets and cookery.
[from Spanish *coco* = grinning face (because the base of the nut looks like a monkey's face)]

cocoon *NOUN* **cocoons** **1** the covering round a chrysalis. **2** a protective wrapping.

cocoon *VERB* **cocoons, cocooning, cocooned** protect something by wrapping it up.
[from French]

cod *NOUN* **cod** a large edible sea fish.
[origin unknown]

coddle *VERB* **coddles, coddling, coddled** cherish and protect carefully.
[origin unknown]

code *NOUN* **codes** **1** a word or phrase used to represent a message in order to keep its meaning secret. **2** a set of signs used in sending messages by machine etc. • *the Morse code.* **3** a set of numbers that represents an area in telephoning • *Do you know the code for Norwich?* **4** a set of laws or rules • *the Highway Code.*

code *VERB* **codes, coding, coded** put a message into code.
[from Latin *codex* = book]

codicil *NOUN* **codicils** an addition to a will.
[from Latin *codicillus* = small document]

codify *VERB* **codifies, codifying, codified** arrange laws or rules into a code or system.
▷ **codification** *noun*
[from *code*]

coeducation *NOUN* educating boys and girls together.
▷ **coeducational** *adjective*
[from *co-* + *education*]

coefficient *NOUN* **coefficients** a number by which another number is multiplied; a factor.
[from *co-* + *efficient* (because the numbers work together)]

coerce (*say* koh-erss) *VERB* **coerces, coercing, coerced** compel someone by using threats or force.
▷ **coercion** *noun*
[from Latin]

coexist *VERB* **coexists, coexisting, coexisted** exist together or at the same time.
▷ **coexistence** *noun* **coexistent** *adjective*
[from *co-* + *exist*]

coffee *NOUN* **coffees** **1** a hot drink made from the roasted ground seeds (**coffee beans**) of a tropical plant. **2** these seeds.
[from Arabic *kahwa*]

coffer *NOUN* **coffers** a large strong box for holding money and valuables.
- **coffers** the funds or financial resources of an organization.
[from Latin *cophinus* = basket, hamper]

coffin *NOUN* **coffins** a long box in which a body is buried or cremated.
[same origin as *coffer*]

cog *NOUN* **cogs** one of a number of tooth-like parts round the edge of a wheel, fitting into and pushing those on another wheel.
[origin unknown]

cogent (*say* koh-jent) *ADJECTIVE* convincing • *a cogent argument.*
[Latin, = compelling]

cogitate *VERB* **cogitates, cogitating, cogitated** think deeply about something.
▷ **cogitation** *noun*
[from Latin]

cognac (*say* kon-yak) *NOUN* **cognacs** brandy, especially from Cognac in France.

cogwheel *NOUN* **cogwheels** a wheel with cogs.

cohere *VERB* **coheres, cohering, cohered** stick to each other in a mass.
▷ **cohesion** *noun* **cohesive** *adjective*
[from *co-* + Latin *haerere* = to stick]

coherent (*say* koh-**heer**-ent) *ADJECTIVE* clear, reasonable, and making sense.
▷ **coherently** *adverb*

coil *NOUN* **coils** something wound into a spiral.

coil *VERB* **coils, coiling, coiled** wind something into a coil.
[same origin as *collect*]

coin *NOUN* **coins** a piece of metal, usually round, used as money.

coin *VERB* **coins, coining, coined** **1** manufacture coins. **2** invent a word or phrase.
[French, = die for stamping coins]

coinage *NOUN* **coinages** **1** coins; a system of money. **2** a new word or phrase.

coincide *VERB* **coincides, coinciding, coincided** **1** happen at the same time as something else. **2** be in the same place. **3** be the same • *My opinion coincided with hers.*
[from *co-* + Latin *incidere* = fall upon or into]

coincidence *NOUN* **coincidences** the happening of similar events at the same time by chance.

coke *NOUN* the solid fuel left when gas and tar have been extracted from coal.
[origin unknown]

col- *PREFIX* with; together. SEE **com-**.

colander *NOUN* **colanders** a bowl-shaped container with holes in it, used for straining water from vegetables etc. after cooking.
[from Latin *colare* = strain]

cold *ADJECTIVE* **1** having or at a low temperature; not warm. **2** not friendly or loving; not enthusiastic.
▷ **coldly** *adverb* **coldness** *noun*
- **get cold feet** have doubts about doing something bold or ambitious.
- **give someone the cold shoulder** be deliberately unfriendly.

cold *NOUN* **colds** **1** lack of warmth; low temperature; cold weather. **2** an infectious illness that makes your nose run, your throat sore, etc.
[from Old English]

cold-blooded *ADJECTIVE* **1** having a body temperature that changes according to the surroundings. **2** callous; deliberately cruel.

cold war *NOUN* a situation where nations are enemies without actually fighting.

colic *NOUN* pain in a baby's stomach.
[from Latin *colicus* = to do with the colon]

collaborate *VERB* **collaborates, collaborating, collaborated** work together on a job.
▷ **collaboration** *noun* **collaborator** *noun*
[from *col-* + Latin *laborare* = to work]

collage (*say* kol-ah*zh*) *NOUN* **collages** a picture made by fixing small objects to a surface.
[French, = gluing]

collapse *VERB* **collapses, collapsing, collapsed** **1** break or fall to pieces; fall in. **2** become very weak or ill. **3** fold up.

collapse *NOUN* **collapses** **1** collapsing. **2** a breakdown.
[from *col-* + Latin *lapsum* = slipped]

collapsible *ADJECTIVE* able to be folded up • *a collapsible umbrella.*

collar *NOUN* **collars** **1** the part of a piece of clothing that goes round your neck. **2** a band that goes round the neck of a dog, cat, horse, etc.

collar *VERB* **collars, collaring, collared** (*informal*) seize or catch someone.
[from Latin *collum* = neck]

collarbone *NOUN* **collarbones** the bone joining the breastbone and shoulder blade.

collate *VERB* **collates, collating, collated** collect and arrange pieces of information in an organized way.
▷ **collation** *noun*
[from Latin]

collateral *ADJECTIVE* additional but less important.

collateral *NOUN* money or property that is used as a guarantee that a loan will be repaid.
[from *col-* + *lateral*]

colleague *NOUN* **colleagues** a person you work with.
[from Latin]

collect[1] (*say* kol-ekt) *VERB* **collects, collecting, collected** **1** bring people or things together from various places. **2** obtain examples of things as a hobby • *She collects stamps.* **3** come together. **4** ask for money or contributions etc. from people. **5** fetch • *Collect your coat from the cleaners.*
▷ **collector** *noun*
[from *col-* + Latin *legere* = assemble, choose]

collect[2] (*say* **kol**-ekt) *NOUN* **collects** a short prayer.
[from Latin *collecta* = a meeting]

collection *NOUN* **collections** **1** collecting. **2** things collected. **3** money collected for a charity etc.

collective *ADJECTIVE* to do with a group taken as a whole • *our collective opinion.*

collective noun *NOUN* **collective nouns** a noun that is singular in form but refers to many individuals taken as a unit, e.g. *army, herd*.

college *NOUN* **colleges** a place where people can continue learning something after they have left school.
[from Latin]

collide *VERB* **collides, colliding, collided** crash into something.
▷ **collision** *noun*
[from Latin *collidere* = clash together]

collie *NOUN* **collies** a dog with a long pointed face.
[origin unknown]

colliery *NOUN* **collieries** a coal mine and its buildings.
[from *coal*]

colloquial (*say* col-**oh**-kwee-al) *ADJECTIVE* suitable for conversation but not for formal speech or writing.
▷ **colloquially** *adverb* **colloquialism** *noun*
[from *col-* + Latin *loqui* = speak]

collusion *NOUN* a secret agreement between two or more people who are trying to deceive or cheat someone.
[from *col-* + Latin *ludere* = to play]

cologne (*say* kol-**ohn**) *NOUN* eau de Cologne or a similar liquid.

colon[1] *NOUN* **colons** a punctuation mark (:), often used to introduce lists.
[from Greek *kolon* = clause]

colon² *NOUN* **colons** the largest part of the intestine.
[from Greek *kolon*]

colonel (*say* ker-nel) *NOUN* **colonels** an army officer in charge of a regiment.
[via French from Italian]

colonial *ADJECTIVE* to do with a colony.

colonialism *NOUN* the policy of acquiring and keeping colonies.

colonize *VERB* **colonizes, colonizing, colonized** establish a colony in a country.
▷ **colonist** *noun* **colonization** *noun*

colonnade *NOUN* **colonnades** a row of columns.
[French]

colony *NOUN* **colonies** **1** an area of land that the people of another country settle in and control. **2** the people of a colony. **3** a group of people or animals of the same kind living close together.
[from Latin *colonia* = farm, settlement]

coloration *NOUN* colouring.

colossal *ADJECTIVE* immense; enormous.

colossus *NOUN* **colossi** **1** a huge statue. **2** a person of immense importance.
[from the bronze statue of Apollo at Rhodes, called the *Colossus of Rhodes*]

colour *NOUN* **colours** **1** the effect produced by waves of light of a particular wavelength. **2** the use of various colours, not only black and white. **3** the colour of someone's skin. **4** a substance used to colour things. **5** the special flag of a ship or regiment.

colour *VERB* **colours, colouring, coloured** **1** put colour on; paint or stain. **2** blush. **3** influence what someone says or believes.
[from Latin]

colour-blind *ADJECTIVE* unable to see the difference between certain colours.

coloured *ADJECTIVE* **1** having colour. **2** having a dark skin.
USAGE The word *coloured*, used to describe people, is often considered to be insulting. It is better to use *black*.

colourful *ADJECTIVE* **1** full of colour. **2** lively; with vivid details.

colouring *NOUN* shade or complexion.

colourless *ADJECTIVE* without colour.

colt *NOUN* **colts** a young male horse.
[origin unknown]

column *NOUN* **columns** **1** a pillar. **2** something long or tall and narrow • *a column of smoke.* **3** a vertical section of a page • *There are two columns on this page.* **4** a regular article in a newspaper.
▷ **columnist** *noun*
[from Latin]

com- *PREFIX* (becoming **col-** before *l*, **cor-** before *r*, **con-** before many other consonants) with; together (as in *combine*, *connect*).
[from Latin *cum* = with]

coma (*say* koh-ma) *NOUN* **comas** a state of deep unconsciousness, especially in someone who is ill or injured.
[from Greek *koma* = deep sleep]

comb *NOUN* **combs** **1** a strip of wood or plastic etc. with teeth, used to tidy hair or hold it in place. **2** something used like this, e.g. to separate strands of wool. **3** the red crest on a fowl's head. **4** a honeycomb.

comb *VERB* **combs, combing, combed** **1** tidy hair with a comb. **2** search thoroughly.
[from Old English]

combat *NOUN* & *VERB* **combats, combating, combated** fight.
[from *com-* + Latin *batuere* = fight]

combatant (*say* kom-ba-tant) *NOUN* **combatants** someone who takes part in a fight.

combination *NOUN* **combinations** **1** combining. **2** a number of people or things that are combined. **3** a series of numbers or letters used to open a combination lock.

combination lock *NOUN* **combination locks** a lock that can be opened only by setting a dial or dials to positions shown by numbers or letters.

combine (*say* komb-I'n) *VERB* **combines, combining, combined** join or mix together.

combine (*say* komb-I'n) *NOUN* **combines** a group of people or firms combining in business.
[from *com-* + Latin *bini* = pair]

combine harvester *NOUN* **combine harvesters** a machine that both reaps and threshes grain.

combustible *ADJECTIVE* able to be set on fire and burn.

combustion *NOUN* the process of burning, a chemical process (accompanied by heat) in which substances combine with oxygen in air.
[from Latin *comburere* = burn up]

come *VERB* **comes, coming, came, come**
1 move towards somewhere • *Come here!* **2** arrive at or reach a place or condition or result • *They came to a city. We came to a decision.* **3** happen • *How did you come to lose it?* **4** occur or be present • *It comes on the next page.* **5** result • *That's what comes of being careless.*
- **come by** obtain.
- **come in for** receive a share of.
- **come to** **1** amount to. **2** become conscious again.
- **come to pass** happen.
[from Old English]

comedian *NOUN* **comedians** someone who entertains people by making them laugh.
[from French]

comedy *NOUN* **comedies** **1** a play or film etc. that makes people laugh. **2** humour.
[from Greek *komos* = having fun + *oide* = song]

comely *ADJECTIVE* good-looking.
[from an old word *becomely* = suitable]

comet *NOUN* **comets** an object moving across the sky with a bright tail of light.
[from Greek *kometes* = long-haired (star)]

comfort *NOUN* **comforts** **1** a comfortable feeling or condition. **2** soothing somebody who is unhappy or in pain. **3** a person or thing that gives comfort.

comfort *VERB* **comforts, comforting, comforted** make a person less unhappy; soothe.
[from Latin *confortare* = strengthen]

comfortable *ADJECTIVE* **1** at ease; free from worry or pain. **2** pleasant to use or wear; making you feel relaxed • *comfortable shoes.*
▷ **comfortably** *adverb*

comfy *ADJECTIVE* (*informal*) comfortable.

comic *ADJECTIVE* making people laugh.
▷ **comical** *adjective* **comically** *adverb*

comic *NOUN* **comics** **1** a paper full of comic strips. **2** a comedian.
[from Greek; related to *comedy*]

comic strip *NOUN* **comic strips** a series of drawings telling a story, especially a funny one.

comma *NOUN* **commas** a punctuation mark (,) used to mark a pause in a sentence or to separate items in a list.
[from Greek *komma* = short clause]

command *NOUN* **commands** **1** a statement telling somebody to do something; an order. **2** authority; control. **3** ability to use something; mastery • *She has a good command of Spanish.*

command *VERB* **commands, commanding, commanded** **1** give a command to somebody; order. **2** have authority over. **3** deserve and get • *They command our respect.*
▷ **commander** *noun*
[from *com-* + Latin *mandare* = entrust or impose a duty]

commandant (*say* kom-an-dant) *NOUN* **commandants** a military officer in charge of a fortress etc.

commandeer *VERB* **commandeers, commandeering, commandeered** take or seize something for military purposes or for your own use.

commandment *NOUN* **commandments** a sacred command, especially one of the Ten Commandments given to Moses.

commando *NOUN* **commandos** a soldier trained for making dangerous raids.
[from Portuguese]

commemorate *VERB* **commemorates, commemorating, commemorated** be a celebration or reminder of some past event or person.
▷ **commemoration** *noun* **commemorative** *adjective*
[from *com-* + Latin *memor* = memory]

commence *VERB* **commences, commencing, commenced** (*formal*) begin.
▷ **commencement** *noun*
[from *com-* + Latin *initiare* = initiate]

commend *VERB* **commends, commending, commended** **1** praise • *He was commended for bravery.* **2** entrust • *We commend him to your care.*
▷ **commendation** *noun*
[same origin as *command*]

commendable *ADJECTIVE* deserving praise.

comment *NOUN* **comments** an opinion given about an event etc. or to explain something.

comment *VERB* **comments, commenting, commented** make a comment.
[from Latin]

commentary *VERB* **commentaries** **1** a description of an event by someone who is watching it, especially for radio or television. **2** a set of explanatory comments on a text.
▷ **commentate** *verb* **commentator** *noun*

commerce *NOUN* trade and the services that assist it, e.g. banking and insurance.
[from *com-* + Latin *merx* = goods for sale, merchandise]

commercial *ADJECTIVE* **1** to do with commerce. **2** paid for by firms etc. whose advertisements are included • *commercial radio.* **3** profitable.
▷ **commercially** *adverb*

commercial *NOUN* **commercials** a broadcast advertisement.

commercialized *ADJECTIVE* changed in order to make more money • *a commercialized resort.*
▷ **commercialization** *noun*

commiserate *VERB* **commiserates, commiserating, commiserated** sympathize.
▷ **commiseration** *noun*
[from *com-* + Latin *miserari* = to pity]

commission *NOUN* **commissions** **1** a task formally given to someone • *a commission to paint a portrait.* **2** an appointment to be an officer in the armed forces. **3** a group of people given authority to do or investigate something. **4** payment to someone for selling your goods etc.
- **out of commission** not in working order.

commission *VERB* **commissions, commissioning, commissioned** give a commission to a person or for a task etc.
[same origin as *commit*]

commissionaire *NOUN* **commissionaires** an attendant in uniform at the entrance to a theatre, large shop, offices, etc.
[French]

commissioner *NOUN* **commissioners** **1** an official appointed by commission. **2** a member of a commission (see *commission* **3**).

commit *VERB* **commits, committing, committed** **1** do or perform • *commit a crime.* **2** place in someone's care or custody • *He was committed to prison.* **3** promise that you will make your time etc. available for a particular purpose • *Don't commit all your spare time to helping him.*
[from *com-* + Latin *mittere* = put, send]

commitment *NOUN* **commitments** **1** the work, belief, and loyalty that a person gives to a system or organization. **2** something that you have to do on a regular basis • *work commitments.*

committal *NOUN* **committals** **1** committing a person to prison etc. **2** giving a body ceremonially for burial or cremation.

committee *NOUN* **committees** a group of people appointed to deal with something.

commode *NOUN* **commodes** a box or chair into which a chamber pot is fitted.
[French, = convenient]

commodious *ADJECTIVE* roomy.
[same origin as *commodity*]

commodity *NOUN* **commodities** a useful thing; a product.
[from Latin *commodus* = convenient]

commodore *NOUN* **commodores** **1** a naval officer ranking next below a rear admiral. **2** the commander of part of a fleet.
[probably from Dutch]

common *ADJECTIVE* **1** ordinary; usual; occurring frequently • *a common weed.* **2** of all or most people • *They worked for the common good.* **3** shared • *Music is their common interest.* **4** vulgar.
▷ **commonly** *adverb* **commonness** *noun*
- **in common** shared by two or more people or things.

common *NOUN* **commons** a piece of land that everyone can use.
[same origin as *commune*[1]]

commoner *NOUN* **commoners** a member of the ordinary people, not of the nobility.

Common Market *NOUN* a former name for the European Union.

commonplace *ADJECTIVE* ordinary; usual.

common room *NOUN* **common rooms** an informal room for students, pupils, or teachers at a school or college.

common sense *NOUN* normal good sense in thinking or behaviour.

commonwealth *NOUN* **1** a group of countries cooperating together. **2** a country made up of an association of states • *the Commonwealth of Australia.*
- **the Commonwealth** **1** an association of Britain and various other countries that used to be part of the British Empire, including Canada, Australia, and New Zealand. **2** the republic set up in Britain by Oliver Cromwell, lasting from 1649 to 1660.
[from *common* + an old sense of *wealth* = welfare]

commotion *NOUN* an uproar; a fuss.
[from *com-* + Latin *motio* = movement, motion]

communal (*say* **kom**-yoo-nal) *ADJECTIVE* shared by several people.
▷ **communally** *adverb*
[same origin as *commune*[1]]

commune[1] (*say* **kom**-yoon) *NOUN* **communes** **1** a group of people living together and sharing everything. **2** a district of local government in France and some other countries.
[from Latin *communis* = common]

commune[2] (*say* ko-**mewn**) *VERB* **communes**, **communing**, **communed** talk together.
[from old French *comuner* = share]

communicant *NOUN* **communicants** **1** a person who communicates with someone. **2** a person who receives Holy Communion.

communicate *VERB* **communicates**, **communicating**, **communicated** **1** pass news, information, etc. to other people. **2** (said about rooms etc.) have a connecting door.
[from Latin *communicare* = tell, share]

communication *NOUN* **communications** **1** communicating. **2** something communicated; a message.
- **communications** *plural noun* links between places (e.g. roads, railways, telephones, radio).

communicative *ADJECTIVE* willing to talk.

communion *NOUN* religious fellowship.
- **Communion** or **Holy Communion** the Christian ceremony in which consecrated bread and wine are given to worshippers.
[same origin as *commune*[1]]

communiqué (*say* ko-**mew**-nik-ay) *NOUN* **communiqués** an official message giving a report.
[French, = communicated]

Communism *NOUN* a political system where the state controls property, production, trade, etc. (COMPARE **capitalism**)
▷ **Communist** *noun*

communism *NOUN* a system where property is shared by the community.
[French, from *commun* = common]

community *NOUN* **communities** **1** the people living in one area. **2** a group with similar interests or origins.
[same origin as *commune*[1]]

commute *VERB* **commutes**, **commuting**, **commuted** **1** travel a fairly long way by train, bus, or car to and from your daily work. **2** alter a punishment to something less severe.
[from *com-* + Latin *mutare* = change]

commuter *NOUN* **commuters** a person who commutes to and from work.

compact[1] *NOUN* **compacts** an agreement or contract.
[from *com-* + *pact*]

compact[2] *ADJECTIVE* **1** closely or neatly packed together. **2** concise.
▷ **compactly** *adverb* **compactness** *noun*

compact *NOUN* **compacts** a small flat container for face powder.

compact *VERB* **compacts**, **compacting**, **compacted** join or press firmly together or into a small space.
[from Latin *compactum* = put together]

compact disc *NOUN* **compact discs** a small plastic disc on which music, information, etc. is stored as digital signals and is read by a laser beam.

companion *NOUN* **companions** **1** a person who you spend time with or travel with. **2** one of a matching pair of things. **3** (in book titles) a guidebook or reference book • *The Oxford Companion to Music.*
▷ **companionship** *noun*
[literally = someone you eat bread with: from *com-* + Latin *panis* = bread]

companionable *ADJECTIVE* sociable.

company *NOUN* **companies** **1** a number of people together. **2** a business firm. **3** having people with you; companionship. **4** visitors • *We've got company.* **5** a section of a battalion.
[same origin as *companion*]

comparable (*say* **kom**-per-a-bul) *ADJECTIVE* able to be compared, similar.
▷ **comparably** *adverb*
[same origin as *compare*]

comparative *ADJECTIVE* comparing a thing with something else • *They live in comparative comfort.*
▷ **comparatively** *adverb*

comparative *NOUN* **comparatives** the form of an adjective or adverb that expresses 'more' • *The comparative of 'big' is 'bigger'.*

compare *VERB* **compares, comparing, compared** **1** put things together so as to tell in what ways they are similar or different. **2** form the comparative and superlative of an adjective or adverb.
- **compare notes** share information.
- **compare with** **1** be similar to. **2** be as good as • *Our art gallery cannot compare with Tate Modern.*
[from *com-* + Latin *par* = equal]
USAGE When *compare* is used with an object, it can be followed by either *to* or *with*. Traditionally, *to* is used when you are showing the similarity between two things: *She compared me to a pig. With* is used when you are looking at the similarities and differences between things: *Just compare this year's profits with last year's.*

comparison *NOUN* **comparisons** comparing.

compartment *NOUN* **compartments** **1** one of the spaces into which something is divided; a separate room or enclosed space. **2** a division of a railway carriage.
[from Latin *compartiri* = share with someone]

compass *NOUN* **compasses** a device that shows direction, with a magnetized needle pointing to the north.
- **compasses** or **pair of compasses** a device for drawing circles, usually with two rods hinged together at one end.
[from old French]

compassion *NOUN* pity or mercy.
▷ **compassionate** *adjective*
compassionately *adverb*
[from *com-* + Latin *passum* = suffered]

compatible *ADJECTIVE* **1** able to live or exist together without trouble. **2** able to be used together • *This printer is not compatible with my computer.*
▷ **compatibly** *adverb* **compatibility** *noun*
[from Latin *compati* = suffer together]

compatriot (*say* kom-**pat**-ri-ot) *NOUN* a person from the same country as another.
[from *com-* + *patriot*]

compel *VERB* **compels, compelling, compelled** force somebody to do something.
[from *com-* + Latin *pellere* = drive]

compendious *ADJECTIVE* giving much information concisely.
[same origin as *compendium*]

compendium *NOUN* **compendiums** or **compendia** **1** an encyclopedia or handbook in one volume. **2** a set of different board games in one box.
[Latin, = a saving, abbreviation]

compensate *VERB* **compensates, compensating, compensated** **1** give a person money etc. to make up for a loss or injury. **2** have a balancing effect • *This victory compensates for our earlier defeats.*
▷ **compensation** *noun*
compensatory *adjective*
[from Latin *compensare* = weigh one thing against another]

A B C D E F G H I J K L M N O P Q R S T U V W X Y Z

compère (*say* kom-pair) *NOUN* **compères** a person who introduces the performers in a show or broadcast.
▷ **compère** *verb*
[French, = godfather]

compete *VERB* **competes, competing, competed** take part in a competition.
[from *com-* + Latin *petere* = aim at]

competent *ADJECTIVE* able to do a particular thing.
▷ **competently** *adverb* **competence** *noun*
[from Latin, = suitable, sufficient]

competition *NOUN* **competitions** **1** a game or race or other contest in which people try to win. **2** competing. **3** the people competing with yourself.
▷ **competitive** *adjective*

competitor *NOUN* **competitors** someone who competes; a rival.

compile *VERB* **compiles, compiling, compiled** put things together into a list or collection, e.g. to form a book.
▷ **compiler** *noun* **compilation** *noun*
[from French]

complacent *ADJECTIVE* smugly satisfied with the way things are, and feeling that no change or action is necessary.
▷ **complacently** *adverb* **complacency** *noun*
[from Latin]

complain *VERB* **complains, complaining, complained** say that you are annoyed or unhappy about something.
[from Latin]

complaint *NOUN* **complaints** **1** a statement complaining about something. **2** an illness.

complement *NOUN* **complements** **1** the quantity needed to fill or complete something • *The ship had its full complement of sailors.* **2** the word or words used after verbs such as *be* and *become* to complete the sense. In *She was brave* and *He became king of England*, the complements are *brave* and *king of England*.

complement *VERB* **complements, complementing, complemented** go well together with something else; make a thing complete • *The hat complements the outfit.*
[same origin as *complete*]
USAGE Do not confuse with **compliment**.

complementary *ADJECTIVE* completing; forming a complement.
USAGE Do not confuse with **complimentary**.

complementary angle *NOUN* **complementary angles** either of two angles that add up to 90°.

complementary medicine *NOUN* alternative medicine.

complete *ADJECTIVE* **1** having all its parts. **2** finished. **3** thorough; in every way • *a complete stranger.*
▷ **completely** *adverb* **completeness** *noun*

complete *VERB* **completes, completing, completed** make a thing complete; add what is needed.
▷ **completion** *noun*
[from Latin *completum* = filled up]

complex *ADJECTIVE* **1** made up of parts. **2** complicated.
▷ **complexity** *noun*

complex *NOUN* **complexes** **1** a set of buildings made up of related parts • *a sports complex.* **2** a group of feelings or ideas that influence a person's behaviour etc. • *a persecution complex.*
[from Latin *complexum* = embraced, plaited]

complexion *NOUN* **complexions** **1** the natural colour and appearance of the skin of the face. **2** the way things seem • *That puts a different complexion on the matter.*
[from old French]

compliant *ADJECTIVE* willing to obey.
▷ **compliance** *noun*

complicate *VERB* **complicates, complicating, complicated** make a thing complex or complicated.
[from *com-* + Latin *plicare* = to fold]

complicated *ADJECTIVE* **1** made up of many parts. **2** difficult to understand or do.

complication *NOUN* **complications** **1** something that complicates things or adds difficulties. **2** a complicated condition.

complicity *NOUN* being involved in a crime etc.
[same origin as *complicate*]

compliment *NOUN* **compliments** something said or done to show that you approve of a person or thing • *pay compliments.*
- **compliments** *plural noun* formal greetings given in a message.

compliment *VERB* **compliments, complimenting, complimented** pay someone a compliment; congratulate.
[via French from Italian]
USAGE Do not confuse with **complement**.

complimentary *ADJECTIVE* **1** expressing a compliment. **2** given free of charge • *complimentary tickets.*
USAGE Do not confuse with **complementary**.

comply *VERB* **complies, complying, complied** obey laws or rules.
[from Italian; related to *complete*]

component *NOUN* **components** each of the parts of which a thing is made up.
[same origin as *compound*¹]

compose *VERB* **composes, composing, composed 1** form or make up • *The class is composed of 20 students.* **2** write music or poetry etc. **3** arrange in good order. **4** make calm • *compose yourself.*
[from French; related to *compound*¹]

composed *ADJECTIVE* calm • *a composed manner.*

composer *NOUN* **composers** a person who composes music etc.

composite (*say* kom-poz-it) *ADJECTIVE* made up of a number of parts or different styles.
[same origin as *compose*]

composition *NOUN* **compositions 1** composing. **2** something composed, especially a piece of music. **3** an essay or story written as a school exercise. **4** the parts that make something • *the composition of the soil.*

compos mentis *ADJECTIVE* in your right mind; sane. (The opposite is **non compos mentis**.)
[Latin, = having control of the mind]

compost *NOUN* **1** decayed leaves and grass etc. used as a fertilizer. **2** a soil-like mixture for growing seedlings, cuttings, etc.
[same origin as *compose*]

composure *NOUN* calmness of manner.

compound¹ *ADJECTIVE* made of two or more parts or ingredients.

compound *NOUN* **compounds** a compound substance.

compound *VERB* **compounds, compounding, compounded** put together; combine.
[from Latin *componere* = put together]

compound² *NOUN* **compounds** a fenced area containing buildings.
[via Portuguese or Dutch from Malay (a language spoken in Malaysia)]

comprehend *VERB* **comprehends, comprehending, comprehended 1** understand. **2** include.
[from *com-* + Latin *prehendere* = take, seize]

comprehensible *ADJECTIVE* understandable.

comprehensive *ADJECTIVE* including all or many kinds of people or things.

comprehensive *NOUN* **comprehensives** a comprehensive school.

comprehensive school *NOUN* **comprehensive schools** a secondary school for all or most of the children of an area.

compress (*say* kom-**press**) *VERB* **compresses, compressing, compressed 1** press together or into a smaller space. **2** alter the form of computer data to reduce the amount of space needed to store it.
▷ **compression** *noun* **compressor** *noun*

compress (*say* **kom**-press) *NOUN* **compresses** a soft pad or cloth pressed on the body to stop bleeding or cool inflammation etc.
[from *com-* + Latin *pressare* = to press]

comprise *VERB* **comprises, comprising, comprised** include; consist of • *The pentathlon comprises five events.*
[from French; related to *comprehend*]
USAGE Do not use *comprise* with *of*. It is incorrect to say 'The group was comprised of 20 men'; correct usage is 'was composed of'.

compromise (*say* **kom**-prom-I'z) *NOUN* **compromises** settling a dispute by each side accepting less than it asked for.

a b c d e f g h i j k l m n o p q r s t u v w x y z

compromise *VERB* **compromises, compromising, compromised** **1** settle by a compromise. **2** expose someone to danger or suspicion etc. • *His confession compromises his sister.*
[from *com-* + Latin *promittere* = to promise]

compulsion *NOUN* **compulsions** a strong and uncontrollable desire to do something.

compulsive *ADJECTIVE* having or resulting from a strong and uncontrollable desire • *a compulsive gambler.*
[same origin as *compel*]
USAGE See *compulsory*.

compulsory *ADJECTIVE* that must be done; not optional • *Wearing seat belts is compulsory.*
[same origin as *compel*]
USAGE Do not confuse **compulsory** with **compulsive**. An action is *compulsory* if a law or rules say that you must do it, but *compulsive* if you want to do it and cannot resist it.

compunction *NOUN* a guilty feeling • *She felt no compunction about hitting the burglar.*
[from *com-* + Latin *punctum* = pricked (by conscience)]

compute *VERB* **computes, computing, computed** calculate.
▷ **computation** *noun*
[from *com-* + Latin *putare* = reckon]

computer *NOUN* **computers** an electronic machine for making calculations, storing and analysing information put into it, or controlling machinery automatically.

computerize *VERB* **computerizes, computerizing, computerized** equip with computers; perform or produce by computer.
▷ **computerization** *noun*

computing *NOUN* the use of computers.

comrade *NOUN* **comrades** a companion who shares in your activities.
▷ **comradeship** *noun*
[from Spanish *camarada* = room-mate]

con[1] *VERB* **cons, conning, conned** (*slang*) swindle.
[short for *confidence trick*]

con[2] *NOUN* **cons** a reason against something • *There are pros and cons.*
[from Latin *contra* = against]

con- *PREFIX* with; together. SEE **com-**.

concave *ADJECTIVE* curved like the inside of a ball or circle. (The opposite is **convex**.)
▷ **concavity** *noun*
[from *con-* + Latin *cavus* = hollow]

conceal *VERB* **conceals, concealing, concealed** hide; keep something secret.
▷ **concealment** *noun*
[from *con-* + Latin *celare* = hide]

concede *VERB* **concedes, conceding, conceded** **1** admit that something is true. **2** grant or allow something • *They conceded us the right to cross their land.* **3** admit that you have been defeated.
[from *con-* + Latin *cedere* = cede]

conceit *NOUN* being too proud of yourself; vanity.
▷ **conceited** *adjective*
[originally = idea, opinion; from *conceive*]

conceivable *ADJECTIVE* able to be imagined or believed.
▷ **conceivably** *adverb*

conceive *VERB* **conceives, conceiving, conceived** **1** become pregnant; form a baby in the womb. **2** form an idea or plan; imagine • *I can't conceive why you want to come.*
[from Latin *concipere* = take in, contain]

concentrate *VERB* **concentrates, concentrating, concentrated** **1** give your full attention or effort to something. **2** bring or come together in one place. **3** make a liquid etc. less dilute.
[from French; related to *centre*]

concentration *NOUN* **concentrations** **1** concentrating. **2** the amount dissolved in each part of a liquid.

concentration camp *NOUN* **concentration camps** a prison camp where political prisoners are kept together, especially one set up by the Nazis during World War II.

concentric *ADJECTIVE* having the same centre • *concentric circles.*
[from Latin; related to *centre*]

concept *NOUN* **concepts** an idea.
▷ **conceptual** *adjective*
[same origin as *conceive*]

conception *NOUN* **conceptions** **1** conceiving. **2** an idea.

concern *VERB* **concerns, concerning, concerned** **1** be important to or affect somebody. **2** worry somebody. **3** be about; have as its subject • *The story concerns a group of rabbits.*

concern *NOUN* **concerns** **1** something that concerns you; a responsibility. **2** worry. **3** a business.
[from Latin]

concerned *ADJECTIVE* **1** worried. **2** involved in or affected by something.

concerning *PREPOSITION* on the subject of; about • *laws concerning seat belts.*

concert *NOUN* **concerts** a musical entertainment.
[same origin as *concerto*]

concerted *ADJECTIVE* done in cooperation with others • *We made a concerted effort.*

concertina *NOUN* **concertinas** a portable musical instrument with bellows, played by squeezing.
[from *concert*]

concerto (*say* kon-chert-oh) *NOUN* **concertos** a piece of music for a solo instrument and an orchestra.
[from Italian *concertare* = harmonize]

concession *NOUN* **concessions** **1** conceding. **2** something conceded. **3** a reduction in price for a certain category of person.
▷ **concessionary** *adjective*
[same origin as *concede*]

conciliate *VERB* **conciliates, conciliating, conciliated** **1** win over an angry or hostile person by friendliness. **2** help people who disagree to come to an agreement.
▷ **conciliation** *noun*
[from Latin; related to *council*]

concise *ADJECTIVE* brief; giving much information in a few words.
▷ **concisely** *adverb* **conciseness** *noun*
[from *con-* + Latin *caedere* = cut]

conclave *NOUN* **conclaves** a private meeting.
[from *con-* + Latin *clavis* = key]

conclude *VERB* **concludes, concluding, concluded** **1** bring or come to an end. **2** decide; form an opinion by reasoning • *The jury concluded that he was guilty.*
[from *con-* + Latin *claudere* = shut]

conclusion *NOUN* **conclusions** **1** an ending. **2** an opinion formed by reasoning.

conclusive *ADJECTIVE* putting an end to all doubt.
▷ **conclusively** *adverb*

concoct *VERB* **concocts, concocting, concocted** **1** make something by putting ingredients together. **2** invent • *We'll have to concoct an excuse.*
▷ **concoction** *noun*
[from *con-* + Latin *coctum* = cooked]

concord *NOUN* friendly agreement or harmony.
[from *con-* + Latin *cor* = heart]

concordance *NOUN* **concordances** **1** agreement. **2** an index of the words used in a book or an author's works.

concourse *NOUN* **concourses** an open area through which people pass, e.g. at an airport.
[same origin as *concur*]

concrete *NOUN* cement mixed with sand and gravel, used in building.

concrete *ADJECTIVE* **1** able to be touched and felt; not abstract. **2** definite • *We need concrete evidence, not theories.*
[from Latin *concretus* = stiff, hard]

concur *VERB* **concurs, concurring, concurred** agree.
▷ **concurrence** *noun*
[from *con-* + Latin *currere* = run]

concurrent *ADJECTIVE* happening or existing at the same time.

concussion *NOUN* a temporary injury to the brain caused by a hard knock.
▷ **concussed** *adjective*
[from Latin *concussum* = shaken violently]

condemn *VERB* **condemns, condemning, condemned** **1** say that you strongly disapprove of something. **2** convict or sentence a criminal • *He was condemned to death.* **3** destine to something unhappy • *She was condemned to a lonely life.* **4** declare that a building is not fit to be used.
▷ **condemnation** *noun*
[from old French; related to *damn*]

condense *VERB* **condenses, condensing, condensed 1** make a liquid denser or more compact. **2** put something into fewer words. **3** change from gas or vapour to liquid • *Steam condenses on windows.*
▷ **condensation** *noun* **condenser** *noun*
[from Latin *condensus* = very thick or dense]

condescend *VERB* **condescends, condescending, condescended 1** behave in a way which shows that you feel superior. **2** allow yourself to do something that seems unsuitable for a person of your high rank.
▷ **condescension** *noun*
[from Latin *condescendere* = stoop, lower yourself]

condiment *NOUN* **condiments** a seasoning (e.g. salt or pepper) for food.
[from Latin]

condition *NOUN* **conditions 1** the state or fitness of a person or thing • *This bicycle is in good condition.* **2** the situation or surroundings etc. that affect something • *working conditions.* **3** something required as part of an agreement.
- **on condition that** only if; on the understanding that something will be done.

condition *VERB* **conditions, conditioning, conditioned 1** put something into a healthy or proper condition. **2** train someone to behave in a particular way or become used to a particular situation.
[from Latin]

conditional *ADJECTIVE* containing a condition (SEE **condition 3**); depending.
▷ **conditionally** *adverb*

conditioner *NOUN* **conditioners** a substance you put on your hair to keep it in good condition.

condole *VERB* **condoles, condoling, condoled** express sympathy.
[from *con-* + Latin *dolere* = grieve]

condolence *NOUN* **condolences** an expression of sympathy, especially for someone who is bereaved.

condom *NOUN* **condoms** a rubber sheath worn on the penis during sexual intercourse as a contraceptive and as a protection against disease.
[origin unknown]

condominium *NOUN* **condominiums** (*American*) an apartment building in which each apartment in owned by the person living in it but there are shared areas such as gardens that are owned by everyone together.
[from Latin *dominium* = property]

condone *VERB* **condones, condoning, condoned** forgive or ignore wrongdoing • *We do not condone violence.*
[from Latin]

condor *NOUN* **condors** a kind of large vulture.
[via Spanish from Quechua (a South American language)]

conducive *ADJECTIVE* helping to cause or produce something • *Noisy surroundings are not conducive to work.*
[same origin as *conduct*]

conduct (*say* kon-**dukt**) *VERB* **conducts, conducting, conducted 1** lead or guide. **2** be the conductor of an orchestra or choir. **3** manage or direct something • *conduct an experiment.* **4** allow heat, light, sound, or electricity to pass along or through. **5** behave • *They conducted themselves with dignity.*

conduct (*say* **kon**-dukt) *NOUN* behaviour.
[from *con-* + Latin *ducere* = to lead]

conduction *NOUN* the conducting of heat or electricity etc. (SEE **conduct 4**).

conductor *NOUN* **conductors 1** a person who directs the performance of an orchestra or choir by movements of the arms. **2** a person who collects the fares on a bus etc. **3** something that conducts heat or electricity etc.
▷ **conductress** *noun*

conduit (*say* kon-dit) *NOUN* **conduits 1** a pipe or channel for liquid. **2** a tube protecting electric wire.
[from French; related to *conduct*]

cone *NOUN* **cones 1** an object that is circular at one end and narrows to a point at the other end. **2** an ice cream cornet. **3** the dry cone-shaped fruit of a pine, fir, or cedar tree.
[from Greek]

confection *NOUN* **confections** something made of various things, especially sweet ones, put together.
[from Latin]

confectioner *NOUN* **confectioners** someone who makes or sells sweets.
▷ **confectionery** *noun*

confederacy *NOUN* **confederacies** a union of states; a confederation.

confederate *ADJECTIVE* allied; joined by an agreement or treaty.

confederate *NOUN* **confederates** **1** a member of a confederacy. **2** an ally; an accomplice.
[from *con-* + Latin *foederatum* = allied]

confederation *NOUN* **confederations** **1** the process of joining in an alliance. **2** a group of people, organizations, or states joined together by an agreement or treaty.

confer *VERB* **confers, conferring, conferred** **1** grant or bestow. **2** hold a discussion before deciding something.
[from *con-* + Latin *ferre* = bring]

conference *NOUN* **conferences** a meeting for holding a discussion.
[same origin as *confer*]

confess *VERB* **confesses, confessing, confessed** state openly that you have done something wrong or have a weakness; admit.
[from Latin]

confession *NOUN* **confessions** **1** admitting that you have done wrong. **2** (in the Roman Catholic Church) an act of telling a priest that you have sinned.

confessional *NOUN* **confessionals** a small room where a priest hears confessions.

confessor *NOUN* **confessors** a priest who hears confessions.

confetti *NOUN* tiny pieces of coloured paper thrown by wedding guests at the bride and bridegroom.
[Italian, = sweets (which were traditionally thrown at Italian weddings)]

confidant *NOUN* (**confidante** is used of a woman) **confidants, confidantes** a person you confide in.
[a different spelling of *confident*]

confide *VERB* **confides, confiding, confided** **1** tell someone a secret • *I decided to confide in my sister.* **2** entrust something to someone.
[from *con-* + Latin *fidere* = to trust]

confidence *NOUN* **confidences** **1** firm trust. **2** a feeling of certainty or boldness; being sure that you can do something. **3** something told confidentially.
- **in confidence** as a secret.
- **in a person's confidence** trusted with his or her secrets.

confidence trick *NOUN* **confidence tricks** swindling a person after persuading him or her to trust you.

confident *ADJECTIVE* showing or feeling confidence; bold.
▷ **confidently** *adverb*
[from Latin; related to *confide*]

confidential *ADJECTIVE* meant to be kept secret.
▷ **confidentially** *adverb* **confidentiality** *noun*

configuration *NOUN* **configurations** **1** a method of arrangement of parts etc. **2** a shape.
[from Latin *configurare* = make according to a pattern]

configure *VERB* **configures, configuring, configring** (*in computing*) **1** arrange something in a particular way. **2** arrange a computer system in a particular way; make software work in the way the user prefers.

confine *VERB* **confines, confining, confined** **1** keep something within limits; restrict • *Please confine your remarks to the subject being discussed.* **2** keep somebody in a place.
[from *con-* + Latin *finis* = limit, end]

confined *ADJECTIVE* narrow or restricted • *a confined space.*

confinement *NOUN* **confinements** **1** confining. **2** the time of giving birth to a baby.

confines (*say* kon-fynz) *PLURAL NOUN* the limits or boundaries of an area.

confirm *VERB* **confirms, confirming, confirmed** **1** prove that something is true or correct. **2** make a thing definite • *Please write to confirm your booking.* **3** make a person a full member of the Christian Church.
▷ **confirmation** *noun* **confirmatory** *adjective*
[from *con-* + Latin *firmare* = strengthen]

confiscate *VERB* **confiscates**, **confiscating**, **confiscated** take something away as a punishment.
▷ **confiscation** *noun*
[from Latin]

conflagration *NOUN* **conflagrations** a great and destructive fire.
[from *con-* + Latin *flagrare* = blaze]

conflict (*say* **kon**-flikt) *NOUN* **conflicts** a fight, struggle, or disagreement.

conflict (*say* kon-**flikt**) *VERB* **conflicts**, **conflicting**, **conflicted** have a conflict; differ or disagree.
[from *con-* = together + Latin *flictum* = struck]

confluence *NOUN* **confluences** the place where two rivers meet.
[from *con-* + Latin *fluens* = flowing]

conform *VERB* **conforms**, **conforming**, **conformed** keep to accepted rules, customs, or ideas.
▷ **conformist** *noun* **conformity** *noun*
[from Latin *conformare* = shape evenly]

confound *VERB* **confounds**, **confounding**, **confounded** **1** astonish or puzzle someone. **2** confuse.
[from Latin]

confront *VERB* **confronts**, **confronting**, **confronted** **1** come or bring face to face, especially in a hostile way. **2** be present and have to be dealt with • *Problems confront us.*
▷ **confrontation** *noun*
[from Latin]

confuse *VERB* **confuses**, **confusing**, **confused** **1** make a person puzzled or muddled. **2** mistake one thing for another.
▷ **confusion** *noun*
[from old French; related to *confound*]

congeal (*say* kon-**jeel**) *VERB* **congeals**, **congealing**, **congealed** become jelly-like instead of liquid, especially in cooling • *congealed blood.*
[from *con-* + Latin *gelare* = freeze]

congenial *ADJECTIVE* pleasant through being similar to yourself or suiting your tastes; agreeable • *a congenial companion.*
▷ **congenially** *adverb*
[from *con-* + *genial*]

congenital (*say* kon-**jen**-it-al) *ADJECTIVE* existing in a person from birth.
▷ **congenitally** *adverb*
[from *con-* + Latin *genitus* = born]

congested *ADJECTIVE* crowded or blocked up • *congested streets; congested lungs.*
▷ **congestion** *noun*
[from Latin *congestum* = heaped up]

conglomerate *NOUN* **conglomerates** a large business group formed by merging several different companies.
[from *con-* + Latin *glomus* = mass]

conglomeration *NOUN* **conglomerations** a mass of different things put together.

congratulate *VERB* **congratulates**, **congratulating**, **congratulated** tell a person that you are pleased about his or her success or good fortune.
▷ **congratulation** *noun* **congratulatory** *adjective*
[from *con-* + Latin *gratulari* = show joy]

congregate *VERB* **congregates**, **congregating**, **congregated** assemble; flock together.
[from *con-* + Latin *gregatum* = herded]

congregation *NOUN* **congregations** a group of people who have come together to take part in religious worship.

Congress *NOUN* the parliament of the USA.

congress *NOUN* **congresses** a conference.
[from *con-* + Latin *-gressus* = going]
WORD FAMILY There are a number of English words that are related to *congress* because part of their original meaning comes from the Latin words *gressus* meaning 'going' or *gressum* meaning 'gone'. These include *digress*, *progress*, *regress*, and *transgress*.

congruent *ADJECTIVE* (*in mathematics*) having exactly the same shape and size • *congruent triangles.*
▷ **congruence** *noun*
[from Latin]

conical *ADJECTIVE* cone-shaped.
▷ **conically** *adverb*

conifer (*say* **kon**-if-er) *NOUN* **conifers** an evergreen tree with cones.
▷ **coniferous** *adjective*
[from *cone* + Latin *ferens* = bearing]

conjecture *NOUN* **conjectures** guesswork or a guess.
▷ **conjecture** *verb* **conjectural** *adjective*
[from Latin]

conjugal (*say* kon-jug-al) *ADJECTIVE* to do with marriage.
[from *con-* + Latin *jugum* = yoke]

conjugate *VERB* **conjugates, conjugating, conjugated** give all the different forms of a verb.
▷ **conjugation** *noun*

conjunction *NOUN* **conjunctions** **1** a word that joins words or phrases or sentences, e.g. *and*, *but*. **2** combination or union • *The four armies acted in conjunction.*
[from Latin *conjunctum* = yoked together]

conjure *VERB* **conjures, conjuring, conjured** perform tricks that look like magic.
▷ **conjuror** *noun*
- **conjure up** produce in your mind • *Mention of the Arctic conjures up visions of snow.*
[from Latin]

conker *NOUN* **conkers** the hard shiny brown nut of the horse chestnut tree.
- **conkers** a game between players who each have a conker threaded on a string.
[from a dialect word = snail shell (because conkers was originally played with snail shells)]

connect *VERB* **connects, connecting, connected** **1** join together; link. **2** think of things or people as being associated with each other.
[from *con-* + Latin *nectere* = bind]

connection *NOUN* **connections** **1** a point where two things are connected; a link • *We all know there is a connection between smoking and cancer.* **2** a train, bus, etc. that leaves a station soon after another arrives, so that passengers can change from one to the other.

conning tower *NOUN* **conning towers** the part on top of a submarine, containing the periscope.
[from an old word *con* = guide a ship]

connive (*say* kon-I'v) *VERB* **connives, conniving, connived**
- **connive at** take no notice of wrongdoing that ought to be reported or punished.
▷ **connivance** *noun*
[from Latin *connivere* = shut the eyes]

connoisseur (*say* kon-a-ser) *NOUN* **connoisseurs** a person with great experience and appreciation of something • *a connoisseur of wine.*
[French, = one who knows]

conquer *VERB* **conquers, conquering, conquered** defeat or overcome.
▷ **conqueror** *noun*
[from old French]

conquest *NOUN* **conquests** **1** a victory over someone. **2** conquered territory.

conscience (*say* kon-shens) *NOUN* **consciences** knowing what is right and wrong, especially in your own actions.
[from Latin *conscientia* = knowledge]

conscientious (*say* kon-shee-en-shus) *ADJECTIVE* careful and honest about doing your work properly.
▷ **conscientiously** *adverb*

conscientious objector *NOUN* **conscientious objectors** a person who refuses to serve in the armed forces because he or she believes it is morally wrong.

conscious (*say* kon-shus) *ADJECTIVE* **1** awake and knowing what is happening. **2** aware of something • *I was not conscious of the time.* **3** done deliberately • *a conscious decision.*
▷ **consciously** *adverb* **consciousness** *noun*
[from Latin *conscius* = knowing]

conscript (*say* kon-skript) *VERB* **conscripts, conscripting, conscripted** make a person join the armed forces.
▷ **conscription** *noun*

conscript (*say* kon-skript) *NOUN* **conscripts** a conscripted person.
[from *con-* + Latin *scriptus* = written in a list, enlisted]

consecrate *VERB* **consecrates, consecrating, consecrated** officially say that a thing, especially a building, is holy.
▷ **consecration** *noun*
[from Latin]

consecutive *ADJECTIVE* following one after another.
▷ **consecutively** *adverb*
[from Latin *consequi* = follow closely]

consensus *NOUN* **consensuses** general agreement; the opinion of most people.
[same origin as *consent*]

consent *NOUN* agreement to what someone wishes; permission.

consent *VERB* **consents**, **consenting**, **consented** say that you are willing to do or allow what someone wishes.
[from *con-* + Latin *sentire* = feel]

consequence *NOUN* **consequences**
1 something that happens as the result of an event or action. **2** importance • *It is of no consequence.*

consequent *ADJECTIVE* happening as a result.
▷ **consequently** *adverb*
[same origin as *consecutive*]

consequential *ADJECTIVE* happening as a result.

conservation *NOUN* conserving; preservation, especially of the natural environment.
▷ **conservationist** *noun*

Conservative *NOUN* **Conservatives** a person who supports the Conservative Party, a British political party that favours private enterprise and freedom from state control.
▷ **Conservative** *adjective*

conservative *ADJECTIVE* **1** liking traditional ways and disliking changes. **2** moderate or cautious; not extreme • *a conservative estimate.*
▷ **conservatively** *adverb* **conservatism** *noun*

conservatory *NOUN* **conservatories** a room with a glass roof and large windows, built against an outside wall of a house with a connecting door from the house.
[from *conserve*]

conserve *VERB* **conserves**, **conserving**, **conserved** prevent something valuable from being changed, spoilt, or wasted.
[from *con-* + Latin *servare* = keep safe]

consider *VERB* **considers**, **considering**, **considered** **1** think carefully about or give attention to something, especially in order to make a decision. **2** have an opinion; think to be • *Consider yourself lucky.*
[from Latin]

considerable *ADJECTIVE* fairly great • *a considerable amount.*
▷ **considerably** *adverb*

considerate *ADJECTIVE* taking care not to inconvenience or hurt others.
▷ **considerately** *adverb*

consideration *NOUN* **considerations**
1 being considerate. **2** careful thought or attention. **3** a fact that must be kept in mind. **4** payment given as a reward.
- **take into consideration** allow for.

considering *PREPOSITION* taking something into consideration • *The car runs well, considering its age.*

consign *VERB* **consigns**, **consigning**, **consigned** hand something over formally; entrust.
[from Latin]

consignment *NOUN* **consignments**
1 consigning. **2** a batch of goods etc. sent to someone.

consist *VERB* **consists**, **consisting**, **consisted** be made up or composed of • *The flat consists of three rooms.*
[from Latin]

consistency *NOUN* **consistencies** **1** being consistent. **2** thickness or stiffness, especially of a liquid.

consistent *ADJECTIVE* **1** keeping to a regular pattern or style; not changing. **2** not contradictory.
▷ **consistently** *adverb*

consolation *NOUN* **consolations**
1 consoling. **2** something that consoles someone.

consolation prize *NOUN* **consolation prizes** a prize given to a competitor who has just missed winning one of the main prizes.

console[1] (*say* kon-**sohl**) *VERB* **consoles**, **consoling**, **consoled** comfort someone who is unhappy or disappointed.
[from *con-* + Latin *solari* = soothe]

console[2] (*say* kon-sohl) *NOUN* **consoles** 1 a panel or unit containing the controls for electrical or other equipment. 2 a frame containing the keyboard and stops etc. of an organ.
[French]

consolidate *VERB* **consolidates, consolidating, consolidated** 1 make or become secure and strong. 2 combine two or more organizations, funds, etc. into one.
▷ **consolidation** *noun*
[from *con-* + Latin *solidare* = make solid]

consonant *NOUN* **consonants** a letter that is not a vowel • *B, c, d, f, etc. are consonants.*
[from *con-* + Latin *sonans* = sounding]

consort (*say* kon-sort) *NOUN* **consorts** a husband or wife, especially of a monarch.

consort (*say* kon-sort) *VERB* **consorts, consorting, consorted** be in someone's company • *He was often seen consorting with criminals.*
[from Latin *consors* = sharer]

consortium *NOUN* **consortia** a combination of countries, companies, or other groups acting together.

conspicuous *ADJECTIVE* easily seen; noticeable.
▷ **conspicuously** *adverb* **conspicuousness** *noun*
[from Latin *conspicere* = look at carefully]

conspiracy *NOUN* **conspiracies** planning with others to do something illegal; a plot.

conspire *VERB* **conspires, conspiring, conspired** take part in a conspiracy.
▷ **conspirator** *noun* **conspiratorial** *adjective*
[from *con-* + Latin *spirare* = breathe]

constable *NOUN* **constables** a police officer of the lowest rank.
[from Latin, originally = officer in charge of the stable]

constabulary *NOUN* **constabularies** a police force.

constant *ADJECTIVE* 1 not changing; happening all the time. 2 faithful or loyal.
▷ **constantly** *adverb* **constancy** *noun*

constant *NOUN* **constants** 1 a thing that does not vary. 2 (*in science and mathematics*) a number or value that does not change.
[from *con-* + Latin *stans* = standing]

constellation *NOUN* **constellations** a group of stars.
[from *con-* + Latin *stella* = star]

constipated *ADJECTIVE* unable to empty the bowels easily or regularly.
▷ **constipation** *noun*
[from Latin *constipare* = cram]

constituency *NOUN* **constituencies** a district represented by a Member of Parliament elected by the people who live there.

constituent *NOUN* **constituents** 1 one of the parts that form a whole thing.
2 someone who lives in a particular constituency.
▷ **constituent** *adjective*
[from Latin, = setting up, constituting]

constitute *VERB* **constitutes, constituting, constituted** make up or form something • *Twelve months constitute a year.*
[from *con-* + Latin *statuere* = set up]

constitution *NOUN* **constitutions** 1 the group of laws or principles that state how a country is to be organized and governed.
2 the nature of the body in regard to healthiness • *She has a strong constitution.*
3 constituting. 4 the composition of something.
▷ **constitutional** *adjective*

constrain *VERB* **constrains, constraining, constrained** force someone to act in a certain way; compel.
[from old French; related to *constrict*]

constraint *NOUN* **constraints**
1 constraining; compulsion. 2 a restriction.

constrict *VERB* **constricts, constricting, constricted** squeeze or tighten something by making it narrower.
▷ **constriction** *noun*
[from *con-* + Latin *strictum* = bound]

construct *VERB* **constructs, constructing, constructed** make something by placing parts together; build.
▷ **constructor** *noun*
[from *con-* + Latin *structum* = built]

A B **C** D E F G H I J K L M N O P Q R S T U V W X Y Z

construction *NOUN* **constructions** **1** constructing. **2** something constructed; a building. **3** two or more words put together to form a phrase or clause or sentence. **4** an explanation or interpretation • *They put a bad construction on our refusal.*

constructive *ADJECTIVE* helpful and positive • *constructive suggestions.*

construe *VERB* **construes, construing, construed** interpret or explain.
[same origin as *construct*]

consul *NOUN* **consuls** **1** a government official appointed to live in a foreign city to help people from his or her own country who visit there. **2** either of the two chief magistrates in ancient Rome.
▷ **consular** *adjective*
[Latin, related to *consult*]

consulate *NOUN* **consulates** the building where a consul works.

consult *VERB* **consults, consulting, consulted** go to a person or book etc. for information or advice.
▷ **consultation** *noun*
[from Latin *consulere* = take advice or counsel]

consultant *NOUN* **consultants** a person who is qualified to give expert advice.

consultative *ADJECTIVE* for consultation • *a consultative committee.*

consume *VERB* **consumes, consuming, consumed** **1** eat or drink something. **2** use up • *Much time was consumed in waiting.* **3** destroy • *Fire consumed the building.*
[from *con-* + Latin *sumere* = take up]

consumer *NOUN* **consumers** a person who buys or uses goods or services.

consummate (*say* kon-sum-ayt) *VERB* **consummates, consummating, consummated** **1** make complete or perfect. **2** complete a marriage by having sexual intercourse.
▷ **consummation** *noun*

consummate (*say* kon-**sum**-at) *ADJECTIVE* perfect; highly skilled • *a consummate artist.*
[from *con-* + Latin *summus* = highest]

consumption *NOUN* **1** consuming. **2** (*old use*) tuberculosis of the lungs.

contact *NOUN* **contacts** **1** touching. **2** being in touch; communication. **3** a person to communicate with when you need information or help.

contact *VERB* **contacts, contacting, contacted** get in touch with a person.
[from *con-* + Latin *tactum* = touched]

contact lens *NOUN* **contact lenses** a tiny lens worn against the eyeball, instead of glasses.

contagion *NOUN* **contagions** a contagious disease.

contagious *ADJECTIVE* spreading by contact with an infected person • *a contagious disease.*
[from *con-* + Latin *tangere* = to touch]

contain *VERB* **contains, containing, contained** **1** have inside • *The box contains chocolates.* **2** consist of • *A gallon contains 8 pints.* **3** restrain; hold back • *Try to contain your laughter.*
[from *con-* + Latin *tenere* = hold]

container *NOUN* **containers** **1** a box or bottle etc. designed to contain something. **2** a large box-like object of standard design in which goods are transported.

contaminate *VERB* **contaminates, contaminating, contaminated** make a thing dirty or impure or diseased etc.; pollute.
▷ **contamination** *noun*
[from Latin; related to *contagion*]

contemplate *VERB* **contemplates, contemplating, contemplated** **1** look at something thoughtfully. **2** consider or think about doing something • *We are contemplating a visit to London.*
▷ **contemplation** *noun*
contemplative *adjective*
[from Latin]

contemporary *ADJECTIVE* **1** belonging to the same period • *Dickens was contemporary with Thackeray.* **2** modern; up-to-date • *contemporary furniture.*

contemporary *NOUN* **contemporaries** a person who is contemporary with another or who is about the same age • *She was my contemporary at college.*
[from *con-* + Latin *tempus* = time]

contempt *NOUN* a feeling of despising a person or thing.
[from Latin]

contemptible *ADJECTIVE* deserving contempt • *Hurting her feelings like that was a contemptible thing to do.*

contemptuous *ADJECTIVE* feeling or showing contempt • *She gave me a contemptuous look.*
▷ **contemptuously** *adverb*

contend *VERB* **contends, contending, contended** **1** struggle in a battle etc. or against difficulties. **2** compete. **3** declare that something is true; assert • *We contend that he is innocent.*
▷ **contender** *noun*
[from *con-* + Latin *tendere* = strive]

content[1] (*say* kon-**tent**) *ADJECTIVE* contented.

content *NOUN* contentment.

content *VERB* **contents, contenting, contented** make a person contented.
[from Latin *contentum* = restrained]

content[2] (*say* **kon**-tent) *NOUN* or **contents** *PLURAL NOUN* what something contains.
[from Latin *contenta* = things contained]

contented *ADJECTIVE* happy with what you have; satisfied.
▷ **contentedly** *adverb*

contention *NOUN* **contentions** **1** contending; arguing. **2** an assertion put forward.

contentment *NOUN* a contented state.

contest (*say* **kon**-test) *NOUN* **contests** a competition; a struggle in which rivals try to obtain something or to do best.

contest (*say* kon-**test**) *VERB* **contests, contesting, contested** **1** compete for or in • *contest an election.* **2** dispute; argue that something is wrong or not legal.
[from Latin]

contestant *NOUN* **contestants** a person taking part in a contest; a competitor.

context *NOUN* **contexts** **1** the words that come before and after a particular word or phrase and help to fix its meaning. **2** the background to an event that helps to explain it.
[from *con-* + Latin *textum* = woven]

contiguous *ADJECTIVE* in contact with; touching.
[same origin as *contingent*]

continent *NOUN* **continents** one of the main masses of land in the world • *The continents are Europe, Asia, Africa, North America, South America, Australia, and Antarctica.*
▷ **continental** *adjective*
- **the Continent** the mainland of Europe, not including the British Isles.
[from Latin *terra continens* = continuous land]

contingency *NOUN* **contingencies** something that may happen but cannot be known for certain.

contingent *ADJECTIVE* **1** depending • *His future is contingent on success in this exam.* **2** possible but not certain • *other contingent events.*

contingent *NOUN* **contingents** a group that forms part of a larger group or gathering.
[from Latin *contingere* = touch, happen to]

continual *ADJECTIVE* happening all the time, usually with breaks in between • *Stop this continual quarrelling!*
▷ **continually** *adverb*
USAGE Do not confuse with **continuous**. *Continual* is used to describe something that happens very frequently (*there were continual interruptions*) while *continuous* is used to describe something that happens without a pause (*there was continuous rain all day*).

continuance *NOUN* continuing.

continue *VERB* **continues, continuing, continued** **1** do something without stopping. **2** begin again after stopping • *The game will continue after lunch.*
▷ **continuation** *noun*
[from Latin]

continuous *ADJECTIVE* going on and on; without a break.
▷ **continuously** *adverb* **continuity** *noun*
USAGE See note at **continual**.

contort *VERB* **contorts, contorting, contorted** twist or force out of the usual shape.
▷ **contortion** *noun*
[from *con-* + Latin *tortum* = twisted]

A B C D E F G H I J K L M N O P Q R S T U V W X Y Z

contortionist *NOUN* **contortionists** a person who can twist his or her body into unusual positions.

contour *NOUN* **contours** **1** a line on a map joining the points that are the same height above sea level. **2** an outline.
[from Latin *contornare* = draw in outline]

contra- *PREFIX* against.
[Latin]

contraband *NOUN* smuggled goods.
[from *contra-* + Italian *banda* = a ban]

contraception *NOUN* preventing pregnancy; birth control.
[from *contra-* + *conception*]

contraceptive *NOUN* **contraceptives** a substance or device that prevents pregnancy.

contract (*say* kon-trakt) *NOUN* **contracts** **1** a formal agreement to do something. **2** a document stating the terms of an agreement.

contract (*say* kon-**trakt**) *VERB* **contracts, contracting, contracted** **1** make or become smaller. **2** make a contract. **3** get an illness • *She contracted measles.*
[from *con-* + Latin *tractum* = pulled]

contraction *NOUN* **contractions** **1** contracting. **2** a shortened form of a word or words. *Can't* is a contraction of *cannot*.

contractor *NOUN* **contractors** a person who makes a contract, especially for building.

contradict *VERB* **contradicts, contradicting, contradicted** **1** say that something said is not true or that someone is wrong. **2** say the opposite of • *These rumours contradict previous ones.*
▷ **contradiction** *noun*
contradictory *adjective*
[from *contra-* + Latin *dicere* = say]

contraflow *NOUN* **contraflows** a flow of road traffic travelling in the opposite direction to the usual flow and close beside it.
[from *contra-* + *flow*]

contralto *NOUN* **contraltos** a female singer with a low voice.
[Italian, from *contra-* + *alto*]

contraption *NOUN* **contraptions** a strange-looking device or machine.
[origin unknown]

contrary *ADJECTIVE* **1** (*say* **kon**-tra-ree) of the opposite kind or direction etc.; opposed. **2** (*say* kon-**trair**-ee) awkward and obstinate.

contrary (*say* **kon**-tra-ree) *NOUN* the opposite.
- **on the contrary** the opposite is true.
[from old French; related to *contra-*]

contrast *NOUN* **contrasts** **1** a difference clearly seen when things are compared. **2** something showing a clear difference.

contrast *VERB* **contrasts, contrasting, contrasted** **1** compare or oppose two things in order to show that they are clearly different. **2** be clearly different when compared.
[from *contra-* + Latin *stare* = to stand]

contravene *VERB* **contravenes, contravening, contravened** act against a rule or law.
▷ **contravention** *noun*
[from *contra-* + Latin *venire* = come]

contretemps (*say* **kawn**-tre-tahn) *NOUN* a trivial disagreement or dispute.
[French, = out of time (in music)]

contribute *VERB* **contributes, contributing, contributed** **1** give money or help jointly with others. **2** write something for a newspaper or magazine etc. **3** help to cause something • *Fatigue contributed to the accident.*
▷ **contribution** *noun* **contributor** *noun*
contributory *adjective*
[from *con-* + Latin *tribuere* = bestow]

contrite *ADJECTIVE* very sorry for having done wrong.
[from Latin *contritus* = ground down]

contrivance *NOUN* **contrivances** an ingenious device.

contrive *VERB* **contrives, contriving, contrived** plan cleverly; find a way of doing or making something.
[from old French]

control *VERB* **controls, controlling, controlled** **1** have the power to make someone or something do what you want. **2** hold something, especially anger, in check; restrain.
▷ **controller** *noun*

control *NOUN* controlling a person or thing; authority.
- **in control** having control of something.
- **out of control** no longer able to be controlled.
[from old French]

controls *PLURAL NOUN* the switches etc. used to control a machine.

control tower *NOUN* **control towers** the building at an airport where people control air traffic by radio.

controversial *ADJECTIVE* causing controversy.

controversy (*say* kon-tro-ver-see or kon-trov-er-see) *NOUN* **controversies** a long argument or disagreement.
[from *contra-* + Latin *versum* = turned]

contusion *NOUN* **contusions** a bruise.
[from Latin]

conundrum *NOUN* **conundrums** a riddle; a hard question.
[origin unknown]

conurbation *NOUN* **conurbations** a large urban area where towns have spread into each other.
[from *con-* + Latin *urbs* = city]

convalesce *VERB* **convalesces, convalescing, convalesced** be recovering from an illness.
▷ **convalescence** *noun*
convalescent *adjective* & *noun*
[from *con-* + Latin *valescere* = grow strong]

convection *NOUN* the passing on of heat within liquid, air, or gas by circulation of the warmed parts.
[from *con-* + Latin *vectum* = carried]

convector *NOUN* **convectors** a heater that circulates warm air by convection.

convene *VERB* **convenes, convening, convened** summon or assemble for a meeting.
▷ **convener** *noun*
[from *con-* + Latin *venire* = come]

convenience *NOUN* **conveniences** **1** being convenient. **2** something that is convenient. **3** a public lavatory.
- **at your convenience** whenever you find convenient; as it suits you.

convenience food *NOUN* **convenience foods** food sold in a form that is already partly prepared and so is easy to use.

convenient *ADJECTIVE* easy to use or deal with or reach.
▷ **conveniently** *adverb*
[from Latin *convenire* = to suit]

convent *NOUN* **convents** a place where nuns live and work.
[same origin as *convene*]

convention *NOUN* **conventions** **1** an accepted way of doing things. **2** a formal assembly.
[from Latin *conventio* = a gathering, agreement]

conventional *ADJECTIVE* **1** done or doing things in the accepted way; traditional. **2** (said about weapons) not nuclear.
▷ **conventionally** *adverb*
conventionality *noun*

converge *VERB* **converges, converging, converged** come to or towards the same point from different directions.
▷ **convergence** *noun* **convergent** *adjective*
[from *con-* + Latin *vergere* = turn]

conversant *ADJECTIVE* (*formal*) familiar with something • *Are you conversant with the rules of this game?*
[from *converse*[1]]

conversation *NOUN* **conversations** talk between people.
▷ **conversational** *adjective*

converse[1] (*say* kon-verss) *VERB* **converses, conversing, conversed** hold a conversation.
[from Latin *conversare* = mix with people]

converse[2] (*say* kon-verss) *ADJECTIVE* opposite; contrary.
▷ **conversely** *adverb*

converse *NOUN* the opposite of something • *In fact, the converse is true.*
[same origin as *convert*]

conversion *NOUN* **conversions** converting.

convert (*say* kon-vert) *VERB* **converts, converting, converted** **1** change. **2** cause a person to change his or her beliefs. **3** kick a goal after scoring a try at rugby football.
▷ **converter** *noun*

A B C D E F G H I J K L M N O P Q R S T U V W X Y Z

convert (*say* kon-vert) *NOUN* **converts** a person who has changed his or her beliefs. [from *con-* + Latin *vertere* = turn]

convertible *ADJECTIVE* able to be converted.
▷ **convertibility** *noun*

convertible *NOUN* **convertibles** a car with a folding roof.

convex *ADJECTIVE* curved like the outside of a ball or circle. (The opposite is **concave**.)
▷ **convexity** *noun*
[from Latin *convexus* = arched]

convey *VERB* **conveys, conveying, conveyed 1** transport. **2** communicate a message or idea.
▷ **conveyor** *noun*
[from old French *conveier* = lead, escort]

conveyance *NOUN* **conveyances 1** conveying. **2** a vehicle for transporting people.

conveyancing *NOUN* transferring the legal ownership of land etc. from one person to another.

conveyor belt *NOUN* **conveyor belts** a continuous moving belt for moving objects from one place to another.

convict (*say* kon-vikt) *VERB* **convicts, convicting, convicted** prove or declare that a certain person is guilty of a crime.

convict (*say* kon-vikt) *NOUN* **convicts** a convicted person who is in prison.
[from *con-* + Latin *victum* = conquered]

conviction *NOUN* **convictions 1** convicting or being convicted of a crime. **2** being convinced. **3** a firm opinion or belief.
- **carry conviction** be convincing.

convince *VERB* **convinces, convincing, convinced** make a person feel certain that something is true.
[from *con-* + Latin *vincere* = conquer]

convivial *ADJECTIVE* sociable and lively.
[from Latin *convivium* = feast]

convoluted *ADJECTIVE* **1** coiled or twisted. **2** complicated.
▷ **convolution** *noun*
[from *con-* + Latin *volutum* = rolled]

convoy *NOUN* **convoys** a group of ships or lorries travelling together.
[same origin as *convey*]

convulse *VERB* **convulses, convulsing, convulsed** cause violent movements or convulsions.
▷ **convulsive** *adjective*
[from *con-* + Latin *vulsum* = pulled]

convulsion *NOUN* **convulsions 1** a violent movement of the body. **2** a violent upheaval.

coo *VERB* **coos, cooing, cooed** make a dove's soft murmuring sound.
▷ **coo** *noun*

cook *VERB* **cooks, cooking, cooked** make food ready to eat by heating it.
- **cook up** (*informal*) if you cook up a story or plan, you invent it.

cook *NOUN* **cooks** a person who cooks.
[from Latin]

cooker *NOUN* **cookers** a stove for cooking food.

cookery *NOUN* the skill of cooking food.

cookie *NOUN* **cookies** (*American*) a sweet biscuit.
[from Dutch *koekje* = little cake]

cool *ADJECTIVE* **1** fairly cold; not hot or warm. **2** calm; not enthusiastic.
▷ **coolly** *adverb* **coolness** *noun*

cool *VERB* **cools, cooling, cooled** make or become cool.
▷ **cooler** *noun*
[from Old English]

coop *NOUN* **coops** a cage for poultry.
[from Latin *cupa* = barrel]

cooped up *ADJECTIVE* having to stay in a place which is small and uncomfortable.

cooperate *VERB* **cooperates, cooperating, cooperated** work helpfully with other people.
▷ **cooperation** *noun* **cooperative** *adjective*
[from *co-* + Latin *operari* = operate]

co-opt *VERB* **co-opts, co-opting, co-opted** invite someone to become a member of a committee etc.
[from *co-* + Latin *optare* = choose]

coordinate *VERB* **coordinates, coordinating, coordinated** organize people or things to work properly together.
▷ **coordination** *noun* **coordinator** *noun*

coordinate *NOUN* **coordinates** either of the pair of numbers or letters used to fix the position of a point on a graph or map.
[from *co-* + Latin *ordinare* = arrange]

coot *NOUN* **coots** a waterbird with a horny white patch on its forehead.
[origin unknown]

cop *VERB* **cops, copping, copped**
- **cop it** get into trouble or be punished.

cop *NOUN* **cops** (*slang*) **1** a police officer. **2** a capture or arrest • *It's a fair cop!*
[from dialect *cap* = capture]

cope *VERB* **copes, coping, coped** manage or deal with something successfully.
[from French; related to *coup*]

copier *NOUN* **copiers** a device for copying things.

coping *NOUN* the top row of stones or bricks in a wall, usually slanted so that rainwater will run off.
[from an old word *cope* = to cover]

copious *ADJECTIVE* plentiful; in large amounts.
▷ **copiously** *adverb*
[same origin as *copy*]

copper[1] *NOUN* **coppers** **1** a reddish-brown metal used to make wire, coins, etc. **2** a reddish-brown colour. **3** a coin made of copper or metal of this colour.
▷ **copper** *adjective*
[via Old English from Latin *cyprium* = Cyprus metal (because the Romans got most of their copper from Cyprus)]

copper[2] *NOUN* **coppers** (*slang*) a policeman.
[from *cop*]

copperplate *NOUN* neat handwriting.
[because the books of examples of this writing for learners to copy were printed from copper plates]

coppice *NOUN* **coppices** a small group of trees.
[from Latin *colpus* = a blow (because from time to time the trees were cut back, and allowed to grow again)]

copra *NOUN* dried coconut kernels.
[via Portuguese and Spanish from Malayalam (a language spoken in southern India)]

copse *NOUN* **copses** a small group of trees.
[a different spelling of *coppice*]

copulate *VERB* **copulates, copulating, copulated** have sexual intercourse with someone.
▷ **copulation** *noun*
[from Latin *copulare* = link or join together]

copy *NOUN* **copies** **1** a thing made to look like another. **2** something written or typed out again from its original form. **3** one of a number of specimens of the same book or newspaper etc.

copy *VERB* **copies, copying, copied** **1** make a copy of something. **2** do the same as someone else; imitate.
[from Latin *copia* = plenty, abundance]

copyright *NOUN* the legal right to print a book, reproduce a picture, record a piece of music, etc.

coquette (*say* ko-ket) *NOUN* **coquettes** a woman who flirts.
▷ **coquettish** *adjective*
[French]

cor- *PREFIX* with; together. SEE **com-**.

coral *NOUN* **1** a hard red, pink, or white substance formed by the skeletons of tiny sea creatures massed together. **2** a pink colour.
[from Greek]

corbel *NOUN* **corbels** a piece of stone or wood that sticks out from a roof to support something.
[from old French]

cord *NOUN* **cords** **1** a long thin flexible strip of twisted threads or strands. **2** a piece of flex. **3** a cord-like structure in the body • *the spinal cord.* **4** corduroy.
[from Greek]
USAGE Do not confuse with **chord**.

cordial *NOUN* **cordials** a fruit-flavoured drink.

cordial *ADJECTIVE* warm and friendly.
▷ **cordially** *adverb* **cordiality** *noun*
[from Latin *cordis* = of the heart (a cordial was originally a drink given to stimulate the heart)]

cordon *NOUN* **cordons** a line of people, ships, fortifications, etc. placed round an area to guard or enclose it.

A B C D E F G H I J K L M N O P Q R S T U V W X Y Z

cordon *VERB* **cordons, cordoning, cordoned** surround with a cordon.
[from French or Italian; related to *cord*]

cordon bleu (*say* kor-dawn **bler**) *ADJECTIVE* (said about cooks and cookery) first-class.
[French, = blue ribbon]

corduroy *NOUN* cotton cloth with velvety ridges.
[from *cord* + *duroy* = a kind of woollen material]

core *NOUN* **cores 1** the part in the middle of something. **2** the hard central part of an apple or pear etc., containing the seeds.
[origin unknown]

corgi *NOUN* **corgis** a small dog with short legs and upright ears.
[from Welsh *cor* = dwarf + *ci* = dog]

cork *NOUN* **corks 1** the lightweight bark of a kind of oak tree. **2** a stopper for a bottle, made of cork or other material.

cork *VERB* **corks, corking, corked** close something with a cork.
[via Dutch and Spanish from Latin]

corkscrew *NOUN* **corkscrews 1** a device for removing corks from bottles. **2** a spiral.

corm *NOUN* **corms** a part of a plant rather like a bulb.
[from Greek]

cormorant *NOUN* **cormorants** a large black seabird.
[from Latin *corvus marinus* = sea raven]

corn[1] *NOUN* **1** the seed of wheat and similar plants. **2** a plant, such as wheat, grown for its grain. **3** (*American & Australian/NZ*) maize.
[from Old English]

corn[2] *NOUN* **corns** a small hard lump on the foot.
[from Latin *cornu* = horn]

cornea *NOUN* **corneas** the transparent covering over the pupil of the eye.
▷ **corneal** *adjective*
[from Latin]

corned beef *NOUN* tinned beef preserved with salt.
[from *corn*[1] (because of the corns (= grains) of coarse salt that were used)]

corner *NOUN* **corners 1** the angle or area where two lines or sides or walls meet or where two streets join. **2** a free hit or kick from the corner of a hockey or football field. **3** a region • *a quiet corner of the world.*

corner *VERB* **corners, cornering, cornered 1** drive someone into a corner or other position from which it is difficult to escape. **2** travel round a corner. **3** obtain possession of all or most of something • *corner the market.*
[from Latin *cornu* = horn, tip]

cornerstone *NOUN* **cornerstones 1** a stone built into the corner at the base of a building. **2** something that is a vital foundation.

cornet *NOUN* **cornets 1** a cone-shaped wafer etc. holding ice cream. **2** a musical instrument rather like a trumpet.
[French, = small horn]

cornflakes *PLURAL NOUN* toasted maize flakes eaten as a breakfast cereal.

cornflour *NOUN* flour made from maize or rice, used in sauces, milk puddings, etc.

cornflower *NOUN* **cornflowers** a plant with blue flowers that grows wild in fields of corn.

cornice *NOUN* **cornices** a band of ornamental moulding on walls just below a ceiling or at the top of a building.
[via French from Italian]

cornucopia *NOUN* **1** a horn-shaped container overflowing with fruit and flowers. **2** a plentiful supply of good things.
[from Latin *cornu* = horn + *copiae* = of plenty]

corny *ADJECTIVE* **cornier, corniest** (*informal*) **1** repeated so often that people are tired of it • *a corny joke.* **2** sentimental.
[originally = rustic, simple: from *corn*[1]]

corollary (*say* ker-**ol**-er-ee) *NOUN* **corollaries** a fact etc. that logically results from another • *The work is difficult and, as a corollary, tiring.*
[from Latin]

corona (*say* kor-**oh**-na) *NOUN* **coronas** a circle of light round something.
[Latin, = crown]

coronary *NOUN* **coronaries** short for **coronary thrombosis**, blockage of an artery carrying blood to the heart.
[from *corona* (because the coronary arteries encircle the heart like a crown)]

coronation *NOUN* **coronations** the crowning of a king or queen.
[same origin as *corona*]

coroner *NOUN* **coroners** an official who holds an inquiry into the cause of a death thought to be from unnatural causes.
[from old French]

coronet *NOUN* **coronets** a small crown.
[from old French]

corporal[1] *NOUN* **corporals** a soldier ranking next below a sergeant.
[via French from Italian]

corporal[2] *ADJECTIVE* to do with the body.
[from Latin *corpus* = body]

corporal punishment *NOUN* punishment by being whipped or beaten.

corporate *ADJECTIVE* shared by members of a group • *corporate responsibility.*
[from Latin *corporare* = unite in one body]

corporation *NOUN* **corporations** **1** a group of people elected to govern a town. **2** a group of people legally authorized to act as an individual in business etc.

corps (*say* kor) *NOUN* **corps** (*say* korz) **1** a special army unit • *the Medical Corps.* **2** a large group of soldiers. **3** a set of people doing the same job • *the diplomatic corps.*
[French, from Latin *corpus* = body]

corps de ballet (*say* kor der bal-ay) *NOUN* the whole group of dancers (not the soloists) in a ballet.
[French]

corpse *NOUN* **corpses** a dead body.
[from Latin *corpus* = body]

corpulent *ADJECTIVE* having a bulky body; fat.
▷ **corpulence** *noun*
[from Latin]

corpuscle *NOUN* **corpuscles** one of the red or white cells in blood.
[from Latin *corpusculum* = little body]

corral (*say* kor-ahl) *NOUN* **corrals** (*American*) an enclosure for horses, cattle, etc.
[from Spanish or Portuguese]

correct *ADJECTIVE* **1** true; accurate; without any mistakes. **2** proper; done or said in an approved way.
▷ **correctly** *adverb* **correctness** *noun*

correct *VERB* **corrects, correcting, corrected** **1** make a thing correct by altering or adjusting it. **2** mark the mistakes in something. **3** point out or punish a person's faults.
▷ **correction** *noun* **corrective** *adjective*
[from *cor-* + Latin *rectus* = straight]

correlate *VERB* **correlates, correlating, correlated** compare or connect things systematically.
▷ **correlation** *noun*
[from *cor-* + *relate*]

correspond *VERB* **corresponds, corresponding, corresponded** **1** write letters to each other. **2** agree; match • *Your story corresponds with his.* **3** be similar or equivalent • *Their assembly corresponds to our parliament.*
[from *cor-* + *respond*]

correspondence *NOUN* **1** letters; writing letters. **2** similarity; agreement.

correspondent *NOUN* **correspondents** **1** a person who writes letters to another. **2** a person employed to gather news and send reports to a newspaper or radio station etc.

corridor *NOUN* **corridors** a passage in a building.
[via French from Italian]

corroborate *VERB* **corroborates, corroborating, corroborated** help to confirm a statement etc.
▷ **corroboration** *noun*
[from *cor-* + Latin *roborare* = strengthen]

corrode *VERB* **corrodes, corroding, corroded** destroy metal gradually by chemical action.
▷ **corrosion** *noun*
[from *cor-* + Latin *rodere* = gnaw]

corrosive *ADJECTIVE* able to corrode something • *corrosive acid.*

corrugated *ADJECTIVE* shaped into alternate ridges and grooves • *corrugated iron.*
[from *cor-* + Latin *ruga* = wrinkle]

corrupt *ADJECTIVE* **1** dishonest; accepting bribes. **2** wicked. **3** decaying.

corrupt *VERB* **corrupts, corrupting, corrupted** **1** cause someone to become dishonest or wicked. **2** spoil; cause something to decay.
▷ **corruption** *noun* **corruptible** *adjective*
[from *cor-* + Latin *ruptum* = broken]

corsair *NOUN* **corsairs** **1** a pirate ship. **2** a pirate.
[from French]

corset *NOUN* **corsets** a close-fitting piece of underwear worn to shape or support the body.
[old French, = small body]

cortège (*say* kort-ay*zh*) *NOUN* **cortèges** a funeral procession.
[French]

cosh *NOUN* **coshes** a heavy weapon for hitting people.
[origin unknown]

cosine *NOUN* **cosines** (in a right-angled triangle) the ratio of the length of a side adjacent to one of the acute angles to the length of the hypotenuse. (COMPARE **sine**)
[from *co-* + *sine*]

cosmetic *NOUN* **cosmetics** a substance (e.g. face powder, lipstick) put on the skin to make it look more attractive.
[from Greek *kosmein* = arrange, decorate]

cosmetic surgery *NOUN* surgery carried out to make people look more attractive.

cosmic *ADJECTIVE* **1** to do with the universe. **2** to do with outer space • *cosmic rays.*
[from *cosmos*]

cosmonaut *NOUN* **cosmonauts** a Russian astronaut.
[from *cosmos* + *astronaut*]

cosmopolitan *ADJECTIVE* from many countries; containing people from many countries.
[from *cosmos* + Greek *polites* = citizen]

cosmos (*say* koz-moss) *NOUN* the universe.
[from Greek, = the world]

Cossack *NOUN* **Cossacks** a member of a people of south Russia, famous as horsemen.

cosset *VERB* **cossets, cosseting, cosseted** pamper; treat someone very kindly and lovingly.
[from old French]

cost *NOUN* **costs** **1** the amount of money needed to buy, do, or make something. **2** the effort or loss needed to achieve something.
- **at all costs** or
- **at any cost** no matter what the cost or difficulty may be.

cost *VERB* **costs, costing, cost** **1** have a certain amount as its price or charge. **2** cause the loss of • *This war has cost many lives.* (*past tense* is **costed**) **3** estimate the cost of something.
[from old French]

costermonger *NOUN* **costermongers** a person who sells fruit etc. from a barrow in the street.
[from old words *costard* = large apple + *monger* = trader]

costly *ADJECTIVE* **costlier, costliest** expensive.
▷ **costliness** *noun*

cost of living *NOUN* the average amount each person in a country spends on food, clothing, and housing.

costume *NOUN* **costumes** **1** clothes, especially for a particular purpose or of a particular place or period. **2** the clothes worn by an actor.
[via French from Italian; related to *custom*]

cosy *ADJECTIVE* **cosier, cosiest** warm and comfortable.
▷ **cosily** *adverb* **cosiness** *noun*

cosy *NOUN* **cosies** a cover placed over a teapot or boiled egg to keep it hot.
[origin unknown]

cot *NOUN* **cots** a baby's bed with high sides.
[from Hindi *khat* = bedstead]

cottage *NOUN* **cottages** a small simple house, especially in the country.
[from Old English]

cottage cheese *NOUN* soft white cheese made from curds of skimmed milk.

cottage pie *NOUN* **cottage pies** a dish of minced meat covered with mashed potato and baked.

cottager *NOUN* **cottagers** a person who lives in a country cottage.

cotton *NOUN* **1** a soft white substance covering the seeds of a tropical plant; the plant itself. **2** thread made from this substance. **3** cloth made from cotton thread.
[via French from Arabic]

cotton wool *NOUN* soft fluffy wadding originally made from cotton.

couch *NOUN* **couches** **1** a long soft seat like a sofa but with only one end raised. **2** a sofa or settee.

couch *VERB* **couches, couching, couched** express in words of a certain kind • *The request was couched in polite terms.*
[from French *coucher* = lay down flat]

cougar (*say* koo-ger) *NOUN* **cougars** (*American*) a puma.
[via French from Guarani (a South American language)]

cough (*say* kof) *VERB* **coughs, coughing, coughed** send out air from the lungs with a sudden sharp sound.

cough *NOUN* **coughs** **1** the act or sound of coughing. **2** an illness that makes you cough.
[imitating the sound]

could *past tense* of **can**².

couldn't (*mainly spoken*) could not.

council *NOUN* **councils** a group of people chosen or elected to organize or discuss something, especially those elected to organize the affairs of a town or county.
[from Latin *concilium* = assembly]
USAGE Do not confuse with **counsel**.

council house *NOUN* **council houses** a house owned and let to tenants by a town council.

councillor *NOUN* **councillors** a member of a town or county council.

council tax *NOUN* **council taxes** a tax paid to a local authority to pay for local services, based on the estimated value of someone's house or flat.

counsel *NOUN* **counsels** **1** advice • *give counsel.* **2** a barrister or group of barristers representing someone in a lawsuit.
- **take counsel with** consult.
USAGE Do not confuse with **council**.

counsel *VERB* **counsels, counselling, counselled** give advice to someone; recommend.
[from Latin *consulere* = consult]

counsellor *NOUN* **counsellors** an adviser.

count¹ *VERB* **counts, counting, counted** **1** say numbers in their proper order. **2** find the total of something by using numbers. **3** include in a total • *There are six of us, counting the dog.* **4** be important • *It's what you do that counts.* **5** regard; consider • *I should count it an honour to be invited.*
- **count on** rely on.

count *NOUN* **counts** **1** counting. **2** a number reached by counting; a total. **3** any of the points being considered, e.g. in accusing someone of crimes • *guilty on all counts.*
[via French from Latin *computare* = compute]

count² *NOUN* **counts** a foreign nobleman.
[from old French]

countdown *NOUN* **countdowns** counting numbers backwards to zero before an event, especially the launching of a space rocket.

countenance *NOUN* **countenances** a person's face; the expression on the face.

countenance *VERB* **countenances, countenancing, countenanced** give approval to; allow • *Will they countenance this plan?*
[from old French]

counter¹ *NOUN* **counters** **1** a flat surface over which customers are served in a shop, bank, etc. **2** a small round playing piece used in certain board games. **3** a device for counting things.
[same origin as *count*¹]

counter² *VERB* **counters, countering, countered** **1** counteract. **2** counter-attack; return an opponent's blow by hitting back.

counter *ADVERB* contrary to something • *This is counter to what we really want.*
[via old French from Latin *contra* = against]

counter- *PREFIX* **1** against; opposing; done in return (as in *counter-attack*). **2** corresponding (as in *countersign*).
[from Latin *contra* = against]

counteract *VERB* **counteracts, counteracting, counteracted** act against something and reduce or prevent its effects.
▷ **counteraction** *noun*
[from *counter-* + *act*]

counter-attack *VERB* **counter-attacks, counter-attacking, counter-attacked** attack to oppose or return an enemy's attack.
▷ **counter-attack** *noun*

counterbalance *NOUN* **counterbalances** a weight or influence that balances another.
▷ **counterbalance** *verb*
[from *counter-* + *balance*]

counterfeit (*say* kownt-er-feet) *ADJECTIVE* fake; not genuine.

counterfeit *NOUN* **counterfeits** a forgery or imitation.

counterfeit *VERB* **counterfeits, counterfeiting, counterfeited** forge or make an imitation of something.
[from old French *countrefait* = made in opposition]

counterfoil *NOUN* **counterfoils** a section of a cheque or receipt etc. that is torn off and kept as a record.
[from *counter-* + an old sense of *foil*[1] = sheet of paper]

countermand *VERB* **countermands, countermanding, countermanded** cancel a command or instruction that has been given.
[from *counter-* + Latin *mandare* = to command]

counterpane *NOUN* **counterpanes** a bedspread.
[from old French]

counterpart *NOUN* **counterparts** a person or thing that corresponds to another • *Their President is the counterpart of our Prime Minister.*

counterpoint *NOUN* a method of combining melodies in harmony.
[from Latin *cantus contrapunctus* = song written opposite (to the original melody)]

countersign *VERB* **countersigns, countersigning, countersigned** add another signature to a document to give it authority.

counterweight *NOUN* a counterbalancing weight or influence.

countess *NOUN* **countesses** the wife or widow of a count or earl; a female count.

countless *ADJECTIVE* too many to count.

countrified *ADJECTIVE* like the country.

country *NOUN* **countries** **1** the land occupied by a nation. **2** all the people of a country. **3** the countryside.

country dance *NOUN* **country dances** a folk dance.

countryman *NOUN* **countrymen** **1** a man who lives in the countryside. **2** a man who belongs to the same country as yourself.

countryside *NOUN* an area with fields, woods, villages, etc. away from towns.

countrywoman *NOUN* **countrywomen** **1** a woman who lives in the countryside. **2** a woman who belongs to the same country as yourself.

county *NOUN* **counties** each of the main areas that a country is divided into for local government.
[originally = the land of a count (*count*[2])]

coup (*say* koo) *NOUN* **coups** a sudden action taken to win power; a clever victory.
[French, = a blow]

coup de grâce (*say* koo der grahs) *NOUN* a stroke or blow that puts an end to something.
[French, = mercy-blow]

coup d'état (*say* koo day-tah) *NOUN* **coups d'état** the sudden overthrow of a government.
[French, = blow of State]

couple *NOUN* **couples** two people or things considered together; a pair.

couple *VERB* **couples, coupling, coupled** fasten or link two things together.
[from Latin *copulare* = link or join together]

couplet *NOUN* **couplets** a pair of lines in rhyming verse.

coupon *NOUN* **coupons** a piece of paper that gives you the right to receive or do something.
[French, = piece cut off]

A B C D E F G H I J K L M N O P Q R S T U V W X Y Z

courage *NOUN* the ability to face danger or difficulty or pain even when you are afraid; bravery.
▷ **courageous** *adjective*
[from Latin *cor* = heart]

courgette (*say* koor-*zh*et) *NOUN* **courgettes** a kind of small vegetable marrow.
[French, = small gourd]

courier (*say* koor-ee-er) *NOUN* **couriers 1** a messenger. **2** a person employed to guide and help a group of tourists.
[old French, = runner]

course *NOUN* **courses 1** the direction in which something goes; a route • *the ship's course.* **2** a series of events or actions etc. • *Your best course is to start again.* **3** a series of lessons, exercises, etc. **4** part of a meal • *the meat course.* **5** a racecourse. **6** a golf course.
- **of course** without a doubt; as we expected.

course *VERB* **courses, coursing, coursed** move or flow freely • *Tears coursed down his cheeks.*
[from Latin *cursus* = running]

court *NOUN* **courts 1** the royal household. **2** a lawcourt; the judges etc. in a lawcourt. **3** an enclosed area for games such as tennis or netball. **4** a courtyard.

court *VERB* **courts, courting, courted** try to win somebody's love or support.
[from old French]

courteous (*say* ker-tee-us) *ADJECTIVE* polite and helpful.
▷ **courteously** *adverb* **courtesy** *noun*
[from old French, = having manners suitable for a royal court]

courtier *NOUN* **courtiers** (*old use*) one of a king's or queen's companions at court.

courtly *ADJECTIVE* dignified and polite.

court martial *NOUN* **courts martial 1** a court for trying people who have broken military law. **2** a trial in this court.
[originally *martial court*]

court-martial *VERB* **court-martials, court-martialling, court-martialled** try a person by a court martial.

courtship *NOUN* **1** courting someone, especially a boyfriend or girlfriend. **2** the mating ritual of some birds and animals.

courtyard *NOUN* **courtyards** a space surrounded by walls or buildings.

cousin *NOUN* **cousins** a child of your uncle or aunt.
[from old French]

cove *NOUN* **coves** a small bay.
[from Old English *cofa* = a hollow]

coven (*say* kuv-en) *NOUN* **covens** a group of witches.
[same origin as *convene*]

covenant (*say* kuv-en-ant) *NOUN* **covenants** a formal agreement; a contract.
[same origin as *convene*]

Coventry *NOUN*
- **send a person to Coventry** refuse to speak to him or her.
[possibly because, during the Civil War, Cavalier prisoners were sent to Coventry (a city in the Midlands): the citizens supported the Roundheads, and would not speak to the Cavaliers]

cover *VERB* **covers, covering, covered 1** place one thing over or round another; conceal. **2** travel a certain distance • *We covered ten miles a day.* **3** aim a gun at or near somebody • *I've got you covered.* **4** protect by insurance or a guarantee • *These goods are covered against fire or theft.* **5** be enough money to pay for something • *£12 should cover my fare.* **6** deal with or include • *The book covers all kinds of farming.*
- **cover up** conceal something, especially an awkward fact or piece of information.

cover *NOUN* **covers 1** a thing used for covering something else; a lid, wrapper, envelope, etc. **2** the binding of a book. **3** something that hides or shelters or protects you.
[from old French]

coverage *NOUN* the amount of time or space given to reporting an event in a newspaper or broadcast.

coverlet *NOUN* **coverlets** a bedspread.
[from old French *covrir lit* = cover the bed]

covert (*say* kuv-ert) *NOUN* **coverts** an area of thick bushes etc. in which birds and animals hide.

covert *ADJECTIVE* done secretly.
[old French, = covered]

cover-up *NOUN* **cover-ups** an attempt to conceal information about something, especially a crime or mistake.

covet (*say* kuv-it) *VERB* **covets, coveting, coveted** wish to have something, especially a thing that belongs to someone else.
▷ **covetous** *adjective*
[from old French; related to *cupidity*]

covey (*say* kuv-ee) *NOUN* **coveys** a group of partridges.
[from old French]

cow[1] *NOUN* **cows** the fully-grown female of cattle or of certain other large animals (e.g. elephant, whale, seal).
[from Old English]

cow[2] *VERB* **cows, cowing, cowed** intimidate; subdue someone by bullying.
[from Old Norse]

coward *NOUN* **cowards** a person who has no courage and shows fear in a shameful way.
▷ **cowardice** *noun* **cowardly** *adjective*
[from old French]

cowboy *NOUN* **cowboys** a man in charge of grazing cattle on a ranch in the USA.

cower *VERB* **cowers, cowering, cowered** crouch or shrink back in fear.
[from old German]

cowl *NOUN* **cowls 1** a monk's hood. **2** a hood-shaped covering, e.g. on a chimney.
[from Old English]

cowshed *NOUN* **cowsheds** a shed for cattle.

cowslip *NOUN* **cowslips** a wild plant with small yellow flowers in spring.
[from Old English]

cox *NOUN* **coxes** a coxswain.
[abbreviation]

coxswain (*say* kok-swayn or kok-sun) *NOUN* **coxswains 1** a person who steers a rowing boat. **2** a sailor with special duties.
[from an old word *cock* = small boat, + *swain*]

coy *ADJECTIVE* pretending to be shy or modest; bashful.
▷ **coyly** *adverb* **coyness** *noun*
[from old French; related to *quiet*]

coyote (*say* koi-oh-ti) *NOUN* **coyotes** a North American mammal, similar to but smaller than a wolf.
[via Mexican Spanish from Nahuatl (an American Indian language) *coyotl*]

crab *NOUN* **crabs** a shellfish with ten legs, the first pair being a set of pincers.
[from Old English]

crab apple *NOUN* **crab apples** a small sour apple.
[probably from a Scandinavian language]

crack *NOUN* **cracks 1** a line on the surface of something where it has broken but not come completely apart. **2** a narrow gap. **3** a sudden sharp noise. **4** a knock • *a crack on the head.* **5** (*informal*) a joke; a wisecrack. **6** a drug made from cocaine.

crack *ADJECTIVE* (*informal*) first-class • *He is a crack shot.*

crack *VERB* **cracks, cracking, cracked** **1** make or get a crack; split. **2** make a sudden sharp noise. **3** break down • *He cracked under the strain.*
- **crack a joke** tell a joke.
- **crack down on** (*informal*) stop something that is illegal or against rules.
- **get cracking** (*informal*) get busy.

[from Old English]

cracker *NOUN* **crackers 1** a paper tube that bangs when pulled apart. **2** a thin biscuit.

crackle *VERB* **crackles, crackling, crackled** make small cracking sounds • *The fire crackled in the grate.*
▷ **crackle** *noun*
[from *crack*]

crackling *NOUN* crisp skin on roast pork.

-cracy *SUFFIX* forms nouns meaning 'ruling' or 'government' (e.g. *democracy*).
[from Greek *-kratia* = rule]

cradle *NOUN* **cradles 1** a small cot for a baby. **2** a supporting framework.

cradle *VERB* **cradles, cradling, cradled** hold gently.
[from Old English]

craft *NOUN* **crafts 1** a job that needs skill, especially with the hands. **2** skill. **3** cunning or trickery. **4** (*plural* **craft**) a ship or boat; an aircraft or spacecraft.
[from Old English]

craftsman *NOUN* **craftsmen** a person who is good at a craft.
▷ **craftsmanship** *noun*

crafty *ADJECTIVE* **craftier, craftiest** cunning.
▷ **craftily** *adverb* **craftiness** *noun*
[originally = skilful: from *craft*]

crag *NOUN* **crags** a steep piece of rough rock.
▷ **craggy** *adjective* **cragginess** *noun*
[a Celtic word]

cram *VERB* **crams, cramming, crammed**
1 push many things into something so that it is very full. **2** learn as many facts as you can in a short time just before an examination.
[from Old English]

cramp *NOUN* **cramps** pain caused by a muscle tightening suddenly.

cramp *VERB* **cramps, cramping, cramped** hinder someone's freedom or growth etc.
[via old French from Germanic]

cramped *ADJECTIVE* in a space that is too small or tight.

cranberry *NOUN* **cranberries** a small sour red berry used for making jelly and sauce.
[from German]

crane *NOUN* **cranes** **1** a machine for lifting and moving heavy objects. **2** a large wading bird with long legs and neck.

crane *VERB* **cranes, craning, craned** stretch your neck to try and see something.
[from Old English]

crane fly *NOUN* **crane flies** a flying insect with very long thin legs.

cranium *NOUN* **craniums** the skull.
[from Greek]

crank *NOUN* **cranks** **1** an L-shaped part used for changing the direction of movement in machinery. **2** a person with strange or fanatical ideas.
▷ **cranky** *adjective*

crank *VERB* **cranks, cranking, cranked** move by means of a crank.
[from Old English]

cranny *NOUN* **crannies** a crevice.
[from old French]

crash *NOUN* **crashes** **1** the loud noise of something breaking or colliding. **2** a violent collision or fall. **3** a sudden drop or failure.

crash *VERB* **crashes, crashing, crashed**
1 make or have a crash; cause to crash.
2 move with a crash. **3** (said about a computer system) stop working suddenly.

crash *ADJECTIVE* intensive • *a crash course.*
[imitating the sound]

crash helmet *NOUN* **crash helmets** a padded helmet worn by cyclists and motorcyclists to protect the head in a crash.

crash landing *NOUN* **crash landings** an emergency landing of an aircraft, which usually damages it.
▷ **crash-land** *verb*

crass *ADJECTIVE* **1** very obvious or shocking; gross • *crass ignorance.* **2** very stupid.
[from Latin *crassus* = thick]

-crat *SUFFIX* forms nouns meaning 'ruler' or 'believer in some type of government'.
[same origin as *-cracy*]

crate *NOUN* **crates** **1** a packing case made of strips of wood. **2** an open container with compartments for carrying bottles.
[origin unknown]

crater *NOUN* **craters** **1** the mouth of a volcano. **2** a bowl-shaped cavity or hollow caused by an explosion or impact.
[from Greek *krater* = bowl]

cravat *NOUN* **cravats** a short wide scarf worn by men round the neck and tucked into an open-necked shirt.
[from French *Cravate* = Croatian (because Croatian soldiers wore linen cravats)]

crave *VERB* **craves, craving, craved**
1 desire strongly. **2** (*formal*) beg for something.
[from Old English]

craven *ADJECTIVE* cowardly.
[from old French *cravanté* = defeated]

craving *NOUN* **cravings** a strong desire; a longing.

crawl *VERB* **crawls, crawling, crawled**
1 move with the body close to the ground or other surface, or on hands and knees.
2 move slowly. **3** be covered with crawling things.
▷ **crawler** *noun*

crawl *NOUN* **1** a crawling movement. **2** a very slow pace. **3** an overarm swimming stroke.
[origin unknown]

crayon *NOUN* **crayons** a stick or pencil of coloured wax etc. for drawing.
[French]

craze *NOUN* **crazes** a temporary enthusiasm.
[probably from Old Norse]

crazed *ADJECTIVE* driven insane.

crazy *ADJECTIVE* **crazier, craziest** **1** insane. **2** very foolish • *this crazy idea.*
▷ **crazily** *adverb* **craziness** *noun*
[from *craze*]

crazy paving *NOUN* paving made of oddly-shaped pieces of stone etc.

creak *NOUN* **creaks** a harsh squeak like that of a stiff door hinge.
▷ **creaky** *adjective*

creak *VERB* **creaks, creaking, creaked** make a creak.
[imitating the sound]

cream *NOUN* **creams** **1** the fatty part of milk. **2** a yellowish-white colour. **3** a food containing or looking like cream • *chocolate cream.* **4** a soft substance • *shoe cream.* **5** the best part.
▷ **creamy** *adjective*

cream *VERB* **creams, creaming, creamed** make creamy; beat butter etc. until it is soft like cream.
- **cream off** remove the best part of something.
[from old French]

crease *NOUN* **creases** **1** a line made in something by folding, pressing, or crushing it. **2** a line on a cricket pitch marking a batsman's or bowler's position.

crease *VERB* **creases, creasing, creased** make a crease or creases in something.
[a different spelling of *crest*]

create *VERB* **creates, creating, created** **1** bring into existence; make or produce, especially something that no one has made before. **2** (*slang*) make a fuss; grumble.
▷ **creation** *noun*
[from Latin]

creative *ADJECTIVE* showing imagination and thought as well as skill • *his creative use of language.*
▷ **creativity** *noun*

creator *NOUN* **creators** a person who creates something.
- **the Creator** God.

creature *NOUN* **creatures** a living being, especially an animal.
[from Latin *creatura* = a created being]

crèche (*say* kresh) *NOUN* **crèches** a place where babies and young children are looked after while their parents are at work.
[French]

credence *NOUN* belief • *Don't give it any credence.*
[from Latin *credentia* = belief]

credentials *PLURAL NOUN* **1** documents showing a person's identity, qualifications, etc. **2** a person's past achievements that make them suitable for something.
[same origin as *credence*]

credible *ADJECTIVE* able to be believed; convincing.
▷ **credibly** *adverb* **credibility** *noun*
[same origin as *credit*]
USAGE Do not confuse with **creditable** or *credulous.*

credit *NOUN* **credits** **1** a source of pride or honour • *a credit to the school.* **2** praise or acknowledgement given for some achievement or good quality • *I must give you credit for persistence.* **3** an arrangement trusting a person to pay for something later on. **4** an amount of money in an account at a bank etc., or entered in a financial account as paid in. (COMPARE **debit**) **5** belief or trust • *I put no credit in this rumour.*
- **credits** a list of people who have helped to produce a film or television programme.

credit *VERB* **credits, crediting, credited** **1** believe. **2** attribute; say that a person has done or achieved something • *Columbus is credited with the discovery of America.* **3** enter something as a credit in a financial account. (COMPARE **debit**)
[from Latin *credere* = believe, trust]

creditable *ADJECTIVE* deserving praise.
▷ **creditably** *adverb*
USAGE Do not confuse with **credible**.

credit card *NOUN* **credit cards** a card authorizing a person to buy on credit.

creditor *NOUN* **creditors** a person to whom money is owed.

credulous *ADJECTIVE* too ready to believe things; gullible.
[from Latin *credulus* = trusting]
USAGE Do not confuse with **credible**.

creed *NOUN* **creeds** a set or formal statement of beliefs.
[from Latin *credo* = I believe]

creek *NOUN* **creeks 1** a narrow inlet. **2** (*American & Australian*) a small stream.
- **up the creek** (*slang*) in difficulties.
[from Old Norse]

creep *VERB* **creeps, creeping, crept 1** move along close to the ground. **2** move quietly. **3** come gradually. **4** prickle with fear • *It makes my flesh creep.*

creep *NOUN* **creeps 1** a creeping movement. **2** (*slang*) an unpleasant person, especially one who seeks to win favour.
- **the creeps** (*informal*) a nervous feeling caused by fear or dislike.
[from Old English]

creeper *NOUN* **creepers** a plant that grows along the ground or up a wall etc.

creepy *ADJECTIVE* **creepier, creepiest** frightening and sinister.

cremate *VERB* **cremates, cremating, cremated** burn a dead body to ashes.
▷ **cremation** *noun*
[from Latin *cremare* = to burn]

crematorium *NOUN* **crematoria** a place where corpses are cremated.

crème de la crème (*say* krem der la krem) *NOUN* the very best of something.
[French, = cream of the cream]

creosote *NOUN* an oily brown liquid used to prevent wood from rotting.
[via German from Greek *kreas* = flesh + *soter* = saviour (because a form of it was used as an antiseptic)]

crêpe (*say* krayp) *NOUN* **crêpes** a thin pancake.
[French]

crêpe paper *NOUN* paper with a wrinkled surface.

crescendo (*say* krish-**end**-oh) *NOUN* **crescendos** a gradual increase in loudness.
[Italian, = increasing]

crescent *NOUN* **crescents 1** a narrow curved shape coming to a point at each end. **2** a curved street.
[originally = the new moon: from Latin *crescens* = growing]

cress *NOUN* a plant with hot-tasting leaves, used in salads and sandwiches.
[from Old English]

crest *NOUN* **crests 1** a tuft of hair, skin, or feathers on an animal's or bird's head. **2** the top of a hill or wave etc. **3** a design used on notepaper etc.
▷ **crested** *adjective*
[from Latin *crista* = tuft, plume]

crestfallen *ADJECTIVE* disappointed or dejected.

cretin (*say* **kret**-in) *NOUN* **cretins** (*slang*) a stupid person.
[via French from Latin *Christianus* = Christian (as a reminder that handicapped people were Christian souls, and should be cared for)]

crevasse (*say* kri-**vass**) *NOUN* **crevasses** a deep open crack, especially in a glacier.
[same origin as *crevice*]

crevice *NOUN* **crevices** a narrow opening, especially in a rock or wall.
[from old French *crever* = burst, split]

crew[1] *NOUN* **crews 1** the people working in a ship or aircraft. **2** a group working together • *the camera crew.*
[from old French]

crew[2] *past tense* of **crow**[2].

crib *NOUN* **cribs 1** a baby's cot. **2** a framework holding fodder for animals. **3** a model representing the Nativity of Jesus Christ. **4** something cribbed. **5** a translation for use by students. **6** cribbage.

crib *VERB* **cribs, cribbing, cribbed** copy someone else's work.
[from Old English]

cribbage *NOUN* a card game.
[origin unknown]

crick *NOUN* **cricks** painful stiffness in the neck or back.
[origin unknown]

cricket[1] *NOUN* a game played outdoors between teams with a ball, bats, and two wickets.
▷ **cricketer** *noun*
[origin unknown]

cricket[2] *NOUN* **crickets** a brown insect like a grasshopper.
[from old French *criquer* = crackle (imitating the sound it makes)]

crime *NOUN* **crimes** **1** an action that breaks the law. **2** law-breaking.
[from Latin]

criminal *NOUN* **criminals** a person who has committed a crime or crimes.
▷ **criminal** *adjective* **criminally** *adverb*

criminology *NOUN* the study of crime.
[from Latin *crimen* = offence, + *-logy*]

crimp *VERB* **crimps, crimping, crimped** press into small ridges.
[origin unknown]

crimson *ADJECTIVE* deep red.
▷ **crimson** *noun*
[from Arabic *kirmiz* = an insect which was used to make crimson dye]

cringe *VERB* **cringes, cringing, cringed** shrink back in fear; cower.
[from Old English *crincan* = yield, fall in battle]

crinkle *VERB* **crinkles, crinkling, crinkled** make or become wrinkled.
▷ **crinkly** *adjective*
[same origin as *cringe*]

crinoline *NOUN* **crinolines** a long skirt worn over a framework that makes it stand out.
[French]

cripple *NOUN* **cripples** a person who is permanently lame.

cripple *VERB* **cripples, crippling, crippled** **1** make a person lame. **2** weaken or damage something seriously.
[from Old English]

crisis *NOUN* **crises** an important and dangerous or difficult situation.
[from Greek]

crisp *ADJECTIVE* **1** very dry so that it breaks with a snap. **2** fresh and stiff • *a crisp £10 note.* **3** cold and dry • *a crisp morning.* **4** brisk and sharp • *a crisp manner.*
▷ **crisply** *adverb* **crispness** *noun*

crisp *NOUN* **crisps** a very thin fried slice of potato, usually sold in packets.
[from Latin]

criss-cross *ADJECTIVE & ADVERB* with crossing lines.
▷ **criss-cross** *verb*
[from *Christ-cross* (the cross on which Christ died)]

criterion (*say* kry-**teer**-ee-on) *NOUN* **criteria** a standard by which something is judged or decided.
[from Greek, = means of judging]
USAGE Note that *criteria* is a plural. It is incorrect to say 'a criteria' or 'this criteria'; correct usage is *this criterion, these criteria.*

critic *NOUN* **critics** **1** a person who gives opinions on books, plays, films, music, etc. **2** a person who criticizes.
[from Greek *krites* = judge]

critical *ADJECTIVE* **1** criticizing. **2** to do with critics or criticism. **3** to do with or at a crisis; very serious.
▷ **critically** *adverb*

criticism *NOUN* **criticisms** **1** criticizing; pointing out faults. **2** the work of a critic.

criticize *VERB* **criticizes, criticizing, criticized** say that a person or thing has faults.

critique (*say* kri-**teek**) *NOUN* an explanation of the good and bad qualities of something such as a literary work or a set of political ideas.
[from Greek *kritikos*]

croak *NOUN* **croaks** a deep hoarse sound like that of a frog.
▷ **croak** *verb*
[imitating the sound]

crochet (*say* **kroh**-shay) *NOUN* a kind of needlework done by using a hooked needle to loop a thread into patterns.
▷ **crochet** *verb*
crochets, crocheting, crocheted [from old French *croc* = hook]

crock[1] *NOUN* **crocks** a piece of crockery.
[from Old English]

crock[2] *NOUN* **crocks** (*informal*) a decrepit person or thing.
[origin unknown]

crockery *NOUN* household china.
[from an old word *crocker* = potter]

crocodile *NOUN* **crocodiles** **1** a large tropical reptile with a thick skin, long tail, and huge jaws. **2** a long line of schoolchildren walking in pairs.
- **crocodile tears** sorrow that is not sincere (so called because the crocodile was said to weep while it ate its victim).
[from Greek]

crocus *NOUN* **crocuses** a small plant with yellow, purple, or white flowers.
[from Greek]

croft *NOUN* **crofts** a small rented farm in Scotland.
▷ **crofter** *noun*
[from Old English]

croissant (*say* **krwah**-sahn) *NOUN* **croissants** a flaky crescent-shaped bread roll.
[French, = crescent]

crone *NOUN* **crones** a very old woman.
[from old French]

crony *NOUN* **cronies** a close friend or companion.
[from Greek]

cronyism *NOUN* the situation in which people in power give jobs to their friends.

crook *NOUN* **crooks** **1** a shepherd's stick with a curved end. **2** something bent or curved. **3** (*informal*) a person who makes a living dishonestly.

crook *ADJECTIVE* (*Australian/NZ*) (*informal*) **1** bad or unwell. **2** dishonest or illegal.

crook *VERB* **crooks**, **crooking**, **crooked** bend • *She crooked her finger.*
[from Old Norse]

crooked *ADJECTIVE* **1** bent or twisted; not straight. **2** dishonest.

croon *VERB* **croons**, **crooning**, **crooned** sing softly and gently.
[imitating the sound]

crop *NOUN* **crops** **1** something grown for food • *a good crop of wheat.* **2** a whip with a loop instead of a lash. **3** part of a bird's throat. **4** a very short haircut.

crop *VERB* **crops**, **cropping**, **cropped** **1** cut or bite off • *Sheep were cropping the grass.* **2** produce a crop.
- **crop up** happen unexpectedly.
[from Old English]

cropper *NOUN* - **come a cropper** (*slang*) **1** have a bad fall. **2** fail badly.
[origin unknown]

croquet (*say* **kroh**-kay) *NOUN* a game played with wooden balls and mallets.
[origin unknown]

crore *NOUN* **crore** (*Indian*) ten million; one hundred lakhs.

crosier (*say* **kroh**-zee-er) *NOUN* **crosiers** a bishop's staff shaped like a shepherd's crook.
[from old French]

cross *NOUN* **crosses** **1** a mark or shape made like **+** or **x**. **2** an upright post with another piece of wood across it, used in ancient times for crucifixion; **the Cross** the cross on which Christ was crucified, used as a symbol of Christianity. **3** a mixture of two different things.

cross *VERB* **crosses**, **crossing**, **crossed** **1** go across something. **2** draw a line or lines across something. **3** make the sign or shape of a cross • *Cross your fingers for luck.* **4** produce something from two different kinds.
- **cross out** draw a line across something because it is unwanted, wrong, etc.

cross *ADJECTIVE* **1** annoyed or bad-tempered. **2** going from one side to another • *There were cross winds on the bridge.*
▷ **crossly** *adverb* **crossness** *noun*
[via Old Norse and old Irish from Latin]

cross- *PREFIX* **1** across; crossing something (as in *crossbar*). **2** from two different kinds (as in *cross-breed*).

crossbar *NOUN* **crossbars** a horizontal bar, especially between two uprights.

crossbow *NOUN* **crossbows** a powerful bow with a mechanism for pulling and releasing the string.
[so called because the bow is mounted across the stock]

cross-breed *VERB* **cross-breeds**, **cross-breeding**, **cross-bred** breed by mating an animal with one of a different kind.
▷ **cross-breed** *noun* (COMPARE **hybrid**)

crosse *NOUN* **crosses** a hooked stick with a net across it, used in lacrosse.
[French]

cross-examine *VERB* **cross-examines, cross-examining, cross-examined** cross-question someone, especially in a lawcourt.
▷ **cross-examination** *noun*

cross-eyed *ADJECTIVE* with eyes that look or seem to look towards the nose.

crossfire *NOUN* lines of gunfire that cross each other.

cross-hatch *VERB* **cross-hatches, cross-hatching, cross-hatched** shade part of a drawing with two sets of parallel lines crossing each other.
▷ **cross-hatching** *noun*

crossing *NOUN* **crossings** a place where people can cross a road or railway.

cross-legged *ADJECTIVE* & *ADVERB* with ankles crossed and knees spread apart.

cross-question *VERB* **cross-questions, cross-questioning, cross-questioned** question someone carefully in order to test answers given to previous questions.

cross-reference *NOUN* **cross-references** a note telling people to look at another part of a book etc. for more information.

crossroads *NOUN* **crossroads** a place where two or more roads cross one another.

cross-section *NOUN* **cross-sections** **1** a drawing of something as if it has been cut through. **2** a typical sample.

crosswise *ADVERB* & *ADJECTIVE* with one thing crossing another.

crossword *NOUN* **crosswords** a puzzle in which words have to be guessed from clues and then written into the blank squares in a diagram.

crotch *NOUN* **crotches** the part between the legs where they join the body; a similar angle in a forked part.
[a different spelling of *crutch*]

crotchet *NOUN* **crotchets** a note in music, which usually represents one beat (written ♩).
[from French, = small hook]

crotchety *ADJECTIVE* bad-tempered.
[from an old meaning of *crotchet* = whim]

crouch *VERB* **crouches, crouching, crouched** lower your body, with your arms and legs bent.
[origin unknown]

croup (*say* kroop) *NOUN* a disease causing a hard cough and difficulty in breathing.
[imitating the sound]

crow[1] *NOUN* **crows** a large black bird.
- **as the crow flies** in a straight line.
[from Old English]

crow[2] *VERB* **crows, crowing, crowed** or **crew** **1** make a shrill cry as a cock does. **2** boast; be triumphant.
▷ **crow** *noun*
[imitating the sound]

crowbar *NOUN* **crowbars** an iron bar used as a lever.
[because the end is shaped like a crow's beak]

crowd *NOUN* **crowds** a large number of people in one place.

crowd *VERB* **crowds, crowding, crowded** **1** come together in a crowd. **2** cram; fill uncomfortably full.
[from Old English]

crown *NOUN* **crowns** **1** an ornamental headdress worn by a king or queen. **2** (often **Crown**) the sovereign • *This land belongs to the Crown.* **3** the highest part • *the crown of the road.* **4** a former coin worth 5 shillings (25p).
- **Crown Prince** or **Crown Princess** the heir to the throne.

crown *VERB* **crowns, crowning, crowned** **1** place a crown on someone as a symbol of royal power or victory. **2** form or cover or decorate the top of something. **3** reward; make a successful end to something • *Our efforts were crowned with victory.* **4** (*slang*) hit someone on the head.
[from Latin *corona* = garland or crown]

Crown Court *NOUN* **Crown Courts** a lawcourt where criminal cases are tried.

crow's nest *NOUN* **crow's nests** a lookout platform high up on a ship's mast.

crucial (*say* kroo-shal) *ADJECTIVE* most important.
▷ **crucially** *adverb*
[from Latin *crucis* = of a cross]

crucible *NOUN* **crucibles** a melting pot for metals.
[from Latin]

crucifix *NOUN* **crucifixes** a model of the Cross or of Jesus Christ on the Cross.
[same origin as *crucify*]

crucify *VERB* **crucifies, crucifying, crucified** put a person to death by nailing or binding the hands and feet to a cross.
▷ **crucifixion** *noun*
[from Latin *crucifigere* = fix to a cross]

crude *ADJECTIVE* **1** in a natural state; not yet refined • *crude oil.* **2** not well finished; rough • *a crude carving.* **3** vulgar.
▷ **crudely** *adverb* **crudity** *noun*
[from Latin *crudus* = raw, rough]

cruel *ADJECTIVE* **crueller, cruellest** causing pain or suffering.
▷ **cruelly** *adverb* **cruelty** *noun*
[from old French; related to *crude*]

cruet *NOUN* **cruets** a set of small containers for salt, pepper, oil, etc. for use at the table.
[from old French]

cruise *NOUN* **cruises** a pleasure trip in a ship.

cruise *VERB* **cruises, cruising, cruised 1** sail or travel at a moderate speed. **2** have a cruise.
[from Dutch *kruisen* = to cross]

cruiser *NOUN* **cruisers 1** a fast warship. **2** a large motor boat.

crumb *NOUN* **crumbs** a tiny piece of bread, etc.
[from Old English]

crumble *VERB* **crumbles, crumbling, crumbled** break or fall into small fragments.
▷ **crumbly** *adjective*

crumble *NOUN* **crumbles** a pudding made with fruit cooked with a crumbly topping • *apple crumble.*
[from Old English; related to *crumb*]

crumpet *NOUN* **crumpets** a soft flat cake made with yeast, eaten toasted with butter.
[origin unknown]

crumple *VERB* **crumples, crumpling, crumpled 1** crush or become crushed into creases. **2** collapse loosely.
[from Old English *crump* = crooked]

crunch *VERB* **crunches, crunching, crunched** crush something noisily, for example between your teeth.

crunch *NOUN* **crunches** a crunching sound.
▷ **crunchy** *adjective*
- **the crunch** (*informal*) a crucial event or turning point.
[imitating the sound]

Crusade *NOUN* **Crusades** a military expedition made by Christians in the Middle Ages to recover Palestine from the Muslims who had conquered it.
▷ **Crusader** *noun*

crusade *NOUN* **crusades** a campaign against something bad.
[from Latin *crux* = cross]

crush *VERB* **crushes, crushing, crushed**
1 press something so that it gets broken or harmed. **2** squeeze tightly. **3** defeat.

crush *NOUN* **crushes 1** a crowd of people pressed together. **2** a drink made with crushed fruit.
[from old French]

crust *NOUN* **crusts 1** the hard outer layer of something, especially bread. **2** the rocky outer layer of the earth.
[from Latin *crusta* = rind, shell]

crustacean (*say* krust-ay-shon) *NOUN* **crustaceans** an animal with a shell, e.g. a crab, lobster, or shrimp.
[same origin as *crust*]

crusty *ADJECTIVE* **crustier, crustiest**
1 having a crisp crust. **2** having a harsh or irritable manner.
▷ **crustiness** *noun*

crutch *NOUN* **crutches** a support like a long walking stick for helping a lame person to walk.
[from Old English]

cry *NOUN* **cries 1** a loud wordless sound expressing pain, grief, joy, etc. **2** a shout.
3 crying • *Have a good cry.*

cry *VERB* **cries, crying, cried 1** shed tears; weep. **2** call out loudly.
[from old French]

crypt *NOUN* **crypts** a room under a church.
[same origin as *cryptic*]

cryptic *ADJECTIVE* hiding its meaning in a puzzling way.
▷ **cryptically** *adverb*
[from Greek *kryptos* = hidden]

cryptogram *NOUN* **cryptograms** something written in cipher.
[from Greek *kryptos* = hidden, + *-gram*]

crystal *NOUN* **crystals** **1** a transparent colourless mineral rather like glass. **2** very clear high-quality glass. **3** a small solid piece of a substance with a symmetrical shape • *ice crystals.*
▷ **crystalline** *adjective*
[from Greek *krystallos* = ice]

crystallize *VERB* **crystallizes, crystallizing, crystallized** **1** form into crystals. **2** become definite in form.
▷ **crystallization** *noun*

crystallized fruit *NOUN* fruit preserved in sugar.

cub *NOUN* **cubs** a young lion, tiger, fox, bear, etc.
[origin unknown]

Cub or **Cub Scout** *NOUN* **Cubs, Cub Scouts** a member of the junior branch of the Scout Association.

cubby hole *NOUN* **cubby holes** a small compartment.
[from an old word *cub* = coop, hutch]

cube *NOUN* **cubes** **1** an object that has six equal square sides, like a box or dice. **2** the number produced by multiplying something by itself twice • *The cube of 3 is 3 x 3 x 3 = 27.*

cube *VERB* **cubes, cubing, cubed** **1** multiply a number by itself twice • *4 cubed is 4 x 4 x 4 = 64.* **2** cut something into small cubes.
[from Greek]

cube root *NOUN* **cube roots** the number that gives a particular number if it is multiplied by itself twice • *The cube root of 27 is 3.*

cubic *ADJECTIVE* three-dimensional.
- **cubic metre, cubic foot, etc.,** the volume of a cube with sides one metre, foot, etc. long, used as a unit of measurement for volume.

cubicle *NOUN* **cubicles** a compartment of a room.
[originally = bedroom: from Latin *cubare* = lie down]

cuboid (*say* kew-boid) *NOUN* **cuboids** an object with six rectangular sides.

cuckoo *NOUN* **cuckoos** a bird that makes a sound like 'cuck-oo'.
[imitating its call]

cucumber *NOUN* **cucumbers** a long green-skinned vegetable eaten raw or pickled.
[from Latin]

cud *NOUN* half-digested food that a cow etc. brings back from its first stomach to chew again.
[from Old English]

cuddle *VERB* **cuddles, cuddling, cuddled** put your arms closely round a person or animal that you love.
▷ **cuddly** *adjective*
[origin unknown]

cudgel *NOUN* **cudgels** a short thick stick used as a weapon.

cudgel *VERB* **cudgels, cudgelling, cudgelled** beat with a cudgel.
- **cudgel your brains** think hard about a problem.
[from Old English]

cue[1] *NOUN* **cues** something said or done that acts as a signal for an actor etc. to say or do something.
[origin unknown]

cue[2] *NOUN* **cues** a long stick for striking the ball in billiards or snooker.
[a different spelling of *queue* (because of its long, thin shape)]

cuff *NOUN* **cuffs** **1** the end of a sleeve that fits round the wrist. **2** hitting somebody with your hand; a slap.
- **off the cuff** without rehearsal or preparation.

cuff *VERB* **cuffs, cuffing, cuffed** hit somebody with your hand.
[origin unknown]

cufflink *NOUN* **cufflinks** each of a pair of fasteners for shirt cuffs, used instead of buttons.

cuisine (*say* kwiz-een) *NOUN* **cuisines** a style of cooking.
[French, = kitchen]

cul-de-sac *NOUN* **culs-de-sac** a street with an opening at one end only; a dead end.
[French, = bottom of a sack]

-cule *SUFFIX* forms diminutives (e.g. *molecule* = little mass).
[from Latin]

culinary *ADJECTIVE* to do with cooking.
[from Latin *culinarius* = to do with the kitchen]

cull *VERB* **culls, culling, culled** 1 select and use • *I've culled lines from several poems.*
2 pick out and kill surplus animals from a flock.
▷ **cull** *noun*
[from Latin *colligere* = collect]

culminate *VERB* **culminates, culminating, culminated** reach its highest or last point.
▷ **culmination** *noun*
[from Latin *culmen* = summit]

culpable *ADJECTIVE* deserving blame.
[from Latin *culpare* = to blame]

culprit *NOUN* **culprits** the person who has done something wrong.
[from old French]

cult *NOUN* **cults** 1 a religious sect. 2 a film, TV programme, rock group, etc. that is very popular with a particular group of people.
[from Latin *cultus* = worship]

cultivate *VERB* **cultivates, cultivating, cultivated** 1 use land to grow crops.
2 grow or develop things by looking after them.
▷ **cultivation** *noun* **cultivator** *noun*
[same origin as *culture*]

cultivated *ADJECTIVE* having good manners and education.

culture *NOUN* **cultures** 1 appreciation and understanding of literature, art, music, etc.
2 the customs and traditions of a people • *West Indian culture.* 3 (*in science*) a quantity of bacteria or cells grown for study.
4 cultivating things.
▷ **cultural** *adjective*
[from Latin *colere* = cultivate, look after, worship]

cultured *ADJECTIVE* educated to appreciate literature, art, music, etc.

cultured pearl *NOUN* **cultured pearls** a pearl formed by an oyster when a speck of grit etc. is put into its shell.

culvert *NOUN* **culverts** a drain that passes under a road or railway etc.
[origin unknown]

cumbersome *ADJECTIVE* clumsy to carry or manage.
[from *encumber* + *-some*]

cumin *NOUN* a plant with spicy seeds that are used for flavouring foods.
[from Greek]

cummerbund *NOUN* **cummerbunds** a broad sash.
[from Urdu]

cumulative *ADJECTIVE* accumulating; increasing by continuous additions.
[from Latin *cumulus* = heap]

cumulus *NOUN* **cumuli** a type of cloud consisting of rounded heaps on a horizontal base.
[Latin = heap]

cunning *ADJECTIVE* 1 clever at deceiving people. 2 cleverly designed or planned.

cunning *NOUN* 1 skill in deceiving people; craftiness. 2 skill or ingenuity.
[from Old Norse]

cup *NOUN* **cups** 1 a small bowl-shaped container for drinking from. 2 anything shaped like a cup. 3 a goblet-shaped ornament given as a prize.
▷ **cupful** *noun*

cup *VERB* **cups, cupping, cupped** form into the shape of a cup • *cup your hands.*
[from Latin]

cupboard *NOUN* **cupboards** a piece of furniture with a door, for storing things.
[originally = sideboard: from *cup* + *board*]

cupidity (*say* kew-**pid**-it-ee) *NOUN* greed for gaining money or possessions.
[from Latin *cupido* = desire]

cupola (*say* **kew**-pol-a) *NOUN* **cupolas** a small dome on a roof.
[Italian]

cur *NOUN* **curs** a scruffy or bad-tempered dog.
[from Old Norse]

curable *ADJECTIVE* able to be cured.

A B C D E F G H I J K L M N O P Q R S T U V W X Y Z

curate *NOUN* **curates** a member of the clergy who helps a vicar.
[from Latin *cura* = care]

curative (*say* kewr-at-iv) *ADJECTIVE* helping to cure illness.

curator (*say* kewr-ay-ter) *NOUN* **curators** a person in charge of a museum or other collection.
[same origin as *cure*]

curb *VERB* **curbs, curbing, curbed** restrain • *You need to curb your impatience.*

curb *NOUN* **curbs** a restraint • *Put a curb on spending.*
[from old French]
USAGE Do not confuse with **kerb**.

curd *NOUN* or **curds** *PLURAL NOUN* a thick substance formed when milk turns sour.
[origin unknown]

curdle *VERB* **curdles, curdling, curdled** form into curds.
- **make someone's blood curdle** horrify or terrify them.

cure *VERB* **cures, curing, cured** **1** get rid of someone's illness. **2** stop something bad. **3** treat something in order to preserve it • *Fish can be cured in smoke.*

cure *NOUN* **cures** **1** something that cures a person or thing; a remedy. **2** curing; being cured • *We cannot promise a cure.*
[from Latin *curare* = care for, cure]

curfew *NOUN* **curfews** a time or signal after which people must remain indoors until the next day.
[from old French *cuevrefeu*, literally = cover fire (from an old law saying that all fires should be covered or put out by a certain time each evening)]

curio *NOUN* **curios** an object that is a curiosity.
[short for *curiosity*]

curiosity *NOUN* **curiosities** **1** being curious. **2** something unusual and interesting.

curious *ADJECTIVE* **1** wanting to find out about things; inquisitive. **2** strange; unusual.
▷ **curiously** *adverb*
[from Latin]

curl *NOUN* **curls** a curve or coil, e.g. of hair.

curl *VERB* **curls, curling, curled** form into curls.
- **curl up** sit or lie with your knees drawn up.
[from old Dutch]

curler *NOUN* **curlers** a device for curling the hair.

curlew *NOUN* **curlews** a wading bird with a long curved bill.
[from old French]

curling *NOUN* a game played on ice with large flat stones.
[from *curl* (because the stones are made to 'curl round' opponents' stones to get to the target)]

curly *ADJECTIVE* having curls.

currant *NOUN* **currants** **1** a small black dried grape used in cookery. **2** a small round red, black, or white berry.
[from old French *raisins de Courauntz* = grapes from Corinth (a city in Greece)]
USAGE Do not confuse with **current**.

currency *NOUN* **currencies** **1** the money in use in a country. **2** the general use of something • *Some words have no currency now.*
[from *current*]

current *ADJECTIVE* happening now; used now.
▷ **currently** *adverb*

current *NOUN* **currents** **1** water or air etc. moving in one direction. **2** the flow of electricity along a wire etc. or through something.
[from Latin *currens* = running]
USAGE Do not confuse with **currant**.

current affairs *PLURAL NOUN* political events in the news at the moment.

curriculum *NOUN* **curricula** a course of study in a school or university.
[Latin, = running, course]

curriculum vitae (*say* veet-I) *NOUN* **curricula vitae** a brief account of a person's education, career, etc., which he or she sends when applying for a job.
[Latin, = course of life]

curry[1] *NOUN* **curries** food cooked with spices that taste hot.
▷ **curried** *adjective*
[from Tamil *kari* = sauce]

curry[2] *VERB* **curries, currying, curried**
- **curry favour** seek to win favour by flattering someone.
[from old French]

curse *NOUN* **curses** **1** a call or prayer for a person or thing to be harmed; the evil produced by this. **2** something very unpleasant. **3** an angry word or words.

curse *VERB* **curses, cursing, cursed** **1** make a curse. **2** use a curse against a person or thing.
- **be cursed with something** suffer from it.
[origin unknown]

cursor *NOUN* **cursors** a movable indicator, usually a flashing light, on a computer screen, showing where new data will go.
[Latin, = runner]

cursory *ADJECTIVE* hasty and not thorough • *a cursory inspection.*
▷ **cursorily** *adverb*
[same origin as *cursor*]

curt *ADJECTIVE* brief and hasty or rude • *a curt reply.*
▷ **curtly** *adverb* **curtness** *noun*
[from Latin *curtus* = cut short]

curtail *VERB* **curtails, curtailing, curtailed**
1 cut short • *The lesson was curtailed.*
2 reduce • *We must curtail our spending.*
▷ **curtailment** *noun*
[from French; related to *curt*]

curtain *NOUN* **curtains** **1** a piece of material hung at a window or door. **2** the large cloth screen hung at the front of a stage.
[from old French]

curtsy *NOUN* **curtsies** a movement of respect made by women and girls, putting one foot behind the other and bending the knees.

curtsy *VERB* **curtsies, curtsying, curtsied** make a curtsy.
[a different spelling of *courtesy*]

curvature *NOUN* **curvatures** curving; a curved shape.

curve *VERB* **curves, curving, curved** bend smoothly.

curve *NOUN* **curves** a curved line or shape.
▷ **curvy** *adjective*
[from Latin]

cushion *NOUN* **cushions** **1** a bag, usually of cloth, filled with soft material so that it is comfortable to sit on or lean against.
2 anything soft or springy that protects or supports something • *The hovercraft travels on a cushion of air.*

cushion *VERB* **cushions, cushioning, cushioned** protect from the effects of a knock or shock etc. • *A pile of boxes cushioned his fall.*
[from old French]

cushy *ADJECTIVE* (*informal*) pleasant and easy • *a cushy job.*
[from Urdu *kushi* = pleasure]

cusp *NOUN* **cusps** **1** a pointed end where two curves meet, e.g. the tips of the crescent moon. **2** (*in astrology*) the time when one sign of the zodiac ends and the next begins.
[from Latin *cuspis* = point]

custard *NOUN* **custards** **1** a sweet yellow sauce made with milk. **2** a pudding made with beaten eggs and milk.
[from old French]

custodian *NOUN* **custodians** a person who has custody of something; a keeper.

custody *NOUN* **1** care and supervision; guardianship. **2** imprisonment.
- **take into custody** arrest.
[from Latin *custos* = guardian]

custom *NOUN* **customs** **1** the usual way of behaving or doing something. **2** regular business from customers.
[from Latin *consuescere* = become accustomed]

customary *ADJECTIVE* according to custom; usual.
▷ **customarily** *adverb*

custom-built *ADJECTIVE* made ac
a customer's order.

customer *NOUN* **customers**
uses a shop, bank, or other b
[originally a person who cu
the same shop etc.]

customs *PLURAL NOUN* **1**
goods brought into a c
a port or airport wher
your luggage.
[= taxes customarily

cut *VERB* **cuts, cutting, cut** **1** divide or wound or separate something by using a knife, axe, scissors, etc. **2** make a thing shorter or smaller; remove part of something • *They are cutting all their prices.* **3** divide a pack of playing cards. **4** hit a ball with a chopping movement. **5** go through or across something. **6** switch off electrical power or an engine etc. **7** (in a film) move to another shot or scene. **8** make a sound recording.
- **cut a corner** pass round it very closely.
- **cut and dried** already decided.
- **cut in** interrupt.

cut *NOUN* **cuts** **1** cutting; the result of cutting. **2** a small wound. **3** (*slang*) a share.
- **be a cut above something** be superior.

[from a Scandinavian language]

cute *ADJECTIVE* (*informal*) **1** attractive. **2** clever.
▷ **cutely** *adverb* **cuteness** *noun*
[from *acute*]

cuticle (*say* kew-tik-ul) *NOUN* **cuticles** the skin round a nail.
[from Latin]

cutlass *NOUN* **cutlasses** a short sword with a broad curved blade.
[same origin as *cutlery*]

cutlery *NOUN* knives, forks, and spoons.
[from Latin *culter* = knife]

cutlet *NOUN* **cutlets** a thick slice of meat for cooking.
[from French]

cut-out *NOUN* **cut-outs** a shape cut out of paper, cardboard, etc.

cut-price *ADJECTIVE* sold at a reduced price.

cutter *NOUN* **cutters** **1** a person or thing that cuts. **2** a small fast sailing ship.

cutting *NOUN* **cuttings** **1** a steep-sided passage cut through high ground for a road or railway. **2** something cut out of a ...ewspaper or magazine. **3** a piece cut from ...lant to form a new plant.

...**efish** *NOUN* **cuttlefish** a sea creature ...n arms, which sends out a black liquid ...ttacked.
...d English]

...orms nouns showing action or ...c. (e.g. *piracy*, *infancy*).
... Greek]

cyanide *NOUN* a very poisonous chemical.
[from Greek]

cycle *NOUN* **cycles** **1** a bicycle or motorcycle. **2** a series of events that are regularly repeated in the same order.
▷ **cyclic** *adjective* **cyclical** *adjective*

cycle *VERB* **cycles, cycling, cycled** ride a bicycle or tricycle.
▷ **cyclist** *noun*
[from Greek *kyklos* = circle]

cyclone *NOUN* **cyclones** a wind that rotates round a calm central area.
▷ **cyclonic** *adjective*
[from Greek *kykloma* = wheel]

cygnet (*say* sig-nit) *NOUN* **cygnets** a young swan.
[from Latin *cycnus* = swan]

cylinder *NOUN* **cylinders** an object with straight sides and circular ends.
▷ **cylindrical** *adjective*
[from Greek *kylindros* = roller]

cymbal *NOUN* **cymbals** a percussion instrument consisting of a metal plate that is hit to make a ringing sound.
[from Greek]
USAGE Do not confuse with **symbol**.

cynic (*say* sin-ik) *NOUN* **cynics** a person who believes that people's reasons for doing things are selfish or bad, and shows this by sneering at them.
▷ **cynical** *adjective* **cynically** *adverb* **cynicism** *noun*
[from Greek *kynikos* = surly]

cypress *NOUN* **cypresses** an evergreen tree with dark leaves.
[from Greek]

cyst (*say* sist) *NOUN* **cysts** an abnormal swelling containing fluid or soft matter.
[from Latin]

czar (*say* zar) *NOUN* **czars** a different spelling of *tsar*.

Dd

dab *NOUN* **dabs** **1** a quick gentle touch, usually with something wet. **2** a small lump • *a dab of butter.*

dab *VERB* **dabs, dabbing, dabbed** touch something quickly and gently.
[imitating the sound of dabbing something wet]

dabble *VERB* **dabbles, dabbling, dabbled** **1** splash something about in water. **2** do something as a hobby • *I dabble in astronomy.*
[from *dab*]

dachshund (*say* daks-huund) *NOUN* **dachshunds** a small dog with a long body and very short legs.
[German, = badger- dog (because dachshunds were used to dig badgers out of their sets)]

dad or **daddy** *NOUN* **dads, daddies** (*informal*) father.
[imitating the sounds a child makes when it first tries to speak]

daddy-long-legs *NOUN* **daddy-long-legs** a crane fly.

daffodil *NOUN* **daffodils** a yellow flower that grows from a bulb.
[from *asphodel*, another plant with yellow flowers]

daft *ADJECTIVE* (*informal*) silly or stupid.
[from Old English]

dag *NOUN* **dags** (*informal*) (*Australian/NZ*) a dirty or untidy person.
[shortening of *daglock* = a piece of dung-coated wool on a sheep's hindquarters]

dagger *NOUN* **daggers** a pointed knife with two sharp edges, used as a weapon.
[from old French]

dahlia (*say* day-lee-a) *NOUN* **dahlias** a garden plant with brightly-coloured flowers.
[named after Andreas *Dahl*, a Swedish botanist]

daily *ADVERB & ADJECTIVE* every day.

dainty *ADJECTIVE* **daintier, daintiest** small, delicate, and pretty.
▷ **daintily** *adverb* **daintiness** *noun*
[via old French from Latin *dignitas* = value, beauty]

dairy *NOUN* **dairies** a place where milk, butter, etc. are produced or sold.

dairy *ADJECTIVE* to do with the production of milk; made from milk • *dairy farming; dairy products.*
[from Old English]

dais (*say* day-iss) *NOUN* **daises** a low platform, especially at the end of a room.
[from old French]

daisy *NOUN* **daisies** a small flower with white petals and a yellow centre.
[from *day's eye* (because the daisy opens in daylight and closes at night)]

dale *NOUN* **dales** a valley.
[from Old English]

dally *VERB* **dallies, dallying, dallied** dawdle or waste time.
[from old French]

dam[1] *NOUN* **dams** a wall built to hold water back.

dam *VERB* **dams, damming, dammed** hold water back with a dam.
[from Old English]

dam[2] *NOUN* **dams** the mother of a horse or dog etc. (COMPARE **sire**)
[from *dame*]

damage *NOUN* harm or injury done to something.

damage *VERB* **damages, damaging, damaged** harm or spoil something.
[from Latin *damnum* = loss]

damages *PLURAL NOUN* money paid as compensation for an injury or loss.

Dame *NOUN* **Dames** the title of a lady who has been given the equivalent of a knighthood.

dame *NOUN* **dames** a comic middle-aged woman in a pantomime, usually played by a man.
[from Latin *domina* = lady]

damn *VERB* **damns, damning, damned** curse or condemn.
[from Latin *damnare* = condemn]

damnation *NOUN* being condemned to hell.

damned *ADJECTIVE* hateful or annoying.

damp *ADJECTIVE* slightly wet; not quite dry.
▷ **damply** *adverb* **dampness** *noun*

damp *NOUN* moisture in the air or on a surface or all through something.

damp *VERB* **damps, damping, damped** **1** make something slightly wet. **2** reduce the strength of something • *The defeat damped their enthusiasm.*
[from a Germanic language]

A B C D E F G H I J K L M N O P Q R S T U V W X Y Z

damp course *NOUN* **damp courses** a layer of material built into a wall to prevent dampness in the ground from rising.

dampen *VERB* **dampens, dampening, dampened 1** make something damp. **2** reduce the strength of something.

damper *NOUN* **dampers 1** a metal plate that can be moved to increase or decrease the amount of air flowing into a fire or furnace etc. **2** (*Australian*) a type of bread made of flour and water, baked in the ashes of a wood fire.
- **put a damper on** reduce people's enthusiasm or enjoyment.
[from *damp*]

damsel *NOUN* **damsels** (*old use*) a young woman.
[from old French]

damson *NOUN* **damsons** a small dark-purple plum.
[from Latin *damascenum prunum* = plum from Damascus (a city in Syria)]

dance *VERB* **dances, dancing, danced** move about in time to music.

dance *NOUN* **dances 1** a set of movements used in dancing. **2** a piece of music for dancing to. **3** a party or gathering where people dance.
▷ **dancer** *noun*
[from old French]

dandelion *NOUN* **dandelions** a yellow wild flower with jagged leaves.
[from French *dent-de-lion* = tooth of a lion (because the jagged edges of the leaves looked like lions' teeth)]

dandruff *NOUN* tiny white flakes of dead skin in a person's hair.
[origin unknown]

D and T *ABBREVIATION* design and technology.

dandy *NOUN* **dandies** a man who likes to look very smart.
[origin unknown]

danger *NOUN* **dangers 1** something that is not safe or could harm you. **2** the possibility of suffering harm or death.
[from old French]

dangerous *ADJECTIVE* likely to kill or harm you.
▷ **dangerously** *adverb*

dangle *VERB* **dangles, dangling, dangled** hang or swing loosely.
[from a Scandinavian language]

dank *ADJECTIVE* damp and chilly.
[from a Scandinavian language]

dapper *ADJECTIVE* dressed neatly and smartly.
[from old German or old Dutch]

dappled *ADJECTIVE* marked with patches of a different colour.
[probably from Old Norse *depill* = spot]

dare *VERB* **dares, daring, dared 1** be brave or bold enough to do something. **2** challenge a person to do something risky.

dare *NOUN* **dares** a challenge to do something risky.
[from Old English]

daredevil *NOUN* **daredevils** a person who is very bold and reckless.

dark *ADJECTIVE* **1** with little or no light. **2** not light in colour • *a dark suit.* **3** having dark hair. **4** sinister or evil.
▷ **darkly** *adverb* **darkness** *noun*

dark *NOUN* **1** absence of light • *Cats can see in the dark.* **2** the time when darkness has come • *She went out after dark.*
[from Old English]

darken *VERB* **darkens, darkening, darkened** make or become dark.

darkroom *NOUN* **darkrooms** a room kept dark for developing and printing photographs.

darling *NOUN* **darlings** someone who is loved very much.
[from Old English *deorling* = little dear]

darn *VERB* **darns, darning, darned** mend a hole by weaving threads across it.

darn *NOUN* **darns** a place that has been darned.
[from Old English *diernan* = hide]

dart *NOUN* **darts 1** an object with a sharp point, thrown at a target. **2** a darting movement. **3** a tapering tuck stitched in something to make it fit.

dart *VERB* **darts, darting, darted** run suddenly and quickly.
[from old French]

darts *NOUN* a game in which darts are thrown at a circular board (a **dartboard**).

dash *VERB* **dashes, dashing, dashed** **1** run quickly; rush. **2** throw a thing violently against something • *The storm dashed the ship against the rocks.*

dash *NOUN* **dashes** **1** a short quick run; a rush. **2** energy or liveliness. **3** a small amount • *Add a dash of brandy.* **4** a short line (-) used in writing or printing.
[origin unknown]

dashboard *NOUN* **dashboards** a panel with dials and controls in front of the driver of a vehicle.
[originally a board on the front of a carriage to keep out mud, which dashed against it]

dashing *ADJECTIVE* lively and showy.

dastardly *ADJECTIVE* contemptible and cowardly.
[originally = dull, stupid: from *dazed*]

data (*say* day-ta) *NOUN* pieces of information.
USAGE Strictly speaking, this word is a plural noun (the singular is *datum*), so it should be used with a plural verb: *Here are the data.* However, the word is widely used nowadays as if it were a singular noun and most people do not regard this as wrong: *Here is the data.*

database *NOUN* **databases** a store of information held in a computer.

date[1] *NOUN* **dates** **1** the time when something happens or happened or was written, stated as the day, month, and year (or any of these). **2** an appointment to meet someone, especially someone of the opposite sex.

date *VERB* **dates, dating, dated** **1** give a date to something. **2** have existed from a particular time • *The church dates from 1684.* **3** seem old-fashioned.
[from Latin *data* = given (at a certain time)]

date[2] *NOUN* **dates** a small sweet brown fruit that grows on a kind of palm tree.
[from Greek]

daub *VERB* **daubs, daubing, daubed** paint or smear something clumsily.
▷ **daub** *noun*
[from Latin *dealbare* = whitewash, plaster]

daughter *NOUN* **daughters** a girl or woman who is someone's child.
[from Old English]

daughter-in-law *NOUN* **daughters-in-law** a son's wife.

daunt *VERB* **daunts, daunting, daunted** make somebody afraid or discouraged.
▷ **daunting** *adjective*
[from Latin *domitare* = to tame]

dauntless *ADJECTIVE* brave; not to be daunted.
▷ **dauntlessly** *adverb*

dauphin (*say* daw-fin) *NOUN* **dauphins** the title of the eldest son of each of the kings of France between 1349 and 1830.
[old French]

dawdle *VERB* **dawdles, dawdling, dawdled** go slowly and lazily.
▷ **dawdler** *noun*
[origin unknown]

dawn *NOUN* **dawns** the time when the sun rises.

dawn *VERB* **dawns, dawning, dawned** **1** begin to grow light in the morning. **2** begin to be realized • *The truth dawned on them.*
[from Old English]

day *NOUN* **days** **1** the 24 hours between midnight and the next midnight. **2** the light part of this time. **3** a particular day • *sports day.* **4** a period of time • *in Queen Victoria's day.*
[from Old English]

daybreak *NOUN* dawn.

daydream *NOUN* **daydreams** pleasant thoughts of something you would like to happen.

daydream *VERB* **daydreams, daydreaming, daydreamed** have daydreams.

daylight *NOUN* **1** the light of day. **2** dawn.

day-to-day *ADJECTIVE* ordinary; happening every day.

dazed *ADJECTIVE* unable to think or see clearly.
▷ **daze** *noun*
[from Old Norse *dasathr* = weary]

dazzle *VERB* **dazzles, dazzling, dazzled** **1** make a person unable to see clearly because of too much bright light. **2** amaze or impress a person by a splendid display.
[from *daze*]

DC *ABBREVIATION* direct current.

de- *PREFIX* **1** removing (as in *defrost*). **2** down, away (as in *descend*). **3** completely (as in *denude*).
[from old French; related to *dis-*]

deacon *NOUN* **deacons** **1** a member of the clergy ranking below bishops and priests. **2** (in some Churches) a church officer who is not a member of the clergy.
▷ **deaconess** *noun*
[from Greek *diakonos* = servant]

dead *ADJECTIVE* **1** no longer alive. **2** not lively. **3** not functioning; no longer in use. **4** exact or complete • *a dead loss.*
[from Old English]

deaden *VERB* **deadens, deadening, deadened** make pain or noise etc. weaker.

dead end *NOUN* **dead ends** **1** a road or passage with one end closed. **2** a situation where there is no chance of making progress.

dead heat *NOUN* **dead heats** a race in which two or more winners finish exactly together.

deadline *NOUN* **deadlines** a time limit.
[originally this meant a line round an American military prison; if prisoners went beyond it they could be shot]

deadlock *NOUN* **deadlocks** a situation in which no progress can be made.
[from *dead* + *lock*[1]]

deadly *ADJECTIVE* **deadlier, deadliest** likely to kill.

deaf *ADJECTIVE* **1** unable to hear. **2** unwilling to hear.
▷ **deafness** *noun*
[from Old English]

deafen *VERB* **deafens, deafening, deafened** make somebody become deaf, especially by a very loud noise.

deafening *ADJECTIVE* extremely loud.

deal[1] *VERB* **deals, dealing, dealt** **1** hand something out; give. **2** give out cards for a card game. **3** do business; buy and sell • *He deals in scrap metal.*
▷ **dealer** *noun*
- **deal with** **1** be concerned with • *This book deals with whales and dolphins.* **2** do what is needed • *I'll deal with the washing-up.*

deal *NOUN* **deals** **1** an agreement or bargain. **2** someone's turn to deal at cards.
- **a good deal** or **a great deal** a large amount.
[from Old English *daelan* = divide, share out]

deal[2] *NOUN* sawn fir or pine wood.
[from old Dutch *dele* = plank]

dean *NOUN* **deans** **1** an important member of the clergy in a cathedral etc. **2** the head of a university, college, or department.
▷ **deanery** *noun*
[from Latin]

dear *ADJECTIVE* **1** loved very much. **2** a polite greeting in letters • *Dear Sir.* **3** expensive.
▷ **dearly** *adverb*
[from Old English]

dearth (*say* derth) *NOUN* **dearths** a scarcity.
[from *dear* (because scarcity made food etc. expensive)]

death *NOUN* **deaths** dying; the end of life.
[from Old English]

deathly *ADJECTIVE & ADVERB* like death.

death trap *NOUN* **death traps** a very dangerous place.

debar *VERB* **debars, debarring, debarred** forbid or ban • *He was debarred from the contest.*
[from *de-* + French *barrer* = to bar]

debase *VERB* **debases, debasing, debased** reduce the quality or value of something.
▷ **debasement** *noun*
[from *de-* + *base*[2]]

debatable *ADJECTIVE* questionable; that can be argued against.

debate *NOUN* **debates** a formal discussion.

debate *VERB* **debates, debating, debated** hold a debate.
▷ **debater** *noun*
[from old French]

debilitating *ADJECTIVE* causing weakness.

debility (*say* dib-il-it-ee) *NOUN* weakness of the body.
[from Latin]

debit *NOUN* **debits** an entry in an account showing how much money is owed. (COMPARE **credit**)

debit *VERB* **debits, debiting, debited** enter something as a debit in an account; remove money from an account.
[from Latin *debitum* = what is owed]

debonair (*say* deb-on-air) *ADJECTIVE* carefree and confident.
[from French *de bon air* = of good disposition]

debris (*say* deb-ree) *NOUN* scattered fragments or wreckage.
[from French *débris* = broken down]

debt (*say* det) *NOUN* **debts** something that you owe someone.
- **in debt** owing money etc.
[same origin as *debit*]

debtor (*say* det-or) *NOUN* **debtors** a person who owes money to someone.

début (*say* day-bew) *NOUN* **débuts** someone's first public appearance.
[from French *débuter* = begin]

deca- *PREFIX* ten (as in *decathlon*).
[from Greek]

decade (*say* dek-ayd) *NOUN* **decades** a period of ten years.
[from old French]

decadent (*say* dek-a-dent) *ADJECTIVE* falling to a lower standard of morality, especially in order to enjoy pleasure.
▷ **decadence** *noun*
[same origin as *decay*]

decaffeinated *ADJECTIVE* (said about coffee or tea) with the caffeine removed.

decamp *VERB* **decamps, decamping, decamped** **1** pack up and leave a camp. **2** go away suddenly or secretly.
[from French]

decant (*say* dik-ant) *VERB* **decants, decanting, decanted** pour wine etc. gently from one container into another.
[from Latin]

decanter (*say* dik-ant-er) *NOUN* **decanters** a decorative glass bottle into which wine etc. is poured for serving.
[from *decant*]

decapitate *VERB* **decapitates, decapitating, decapitated** cut someone's head off; behead.
▷ **decapitation** *noun*
[from *de-* + Latin *caput* = head]

decathlon *NOUN* **decathlons** an athletic contest in which each competitor takes part in ten events.
[from *deca-* + Greek *athlon* = contest]

decay *VERB* **decays, decaying, decayed** **1** go bad; rot. **2** become less good or less strong.
▷ **decay** *noun*
[from old French *decaoir* = fall down]

decease (*say* dis-eess) *NOUN* (*formal*) death.
[from *de-* + Latin *cedere* = go]

deceased *ADJECTIVE* dead.

deceit (*say* dis-eet) *NOUN* **deceits** making a person believe something that is not true.
▷ **deceitful** *adjective* **deceitfully** *adverb*

deceive *VERB* **deceives, deceiving, deceived** make a person believe something that is not true.
▷ **deceiver** *noun*
[from Latin]

December *NOUN* the twelfth month of the year.
[from Latin *decem* = ten, because it was the tenth month of the ancient Roman calendar]

decent *ADJECTIVE* **1** respectable and honest. **2** reasonable or adequate. **3** (*informal*) kind.
▷ **decently** *adverb* **decency** *noun*
[from Latin]

deception *NOUN* **deceptions** deceiving someone.
▷ **deceptive** *adjective* **deceptively** *adverb*

deci- (*say* dess-ee) *PREFIX* one-tenth (as in *decimetre*).
[same origin as *decimal*]

decibel (*say* dess-ib-el) *NOUN* **decibels** a unit for measuring the loudness of sound.
[originally one- tenth of the unit called a *bel*]

decide *VERB* **decides, deciding, decided**
1 make up your mind; make a choice.
2 settle a contest or argument.
▷ **decider** *noun*
[from Latin]

decided *ADJECTIVE* **1** having clear and definite opinions. **2** noticeable • *a decided difference.*
▷ **decidedly** *adverb*

deciduous (*say* dis-id-yoo-us) *ADJECTIVE* a deciduous tree is one that loses its leaves in autumn.
[from Latin *decidere* = fall off]

decimal *ADJECTIVE* using tens or tenths.

decimal *NOUN* **decimals** a decimal fraction.
[from Latin *decimus* = tenth]

decimal currency *NOUN* **decimal currencies** a currency in which each unit is ten or one hundred times the value of the one next below it.

decimal fraction *NOUN* **decimal fractions** a fraction with tenths shown as numbers after a dot ($\frac{1}{3}$ is 0.3; $\frac{11}{2}$ is 1.5).

decimalize *VERB* **decimalizes, decimalizing, decimalized 1** express something as a decimal. **2** change something, especially coinage, to a decimal system.
▷ **decimalization** *noun*

decimal point *NOUN* **decimal points** the dot in a decimal fraction.

decimate (*say* dess-im-ayt) *VERB* **decimates, decimating, decimated** kill or destroy a large part of • *The famine decimated the population.*
[from Latin *decimare* = kill every tenth man (this was the ancient Roman punishment for an army guilty of mutiny or other serious crime)]

decipher (*say* dis-I-fer) *VERB* **deciphers, deciphering, deciphered 1** work out the meaning of a coded message. **2** work out the meaning of something written badly.
▷ **decipherment** *noun*

decision *NOUN* **decisions 1** deciding; what you have decided. **2** determination.

decisive (*say* dis-I-siv) *ADJECTIVE* **1** that settles or ends something • *a decisive battle.* **2** able to make decisions quickly and firmly.
▷ **decisively** *adverb* **decisiveness** *noun*

deck *NOUN* **decks 1** a floor on a ship or bus. **2** a pack of playing cards. **3** a turntable on a record player.

deck *VERB* **decks, decking, decked** decorate with something • *The front of the house was decked with flags and balloons.*
[from old Dutch *dec* = a covering]

deckchair *NOUN* **deckchairs** a folding chair with a canvas or plastic seat.
[because they were used on the decks of passenger ships]

declaim *VERB* **declaims, declaiming, declaimed** make a speech etc. loudly and dramatically.
▷ **declamation** *noun*
[from *de-* + Latin *clamare* = to shout]

declare *VERB* **declares, declaring, declared 1** say something clearly or firmly. **2** tell customs officials that you have goods on which you ought to pay duty. **3** end a cricket innings before all the batsmen are out.
▷ **declaration** *noun*
- **declare war** announce that you are starting a war against someone.
[from *de-* + Latin *clarare* = make clear]

decline *VERB* **declines, declining, declined 1** refuse. **2** become weaker or smaller. **3** slope downwards. **4** state the forms of a noun, pronoun, or adjective that correspond to particular cases, numbers, and genders.

decline *NOUN* **declines** a gradual decrease or loss of strength.
[from *de-* + Latin *clinare* = bend]

decode *VERB* **decodes, decoding, decoded** work out the meaning of something written in code.
▷ **decoder** *noun*

decompose *VERB* **decomposes, decomposing, decomposed** decay or rot.
▷ **decomposition** *noun*

decompression *NOUN* reducing air pressure.

decontamination *NOUN* getting rid of poisonous chemicals or radioactive material from a place, clothes, etc.

décor (*say* day-kor) *NOUN* the style of furnishings and decorations used in a room etc.
[French, from *décorer* = decorate]

decorate *VERB* **decorates, decorating, decorated 1** make something look more beautiful or colourful. **2** put fresh paint or paper on walls. **3** give somebody a medal.
▷ **decoration** *noun* **decorator** *noun* **decorative** *adjective*
[from Latin *decor* = beauty]

decorous (*say* dek-er-us) *ADJECTIVE* polite and dignified.
▷ **decorously** *adverb*
[from Latin *decorus* = suitable, proper]

decorum (*say* dik-or-um) *NOUN* polite and dignified behaviour.
[same origin as *decorous*]

decoy (*say* dee-koi) *NOUN* **decoys** something used to tempt a person or animal into a trap or into danger.

decoy (*say* dik-oi) *VERB* **decoys, decoying, decoyed** tempt a person or animal into a trap etc.
[from Dutch]

decrease *VERB* **decreases, decreasing, decreased** make or become smaller or fewer.

decrease *NOUN* **decreases** decreasing; the amount by which something decreases.
[from *de-* + Latin *crescere* = grow]

decree *NOUN* **decrees** an official order or decision.

decree *VERB* **decrees, decreeing, decreed** make a decree.
[from Latin *decretum* = what has been decided]

decrepit (*say* dik-rep-it) *ADJECTIVE* old and weak.
▷ **decrepitude** *noun*
[from Latin *decrepitus* = creaking]

dedicate *VERB* **dedicates, dedicating, dedicated** **1** devote all your time or energy to something • *She dedicated her life to nursing.* **2** name a person as a mark of respect, e.g. at the beginning of a book.
▷ **dedication** *noun*
[from Latin]

deduce *VERB* **deduces, deducing, deduced** work something out by reasoning from facts that you know are true.
▷ **deducible** *adjective*
[from *de-* + Latin *ducere* = to lead]

deduct *VERB* **deducts, deducting, deducted** subtract part of something.
[same origin as *deduce*]

deductible *ADJECTIVE* able to be deducted.

deduction *NOUN* **deductions** **1** deducting; something deducted. **2** deducing; something deduced.

deed *NOUN* **deeds** **1** something that someone has done; an act. **2** a legal document.
[from Old English]

deem *VERB* **deems, deeming, deemed** (*formal*) consider • *I should deem it an honour to be invited.*
[from Old English]

deep *ADJECTIVE* **1** going a long way down or back or in • *a deep well;* • *deep cupboards.* **2** measured from top to bottom or front to back • *a hole six feet deep.* **3** intense or strong • *deep colours;* • *deep feelings.* **4** low-pitched, not shrill • *a deep voice.*
▷ **deeply** *adverb* **deepness** *noun*
[from Old English]

deepen *VERB* **deepens, deepening, deepened** make or become deeper.

deep-freeze *NOUN* **deep-freezes** a freezer.

deer *NOUN* **deer** a fast-running graceful animal, the male of which usually has antlers.
[from Old English *deor* = an animal]

deface *VERB* **defaces, defacing, defaced** spoil the surface of something, e.g. by scribbling on it.
▷ **defacement** *noun*
[from old French]

defame *VERB* **defames, defaming, defamed** attack a person's good reputation; slander or libel.
▷ **defamation** (*say* def-a-may-shon) *noun* **defamatory** (*say* dif-am-a-ter-ee) *adjective*
[from *de-* + Latin *fama* = fame, reputation]

default *VERB* **defaults, defaulting, defaulted** fail to do what you have agreed to do, especially to pay back a loan.
▷ **defaulter** *noun*

default *NOUN* **defaults** **1** failure to do something. **2** (*in computing*) what a computer does unless you give it another command.
- **by default** because something has failed to happen.
[from old French]

defeat *VERB* **defeats, defeating, defeated** **1** win a victory over someone. **2** baffle; be too difficult for someone.

A B C D E F G H I J K L M N O P Q R S T U V W X Y Z

defeat *NOUN* **defeats** **1** defeating someone. **2** being defeated; a lost game or battle.
[from Latin *disfacere* = undo, destroy]

defeatist *NOUN* **defeatists** a person who expects to be defeated.
▷ **defeatism** *noun*

defecate (*say* dee-fik-ayt) *VERB* **defecates, defecating, defecated** get rid of faeces from your body.
▷ **defecation** *noun*
[from *de-* + *faeces*]

defect (*say* dif-ekt or dee-fekt) *NOUN* **defects** a flaw.

defect (*say* dif-ekt) *VERB* **defects, defecting, defected** desert your own country etc. and join the enemy.
▷ **defection** *noun* **defector** *noun*
[from Latin *deficere* = fail, leave, undo]

defective *ADJECTIVE* having defects; incomplete.
▷ **defectiveness** *noun*

defence *NOUN* **defences** **1** defending something. **2** all the soldiers, weapons, etc. that a country uses to protect itself from attack • *spending on defence.* **3** something that defends or protects. **4** the case put forward by or on behalf of a defendant in a lawsuit. **5** the players in a defending position in a game.

defenceless *ADJECTIVE* having no defences.

defend *VERB* **defends, defending, defended** **1** protect, especially against an attack or accusation. **2** try to prove that a statement is true or that an accused person is not guilty.
▷ **defender** *noun*
[from Latin]

defendant *NOUN* **defendants** a person accused of something in a lawcourt.

defensible *ADJECTIVE* able to be defended.
▷ **defensibility** *noun*

defensive *ADJECTIVE* **1** used or done for defence; protective. **2** anxious about being criticized.
▷ **defensively** *adverb*
- **on the defensive** ready to defend yourself against criticism.

defer[1] *VERB* **defers, deferring, deferred** postpone.
▷ **deferment** *noun* **deferral** *noun*
[from old French; related to *differ*]

defer[2] *VERB* **defers, deferring, deferred** give way to a person's wishes or authority; yield.
[from Latin]

deference (*say* def-er-ens) *NOUN* polite respect.
▷ **deferential** (*say* def-er-en-shal) *adjective* **deferentially** *adverb*
[from *defer*[2]]

defiant *ADJECTIVE* defying; openly disobedient.
▷ **defiantly** *adverb* **defiance** *noun*

deficiency *NOUN* **deficiencies** **1** a lack or shortage. **2** a defect.
▷ **deficient** *adjective*
[same origin as *defect*]

deficit (*say* def-iss-it) *NOUN* **deficits** **1** the amount by which a total is smaller than what is required. **2** the amount by which spending is greater than income.
[same origin as *defect*]

defile *VERB* **defiles, defiling, defiled** make a thing dirty or impure.
▷ **defilement** *noun*
[from an old word *defoul*]

define *VERB* **defines, defining, defined** **1** explain what a word or phrase means. **2** show clearly what something is; specify. **3** show a thing's outline.
▷ **definable** *adjective*
[from *de-* + Latin *finis* = limit]

definite *ADJECTIVE* **1** clearly stated; exact • *Fix a definite time.* **2** certain or settled • *Is it definite that we are to move?*
[from Latin *definitus* = defined]

definite article *NOUN* **definite articles** the word 'the'.

definitely *ADVERB* without doubt.

definition *NOUN* **definitions** **1** a statement of what a word or phrase means or of what a thing is. **2** being distinct; clearness of outline (e.g. in a photograph).

definitive (*say* dif-in-it-iv) *ADJECTIVE* **1** finally settling something; conclusive • *a definitive victory.* **2** not able to be bettered • *the definitive history of the British cinema.*

deflate *VERB* **deflates, deflating, deflated** **1** let out air from a tyre or balloon etc. **2** make someone feel less proud or less confident. **3** reduce or reverse inflation.
▷ **deflation** *noun* **deflationary** *adjective*
[from *de-* + *inflate*]

deflect *VERB* **deflects, deflecting, deflected** make something turn aside.
▷ **deflection** *noun* **deflector** *noun*
[from *de-* + Latin *flectere* = to bend]

deforest *VERB* **deforests, deforesting, deforested** clear away the trees from an area.
▷ **deforestation** *noun*

deform *VERB* **deforms, deforming, deformed** spoil a thing's shape or appearance.
▷ **deformation** *noun*
[from *de-* + Latin *forma* = shape, form]

deformed *ADJECTIVE* badly or abnormally shaped.
▷ **deformity** *noun*

defraud *VERB* **defrauds, defrauding, defrauded** take something from a person by fraud; cheat or swindle.
[from *de-* + Latin *fraudere* = defraud]

defray *VERB* **defrays, defraying, defrayed** provide money to pay costs or expenses.
▷ **defrayal** *noun*
[from *de-* + old French *frais* = cost]

defrost *VERB* **defrosts, defrosting, defrosted** **1** thaw out something frozen. **2** remove the ice and frost from a refrigerator or windscreen.

deft *ADJECTIVE* skilful and quick.
▷ **deftly** *adverb* **deftness** *noun*
[from Old English]

defunct *ADJECTIVE* no longer in use or existing.
[from Latin *defunctus* = finished]

defuse *VERB* **defuses, defusing, defused** **1** remove the fuse from a bomb so that it cannot explode. **2** make a situation less dangerous or tense.

defy *VERB* **defies, defying, defied** **1** resist something openly; refuse to obey • *They defied the law.* **2** challenge a person to do something you believe cannot be done • *I defy you to prove this.* **3** prevent something being done • *The door defied all efforts to open it.*
[from *de-* + Latin *fidus* = faithful]

degenerate *VERB* **degenerates, degenerating, degenerated** become worse or lower in standard.
▷ **degeneration** *noun*

degenerate *ADJECTIVE* having become immoral or bad.
▷ **degeneracy** *noun*
[from Latin]

degrade *VERB* **degrades, degrading, degraded** **1** humiliate or dishonour someone. **2** reduce to a simpler molecular form.
▷ **degradation** (*say* deg-ra-day-shon) *noun*
[from *de-* + Latin *gradus* = grade]

degree *NOUN* **degrees** **1** a unit for measuring temperature. **2** a unit for measuring angles. **3** extent • *to some degree.* **4** an award to someone at a university or college who has successfully finished a course.
[from *de-* + Latin *gradus* = grade]

dehydrated *ADJECTIVE* dried up, with all moisture removed.
▷ **dehydration** *noun*
[from *de-* + Greek *hydor* = water]

de-ice *VERB* **de-ices, de-icing, de-iced** remove ice from a windscreen etc.
▷ **de-icer** *noun*

deign (*say* dayn) *VERB* **deigns, deigning, deigned** be gracious enough to do something; condescend.
[from Latin]

deity (*say* dee-it-ee or day-it-ee) *NOUN* **deities** a god or goddess.
[from Latin *deus* = god]

déjà vu (*say* day-*zha* vew) *NOUN* a feeling that you have already experienced what is happening now.
[French, = already seen]

dejected *ADJECTIVE* sad or depressed.
▷ **dejectedly** *adverb* **dejection** *noun*
[from *de-* + Latin *-jectum* = cast]

delay *VERB* **delays, delaying, delayed**
1 make someone or something late.
2 postpone.

delay *NOUN* **delays** delaying; the time for which something is delayed • *a two-hour delay.*
[from old French]

delectable *ADJECTIVE* delightful or delicious.
▷ **delectably** *adverb*
[same origin as *delight*]

delegate (*say* del-ig-at) *NOUN* **delegates** a person who represents others and acts on their instructions.

delegate (*say* del-ig-ayt) *VERB* **delegates, delegating, delegated** **1** give someone a task or duty to do on your behalf • *I'm going to delegate this job to my assistant.* **2** appoint someone as a delegate • *We delegated Jones to represent us.*
[from Latin *delegare* = entrust]

delegation (*say* del-ig-ay-shon) *NOUN* **delegations** **1** delegating. **2** a group of delegates.

delete (*say* dil-eet) *VERB* **deletes, deleting, deleted** cross out or remove something written or printed or stored on a computer.
▷ **deletion** *noun*
[from Latin]

deliberate (*say* dil-ib-er-at) *ADJECTIVE*
1 done on purpose; intentional. **2** slow and careful.
▷ **deliberately** *adverb*

deliberate (*say* dil-ib-er-ayt) *VERB* **deliberates, deliberating, deliberated** discuss or think carefully.
▷ **deliberation** *noun*
[from *de-* + Latin *librare* = weigh]

deliberative *ADJECTIVE* for deliberating or discussing things.

delicacy *NOUN* **delicacies** **1** being delicate.
2 a delicious food.

delicate *ADJECTIVE* **1** fine and graceful • *delicate embroidery.* **2** fragile and easily damaged. **3** pleasant and not strong or intense. **4** becoming ill easily. **5** using or needing great care • *a delicate situation.*
▷ **delicately** *adverb* **delicateness** *noun*
[from Latin]

delicatessen *NOUN* **delicatessens** a shop that sells cooked meats, cheeses, salads, etc.
[from German, = delicacies to eat]

delicious *ADJECTIVE* tasting or smelling very pleasant.
▷ **deliciously** *adverb*
[from Latin]

delight *VERB* **delights, delighting, delighted** **1** please someone greatly.
2 take great pleasure in something.

delight *NOUN* **delights** great pleasure.
▷ **delightful** *adjective* **delightfully** *adverb*
[from Latin *delectare* = entice]

delinquent (*say* dil-ing-kwent) *NOUN* **delinquents** a young person who breaks the law.
▷ **delinquent** *adjective* **delinquency** *noun*
[from Latin *delinquere* = offend]

delirious (*say* di-li-ri-us) *ADJECTIVE*
1 affected with delirium. **2** extremely excited or enthusiastic.
▷ **deliriously** *adverb*
[same origin as *delirium*]

delirium (*say* dil-irri-um) *NOUN* **1** a state of mental confusion and agitation during a feverish illness. **2** wild excitement.
[Latin, = deranged]

deliver *VERB* **delivers, delivering, delivered** **1** take letters or goods etc. to someone's house or place of work. **2** give a speech or lecture etc. **3** help with the birth of a baby. **4** aim or strike a blow or an attack. **5** rescue; set free.
▷ **deliverer** *noun* **deliverance** *noun* **delivery** *noun*
[from *de-* + Latin *liberare* = set free]

dell *NOUN* **dells** a small valley with trees.
[from Old English]

delphinium *NOUN* **delphiniums** a garden plant with tall spikes of flowers, usually blue.
[from Greek]

delta *NOUN* **deltas** a triangular area at the mouth of a river where it spreads into branches.
[shaped like the Greek letter delta (= D), written D]

delude *VERB* **deludes, deluding, deluded** deceive or mislead someone.
[from Latin *deludere* = play unfairly]

deluge *NOUN* **deluges** **1** a large flood. **2** a heavy fall of rain. **3** something coming in great numbers • *a deluge of questions.*

deluge *VERB* **deluges, deluging, deluged** overwhelm by a deluge.
[from old French]

delusion *NOUN* **delusions** a false belief.

de luxe *ADJECTIVE* of very high quality.
[French, = of luxury]

delve *VERB* **delves, delving, delved** search deeply, e.g. for information • *delving into history.*
[from Old English]

demagogue (*say* dem-a-gog) *NOUN* **demagogues** a leader who wins support by making emotional speeches rather than by careful reasoning.
[from Greek *demos* = people + *agogos* = leading]

demand *VERB* **demands, demanding, demanded** **1** ask for something firmly or forcefully. **2** need • *This work demands great skill.*

demand *NOUN* **demands** **1** a firm or forceful request. **2** a desire to have or buy something • *There is a great demand for computers.*
- **in demand** wanted or needed.
[from *de-* + Latin *mandare* = to order]

demanding *ADJECTIVE* **1** needing skill or effort • *a demanding job.* **2** needing a lot of attention • *a demanding child.*

demarcation (*say* dee-mar-kay-shon) *NOUN* marking the boundary or limits of something.
[from Spanish]

demean *VERB* **demeans, demeaning, demeaned** lower a person's dignity • *I wouldn't demean myself to ask for it!*
[from *de-* + *mean*[2]]

demeanour (*say* dim-een-er) *NOUN* **demeanours** a person's behaviour or manner.
[from old French]

demented *ADJECTIVE* driven mad; crazy.
[from *de-* + Latin *mentis* = of the mind]

demerara (*say* dem-er-air-a) *NOUN* light-brown cane sugar.
[named after Demerara in Guyana, South America]

demerit *NOUN* **demerits** a fault or defect.
[from old French]

demi- *PREFIX* half (as in *demisemiquaver*).
[from French]

demigod *NOUN* **demigods** a partly divine being.

demise (*say* dim-I'z) *NOUN* (*formal*) death.
[from old French]

demisemiquaver *NOUN* **demisemiquavers** a note in music, equal in length to one-eighth of a crotchet.

demist *VERB* **demists, demisting, demisted** remove misty condensation from a windscreen etc.
▷ **demister** *noun*

demo *NOUN* **demos** (*informal*) a demonstration.

democracy *NOUN* **democracies** **1** government of a country by representatives elected by the whole people. **2** a country governed in this way.
▷ **democrat** *noun* **democratic** *adjective* **democratically** *adverb*
[from Greek *demos* = people, + *-cracy*]

Democrat *NOUN* **Democrats** a member of the Democratic Party in the USA.

demography (*say* dim-og-ra-fee) *NOUN* the changing number of births, deaths, diseases etc. in a country over a period of time; the scientific study of these changes.
▷ **demographic** *adjective*
[from Greek *demos* = people + *-graphy*]

demolish *VERB* **demolishes, demolishing, demolished** **1** knock a building down and break it up. **2** destroy something completely.
▷ **demolition** *noun*
[from *de-* + Latin *moliri* = build]

demon *NOUN* **demons** **1** a devil; an evil spirit. **2** a fierce or forceful person.
▷ **demonic** (*say* dim-on-ik) *adjective*
[from Greek *daimon* = a spirit]

demonstrable (*say* dem-on-strab-ul) *ADJECTIVE* able to be shown or proved.
▷ **demonstrably** *adverb*

A B C D E F G H I J K L M N O P Q R S T U V W X Y Z

demonstrate *VERB* **demonstrates, demonstrating, demonstrated** **1** show or prove something. **2** take part in a demonstration.
▷ **demonstrator** *noun*
[from *de-* + Latin *monstrare* = to show]

demonstration *NOUN* **demonstrations** **1** demonstrating; showing how to do or work something. **2** a march or meeting held to show everyone what you think about something.

demonstrative (*say* dim-on-strat-iv) *ADJECTIVE* **1** showing or proving something. **2** showing feelings or affections openly. **3** (*in grammar*) pointing out the person or thing referred to. *This, that, these,* and *those* are demonstrative adjectives and pronouns.
▷ **demonstratively** *adverb* **demonstrativeness** *noun*

demoralize *VERB* **demoralizes, demoralizing, demoralized** dishearten someone; weaken someone's confidence or morale.
▷ **demoralization** *noun*
[from *de-* + *morale*]

demote *VERB* **demotes, demoting, demoted** reduce a person to a lower position or rank.
▷ **demotion** *noun*
[from *de-* + *promote*]

demur (*say* dim-er) *VERB* **demurs, demurring, demurred** raise objections.
[from Latin *demorari* = delay]

demure *ADJECTIVE* shy and modest.
▷ **demurely** *adverb* **demureness** *noun*
[origin unknown]

den *NOUN* **dens** **1** a lair. **2** a person's private room. **3** a place where something illegal happens • *a gambling den.*
[from Old English]

deniable *ADJECTIVE* able to be denied.

denial *NOUN* **denials** denying or refusing something.

denier (*say* den-yer) *NOUN* **deniers** a unit for measuring the fineness of silk, rayon, or nylon thread.
[French]

denigrate *VERB* **denigrates, denigrating, denigrated** blacken the reputation of someone or something.
▷ **denigration** *noun*
[from *de-* + Latin *nigare* = blacken]

denim *NOUN* a kind of strong, usually blue, cotton cloth used to make jeans etc.
[from French *serge de Nim* = serge from Nîmes (a town in southern France)]

denizen (*say* den-iz-en) *NOUN* **denizens** an inhabitant • *Monkeys are denizens of the jungle.*
[from old French *deinz* = within]

denomination *NOUN* **denominations** **1** a name or title. **2** a religious group with a special name • *Baptists, Methodists, and other denominations.* **3** a unit of weight or of money • *coins of small denomination.*
[from *de-* + Latin *nominare* = to name]

denominator *NOUN* **denominators** the number below the line in a fraction, showing how many parts the whole is divided into, e.g. 4 in $\frac{1}{4}$. (COMPARE **numerator**)

denote *VERB* **denotes, denoting, denoted** mean or indicate • *In road signs, P denotes a car park.*
▷ **denotation** *noun*
[from *de-* + Latin *notare* = mark out]

dénouement (*say* day-noo-mahn) *NOUN* **dénouements** the final outcome of a plot or story, revealed at the end.
[French, = unravelling]

denounce *VERB* **denounces, denouncing, denounced** speak strongly against something; accuse • *They denounced him as a spy.*
▷ **denunciation** *noun*
[from *de-* + Latin *nuntiare* = announce]

dense *ADJECTIVE* **1** thick; packed close together • *dense fog; dense crowds.* **2** (*informal*) stupid.
▷ **densely** *adverb*
[from Latin]

density *NOUN* **densities** **1** thickness. **2** (*in science*) the proportion of mass to volume.

dent *NOUN* **dents** a hollow left in a surface where something has pressed or hit it.

dent *VERB* **dents, denting, dented** make a dent in something.
[a different spelling of *dint*]

dental *ADJECTIVE* to do with the teeth or with dentistry.
[from Latin *dentalis* = to do with a tooth]

dentist *NOUN* **dentists** a person who is trained to treat teeth, fill or extract them, fit false ones, etc.
▷ **dentistry** *noun*
[from French *dent* = tooth]

denture *NOUN* **dentures** a set of false teeth.
[French]

denude *VERB* **denudes, denuding, denuded** make bare or naked; strip something away.
▷ **denudation** *noun*
[from *de-* + Latin *nudare* = to bare]

denunciation *NOUN* **denunciations** denouncing.

deny *VERB* **denies, denying, denied 1** say that something is not true. **2** refuse to give or allow something • *deny a request.*
- **deny yourself** go without pleasures.
[from *de-* + Latin *negare* = say no]

deodorant (*say* dee-**oh**-der-ant) *NOUN* **deodorants** a substance that removes smells.

deodorize *VERB* **deodorizes, deodorizing, deodorized** remove smells.
▷ **deodorization** *noun*
[from *de-* + Latin *odor* = a smell]

depart *VERB* **departs, departing, departed** go away; leave.
[from old French *départir* = separate]

department *NOUN* **departments** one section of a large organization or shop.
▷ **departmental** *adjective*
[from French *département* = division]

department store *NOUN* **department stores** a large shop that sells many different kinds of goods.

departure *NOUN* **departures** departing.

depend *VERB* **depends, depending, depended**
- **depend on 1** rely on • *We depend on your help.* **2** be controlled by something else • *It all depends on the weather.*
[from *de-* + Latin *pendere* = hang]

dependable *ADJECTIVE* reliable.

dependant *NOUN* **dependants** a person who depends on another, especially financially • *She has two dependants.*
USAGE Note that the spelling ends in *-ant* for this noun but *-ent* for the adjective *dependent.*

dependency *NOUN* **dependencies**
1 dependence. **2** a country that is controlled by another.

dependent *ADJECTIVE* depending • *She has two dependent children; they are dependent on her.*
▷ **dependence** *noun*
USAGE See note at **dependant**.

depict *VERB* **depicts, depicting, depicted**
1 show something in a painting or drawing etc. **2** describe.
▷ **depiction** *noun*
[from *de-* + Latin *pictum* = painted]

deplete (*say* dip-**leet**) *VERB* **depletes, depleting, depleted** reduce the amount of something by using up large amounts.
▷ **depletion** *noun*
[from *de-* + Latin *-pletum* = filled]

deplore *VERB* **deplores, deploring, deplored** be very upset or annoyed by something.
▷ **deplorable** *adjective* **deplorably** *adverb*
[from *de-* + Latin *plorare* = weep]

deploy *VERB* **deploys, deploying, deployed 1** place troops or weapons in good positions so that they are ready to be used effectively. **2** use something effectively.
▷ **deployment** *noun*
[from French]

deport *VERB* **deports, deporting, deported** send an unwanted foreign person out of a country.
▷ **deportation** *noun*
[from *de-* + Latin *portare* = carry]

deportment *NOUN* a person's manner of standing, walking, and behaving.
[from old French]

depose *VERB* **deposes, deposing, deposed** remove a person from power.
[from old French *deposer* = put down]

deposit *NOUN* **deposits 1** an amount of money paid into a bank etc. **2** money paid as a first instalment. **3** a layer of solid matter in or on the earth.

deposit *VERB* **deposits, depositing, deposited** **1** put something down. **2** pay money as a deposit.
▷ **depositor** *noun*
[from *de-* + Latin *positum* = placed]

deposition *NOUN* **depositions** a written piece of evidence, given under oath.

depot (*say* dep-oh) *NOUN* **depots** **1** a place where things are stored. **2** a place where buses or trains are kept and repaired. **3** a headquarters.
[same origin as *deposit*]

depraved *ADJECTIVE* behaving wickedly; of bad character.
▷ **depravity** *noun*
[from *de-* + Latin *pravus* = perverse, wrong]

deprecate (*say* dep-rik-ayt) *VERB* **deprecates, deprecating, deprecated** say that you disapprove of something.
▷ **deprecation** *noun*
[from Latin *deprecari* = keep away misfortune by prayer]
USAGE Do not confuse with **depreciate**.

depreciate (*say* dip-ree-shee-ayt) *VERB* **depreciates, depreciating, depreciated** make or become lower in value.
▷ **depreciation** *noun*
[from *de-* + Latin *pretium* = price]
USAGE Do not confuse with **deprecate**.

depredation (*say* dep-rid-ay-shon) *NOUN* **depredations** the act of plundering or damaging something. (COMPARE **predator**)
[from *de-* + Latin *praedere* = to plunder]

depress *VERB* **depresses, depressing, depressed** **1** make somebody sad. **2** lower the value of something • *Threat of war depressed prices.* **3** press down • *Depress the lever.*
▷ **depressive** *adjective*
[from Latin *depressum* = pressed down]

depression *NOUN* **depressions** **1** a feeling of great sadness or hopelessness, often with physical symptoms. **2** a long period when trade is very slack because no one can afford to buy things, with widespread unemployment. **3** a shallow hollow in the ground or on a surface. **4** an area of low air pressure which may bring rain. **5** pressing something down.

deprive *VERB* **deprives, depriving, deprived** take or keep something away from somebody.
▷ **deprival** *noun* **deprivation** *noun*
[from *de-* + Latin *privare* = rob]

depth *NOUN* **depths** **1** being deep; how deep something is. **2** the deepest or lowest part.
- **in depth** thoroughly.
- **out of your depth** **1** in water that is too deep to stand in. **2** trying to do something that is too difficult for you.
[from *deep*]

deputation *NOUN* **deputations** a group of people sent as representatives of others.

depute (*say* dip-yoot) *VERB* **deputes, deputing, deputed** **1** appoint a person to do something • *We deputed John to take the message.* **2** assign or delegate a task to someone • *We deputed the task to him.*
[from old French]

deputize *VERB* **deputizes, deputizing, deputized** act as someone's deputy.

deputy *NOUN* **deputies** a person appointed to act as a substitute for another.
[from French *deputé* = deputed]

derail *VERB* **derails, derailing, derailed** cause a train to leave the rails.
▷ **derailment** *noun*
[from *de-* + French *rail* = rail]

deranged *ADJECTIVE* insane.
▷ **derangement** *noun*
[from *de-* + French *rang* = rank]

derby (*say* dar-bi) *NOUN* **derbies** a sports match between two teams from the same city or area.
[from the name of the Earl of *Derby*, who in 1780 founded the famous horse race called the Derby which is run at Epsom in Surrey]

derelict (*say* derri-likt) *ADJECTIVE* abandoned and left to fall into ruin.
▷ **dereliction** *noun*
[from *de-* + Latin *relictum* = left behind]

deride *VERB* **derides, deriding, derided** laugh at with contempt or scorn; ridicule.
[from *de-* + Latin *ridere* = to laugh]

de rigueur (*say* der rig-er) *ADJECTIVE* proper; required by custom or etiquette.
[French, literally = of strictness]

derision *NOUN* scorn or ridicule.
▷ **derisive** (*say* dir-I-siv) *adjective*
derisively *adverb*
[same origin as *deride*]

derisory *ADJECTIVE* **1** scornful. **2** so small that it is ridiculous • *a derisory offer.*
[same origin as *deride*]

derivation *NOUN* **derivations** **1** deriving. **2** the origin of a word from another language or from a simple word to which a prefix or suffix is added; etymology.

derivative *ADJECTIVE* derived from something; not original.
▷ **derivative** *noun*

derive *VERB* **derives, deriving, derived** **1** obtain something from a source • *She derived great enjoyment from music.* **2** form or originate from something • *Some English words are derived from Latin words.*
[from *de-* + Latin *rivus* = a stream]

dermatology *NOUN* the study of the skin and its diseases.
▷ **dermatologist** *noun*
[from Greek *derma* = skin, + *-logy*]

dermis *NOUN* the layer of skin below the epidermis.
[Latin, from Greek *derma* = skin]

derogatory (*say* di-rog-at-er-ee) *ADJECTIVE* scornful or disparaging.
[from Latin *derogare* = make smaller]

derrick *NOUN* **derricks** **1** a kind of crane for lifting things. **2** a tall framework holding the machinery used in drilling an oil well etc.
[originally a gallows; Derrick was the surname of a London hangman]

derv *NOUN* diesel fuel for lorries etc.
[from the initials of 'diesel- engined road vehicle']

dervish *NOUN* **dervishes** a member of a Muslim religious group who vowed to live a life of poverty.
[from Persian *darvish* = poor]

descant *NOUN* **descants** a tune sung or played above the main tune.
[from *dis-* + Latin *cantus* = song]

descend *VERB* **descends, descending, descended** go down.
- **be descended from** have as an ancestor; come by birth from a certain person or family.
[from *de-* + Latin *scandere* = climb]

descendant *NOUN* **descendants** a person who is descended from someone.

descent *NOUN* **descents** descending.

describe *VERB* **describes, describing, described** **1** say what someone or something is like. **2** draw in outline; move in a pattern • *The orbit of the Earth around the Sun describes an ellipse.*
▷ **description** *noun* **descriptive** *adjective*
[from *de-* + Latin *scribere* = write]

desecrate (*say* dess-ik-rayt) *VERB* **desecrates, desecrating, desecrated** treat a sacred thing without respect.
▷ **desecration** *noun*
[from *de-* + *consecrate*]

desert (*say* dez-ert) *NOUN* **deserts** a large area of dry often sandy land.

desert (*say* diz-ert) *VERB* **deserts, deserting, deserted** **1** leave a person or place without intending to return. **2** run away from the army.
▷ **deserter** *noun* **desertion** *noun*
[from Latin *desertus* = abandoned]

desert island *NOUN* **desert islands** an uninhabited island.

deserts (*say* diz-erts) *PLURAL NOUN* what a person deserves • *He got his deserts.*
[from *deserve*]

deserve *VERB* **deserves, deserving, deserved** have a right to something; be worthy of something.
▷ **deservedly** *adverb*
[from Latin *deservire* = serve someone well]

desiccated *ADJECTIVE* dried • *desiccated coconut.*
[from Latin]
USAGE Note the spelling of this word. It has one 's' and two 'c's.

design *NOUN* **designs** **1** a drawing that shows how something is to be made. **2** the way something is made or arranged. **3** lines and shapes that form a decoration; a pattern. **4** a mental plan or scheme.
- **have designs on** plan to get hold of.

design *VERB* **designs, designing, designed** 1 draw a design for something. 2 plan or intend something for a special purpose.
▷ **designer** *noun*
[from *de-* + Latin *signare* = mark out]

designate *VERB* **designates, designating, designated** mark or describe as something particular • *They designated the river as the boundary.*
▷ **designation** *noun*

designate *ADJECTIVE* appointed to a job but not yet doing it • *the bishop designate.*
[same origin as *design*]

desirable *ADJECTIVE* 1 causing people to desire it; worth having. 2 worth doing; advisable.
▷ **desirability** *noun*

desire *NOUN* **desires** a feeling of wanting something very much.
▷ **desirous** *adjective*

desire *VERB* **desires, desiring, desired** have a desire for something.
[from Latin]

desist (*say* diz-ist) *VERB* **desists, desisting, desisted** stop doing something.
[from Latin]

desk *NOUN* **desks** 1 a piece of furniture with a flat top and often drawers, used when writing or doing work. 2 a counter at which a cashier or receptionist sits.
[from Latin]

desktop *ADJECTIVE* small enough to use on a desk • *a desktop computer.*

desolate *ADJECTIVE* 1 lonely and sad. 2 uninhabited.
▷ **desolation** *noun*
[from Latin *desolare* = abandon]

despair *NOUN* a feeling of hopelessness.

despair *VERB* **despairs, despairing, despaired** feel despair.
[from *de-* + Latin *sperare* = to hope]

despatch *VERB* **despatches, despatching, despatched** a different spelling of *dispatch*.
▷ **despatch** *noun*

desperado (*say* dess-per-ah-doh) *NOUN* **desperadoes** a reckless criminal.
[from *desperate*]

desperate *ADJECTIVE* 1 extremely serious or hopeless • *a desperate situation.* 2 having a great need or desire for something • *She is desperate to get a ticket.* 3 reckless and ready to do anything.
▷ **desperately** *adverb* **desperation** *noun*
[same origin as *despair*]

despicable *ADJECTIVE* deserving to be despised; contemptible.

despise *VERB* **despises, despising, despised** think someone or something is inferior or worthless.
[from *de-* + Latin *-spicere* = to look]

despite *PREPOSITION* in spite of.
[same origin as *despise*]

despondent *ADJECTIVE* sad or gloomy.
▷ **despondently** *adverb* **despondency** *noun*
[from Latin *despondere* = give up, resign]

despot (*say* dess-pot) *NOUN* **despots** a tyrant.
▷ **despotism** *noun* **despotic** (*say* dis-pot-ik) *adjective*
[from Greek *despotes* = master]

dessert (*say* diz-ert) *NOUN* **desserts** fruit or a sweet food served as the last course of a meal.
[from French *desservir* = clear the table]

dessertspoon *NOUN* **dessertspoons** a medium-sized spoon used for eating puddings etc.

destination *NOUN* **destinations** the place to which a person or thing is travelling.
[same origin as *destiny*]

destined *ADJECTIVE* having as a destiny; intended.

destiny *NOUN* **destinies** what will happen or has happened to somebody or something; fate.
[from Latin *destinare* = fix, settle]

destitute *ADJECTIVE* left without anything; living in extreme poverty.
▷ **destitution** *noun*
[from Latin *destitutus* = left in the lurch]

destroy *VERB* **destroys, destroying, destroyed** ruin or put an end to something.
▷ **destruction** *noun* **destructive** *adjective*
[from *de-* + Latin *struere* = pile up]

destroyer *NOUN* **destroyers** a fast warship.

desultory (*say* dess-ul-ter-ee) *ADJECTIVE* half-hearted, without enthusiasm or a definite plan • *desultory talk.*
[from Latin *desultorius* = like an acrobat (someone who leaps about)]

detach *VERB* **detaches, detaching, detached** unfasten or separate.
▷ **detachable** *adjective*
[from *de-* + *attach*]

detached *ADJECTIVE* **1** separated. **2** (said about a house) not joined to another. **3** impartial; not involved in something.

detachment *NOUN* **detachments** **1** being impartial. **2** a small group of soldiers sent away from a larger group for a special duty.

detail *NOUN* **details** **1** a very small part of a design or plan or decoration etc. **2** a small piece of information.
▷ **detailed** *adjective*
- **in detail** describing or dealing with everything fully.
[from *de-* + French *tailler* = cut in pieces]

detain *VERB* **detains, detaining, detained** **1** keep someone waiting. **2** keep someone at a place.
▷ **detention** *noun*
[from *de-* + Latin *tenere* = hold]

detainee *NOUN* **detainees** a person who is officially detained or kept in custody.

detect *VERB* **detects, detecting, detected** discover.
▷ **detection** *noun* **detector** *noun*
[from *de-* + Latin *tegere* = cover]

detective *NOUN* **detectives** a person who investigates crimes.

detention *NOUN* **detentions** **1** detaining; being detained. **2** being made to stay late in school as a punishment.
[same origin as *detain*]

deter *VERB* **deters, deterring, deterred** discourage or prevent a person from doing something.
[from *de-* + Latin *terrere* = frighten]

detergent *NOUN* **detergents** a substance used for cleaning or washing things.
[from *de-* + Latin *tergere* = to clean]

deteriorate (*say* dit-eer-ee-er-ayt) *VERB* **deteriorates, deteriorating, deteriorated** become worse.
▷ **deterioration** *noun*
[from Latin *deterior* = worse]

determination *NOUN* **1** the firm intention to achieve what you have decided to achieve. **2** determining or deciding something.

determine *VERB* **determines, determining, determined** **1** decide • *His punishment is still to be determined.* **2** cause or influence • *Income determines your standard of living.* **3** find out; calculate • *Can you determine the height of the mountain?*
[from *de-* + Latin *terminare* = to limit]

determined *ADJECTIVE* full of determination; with your mind firmly made up.

determiner *NOUN* **determiners** (*in grammar*) a word (such as *a*, *the*, *many*) that modifies a noun.

deterrent *NOUN* **deterrents** something that may deter people, e.g. a nuclear weapon that deters countries from making war on the one that has it.
▷ **deterrence** *noun*

detest *VERB* **detests, detesting, detested** dislike something very much; loathe.
▷ **detestable** *adjective* **detestation** *noun*
[from Latin]

detonate (*say* det-on-ayt) *VERB* **detonates, detonating, detonated** explode or cause something to explode.
▷ **detonation** *noun* **detonator** *noun*
[from *de-* + Latin *tonare* = to thunder]

detour (*say* dee-toor) *NOUN* **detours** a roundabout route instead of the normal one.
[from French *détourner* = turn away]

detract *VERB* **detracts, detracting, detracted** lessen the amount or value • *It will not detract from our pleasure.*
▷ **detraction** *noun*
[from *de-* + Latin *tractus* = pulled]

detriment (*say* det-rim-ent) *NOUN* harm or disadvantage • *She worked long hours, to the detriment of her health.*
[from Latin *detrimentum* = worn away]

detrimental (*say* det-rim-en-tal) *ADJECTIVE* harmful or disadvantageous.
▷ **detrimentally** *adverb*

de trop (*say* der troh) *ADJECTIVE* not wanted; unwelcome.
[French, = too much]

deuce *NOUN* **deuces** a score in tennis where both sides have 40 points and must gain two consecutive points to win.
[from old French *deus* = two]

devalue *VERB* **devalues, devaluing, devalued** **1** reduce a thing's value. **2** reduce the value of a country's currency in relation to other currencies or to gold.
▷ **devaluation** *noun*

devastate *VERB* **devastates, devastating, devastated** **1** ruin or cause great destruction to something. **2** cause great shock or grief.
▷ **devastating** *adjective* **devastation** *noun*
[from Latin]

develop *VERB* **develops, developing, developed** **1** make or become bigger or better. **2** come gradually into existence • *Storms developed.* **3** begin to have or use • *They developed bad habits.* **4** use an area of land for building houses, shops, factories, etc. **5** treat photographic film with chemicals so that pictures appear.
▷ **developer** *noun* **development** *noun* **developmental** *adjective*
[from French]

developing country *NOUN* **developing countries** a poor country that is building up its industry and trying to improve its living conditions.

deviate (*say* dee-vee-ayt) *VERB* **deviates, deviating, deviated** turn aside from a course or from what is usual or true.
▷ **deviation** *noun*
[from *de-* + Latin *via* = way]

device *NOUN* **devices** **1** something made for a particular purpose • *a device for opening tins.* **2** a design used as a decoration or emblem.
- **leave someone to their own devices** leave them to do as they wish.
[same origin as *devise*]

devil *NOUN* **devils** **1** an evil spirit. **2** a wicked, cruel, or annoying person.
▷ **devilish** *adjective* **devilry** *noun*
[via Old English from Latin]

devilment *NOUN* mischief.

devious (*say* dee-vee-us) *ADJECTIVE* **1** roundabout; not direct • *a devious route.* **2** not straightforward; underhand.
▷ **deviously** *adverb* **deviousness** *noun*
[same origin as *deviate*]

devise *VERB* **devises, devising, devised** invent or plan.
[from old French]

devoid *ADJECTIVE* lacking or without something • *His work is devoid of merit.*
[from *de-* + old French *voider* = make void]

devolution *NOUN* handing over power from central government to local or regional government.
[same origin as *devolve*]

devolve *VERB* **devolves, devolving, devolved** pass or be passed to a deputy or successor.
[from Latin *devolvere* = roll down]

devote *VERB* **devotes, devoting, devoted** give completely • *He devoted his time to sport.*
[from *de-* + Latin *vovere* = to vow]

devoted *ADJECTIVE* very loving or loyal.

devotee (*say* dev-o-tee) *NOUN* **devotees** a person who is devoted to something; an enthusiast.

devotion *NOUN* great love or loyalty.

devotions *PLURAL NOUN* prayers.

devour *VERB* **devours, devouring, devoured** eat or swallow something hungrily or greedily.
[from *de-* + Latin *vorare* = to swallow]

devout *ADJECTIVE* earnestly religious or sincere.
▷ **devoutly** *adverb* **devoutness** *noun*
[same origin as *devote*]

dew *NOUN* tiny drops of water that form during the night on surfaces of things in the open air.
▷ **dewdrop** *noun* **dewy** *adjective*
[from Old English]

dexterity (*say* deks-terri-tee) NOUN skill in handling things.
[from Latin *dexter* = on the right-hand side]

dhoti NOUN **dhotis** the loincloth worn by male Hindus.
[Hindi]

di-[1] PREFIX two; double (as in *dioxide*).
[from Greek *dis* = twice]

di-[2] PREFIX **1** not; the reverse of. **2** apart; separated. SEE **dis-**.

dia- PREFIX through (as in *diarrhoea*); across (as in *diagonal*).
[from Greek *dia* = through]

diabetes (*say* dy-a-**bee**-teez) NOUN a disease in which there is too much sugar in a person's blood.
▷ **diabetic** (*say* dy-a-**bet**-ik) *adjective* & *noun*
[from Greek]

diabolical ADJECTIVE **1** like a devil; very wicked. **2** very clever or annoying.
[from Latin *diabolus* = devil]

diadem (*say* **dy**-a-dem) NOUN **diadems** a crown or headband worn by a royal person.
[from Greek]

diagnose VERB **diagnoses, diagnosing, diagnosed** find out what disease a person has or what is wrong.
▷ **diagnosis** *noun* **diagnostic** *adjective*
[from *dia-* + Greek *gignoskein* = know]

diagonal (*say* dy-**ag**-on-al) NOUN **diagonals** a straight line joining opposite corners.
▷ **diagonal** *adjective* **diagonally** *adverb*
[from *dia-* + Greek *gonia* = angle]

diagram NOUN **diagrams** a kind of drawing or picture that shows the parts of something or how it works.
[from *dia-* + *-gram*]

dial NOUN **dials** a circular object with numbers or letters round it.

dial VERB **dials, dialling, dialled** telephone a number by turning a telephone dial or pressing numbered buttons.
[from Latin *diale* = clock-face, from *dies* = day]

dialect NOUN **dialects** the words and pronunciations used by people in one district but not in the rest of a country.
[from Greek *dialektos* = way of speaking]

dialogue NOUN **dialogues** **1** the words spoken by characters in a play, film, or story. **2** a conversation.
[from Greek]

dialysis (*say* dy-**al**-iss-iss) NOUN a way of removing harmful substances from the blood by letting it flow through a machine.
[from *dia-* + Greek *lysis* = loosening]

diameter (*say* dy-**am**-it-er) NOUN **diameters** **1** a line drawn straight across a circle or sphere and passing through its centre. **2** the length of this line.
[from Greek *diametros* = measuring across]

diametrically ADVERB completely
• *diametrically opposite.*

diamond NOUN **diamonds** **1** a very hard precious stone, a form of carbon, that looks like clear glass. **2** a shape with four equal sides and four angles that are not right angles. **3** a playing card with red diamond shapes on it.
[from Greek *adamas* = adamant (= a very hard stone)]

diamond wedding NOUN **diamond weddings** a couple's 60th wedding anniversary.

diaper NOUN **diapers** (*American*) a baby's nappy.
[from medieval Greek *diaspros* = made of white cloth]

diaphanous (*say* dy-**af**-an-us) ADJECTIVE (said about fabric) almost transparent.
[from *dia-* + Greek *phainein* = to show]

diaphragm (*say* **dy**-a-fram) NOUN **diaphragms** **1** the muscular layer inside the body that separates the chest from the abdomen and is used in breathing. **2** a dome-shaped contraceptive device that fits over the cervix.
[from *dia-* + Greek *phragma* = fence]

diarist NOUN **diarists** a person who keeps a diary.

diarrhoea (*say* dy-a-**ree**-a) NOUN too frequent and too watery emptying of the bowels.
[from *dia-* + Greek *rhoia* = a flow]

diary NOUN **diaries** a book in which someone writes down what happens each day.
[from Latin *dies* = day]

diatribe *NOUN* **diatribes** a strong verbal attack.
[French]

dice *NOUN* (strictly this is the plural of **die**², but it is often used as a singular, plural **dice**) a small cube marked with dots (1 to 6) on its sides, used in games.

dice *VERB* **dices, dicing, diced** **1** play gambling games using dice. **2** cut meat, vegetables, etc. into small cubes.
[plural of *die*²]

dictate *VERB* **dictates, dictating, dictated** **1** speak or read something aloud for someone else to write down. **2** give orders in a bossy way.
▷ **dictation** *noun*
[from Latin *dictare* = keep saying]

dictates (*say* dik-tayts) *PLURAL NOUN* orders or commands.

dictator *NOUN* **dictators** a ruler who has unlimited power.
▷ **dictatorial** (*say* dik-ta-tor-ee-al) *adjective*
dictatorship *noun*

diction *NOUN* **1** a person's way of speaking words • *clear diction.* **2** a writer's choice of words.
[from Latin *dictio* = saying, word]
USAGE There are a number of English words that are related to *diction* because part of their original meaning comes from the Latin words *dicere* meaning 'to say or speak' or *dictio* meaning 'saying or word'. These include *benediction, contradict, dictate, dictator, dictionary, edict, interdict*, and *predict*.

dictionary *NOUN* **dictionaries** a book that contains words in alphabetical order so that you can find out how to spell them and what they mean.
[same origin as *diction*]

didactic (*say* dy-dak-tik) *ADJECTIVE* having the manner of someone who is lecturing people.
▷ **didactically** *adverb*
[from Greek *didaktikos* = teaching]

diddle *VERB* **diddles, diddling, diddled** (*slang*) cheat or swindle.
[origin unknown]

didgeridoo *NOUN* **didgeridoos** an Australian Aboriginal musical instrument which consists of a long thin pipe that you blow into to make a low humming sound.
[from an Aboriginal language]

didn't (*mainly spoken*) did not.

die¹ *VERB* **dies, dying, died** **1** stop living or existing. **2** stop burning or functioning • *The fire had died down.*
- **be dying for** or **to** (*informal*) want to have or do something very much • *We are all dying to see you again.*
[from Old Norse]

die² *NOUN* singular of **dice**.
[from old French]

die³ *NOUN* **dies** a device that stamps a design on coins etc. or that cuts or moulds metal.
[from old French]

diehard *NOUN* **diehards** a person who obstinately refuses to give up old ideas or policies.
[from *die hard* = die painfully]

diesel (*say* dee-zel) *NOUN* **diesels** **1** an engine that works by burning oil in compressed air. **2** fuel for this kind of engine.
[named after R. *Diesel*, a German engineer, who invented it]

diet¹ *NOUN* **diets** **1** special meals that someone eats in order to be healthy or to become less fat. **2** the sort of foods usually eaten by a person or animal.

diet *VERB* **diets, dieting, dieted** keep to a diet.
[from Greek *diaita* = way of life]

diet² *NOUN* **diets** the parliament of certain countries (e.g. Japan).
[from Latin *dieta* = day's business]

dietitian (*say* dy-it-ish-an) *NOUN* **dietitians** an expert in diet and nutrition.

dif- *PREFIX* **1** not; the reverse of. **2** apart; separated. SEE **dis-**.

differ *VERB* **differs, differing, differed** **1** be different. **2** disagree.
[from *dif-* + Latin *ferre* = carry]

difference *NOUN* **differences** **1** being different; the way in which things differ. **2** the remainder left after one number is subtracted from another • *The difference between 8 and 3 is 5.* **3** a disagreement.

different *ADJECTIVE* **1** unlike; not the same. **2** separate or distinct • *I called on three different occasions.*
▷ **differently** *adverb*

USAGE It is regarded as more acceptable to say *different from* rather than *different to*, which is common in less formal use. The phrase *different than* is used in American English but not in standard British English.

differential *NOUN* **differentials** **1** a difference in wages between one group of workers and another. **2** a differential gear.

differential gear *NOUN* **differential gears** a system of gears that makes a vehicle's driving wheels revolve at different speeds when going round corners.

differentiate *VERB* **differentiates, differentiating, differentiated** **1** be a difference between things; make one thing different from another • *What are the features that differentiate one breed from another?* **2** distinguish; recognize differences • *We do not differentiate between them.*
▷ **differentiation** *noun*

difficult *ADJECTIVE* needing a lot of effort or skill; not easy.
[from *dif-* + Latin *facilis* = easy]

difficulty *NOUN* **difficulties** **1** being difficult. **2** something that causes a problem.

diffident (*say* dif-id-ent) *ADJECTIVE* shy and not self-confident; hesitating to put yourself or your ideas forward.
▷ **diffidently** *adverb* **diffidence** *noun*
[from *dif-* + Latin *fidentia* = confidence]

diffract *VERB* **diffracts, diffracting, diffracted** break up a beam of light etc.
▷ **diffraction** *noun*
[from *dif-* + Latin *fractum* = broken]

diffuse (*say* dif-yooz) *VERB* **diffuses, diffusing, diffused** **1** spread something widely or thinly • *diffused lighting.* **2** mix slowly • *diffusing gases.*
▷ **diffusion** *noun*

diffuse (*say* dif-yooss) *ADJECTIVE* **1** spread widely; not concentrated. **2** using many words; not concise.
▷ **diffusely** *adverb* **diffuseness** *noun*
[from *dif-* + Latin *fusum* = poured]

dig *VERB* **digs, digging, dug** **1** break up soil and move it; make a hole or tunnel by moving soil. **2** poke something in • *Dig a knife into it.* **3** seek or discover by investigating • *We dug up some facts.*
▷ **digger** *noun*

dig *NOUN* **digs** **1** a piece of digging, especially an archaeological excavation. **2** a poke. **3** an unpleasant remark.
[probably from Old English]

digest (*say* dy-jest) *VERB* **digests, digesting, digested** **1** soften and change food in the stomach etc. so that the body can absorb it. **2** take information into your mind and think it over.
▷ **digestible** *adjective* **digestion** *noun*

digest (*say* dy-jest) *NOUN* **digests** a summary of news, information, etc.
[from Latin]

digestive *ADJECTIVE* to do with digestion • *the digestive system.*

digestive biscuit *NOUN* **digestive biscuits** a wholemeal biscuit (because it is supposed to be easy to digest).

digger *NOUN* **diggers** (*informal*) (*Australian/NZ*) a friendly form of address for a man.
[from *digger* = miner]

digit (*say* dij-it) *NOUN* **digits** **1** any of the numbers from 0 to 9. **2** a finger or toe.
[from Latin *digitus* = finger or toe]

digital *ADJECTIVE* **1** to do with or using digits. **2** (said about a watch or clock) showing the time with a row of figures. **3** (said about a computer, recording, etc.) storing the data or sound as a series of binary digits.

dignified *ADJECTIVE* having dignity.

dignitary *NOUN* **dignitaries** an important official.
[same origin as *dignity*]

dignity *NOUN* a calm and serious manner.
- **beneath your dignity** not considered worthy enough for you to do.
[from Latin *dignus* = worthy]

digress *VERB* **digresses, digressing, digressed** stray from the main subject.
▷ **digression** *noun*
[from *di-*[2] + Latin *gressum* = gone]

dike *NOUN* **dikes** **1** a long wall or embankment to hold back water and prevent flooding. **2** a ditch for draining water from land.
[from Old Norse]

dilapidated *ADJECTIVE* falling to pieces.
▷ **dilapidation** *noun*
[from Latin]

dilate *VERB* **dilates, dilating, dilated** make or become wider or larger.
▷ **dilation** *noun*
[from *di-*[2] + Latin *latus* = wide]

dilatory (*say* dil-at-er-ee) *ADJECTIVE* slow in doing something; not prompt.
[from Latin *dilator* = someone who delays]

dilemma (*say* dil-em-a) *NOUN* **dilemmas** a situation where someone has to choose between two or more possible actions, either of which would bring difficulties.
[from Greek, = double proposal]
USAGE Do not use *dilemma* to mean simply a problem or difficult situation. There should be some idea of choosing between two (or perhaps more) things.

diligent (*say* dil-ij-ent) *ADJECTIVE* hard-working.
▷ **diligently** *adverb* **diligence** *noun*
[from Latin *diligens* = careful, conscientious]

dilute *VERB* **dilutes, diluting, diluted** make a liquid weaker by adding water or other liquid.
▷ **dilution** *noun*

dilute *ADJECTIVE* diluted • *a dilute acid.*
[from Latin *diluere* = wash away]

dim *ADJECTIVE* **dimmer, dimmest** **1** not bright or clear; only faintly lit. **2** (*informal*) stupid.
▷ **dimly** *adverb* **dimness** *noun*

dim *VERB* **dims, dimming, dimmed** make or become dim.
▷ **dimmer** *noun*
[from Old English]

dime *NOUN* **dimes** (*American*) a ten-cent coin.
[from Latin *decem* = ten]

dimension *NOUN* **dimensions** **1** a measurement such as length, width, area, or volume. **2** size or extent.
▷ **dimensional** *adjective*
[from Latin *dimensio* = measuring out]

diminish *VERB* **diminishes, diminishing, diminished** make or become smaller.
▷ **diminution** *noun*
[same origin as *diminutive*]

diminutive (*say* dim-in-yoo-tiv) *ADJECTIVE* very small.
[from Latin *diminuere* = lessen]

dimple *NOUN* **dimples** a small hollow or dent, especially in the skin.
▷ **dimpled** *adjective*
[probably from Old English]

din *NOUN* a loud annoying noise.
[from Old English]

dine *VERB* **dines, dining, dined** (*formal*) have dinner.
▷ **diner** *noun*
[from old French *disner*]

diner *NOUN* **diners** (*American*) a small, inexpensive restaurant.

dinghy (*say* ding-ee) *NOUN* **dinghies** a kind of small boat.
[from Hindi *dingi* = a small river boat]

dingo *NOUN* **dingoes** an Australian wild dog.
[from an Australian Aboriginal word]

dingy (*say* din-jee) *ADJECTIVE* dirty-looking.
▷ **dingily** *adverb* **dinginess** *noun*
[origin unknown]

dinkum *ADJECTIVE* (*informal*) (*Australian/NZ*) genuine, real, or honest.
- **fair dinkum**
used for emphasis or to query whether something is true.
[origin unknown]

dinner *NOUN* **dinners** **1** the main meal of the day, either at midday or in the evening. **2** a formal evening meal in honour of something.
[same origin as *dine*]

dinosaur (*say* dy-noss-or) *NOUN* **dinosaurs** a prehistoric reptile, often of enormous size.
[from Greek *deinos* = terrible + *sauros* = lizard]

dint *NOUN* **dints** - **by dint of** by means of; using • *I got through the exam by dint of a good memory and a lot of luck.*
[from Old English]

diocese (*say* dy-oss-iss) NOUN **dioceses** a district under the care of a bishop.
▷ **diocesan** (*say* dy-oss-iss-an) *adjective*
[from Latin]

dioxide NOUN an oxide with two atoms of oxygen to one of another element • *carbon dioxide.*
[from *di-* ¹ + *oxide*]

dip VERB **dips, dipping, dipped** put down or go down, especially into a liquid.

dip NOUN **dips** **1** dipping. **2** a downward slope. **3** a quick swim. **4** a substance into which things are dipped.
[from Old English]

diphtheria (*say* dif-theer-ee-a) NOUN a serious disease that causes inflammation in the throat.
[from Greek *diphthera* = skin (because a tough skin forms on the throat membrane)]

diphthong (*say* dif-thong) NOUN **diphthongs** a compound vowel sound made up of two sounds, e.g. *oi* in *point*, (made up of 'aw' + 'ee') or *ou* in *loud* ('ah' + 'oo').
[from *di-* ¹ + Greek *phthongos* = sound]

diploma NOUN **diplomas** a certificate awarded by a college etc. for skill in a particular subject.
[Latin, from Greek, literally = folded paper]

diplomacy NOUN **1** the work of making agreements with other countries. **2** skill in dealing with people and gently persuading them to agree to things; tact.

diplomat NOUN **diplomats** **1** a person employed in diplomacy on behalf of his or her country. **2** a tactful person.
[from Latin *diploma* = an official letter given to travellers, saying who they were]

diplomatic ADJECTIVE **1** to do with diplomats or diplomacy. **2** tactful.
▷ **diplomatically** *adverb*

dipper NOUN **dippers** **1** a kind of bird that dives for its food. **2** a ladle.
[from *dip*]

dire ADJECTIVE dreadful or serious • *in dire need.*
[from Latin]

direct ADJECTIVE **1** as straight as possible. **2** going straight to the point; frank. **3** exact • *the direct opposite.*
▷ **directness** *noun*

direct VERB **directs, directing, directed** **1** tell someone the way. **2** guide or aim in a certain direction. **3** control or manage. **4** order • *He directed his troops to advance.*
[from Latin *directus* = kept straight]

direct current NOUN electric current flowing only in one direction.

direction NOUN **directions** **1** the line along which something moves or faces. **2** directing.
▷ **directional** *adjective*

directions PLURAL NOUN information on how to use or do something or how to get somewhere.

directive NOUN **directives** a command.

directly ADVERB **1** by a direct route • *Go directly to the shop.* **2** immediately • *I want you to come directly.*

direct object NOUN **direct objects** (*in grammar*) the word that receives the action of the verb. In *she hit him*, 'him' is the direct object.

director NOUN **directors** **1** a person who is in charge of something, especially one of a group of people managing a company. **2** a person who decides how a film, programme, or play should be made or performed.

directory NOUN **directories** **1** a book containing a list of people with their telephone numbers, addresses, etc. **2** (*in computing*) a file containing a group of other files.
[from Latin *directorius* = guiding]

direct speech NOUN someone's words written down exactly in the way they were said.

dirge NOUN **dirges** a slow sad song.
[from the first word of a song, which used to be part of the Roman Catholic service for a dead person]

dirk NOUN **dirks** a kind of dagger.
[origin unknown]

dirt NOUN earth or soil; anything that is not clean.
[from Old Norse]

dirty *ADJECTIVE* **dirtier, dirtiest 1** not clean; soiled. **2** unfair; dishonourable • *a dirty trick.* **3** indecent; obscene.
▷ **dirtily** *adverb* **dirtiness** *noun*

dis- *PREFIX* (changing to **dif-** before words beginning with *f*, and to **di-** before some consonants) **1** not; the reverse of (as in *dishonest*). **2** apart; separated (as in *disarm, disperse*).
[from Latin]

disabled *ADJECTIVE* unable to use part of your body properly because of illness or injury.
▷ **disability** *noun* **disablement** *noun*

disadvantage *NOUN* **disadvantages** something that hinders or is unhelpful.
▷ **disadvantaged** *adjective* **disadvantageous** *adjective*

disagree *VERB* **disagrees, disagreeing, disagreed 1** have or express a different opinion from someone. **2** have a bad effect • *Rich food disagrees with me.*
▷ **disagreement** *noun*
[from old French]

disagreeable *ADJECTIVE* unpleasant.
[from old French]

disappear *VERB* **disappears, disappearing, disappeared** stop being visible; vanish.
▷ **disappearance** *noun*

disappoint *VERB* **disappoints, disappointing, disappointed** fail to do what someone hopes for.
▷ **disappointment** *noun*
[originally = to dismiss someone from an important position: from *dis-* + *appoint*]

disapprove *VERB* **disapproves, disapproving, disapproved** have an unfavourable opinion of something; not approve.
▷ **disapproval** *noun*

disarm *VERB* **disarms, disarming, disarmed 1** reduce the size of armed forces. **2** take away someone's weapons. **3** overcome a person's anger or doubt • *Her friendliness disarmed their suspicions.*
▷ **disarming** *adjective*
[from old French]

disarmament *NOUN* reduction of a country's armed forces or weapons.

disarray *NOUN* disorder.
[from old French]

disassemble *VERB* **disassembles, disassembling, disassembled** take something to pieces.

disaster *NOUN* **disasters 1** a very bad accident or misfortune. **2** a complete failure.
▷ **disastrous** *adjective* **disastrously** *adverb*
[via French from Italian]

disband *VERB* **disbands, disbanding, disbanded** break up • *The choir disbanded last year.*
[from old French]

disbelief *NOUN* refusal or unwillingness to believe something.
▷ **disbelieve** *verb*

disburse *VERB* **disburses, disbursing, disbursed** pay out money.
▷ **disbursement** *noun*
[from *dis-* + French *bourse* = purse]

disc *NOUN* **discs 1** any round flat object. **2** a layer of cartilage between vertebrae in the spine. **3** a CD or record.
[from Latin *discus* = disc]

discard *VERB* **discards, discarding, discarded** throw something away; put something aside because it is useless or unwanted.
[originally = to throw out an unwanted playing card from a hand: from *dis-* + *card*]

discern (*say* dis-sern) *VERB* **discerns, discerning, discerned** perceive; see or recognize clearly.
▷ **discernible** *adjective* **discernment** *noun*
[from *dis-* + Latin *cernere* = to separate]

discerning *ADJECTIVE* perceptive; showing good judgement.

discharge *VERB* **discharges, discharging, discharged 1** release a person. **2** send something out • *The engine was discharging smoke.* **3** pay or do what was agreed • *discharge the debt.*

discharge *NOUN* **discharges 1** discharging. **2** something that is discharged.
[from Latin *discarricare* = unload]

disciple *NOUN* **disciples** **1** a person who accepts the teachings of another whom he or she regards as a leader. **2** any of the original followers of Jesus Christ.
[from Latin *discipulus* = learner]

disciplinarian *NOUN* **disciplinarians** a person who believes in strict discipline.

discipline *NOUN* **disciplines** **1** orderly and obedient behaviour. **2** a subject for study.
▷ **disciplinary** (*say* dis-ip-lin-er-ee) *adjective*

discipline *VERB* **disciplines, disciplining, disciplined** **1** train to be orderly and obedient. **2** punish.
[from Latin *disciplina* = training]

disc jockey *NOUN* **disc jockeys** a person who introduces and plays records.

disclaim *VERB* **disclaims, disclaiming, disclaimed** say that you are not responsible for or have no knowledge of something.
▷ **disclaimer** *noun*
[from old French]

disclose *VERB* **discloses, disclosing, disclosed** reveal.
▷ **disclosure** *noun*
[from old French *desclore* = open up]

disco *NOUN* **discos** a place where CDs or records are played for dancing.
[from French *discothèque* = record- library]

discolour *VERB* **discolours, discolouring, discoloured** spoil a thing's colour; stain.
▷ **discoloration** *noun*
[from *dis-* + Latin *colorare* = to colour]

discomfit *VERB* **discomfits, discomfiting, discomfited** make a person feel uneasy; disconcert.
▷ **discomfiture** *noun*
[from old French *desconfit* = defeated]

discomfort *NOUN* being uncomfortable.
[from old French]

disconcert (*say* dis-kon-**sert**) *VERB* **disconcerts, disconcerting, disconcerted** make a person feel uneasy.
[from *dis-* + French *concerter* = make harmonious]

disconnect *VERB* **disconnects, disconnecting, disconnected** break a connection; detach • *The phone has been disconnected.*
▷ **disconnection** *noun*

disconnected *ADJECTIVE* not having a connection between its parts.

disconsolate (*say* dis-**kon**-sol-at) *ADJECTIVE* disappointed.
[from *dis-* + Latin *consolatus* = consoled]

discontent *NOUN* lack of contentment; dissatisfaction.
▷ **discontented** *adjective*
discontentment *noun*

discontinue *VERB* **discontinues, discontinuing, discontinued** put an end to something.
[from *dis-* + Latin *continuare* = continue]

discord *NOUN* **discords** **1** disagreement; quarrelling. **2** musical notes sounded together and producing a harsh or unpleasant sound.
▷ **discordant** *adjective*
[from *dis-* + Latin *cordis* = of the heart]

discotheque (*say* **dis**-ko-tek) *NOUN* **discotheques** a disco.
[French, = record- library]

discount *NOUN* **discounts** an amount by which a price is reduced.

discount *VERB* **discounts, discounting, discounted** ignore or disregard something • *We cannot discount the possibility.*
[from old French]

discourage *VERB* **discourages, discouraging, discouraged** **1** take away someone's enthusiasm or confidence. **2** try to persuade someone not to do something.
▷ **discouragement** *noun*
[from old French]

discourse *NOUN* **discourses** a formal speech or piece of writing about something.

discourse *VERB* **discourses, discoursing, discoursed** speak or write at length about something.
[from Latin *discursus* = running to and fro]

discourteous *ADJECTIVE* not courteous; rude.
▷ **discourteously** *adverb* **discourtesy** *noun*

discover *VERB* **discovers, discovering, discovered** **1** find or find out. **2** be the first person to find something.
▷ **discoverer** *noun* **discovery** *noun*
[from *dis-* + Latin *cooperire* = to cover]

A B C D E F G H I J K L M N O P Q R S T U V W X Y Z

discredit *VERB* **discredits, discrediting, discredited 1** cause something to be doubted. **2** damage someone's reputation.

discredit *NOUN* damage to someone's reputation.
▷ **discreditable** *adjective*
[from *dis-* + *credit*]

discreet *ADJECTIVE* **1** not giving away secrets. **2** not showy.
▷ **discreetly** *adverb*
[from Latin *discernere* = be discerning]
USAGE Do not confuse with **discrete**.

discrepancy (*say* dis-**krep**-an-see) *NOUN* **discrepancies** lack of agreement between things which should be the same • *There are several discrepancies in the two accounts.*
[from Latin *discrepantia* = discord]

discrete *ADJECTIVE* separate; distinct from each other.
[from Latin *discretus* = separated]
USAGE Do not confuse with **discreet**.

discretion (*say* dis-**kresh**-on) *NOUN* **1** being discreet; keeping secrets • *I hope I can count on your discretion.* **2** freedom to decide things and take action according to your own judgement • *You can use your discretion.*
[from *discreet*]

discriminate *VERB* **discriminates, discriminating, discriminated 1** notice the differences between things; prefer one thing to another. **2** treat people differently or unfairly, e.g. because of their race, sex, or religion.
▷ **discrimination** *noun*
[same origin as *discern*]

discus *NOUN* **discuses** a thick heavy disc thrown in athletic contests.
[Latin]

discuss *VERB* **discusses, discussing, discussed** talk with other people about a subject.
▷ **discussion** *noun*
[from Latin]

disdain *NOUN* scorn or contempt.
▷ **disdainful** *adjective* **disdainfully** *adverb*

disdain *VERB* **disdains, disdaining, disdained 1** regard or treat with disdain. **2** not do something because of disdain • *She disdained to reply.*
[from *dis-* + Latin *dignare* = deign]

disease *NOUN* **diseases** an unhealthy condition; an illness.
▷ **diseased** *adjective*
[from *dis-* + *ease*]

disembark *VERB* **disembarks, disembarking, disembarked** get off a ship or aircraft.
▷ **disembarkation** *noun*
[from French]

disembodied *ADJECTIVE* freed from the body • *a disembodied spirit.*

disembowel *VERB* **disembowels, disembowelling, disembowelled** take out the bowels or inside parts of something.
[from *dis-* + *em-* + *bowel*]

disengage *VERB* **disengages, disengaging, disengaged** disconnect or detach.

disentangle *VERB* **disentangles, disentangling, disentangled** free from tangles or confusion.

disfavour *NOUN* disapproval or dislike.

disfigure *VERB* **disfigures, disfiguring, disfigured** spoil a person's or thing's appearance.
▷ **disfigurement** *noun*
[from *dis-* + Latin *figura* = a shape]

disgorge *VERB* **disgorges, disgorging, disgorged** pour or send out • *The pipe disgorged its contents.*
[from *dis-* + French *gorge* = throat]

disgrace *NOUN* **1** shame; loss of approval or respect. **2** something that causes shame.
▷ **disgraceful** *adjective* **disgracefully** *adverb*

disgrace *VERB* **disgraces, disgracing, disgraced** bring disgrace upon someone.
[from *dis-* + Latin *gratia* = grace]

disgruntled *ADJECTIVE* discontented or resentful.
[from *dis-* = thoroughly + *gruntle* = grunt softly]

disguise *VERB* **disguises, disguising, disguised 1** make a person or thing look different in order to deceive people. **2** conceal your feelings.

disguise *NOUN* **disguises** something used for disguising.
[from *dis-* + *guise*]

disgust *NOUN* a feeling that something is very unpleasant or disgraceful.

disgust *VERB* **disgusts, disgusting, disgusted** cause disgust.
▷ **disgusted** *adjective* **disgusting** *adjective*
[from *dis-* + Latin *gustare* = to taste]

dish *NOUN* **dishes** **1** a plate or bowl for food. **2** food prepared for eating. **3** a satellite dish.

dish *VERB* **dishes, dishing, dished**
(*informal*)
- **dish out** give out portions of something to people.
[from Old English]

dishcloth *NOUN* **dishcloths** a cloth for washing dishes.

dishearten *VERB* **disheartens, disheartening, disheartened** cause a person to lose hope or confidence.

dishevelled (*say* dish-ev-eld) *ADJECTIVE* ruffled and untidy.
▷ **dishevelment** *noun*
[from *dis-* + old French *chevel* = hair]

dishonest *ADJECTIVE* not honest.
▷ **dishonestly** *adverb* **dishonesty** *noun*
[from old French]

dishonour *NOUN* & *VERB* **dishonours, dishonouring, dishonoured** disgrace.
▷ **dishonour** *noun* **dishonourable** *adjective*
[from old French]

dishwasher *NOUN* **dishwashers** a machine for washing dishes etc. automatically.

disillusion *VERB* **disillusions, disillusioning, disillusioned** get rid of someone's pleasant but wrong beliefs.
▷ **disillusionment** *noun*

disincentive *NOUN* **disincentives** something that discourages an action or effort.

disinclination *NOUN* unwillingness.

disinclined *ADJECTIVE* unwilling to do something.

disinfect *VERB* **disinfects, disinfecting, disinfected** destroy the germs in something.
▷ **disinfection** *noun*
[from French]

disinfectant *NOUN* **disinfectants** a substance used for disinfecting things.
[from French]

disinherit *VERB* **disinherits, disinheriting, disinherited** deprive a person of the right to inherit something.

disintegrate *VERB* **disintegrates, disintegrating, disintegrated** break up into small parts or pieces.
▷ **disintegration** *noun*

disinter *VERB* **disinters, disinterring, disinterred** dig up something that is buried.
[from French]

disinterested *ADJECTIVE* not influenced by hope of gaining something yourself; impartial • *She gave us some disinterested advice.*

USAGE It is not accepted as part of standard English to use this word as if it meant 'not interested' or 'bored'. If this is what you mean, use *uninterested.*

disjointed *ADJECTIVE* (said about talk or writing) not having parts that fit together well and so difficult to understand.
[from *dis-* + Latin *jungere* = join]

disk *NOUN* **disks** a computer storage device consisting of magnetically coated plates.
[the American spelling of *disc*]

dislike *NOUN* **dislikes** a feeling of not liking somebody or something.

dislike *VERB* **dislikes, disliking, disliked** not to like somebody or something.
[from *dis-* + *like*[1]]

dislocate *VERB* **dislocates, dislocating, dislocated** **1** move or force a bone from its proper position in one of the joints. **2** disrupt • *Fog dislocated the traffic.*
▷ **dislocation** *noun*
[from *dis-* + Latin *locare* = to place]

dislodge *VERB* **dislodges, dislodging, dislodged** move or force something from its place.
[from French]

disloyal *ADJECTIVE* not loyal.
▷ **disloyally** *adverb* **disloyalty** *noun*
[from French]

dismal *ADJECTIVE* **1** gloomy. **2** of poor quality.
▷ **dismally** *adverb*
[from Latin *dies mali* = unlucky days]

A B C D E F G H I J K L M N O P Q R S T U V W X Y Z

dismantle *VERB* **dismantles, dismantling, dismantled** take something to pieces.
[from *dis-* + old French *manteler* = fortify]

dismay *NOUN* a feeling of surprise and discouragement.
▷ **dismayed** *adjective*
[from *dis-* + *may*[1]]

dismember *VERB* **dismembers, dismembering, dismembered** tear or cut the limbs from a body.
[from old French]

dismiss *VERB* **dismisses, dismissing, dismissed** **1** send someone away. **2** tell a person that you will no longer employ him or her. **3** put something out of your thoughts because it is not worth thinking about. **4** get a batsman or cricket side out.
▷ **dismissal** *noun* **dismissive** *adjective*
[from *dis-* + Latin *missum* = sent]

dismount *VERB* **dismounts, dismounting, dismounted** get off a horse or bicycle.

disobedient *ADJECTIVE* not obedient.
▷ **disobediently** *adverb* **disobedience** *noun*
[from old French]

disobey *VERB* **disobeys, disobeying, disobeyed** not to obey; disregard orders.
[from old French]

disorder *NOUN* **disorders** **1** untidiness. **2** a disturbance. **3** an illness.
▷ **disorderly** *adjective*

disorganized *ADJECTIVE* muddled and badly organized.
▷ **disorganization** *noun*
[from French]

disown *VERB* **disowns, disowning, disowned** refuse to acknowledge that a person or thing has any connection with you.

disparage (*say* dis-pa-rij) *VERB* **disparages, disparaging, disparaged** declare that something is small or unimportant; belittle.
▷ **disparagement** *noun*
[from *dis-* + old French *parage* = equality in rank]

disparity *NOUN* **disparities** difference or inequality.
[from *dis-* + Latin *paritas* = equality]

dispassionate *ADJECTIVE* calm and impartial.
▷ **dispassionately** *adverb*

dispatch *VERB* **dispatches, dispatching, dispatched** **1** send off to a destination. **2** kill.

dispatch *NOUN* **dispatches** **1** dispatching. **2** a report or message sent. **3** promptness; speed.
[from Italian or Spanish]

dispatch box *NOUN* **dispatch boxes** a container for carrying official documents.

dispatch rider *NOUN* **dispatch riders** a messenger who travels by motorcycle.

dispel *VERB* **dispels, dispelling, dispelled** drive away; scatter • *Wind dispels fog.*
[from *dis-* + Latin *pellere* = to drive]

dispensary *NOUN* **dispensaries** a place where medicines are dispensed.

dispense *VERB* **dispenses, dispensing, dispensed** **1** distribute; deal out. **2** prepare medicine according to prescriptions.
▷ **dispensation** *noun*
- **dispense with** do without something.
[from Latin *dispensare* = weigh out]

dispenser *NOUN* **dispensers** a device that supplies a quantity of something • *a cash dispenser.*

disperse *VERB* **disperses, dispersing, dispersed** scatter.
▷ **dispersal** *noun* **dispersion** *noun*
[from Latin *dispersum* = scattered]

displace *VERB* **displaces, displacing, displaced** **1** shift from its place. **2** take a person's or thing's place.
▷ **displacement** *noun*

display *VERB* **displays, displaying, displayed** show; arrange something so that it can be clearly seen.

display *NOUN* **displays** **1** the displaying of something; an exhibition. **2** an electronic device for visually presenting data. **3** something displayed.
[from *dis-* = separately + Latin *plicare* = to fold]

displease *VERB* **displeases, displeasing, displeased** annoy or not please someone.
▷ **displeasure** *noun*
[from old French]

disposable *ADJECTIVE* made to be thrown away after it has been used • *disposable nappies.*

disposal *NOUN* getting rid of something.
- **at your disposal** for you to use; ready for you.

dispose *VERB* **disposes, disposing, disposed** 1 make a person ready or willing to do something • *I feel disposed to help him.* 2 place in position; arrange • *Dispose your troops in two lines.*
- **be well disposed** be friendly.
- **dispose of** get rid of.
[from old French; related to *deposit*]

disposition *NOUN* **dispositions** 1 a person's nature or qualities. 2 arrangement.

disproportionate *ADJECTIVE* out of proportion; too large or too small.

disprove *VERB* **disproves, disproving, disproved** show that something is not true. [from old French]

disputation *NOUN* **disputations** a debate or argument.

dispute *VERB* **disputes, disputing, disputed** 1 argue; debate. 2 quarrel. 3 raise an objection to • *We dispute their claim.*

dispute *NOUN* **disputes** 1 an argument or debate. 2 a quarrel.
- **in dispute** being argued about.
[from *dis-* + Latin *putare* = settle]

disqualify *VERB* **disqualifies, disqualifying, disqualified** bar someone from a competition etc. because he or she has broken the rules or is not properly qualified to take part.
▷ **disqualification** *noun*

disquiet *NOUN* anxiety or worry.
▷ **disquieting** *adjective*

disregard *VERB* **disregards, disregarding, disregarded** ignore.

disregard *NOUN* the act of ignoring something.

disrepair *NOUN* bad condition caused by not doing repairs • *The old mill is in a state of disrepair.*

disreputable *ADJECTIVE* not respectable. [from *disrepute*]

disrepute *NOUN* bad reputation.

disrespect *NOUN* lack of respect; rudeness.
▷ **disrespectful** *adjective*
disrespectfully *adverb*

disrupt *VERB* **disrupts, disrupting, disrupted** put into disorder; interrupt a continuous flow • *Fog disrupted traffic.*
▷ **disruption** *noun* **disruptive** *adjective*
[from *dis-* + Latin *ruptum* = broken]

dissatisfied *ADJECTIVE* not satisfied.
▷ **dissatisfaction** *noun*

dissect (*say* dis-sekt) *VERB* **dissects, dissecting, dissected** cut something up in order to examine it.
▷ **dissection** *noun*
[from *dis-* + Latin *sectum* = cut]

disseminate *VERB* **disseminates, disseminating, disseminated** spread ideas etc. widely.
▷ **dissemination** *noun*
[from *dis-* + Latin *seminare* = sow (scatter seeds)]

dissent *NOUN* disagreement.

dissent *VERB* **dissents, dissenting, dissented** disagree.
[from *dis-* + Latin *sentire* = feel]

dissertation *NOUN* **dissertations** a long essay on an academic subject, written as part of a university degree.
[from Latin *dissertare* = examine, discuss]

disservice *NOUN* a harmful action done by someone who was intending to help.

dissident *NOUN* **dissidents** a person who disagrees, especially someone who opposes their government.
▷ **dissident** *adjective* **dissidence** *noun*
[from Latin *dissidere* = sit by yourself]

dissipate *VERB* **dissipates, dissipating, dissipated** 1 disappear or scatter. 2 waste or squander something.
▷ **dissipation** *noun*
[from Latin *dissipatus* = scattered]

dissociate *VERB* **dissociates, dissociating, dissociated** separate something in your thoughts.
▷ **dissociation** *noun*
[from Latin]

dissolute *ADJECTIVE* having an immoral way of life.
[from Latin *dissolutus* = loose]

dissolution *NOUN* **dissolutions** **1** putting an end to a marriage or partnership etc. **2** formally ending a parliament or assembly. [from Latin]

dissolve *VERB* **dissolves, dissolving, dissolved** **1** mix something with a liquid so that it becomes part of the liquid. **2** make or become liquid; melt. **3** put an end to a marriage or partnership. **4** formally end a parliament or assembly • *Parliament was dissolved and a general election was held.* [from *dis-* = separate + Latin *solvere* = loosen]

dissuade *VERB* **dissuades, dissuading, dissuaded** persuade somebody not to do something.
▷ **dissuasion** *noun*
[from *dis-* + Latin *suadere* = persuade]

distaff *NOUN* **distaffs** a stick holding raw wool etc. for spinning into yarn. [from Old English]

distance *NOUN* **distances** the amount of space between two places.
- **in the distance** far away but visible.

distant *ADJECTIVE* **1** far away. **2** not friendly; not sociable. **3** not closely related • *distant cousins.*
▷ **distantly** *adverb*
[from *dis-* + Latin *stans* = standing]

distaste *NOUN* dislike.

distasteful *ADJECTIVE* unpleasant.

distemper *NOUN* **1** a disease of dogs and certain other animals. **2** a kind of paint. [from Latin]

distend *VERB* **distends, distending, distended** make or become swollen because of pressure from inside.
▷ **distension** *noun*
[from *dis-* + Latin *tendere* = stretch]

distil *VERB* **distils, distilling, distilled** purify a liquid by boiling it and condensing the vapour.
▷ **distillation** *noun*
[from *dis-* + Latin *stillare* = drip down]

distiller *NOUN* **distillers** a person or firm that makes alcoholic drinks (e.g. whisky) by distillation.
▷ **distillery** *noun*

distinct *ADJECTIVE* **1** easily heard or seen; noticeable. **2** clearly separate or different.
▷ **distinctly** *adverb* **distinctness** *noun*
[from Latin *distinctus* = separated]
USAGE See note at **distinctive**.

distinction *NOUN* **distinctions** **1** a difference. **2** excellence or honour. **3** an award for excellence; a high mark in an examination.

distinctive *ADJECTIVE* that distinguishes one thing from another or others • *The school has a distinctive uniform.*
▷ **distinctively** *adverb*
USAGE Do not confuse this word with **distinct**. A **distinct** mark is a clear mark; a *distinctive* mark is one that is not found anywhere else.

distinguish *VERB* **distinguishes, distinguishing, distinguished** **1** make or notice differences between things. **2** see or hear something clearly. **3** bring honour to • *He distinguished himself by his bravery.*
▷ **distinguishable** *adjective*
[from Latin *distinguere* = to separate]

distinguished *ADJECTIVE* **1** excellent and famous. **2** dignified in appearance.

distort *VERB* **distorts, distorting, distorted** **1** pull or twist out of its normal shape. **2** misrepresent; give a false account of something • *distort the truth.*
▷ **distortion** *noun*
[from *dis-* + Latin *tortum* = twisted]

distract *VERB* **distracts, distracting, distracted** take a person's attention away from something.
[from *dis-* + Latin *tractum* = pulled]

distracted *ADJECTIVE* greatly upset by worry or distress; distraught.

distraction *NOUN* **distractions** **1** something that distracts a person's attention. **2** an amusement. **3** great worry or distress.

distraught (*say* dis-**trawt**) *ADJECTIVE* greatly upset by worry or distress. [same origin as *distract*]

distress *NOUN* **distresses** great sorrow, pain, or trouble.

distress *VERB* **distresses, distressing, distressed** cause distress to a person. [from old French]

distribute *VERB* **distributes, distributing, distributed** 1 deal or share out. 2 spread or scatter.
▷ **distribution** *noun* **distributor** *noun*
[from *dis-* = + Latin *tributum* = given]

district *NOUN* **districts** part of a town or country.
[French]

distrust *NOUN* lack of trust; suspicion.
▷ **distrustful** *adjective*

distrust *VERB* **distrusts, distrusting, distrusted** not to trust.

disturb *VERB* **disturbs, disturbing, disturbed** 1 spoil someone's peace or rest. 2 cause someone to worry. 3 move a thing from its position.
▷ **disturbance** *noun*
[from *dis-* = thoroughly + Latin *turbare* = confuse, upset]

disuse *NOUN* the state of being no longer used.

disused *ADJECTIVE* no longer used.

ditch *NOUN* **ditches** a trench dug to hold water or carry it away, or to serve as a boundary.

ditch *VERB* **ditches, ditching, ditched** 1 (*informal*) bring an aircraft down in a forced landing on the sea. 2 (*informal*) abandon or discard something.
[from Old English]

dither *VERB* **dithers, dithering, dithered** hesitate nervously.
[origin unknown]

ditto *NOUN* (used in lists) the same again.
[from Italian *detto* = said]

ditty *NOUN* **ditties** a short song.
[from old French]

divan *NOUN* **divans** a bed or couch without a raised back or sides.
[Persian, = cushioned bench]

dive *VERB* **dives, diving, dived** 1 go under water, especially head first. 2 move down quickly.
▷ **dive** *noun*
[from Old English]

diver *NOUN* **divers** 1 someone who dives. 2 a person who works under water in a special suit with an air supply. 3 a bird that dives for its food.

diverge *VERB* **diverges, diverging, diverged** go aside or in different directions.
▷ **divergent** *adjective* **divergence** *noun*
[from Latin]

divers (*say* dy-verz) *ADJECTIVE* (*old use*) various.
[from Latin *diversus* = diverted]

diverse (*say* dy-verss) *ADJECTIVE* varied; of several different kinds.
▷ **diversity** *noun*
[a different spelling of *divers*]

diversify *VERB* **diversifies, diversifying, diversified** make or become varied; involve yourself in different kinds of things.
▷ **diversification** *noun*

diversion *NOUN* **diversions** 1 diverting something from its course. 2 an alternative route for traffic when a road is closed. 3 a recreation or entertainment.
▷ **diversionary** *adjective*

divert *VERB* **diverts, diverting, diverted** 1 turn something aside from its course. 2 entertain or amuse.
▷ **diverting** *adjective*
[from *di-*[2] + Latin *vertere* = to turn]

divest *VERB* **divests, divesting, divested** take away; deprive • *They divested him of power.*
[from *di-*[2] + Latin *vestire* = clothe]

divide *VERB* **divides, dividing, divided** 1 separate from something or into smaller parts; split up. 2 find how many times one number is contained in another • *Divide six by three* ($6 \div 3 = 2$).
▷ **divider** *noun*
[from Latin]

dividend *NOUN* **dividends** 1 a share of a business's profit. 2 a number that is to be divided by another. (COMPARE **divisor**)
[from Latin *dividendum* = something to be divided]

dividers *PLURAL NOUN* a pair of compasses for measuring distances.

divine *ADJECTIVE* 1 belonging to or coming from God. 2 like a god. 3 (*informal*) excellent; extremely beautiful.
▷ **divinely** *adverb*

divine *VERB* **divines, divining, divined** prophesy or guess what is about to happen.
[from Latin *divus* = god]

divinity *NOUN* **divinities** **1** being divine. **2** a god or goddess. **3** the study of religion.

division *NOUN* **divisions** **1** dividing. **2** a dividing line; a partition. **3** one of the parts into which something is divided. **4** (in Parliament) separation of members into two sections for counting votes.
▷ **divisional** *adjective*
[from Latin *dividere* = divide]

divisive (*say* div-I-siv) *ADJECTIVE* causing disagreement within a group.

divisor *NOUN* **divisors** a number by which another is to be divided. (COMPARE *dividend* **2**)

divorce *NOUN* **divorces** the legal ending of a marriage.

divorce *VERB* **divorces**, **divorcing**, **divorced** **1** end a marriage by divorce. **2** separate; think of things separately.
[French; related to *divert*]

divulge *VERB* **divulges**, **divulging**, **divulged** reveal information.
▷ **divulgence** *noun*
[from *di-*[2] + Latin *vulgare* = publish]

Diwali (*say* di-wah-lee) *NOUN* a Hindu religious festival at which lamps are lit, held in October or November.
[from Sanskrit *dipavali* = row of lights]

DIY *ABBREVIATION* do-it-yourself.

dizzy *ADJECTIVE* **dizzier**, **dizziest** having or causing the feeling that everything is spinning round; giddy.
▷ **dizzily** *adverb* **dizziness** *noun*
[from Old English]

DJ *ABBREVIATION* disc jockey.

DNA *ABBREVIATION* deoxyribonucleic acid; a substance in chromosomes that stores genetic information.

do *VERB* **does**, **doing**, **did**, **done** This word has many different uses, most of which mean performing or dealing with something (*Do your best. I can't do this. She is doing well at school*) or being suitable or enough (*This will do*). The verb is also used with other verbs **1** in questions (*Do you want this?*), **2** in statements with 'not' (*He does not want it*), **3** for emphasis (*I do like nuts*), **4** to avoid repeating a verb that has just been used (*We work as hard as they do*).
- **do away with** get rid of.
- **do up** **1** fasten • *Do your coat up.* **2** repair or redecorate • *Do up the spare room.*

do *NOUN* **dos** (*informal*) a party or other social event.
[from Old English]

docile (*say* doh-syl) *ADJECTIVE* willing to obey.
▷ **docilely** *adverb* **docility** *noun*
[from Latin *docilis* = easily taught]

dock[1] *NOUN* **docks** a part of a harbour where ships are loaded, unloaded, or repaired.

dock *VERB* **docks**, **docking**, **docked** **1** bring or come into a dock. **2** when two spacecraft dock, they join together in space.
[from old German or old Dutch]

dock[2] *NOUN* an enclosure for the prisoner on trial in a lawcourt.
[from Flemish *dok* = cage]

dock[3] *NOUN* a weed with broad leaves.
[from Old English]

dock[4] *VERB* **docks**, **docking**, **docked** **1** cut short an animal's tail. **2** reduce or take away part of someone's wages or supplies etc.
[origin unknown]

docker *NOUN* **dockers** a labourer who loads and unloads ships.

docket *NOUN* **dockets** a document or label listing the contents of a package.
[origin unknown]

dockyard *NOUN* **dockyards** an open area with docks and equipment for building or repairing ships.

doctor *NOUN* **doctors** **1** a person who is trained to treat sick or injured people. **2** a person who holds an advanced degree (a **doctorate**) at a university • *Doctor of Music.*
[Latin, = teacher]

doctrine *NOUN* **doctrines** a belief held by a religious, political, or other group.
▷ **doctrinal** *adjective*
[from Latin *doctrina* = teaching]

document *NOUN* **documents** **1** a written or printed paper giving information or evidence about something. **2** (*in computing*) a computer file that contains text or images and that has a name • *Save the document before logging off.*
▷ **documentation** *noun*
[from Latin *documentum* = lesson, official paper]

documentary *ADJECTIVE* **1** consisting of documents • *documentary evidence.* **2** showing real events or situations.

documentary *NOUN* **documentaries** a film giving information about real events.
[same origin as *document*]

dodder *VERB* **dodders, doddering, doddered** walk unsteadily, especially because of old age.
▷ **doddery** *adjective*
[origin unknown]

dodge *VERB* **dodges, dodging, dodged** move quickly to avoid someone or something.

dodge *NOUN* **dodges** **1** a dodging movement. **2** (*informal*) a trick; a clever way of doing something.
[origin unknown]

dodgem *NOUN* **dodgems** a small electrically driven car at a funfair, in which each driver tries to bump some cars and dodge others.
[from *dodge* + *'em* (them)]

dodgy *ADJECTIVE* (*informal*) **1** awkward or tricky. **2** not working properly. **3** dishonest.
[from *dodge* = a trick]

dodo *NOUN* **dodos** a large heavy bird that used to live on an island in the Indian Ocean but has been extinct for over 200 years.
[from Portuguese *doudo* = fool (because the bird had no fear of man)]

doe *NOUN* **does** a female deer, rabbit, or hare.
[from Old English]

doer *NOUN* **doers** a person who does things.

doesn't (*mainly spoken*) does not.

doff *VERB* **doffs, doffing, doffed** take off • *He doffed his hat.*
[from *do off*; compare *don*]

dog *NOUN* **dogs** a four-legged animal that barks, often kept as a pet.

dog *VERB* **dogs, dogging, dogged** follow closely or persistently • *Reporters dogged his footsteps.*
[from Old English]

doge (*say* dohj) *NOUN* **doges** the elected ruler of the former republics of Venice and Genoa.
[from Latin *dux* = leader]

dog-eared *ADJECTIVE* (said about a book) having the corners of the pages bent from constant use.

dogfish *NOUN* **dogfish** a kind of small shark.

dogged (*say* dog-id) *ADJECTIVE* persistent or obstinate.
▷ **doggedly** *adverb*
[from *dog*]

doggerel *NOUN* bad verse.
[origin unknown]

dogma *NOUN* **dogmas** a belief or principle that a Church or other authority declares is true and must be accepted.
[Greek, = opinion, decree]

dogmatic *ADJECTIVE* expressing ideas in a very firm authoritative way.
▷ **dogmatically** *adverb*
[from *dogma*]

dogsbody *NOUN* **dogsbodies** (*informal*) a person who is given boring or unimportant jobs to do.

doh *NOUN* a name for the keynote of a scale in music, or the note C.
[Italian]

doily *NOUN* **doilies** a small ornamental table-mat, made of paper or lace.
[named after a Mr *Doily* or *Doyley*, who sold household linen]

do-it-yourself *ADJECTIVE* suitable for an amateur to do or make at home.

doldrums *PLURAL NOUN* **1** the ocean regions near the equator where there is little or no wind. **2** a time of depression or inactivity.
[origin unknown]

dole *VERB* **doles, doling, doled**
- **dole out** distribute.

dole *NOUN* (*informal*) money paid by the state to unemployed people.
[from Old English]

doleful *ADJECTIVE* sad or sorrowful.
▷ **dolefully** *adverb*
[from an old word *dole* = grief]

doll *NOUN* **dolls** a toy model of a person.
[pet form of *Dorothy*]

dollar *NOUN* **dollars** a unit of money in the USA and some other countries.
[from German *thaler* = a silver coin]

dollop *NOUN* **dollops** (*informal*) a lump of something soft.
[perhaps from a Scandinavian language]

dolly *NOUN* **dollies** (*informal*) a doll.

dolphin *NOUN* **dolphins** a sea animal like a small whale with a beaklike snout.
[from Greek]

-dom *SUFFIX* forms nouns showing rank, office, territory, or condition (e.g. *kingdom*, *freedom*).
[from Old English]

domain (*say* dom-ayn) *NOUN* **domains 1** a kingdom. **2** an area of knowledge, interest, etc.
[from French; related to *dominion*]

dome *NOUN* **domes** a roof shaped like the top half of a ball.
▷ **domed** *adjective*
[via French from Italian]

domestic *ADJECTIVE* **1** to do with the home or household. **2** (said about animals) kept by people, not wild.
▷ **domestically** *adverb*
[from Latin *domesticus* = to do with the home]

domesticated *ADJECTIVE* (said about animals) trained to live with and be kept by humans.

domicile (*say* dom-iss-syl) *NOUN* **domiciles** (*formal*) the place where someone lives; residence.
▷ **domiciled** *adjective*
[from Latin *domus* = home]

dominate *VERB* **dominates, dominating, dominated 1** control by being stronger or more powerful. **2** be conspicuous or prominent • *The mountain dominated the whole landscape.*
▷ **dominant** *adjective* **dominance** *noun* **domination** *noun*
[from Latin *dominus* = master]

domineer *VERB* **domineers, domineering, domineered** behave in a dominating way.
▷ **domineering** *adjective*
[same origin as *dominate*]

dominion *NOUN* **dominions 1** authority to rule others; control. **2** an area over which someone rules; a domain.
[from Latin *dominium* = property]

domino *NOUN* **dominoes** a small flat oblong piece of wood or plastic with dots (1 to 6) or a blank space at each end, used in the game of dominoes.
[French]

don *VERB* **dons, donning, donned** put on • *don a cloak.*
[from *do on*; compare *doff*]

donate *VERB* **donates, donating, donated** present money or a gift to a fund or institution etc.
▷ **donation** *noun*
[from Latin *donum* = gift]

donga *NOUN* **dongas** (*S. African*) **1** a ditch caused by erosion. **2** a dry water channel.
[from Xhosa (a S. African language) and Zulu (a S. African language) *udonga*]

donkey *NOUN* **donkeys** an animal that looks like a small horse with long ears.
[origin unknown]

donor *NOUN* **donors** someone who gives something • *a blood donor.*
[from old French]

don't (*mainly spoken*) do not.

doodle *VERB* **doodles, doodling, doodled** scribble or draw absent-mindedly.
▷ **doodle** *noun*
[from old German]

doom *NOUN* a grim fate that you cannot avoid, especially death or destruction • *a sense of impending doom.*

doom *VERB* **dooms, dooming, doomed** destine to a grim fate.
[from Old English]

doomed *ADJECTIVE* **1** destined to a grim fate. **2** bound to fail or be destroyed.

doomsday *NOUN* the day of the Last Judgement; the end of the world.
[from *doom* in an old sense = judgement]

door *NOUN* **doors** a movable barrier on hinges (or one that slides or revolves), used to open or close an entrance; the entrance itself.
▷ **doorknob** *noun* **doormat** *noun*
[from Old English]

doorstep *NOUN* **doorsteps** the step or piece of ground just outside a door.

door-to-door *ADJECTIVE* done at each house in turn.

doorway *NOUN* **doorways** the opening into which a door fits.

dope *NOUN* **dopes** **1** (*informal*) a drug, especially one taken or given illegally. **2** (*informal*) a stupid person.
▷ **dopey** *adjective*

dope *VERB* **dopes, doping, doped** (*informal*) give a drug to a person or animal.
[from Dutch *doop* = sauce]

dormant *ADJECTIVE* **1** sleeping. **2** living or existing but not active; not extinct • *a dormant volcano.*
[French, = sleeping]

dormitory *NOUN* **dormitories** a room for several people to sleep in, especially in a school or institution.
[from Latin *dormire* = to sleep]

dormouse *NOUN* **dormice** an animal like a large mouse that hibernates in winter.
[origin unknown]

dorp *NOUN* **dorps** (*S. African*) a village or small country town in South Africa.
[from Dutch]

dorsal *ADJECTIVE* to do with or on the back • *Some fish have a dorsal fin.*
[from Latin *dorsum* = the back]

dosage *NOUN* **dosages** **1** the giving of medicine in doses. **2** the size of a dose.

dose *NOUN* **doses** an amount of medicine taken at one time.

dose *VERB* **doses, dosing, dosed** give a dose of medicine to a person or animal.
[from Greek *dosis* = something given]

dossier (*say* **doss**-ee-er or **doss**-ee-ay) **dossiers** a set of documents containing information about a person or event.
[French]

dot *NOUN* **dots** a tiny spot.

dot *VERB* **dots, dotting, dotted** mark something with dots.
[from Old English]

dotage (*say* **doh**-tij) *NOUN* a condition of weakness of mind caused by old age • *He is in his dotage.*
[from *dote*]

dote *VERB* **dotes, doting, doted**
- **dote on** be very fond of.
[from old Dutch *doten* = to be silly]

dotty *ADJECTIVE* **dottier, dottiest** (*informal*) crazy or silly.
▷ **dottiness** *noun*
[origin unknown]

double *ADJECTIVE* **1** twice as much; twice as many. **2** having two things or parts that form a pair • *a double-barrelled gun.* **3** suitable for two people • *a double bed.*
▷ **doubly** *adverb*

double *NOUN* **doubles** **1** a double quantity or thing. **2** a person or thing that looks exactly like another.
- **doubles** a game of tennis etc. between two pairs of players.

double *VERB* **doubles, doubling, doubled** **1** make or become twice as much or as many. **2** bend or fold in two. **3** turn back sharply • *The fox doubled back on its tracks.*
[from old French]

double bass *NOUN* **double basses** a musical instrument with strings, like a large cello.
[from *double* + *bass*[1]]

double-cross *VERB* **double-crosses, double-crossing, double-crossed** deceive or cheat someone who thinks you are working with them.

double-decker *NOUN* **double-deckers** a bus with two floors, one above the other.

double entendre *NOUN* **double entendres** a word or phrase with two meanings, one of which is sexual or rude.
[French, = double understanding]

doublet *NOUN* **doublets** a man's close-fitting jacket worn in the 15th-17th centuries.
[from old French]

doubt *NOUN* **doubts** a feeling of not being sure about something.

A B C D E F G H I J K L M N O P Q R S T U V W X Y Z

doubt *VERB* **doubts, doubting, doubted** feel doubt.
▷ **doubter** *noun*
[from Latin *dubitare* = hesitate]

doubtful *ADJECTIVE* **1** feeling doubt. **2** making you feel doubt.
▷ **doubtfully** *adverb*

doubtless *ADVERB* certainly.

dough *NOUN* **1** a thick mixture of flour and water used for making bread, pastry, etc. **2** (*slang*) money.
▷ **doughy** *adjective*
[from Old English]

doughnut *NOUN* **doughnuts** a round bun that has been fried and covered in sugar.

doughty (*say* dow-tee) *ADJECTIVE* brave.
[from Old English]

dour (*say* doo-er) *ADJECTIVE* stern and gloomy-looking.
▷ **dourly** *adverb*
[from Scottish Gaelic *dur* = dull, obstinate]

douse *VERB* **douses, dousing, doused** **1** put into water; pour water over something. **2** put out • *douse the light.*
[origin unknown]

dove *NOUN* **doves** a kind of pigeon.
[from Old Norse]

dovetail *NOUN* **dovetails** a wedge-shaped joint used to join two pieces of wood.

dovetail *VERB* **dovetails, dovetailing, dovetailed** **1** join pieces of wood with a dovetail. **2** fit neatly together • *My plans dovetailed with hers.*
[because the wedge- shape looks like a dove's tail]

dowager *NOUN* **dowagers** a woman who holds a title or property after her husband has died • *the dowager duchess.*
[from old French *douage* = widow's share]

dowdy *ADJECTIVE* **dowdier, dowdiest** shabby; unfashionable.
▷ **dowdily** *adverb*
[origin unknown]

dowel *NOUN* **dowels** a headless wooden or metal pin for holding together two pieces of wood, stone, etc.
▷ **dowelling** *noun*
[probably from old German]

down[1] *ADVERB* **1** to or in a lower place or position or level • *It fell down.* **2** to a source or place etc. • *Track them down.* **3** in writing • *Take down these instructions.* **4** as a payment • *We will pay £50 down and the rest later.*

down *PREPOSITION* downwards through or along or into • *Pour it down the drain.*

down *ADJECTIVE* unhappy or depressed • *He's feeling down at the moment.*
- **be down on** disapprove of • *She is down on smoking.*
[from Old English *adune*]

down[2] *NOUN* very fine soft feathers or hair.
▷ **downy** *adjective*
[from Old Norse]

down[3] *NOUN* **downs** a grass-covered hill • *the South Downs.*
▷ **downland** *noun*
[from Old English *dun*]

downcast *ADJECTIVE* **1** looking downwards • *downcast eyes.* **2** dejected.

downfall *NOUN* **downfalls** **1** a fall from power or prosperity. **2** a heavy fall of rain or snow.

downgrade *VERB* **downgrades, downgrading, downgraded** make a person or thing less important or valuable • *He wants to downgrade local government.*

downhill *ADVERB* & *ADJECTIVE* down a slope.

download *VERB* **downloads, downloading, downloaded** transfer data from a large computer system to a smaller one.

downpour *NOUN* **downpours** a heavy fall of rain.

downright *ADVERB* & *ADJECTIVE* complete or completely • *a downright lie.*

Down's syndrome *NOUN* a medical condition caused by a chromosome defect that causes intellectual impairment and physical abnormalities such as short stature and a broad flattened skull.

downstairs *ADVERB* & *ADJECTIVE* to or on a lower floor.

downstream *ADJECTIVE* & *ADVERB* in the direction in which a stream flows.

down-to-earth *ADJECTIVE* sensible and practical.

downtown *ADVERB* (*esp. American*) towards or in the centre of a town or city • *Let's go to a movie downtown.*

downward *ADJECTIVE & ADVERB* going towards what is lower.
▷ **downwards** *adverb*

dowry *NOUN* **dowries** property or money brought by a bride to her husband when she marries him.
[from old French; related to *endow*]

doze *VERB* **dozes, dozing, dozed** sleep lightly.

doze *NOUN* a light sleep.
▷ **dozy** *adjective*
[origin unknown]

dozen *NOUN* **dozens** a set of twelve.
[from old French]
USAGE Correct use is *ten dozen* (not *ten dozens*).

drab *ADJECTIVE* **drabber, drabbest 1** not colourful. **2** dull or uninteresting • *a drab life.*
▷ **drably** *adverb* **drabness** *noun*
[from old French]

Draconian (*say* drak-**oh**-nee-an) *ADJECTIVE* very harsh • *Draconian laws.*
[named after *Draco*, who established very severe laws in ancient Athens]

draft *NOUN* **drafts 1** a rough sketch or plan. **2** a written order for a bank to pay out money.

draft *VERB* **drafts, drafting, drafted**
1 prepare a draft. **2** select for a special duty • *She was drafted to our office in Paris.*
[a different spelling of *draught*]
USAGE This is also the American spelling of *draught.*

drag *VERB* **drags, dragging, dragged 1** pull something heavy along. **2** search a river or lake etc. with nets and hooks. **3** continue slowly in a boring manner.

drag *NOUN* **1** something that is tedious or a nuisance. **2** (*slang*) women's clothes worn by men.
[from Old Norse]

dragon *NOUN* **dragons 1** a mythological monster, usually with wings and able to breathe out fire. **2** a fierce person, especially a woman.
[from Greek *drakon* = serpent]

dragonfly *NOUN* **dragonflies** an insect with a long thin body and two pairs of transparent wings.

dragoon *NOUN* **dragoons** a member of certain cavalry regiments.

dragoon *VERB* **dragoons, dragooning, dragooned** force someone into doing something.
[same origin as *dragon*]

drain *NOUN* **drains 1** a pipe or ditch for taking away water or other liquid.
2 something that takes away strength or resources.
▷ **drainpipe** *noun*

drain *VERB* **drains, draining, drained**
1 take away water etc. through a drain.
2 flow or trickle away. **3** empty liquid out of a container. **4** take away strength etc.; exhaust.
▷ **drainage** *noun*
[from Old English]

drake *NOUN* **drakes** a male duck.
[from West Germanic]

drama *NOUN* **dramas 1** a play. **2** writing or performing plays. **3** a series of exciting events.
[from Greek]

dramatic *ADJECTIVE* **1** to do with drama.
2 exciting and impressive • *a dramatic change.*
▷ **dramatics** *plural noun* **dramatically** *adverb*

dramatis personae (*say* dram-a-tis per-**sohn**-I) *PLURAL NOUN* the characters in a play.
[Latin, = persons of the drama]

dramatist *NOUN* **dramatists** a person who writes plays.

dramatize *VERB* **dramatizes, dramatizing, dramatized 1** make a story etc. into a play.
2 make something seem exciting.
▷ **dramatization** *noun*

drape *VERB* **drapes, draping, draped** hang cloth etc. loosely over something.
[from French *drap* = cloth]

draper *NOUN* **drapers** (*old use*) a shopkeeper who sells cloth or clothes.
[same origin as *drape*]

drapery *NOUN* **draperies** cloth arranged in loose folds.
[same origin as *drape*]

drastic *ADJECTIVE* having a strong or violent effect.
▷ **drastically** *adverb*
[from Greek]

draught (*say* drahft) *NOUN* **draughts** **1** a current of usually cold air indoors. **2** a haul of fish in a net. **3** the depth of water needed to float a ship. **4** a swallow of liquid.
▷ **draughty** *adjective*
[from Old Norse]

draughts *NOUN* a game played with 24 round pieces on a chessboard.
[from *draught* in an old sense = way of moving]

draughtsman *NOUN* **draughtsmen** **1** a person who makes drawings. **2** a piece used in the game of draughts.
[*draught* is an old spelling of *draft*]

draw *VERB* **draws**, **drawing**, **drew**, **drawn** **1** produce a picture or outline by making marks on a surface. **2** pull. **3** take out • *draw water.* **4** attract • *The fair drew large crowds.* **5** end a game or contest with the same score on both sides. **6** move or come • *The ship drew nearer.* **7** write out a cheque to be cashed.
- **draw a conclusion** form an opinion about something by thinking about the evidence.

draw *NOUN* **draws** **1** the drawing of lots (SEE **lot**). **2** the drawing out of a gun • *He was quick on the draw.* **3** an attraction. **4** a drawn game.
[from Old English]
USAGE Do not confuse this word with **drawer**.

drawback *NOUN* **drawbacks** a disadvantage.
[from *draw back* = hesitate]

drawbridge *NOUN* **drawbridges** a bridge over a moat, hinged at one end so that it can be raised or lowered.

drawer *NOUN* **drawers** **1** a sliding box-like compartment in a piece of furniture. **2** a person who draws something. **3** someone who draws (= writes out) a cheque.

drawing *NOUN* **drawings** a picture or outline drawn.

drawing pin *NOUN* **drawing pins** a short pin with a flat top to be pressed with your thumb, used for fastening paper etc. to a surface.

drawing room *NOUN* **drawing rooms** a sitting room.
[short for *withdrawing room* = a private room in a hotel etc., to which guests could withdraw]

drawl *VERB* **drawls**, **drawling**, **drawled** speak very slowly or lazily.

drawl *NOUN* **drawls** a drawling way of speaking.
[from old German or old Dutch *dralen* = delay]

dray *NOUN* **drays** a strong low flat cart for carrying heavy loads.
[from Middle English; related to *draw*]

dread *NOUN* great fear.

dread *VERB* **dreads**, **dreading**, **dreaded** fear something greatly.
▷ **dreaded** *adjective*
[from Old English]

dreadful *ADJECTIVE* (*informal*) very bad • *dreadful weather.*
▷ **dreadfully** *adverb*

dreadlocks *PLURAL NOUN* hair worn in many ringlets or plaits, especially by Rastafarians.
[from *dread* + *lock*[2] (because the style was copied from pictures of Ethiopian warriors)]

dream *NOUN* **dreams** **1** a series of pictures or events in a sleeping person's mind. **2** something imagined; an ambition or ideal.
▷ **dreamy** *adjective* **dreamily** *adverb*

dream *VERB* **dreams**, **dreaming**, **dreamt** or **dreamed** **1** have a dream or dreams. **2** have an ambition. **3** think something might happen • *I never dreamt she would leave.*
- **dream up** invent or imagine a plan, idea, etc.
▷ **dreamer** *noun*
[from Middle English]

dreary *ADJECTIVE* **drearier**, **dreariest** **1** dull or boring. **2** gloomy.
▷ **drearily** *adverb* **dreariness** *noun*
[from Old English]

dredge *VERB* **dredges**, **dredging**, **dredged** drag something up, especially by scooping at the bottom of a river or the sea.
▷ **dredger** *noun*
[origin unknown]

dregs *PLURAL NOUN* the last drops of a liquid at the bottom of a glass, barrel, etc., together with any sediment.
[from a Scandinavian language]

drench *VERB* **drenches, drenching, drenched** make wet all through; soak.
[from Old English]

dress *NOUN* **dresses** **1** a woman's or girl's piece of clothing with a bodice and skirt. **2** clothes; costume • *fancy dress.*

dress *VERB* **dresses, dressing, dressed** **1** put clothes on. **2** arrange a display in a window etc.; decorate • *dress the shop windows.* **3** prepare food for cooking or eating. **4** put a dressing on a wound.
▷ **dresser** *noun*
[from French *dresser* = prepare]

dressage (*say* **dress**-ah*zh*) *NOUN* the training of a horse to perform various manoeuvres in order to show its obedience.
[French, = training]

dresser *NOUN* **dressers** a sideboard with shelves at the top for dishes etc.
[same origin as *dress*]

dressing *NOUN* **dressings** **1** a bandage, plaster, or ointment etc. for a wound. **2** a sauce of oil, vinegar, etc. for a salad. **3** manure or other fertilizer for spreading on the soil.

dressing gown *NOUN* **dressing gowns** a loose garment for wearing when you are not fully dressed.

dressmaker *NOUN* **dressmakers** a woman who makes women's clothes.
▷ **dressmaking** *noun*

dress rehearsal *NOUN* **dress rehearsals** the final rehearsal of a play at which the cast wear their costumes.

drey *NOUN* **dreys** a squirrel's nest.
[origin unknown]

dribble *VERB* **dribbles, dribbling, dribbled** **1** let saliva trickle out of your mouth. **2** (said about a liquid) flow in drops. **3** move the ball forward in football or hockey with slight touches of your feet or stick.
▷ **dribble** *noun*
[from *drib*, a different spelling of *drip*]

drier *NOUN* **driers** a device for drying hair, laundry, etc.

drift *VERB* **drifts, drifting, drifted** **1** be carried gently along by water or air. **2** move along slowly and casually. **3** live casually with no definite objective.
▷ **drifter** *noun*

drift *NOUN* **drifts** **1** a drifting movement. **2** a mass of snow or sand piled up by the wind. **3** the general meaning of what someone says.
[from Old Norse]

driftwood *NOUN* wood floating on the sea or washed ashore by it.

drill *NOUN* **drills** **1** a tool for making holes; a machine for boring holes or wells. **2** repeated exercises, e.g. in military training.

drill *VERB* **drills, drilling, drilled** **1** make a hole etc. with a drill. **2** teach someone to do something by making them do repeated exercises.
[from old Dutch]

drily *ADVERB* in a dry way.

drink *VERB* **drinks, drinking, drank, drunk** **1** swallow liquid. **2** drink a lot of alcoholic drinks.
▷ **drinker** *noun*

drink *NOUN* **drinks** **1** a liquid for drinking; an amount of liquid swallowed. **2** an alcoholic drink.
[from Old English]

drip *VERB* **drips, dripping, dripped** fall or let something fall in drops.

drip *NOUN* **drips** **1** liquid falling in drops; the sound it makes. **2** apparatus for dripping liquid into the veins of a sick person.
[from Old English]

drip-dry *ADJECTIVE* made of material that dries easily and does not need ironing.

dripping *NOUN* fat melted from roasted meat and allowed to set.
[from *drip*]

drive *VERB* **drives, driving, drove, driven** **1** make something or someone move. **2** operate a motor vehicle or a train etc. **3** force or compel someone to do something • *Hunger drove them to steal.* **4** force someone into a state • *She is driving me crazy.* **5** rush; move rapidly • *Rain drove against the window.*
▷ **driver** *noun*

drive *NOUN* **drives** **1** a journey in a vehicle. **2** a hard stroke in cricket or golf etc. **3** the transmitting of power to machinery • *four-wheel drive.* **4** energy or enthusiasm. **5** an organized effort • *a sales drive.* **6** a track for vehicles through the grounds of a house. [from Old English]

drive-in *ADJECTIVE* that you can use without getting out of your car.

drivel *NOUN* silly talk; nonsense. [from Old English *dreflian* = dribble]

drizzle *NOUN* very fine rain. [from Old English *dreosan* = to fall]

droll *ADJECTIVE* amusing in an odd way. [from French]

dromedary *NOUN* **dromedaries** a camel with one hump, bred for riding on. [from Greek *dromas* = runner]

drone *VERB* **drones, droning, droned** **1** make a deep humming sound. **2** talk in a boring voice.

drone *NOUN* **drones** **1** a droning sound. **2** a male bee. [from Old English]

drool *VERB* **drools, drooling, drooled** dribble.
- **drool over** be very emotional about liking something.
[from *drivel*]

droop *VERB* **droops, drooping, drooped** hang down weakly. [from Old Norse]

drop *NOUN* **drops** **1** a tiny amount of liquid. **2** a fall or decrease. **3** a descent. **4** a small round sweet. **5** a hanging ornament.

drop *VERB* **drops, dropping, dropped** **1** fall. **2** let something fall. **3** become lower or less. **4** abandon or stop dealing with something • *Let's just drop the subject!* **5** put down a passenger etc. • *Drop me at the station.*
- **drop in** visit someone casually.
- **drop out** stop taking part in something. **drop-out***noun*
[from Old English]

droplet *NOUN* **droplets** a small drop.

droppings *PLURAL NOUN* the dung of animals or birds.

drought (*say* drout) *NOUN* **droughts** a long period of dry weather. [from Old English]

drove *NOUN* **droves** a moving herd or flock.
- **droves** a large number of people.
[from Old English; related to *drive*]

drown *VERB* **drowns, drowning, drowned** **1** die or kill by suffocation under water. **2** flood or drench. **3** make so much noise that another sound cannot be heard. [from Old Norse]

drowsy *ADJECTIVE* sleepy.
▷ **drowsily** *adverb* **drowsiness** *noun*
[from Old English]

drubbing *NOUN* **drubbings** a severe defeat. [from Arabic *daraba* = beat]

drudge *NOUN* **drudges** a person who does hard or boring work.
▷ **drudgery** *noun*
[origin unknown]

drug *NOUN* **drugs** **1** a substance used in medicine. **2** a substance that affects your senses or your mind, e.g. a narcotic or stimulant, especially one causing addiction • *a drug addict.*

drug *VERB* **drugs, drugging, drugged** give a drug to someone, especially to make them unconscious. [from French]

drugstore *NOUN* **drugstores** (*American*) a pharmacy that also sells cosmetics and other articles.

Druid (*say* droo-id) *NOUN* **Druids** a priest of an ancient Celtic religion in Britain and France.

drum *NOUN* **drums** **1** a musical instrument made of a cylinder with a skin or parchment stretched over one or both ends. **2** a cylindrical object or container • *an oil drum.*

drum *VERB* **drums, drumming, drummed** **1** play a drum or drums. **2** tap repeatedly on something.
▷ **drummer** *noun*
- **drum into** drive a lesson, facts etc. into a person's mind by constant repetition.
[imitating the sound]

drumstick *NOUN* **drumsticks** **1** a stick for beating a drum. **2** the lower part of a cooked bird's leg.

drunk *ADJECTIVE* not able to control your behaviour through drinking too much alcohol.

drunk *NOUN* **drunks** a person who is drunk.
[past participle of *drink*]

drunkard *NOUN* **drunkards** a person who is often drunk.

drunken *ADJECTIVE* **1** drunk • *a drunken man.* **2** caused by drinking alcohol • *a drunken brawl.*

dry *ADJECTIVE* **drier, driest** **1** without water or moisture. **2** thirsty. **3** boring or dull. **4** (said about remarks or humour) said in a matter-of-fact or ironical way • *dry wit.*
▷ **drily** *adverb* **dryness** *noun*

dry *VERB* **dries, drying, dried** make or become dry.
[from Old English]

dryad *NOUN* **dryads** a wood nymph.
[from Greek *drys* = tree]

dry-cleaning *NOUN* a method of cleaning clothes etc. using a liquid that evaporates quickly.

dry dock *NOUN* **dry docks** a dock that can be emptied of water so that ships can float in and then be repaired.

dual *ADJECTIVE* composed of two parts; double.
[from Latin *duo* = two]
USAGE Do not confuse this word with **duel**.

dual carriageway *NOUN* **dual carriageways** a road with a dividing strip between lanes of traffic in opposite directions.

dub[1] *VERB* **dubs, dubbing, dubbed** **1** make someone a knight by touching him on the shoulder with a sword. **2** give a person or thing a nickname.
[from old French *adober* = equip with armour]

dub[2] *VERB* **dubs, dubbing, dubbed** change or add new sound to the soundtrack of a film or to a recording.
[short for *double*]

dubbin *NOUN* thick grease used to soften leather and make it waterproof.
[from old French]

dubious (*say* dew-bee-us) *ADJECTIVE* doubtful.
▷ **dubiously** *adverb*
[from Latin *dubium* = doubt]

ducal *ADJECTIVE* to do with a duke.

ducat (*say* duk-at) *NOUN* **ducats** a former gold coin used in Europe.
[from Latin]

duchess *NOUN* **duchesses** a duke's wife or widow.
[from Latin]

duchy *NOUN* **duchies** the territory of a duke • *the duchy of Cornwall.*
[from old French]

duck *NOUN* **ducks** **1** a swimming bird with a flat beak; the female of this. **2** a batsman's score of nought at cricket. **3** a ducking movement.

duck *VERB* **ducks, ducking, ducked** **1** bend down quickly to avoid something. **2** go or push quickly under water. **3** dodge; avoid doing something.
[from Old English]

duckling *NOUN* **ducklings** a young duck.

duct *NOUN* **ducts** a tube or channel through which liquid, gas, air, or cables can pass.
[from Latin *ductus* = leading]
WORD FAMILY There are a number of English words that are related to *duct* because part of their original meaning comes from the Latin words *ducere* meaning 'to lead' or *ductus* meaning 'leading'. These include *abduct, conducive, conduct, deduce, deduct, ductile, induce, introduce, produce,* and *reduce.*

ductile *ADJECTIVE* (said about metal) able to be drawn out into fine strands.
[from Latin]

dud *NOUN* **duds** (*slang*) something that is useless or a fake or fails to work.
[origin unknown]

dudgeon (*say* duj-on) *NOUN*
- **in high dudgeon** indignant.
[origin unknown]

A B C D E F G H I J K L M N O P Q R S T U V W X Y Z

due *ADJECTIVE* **1** expected; scheduled to do something or to arrive • *The train is due in ten minutes.* **2** owing; needing to be paid. **3** that ought to be given; rightful • *Treat her with due respect.*
- **due to** as a result of.
USAGE Traditionally, correct use is as in *His lateness was due to an accident.* Some people object to the use of 'due to' without a preceding noun (e.g. 'lateness') to which it refers. However, such uses as 'He was late, due to an accident' are nowadays widely regarded as acceptable. But if you prefer, you can use *because of* or *owing to* instead.

due *ADVERB* exactly • *We sailed due east.*

due *NOUN* **dues** **1** something you deserve or have a right to; proper respect • *Give him his due.* **2** a fee • *harbour dues.*
[from French *dû* = what is owed]

duel *NOUN* **duels** a fight between two people, especially with pistols or swords.
▷ **duelling** *noun* **duellist** *noun*
[from Italian]
USAGE Do not confuse this word with **dual**.

duet *NOUN* **duets** a piece of music for two players or singers.
[from Italian *duo* = two]

duff *ADJECTIVE* (*slang*) worthless or broken.
[origin unknown]

duffel coat *NOUN* **duffel coats** a thick overcoat with a hood, fastened with toggles.
[named after *Duffel*, a town in Belgium, where the cloth for it was made]

duffer *NOUN* **duffers** (*informal*) a person who is stupid or not good at doing something.
[origin unknown]

dugout *NOUN* **dugouts** **1** an underground shelter. **2** a canoe made by hollowing out a tree trunk.

duke *NOUN* **dukes** a member of the highest rank of noblemen.
▷ **dukedom** *noun*
[from Latin *dux* = leader]

dulcet (*say* dul-sit) *ADJECTIVE* sweet-sounding.
[from Latin *dulcis* = sweet]

dulcimer *NOUN* **dulcimers** a musical instrument with strings that are struck by two small hammers.
[from old French]

dull *ADJECTIVE* **1** not bright or clear • *dull weather.* **2** stupid. **3** boring • *a dull concert.* **4** not sharp • *a dull pain; a dull thud.*
▷ **dully** *adverb* **dullness** *noun*
[from Old English]

dullard *NOUN* **dullards** a stupid person.

duly *ADVERB* in the due or proper way.
[from *due*]

dumb *ADJECTIVE* **1** without the ability to speak. **2** silent. **3** (*informal*) stupid.
▷ **dumbly** *adverb* **dumbness** *noun*
[from Old English]

dumbfounded *ADJECTIVE* unable to say anything because you are so astonished.
[from *dumb* + *confound*]

dummy *NOUN* **dummies** **1** something made to look like a person or thing. **2** an imitation teat given to a baby to suck.
[from *dumb*]

dump *NOUN* **dumps** **1** a place where something (especially rubbish) is left or stored. **2** (*informal*) a dull or unattractive place.

dump *VERB* **dumps, dumping, dumped** **1** get rid of something that is not wanted. **2** put something down carelessly.
[from a Scandinavian language]

dumpling *NOUN* **dumplings** a lump of dough cooked in a stew etc. or baked with fruit inside.
[same origin as *dumpy*]

dumps *PLURAL NOUN* (*informal*)
- **in the dumps** depressed or unhappy.
[from old Dutch *domp* = mist, dampness]

dumpy *ADJECTIVE* short and fat.
[from an old word *dump* = dumpy person]

dunce *NOUN* **dunces** a person who is slow at learning.
[from John *Duns* Scotus, a Scottish philosopher in the Middle Ages (because his opponents said that his followers could not understand new ideas)]

dune *NOUN* **dunes** a mound of loose sand shaped by the wind.
[via old French from Dutch]

dung *NOUN* solid waste matter excreted by an animal.
[from Old English]

dungarees *PLURAL NOUN* trousers with a piece in front covering your chest, held up by straps over your shoulders.
[from Hindi *dungri* = the cloth they were made of]

dungeon (*say* dun-jon) *NOUN* **dungeons** an underground cell for prisoners.
[from old French]

dunk *VERB* **dunks, dunking, dunked** dip something into liquid.
[from German]

duo (*say* dew-oh) *NOUN* **duos** a pair of people, especially playing music.
[Latin = two]

duodenum (*say* dew-o-**deen**-um) *NOUN* **duodenums** the part of the small intestine that is just below the stomach.
▷ **duodenal** *adjective*
[from Latin *duodecim* = twelve (because its length is about twelve times the breadth of a finger)]

dupe *VERB* **dupes, duping, duped** deceive.
[French]

duplex (*say* dew-pleks) *NOUN* **duplexes** **1** (*American*) a residential building divided into two apartments. **2** (*American & Australian*) a semi-detached house.
[from Latin]

duplicate (*say* **dyoop**-lik-at) *NOUN* **duplicates** **1** something that is exactly the same as something else. **2** an exact copy.

duplicate (*say* **dyoop**-lik-ayt) *VERB* **duplicates, duplicating, duplicated** make or be a duplicate.
▷ **duplication** *noun* **duplicator** *noun*
[from Latin *duplex* = double]

duplicity (*say* dew-**plis**-it-ee) *NOUN* deceitfulness.
[same origin as *duplicate*]

durable *ADJECTIVE* strong and likely to last.
▷ **durably** *adverb* **durability** *noun*
[from Latin *durare* = endure]

duration *NOUN* the length of time something lasts.
[same origin as *durable*]

duress (*say* dewr-ess) *NOUN* the use of force or threats to get what you want.
[from Latin *durus* = hard]

during *PREPOSITION* while something else is going on.
[from Latin *durans* = lasting, enduring]

dusk *NOUN* **dusks** twilight in the evening.
[from Old English]

dusky *ADJECTIVE* dark or shadowy.

dust *NOUN* tiny particles of earth or other solid material.

dust *VERB* **dusts, dusting, dusted** **1** wipe away dust. **2** sprinkle with dust or something powdery.
[from Old English]

dustbin *NOUN* **dustbins** a bin for household rubbish.

duster *NOUN* **dusters** a cloth for dusting things.

dustman *NOUN* **dustmen** a person employed to empty dustbins and take away household rubbish.

dustpan *NOUN* **dustpans** a pan into which dust is brushed from a floor.

dusty *ADJECTIVE* **dustier, dustiest** **1** covered with dust. **2** like dust.

dutiful *ADJECTIVE* doing your duty; obedient.
▷ **dutifully** *adverb*
[from *duty* + *-ful*]

duty *NOUN* **duties** **1** what you ought to do or must do. **2** a task that must be done. **3** a tax charged on imports and on certain other things.
- **on** or **off duty** actually doing (or not doing) what is your regular work.
[same origin as *due*]

duty-free *ADJECTIVE* (said about goods) on which duty is not charged.

duvet (*say* **doo**-vay) *NOUN* **duvets** a kind of quilt used instead of other bedclothes.
[French, = *down*²]

DVD *ABBREVIATION* digital videodisc; a disc used for storing large amounts of audio or video information, especially films.

dwarf *NOUN* **dwarfs** or **dwarves** a very small person or thing.

dwarf *VERB* **dwarfs, dwarfing, dwarfed** make something seem small by contrast • *The ocean liner dwarfed the tugs that were towing it.*
[from Old English]

dwell *VERB* **dwells, dwelling, dwelt** live somewhere.
▷ **dweller** *noun*
- **dwell on** think or talk about something for a long time.
[from Old English]

dwelling *NOUN* **dwellings** a house etc. to live in.

dwindle *VERB* **dwindles, dwindling, dwindled** get smaller gradually.
[from Old English]

dye *VERB* **dyes, dyeing, dyed** colour something by putting it into a liquid.
▷ **dyer** *noun*

dye *NOUN* **dyes** a substance used to dye things.
[from Old English]

dyke *NOUN* **dykes** a different spelling of *dike*.

dynamic *ADJECTIVE* **1** energetic or forceful. **2** (said about a force) producing motion.
▷ **dynamically** *adverb*
[from Greek *dynamis* = power]

dynamics *NOUN* **1** the scientific study of force and motion. **2** (*in music*) the different levels of loudness and softness in a piece of music.

dynamite *NOUN* **1** a powerful explosive. **2** something likely to make people very excited or angry.
[same origin as *dynamic*]

dynamo *NOUN* **dynamos** a machine that makes electricity.

dynasty (*say* **din**-a-stee) *NOUN* **dynasties** a line of rulers or powerful people all from the same family.
▷ **dynastic** *adjective*
[same origin as *dynamic*]

dys- *PREFIX* bad; difficult.
[from Greek]

dysentery (*say* **dis**-en-tree) *NOUN* a disease causing severe diarrhoea.
[from *dys-* + Greek *entera* = bowels]

dyslexia (*say* dis-**leks**-ee-a) *NOUN* special difficulty in being able to read and spell, caused by a brain condition.
▷ **dyslexic** *adjective*
[from *dys-* + Greek *lexis* = speech (which was confused with Latin *legere* = read)]

dyspepsia (*say* dis-**pep**-see-a) *NOUN* indigestion.
▷ **dyspeptic** *adjective*
[from *dys-* + Greek *peptikos* = able to digest]

dystrophy (*say* **dis**-trof-ee) *NOUN* a disease that weakens the muscles.
[from *dys-* + Greek *-trophia* = nourishment]

Ee

E. *ABBREVIATION* east; eastern.

e- *PREFIX* **1** out; away. **2** up, upwards; thoroughly. **3** formerly. SEE **ex-**.

each *ADJECTIVE* & *PRONOUN* every; every one • *each child; each of you.*
[from Old English]
USAGE In standard English, the pronoun *each* should be used with a singular verb and singular pronouns: • *Each has chosen her own outfit.*

eager *ADJECTIVE* strongly wanting to do something; enthusiastic.
▷ **eagerly** *adverb* **eagerness** *noun*
[from Latin]

eagle *NOUN* **eagles** a large bird of prey with very strong sight.
[from Latin]

ear[1] *NOUN* **ears** **1** the organ of the body that is used for hearing. **2** hearing ability • *She has a good ear for music.*
[from Old English *eare*]

ear[2] *NOUN* **ears** the spike of seeds at the top of a stalk of corn.
[from Old English *ear*]

earache *NOUN* pain in the ear.

eardrum *NOUN* **eardrums** a membrane in the ear that vibrates when sounds reach it.

earl *NOUN* **earls** a British nobleman.
▷ **earldom** *noun*
[from Old English]

early *ADJECTIVE & ADVERB* **earlier, earliest**
1 before the usual or expected time. **2** near the beginning • *early in the book.*
▷ **earliness** *noun*
[from *ere* + *-ly*]

earmark *VERB* **earmarks, earmarking, earmarked** put something aside for a particular purpose.
[from the custom of marking an animal's ear to identify it]

earn *VERB* **earns, earning, earned** get something by working or in return for what you have done.
[from Old English]

earnest *ADJECTIVE* showing serious feelings or intentions.
▷ **earnestly** *adverb* **earnestness** *noun*
- **in earnest** **1** more seriously or with more determination • *We began to shovel the snow in earnest.* **2** meaning what you say.
[from Old English]

earnings *PLURAL NOUN* money earned.

earphone *NOUN* **earphones** a listening device that fits over the ear.
[from *ear* + Greek *phone* = sound]

earring *NOUN* **earrings** an ornament worn on the ear.

earshot *NOUN* the distance within which a sound can be heard.
[from *ear* + *shot* in the sense 'as far as something can reach']

earth *NOUN* **earths** **1** the planet (*Earth*) that we live on. **2** the ground; soil. **3** the hole where a fox or badger lives. **4** connection to the ground to complete an electrical circuit.

earth *VERB* **earths, earthing, earthed** connect an electrical circuit to the ground.
[from Old English]

earthenware *NOUN* pottery made of coarse baked clay.

earthly *ADJECTIVE* concerned with life on earth rather than with life after death.

earthquake *NOUN* **earthquakes** a violent movement of part of the earth's surface.

earthworm *NOUN* **earthworms** a worm that lives in the soil.

earthy *ADJECTIVE* **1** like earth or soil. **2** crude and vulgar.

earwig *NOUN* **earwigs** a crawling insect with pincers at the end of its body.
[so named because it was thought to crawl into people's ears]

ease *NOUN* freedom from trouble or effort or pain • *She climbed the tree with ease.*

ease *VERB* **eases, easing, eased** **1** make less painful or less tight or troublesome. **2** move gently into position. **3** become less severe • *The pressure eased.*
[from French]

easel *NOUN* **easels** a stand for supporting a blackboard or a painting.
[from Dutch *ezel* = donkey (which carries a load)]

easily *ADVERB* **1** without difficulty; with ease. **2** by far • *easily the best.* **3** very likely • *He could easily be lying.*

east *NOUN* **1** the direction where the sun rises. **2** the eastern part of a country, city, etc.

east *ADJECTIVE & ADVERB* towards or in the east; coming from the east.
▷ **easterly** *adjective* **eastern** *adjective* **easterner** *noun* **easternmost** *adjective*
[from Old English]

Easter *NOUN* the Sunday (in March or April) when Christians commemorate the resurrection of Christ; the days around it.
[named after *Eastre*, an Anglo-Saxon goddess whose feast was celebrated in spring]

eastward *ADJECTIVE & ADVERB* towards the east.
▷ **eastwards** *adverb*

easy *ADJECTIVE* **easier, easiest** able to be done or used or understood without trouble.
▷ **easiness** *noun*

easy *ADVERB* with ease; comfortably • *Take it easy!*
[from French]

easy chair *NOUN* **easy chairs** a comfortable armchair.

eat *VERB* **eats, eating, ate, eaten** **1** chew and swallow as food. **2** have a meal • *When do we eat?* **3** use up; destroy gradually • *Extra expenses ate up our savings.*
[from Old English]

eatable *ADJECTIVE* fit to be eaten.

eau de Cologne (*say* oh der kol-**ohn**) *NOUN* a perfume first made at Cologne. [French, = water of Cologne]

eaves *PLURAL NOUN* the overhanging edges of a roof.
[from Old English]

eavesdrop *VERB* **eavesdrops, eavesdropping, eavesdropped** listen secretly to a private conversation.
▷ **eavesdropper** *noun*
[as if you are listening outside a wall, where water drops from the eaves]

ebb *NOUN* **ebbs** **1** the movement of the tide when it is going out, away from the land.
2 a low point • *Our courage was at a low ebb.*

ebb *VERB* **ebbs, ebbing, ebbed** **1** flow away from the land. **2** weaken; become less • *strength ebbed.*
[from Old English]

ebony *NOUN* a hard black wood.
[from Greek]

ebullient (*say* i-**bul**-ient) *ADJECTIVE* cheerful, full of high spirits.
▷ **ebullience** *noun*
[from *ex-* + Latin *bullire* = boil]

EC *ABBREVIATION* European Community.

eccentric (*say* ik-**sen**-trik) *ADJECTIVE* behaving strangely.
▷ **eccentrically** *adverb* **eccentricity** (*say* ek-sen-**triss**-it-ee) *noun*
[from Greek *ekkentros* = away from the centre]

ecclesiastical (*say* ik-lee-zee-ast-ik-al) *ADJECTIVE* to do with the Church or the clergy.
[from Greek *ekklesia* = church]

echo *NOUN* **echoes** a sound that is heard again as it is reflected off something.

echo *VERB* **echoes, echoing, echoed**
1 make an echo. **2** repeat a sound or saying.
[from Greek *eche* = sound]

éclair (*say* ay-**klair**) *NOUN* **éclairs** a finger-shaped cake of pastry with a creamy filling.
[French]

eclipse *NOUN* **eclipses** the blocking of the sun's or moon's light when the moon or the earth is in the way.

eclipse *VERB* **eclipses, eclipsing, eclipsed**
1 block the light and cause an eclipse.
2 seem better or more important than others • *Her performance eclipsed the rest of the team.*
[from Greek]

eco- *PREFIX* to do with ecology or the environment.
[from *ecology*]

ecology (*say* ee-**kol**-o-jee) *NOUN* the study of living things in relation to each other and to where they live.
▷ **ecological** *adjective* **ecologically** *adverb* **ecologist** *noun*
[from Greek *oikos* = house, + *-logy*]

economic (*say* ee-kon-**om**-ik) *ADJECTIVE* **1** to do with economy or economics.
2 profitable.

economical *ADJECTIVE* using as little as possible.
▷ **economically** *adverb*

economics *NOUN* the study of how money is used and how goods and services are provided and used.
▷ **economist** *noun*

economize *VERB* **economizes, economizing, economized** be economical; use or spend less • *We need to economize on fuel.*

economy *NOUN* **economies** **1** a country's or household's income (e.g. from what it sells or earns) and the way this is spent (e.g. on goods and services). **2** being economical. **3** a saving • *You need to make economies.*
[from Greek *oikos* = house + *-nomia* = management]

ecosystem (*say* ee-koh-sis-tum) *NOUN* **ecosystems** all the plants and animals in a particular area considered in terms of their relationship with their environment.

ecstasy (*say* **ek**-sta-see) *NOUN* **1** a feeling of great delight. **2** an illegal drug that makes people feel very energetic and can cause hallucinations.
▷ **ecstatic** (*say* ik-**stat**-ik) *adjective* **ecstatically** *adverb*
[from Greek, = standing outside yourself]

ecumenical (*say* ee-kew-men-ikal) *ADJECTIVE* **1** to do with or including all the Christian Churches. **2** to do with the unity of the whole Christian Church • *the ecumenical movement.*
[from Greek *oikoumene* = the inhabited world]

eczema (*say* eks-im-a) *NOUN* a skin disease causing rough itching patches.
[from Greek]

-ed *SUFFIX* can form a past tense or past participle of a verb (e.g. *paint/painted*), or an adjective (e.g. *diseased*).
[from Old English]

eddy *NOUN* **eddies** a swirling patch of water or air or smoke etc.

eddy *VERB* **eddies, eddying, eddied** swirl.
[from Old English]

edge *NOUN* **edges** **1** the part along the side or end of something. **2** the sharp part of a knife or axe or other cutting instrument.
- **be on edge** be tense and irritable.

edge *VERB* **edges, edging, edged** **1** be the edge or border of something. **2** put a border on. **3** move gradually • *He edged away.*
[from Old English]

edgeways *ADVERB* with the edge forwards or outwards.

edgy *ADJECTIVE* tense and irritable.
▷ **edginess** *noun*

edible *ADJECTIVE* suitable for eating, not poisonous • *edible fruits.*
[from Latin *edere* = eat]

edict (*say* ee-dikt) *NOUN* **edicts** an official command.
[from *e-* + Latin *dictum* = said]

edifice (*say* ed-if-iss) *NOUN* **edifices** a large building.
[from Latin *aedis* = temple]

edify *VERB* **edifies, edifying, edified** be an improving influence on a person's mind.
▷ **edification** *noun*
[from Latin]

edit *VERB* **edits, editing, edited** **1** be the editor of a newspaper or other publication. **2** make written material ready for publishing. **3** choose and put the parts of a film or tape recording etc. into order.
[from *editor*]

edition *NOUN* **editions** **1** the form in which something is published • *a paperback edition.* **2** all the copies of a book etc. issued at the same time • *the first edition.* **3** an individual television or radio programme in a series.

editor *NOUN* **editors** **1** the person in charge of a newspaper or a section of it. **2** a person who edits something.
[Latin, = producer]

editorial *ADJECTIVE* to do with editing or editors.

editorial *NOUN* **editorials** a newspaper article giving the editor's comments on something.

educate *VERB* **educates, educating, educated** provide people with education.
▷ **educative** *adjective* **educator** *noun*
[from Latin]

educated *ADJECTIVE* showing a high standard of knowledge and culture, as a result of a good education.

education *NOUN* the process of training people's minds and abilities so that they acquire knowledge and develop skills.
▷ **educational** *adjective* **educationally** *adverb* **educationist** *noun*

-ee *SUFFIX* forms nouns meaning 'person affected by or described as' (e.g. *absentee, employee, refugee*).
[from French]

eel *NOUN* **eels** a long fish that looks like a snake.
[from Old English]

eerie *ADJECTIVE* **eerier, eeriest** strange in a frightening or mysterious way.
▷ **eerily** *adverb* **eeriness** *noun*
[from Old English]

ef- *PREFIX* **1** out; away. **2** up, upwards; thoroughly. **3** formerly. SEE **ex-**.

efface *VERB* **effaces, effacing, effaced** wipe or rub out.
▷ **effacement** *noun*
[from French]

effect *NOUN* **effects** **1** a change that is produced by an action or cause; a result. **2** an impression that is produced by something • *a cheerful effect.*

effect *VERB* **effects, effecting, effected** make something happen • *We want to effect a change.*
[from *ef-* + Latin *-fectum* = done]
USAGE Do not confuse with **affect**.

effective *ADJECTIVE* **1** producing the effect that is wanted. **2** impressive and striking.
▷ **effectively** *adverb* **effectiveness** *noun*

effectual *ADJECTIVE* producing the result desired.
▷ **effectually** *adverb*

effeminate *ADJECTIVE* (said about a man) having qualities that are thought to be feminine.
▷ **effeminacy** *noun*
[from Latin]

effervesce (*say* ef-er-vess) *VERB* **effervesces, effervescing, effervesced** give off bubbles of gas; fizz.
▷ **effervescent** *adjective* **effervescence** *noun*
[from *ef-* + Latin *fervescere* = come to the boil]

efficacious (*say* ef-ik-ay-shus) *ADJECTIVE* able to produce the result desired.
▷ **efficacy** (*say* ef-ik-a-see) *noun*
[from Latin *efficere* = succeed in doing]

efficient *ADJECTIVE* doing work well; effective.
▷ **efficiently** *adverb* **efficiency** *noun*
[same origin as *efficacious*]

effigy *NOUN* **effigies** a model or sculptured figure.
[from Latin *effingere* = to form]

effort *NOUN* **efforts** **1** the use of energy; the energy used. **2** something difficult or tiring. **3** an attempt • *This painting is a good effort.*
[from old French]

effortless *ADJECTIVE* done with little or no effort.
▷ **effortlessly** *adverb*

effusive *ADJECTIVE* making a great show of affection or enthusiasm.
▷ **effusively** *adverb* **effusiveness** *noun*
[from Latin *effundere* = pour out]

e.g. *ABBREVIATION* for example.
[short for Latin *exempli gratia* = for the sake of an example]

egalitarian (*say* ig-al-it-air-ee-an) *ADJECTIVE* believing that everybody is equal and that nobody should be given special privileges.
[from French *égal* = equal]

egg[1] *NOUN* **eggs** **1** a more or less round object produced by the female of birds, fishes, reptiles, and insects, which may develop into a new individual if fertilized. **2** a hen's or duck's egg used as food. **3** an ovum.
[from Old Norse]

egg[2] *VERB* **eggs, egging, egged** encourage someone with taunts or dares etc. • *We egged him on.*
[from Old Norse *eggja* = sharpen]

eggplant *NOUN* **eggplants** (*American*) an aubergine.
[because of the aubergine's shape]

ego (*say* eeg-oh) *NOUN* **egos** a person's self or self-respect.
[Latin, = I]

egotist (*say* eg-oh-tist) *NOUN* **egotists** a conceited person who is always talking about himself or herself.
▷ **egotism** *noun* **egotistic** *adjective*
[from *ego* + *-ist*]

Eid (*say* eed) *NOUN* a Muslim festival marking the end of the fast of Ramadan.
[from Arabic *'id* = feast]

eiderdown *NOUN* **eiderdowns** a quilt stuffed with soft material.
[originally the soft down of the *eider*, a kind of duck]

eight *ADJECTIVE* & *NOUN* **eights** the number 8.
▷ **eighth** *adjective* & *noun*
[from Old English]

eighteen *ADJECTIVE* & *NOUN* **eighteens** the number 18.
▷ **eighteenth** *adjective* & *noun*
[from Old English]

eighty *NOUN* & *ADJECTIVE* **eighties** the number 80.
▷ **eightieth** *adjective* & *noun*
[from Old English]

eisteddfod (*say* I-steth-vod) *NOUN* **eisteddfods** or **eisteddfodau** an annual Welsh gathering of poets and musicians for competitions.
[Welsh, = session]

either *ADJECTIVE & PRONOUN* **1** one or the other of two • *Either team can win; either of them.* **2** both of two • *There are fields on either side of the river.*

either *ADVERB* also; similarly • *If you won't go, I won't either.*

either *CONJUNCTION (used with* or*)* the first of two possibilities • *He is either ill or drunk. Either come right in or go away.*
[from Old English]

ejaculate *VERB* **ejaculates, ejaculating, ejaculated** **1** (said about a man) produce semen from the penis. **2** (*formal*) suddenly say something.
▷ **ejaculation** *noun*
[from *e-* + Latin *jacere* = to throw]

eject *VERB* **ejects, ejecting, ejected** **1** send something out forcefully. **2** force someone to leave. **3** (said about a pilot) be thrown out of an aircraft in a special seat in an emergency.
▷ **ejection** *noun* **ejector** *noun*
[from *e-* + Latin *-jectum* = thrown]

eke (*say* eek) *VERB* **ekes, eking, eked**
- **eke out** manage to make something last as long as possible by only using small amounts of it.
[from Old English]

elaborate (*say* il-ab-er-at) *ADJECTIVE* having many parts or details; complicated.
▷ **elaborately** *adverb* **elaborateness** *noun*

elaborate (*say* il-ab-er-ayt) *VERB* **elaborates, elaborating, elaborated** explain or work something out in detail.
▷ **elaboration** *noun*
[from *e-* + Latin *laborare* = to work]

elapse *VERB* **elapses, elapsing, elasped** (said about time) pass.
[from *e-* + Latin *lapsum* = slipped]

elastic *NOUN* cord or material woven with strands of rubber etc. so that it can stretch.

elastic *ADJECTIVE* able to be stretched or squeezed and then go back to its original length or shape.
▷ **elasticity** *noun*
[from Greek]

elated *ADJECTIVE* feeling very pleased.
▷ **elation** *noun*
[from *e-* + Latin *latum* = carried]

elbow *NOUN* **elbows** the joint in the middle of the arm.

elbow *VERB* **elbows, elbowing, elbowed** push with the elbow.
[from Old English]

elder[1] *ADJECTIVE* older • *my elder brother.*

elder *NOUN* **elders** **1** an older person • *Respect your elders!* **2** an official in certain Churches.
[an old spelling of *older*]

elder[2] *NOUN* **elders** a tree with white flowers and black berries.
▷ **elderberry** *noun*
[from Old English]

elderly *ADJECTIVE* rather old.
[from *elder*[1] + *-ly*]

eldest *ADJECTIVE* oldest.
[an old spelling of *oldest*]

elect *VERB* **elects, electing, elected** **1** choose by voting. **2** choose to do something; decide.

elect *ADJECTIVE* chosen by a vote but not yet in office • *the president elect.*
[from *e-* + Latin *lectum* = chosen]

election *NOUN* **elections** electing; the process of electing Members of Parliament.

elector *NOUN* **electors** a person who has the right to vote in an election.
▷ **electoral** *adjective*

electorate *NOUN* **electorates** all the electors.

electric *ADJECTIVE* **1** to do with or worked by electricity. **2** causing sudden excitement • *The news had an electric effect.*
▷ **electrical** *adjective* **electrically** *adverb*
[from Greek *elektron* = amber (which is easily given a charge of static electricity)]

electric chair *NOUN* an electrified chair used for capital punishment in the USA.

electrician *NOUN* **electricians** a person whose job is to deal with electrical equipment.

electricity *NOUN* a form of energy carried by certain particles of matter (electrons and protons), used for lighting and heating and for making machines work.

electrify *VERB* **electrifies**, **electrifying**, **electrified** **1** give an electric charge to something. **2** supply something with electric power; cause something to work with electricity. **3** thrill with sudden excitement.
▷ **electrification** *noun*

electro- *PREFIX* to do with or using electricity.

electrocute *VERB* **electrocutes**, **electrocuting**, **electrocuted** kill by electricity.
▷ **electrocution** *noun*
[from *electro-* + *execute*]

electrode *NOUN* **electrodes** a solid conductor through which electricity enters or leaves a vacuum tube.
[from *electro-* + Greek *hodos* = way]

electromagnet *NOUN* **electromagnets** a magnet worked by electricity.
▷ **electromagnetic** *adjective*

electron *NOUN* **electrons** a particle of matter with a negative electric charge.
[same origin as *electric*]

electronic *ADJECTIVE* produced or worked by a flow of electrons.
▷ **electronically** *adverb*

electronic mail *NOUN* a system of sending messages and data from one computer to another by means of a network.

electronics *NOUN* the use or study of electronic devices.

elegant *ADJECTIVE* graceful and dignified.
▷ **elegantly** *adverb* **elegance** *noun*
[from Latin]

elegiac *ADJECTIVE* expressing sadness or sorrow.

elegy (*say* el-ij-ee) *NOUN* **elegies** a sorrowful or serious poem.
[from Greek]

element *NOUN* **elements** **1** each of about 100 substances that cannot be split up into simpler substances, composed of atoms that have the same number of protons. **2** each of the parts that make up a whole thing. **3** a basic or elementary principle • *the elements of algebra.* **4** a wire or coil that gives out heat in an electric fire or cooker etc. **5** the environment or circumstances that suit you best • *Karen is really in her element at parties.*
- **the elements** the forces of weather, such as rain, wind, and cold.
[from Latin]

elementary *ADJECTIVE* dealing with the simplest stages of something; easy.

elephant *NOUN* **elephants** a very large animal with a trunk, large ears, and tusks.
[from Greek *elephas* = ivory (which its tusks are made of)]

elephantine (*say* el-if-ant-I'n) *ADJECTIVE* **1** very large. **2** clumsy and slow-moving.

elevate *VERB* **elevates**, **elevating**, **elevated** lift or raise something to a higher position.
▷ **elevation** *noun*
[from *e-* + Latin *levare* = to lift]

elevator *NOUN* **elevators** **1** something that raises things. **2** (*American*) a lift.

eleven *ADJECTIVE* & *NOUN* **elevens** the number 11.
▷ **eleventh** *adjective* & *noun*
[from Old English]

elf *NOUN* **elves** (in fairy tales) a small being with magic powers.
▷ **elfin** *adjective*
[from Old English]

elicit (*say* ill-iss-it) *VERB* **elicits**, **eliciting**, **elicited** draw out information by reasoning or questioning.
[from Latin]
USAGE Do not confuse with **illicit**.

elide *VERB* **elides**, **eliding**, **elided** omit part of a word by elision.

eligible (*say* el-ij-ib-ul) *ADJECTIVE* qualified or suitable for something.
▷ **eligibility** *noun*
[from Latin *eligere* = choose]

eliminate *VERB* **eliminates**, **eliminating**, **eliminated** get rid of something.
▷ **elimination** *noun*
[from *e-* + Latin *limen* = entrance]

elision (*say* il-**lizh**-on) *NOUN* omitting part of a word in pronouncing it, e.g. in saying *I'm* for *I am*.
[from Latin *elidere* = to push out]

élite (*say* ay-**leet**) *NOUN* a group of people given privileges which are not given to others.
[from old French *élit* = chosen]

elixir (*say* il-**iks**-er) *NOUN* **elixirs** a liquid that is believed to have magic powers, such as restoring youth to someone who is old.
[from Arabic *al-iksir* = substance that would cure illness and change metals into gold]

Elizabethan (*say* il-iz-a-**beeth**-an) *ADJECTIVE* from the time of Queen Elizabeth I (1558-1603).
▷ **Elizabethan** *noun*

elk *NOUN* **elks** a large kind of deer.
[from Old English]

ellipse (*say* il-**ips**) *NOUN* **ellipses** an oval shape.
[same origin as *elliptical*]

ellipsis *NOUN* omitting a word or words from a sentence, usually so that the sentence can still be understood.
[same origin as *elliptical*]

elliptical (*say* il-**ip**-tik-al) *ADJECTIVE* **1** shaped like an ellipse. **2** with some words omitted • *an elliptical phrase.*
▷ **elliptically** *adverb*
[from Greek *elleipsis* = fault]

elm *NOUN* **elms** a tall tree with rough leaves.
[from Old English]

elocution (*say* el-o-**kew**-shon) *NOUN* the art of speaking clearly and correctly.
[same origin as *eloquent*]

elongated *ADJECTIVE* made longer; lengthened.
▷ **elongation** *noun*
[from *e-* + Latin *longus* = long]

elope *VERB* **elopes, eloping, eloped** run away secretly to get married.
▷ **elopement** *noun*
[from old French]

eloquent *ADJECTIVE* speaking fluently and expressing ideas vividly.
▷ **eloquently** *adverb* **eloquence** *noun*
[from *e-* + Latin *loqui* = speak]

else *ADVERB* **1** besides; other • *Nobody else knows.* **2** otherwise; if not • *Run or else you'll be late.*
[from Old English]

elsewhere *ADVERB* somewhere else.

elucidate (*say* il-**oo**-sid-ayt) *VERB* **elucidates, elucidating, elucidated** make something clear by explaining it.
▷ **elucidation** *noun*
[from *e-* + Latin *lucidus* = clear]

elude (*say* il-**ood**) *VERB* **eludes, eluding, eluded** **1** avoid being caught by someone • *The fox eluded the hounds.* **2** be too difficult for you to remember or understand • *I'm afraid the name eludes me.*
▷ **elusive** *adjective*
[from *e-* + Latin *ludere* = to play]
USAGE Do not confuse with **allude**.

em- *PREFIX* **1** in; into. **2** on. SEE **en-**.

emaciated (*say* im-**ay**-see-ay-tid) *ADJECTIVE* very thin from illness or starvation.
▷ **emaciation** *noun*
[from *e-* + Latin *macies* = leanness]

email *NOUN* electronic mail.
▷ **email** *verb*

emanate (*say* **em**-an-ayt) *VERB* **emanates, emanating, emanated** come from a source.
[from *e-* + Latin *manare* = to flow]

emancipate (*say* im-**an**-sip-ayt) *VERB* **emancipates, emancipating, emancipated** set free from slavery or other restraints.
▷ **emancipation** *noun*
[from *e-* + Latin *mancipium* = slave]

embalm *VERB* **embalms, embalming, embalmed** preserve a corpse from decay by using spices or chemicals.
[from *em-* + *balm*]

embankment *NOUN* **embankments** a long bank of earth or stone to hold back water or support a road or railway.
[from *em-* + *bank*[1]]

embargo *NOUN* **embargoes** an official ban, especially on trade with a country.
[from Spanish *embargar* = restrain]

embark *VERB* **embarks, embarking, embarked** put or go on board a ship or aircraft.
▷ **embarkation** *noun*
- **embark on** begin • *They embarked on a dangerous exercise.*
[from *em-* + French *barque* = a sailing ship]

embarrass *VERB* **embarrasses, embarrassing, embarrassed** make someone feel awkward or ashamed.
▷ **embarrassment** *noun*
[via French from Spanish]

embassy *NOUN* **embassies** **1** an ambassador and his or her staff. **2** the building where they work.
[from old French; related to *ambassador*]

embed *VERB* **embeds, embedding, embedded** fix firmly in something solid.

embellish *VERB* **embellishes, embellishing, embellished** ornament something; add details to it.
▷ **embellishment** *noun*
[from *em-* + French *bel* = beautiful]

embers *PLURAL NOUN* small pieces of glowing coal or wood in a dying fire.
[from Old English]

embezzle *VERB* **embezzles, embezzling, embezzled** take dishonestly money that was left in your care.
▷ **embezzlement** *noun*
[from old French]

emblazon *VERB* **emblazons, emblazoning, emblazoned** **1** decorate something with a coat of arms. **2** decorate something with bright or eye-catching designs or words.
[from *em-* + French *blason* = shield]

emblem *NOUN* **emblems** a symbol that represents something • *The crown is a royal emblem.*
▷ **emblematic** *adjective*
[from Latin]

embody *VERB* **embodies, embodying, embodied** **1** express principles or ideas in a visible form • *The house embodies our idea of a modern home.* **2** include or contain • *Parts of the old treaty are embodied in the new one.*
▷ **embodiment** *noun*

emboss *VERB* **embosses, embossing, embossed** decorate a flat surface with a raised design.
[from *em-* + old French *boce* = *boss*²]

embrace *VERB* **embraces, embracing, embraced** **1** hold someone closely in your arms. **2** include a number of things. **3** accept or adopt a cause or belief.

embrace *NOUN* **embraces** a hug.
[from *em-* + Latin *bracchium* = an arm]

embrocation *NOUN* a lotion for rubbing on parts of the body that ache.
[from Greek]

embroider *VERB* **embroiders, embroidering, embroidered** **1** decorate cloth with needlework. **2** add made-up details to a story to make it more interesting.
▷ **embroidery** *noun*
[from old French]

embroil *VERB* **embroils, embroiling, embroiled** involve in an argument or quarrel.
[from old French]

embryo (*say* em-bree-oh) *NOUN* **embryos** **1** a baby or young animal as it starts to grow in the womb; a young bird growing in an egg. **2** anything in its earliest stages of development.
▷ **embryonic** (*say* em-bree-on-ik) *adjective*
[from *em-* + Greek *bryein* = grow]

emend *VERB* **emends, emending, emended** remove errors from a piece of writing.
[from *e-* + Latin *menda* = a fault]

emerald *NOUN* **emeralds** **1** a bright-green precious stone. **2** its colour.
[from old French]

emerge *VERB* **emerges, emerging, emerged** **1** come out or appear. **2** become known.
▷ **emergence** *noun* **emergent** *adjective*
[from *e-* + Latin *mergere* = plunge]

emergency *NOUN* **emergencies** a sudden serious happening needing prompt action.
[same origin as *emerge*]

emery paper *NOUN* paper with a gritty coating like sandpaper.
[from Greek]

emetic (*say* im-et-ik) *NOUN* **emetics** a medicine used to make a person vomit.
[from Greek]

emigrate *VERB* **emigrates, emigrating, emigrated** leave your own country and go and live in another.
▷ **emigration** *noun* **emigrant** *noun*
[from *e-* + Latin *migrare* = migrate]
USAGE People are *emigrants* from the country they leave and *immigrants* in the country where they settle.

eminent *ADJECTIVE* famous and respected.
▷ **eminently** *adverb* **eminence** *noun*
[from Latin]

emir (*say* em-eer) *NOUN* **emirs** a Muslim ruler.
[from Arabic *amir* = ruler]

emission *NOUN* **emissions** **1** emitting something. **2** something that is emitted, especially fumes or radiation.

emit *VERB* **emits, emitting, emitted** send out light, heat, fumes, etc.
[from *e-* + Latin *mittere* = send]

emolument (*say* im-ol-yoo-ment) *NOUN* **emoluments** (*formal*) payment for work; a salary.
[from Latin]

emotion *NOUN* **emotions** a strong feeling in the mind, such as love, anger, or hate.
▷ **emotional** *adjective* **emotionally** *adverb*
[from French]

emotive *ADJECTIVE* causing emotion.

empathy *NOUN* the ability to understand and share in someone else's feelings.
▷ **empathize** *verb*
[from *em-* + Greek *pathos* = feeling]

emperor *NOUN* **emperors** a man who rules an empire.
[from Latin *imperator* = commander]

emphasis (*say* em-fa-sis) *NOUN* **emphases** **1** special importance given to something. **2** stress put on a word or part of a word.
[from *em-* + Greek *phanein* = to show]

emphasize *VERB* **emphasizes, emphasizing, emphasized** put emphasis on something.

emphatic (*say* im-fat-ik) *ADJECTIVE* using emphasis.
▷ **emphatically** *adverb*

empire *NOUN* **empires** **1** a group of countries controlled by one person or government. **2** a large business organization controlled by one person or group.
[from Latin]

empirical *ADJECTIVE* based on observation or experiment, not on theory.
[from Greek *empeiria* = experience]

employ *VERB* **employs, employing, employed** **1** pay a person to work for you. **2** make use of • *Our doctor employs the most modern methods.*
▷ **employer** *noun* **employment** *noun*
[from French]

employee *NOUN* **employees** a person employed by someone else.

emporium (*say* em-por-ee-um) *NOUN* **emporias** or **emporiums** a large shop.
[from Greek *emporos* = merchant]

empower *VERB* **empowers, empowering, empowered** give someone the power to do something; authorize.

empress *NOUN* **empresses** **1** a woman who rules an empire. **2** an emperor's wife.
[from old French]

empty *ADJECTIVE* **1** with nothing in it. **2** with nobody in it. **3** with no meaning or no effect • *empty promises.*
▷ **emptily** *adverb* **emptiness** *noun*

empty *VERB* **empties, emptying, emptied** make or become empty.
[from Old English]

EMU *ABBREVIATION* Economic and Monetary Union.

emu *NOUN* **emus** a large Australian bird rather like an ostrich.
[from Portuguese]

emulate *VERB* **emulates, emulating, emulated** try to do as well as someone or something, especially by imitating them • *He is emulating his father.*
▷ **emulation** *noun*
[from Latin *aemulus* = a rival]

emulsion *NOUN* **emulsions** **1** a creamy or slightly oily liquid. **2** a kind of water-based paint. **3** the coating on photographic film which is sensitive to light.
[from Latin]

en- *PREFIX* (changing to **em-** before words beginning with *b*, *m*, or *p*) **1** in; into. **2** on. [from Latin or Greek, = in]

enable *VERB* **enables, enabling, enabled** give the means or ability to do something.

enact *VERB* **enacts, enacting, enacted** **1** make a law by a formal process • *Parliament enacted new laws against drugs.* **2** perform • *enact a play.*
▷ **enactment** *noun*

enamel *NOUN* **enamels** **1** a shiny substance for coating metal. **2** paint that dries hard and shiny. **3** the hard shiny surface of teeth.

enamel *VERB* **enamels, enamelling, enamelled** coat or decorate with enamel. [from old French]

enamoured (*say* in-**am**-erd) *ADJECTIVE* very fond of someone or something. [from *en-* + French *amour* = love]

en bloc (*say* ahn **blok**) *ADVERB* all at the same time; in a block. [French]

encamp *VERB* **encamps, encamping, encamped** settle in a camp.

encampment *NOUN* **encampments** a camp.

encapsulate *VERB* **encapsulates, encapsulating, encapsulated** express an idea or set of ideas concisely. [from *en-* + *capsule*]

encase *VERB* **encases, encasing, encased** enclose something in a case. [from *en-* + *case*[1]]

enchant *VERB* **enchants, enchanting, enchanted** **1** put someone under a magic spell. **2** fill someone with intense delight.
▷ **enchanter** *noun* **enchantment** *noun* **enchantress** *noun*
[from old French; related to *incantation*]

encircle *VERB* **encircles, encircling, encircled** surround.
▷ **encirclement** *noun*

enclave *NOUN* **enclaves** a country's territory lying entirely within the boundaries of another country. [from *en-* + Latin *clavis* = key]

enclose *VERB* **encloses, enclosing, enclosed** **1** put a wall or fence round; shut in on all sides. **2** put something into a box or envelope etc. [from old French; related to *include*]

enclosure *NOUN* **enclosures** **1** enclosing. **2** an enclosed area. **3** something enclosed with a letter or parcel.

encompass *VERB* **encompasses, encompassing, encompassed** **1** surround. **2** contain or include. [from *en-* + *compass* in an old sense = circle]

encore (*say* **on**-kor) *NOUN* **encores** an extra item performed at a concert etc. after previous items have been applauded. [French]

encounter *VERB* **encounters, encountering, encountered** **1** meet someone unexpectedly. **2** experience • *We encountered some difficulties.*

encounter *NOUN* **encounters** **1** an unexpected meeting. **2** a battle. [from *en-* + Latin *contra* = against]

encourage *VERB* **encourages, encouraging, encouraged** **1** give confidence or hope; hearten. **2** try to persuade; urge. **3** stimulate; help to develop • *We need to encourage healthy eating.*
▷ **encouragement** *noun*
[from *en-* + old French *corage* = courage]

encroach *VERB* **encroaches, encroaching, encroached** intrude upon someone's rights; go further than the proper limits • *The extra work would encroach on their free time.*
▷ **encroachment** *noun*
[from *en-* + French *crochier* = to hook]

encrust *VERB* **encrusts, encrusting, encrusted** cover with a crust or layer.
▷ **encrustation** *noun*
[from Latin]

encrypt *VERB* **encrypts, encrypting, encrypted** put information into a special code in order to stop people reading it if they are not allowed to.
▷ **encryption** *noun*

encumber *VERB* **encumbers, encumbering, encumbered** be a burden to; hamper.
▷ **encumbrance** *noun*
[from *en-* + old French *combre* = dam]

encyclopedia *NOUN* **encyclopedias** a book or set of books containing all kinds of information.
[from Greek *enkyklopaideia* = general education]

encyclopedic *ADJECTIVE* giving information about many different things.

end *NOUN* **ends** **1** the last part or extreme point of something. **2** the half of a sports pitch or court defended or occupied by one team or player. **3** destruction or death. **4** purpose • *She did it to gain her own ends.*

end *VERB* **ends, ending, ended** bring or come to an end.
[from Old English]

endanger *VERB* **endangers, endangering, endangered** cause danger to.

endangered species *NOUN* **endangered species** a species in danger of extinction.

endear *VERB* **endears, endearing, endeared** if you endear yourself to someone, you make them fond of you.
▷ **endearing** *adjective*

endearment *NOUN* **endearments** a word or phrase that expresses love or affection.

endeavour (*say* in-**dev**-er) *VERB* **endeavours, endeavouring, endeavoured** attempt.

endeavour *NOUN* **endeavours** an attempt.
[from an old phrase *put yourself in devoir* = do your best (from French *devoir* = duty)]

endemic (*say* en-**dem**-ik) *ADJECTIVE* (said about a disease) often found in a certain area or group of people.
[from *en-* + Greek *demos* = people]

ending *NOUN* **endings** the last part.

endless *ADJECTIVE* **1** never stopping. **2** with the ends joined to make a continuous strip for use in machinery etc. • *an endless belt.*
▷ **endlessly** *adverb*

endorse *VERB* **endorses, endorsing, endorsed** **1** sign your name on the back of a cheque or document. **2** make an official entry on a licence about an offence committed by its holder. **3** confirm or give your approval to something.
▷ **endorsement** *noun*
[from Latin *in dorsum* = on the back]

endow *VERB* **endows, endowing, endowed** **1** provide a source of income to establish something • *She endowed a scholarship.* **2** provide with an ability or quality • *He was endowed with great talent.*
▷ **endowment** *noun*
[from old French; related to *dowry*]

endurance *NOUN* the ability to put up with difficulty or pain for a long period.

endure *VERB* **endures, enduring, endured** **1** suffer or put up with difficulty or pain etc. **2** continue to exist; last.
▷ **endurable** *adjective*
[from *en-* + Latin *durus* = hard]

enemy *NOUN* **enemies** **1** one who hates and opposes or seeks to harm another. **2** a nation or army etc. at war with another.
[from old French]

energetic *ADJECTIVE* full of energy.
▷ **energetically** *adverb*

energy *NOUN* **energies** **1** strength to do things, liveliness. **2** the ability of matter or radiation to do work. Energy is measured in joules. **3** power obtained from fuel and other resources and used for light and heat, the operation of machinery etc.
[from *en-* + Greek *ergon* = work]

enfold *VERB* **enfolds, enfolding, enfolded** surround or be wrapped round something.

enforce *VERB* **enforces, enforcing, enforced** compel people to obey a law or rule.
▷ **enforcement** *noun* **enforceable** *adjective*
[from old French]

enfranchise *VERB* **enfranchises, enfranchising, enfranchised** give people the right to vote in elections.
▷ **enfranchisement** *noun*
[from *en-* + old French *franc* = free]

A B C D E F G H I J K L M N O P Q R S T U V W X Y Z

engage *VERB* **engages, engaging, engaged** **1** arrange to employ or use • *Engage a typist.* **2** occupy the attention of • *They engaged her in conversation.* **3** begin a battle with • *We engaged the enemy.*
[from old French]

engaged *ADJECTIVE* **1** having promised to marry somebody. **2** in use; occupied.

engagement *NOUN* **engagements** **1** engaging something. **2** a promise to marry somebody. **3** an arrangement to meet somebody or do something. **4** a battle.

engaging *ADJECTIVE* attractive or charming.

engine *NOUN* **engines** **1** a machine that provides power. **2** a vehicle that pulls a railway train; a locomotive.
[from old French; related to *ingenious*]

engineer *NOUN* **engineers** an expert in engineering.

engineer *VERB* **engineers, engineering, engineered** plan and construct or cause to happen • *He engineered a meeting between them.*

engineering *NOUN* the design and building or control of machinery or of structures such as roads and bridges.

engrave *VERB* **engraves, engraving, engraved** carve words or lines etc. on a surface.
▷ **engraver** *noun* **engraving** *noun*
[from *en-* + Old English *grafan* = carve]

engross *VERB* **engrosses, engrossing, engrossed** occupy a person's whole attention • *He was engrossed in his book.*
[originally = to buy up all of something: from French *en gros* = wholesale]

engulf *VERB* **engulfs, engulfing, engulfed** flow over and cover; swamp.

enhance *VERB* **enhances, enhancing, enhanced** make a thing more attractive; increase its value.
▷ **enhancement** *noun*
[from old French]

enigma (*say* in-ig-ma) *NOUN* **enigmas** something very difficult to understand; a puzzle.
[from Greek]

enigmatic (*say* en-ig-mat-ik) *ADJECTIVE* mysterious and puzzling.
▷ **enigmatically** *adverb*

enjoy *VERB* **enjoys, enjoying, enjoyed** get pleasure from something.
▷ **enjoyable** *adjective* **enjoyment** *noun*
[from *en-* + old French *joir* = rejoice]

enlarge *VERB* **enlarges, enlarging, enlarged** make bigger.
▷ **enlargement** *noun*
[from old French]

enlighten *VERB* **enlightens, enlightening, enlightened** give more knowledge or information to a person.
▷ **enlightenment** *noun*
[from *en-* + *lighten*[1]]

enlist *VERB* **enlists, enlisting, enlisted** **1** join the armed forces. **2** obtain someone's support or services etc. • *enlist their help.*
▷ **enlistment** *noun*
[from *en-* + *list*[1]]

enliven *VERB* **enlivens, enlivening, enlivened** make something more lively.
▷ **enlivenment** *noun*

en masse (*say* ahn mass) *ADVERB* all together.
[French, = in a mass]

enmity *NOUN* being somebody's enemy; hostility.
[from old French]

enormity *NOUN* **enormities** **1** great wickedness • *the enormity of this crime.* **2** great size; hugeness • *the enormity of their task.*
[same origin as *enormous*]

USAGE Many people regard the use of sense 2 as incorrect, though it is very common. In formal writing it is probably best to avoid it and to use *magnitude* instead.

enormous *ADJECTIVE* very large; huge.
▷ **enormously** *adverb* **enormousness** *noun*
[from *e-* + Latin *norma* = standard]

enough *ADJECTIVE, NOUN, & ADVERB* as much or as many as necessary • *enough food; I have had enough; Are you warm enough?*
[from Old English]

en passant (*say* ahn pas-ahn) *ADVERB* by the way.
[French, = in passing]

enquire *VERB* **enquires, enquiring, enquired** 1 ask for information • *He enquired if I was well.* 2 investigate something carefully.
[same origin as *inquire*]
USAGE See the note at **inquire**.

enquiry *NOUN* **enquiries** 1 a question. 2 an investigation.

enrage *VERB* **enrages, enraging, enraged** make someone very angry.
[from old French]

enrapture *VERB* **enraptures, enrapturing, enraptured** fill someone with intense delight.

enrich *VERB* **enriches, enriching, enriched** make richer.
▷ **enrichment** *noun*
[from old French]

enrol *VERB* **enrols, enrolling, enrolled** 1 become a member of a society etc. 2 make someone into a member.
▷ **enrolment** *noun*
[from *en-* + old French *rolle* = roll]

en route (*say* ahn **root**) *ADVERB* on the way.
[French]

ensconce *VERB* **ensconces, ensconcing, ensconced** settle comfortably • *ensconced in a chair.*
[from *en-* + an old word *sconce* = a shelter]

ensemble (*say* on-sombl) *NOUN* **ensembles** 1 a group of things that go together. 2 a group of musicians. 3 a matching outfit of clothes.
[French]

enshrine *VERB* **enshrines, enshrining, enshrined** preserve an idea, memory, etc. with love or respect • *His memory is enshrined in our hearts.*

ensign *NOUN* **ensigns** a military or naval flag.
[from old French; related to *insignia*]

enslave *VERB* **enslaves, enslaving, enslaved** make a slave of someone; force someone into slavery.
▷ **enslavement** *noun*

ensue *VERB* **ensues, ensuing, ensued** happen afterwards or as a result.
[from old French]

ensure *VERB* **ensures, ensuring, ensured** make certain of; guarantee • *Good food will ensure good health.*
[from old French]
USAGE Do not confuse with **insure**.

entail *VERB* **entails, entailing, entailed** make a thing necessary; involve • *This plan entails danger.*
▷ **entailment** *noun*
[from *en-* + old French *taillir* = bequeath]

entangle *VERB* **entangles, entangling, entangled** tangle.
▷ **entanglement** *noun*

entente (*say* on-**tont**) *NOUN* **ententes** a friendly understanding between countries.
[French]

enter *VERB* **enters, entering, entered** 1 come in or go in. 2 put something into a list or book. 3 key something into a computer. 4 register as a competitor.
[from Latin *intra* = within]

enterprise *NOUN* **enterprises** 1 being enterprising; adventurous spirit. 2 an undertaking or project. 3 business activity • *private enterprise.*
[from *en-* + Latin *prehendere* = take]

enterprising *ADJECTIVE* willing to undertake new or adventurous projects.

entertain *VERB* **entertains, entertaining, entertained** 1 amuse. 2 have people as guests and give them food and drink. 3 consider • *He refused to entertain the idea.*
▷ **entertainer** *noun*
[from old French]

entertainment *NOUN* **entertainments** 1 entertaining; being entertained. 2 something performed before an audience to amuse or interest them.

enthral (*say* in-**thrawl**) *VERB* **enthrals, enthralling, enthralled** hold someone spellbound; fascinate.

enthusiasm *NOUN* **enthusiasms** a strong liking, interest, or excitement.
▷ **enthusiast** *noun*
[from Greek *enthousiazein* = be possessed by a god]

enthusiastic *ADJECTIVE* full of enthusiasm.
▷ **enthusiastically** *adverb*

entice *VERB* **entices, enticing, enticed** attract or persuade by offering something pleasant.
▷ **enticement** *noun*
[from old French]

entire *ADJECTIVE* whole or complete.
▷ **entirely** *adverb*
[from old French; related to *integer*]

entirety (*say* int-I-rit-ee) *NOUN* the whole of something.
- **in its entirety** in its complete form.

entitle *VERB* **entitles, entitling, entitled** give the right to have something • *This coupon entitles you to a ticket.*
▷ **entitlement** *noun*
[from old French]

entitled *ADJECTIVE* having as a title • *a short poem entitled 'Spring'.*

entity *NOUN* **entities** something that exists separately from other things • *A language is a living entity.*
[from Latin *entitas*]

entomb (*say* in-toom) *VERB* **entombs, entombing, entombed** place in a tomb.
▷ **entombment** *noun*
[from old French]

entomology (*say* en-tom-**ol**-o-jee) *NOUN* the study of insects.
▷ **entomologist** *noun*
[from Greek *entomon* = insect, + *-logy*]

entourage (*say* on-toor-**ah***zh*) *NOUN* the people who accompany an important person.
[from French *entourer* = surround]

entrails *PLURAL NOUN* the intestines.
[from French]

entrance[1] (*say* **en**-trans) *NOUN* **entrances** **1** the way into a place. **2** entering • *Her entrance is the signal for applause.*
[from old French]

entrance[2] (*say* in-**trahns**) *VERB* **entrances, entrancing, entranced** fill with intense delight; enchant.
[from *en-* + *trance*]

entrant *NOUN* **entrants** someone who enters for an examination or competition.
[from French]

entreat *VERB* **entreats, entreating, entreated** request earnestly; beg.
[from old French]

entreaty *NOUN* **entreaties** an earnest request.

entrench *VERB* **entrenches, entrenching, entrenched** **1** fix or establish firmly • *These ideas are entrenched in his mind.* **2** settle in a well-defended position.
▷ **entrenchment** *noun*

entrepreneur (*say* on-tru-pren-**er**) *NOUN* **entrepreneurs** a person who starts a new business or sets up business deals, especially risky ones, in order to make a profit.
▷ **entrepreneurial** *adjective*
[from French *entreprendre* = to undertake]

entrust *VERB* **entrusts, entrusting, entrusted** place a person or thing in someone's care.

entry *NOUN* **entries** **1** an entrance. **2** something entered in a list, diary, or reference book. **3** something entered in a competition • *Send your entries to this address.*

entwine *VERB* **entwines, entwining, entwined** twine round.

enumerate *VERB* **enumerates, enumerating, enumerated** count; list one by one.
[from *e-* + Latin *numerare* = to number]

envelop (*say* en-**vel**-op) *VERB* **envelops, enveloping, enveloped** cover or wrap round something completely.
[from old French]

envelope (*say* **en**-vel-ohp) *NOUN* **envelopes** a wrapper or covering, especially a folded cover for a letter.
[from French]

enviable *ADJECTIVE* likely to be envied.

envious *ADJECTIVE* feeling envy.
▷ **enviously** *adverb*

environment *NOUN* **environments** **1** surroundings, especially as they affect people's lives. **2** the natural world of the land, sea, and air.
▷ **environmental** *adjective*
[from old French *environer* = surround, enclose]

environmentalist *NOUN* **environmentalists** a person who wishes to protect or improve the environment.

environmentally-friendly *ADJECTIVE* not harmful to the environment.

environs (*say* in-vy-ronz) PLURAL NOUN the surrounding districts • *They all lived in the environs of Liverpool.*
[same origin as *environment*]

envisage (*say* in-viz-ij) VERB **envisages, envisaging, envisaged** picture in the mind; imagine as being possible • *It is difficult to envisage such a change.*
[from *en-* + Latin *visus* = sight]

envoy NOUN **envoys** an official representative, especially one sent by one government to another.
[from French *envoyé* = sent]

envy NOUN **1** a feeling of discontent you have when someone possesses things that you would like to have for yourself.
2 something causing this • *Their car is the envy of all their friends.*

envy VERB **envies, envying, envied** feel envy towards someone.
[from French; related to *invidious*]

enzyme NOUN **enzymes** a kind of substance that assists chemical processes.
[from Greek *enzymos* = leavened]

epaulette (*say* ep-al-et) NOUN **epaulettes** an ornamental flap on the shoulder of a coat.
[French, = little shoulder]

ephemeral (*say* if-em-er-al) ADJECTIVE lasting only a very short time.
[from Greek *ephemeros* = lasting a day]

epi- PREFIX on; above; in addition.
[from Greek *epi* = on]

epic NOUN **epics 1** a long poem or story about heroic deeds or history. **2** a spectacular film.
[from Greek *epos* = song]

epicentre NOUN **epicentres** the point where an earthquake reaches the earth's surface.
[from *epi-* + Greek *kentros* = centre]

epidemic NOUN **epidemics** an outbreak of a disease that spreads quickly among the people of an area.
[from *epi-* + Greek *demos* = people]

epidermis NOUN the outer layer of the skin.
[from *epi-* + Greek *derma* = skin]

epigram NOUN **epigrams** a short witty saying.
[from *epi-* + *-gram*]

epilepsy NOUN a disease of the nervous system, causing convulsions.
▷ **epileptic** *adjective* & *noun*
[from Greek *epilambanein* = seize, attack]

epilogue (*say* ep-il-og) NOUN **epilogues** a short section at the end of a book or play.
[from *epi-* + Greek *logos* = speech]

Epiphany (*say* ip-if-an-ee) NOUN a Christian festival on 6 January, commemorating the showing of the infant Christ to the 'wise men' from the East.
[from Greek *epiphanein* = to show clearly]

episcopal (*say* ip-iss-kop-al) ADJECTIVE **1** to do with a bishop or bishops. **2** (said about a Church) governed by bishops.
[from Latin *episcopus* = bishop]

episode NOUN **episodes 1** one event in a series of happenings. **2** one programme in a radio or television serial.
[from Greek]

epistle NOUN **epistles** a letter, especially one forming part of the New Testament.
[from *epi-* + Greek *stellein* = send]

epitaph NOUN **epitaphs** words written on a tomb or describing a person who has died.
[from *epi-* + Greek *taphos* = tomb]

epithet NOUN **epithets** an adjective; words expressing something special about a person or thing, e.g. 'the Great' in *Alfred the Great*.
[from Greek *epithetos* = attributed]

epitome (*say* ip-it-om-ee) NOUN a person or thing that is a perfect example of something • *She is the epitome of kindness.*
[from Greek *epitome* = shortening]

epoch (*say* ee-pok) NOUN **epochs** an era.
- **epoch-making** *adjective* very important.
[from Greek]

equable (*say* ek-wa-bul) ADJECTIVE **1** calm and not likely to get annoyed • *She has an equable manner.* **2** (said about a climate) moderate, neither too hot nor too cold.
[from Latin]

equal ADJECTIVE **1** the same in amount, size, or value. **2** having the necessary strength, courage, or ability etc. • *She was equal to the task.*
▷ **equally** *adverb*

equal NOUN **equals** a person or thing that is equal to another • *She has no equal.*

A B C D E F G H I J K L M N O P Q R S T U V W X Y Z

equal *VERB* **equals, equalling, equalled**
1 be the same in amount, size, or value.
2 match or be as good • *No one has yet equalled this score.*
[from Latin]

equality *NOUN* being equal.

equalize *VERB* **equalizes, equalizing, equalized** make things equal.
▷ **equalization** *noun*

equalizer *NOUN* **equalizers** a goal or point that makes the score equal.

equanimity (*say* ekwa-**nim**-it-ee) *NOUN* calmness of mind or temper.
[from *equi-* + Latin *animus* = mind]

equate *VERB* **equates, equating, equated** say things are equal or equivalent.
[from Latin *aequus* = equal]

equation *NOUN* **equations** (*in mathematics*) a statement that two amounts etc. are equal, e.g. 3 + 4 = 2 + 5.

equator *NOUN* **equators** an imaginary line round the Earth at an equal distance from the North and South Poles.
[from Latin *circulus aequator diei et noctis* = circle equalizing day and night]

equatorial (*say* ek-wa-**tor**-ee-al) *ADJECTIVE* to do with or near the equator.

equerry (*say* **ek**-wer-ee) *NOUN* **equerries** a personal attendant of a member of the British royal family.
[from Latin *scutarius* = shield-bearer]

equestrian (*say* ik-**wes**-tree-an) *ADJECTIVE* to do with horse riding.
[same origin as *equine*]

equi- *PREFIX* equal; equally.
[from Latin *aequus* = equal]

equidistant (*say* ee-kwi-**dis**-tant) *ADJECTIVE* at an equal distance.
[from *equi-* + *distant*]

equilateral (*say* ee-kwi-**lat**-er-al) *ADJECTIVE* (said about a triangle) having all sides equal.

equilibrium (*say* ee-kwi-**lib**-ree-um) *NOUN* **1** a balance between different forces, influences, etc. **2** a balanced state of mind.
[from *equi-* + Latin *libra* = balance]

equine (*say* **ek**-wyn) *ADJECTIVE* to do with or like a horse.
[from Latin *equus* = horse]

equinox (*say* **ek**-win-oks) *NOUN* **equinoxes** the time of year when day and night are equal in length (about 20 March in spring, about 22 September in autumn).
▷ **equinoctial** *adjective*
[from *equi-* + Latin *nox* = night]

equip *VERB* **equips, equipping, equipped** supply with what is needed.
[from French]

equipment *NOUN* the things needed for a particular purpose.

equity (*say* **ek**-wit-ee) *NOUN* fairness.
▷ **equitable** *adjective*
[from Latin]

equivalent *ADJECTIVE* equal in importance, meaning, value, etc.
▷ **equivalence** *noun*
[from *equi-* + Latin *valens* = worth]

equivocal (*say* ik-**wiv**-ok-al) *ADJECTIVE* able to be interpreted in two ways and deliberately vague; ambiguous.
▷ **equivocally** *adverb*
[from *equi-* + Latin *vocare* = to call]

-er[1] or **-ier** *SUFFIX* can form the comparative of adjectives and adverbs (e.g. *high/higher, lazy/lazier*).
[from Old English *-re*]

-er[2] *SUFFIX* can form nouns meaning 'a person or thing that does something' (e.g. *farmer, computer*).
[from Old English *-ere*; in a few words (e.g. *butler, mariner*) from Latin: compare *or*]

era (*say* **eer**-a) *NOUN* **eras** a period of history.
[from Latin]

eradicate *VERB* **eradicates, eradicating, eradicated** get rid of something; remove all traces of it.
▷ **eradication** *noun*
[from Latin *eradicare* = root out]

erase *VERB* **erases, erasing, erased** **1** rub something out. **2** wipe out a recording on magnetic tape.
▷ **eraser** *noun*
[from *e-* + Latin *rasum* = scraped]

erasure *NOUN* **erasures** **1** erasing. **2** the place where something has been erased.

ere (*say* air) *PREPOSITION* & *CONJUNCTION* (*old use*) before.
[from Old English]

erect *ADJECTIVE* standing straight up.

erect *VERB* **erects, erecting, erected** set up or build something.
▷ **erection** *noun*
[from Latin]

ermine *NOUN* **ermines** **1** a kind of weasel with brown fur that turns white in winter. **2** this valuable white fur.
[from French]

erode *VERB* **erodes, eroding, eroded** wear away • *Water eroded the rocks.*
[from *e-* + Latin *rodere* = gnaw]

erosion *NOUN* the wearing away of the earth's surface by the action of water, wind, etc.

erotic *ADJECTIVE* arousing sexual feelings.
▷ **erotically** *adverb*
[from Greek *eros* = sexual love]

err (*say* er) *VERB* **errs, erring, erred** **1** make a mistake. (COMPARE **error**) **2** do wrong.
[from Latin *errare* = wander]

errand *NOUN* **errands** a short journey to take a message or fetch goods etc.
[from Old English]

errant (*say* e-rant) *ADJECTIVE* **1** misbehaving. **2** wandering; travelling in search of adventure • *a knight errant.*
[same origin as *err*]

erratic (*say* ir-at-ik) *ADJECTIVE* **1** not regular. **2** not reliable.
▷ **erratically** *adverb*
[from Latin *erraticus* = wandering]

erroneous (*say* ir-oh-nee-us) *ADJECTIVE* incorrect.
▷ **erroneously** *adverb*
[same origin as *err*]

error *NOUN* **errors** a mistake.
[same origin as *err*]

erudite (*say* e-rew-dyt) *ADJECTIVE* having great knowledge or learning.
▷ **eruditely** *adverb* **erudition** *noun*
[from Latin *erudire* = instruct]

erupt *VERB* **erupts, erupting, erupted** **1** burst out. **2** when a volcano erupts, it shoots out lava.
▷ **eruption** *noun*
[from *e-* + Latin *ruptum* = burst]

escalate *VERB* **escalates, escalating, escalated** make or become greater, more serious or more intense • *The riots escalated into a war.*
▷ **escalation** *noun*
[from *escalator*]

escalator *NOUN* **escalators** a staircase with an endless line of steps moving up or down.
[from French *escalade* = scaling a wall with ladders]

escapade (*say* es-ka-**payd**) *NOUN* **escapades** a reckless adventure.
[French, = an escape]

escape *VERB* **escapes, escaping, escaped** **1** get yourself free; get out or away. **2** avoid something • *He escaped punishment.* **3** be forgotten • *Her name escapes me for the moment.*

escape *NOUN* **escapes** **1** escaping. **2** a way to escape.
[from French]

escapism *NOUN* escaping from the difficulties of life by thinking about or doing more pleasant things.
▷ **escapist** *adjective*

escarpment *NOUN* **escarpments** a steep slope at the edge of some high level ground.
[from French]

escort (*say* ess-kort) *NOUN* **escorts** a person or group accompanying a person or thing, especially to give protection.

escort (*say* iss-**kort**) *VERB* **escorts, escorting, escorted** act as an escort to somebody or something.
[from French]

Eskimo *NOUN* **Eskimos** or **Eskimo** a member of a people living near the Arctic coast of North America, Greenland, and Siberia.
[from a Native American word]
USAGE It is becoming less common to refer to these peoples as *Eskimos*. Many people who live in northern Canada and Greenland dislike the word and prefer the term *Inuit*. The name for those who live in Alaska and Asia is *Yupik*.

especial *ADJECTIVE* special.
[from French]

especially *ADVERB* specially; more than anything else.

espionage (*say* ess-pee-on-ah*zh*) NOUN spying.
[from French *espion* = spy]

esplanade NOUN **esplanades** a flat open area used as a promenade, especially by the sea.
[French]

espresso NOUN **espressos** coffee made by forcing steam through ground coffee beans.
[Italian, = pressed out]

esprit de corps (*say* es-pree der **kor**) NOUN loyalty to your group.
[French, = spirit of the body]

espy VERB **espies, espying, espied** catch sight of.
[from old French]

Esq. ABBREVIATION (short for **Esquire**) a title written after a man's surname where no title is used before his name.
[an *esquire* was originally a knight's attendant; from Latin *scutarius* = shield-bearer)]

-esque SUFFIX forms adjectives meaning 'like' or 'in the style of' (e.g. *picturesque*).
[French]

-ess SUFFIX forms feminine nouns (e.g. *lioness, princess*).
[from French]

essay (*say* ess-ay) NOUN **essays** **1** a short piece of writing in prose. **2** an attempt.

essay (*say* ess-ay) VERB **essays, essaying, essayed** attempt.
[from French]

essence NOUN **essences** **1** the most important quality or element of something. **2** a concentrated liquid.
[from Latin *esse* = to be]

essential ADJECTIVE not able to be done without.
▷ **essentially** *adverb*

essential NOUN **essentials** an essential thing.
[same origin as *essence*]

-est or **-iest** SUFFIX can form the superlative of adjectives and adverbs (e.g. *high/highest, lazy/laziest*).
[from Old English]

establish VERB **establishes, establishing, established** **1** set up a business, government, or relationship etc. on a firm basis. **2** show something to be true; prove • *He established his innocence.*
- **the established Church** a country's national Church, officially recognized as such by law.
[from old French; related to *stable*[1]]

establishment NOUN **establishments** **1** establishing something. **2** a business firm or other institution.
- **the Establishment** the people in a country in positions of power and influence.

estate NOUN **estates** **1** an area of land with a set of houses or factories on it. **2** a large area of land owned by one person. **3** all that a person owns when he or she dies. **4** (*old use*) a condition or status • *the holy estate of matrimony.*
[from old French; related to *state*]

estate agent NOUN **estate agents** a person whose business is selling or letting houses and land.

estate car NOUN **estate cars** a car with a door or doors at the back, and rear seats that can be removed or folded away.

esteem VERB **esteems, esteeming, esteemed** think that a person or thing is excellent.

esteem NOUN respect and admiration.
[same origin as *estimate*]

ester NOUN **esters** a kind of chemical compound.
[German]

estimable ADJECTIVE worthy of esteem.

estimate (*say* ess-tim-at) NOUN **estimates** a rough calculation or guess about an amount or value.

estimate (*say* ess-tim-ayt) VERB **estimates, estimating, estimated** make an estimate.
▷ **estimation** *noun*
[from Latin *aestimare* = to put a value on something]

estranged ADJECTIVE unfriendly after having been friendly or loving.
▷ **estrangement** *noun*
[from Latin *extraneare* = treat someone as a stranger]

estuary (*say* ess-tew-er-ee) *NOUN* **estuaries** the mouth of a river where it reaches the sea and the tide flows in and out.
[from Latin *aestus* = tide]

etc. *ABBREVIATION* (short for **et cetera**) and other similar things; and so on.
[from Latin *et* = and + *cetera* = the other things]

etch *VERB* **etches**, **etching**, **etched**
1 engrave a picture with acid on a metal plate, especially for printing. **2** if something is etched on your mind or memory, it has made a deep impression and you will never forget it.
▷ **etcher** *noun*
[from Dutch]

etching *NOUN* **etchings** a picture printed from an etched metal plate.

eternal *ADJECTIVE* lasting for ever; not ending or changing.
▷ **eternally** *adverb* **eternity** *noun*
[from old French]

ether (*say* ee-ther) *NOUN* **1** a colourless liquid that evaporates easily into fumes that are used as an anaesthetic. **2** the upper air.
[from Greek]

ethereal (*say* ith-eer-ee-al) *ADJECTIVE* light and delicate.
▷ **ethereally** *adverb*
[from Latin *aetherius* = belonging to the upper air]

ethical (*say* eth-ik-al) *ADJECTIVE* **1** to do with ethics. **2** morally right; honourable.
▷ **ethically** *adverb*

ethics (*say* eth-iks) *PLURAL NOUN* standards of right behaviour; moral principles.
[from Greek *ethos* = character]

ethnic *ADJECTIVE* belonging to a particular racial group within a larger set of people.
[from Greek *ethnos* = nation]

ethnic cleansing *NOUN* the mass killing of people from other ethnic or religious groups within a certain area.

etiquette (*say* et-ik-et) *NOUN* the rules of correct behaviour.
[from French]

-ette *SUFFIX* forms diminutives which mean 'little' (e.g. *cigarette, kitchenette*).
[from French]

etymology (*say* et-im-ol-oj-ee) *NOUN* **etymologies** **1** an account of the origin of a word and its meaning. **2** the study of the origins of words.
▷ **etymological** *adjective*
[from Greek *etymon* = original word, + *-logy*]

EU *ABBREVIATION* European Union.

eu- (*say* yoo) *PREFIX* well.
[from Greek]

eucalyptus (*say* yoo-kal-ip-tus) *NOUN* **eucalyptuses** **1** a kind of evergreen tree. **2** a strong-smelling oil obtained from its leaves.
[from Greek]

Eucharist (*say* yoo-ker-ist) *NOUN* the Christian sacrament in which bread and wine are consecrated and swallowed, commemorating the Last Supper of Christ and his disciples.
[from Greek *eucharistia* = thanksgiving]

eulogy (*say* yoo-loj-ee) *NOUN* **eulogies** a piece of praise for a person or thing.
[from *eu-* + Greek *-logia* = speaking]

eunuch (*say* yoo-nuk) *NOUN* **eunuchs** a man who has been castrated.
[from Greek]

euphemism (*say* yoo-fim-izm) *NOUN* **euphemisms** a mild word or phrase used instead of an offensive or frank one; *'to pass away'* is a euphemism for *'to die'*.
▷ **euphemistic** *adjective* **euphemistically** *adverb*
[from *eu-* + Greek *pheme* = speech]

euphonium (*say* yoof-oh-nee-um) *NOUN* **euphoniums** a large brass wind instrument.
[from *eu-* + Greek *phone* = sound]

euphoria (*say* yoo-for-ee-a) *NOUN* a feeling of general happiness.
[from Greek]

Eurasian *ADJECTIVE* having European and Asian parents or ancestors.
▷ **Eurasian** *noun*
[from European + *Asian*]

eureka (*say* yoor-eek-a) *INTERJECTION* I have found it!
[Greek]

euro *NOUN* **euros** or **euro** the single currency introduced in the EU in 1999.

European ADJECTIVE to do with Europe or its people.
▷ **European** *noun*

euthanasia (*say* yooth-an-ay-zee-a) NOUN causing somebody to die gently and without pain, especially when they are suffering from a painful incurable disease.
[from *eu-* + Greek *thanatos* = death]

evacuate VERB **evacuates, evacuating, evacuated** 1 move people away from a dangerous place. 2 make a thing empty of air or other contents.
▷ **evacuation** *noun*
[from *e-* + Latin *vacuus* = empty]

evacuee NOUN **evacuees** a person who has been evacuated.

evade VERB **evades, evading, evaded** avoid a person or thing by cleverness or trickery.
[from *e-* + Latin *vadere* = go]

evaluate VERB **evaluates, evaluating, evaluated** estimate the value of something; assess.
▷ **evaluation** *noun*
[from French]

Evangelist NOUN **Evangelists** any of the writers (Matthew, Mark, Luke, John) of the four Gospels.
[from Greek *euangelion* = good news]

evangelist NOUN **evangelists** a person who preaches the Christian faith enthusiastically.
▷ **evangelism** *noun* **evangelical** *adjective*
[from Greek, = announce good news (*eu* = well, *angelos* = messenger)]

evaporate VERB **evaporates, evaporating, evaporated** 1 change from liquid into steam or vapour. 2 cease to exist • *Their enthusiasm had evaporated.*
▷ **evaporation** *noun*
[from *e-* = out + Latin *vapor* = steam]

evasion NOUN **evasions** 1 evading. 2 an evasive answer or excuse.
[from Latin]

evasive ADJECTIVE trying to avoid answering something; not frank or straightforward.
▷ **evasively** *adverb* **evasiveness** *noun*
[from Latin]

eve NOUN **eves** 1 the day or evening before an important day or event • *Christmas Eve.* 2 (*old use*) evening.
[from *even*²]

even¹ ADJECTIVE 1 level and smooth. 2 not varying. 3 calm; not easily upset • *an even temper.* 4 equal • *Our scores were even.* 5 able to be divided exactly by two • *Six and fourteen are even numbers.* (COMPARE **odd**)
▷ **evenly** *adverb* **evenness** *noun*
- **get even** take revenge.

even VERB **evens, evening, evened** make or become even.

even ADVERB (used to emphasize a word or statement) • *She ran even faster.*
- **even so** although that is correct.
[from Old English *efen*]

even² NOUN (*old use*) evening.
[from Old English *aefen*]

even-handed ADJECTIVE fair and impartial.

evening NOUN **evenings** the time at the end of the day before most people go to bed.
[from Old English]

evensong NOUN the service of evening prayer in the Church of England.
[from *even*² + *song*]

event NOUN **events** 1 something that happens, especially something important. 2 a race or competition that forms part of a sports contest.
[from Latin *evenire* = happen]

eventful ADJECTIVE full of happenings.

eventual ADJECTIVE happening at last • *his eventual success.*
▷ **eventually** *adverb*
[from Latin *eventus* = result, event]

eventuality (*say* iv-en-tew-al-it-ee) NOUN **eventualities** something that may happen.
[from *eventual*]

ever ADVERB 1 at any time • *the best thing I ever did.* 2 always • *ever hopeful.* 3 (*informal*) used for emphasis • *Why ever didn't you tell me?*
[from Old English]

evergreen ADJECTIVE having green leaves all the year.
▷ **evergreen** *noun*

everlasting ADJECTIVE lasting for ever or for a very long time.

every *ADJECTIVE* each without any exceptions
• *We enjoyed every minute.*
- **every one** each one.
- **every other day** or **week, etc.** each alternate one; every second one.
[from Old English]
USAGE Follow with a singular verb, e.g. *Every one of them is growing* (not 'are growing').

everybody *PRONOUN* every person.

everyday *ADJECTIVE* ordinary; usual
• *everyday clothes.*

everyone *PRONOUN* everybody.

everything *PRONOUN* **1** all things; all. **2** the only or most important thing • *Beauty is not everything.*

everywhere *ADVERB* in every place.

evict *VERB* **evicts, evicting, evicted** make people move out from where they are living.
▷ **eviction** *noun*
[from Latin *evictum* = expelled]

evidence *NOUN* **1** anything that gives people reason to believe something.
2 statements made or objects produced in a lawcourt to prove something.
[same origin as *evident*]

evident *ADJECTIVE* obvious; clearly seen.
▷ **evidently** *adverb*
[from *e-* + Latin *videre* = see]

evil *ADJECTIVE* morally bad; wicked.
▷ **evilly** *adverb*

evil *NOUN* **evils** **1** wickedness. **2** something unpleasant or harmful.
[from Old English]

evoke *VERB* **evokes, evoking, evoked** produce or inspire a memory or feelings etc.
• *The photographs evoked happy memories.*
▷ **evocation** *noun* **evocative** *adjective*
[from *e-* + Latin *vocare* = call]

evolution (*say* ee-vol-oo-shon) *NOUN*
1 gradual change into something different.
2 the development of animals and plants from earlier or simpler forms of life.
▷ **evolutionary** *adjective*

evolve *VERB* **evolves, evolving, evolved** develop gradually or naturally.
[from *e-* + Latin *volvere* = to roll]

ewe (*say* yoo) *NOUN* **ewes** a female sheep.
[from Old English]

ewer (*say* yoo-er) *NOUN* **ewers** a large water jug.
[from old French]

ex- *PREFIX* (changing to **ef-** before words beginning with *f*; shortened to **e-** before many consonants) **1** out; away (as in *extract*). **2** up, upwards; thoroughly (as in *extol*). **3** formerly (as in *ex-president*).
[from Latin *ex* = out of]

exacerbate (*say* eks-ass-er-bayt) *VERB* **exacerbates, exacerbating, exacerbated** make a pain or disease or other problem worse.
[from *ex-* + Latin *acerbus* = harsh, bitter]

exact *ADJECTIVE* **1** correct. **2** clearly stated; giving all details • *exact instructions.*
▷ **exactly** *adverb* **exactness** *noun*

exact *VERB* **exacts, exacting, exacted** insist on something and obtain it • *He exacted obedience from the recruits.*
▷ **exaction** *noun*
[from *ex-* + Latin *actum* = performed]

exacting *ADJECTIVE* making great demands
• *an exacting task.*

exactitude *NOUN* exactness.

exaggerate *VERB* **exaggerates, exaggerating, exaggerated** make something seem bigger, better, or worse etc. than it really is.
▷ **exaggeration** *noun*
[from *ex-* + Latin *aggerare* = heap up]

exalt (*say* ig-zawlt) *VERB* **exalts, exalting, exalted** **1** raise in rank or status etc.
2 praise highly. **3** delight or elate.
▷ **exaltation** *noun*
[from *ex-* + Latin *altus* = high]

exam *NOUN* **exams** (*informal*) an examination.

examination *NOUN* **examinations** **1** a test of a person's knowledge or skill.
2 examining something; an inspection • *a medical examination.*

examine *VERB* **examines, examining, examined** **1** test a person's knowledge or skill. **2** look at something closely or in detail.
▷ **examiner** *noun*
[from Latin *examinare* = weigh accurately]

examinee *NOUN* **examinees** a person being tested in an examination.

example *NOUN* **examples** 1 anything that shows what others of the same kind are like or how they work. 2 a person or thing good enough to be worth imitating.
[from Latin]

exasperate *VERB* **exasperates, exasperating, exasperated** annoy someone greatly.
▷ **exasperation** *noun*
[from *ex-* + Latin *asper* = rough]

excavate *VERB* **excavates, excavating, excavated** dig out; uncover by digging.
▷ **excavation** *noun* **excavator** *noun*
[from *ex-* + Latin *cavus* = hollow]

exceed *VERB* **exceeds, exceeding, exceeded** 1 be greater than; surpass. 2 do more than you need or ought to do; go beyond a thing's limits • *He has exceeded his authority.*
[from *ex-* + Latin *cedere* = go]

exceedingly *ADVERB* very; extremely.

excel *VERB* **excels, excelling, excelled** be better than others at doing something.
[from *ex-* + Latin *celsus* = lofty]

Excellency *NOUN* **Excellencies** the title of high officials such as ambassadors and governors.
[from Latin]

excellent *ADJECTIVE* extremely good.
▷ **excellently** *adverb* **excellence** *noun*
[from Latin]

except *PREPOSITION* excluding; not including • *They all left except me.*

except *VERB* **excepts, excepting, excepted** exclude; leave out • *I blame you all, no one is excepted.*
[from *ex-* + Latin *-ceptum* = taken]
USAGE Do not confuse with **accept**.

excepting *PREPOSITION* except.

exception *NOUN* **exceptions** a person or thing that is left out or does not follow the general rule.
- **take exception** raise objections to something.
- **with the exception of** except.

exceptional *ADJECTIVE* 1 very unusual. 2 outstandingly good.
▷ **exceptionally** *adverb*

excerpt (*say* ek-serpt) *NOUN* **excerpts** a passage taken from a book or speech or film etc.
[from Latin *excerptum* = plucked out]

excess *NOUN* **excesses** too much of something.
- **in excess of** more than.
[same origin as *exceed*]

excessive *ADJECTIVE* too much or too great.
▷ **excessively** *adverb*

exchange *VERB* **exchanges, exchanging, exchanged** give something and receive something else for it.

exchange *NOUN* **exchanges** 1 exchanging. 2 a place where things (especially stocks and shares) are bought and sold • *a stock exchange.* 3 a place where telephone lines are connected to each other when a call is made.
[from old French]

exchequer *NOUN* **exchequers** a national treasury into which public funds (such as taxes) are paid.
[from Latin *scaccarium* = chessboard (because the Norman kings kept their accounts by means of counters placed on a chequered tablecloth)]

excise[1] (*say* **eks**-I'z) *NOUN* a tax charged on certain goods and licences etc.
[from old Dutch *excijs* = tax]

excise[2] (*say* iks-**I'z**) *VERB* **excises, excising, excised** remove something by cutting it away • *The surgeon excised the tumour.*
[from *ex-* + Latin *caesum* = cut]

excitable *ADJECTIVE* easily excited.

excite *VERB* **excites, exciting, excited** 1 make someone eager and enthusiastic about something • *The thought of finding gold excited them.* 2 cause a feeling or reaction • *The invention excited great interest.*
▷ **excitedly** *adverb*
[from *ex-* + Latin *citum* = woken, stirred]

excitement *NOUN* **excitements** a strong feeling of eagerness or pleasure.

exclaim *VERB* **exclaims, exclaiming, exclaimed** shout or cry out in eagerness or surprise.
[from *ex-* + Latin *clamare* = cry]

exclamation *NOUN* **exclamations** **1** exclaiming. **2** a word or words cried out expressing joy or pain or surprise etc.

exclamation mark *NOUN* **exclamation marks** the punctuation mark (!) placed after an exclamation.

exclude *VERB* **excludes, excluding, excluded** **1** keep somebody or something out. **2** leave something out • *Do not exclude the possibility of rain.*
▷ **exclusion** *noun*
[from *ex-* + Latin *claudere* = shut]

exclusive *ADJECTIVE* **1** allowing only certain people to be members etc. • *an exclusive club.* **2** not shared with others • *This newspaper has an exclusive report.*
▷ **exclusively** *adverb* **exclusiveness** *noun*
- **exclusive of** excluding, not including • *This is the price exclusive of meals.*
[same origin as *exclude*]

excommunicate *VERB* **excommunicates, excommunicating, excommunicated** cut off a person from membership of a Church.
▷ **excommunication** *noun*
[from Latin *excommunicare* = put out of the community]

excrement (*say* eks-krim-ent) *NOUN* waste matter excreted from the bowels.
[same origin as *excrete*]

excrescence (*say* iks-kress-ens) *NOUN* **excrescences** **1** a growth or lump on a plant or animal's body. **2** an ugly addition or part.
[from *ex-* + Latin *crescens* = growing]

excrete *VERB* **excretes, excreting, excreted** get rid of waste matter from the body.
▷ **excretion** *noun* **excretory** *adjective*
[from *ex-* + Latin *cretum* = separated]

excruciating (*say* iks-kroo-shee-ayt-ing) *ADJECTIVE* extremely painful; agonizing.
▷ **excruciatingly** *adverb*
[from *ex-* + Latin *cruciatum* = tortured]

excursion *NOUN* **excursions** a short journey made for pleasure.
[from *ex-* + Latin *cursus* = course]

excusable *ADJECTIVE* able to be excused.
▷ **excusably** *adverb*

excuse (*say* iks-kewz) *VERB* **excuses, excusing, excused** **1** forgive. **2** allow someone not to do something or to leave a room etc. • *Please may I be excused swimming?*

excuse (*say* iks-kewss) *NOUN* **excuses** a reason given to explain why something wrong has been done.
[from *ex-* + Latin *causa* = accusation]

execrable (*say* eks-ik-rab-ul) *ADJECTIVE* very bad or unpleasant.
[from Latin *execrari* = to curse]

execute *VERB* **executes, executing, executed** **1** put someone to death as a punishment. **2** perform or produce something • *She executed the somersault perfectly.*
▷ **execution** *noun*
[from Latin *executare* = to carry out]

executioner *NOUN* **executioners** an official who executes a condemned person.

executive (*say* ig-zek-yoo-tiv) *NOUN* **executives** a senior person with authority in a business or government organization.

executive *ADJECTIVE* having the authority to carry out plans or laws.

executor (*say* ig-zek-yoo-ter) *NOUN* **executors** a person appointed to carry out the instructions in someone's will.

exemplary (*say* ig-zem-pler-ee) *ADJECTIVE* very good; being an example to others • *His conduct was exemplary.*
[from Latin *exemplum* = example]

exemplify *VERB* **exemplifies, exemplifying, exemplified** be an example of something.
[same origin as *exemplary*]

exempt *ADJECTIVE* not having to do something that others have to do • *Charities are exempt from paying tax.*

exempt *VERB* **exempts, exempting, exempted** make someone or something exempt.
▷ **exemption** *noun*
[from Latin *exemptus* = taken out]

exercise *NOUN* **exercises** **1** using your body to make it strong and healthy. **2** a piece of work done for practice.

A B C D E F G H I J K L M N O P Q R S T U V W X Y Z

exercise *VERB* **exercises, exercising, exercised** **1** do exercises. **2** give exercise to an animal. **3** use • *You must exercise more patience.*
[from Latin *exercere* = keep someone working]

exert *VERB* **exerts, exerting, exerted** use power or influence etc. • *He exerted all his strength.*
▷ **exertion** *noun*
- **exert yourself** make an effort.
[from Latin]

exeunt (*say* eks-ee-unt) *VERB* (in stage directions) they leave the stage.
[Latin, = they go out]

ex gratia (*say* eks gray-sha) *ADJECTIVE* given without being legally obliged to be given • *an ex gratia payment.*
[Latin, = from favour]

exhale *VERB* **exhales, exhaling, exhaled** breathe out.
▷ **exhalation** *noun*
[from *ex-* + Latin *halare* = breathe]

exhaust *VERB* **exhausts, exhausting, exhausted** **1** make somebody very tired. **2** use up something completely.
▷ **exhaustion** *noun*

exhaust *NOUN* **exhausts** **1** the waste gases or steam from an engine. **2** the pipe etc. through which they are sent out.
[from *ex-* + Latin *haustum* = drained]

exhaustive *ADJECTIVE* thorough; trying everything possible • *We made an exhaustive search.*
▷ **exhaustively** *adverb*

exhibit *VERB* **exhibits, exhibiting, exhibited** show or display something in public.
▷ **exhibitor** *noun*

exhibit *NOUN* **exhibits** something on display in a gallery or museum.
[from *ex-* + Latin *habere* = hold]

exhibition *NOUN* **exhibitions** a collection of things put on display for people to look at.

exhibitionist *NOUN* **exhibitionists** a person who behaves in a way that is meant to attract attention.
▷ **exhibitionism** *noun*

exhilarate (*say* ig-zil-er-ayt) *VERB* **exhilarates, exhilarating, exhilarated** make someone very happy and excited.
▷ **exhilaration** *noun*
[from *ex-* + Latin *hilaris* = cheerful]

exhort (*say* ig-zort) *VERB* **exhorts, exhorting, exhorted** try hard to persuade someone to do something.
▷ **exhortation** *noun*
[from *ex-* + Latin *hortari* = encourage]

exhume (*say* ig-zewm) *VERB* **exhumes, exhuming, exhumed** dig up a body that has been buried.
▷ **exhumation** *noun*
[from *ex-* + Latin *humare* = bury]

exile *VERB* **exiles, exiling, exiled** banish.

exile *NOUN* **exiles** **1** having to live away from your own country • *He was in exile for ten years.* **2** a banished person.
[from Latin]

exist *VERB* **exists, existing, existed** **1** be present as part of what is real • *Do ghosts exist?* **2** stay alive • *We cannot exist without food.*
▷ **existence** *noun* **existent** *adjective*
[from *ex-* + Latin *sistere* = stand]

exit *NOUN* **exits** **1** the way out of a building. **2** going off the stage • *The actress made her exit.*

exit *VERB* (in stage directions) he or she leaves the stage.
[Latin, = he or she goes out]

exodus *NOUN* **exoduses** the departure of many people.
[from Greek *exodos* = a way out]

exonerate *VERB* **exonerates, exonerating, exonerated** declare or prove that a person is not to blame for something.
▷ **exoneration** *noun*
[from *ex-* + Latin *onus* = a burden]

exorbitant *ADJECTIVE* much too great; excessive • *exorbitant prices.*
[from *ex-* + Latin *orbita* = orbit]

exorcize *VERB* **exorcizes, exorcizing, exorcized** drive out an evil spirit.
▷ **exorcism** *noun* **exorcist** *noun*
[from Greek]

exotic *ADJECTIVE* **1** very unusual • *exotic clothes.* **2** from another part of the world • *exotic plants.*
▷ **exotically** *adverb*
[from Greek *exo* = outside]

expand *VERB* **expands, expanding, expanded** make or become larger or fuller.
▷ **expansion** *noun* **expansive** *adjective*
[from *ex-* + Latin *pandere* = to spread]

expanse *NOUN* **expanses** a wide area.
[same origin as *expand*]

expatriate (*say* eks-pat-ree-at) *NOUN* **expatriates** a person living away from his or her own country.
[from *ex-* + Latin *patria* = native land]

expect *VERB* **expects, expecting, expected** **1** think or believe that something will happen or that someone will come. **2** think that something ought to happen • *She expects obedience.*
[from *ex-* + Latin *spectare* = to look]

expectant *ADJECTIVE* **1** expecting something to happen; hopeful. **2** an expectant mother is a woman who is pregnant.
▷ **expectantly** *adverb* **expectancy** *noun*

expectation *NOUN* **expectations** **1** expecting something; being hopeful. **2** something you expect to happen or get.

expecting *ADJECTIVE* (*informal*) (said about a woman) pregnant.

expedient (*say* iks-pee-dee-ent) *ADJECTIVE* **1** suitable or convenient. **2** useful and practical though perhaps unfair.
▷ **expediently** *adverb* **expediency** *noun*

expedient *NOUN* **expedients** a means of doing something, especially when in difficulty.
[same origin as *expedite*]

expedite (*say* eks-pid-dyt) *VERB* **expedites, expediting, expedited** make something happen more quickly.
[from Latin *expedire* = free someone's feet]

expedition *NOUN* **expeditions** **1** a journey made in order to do something • *a climbing expedition.* **2** speed or promptness.
▷ **expeditionary** *adjective*
[from French; related to *expedite*]

expeditious (*say* eks-pid-**ish**-us) *ADJECTIVE* quick and efficient.
▷ **expeditiously** *adverb*

expel *VERB* **expels, expelling, expelled** **1** send or force something out • *This fan expels stale air.* **2** make a person leave a school or country etc.
▷ **expulsion** *noun*
[from *ex-* + Latin *pellere* = drive]

expend *VERB* **expends, expending, expended** spend; use up.
[from *ex-* + Latin *pendere* = pay]

expendable *ADJECTIVE* able to be sacrificed or got rid of in order to gain something.

expenditure *NOUN* **expenditures** the spending or using up of money or effort etc.

expense *NOUN* **expenses** the cost of doing something.
[from old French; related to *expend*]

expensive *ADJECTIVE* costing a lot.
▷ **expensively** *adverb* **expensiveness** *noun*

experience *NOUN* **experiences** **1** what you learn from doing or seeing things. **2** something that has happened to you.

experience *VERB* **experiences, experiencing, experienced** have something happen to you.
[same origin as *experiment*]

experienced *ADJECTIVE* having great skill or knowledge from much experience.

experiment *NOUN* **experiments** a test made in order to find out what happens or to prove something.
▷ **experimental** *adjective* **experimentally** *adverb*

experiment *VERB* **experiments, experimenting, experimented** carry out an experiment.
▷ **experimentation** *noun*
[from Latin *experiri* = to test]

expert *NOUN* **experts** a person with great knowledge or skill in something.

expert *ADJECTIVE* having great knowledge or skill.
▷ **expertly** *adverb* **expertness** *noun*
[from Latin *expertus* = experienced]

expertise (*say* eks-per-**teez**) *NOUN* expert ability.
[French]

expiate (*say* eks-pee-ayt) *VERB* **expiates, expiating, expiated** make up for something wrong you have done; atone for something.
▷ **expiation** *noun*
[from Latin]

expire *VERB* **expires, expiring, expired** **1** come to an end; stop being usable • *Your season ticket has expired.* **2** die. **3** breathe out air.
▷ **expiration** *noun* **expiry** *noun*
[from *ex-* + Latin *spirare* = breathe]

explain *VERB* **explains, explaining, explained** **1** make something clear to somebody else; show its meaning. **2** account for something • *That explains his absence.*
▷ **explanation** *noun*
[from *ex-* + Latin *planare* = make level or plain]

explanatory (*say* iks-plan-at-er-ee) *ADJECTIVE* giving an explanation.

explicit (*say* iks-pliss-it) *ADJECTIVE* stated or stating something openly and exactly. (COMPARE **implicit**)
▷ **explicitly** *adverb*
[from Latin *explicitus* = unfolded]

explode *VERB* **explodes, exploding, exploded** **1** burst or suddenly release energy with a loud noise. **2** cause a bomb to go off. **3** increase suddenly or quickly.
[originally = to drive a player off the stage by clapping or hissing; from *ex-* + Latin *plaudere* = clap]

exploit (*say* eks-ploit) *NOUN* **exploits** a brave or exciting deed.

exploit (*say* iks-ploit) *VERB* **exploits, exploiting, exploited** **1** use or develop resources. **2** use a person or thing selfishly.
▷ **exploitation** *noun*
[from old French]

exploratory (*say* iks-plorra-ter-ee) *ADJECTIVE* for the purpose of exploring.

explore *VERB* **explores, exploring, explored** **1** travel through a country etc. in order to learn about it. **2** examine a subject or idea carefully • *We explored the possibilities.*
▷ **exploration** *noun* **explorer** *noun*
[from Latin *explorare* = search out]

explosion *NOUN* **explosions** **1** the exploding of a bomb etc.; the noise made by exploding. **2** a sudden great increase.

explosive *ADJECTIVE* able to explode.

explosive *NOUN* **explosives** an explosive substance.

exponent *NOUN* **exponents** **1** a person who puts forward an idea etc. **2** someone who is good at an activity. **3** (*in mathematics*) the raised number etc. written to the right of another (e.g. 3 in 2^3) showing how many times the first one is to be multiplied by itself; index.

export *VERB* **exports, exporting, exported** send goods abroad to be sold.
▷ **exportation** *noun* **exporter** *noun*

export *NOUN* **exports** **1** exporting things. **2** something exported.
[from *ex-* + Latin *portare* = carry]

expose *VERB* **exposes, exposing, exposed** **1** reveal or uncover. **2** allow light to reach a photographic film so as to take a picture.
[from old French]

expostulate *VERB* **expostulates, expostulating, expostulated** make a protest.
▷ **expostulation** *noun*
[from *ex-* + Latin *postulare* = demand]

exposure *NOUN* **exposures** **1** the harmful effects of being exposed to cold weather without enough protection. **2** exposing film to the light so as to take a picture, or a piece of film exposed in this way.

expound *VERB* **expounds, expounding, expounded** describe or explain something in detail.
[from Latin *exponere* = put out, publish]

express *ADJECTIVE* **1** going or sent quickly. **2** clearly stated • *This was done against my express orders.*

express *NOUN* **expresses** a fast train stopping at only a few stations.

express *VERB* **expresses, expressing, expressed** **1** put ideas etc. into words; make your feelings known. **2** press or squeeze out • *Express the juice.*
[from old French]

expression *NOUN* **expressions** **1** the look on a person's face that shows his or her feelings. **2** a word or phrase. **3** a way of speaking or of playing music etc. so as to show your feelings. **4** expressing • *this expression of opinion.*

expressive *ADJECTIVE* full of expression.

expressly *ADVERB* **1** clearly and plainly • *This was expressly forbidden.* **2** specially • *designed expressly for children.*

expressway *NOUN* **expressways** (*American*) a motorway that goes through or around a city.

expulsion *NOUN* **expulsions** expelling or being expelled.

expunge *VERB* **expunges, expunging, expunged** erase; wipe out.
[from Latin]

exquisite (*say* eks-kwiz-it) *ADJECTIVE* very beautiful.
▷ **exquisitely** *adverb*
[from Latin *exquisitus* = sought out]

extemporize *VERB* **extemporizes, extemporizing, extemporized** speak or produce or do something without advance preparation.
▷ **extemporization** *noun*
[from Latin *ex tempore* = on the spur of the moment]

extend *VERB* **extends, extending, extended** **1** stretch out. **2** make something become longer or larger. **3** offer or give • *Extend a warm welcome to our friends.*
▷ **extendible** *adjective*
[from *ex-* + Latin *tendere* = to stretch]

extension *NOUN* **extensions** **1** extending or being extended. **2** something added on; an addition to a building. **3** one of a set of telephones in an office or house etc.

extensive *ADJECTIVE* covering a large area or range • *extensive gardens.*
▷ **extensively** *adverb* **extensiveness** *noun*

extent *NOUN* **extents** **1** the area or length over which something extends. **2** the amount, level, or scope of something • *the full extent of his power.*
[from Latin *extenta* = extended]

extenuating *ADJECTIVE* making a crime seem less great by providing a partial excuse • *There were extenuating circumstances.*
▷ **extenuation** *noun*
[from Latin *extenuare* = reduce]

exterior *ADJECTIVE* outer.

exterior *NOUN* **exteriors** the outside of something.
[Latin, = further out]

exterminate *VERB* **exterminates, exterminating, exterminated** destroy or kill all the members or examples.
▷ **extermination** *noun* **exterminator** *noun*
[originally = banish; from *ex-* + Latin *terminus* = boundary]

external *ADJECTIVE* outside.
▷ **externally** *adverb*
[from Latin]

extinct *ADJECTIVE* **1** not existing any more • *The dodo is an extinct bird.* **2** not burning; not active • *an extinct volcano.*
[same origin as *extinguish*]

extinction *NOUN* **1** making or becoming extinct. **2** extinguishing; being extinguished.

extinguish *VERB* **extinguishes, extinguishing, extinguished** **1** put out a fire or light. **2** put an end to; destroy • *Our hopes of victory were extinguished.*
[from *ex-* + Latin *stinguere* = quench]

extinguisher *NOUN* **extinguishers** a portable device for sending out water, chemicals, or gases to extinguish a fire.

extol *VERB* **extols, extolling, extolled** praise.
[from *ex-* + Latin *tollere* = raise]

extort *VERB* **extorts, extorting, extorted** obtain something by force or threats.
▷ **extortion** *noun*
[from *ex-* + Latin *tortum* = twisted]

extortionate *ADJECTIVE* charging or demanding far too much.
[from *extort*]

extra *ADJECTIVE* additional; more than is usual • *extra strength.*

extra *ADVERB* more than usually • *extra strong.*

extra *NOUN* **extras** **1** an extra person or thing. **2** a person acting as part of a crowd in a film or play.
[probably from *extraordinary*]

extra- *PREFIX* outside; beyond (as in *extraterrestrial*).
[from Latin]

extract (*say* iks-**trakt**) *VERB* **extracts, extracting, extracted** take out; remove.
▷ **extractor** *noun*

extract (*say* **eks**-trakt) *NOUN* **extracts** **1** a passage taken from a book, speech, film, etc. **2** a substance separated or obtained from another.
[from *ex-* + Latin *tractum* = pulled]

extraction *NOUN* **1** extracting. **2** someone's descent • *He is of Chinese extraction.*

extradite *VERB* **extradites, extraditing, extradited** hand over an accused person to the police of the country where the crime was committed.
▷ **extradition** (*say* eks-tra-**dish**-on) *noun*
[from *ex-* + Latin *tradere* = hand over]

extraneous (*say* iks-**tray**-nee-us) *ADJECTIVE* **1** added from outside. **2** not belonging to the matter in hand; irrelevant.
[from Latin]

extraordinary *ADJECTIVE* very unusual or strange.
▷ **extraordinarily** *adverb*
[from Latin *extra ordinem* = out of the ordinary]

extrapolate (*say* iks-**trap**-ol-ayt) *VERB* **extrapolates, extrapolating, extrapolated** draw conclusions from known facts about something unknown or beyond the range of the known facts.
[from *extra-* and *interpolate*]

extrasensory *ADJECTIVE* outside the range of the known human senses.

extraterrestrial *ADJECTIVE* from beyond the earth's atmosphere; from outer space.

extraterrestrial *NOUN* **extraterrestrials** a being from outer space.

extravagant *ADJECTIVE* spending or using too much.
▷ **extravagantly** *adverb* **extravagance** *noun*
[from *extra-* + Latin *vagans* = wandering]

extravaganza *NOUN* **extravaganzas** a very spectacular show.
[from Italian; related to *extravagant*]

extreme *ADJECTIVE* **1** very great or intense • *extreme cold.* **2** furthest away • *the extreme north.* **3** going to great lengths in actions or opinions; not moderate.
▷ **extremely** *adverb*

extreme *NOUN* **extremes** **1** something extreme. **2** either end of something.
[from Latin *extremus* = furthest out]

extremist *NOUN* **extremists** a person who holds extreme (not moderate) opinions in political or other matters.

extremity (*say* iks-**trem**-it-ee) *NOUN* **extremities** **1** an extreme point; the very end. **2** an extreme need or feeling or danger etc.

extricate (*say* **eks**-trik-ayt) *VERB* **extricates, extricating, extricated** free from a difficult position or situation.
▷ **extrication** *noun*
[from *ex-* + Latin *tricae* = entanglements]

extrovert *NOUN* **extroverts** a person who is generally friendly and likes company. (The opposite is **introvert**)
[from *extro-* = outside + Latin *vertere* = to turn]

extrude *VERB* **extrudes, extruding, extruded** push or squeeze out.
▷ **extrusion** *noun*
[from *ex-* + Latin *trudere* = to push]

exuberant (*say* ig-**zew**-ber-ant) *ADJECTIVE* very lively and cheerful.
▷ **exuberantly** *adverb* **exuberance** *noun*
[from Latin *exuberare* = grow thickly]

exude *VERB* **exudes, exuding, exuded** **1** give off moisture, a smell, etc. **2** display a feeling or quality openly • *She exuded confidence.*
[from *ex-* + Latin *sudare* = to sweat]

exult *VERB* **exults, exulting, exulted** rejoice greatly.
▷ **exultant** *adjective* **exultation** *noun*
[from Latin *exsilire* = leap up]

eye *NOUN* **eyes** **1** the organ of the body that is used for seeing. **2** the power of seeing • *She has sharp eyes.* **3** the small hole in a needle. **4** the centre of a storm.

eye *VERB* **eyes, eyeing, eyed** look at something with interest.
[from Old English]

eyeball *NOUN* **eyeballs** the ball-shaped part of the eye inside the eyelids.

eyebrow *NOUN* **eyebrows** the fringe of hair growing on the face above the eye.

eye-catching *ADJECTIVE* striking or attractive.

eyelash *NOUN* **eyelashes** one of the short hairs that grow on an eyelid.

eyelid *NOUN* **eyelids** either of the two folds of skin that can close over the eyeball.

eyepiece *NOUN* **eyepieces** the lens of a telescope or microscope etc. that you put to your eye.

eyesight *NOUN* the ability to see.

eyesore *NOUN* **eyesores** something that is ugly to look at.

eyewitness *NOUN* **eyewitnesses** a person who actually saw an accident or crime etc.

eyrie (*say* I-ree) *NOUN* **eyries** the nest of an eagle or other bird of prey.
[from Latin]

Ff

fable *NOUN* **fables** a short story that teaches about behaviour, often with animals as characters.
[from Latin *fabula* = story]

fabric *NOUN* **fabrics** **1** cloth. **2** the basic framework of something, especially the walls, floors, and roof of a building.
[from Latin]

fabricate *VERB* **fabricates, fabricating, fabricated** **1** construct or manufacture something. **2** invent • *fabricate an excuse.*
▷ **fabrication** *noun*
[from Latin *fabricare* = to make or forge]

fabulous *ADJECTIVE* **1** wonderful. **2** incredibly great • *fabulous wealth.* **3** told of in fables and myths.
▷ **fabulously** *adverb*
[same origin as *fable*]

façade (*say* fas-**ahd**) *NOUN* **façades** **1** the front of a building. **2** an outward appearance, especially a deceptive one.
[French; related to *face*]

face *NOUN* **faces** **1** the front part of the head. **2** the expression on a person's face. **3** the front or upper side of something. **4** a surface • *A cube has six faces.*

face *VERB* **faces, facing, faced** **1** look or have the front towards something • *Our room faced the sea.* **2** meet and have to deal with something; encounter • *Explorers face many dangers.* **3** cover a surface with a layer of different material.
[from Latin *facies* = appearance]

facelift *NOUN* **facelifts** surgery to remove wrinkles by tightening the skin of the face, done to make someone look younger.

facet (*say* **fas**-it) *NOUN* **facets** **1** one of the many sides of a cut stone or jewel. **2** one aspect of a situation or problem.
[from French *facette* = small face]

facetious (*say* fas-**ee**-shus) *ADJECTIVE* trying to be funny at an unsuitable time • *facetious remarks.*
▷ **facetiously** *adverb*
[from Latin *facetus* = witty]

facial (*say* **fay**-shal) *ADJECTIVE* to do with the face.

facile (*say* **fas**-I'll) *ADJECTIVE* done or produced easily or with little thought or care.
[from Latin *facilis* = easy]

facilitate (*say* fas-**il**-it-ayt) *VERB* **facilitates, facilitating, facilitated** make something easier to do.
▷ **facilitation** *noun*

facility (*say* fas-**il**-it-ee) *NOUN* **facilities** **1** something that provides you with the means to do things • *There are sports facilities.* **2** ease or skill in doing something • *She reads music with great facility.*

facsimile (*say* fak-**sim**-il-ee) *NOUN* **facsimiles** **1** an exact reproduction of a document etc. **2** a fax.
[from Latin *fac* = make + *simile* = a likeness]

A B C D E F G H I J K L M N O P Q R S T U V W X Y Z

fact *NOUN* **facts** something that is certainly true.
- **the facts of life** information about how babies are conceived.
[from Latin *factum* = thing done]

faction *NOUN* **factions** a small united group within a larger one, especially in politics.
[from Latin]

-faction *SUFFIX* forms nouns (e.g. *satisfaction*) from verbs that end in *-fy*.
[from Latin]

factor *NOUN* **factors** **1** something that helps to bring about a result • *Hard work was a factor in her success.* **2** a number by which a larger number can be divided exactly • *2 and 3 are factors of 6.*
[from Latin *facere* = do or make]
WORD FAMILY There are a number of English words that are related to *factor* because part of their original meaning comes from the Latin word *facere* meaning 'to do or make'. These include *benefactor*, *fact*, *factory*, *malefactor*, and *satisfaction*.

factory *NOUN* **factories** a large building where machines are used to make things.
[from Latin *factorium* = place where things are made]

factotum (*say* fakt-**oh**-tum) *NOUN* **factotums** a servant or assistant who does all kinds of work.
[from Latin *fac* = do + *totum* = everything]

factual *ADJECTIVE* based on facts; containing facts.
▷ **factually** *adverb*

faculty *NOUN* **faculties** **1** any of the powers of the body or mind (e.g. sight, speech, understanding). **2** a department teaching a particular subject in a university or college • *the faculty of music.*
[same origin as *facile*]

fad *NOUN* **fads** **1** a person's particular like or dislike. **2** a temporary fashion or craze.
▷ **faddy** *adjective*
[originally a dialect word; origin unknown]

fade *VERB* **fades, fading, faded** **1** lose colour or freshness or strength. **2** disappear gradually. **3** make a sound etc. become gradually weaker (*fade it out*) or stronger (*fade it in* or *up*).
[from old French]

faeces (*say* fee-seez) *PLURAL NOUN* solid waste matter passed out of the body.
[plural of Latin *faex* = dregs]

fag *NOUN* **fags** **1** something that is tiring or boring. **2** (*informal*) a cigarette.
- **fagged out** tired out; exhausted.
[origin unknown]

faggot *NOUN* **faggots** **1** a meat ball made with chopped liver and baked. **2** a bundle of sticks bound together, used for firewood.
[from Greek *phakelos* = bundle]

Fahrenheit *ADJECTIVE* measuring temperature on a scale where water freezes at 32° and boils at 212°.
[named after G. D. *Fahrenheit*, a German scientist, who invented the mercury thermometer]

fail *VERB* **fails, failing, failed** **1** try to do something but be unable to do it. **2** become weak or useless; break down • *The brakes failed.* **3** not do something • *He failed to warn me.* **4** not get enough marks to pass an examination. **5** judge that someone has not passed an examination.

fail *NOUN* **fails** not being successful in an examination • *Alex got four passes and one fail.*
- **without fail** for certain; whatever happens.
[from Latin *fallere* = disappoint, deceive]

failing *NOUN* **failings** a weakness or a fault.

failure *NOUN* **failures** **1** not being able to do something. **2** a person or thing that has failed.

faint *ADJECTIVE* **1** pale or dim; not distinct. **2** weak or giddy; nearly unconscious. **3** slight • *a faint hope.*
▷ **faintly** *adverb* **faintness** *noun*

faint *VERB* **faints, fainting, fainted** become unconscious for a short time.
[same origin as *feint*]
USAGE Do not confuse with **feint**.

fair[1] *ADJECTIVE* **1** right or just; according to the rules • *a fair fight.* **2** (said about hair or skin) light in colour; (said about a person) having fair hair. **3** (*old use*) beautiful. **4** fine or favourable • *fair weather.* **5** moderate; quite good • *a fair number of people.*
▷ **fairness** *noun*

fair *ADVERB* fairly • *Play fair!*
[from Old English]

fair² *NOUN* **fairs** **1** a group of outdoor entertainments such as roundabouts, sideshows, and stalls. **2** an exhibition or market.
▷ **fairground** *noun*
[from Latin *feriae* = holiday]

fairly *ADVERB* **1** justly; according to the rules. **2** moderately • *It is fairly hard.*

fairy *NOUN* **fairies** an imaginary very small creature with magic powers.
▷ **fairyland** *noun* **fairy tale** *noun*
[from an old word *fay*, from Latin *fata* = the Fates, three goddesses who were believed to control people's lives]

fait accompli *NOUN* **faits accomplis** a thing that has already been done and so is past arguing about.
[French, = accomplished fact]

faith *NOUN* **faiths** **1** strong belief or trust. **2** a religion.
- **in good faith** with honest intentions.
[from old French; related to *fidelity*]

faithful *ADJECTIVE* **1** loyal and trustworthy. **2** true to the facts • *a faithful account.* **3** sexually loyal to one partner.
▷ **faithfully** *adverb* **faithfulness** *noun*
- **Yours faithfully** see *yours*.

fake *NOUN* **fakes** something that looks genuine but is not; a forgery.

fake *VERB* **fakes, faking, faked** **1** make something that looks genuine, in order to deceive people. **2** pretend • *He used to fake illness to miss games.*
▷ **faker** *noun*
[originally slang; origin unknown]

fakir (*say* fay-keer) *NOUN* **fakirs** a Muslim or Hindu religious beggar regarded as a holy man.
[Arabic, = a poor man]

falcon *NOUN* **falcons** a kind of hawk often used in the sport of hunting other birds or game.
▷ **falconry** *noun*
[Latin]

fall *VERB* **falls, falling, fell, fallen** **1** come or go down without being pushed or thrown etc. **2** decrease; become lower • *Prices fell.* **3** be captured or overthrown • *The city fell.* **4** die in battle. **5** happen • *Silence fell.* **6** become • *She fell asleep.*
- **fall back** retreat.
- **fall back on** use for support or in an emergency.
- **fall for** **1** be attracted by a person. **2** be taken in by a deception.
- **fall out** quarrel.
- **fall through** fail • *Our plans fell through.*

fall *NOUN* **falls** **1** the action of falling. **2** (*American*) autumn, when leaves fall.
[from Old English]

fallacy (*say* fal-a-see) *NOUN* **fallacies** a false or mistaken idea or belief.
▷ **fallacious** (*say* fal-ay-shus) *adjective*
[same origin as *fail*]

fallible (*say* fal-ib-ul) *ADJECTIVE* liable to make mistakes; not infallible • *All people are fallible.*
▷ **fallibility** *noun*
[same origin as *fail*]

Fallopian tube *NOUN* **Fallopian tubes** one of the two tubes in a woman's body along which the eggs travel from the ovaries to the uterus.
[named after Gabriele *Fallopio*, a 16th-century Italian anatomist]

fallout *NOUN* particles of radioactive material carried in the air after a nuclear explosion.

fallow *ADJECTIVE* (said about land) ploughed but left without crops in order to restore its fertility.
[from Old English *falu* = pale brown (because of the colour of the bare earth)]

fallow deer *NOUN* **fallow deer** a kind of light-brown deer.
[same origin as *fallow*]

falls *PLURAL NOUN* a waterfall.

false *ADJECTIVE* **1** untrue or incorrect. **2** not genuine; artificial • *false teeth.* **3** treacherous or deceitful.
▷ **falsely** *adverb* **falseness** *noun* **falsity** *noun*
[same origin as *fail*]

falsehood *NOUN* **falsehoods** **1** a lie. **2** telling lies.

falsetto *NOUN* **falsettos** a man's voice forced into speaking or singing higher than is natural.
[Italian]

falsify *VERB* **falsifies, falsifying, falsified** alter a thing dishonestly.
▷ **falsification** *noun*

falter *VERB* **falters, faltering, faltered** **1** hesitate when you move or speak. **2** become weaker; begin to give way • *His courage began to falter.*
[origin unknown]

fame *NOUN* being famous.
▷ **famed** *adjective*
[from Latin *fama* = report, rumour]

familiar *ADJECTIVE* **1** well-known; often seen or experienced. **2** knowing something well • *Are you familiar with this book?* **3** very friendly.
▷ **familiarly** *adverb* **familiarity** *noun*
[from Latin *familias* = family]

familiarize *VERB* **familiarizes, familiarizing, familiarized** make yourself familiar with something.
▷ **familiarization** *noun*

family *NOUN* **families** **1** parents and their children, sometimes including grandchildren and other relations. **2** a group of things that are alike in some way. **3** a group of related plants or animals • *Lions belong to the cat family.*
[from Latin]

family planning *NOUN* the use of contraceptives to control pregnancies; birth control.

family tree *NOUN* **family trees** a diagram showing how people in a family are related.

famine *NOUN* **famines** a very bad shortage of food in an area.
[from Latin *fames* = hunger]

famished *ADJECTIVE* very hungry.
[same origin as *famine*]

famous *ADJECTIVE* known to very many people.
[same origin as *fame*]

famously *ADVERB* (*informal*) very well • *They get on famously.*

fan[1] *NOUN* **fans** a device or machine for making air move about so as to cool people or things.

fan *VERB* **fans, fanning, fanned** send a current of air on something.
- **fan out** spread out in the shape of a fan.
[from Latin]

fan[2] *NOUN* **fans** an enthusiastic admirer or supporter.
[short for *fanatic*]

fanatic *NOUN* **fanatics** a person who is very enthusiastic or too enthusiastic about something.
▷ **fanatical** *adjective* **fanatically** *adverb* **fanaticism** *noun*
[from Latin *fanaticus* = inspired by a god]

fanciful *ADJECTIVE* **1** imagining things. **2** imaginary.

fancy *NOUN* **fancies** **1** a liking or desire for something. **2** imagination.

fancy *ADJECTIVE* decorated or elaborate; not plain.

fancy *VERB* **fancies, fancying, fancied** **1** have a liking or desire for something. **2** imagine. **3** believe • *I fancy it's raining.*
[short for *fantasy*]

fancy dress *NOUN* unusual costume worn for a party, often to make you look like a famous person.

fanfare *NOUN* **fanfares** a short piece of loud music played on trumpets.
[French]

fang *NOUN* **fangs** a long sharp tooth.
[from Old English]

fanlight *NOUN* **fanlights** a window above a door.
[because many of these are fan-shaped]

fantasia (*say* fan-tay-zee-a) *NOUN* **fantasias** an imaginative piece of music or writing.
[Italian; related to *fantastic*]

fantasize *VERB* **fantasizes, fantasizing, fantasized** imagine something pleasant or strange that you would like to happen.
[from *fantasy*]

fantastic *ADJECTIVE* **1** (*informal*) excellent. **2** strange or unusual. **3** designed in a very fanciful way.
▷ **fantastically** *adverb*
[from Greek *phantazesthai* = imagine]

fantasy *NOUN* **fantasies** something imaginary or fantastic.
[same origin as *fantastic*]

far *ADVERB* **1** at or to a great distance • *We didn't go far.* **2** much; by a great amount • *This is far better.*

far *ADJECTIVE* distant or remote • *On the far side of the river.*
[from Old English]

farce *NOUN* **farces** **1** an exaggerated comedy. **2** a situation or series of events that is ridiculous or a pretence • *The trial was a complete farce.*
▷ **farcical** *adjective*
[French, literally = stuffing (the name given to a comic interlude between acts of a play)]

fare *NOUN* **fares** **1** the price charged for a passenger to travel. **2** food and drink • *There was only very plain fare.*

fare *VERB* **fares, faring, fared** get along; progress • *How did they fare?*
[from Old English]

farewell *INTERJECTION* & *NOUN* **farewells** goodbye.

far-fetched *ADJECTIVE* unlikely, difficult to believe.

farm *NOUN* **farms** **1** an area of land where someone grows crops or keeps animals for food or other use. **2** the farmer's house.
▷ **farmhouse** *noun* **farmyard** *noun*

farm *VERB* **farms, farming, farmed** **1** grow crops or keep animals for food etc. **2** use land for growing crops; cultivate.
[from French]

farmer *NOUN* **farmers** a person who owns or manages a farm.

farrier (*say* fa-ree-er) *NOUN* **farriers** a smith who shoes horses.
▷ **farriery** *noun*
[from Latin *ferrum* = iron, an iron horseshoe]

farrow *NOUN* **farrows** a litter of young pigs.
[from Old English]

farther *ADVERB* & *ADJECTIVE* at or to a greater distance; more distant.
[a different spelling of *further*]
USAGE *Farther* and *farthest* are used only in connection with distance (e.g. *She lives farther from the school than I do*), but even in such cases many people prefer to use *further*. Only *further* can be used to mean 'additional', e.g. in *We must make further inquiries.* If you are not sure which is right, use *further*.

farthest *ADVERB* & *ADJECTIVE* at or to the greatest distance; most distant.
USAGE See the note at **farther**.

farthing *NOUN* **farthings** a former British coin worth one-quarter of a penny.
[from Old English *feorthing* = one-fourth]

fascinate *VERB* **fascinates, fascinating, fascinated** be very attractive or interesting to somebody.
▷ **fascination** *noun* **fascinator** *noun*
[from Latin *fascinum* = a spell]

Fascist (*say* fash-ist) *NOUN* **Fascists** a person who supports an extreme right-wing dictatorial type of government.
▷ **Fascism** *noun*
[from Latin *fasces*, the bundle of rods with an axe through it, carried before a magistrate in ancient Rome as a symbol of his power to punish people]

fashion *NOUN* **fashions** **1** the style of clothes or other things that most people like at a particular time. **2** a way of doing something • *Continue in the same fashion.*

fashion *VERB* **fashions, fashioning, fashioned** make something in a particular shape or style.
[via old French from Latin *facere* = make or do]

fashionable *ADJECTIVE* following the fashion of the time; popular.
▷ **fashionably** *adverb*

fast[1] *ADJECTIVE* **1** moving or done quickly; rapid. **2** allowing fast movement • *a fast road.* **3** showing a time later than the correct time • *Your watch is fast.* **4** firmly fixed or attached. **5** not likely to fade • *fast colours.*
▷ **fastness** *noun*

fast *ADVERB* **1** quickly • *Run fast!* **2** firmly • *His leg was stuck fast in the mud.*
- **fast asleep** in a deep sleep.
[from Old English *faest*]

fast[2] *VERB* **fasts, fasting, fasted** go without food.
▷ **fast** *noun*
[from Old English *faestan*]

A B C D E **F** G H I J K L M N O P Q R S T U V W X Y Z

fasten *VERB* **fastens, fastening, fastened** fix one thing firmly to another.
▷ **fastener** *noun* **fastening** *noun*
[from Old English]

fast food *NOUN* restaurant food that is quickly prepared and served.

fastidious *ADJECTIVE* **1** fussy and hard to please. **2** very careful about small details of dress or cleanliness.
▷ **fastidiously** *adverb* **fastidiousness** *noun*
[from Latin *fastidium* = loathing]

fat *NOUN* **fats** **1** the white greasy part of meat. **2** oil or grease used in cooking.
- **the fat of the land** the best food.

fat *ADJECTIVE* **fatter, fattest** **1** having a very thick round body. **2** thick • *a fat book.* **3** full of fat.
▷ **fatness** *noun*
[from Old English]

fatal *ADJECTIVE* causing death or disaster • *a fatal accident.*
▷ **fatally** *adverb*
[from Latin *fatalis* = by fate]

fatalist *NOUN* **fatalists** a person who accepts whatever happens and thinks it could not have been avoided.
▷ **fatalism** *noun* **fatalistic** *adjective*
[from *fatal*, in an old sense = decreed by fate]

fatality (*say* fa-tal-it-ee) *NOUN* **fatalities** a death caused by an accident, war, or other disaster.

fate *NOUN* **fates** **1** a power that is thought to make things happen. **2** what will happen or has happened to somebody or something; destiny.
[from Latin *fatum*, literally = that which has been spoken]

fated *ADJECTIVE* destined by fate; doomed.

fateful *ADJECTIVE* bringing events that are important and usually unpleasant • *How well she remembered that fateful day.*
▷ **fatefully** *adverb*

father *NOUN* **fathers** **1** a male parent. **2** the title of certain priests.
▷ **fatherly** *adjective*

father *VERB* **fathers, fathering, fathered** be the father of • *He fathered six children.*
[from Old English]

father-in-law *NOUN* **fathers-in-law** the father of a married person's husband or wife.

fathom *NOUN* **fathoms** a unit used to measure the depth of water, equal to 1.83 metres or 6 feet.

fathom *VERB* **fathoms, fathoming, fathomed** **1** measure the depth of something. **2** get to the bottom of something; work it out.
▷ **fathomless** *adjective*
[from Old English]

fatigue *NOUN* **1** tiredness. **2** weakness in metals, caused by stress.
▷ **fatigued** *adjective*
[from Latin *fatigare* = make weary]

fatten *VERB* **fattens, fattening, fattened** make or become fat.

fatty *ADJECTIVE* like fat; containing fat.

fatuous *ADJECTIVE* silly or foolish.
▷ **fatuously** *adverb* **fatuousness** *noun* **fatuity** *noun*
[from Latin]

fatwa *NOUN* **fatwas** a ruling on a religious matter given by an Islamic authority.
[Arabic]

faucet *NOUN* **faucets** (*American*) a tap.
[from old French]

fault *NOUN* **faults** **1** anything that makes a person or thing imperfect; a flaw or mistake. **2** the responsibility for something wrong • *It wasn't your fault.* **3** a break in a layer of rock, caused by movement of the earth's crust.
- **at fault** responsible for a mistake or failure.

fault *VERB* **faults, faulting, faulted** find faults in something.
[from old French; related to *fail*]

faultless *ADJECTIVE* without a fault.
▷ **faultlessly** *adverb* **faultlessness** *noun*

faulty *ADJECTIVE* having a fault or faults.
▷ **faultily** *adverb*

faun *NOUN* **fauns** an ancient country god with a goat's legs, horns, and tail.
[from the name of *Faunus*, an ancient Roman country god (see *fauna*)]

fauna *NOUN* the animals of a certain area or period of time. (COMPARE **flora**)
[from the name of *Fauna*, an ancient Roman country goddess, sister of Faunus (see *faun*)]

faux pas (*say* foh pah) *NOUN* **faux pas** an embarrassing blunder.
[French, = false step]

favour *NOUN* **favours** **1** a kind or helpful act. **2** approval or goodwill. **3** friendly support shown to one person or group but not to another • *without fear or favour.*
- **be in favour of** like or support.

favour *VERB* **favours, favouring, favoured** be in favour of something; show favour to a person.
[from Latin]

favourable *ADJECTIVE* **1** helpful or advantageous. **2** showing approval.
▷ **favourably** *adverb*

favourite *ADJECTIVE* liked more than others.

favourite *NOUN* **favourites** **1** a person or thing that someone likes most. **2** a competitor that is generally expected to win.

favouritism *NOUN* unfairly being kinder to one person than to others.

fawn[1] *NOUN* **fawns** **1** a young deer. **2** a light-brown colour.
[from old French; related to *foetus*]

fawn[2] *VERB* **fawns, fawning, fawned** get someone to like you by flattering or praising them too much.
[from Old English]

fax *NOUN* **faxes** **1** a machine that sends an exact copy of a document electronically. **2** a copy produced by this.

fax *VERB* **faxes, faxing, faxed** send a copy of a document using a fax machine.
[from *facsimile*]

faze *VERB* **fazes, fazing, fazed** (*informal*) make someone feel confused or shocked, so that they do not know what to do • *She wasn't fazed by his criticisms.*
[from Old English *fezian* = to drive away]

fear *NOUN* **fears** a feeling that something unpleasant may happen.

fear *VERB* **fears, fearing, feared** feel fear; be afraid of somebody or something.
[from Old English]

fearful *ADJECTIVE* **1** feeling fear; afraid. **2** causing fear or horror • *a fearful monster.* **3** (*informal*) very great or bad.
▷ **fearfully** *adverb*

fearless *ADJECTIVE* without fear.
▷ **fearlessly** *adverb* **fearlessness** *noun*

fearsome *ADJECTIVE* frightening.

feasible *ADJECTIVE* **1** able to be done; possible. **2** likely or probable • *a feasible explanation.*
▷ **feasibly** *adverb* **feasibility** *noun*
[from French *faire* = do]
USAGE The use of *feasible* to mean 'likely or probable' has not become generally accepted in standard English, so it is better to avoid it in writing or formal situations.

feast *NOUN* **feasts** **1** a large splendid meal. **2** a religious festival.
▷ **feast** *verb*
[from old French; related to *fête*]

feat *NOUN* **feats** a brave or clever deed.
[from old French; related to *fact*]

feather *NOUN* **feathers** one of the very light coverings that grow from a bird's skin.
▷ **feathery** *adjective*

feather *VERB* **feathers, feathering, feathered** cover or line something with feathers.
[from Old English]

featherweight *NOUN* **featherweights** **1** a person who weighs very little. **2** a boxer weighing between 54 and 57 kg.

feature *NOUN* **features** **1** any part of the face (e.g. mouth, nose, eyes). **2** an important or noticeable part; a characteristic. **3** a special newspaper article or programme that deals with a particular subject. **4** the main film in a cinema programme.

feature *VERB* **features, featuring, featured** make or be a noticeable part of something.
[from Latin *factura* = a creation]

February *NOUN* the second month of the year.
[named after *februa*, the ancient Roman feast of purification held in this month]

A B C D E F G H I J K L M N O P Q R S T U V W X Y Z

feckless *ADJECTIVE* not having the determination to achieve anything in life; irresponsible.
[from Scots *feck* = effect, + *-less*]

fed *past tense* of **feed**.
- **fed up** (*informal*) depressed, unhappy, or bored.

federal *ADJECTIVE* to do with a system in which several states are ruled by a central government but are responsible for their own internal affairs.
[from Latin *foederis* = of a treaty]

federation *NOUN* **federations** a group of federal states.

fee *NOUN* **fees** a charge for something.
[from old French]

feeble *ADJECTIVE* weak; without strength.
▷ **feebly** *adverb* **feebleness** *noun*
[from Latin *flebilis* = wept over]

feed *VERB* **feeds, feeding, fed** **1** give food to a person or animal. **2** take food. **3** supply something to a machine etc. • *We fed all the figures into the database.*
▷ **feeder** *noun*

feed *NOUN* food for animals or babies.
[from Old English]

feedback *NOUN* **1** the response you get from people to something you have done. **2** the harsh noise produced when some of the sound from an amplifier goes back into it.

feel *VERB* **feels, feeling, felt** **1** touch something to find out what it is like. **2** be aware of something; have an opinion. **3** experience an emotion. **4** give a certain sensation • *It feels warm.*
- **feel like** want.

feel *NOUN* the sensation caused by feeling something • *I like the feel of silk.*
[from Old English]

feeler *NOUN* **feelers** **1** a long thin projection on an insect's or crustacean's body, used for feeling; an antenna. **2** a cautious question or suggestion etc. to test people's reactions.

feeling *NOUN* **feelings** **1** the ability to feel things; the sense of touch. **2** what a person feels in the mind; emotion • *I didn't mean to hurt your feelings.* **3** what you think about something • *I have a feeling that we are going to win.*

feign (*say* fayn) *VERB* **feigns, feigning, feigned** pretend.
[from Latin *fingere* = to form or plan]

feint (*say* faynt) *NOUN* **feints** a pretended attack or punch meant to deceive an opponent.

feint *VERB* **feints, feinting, feinted** make a feint.
[old French, = feigned]
USAGE Do not confuse with **faint**.

felicity *NOUN* **1** great happiness. **2** a pleasing manner or style • *He expressed himself with great felicity.*
▷ **felicitous** *adjective* **felicitously** *adverb*
[from Latin *felix* = happy]

feline (*say* feel-I'n) *ADJECTIVE* to do with cats; cat-like.
[from Latin *feles* = cat]

fell[1] *past tense* of **fall**.

fell[2] *VERB* **fells, felling, felled** make something fall; cut or knock down • *They were felling the trees.*
[from Old English]

fell[3] *NOUN* **fells** a piece of wild hilly country, especially in the north of England.
[from Old Norse]

fellow *NOUN* **fellows** **1** a friend or companion; one who belongs to the same group. **2** a man or boy. **3** a member of a learned society.

fellow *ADJECTIVE* of the same group or kind • *Her fellow teachers supported her.*
[from Old Norse]

fellowship *NOUN* **fellowships** **1** friendship. **2** a group of friends; a society.

felon (*say* fel-on) *NOUN* **felons** a criminal.
[from Latin *felo* = an evil person]

felony (*say* fel-on-ee) *NOUN* **felonies** a serious crime.
[from French]

felt[1] *past tense* of **feel**.

felt[2] *NOUN* a thick fabric made of fibres of wool or fur etc. pressed together.
[from Old English]

female *ADJECTIVE* of the sex that can bear offspring or produce eggs or fruit.

female *NOUN* **females** a female person, animal, or plant.
[from Latin *femina* = woman]

feminine *ADJECTIVE* **1** to do with or like women; suitable for women. **2** (in some languages) belonging to the class of words which includes the words referring to women.
▷ **femininity** *noun*
[same origin as *female*]

feminist *NOUN* **feminists** a person who believes that women should have the same rights and status as men.
▷ **feminism** *noun*

femur (*say* fee-mer) *NOUN* **femurs** the thigh bone.
[Latin]

fen *NOUN* **fens** an area of low-lying marshy or flooded ground.
[from Old English]

fence *NOUN* **fences** **1** a barrier made of wood or wire etc. round an area. **2** a structure for a horse to jump over. **3** a person who buys stolen goods and sells them again.

fence *VERB* **fences, fencing, fenced** **1** put a fence round or along something. **2** fight with long narrow swords (called *foils*) as a sport.
▷ **fencer** *noun*
[shortened from *defence*]

fend *VERB* **fends, fending, fended**
- **fend for yourself** take care of yourself.
- **fend off** keep a person or thing away from yourself.
[shortened from *defend*]

fender *NOUN* **fenders** **1** something placed round a fireplace to stop coals from falling into the room. **2** something hung over the side of a boat to protect it from knocks.
[from *fend*]

fennel *NOUN* a herb with yellow flowers.
[Old English from Latin]

feral *ADJECTIVE* wild and untamed • *feral cats.*
[from Latin *fera* = wild animal]

ferment (*say* fer-ment) *VERB* **ferments, fermenting, fermented** bubble and change chemically by the action of a substance such as yeast.
▷ **fermentation** *noun*
USAGE Do not confuse with **foment**.

ferment (*say* fer-ment) *NOUN* **1** fermenting. **2** an excited or agitated condition.
[from Latin *fermentum* = yeast]

fern *NOUN* **ferns** a plant with feathery leaves and no flowers.
[from Old English]

ferocious *ADJECTIVE* fierce or savage.
▷ **ferociously** *adverb* **ferocity** *noun*
[from Latin *ferox* = fierce]

-ferous or **-iferous** *SUFFIX* form nouns meaning 'carrying' or 'providing' (e.g. *carboniferous*).
[from Latin *ferre* = carry]

ferret *NOUN* **ferrets** a small weasel-like animal used for catching rabbits and rats.
▷ **ferrety** *adjective*

ferret *VERB* **ferrets, ferreting, ferreted** **1** hunt with a ferret. **2** search for something; rummage.
[from Latin *fur* = thief]

ferric or **ferrous** *ADJECTIVES* containing iron.
[from Latin *ferrum* = iron]

ferry *NOUN* **ferries** a boat or ship used for transporting people or things across a short stretch of water.

ferry *VERB* **ferries, ferrying, ferried** transport people or things across water or for a short distance.
[from Old Norse]

fertile *ADJECTIVE* **1** producing good crops • *fertile soil.* **2** able to produce offspring. **3** able to produce ideas • *a fertile imagination.*
▷ **fertility** *noun*
[from Latin]

fertilize *VERB* **fertilizes, fertilizing, fertilized** **1** add substances to the soil to make it more fertile. **2** put pollen into a plant or sperm into an egg or female animal so that it develops seed or young.
▷ **fertilization** *noun*

fertilizer *NOUN* **fertilizers** chemicals or manure added to the soil to make it more fertile.

fervent or **fervid** *ADJECTIVES* showing warm or strong feeling.
▷ **fervently** *adverb* **fervency** *noun* **fervour** *noun*
[from Latin *fervens* = boiling]

fester *VERB* **festers, festering, festered** **1** become septic and filled with pus. **2** cause resentment for a long time.
[from old French]

festival *NOUN* **festivals** **1** a time of celebration, especially for religious reasons. **2** an organized series of concerts, films, performances, etc., especially one held every year.
[from Latin]

festive *ADJECTIVE* **1** to do with a festival. **2** suitable for a festival; joyful.
▷ **festively** *adverb*

festivity *NOUN* **festivities** a festive occasion or celebration.

festoon *NOUN* **festoons** a chain of flowers or ribbons etc. hung as a decoration.

festoon *VERB* **festoons, festooning, festooned** decorate something with ornaments.
[via French from Italian *festone* = festive ornament]

fetch *VERB* **fetches, fetching, fetched** **1** go for and bring back • *fetch some milk; fetch a doctor.* **2** be sold for a particular price • *The chairs fetched £20.*
[from Old English]

fete (*say* fayt) *NOUN* **fetes** an outdoor entertainment with stalls and sideshows.

fete *VERB* **fetes, feting, feted** honour a person with celebrations.
[from old French *feste* = feast]

fetish *NOUN* **fetishes** **1** an object supposed to have magical powers. **2** something that a person has an obsession about.
[via French from Portuguese]

fetlock *NOUN* **fetlocks** the part of a horse's leg above and behind the hoof.
[from a Germanic language; related to *foot*]

fetter *NOUN* **fetters** a chain or shackle put round a prisoner's ankle.

fetter *VERB* **fetters, fettering, fettered** put fetters on a prisoner.
[from Old English]

fettle *NOUN*
- **in fine fettle** in good health.
[from Old English]

feud (*say* fewd) *NOUN* **feuds** a long-lasting quarrel, especially between two families.
[via old French from Germanic; related to *foe*]

feudal (*say* few-dal) *ADJECTIVE* to do with the system used in the Middle Ages in which people could farm land in exchange for work done for the owner.
▷ **feudalism** *noun*
[from Latin]

fever *NOUN* **fevers** **1** an abnormally high body temperature, usually with an illness. **2** excitement or agitation.
▷ **fevered** *adjective* **feverish** *adjective* **feverishly** *adverb*
[from Latin]

few *ADJECTIVE* not many.
USAGE Note that *fewer* means 'not so many', while *less* means 'not so much'. It is widely regarded as incorrect to use *less* when you mean *fewer*.

few *NOUN* a small number of people or things.
- **quite a few** or **a good few** a fairly large number
[from Old English]

fez *NOUN* **fezzes** a high flat-topped red hat with a tassel, worn by Muslim men in some countries.
[named after *Fez*, a town in Morocco, where fezzes were made]

fiancé (*say* fee-ahn-say) *NOUN* **fiancés** a man who is engaged to be married.
[French, = betrothed]

fiancée (*say* fee-ahn-say) *NOUN* **fiancées** a woman who is engaged to be married.

fiasco (*say* fee-as-koh) *NOUN* **fiascos** a complete failure.
[Italian]

fib *NOUN* **fibs** a lie about something unimportant.
▷ **fibber** *noun* **fibbing** *noun*
[related to *fable*]

fibre *NOUN* **fibres** **1** a very thin thread. **2** a substance made of thin threads. **3** indigestible material in certain foods that stimulates the action of the intestines.
▷ **fibrous** *adjective*
[from Latin]

fibreglass *NOUN* **1** fabric made from glass fibres. **2** plastic containing glass fibres.

fickle *ADJECTIVE* constantly changing; not loyal to one person or group etc.
▷ **fickleness** *noun*
[from Old English]

fiction *NOUN* **fictions** **1** writings about events that have not really happened; stories and novels. **2** something imagined or untrue.
▷ **fictional** *adjective*
[same origin as *feign*]

fictitious *ADJECTIVE* imagined or untrue.

fiddle *NOUN* **fiddles** **1** (*informal*) a violin. **2** (*slang*) a swindle.

fiddle *VERB* **fiddles, fiddling, fiddled** **1** (*informal*) play the violin. **2** fidget or tinker with something, using your fingers. **3** (*slang*) alter accounts or records dishonestly.
▷ **fiddler** *noun*
[from Old English]

fiddly *ADJECTIVE* small and awkward to use or do.

fidelity *NOUN* **1** faithfulness or loyalty. **2** accuracy; the exactness with which sound is reproduced.
[from Latin *fides* = faith]

fidget *VERB* **fidgets, fidgeting, fidgeted** make small restless movements.
▷ **fidgety** *adjective*

fidget *NOUN* **fidgets** a person who fidgets.
[origin unknown]

field *NOUN* **fields** **1** a piece of land with grass or crops growing on it. **2** an area of interest or study • *recent advances in the field of genetics.* **3** those who are taking part in a race or outdoor game etc.

field *VERB* **fields, fielding, fielded** **1** stop or catch the ball in cricket etc. **2** be on the side not batting in cricket etc. **3** put a team into a match etc. • *They fielded their best players.*
▷ **fielder** *noun* **fieldsman** *noun*
[from Old English]

field events *PLURAL NOUN* athletic sports other than track races, such as jumping and throwing events.

Field Marshal *NOUN* **Field Marshals** an army officer of the highest rank.

fieldwork *NOUN* practical work or research done in various places, not in a library or museum or laboratory etc.

fiend (*say* feend) *NOUN* **fiends** **1** an evil spirit; a devil. **2** a very wicked or cruel person. **3** an enthusiast • *a fresh-air fiend.*
[from Old English]

fiendish *ADJECTIVE* **1** very wicked or cruel. **2** extremely difficult or complicated.

fierce *ADJECTIVE* **1** angry and violent or cruel. **2** intense • *fierce heat.*
▷ **fiercely** *adverb* **fierceness** *noun*
[from Latin *ferus* = untamed]

fiery *ADJECTIVE* **1** full of flames or heat. **2** full of emotion. **3** easily made angry.

fife *NOUN* **fifes** a small shrill flute.
[from German *Pfeife* = pipe]

fifteen *NOUN & ADJECTIVE* **fifteens** **1** the number 15. **2** a team in rugby union football.
▷ **fifteenth** *adjective & noun*
[from Old English]

fifth *ADJECTIVE & NOUN* **fifths** next after the fourth.
▷ **fifthly** *adverb*
[from Old English]

fifty *NOUN & ADJECTIVE* **fifties** the number 50.
▷ **fiftieth** *adjective & noun*
[from Old English]

fifty-fifty *ADJECTIVE & ADVERB* **1** shared equally between two people or groups • *We'll split the money fifty-fifty.* **2** evenly balanced • *a fifty-fifty chance.*

fig *NOUN* **figs** a soft fruit full of small seeds.
[from Latin]

fight *NOUN* **fights** **1** a struggle against somebody using hands, weapons, etc. **2** an attempt to achieve or overcome something • *the fight against poverty.*

fight *VERB* **fights, fighting, fought** **1** have a fight. **2** attempt to achieve or overcome something.
▷ **fighter** *noun*
[from Old English]

figment *NOUN* **figments** something imagined • *a figment of the imagination.*
[from Latin; related to *feign*]

figurative *ADJECTIVE* using a figure of speech; metaphorical, not literal.
▷ **figuratively** *adverb*

A B C D E F G H I J K L M N O P Q R S T U V W X Y Z

figure *NOUN* **figures** **1** the symbol of a number. **2** an amount or value. **3** a diagram or illustration. **4** a shape. **5** the shape of a person's, especially a woman's, body. **6** a person. **7** a representation of a person or animal in painting, sculpture, etc.

figure *VERB* **figures, figuring, figured** appear or take part in something • *She figures in some of the stories about King Arthur.*
- **figure out** work something out.
[from Latin]

figurehead *NOUN* **figureheads** **1** a carved figure decorating the prow of a sailing ship. **2** a person who is head of a country or organization but has no real power.

figure of speech *NOUN* **figures of speech** a word or phrase used for special effect and not intended literally, e.g. *'flood of letters'*.

filament *NOUN* **filaments** a thread or thin wire, especially one in a light bulb.
[from Latin *filum* = thread]

filch *VERB* **filches, filching, filched** steal something slyly; pilfer.
[origin unknown]

file[1] *NOUN* **files** a metal tool with a rough surface that is rubbed on things to shape them or make them smooth.

file *VERB* **files, filing, filed** shape or smooth something with a file.
[from Old English]

file[2] *NOUN* **files** **1** a folder or box etc. for keeping papers in order. **2** a collection of data stored under one name in a computer. **3** a line of people one behind the other.

file *VERB* **files, filing, filed** **1** put something into a file. **2** walk in a file • *They filed out.*
[from Latin *filum* = thread (because a string or wire was put through papers to hold them in order)]

filial (*say* fil-ee-al) *ADJECTIVE* to do with a son or daughter.
[from Latin *filius* = son, *filia* = daughter]

filibuster *VERB* **filibusters, filibustering, filibustered** try to delay or prevent the passing of a law by making long speeches.
▷ **filibuster** *noun*
[from Dutch *vrijbuiter* = pirate]

filigree *NOUN* ornamental lace-like work of twisted metal wire.
[from Latin *filum* = thread + *granum* = grain]

filings *PLURAL NOUN* tiny pieces of metal rubbed off by a file • *iron filings.*

fill *VERB* **fills, filling, filled** **1** make or become full. **2** block up a hole or cavity. **3** hold a position, or appoint a person to a vacant post.
▷ **filler** *noun*
- **fill in** put answers or other information in a form or document.

fill *NOUN* enough to fill a person or thing • *We ate our fill.*
[from Old English]

fillet *NOUN* **fillets** a piece of fish or meat without bones.

fillet *VERB* **fillets, filleting, filleted** remove the bones from fish or meat.
[from French]

filling *NOUN* **fillings** **1** something used to fill a hole or gap, e.g. in a tooth. **2** something put in pastry to make a pie, or between layers of bread to make a sandwich.

filling station *NOUN* **filling stations** a place where petrol is sold from pumps.

filly *NOUN* **fillies** a young female horse.
[from Old Norse]

film *NOUN* **films** **1** a motion picture, such as those shown in cinemas or on television. **2** a rolled strip or sheet of thin plastic coated with material that is sensitive to light, used for taking photographs or making a motion picture. **3** a very thin layer • *a film of grease.*

film *VERB* **films, filming, filmed** record something on film; make a film of a story etc.
[from Old English *filmen* = thin skin]

filmy *ADJECTIVE* **filmier, filmiest** thin and almost transparent.
▷ **filminess** *noun*

filter *NOUN* **filters** **1** a device for holding back dirt or other unwanted material from a liquid or gas etc. that passes through it. **2** a system for filtering traffic.

filter *VERB* **filters, filtering, filtered** **1** pass through a filter. **2** move gradually • *They filtered into the hall; News began to filter out.* **3** move in a particular direction while other traffic is held up.
[from old French]

filth *NOUN* disgusting dirt.
[from Old English]

filthy *ADJECTIVE* **filthier, filthiest** 1 disgustingly dirty. 2 obscene or offensive.
▷ **filthiness** *noun*

fin *NOUN* **fins** 1 a thin flat part sticking out from a fish's body, that helps it to swim. 2 a small part that sticks out on an aircraft or rocket, for helping its balance.
[from Old English]

final *ADJECTIVE* 1 coming at the end; last. 2 that puts an end to an argument etc. • *You must go, and that's final!*
▷ **finally** *adverb* **finality** *noun*

final *NOUN* **finals** the last in a series of contests.
[from Latin *finis* = end]

finale (*say* fin-ah-lee) *NOUN* **finales** the final section of a piece of music or entertainment.
[Italian; related to *final*]

finalist *NOUN* **finalists** a competitor in a final.

finalize *VERB* **finalizes, finalizing, finalized** put something into its final form.
▷ **finalization** *noun*

finance *NOUN* 1 the use or management of money. 2 the money used to pay for something.
- **finances** *plural noun* money resources; funds.

finance *VERB* **finances, financing, financed** provide the money for something.
▷ **financier** *noun*
[from old French *finer* = settle a debt]

financial *ADJECTIVE* to do with finance.
▷ **financially** *adverb*

finch *NOUN* **finches** a small bird with a short stubby bill.
[from Old English]

find *VERB* **finds, finding, found** 1 get or see something by looking for it or by chance. 2 learn something by experience • *He found that digging was hard work.* 3 decide and give a verdict • *The jury found him guilty.*
- **find out** get or discover some information.

find *NOUN* **finds** something found.
[from Old English]

findings *PLURAL NOUN* the conclusions reached from an investigation.

fine[1] *ADJECTIVE* 1 of high quality; excellent. 2 dry and clear; sunny • *fine weather.* 3 very thin; consisting of small particles. 4 in good health; well • *I'm fine.*
▷ **finely** *adverb* **fineness** *noun*

fine *ADVERB* 1 finely • *chop it fine.* 2 (*informal*) very well • *That will suit me fine.*
[same origin as *finish*]

fine[2] *NOUN* **fines** money which has to be paid as a punishment.

fine *VERB* **fines, fining, fined** make somebody pay a fine.
[from Latin *finis* = end (in the Middle Ages it referred to the sum paid to settle a lawsuit)]

fine arts *PLURAL NOUN* painting, sculpture, and music.

finery *NOUN* fine clothes or decorations.

finesse (*say* fin-ess) *NOUN* skill and elegance in doing something.
[French, = fineness]

finger *NOUN* **fingers** 1 one of the separate parts of the hand. 2 a narrow piece of something • *fish fingers.*

finger *VERB* **fingers, fingering, fingered** touch or feel something with your fingers.
[from Old English]

fingernail *NOUN* **fingernails** the hard covering at the end of a finger.

fingerprint *NOUN* **fingerprints** a mark made by the tiny ridges on the fingertip, used as a way of identifying someone.

fingertip *NOUN* **fingertips** the tip of a finger.
- **have something at your fingertips** be very familiar with a subject etc.

finicky *ADJECTIVE* fussy about details; hard to please.
[origin unknown]

finish *VERB* **finishes, finishing, finished** bring or come to an end.

finish *NOUN* **finishes** 1 the last stage of something; the end. 2 the surface or coating on woodwork etc.
[from Latin *finis* = end]

finite (*say* fy-nyt) *ADJECTIVE* limited; not infinite • *We have only a finite supply of coal.*
[from Latin *finitus* = finished]

A B C D E F G H I J K L M N O P Q R S T U V W X Y Z

finite verb *NOUN* **finite verbs** a verb that agrees with its subject in person and number; 'was', 'went', and 'says' are finite verbs; 'going' and 'to say' are not.

fiord (*say* fee-**ord**) *NOUN* **fiords** an inlet of the sea between high cliffs, as in Norway. [Norwegian]

fir *NOUN* **firs** an evergreen tree with needle-like leaves, that produces cones. [from Old Norse]

fire *NOUN* **fires 1** the process of burning that produces light and heat. **2** coal and wood etc. burning in a grate or furnace to give heat. **3** a device using electricity or gas to heat a room. **4** the shooting of guns • *Hold your fire!*
- **on fire** burning.
- **set fire to** start something burning.

fire *VERB* **fires, firing, fired 1** set fire to. **2** bake pottery or bricks etc. in a kiln. **3** shoot a gun; send out a bullet or missile. **4** dismiss someone from a job. **5** excite • *fire them with enthusiasm.*
▷ **firer** *noun*
[from Old English]

firearm *NOUN* **firearms** a small gun; a rifle, pistol, or revolver.

firebrand *NOUN* **firebrands** a person who stirs up trouble.

fire brigade *NOUN* **fire brigades** a team of people organized to fight fires.

fire drill *NOUN* **fire drills** a rehearsal of the procedure that needs to be followed in case of a fire.

fire engine *NOUN* **fire engines** a large vehicle that carries firefighters and equipment to put out large fires.

fire escape *NOUN* **fire escapes** a special staircase by which people may escape from a burning building.

fire extinguisher *NOUN* **fire extinguishers** a metal cylinder from which water or foam can be sprayed to put out a fire.

firefighter *NOUN* **firefighters** a member of a fire brigade.

firefly *NOUN* **fireflies** a kind of beetle that gives off a glowing light.

fireman *NOUN* **firemen** a member of a fire brigade.

fireplace *NOUN* **fireplaces** an open structure for holding a fire in a room.

fireside *NOUN* **firesides** the part of the room near a fireplace.

firewood *NOUN* wood for use as fuel.

firework *NOUN* **fireworks** a device containing chemicals that burn or explode attractively and noisily.

firing squad *NOUN* **firing squads** a group of soldiers given the duty of shooting a condemned person.

firm *NOUN* **firms** a business organization.

firm *ADJECTIVE* **1** not giving way when pressed; hard or solid. **2** steady; not shaking or moving. **3** definite and not likely to change • *a firm belief.*
▷ **firmly** *adverb* **firmness** *noun*

firm *ADVERB* firmly • *Stand firm!*

firm *VERB* **firms, firming, firmed** make something become firm.
[from Latin]

firmament *NOUN* (*poetical use*) the sky with its clouds and stars.
[same origin as *firm*]

first *ADJECTIVE* coming before all others in time or order or importance.
▷ **firstly** *adverb*

first *ADVERB* before everything else • *Finish this work first.*

first *NOUN* **firsts** a person or thing that is first.
[from Old English]

first aid *NOUN* treatment given to an injured person before a doctor comes.

first-class *ADJECTIVE* **1** using the best class of a sevice • *first-class post.* **2** excellent.

first-hand *ADJECTIVE* & *ADVERB* obtained directly, rather than from other people or from books • *first-hand experience.*

firth *NOUN* **firths** an estuary or inlet of the sea on the coast of Scotland.
[from Old Norse *fjorthr* = fiord]

fiscal *ADJECTIVE* to do with public finances.
[from Latin *fiscus* = treasury]

fish *NOUN* **fish** or **fishes** an animal with gills and fins that always lives and breathes in water.

fish *VERB* **fishes, fishing, fished 1** try to catch fish. **2** search for something; try to get something • *He is only fishing for compliments.*
[from Old English]

fisherman *NOUN* **fishermen** a person who tries to catch fish.

fishery *NOUN* **fisheries 1** the part of the sea where fishing is carried on. **2** the business of fishing.

fishmonger *NOUN* **fishmongers** a shopkeeper who sells fish.
[from *fish* + an old word *monger* = trader]

fishy *ADJECTIVE* **fishier, fishiest 1** smelling or tasting of fish. **2** (*informal*) causing doubt or suspicion • *a fishy excuse.*
▷ **fishily** *adverb* **fishiness** *noun*

fissile *ADJECTIVE* **1** likely to split. **2** capable of undergoing nuclear fission.
[same origin as *fission*]

fission *NOUN* **1** splitting something. **2** splitting the nucleus of an atom so as to release energy.
[from Latin *fissum* = split]

fissure (*say* **fish**-er) *NOUN* **fissures** a narrow opening made where something splits.
[same origin as *fission*]

fist *NOUN* **fists** a tightly closed hand with the fingers bent into the palm.
[from Old English]

fisticuffs *NOUN* (*old use*) fighting with the fists.
[from *fist* + *cuff* = slap]

fit[1] *ADJECTIVE* **fitter, fittest 1** suitable or good enough • *a meal fit for a king.* **2** healthy, in good physical condition • *Keep fit!* **3** ready or likely • *They worked till they were fit to collapse.*
▷ **fitness** *noun*

fit *VERB* **fits, fitting, fitted 1** be the right size and shape for something; be suitable. **2** put something into place • *Fit a lock on the door.* **3** alter something to make it the right size and shape. **4** make suitable for something • *His training fits him for the job.*
▷ **fitter** *noun*

fit *NOUN* the way something fits • *a good fit.*
[origin unknown]

fit[2] *NOUN* **fits 1** a sudden illness, especially one that makes you move violently or become unconscious. **2** an outburst • *a fit of rage.*
[from Old English]

fitful *ADJECTIVE* happening in short periods, not steadily.
▷ **fitfully** *adverb*
[from *fit*[2] + *-ful*]

fitment *NOUN* **fitments** a piece of fixed furniture etc.
[from *fit*[1]]

fitting *ADJECTIVE* proper or appropriate • *This statue is a fitting memorial to an extraordinary woman.*

fitting *NOUN* **fittings** having a piece of clothing fitted • *I needed several fittings.*

fittings *PLURAL NOUN* the fixtures and fitments of a building.

five *NOUN* & *ADJECTIVE* **fives** the number 5.
[from Old English]

fiver *NOUN* **fivers** (*informal*) a five-pound note; £5.

fives *NOUN* a game in which a ball is hit with gloved hands or a bat against the walls of a court.
[origin unknown]

fix *VERB* **fixes, fixing, fixed 1** fasten or place firmly. **2** make permanent and unable to change. **3** decide or arrange • *We fixed a date for the party.* **4** repair; put into working condition • *He is fixing my bike.*
▷ **fixer** *noun*
– **fix up** arrange or organize something.

fix *NOUN* **fixes 1** (*informal*) an awkward situation • *I'm in a fix.* **2** finding the position of something, by using a compass, radar, etc. **3** (*slang*) an addict's dose of a drug.
[from Latin]

fixation *NOUN* **fixations** a strong interest or a concentration on one idea etc.; an obsession.

fixative *NOUN* **fixatives** a substance used to keep something in position or make it permanent.

fixedly *ADVERB* with a fixed expression.

fixity *NOUN* a fixed condition; permanence.

fixture *NOUN* **fixtures** **1** something fixed in its place. **2** a sports event planned for a particular day.

fizz *VERB* **fizzes, fizzing, fizzed** make a hissing or spluttering sound; produce a lot of small bubbles.
[imitating the sound]

fizzle *VERB* **fizzles, fizzling, fizzled** make a slight fizzing sound.
- **fizzle out** end feebly or unsuccessfully.
[from *fizz*]

fizzy *ADJECTIVE* (said about a drink) having a lot of small bubbles.
▷ **fizziness** *noun*

fjord (*say* fee-ord) *NOUN* **fjords** a different spelling of *fiord*.

flabbergasted *ADJECTIVE* greatly astonished.
[origin unknown]

flabby *ADJECTIVE* fat and soft, not firm.
▷ **flabbily** *adverb* **flabbiness** *noun*
[related to *flap*]

flaccid (*say* flass-id or flak-sid) *ADJECTIVE* soft and limp.
▷ **flaccidly** *adverb* **flaccidity** *noun*
[from Latin *flaccus* = flabby]

flag[1] *NOUN* **flags** **1** a piece of cloth with a coloured pattern or shape on it, used as a sign or signal. **2** a small piece of paper or plastic that looks like a flag.
▷ **flagpole** *noun* **flagstaff** *noun*

flag *VERB* **flags, flagging, flagged** **1** become weak; droop. **2** signal with a flag or by waving.
[from an old word *flag* = drooping]

flag[2] *NOUN* **flags** a flagstone.
[from Old Norse *flaga* = slab of stone]

flagon *NOUN* **flagons** a large bottle or container for wine or cider etc.
[from Latin *flasco* = flask]

flagrant (*say* flay-grant) *ADJECTIVE* very bad and noticeable • *flagrant disobedience.*
▷ **flagrantly** *adverb* **flagrancy** *noun*
[from Latin *flagrans* = blazing]

flagship *NOUN* **flagships** **1** a ship that carries an admiral and flies his flag. **2** a company's best or most important product, store, etc.

flagstone *NOUN* **flagstones** a flat slab of stone used for paving.
[from *flag*[2] + *stone*]

flail *NOUN* **flails** an old-fashioned tool for threshing grain.

flail *VERB* **flails, flailing, flailed** beat as if with a flail; wave about wildly.
[from Latin *flagellum* = a whip]

flair *NOUN* a natural ability or talent • *Ian has a flair for languages.*
[French, = power to smell things]
USAGE Do not confuse with **flare**.

flak *NOUN* **1** shells fired by anti-aircraft guns. **2** strong criticism.
[short for German *Fliegerabwehrkanone* = aircraft- defence- cannon]

flake *NOUN* **flakes** **1** a very light thin piece of something. **2** a small flat piece of falling snow.
▷ **flaky** *adjective*

flake *VERB* **flakes, flaking, flaked** come off in flakes.
[origin unknown]

flamboyant *ADJECTIVE* very showy in appearance or manner.

flamboyant *NOUN* **flamboyants** a tree from Madagascar with bright red flowers, often planted as a street tree in tropical countries.
[from French, meaning 'flaming, blazing']

flame *NOUN* **flames** a tongue-shaped portion of fire or burning gas.

flame *VERB* **flames, flaming, flamed** **1** produce flames. **2** become bright red.
[from old French]

flamenco (*say* fla-menk-oh) *NOUN* **flamencos** a lively Spanish style of guitar playing and dance.
[from Spanish, = Flemish, 'like a gypsy']

flamingo *NOUN* **flamingoes** a wading bird with long legs, a long neck, and pinkish feathers.
[from Spanish]

flammable *ADJECTIVE* able to be set on fire.
▷ **flammability** *noun*
[from Latin *flamma* = flame]
USAGE See note at **inflammable**.

flan *NOUN* **flans** a pastry or sponge shell with no cover over the filling.
[French]

flank *NOUN* **flanks** the side of something, especially an animal's body or an army.

flank *VERB* **flanks, flanking, flanked** be positioned at the side of something.
▷ **flanker** *noun*
[from old French]

flannel *NOUN* **flannels 1** a soft cloth for washing yourself. **2** a soft woollen material.
[from Welsh *gwlanen* = woollen]

flap *VERB* **flaps, flapping, flapped 1** wave about. **2** (*informal*) panic or fuss about something.

flap *NOUN* **flaps 1** a part that is fixed at one edge onto something else, often to cover an opening. **2** the action or sound of flapping. **3** (*informal*) a panic or fuss • *Don't get in a flap.*
[imitating the sound]

flapjack *NOUN* a cake made from oats and golden syrup.
[from *flap* + the name *Jack*]

flare *VERB* **flares, flaring, flared 1** blaze with a sudden bright flame. **2** become angry suddenly. **3** become gradually wider • *flaring nostrils.*

flare *NOUN* **flares 1** a sudden bright flame or light, especially one used as a signal. **2** a gradual widening, especially in skirts or trousers.
[origin unknown]
USAGE Do not confuse with **flair**.

flash *NOUN* **flashes 1** a sudden bright flame or light. **2** a device for making a sudden bright light for taking photographs. **3** a sudden display of anger, wit, etc. **4** a short item of news.

flash *VERB* **flashes, flashing, flashed 1** make a flash. **2** appear suddenly; move quickly • *The train flashed past us.*
[origin unknown]

flashback *NOUN* **flashbacks** going back in a film or story to something that happened earlier.

flashy *ADJECTIVE* gaudy or showy.

flask *NOUN* **flasks 1** a bottle with a narrow neck. **2** a vacuum flask.
[via Old English from Latin; related to *flagon*]

flat *ADJECTIVE* **flatter, flattest 1** with no curves or bumps; smooth and level. **2** spread out; lying at full length • *Lie flat on the ground.* **3** (said about a tyre) with no air inside. **4** (said about feet) without the normal arch underneath. **5** absolute • *a flat refusal.* **6** dull; not changing. **7** (said about a drink) no longer fizzy. **8** (said about a battery) unable to produce any more electric current. **9** (*in music*) one semitone lower than the natural note • *E flat.*
▷ **flatly** *adverb* **flatness** *noun*

flat *ADVERB* **1** so as to be flat • *Press it flat.* **2** (*informal*) exactly • *in ten seconds flat.* **3** (*in music*) below the correct pitch.
– **flat out** as fast as possible.

flat *NOUN* **flats 1** a set of rooms for living in, usually on one floor of a building. **2** (*in music*) a note one semitone lower than the natural note; the sign (♭) that indicates this. **3** a punctured tyre.
[from Old Norse]

flatten *VERB* **flattens, flattening, flattened** make or become flat.

flatter *VERB* **flatters, flattering, flattered 1** praise somebody more than he or she deserves. **2** make a person or thing seem better or more attractive than they really are.
▷ **flatterer** *noun* **flattery** *noun*
[from Old French *flater* = smooth down]

flaunt *VERB* **flaunts, flaunting, flaunted** display something proudly in a way that annoys people; show it off • *He liked to flaunt his expensive clothes and cars.*
[origin unknown]
USAGE Do not confuse this word with **flout**, which has a different meaning.

flavour *NOUN* **flavours** the taste of something.

flavour *VERB* **flavours, flavouring, flavoured** give something a flavour; season it.
▷ **flavouring** *noun*
[from old French]

flaw *NOUN* **flaws** something that makes a person or thing imperfect.
▷ **flawed** *adjective*
[origin unknown]

flawless *ADJECTIVE* without a flaw; perfect.
▷ **flawlessly** *adverb* **flawlessness** *noun*

flax *NOUN* a plant that produces fibres from which linen is made and seeds from which linseed oil is obtained.
[from Old English]

flaxen *ADJECTIVE* pale yellow like flax fibres • *flaxen hair.*

flay *VERB* **flays, flaying, flayed** strip the skin from an animal.
[from Old English]

flea *NOUN* **fleas** a small jumping insect that sucks blood.
[from Old English]

flea market *NOUN* **flea markets** a street market that sells cheap or second-hand goods.

fleck *NOUN* **flecks** **1** a very small patch of colour. **2** a particle; a speck • *flecks of dirt.*
▷ **flecked** *adjective*
[origin unknown]

fledged *ADJECTIVE* (said about young birds) having grown feathers and able to fly.
[from Old English]

fledgeling *NOUN* **fledgelings** a young bird that is just fledged.
[from *fledge* = become fledged, + *-ling*]

flee *VERB* **flees, fleeing, fled** run or hurry away from something.
[from Old English]

fleece *NOUN* **fleeces** **1** the woolly hair of a sheep or similar animal. **2** a warm piece of clothing made from a soft fabric.
▷ **fleecy** *adjective*

fleece *VERB* **fleeces, fleecing, fleeced** **1** shear the fleece from a sheep. **2** swindle a person out of some money.
[from Old English]

fleet[1] *NOUN* **fleets** a number of ships, aircraft, or vehicles owned by one country or company.
[from Old English]

fleet[2] *ADJECTIVE* moving swiftly; nimble.
[from Old Norse]

fleeting *ADJECTIVE* passing quickly; brief.

Flemish *ADJECTIVE* to do with Flanders in Belgium or its people or language.
▷ **Flemish** *noun*

flesh *NOUN* **1** the soft substance of the bodies of people and animals, consisting of muscle and fat. **2** the body as opposed to the mind or soul. **3** the pulpy part of fruits and vegetables.
▷ **fleshy** *adjective*
[from Old English]

flex *VERB* **flexes, flexing, flexed** bend or stretch something that is flexible • *Try flexing your muscles.*

flex *NOUN* **flexes** flexible insulated wire for carrying electric current.
[from Latin *flexum* = bent]

flexible *ADJECTIVE* **1** easy to bend or stretch. **2** able to be changed or adapted • *Our plans are flexible.*
▷ **flexibility** *noun*

flick *NOUN* **flicks** a quick light hit or movement.

flick *VERB* **flicks, flicking, flicked** hit or move with a flick.
[from Middle English]

flicker *VERB* **flickers, flickering, flickered** **1** burn or shine unsteadily. **2** move quickly to and fro.

flicker *NOUN* **flickers** a flickering light or movement.
[from Old English]

flick knife *NOUN* **flick knives** a knife with a blade that springs out when a button is pressed.

flier *NOUN* **fliers** a different spelling of *flyer*.

flight[1] *NOUN* **flights** **1** flying. **2** a journey in an aircraft. **3** a series of stairs. **4** a group of flying birds or aircraft. **5** the feathers or fins on a dart or arrow.
[from Old English]

flight[2] *NOUN* **flights** fleeing; an escape.
[from Middle English]

flight recorder *NOUN* **flight recorders** an electronic device in an aircraft that records technical information about its flight. It may be used after an accident to help find the cause.

flighty *ADJECTIVE* **flightier, flightiest** silly and frivolous.
▷ **flightiness** *noun*
[from *flight*[1]]

flimsy *ADJECTIVE* **flimsier, flimsiest** made of something thin or weak.
▷ **flimsily** *adverb* **flimsiness** *noun*
[origin unknown]

flinch *VERB* **flinches, flinching, flinched** move or shrink back because you are afraid; wince.
▷ **flinch** *noun*
[via old French from Germanic]

fling *VERB* **flings, flinging, flung** throw something violently or carelessly.

fling *NOUN* **flings** **1** a short time of enjoyment • *a final fling before the exams.* **2** a brief romantic affair. **3** a vigorous dance • *the Highland fling.*
[origin unknown]

flint *NOUN* **flints** **1** a very hard kind of stone. **2** a piece of flint or hard metal used to produce sparks.
▷ **flinty** *adjective*
[from Old English]

flip *VERB* **flips, flipping, flipped** **1** flick. **2** (*slang*) become crazy or very angry.

flip *NOUN* **flips** a flipping movement.
[origin unknown]

flippant *ADJECTIVE* not showing proper seriousness.
▷ **flippantly** *adverb* **flippancy** *noun*
[from *flip*]

flipper *NOUN* **flippers** **1** a limb that water animals use for swimming. **2** a kind of flat rubber shoe, shaped like a duck's foot, that you wear on your feet to help you to swim.
[from *flip*]

flirt *VERB* **flirts, flirting, flirted** **1** behave as though you are sexually attracted to someone to amuse yourself. **2** take an interest in an idea without being too serious about it.
- **flirt with danger** or **death** risk danger.
▷ **flirtation** *noun*

flirt *NOUN* **flirts** a person who flirts.
▷ **flirtatious** *adjective* **flirtatiously** *adverb*
[origin unknown]

flit *VERB* **flits, flitting, flitted** fly or move lightly and quickly.
▷ **flit** *noun*
[from Old Norse]

flitter *VERB* **flitters, flittering, flittered** flit about.
▷ **flitter** *noun*

float *VERB* **floats, floating, floated** **1** stay or move on the surface of a liquid or in air. **2** make something float. **3** launch a business by getting financial support from the sale of shares.
▷ **floater** *noun*

float *NOUN* **floats** **1** a device designed to float. **2** a vehicle with a platform used for delivering milk or for carrying a display in a parade etc. **3** a small amount of money kept for paying small bills or giving change etc.
[from Old English]

floating voter *NOUN* **floating voters** a person who does not support any political party permanently.

flock[1] *NOUN* **flocks** a group of sheep, goats, or birds.

flock *VERB* **flocks, flocking, flocked** gather or move in a crowd.
[from Old English]

flock[2] *NOUN* **flocks** a tuft of wool or cotton etc.
[from Latin]

floe *NOUN* **floes** a sheet of floating ice.
[from Norwegian *flo* = layer]

flog *VERB* **flogs, flogging, flogged** **1** beat a person or animal hard with a whip or stick as a punishment. **2** (*slang*) sell.
▷ **flogging** *noun*
[from Latin]

flood *NOUN* **floods** **1** a large amount of water spreading over a place that is usually dry. **2** a great amount • *a flood of requests.* **3** the movement of the tide when it is coming in towards the land.

flood *VERB* **floods, flooding, flooded** **1** cover with a flood. **2** come in great amounts • *Letters flooded in.*
[from Old English]

floodlight *NOUN* **floodlights** a lamp that makes a broad bright beam to light up a stage, stadium, important building, etc.
▷ **floodlit** *adjective*

A B C D E F G H I J K L M N O P Q R S T U V W X Y Z

floor *NOUN* **floors** **1** the part of a room that people walk on. **2** a storey of a building; all the rooms at the same level.
USAGE In Britain, the *ground floor* of a building is the one at street level, and the one above it is the *first floor*. In the USA, the *first floor* is the one at street level, and the one above it is the *second floor*.

floor *VERB* **floors, flooring, floored** **1** put a floor into a building. **2** knock a person down. **3** baffle somebody.
[from Old English]

floorboard *NOUN* **floorboards** one of the boards forming the floor of a room.

flop *VERB* **flops, flopping, flopped** **1** fall or sit down clumsily. **2** hang or sway heavily and loosely. **3** (*slang*) be a failure.

flop *NOUN* **flops** **1** a flopping movement or sound. **2** (*slang*) a failure.
[a different spelling of *flap*]

floppy *ADJECTIVE* hanging loosely; not firm or rigid.
▷ **floppiness** *noun*

floppy disk *NOUN* **floppy disks** a flexible disc holding data for use in a computer.

flora *NOUN* the plants of a particular area or period. (COMPARE **fauna**)
[from the name of *Flora*, the ancient Roman goddess of flowers; her name comes from Latin *flores* = flowers]

floral *ADJECTIVE* to do with flowers.
[same origin as *flora*]

florid (*say* flo-rid) *ADJECTIVE* **1** red and flushed • *a florid complexion.* **2** elaborate and ornate • *florid language.*
[same origin as *flora*]

florin *NOUN* **florins** **1** a former British coin worth two shillings (10p). **2** a Dutch guilder.
[from Italian *fiore* = flower; the name was originally given to an Italian coin which had a lily on one side]

florist *NOUN* **florists** a shopkeeper who sells flowers.
[same origin as *flora*]

floss *NOUN* **1** silky thread or fibres. **2** a soft medicated thread pulled between the teeth to clean them.
▷ **flossy** *adjective*
[from old French]

flotation *NOUN* **flotations** **1** offering shares in a company on the stock market in order to launch or finance it. **2** floating something.

flotilla (*say* flot-il-a) *NOUN* **flotillas** a fleet of boats or small ships.
[Spanish, = little fleet]

flotsam *NOUN* wreckage or cargo found floating after a shipwreck.
- **flotsam and jetsam** odds and ends.
[from old French *floter* = float]

flounce[1] *VERB* **flounces, flouncing, flounced** go in an impatient or annoyed manner • *She flounced out of the room.*
▷ **flounce** *noun*
[origin unknown]

flounce[2] *NOUN* **flounces** a wide frill.
[from old French]

flounder[1] *VERB* **flounders, floundering, floundered** **1** move clumsily and with difficulty. **2** make mistakes or become confused when trying to do something.
[from old French]

flounder[2] *NOUN* **flounder** a small flat edible sea fish.
[from Old French]

flour *NOUN* a fine powder of wheat or other grain, used in cooking.
▷ **floury** *adjective*
[old spelling of *flower*]

flourish *VERB* **flourishes, flourishing, flourished** **1** grow or develop strongly. **2** be successful; prosper. **3** wave something about dramatically.

flourish *NOUN* **flourishes** a showy or dramatic sweeping movement, curve, or passage of music.
[from Latin *florere* = to flower]

flout *VERB* **flouts, flouting, flouted** disobey a rule or instruction openly and scornfully • *She shaved her head one day, just because she loved to flout convention.*
[probably from Dutch *fluiten* = whistle, hiss]
USAGE Do not confuse this word with **flaunt**, which has a different meaning.

flow *VERB* **flows, flowing, flowed** **1** move along smoothly or continuously. **2** gush out • *Water flowed from the tap.* **3** hang loosely • *flowing hair.* **4** (said about the tide) come in towards the land.

flow *NOUN* **flows** **1** a flowing movement or mass. **2** a steady continuous stream of something • *a flow of ideas.* **3** the movement of the tide when it is coming in towards the land • *the ebb and flow of the tide.*
[from Old English]

flow chart *NOUN* **flow charts** a diagram that shows how the different stages of a process or parts of a system are connected.

flower *NOUN* **flowers** **1** the part of a plant from which seed and fruit develops. **2** a blossom and its stem used for decoration, usually in groups. (COMPARE **flora**)

flower *VERB* **flowers, flowering, flowered** produce flowers.
[from old French; related to *flora*]

flowerpot *NOUN* **flowerpots** a pot in which a plant may be grown.

flowery *ADJECTIVE* **1** full of flowers. **2** (said about language) elaborate, full of ornamental phrases.

flu *NOUN* influenza.

fluctuate *VERB* **fluctuates, fluctuating, fluctuated** rise and fall; vary • *Prices fluctuated.*
▷ **fluctuation** *noun*
[from Latin *fluctus* = a wave]

flue *NOUN* **flues** a pipe or tube through which smoke or hot gases are drawn off.
[origin unknown]

fluent (*say* floo-ent) *ADJECTIVE* **1** skilful at speaking clearly and without hesitating. **2** able to speak a foreign language easily and well.
▷ **fluently** *adverb* **fluency** *noun*
[from Latin *fluens* = flowing]

fluff *NOUN* a fluffy substance.

fluff *VERB* **fluffs, fluffing, fluffed** (*informal*) make a mistake.
- **fluff up** make something softer and rounder by patting it.
[probably from Flemish]

fluffy *ADJECTIVE* having a mass of soft fur or fibres.
▷ **fluffiness** *noun*

fluid *NOUN* **fluids** a substance that is able to flow freely as liquids and gases do.

fluid *ADJECTIVE* **1** able to flow freely. **2** not fixed • *My plans for Christmas are fluid.*
▷ **fluidity** *noun*
[from Latin *fluere* = to flow]

fluke *NOUN* **flukes** a success that you achieve by unexpected good luck.
[origin unknown]

flummox *VERB* **flummoxes, flummoxing, flummoxed** (*informal*) baffle.
[origin unknown]

fluorescent (*say* floo-er-ess-ent) *ADJECTIVE* creating light from radiation • *a fluorescent lamp.*
▷ **fluorescence** *noun*
[from *fluorspar*, a fluorescent mineral]

fluoridation *NOUN* adding fluoride to drinking water in order to help prevent tooth decay.

fluoride *NOUN* a chemical substance that is thought to prevent tooth decay.
[from Latin]

flurry *NOUN* **flurries** **1** a sudden whirling gust of wind, rain, or snow. **2** a short period of activity or excitement.
[from an old word *flurr* = to throw about]

flush[1] *VERB* **flushes, flushing, flushed** **1** blush. **2** clean or remove something with a fast flow of water.

flush *NOUN* **flushes** **1** a blush. **2** a fast flow of water. **3** (in card games) a hand of cards of the same suit.
[imitating the sound of water]

flush[2] *ADJECTIVE* **1** level with the surrounding surface • *The doors are flush with the walls.* **2** having plenty of money.
[origin unknown]

fluster *VERB* **flusters, flustering, flustered** make somebody nervous and confused.
▷ **fluster** *noun*
[origin unknown]

flute *NOUN* **flutes** a musical instrument consisting of a long pipe with holes that are stopped by fingers or keys.
[from old French]

flutter *VERB* **flutters, fluttering, fluttered** **1** flap wings quickly. **2** move or flap quickly and irregularly.

flutter *NOUN* **flutters** **1** a fluttering movement. **2** a nervously excited condition. **3** (*informal*) a small bet • *Have a flutter!*
[from Old English]

flux *NOUN* **fluxes** continual change or flow.
[from Latin *fluxus* = flowing]

fly[1] *NOUN* **flies** **1** a small flying insect with two wings. **2** a real or artificial fly used as bait in fishing.
[from Old English *flycge*]

fly[2] *VERB* **flies, flying, flew, flown** **1** move through the air by means of wings or in an aircraft. **2** travel through the air or through space. **3** wave in the air • *Flags were flying.* **4** make something fly • *They flew model aircraft.* **5** move or pass quickly • *Time flies.* **6** flee from • *You must fly the country!*
▷ **flyer** *noun*

fly *NOUN* **flies** the front opening of a pair of trousers.
[from Old English *fleogan*]

flying saucer *NOUN* **flying saucers** a mysterious saucer-shaped object reported to have been seen in the sky and believed by some people to be an alien spacecraft.

flying squad *NOUN* **flying squads** a team of police officers organized so that they can move rapidly.

flyleaf *NOUN* **flyleaves** a blank page at the beginning or end of a book.

flyover *NOUN* **flyovers** a bridge that carries one road or railway over another.

flywheel *NOUN* **flywheels** a heavy wheel used to regulate machinery.

foal *NOUN* **foals** a young horse.

foal *VERB* **foals, foaling, foaled** give birth to a foal.
[from Old English]

foam *NOUN* **1** a white mass of tiny bubbles on a liquid; froth. **2** a spongy kind of rubber or plastic.
▷ **foamy** *adjective*

foam *VERB* **foams, foaming, foamed** form bubbles or froth.
[from Old English]

fob[1] *NOUN* **fobs** **1** a chain for a pocket watch. **2** a tab on a key ring.
[probably from German]

fob[2] *VERB* **fobs, fobbing, fobbed**
- **fob off** get rid of someone by an excuse or a trick.
[from German]

focal *ADJECTIVE* to do with or at a focus.

focus *NOUN* **focuses** or **foci** **1** the distance from an eye or lens at which an object appears clearest. **2** the point at which rays etc. seem to meet. **3** something that is a centre of interest or attention etc.
- **in focus** appearing clearly.
- **out of focus** not appearing clearly.

focus *VERB* **focuses, focusing, focused** **1** adjust the focus of your eye or a lens so that objects appear clearly. **2** concentrate • *She focused her attention on it.*
[Latin, = hearth (the central point of a household)]

fodder *NOUN* food for horses and farm animals.
[from Old English]

foe *NOUN* **foes** (*old use*) an enemy.
[from Old English]

foetus (*say* fee-tus) *NOUN* **foetuses** a developing embryo, especially an unborn human baby.
▷ **foetal** *adjective*
[Latin]

fog *NOUN* thick mist.
▷ **foggy** *adjective*
[origin unknown]

foghorn *NOUN* **foghorns** a loud horn for warning ships in fog.

fogy *NOUN* **fogies** - **old fogy** a person with old-fashioned ideas.
[origin unknown]

foible *NOUN* **foibles** a slight peculiarity in someone's character or tastes.
[from old French; related to *feeble*]

foil[1] *NOUN* **foils** **1** a very thin sheet of metal. **2** a person or thing that makes another look better in contrast.
[same origin as *foliage*]

foil[2] *NOUN* **foils** a long narrow sword used in the sport of fencing.
[origin unknown]

foil[3] *VERB* **foils, foiling, foiled** prevent something from being successful • *We foiled his evil plan.*
[from old French *fouler* = trample]

foist *VERB* **foists, foisting, foisted** make a person accept something inferior or unwelcome • *They foisted the job on me.* [from Dutch]

fold[1] *VERB* **folds, folding, folded** bend or move so that one part lies on another part.

fold *NOUN* **folds** a line where something is folded.
[from Old English *fealdan*]

fold[2] *NOUN* **folds** an enclosure for sheep.
[from Old English *fald*]

-fold *SUFFIX* forms adjectives and adverbs meaning 'multiplied by' (e.g. *twofold, fourfold, manifold*).
[from Old English]

folder *NOUN* **folders** a folding cover for loose papers.

foliage *NOUN* the leaves of a tree or plant.
[from Latin *folium* = leaf]

folk *PLURAL NOUN* people.
[from Old English]

folk dance *NOUNS* **folk dances** a dance in the traditional style of a country.

folklore *NOUN* old beliefs and legends.

folk music *NOUN* the traditional music of a country.

folk song *NOUN* **folk songs** a song in the traditional style of a country.

follow *VERB* **follows, following, followed** **1** go or come after. **2** do a thing after something else. **3** take a person or thing as a guide or example. **4** take an interest in the progress of events or a sport or team etc. **5** understand • *Did you follow what he said?* **6** result from something.
▷ **follower** *noun*
[from Old English]

following *PREPOSITION* after, as a result of • *Following the burglary, we had new locks fitted.*

folly *NOUN* **follies** foolishness; a foolish action etc.
[from French *folie* = madness]

foment (*say* fo-ment) *VERB* **foments, fomenting, fomented** arouse or stimulate deliberately • *foment trouble.*
▷ **fomentation** *noun*
[from Latin *fomentum* = poultice]
USAGE Do not confuse with **ferment**.

fond *ADJECTIVE* **1** loving or liking a person or thing. **2** foolishly hopeful • *fond hopes.*
▷ **fondly** *adverb* **fondness** *noun*
[from an old word *fon* = fool]

fondle *VERB* **fondles, fondling, fondled** touch or stroke lovingly.
[from *fond*]

font *NOUN* **fonts** a basin (often of carved stone) in a church, to hold water for baptism.
[from Latin *fontis* = of a spring]

food *NOUN* **foods** any substance that a plant or animal can take into its body to help it to grow and be healthy.
[from Old English]

food chain *NOUN* **food chains** a series of plants and animals each of which serves as food for the one above it in the series.

foodstuff *NOUN* **foodstuffs** something that can be used as food.

food technology *NOUN* the study of foods, what they are made of, and how they are prepared.

fool *NOUN* **fools** **1** a stupid person; someone who acts unwisely. **2** a jester or clown • *Stop playing the fool.* **3** a creamy pudding with crushed fruit in it • *gooseberry fool.*
- **fool's errand** a useless errand.
- **fool's paradise** happiness that comes only from being mistaken about something.

fool *VERB* **fools, fooling, fooled** **1** behave in a joking way; play about. **2** trick or deceive someone.
[from old French]

foolery *NOUN* foolish acts or behaviour.

foolhardy *ADJECTIVE* bold but foolish; reckless.
▷ **foolhardiness** *noun*
[from old French *fol* = foolish + *hardi* = bold]

foolish *ADJECTIVE* without good sense or judgement; unwise.
▷ **foolishly** *adverb* **foolishness** *noun*

foolproof *ADJECTIVE* easy to use or do correctly.

foot *NOUN* **feet** **1** the lower part of the leg below the ankle. **2** any similar part, e.g. one used by certain animals to move or attach themselves to things. **3** the lowest part • *the foot of the hill.* **4** a measure of length, 12 inches or about 30 centimetres • *a ten-foot pole; it is ten feet long*. **5** a unit of rhythm in a line of poetry, e.g. each of the four divisions in *Jack / and Jill / went up / the hill.*
- **on foot** walking.
[from Old English]

footage *NOUN* a length of film.

foot-and-mouth disease *NOUN* a serious contagious disease that affects cattle, sheep, and other animals.

football *NOUN* **footballs** **1** a game played by two teams which try to kick an inflated leather ball into their opponents' goal. **2** the ball used in this game.
▷ **footballer** *noun*

foothill *NOUN* **foothills** a low hill near the bottom of a mountain or range of mountains.

foothold *NOUN* **footholds** **1** a place to put your foot when climbing. **2** a small but firm position from which further progress can be made.

footing *NOUN* **1** having your feet placed on something; a foothold • *He lost his footing and slipped.* **2** the status or nature of a relationship • *We are on a friendly footing with that country.*

footlights *PLURAL NOUN* a row of lights along the front of the floor of a stage.

footman *NOUN* **footmen** a male servant who opens doors, serves at table, etc.
[originally a servant who accompanied his master on foot]

footnote *NOUN* **footnotes** a note printed at the bottom of the page.

footpath *NOUN* **footpaths** a path for pedestrians.

footprint *NOUN* **footprints** a mark made by a foot or shoe.

footsore *ADJECTIVE* having feet that are painful or sore from walking.

footstep *NOUN* **footsteps** **1** a step taken in walking or running. **2** the sound of this.

footstool *NOUN* **footstools** a stool for resting your feet on when you are sitting.

footwear *NOUN* shoes, boots, and other coverings for the feet.

for *PREPOSITION* This word is used to show **1** purpose or direction (*This letter is for you; We set out for home*), **2** distance or time (*Walk for six miles or two hours*), **3** price or exchange (*We bought it for £5; New lamps for old*), **4** cause (*She was fined for speeding*), **5** defence or support (*He fought for his country; Are you for us or against us?*), **6** reference (*For all her wealth, she is bored*), **7** similarity or correspondence (*We took him for a fool*),
- **for ever** for all time; always.

for *CONJUNCTION* because • *They hesitated, for they were afraid.*
[from Old English]

for- *PREFIX* **1** away, off (as in *forgive*). **2** prohibiting (as in *forbid*). **3** abstaining or neglecting (as in *forgo, forsake*).
[from Old English]

forage *NOUN* **1** food for horses and cattle. **2** the action of foraging.

forage *VERB* **forages, foraging, foraged** go searching for something, especially food or fuel.
[via French from Germanic]

foray *NOUN* **forays** a sudden attack or raid.
[from old French; related to *forage*]

forbear *VERB* **forbears, forbearing, forbore, forborne** **1** refrain from something • *We forbore to mention it.* **2** be patient or tolerant.
▷ **forbearance** *noun*
[from Old English]

forbid *VERB* **forbids, forbidding, forbade, forbidden** **1** order someone not to do something. **2** refuse to allow • *We shall forbid the marriage.*
[from Old English]

forbidding *ADJECTIVE* looking stern or unfriendly.

force *NOUN* **forces** **1** strength or power. **2** (*in science*) an influence, which can be measured, that causes something to move. **3** an organized group of police, soldiers, etc.
- **in** or **into force** in or into effectiveness • *The new law comes into force next week.*
- **the forces** a country's armed forces.

force *VERB* **forces, forcing, forced 1** use force in order to get or do something, or to make somebody obey. **2** break something open by force. **3** cause plants to grow or bloom earlier than is normal • *You can force them in a greenhouse.*
[from Latin *fortis* = strong]

forceful *ADJECTIVE* strong and vigorous.
▷ **forcefully** *adverb*

forceps *NOUN* **forceps** pincers or tongs used by dentists, surgeons, etc.
[Latin]

forcible *ADJECTIVE* done by force; forceful.
▷ **forcibly** *adverb*

ford *NOUN* **fords** a shallow place where you can walk across a river.

ford *VERB* **fords, fording, forded** cross a river at a ford.
[from Old English]

fore *ADJECTIVE & ADVERB* at or towards the front • *fore and aft.*

fore *NOUN* the front part.
- **to the fore** to or at the front; in or to a prominent position.
[from Old English]

fore- *PREFIX* before (as in *forecast*); in front (as in *foreleg*).

forearm[1] *NOUN* **forearms** the arm from the elbow to the wrist or fingertips.
[from *fore-* + *arm*[1]]

forearm[2] *VERB* **forearms, forearming, forearmed** prepare in advance against possible danger.
[from *fore-* + *arm*[2]]

forebears *PLURAL NOUN* ancestors.
[from *fore-* + *be-er* = someone or something that is]

foreboding *NOUN* a feeling that trouble is coming.
[from *fore-* + *bode*]

forecast *NOUN* **forecasts** a statement that tells in advance what is likely to happen.

forecast *VERB* **forecasts, forecasting, forecast** make a forecast.
▷ **forecaster** *noun*
[from *fore-* + *cast*]

forecastle (*say* foh-ksul) *NOUN* **forecastles** the forward part of certain ships.
[from *fore-* + *castle* (because originally this part was raised up like a castle to command your own or an enemy's deck)]

forecourt *NOUN* **forecourts** an enclosed area in front of a building etc.

forefathers *PLURAL NOUN* ancestors.

forefinger *NOUN* **forefingers** the finger next to the thumb.

forefoot *NOUN* **forefeet** an animal's front foot.

forefront *NOUN* the very front.

foregoing *ADJECTIVE* preceding; previously mentioned.
USAGE Note the spelling of this word. It has an 'e' in it, whereas *forgo*, meaning 'give up', does not.

foregone conclusion *NOUN* **foregone conclusions** a result that can be foreseen easily or is bound to happen.

foreground *NOUN* the part of a scene, picture, or view that is nearest to you.

forehand *NOUN* **forehands** a stroke made in tennis etc. with the palm of the hand turned forwards.

forehead (*say* forrid or for-hed) *NOUN* **foreheads** the part of the face above the eyes.

foreign *ADJECTIVE* **1** belonging to or in another country. **2** not belonging naturally to a place or to someone's nature • *Lying is foreign to her nature.*
[from old French]

foreigner *NOUN* **foreigners** a person from another country.

foreleg *NOUN* **forelegs** an animal's front leg.

foreman *NOUN* **foremen 1** a worker in charge of a group of other workers. **2** a member of a jury who is in charge of the jury's discussions and who speaks on its behalf.

foremost *ADJECTIVE & ADVERB* first in position or rank; most important.

forensic (*say* fer-en-sik) *ADJECTIVE* to do with or used in lawcourts.
[from Latin; related to *forum*]

forensic medicine *NOUN* medical knowledge needed in legal matters or in solving crimes.

forerunner *NOUN* **forerunners** a person or thing that comes before another; a sign of what is to come.

foresee *VERB* **foresees, foreseeing, foresaw, foreseen** realize what is going to happen.

F

foreseeable *ADJECTIVE* able to be foreseen.

foreshadow *VERB* **foreshadows, foreshadowing, foreshadowed** be a sign of something that is to come.

foreshorten *VERB* **foreshortens, foreshortening, foreshortened** show an object in a drawing etc. with some lines shortened to give an effect of distance or depth.

foresight *NOUN* the ability to foresee and prepare for future needs.

foreskin *NOUN* **foreskins** the fold of skin covering the end of the penis.

forest *NOUN* **forests** trees and undergrowth covering a large area.
▷ **forested** *adjective*
[from old French]

forestall *VERB* **forestalls, forestalling, forestalled** prevent somebody or something by taking action first.
[from Old English *foresteall* = an ambush]

forestry *NOUN* planting forests and looking after them.
▷ **forester** *noun*

foretaste *NOUN* **foretastes** an experience of something that is to come in the future.

foretell *VERB* **foretells, foretelling, foretold** tell in advance; prophesy.

forethought *NOUN* careful thought and planning for the future.

forewarn *VERB* **forewarns, forewarning, forewarned** warn someone beforehand.

forewoman *NOUN* **forewomen** **1** a female worker in charge of other workers. **2** a female member of a jury who is in charge of the jury's discussions and who speaks on its behalf.

foreword *NOUN* **forewords** a preface.

forfeit (*say* for-fit) *VERB* **forfeits, forfeiting, forfeited** pay or give up something as a penalty.
▷ **forfeiture** *noun*

forfeit *NOUN* **forfeits** something forfeited.
[from old French]

forge[1] *NOUN* **forges** a place where metal is heated and shaped; a blacksmith's workshop.

forge *VERB* **forges, forging, forged**
1 shape metal by heating and hammering.
2 copy something in order to deceive people.
▷ **forger** *noun* **forgery** *noun*
[from old French]

forge[2] *VERB* **forges, forging, forged**
- **forge ahead** move forward by a strong effort.
[probably a different spelling of *force*]

forget *VERB* **forgets, forgetting, forgot, forgotten** **1** fail to remember. **2** stop thinking about • *Forget your troubles.*
- **forget yourself** behave rudely or thoughtlessly.
[from Old English]

forgetful *ADJECTIVE* tending to forget.
▷ **forgetfully** *adverb* **forgetfulness** *noun*

forget-me-not *NOUN* **forget-me-nots** a plant with small blue flowers.
[because in the Middle Ages the flower was worn by lovers]

forgive *VERB* **forgives, forgiving, forgave, forgiven** stop feeling angry with somebody about something.
▷ **forgiveness** *noun*
[from Old English]

forgo *VERB* **forgoes, forgoing, forwent, forgone** give something up; go without.
[from *for-* + go]
USAGE See note at **foregoing**.

fork *NOUN* **forks** **1** a small device with prongs for lifting food to your mouth. **2** a large device with prongs used for digging or lifting things. **3** a place where something separates into two or more parts • *a fork in the road.*

fork *VERB* **forks, forking, forked** **1** lift or dig with a fork. **2** form a fork by separating into two branches. **3** follow one of these branches • *Fork left.*
- **fork out** (*slang*) pay out money.
[via Old English from Latin]

fork-lift truck *NOUN* **fork-lift trucks** a truck with two metal bars at the front for lifting and moving heavy loads.

forlorn *ADJECTIVE* left alone and unhappy.
- **forlorn hope** the only faint hope left.
[from *for-* + an old word *lorn* = lost]

form *NOUN* **forms** **1** the shape, appearance, or condition of something. **2** the way something exists • *Ice is a form of water.* **3** a class in school. **4** a bench. **5** a piece of paper with spaces to be filled in.

form *VERB* **forms, forming, formed**
1 shape or construct something; create.
2 come into existence; develop • *Icicles formed.*
[from Latin]
WORD FAMILY There are a number of English words that are related to *form* because part of their original meaning comes from the Latin words *formare* meaning 'to form' or *forma* meaning 'a shape or form'. These include *conform, deform, formal, format, formation, formula, reform,* and *transform.*

formal *ADJECTIVE* **1** strictly following the accepted rules or customs; ceremonious • *a formal occasion; formal dress.* **2** rather serious and stiff in your manner.
▷ **formally** *adverb*
[from Latin *formalis* = having a set form]

formality *NOUN* **formalities** **1** formal behaviour. **2** something done to obey a rule or custom.

format *NOUN* **formats** **1** the shape and size of something. **2** the way something is arranged or organized. **3** (*in computing*) the way data is organized for processing or storage by a computer.

format *VERB* **formats, formatting, formatted** (*in computing*) organize data in the correct format.
[from Latin *formatus* = formed, shaped]

formation *NOUN* **formations** **1** the act of forming something. **2** a thing formed. **3** a special arrangement or pattern • *flying in formation.*
[from Latin *formare* = to mould]

formative *ADJECTIVE* forming or developing something.

former *ADJECTIVE* of an earlier time.
▷ **formerly** *adverb*
- **the former** the first of two people or things just mentioned.
[from Old English; related to *fore*]

formidable (*say* for-mid-a-bul) *ADJECTIVE*
1 difficult to deal with or do • *a formidable task.* **2** fearsome or frightening.
▷ **formidably** *adverb*
[from Latin *formidare* = to fear]

formula *NOUN* **formulae** **1** a set of chemical symbols showing what a substance consists of. **2** a rule or statement expressed in symbols or numbers. **3** a list of substances needed for making something. **4** a fixed wording for a ceremony etc. **5** one of the groups into which racing cars are placed according to the size of their engines • *Formula One.*
[Latin, = small form]

formulate *VERB* **formulates, formulating, formulated** express an idea or plan clearly and exactly.
▷ **formulation** *noun*
[from *formula*]

fornication *NOUN* (*formal*) sexual intercourse between people who are not married to each other.
[from Latin *fornix* = brothel]

forsake *VERB* **forsakes, forsaking, forsook, forsaken** abandon.
[from Old English]

fort *NOUN* **forts** a fortified building.
[from Latin *fortis* = strong]

forth *ADVERB* **1** out; into view. **2** onwards or forwards • *from this day forth.*
- **and so forth** and so on.
[from Old English]

forthcoming *ADJECTIVE* **1** happening soon • *forthcoming events.* **2** made available when needed • *Money for the trip was not forthcoming.* **3** willing to give information.

forthright *ADJECTIVE* frank and outspoken.

forthwith *ADVERB* immediately.

fortification *NOUN* **fortifications** **1** fortifying something. **2** a wall or building constructed to make a place strong against attack.

fortify *VERB* **fortifies, fortifying, fortified** **1** make a place strong against attack, especially by building fortifications. **2** strengthen.
[same origin as *fort*]

fortissimo *ADVERB* (*in music*) very loudly.
[Italian]

fortitude *NOUN* courage in bearing pain or trouble.
[from Latin *fortis* = strong]

fortnight *NOUN* **fortnights** a period of two weeks.
▷ **fortnightly** *adverb* & *adjective*
[from Old English *feowertene niht* = fourteen nights]

fortress *NOUN* **fortresses** a fortified building or town.
[from French *forteresse* = strong place]

fortuitous (*say* for-tew-it-us) *ADJECTIVE* happening by chance; accidental.
▷ **fortuitously** *adverb*
[from Latin *forte* = by chance]
USAGE Note that *fortuitous* does not mean the same as *fortunate*.

fortunate *ADJECTIVE* lucky.
▷ **fortunately** *adverb*
[same origin as *fortune*]

fortune *NOUN* **fortunes** **1** luck, especially good luck. **2** a great amount of money.
- **tell someone's fortune** predict what will happen to them in the future.
[from Latin *fortuna* = luck]

forty *NOUN* & *ADJECTIVE* **forties** the number 40.
▷ **fortieth** *adjective* & *noun*
- **forty winks** a short sleep; a nap.
[from Old English]

forum *NOUN* **forums** **1** the public square in an ancient Roman city. **2** a meeting where a public discussion is held.
[Latin]

forward *ADJECTIVE* **1** going forwards. **2** placed in the front. **3** having made more than the normal progress. **4** too eager or bold.
▷ **forwardness** *noun*

forward *ADVERB* forwards.

forward *NOUN* **forwards** a player in the front line of a team in football, hockey, etc.

forward *VERB* **forwards, forwarding, forwarded** **1** send on a letter etc. to a new address. **2** help something to improve or make progress.
[from Old English]

forwards *ADVERB* **1** to or towards the front. **2** in the direction you are facing.

fossick *VERB* **fossicks, fossicking, fossicked** (*Australian/NZ*) **1** turn things over or move them about while looking for something. **2** search for gold or precious stones in streams or old mines.
[origin unknown]

fossil *NOUN* **fossils** the remains or traces of a prehistoric animal or plant that has been buried in the ground for a very long time and become hardened in rock.
▷ **fossilized** *adjective*
[from Latin *fossilis* = dug up]

fossil fuel *NOUN* **fossil fuels** a natural fuel such as coal or gas formed in the geological past.

fossilize *VERB* **fossilizes, fossilizing, fossilized** turn into a fossil.
▷ **fossilization** *noun*

foster *VERB* **fosters, fostering, fostered** **1** bring up someone else's child as if he or she was your own. **2** help to grow or develop.
▷ **foster child** *noun* **foster parent** *noun*
[from Old English]

foul *ADJECTIVE* **1** disgusting; tasting or smelling unpleasant. **2** (said about weather) rough; stormy. **3** unfair; breaking the rules of a game. **4** colliding or entangled with something.
▷ **foully** *adverb* **foulness** *noun*

foul *NOUN* **fouls** an action that breaks the rules of a game.

foul *VERB* **fouls, fouling, fouled** **1** make or become foul • *Smoke had fouled the air.* **2** commit a foul against a player in a game. [from Old English]

foul play *NOUN* a violent crime, especially murder.

found[1] *past tense* of **find.**

found[2] *VERB* **founds, founding, founded** **1** establish; provide money for starting • *They founded a hospital.* **2** base • *This novel is founded on fact.* [from Latin *fundus* = bottom]

foundation *NOUN* **foundations** **1** the solid base on which a building is built up. **2** the basis for something. **3** the founding of something. **4** a fund of money set aside for a charitable purpose.
▷ **foundation stone** *noun*

founder[1] *NOUN* **founders** a person who founds something • *the founder of the hospital.*

founder[2] *VERB* **founders, foundering, foundered** **1** fill with water and sink • *The ship foundered.* **2** stumble or fall. **3** fail completely • *Their plans foundered.* [same origin as *found*[2]]

foundling *NOUN* **foundlings** a child found abandoned, whose parents are not known.

foundry *NOUN* **foundries** a factory or workshop where metal or glass is made. [from *found*[2]]

fount *NOUN* **founts** (*poetical use*) a fountain.

fountain *NOUN* **fountains** an ornamental structure in which a jet of water shoots up into the air. [same origin as *font*]

fountain pen *NOUN* **fountain pens** a pen that can be filled with a supply of ink.

four *NOUN* & *ADJECTIVE* **fours** the number 4.
- **on all fours** on hands and knees. [from Old English]

fourteen *NOUN* & *ADJECTIVE* **fourteens** the number 14.
▷ **fourteenth** *adjective* & *noun* [from Old English]

fourth *ADJECTIVE* next after the third.
▷ **fourthly** *adverb*

fourth *NOUN* **fourths** **1** the fourth person or thing. **2** one of four equal parts; a quarter. [from Old English]

fowl *NOUN* **fowls** a bird, especially one kept on a farm etc. for its eggs or meat. [from Old English]

fox *NOUN* **foxes** a wild animal that looks like a dog with a long furry tail.
▷ **foxy** *adjective*

fox *VERB* **foxes, foxing, foxed** deceive or puzzle someone. [from Old English]

foxglove *NOUN* **foxgloves** a tall plant with flowers like the fingers of gloves.

foyer (*say* foy-ay) *NOUN* **foyers** the entrance hall of a theatre, cinema, or hotel. [French, = hearth, home]

fraction *NOUN* **fractions** **1** a number that is not a whole number, e.g. $\frac{1}{2}$, 0.5. **2** a tiny part.
▷ **fractional** *adjective* **fractionally** *adverb* [Latin, = breaking]

fractious (*say* frak-shus) *ADJECTIVE* irritable.
▷ **fractiously** *adverb* **fractiousness** *noun* [from *fraction*]

fracture *NOUN* **fractures** the breaking of something, especially of a bone.

fracture *VERB* **fractures, fracturing, fractured** break. [from Latin *fractus* = broken]

fragile *ADJECTIVE* easy to break or damage.
▷ **fragility** *noun* [from Latin]

fragment *NOUN* **fragments** **1** a small piece broken off. **2** a small part.
▷ **fragmentary** *adjective* **fragmentation** *noun* **fragmented** *adjective* [from Latin]

fragrant *ADJECTIVE* having a pleasant smell.
▷ **fragrance** *noun* [from Latin *fragrare* = smell sweet]

frail *ADJECTIVE* **1** (said about people) not strong or healthy • *a frail old man.* **2** (said about things) fragile.
▷ **frailty** *noun* [from Latin *fragilis* = fragile]

frame *NOUN* **frames** **1** a holder that fits round the outside of a picture. **2** a rigid structure that supports something. **3** a human or animal body • *He has a small frame.* **4** a single exposure on a cinema film.
- **frame of mind** the way you think or feel for a while.

frame *VERB* **frames, framing, framed** **1** put a frame on or round. **2** construct • *They framed the question badly.* **3** make an innocent person seem guilty by arranging false evidence.
▷ **frame-up** *noun*
[from Old English]

framework *NOUN* **frameworks** **1** a frame supporting something. **2** a basic plan or system.

franc *NOUN* **francs** a unit of money in Switzerland. Formerly also used in France, Belgium, and some other countries until replaced by the euro.
[from Latin *Francorum rex* = King of the Franks, which was stamped on French gold coins in the Middle Ages]

franchise *NOUN* **franchises** **1** the right to vote in elections. **2** a licence to sell a firm's goods or services in a certain area.
[same origin as *frank*]

frank *ADJECTIVE* making your thoughts and feelings clear to people; candid.
▷ **frankly** *adverb* **frankness** *noun*

frank *VERB* **franks, franking, franked** mark a letter or parcel automatically in a machine to show that postage has been paid.
[from Latin *francus* = free]

frankincense *NOUN* a sweet-smelling gum burnt as incense.
[from old French *franc encens* = finest incense]

frantic *ADJECTIVE* wildly agitated or excited.
▷ **frantically** *adverb*
[from old French; related to *frenzy*]

fraternal (*say* fra-tern-al) *ADJECTIVE* to do with brothers; brotherly.
▷ **fraternally** *adverb*
[from Latin *frater* = brother]

fraternity *NOUN* **fraternities** **1** a brotherly feeling. **2** a group of people who have the same interests or occupation • *the medical fraternity.*

fraternize *VERB* **fraternizes, fraternizing, fraternized** associate with other people in a friendly way.
▷ **fraternization** *noun*
[same origin as *fraternal*]

fraud *NOUN* **frauds** **1** the crime of swindling people. **2** a dishonest trick. **3** an impostor; a person or thing that is not what it pretends to be.
[from Latin]

fraudulent (*say* fraw-dew-lent) *ADJECTIVE* involving fraud; deceitful or dishonest.
▷ **fraudulently** *adverb* **fraudulence** *noun*

fraught *ADJECTIVE* **1** filled with • *The situation is fraught with danger.* **2** tense or upset • *I'm feeling rather fraught this morning.*
[from old Dutch *vrachten* = load a ship]

fray[1] *NOUN* **frays** a fight or conflict • *ready for the fray.*
[shortened from *affray*]

fray[2] *VERB* **frays, fraying, frayed** **1** make or become ragged so that loose threads show. **2** (said about tempers or nerves) become strained or upset.
[from French; related to *friction*]

freak *NOUN* **freaks** a very strange or abnormal person, animal, or thing.
▷ **freakish** *adjective*
[origin unknown]

freckle *NOUN* **freckles** a small brown spot on the skin.
▷ **freckled** *adjective*
[from Old Norse]

free *ADJECTIVE* **freer, freest** **1** able to do what you want to do or go where you want to go. **2** not costing anything. **3** not fixed • *Leave one end free.* **4** not having or being affected by something • *The harbour is free of ice.* **5** available; not being used or occupied. **6** generous • *She is very free with her money.*
▷ **freely** *adverb*

free *VERB* **frees, freeing, freed** set free.
[from Old English]

freedom *NOUN* **freedoms** being free; independence.

freehand *ADJECTIVE* & *ADVERB* (said about a drawing) done without a ruler or compasses, or without tracing it • *Draw a circle freehand.*

freehold *NOUN* possessing land or a house as its absolute owner, not as a tenant renting from a landlord.

Freemason *NOUN* **Freemasons** a member of a certain secret society.
▷ **Freemasonry** *noun*
[originally, a society of stonemasons]

free-range *ADJECTIVE* **1** free-range hens are not kept in small cages but are allowed to move about freely. **2** free-range eggs are ones laid by these hens.

freeway *NOUN* **freeways** (*American*) a dual-carriageway main road.

freewheel *VERB* **freewheels, freewheeling, freewheeled** ride a bicycle without pedalling.

freeze *VERB* **freezes, freezing, froze, frozen** **1** turn into ice; become covered with ice. **2** make or be very cold. **3** keep wages or prices etc. at a fixed level. **4** suddenly stand completely still.

freeze *NOUN* **freezes** **1** a period of freezing weather. **2** the freezing of prices etc.
[from Old English]

freezer *NOUN* **freezers** a refrigerator in which food can be frozen quickly and stored.

freezing point *NOUN* **freezing points** the temperature at which a liquid freezes.

freight (*say* frayt) *NOUN* goods transported as cargo.
[from old Dutch; related to *fraught*]

freighter (*say* fray-ter) *NOUN* **freighters** a ship or aircraft carrying mainly cargo.

French window *NOUN* **French windows** a long window that serves as a door on an outside wall.

frenzy *NOUN* wild excitement or agitation.
▷ **frenzied** *adjective* **frenziedly** *adverb*
[from Greek *phren* = the mind]

frequency *NOUN* **frequencies** **1** being frequent. **2** how often something happens. **3** the number of vibrations made each second by a wave of sound, radio, or light.

frequent (*say* freek-went) *ADJECTIVE* happening often.
▷ **frequently** *adverb*

frequent (*say* frik-went) *VERB* **frequents, frequenting, frequented** be in or go to a place often • *They frequented the club.*
[from Latin *frequens* = crowded]

fresco *NOUN* **frescoes** or **frescos** a picture painted on a wall or ceiling before the plaster is dry.
[from Italian *affresco* = on the fresh (plaster)]

fresh *ADJECTIVE* **1** newly made or produced or arrived; not stale • *fresh bread.* **2** not tinned or preserved • *fresh fruit.* **3** cool and clean • *fresh air.* **4** (said about water) not salty.
▷ **freshly** *adverb* **freshness** *noun*
[from Old English]

freshen *VERB* **freshens, freshening, freshened** make or become fresh.

freshman *NOUN* **freshmen** (*American*) a first-year university or high-school student.

freshwater *ADJECTIVE* living in rivers or lakes, not the sea.

fret[1] *VERB* **frets, fretting, fretted** worry or be upset about something.
▷ **fretful** *adjective* **fretfully** *adverb*
[from Old English]

fret[2] *NOUN* **frets** a bar or ridge on the fingerboard of a guitar etc.
[origin unknown]

fretsaw *NOUN* **fretsaws** a very narrow saw used for making fretwork.

fretwork *NOUN* cutting decorative patterns in wood; wood cut in this way.
[from French *frete* = trellis]

friar *NOUN* **friars** a man who is a member of a Roman Catholic religious order and has vowed to live a life of poverty.
▷ **friary** *noun*
[from French *frère* = brother]

friction *NOUN* **1** rubbing of one thing against another. **2** bad feeling between people; quarrelling.
▷ **frictional** *adjective*
[from Latin *fricare* = to rub]

Friday *NOUN* the day of the week following Thursday.
[from Old English *Frigedaeg* = day of Frigga, a Norse goddess]

fridge *NOUN* **fridges** (*informal*) a refrigerator.

A B C D E F G H I J K L M N O P Q R S T U V W X Y Z

friend *NOUN* **friends** **1** a person you like who likes you. **2** a helpful or kind person.
[from Old English]

friendless *ADJECTIVE* without a friend.

friendly *ADJECTIVE* **friendlier, friendliest** behaving like a friend.
▷ **friendliness** *noun*

friendship *NOUN* **friendships** being friends.

frieze (*say* freez) *NOUN* **friezes** a strip of designs or pictures round the top of a wall.
[from Latin]

frigate *NOUN* **frigates** a small warship.
[via French from Italian]

fright *NOUN* **frights** **1** sudden great fear. **2** a person or thing that looks ridiculous.
[from Old English]

frighten *VERB* **frightens, frightening, frightened** make or become afraid.
- **be frightened of** be afraid of.

frightful *ADJECTIVE* awful; very great or bad.
▷ **frightfully** *adverb*

frigid *ADJECTIVE* **1** extremely cold. **2** unfriendly; not affectionate.
▷ **frigidly** *adverb* **frigidity** *noun*
[from Latin *frigidus* = cold]

frill *NOUN* **frills** **1** a decorative gathered or pleated trimming on a dress, curtain, etc. **2** something extra that is pleasant but unnecessary • *a simple hotel with no frills.*
▷ **frilled** *adjective* **frilly** *adjective*
[from Flemish]

fringe *NOUN* **fringes** **1** a decorative edging with many threads hanging down loosely. **2** a straight line of hair hanging down over the forehead. **3** the edge of something.
▷ **fringed** *adjective*
[from old French]

frisk *VERB* **frisks, frisking, frisked** **1** jump or run about playfully. **2** search somebody by running your hands over his or her clothes.
[from old French *frisque* = lively]

frisky *ADJECTIVE* playful or lively.
▷ **friskily** *adverb* **friskiness** *noun*

fritter[1] *NOUN* **fritters** a slice of meat, potato, or fruit coated in batter and fried.
[from Latin *frictum* = fried]

fritter[2] *VERB* **fritters, frittering, frittered** waste something gradually; spend money or time on trivial things.
[from an old word *fritters* = fragments]

frivolous *ADJECTIVE* seeking pleasure in a light-hearted way; not serious.
▷ **frivolously** *adverb* **frivolity** *noun*
[from Latin]

frizzle *VERB* **frizzles, frizzling, frizzled** **1** fry with a spluttering noise. **2** shrivel something by burning it.
[from *fry*[1]]

frizzy *ADJECTIVE* (said about hair) in tight curls.
▷ **frizziness** *noun*
[from French]

fro *ADVERB*
- **to and fro** backwards and forwards.
[from Old Norse]

frock *NOUN* **frocks** a girl's or woman's dress.
[from old French]

frog *NOUN* **frogs** a small jumping animal that can live both in water and on land.
- **a frog in your throat** hoarseness.
[from Old English]

frogman *NOUN* **frogmen** a swimmer equipped with a rubber suit, flippers, and breathing apparatus for swimming and working underwater.

frolic *NOUN* **frolics** a lively cheerful game or entertainment.
▷ **frolicsome** *adjective*

frolic *VERB* **frolics, frolicking, frolicked** play about in a lively cheerful way.
[from Dutch *vrolijk* = joyously]

from *PREPOSITION* This word is used to show **1** starting point in space or time or order (*We flew from London to Paris. We work from 9 to 5 o'clock. Count from one to ten*), **2** source or origin (*Get water from the tap*), **3** separation or release (*Take the gun from him. She was freed from prison*), **4** difference (*Can you tell margarine from butter?*), **5** cause (*I suffer from headaches*).
[from Old English]

frond *NOUN* **fronds** a leaf-like part of a fern, palm tree, etc.
[from Latin *frondis* = of a leaf]

front *NOUN* **fronts 1** the part or side that comes first or is the most important or furthest forward. **2** a road or promenade along the seashore. **3** the place where fighting is happening in a war. **4** (in weather systems) the forward edge of an approaching mass of air.
▷ **frontal** *adjective*

front *ADJECTIVE* of the front; in front.
[from Latin *frons* = forehead, front]

frontage *NOUN* **frontages** the front of a building; the land beside this.

frontier *NOUN* **frontiers** the boundary between two countries or regions.
[from old French; related to *front*]

frontispiece *NOUN* **frontispieces** an illustration opposite the title page of a book.
[from French]

frost *NOUN* **frosts 1** powdery ice that forms on things in freezing weather. **2** weather with a temperature below freezing point.

frost *VERB* **frosts, frosting, frosted** cover with frost or frosting.
[from Old English]

frostbite *NOUN* harm done to the body by very cold weather.
▷ **frostbitten** *adjective*

frosted glass *NOUN* glass made cloudy so that you cannot see through it.

frosting *NOUN* sugar icing for cakes.

frosty *ADJECTIVE* **frostier, frostiest 1** cold with frost. **2** unfriendly and unwelcoming • *a frosty look.*
▷ **frostily** *adverb*

froth *NOUN* a white mass of tiny bubbles on a liquid.
▷ **frothy** *adjective*
[from Old Norse]

frown *VERB* **frowns, frowning, frowned** wrinkle your forehead because you are angry or worried.

frown *NOUN* **frowns** a frowning movement or look.
[from old French]

frugal (*say* froo-gal) *ADJECTIVE* **1** spending very little money. **2** costing very little money; not plentiful • *a frugal meal.*
▷ **frugally** *adverb* **frugality** *noun*
[from Latin]

fruit *NOUN* **fruits** or **fruit 1** the seed container that grows on a tree or plant and is often used as food. **2** the result of doing something • *the fruits of his efforts.*
▷ **fruity** *adjective*

fruit *VERB* **fruits, fruiting, fruited** produce fruit.
[same origin as *fruition*]

fruitful *ADJECTIVE* producing good results • *fruitful discussions.*
▷ **fruitfully** *adverb*

fruition (*say* froo-**ish**-on) *NOUN* the achievement of what was hoped or worked for • *Our plans never came to fruition.*
[from Latin *frui* = enjoy]

fruitless *ADJECTIVE* producing no results.
▷ **fruitlessly** *adverb*

fruit machine *NOUN* **fruit machines** a gambling machine worked by putting a coin in a slot.

frustrate *VERB* **frustrates, frustrating, frustrated** prevent somebody from doing something; prevent something from being successful • *A lack of money has frustrated our plans.*
▷ **frustration** *noun*
[from Latin *frustra* = in vain]

fry[1] *VERB* **fries, frying, fried** cook something in very hot fat.
▷ **fryer** *noun*
[from Latin]

fry[2] *PLURAL NOUN* very young fishes.
[from Old Norse]

frying pan *NOUN* **frying pans** a shallow pan for frying things.

fuchsia (*say* few-sha) *NOUN* **fuchsias** an ornamental plant with flowers that hang down.
[named after Leonard *Fuchs*, a German botanist]

fudge[1] *NOUN* a soft sugary sweet.
[origin unknown]

fudge[2] *VERB* **fudges, fudging, fudged** avoid giving clear and accurate information, or a clear answer • *People accuse us of fudging the issue.*
[origin unknown]

fuel *NOUN* **fuels** something that is burnt to produce heat or power.

fuel *VERB* **fuels, fuelling, fuelled** supply something with fuel.
[from old French; related to *focus*]

fug *NOUN* (*informal*) a stuffy atmosphere in a room.
▷ **fuggy** *adjective* **fugginess** *noun*
[originally slang: origin unknown]

fugitive (*say* few-jit-iv) *NOUN* **fugitives** a person who is running away from something.
[from Latin *fugere* = flee]

fugue (*say* fewg) *NOUN* **fugues** a piece of music in which tunes are repeated in a pattern.
[via French from Italian]

-ful *SUFFIX* forms **1** adjectives meaning 'full of' or 'having this quality' (e.g. *beautiful, truthful*), **2** nouns meaning 'the amount required to fill something' (e.g. *handful*).
[from *full*]

fulcrum *NOUN* **fulcrums** or **fulcra** the point on which a lever rests.
[Latin]

fulfil *VERB* **fulfils, fulfilling, fulfilled** **1** do what is required; satisfy; carry out • *You must fulfil your promises.* **2** make something come true • *It fulfilled an ancient prophecy.* **3** give you satisfaction.
▷ **fulfilment** *noun*
[from Old English *fullfyllan* = fill up, satisfy]

full *ADJECTIVE* **1** containing as much or as many as possible. **2** having many people or things • *full of ideas.* **3** complete • *the full story.* **4** the greatest possible • *at full speed.* **5** fitting loosely; with many folds • *a full skirt.*
▷ **fully** *adverb* **fullness** *noun*
- **in full** with nothing left out • *We have paid in full.*

full *ADVERB* completely and directly • *It hit him full in the face.*
[from Old English]

full-blown *ADJECTIVE* fully developed.

full moon *NOUN* **full moons** the moon when you can see the whole of it as a bright disc.

full stop *NOUN* **full stops** the dot used as a punctuation mark at the end of a sentence or an abbreviation.

full-time *ADJECTIVE* & *ADVERB* for all the normal working hours of the day • *a full-time job.*

fully *ADVERB* completely.

fully-fledged *ADJECTIVE* fully trained or developed • *a fully-fledged engineer.*

fulsome *ADJECTIVE* praising something or thanking someone too much or too · emotionally; excessive.
[Middle English, = plentiful, from *full*]
USAGE Note that *fulsome praise* does not mean 'generous praise', but rather 'excessive praise'.

fumble *VERB* **fumbles, fumbling, fumbled** hold or handle something clumsily.
[from German or Dutch]

fumes *PLURAL NOUN* strong-smelling smoke or gas.

fume *VERB* **fumes, fuming, fumed** **1** give off fumes. **2** be very angry.
[from Latin *fumus* = smoke]

fumigate (*say* few-mig-ayt) *VERB* **fumigates, fumigating, fumigated** disinfect something by fumes.
▷ **fumigation** *noun*

fun *NOUN* amusement or enjoyment.
- **make fun of** make people laugh at a person or thing.
[origin unknown]

function *NOUN* **functions** **1** what somebody or something is there to do • *The function of a knife is to cut things.* **2** an important event or party. **3** a basic operation in a computer or calculator. **4** a variable quantity whose value depends on the value of other variable quantities • *X is a function of Y and Z.*

function *VERB* **functions, functioning, functioned** perform a function; work properly.
[from Latin *functum* = performed]

functional *ADJECTIVE* **1** working properly. **2** practical without being decorative or luxurious.
▷ **functionally** *adverb*

fund *NOUN* **funds** **1** money collected or kept for a special purpose. **2** a stock or supply.

fund *VERB* **funds, funding, funded** supply with money.
[same origin as *found*[2]]

fundamental *ADJECTIVE* basic.
▷ **fundamentally** *adverb*
[from Latin *fundamentum* = foundation]

funeral *NOUN* **funerals** the ceremony when a dead person is buried or cremated.
[from Latin *funeris* = of a burial]

funereal (*say* few-**neer**-ee-al) *ADJECTIVE* gloomy or depressing.
[same origin as *funeral*]

funfair *NOUN* **funfairs** a fair consisting of amusements and sideshows.

fungus *NOUN* **fungi** (*say* **fung**-I) a plant without leaves or flowers that grows on other plants or on decayed material, such as mushrooms and toadstools.
[Latin]

funk[1] *VERB* **funks, funking, funked** (*old-fashioned use*) be afraid of doing something and avoid it.
[origin unknown]

funk[2] *NOUN* a style of popular music with a strong rhythm, based on jazz and blues.
[origin unknown]

funnel *NOUN* **funnels 1** a metal chimney on a ship or steam engine. **2** a tube that is wide at the top and narrow at the bottom to help you pour things into a narrow opening.
[from Latin *fundere* = pour]

funny *ADJECTIVE* **funnier, funniest 1** that makes you laugh or smile. **2** strange or odd • *a funny smell.*
▷ **funnily** *adverb*

funny bone *NOUN* **funny bones** part of your elbow which produces a tingling feeling if you knock it.

fur *NOUN* **furs 1** the soft hair that covers some animals. **2** animal skin with the fur on it, used for clothing; fabric that looks like animal fur.
[from old French]

furbish *VERB* **furbishes, furbishing, furbished** polish or clean; renovate.
[via old French from Germanic]

furious *ADJECTIVE* **1** very angry. **2** violent or intense • *furious heat.*
▷ **furiously** *adverb*
[from Latin]

furl *VERB* **furls, furling, furled** roll up a sail, flag, or umbrella.
[from old French *ferlier* = bind firmly]

furlong *NOUN* **furlongs** one-eighth of a mile, 220 yards.
[from Old English *furlang* = 'furrow long'; the length of a furrow in a common field]

furniture *NOUN* tables, chairs, and other movable things that you need in a house or school or office etc.

furore (*say* few-**ror**-ee) *NOUN* an excited or angry uproar.
[from Latin *furor* = madness]

furrow *NOUN* **furrows 1** a long cut in the ground made by a plough or other implement. **2** a groove. **3** a deep wrinkle in the skin.

furrow *VERB* **furrows, furrowing, furrowed** make furrows in something.
[from Old English]

furry *ADJECTIVE* like fur; covered with fur.

further *ADVERB & ADJECTIVE* **1** at or to a greater distance; more distant. **2** more; additional • *We made further enquiries.*
USAGE See the note at **farther**.

further *VERB* **furthers, furthering, furthered** help something to progress • *This success will further your career.*
▷ **furtherance** *noun*
[from Old English]

further education *NOUN* education for people above school age.

furthermore *ADVERB* also; moreover.

furthest *ADVERB & ADJECTIVE* at or to the greatest distance; most distant.
USAGE See the note at **farther**.

furtive *ADJECTIVE* stealthy; trying not to be seen.
▷ **furtively** *adverb* **furtiveness** *noun*
[from Latin *furtivus* = stolen]

fury *NOUN* **furies** wild anger; rage.
[from Latin *furia* = rage; an avenging spirit]

furze *NOUN* gorse.
[from Old English]

fuse[1] *NOUN* **fuses** a safety device containing a short piece of wire that melts if too much electricity is passed through it.

fuse *VERB* **fuses, fusing, fused 1** stop working because a fuse has melted. **2** blend together, especially through melting.
[from Latin *fusum* = melted]

a b c d e f g h i j k l m n o p q r s t u v w x y z

fuse[2] *NOUN* **fuses** a length of material that burns easily, used for setting off an explosive.
[from Latin *fusus* = spindle (because originally the material was put in a tube)]

fuselage (*say* few-zel-ahzh) *NOUN* **fuselages** the body of an aircraft.
[French, = shaped like a spindle]

fusillade (*say* few-zil-ayd) *NOUN* **fusillades** a great outburst of firing guns or questions etc.
[French, from *fusiller* = shoot]

fusion *NOUN* **1** the action of blending or uniting things. **2** the uniting of atomic nuclei, usually releasing energy.

fuss *NOUN* **fusses 1** unnecessary excitement or bustle. **2** an agitated protest.
- **make a fuss of** treat someone with great kindness and attention.

fuss *VERB* **fusses**, **fussing**, **fussed** make a fuss about something.
[origin unknown]

fussy *ADJECTIVE* **fussier**, **fussiest 1** fussing; inclined to make a fuss. **2** choosing very carefully; hard to please. **3** full of unnecessary details or decorations.
▷ **fussily** *adverb* **fussiness** *noun*

fusty *ADJECTIVE* **fustier**, **fustiest** smelling stale or stuffy.
▷ **fustiness** *noun*
[from old French]

futile (*say* few-tyl) *ADJECTIVE* useless; having no result.
▷ **futility** *noun*
[from Latin *futilis* = leaking]

futon (*say* foo-ton) *NOUN* **futons** a seat with a mattress that rolls out to form a bed.
[Japanese]

future *NOUN* **1** the time that will come; what is going to happen then. **2** (*in grammar*) the tense of a verb that indicates something happening in the future, expressed by using 'shall', 'will', or 'be going to'.

future *ADJECTIVE* belonging or referring to the future.
[from Latin]

futuristic *ADJECTIVE* very modern, as if belonging to the future rather than the present • *futuristic buildings.*

fuzz *NOUN* something fluffy or frizzy.
[probably from Dutch]

fuzzy *ADJECTIVE* **1** like fuzz; covered with fuzz. **2** blurred; not clear.
▷ **fuzzily** *adverb* **fuzziness** *noun*

-fy *SUFFIX* forms verbs meaning 'make' or 'bring into a certain condition' (e.g. *beautify, purify*).
[from Latin *-ficare* = make]

Gg

gabardine *NOUN* a raincoat made of a strong fabric woven in a slanting pattern.
[from old French *gauvardine*, a kind of cloak]

gabble *VERB* **gabbles**, **gabbling**, **gabbled** talk so quickly that it is difficult to know what is being said.
[from old Dutch]

gable *NOUN* **gables** the pointed part at the top of an outside wall, between two sloping roofs.
▷ **gabled** *adjective*
[from Old Norse]

gad *VERB* **gads**, **gadding**, **gadded**
- **gad about** go about in search of pleasure.
▷ **gadabout** *noun*
[from Old English]

gadget *NOUN* **gadgets** any small useful tool.
▷ **gadgetry** *noun*
[originally a sailors' word; origin unknown]

Gaelic (*say* gay-lik) *NOUN* the Celtic languages of Scotland and Ireland.

gaff *NOUN* **gaffs** a stick with a metal hook for landing large fish.
- **blow the gaff** reveal a plot or secret.
[from French]

gaffe *NOUN* **gaffes** an embarrassing blunder.
[from French]

gag *NOUN* **gags 1** something put into a person's mouth or tied over it to prevent him or her speaking. **2** a joke.

gag *VERB* **gags, gagging, gagged 1** put a gag on a person. **2** prevent someone from making comments • *We cannot gag the press.* **3** retch.
[imitating the sound of someone retching]

gaggle *NOUN* **gaggles** a flock of geese.
[imitating the noise that a goose makes]

gaiety *NOUN* **1** cheerfulness. **2** brightly coloured appearance.
USAGE See *gay* for origin and usage note.

gaily *ADVERB* in a cheerful way.

gain *VERB* **gains, gaining, gained 1** get something that you did not have before; obtain. **2** a clock or watch gains when it becomes ahead of the correct time.
3 reach; arrive at • *At last we gained the shore.*
- **gain on** come closer to a person or thing when chasing them or in a race.

gain *NOUN* **gains** something gained; a profit or improvement.
▷ **gainful** *adjective*
[via old French from Germanic]

gait *NOUN* **gaits** a way of walking or running • *He walked with a shuffling gait.*
[from Old Norse *gata* = a road]

gaiter *NOUN* **gaiters** a leather or cloth covering for the lower part of the leg.
[from French]

gala (*say* gah-la) *NOUN* **galas 1** a festival or celebration. **2** a set of sports contests.
[from old French *galer* = celebrate]

galaxy *NOUN* **galaxies** a very large group of stars.
▷ **galactic** (*say* ga-**lak**-tik) *adjective*
[originally = the Milky Way: from Greek *galaxias* = milky]

gale *NOUN* **gales** a very strong wind.
[origin unknown]

gall[1] (*say* gawl) *NOUN* **1** boldness or impudence. **2** bitterness of feeling. **3** (*old use*) bile.
[from Old English *gealla*]

gall[2] (*say* gawl) *NOUN* **galls** a sore spot on an animal's skin.

gall *VERB* **galls, galling, galled 1** rub a sore.
2 annoy or humiliate someone.
[from Old English *gealle*]

gallant (*say* **gal**-lant) *ADJECTIVE* **1** brave or heroic • *a gallant effort.* **2** courteous towards women. **3** (*old use*) fine and stately • *our gallant ship.*
▷ **gallantly** *adverb* **gallantry** *noun*
[originally = spendidly dressed: from old French *galant* = celebrating]

gall bladder *NOUN* **gall bladders** an organ attached to the liver, in which bile is stored.

galleon *NOUN* **galleons** a large Spanish sailing ship used in the 16th-17th centuries.
[same origin as *galley*]

gallery *NOUN* **galleries 1** a room or building for showing works of art. **2** a platform jutting out from the wall in a church or hall.
3 the highest balcony in a cinema or theatre.
4 a long room or passage.
[from Italian *galleria* = gallery, church porch, perhaps from *Galilee* (a church porch furthest from the altar was called a *galilee*, as Galilee was the province furthest from Jerusalem)]

galley *NOUN* **galleys 1** an ancient type of ship driven by oars. **2** the kitchen in a ship or aircraft.
[from Latin or Greek *galea*]

galling (*say* **gawl**-ing) *ADJECTIVE* annoying or humiliating.
[from *gall*[2]]

gallivant *VERB* **gallivants, gallivanting, gallivanted** go out or wander about in search of pleasure.
[origin unknown]

gallon *NOUN* **gallons** a unit used to measure liquids, 8 pints or 4.546 litres.
[from old French]

gallop *NOUN* **gallops 1** the fastest pace that a horse can go. **2** a fast ride on a horse.

gallop *VERB* **gallops, galloping, galloped** go or ride at a gallop.
[from old French; related to *wallop*]

gallows *NOUN* **gallows** or **gallowses** a framework with a noose for hanging criminals.
[from Old English]

galore *ADVERB* in great numbers; in a large amount • *bargains galore.*
[from Irish]

galoshes *PLURAL NOUN* a pair of waterproof shoes worn over ordinary shoes.
[from old French]

galvanize *VERB* **galvanizes, galvanizing, galvanized** **1** stimulate someone into sudden activity. **2** coat iron with zinc to protect it from rust.
▷ **galvanization** *noun*
[named after an Italian scientist, Luigi *Galvani*, who discovered that muscles move because of electricity in the body]

gambit *NOUN* **gambits** **1** a kind of opening move in chess. **2** an action or remark intended to gain an advantage.
[from Italian *gambetto* = tripping up]

gamble *VERB* **gambles, gambling, gambled** **1** bet on the result of a game, race, or other event. **2** take great risks in the hope of gaining something.
▷ **gambler** *noun*

gamble *NOUN* **gambles** **1** a bet or chance • *a gamble on the lottery.* **2** a risky attempt.
[from Old English *gamenian* = play games]

gambol *VERB* **gambols, gambolling, gambolled** jump or skip about in play.
[from French]

game *NOUN* **games** **1** a form of play or sport, especially one with rules • *a game of football; a computer game.* **2** a section of a long game such as tennis or whist. **3** a scheme or plan; a trick • *Whatever his game is, he won't succeed.* **4** wild animals or birds hunted for sport or food.
- **give the game away** reveal a secret.

game *ADJECTIVE* **1** able and willing to do something • *Are you game for a swim?* **2** brave.
▷ **gamely** *adverb*
[from Old English]

gamekeeper *NOUN* **gamekeepers** a person employed to protect game birds and animals, especially from poachers.

gameplay *NOUN* the design of a computer game and how it is played.

games *PLURAL NOUN* **1** a meeting for sporting contests • *the Olympic Games.* **2** athletics or sports as a subject taught at school.

gaming *NOUN* gambling.

gamma *NOUN* the third letter of the Greek alphabet, equivalent to Roman *G, g*.

gamma rays *PLURAL NOUN* very short X-rays emitted by radioactive substances.

gammon *NOUN* a kind of ham.
[from old French]

gamut (*say* gam-ut) *NOUN* the whole range or scope of anything • *He ran the whole gamut of emotions from joy to despair.*
[related to *gamma*]

gander *NOUN* **ganders** a male goose.
[from Old English]

gang *NOUN* **gangs** **1** a group of people who do things together. **2** a group of criminals.

gang *VERB* **gangs, ganging, ganged**
- **gang up on** form a group to fight or oppose someone.
[from Old Norse]

gangling *ADJECTIVE* tall, thin, and awkward-looking.
[from Old English]

gangplank *NOUN* **gangplanks** a plank placed so that people can walk into or out of a boat.
[from Old Norse *gangr* = walking, going]

gangrene (*say* gang-green) *NOUN* decay of body tissue in a living person.
[from Greek]

gangster *NOUN* **gangsters** a member of a gang of violent criminals.

gangway *NOUN* **gangways** **1** a gap left for people to pass between rows of seats or through a crowd. **2** a movable bridge placed so that people can walk onto or off a ship.
[same origin as *gangplank*]

gannet *NOUN* **gannets** a large seabird which catches fish by flying above the sea and then diving in.
[from Old English]

gaol (*say* jayl) *NOUN* **gaols** a different spelling of *jail*.
▷ **gaol** *verb* **gaoler** *noun*

gap *NOUN* **gaps** **1** a break or opening in something continuous such as a hedge or fence. **2** an interval. **3** a wide difference in ideas.
[from Old Norse]

gape *VERB* **gapes, gaping, gaped** **1** have your mouth open. **2** stare with your mouth open. **3** be open wide.
[from Old Norse]

garage (*say* ga-rah*zh* or ga-rij) *NOUN* **garages 1** a building in which a motor vehicle or vehicles may be kept. **2** a place where motor vehicles are repaired or serviced and where petrol is sold.
[French, = a shelter]

garb *NOUN* special clothing.

garb *VERB* **garbs**, **garbing**, **garbed** (*old use*) or (*poetical use*) dress.
[via old French and Italian from Germanic]

garbage *NOUN* rubbish, especially household rubbish.
[from old French]

garble *VERB* **garbles**, **garbling**, **garbled** give a confused account of a story or message so that it is misunderstood.
[from Arabic *garbala* = sift, select (because the real facts are 'sifted out')]

garden *NOUN* **gardens** a piece of ground where flowers, fruit, or vegetables are grown.
▷ **gardener** *noun* **gardening** *noun*
[via old French from Germanic]

gargantuan (*say* gar-gan-tew-an) *ADJECTIVE* gigantic.
[from *Gargantua*, the name of a giant in a book by Rabelais]

gargle *VERB* **gargles**, **gargling**, **gargled** hold a liquid at the back of the mouth and breathe air through it to wash the inside of the throat.
▷ **gargle** *noun*
[from French *gargouille* = throat]

gargoyle *NOUN* **gargoyles** an ugly or comical face or figure carved on a building, especially on a waterspout.
[from French *gargouille* = throat (because the water passes through the throat of the figure)]

garish (*say* gair-ish) *ADJECTIVE* too bright or highly coloured; gaudy.
▷ **garishly** *adverb*
[origin unknown]

garland *NOUN* **garlands** a wreath of flowers worn or hung as a decoration.
▷ **garland** *verb*
[from old French]

garlic *NOUN* a plant with a bulb divided into smaller bulbs (cloves), which have a strong smell and taste and are used for flavouring food.
[from Old English]

garment *NOUN* **garments** a piece of clothing.
[from French *garnement* = equipment]

garner *VERB* **garners**, **garnering**, **garnered** (*formal or poetical use*) store up; gather or collect.
[from Latin *granarium* = granary]

garnet *NOUN* **garnets** a dark-red stone used as a gem.
[from old Dutch]

garnish *VERB* **garnishes**, **garnishing**, **garnished** decorate something, especially food.

garnish *NOUN* something used to decorate food or give it extra flavour.
[via old French from Germanic]

garret *NOUN* **garrets** an attic.
[from old French *garite* = watchtower]

garrison *NOUN* **garrisons 1** troops who stay in a town or fort to defend it. **2** the building they occupy.
▷ **garrison** *verb*
[from old French *garison* = defence]

garrotte (*say* ga-rot) *NOUN* **garrottes 1** a metal collar for strangling a person condemned to death, formerly used in Spain. **2** a cord or wire used for strangling a victim.

garrotte *VERB* **garrottes**, **garrotting**, **garrotted** strangle with a garrotte.
[from Spanish]

garrulous (*say* ga-rool-us) *ADJECTIVE* talkative.
▷ **garrulousness** *noun*
[from Latin *garrire* = to chatter]

garter *NOUN* **garters** a band of elastic to hold up a sock or stocking.
[from old French]

gas[1] *NOUN* **gases 1** a substance, such as oxygen, that can move freely and is not liquid or solid at ordinary temperatures. **2** a gas that can be burned, used for lighting, heating, or cooking.

gas *VERB* **gasses, gassing, gassed** **1** kill or injure someone with gas. **2** (*informal*) talk idly for a long time.
[an invented word suggested by the Greek word *chaos*]

gas[2] *NOUN* (*informal*) (*American*) short for gasoline.
[abbreviation]

gas chamber *NOUN* **gas chambers** a room that can be filled with poisonous gas to kill people or animals.

gaseous (*say* gas-ee-us) *ADJECTIVE* in the form of a gas.

gash *NOUN* **gashes** a long deep cut or wound.

gash *VERB* **gashes, gashing, gashed** make a gash in something.
[from old French]

gasket *NOUN* **gaskets** a flat ring or strip of soft material for sealing a joint between metal surfaces.
[origin unknown]

gasoline *NOUN* (*American*) petrol.
[from *gas* + Latin *oleum* = oil]

gasometer (*say* gas-om-it-er) *NOUN* **gasometers** a large round tank in which gas is stored.
[from French *gazomètre* = a container for measuring gas]

gasp *VERB* **gasps, gasping, gasped**
1 breathe in suddenly when you are shocked or surprised. **2** struggle to breathe with your mouth open when you are tired or ill.
3 speak in a breathless way.
▷ **gasp** *noun*
[from Old Norse]

gassy *ADJECTIVE* fizzy.

gastric *ADJECTIVE* to do with the stomach.
[from Greek *gaster* = stomach]

gastronomy (*say* gas-tron-om-ee) *NOUN* the art or science of good eating.
▷ **gastronomic** *adjective*
[from Greek *gaster* = stomach + *-nomia* = management]

gastropod *NOUN* **gastropods** an animal (e.g. a snail) that moves by means of a fleshy 'foot' on its stomach.
[from Greek *gaster* = stomach + *podos* = of the foot]

gate *NOUN* **gates** **1** a movable barrier, usually on hinges, used as a door in a wall or fence. **2** a barrier for controlling the flow of water in a dam or lock. **3** a place where you wait before you board an aircraft. **4** the number of people attending a football match etc.
[from Old English]

gateau (*say* gat-oh) *NOUN* **gateaus** or **gateaux** a large rich cream cake.
[French]

gatecrash *VERB* **gatecrashes, gatecrashing, gatecrashed** go to a private party without being invited.
▷ **gatecrasher** *noun*

gateway *NOUN* **gateways** **1** an opening containing a gate. **2** a way to reach something • *the gateway to success.*

gather *VERB* **gathers, gathering, gathered** **1** come or bring together.
2 collect; obtain gradually • *We've been gathering information.* **3** collect as harvest; pick • *Gather the corn when it is ripe; gather flowers.* **4** understand or learn • *I gather you've been on holiday.* **5** pull cloth into folds by running a thread through it.
- **gather speed** move gradually faster.
[from Old English]

gathering *NOUN* **gatherings** an assembly or meeting of people; a party.

gaudy *ADJECTIVE* too showy and bright.
▷ **gaudily** *adverb* **gaudiness** *noun*
[from Latin *gaudere* = rejoice]

gauge (*say* gayj) *NOUN* **gauges** **1** a standard measurement. **2** the distance between a pair of rails on a railway. **3** a measuring instrument.

gauge *VERB* **gauges, gauging, gauged**
1 measure. **2** estimate; form a judgement.
[from old French]

gaunt *ADJECTIVE* lean and haggard.
▷ **gauntness** *noun*
[origin unknown]

gauntlet[1] *NOUN* **gauntlets** a glove with a wide cuff covering the wrist.
- **throw down the gauntlet** offer a challenge.
[from French *gant* = glove]

gauntlet[2] *NOUN*
- **run the gauntlet** have to face criticism or hostility from a lot of people.
[from a former military and naval punishment in which the victim was made to pass between two rows of men who struck him as he passed; the word is from Swedish *gatlopp* = passage]

gauze *NOUN* **1** thin transparent woven material. **2** fine wire mesh.
▷ **gauzy** *adjective*
[from *Gaza*, a town in Palestine, where it was first made]

gay *ADJECTIVE* **1** homosexual. **2** cheerful. **3** brightly coloured.
▷ **gayness** *noun*
[from French]
USAGE Nowadays the most common meaning of *gay* is 'homosexual'. The older meanings 'cheerful' and 'brightly coloured' can still be used but are becoming less and less common in everyday use. *Gayness* is the noun from meaning 1 of *gay*. The noun that relates to the other two meanings is *gaiety*.

gaze *VERB* **gazes, gazing, gazed** look at something steadily for a long time.

gaze *NOUN* **gazes** a long steady look.
[origin unknown]

gazelle *NOUN* **gazelles** or **gazelle** a small antelope, usually fawn and white, from Africa or Asia.
[via old French from Arabic]

gazette *NOUN* **gazettes 1** a newspaper. **2** an official journal.
[from Italian *gazetta de la novità* = a halfpenny worth of news (a *gazetta* was a Venetian coin of small value)]

gazetteer (*say* gaz-it-eer) *NOUN* **gazetteers** a list of place names.
[originally = journalist; the first gazetteer was intended to help journalists]

GCSE *ABBREVIATION* General Certificate of Secondary Education.

gear *NOUN* **gears 1** a cogwheel, especially one of a set in a motor vehicle that turn power from the engine into movement of the wheels. **2** equipment or apparatus • *camping gear*.

gear *VERB* **gears, gearing, geared**
- **gear to** make something match or be suitable for something else • *Health care should be geared to people's needs, not to whether they can pay.*
- **gear up** get ready for • *We were all geared up to play cricket, but then it rained.*
[from Old Norse]

gearbox *NOUN* **gearboxes** a case enclosing gears.

Geiger counter (*say* gy-ger) *NOUN* **Geiger counters** an instrument that detects and measures radioactivity.
[named after a German scientist, H. W. *Geiger*, who helped to develop it]

gel *NOUN* **gels** a jelly-like substance, especially one used to give a style to hair.

gelatine *NOUN* a clear jelly-like substance made by boiling animal tissue and used to make jellies and other foods and in photographic film.
▷ **gelatinous** (*say* jil-at-in-us) *adjective*
[from Italian *gelata* = jelly]

geld *VERB* **gelds, gelding, gelded** castrate or spay an animal.
[from Old Norse]

gelding *NOUN* **geldings** a castrated horse or other male animal.

gelignite (*say* jel-ig-nyt) *NOUN* a kind of explosive.
[from *gelatine* + Latin *lignum* = wood (because gelignite contains wood pulp)]

gem *NOUN* **gems 1** a precious stone. **2** an excellent person or thing.
[via Old English from Latin]

-gen *SUFFIX* used in scientific language to form nouns meaning 'producing' or 'produced' (e.g. *oxygen*, *hydrogen*).

gender *NOUN* **genders 1** the group in which a noun is classed in the grammar of some languages, e.g. masculine, feminine, or neuter. **2** a person's sex • *Jobs should be open to all, regardless of race or gender.*
[from Latin *genus* = a kind]

gene (*say* jeen) *NOUN* **genes** the part of a living cell that controls which characteristics (such as the colour of hair or eyes) are inherited from parents.
[from Greek *genos* = kind, race]

A B C D E F **G** H I J K L M N O P Q R S T U V W X Y Z

genealogy (*say* jeen-ee-al-o-jee) NOUN **genealogies 1** a list or diagram showing how people are descended from an ancestor. **2** the study of family history and ancestors.
▷ **genealogical** (*say* jeen-ee-a-loj-ik-al) *adjective*
[from Greek *genea* = race of people, + *-logy*]

genera (*say* jen-e-ra) PLURAL NOUN plural of **genus**.

general ADJECTIVE **1** to do with or involving most people or things • *This drug is now in general use.* **2** not detailed; broad • *I've got the general idea.* **3** chief or head • *the general manager.*
- **in general** as a general rule; usually.

general NOUN **generals** a senior army officer.
[from Latin]

general election NOUN **general elections** an election of Members of Parliament for the whole country.

generality NOUN **generalities 1** being general. **2** a general statement without exact details.

generalize VERB **generalizes, generalizing, generalized** make a statement that is true in most cases.
▷ **generalization** *noun*

generally ADVERB **1** usually. **2** in a general sense; without regard to details • *I was speaking generally.*

general practitioner NOUN **general practitioners** a doctor who treats all kinds of diseases. He or she is the first doctor that people see when they are ill.

generate VERB **generates, generating, generated** produce or create.
[from Latin *generatus* = fathered]

generation NOUN **generations**
1 generating. **2** a single stage in a family • *Three generations were included: children, parents, and grandparents.* **3** all the people born at about the same time • *our parents' generation.*

generator NOUN **generators 1** an apparatus for producing gases or steam. **2** a machine for converting mechanical energy into electricity.

generic (*say* jin-e-rik) ADJECTIVE belonging to a whole class, group, or genus.
▷ **generically** *adverb*

generous ADJECTIVE **1** willing to give things or share them. **2** given freely; plentiful • *a generous helping.*
▷ **generously** *adverb* **generosity** *noun*
[from Latin *generosus* = noble]

genesis NOUN the beginning or origin of something.
[Greek, = creation or origin]

genetic (*say* jin-et-ik) ADJECTIVE **1** to do with genes. **2** to do with characteristics inherited from parents or ancestors.
▷ **genetically** *adverb*
[from *genesis*]

genetics NOUN the study of genes and genetic behaviour.

genial (*say* jee-nee-al) ADJECTIVE kindly and cheerful.
▷ **genially** *adverb* **geniality** (*say* jee-nee-al-it-ee) *noun*
[from Latin *genialis* = joyous]

genie (*say* jee-nee) NOUN **genii** (*say* jee-nee-y) (in Arabian tales) a spirit with strange powers, especially one who can grant wishes.
[same origin as *genius*]

genital (*say* jen-it-al) ADJECTIVE to do with animal reproduction or reproductive organs.
[from old French; related to *generate*]

genitals (*say* jen-it-alz) PLURAL NOUN external sexual organs.

genius NOUN **geniuses 1** an unusually clever person; a person with very great creativity or natural ability. **2** unusual cleverness; very great creativity or natural ability • *He has a real genius for music.*
[Latin, = a spirit]

genocide (*say* jen-o-syd) NOUN deliberate extermination of a race of people.
[from Greek *genos* = kind, race, + *-cide*]

genome (*say* jen-ohm) NOUN **genomes** (*in science*) all the genes in one cell of a living thing • *the human genome.*
[from Greek *genus* = type, + *chromosome*]

genre (*say* zhahnr) NOUN **genres** a particular kind or style of art or literature, e.g. epic, romance, or western.
[French, = a kind]

gent NOUN **gents** (*informal*) a gentleman; a man.

genteel (*say* jen-**teel**) ADJECTIVE trying to seem polite and refined.
▷ **genteelly** *adverb* **gentility** (*say* jen-**til**-it-ee) *noun*
[from French; related to *gentle*]

gentile NOUN **gentiles** a person who is not Jewish.
[from Latin *gens* = clan or race]

gentle ADJECTIVE **1** mild or kind; not rough. **2** not harsh or severe • *a gentle breeze.*
▷ **gently** *adverb* **gentleness** *noun*
[from Latin *gentilis* = from a good family]

gentleman NOUN **gentlemen 1** a well-mannered or honourable man. **2** a man of good social position. **3** (*in polite use*) a man.

gentry PLURAL NOUN (*old use*) upper-class people.

genuine ADJECTIVE real; not faked or pretending.
▷ **genuinely** *adverb* **genuineness** *noun*
[from Latin *genu* = knee (because a father would take a baby onto his knee to show that he accepted it as his)]

genus (*say* **jee**-nus) NOUN **genera** (*say* **jen**-er-a) a group of similar animals or plants • *Lions and tigers belong to the same genus.*
[Latin, = family or race]

geo- PREFIX earth.
[from Greek *ge* = earth]

geography (*say* jee-**og**-ra-fee) NOUN the study of the earth's surface and of its climate, peoples, and products.
▷ **geographer** *noun* **geographical** *adjective* **geographically** *adverb*
[from *geo-* + *-graphy*]

geology (*say* jee-**ol**-o-jee) NOUN the study of the structure of the earth's crust and its layers.
▷ **geological** *adjective* **geologically** *adverb* **geologist** *noun*
[from *geo-* + *-logy*]

geometry (*say* jee-**om**-it-ree) NOUN the study of lines, angles, surfaces, and solids in mathematics.
▷ **geometric** *adjective* **geometrical** *adjective* **geometrically** *adverb*
[from *geo-* + Greek *-metria* = measurement]

Georgian ADJECTIVE belonging to the time of the kings George I-IV (1714-1830) or George V-VI (1910-52).

geranium NOUN **geraniums** a garden plant with red, pink, or white flowers.
[from Greek]

gerbil (*say* **jer**-bil) NOUN **gerbils** a small brown rodent with long hind legs, often kept as a pet.
[from Latin]

geriatric (*say* je-ree-**at**-rik) ADJECTIVE to do with the care of old people and their health.
[from Greek *geras* = old age + *iatros* = doctor]

germ NOUN **germs 1** a micro-organism, especially one that can cause disease. **2** a tiny living structure from which a plant or animal may develop. **3** part of the seed of a cereal plant.
[from Latin *germen* = seed or sprout]

Germanic NOUN **1** a group of languages spoken in northern Europe and Scandinavia. **2** an unrecorded language believed to be the ancestor of this group.

German measles NOUN rubella.

German shepherd dog NOUN **German shepherd dogs** a large strong dog, often used by the police.

germicide NOUN **germicides** a substance that kills germs.
[from *germ* + *-cide*]

germinate VERB **germinates, germinating, germinated** when a seed germinates, it begins to develop, and roots and shoots grow from it.
▷ **germination** *noun*
[same origin as *germ*]

gerund (*say* **je**-rund) NOUN **gerunds** a form of a verb (in English ending in *-ing*) that functions as a noun, e.g. *scolding* in *what is the use of my scolding him?*
[from Latin *gerundum* = doing]

gestation (*say* jes-tay-shun) *NOUN* the process of carrying a foetus in the womb between conception and birth; the time this takes.
[from Latin *gestare* = carry]

gesticulate (*say* jes-tik-yoo-layt) *VERB* **gesticulates, gesticulating, gesticulated** make expressive movements with your hands and arms.
▷ **gesticulation** *noun*
[same origin as *gesture*]

gesture (*say* jes-cher) *NOUN* **gestures 1** a movement that expresses what a person feels. **2** an action that shows goodwill • *It would be a nice gesture to send her some flowers.*

gesture *VERB* **gestures, gesturing, gestured** tell a person something by making a gesture • *She gestured me to be quiet.*
[from Latin *gestus* = action, way of standing or moving]

get *VERB* **gets, getting, got**
This word has many different uses, including **1** obtain or receive • *She got first prize.* **2** become • *Don't get angry!* **3** reach a place • *We got there by midnight.* **4** put or move • *I can't get my shoe on.* **5** prepare • *Will you get the tea?* **6** persuade or order • *Get him to wash up.* **7** catch or suffer from an illness. **8** (*informal*) understand • *Do you get what I mean?*
- **get away with 1** escape with something. **2** avoid being punished for what you have done.
- **get by** (*informal*) manage.
- **get on 1** make progress. **2** be friendly with somebody.
- **get over** recover from an illness etc.
- **get up 1** stand up. **2** get out of bed in the morning. **3** prepare or organize • *We got up a concert.*
- **get your own back** (*informal*) have your revenge.
- **have got to** must.
[from Old Norse]

getaway *NOUN* **getaways** an escape after committing a crime • *They made their getaway in a stolen car.*

geyser (*say* gee-zer or gy-zer) *NOUN* **geysers 1** a natural spring that shoots up columns of hot water. **2** a kind of water heater.
[from *Geysir* = gusher, the name of a geyser in Iceland]

ghastly *ADJECTIVE* **1** very unpleasant or bad. **2** looking pale and ill.
▷ **ghastliness** *noun*
[from Old English *gaestan* = terrify]

gherkin (*say* ger-kin) *NOUN* **gherkins** a small cucumber used for pickling.
[via Dutch from Greek]

ghetto (*say* get-oh) *NOUN* **ghettos** an area of a city, often a slum area, where a group of people live who are treated unfairly in comparison with others.
[probably from Italian *getto* = foundry (because the first ghetto was established in 1516 in the site of a foundry in Venice)]

ghost *NOUN* **ghosts** the spirit of a dead person that appears to the living.
▷ **ghostly** *adjective*
[from Old English]

ghoulish (*say* gool-ish) *ADJECTIVE* enjoying things that are grisly or unpleasant.
▷ **ghoulishly** *adverb* **ghoulishness** *noun*
[from Arabic *gul* = a demon that eats dead bodies]

giant *NOUN* **giants 1** (in myths or fairy tales) a creature like a huge man. **2** a man, animal, or plant that is much larger than the usual size.
[from Greek]

gibber (*say* jib-er) *VERB* **gibbers, gibbering, gibbered** make quick meaningless sounds, especially when shocked or terrified.
[imitating the sound]

gibberish (*say* jib-er-ish) *NOUN* meaningless speech; nonsense.
[probably from *gibber* + *-ish*]

gibbet (*say* jib-it) *NOUN* **gibbets 1** a gallows. **2** an upright post with an arm from which a criminal's body was hung after execution, as a warning to others.
[from old French]

gibbon *NOUN* **gibbons** a small ape from south-east Asia. Gibbons have very long arms to help them swing through the trees where they live.
[French]

gibe (*say* jyb) *NOUN* **gibes** a remark that is meant to hurt someone's feelings or make them look silly.

gibe *VERB* **gibes, gibing, gibed** make a hurtful remark; taunt, mock.
[origin unknown]

giblets (*say* jib-lits) *PLURAL NOUN* the parts of the inside of a bird, such as the heart, liver, etc., that are taken out before it is cooked.
[from old French]

giddy *ADJECTIVE* **1** feeling that everything is spinning round and that you might fall. **2** causing this feeling • *We looked down from the giddy height of the cliff.*
▷ **giddily** *adverb* **giddiness** *noun*
[from Old English]

gift *NOUN* **gifts 1** a present. **2** a natural talent • *She has a gift for music.*
[from Old Norse]

gifted *ADJECTIVE* having a special talent.

gig *NOUN* **gigs** (*informal*) a live performance by a musician, comedian, etc.
[origin unknown]

gigabyte (*say* gi-ga-byt or ji-ga-byt) *NOUN* **gigabytes** (*in computing*) a unit of information equal to one thousand million bytes, or (more precisely) 2^{30} bytes.
[from Greek *gigas* = giant + *byte*]

gigantic (*say* jy-gan-tik) *ADJECTIVE* extremely large; huge.
[from Latin *gigantis* = of a giant]

giggle *VERB* **giggles, giggling, giggled** laugh in a silly way.

giggle *NOUN* **giggles 1** a silly laugh. **2** (*informal*) something amusing; a bit of fun.
[imitating the sound]

gild *VERB* **gilds, gilding, gilded** cover something with a thin layer of gold or gold paint.
[from Old English]

gills *PLURAL NOUN* the part of the body through which fishes and certain other water animals breathe.
[from Old Norse]

gilt *NOUN* a thin covering of gold or gold paint.

gilt *ADJECTIVE* gilded; gold-coloured.
[the old past tense of *gild*]

gimlet *NOUN* **gimlets** a small tool with a screw-like tip for boring holes.
[via old French from Germanic]

gimmick *NOUN* **gimmicks** something unusual or silly done or used just to attract people's attention.
[originally American; origin unknown]

gin[1] *NOUN* a colourless alcoholic drink flavoured with juniper berries.
[from the name of *Geneva*, a city in Switzerland]

gin[2] *NOUN* **gins 1** a kind of trap for catching animals. **2** a machine for separating the fibres of the cotton plant from its seeds.
[from old French *engin* = engine]

ginger *NOUN* **1** the hot-tasting root of a tropical plant, or a flavouring made from this root, used especially in drinks and Eastern cooking. **2** liveliness or energy. **3** a reddish-yellow colour.
▷ **ginger** *adjective*

ginger *VERB* **gingers, gingering, gingered** make something more lively • *This will ginger things up!*
[via Old English, Latin, and Greek from Dravidian (a group of languages spoken in southern India)]

gingerbread *NOUN* a ginger-flavoured cake or biscuit.

gingerly *ADVERB* cautiously.
[origin unknown]

gipsy *NOUN* **gipsies** a different spelling of *gypsy*.

giraffe *NOUN* **giraffe** or **giraffes** an African animal with long legs and a very long neck, the world's tallest mammal.
[from Arabic]

gird *VERB* **girds, girding, girded 1** fasten with a belt or band • *He girded on his sword.* **2** prepare for an effort • *It is time to gird yourself for action.*
[from Old English]

girder *NOUN* **girders** a metal beam supporting part of a building or a bridge.
[from an old meaning of *gird* = brace or strengthen]

girdle *NOUN* **girdles 1** a belt or cord worn round the waist. **2** a woman's elastic corset covering from the waist to the thigh.
[from Old English]

girl *NOUN* **girls 1** a female child. **2** a young woman.
▷ **girlhood** *noun* **girlish** *adjective*
[origin unknown]

girlfriend *NOUN* **girlfriends** a person's regular female friend or lover.

giro (*say* jy-roh) *NOUN* a system of sending money directly from one bank account or post office account to another.
[via German from Italian]

girt *ADJECTIVE* (*old use*) girded.
[old past tense of *gird*]

girth *NOUN* **girths 1** the distance round something. **2** a band passing under a horse's body to hold the saddle in place.
[from Old Norse]

gist (*say* jist) *NOUN* the essential points or general sense of what someone says.
[from old French]

give *VERB* **gives, giving, gave, given 1** let someone have something. **2** make or do something • *He gave a laugh.* **3** be flexible or springy; bend or collapse when pressed.
▷ **giver** *noun*
- **give in** acknowledge that you are defeated; yield.
- **give up 1** stop trying. **2** end a habit.
[from Old English]

given *ADJECTIVE* named or stated in advance • *All the people in a given area.*

gizzard *NOUN* **gizzards** a bird's second stomach, in which food is ground up.
[from old French]

glacé (*say* glas-ay) *ADJECTIVE* iced with sugar; crystallized.
[French, = iced]

glacial (*say* glay-shal) *ADJECTIVE* icy; made of or produced by ice.
▷ **glacially** *adverb*
[from Latin *glacies* = ice]

glaciation (*say* glay-see-ay-shun) *NOUN* the process or state of being covered with glaciers or ice sheets.
▷ **glaciated** *adjective*

glacier (*say* glas-ee-er) *NOUN* **glaciers** a mass of ice that moves very slowly down a mountain valley.
[same origin as *glacial*]

glad *ADJECTIVE* **1** pleased; expressing joy. **2** giving pleasure • *We brought the glad news.*
▷ **gladly** *adverb* **gladness** *noun*
- **glad of** grateful for or pleased with something.
[from Old English]

gladden *VERB* **gladdens, gladdening, gladdened** make a person glad.

glade *NOUN* **glades** an open space in a forest.
[origin unknown]

gladiator (*say* glad-ee-ay-ter) *NOUN* **gladiators** a man trained to fight for public entertainment in ancient Rome.
▷ **gladiatorial** (*say* glad-ee-at-or-ee-al) *adjective*
[from Latin *gladius* = sword]

glamorize *VERB* **glamorizes, glamorizing, glamorized** make something seem glamorous or romantic.

glamorous *ADJECTIVE* excitingly attractive.

glamour *NOUN* attractiveness, romantic charm.
[from an old meaning of *grammar* = magic]

glance *VERB* **glances, glancing, glanced 1** look at something briefly. **2** strike something at an angle and slide off it • *The ball glanced off his bat.*
▷ **glance** *noun*
[origin unknown]

gland *NOUN* **glands** an organ of the body that separates substances from the blood so that they can be used or secreted (passed out of the body).
▷ **glandular** *adjective*
[from Latin]

glare *VERB* **glares, glaring, glared 1** shine with a bright or dazzling light. **2** stare angrily or fiercely.
▷ **glare** *noun*
[from old German or old Dutch]

glaring *ADJECTIVE* very obvious • *a glaring error.*

glasnost *NOUN* the open reporting of news or giving of information, especially in the former Soviet Union.
[Russian, = openness]

A B C D E F G H I J K L M N O P Q R S T U V W X Y Z

glass *NOUN* **glasses** **1** a hard brittle substance that is usually transparent. **2** a container made of glass for drinking from. **3** a mirror. **4** a lens.
▷ **glassy** *adjective*
[from Old English]

glasses *PLURAL NOUN* **1** a pair of lenses in a frame, worn over the eyes to help improve eyesight. **2** binoculars.

glaze *VERB* **glazes, glazing, glazed** **1** fit a window or building with glass. **2** give a shiny surface to something. **3** become glassy.

glaze *NOUN* **glazes** a shiny surface or coating, especially on pottery or food.
[from *glass*]

glazier (*say* glay-zee-er) *NOUN* **glaziers** a person whose job is to fit glass in windows.

gleam *NOUN* **gleams** **1** a beam of soft light, especially one that comes and goes. **2** a small amount of hope, humour, etc.

gleam *VERB* **gleams, gleaming, gleamed** shine brightly, especially after cleaning or polishing.
[from Old English]

glean *VERB* **gleans, gleaning, gleaned** **1** pick up grain left by harvesters. **2** gather bit by bit • *glean some information.*
▷ **gleaner** *noun*
[via Latin from a Celtic language]

glee *NOUN* great delight.
▷ **gleeful** *adjective* **gleefully** *adverb*
[from Old English]

glen *NOUN* **glens** a narrow valley, especially in Scotland.
[from Scottish Gaelic or Irish]

glib *ADJECTIVE* speaking or writing readily but not sincerely or thoughtfully.
▷ **glibly** *adverb* **glibness** *noun*
[from an old word *glibbery* = slippery]

glide *VERB* **glides, gliding, glided** **1** move along smoothly. **2** fly without using an engine. **3** birds glide when they fly without beating their wings.
▷ **glide** *noun*
[from Old English]

glider *NOUN* **gliders** an aircraft without an engine that flies by floating on warm air currents called thermals.

glimmer *NOUN* **glimmers** **1** a faint light. **2** a small sign or trace of something • *a glimmer of hope.*

glimmer *VERB* **glimmers, glimmering, glimmered** shine with a faint, flickering light.
[probably from a Scandinavian language]

glimpse *NOUN* **glimpses** a brief view.

glimpse *VERB* **glimpses, glimpsing, glimpsed** see something briefly.
[probably from Old English]

glint *NOUN* **glints** a very brief flash of light.

glint *VERB* **glints, glinting, glinted** shine with a flash of light.
[probably from a Scandinavian language]

glisten (*say* glis-en) *VERB* **glistens, glistening, glistened** shine like something wet or oily.
[from Old English]

glitter *VERB* **glitters, glittering, glittered** shine with tiny flashes of light; sparkle.

glitter *NOUN* tiny sparkling pieces used for decoration.
[from Old Norse]

gloaming *NOUN* (*Scottish*) the evening twilight.
[from Old English]

gloat *VERB* **gloats, gloating, gloated** be pleased in an unkind way that you have succeeded or that someone else has been hurt or upset.
[origin unknown]

global *ADJECTIVE* **1** to do with the whole world; worldwide. **2** to do with the whole of a system.
▷ **globally** *adverb*
[from *globe*]

globalization *NOUN* the process by which a business or organization becomes international.
[from Latin *globus* = sphere]

global warming *NOUN* the increase in the temperature of the earth's atmosphere, caused by the greenhouse effect.

globe *NOUN* **globes** **1** something shaped like a ball, especially one with a map of the whole world on it. **2** the world • *She has travelled all over the globe.* **3** a hollow round glass object.
[from Latin]

globular (*say* glob-yoo-ler) *ADJECTIVE* shaped like a globe.
[same origin as *globule*]

globule (*say* glob-yool) *NOUN* **globules** a small rounded drop.
[from Latin *globulus* = small globe]

gloom *NOUN* **1** darkness. **2** sadness or despair.
[origin unknown]

gloomy *ADJECTIVE* **gloomier**, **gloomiest** **1** almost dark. **2** depressed or depressing.
▷ **gloomily** *adverb* **gloominess** *noun*

G

glorify *VERB* **glorifies**, **glorifying**, **glorified** **1** give great praise or great honour to. **2** make a thing seem more splendid or attractive than it really is • *It is a film that glorifies war.*
▷ **glorification** *noun*

glorious *ADJECTIVE* splendid or magnificent.
▷ **gloriously** *adverb*

glory *NOUN* **glories 1** fame and honour. **2** praise. **3** beauty or magnificence.

glory *VERB* **glories**, **glorying**, **gloried** rejoice; pride yourself • *They gloried in victory.*
[from Latin]

gloss[1] *NOUN* **glosses** the shine on a smooth surface.

gloss *VERB* **glosses**, **glossing**, **glossed** make a thing glossy.
[origin unknown]

gloss[2] *VERB* **glosses**, **glossing**, **glossed**
- **gloss over** mention a fault or mistake only briefly to make it seem less serious than it really is.
[from old French *gloser* = flatter or deceive]

glossary *NOUN* **glossaries** a list of difficult words with their meanings explained • *There is a glossary at the back of the book.*
[from Greek *glossa* = tongue, language]

gloss paint *NOUN* **gloss paints** a paint with a glossy finish.

glossy *ADJECTIVE* **glossier**, **glossiest** smooth and shiny.
▷ **glossily** *adverb* **glossiness** *noun*

glove *NOUN* **gloves** a covering for the hand, usually with separate divisions for each finger and thumb.
▷ **gloved** *adjective*
[from Old English]

glow *NOUN* **1** brightness and warmth without flames. **2** a warm or cheerful feeling • *We felt a glow of pride.*

glow *VERB* **glows**, **glowing**, **glowed** shine with a soft, warm light.
[from Old English]

glower (*rhymes with* **flower**) *VERB* **glowers**, **glowering**, **glowered** stare angrily; scowl.
[origin unknown]

glowing *ADJECTIVE* very enthusiastic or favourable • *a glowing report.*

glow-worm *NOUN* **glow-worms** a kind of beetle whose tail gives out a green light.

glucose *NOUN* a form of sugar found in fruit juice and honey.
[same origin as *glycerine*]

glue *NOUN* **glues** a sticky substance used for joining things together.
▷ **gluey** *adjective*

glue *VERB* **glues**, **gluing**, **glued** **1** stick with glue. **2** attach or hold closely • *His ear was glued to the keyhole.*
[from French; related to *gluten*]

glum *ADJECTIVE* miserable or depressed.
▷ **glumly** *adverb* **glumness** *noun*
[from dialect *glum* = to frown]

glut *NOUN* **gluts** an excessive supply.
[from Latin *gluttire* = to swallow]

gluten (*say* gloo-ten) *NOUN* a sticky protein substance in flour.
[Latin, = glue]

glutinous (*say* gloo-tin-us) *ADJECTIVE* glue-like or sticky.
[same origin as *gluten*]

glutton *NOUN* **gluttons** a person who eats too much.
▷ **gluttonous** *adjective* **gluttony** *noun*
- **glutton for punishment** a person who seems to enjoy doing something difficult or unpleasant.
[from old French; related to *glut*]

glycerine (*say* glis-er-een) *NOUN* a thick sweet colourless liquid used in ointments and medicines and in explosives.
[from Greek *glykys* = sweet]

gm *ABBREVIATION* gram.

GMT *ABBREVIATION* Greenwich Mean Time.

gnarled (*say* narld) *ADJECTIVE* twisted and knobbly, like an old tree.
[from old German or old Dutch]

gnash (*say* nash) *VERB* **gnashes, gnashing, gnashed** grind your teeth together.
[origin unknown]

gnat (*say* nat) *NOUN* **gnats** a tiny fly that bites.
[from Old English]

gnaw (*say* naw) *VERB* **gnaws, gnawing, gnawed** keep on biting something hard so that it wears away.
[from Old English]

gnome (*say* nohm) *NOUN* **gnomes** a kind of dwarf in fairy tales, usually living underground.
[from Latin]

gnu (*say* noo) *NOUN* **gnu** or **gnus** a large ox-like antelope.
[from Khoisan (a group of languages spoken in southern Africa)]

GNVQ *ABBREVIATION* General National Vocational Qualification.

go *VERB* **goes, going, went, gone**
This word has many uses, including **1** move from one place to another • *Where are you going?* **2** leave • *I must go.* **3** lead from one place to another • *The road goes to Bristol.* **4** become • *Milk went sour.* **5** make a sound • *The gun went bang.* **6** belong in some place or position • *Plates go on that shelf.* **7** be sold • *The house went very cheaply.*
- **go off** **1** explode. **2** become stale. **3** stop liking something.
- **go on** continue.
- **go out** stop burning or shining.
- **go through** experience something unpleasant or difficult.

go *NOUN* **goes 1** a turn or try • *May I have a go?* **2** (*informal*) energy or liveliness • *She is full of go.*
- **make a go of** make a success of something.
- **on the go** active; always working or moving.
[from Old English]

goad *NOUN* **goads** a stick with a pointed end for prodding cattle to move onwards.

goad *VERB* **goads, goading, goaded** stir into action by being annoying • *He goaded me into fighting.*
[from Old English]

go-ahead *NOUN* permission to proceed.

go-ahead *ADJECTIVE* adventurous and willing to try new methods.

goal *NOUN* **goals 1** the place where a ball must go to score a point in football, hockey, etc. **2** a point scored in this way. **3** something that you are trying to reach or achieve.
[origin unknown]

goalkeeper *NOUN* **goalkeepers** the player who stands in the goal to try and keep the ball from entering.

goat *NOUN* **goats** a mammal with horns and a beard, closely related to the sheep. Domestic goats are kept for their milk.
[from Old English]

gobble *VERB* **gobbles, gobbling, gobbled** eat quickly and greedily.
[from old French *gober* = to swallow]

gobbledegook *NOUN* (*slang*) the pompous and technical language used by officials that is difficult to understand.
[imitation of the sound a turkeycock makes]

go-between *NOUN* **go-betweens** a person who acts as a messenger or negotiator between others.

goblet *NOUN* **goblets** a drinking glass with a long stem and a base.
[from French *gobelet* = little cup]

goblin *NOUN* **goblins** a mischievous ugly elf.
[from old French]

God *NOUN* the creator of the universe in Christian, Jewish, and Muslim belief.
[from Old English]

god *NOUN* **gods** a male being that is worshipped • *Mars was a Roman god.*

godchild *NOUN* **godchildren** a child that a godparent promises to see brought up as a Christian.
▷ **god-daughter** *noun* **godson** *noun*

goddess *NOUN* **goddesses** a female being that is worshipped.

godhead *NOUN* the divine nature of God.
[from *god* + Old English *-had* = -hood]

A B C D E F **G** H I J K L M N O P Q R S T U V W X Y Z

godly *ADJECTIVE* **godlier**, **godliest** sincerely religious.
▷ **godliness** *noun*

godparent *NOUN* **godparents** a person at a child's christening who promises to see that it is brought up as a Christian.
▷ **godfather** *noun* **godmother** *noun*

godsend *NOUN* **godsends** a piece of unexpected good luck.
[from an old phrase *God's send* = what God has sent]

gogga *NOUN* **goggas** (*informal*) (*S. African*) an insect or any small flying or crawling creature.
[from Afrikaans]

goggle *VERB* **goggles**, **goggling**, **goggled** stare with wide-open eyes.
[origin unknown]

goggles *PLURAL NOUN* large spectacles for protecting your eyes from wind, water, dust, etc.
[from *goggle*]

going *present participle* of **go**.
- **be going to do something** be ready or likely to do it.

going *NOUN*
- **good going** quick progress • *It was good going to get home before dark.*

go-kart *NOUN* **go-karts** a kind of miniature racing car.

gold *NOUN* **golds 1** a precious yellow metal. **2** a deep yellow colour. **3** a gold medal, awarded as first prize.
▷ **gold** *adjective*
[from Old English]

golden *ADJECTIVE* **1** made of gold. **2** coloured like gold. **3** precious or excellent • *a golden opportunity.*

golden wedding *NOUN* **golden weddings** a couple's fiftieth wedding anniversary.

goldfinch *NOUN* **goldfinches** a bird with yellow feathers in its wings.

goldfish *NOUN* **goldfish** a small red or orange fish, often kept as a pet.

gold leaf *NOUN* gold that has been beaten into a very thin sheet.

goldsmith *NOUN* **goldsmiths** a person who makes things in gold.

golf *NOUN* an outdoor game played by hitting a small white ball with a club into a series of holes on a specially prepared ground (a
- **golf course** or
- **golf links**) and taking as few strokes as possible.
▷ **golfer** *noun* **golfing** *noun*
[origin unknown]

-gon *SUFFIX* used to form nouns meaning 'having a certain number of angles (and sides)' (e.g. *hexagon*).
[from Greek *gonia* = angle]

gondola (*say* gond-ol-a) *NOUN* **gondolas** a boat with high pointed ends used on the canals in Venice.
[Italian]

gondolier *NOUN* **gondoliers** the person who moves a gondola along with a pole.

gong *NOUN* **gongs** a large metal disc that makes an echoing sound when it is hit.
[from Malay (a language spoken in Malaysia)]

good *ADJECTIVE* **better**, **best 1** having the right qualities; of the kind that people like • *a good book.* **2** kind • *It was good of you to help us.* **3** well-behaved • *Be a good boy.* **4** skilled or talented • *a good pianist.* **5** healthy; giving benefit • *Exercise is good for you.* **6** thorough • *Give it a good clean.* **7** large; considerable • *It's a good distance from the shops.*

good *NOUN* **1** something good • *Do good to others.* **2** benefit • *It's for your own good.*
- **for good** for ever.
- **no good** useless.
[from Old English]
USAGE In standard English, *good* cannot be used as an adverb. You can say *She's a good player* but not *She played good.* The adverb that goes with *good* is *well.*

goodbye *INTERJECTION* a word used when you leave somebody or at the end of a phone call.
[short for *God be with you*]

Good Friday *NOUN* the Friday before Easter, when Christians commemorate the Crucifixion of Christ.

good-looking *ADJECTIVE* attractive or handsome.

goodness *NOUN* **1** being good. **2** the good part of something.

goods *PLURAL NOUN* **1** things that are bought and sold. **2** things that are carried on trains or lorries.

goodwill *NOUN* a kindly feeling towards another person.

goody *NOUN* **goodies** (*informal*) **1** something good or attractive, especially to eat. **2** a good person, especially one of the heroes in a story.

gooey *ADJECTIVE* sticky or slimy.

goose *NOUN* **geese** a long-necked water bird with webbed feet, larger than a duck. [from Old English]

gooseberry *NOUN* **gooseberries 1** a small green fruit that grows on a prickly bush. **2** (*informal*) an unwanted extra person. [probably from French dialect *gozell*]

goose pimples or **goosebumps** *PLURAL NOUN* skin that has turned rough with small bumps on it because a person is cold or afraid.
[because it looks like the skin of a plucked goose]

gore[1] *VERB* **gores, goring, gored** wound by piercing with a horn or tusk.
[origin unknown]

gore[2] *NOUN* thickened blood from a cut or wound.
[from Old English *gor* = filth or slime]

gorge *NOUN* **gorges** a narrow valley with steep sides.

gorge *VERB* **gorges, gorging, gorged** eat greedily; stuff with food.
[French, = throat]

gorgeous *ADJECTIVE* magnificent or beautiful.
▷ **gorgeously** *adverb*
[from old French]

gorilla *NOUN* **gorillas** a large powerful African ape, the largest of all the apes.
[from Latin, probably from an African word = hairy woman]
USAGE Do not confuse with **guerrilla**, which can be pronounced in the same way.

gorse *NOUN* a prickly bush with small yellow flowers.
[from Old English]

gory *ADJECTIVE* **1** covered with blood. **2** with much bloodshed • *a gory battle.*

gosh *INTERJECTION* an exclamation of surprise.
[used to avoid saying 'God']

gosling *NOUN* **goslings** a young goose.
[from Old Norse]

gospel *NOUN* **1** the teachings of Jesus Christ. **2** something you can safely believe to be true.
- **the Gospels** the first four books of the New Testament, telling of the life and teachings of Jesus Christ.
[from Old English *god* = good + *spel* = news]

gospel music *NOUN* a style of black American religious singing.

gossamer *NOUN* **1** fine cobwebs made by small spiders. **2** any fine delicate material.
[from *goose summer*, a period of fine weather in the autumn (when geese were eaten), when gossamer is very common]

gossip *VERB* **gossips, gossiping, gossiped** talk a lot about other people.

gossip *NOUN* **gossips 1** talk, especially rumours, about other people. **2** a person who enjoys gossiping.
▷ **gossipy** *adjective*
[from Old English *godsibb* = close friend (literally = god- brother or sister), someone to gossip with]

got *past tense* of **get**
- **have got** possess • *Have you got a car?*
- **have got to** must.

Gothic *NOUN* the style of building common in the 12th-16th centuries, with pointed arches and much decorative carving.
[from the *Goths*, whom the Romans regarded as barbarians (because some people thought this style was barbaric compared to Greek or Roman styles)]

gouge (*say* gowj) *VERB* **gouges, gouging, gouged** scoop or force out by pressing.
[from Latin *gubia* = a kind of chisel]

goulash (*say* goo-lash) *NOUN* a Hungarian meat stew seasoned with paprika.
[from Hungarian *gulyáshús* = herdsman's meat]

gourd (*say* goord) *NOUN* **gourds** the rounded hard-skinned fruit of a climbing plant.
[from old French]

a b c d e f g h i j k l m n o p q r s t u v w x y z

A B C D E F G H I J K L M N O P Q R S T U V W X Y Z

gourmet (*say* goor-may) *NOUN* **gourmets** a person who understands and appreciates good food and drink.
[French, = wine taster]

gout *NOUN* a disease that causes painful inflammation (heat and swelling) of the toes, knees, and fingers.
▷ **gouty** *adjective*
[from old French or Latin]

govern *VERB* **governs, governing, governed** be in charge of the public affairs of a country or region.
[from Latin *gubernare* = steer or direct]

governess *NOUN* **governesses** a woman employed to teach children in a private household.

government *NOUN* **governments 1** the group of people who are in charge of the public affairs of a country. **2** the process of governing.
▷ **governmental** *adjective*

governor *NOUN* **governors 1** a person who governs a state or a colony etc. **2** a member of the governing body of a school or other institution. **3** the person in charge of a prison.

governor-general *NOUN* **governor-generals** the representative of Britain in some countries in the Commonwealth.

gown *NOUN* **gowns 1** a woman's long dress. **2** a loose robe worn by lawyers, members of a university, etc.
[from Latin *gunna* = a fur- lined robe]

GP *ABBREVIATION* general practitioner.

grab *VERB* **grabs, grabbing, grabbed** take hold of something firmly or suddenly.
[from old German or old Dutch]

grace *NOUN* **1** beauty, especially of movement. **2** goodwill or favour. **3** dignity or good manners • *At least he had the grace to apologize.* **4** a short prayer of thanks before or after a meal. **5** the title of a duke, duchess, or archbishop • *His Grace the Duke of Kent.*

grace *VERB* **graces, gracing, graced** bring honour or dignity to something • *The mayor himself graced us with his presence.*
[from Latin *gratus* = pleasing]

graceful *ADJECTIVE* beautiful and elegant in movement or shape.
▷ **gracefully** *adverb* **gracefulness** *noun*

gracious *ADJECTIVE* behaving kindly and honourably.
▷ **graciously** *adverb* **graciousness** *noun*

grade *NOUN* **grades 1** a step in a scale of quality or value or rank. **2** a mark showing the quality of a student's work.

grade *VERB* **grades, grading, graded** sort or divide into grades.
[from Latin *gradus* = a step]

gradient (*say* gray-dee-ent) *NOUN* **gradients** a slope or the steepness of a slope.
[from *grade*]

gradual *ADJECTIVE* happening slowly but steadily.
▷ **gradually** *adverb*

graduate (*say* grad-yoo-ayt) *VERB* **graduates, graduating, graduated 1** get a university or college degree. **2** divide something into graded sections; mark something with units of measurement.
▷ **graduation** *noun*

graduate (*say* grad-yoo-at) *NOUN* **graduates** a person who has a university or college degree.
[same origin as *grade*]

graffiti *NOUN* words or drawings scribbled or sprayed on a wall.
[Italian, = scratchings]
USAGE Strictly speaking, this word is a plural noun (the singular is *graffito*), so it should be used with a plural verb: *There are graffiti all over the wall.* However, the word is widely used nowadays as if it were a singular noun and most people do not regard this as wrong: *There is graffiti all over the wall.*

graft *NOUN* **grafts 1** a shoot from one plant or tree fixed into another to form a new growth. **2** a piece of living tissue transplanted by a surgeon to replace what is diseased or damaged • *a skin graft.*

graft *VERB* **grafts, grafting, grafted** insert or transplant as a graft.
[from Greek *grapheion* = pointed writing stick (because of the pointed shape of the end of the shoot)]

grain *NOUN* **grains 1** a small hard seed or similar particle. **2** cereal plants when they are growing or after being harvested. **3** a very small amount • *a grain of truth.* **4** the pattern of lines made by the fibres in a piece of wood or paper.
▷ **grainy** *adjective*
[from Latin]

gram *NOUN* **grams** a unit of mass or weight in the metric system.
[from Latin *gramma* = a small weight]

-gram *SUFFIX* used to form nouns meaning something written or drawn etc. (e.g. *diagram*).
[from Greek *gramma* = thing written]

grammar *NOUN* **grammars 1** the rules for using words correctly. **2** a book about these rules.
[from Greek, = the art of letters]

grammar school *NOUN* **grammar schools** a secondary school for children with academic ability.

grammatical *ADJECTIVE* following the rules of grammar.
▷ **grammatically** *adverb*

gramophone *NOUN* **gramophones** (*old use*) a record player.
[altered from 'phonogram' (the name given to the first record player, from Greek *phone* = a sound, + *-gram*)]

grampus *NOUN* **grampuses** a large dolphin-like sea animal.
[from Latin *craspiscis* = fat fish]

granary *NOUN* **granaries** a storehouse for grain.
[from Latin]

grand *ADJECTIVE* **1** splendid and impressive. **2** most important or highest-ranking. **3** including everything; complete.
▷ **grandly** *adverb* **grandness** *noun*
[from Latin *grandis* = fully- grown]

grandad *NOUN* **grandads** (*informal*) grandfather.

grandchild *NOUN* **grandchildren** the child of a person's son or daughter.
▷ **granddaughter** *noun* **grandson** *noun*

grandeur (*say* grand-yer) *NOUN* impressive beauty; splendour.
[from French]

grandfather *NOUN* **grandfathers** the father of a person's father or mother.

grandfather clock *NOUN* **grandfather clocks** a clock in a tall wooden case.

grandiose (*say* grand-ee-ohss) *ADJECTIVE* large and impressive; trying to seem impressive.
[via French from Italian]

grandma *NOUN* (*informal*) grandmother.

grandmother *NOUN* **grandmothers** the mother of a person's father or mother.

grandpa *NOUN* (*informal*) grandfather.

grandparent *NOUN* **grandparents** a grandfather or grandmother.

grand piano *NOUN* **grand pianos** a large piano with the strings fixed horizontally.

grandstand *NOUN* **grandstands** a building with a roof and rows of seats for spectators at a racecourse or sports ground.

grand total *NOUN* the sum of other totals.

grange *NOUN* **granges** a large country house.
[originally = barn: from French, related to *grain*]

granite *NOUN* a very hard kind of rock used for building.
[from Italian *granito* = granular (because of the small particles you can see in the rock)]

granny *NOUN* **grannies** (*informal*) grandmother.

granny knot *NOUN* **granny knots** a reef knot with the strings crossed the wrong way.

grant *VERB* **grants, granting, granted** **1** give or allow someone what he or she has asked for • *We have decided to grant your request.* **2** admit; agree that something is true.
- **take for granted 1** assume that something is true or will happen. **2** be so used to having something that you no longer appreciate it.

grant *NOUN* **grants** a sum of money awarded for a special purpose.
[from old French]

Granth (*say* grunt) *NOUN* the sacred scriptures of the Sikhs.
[from Sanskrit]

granular *ADJECTIVE* like grains.
[from *granule*]

A B C D E F G H I J K L M N O P Q R S T U V W X Y Z

granulated *ADJECTIVE* in grains • *granulated sugar.*

granule *NOUN* **granules** a small grain.
[from Latin]

grape *NOUN* **grapes** a small green or purple berry that grows in bunches on a vine. Grapes are used to make wine.
[from old French]

grapefruit *NOUN* **grapefruit** a large round yellow citrus fruit.
[because they grow in clusters, like grapes]

grapevine *NOUN* **grapevines 1** a vine on which grapes grow. **2** a way by which news spreads unofficially, with people passing it on from one to another.

graph *NOUN* **graphs** a diagram showing how two quantities or variables are related.
[from Greek *graphein* = to write or draw]

-graph *SUFFIX* used to form nouns and verbs meaning **1** something written, drawn, or recorded in some way (e.g. *photograph*). **2** a machine which records (e.g. *telegraph*, *seismograph*).
[same origin as *graph*]

WORD FAMILY There are a number of English words that are related to *graph* because part of their original meaning comes from the Greek word *graphein* meaning 'to write or draw'. These include *autograph*, *graphic*, *graphite*, *photograph*, *seismograph*, and *telegraph*.

graphic *ADJECTIVE* **1** to do with drawing or painting • *a graphic artist.* **2** giving a lively description.
▷ **graphically** *adverb*
[same origin as *graph*]

graphics *PLURAL NOUN* diagrams, lettering, and drawings, especially pictures that are produced by a computer.

graphite *NOUN* a soft black form of carbon used for the lead in pencils, as a lubricant, and in nuclear reactors.
[from Greek *graphein* = to write or draw (because pencil lead is made of graphite)]

graph paper *NOUN* paper printed with small squares, used for drawing graphs.

-graphy *SUFFIX* used to form names of **1** sciences (e.g. *geography*), **2** methods of writing, drawing, or recording (e.g. *photography*).
[same origin as *graph*]

grapnel *NOUN* **grapnels** a heavy metal device with claws for hooking things.
[via old French from Germanic]

grapple *VERB* **grapples, grappling, grappled 1** struggle or wrestle. **2** seize or hold firmly. **3** try to deal with a problem • *I've been grappling with this essay all day.*
[from old French; related to *grapnel*]

grasp *VERB* **grasps, grasping, grasped 1** seize and hold firmly. **2** understand.

grasp *NOUN* **1** a person's understanding of something • *a good grasp of electronics.* **2** a firm hold.
[origin unknown]

grasping *ADJECTIVE* greedy for money or possessions.

grass *NOUN* **grasses 1** a plant with green blades and stalks that are eaten by animals. **2** ground covered with grass; lawn.
▷ **grassy** *adjective*
[from Old English]

grasshopper *NOUN* **grasshoppers** a jumping insect that makes a shrill noise.

grassland *NOUN* **grasslands** a wide area covered in grass with few trees.

grass roots *PLURAL NOUN* the ordinary people in a political party or other group.

grate[1] *NOUN* **grates 1** a metal framework that keeps fuel in a fireplace. **2** a fireplace.
[from old French or Spanish]

grate[2] *VERB* **grates, grating, grated 1** shred something into small pieces by rubbing it on a rough surface. **2** make an unpleasant noise by rubbing. **3** sound harshly.
- **grate on** have an irritating effect.
[via old French from Germanic]

grateful *ADJECTIVE* feeling or showing that you are thankful for something that has been done for you.
▷ **gratefully** *adverb*
[from Latin *gratus* = thankful, pleasing]

grater *NOUN* **graters** a device with a jagged surface for grating food.

gratify *VERB* **gratifies, gratifying, gratified** **1** give pleasure. **2** satisfy a feeling or desire • *Please gratify our curiosity.*
▷ **gratifying** *adjective* **gratification** *noun*
[from Latin *gratus* = pleasing]

grating *NOUN* **gratings** a framework of metal bars placed across an opening.
[from *grate*[1]]

gratis (*say* gray-tiss) *ADVERB* & *ADJECTIVE* free of charge • *You can have the leaflet gratis.*
[Latin, = out of kindness]

gratitude *NOUN* being grateful.

gratuitous (*say* gra-tew-it-us) *ADJECTIVE* done without good reason; uncalled for.
▷ **gratuitously** *adverb*

gratuity (*say* gra-tew-it-ee) *NOUN* **gratuities** money given in gratitude; a tip.
[from Latin *gratuitas* = gift]

grave[1] *NOUN* **graves** the place where a corpse is buried.
[from Old English]

grave[2] *ADJECTIVE* serious or solemn.
▷ **gravely** *adverb*
[from Latin *gravis* = heavy]

grave accent (*rhymes with* **starve**) *NOUN* **grave accents** a backward-sloping mark over a vowel, as in *vis-à-vis*.
[from French; related to *grave*[2]]

gravel *NOUN* small stones mixed with coarse sand, used to make paths.
▷ **gravelled** *adjective* **gravelly** *adjective*
[from old French]

graven (*say* gray-ven) *ADJECTIVE* (*old use*) carved.
[from Old English *grafan* = dig out]

gravestone *NOUN* **gravestones** a stone monument over a grave.

graveyard *NOUN* **graveyards** a burial ground.

gravitate *VERB* **gravitates, gravitating, gravitated** move or be attracted towards something.

gravitation *NOUN* **1** gravitating. **2** the force of gravity.
▷ **gravitational** *adjective*

gravity *NOUN* **1** the force that pulls all objects in the universe towards each other. **2** the force that pulls everything towards the earth. **3** seriousness.
[same origin as *grave*[2]]

gravy *NOUN* a hot brown sauce made from meat juices.
[from old French]

graze *VERB* **grazes, grazing, grazed** **1** feed on growing grass. **2** scrape your skin slightly • *I grazed my elbow on the wall.* **3** touch something lightly in passing.

graze *NOUN* **grazes** a raw place where skin has been scraped.
[from Old English *graes* = grass]

grease *NOUN* **1** any thick oily substance. **2** melted fat.
▷ **greasy** *adjective*

grease *VERB* **greases, greasing, greased** put grease on something.
[from Latin *crassus* = thick, fat]

great *ADJECTIVE* **1** very large; much above average. **2** very important or talented • *a great composer.* **3** (*informal*) very good or enjoyable • *It's great to see you again.*
4 older or younger by one generation
• *great-grandfather.*
▷ **greatly** *adverb* **greatness** *noun*
[from Old English]

Great Britain *NOUN* the island made up of England, Scotland, and Wales, with the small adjacent islands.
USAGE See the note at **Britain**.

grebe (*say* greeb) *NOUN* **grebes** a kind of diving bird.
[from French]

greed *NOUN* being greedy.
[from *greedy*]

greedy *ADJECTIVE* **greedier, greediest** wanting more food, money, or other things than you need.
▷ **greedily** *adverb* **greediness** *noun*
[from Old English]

green *NOUN* **greens** **1** the colour of grass, leaves, etc. **2** an area of grassy land • *the village green; a putting green.*

green *ADJECTIVE* **1** of the colour green. **2** concerned with protecting the natural environment. **3** inexperienced and likely to make mistakes.
▷ **greenness** *noun*
[from Old English]

green belt *NOUN* **green belts** an area kept as open land round a city.

greenery *NOUN* green leaves or plants.

greenfield *ADJECTIVE* a greenfield site is a piece of land that has not yet had buildings on it, though there may be plans to build on it. (COMPARE **brownfield**)

greenfly *NOUN* **greenfly** a small green insect that sucks the juices from plants.

greengrocer *NOUN* **greengrocers** a person who keeps a shop that sells fruit and vegetables.
▷ **greengrocery** *noun*

greenhouse *NOUN* **greenhouses** a glass building where plants are protected from cold.

greenhouse effect *NOUN* the warming up of the earth's surface when heat from the sun is trapped in the earth's atmosphere by gases such as carbon dioxide and methane.

greenhouse gas *NOUN* **greenhouse gases** any of the gases, especially carbon dioxide and methane, that are found in the earth's atmosphere and contribute to the greenhouse effect.

greens *PLURAL NOUN* green vegetables, such as cabbage and spinach.

Greenwich Mean Time (*say* gren-ich) *NOUN* the time on the line of longitude which passes through Greenwich in London, used as a basis for calculating time throughout the world.

greet *VERB* **greets, greeting, greeted** **1** speak to a person who arrives. **2** receive • *They greeted the song with applause.* **3** present itself to • *A strange sight greeted our eyes.*
[from Old English]

greeting *NOUN* **greetings** words or actions used to greet somebody.

greetings *PLURAL NOUN* good wishes • *a greetings card.*

gregarious (*say* grig-air-ee-us) *ADJECTIVE* **1** fond of company. **2** living in flocks or communities.
▷ **gregariously** *adverb* **gregariousness** *noun*
[from Latin *gregis* = of a herd]

grenade (*say* grin-ayd) *NOUN* **grenades** a small bomb, usually thrown by hand.
[from old French *pome grenate* = pomegranate (because of the shape of the grenade)]

grey *NOUN* **greys** the colour between black and white, like ashes or dark clouds.
▷ **grey** *adjective* **greyness** *noun*
[from Old English]

greyhound *NOUN* **greyhounds** a slender dog with smooth hair, used in racing.
[from Old English *grighund*, probably = bitch-hound]

grid *NOUN* **grids** **1** a framework or pattern of bars or lines crossing each other. **2** a network of cables or wires for carrying electricity over a large area.
[from *gridiron*]

griddle *NOUN* **griddles** a round iron plate for cooking things on.
[from old French *gredil* = gridiron]

gridiron *NOUN* **gridirons** a framework of bars for cooking on.
[from *griddle*]

grid reference *NOUN* **grid references** a set of numbers that allows you to describe the exact position of something on a map.

grief *NOUN* deep sorrow, especially at a person's death.
- **come to grief** suffer a disaster.
[same origin as *grieve*]

grievance *NOUN* **grievances** something that people are discontented about.
[old French, = injury or hardship]

grieve *VERB* **grieves, grieving, grieved** **1** feel deep sorrow, especially at a person's death. **2** make a person feel very sad.
[from old French *grever* = to burden; related to *grave*²]

grievous (*say* gree-vus) *ADJECTIVE* **1** causing grief. **2** serious.
▷ **grievously** *adverb*

griffin *NOUN* **griffins** a creature in fables, with an eagle's head and wings on a lion's body.
[from old French]

grill *NOUN* **grills 1** a heated element on a cooker, for sending heat downwards. **2** food cooked under this. **3** a grille.

grill *VERB* **grills, grilling, grilled 1** cook under a grill. **2** question closely and severely • *The police grilled him for an hour.*
[same origin as *griddle*]

grille *NOUN* **grilles** a metal grating covering a window or similar opening.
[from French]

grim *ADJECTIVE* **grimmer, grimmest 1** stern or severe. **2** unpleasant or unattractive • *a grim prospect.*
▷ **grimly** *adverb* **grimness** *noun*
[from Old English]

grimace (*say* grim-ayss or grim-as) *NOUN* **grimaces** a twisted expression on the face made in pain or disgust.

grimace *VERB* **grimaces, grimacing, grimaced** make a grimace.
[from Spanish *grima* = fright]

grime *NOUN* dirt in a layer on a surface or on the skin.
▷ **grimy** *adjective*
[from old German or old Dutch]

grin *NOUN* **grins** a broad smile showing your teeth.

grin *VERB* **grins, grinning, grinned** smile broadly showing your teeth.
[from Old English]

grind *VERB* **grinds, grinding, ground 1** crush something into tiny pieces or powder. **2** sharpen or smooth something by rubbing it on a rough surface. **3** rub harshly together • *He ground his teeth in fury.*
▷ **grinder** *noun*
- **grind to a halt** stop suddenly with a loud noise.
[from Old English]

grindstone *NOUN* **grindstones** a thick round rough revolving stone for sharpening or grinding things.
- **keep your nose to the grindstone** keep working hard.

grip *VERB* **grips, gripping, gripped 1** hold something firmly. **2** hold a person's attention • *The opening chapter really gripped me.*
▷ **gripping** *adjective*

grip *NOUN* **grips 1** a firm hold. **2** a handle, especially on a sports racket, bat, etc. **3** a travelling bag. **4** control or power • *The country is in the grip of lottery fever.*
- **get to grips with** begin to deal with successfully.
[from Old English]

gripe *VERB* **gripes, griping, griped** (*informal*) grumble or complain.

gripe *NOUN* **gripes** a complaint.
[from Old English]

grisly *ADJECTIVE* **grislier, grisliest** causing horror or disgust; gruesome.
[from Old English]

grist *NOUN* corn for grinding.
- **grist to the mill** experience or knowledge that you can make use of.
[from Old English]

gristle *NOUN* tough rubbery tissue in meat.
▷ **gristly** *adjective*
[from Old English]

grit *NOUN* **1** tiny pieces of stone or sand. **2** courage and endurance.
▷ **gritty** *adjective* **grittiness** *noun*

grit *VERB* **grits, gritting, gritted 1** spread a road or path with grit. **2** clench your teeth when in pain or trouble.
[from Old English]

grizzle *VERB* **grizzles, grizzling, grizzled** whimper or whine.
[origin unknown]

grizzled *ADJECTIVE* streaked with grey hairs.
[from old French *grisel* = grey]

grizzly *ADJECTIVE* grey-haired.

grizzly bear *NOUN* **grizzly bears** a large fierce bear of North America.
[from *grizzled* (the bear has brown fur with white- tipped hairs)]

groan *VERB* **groans, groaning, groaned 1** make a long deep sound in pain, distress, or disapproval. **2** creak loudly under a heavy load.
▷ **groan** *noun* **groaner** *noun*
[from Old English]

a b c d e f g h i j k l m n o p q r s t u v w x y z

grocer *NOUN* **grocers** a person who keeps a shop that sells food and household goods. [originally = wholesaler; from Latin *grossus* = gross (because a wholesaler buys goods *in the gross* = in large quantities)]

groceries *PLURAL NOUN* goods sold by a grocer.

grocery *NOUN* **groceries** a grocer's shop.

grog *NOUN* (*Australian/NZ*) alcoholic drink.

groggy *ADJECTIVE* **groggier**, **groggiest** dizzy and unsteady, especially after illness or injury.
▷ **groggily** *adverb* **grogginess** *noun*
[originally = drunk: from *grog*]

groin *NOUN* the hollow between your thigh and the trunk of the body.
[origin unknown]

groom *NOUN* **grooms 1** a person whose job is to look after horses. **2** a bridegroom.

groom *VERB* **grooms**, **grooming**, **groomed 1** clean and brush a horse or other animal. **2** make something neat and trim. **3** train a person for a certain job or position • *Evans is being groomed for the captaincy.*
[origin unknown]

groove *NOUN* **grooves** a long narrow furrow or channel cut in the surface of something.
▷ **grooved** *adjective*
[from old Dutch *groeve* = furrow or ditch]

grope *VERB* **gropes**, **groping**, **groped** feel about for something you cannot see.
[from Old English]

gross (*say* grohss) *ADJECTIVE* **1** fat and ugly. **2** very obvious or shocking • *gross stupidity.* **3** having bad manners; vulgar. **4** (*informal*) disgusting. **5** total; without anything being deducted • *our gross income.* (COMPARE *net*²)
▷ **grossly** *adverb* **grossness** *noun*

gross *NOUN* **gross** twelve dozen (144) of something • *ten gross.*
[from Latin]

grotesque (*say* groh-**tesk**) *ADJECTIVE* fantastically ugly or very strangely shaped.
▷ **grotesquely** *adverb* **grotesqueness** *noun*
[via French from Italian]

grotto *NOUN* **grottoes 1** an attractive cave. **2** an artificial cave, especially one that is brightly decorated.
[from Italian; related to *crypt*]

ground¹ *past tense* of **grind**.

ground² *NOUN* **grounds 1** the solid surface of the earth. **2** a sports field. **3** land of a certain kind • *marshy ground.* **4** the amount of a subject that is dealt with • *The course covers a lot of ground.*

ground *VERB* **grounds**, **grounding**, **grounded 1** prevent a plane from flying • *All aircraft are grounded because of the fog.* **2** stop a child from going out, as a punishment. **3** give a good basic training • *Ground them in the rules of spelling.* **4** base • *This theory is grounded on reliable evidence.*
[from Old English]

ground control *NOUN* the people and machinery that control and monitor an aircraft or spacecraft from the ground.

grounding *NOUN* basic training or instruction.

groundless *ADJECTIVE* without reason • *Your fears are groundless.*

grounds *PLURAL NOUN* **1** the gardens of a large house. **2** solid particles that sink to the bottom • *coffee grounds.* **3** reasons • *There are grounds for suspicion.*

groundsheet *NOUN* **groundsheets** a piece of waterproof material for spreading on the ground, especially in a tent.

groundsman *NOUN* **groundsmen** a person whose job is to look after a sports ground.

groundwork *NOUN* work that lays the basis for something.

group *NOUN* **groups 1** a number of people, animals, or things that come together or belong together in some way. **2** a band of musicians.

group *VERB* **groups**, **grouping**, **grouped** put together or come together in a group or groups.
[via French and Italian from Germanic]

grouse¹ *NOUN* **grouse** a bird with feathered feet, hunted as game.
[origin unknown]

grouse² *VERB* **grouses**, **grousing**, **groused** (*informal*) grumble or complain.
▷ **grouse** *noun* **grouser** *noun*
[origin unknown]

grove *NOUN* **groves** a group of trees; a small wood.
[from Old English]

grovel *VERB* **grovels, grovelling, grovelled** **1** crawl on the ground, especially in a show of fear or humility. **2** act in an excessively humble way, for example by apologizing a lot.
▷ **groveller** *noun*
[from Old Norse *a grufu* = face downwards]

grow *VERB* **grows, growing, grew, grown** **1** become bigger or greater. **2** develop. **3** cultivate; plant and look after • *She grows roses.* **4** become • *He grew rich.*
▷ **grower** *noun*
- **grow up** become an adult.
[from Old English]

growl *VERB* **growls, growling, growled** make a deep angry sound in the throat.
▷ **growl** *noun*
[imitating the sound]

grown-up *NOUN* **grown-ups** an adult person.
▷ **grown-up** *adjective*

growth *NOUN* **growths 1** growing or developing. **2** something that has grown. **3** a lump that has grown on or inside a person's body; a tumour.

grub *NOUN* **grubs 1** a tiny worm-like creature that will become an insect; a larva. **2** (*slang*) food.

grub *VERB* **grubs, grubbing, grubbed** **1** dig up by the roots. **2** turn things over or move them about while looking for something; rummage.
[origin unknown]

grubby *ADJECTIVE* **grubbier, grubbiest** rather dirty.
▷ **grubbiness** *noun*

grudge *NOUN* **grudges** a feeling of resentment or ill will • *She isn't the sort of person who bears a grudge.*

grudge *VERB* **grudges, grudging, grudged** resent having to give or allow something.
[from old French *grouchier* = grumble]

gruelling *ADJECTIVE* exhausting.
[from old French]

gruesome *ADJECTIVE* horrible or disgusting.
[from an old word *grue* = to shudder]

gruff *ADJECTIVE* having a rough unfriendly voice or manner.
▷ **gruffly** *adverb* **gruffness** *noun*
[from Dutch *grof* = coarse or rude]

grumble *VERB* **grumbles, grumbling, grumbled** complain in a bad-tempered way.
▷ **grumble** *noun* **grumbler** *noun*
[origin unknown]

grumpy *ADJECTIVE* bad-tempered.
▷ **grumpily** *adverb* **grumpiness** *noun*
[imitating the muttering noises made by a grumpy person]

grunt *VERB* **grunts, grunting, grunted** **1** make a pig's gruff snort. **2** speak or say gruffly.
▷ **grunt** *noun*
[from Old English *grunnettan*, imitating the sound]

guarantee *NOUN* **guarantees** a formal promise to do something or to repair something you have sold if it breaks or goes wrong.

guarantee *VERB* **guarantees, guaranteeing, guaranteed** **1** give a guarantee; promise. **2** make it certain that something will happen • *Money does not guarantee happiness.*
▷ **guarantor** *noun*
[from Spanish]

guard *VERB* **guards, guarding, guarded** **1** protect; keep safe. **2** watch over and prevent from escaping.
- **guard against** try to prevent something happening.

guard *NOUN* **guards 1** guarding; protection • *Keep the prisoners under close guard.* **2** someone who guards a person or place. **3** a group of soldiers or police officers etc. acting as a guard. **4** a railway official in charge of a train. **5** a protecting device • *a fireguard.*
- **on guard** alert for possible danger or difficulty.
[via old French from Germanic; related to *ward*]

A B C D E F G H I J K L M N O P Q R S T U V W X Y Z

guardian *NOUN* **guardians 1** someone who guards. **2** a person who is legally in charge of a child whose parents cannot look after him or her.
▷ **guardianship** *noun*
[via old French from Germanic; related to *warden*]

guerrilla (*say* ger-**il**-a) *NOUN* **guerrillas** a member of a small unofficial army who fights by making surprise attacks.
[Spanish, = little war]
USAGE Do not confuse with **gorilla**.

guess *NOUN* **guesses** an opinion or answer that you give without making careful calculations or without certain knowledge.

guess *VERB* **guesses, guessing, guessed** make a guess.
▷ **guesser** *noun*
[probably from old German or old Dutch]

guesswork *NOUN* something you do by guessing.

guest *NOUN* **guests 1** a person who is invited to visit or stay at another's house. **2** a person staying at a hotel. **3** a person who takes part in another's show as a visiting performer.
[from Old Norse]

guest house *NOUN* **guest houses** a kind of small hotel.

guffaw *VERB* **guffaws, guffawing, guffawed** laugh noisily.
▷ **guffaw** *noun*
[imitating the sound]

guidance *NOUN* **1** guiding. **2** advising or advice on problems.

Guide *NOUN* **Guides** a member of the Girl Guides Association, an organization for girls.

guide *NOUN* **guides 1** a person who shows others the way or points out interesting sights. **2** a book giving information about a place or subject.

guide *VERB* **guides, guiding, guided** show someone the way or how to do something.
[via old French from Germanic; related to *wit*]

guidebook *NOUN* **guidebooks** a book of information about a place, for travellers or visitors.

guided missile *NOUN* **guided missiles** an explosive rocket that is guided to its target by remote control or by equipment inside it.

guide dog *NOUN* **guide dogs** a dog trained to lead a blind person.

guideline *NOUN* **guidelines** guidelines are rules or information about how something should be done or what action should be taken.

guidelines *PLURAL NOUN* statements that give general advice about how something should be done.

guild (*say* gild) *NOUN* **guilds** a society of people with similar skills or interests.
[from old German or old Dutch]

guilder (*say* **gild**-er) *NOUN* **guilders** a Dutch coin.
[from Dutch]

guile (*rhymes with* **mile**) *NOUN* craftiness.
[via old French from Old Norse]

guillotine (*say* **gil**-ot-een) *NOUN* **guillotines 1** a machine with a heavy blade for beheading criminals, used in France. **2** a machine with a long blade for cutting paper or metal.

guillotine *VERB* **guillotines, guillotining, guillotined** cut with a guillotine.
[named after Dr *Guillotin*, who suggested its use in France in 1789]

guilt *NOUN* **1** the fact that you have committed an offence. **2** a feeling that you are to blame for something that has happened.
[from Old English *gylt* = a crime or sin]

guilty *ADJECTIVE* **1** having done wrong • *He was found guilty of murder.* **2** feeling or showing guilt • *a guilty conscience.*
▷ **guiltily** *adverb*

guinea (*say* **gin**-ee) *NOUN* **guineas 1** a former British gold coin worth 21 shillings (£1.05). **2** this amount of money.
[originally = a coin used by British traders in Africa: named after *Guinea* in west Africa]

guinea pig *NOUN* **guinea pigs 1** a small furry animal without a tail. **2** a person who is used as the subject of an experiment.
[from *Guinea* in west Africa, probably by mistake for Guiana, in South America, where the guinea pig comes from]

guise (*say* guys) *NOUN* **guises** an outward disguise or pretence.
[via old French from Germanic; related to *wise*]

guitar *NOUN* **guitars** a musical instrument played by plucking its strings.
▷ **guitarist** *noun*
[from Greek *kithara*, a small harp]

gulf *NOUN* **gulfs 1** a large area of the sea that is partly surrounded by land. **2** a wide gap; a great difference.
[from Greek]

gull *NOUN* **gulls** a seagull.
[a Celtic word]

gullet *NOUN* **gullets** the tube from the throat to the stomach.
[from old French *gole* = throat]

gullible *ADJECTIVE* easily deceived.
[from an old word *gull* = fool or deceive]

gully *NOUN* **gullies** a narrow channel that carries water.
[same origin as *gullet*]

gulp *VERB* **gulps, gulping, gulped**
1 swallow hastily or greedily. **2** make a loud swallowing noise, especially because of fear.

gulp *NOUN* **gulps 1** the act of gulping. **2** a large mouthful of liquid.
[imitating the sound]

gum[1] *NOUN* **gums** the firm flesh in which your teeth are rooted.
[from Old English]

gum[2] *NOUN* **gums 1** a sticky substance produced by some trees and shrubs, used as glue. **2** a sweet made with gum or gelatine • *a fruit gum.* **3** chewing gum. **4** a gum tree.
▷ **gummy** *adjective*

gum *VERB* **gums, gumming, gummed**
cover or stick something with gum.
[via old French, Latin, and Greek from Egyptian]

gumption *NOUN* (*informal*) common sense.
[origin unknown]

gum tree *NOUN* **gum trees** a eucalyptus.

gun *NOUN* **guns 1** a weapon that fires shells or bullets from a metal tube. **2** a starting pistol. **3** a device that forces a substance out of a tube • *a grease gun.*
▷ **gunfire** *noun* **gunshot** *noun*

gun *VERB* **guns, gunning, gunned**
- **gun down** shoot someone with a gun.
[probably from the Swedish girl's name *Gunnhildr*, from *gunnr* = war]

gunboat *NOUN* **gunboats** a small warship.

gunman *NOUN* **gunmen** a criminal with a gun.

gunner *NOUN* **gunners** a person in the armed forces who operates a large gun.

gunnery *NOUN* the making or use of large guns.

gunpowder *NOUN* an explosive made from a powdered mixture of potassium nitrate, charcoal, and sulphur.

gunwale (*say* gun-al) *NOUN* **gunwales** the upper edge of a small ship's or boat's side.
[from *gun* + *wale* = a ridge (because it was formerly used to support guns)]

gurdwara *NOUN* **gurdwaras** a Sikh temple.
[from Sanskrit *guru* = teacher + *dvara* = door]

gurgle *VERB* **gurgles, gurgling, gurgled**
make a low bubbling sound.
▷ **gurgle** *noun*
[imitating the sound]

guru *NOUN* **gurus 1** a Hindu religious leader. **2** an influential teacher; a mentor.
[from Sanskrit]

gush *VERB* **gushes, gushing, gushed 1** flow suddenly or quickly. **2** talk too enthusiastically or emotionally.
▷ **gush** *noun*
[imitating the sound]

gust *NOUN* **gusts** a sudden rush of wind, rain, or smoke.
▷ **gusty** *adjective* **gustily** *adverb*

gust *VERB* **gusts, gusting, gusted** blow in gusts.
[from Old Norse]

gusto *NOUN* great enjoyment; zest.
[Italian, from Latin *gustus* = a taste]

gut *NOUN* **guts** the lower part of the digestive system; the intestine.

gut *VERB* **guts, gutting, gutted 1** remove the guts from a dead fish or other animal. **2** remove or destroy the inside of something • *The fire gutted the factory.*
[from Old English]

guts *PLURAL NOUN* **1** the digestive system; the insides of a person or thing. **2** (*informal*) courage.

gutted *ADJECTIVE* (*informal*) extremely disappointed or upset.

gutter *NOUN* **gutters** a long narrow channel at the side of a street, or along the edge of a roof, for carrying away rainwater.

gutter *VERB* **gutters, guttering, guttered** a candle gutters when it burns unsteadily so that melted wax runs down.
[from Latin *gutta* = a drop]

guttural (*say* gut-er-al) *ADJECTIVE* throaty and harsh-sounding • *a guttural voice.*
[from Latin *guttur* = throat]

guy[1] *NOUN* **guys 1** a figure representing Guy Fawkes, burnt on 5 November in memory of the Gunpowder Plot which planned to blow up Parliament on that day in 1605.
2 (*informal*) a man.

guy[2] or **guy-rope** *NOUN* **guys, guy-ropes** a rope used to hold something in place, especially a tent.
[probably from old German]

guzzle *VERB* **guzzles, guzzling, guzzled** eat or drink greedily.
▷ **guzzler** *noun*
[from old French]

gym (*say* jim) *NOUN* **gyms** (*informal*) **1** a gymnasium. **2** gymnastics.

gymkhana (*say* jim-**kah**-na) *NOUN* **gymkhanas** a series of horse-riding contests and other sports events.
[from Urdu]

gymnasium *NOUN* **gymnasia, gymnasiums** a place equipped for gymnastics.
[from Greek *gymnos* = naked (because Greek men exercised naked)]

gymnast *NOUN* **gymnasts** an expert in gymnastics.

gymnastics *PLURAL NOUN* exercises performed to develop the muscles or to show the performer's agility.
▷ **gymnastic** *adjective*

gynaecology (*say* guy-ni-**kol**-o-ji) *NOUN* the branch of medicine concerned with the diseases and disorders of women's bodies, especially with the reproductive system.
[from Greek *gynaikos* = of a woman, + *-ology*]

gypsy *NOUN* **gypsies** a member of a community of people, also called travellers, who live in caravans or similar vehicles and travel from place to place.
[from *Egyptian*, because gypsies were originally thought to have come from Egypt]

gyrate (*say* jy-rayt) *VERB* **gyrates, gyrating, gyrated** revolve; move in circles or spirals.
▷ **gyration** *noun*
[from Greek *gyros* = a ring or circle]

gyroscope (*say* jy-ro-skohp) *NOUN* **gyroscopes** a device used in navigation, that keeps steady because of a heavy wheel spinning inside it.
[same origin as *gyrate*]

Hh

haberdashery *NOUN* small articles used in sewing, e.g. ribbons, buttons, thread.
▷ **haberdasher** *noun*
[origin unknown]

habit *NOUN* **habits 1** something that you do without thinking because you have done it so often; a settled way of behaving.
2 something that is hard to give up • *a smoking habit.* **3** the long dress worn by a monk or nun.
▷ **habitual** *adjective* **habitually** *adverb*
[from Latin]

habitat *NOUN* **habitats** where an animal or plant lives naturally.
[Latin, literally = inhabits]

habitation *NOUN* **habitations 1** a place to live in. **2** inhabiting a place.
[from Latin *habitare* = inhabit]

hack[1] *VERB* **hacks, hacking, hacked 1** chop or cut roughly. **2** (*informal*) break into a computer system.
[from Old English]

hack[2] *NOUN* **hacks** a horse for ordinary riding.
[from *Hackney*, in London (because many horses used to be kept on Hackney Marshes)]

hacker *NOUN* **hackers** a person who breaks into a computer system, especially that of a company or government.

hackles *PLURAL NOUN*
- **make someone's hackles rise** make someone angry or indignant.
[*hackles* are the long feathers on some birds' necks]

hackneyed *ADJECTIVE* used so often that it is no longer interesting.
[same origin as *hack*^{2}: hack or hackney was used to mean a hired horse, one that everyone used]

hacksaw *NOUN* **hacksaws** a saw for cutting metal.

haddock *NOUN* **haddock** a sea fish like cod but smaller, used as food.
[from old French]

hadn't (*mainly spoken*) had not.

haemoglobin (*say* heem-a-**gloh**-bin) *NOUN* the red substance that carries oxygen in the blood.
[from Greek *haima* = blood + *globule* (because of the shape of haemoglobin cells)]

haemophilia (*say* heem-o-**fil**-ee-a) *NOUN* a disease that causes people to bleed dangerously from even a slight cut.
▷ **haemophiliac** *noun*
[from Greek *haima* = blood + *philia* = loving]

haemorrhage (*say* **hem**-er-ij) *NOUN* bleeding, especially inside a person's body.
[from Greek *haima* = blood + *rhegnunai* = burst]

hag *NOUN* **hags** an ugly old woman.
[from Old English]

haggard *ADJECTIVE* looking ill or very tired.
[from old French]

haggis *NOUN* **haggises** a Scottish food made from sheep's offal.
[probably from Old Norse]

haggle *VERB* **haggles**, **haggling**, **haggled** argue about a price or agreement.
[from Old Norse]

haiku (*say* **hy**-koo) *NOUN* **haiku** a Japanese form of poem, written in three lines of five, seven, and five syllables.
[from Japanese *haikai no ku* = light or comic verse]

hail^1 *NOUN* frozen drops of rain.
▷ **hail** *verb* **hailstone** *noun* **hailstorm** *noun*
[from Old English]

hail^2 *INTERJECTION* (*old use*) an exclamation of greeting.

hail *VERB* **hails**, **hailing**, **hailed** call out to somebody.
- **hail from** come from • *He hails from Ireland.*
[from Old Norse]

hair *NOUN* **hairs 1** a soft covering that grows on the heads and bodies of people and animals. **2** one of the threads that make up this covering.
▷ **hairbrush** *noun*
- **keep your hair on** (*informal*) do not lose your temper.
- **split hairs** make petty or unimportant distinctions of meaning.
▷ **hair-splitting** *noun*
[from Old English]

haircut *NOUN* **haircuts 1** cutting a person's hair when it gets too long. **2** the style in which someone's hair is cut.

hairdresser *NOUN* **hairdressers** a person whose job is to cut and arrange people's hair.

hairpin *NOUN* **hairpins** a U-shaped pin for keeping hair in place.

hairpin bend *NOUN* **hairpin bends** a sharp bend in a road.

hair-raising *ADJECTIVE* terrifying.

hairstyle *NOUN* **hairstyles** a way or style of arranging your hair.

hairy *ADJECTIVE* **1** with a lot of hair. **2** (*informal*) dangerous or risky.

hajj *NOUN* the pilgrimage to Mecca which all Muslims are expected to make at least once.
[Arabic, = pilgrimage]

haka *NOUN* **hakas** a traditional Maori war dance in which the dancers also sing.
[from Maori]

hake *NOUN* **hake** a sea fish used as food.
[from Old English]

halal *NOUN* meat prepared according to Muslim law.
[Arabic, = according to religious law]

halcyon (*say* **hal**-see-on) *ADJECTIVE* happy and peaceful • *halcyon days.*
[from Greek *alkyon* = a bird which was once believed to build its nest on the sea, which magically stayed calm]

hale *ADJECTIVE* strong and healthy • *hale and hearty.*
[from Old English *hal* = whole]

half *NOUN* **halves** one of the two equal parts or amounts into which something is or can be divided.

half *ADVERB* partly; not completely • *This meat is only half cooked.*
- **not half** (*slang*) extremely • *Was she cross? Not half!*
[from Old English]

half-baked *ADJECTIVE* (*informal*) not properly planned or thought out.

half-brother *NOUN* **half-brothers** a brother to whom you are related by one parent but not by both parents.

half-hearted *ADJECTIVE* not very enthusiastic.
▷ **half-heartedly** *adverb*

half-life *NOUN* **half-lives** the time taken for the radioactivity of a substance to fall to half its original value.

half mast *NOUN* a point about halfway up a flagpole, to which a flag is lowered as a mark of respect for a person who has died.

halfpenny (*say* **hayp**-nee) *NOUN* **halfpennies** for separate coins, **halfpence** for a sum of money a former coin worth half a penny.

half-sister *NOUN* **half-sisters** a sister to whom you are related by one parent but not by both parents.

half-term *NOUN* **half-terms** a short holiday in the middle of a term.

half-time *NOUN* the point or interval halfway through a game.

halfway *ADJECTIVE* & *ADVERB* at a point half the distance or amount between two places or times.

half-witted *ADJECTIVE* stupid.
▷ **half-wit** *noun*

halibut *NOUN* **halibut** a large flat fish used as food.
[from *holy* + *butt*, a dialect word = flatfish (because it was eaten on Christian holy days, when meat was forbidden)]

hall *NOUN* **halls 1** a space or passage just inside the front entrance of a house. **2** a very large room or building used for meetings, concerts, etc. **3** a large country house.
[from Old English]

hallelujah *INTERJECTION* & *NOUN* **hallelujahs** alleluia.

hallmark *NOUN* **hallmarks 1** an official mark made on gold, silver, and platinum to show its quality. **2** a characteristic by which something is easily recognized.
[because the first such marks were made at the Goldsmiths' Hall in London]

hallo *INTERJECTION* hello.
[origin unknown]

hallowed *ADJECTIVE* honoured as being holy.
[from Old English]

Hallowe'en *NOUN* 31 October, traditionally a time when ghosts and witches are believed to appear.
[from *All Hallow Even*, the evening before the Christian festival honouring all the *hallows* = saints]

hallucination *NOUN* **hallucinations** something you think you can see or hear that is not really there.
▷ **hallucinate** *verb*
[from Latin *alucinari* = wander in your mind]

halo *NOUN* **haloes** a circle of light round something, especially round the head of a saint etc. in paintings.
[from Greek]

halt *VERB* **halts, halting, halted** stop.

halt *NOUN* **halts 1** a stop or standstill • *Work came to a halt.* **2** a small stopping place on a railway.
[from German]

halter *NOUN* **halters** a rope or strap put round a horse's head so that it can be led or fastened to something.
[from Old English]

halting *ADJECTIVE* slow and uncertain • *He has a halting walk.*
▷ **haltingly** *adverb*

halve *VERB* **halves, halving, halved** **1** divide something into halves. **2** reduce something to half its size.
[from *half*]

ham *NOUN* **hams 1** meat from a pig's leg. **2** (*slang*) an actor who overacts. **3** (*informal*) someone who operates a radio to send and receive messages as a hobby.
[from Old English]

hamburger *NOUN* **hamburgers** a flat round cake of minced beef served fried, often in a bread roll.
[named after Hamburg in Germany (not after *ham*)]

hamlet *NOUN* **hamlets** a small village.
[via old French from old German]

hammer *NOUN* **hammers** a tool with a heavy metal head used for driving nails in, breaking things, etc.

hammer *VERB* **hammers, hammering, hammered** **1** hit something with a hammer. **2** knock loudly • *Someone was hammering on the door.* **3** (*informal*) defeat.
[from Old English]

hammock *NOUN* **hammocks** a bed made of a strong net or piece of cloth hung by cords.
[via Spanish from Taino (a South American language)]

hamper[1] *NOUN* **hampers** a large box-shaped basket with a lid.
[from old French]

hamper[2] *VERB* **hampers, hampering, hampered** hinder; prevent from moving or working freely.
[origin unknown]

hamster *NOUN* **hamsters** a small furry animal with cheek pouches for carrying grain.
[from German]

hamstring *NOUN* **hamstrings** any of the five tendons at the back of a person's knee.
[from *ham* and *string*]

hand *NOUN* **hands 1** the end part of the arm below the wrist. **2** a pointer on a clock or dial. **3** a worker; a member of a ship's crew • *All hands on deck!* **4** the cards held by one player in a card game. **5** side or direction • *the right-hand side; on the other hand.* **6** help or aid • *Give me a hand with these boxes.*
- **at hand** near.
- **by hand** using your hand or hands.
- **give** or **receive a big hand** applaud or be applauded.
- **hands down** winning easily.
- **in good hands** in the care or control of someone who can be trusted.
- **in hand** in your possession; being dealt with.
- **on hand** available.
- **out of hand** out of control.

hand *VERB* **hands, handing, handed** give or pass something to somebody • *Hand it over.*
- **hand down** pass something from one generation to the next.

[from Old English]

handbag *NOUN* **handbags** a small bag for holding a purse and personal articles.

handbook *NOUN* **handbooks** a small book that gives useful facts about something.

handcuff *NOUN* **handcuffs** one of a pair of metal rings linked by a chain, for fastening wrists together.

handcuff *VERB* **handcuffs, handcuffing, handcuffed** fasten with handcuffs.

handful *NOUN* **handfuls 1** as much as can be carried in one hand. **2** a few people or things. **3** (*informal*) a troublesome person or task.

handicap *NOUN* **handicaps 1** a disadvantage. **2** a physical or mental disability.
▷ **handicapped** *adjective*
[from *hand in cap* (from an old game in which forfeit money was deposited in a cap)]

handicraft *NOUN* **handicrafts** artistic work done with the hands, e.g. woodwork, needlework.

handily *ADVERB* in a handy way.

handiwork *NOUN* **1** something made by hand. **2** something done • *Is this mess your handiwork?*

handkerchief *NOUN* **handkerchiefs** a small square of cloth for wiping the nose or face.
[from *hand* + *kerchief*]

handle *NOUN* **handles** the part of a thing by which it is held, carried, or controlled.

handle *VERB* **handles, handling, handled** **1** touch or feel something with your hands. **2** deal with; manage • *Will you handle the catering?*
▷ **handler** *noun*
[from Old English]

handlebar *NOUN* or **handlebars** *PLURAL NOUN* the bar, with a handle at each end, that steers a bicycle or motorcycle etc.

handout *NOUN* **handouts 1** money given to a needy person. **2** a sheet of information given out in a lesson, lecture, etc.

handrail *NOUN* **handrails** a narrow rail for people to hold as a support.

handset *NOUN* **handsets 1** the part of a telephone that you hold up to speak into and listen to. **2** a hand-held control device for a piece of electronic equipment.

handshake *NOUN* **handshakes** shaking hands with someone as a greeting or to show you agree to something.

handsome *ADJECTIVE* **1** good-looking. **2** generous • *a handsome offer.*
▷ **handsomely** *adverb*
[originally = easy to handle or use: from *hand* + *-some*]

hands-on *ADJECTIVE* involving actual experience of using equipment or doing something.

handstand *NOUN* **handstands** balancing on your hands with your feet in the air.

handwriting *NOUN* writing done by hand; a person's style of writing.
▷ **handwritten** *adjective*

handy *ADJECTIVE* **handier, handiest** **1** convenient or useful. **2** good at using the hands.
▷ **handily** *adverb* **handiness** *noun*

handyman *NOUN* **handymen** a person who does household repairs or odd jobs.

hang *VERB* **hangs, hanging, hung** **1** fix the top or side of something to a hook or nail etc.; be supported in this way. **2** stick wallpaper to a wall. **3** decorate with drapery or hanging ornaments etc. • *The tree was hung with lights.* **4** droop or lean • *People hung over the gate.* **5** remain in the air or as something unpleasant • *Smoke hung over the city. The threat is still hanging over him.* with *past tense* & *past participle* **hanged 6** execute someone by hanging them from a rope that tightens round the neck • *He was hanged in 1950.*
- **hang about 1** loiter. **2** not go away.
- **hang back** hesitate to go forward or to do something.
- **hang on 1** hold tightly. **2** (*informal*) wait.
- **hang up** end a telephone conversation by putting back the receiver.

hang *NOUN*
- **get the hang of** (*informal*) learn how to do or use something.

[from Old English]

hangar *NOUN* **hangars** a large shed where aircraft are kept.
[French, originally = a shed]

hanger *NOUN* **hangers** a device on which to hang things • *a coat hanger.*

hang-glider *NOUN* **hang-gliders** a framework in which a person can glide through the air.
▷ **hang-gliding** *noun*

hangman *NOUN* **hangmen** a man whose job it is to hang people condemned to death.

hangover *NOUN* **hangovers** an unpleasant feeling after drinking too much alcohol.

hank *NOUN* **hanks** a coil or piece of wool, thread, etc.
[from Old Norse]

hanker *VERB* **hankers, hankering, hankered** feel a longing for something.
[origin unknown]

hanky *NOUN* **hankies** (*informal*) a handkerchief.

Hanukkah (*say* **hah**-noo-ka) *NOUN* the eight-day Jewish festival of lights beginning in December.
[Hebrew, = consecration]

haphazard *ADJECTIVE* done or chosen at random, not by planning.
[from an old word *hap* = luck, + *hazard*]

hapless *ADJECTIVE* having no luck.
[from an old word *hap* = luck, + *-less*]

happen *VERB* **happens**, **happening**, **happened** **1** take place; occur. **2** do something by chance • *I happened to see him.*
[from an old word *hap* = luck]

happening *NOUN* **happenings** something that happens; an event.

happy *ADJECTIVE* **happier**, **happiest** **1** pleased or contented. **2** fortunate • *a happy coincidence.* **3** willing • *I'd be happy to help.*
▷ **happily** *adverb* **happiness** *noun*
[same origin as *happen*]

hara-kiri *NOUN* a form of suicide formerly used by Japanese officers when in disgrace.
[from Japanese *hara* = belly + *kiri* = cutting]

harangue (*say* ha-rang) *VERB* **harangues**, **haranguing**, **harangued** make a long aggressive speech to somebody.
▷ **harangue** *noun*
[from Latin]

harass (*say* ha-ras) *VERB* **harasses**, **harassing**, **harassed** trouble or annoy somebody often.
▷ **harassment** (*say* ha-ras-ment) *noun*
[from French *harer* = set a dog on someone]

harbour *NOUN* **harbours** a place where ships can shelter or unload.

harbour *VERB* **harbours**, **harbouring**, **harboured** **1** keep in your mind • *I think she still harbours a grudge against them.* **2** give shelter to somebody, especially a criminal.
[from Old English]

hard *ADJECTIVE* **1** firm or solid; not soft. **2** difficult • *hard sums.* **3** severe or stern. **4** causing suffering • *hard luck.* **5** using great effort • *a hard worker.* **6** (said about drugs) strong and addictive.
▷ **hardness** *noun*
- **hard of hearing** slightly deaf.
- **hard up** (*informal*) short of money.

hard *ADVERB* **1** so as to be hard • *The ground froze hard.* **2** with great effort; intensively • *We worked hard.* • *It is raining hard.* **3** with difficulty • *hard-earned cash.*
[from Old English]

hardback *NOUN* **hardbacks** a book bound in stiff covers.

hardboard *NOUN* stiff board made of compressed wood pulp.

hard disk *NOUN* **hard disks** a disk fixed inside a computer, able to store large amounts of data.

harden *VERB* **hardens**, **hardening**, **hardened** make or become hard.
▷ **hardener** *noun*

hard-hearted *ADJECTIVE* unsympathetic.

hardly *ADVERB* only just; only with difficulty • *She can hardly walk.*
USAGE It is not acceptable in standard English to use 'not' with *hardly*, as in 'she can't hardly walk'.

hardship *NOUN* **hardships** difficult conditions that cause discomfort or suffering • *a life of hardship.*

hard shoulder *NOUN* **hard shoulders** a strip at the edge of a motorway where vehicles can stop in an emergency.

hardware *NOUN* **1** metal implements and tools etc.; machinery. **2** the machinery of a computer as opposed to the software. (COMPARE **software**)

hard water *NOUN* water containing minerals that prevent soap from making much lather.

hard-wearing *ADJECTIVE* able to stand a lot of wear.

hardwood *NOUN* **hardwoods** hard heavy wood from deciduous trees, e.g. oak and teak.

hardy *ADJECTIVE* **hardier**, **hardiest** able to endure cold or difficult conditions.
▷ **hardiness** *noun*
[from French *hardi* = bold or daring]

hare *NOUN* **hares** an animal like a rabbit but larger.
[from Old English]

harem (*say* har-eem) *NOUN* **harems** the part of a Muslim palace or house where the women live; the women living there.
[from Arabic *harim* = forbidden]

hark *VERB* **harks, harking, harked** listen.
- **hark back** return to an earlier subject.
[probably from Old English; *hark back* from a call telling hounds to retrace their steps to find a lost scent]

harlequin *ADJECTIVE* in mixed colours.
[from *Arlecchino*, the name of a character in Italian comedies whose clothes were of several colours]

harm *VERB* **harms, harming, harmed** damage or injure.

harm *NOUN* damage or injury.
▷ **harmful** *adjective* **harmless** *adjective*
[from Old English]

harmonic *ADJECTIVE* to do with harmony in music.

harmonica *NOUN* **harmonicas** a mouth organ.
[from Latin *harmonicus* = to do with melody]

harmonious *ADJECTIVE* **1** combining together in a pleasant, attractive, or effective way. **2** sounding pleasant. **3** peaceful and friendly.

harmonize *VERB* **harmonizes, harmonizing, harmonized** combine together in a pleasant, attractive, or effective way.
▷ **harmonization** *noun*

harmony *NOUN* **harmonies 1** a pleasant combination, especially of musical notes. **2** being friendly to each other and not quarrelling.
[from Latin *harmonia* = agreement]

harness *NOUN* **harnesses** the straps put round a horse's head and neck for controlling it.

harness *VERB* **harnesses, harnessing, harnessed 1** put a harness on a horse. **2** control and use something • *Could we harness the power of the wind?*
[via French from Old Norse]

harp *NOUN* **harps** a musical instrument made of strings stretched across a frame and plucked with the fingers.
▷ **harpist** *noun*

harp *VERB* **harps, harping, harped** keep on talking about something in a tiresome way • *He keeps harping on about all the work he has to do.*
[from Old English]

harpoon *NOUN* **harpoons** a spear attached to a rope, used for catching whales etc.
▷ **harpoon** *verb*
[from French]

harpsichord *NOUN* **harpsichords** an instrument like a piano but with strings that are plucked (not struck) by a mechanism.
[from Latin *harpa* = harp + *chorda* = string]

harrow *NOUN* **harrows** a heavy device pulled over the ground to break up the soil.
[from Old Norse]

harrowing *ADJECTIVE* very upsetting or distressing.
[as if a harrow had been pulled over you]

harry *VERB* **harries, harrying, harried** harass or worry.
[from Old English]

harsh *ADJECTIVE* **1** rough and unpleasant. **2** severe or cruel.
▷ **harshly** *adverb* **harshness** *noun*
[from old German *horsch* = rough or hairy]

hart *NOUN* **harts** a male deer.
(COMPARE **hind**[2])
[from Old English]

harvest *NOUN* **harvests 1** the time when farmers gather in the corn, fruit, or vegetables that they have grown. **2** the crop that is gathered in.

harvest *VERB* **harvests, harvesting, harvested** gather in a crop; reap.
▷ **harvester** *noun*
[from Old English]

hash[1] *NOUN* a mixture of small pieces of meat and vegetables, usually fried.
- **make a hash of** (*informal*) make a mess of something; bungle.
[from French *hacher* = cut up small]

hash[2] *NOUN* the symbol #.
[probably from *hatch*[3]]

hashish *NOUN* a drug made from hemp.
[from Arabic]

hasn't (*mainly spoken*) has not.

hassle *NOUN* (*informal*) something that is difficult or troublesome.
[origin unknown]

hassock *NOUN* **hassocks** a small thick cushion for kneeling on in church.
[origin unknown]

haste *NOUN* a hurry.
- **make haste** act quickly.
[via old French from Germanic]

hasten *VERB* **hastens, hastening, hastened** hurry.

hasty *ADJECTIVE* hurried; done too quickly.
▷ **hastily** *adverb* **hastiness** *noun*

hat *NOUN* **hats** a covering for the head, worn out of doors.
- **keep something under your hat** keep it a secret.
[from Old English]

hatch[1] *NOUN* **hatches** an opening in a floor, wall, or door, usually with a covering.
[from Old English]

hatch[2] *VERB* **hatches, hatching, hatched** **1** break out of an egg. **2** keep an egg warm until a baby bird comes out. **3** plan • *They hatched a plot.*
[origin unknown]

hatch[3] *VERB* **hatches, hatching, hatched** shade part of a drawing with close parallel lines.
▷ **hatching** *noun*
[from old French *hacher* = inlay with strips of metal]

hatchback *NOUN* **hatchbacks** a car with a sloping back hinged at the top.

hatchet *NOUN* **hatchets** a small axe.
[via old French and Latin from Germanic]

hate *VERB* **hates, hating, hated** dislike very strongly.

hate *NOUN* extreme dislike.
[from Old English]

hateful *ADJECTIVE* arousing hatred.

hatred *NOUN* extreme dislike.

hatter *NOUN* **hatters** a person who makes hats.

hat-trick *NOUN* **hat-tricks** getting three goals, wickets, or victories one after the other.

haughty *ADJECTIVE* **haughtier, haughtiest** proud of yourself and looking down on other people.
▷ **haughtily** *adverb* **haughtiness** *noun*
[from French *haut* = high]

haul *VERB* **hauls, hauling, hauled** pull or drag with great effort.
▷ **haulage** *noun*

haul *NOUN* **hauls 1** hauling. **2** the amount obtained by an effort; booty • *The thieves made a haul of £2 million.* **3** a distance to be covered • *a long haul.*
[via old French from Old Norse]

haulage *NOUN* **1** transporting goods. **2** a charge for this.

haunch *NOUN* **haunches** the buttock and top part of the thigh.
[via old French from Germanic]

haunt *VERB* **haunts, haunting, haunted** **1** (said about ghosts) appear often in a place or to a person. **2** visit a place often. **3** stay in your mind • *The memory haunts me still.*
▷ **haunted** *adjective*

haunt *NOUN* **haunts** a place that you often visit.
[via old French from Germanic]

haunting *ADJECTIVE* so beautiful and sad that it stays in your mind • *a haunting tune.*

have *VERB* **has, having, had**
This word has many uses, including
1 possess or own • *We have two dogs.*
2 contain • *This tin has sweets in it.*
3 experience • *He had a shock.* **4** be obliged to do something • *We have to go now.*
5 allow • *I won't have him bullied.* **6** receive or accept • *Will you have a sweet?* **7** get something done • *I'm having my watch mended.* **8** (*slang*) cheat or deceive • *We've been had!*
- **have somebody on** (*informal*) fool him or her.

have *AUXILIARY VERB* used to form the past tense of verbs, e.g. *He has gone.*
[from Old English]

haven *NOUN* **havens** a safe place or refuge.
[from Old Norse]

haven't (*mainly spoken*) have not.

haversack *NOUN* **haversacks** a strong bag carried on your back or over your shoulder.
[from old German *Habersack* = oat- bag (in which the German cavalry carried oats for their horses)]

A B C D E F G **H** I J K L M N O P Q R S T U V W X Y Z

havoc *NOUN* great destruction or disorder.
- **play havoc with** disrupt something completely.
[from old French *havot*, an order to begin looting]

haw *NOUN* **haws** a hawthorn berry.
[from Old English]

hawk[1] *NOUN* **hawks** a bird of prey with very strong eyesight.
[from Old English]

hawk[2] *VERB* **hawks, hawking, hawked** carry goods about and try to sell them.
▷ **hawker** *noun*
[from Dutch]

hawthorn *NOUN* **hawthorns** a thorny tree with small red berries (called *haws*).

hay *NOUN* dried grass for feeding to animals.
[from Old English]

hay fever *NOUN* irritation of the nose, throat, and eyes, caused by pollen or dust.

haystack or **hayrick** *NOUN* **haystacks, hayricks** a large neat pile of hay packed for storing.

haywire *ADJECTIVE* (*informal*) out of control.
[because wire for tying up hay bales was often used for makeshift repairs]

hazard *NOUN* **hazards 1** a danger or risk. **2** an obstacle on a golf course.
▷ **hazardous** *adjective*

hazard *VERB* **hazards, hazarding, hazarded** put at risk.
- **hazard a guess** make a guess.
[via French from Persian or Turkish *zar* = dice]

haze *NOUN* thin mist.
[origin unknown]

hazel *NOUN* **hazels 1** a bush with small nuts. **2** a light brown colour.
▷ **hazelnut** *noun*
[from Old English]

hazy *ADJECTIVE* **1** misty. **2** vague or uncertain.
▷ **hazily** *adverb* **haziness** *noun*

H-bomb *NOUN* **H-bombs** a hydrogen bomb.

he *PRONOUN* **1** the male person or animal being talked about. **2** a person (male or female) • *He who hesitates is lost.*
[from Old English]

head *NOUN* **heads 1** the part of the body containing the brains, eyes, and mouth. **2** your brains or mind; intelligence • *Use your head!* **3** a talent or ability • *She has a good head for figures.* **4** the side of a coin on which someone's head is shown • *Heads or tails?* **5** a person • *It costs £5 a head.* **6** the top or front of something • *a pinhead; at the head of the procession.* **7** the chief; the person in charge. **8** a headteacher.
- **come to a head** reach a crisis point.
- **keep your head** stay calm.
- **off the top of your head** without preparation or thinking carefully.

head *VERB* **heads, heading, headed 1** be at the top or front of something. **2** hit a ball with your head. **3** move in a particular direction • *We headed for the coast.* **4** force someone to turn aside by getting in front of them • *Let's see if we can head him off.*
[from Old English]

headache *NOUN* **headaches 1** a pain in the head. **2** (*informal*) a worrying problem.

headdress *NOUN* **headdresses** a covering or decoration for the head.

header *NOUN* **headers** heading the ball in football.

heading *NOUN* **headings** a word or words put at the top of a piece of printing or writing.

headland *NOUN* **headlands** a large piece of high land that sticks out into the sea.

headlight *NOUN* **headlights** a powerful light at the front of a car, engine, etc.

headline *NOUN* **headlines** a heading in a newspaper.
- **the headlines** the main items of news.

headlong *ADVERB* & *ADJECTIVE* **1** falling head first. **2** in a hasty or thoughtless way.

headmaster *NOUN* **headmasters** a male headteacher.

headmistress *NOUN* **headmistresses** a female headteacher.

head-on *ADVERB* & *ADJECTIVE* with the front parts colliding • *a head-on collision.*

headphones *PLURAL NOUN* a pair of earphones on a band that fits over the head.

headquarters *NOUN & PLURAL NOUN* the place from which an organization is controlled.

headstone *NOUN* **headstones** a stone set up on a grave.

headstrong *ADJECTIVE* determined to do as you want.

headteacher *NOUN* **headteachers** the person in charge of a school.

headway *NOUN*
- **make headway** make progress.

heal *VERB* **heals, healing, healed** **1** make or become healthy flesh again • *The wound healed slowly.* **2** (*old use*) cure • *healing the sick.*
[from Old English]

health *NOUN* **1** the condition of a person's body or mind • *His health is bad.* **2** being healthy • *in sickness and in health.*
[from Old English]

health food *NOUN* **health foods** food that contains only natural substances and is thought to be good for your health.

healthy *ADJECTIVE* **healthier, healthiest** **1** being well; free from illness. **2** producing good health • *Fresh air is healthy.*
▷ **healthily** *adverb* **healthiness** *noun*

heap *NOUN* **heaps** a pile, especially an untidy one.
- **heaps** *plural noun* (*informal*) a great amount; plenty • *There's heaps of time.*

heap *VERB* **heaps, heaping, heaped** **1** make things into a heap. **2** put on large amounts • *She heaped the plate with food.*
[from Old English]

hear *VERB* **hears, hearing, heard** **1** take in sounds through the ears. **2** receive news or information. **3** listen to and try a case in a lawcourt.
▷ **hearer** *noun*
- **hear! hear!** (in a debate) I agree.
- **not hear of** refuse to allow something • *He wouldn't hear of my paying for it.*
[from Old English]

hearing *NOUN* **hearings** **1** the ability to hear. **2** a chance to be heard; a trial in a lawcourt.

hearing aid *NOUN* **hearing aids** a device to help a deaf person to hear.

hearsay *NOUN* something heard, e.g. in a rumour or gossip.

hearse *NOUN* **hearses** a vehicle for taking the coffin to a funeral.
[from old French]

heart *NOUN* **hearts** **1** the organ of the body that makes the blood circulate. **2** a person's feelings or emotions; sympathy. **3** enthusiasm or courage • *We must take heart.* **4** the middle or most important part. **5** a curved shape representing a heart. **6** a playing card with red heart shapes on it.
- **break a person's heart** make him or her very unhappy.
- **by heart** memorized.
[from Old English]

heart attack *NOUN* **heart attacks** a sudden failure of the heart to work properly, which results in great pain or sometimes death.

heartbroken *ADJECTIVE* very unhappy.

hearten *VERB* **heartens, heartening, heartened** make a person feel encouraged.

heart failure *NOUN* gradual failure of the heart to work properly, especially as a cause of death.

heartfelt *ADJECTIVE* felt deeply.

hearth *NOUN* **hearths** the floor of a fireplace, or the area in front of it.
[from Old English]

heartland *NOUN* the central or most important region.

heartless *ADJECTIVE* without pity or sympathy.

hearty *ADJECTIVE* **1** strong and vigorous. **2** enthusiastic and sincere • *hearty congratulations.* **3** (said about a meal) large.
▷ **heartily** *adverb* **heartiness** *noun*

heat *NOUN* **heats** **1** hotness or (in scientific use) the form of energy causing this. **2** hot weather. **3** strong feeling, especially anger. **4** a race or contest to decide who will take part in the final.
- **on heat** (said about a female mammal) ready for mating.

heat *VERB* **heats, heating, heated** make or become hot.
[from Old English]

heater *NOUN* **heaters** a device for heating something.

heath *NOUN* **heaths** flat land with low shrubs.
[from Old English]

heathen *NOUN* **heathens** a person who does not believe in any of the world's chief religions.
[from Old English]

heather *NOUN* an evergreen plant with small purple, pink, or white flowers.
[from Old English]

heatwave *NOUN* **heatwaves** a long period of hot weather.

heave *VERB* **heaves, heaving, heaved** (when used of ships **hove**) **1** lift or move something heavy. **2** (*informal*) throw. **3** rise and fall. **4** if your stomach heaves, you feel like vomiting.
▷ **heave** *noun*
- **heave into view** (said about a ship) come into view.
- **heave a sigh** utter a deep sigh.
- **heave to** (said about a ship) stop without mooring or anchoring.
[from Old English]

heaven *NOUN* **heavens 1** the place where God and angels are thought to live. **2** a very pleasant place or condition.
- **the heavens** the sky.
[from Old English]

heavenly *ADJECTIVE* **1** to do with heaven. **2** in the sky • *Stars are heavenly bodies.* **3** (*informal*) very pleasing.

heavy *ADJECTIVE* **heavier, heaviest**
1 weighing a lot; difficult to lift or carry. **2** great in amount or force • *heavy rain; a heavy penalty*. **3** needing much effort • *heavy work.* **4** full of sadness or worry • *with a heavy heart.*
▷ **heavily** *adverb* **heaviness** *noun*
[from Old English]

heavy industry *NOUN* **heavy industries** industry producing metal, large machines, etc.

heavyweight *NOUN* **heavyweights 1** a heavy person. **2** a boxer of the heaviest weight.
▷ **heavyweight** *adjective*

Hebrew *NOUN* the language of the Jews in ancient Palestine and modern Israel.

heckle *VERB* **heckles, heckling, heckled** interrupt a speaker with awkward questions.
▷ **heckler** *noun*
[originally, to use a *heckle* = a steel comb for hemp or flax]

hectare (*say* **hek**-tar) *NOUN* **hectares** a unit of area equal to 10,000 square metres or nearly 2 acres.
[from Greek *hekaton* = hundred, + French *are* = a hundred square metres]

hectic *ADJECTIVE* full of activity.
[from Greek]

hecto- *PREFIX* one hundred (as in *hectogram* = 100 grams).
[from Greek]

hector *VERB* **hectors, hectoring, hectored** talk to someone in a bullying way.
[from a gang of young bullies in London in the 17th century who named themselves after Hector, a hero in Greek legend]

hedge *NOUN* **hedges** a row of bushes forming a barrier or boundary.

hedge *VERB* **hedges, hedging, hedged**
1 surround with a hedge or other barrier. **2** make or trim a hedge. **3** avoid giving a definite answer.
▷ **hedger** *noun*
- **hedge your bets** avoid committing yourself when you are faced with a difficult choice.
[from Old English]

hedgehog *NOUN* **hedgehogs** a small animal covered with long prickles.
[because of the grunting noises it makes]

hedgerow *NOUN* **hedgerows** a hedge of bushes bordering a field.

heed *VERB* **heeds, heeding, heeded** pay attention to.

heed *NOUN*
- **take** or **pay heed** give attention to something.
▷ **heedful** *adjective* **heedless** *adjective*
[from Old English]

hee-haw *NOUN* **hee-haws** a donkey's bray.
[imitating the sound]

heel[1] *NOUN* **heels 1** the back part of the foot. **2** the part round or under the heel of a sock or shoe etc.
- **take to your heels** run away.

heel *VERB* **heels, heeling, heeled 1** repair the heel of a shoe. **2** kick a ball with your heel.
[from Old English *hela*]

heel[2] *VERB* **heels, heeling, heeled** (said about a ship) lean over to one side.
[from Old English *hieldan*]

hefty *ADJECTIVE* **heftier, heftiest** large and strong.
▷ **heftily** *adverb*
[probably from a Scandinavian language]

Hegira (*say* hej-ir-a) *NOUN* the flight of Muhammad from Mecca in AD622. The Muslim era is reckoned from this date.
[from Arabic *hijra* = departure from your home or country]

heifer (*say* hef-er) *NOUN* **heifers** a young cow.
[from Old English]

height *NOUN* **heights 1** how high something is; the distance from the base to the top or from head to foot. **2** a high place. **3** the highest or most intense part • *at the height of the holiday season.*
[from Old English]

heighten *VERB* **heightens, heightening, heightened** make or become higher or more intense.

heinous (*say* hay-nus or hee-nus) *ADJECTIVE* very wicked • *a heinous crime.*
[from old French *hair* = to hate]

heir (*say as* air) *NOUN* **heirs** a person who inherits something.
[from Latin]

heir apparent *NOUN* **heirs apparent** an heir whose right to inherit cannot be set aside even if someone with a stronger right is born.

heiress (*say* air-ess) *NOUN* **heiresses** a female heir, especially to great wealth.

heirloom (*say* air-loom) *NOUN* **heirlooms** a valued possession that has been handed down in a family for several generations.
[from *heir* + Old English *geloma* = tool]

heir presumptive *NOUN* **heirs presumptive** an heir whose right to inherit may be set aside if someone with a stronger right is born.

helicopter *NOUN* **helicopters** a kind of aircraft with a large horizontal propeller or rotor.
[from *helix* + Greek *pteron* = wing]

heliotrope *NOUN* **heliotropes** a plant with small fragrant purple flowers.
[from Greek *helios* = sun + *trope* = turning (because the plant turns its flowers to the sun)]

helium (*say* hee-lee-um) *NOUN* a light colourless gas that does not burn.
[from Greek *helios* = sun]

helix (*say* hee-liks) *NOUN* **helices** (*say* hee-liss-eez) a spiral.
[Greek, = coil]

hell *NOUN* **1** a place where, in some religions, wicked people are thought to be punished after they die. **2** a very unpleasant place. **3** (*informal*) an exclamation of anger.
- **hell for leather** (*informal*) at high speed.
[from Old English]

hellish *ADJECTIVE* (*informal*) very difficult or unpleasant.

hello *INTERJECTION* a word used to greet somebody or to attract their attention.

helm *NOUN* **helms** the handle or wheel used to steer a ship.
▷ **helmsman** *noun*
[from Old English]

helmet *NOUN* **helmets** a strong covering worn to protect the head.
[old French, from Old English]

help *VERB* **helps, helping, helped 1** do something useful for someone. **2** benefit; make something better or easier • *This will help you to sleep.* **3** if you cannot help doing something, you cannot avoid doing it • *I can't help coughing.* **4** serve food etc. to somebody.
▷ **helper** *noun*

help *NOUN* **1** helping somebody. **2** a person or thing that helps.
[from Old English]

helpful *ADJECTIVE* giving help; useful.
▷ **helpfully** *adverb* **helpfulness** *noun*

helping *NOUN* **helpings** a portion of food.

a b c d e f g h i j k l m n o p q r s t u v w x y z

helpless *ADJECTIVE* not able to do things.
▷ **helplessly** *adverb* **helplessness** *noun*

helpline *NOUN* **helplines** a telephone service giving advice on problems.

helpmate *NOUN* **helpmates** a helper.

helter-skelter *ADVERB* in great haste.

helter-skelter *NOUN* **helter-skelters** a spiral slide at a fair.
[vaguely imitating the sound of many running feet]

hem *NOUN* **hems** the edge of a piece of cloth that is folded over and sewn down.

hem *VERB* **hems, hemming, hemmed** put a hem on something.
- **hem in** surround and restrict.
[from Old English]

hemisphere *NOUN* **hemispheres 1** half a sphere. **2** half the earth • *Australia is in the southern hemisphere.*
▷ **hemispherical** *adjective*
[from Greek *hemi-* = half, + *sphere*]

hemlock *NOUN* a poisonous plant or poison made from it.
[from Old English]

hemp *NOUN* **1** a plant that produces coarse fibres from which cloth and ropes are made. **2** the drug cannabis, made from this plant.
▷ **hempen** *adjective*
[from Old English]

hen *NOUN* **hens 1** a female bird. **2** a female fowl.
[from Old English]

hence *ADVERB* **1** henceforth. **2** therefore. **3** (*old use*) from here.
[from Old English]

henceforth *ADVERB* from now on.

henchman *NOUN* **henchmen** a trusty supporter.
[origin unknown]

henna *NOUN* a reddish-brown dye, especially used for colouring hair.
[from Arabic]

hepatitis *NOUN* inflammation of the liver.
[from Greek *hepar* = liver, + *-itis*]

hepta- *PREFIX* seven.
[from Greek]

heptagon *NOUN* **heptagons** a flat shape with seven sides and seven angles.
▷ **heptagonal** *adjective*
[from *hepta-* + Greek *gonia* = angle]

heptathlon *NOUN* **heptathlons** an athletic contest in which each competitor takes part in seven events.

her *PRONOUN* the form of *she* used as the object of a verb or after a preposition.

her *ADJECTIVE* belonging to her • *her book.*
[from Old English]

herald *NOUN* **heralds 1** an official in former times who made announcements and carried messages for a king or queen. **2** a person or thing that is a sign of something to come • *Spring is the herald of summer.*

herald *VERB* **heralds, heralding, heralded** show that something is coming.
[via old French from Germanic]

heraldry *NOUN* the study of coats of arms.
▷ **heraldic** (*say* hir-**al**-dik) *adjective*
[because a herald (sense 1) decided who could have a coat of arms and what should be on it]

herb *NOUN* **herbs** a plant used for flavouring or for making medicine.
▷ **herbal** *adjective*
[from Latin]

herbaceous (*say* her-**bay**-shus) *ADJECTIVE* **1** containing many flowering plants • *a herbaceous border.* **2** to do with or like herbs.

herbivorous (*say* her-**biv**-er-us) *ADJECTIVE* plant-eating. (COMPARE **carnivorous**)
▷ **herbivore** *noun*
[from Latin *herba* = grass, + *-vorous*]

herculean (*say* her-kew-**lee**-an) *ADJECTIVE* needing great strength or effort • *a herculean task.*
[from *Hercules*, a hero in ancient Greek legend]

herd *NOUN* **herds 1** a group of cattle or other animals that feed together. **2** a mass of people; a mob.
▷ **herdsman** *noun*

herd *VERB* **herds, herding, herded 1** gather or move or send in a herd • *We all herded into the dining room.* **2** look after a herd of animals.
[from Old English]

here *ADVERB* in or to this place etc.
- **here and there** in various places or directions.
[from Old English]

hereafter *ADVERB* from now on; in future.

hereby *ADVERB* by this act or decree etc.

hereditary *ADJECTIVE* **1** inherited • *a hereditary disease.* **2** inheriting a position • *Our Queen is a hereditary monarch.*
[from Latin]

heredity (*say* hir-**ed**-it-ee) *NOUN* the process of inheriting physical or mental characteristics from parents or ancestors.
[from Latin *heredis* = to do with an heir]

heresy (*say* **herri**-see) *NOUN* **heresies** an opinion that disagrees with the beliefs generally accepted by the Christian Church or other authority.
[from Greek *hairesis* = choice]

heretic (*say* **herri**-tik) *NOUN* **heretics** a person who supports a heresy.
▷ **heretical** (*say* hi-**ret**-ik-al) *adjective*
[from Greek]

heritage *NOUN* the things that someone has inherited.
[from Latin *hereditare* = inherit]

hermaphrodite (*say* her-**maf**-ro-dyt) *NOUN* **hermaphrodites** an animal, flower, or person that has both male and female sexual organs or characteristics.
[from Greek *hermaphroditos*, originally the name of the son of the gods Hermes and Aphrodite, who became joined in one body with a nymph]

hermetically *ADVERB* so as to be airtight • *The tin is hermetically sealed.*
[from Latin]

hermit *NOUN* **hermits** a person who lives alone and keeps away from people.
[from Greek *eremos* = alone or deserted]

hermitage *NOUN* **hermitages** a hermit's home.

hernia *NOUN* **hernias** a condition in which an internal part of the body pushes through a weak point in another part.
[Latin]

hero *NOUN* **heroes 1** a man or boy who is admired for doing something very brave or great. **2** the chief male character in a story etc.
▷ **heroic** *adjective* **heroically** *adverb* **heroism** *noun*
[from Greek *heros* = a very strong or brave man, whom the gods love]

heroin *NOUN* a very strong drug, made from morphine.
[from Greek]

heroine *NOUN* **heroines 1** a woman or girl who is admired for doing something very brave or great. **2** the chief female character in a story etc.
[Greek, feminine of *heros* = hero]

heron *NOUN* **herons** a wading bird with long legs and a long neck.
[via old French from Germanic]

herring *NOUN* **herring** or **herrings** a sea fish used as food.
[from Old English]

herringbone *NOUN* a zigzag pattern.
[because it looks like the spine and ribs of a herring]

hers *POSSESSIVE PRONOUN* belonging to her • *Those books are hers.*
[from *her*]
USAGE It is incorrect to write *her's*.

herself *PRONOUN* she or her and nobody else. The word is used to refer back to the subject of a sentence (e.g. *She cut herself*) or for emphasis (e.g. *She herself has said it*).
- **by herself** alone; on her own.

hertz *NOUN* **hertz** a unit of frequency of electromagnetic waves, equal to one cycle per second.
[named after a German scientist, H. R. *Hertz*, who discovered radio waves]

hesitant *ADJECTIVE* hesitating.
▷ **hesitantly** *adverb* **hesitancy** *noun*

hesitate *VERB* **hesitates**, **hesitating**, **hesitated** be slow or uncertain in speaking, moving, etc.
▷ **hesitation** *noun*
[from Latin *haesitare* = get stuck]

hessian *NOUN* a type of strong coarse cloth, used for making sacks.
[named after *Hesse*, in Germany, where it was made]

A B C D E F G H I J K L M N O P Q R S T U V W X Y Z

hetero- *PREFIX* other; different.
[from Greek *heteros* = other]

heterogeneous (*say* het-er-o-**jeen**-ee-us) *ADJECTIVE* composed of people or things of different kinds.
[from *hetero-* + Greek *genos* = a kind]

heterosexual *ADJECTIVE* attracted to people of the opposite sex; not homosexual.
▷ **heterosexual** *noun*

hew *VERB* **hews, hewing, hewn** chop or cut with an axe or sword etc.
[from Old English]

hexa- *PREFIX* six.
[from Greek]

hexagon *NOUN* **hexagons** a flat shape with six sides and six angles.
▷ **hexagonal** *adjective*
[from *hexa-* + Greek *gonia* = angle]

hey *INTERJECTION* an exclamation used to attract attention or to express surprise or interest.

heyday *NOUN* the time of a thing's greatest success or prosperity.
[from *hey-day*, an expression of joy]

hi *INTERJECTION* an exclamation used as a friendly greeting.

hiatus (*say* hy-**ay**-tus) *NOUN* **hiatuses** a gap in something that is otherwise continuous.
[Latin, = gaping]

hibernate *VERB* **hibernates, hibernating, hibernated** spend the winter in a state like deep sleep.
▷ **hibernation** *noun*
[from Latin *hibernus* = wintry]

hiccup *NOUN* **hiccups 1** a high gulping sound made when your breath is briefly interrupted. **2** a brief hitch or setback.
▷ **hiccup** *verb*
[imitating the sound]

hickory *NOUN* **hickories** a tree rather like the walnut tree.
[from a Native American language]

hide[1] *VERB* **hides, hiding, hid, hidden 1** get into a place where you cannot be seen. **2** keep a person or thing from being seen. **3** keep a thing secret.
[from Old English *hydan*]

hide[2] *NOUN* **hides** an animal's skin.
[from Old English *hyd*]

hide-and-seek *NOUN* a game in which one person looks for others who are hiding.

hidebound *ADJECTIVE* narrow-minded.
[originally used of underfed cattle, with skin stretched tight over their bones, later of a tree whose bark was so tight it could not grow]

hideous *ADJECTIVE* very ugly or unpleasant.
▷ **hideously** *adverb*
[from old French]

hideout *NOUN* **hideouts** a place where somebody hides.

hiding[1] *NOUN* being hidden • *She went into hiding.*
▷ **hiding place** *noun*

hiding[2] *NOUN* **hidings** a thrashing or beating.
[from an old word *hide* = to beat the hide (skin)]

hierarchy (*say* **hyr**-ark-ee) *NOUN* **hierarchies** an organization that ranks people one above another according to the power or authority that they hold.
[from Greek *hieros* = sacred, + *-archy*]

hieroglyphics (*say* hyr-o-**glif**-iks) *PLURAL NOUN* pictures or symbols used in ancient Egypt to represent words.
[from Greek *hieros* = sacred + *glyphe* = carving]

hi-fi *NOUN* **hi-fis** (*informal*) **1** high fidelity. **2** equipment for reproducing recorded sound with very little distortion.

higgledy-piggledy *ADVERB & ADJECTIVE* completely mixed up; in great disorder.
[nonsense word based on *pig* (because of the way pigs huddle together)]

high *ADJECTIVE* **1** reaching a long way upwards • *high hills.* **2** far above the ground or above sea level • *high clouds.* **3** measuring from top to bottom • *The post is two metres high.* **4** above average level in importance, quality, amount, etc. • *high rank; high prices.* **5** (said about meat) beginning to go bad. **6** (*informal*) affected by a drug.
- **it is high time** it is past the time when something should have happened • *It's high time we left.*

high *ADVERB* at or to a high level or position etc. • *They flew high above us.*
[from Old English]

highbrow *ADJECTIVE* intellectual.
[from *highbrowed* = having a high forehead (thought to be a sign of intelligence)]

Higher *NOUN* **Highers** the advanced level of the Scottish Certificate of Education.

higher *ADJECTIVE* & *ADVERB* more high.

higher education *NOUN* education at a university or college.

high explosive *NOUN* **high explosives** a powerful explosive.

high fidelity *NOUN* reproducing recorded sound with very little distortion.

high jump *NOUN* an athletic contest in which competitors try to jump over a high bar.

highlands *PLURAL NOUN* mountainous country.
▷ **highland** *adjective* **highlander** *noun*

highlight *NOUN* **highlights 1** the most interesting part of something • *The highlight of the holiday was the trip to Pompeii.* **2** a light area in a painting etc. **3** a light-coloured streak in a person's hair.

highlight *VERB* **highlights, highlighting, highlighted** draw special attention to something.

highlighter *NOUN* **highlighters** a felt-tip pen that you use to spread bright colour over lines of text to draw attention to them.

highly *ADVERB* **1** extremely • *highly amusing.* **2** very favourably • *We think highly of her.*

highly-strung *ADJECTIVE* nervous and easily upset.

Highness *NOUN* **Highnesses** the title of a prince or princess.

high-pitched *ADJECTIVE* high in sound.

high-rise *ADJECTIVE* with many storeys.

high road *NOUN* **high roads** a main road.

high school *NOUN* **high schools** a secondary school.

high spirits *PLURAL NOUN* cheerful and lively behaviour.
▷ **high-spirited** *adjective*

high street *NOUN* **high streets** a town's main street.

high-tech *ADJECTIVE* using the most advanced technology, especially electronic devices and computers.
[short for 'high technology']

highway *NOUN* **highways** a main road or route.

highwayman *NOUN* **highwaymen** a man who robbed travellers on highways in former times.

hijack *VERB* **hijacks, hijacking, hijacked** seize control of an aircraft or vehicle during a journey.
▷ **hijack** *noun* **hijacker** *noun*
[origin unknown]

hike *NOUN* **hikes** a long walk.
▷ **hike** *verb* **hiker** *noun*
[origin unknown]

hilarious *ADJECTIVE* very funny.
▷ **hilariously** *adverb* **hilarity** *noun*
[from Greek *hilaros* = cheerful]

hill *NOUN* **hills** a piece of land that is higher than the ground around it.
▷ **hillside** *noun* **hilly** *adjective*
[from Old English]

hillock *NOUN* **hillocks** a small hill; a mound.
[from *hill* + Old English *-oc* = small]

hilt *NOUN* **hilts** the handle of a sword, dagger, or knife.
- **to the hilt** completely.
[from Old English]

him *PRONOUN* the form of *he* used as the object of a verb or after a preposition.
[from Old English]

himself *PRONOUN* he or him and nobody else. (COMPARE **herself**)

hind[1] *ADJECTIVE* at the back • *the hind legs.*
[probably from *behind*]

hind[2] *NOUN* **hinds** a female deer. (COMPARE **hart**)
[from Old English]

hinder *VERB* **hinders, hindering, hindered** get in someone's way or make things difficult for them.
▷ **hindrance** *noun*
[from Old English]

Hindi *NOUN* one of the languages of India.

hindmost *ADJECTIVE* furthest behind.

hindquarters *PLURAL NOUN* an animal's hind legs and rear parts.

A B C D E F G **H** I J K L M N O P Q R S T U V W X Y Z

hindsight *NOUN* looking back on an event with knowledge or understanding that you did not have at the time.

Hindu *NOUN* **Hindus** a person who believes in Hinduism, which is one of the religions of India.

hinge *NOUN* **hinges** a joining device on which a lid or door etc. turns when it opens.

hinge *VERB* **hinges, hinging, hinged 1** fix something with a hinge. **2** depend • *Everything hinges on this meeting.*
[Middle English, related to *hang*]

hint *NOUN* **hints 1** a slight indication or suggestion • *Give me a hint of what you want.* **2** a useful idea or piece of advice • *household hints.*

hint *VERB* **hints, hinting, hinted** make a hint.
[from an old word *hent* = getting hold, especially of an idea]

hinterland *NOUN* **hinterlands** the district lying inland beyond a coast or port etc.
[German, = land behind]

hip[1] *NOUN* **hips** the bony part at the side of the body between the waist and the thigh.
[from Old English *hype*]

hip[2] *NOUN* **hips** the fruit of the wild rose.
[from Old English *heope*]

hip hop *NOUN* a type of modern dance music with spoken words and a steady beat, played on electronic instruments.

hippie *NOUN* **hippies** (*informal*) a young person who joins with others to live in an unconventional way, often based on ideas of peace and love. Hippies first appeared in the 1960s.
[from American slang *hip* = aware of and understanding new music, fashions, and attitudes]

hippo *NOUN* **hippos** (*informal*) a hippopotamus.

hippopotamus *NOUN* **hippopotamuses** a very large African animal that lives near water.
[from Greek *hippos ho potamios* = horse of the river]

hire *VERB* **hires, hiring, hired 1** pay to borrow something. **2** lend for payment • *He hires out bicycles.*
▷ **hirer** *noun*

hire *NOUN* hiring • *for hire.*
[from Old English]

hire purchase *NOUN* buying something by paying for it in instalments.

hirsute (*say* **herss**-yoot) *ADJECTIVE* (*formal*) hairy.
[from Latin *hirsutus* = rough or shaggy]

his *ADJECTIVE* & *POSSESSIVE PRONOUN* belonging to him • *That is his book. That book is his.*
[from Old English]

hiss *VERB* **hisses, hissing, hissed** make a sound like an *s* • *The snakes were hissing.*
▷ **hiss** *noun*
[imitating the sound]

histogram *NOUN* **histograms** a chart showing amounts as rectangles of varying sizes.
[from Greek *histos* = mast, + *-gram*]

historian *NOUN* **historians** a person who writes or studies history.

historic *ADJECTIVE* famous or important in history; likely to be remembered • *a historic town; a historic meeting.*
USAGE Do not confuse with **historical**.

historical *ADJECTIVE* **1** to do with history. **2** that actually existed or took place in the past • *The novel is based on historical events.*
▷ **historically** *adverb*
USAGE Do not confuse with **historic**.

history *NOUN* **histories 1** what happened in the past. **2** study of past events. **3** a description of important events.
[from Greek *historia* = learning or finding out]

hit *VERB* **hits, hitting, hit 1** come forcefully against a person or thing; knock or strike. **2** have a bad effect on • *Famine has hit the poor countries.* **3** reach • *I can't hit that high note.*
- **hit it off** get on well with someone.
- **hit on** discover something suddenly or by chance.

hit *NOUN* **hits 1** hitting; a knock or stroke. **2** a shot that hits the target. **3** a success. **4** a successful song, show, etc.
[from Old Norse]

hit-and-run *ADJECTIVE* a hit-and-run driver is one who injures someone in an accident and drives off without stopping.

hitch *VERB* **hitches, hitching, hitched**
1 raise or pull with a slight jerk. **2** fasten with a loop or hook etc. **3** hitch-hike.

hitch *NOUN* **hitches 1** a slight difficulty causing delay. **2** a hitching movement. **3** a knot.
[origin unknown]

hitch-hike *VERB* **hitch-hikes, hitch-hiking, hitch-hiked** travel by getting lifts from passing vehicles.
▷ **hitch-hiker** *noun*

hi-tech *ADJECTIVE* a different spelling of *high-tech*.

hither *ADVERB* to or towards this place.
[from Old English]

hitherto *ADVERB* until this time.

HIV *ABBREVIATION* human immunodeficiency virus; a virus that causes Aids.
[from the initial letters of *human immunodeficiency virus*]

hive *NOUN* **hives 1** a beehive. **2** the bees living in a beehive.
- **hive of industry** a place full of people working busily.
[from Old English]

ho *INTERJECTION* an exclamation of triumph, surprise, etc.

hoard *NOUN* **hoards** a carefully saved store of money, treasure, food, etc.

hoard *VERB* **hoards, hoarding, hoarded** store something away.
▷ **hoarder** *noun*
[from Old English]
USAGE Do not confuse with **horde**.

hoarding *NOUN* **hoardings** a tall fence covered with advertisements.
[from old French]

hoar frost *NOUN* a white frost.
[from Old English *har* = grey-haired, + *frost*]

hoarse *ADJECTIVE* having a rough or croaking voice.
▷ **hoarsely** *adverb* **hoarseness** *noun*
[from Old English]

hoary *ADJECTIVE* **1** white or grey from age • *hoary hair*. **2** old • *hoary jokes*.
[from Old English]

hoax *VERB* **hoaxes, hoaxing, hoaxed** deceive somebody as a joke.
▷ **hoax** *noun* **hoaxer** *noun*
[probably from *hocus-pocus*, used by conjurors as a 'magic' word]

hob *NOUN* **hobs** a flat surface on a cooker or beside a fireplace, where food etc. can be cooked or kept warm.
[a different spelling of *hub*]

hobble *VERB* **hobbles, hobbling, hobbled** limp or walk with difficulty.
[probably from old German]

hobby *NOUN* **hobbies** something you do for pleasure in your spare time.
[from *hobby horse*]

hobby horse *NOUN* **hobby horses 1** a stick with a horse's head, used as a toy. **2** a subject that a person likes to talk about whenever he or she gets the chance.
[from *hobby*, a pet form of the name Robert, often used for ponies, + *horse*]

hobgoblin *NOUN* **hobgoblins** a mischievous or evil spirit.
[from *hob*, a pet form of the name Robert, + *goblin*]

hobnob *VERB* **hobnobs, hobnobbing, hobnobbed** spend time together in a friendly way • *She's been hobnobbing with rock stars*.
[from an old phrase *drink hob and nob* = drink to each other]

hock *NOUN* **hocks** the middle joint of an animal's hind leg.
[from Old English]

hockey *NOUN* a game played by two teams with curved sticks and a hard ball.
[origin unknown]

hoe *NOUN* **hoes** a tool for scraping up weeds.

hoe *VERB* **hoes, hoeing, hoed** scrape or dig with a hoe.
[via old French from Germanic]

hog *NOUN* **hogs 1** a male pig. **2** (*informal*) a greedy person.
- **go the whole hog** (*slang*) do something completely or thoroughly.

hog *VERB* **hogs, hogging, hogged** (*informal*) take more than your fair share of something.
[probably from a Celtic language]

A B C D E F G H I J K L M N O P Q R S T U V W X Y Z

Hogmanay *NOUN* New Year's Eve in Scotland.
[from old French]

hoi polloi *NOUN* the ordinary people; the masses.
[Greek, = the many]

hoist *VERB* **hoists, hoisting, hoisted** lift something up, especially by using ropes or pulleys.
[probably from Dutch]

hold *VERB* **holds, holding, held 1** have and keep, especially in your hands. **2** have room for • *The jug holds two pints.* **3** support • *This plank won't hold my weight.* **4** stay the same; continue • *Will the fine weather hold?* **5** believe or consider • *We shall hold you responsible.* **6** cause something to take place • *hold a meeting.* **7** restrain someone or stop them getting away • *The police are holding three men for the robbery.*
- **hold forth** make a long speech.
- **hold it** stop; wait a minute.
- **hold out 1** refuse to give in. **2** last or continue.
- **hold up 1** hinder. **2** stop and rob somebody by threats or force.
- **hold with** approve of • *We don't hold with bullying.*
- **hold your tongue** (*informal*) stop talking.

hold *NOUN* **holds 1** holding something; a grasp. **2** something to hold on to for support. **3** the part of a ship where cargo is stored, below the deck.
- **get hold of 1** grasp. **2** obtain. **3** make contact with a person.

[from Old English]

holdall *NOUN* **holdalls** a large portable bag or case.

holder *NOUN* **holders** a person or thing that holds something.

hold-up *NOUN* **hold-ups 1** a delay. **2** a robbery with threats or force.

hole *NOUN* **holes 1** a hollow place; a gap or opening. **2** a burrow. **3** one of the small holes into which you have to hit the ball in golf. **4** (*informal*) an unpleasant place.
▷ **holey** *adjective*
- **in a hole** in an awkward situation.

hole *VERB* **holes, holing, holed 1** make a hole or holes in something. **2** hit a golf ball into one of the holes.
[from Old English]

Holi *NOUN* a Hindu festival held in the spring.
[Hindi]

holiday *NOUN* **holidays 1** a day or time when people do not go to work or to school. **2** a time when you go away to enjoy yourself.
[from *holy* + *day* (because holidays were originally religious festivals)]

holiness *NOUN* being holy or sacred.
- **His Holiness** the title of the pope.

hollow *ADJECTIVE* with an empty space inside; not solid.
▷ **hollowly** *adverb*

hollow *ADVERB* completely • *We beat them hollow.*

hollow *NOUN* **hollows** a hollow or sunken place.

hollow *VERB* **hollows, hollowing, hollowed** make a thing hollow.
[from Old English]

holly *NOUN* **hollies** an evergreen bush with shiny prickly leaves and red berries.
[from Old English]

hollyhock *NOUN* **hollyhocks** a plant with large flowers on a very tall stem.
[from Old English]

holocaust *NOUN* **holocausts** an immense destruction, especially by fire • *the nuclear holocaust.*
- **the Holocaust** the mass murder of Jews by the Nazis from 1939 to 1945.

[from Greek *holos* = whole + *kaustos* = burnt]

hologram *NOUN* **holograms** a type of photograph made by laser beams that produces a three-dimensional image.
[from Greek *holos* = whole, + *-gram*]

holster *NOUN* **holsters** a leather case in which a pistol or revolver is carried.
[probably from Dutch]

holy *ADJECTIVE* **holier, holiest 1** belonging or devoted to God. **2** consecrated • *holy water.*
▷ **holiness** *noun*
[from Old English]

homage *NOUN* **homages** an act or expression of respect or honour • *We paid homage to his achievements.*
[from old French]

home *NOUN* **homes 1** the place where you live. **2** the place where you were born or where you feel you belong. **3** a place where those who need help are looked after • *an old people's home.* **4** the place to be reached in a race or in certain games.

home *ADJECTIVE* **1** to do with your own home or country • *home industries.* **2** played on a team's own ground • *a home match.*

home *ADVERB* **1** to or at home • *Is she home yet?* **2** to the point aimed at • *Push the bolt home.*
- **bring something home to somebody** make him or her realize it.

home *VERB* **homes, homing, homed** make for a target • *The missile homed in.*
[from Old English]

home economics *NOUN* the study of cookery and how to run a home.

homeland *NOUN* **homelands** a person's native country.

homeless *ADJECTIVE* having no home.
▷ **homelessness** *noun*

homely *ADVERB* simple and ordinary • *a homely meal.*
▷ **homeliness** *noun*

home-made *ADJECTIVE* made at home, not bought from a shop.

homeopath *NOUN* **homeopaths** a person who practises homeopathy.

homeopathy *NOUN* the treatment of disease by tiny doses of drugs that in a healthy person would produce symptoms of the disease.
▷ **homeopathic** *adjective*
[from Greek *homoios* = similar + *-pathos* = suffering]

home page *NOUN* **home pages** a person's or organization's introductory page on the World Wide Web.

homesick *ADJECTIVE* sad because you are away from home.
▷ **homesickness** *noun*

homestead *NOUN* **homesteads** a farmhouse, usually with the land and buildings round it.
[from *home* + Old English *stede* = a place]

homeward *ADJECTIVE* & *ADVERB* going towards home.
▷ **homewards** *adverb*

homework *NOUN* school work that has to be done at home.

homicide *NOUN* **homicides** the killing of one person by another.
▷ **homicidal** *adjective*
[from Latin *homo* = person, + *-cide*]

homily *NOUN* **homilies** a lecture about behaviour.
[from Greek *homilia* = sermon]

homing *ADJECTIVE* trained to fly home • *a homing pigeon.*

homo- *PREFIX* same.
[from Greek]

homogeneous (*say* **hom**-o-**jeen**-ee-us) *ADJECTIVE* formed of people or things of the same kind.
[from *homo-* + Greek *genos* = a kind]

homograph *NOUN* **homographs** a word that is spelt like another but has a different meaning or origin, e.g. *bat* (a flying animal) and *bat* (for hitting a ball).
[from *homo-* + *-graph*]

homonym (*say* **hom**-o-nim) *NOUN* **homonyms** a homograph or homophone.
[from *homo-* + Greek *onyma* = name]

homophone *NOUN* **homophones** a word with the same sound as another, e.g. *son, sun.*
[from *homo-* + Greek *phone* = sound]

Homo sapiens *NOUN* human beings regarded as a species of animal.
[Latin, = wise man or person]

homosexual *ADJECTIVE* attracted to people of the same sex.
▷ **homosexual** *noun* **homosexuality** *noun*

honest *ADJECTIVE* not stealing or cheating or telling lies; truthful.
▷ **honestly** *adverb* **honesty** *noun*
[from old French; related to *honour*]

honey *NOUN* a sweet sticky food made by bees.
[from Old English]

honeycomb *NOUN* **honeycombs** a wax structure of small six-sided sections made by bees to hold their honey and eggs.

honeycombed *ADJECTIVE* with many holes or tunnels.

honeymoon *NOUN* **honeymoons** a holiday spent together by a newly-married couple. [from *honey* + *moon* (because the first intensely passionate feelings gradually wane)]

honeysuckle *NOUN* a climbing plant with fragrant yellow or pink flowers. [because people sucked the flowers for their sweet nectar]

honk *NOUN* **honks** a loud sound like that made by a goose or an old-fashioned car horn.
▷ **honk** *verb*
[imitating the sound]

honorary *ADJECTIVE* **1** given or received as an honour • *an honorary degree.* **2** unpaid • *the honorary treasurer of the club.*
USAGE Do not confuse with **honourable**.

honour *NOUN* **honours 1** great respect or reputation. **2** a person or thing that brings honour. **3** something a person is proud to do • *It is an honour to meet you.* **4** honesty and loyalty • *a man of honour.* **5** an award given as a mark of respect.
- **in honour of** as an expression of respect for.

honour *VERB* **honours, honouring, honoured 1** feel or show honour for a person. **2** keep to the terms of an agreement or promise. **3** acknowledge and pay a cheque etc.
[from Latin]

honourable *ADJECTIVE* deserving honour; honest and loyal.
▷ **honourably** *adverb*
USAGE Do not confuse with **honorary**.

hood *NOUN* **hoods 1** a covering of soft material for the head and neck. **2** a folding roof or cover. **3** (*American*) the bonnet of a car.
▷ **hooded** *adjective*
[from Old English *hod*]

-hood *SUFFIX* forms nouns meaning condition or quality (e.g. *childhood*). [from Old English]

hoodwink *VERB* **hoodwinks, hoodwinking, hoodwinked** deceive. [originally = to blindfold with a hood: from *hood* + an old sense of *wink* = close the eyes]

hoof *NOUN* **hoofs** or **hooves** the horny part of the foot of a horse etc.
[from Old English]

hook *NOUN* **hooks** a bent or curved piece of metal etc. for hanging things on or for catching hold of something.

hook *VERB* **hooks, hooking, hooked**
1 fasten something with or on a hook.
2 catch a fish etc. with a hook. **3** hit a ball in a curving path.
- **be hooked on something** (*informal*) be addicted to it.
[from Old English]

hookah *NOUN* **hookahs** an oriental tobacco pipe with a long tube passing through a jar of water.
[via Urdu from Arabic *hukka* = box or jar]

hooked *ADJECTIVE* hook-shaped.

hooligan *NOUN* **hooligans** a rough and violent young person.
▷ **hooliganism** *noun*
[the surname of a rowdy Irish family in a cartoon]

hoop *NOUN* **hoops** a ring made of metal or wood.
[from Old English]

hoopla *NOUN* a game in which people try to throw hoops round an object, which they then win as a prize.

hooray *INTERJECTION* a different spelling of *hurray*.

hoot *NOUN* **hoots 1** the sound made by an owl or a vehicle's horn or a steam whistle. **2** a cry of scorn or disapproval. **3** laughter. **4** something funny.
▷ **hoot** *verb* **hooter** *noun*
[imitating the sound]

Hoover *NOUN* **Hoovers** (*trademark*) a vacuum cleaner.

hoover *VERB* **hoovers, hoovering, hoovered** clean a carpet with a vacuum cleaner.

hop[1] *VERB* **hops, hopping, hopped 1** jump on one foot. **2** (said about an animal) spring from all feet at once. **3** (*informal*) move quickly • *Here's the car-hop in!*
- **hop it** (*slang*) go away.

hop *NOUN* **hops** a hopping movement.
[from Old English]

hop[2] *NOUN* **hops** a climbing plant used to give beer its flavour.
[from old German or old Dutch]

hope *NOUN* **hopes 1** the feeling of wanting something to happen, and thinking that it will happen. **2** a person or thing that gives hope • *You are our only hope.*

hope *VERB* **hopes, hoping, hoped** feel hope; want and expect something.
[from Old English]

hopeful *ADJECTIVE* **1** feeling hope. **2** likely to be good or successful.

hopefully *ADVERB* **1** it is to be hoped; I hope that • *Hopefully we will be there by lunchtime.* **2** in a hopeful way • *'Can I come too?', she asked hopefully.*
USAGE Some people say it is incorrect to use *hopefully* to mean 'I hope that' or 'let's hope', and say that it should only be used to mean 'in a hopeful way'. This first use is very common in informal language but you should probably avoid it when you are writing or speaking formally.

hopeless *ADJECTIVE* **1** without hope. **2** very bad at something.
▷ **hopelessly** *adverb* **hopelessness** *noun*

hopper *NOUN* **hoppers** a large funnel-shaped container.

hopscotch *NOUN* a game of hopping into squares drawn on the ground.
[from *hop* + an old word *scotch* = a cut or scratch]

horde *NOUN* **hordes** a large group or crowd.
[via Polish from Turkish *ordu* = royal camp]
USAGE Do not confuse with **hoard**.

horizon *NOUN* **horizons** the line where the earth and the sky seem to meet.
[from Greek *horizein* = form a boundary]

horizontal *ADJECTIVE* level, so as to be parallel to the horizon; going across from left to right. (The opposite is **vertical**.)
▷ **horizontally** *adverb*

hormone *NOUN* **hormones** a substance produced by glands in the body and carried by the blood to stimulate other organs in the body.
▷ **hormonal** *adjective*
[from Greek *horman* = set something going]

horn *NOUN* **horns 1** a hard substance that grows into a point on the head of a bull, cow, ram, etc. **2** a pointed part. **3** a brass instrument played by blowing. **4** a device for making a warning sound.
▷ **horned** *adjective* **horny** *adjective*
[from Old English]

hornet *NOUN* **hornets** a large kind of wasp.
[from Old English]

hornpipe *NOUN* **hornpipes** a sailors' dance.
[originally = a wind instrument made of horn, which was played to dance to]

horoscope *NOUN* **horoscopes** an astrologer's forecast of future events.
[from Greek *hora* = hour (of birth) + *skopos* = observer]

horrendous *ADJECTIVE* extremely unpleasant.
[from Latin *horrendus* = making your hair stand on end]

horrible *ADJECTIVE* **1** horrifying. **2** very unpleasant or nasty.
▷ **horribly** *adverb*
[from Latin]

horrid *ADJECTIVE* horrible.
▷ **horridly** *adverb*
[from Latin *horridus* = rough, shaggy, or wild]

horrific *ADJECTIVE* horrifying.
▷ **horrifically** *adverb*
[from Latin]

horrify *VERB* **horrifies, horrifying, horrified 1** make somebody feel very afraid or disgusted. **2** shock.
[from Latin *horrificare* = make someone shiver with cold or fear]

horror *NOUN* **horrors 1** great fear or disgust. **2** a person or thing causing horror.
[from Latin]

hors-d'oeuvre (*say* or-**dervr**) *NOUN* **hors-d'oeuvres** food served as an appetizer at the start of a meal.
[French, = outside the work]

horse *NOUN* **horses 1** a large four-legged animal used for riding on and for pulling carts etc. **2** a framework for hanging clothes on to dry. **3** a vaulting horse.
- **on horseback** mounted on a horse.
[from Old English]

horse chestnut *NOUN* **horse chestnuts** a large tree that produces dark-brown nuts (conkers).

horseman *NOUN* **horsemen** a man who rides a horse, especially a skilled rider.
▷ **horsemanship** *noun*

horseplay *NOUN* rough play.

horsepower *NOUN* a unit for measuring the power of an engine, equal to 746 watts.
[because the unit was based on the amount of work a horse could do]

horseshoe *NOUN* **horseshoes** a U-shaped piece of metal nailed to a horse's hoof.

horsewoman *NOUN* **horsewomen** a woman who rides a horse, especially a skilled rider.

horticulture *NOUN* the art of cultivating gardens.
▷ **horticultural** *adjective*
[from Latin *hortus* = garden, + *culture*]

hose *NOUN* **hoses 1** a flexible tube for taking water to something. **2** (*old use*) breeches • *doublet and hose.*

hose *VERB* **hoses, hosing, hosed** water or spray with a hose.
[from Old English]

hosiery *NOUN* (in shops) socks, stockings, and tights.
[from *hose*]

hospice (*say* hosp-iss) *NOUN* **hospices** a nursing home for people who are very ill or dying.
[from Latin *hospitium* = hospitality or lodgings]

hospitable *ADJECTIVE* welcoming; liking to give hospitality.
▷ **hospitably** *adverb*
[from Latin]

hospital *NOUN* **hospitals** a place providing medical and surgical treatment for people who are ill or injured.
[from Latin *hospitalis* = hospitable]

hospitality *NOUN* welcoming guests or strangers and giving them food and entertainment.
[from Latin]

host[1] *NOUN* **hosts 1** a person who has guests and looks after them. **2** the presenter of a television or radio programme.

host *VERB* **hosts, hosting, hosted** organize a party, event, etc. and look after the people who come.
[from Latin *hospes*]

host[2] *NOUN* **hosts** a large number of people or things.
[from Latin *hostis* = enemy or army]

host[3] *NOUN* **hosts** the bread consecrated at Holy Communion.
[from Latin *hostia* = sacrifice]

hostage *NOUN* **hostages** a person who is held prisoner until the holder's demands are met.
[from old French]

hostel *NOUN* **hostels** a building where travellers, students, or other groups can stay or live.
[from old French; related to *hospital*]

hostess *NOUN* **hostesses** a woman who has guests and looks after them.
[from old French]

hostile *ADJECTIVE* **1** unfriendly • *a hostile glance.* **2** opposed to something. **3** to do with an enemy • *hostile aircraft.*
▷ **hostility** *noun*
[same origin as *host*[2]]

hot *ADJECTIVE* **hotter, hottest 1** having great heat or a high temperature. **2** giving a burning sensation when tasted.
3 passionate or excitable • *a hot temper.*
▷ **hotly** *adverb* **hotness** *noun*
- **in hot water** (*informal*) in trouble or disgrace.

hot *VERB* **hots, hotting, hotted**
- **hot up** (*informal*) make or become hot or hotter or more exciting.
[from Old English]

hot cross bun *NOUN* **hot cross buns** a spicy bun marked with a cross, eaten at Easter.

hot dog *NOUN* **hot dogs** a hot sausage in a bread roll.

hotel *NOUN* **hotels** a building where people pay to have meals and stay for the night. [from French; related to *hostel*]

hotfoot *ADVERB* in eager haste.

hothead *NOUN* **hotheads** an impetuous person.
▷ **hotheaded** *adjective*

hothouse *NOUN* **hothouses** a heated greenhouse.

hotplate *NOUN* **hotplates** a heated surface for cooking food etc. or keeping it hot.

hotpot *NOUN* **hotpots** a kind of stew.

hot-water bottle *NOUN* **hot-water bottles** a container that is filled with hot water and used to warm a bed.

hound *NOUN* **hounds** a dog used in hunting or racing.

hound *VERB* **hounds, hounding, hounded** pursue or harass someone.
[from Old English]

hour *NOUN* **hours 1** one twenty-fourth part of a day and night; sixty minutes. **2** a particular time • *Why are you up at this hour?*
- **hours** *plural noun* a fixed period for work • *Office hours are 9 a.m. to 5 p.m.*
[from Greek]

hourglass *NOUN* **hourglasses** a glass container with a very narrow part in the middle through which sand runs from the top half to the bottom half, taking one hour.

hourly *ADVERB* & *ADJECTIVE* every hour.

house (*say* howss) *NOUN* **houses 1** a building made for people to live in, usually designed for one family. **2** a building or establishment for a special purpose • *the opera house.* **3** a building for a government assembly; the assembly itself • *the House of Commons; the House of Lords.* **4** one of the divisions in some schools for sports competitions etc. **5** a family or dynasty • *the royal house of Tudor.*

house (*say* howz) *VERB* **houses, housing, housed** provide accommodation or room for someone or something.
[from Old English]

houseboat *NOUN* **houseboats** a barge-like boat for living in.

household *NOUN* **households** all the people who live together in the same house. [from *house* + an old sense of *hold* = possession]

householder *NOUN* **householders** a person who owns or rents a house.

housekeeper *NOUN* **housekeepers** a person employed to look after a household.

housekeeping *NOUN* **1** looking after a household. **2** the money for a household's food and other necessities.

housemaid *NOUN* **housemaids** a woman servant in a house, especially one who cleans rooms.

house plant *NOUN* **house plants** a plant grown indoors.

house-proud *ADJECTIVE* very careful to keep a house clean and tidy.

house-trained *ADJECTIVE* (said about an animal) trained to be clean in the house.

house-warming *NOUN* **house-warmings** a party to celebrate moving into a new home.

housewife *NOUN* **housewives** a woman who does the housekeeping for her family.

housework *NOUN* the regular work that has to be done in a house, such as cleaning and cooking.

housing *NOUN* **housings**
1 accommodation; houses. **2** a stiff cover or guard for a piece of machinery.

housing estate *NOUN* **housing estates** a set of houses planned and built together in one area.

hove *past tense* of **heave** (when used of ships).

hovel *NOUN* **hovels** a small shabby house. [origin unknown]

hover *VERB* **hovers, hovering, hovered**
1 stay in one place in the air. **2** wait about near someone or something.
[origin unknown]

hovercraft *NOUN* **hovercraft** a vehicle that travels just above the surface of land or water, supported by a strong current of air sent downwards from its engines.

how *ADVERB* **1** in what way; by what means • *How did you do it?* **2** to what extent or amount etc. • *How high can you jump?* **3** in what condition • *How are you?*
- **how about** would you like • *How about a game of football?*
- **how do you do?** a formal greeting.
[from Old English]

however *ADVERB* **1** in whatever way; to whatever extent • *You will never catch him, however hard you try.* **2** all the same; nevertheless • *Later, however, he decided to go.*

howl *NOUN* **howls** a long loud sad-sounding cry or sound, such as that made by a dog or wolf.

howl *VERB* **howls, howling, howled** **1** make a howl. **2** weep loudly.
[imitating the sound]

howler *NOUN* **howlers** (*informal*) a foolish mistake.

HQ *ABBREVIATION* headquarters.

hub *NOUN* **hubs 1** the central part of a wheel. **2** the central point of interest or activity.
[origin unknown]

hubbub *NOUN* a loud confused noise of voices.
[probably from Irish]

huddle *VERB* **huddles, huddling, huddled** **1** crowd together with other people, often for warmth. **2** curl your body closely.
▷ **huddle** *noun*
[origin unknown]

hue[1] *NOUN* **hues** a colour or tint.
[from Old English]

hue[2] *NOUN*
- **hue and cry** a general outcry of demand, alarm, or protest.
[from old French *huer* = to shout]

huff *NOUN*
- **in a huff** offended or sulking about something • *She went away in a huff.*
▷ **huffy** *adjective*

huff *VERB* **huffs, huffing, huffed** blow • *huffing and puffing.*
[imitating the sound]

hug *VERB* **hugs, hugging, hugged** **1** clasp someone tightly in your arms. **2** keep close to something • *The ship hugged the shore.*

hug *NOUN* **hugs** a tight embrace.
[probably from a Scandinavian language]

huge *ADJECTIVE* extremely large; enormous.
▷ **hugely** *adverb* **hugeness** *noun*
[from old French]

hulk *NOUN* **hulks 1** the body or wreck of an old ship. **2** a large clumsy person or thing.
▷ **hulking** *adjective*
[from Old English]

hull *NOUN* **hulls** the framework of a ship.
[from Old English]

hullabaloo *NOUN* **hullabaloos** an uproar.
[origin unknown]

hullo *INTERJECTION* hello.

hum *VERB* **hums, humming, hummed** **1** sing a tune with your lips closed. **2** make a low continuous sound like that of a bee.

hum *NOUN* **hums** a humming sound.
[imitating the sound]

human *ADJECTIVE* to do with human beings.

human *NOUN* **humans** a human being.
[from Latin]

human being *NOUN* **human beings** a man, woman, or child.

humane (*say* hew-**mayn**) *ADJECTIVE* kind-hearted and merciful.
▷ **humanely** *adverb*
[old spelling of *human*]

humanist *NOUN* **humanists** a person who is concerned with people's needs and with finding rational ways to solve human problems, rather than using religious belief.
▷ **humanism** *noun*

humanitarian *ADJECTIVE* concerned with people's welfare and the reduction of suffering.
▷ **humanitarian** *noun*

humanity *NOUN* **1** human beings; people. **2** being human. **3** being humane.
- **humanities** *plural noun* arts subjects such as history, literature, and music, not sciences.

humanize *VERB* **humanizes, humanizing, humanized** make human or humane.
▷ **humanization** *noun*

humble *ADJECTIVE* **1** modest; not proud or showy. **2** of low rank or importance.
▷ **humbly** *adverb* **humbleness** *noun*

humble *VERB* **humbles, humbling, humbled** make someone feel humble.
[from Latin *humilis* = near the ground, low]

humbug *NOUN* **humbugs 1** insincere or dishonest talk or behaviour. **2** a hard peppermint sweet.
[origin unknown]

humdrum *ADJECTIVE* dull and not exciting; commonplace.
[origin unknown]

humid (*say* hew-mid) *ADJECTIVE* (said about air) warm and damp.
▷ **humidity** *noun*
[from Latin]

humiliate *VERB* **humiliates, humiliating, humiliated** make a person feel disgraced or ashamed.
▷ **humiliation** *noun*
[same origin as *humble*]

humility *NOUN* being humble.
[same origin as *humble*]

hummingbird *NOUN* **hummingbirds** a small tropical bird that makes a humming sound by beating its wings rapidly.

humorist *NOUN* **humorists** a humorous writer.

humorous *ADJECTIVE* full of humour; amusing.

humour *NOUN* **1** being amusing; what makes people laugh. **2** the ability to enjoy comical things • *a sense of humour.* **3** a person's mood • *in a good humour.*

humour *VERB* **humours, humouring, humoured** keep a person contented by doing what he or she wants.
[from Latin]

hump *NOUN* **humps 1** a rounded lump or mound. **2** an abnormal outward curve at the top of a person's back.

hump *VERB* **humps, humping, humped** carry something heavy with difficulty.
[probably from old German or Dutch]

humpback bridge *NOUN* **humpback bridges** a small bridge that steeply curves upwards in the middle.

humus (*say* hew-mus) *NOUN* rich earth made by decayed plants.
[Latin, = soil]

hunch[1] *NOUN* **hunches** a feeling that you can guess what is going to happen.
[origin unknown]

hunch[2] *VERB* **hunches, hunching, hunched** bend your shoulders upward so that your back is rounded.
[origin unknown]

hunchback *NOUN* **hunchbacks** someone with a hump on their back.
▷ **hunchbacked** *adjective*

hundred *NOUN* & *ADJECTIVE* **hundreds** the number 100.
▷ **hundredth** *adjective* & *noun*
[from Old English]

hundredfold *ADJECTIVE* & *ADVERB* one hundred times as much or as many.

hundredweight *NOUN* **hundredweight** a unit of weight equal to 112 pounds (about 50.8 kilograms).
[probably originally = 100 pounds]

hunger *NOUN* **1** the feeling that you have when you have not eaten for some time; need for food. **2** a strong desire for something.

hunger *VERB* **hungers, hungering, hungered** have a strong desire for something.
[from Old English]

hunger strike *NOUN* **hunger strikes** refusing to eat, as a way of making a protest.

hungry *ADJECTIVE* **hungrier, hungriest** feeling hunger.
▷ **hungrily** *adverb*

hunk *NOUN* **hunks 1** a large piece of something. **2** (*informal*) a muscular, good-looking man.
[probably from old Dutch]

hunt *VERB* **hunts, hunting, hunted 1** chase and kill animals for food or as a sport. **2** search for something.
▷ **hunter** *noun* **huntsman** *noun*

hunt *NOUN* **hunts 1** hunting. **2** a group of hunters.
[from Old English]

hurdle *NOUN* **hurdles 1** an upright frame to be jumped over in hurdling. **2** an obstacle or difficulty.
[from Old English]

hurdling *NOUN* racing in which the runners jump over hurdles.
▷ **hurdler** *noun*

hurl *VERB* **hurls, hurling, hurled** throw something with great force.
[origin unknown]

hurly-burly *NOUN* a rough bustle of activity.
[from *hurl*]

hurray or **hurrah** *INTERJECTION* a shout of joy or approval; a cheer.
[origin unknown]

hurricane *NOUN* **hurricanes** a storm with violent wind.
[via Spanish and Portuguese from Taino (a South American language)]

hurry *VERB* **hurries, hurrying, hurried**
1 move quickly; do something quickly. **2** try to make somebody or something be quick.
▷ **hurried** *adjective* **hurriedly** *adverb*

hurry *NOUN* hurrying; a need to hurry.
[origin unknown]

hurt *VERB* **hurts, hurting, hurt 1** cause pain or injury to someone. **2** suffer pain • *My leg hurts.* **3** upset or offend • *I'm sorry if I hurt your feelings.*

hurt *NOUN* physical or mental pain or injury.
▷ **hurtful** *adjective*
[from old French]

hurtle *VERB* **hurtles, hurtling, hurtled** move rapidly • *The train hurtled along.*
[from an old sense of *hurt* = knock or dash against something]

husband *NOUN* **husbands** the man to whom a woman is married.

husband *VERB* **husbands, husbanding, husbanded** manage money, strength, etc. economically and try to save it.
[from Old Norse *husbondi* = master of the house]

husbandry *NOUN* **1** farming.
2 management of resources.
[from *husband*]

hush *VERB* **hushes, hushing, hushed** make or become silent or quiet.
- **hush up** prevent something from becoming generally known.

hush *NOUN* silence.
[imitating the soft hissing sound you make to get someone to be quiet]

hush-hush *ADJECTIVE* (*informal*) highly secret or confidential.

husk *NOUN* **husks** the dry outer covering of some seeds and fruits.
[probably from old German]

husky[1] *ADJECTIVE* **huskier, huskiest**
1 hoarse. **2** big and strong; burly.
▷ **huskily** *adverb* **huskiness** *noun*
[from *husk*]

husky[2] *NOUN* **huskies** a large dog used in the Arctic for pulling sledges.
[from a Native American word meaning 'Eskimo']

hustings *PLURAL NOUN* political speeches and campaigning just before an election.
[from Old Norse]

hustle *VERB* **hustles, hustling, hustled**
1 hurry. **2** push or shove rudely.
[from Dutch *husselen* = shake or toss]

hut *NOUN* **huts** a small roughly-made house or shelter.
[via French from old German]

hutch *NOUN* **hutches** a box-like cage for a pet rabbit etc.
[from Latin]

hyacinth *NOUN* **hyacinths** a fragrant flower that grows from a bulb.
[because, in Greek legend, the flower sprang from the blood of *Hyacinthus*, a youth who was accidentally killed by Apollo]

hybrid *NOUN* **hybrids 1** a plant or animal produced by combining two different species or varieties. **2** something that combines parts or characteristics of two different things.
[from Latin]

hydr- *PREFIX* **1** water. **2** containing hydrogen. SEE **hydro-**.

hydra *NOUN* **hydras** or **hydrae** a microscopic freshwater animal with a tubular body.
[named after the Hydra in Greek mythology, a water snake with many heads that grew again if cut off]

hydrangea (*say* hy-**drayn**-ja) *NOUN* **hydrangeas** a shrub with pink, blue, or white flowers growing in large clusters.
[from *hydr-* + Greek *angeion* = container (because the seed capsule is shaped like a cup)]

hydrant *NOUN* **hydrants** a special water tap to which a large hose can be attached for fire-fighting or street-cleaning etc.
[same origin as *hydro-*]

hydraulic *ADJECTIVE* worked by the force of water or other fluid • *hydraulic brakes.*
[from *hydr-* + Greek *aulos* = pipe]

hydro- *PREFIX* (**hydr-** before a vowel) **1** water (as in *hydroelectric*). **2** (in chemical names) containing hydrogen (as in *hydrochloric*).
[from Greek *hydor* = water]

hydrochloric acid *NOUN* a colourless acid containing hydrogen and chlorine.

hydroelectric *ADJECTIVE* using water power to produce electricity.
▷ **hydroelectricity** *noun*

hydrofoil *NOUN* **hydrofoils** a boat designed to skim over the surface of water.
[from *hydro-* + *foil*[1]]

hydrogen *NOUN* a lightweight gas that combines with oxygen to form water.
[from *hydro-* + *-gen* = producing]

hydrogen bomb *NOUN* **hydrogen bombs** a very powerful bomb using energy created by the fusion of hydrogen nuclei.

hydrolysis *NOUN* the chemical reaction of a substance with water, usually resulting in decomposition.
[from *hydro-* + Greek *lysis* = loosening]

hydrophobia *NOUN* abnormal fear of water, as in someone suffering from rabies.
[from *hydro-* + *phobia*]

hyena *NOUN* **hyenas** a wild animal that looks like a wolf and makes a shrieking howl.
[from Greek]

hygiene (*say* hy-jeen) *NOUN* keeping things clean in order to remain healthy and prevent disease.
▷ **hygienic** *adjective* **hygienically** *adverb*
[from Greek *hygies* = healthy]

hymn *NOUN* **hymns** a religious song, usually one praising God.
▷ **hymn book** *noun*
[from Greek]

hymnal *NOUN* **hymnals** a hymn book.

hype *NOUN* (*informal*) extravagant publicity or advertising.
[origin unknown]

hyper- *PREFIX* over or above; excessive.
[from Greek *hyper* = over]

hyperactive *ADJECTIVE* unable to relax and always moving about or doing things.

hyperbola (*say* hy-**per**-bol-a) *NOUN* **hyperbolas** (*in mathematics*) a kind of curve.
[same origin as *hyperbole*]

hyperbole (*say* hy-**per**-bol-ee) *NOUN* **hyperboles** a dramatic exaggeration that is not meant to be taken literally, e.g. 'I've got a stack of work a mile high'.
[from *hyper-* + Greek *bole* = a throw]

hyperlink *NOUN* **hyperlinks** a place in a computer document that is linked to another computer document • *Click on the hyperlink.*

hypermarket *NOUN* **hypermarkets** a very large supermarket, usually outside a town.

hypertext *NOUN* **hypertexts** a computer document that contains links that allow the user to move from one document to another.

hyphen *NOUN* **hyphens** a short dash used to join words or parts of words together (e.g. in *hitch-hiker*).
[from Greek, = together]

hyphenate *VERB* **hyphenates**, **hyphenating**, **hyphenated** join or spell with a hyphen.
▷ **hyphenation** *noun*

hypnosis (*say* hip-**noh**-sis) *NOUN* a condition like a deep sleep in which a person's actions may be controlled by someone else.
[from Greek *hypnos* = sleep]

hypnotize *VERB* **hypnotizes**, **hypnotizing**, **hypnotized** produce hypnosis in somebody.
▷ **hypnotism** *noun* **hypnotic** *adjective* **hypnotist** *noun*

hypo- *PREFIX* below; under.
[from Greek *hypo* = under]

hypochondriac (*say* hy-po-**kon**-dree-ak) *NOUN* **hypochondriacs** a person who constantly imagines that he or she is ill.
▷ **hypochondria** *noun*
[from Greek *hypochondrios* = under the breastbone (because the organs there were once thought to be the source of depression and anxiety)]

hypocrite (*say* **hip**-o-krit) *NOUN* **hypocrites** a person who pretends to be more virtuous than he or she really is.
▷ **hypocrisy** (*say* hip-**ok**-riss-ee) *noun* **hypocritical** *adjective*
[from Greek *hypokrites* = actor or pretender]

hypodermic *ADJECTIVE* injecting something under the skin • *a hypodermic syringe.*
[from *hypo-* + Greek *derma* = skin]

hypotenuse (*say* hy-**pot**-i-newz) *NOUN* **hypotenuses** the side opposite the right angle in a right-angled triangle.
[from Greek]

hypothermia *NOUN* the condition of having a body temperature well below normal.
[from *hypo-* + Greek *therme* = heat]

hypothesis (*say* hy-**poth**-i-sis) *NOUN* **hypotheses** a suggestion or guess that tries to explain something but has not yet been proved to be true or correct.
[from *hypo-* + Greek *thesis* = placing]

hypothetical (*say* hy-po-**thet**-ikal) *ADJECTIVE* based on a theory or possibility, not on proven facts.

hysterectomy (*say* hist-er-**ek**-tom-ee) *NOUN* **hysterectomies** surgical removal of the womb.
[from Greek *hystera* = womb, + *-ectomy* = cutting out]

hysteria *NOUN* wild uncontrollable excitement, panic, or emotion.
[from Greek *hystera* = womb (once thought to be the cause of hysteria)]

hysterical *ADJECTIVE* **1** in a state of hysteria. **2** (*informal*) extremely funny.
▷ **hysterically** *adverb*

hysterics (*say* hiss-**te**-riks) *PLURAL NOUN* a fit of hysteria.
- **in hysterics** (*informal*) laughing a lot.

Ii

I *PRONOUN* a word used by a person to refer to himself or herself.
[from Old English]

-ible SEE **-able**.

-ic *SUFFIX* forms **1** adjectives, some of which are used as nouns (e.g. *comic*, *domestic*, *public*), **2** names of arts (e.g. *music*, *magic*).
[from Latin *-icus* or Greek *-ikos*]

-ical *SUFFIX* forms adjectives from or similar to words ending in *-ic* (e.g. *comical*, *musical*).

ice *NOUN* **ices 1** frozen water, a brittle transparent solid substance. **2** an ice cream.

ice *VERB* **ices**, **icing**, **iced 1** make or become icy. **2** put icing on a cake.
[from Old English]

ice age *NOUN* **ice ages** a period in the past when most of the earth's surface was covered with ice.

iceberg *NOUN* **icebergs** a large mass of ice floating in the sea with most of it under water.
[from Dutch]

ice cap *NOUN* **ice caps** a permanent covering of ice and snow at the North or South Pole.

ice cream *NOUN* **ice creams** a sweet creamy frozen food.

ice hockey *NOUN* a form of hockey played on ice.

ice lolly *NOUN* **ice lollies** frozen juice on a small stick.

ice rink *NOUN* **ice rinks** a place made for skating.

-ician *SUFFIX* forms nouns meaning 'person skilled in something' (e.g. *musician*).

icicle *NOUN* **icicles** a pointed hanging piece of ice formed when dripping water freezes. [from Old English]

icing *NOUN* a sugary substance for decorating cakes.

-icity *SUFFIX* forms nouns (e.g. *publicity*) from words ending in *-ic*.

icon (*say* I-kon) *NOUN* **icons 1** a sacred painting or mosaic of a holy person. **2** a small symbol or picture on a computer screen, representing a program, window, etc. that you can select.
[from Greek *eikon* = image]

-ics *SUFFIX* forms nouns which are plural in form but are often used with a singular verb (e.g. *mathematics*, *gymnastics*).

ICT *ABBREVIATION* information and communication technology.

icy *ADJECTIVE* **icier**, **iciest 1** covered with ice. **2** very cold.
▷ **icily** *adverb* **iciness** *noun*

Id *NOUN* a different spelling of *Eid*.

idea *NOUN* **ideas 1** a plan or thought formed in the mind. **2** an opinion or belief. **3** a feeling that something is likely.
[Greek]

ideal *ADJECTIVE* perfect; completely suitable.
▷ **ideally** *adverb*

ideal *NOUN* **ideals** a person or thing regarded as perfect or as worth trying to achieve.
[from Latin, related to *idea*]

idealist *NOUN* **idealists** a person who has high ideals and wishes to achieve them.
▷ **idealism** *noun* **idealistic** *adjective*

identical *ADJECTIVE* exactly the same.
▷ **identically** *adverb*
[same origin as *identity*]

identification *NOUN* **1** any document, such as a passport or driving licence, that proves who you are. **2** identifying someone or something.

identify *VERB* **identifies**, **identifying**, **identified 1** recognize as being a certain person or thing. **2** treat something as being identical to something else • *Don't identify wealth with happiness.* **3** think of yourself as sharing someone's feelings etc. • *We can identify with the hero of this play.*
▷ **identifiable** *adjective*

identity *NOUN* **identities 1** who or what a person or thing is. **2** being identical; sameness. **3** distinctive character.
[from Latin *idem* = same]

ideology (*say* I-dee-ol-o-jee) *NOUN* **ideologies** a set of beliefs and aims, especially in politics • *a socialist ideology.*
▷ **ideological** *adjective*
[from *idea* + *-ology*]

idiocy *NOUN* **1** being an idiot. **2** stupid behaviour.

idiom *NOUN* **idioms** a phrase that means something different from the meanings of the words in it, e.g. *in hot water* (= in disgrace) *hell for leather* (= at high speed).
▷ **idiomatic** *adjective* **idiomatically** *adverb*
[from Greek *idios* = your own]

idiosyncrasy (*say* id-ee-o-**sink**-ra-see) *NOUN* **idiosyncrasies** one person's own way of behaving or doing something.
[from Greek *idios* = your own + *syn-* + *krasis* = mixture]

idiot *NOUN* **idiots** a stupid or foolish person.
▷ **idiocy** *noun* **idiotic** *adjective* **idiotically** *adverb*
[from Greek *idiotes* = private citizen, uneducated person]

idle *ADJECTIVE* **1** doing no work; lazy. **2** not in use • *The machines were idle.* **3** useless; with no special purpose • *idle gossip.*
▷ **idly** *adverb* **idleness** *noun*

idle *VERB* **idles**, **idling**, **idled 1** be idle. **2** (said about an engine) work slowly.
▷ **idler** *noun*
[from Old English]

idol *NOUN* **idols 1** a statue or image that is worshipped as a god. **2** a famous person who is widely admired.
[from Greek *eidolon* = image]

idolatry *NOUN* **1** worship of idols. **2** idolizing someone.
▷ **idolatrous** *adjective*
[from *idol* + Greek *latreia* = worship]

idolize *VERB* **idolizes**, **idolizing**, **idolized** admire someone greatly.
▷ **idolization** *noun*

idyll (*say* **id**-il) *NOUN* **idylls 1** a beautiful or peaceful scene or situation. **2** a poem describing a peaceful or romantic scene.
▷ **idyllic** (*say* id-**il**-ik) *adjective*
[from Greek *eidyllion* = little picture]

i.e. *ABBREVIATION* that is • *The world's highest mountain (i.e. Mount Everest) is in the Himalayas.*
[short for Latin *id est* = that is]
USAGE Do not confuse with **e.g.**

-ie *SUFFIX* , SEE **-y**.

-ier *SUFFIX* , SEE **-er**.

-iest *SUFFIX* , SEE **-est**.

if *CONJUNCTION* **1** on condition that; supposing that • *He will do it if you pay him.* **2** even though • *I'll finish this job if it kills me.* **3** whether • *Do you know if lunch is ready?*
- **if only** I wish • *If only I were rich!*
[from Old English]

-iferous *SUFFIC* , SEE **-ferous**.

-ification *SUFFIX* forms nouns of action (e.g. *purification*) from verbs that end in *-ify*.
[from Latin *-ficare* = make]

igloo *NOUN* **igloos** an Inuit round house built of blocks of hard snow.
[from Inuit *iglu* = house]

igneous *ADJECTIVE* (said about rock) formed when hot liquid rock from a volcano cools and becomes hard.
[from Latin *igneus* = fiery]

ignite *VERB* **ignites**, **igniting**, **ignited 1** set fire to something. **2** catch fire.
[from Latin *ignis* = fire]

ignition *NOUN* **ignitions 1** igniting. **2** the part of a motor engine that starts the fuel burning.

ignoble *ADJECTIVE* not noble; shameful.
[from Latin]

ignominious *ADJECTIVE* humiliating; bringing disgrace.
▷ **ignominy** *noun*
[from Latin]

ignoramus *NOUN* **ignoramuses** an ignorant person.
[Latin, = we do not know]

ignorant *ADJECTIVE* **1** not knowing about something. **2** knowing very little.
▷ **ignorantly** *adverb* **ignorance** *noun*
[same origin as *ignore*]

ignore *VERB* **ignores**, **ignoring**, **ignored** take no notice of a person or thing.
[from Latin *ignorare* = not know]

iguana (*say* ig-**wah**-na) *NOUN* **iguanas** a large tree-climbing tropical lizard.
[via Spanish from Arawak (a South American language)]

il- *PREFIX* **1** in; into. **2** on; towards. **3** not. SEE **in-**.

ilk *NOUN*
- **of that ilk** (*informal*) of that kind.
[from Old English *ilca* = same]

ill *ADJECTIVE* **1** unwell; in bad health. **2** bad or harmful • *There were no ill effects.*

ill *ADVERB* badly • *She was ill-treated.*
- **ill at ease** uncomfortable or embarrassed.
[from Old Norse]

illegal *ADJECTIVE* not legal; against the law.
▷ **illegally** *adverb* **illegality** *noun*

illegible *ADJECTIVE* impossible to read.
▷ **illegibly** *adverb* **illegibility** *noun*

illegitimate *ADJECTIVE* born of parents who are not married to each other.
▷ **illegitimately** *adverb* **illegitimacy** *noun*

ill-fated *ADJECTIVE* bound to fail; unlucky.

illicit *ADJECTIVE* done in a way that is against the law; not allowed.
▷ **illicitly** *adverb*
[from *il-* + Latin *licitus* = allowed]
USAGE Do not confuse with **elicit**.

illiterate *ADJECTIVE* unable to read or write.
▷ **illiterately** *adverb* **illiteracy** *noun*

illness *NOUN* **illnesses 1** being ill. **2** a particular form of bad health; a disease.

illogical *ADJECTIVE* not logical; not reasoning correctly.
▷ **illogically** *adverb* **illogicality** *noun*

ills *PLURAL NOUN* problems and difficulties.

illuminate *VERB* **illuminates**, **illuminating**, **illuminated 1** light something up. **2** decorate streets etc. with lights. **3** decorate a manuscript with coloured designs. **4** clarify or help to explain something.
▷ **illumination** *noun*
[from *il-* + Latin *lumen* = light]

illusion *NOUN* **illusions 1** something that seems to be real or actually happening but is not, especially something that deceives the eye. **2** a false idea or belief. (COMPARE **delusion**)

▷ **illusory** *adjective*

[from Latin *illudere* = mock]

illusionist *NOUN* **illusionists** a conjuror.

illustrate *VERB* **illustrates, illustrating, illustrated** **1** show something by pictures, examples, etc. **2** put illustrations in a book.

▷ **illustrator** *noun*

[from Latin *illustrare* = add light or brilliance]

illustration *NOUN* **illustrations 1** a picture in a book etc. **2** an example that helps to explain something. **3** illustrating something.

illustrious *ADJECTIVE* famous and distinguished.

[from Latin]

ill will *NOUN* unkind feelings towards a person.

im- *PREFIX* **1** in; into. **2** on; towards. **3** not. SEE **in-**.

image *NOUN* **images 1** a picture or statue of a person or thing. **2** the appearance of something as seen in a mirror or through a lens etc. **3** a person or thing that is very much like another • *He is the image of his father.* **4** a word or phrase that describes something in an imaginative way. **5** a person's public reputation.

[from Latin]

imagery *NOUN* a writer's or speaker's use of words to produce pictures in the mind of the reader or hearer.

imaginable *ADJECTIVE* able to be imagined.

imaginary *ADJECTIVE* existing only in the imagination; not real.

imagination *NOUN* **imaginations** the ability to imagine things, especially in a creative or inventive way.

imaginative *ADJECTIVE* having or showing imagination.

imagine *VERB* **imagines, imagining, imagined** **1** form pictures or ideas in your mind. **2** suppose or think • *I don't imagine there'll be any tickets left.*

[from Latin]

imam *NOUN* **imams** a Muslim religious leader.

[Arabic, = leader]

imbalance *NOUN* lack of balance.

imbecile (*say* imb-i-seel) *NOUN* **imbeciles** an idiot.

▷ **imbecile** *adjective* **imbecility** *noun*

[from Latin]

imbibe *VERB* **imbibes, imbibing, imbibed** (*formal*) drink.

[from *im-* + Latin *bibere* = drink]

imitate *VERB* **imitates, imitating, imitated** copy or mimic something.

▷ **imitation** *noun* **imitator** *noun* **imitative** *adjective*

[from Latin]

immaculate *ADJECTIVE* **1** perfectly clean; spotless. **2** without any fault or blemish.

▷ **immaculately** *adverb*

[from *im-* + Latin *macula* = spot or blemish]

immaterial *ADJECTIVE* **1** unimportant; not mattering • *It is immaterial whether he goes or stays.* **2** having no physical body • *as immaterial as a ghost.*

immature *ADJECTIVE* not mature.

▷ **immaturity** *noun*

immediate *ADJECTIVE* **1** happening or done without any delay. **2** nearest; with nothing or no one between • *our immediate neighbours.*

▷ **immediately** *adverb* **immediacy** *noun*

[from *im-* + Latin *mediatus* = coming between]

immemorial *ADJECTIVE* going further back in time than what can be remembered • *from time immemorial.*

[from *im-* + Latin *memoria* = memory]

immense *ADJECTIVE* exceedingly great; huge.

▷ **immensely** *adverb* **immensity** *noun*

[from *im-* + Latin *mensum* = measured]

immerse *VERB* **immerses, immersing, immersed** **1** put something completely into a liquid. **2** absorb or involve deeply • *She was immersed in her work.*

▷ **immersion** *noun*

[from *im-* + Latin *mersum* = dipped]

A B C D E F G H I J K L M N O P Q R S T U V W X Y Z

immersion heater *NOUN* **immersion heaters** a device that heats up water by means of an electric element immersed in the water in a tank.

immigrate *VERB* **immigrates, immigrating, immigrated** come into a country to live there.
▷ **immigration** *noun* **immigrant** *noun*
USAGE See the note at **emigrate**.

imminent *ADJECTIVE* likely to happen at any moment • *an imminent storm.*
▷ **imminence** *noun*
[from Latin *imminere* = hang over]

immobile *ADJECTIVE* not moving; immovable.
▷ **immobility** *noun*

immobilize *VERB* **immobilizes, immobilizing, immobilized** stop a thing from moving or working.
▷ **immobilization** *noun*

immodest *ADJECTIVE* **1** without modesty; indecent. **2** conceited.

immoral *ADJECTIVE* morally wrong; wicked.
▷ **immorally** *adverb* **immorality** *noun*

immortal *ADJECTIVE* **1** living for ever; not mortal. **2** famous for all time.
▷ **immortal** *noun* **immortality** *noun*

immortalize *VERB* **immortalizes, immortalizing, immortalized** make someone famous for all time.

immovable *ADJECTIVE* unable to be moved.
▷ **immovably** *adverb*

immune *ADJECTIVE* safe from danger or attack, especially from disease • *immune from* (or *against* or *to*) *infection* etc.
▷ **immunity** *noun*
[from Latin *immunis* = exempt]

immune system *NOUN* **immune systems** the body's means of resisting infection.

immunize *VERB* **immunizes, immunizing, immunized** make a person immune from a disease etc., e.g. by vaccination.
▷ **immunization** *noun*

immutable (*say* i-mewt-a-bul) *ADJECTIVE* unchangeable.
▷ **immutably** *adverb*

imp *NOUN* **imps 1** a small devil. **2** a mischievous child.
▷ **impish** *adjective*
[from Old English]

impact *NOUN* **impacts 1** a collision; the force of a collision. **2** an influence or effect • *the impact of computers on our lives.*
[from *im-* + Latin *pactum* = driven]

impair *VERB* **impairs, impairing, impaired** damage or weaken something • *Smoking impairs health.*
▷ **impairment** *noun*
[from *im-* + Latin *pejor* = worse]

impala (*say* im-pah-la) *NOUN* **impala** a small African antelope.
[from Zulu]

impale *VERB* **impales, impaling, impaled** pierce or fix something on a sharp pointed object.
[from *im-* + Latin *palus* = a stake]

impart *VERB* **imparts, imparting, imparted 1** tell • *She imparted the news to her brother.* **2** give • *Lemon imparts a sharp flavour to drinks.*
[from Latin *impartire* = give someone part of something]

impartial *ADJECTIVE* not favouring one side more than the other; not biased.
▷ **impartially** *adverb* **impartiality** *noun*

impassable *ADJECTIVE* not able to be travelled along or over • *The road is impassable because of flooding.*

impasse (*say* am-pahss) *NOUN* **impasses** a situation in which no progress can be made; a deadlock.
[French, = impassable place]

impassive *ADJECTIVE* not showing any emotion • *His face remained impassive as the charges were read out.*
▷ **impassively** *adverb*
[from *im-* + an old sense of *passive* = suffering]

impasto (*say* im-past-oh) *NOUN* (*in art*) the technique of applying paint so thickly that it stands out from the surface of the picture.
[from Italian]

impatient *ADJECTIVE* **1** not patient; in a hurry. **2** eager to do something and not wanting to wait.
▷ **impatiently** *adverb* **impatience** *noun*

impeach *VERB* **impeaches, impeaching, impeached** bring a person to trial for a serious crime against his or her country.
▷ **impeachment** *noun*
[from old French; related to *impede*]

impeccable *ADJECTIVE* faultless.
▷ **impeccably** *adverb*
[from *im-* + Latin *peccare* = to sin]

impede *VERB* **impedes, impeding, impeded** hinder or get in the way.
[from Latin *impedire* = shackle the feet]

impediment *NOUN* **impediments 1** a hindrance. **2** a defect • *He has a speech impediment* (= a lisp or stammer).
[same origin as *impede*]

impel *VERB* **impels, impelling, impelled 1** urge or drive someone to do something • *Curiosity impelled her to investigate.* **2** drive forward; propel.
[from *im-* + Latin *pellere* = to drive]

impending *ADJECTIVE* soon to happen; imminent.
[from *im-* + Latin *pendere* = hang]

impenetrable *ADJECTIVE* **1** impossible to get through. **2** incomprehensible.

impenitent *ADJECTIVE* not regretting at all something wrong you have done; unrepentant.

imperative *ADJECTIVE* **1** expressing a command. **2** essential • *Speed is imperative.*

imperative *NOUN* **imperatives** a command; the form of a verb used in making commands (e.g. 'come' in *Come here!*).
[from Latin *imperare* = to command]

imperceptible *ADJECTIVE* too small or gradual to be noticed.

imperfect *ADJECTIVE* **1** not perfect. **2** (said about a tense of a verb) showing a continuous action, e.g. *She was singing.*
▷ **imperfectly** *adverb* **imperfection** *noun*

imperial *ADJECTIVE* **1** to do with an empire or its rulers. **2** (said about weights and measures) fixed by British law; non-metric • *an imperial gallon.*
▷ **imperially** *adverb*
[from Latin *imperium* = supreme power]

imperialism *NOUN* the policy of extending a country's empire or its influence; colonialism.
▷ **imperialist** *noun*

imperious *ADJECTIVE* haughty and bossy.
[same origin as *imperial*]

impermeable *ADJECTIVE* not allowing liquid to pass through it.

impersonal *ADJECTIVE* **1** not affected by personal feelings; showing no emotion. **2** not referring to a particular person.
▷ **impersonally** *adverb*

impersonate *VERB* **impersonates, impersonating, impersonated** pretend to be another person.
▷ **impersonation** *noun* **impersonator** *noun*
[from *im-* + Latin *persona* = person]

impertinent *ADJECTIVE* insolent; not showing proper respect.
▷ **impertinently** *adverb* **impertinence** *noun*

imperturbable *ADJECTIVE* not excitable; calm.
▷ **imperturbably** *adverb*

impervious *ADJECTIVE* **1** not allowing water, heat, etc. to pass through • *impervious to water.* **2** not able to be affected by something • *impervious to criticism.*
[from *im-* + Latin *per* = through + *via* = way]

impetuous *ADJECTIVE* acting hastily without thinking.
[same origin as *impetus*]

impetus *NOUN* **1** the force that makes an object start moving and that keeps it moving. **2** the influence that causes something to develop more quickly • *The ceasefire gave an impetus to peace talks.*
[Latin, = an attack]

impiety *NOUN* lack of reverence.
▷ **impious** (*say* imp-ee-us) *adjective*

impinge *VERB* **impinges, impinging, impinged 1** have an impact on; influence • *The economic recession impinged on all aspects of our lives.* **2** encroach or trespass.
[from *im-* + Latin *pangere* = drive in]

implacable *ADJECTIVE* not able to be placated; relentless.
▷ **implacably** *adverb*
[from *im-* + *placate* + *-able*]

implant *VERB* **implants, implanting, implanted** insert; fix something in.
▷ **implantation** *noun*

implant *NOUN* **implants** an organ or piece of tissue inserted in the body.
[from *im-* + Latin *plantare* = to plant]

implement *NOUN* **implements** a tool.

implement *VERB* **implements, implementing, implemented** put into action • *We shall implement these plans next month.*
▷ **implementation** *noun*
[from Latin]

implicate *VERB* **implicates, implicating, implicated** involve a person in a crime etc.; show that a person is involved • *His evidence implicates his sister.*
[from Latin *implicare* = to fold in]

implication *NOUN* **implications** **1** implicating. **2** implying; something that is implied.

implicit (*say* im-**pliss**-it) *ADJECTIVE* **1** implied but not stated openly. (COMPARE **explicit**) **2** absolute or unquestioning • *She expects implicit obedience.*
▷ **implicitly** *adverb*
[from Latin *implicitus* = entangled]

implode *VERB* **implodes, imploding, imploded** burst or explode inwards.
▷ **implosion** *noun*
[from *in-* = in, on the model of *explode*]

implore *VERB* **implores, imploring, implored** beg somebody to do something.
[from Latin *implorare* = ask tearfully]

imply *VERB* **implies, implying, implied** suggest something without actually saying it.
▷ **implication** *noun*
[from old French; related to *implicate*]
USAGE See note at **infer**.

impolite *ADJECTIVE* not polite.

imponderable *ADJECTIVE* not able to be judged or estimated.
[from *im-* + Latin *ponderabilis* = able to be weighed]

import *VERB* **imports, importing, imported** bring in goods etc. from another country.

import *NOUN* **imports** **1** importing; something imported. **2** (*formal*) meaning or importance • *The message was of great import.*
[from *im-* + Latin *portare* = carry]

important *ADJECTIVE* **1** having or able to have a great effect. **2** having great authority or influence.
▷ **importantly** *adverb* **importance** *noun*
[from Latin]

impose *VERB* **imposes, imposing, imposed** put or inflict • *It imposes a strain upon us.*
- **impose on somebody** put an unfair burden on him or her.
[from *im-* + Latin *positum* = placed]

imposing *ADJECTIVE* impressive.

imposition *NOUN* **impositions** **1** something imposed; an unfair burden or inconvenience. **2** imposing something.

impossible *ADJECTIVE* **1** not possible. **2** (*informal*) very annoying; unbearable • *He really is impossible!*
▷ **impossibly** *adverb* **impossibility** *noun*

impostor *NOUN* **impostors** a person who dishonestly pretends to be someone else.
[from French]

impotent *ADJECTIVE* **1** powerless; unable to take action. **2** (said about a man) unable to have sexual intercourse.
▷ **impotently** *adverb* **impotence** *noun*

impound *VERB* **impounds, impounding, impounded** confiscate; take possession of.
[from *im-* + *pound*[2]]

impoverish *VERB* **impoverishes, impoverishing, impoverished** **1** make a person poor. **2** make a thing poor in quality • *impoverished soil.*
▷ **impoverishment** *noun*
[from *im-* + old French *povre* = poor]

impracticable *ADJECTIVE* not able to be done in practice.

impractical *ADJECTIVE* not practical.

imprecise *ADJECTIVE* not precise.

impregnable *ADJECTIVE* strong enough to be safe against attack.
[from *im-* + old French *prendre* = take]

impregnate *VERB* **impregnates, impregnating, impregnated** **1** fertilize; make pregnant. **2** saturate; fill throughout • *The air was impregnated with the scent.*
▷ **impregnation** *noun*
[from *im-* + Latin *pregnare* = be pregnant]

impresario *NOUN* **impresarios** a person who organizes concerts, shows, etc.
[Italian, from *impresa* = an undertaking]

impress *VERB* **impresses, impressing, impressed** **1** make a person admire something or think it is very good. **2** fix something firmly in the mind • *He impressed on them the need for secrecy.* **3** press a mark into something.
[from *im-* + old French *presser* = to press]

impression *NOUN* **impressions** **1** an effect produced on the mind • *The book made a big impression on me.* **2** a vague idea. **3** an imitation of a person or a sound. **4** a reprint of a book.

impressionable *ADJECTIVE* easily influenced or affected.

impressionism *NOUN* a style of painting that gives the general effect of a scene etc. but without details.

impressionist *NOUN* **impressionists** **1** a painter in the style of impressionism. **2** an entertainer who does impressions of famous people.

impressive *ADJECTIVE* making a strong impression; seeming to be very good.

imprint *NOUN* **imprints** a mark pressed into or on something.
[from Latin *imprimere* = press in]

imprison *VERB* **imprisons, imprisoning, imprisoned** put someone in prison; shut someone up in a place.
▷ **imprisonment** *noun*
[from old French]

improbable *ADJECTIVE* unlikely.
▷ **improbably** *adverb* **improbability** *noun*

impromptu *ADJECTIVE & ADVERB* done without any rehearsal or preparation.
[from Latin *in promptu* = in readiness]

improper *ADJECTIVE* **1** unsuitable or wrong. **2** indecent.
▷ **improperly** *adverb* **impropriety** (*say* im-pro-**pry**-it-ee) *noun*

improper fraction *NOUN* **improper fractions** a fraction that is greater than 1, with the numerator greater than the denominator, e.g. $\frac{5}{3}$.

improve *VERB* **improves, improving, improved** make or become better.
▷ **improvement** *noun*
[from old French *emprouer* = make a profit]

improvident *ADJECTIVE* not providing or planning for the future; not thrifty.

improvise *VERB* **improvises, improvising, improvised** **1** compose or perform something without any rehearsal or preparation. **2** make something quickly with whatever is available.
▷ **improvisation** *noun*
[from *im-* + Latin *provisus* = provided for]

imprudent *ADJECTIVE* unwise or rash.

impudent *ADJECTIVE* cheeky or disrespectful.
▷ **impudently** *adverb* **impudence** *noun*
[from *im-* + Latin *pudens* = ashamed]

impulse *NOUN* **impulses** **1** a sudden desire to do something • *I did it on impulse.* **2** a push or impetus. **3** (*in science*) a force acting on something for a very short time • *electrical impulses.*
[same origin as *impel*]

impulsive *ADJECTIVE* done or acting on impulse, not after careful thought.
▷ **impulsively** *adverb* **impulsiveness** *noun*

impunity (*say* im-pewn-it-ee) *NOUN* freedom from punishment or injury.
[from *im-* + Latin *poena* = penalty]

impure *ADJECTIVE* not pure.
▷ **impurity** *noun*

impute *VERB* **imputes, imputing, imputed** (*formal*) regard someone as being responsible for something; attribute.
▷ **imputation** *noun*
[from old French]

in *PREPOSITION* This word is used to show position or condition, e.g. **1** at or inside; within the limits of something (*in a box*; *in two hours*), **2** into (*He fell in a puddle*), **3** arranged as; consisting of (*a serial in four parts*), **4** occupied with; a member of (*He is in the army*), **5** by means of (*We paid in cash*).
- **in all** in total number; altogether.

in *ADVERB* **1** so as to be in something or inside (*Get in*), **2** inwards (*The top caved in*), **3** at home; indoors (*Is anybody in?*), **4** in action; (in cricket) batting; (said about a fire) burning, **5** having arrived (*The train is in*).
- **in for** likely to get • *You're in for a shock.*
- **in on** (*informal*) aware of or sharing in • *I want to be in on this project.*
[from Old English]

in- *PREFIX* (changing to **il-** before *l*, **im-** before *b*, *m*, *p*, **ir-** before *r*) **1** in; into; on; towards (as in *include*, *invade*). **2** not (as in *incorrect*, *indirect*).
[usually from Latin; in a few words from Germanic *un-*]

inability *NOUN* being unable.

inaccessible *ADJECTIVE* not able to be reached.

inaccurate *ADJECTIVE* not accurate.

inactive *ADJECTIVE* not active.
▷ **inaction** *noun* **inactivity** *noun*

inadequate *ADJECTIVE* **1** not enough. **2** not able to cope or deal with something.
▷ **inadequately** *adverb* **inadequacy** *noun*

inadvertent *ADJECTIVE* unintentional.
[from *in-* + Latin *advertentia* = directing towards]

inadvisable *ADJECTIVE* not advisable.

inalienable *ADJECTIVE* that cannot be taken away • *an inalienable right.*
[from *in-* + *alienate* + *-able*]

inane *ADJECTIVE* silly; without sense.
▷ **inanely** *adverb* **inanity** *noun*
[from Latin *inanis* = empty]

inanimate *ADJECTIVE* **1** not living. **2** showing no sign of life.

inappropriate *ADJECTIVE* not appropriate.

inarticulate *ADJECTIVE* **1** not able to speak or express yourself clearly • *inarticulate with rage.* **2** not expressed in words • *an inarticulate cry.*

inattentive *ADJECTIVE* not listening or paying attention.
▷ **inattention** *noun*

inaudible *ADJECTIVE* not able to be heard.
▷ **inaudibly** *adverb* **inaudibility** *noun*

inaugurate *VERB* **inaugurates, inaugurating, inaugurated** **1** start or introduce something new and important. **2** formally establish a person in office • *inaugurate a new President.*
▷ **inaugural** *adjective* **inauguration** *noun*
[from Latin]

inauspicious *ADJECTIVE* not auspicious; unlikely to be successful.

inborn *ADJECTIVE* present in a person or animal from birth • *an inborn ability.*

inbred *ADJECTIVE* **1** inborn. **2** produced by inbreeding.

inbreeding *NOUN* breeding from closely related individuals.

incalculable *ADJECTIVE* not able to be calculated or predicted.
[from *in-* + *calculate* + *-able*]

in camera *ADVERB* in a judge's private room, not in public.
[Latin, = in the room]

incandescent *ADJECTIVE* giving out light when heated; shining.
▷ **incandescence** *noun*
[from *in-* + Latin *candescere* = become white]

incantation *NOUN* **incantations** a spoken spell or charm; the chanting of this.
[from *in-* = in + Latin *cantare* = sing]

incapable *ADJECTIVE* not able to do something • *They seem incapable of understanding how serious the situation is.*

incapacitate *VERB* **incapacitates, incapacitating, incapacitated** make a person or thing unable to do something; disable.
[from *in-* + *capacity* + *-ate*]

incapacity *NOUN* inability; lack of sufficient strength or power.

incarcerate *VERB* **incarcerates, incarcerating, incarcerated** shut in or imprison a person.
▷ **incarceration** *noun*
[from *in-* + Latin *carcer* = prison]

incarnate *ADJECTIVE* having a body or human form • *a devil incarnate.*
▷ **incarnation** *noun*
- **the Incarnation** (in Christian teaching) God's taking a human form as Jesus Christ.
[from *in-* + Latin *carnis* = of flesh]

A B C D E F G H I J K L M N O P Q R S T U V W X Y Z

incautious *ADJECTIVE* rash.

incendiary *ADJECTIVE* starting or designed to start a fire • *an incendiary bomb.*
[same origin as *incense*]

incense (*say* **in**-sens) *NOUN* a substance making a spicy smell when it is burnt.

incense (*say* in-**sens**) *VERB* **incenses, incensing, incensed** make a person angry.
[from Latin *incendere* = set fire to]

incentive *NOUN* **incentives** something that encourages a person to do something or to work harder.
[from Latin *incentivus* = setting the tune]

inception *NOUN* the beginning of something.
[same origin as *incipient*]

incessant *ADJECTIVE* continuing without a pause; unceasing.
[from *in-* + Latin *cessare* = cease]

incest *NOUN* sexual intercourse between two people who are so closely related that they cannot marry each other.
▷ **incestuous** *adjective*
[from *in-* + Latin *castus* = pure]

inch *NOUN* **inches** a measure of length, one-twelfth of a foot (about $2\frac{1}{2}$ centimetres).

inch *VERB* **inches, inching, inched** move slowly and gradually • *I inched along the ledge.*
[from Old English]

incidence *NOUN* the extent or frequency of something • *What is the incidence of heart disease in the population?*
[from Latin *incidens* = happening]

incident *NOUN* **incidents** an event.
[from Latin *incidere* = fall upon or happen to]

incidental *ADJECTIVE* happening as a minor part of something else • *incidental expenses.*
[from *incident*]

incidentally *ADVERB* by the way.

incinerate *VERB* **incinerates, incinerating, incinerated** destroy something by burning.
▷ **incineration** *noun*
[from *in-* + Latin *cineris* = of ashes]

incinerator *NOUN* **incinerators** a device for burning rubbish.

incipient (*say* in-**sip**-ee-ent) *ADJECTIVE* just beginning • *incipient decay.*
[from Latin *incipere* = begin]

incise *VERB* **incises, incising, incised** cut or engrave something into a surface.
[from *in-* + Latin *caesum* = cut]

incision *NOUN* **incisions** a cut, especially one made in a surgical operation.

incisive *ADJECTIVE* clear and sharp • *incisive comments.*
[same origin as *incise*]

incisor (*say* in-**sy**-zer) *NOUN* **incisors** each of the sharp-edged front teeth in the upper and lower jaws.
[same origin as *incise*]

incite *VERB* **incites, inciting, incited** urge a person to do something; stir up • *They incited a riot.*
▷ **incitement** *noun*
[from *in-* = towards + Latin *citare* = rouse]

incivility *NOUN* rudeness or discourtesy.
[from *in-* + *civility*]

inclement *ADJECTIVE* (*formal*) cold, wet, or stormy • *inclement weather.*
[from *in-* + Latin *clemens* = mild]

inclination *NOUN* **inclinations 1** a tendency. **2** a liking or preference. **3** a slope or slant.

incline (*say* in-**klyn**) *VERB* **inclines, inclining, inclined 1** lean or slope. **2** bend the head or body forward, as in a nod or bow. **3** cause or influence • *Her frank manner inclines me to believe her.*
– **be inclined** have a tendency or willingness • *The door is inclined to bang.* • *I'm inclined to agree with you.*

incline (*say* **in**-klyn) *NOUN* **inclines** a slope.
[from Latin *inclinare* = to bend]

include *VERB* **includes, including, included** make or consider something as part of a group of things.
▷ **inclusion** *noun*
[from Latin *includere* = enclose]

inclusive *ADJECTIVE* including everything; including all the things mentioned • *Read pages 20 to 28 inclusive.*

incognito (*say* in-kog-neet-oh or in-kog-nit-oh) *ADJECTIVE & ADVERB* with your name or identity concealed • *The film star was travelling incognito.*
[Italian, from *in-* + Latin *cognitus* = known]

incoherent *ADJECTIVE* not speaking or reasoning in an orderly way.

incombustible *ADJECTIVE* unable to be set on fire.
[from *in-* + Latin *combustibilis* = combustible]

income *NOUN* **incomes** money received regularly from doing work or from investments.
[from *in* (adverb) + *come*]

income tax *NOUN* tax charged on income.

incoming *ADJECTIVE* **1** coming in • *incoming telephone calls.* **2** about to take over from someone else • *the incoming chairman.*

incomparable (*say* in-komp-er-abul) *ADJECTIVE* without an equal; unsurpassed • *incomparable beauty.*
[from *in-* + Latin *comparabilis* = comparable]

incompatible *ADJECTIVE* not able to exist or be used together.

incompetent *ADJECTIVE* not able or skilled enough to do something properly.

incomplete *ADJECTIVE* not complete.

incomprehensible *ADJECTIVE* not able to be understood.
▷ **incomprehension** *noun*
[from *in-* + Latin *comprehensibilis* = comprehensible]

inconceivable *ADJECTIVE* not able to be imagined; most unlikely.

inconclusive *ADJECTIVE* not conclusive.

incongruous *ADJECTIVE* out of place or unsuitable.
▷ **incongruously** *adverb* **incongruity** *noun*
[from *in-* + Latin *congruus* = agreeing or suitable]

inconsiderable *ADJECTIVE* of small value.

inconsiderate *ADJECTIVE* not considerate towards other people.

inconsistent *ADJECTIVE* not consistent.
▷ **inconsistently** *adverb* **inconsistency** *noun*

inconsolable *ADJECTIVE* not able to be consoled; very sad.

inconspicuous *ADJECTIVE* not attracting attention or clearly visible.
▷ **inconspicuously** *adverb*

incontinent *ADJECTIVE* not able to control the bladder or bowels.
▷ **incontinence** *noun*
[from *in-* + Latin *continentia* = restraining, keeping in]

incontrovertible *ADJECTIVE* unable to be denied; indisputable.
[from *in-* + Latin *controversus* = disputed]

inconvenience *NOUN* **inconveniences** being inconvenient.

inconvenience *VERB* **inconveniences, inconveniencing, inconvenienced** cause inconvenience or slight difficulty to someone.

inconvenient *ADJECTIVE* not convenient.

incorporate *VERB* **incorporates, incorporating, incorporated** include something as a part of something larger.
▷ **incorporation** *noun*
[from *in-* + Latin *corpus* = body]

incorporated *ADJECTIVE* (said about a business firm) formed into a legal corporation.

incorrect *ADJECTIVE* not correct.
▷ **incorrectly** *adverb*

incorrigible *ADJECTIVE* not able to be reformed • *an incorrigible liar.*
[from *in-* + Latin *corrigere* = to correct]

incorruptible *ADJECTIVE* **1** not able to decay. **2** not able to be bribed.

increase *VERB* **increases, increasing, increased** make or become larger or more.

increase *NOUN* **increases** increasing; the amount by which a thing increases.
[from *in-* + Latin *crescere* = grow]

increasingly *ADVERB* more and more.

incredible *ADJECTIVE* unbelievable.
▷ **incredibly** *adverb* **incredibility** *noun*
USAGE Do not confuse with **incredulous**.

incredulous *ADJECTIVE* not believing somebody; showing disbelief.
▷ **incredulously** *adverb* **incredulity** *noun*
USAGE Do not confuse with **incredible**.

increment (*say* in-krim-ent) *NOUN* **increments** an increase; an added amount.
▷ **incremental** *adjective*
[from Latin *incrementum* = growth]

incriminate *VERB* **incriminates, incriminating, incriminated** show a person to have been involved in a crime etc.
▷ **incrimination** *noun*
[from *in-* + Latin *criminare* = accuse of a crime]

incrustation *NOUN* **incrustations** encrusting; a crust or deposit that forms on a surface.
[from *in-* + Latin *crustare* = form a crust]

incubate *VERB* **incubates, incubating, incubated** **1** hatch eggs by keeping them warm. **2** cause bacteria or a disease to develop.
▷ **incubation** *noun*
[from *in-* + Latin *cubare* = lie]

incubation period *NOUN* **incubation periods** the time it takes for symptoms of a disease to be seen in an infected person.

incubator *NOUN* **incubators** **1** a device in which a baby born prematurely can be kept warm and supplied with oxygen. **2** a device for incubating eggs etc.

incumbent *ADJECTIVE* if it is incumbent on you to do something, it is your duty to do it • *It is incumbent on you to warn people of the danger.*

incumbent *NOUN* **incumbents** a person who holds a particular office or position.
[from *in-* + Latin *-cumbens* = lying]

incur *VERB* **incurs, incurring, incurred** bring something on yourself • *I hope you don't incur too much expense.*
[from *in-* + Latin *currere* = to run]

incurable *ADJECTIVE* not able to be cured.
▷ **incurably** *adverb*

incurious *ADJECTIVE* feeling or showing no curiosity about something.

incursion *NOUN* **incursions** a raid or brief invasion.
[same origin as *incur*]

indebted *ADJECTIVE* owing money or gratitude to someone.
[from old French]

indecent *ADJECTIVE* not decent; improper.
▷ **indecently** *adverb* **indecency** *noun*

indecipherable *ADJECTIVE* not able to be deciphered.

indecision *NOUN* being unable to make up your mind; hesitation.

indecisive *ADJECTIVE* not decisive.

indeed *ADVERB* **1** used to strengthen a meaning • *It's very cold indeed.* **2** really; truly • *I am indeed surprised.* **3** admittedly • *It is, indeed, his first attempt.*
[from *in deed* = in action or fact]

indefensible *ADJECTIVE* unable to be defended or justified • *an indefensible decision.*

indefinable *ADJECTIVE* unable to be defined or described clearly.

indefinite *ADJECTIVE* not definite; vague.

indefinite article *NOUN* **indefinite articles** the word 'a' or 'an'.

indefinitely *ADVERB* for an indefinite or unlimited time.

indelible *ADJECTIVE* impossible to rub out or remove.
▷ **indelibly** *adverb*
[from *in-* + Latin *delere* = destroy]

indelicate *ADJECTIVE* **1** slightly indecent. **2** tactless.
▷ **indelicacy** *noun*

indent *VERB* **indents, indenting, indented** **1** make notches or recesses in something. **2** start a line of writing or printing further in from the margin than other lines • *Always indent the first line of a new paragraph.* **3** place an official order for goods or stores.
▷ **indentation** *noun*
[from *in-* + Latin *dens* = tooth (because the indentations looked like teeth)]

indenture *NOUN* an agreement binding an apprentice to work for a certain employer.
▷ **indentured** *adjective*
[same origin as *indent* (because each copy of the agreement had notches cut into it, so that the copies could be fitted together to show that they were genuine)]

independent *ADJECTIVE* **1** not dependent on any other person or thing for help, money, or support. **2** (said about a country) governing itself. **3** not connected or involved with something.
▷ **independently** *adverb* **independence** *noun*

indescribable *ADJECTIVE* unable to be described.
▷ **indescribably** *adverb*

indestructible *ADJECTIVE* unable to be destroyed.
▷ **indestructibility** *noun*
[from *in-* + Latin *destruere* = destroy]

indeterminate *ADJECTIVE* not fixed or decided exactly; left vague.
[from *in-* + Latin *determinare* = define or determine]

index *NOUN* **1** (*plural* **indexes**) an alphabetical list of things, especially at the end of a book. **2** a number showing how prices or wages have changed from a previous level. **3** (*in mathematics*) (*plural* **indices**) the raised number etc. written to the right of another (e.g. 3 in 2^3) showing how many times the first one is to be multiplied by itself.

index *VERB* **indexes, indexing, indexed** make an index to a book etc.; put something into an index.
[Latin, = pointer]

index finger *NOUN* **index fingers** the forefinger.

Indian *ADJECTIVE* **1** to do with India or its people. **2** to do with Native Americans.
▷ **Indian** *noun*
USAGE The preferred term for the descendants of the original inhabitants of North and South America is *Native American*. *American Indian* is usually acceptable but the term *Red Indian* is now regarded as offensive and should not be used.

Indian summer *NOUN* **Indian summers** a period of warm weather in late autumn.

india rubber *NOUN* **india rubbers** a rubber.
[because it was made of rubber from India]

indicate *VERB* **indicates, indicating, indicated** **1** point something out or make it known. **2** be a sign of. **3** when drivers indicate, they signal which direction they are turning by using their indicators.
▷ **indication** *noun*
[from Latin; related to *index*]

indicative *ADJECTIVE* giving an indication.

indicative *NOUN* the form of a verb used in making a statement (e.g. 'he said' or 'he is coming'), not in a command, question, or wish.

indicator *NOUN* **indicators 1** a thing that indicates or points to something. **2** a flashing light used to signal that a motor vehicle is turning. **3** (*in science*) a chemical compound (such as litmus) that changes colour in the presence of a particular substance or condition.

indict (*say* ind-I't) *VERB* **indicts, indicting, indicted** charge a person with having committed a crime.
▷ **indictment** *noun*
[from Latin *indicere* = proclaim]

indie *ADJECTIVE* used to describe popular music played by groups that are not well-known, that is produced by small independent companies • *indie bands*
[short for *independent*]

indifferent *ADJECTIVE* **1** not caring about something; not interested. **2** not very good • *an indifferent cricketer.*
▷ **indifferently** *adverb* **indifference** *noun*
[from *in-* + Latin *differre* = recognize differences]

indigenous (*say* in-dij-in-us) *ADJECTIVE* growing or originating in a particular country; native • *The koala bear is indigenous to Australia.*
[from Latin *indigena* = born in a country]

indigent (*say* in-dij-ent) *ADJECTIVE* poor or needy.
[from Latin]

indigestible *ADJECTIVE* difficult or impossible to digest.

indigestion *NOUN* pain or discomfort caused by difficulty in digesting food.
[from *in-* + Latin *digerere* = digest]

indignant *ADJECTIVE* angry at something that seems unfair or wicked.
▷ **indignantly** *adverb* **indignation** *noun*
[from Latin *indignari* = regard as unworthy]

indignity *NOUN* **indignities** treatment that makes a person feel undignified or humiliated; an insult.
[from *in-* + Latin *dignus* = worthy]

indigo *NOUN* a deep-blue colour.
[from Greek *indikon* = something from India]

indirect *ADJECTIVE* not direct.
▷ **indirectly** *adverb*

indirect speech *NOUN* a speaker's words given in a changed form reported by someone else, as in *He said that he would come* (reporting the words 'I will come').

indiscreet *ADJECTIVE* **1** not discreet; revealing secrets. **2** not cautious; rash.
▷ **indiscreetly** *adverb* **indiscretion** *noun*

indiscriminate *ADJECTIVE* showing no discrimination; not making a careful choice.
▷ **indiscriminately** *adverb*

indispensable *ADJECTIVE* not able to be dispensed with; essential.
▷ **indispensability** *noun*

indisposed *ADJECTIVE* **1** slightly unwell. **2** unwilling • *They seem indisposed to help us.*
▷ **indisposition** *noun*

indisputable *ADJECTIVE* undeniable.
[from *in-* + Latin *disputare* = dispute]

indistinct *ADJECTIVE* not distinct.
▷ **indistinctly** *adverb* **indistinctness** *noun*

indistinguishable *ADJECTIVE* not able to be told apart; not distinguishable.

individual *ADJECTIVE* **1** of or for one person. **2** single or separate • *Count each individual word.*
▷ **individually** *adverb*

individual *NOUN* **individuals** one person, animal, or plant.
[from *in-* + Latin *dividuus* = able to be divided]

individuality *NOUN* the things that make one person or thing different from another; distinctive identity.

indivisible *ADJECTIVE* not able to be divided or separated.
▷ **indivisibly** *adverb*
[from *in-* + Latin *divisum* = divided]

indoctrinate *VERB* **indoctrinates, indoctrinating, indoctrinated** fill a person's mind with particular ideas or beliefs, so that he or she comes to accept them without thinking.
▷ **indoctrination** *noun*
[from *in-* = in, + *doctrine*]

indolent *ADJECTIVE* lazy.
▷ **indolently** *adverb* **indolence** *noun*
[from *in-* + Latin *dolere* = suffer pain or trouble]

indomitable *ADJECTIVE* not able to be overcome or conquered.
[from *in-* + Latin *domitare* = to tame]

indoor *ADJECTIVE* used or placed or done etc. inside a building • *indoor games.*

indoors *ADVERB* inside a building.

indubitable (*say* in-dew-bit-a-bul) *ADJECTIVE* not able to be doubted; certain.
▷ **indubitably** *adverb*
[from *in-* + Latin *dubitare* = to doubt]

induce *VERB* **induces, inducing, induced** **1** persuade. **2** produce or cause • *Some substances induce sleep.* **3** if a pregnant woman is induced, labour is brought on artificially with the use of drugs.
▷ **induction** *noun*
[from *in-* + Latin *ducere* = to lead]

inducement *NOUN* **inducements** an incentive.

indulge *VERB* **indulges, indulging, indulged** allow a person to have or do what he or she wants.
- **indulge in** allow yourself to have or do something that you enjoy.
[from Latin]

indulgent *ADJECTIVE* allowing someone to have or do whatever they want; kind and lenient.
▷ **indulgence** *noun*

industrial *ADJECTIVE* to do with industry; working or used in industry.
▷ **industrially** *adverb*

industrial action *NOUN* ways for workers to protest, such as striking or working to rule.

industrialist *NOUN* **industrialists** a person who owns or manages an industrial business.

industrialized *ADJECTIVE* (said about a country or district) having many industries.
▷ **industrialization** *noun*

Industrial Revolution *NOUN* the expansion of British industry by the use of machines in the late 18th and early 19th century.

A B C D E F G H I J K L M N O P Q R S T U V W X Y Z

industrious *ADJECTIVE* working hard.
▷ **industriously** *adverb*

industry *NOUN* **industries 1** making or producing goods, especially in factories. **2** a particular branch of this, or any business activity • *the motor industry*; *the tourist industry*. **3** being industrious.
[from Latin *industria* = hard work]

inebriated *ADJECTIVE* drunk.
[from *in-* + Latin *ebrius* = drunk]

inedible *ADJECTIVE* not edible.

ineffective *ADJECTIVE* not effective; inefficient.
▷ **ineffectively** *adverb*

ineffectual *ADJECTIVE* not achieving anything.

inefficient *ADJECTIVE* not efficient.
▷ **inefficiently** *adverb* **inefficiency** *noun*

inelegant *ADJECTIVE* not elegant.

ineligible *ADJECTIVE* not eligible.

inept *ADJECTIVE* lacking any skill; clumsy.
▷ **ineptly** *adverb* **ineptitude** *noun*
[from *in-* + Latin *aptus* = apt]

inequality *NOUN* **inequalities** not being equal.

inequity *NOUN* **inequities** unfairness.
▷ **inequitable** *adjective*

inert *ADJECTIVE* not moving or reacting.
▷ **inertly** *adverb*
[from Latin *iners* = idle]

inert gas *NOUN* **inert gases** a gas that almost never combines with other substances.

inertia (*say* in-**er**-sha) *NOUN* **1** being inert or slow to take action. **2** (*in science*) the tendency for a moving thing to keep moving in a straight line.
[same origin as *inert*]

inescapable *ADJECTIVE* unavoidable.

inessential *ADJECTIVE* not essential.

inestimable *ADJECTIVE* too great or precious to be able to be estimated.

inevitable *ADJECTIVE* unavoidable; sure to happen.
▷ **inevitably** *adverb* **inevitability** *noun*
[from *in-* + Latin *evitare* = avoid]

inexact *ADJECTIVE* not exact.

inexcusable *ADJECTIVE* not excusable.

inexhaustible *ADJECTIVE* so great that it cannot be used up completely • *Ben has an inexhaustible supply of jokes.*

inexorable (*say* in-**eks**-er-a-bul) *ADJECTIVE* **1** relentless. **2** not able to be persuaded by requests or entreaties.
▷ **inexorably** *adverb*
[from *in-* + Latin *exorare* = plead]

inexpensive *ADJECTIVE* not expensive; cheap.
▷ **inexpensively** *adverb*

inexperience *NOUN* lack of experience.
▷ **inexperienced** *adjective*

inexpert *ADJECTIVE* unskilful.
[from Latin *inexpertus* = inexperienced]

inexplicable *ADJECTIVE* impossible to explain.
▷ **inexplicably** *adverb*
[from *in-* + Latin *explicare* = unfold]

in extremis (*say* eks-**treem**-iss) *ADVERB* at the point of death; in very great difficulties.
[Latin, = in the greatest danger]

infallible *ADJECTIVE* **1** never wrong. **2** never failing • *an infallible remedy.*
▷ **infallibly** *adverb* **infallibility** *noun*
[from *in-* + Latin *fallere* = deceive]

infamous (*say* **in**-fam-us) *ADJECTIVE* having a bad reputation; wicked.
▷ **infamously** *adverb* **infamy** *noun*
[from *in-* + Latin *fama* = good reputation, fame]

infancy *NOUN* **1** early childhood; babyhood. **2** an early stage of development.

infant *NOUN* **infants** a baby or young child.
[from Latin *infans* = unable to speak]

infantile *ADJECTIVE* **1** to do with infants. **2** very childish.

infantry *NOUN* soldiers who fight on foot. (COMPARE **cavalry**)
[from Italian *infante* = a youth]

infatuated *ADJECTIVE* filled with foolish or unreasoning love.
▷ **infatuation** *noun*
[from *in-* + Latin *fatuus* = foolish]

infect *VERB* **infects, infecting, infected** pass on a disease or bacteria to a person, animal, or plant.
[from Latin *infectum* = tainted]

infection *NOUN* **infections 1** infecting. **2** an infectious disease or condition.

infectious *ADJECTIVE* **1** (said about a disease) able to be spread by air or water etc. (COMPARE **contagious**) **2** quickly spreading to others • *His fear was infectious.*

infer *VERB* **infers, inferring, inferred** form an opinion or work something out from what someone says or does, even though they do not actually say it • *I infer from your luggage that you are going on holiday.*
▷ **inference** *noun*
[from *in-* + Latin *ferre* = bring]
USAGE Do not confuse with **imply**. Remember that **imply** and *infer* are a pair of words with opposite meanings, in the same way that *lend* means the opposite of *borrow* and *teach* the opposite of *learn*. Don't say 'What exactly are you inferring?' when you mean 'What exactly are you implying?'

inferior *ADJECTIVE* less good or less important; low or lower in position, quality, etc.
▷ **inferiority** *noun*

inferior *NOUN* **inferiors** a person who is lower in position or rank than someone else.
[Latin, = lower]

infernal *ADJECTIVE* **1** to do with or like hell • *the infernal regions.* **2** (*informal*) detestable or tiresome • *Stop that infernal noise.*
▷ **infernally** *adverb*
[from Latin *infernus* = below, used by Christians to mean 'hell']

inferno *NOUN* **infernos** a raging fire.
[same origin as *infernal*]

infertile *ADJECTIVE* not fertile.
▷ **infertility** *noun*

infest *VERB* **infests, infesting, infested** (said about pests) be numerous and troublesome in a place.
▷ **infestation** *noun*
[from Latin *infestus* = hostile]

infidel (*say* in-fid-el) *NOUN* **infidels** (*old use*) a person who does not believe in a religion.
[from *in-* + Latin *fidelis* = faithful]

infidelity *NOUN* unfaithfulness.
[same origin as *infidel*]

infiltrate *VERB* **infiltrates, infiltrating, infiltrated** get into a place or organization gradually and without being noticed.
▷ **infiltration** *noun* **infiltrator** *noun*
[from *in-* + Latin *filtrare* = to filter]

infinite *ADJECTIVE* **1** endless; without a limit. **2** too great to be measured.
▷ **infinitely** *adverb*
[from Latin *infinitus* = unlimited]

infinitesimal *ADJECTIVE* extremely small.
▷ **infinitesimally** *adverb*
[from Latin]

infinitive *NOUN* **infinitives** (*in grammar*) the form of a verb that does not change to indicate a particular tense or number or person, in English used with or without *to*, e.g. *go* in 'Let him go' or 'Allow him to go'.
[from *in-* + Latin *finitivus* = definite]

infinity *NOUN* an infinite number or distance or time.

infirm *ADJECTIVE* weak, especially from old age or illness.
▷ **infirmity** *noun*
[from *in-* + Latin *firmus* = firm]

infirmary *NOUN* **infirmaries 1** a hospital. **2** a place where sick people are cared for in a school or monastery etc.

inflame *VERB* **inflames, inflaming, inflamed 1** produce strong feelings or anger in people. **2** cause redness, heat, and swelling in a part of the body.
[from *in-* + Latin *flamma* = flame]

inflammable *ADJECTIVE* able to be set on fire.
[same origin as *inflame*]
USAGE This word means the same as *flammable*. If you want to say that something is not able to be set on fire, use *non-flammable*.

inflammation *NOUN* painful redness or swelling in a part of the body.

inflammatory *ADJECTIVE* likely to make people angry • *inflammatory leaflets.*

inflatable *ADJECTIVE* able to be inflated.

inflate *VERB* **inflates, inflating, inflated 1** fill something with air or gas so that it expands. **2** increase something too much. **3** raise prices or wages etc. more than is justifiable.
[from *in-* + Latin *flatum* = blown]

A B C D E F G H I J K L M N O P Q R S T U V W X Y Z

inflation *NOUN* **1** inflating. **2** a general rise in prices and fall in the purchasing power of money.
▷ **inflationary** *adjective*

inflect *VERB* **inflects, inflecting, inflected**
1 (*in grammar*) change the ending or form of a word to show its tense or its grammatical relation to other words, e.g. *sing* changes to *sang* or *sung*, *child* changes to *children*. **2** alter the voice in speaking.
[originally = bend inwards: from *in-* + Latin *flectere* = to bend]

inflection *NOUN* **inflections** (*in grammar*) an ending or form of a word used to inflect, e.g. **-ed**.

inflexible *ADJECTIVE* not able to be bent or changed or persuaded.
▷ **inflexibly** *adverb* **inflexibility** *noun*
[from *in-* + Latin *flexibilis* = flexible]

inflexion *NOUN* **inflexions** a different spelling of *inflection*.

inflict *VERB* **inflicts, inflicting, inflicted**
make a person suffer something • *She inflicted a severe blow on him.*
▷ **infliction** *noun*
[from *in-* + Latin *flictum* = struck]

inflow *NOUN* flowing in; what flows in.

influence *NOUN* **influences 1** the power to affect other people or things. **2** a person or thing with this power.

influence *VERB* **influences, influencing, influenced** have an influence on a person or thing • *The tides are influenced by the moon.*
[from *in-* + Latin *fluentia* = flowing]

influential *ADJECTIVE* having great influence.

influenza *NOUN* an infectious disease that causes fever, catarrh, and pain.
[Italian, literally = influence]

influx *NOUN* a flowing in, especially of people or things coming in.
[from Latin]

inform *VERB* **informs, informing, informed** give information to somebody.
▷ **informant** *noun*
[from Latin *informare* = form an idea of something]

informal *ADJECTIVE* not formal.
▷ **informally** *adverb* **informality** *noun*
USAGE In this dictionary, words marked *informal* are used in talking but not when you are writing or speaking formally.

information *NOUN* facts told or heard or discovered, or put into a computer etc.
[from Latin *informatio* = idea]

information technology *NOUN* the study or use of ways of storing, arranging, and giving out information, especially computers and telecommunications.

informative *ADJECTIVE* giving a lot of useful information.

informed *ADJECTIVE* knowing about something.

informer *NOUN* **informers** a person who gives information against someone, especially to the police.

infra- *PREFIX* below.
[Latin]

infra-red *ADJECTIVE* below or beyond red in the spectrum.

infrastructure *NOUN* **infrastructures** the basic services and systems that a country needs in order for its society and economy to work properly, such as buildings, roads, transport, and power supplies.
[from *infra-* + *structure*]

infrequent *ADJECTIVE* not frequent.

infringe *VERB* **infringes, infringing, infringed 1** break a rule, law, or agreement. **2** encroach on a person's rights.
▷ **infringement** *noun*
[from *in-* + Latin *frangere* = break]

infuriate *VERB* **infuriates, infuriating, infuriated** make a person very angry.
▷ **infuriation** *noun*
[from *in-* + Latin *furia* = fury]

infuse *VERB* **infuses, infusing, infused**
1 add or inspire with a feeling • *She infused them all with courage.* **2** soak or steep tea or herbs etc. in a liquid to extract the flavour.
▷ **infusion** *noun*
[from Latin *infusum* = poured in]

-ing *SUFFIX* forms nouns and adjectives showing the action of a verb (e.g. *hearing*, *tasting*, *telling*).

ingenious *ADJECTIVE* **1** clever at inventing things. **2** cleverly made.
▷ **ingeniously** *adverb* **ingenuity** *noun*
[from Latin *ingenium* = genius]
USAGE Do not confuse with **ingenuous**.

ingenuous *ADJECTIVE* without cunning; innocent.
▷ **ingenuously** *adverb* **ingenuousness** *noun*
[from Latin *ingenuus* = inborn]
USAGE Do not confuse with **ingenious**.

ingot *NOUN* **ingots** a lump of gold or silver etc. that is cast in a brick shape.
[from *in-* + Old English *geotan* = pour]

ingrained *ADJECTIVE* **1** (said about feelings or habits) deeply fixed. **2** (said about dirt) marking a surface deeply.
[from *in the grain* (of wood)]

ingratiate *VERB* **ingratiates**, **ingratiating**, **ingratiated**
- **ingratiate yourself** get yourself into favour with someone, especially by flattering them or always agreeing with them.
▷ **ingratiation** *noun*
[from Latin *in gratiam* = into favour]

ingratitude *NOUN* lack of gratitude.

ingredient *NOUN* **ingredients** one of the parts of a mixture; one of the things used in a recipe.
[from Latin *ingrediens* = going in]

inhabit *VERB* **inhabits**, **inhabiting**, **inhabited** live in a place.
▷ **inhabitant** *noun*
[from *in-* + Latin *habitare* = occupy]

inhale *VERB* **inhales**, **inhaling**, **inhaled** breathe in.
▷ **inhalation** *noun*
[from *in-* + Latin *halare* = breathe]

inhaler *NOUN* **inhalers** a device used for relieving asthma etc. by inhaling.

inherent (*say* in-**heer**-ent) *ADJECTIVE* existing in something as one of its natural or permanent qualities.
▷ **inherently** *adverb* **inherence** *noun*
[from *in-* + Latin *haerere* = to stick]

inherit *VERB* **inherits**, **inheriting**, **inherited** **1** receive money, property, or a title etc. when its previous owner dies. **2** get certain qualities etc. from parents or predecessors.
▷ **inheritance** *noun* **inheritor** *noun*
[from *in-* + Latin *heres* = heir]

inhibit *VERB* **inhibits**, **inhibiting**, **inhibited** hinder or restrain something.

inhibition *NOUN* **inhibitions** a feeling of embarrassment or worry that prevents you from doing something or expressing your emotions.
▷ **inhibited** *adjective*
[from *in-* + Latin *habere* = to hold]

inhospitable *ADJECTIVE* **1** unfriendly to visitors. **2** giving no shelter or good weather.

inhuman *ADJECTIVE* cruel; without pity or kindness.
▷ **inhumanity** *noun*
[from *in-* + Latin *humanus* = human]

inhumane *ADJECTIVE* not humane.

inimitable *ADJECTIVE* impossible to imitate.

iniquitous *ADJECTIVE* very unjust.
▷ **iniquity** *noun*
[from *in-* + Latin *aequus* = equal or fair]

initial *NOUN* **initials** the first letter of a word or name.

initial *VERB* **initials**, **initialling**, **initialled** mark or sign something with the initials of your names.

initial *ADJECTIVE* at the beginning • *the initial stages.*
▷ **initially** *adverb*
[from Latin *initium* = the beginning]

initiate *VERB* **initiates**, **initiating**, **initiated** **1** start something. **2** admit a person as a member of a society or group, often with special ceremonies.
▷ **initiation** *noun* **initiator** *noun*
[same origin as *initial*]

initiative (*say* in-**ish**-a-tiv) *NOUN* **1** the power or right to get something started. **2** the ability to make decisions and take action on your own without being told what to do.
- **take the initiative** take action to start something happening.

inject *VERB* **injects, injecting, injected** **1** put a medicine or drug into the body by means of a hollow needle. **2** put liquid into something by means of a syringe etc. **3** add a new quality • *Try to inject some humour into the story.*
▷ **injection** *noun*
[from *in-* + Latin *jacere* = to throw]
WORD FAMILY There are a number of English words that are related to *inject* because part of their original meaning comes from the Latin word *jacere* meaning 'to throw'. These include *abject, conjecture, dejected, eject, interject, project, projectile, reject,* and *subject.*

injudicious *ADJECTIVE* unwise.

injunction *NOUN* **injunctions** a command given with authority, e.g. by a lawcourt.
[from Latin]

injure *VERB* **injures, injuring, injured** harm or hurt someone.
▷ **injury** *noun* **injurious** (*say* in-joor-ee-us) *adjective*
[originally = treat someone unfairly: from *in-* + Latin *juris* = of right]

injustice *NOUN* **injustices 1** lack of justice. **2** an unjust action or treatment.

ink *NOUN* **inks** a black or coloured liquid used in writing and printing.
[from Greek]

inkling *NOUN* **inklings** a slight idea or suspicion • *I had no inkling of your artistic talents.*
[origin unknown]

inky *ADJECTIVE* **1** stained with ink. **2** black like ink • *inky darkness.*

inland *ADJECTIVE & ADVERB* in or towards the interior of a country; away from the coast.

Inland Revenue *NOUN* the government department responsible for collecting taxes and similar charges inland (not at a port).

in-laws *PLURAL NOUN* (*informal*) relatives by marriage.
[from French *en loi de mariage* = in law of marriage]

inlay *VERB* **inlays, inlaying, inlaid** set pieces of wood or metal etc. into a surface to form a design.
▷ **inlay** *noun*
[from *in-* + *lay*[1]]

inlet *NOUN* **inlets** a strip of water reaching into the land from a sea or lake.

inmate *NOUN* **inmates** one of the occupants of a prison, hospital, or other institution.
[originally = a lodger: from *inn* + *mate*[1]]

in memoriam *PREPOSITION* in memory of.
[Latin]

inmost *ADJECTIVE* most inward.

inn *NOUN* **inns** a hotel or public house, especially in the country.
▷ **innkeeper** *noun*
[from Old English]

innards *PLURAL NOUN* (*informal*) the internal organs of a person or animal; the inner parts of a machine.

innate *ADJECTIVE* inborn or natural.
[from *in-* + Latin *natus* = born]

inner *ADJECTIVE* inside; nearer to the centre.
▷ **innermost** *adjective*

innings *NOUN* **innings** the time when a cricket team or player is batting.
[from an old verb *in* = put or get in, + *-ing*]

innocent *ADJECTIVE* **1** not guilty. **2** not wicked; lacking experience of evil. **3** harmless.
▷ **innocently** *adverb* **innocence** *noun*
[from *in-* + Latin *nocens* = doing harm]

innocuous *ADJECTIVE* harmless.
[from *in-* + Latin *nocuus* = harmful]

innovation *NOUN* **innovations** **1** introducing new things or new methods. **2** a completely new process or way of doing things that has just been introduced.
▷ **innovative** *adjective* **innovator** *noun*
[from *in-* + Latin *novus* = new]

innuendo *NOUN* **innuendoes** indirect reference to something insulting or rude.
[Latin, = by nodding at or pointing to]

innumerable *ADJECTIVE* too many to be counted.
[from *in-* + Latin *numerare* = to count or number]

inoculate *VERB* **inoculates, inoculating, inoculated** inject or treat someone with a vaccine or serum as a protection against a disease.
▷ **inoculation** *noun*
[from Latin *inoculare* = implant]
USAGE Note the spelling of this word. It has one 'n' and one 'c'.

inoffensive *ADJECTIVE* harmless.

inordinate *ADJECTIVE* excessive.
▷ **inordinately** *adverb*
[from *in-* + Latin *ordinare* = ordain]

inorganic *ADJECTIVE* not of living organisms; of mineral origin.

in-patient *NOUN* **in-patients** a patient who stays at a hospital for treatment.

input *NOUN* what is put into something, especially data put into a computer.
▷ **input** *verb*

inquest *NOUN* **inquests** an official inquiry to find out how a person died.
[from old French; related to *inquire*]

inquire *VERB* **inquires, inquiring, inquired** **1** investigate something carefully. **2** ask for information.
[from *in-* + Latin *quaerere* = seek]
USAGE You can spell this word *inquire* or *enquire* in either of its meanings. It is probably more common for *inquire* to be used for 'investigate' and *enquire* to be used for 'ask for information', but there is no real need to follow this distinction.

inquiry *NOUN* **inquiries 1** an official investigation. **2** a question.

inquisition *NOUN* **inquisitions** a detailed questioning or investigation.
▷ **inquisitor** *noun*
- **the Inquisition** a council of the Roman Catholic Church in the Middle Ages, especially the very severe one in Spain, set up to discover and punish heretics.
[same origin as *inquire*]

inquisitive *ADJECTIVE* always asking questions or trying to find out things.
▷ **inquisitively** *adverb*
[same origin as *inquire*]

inroads *PLURAL NOUN*
- **make inroads on** or **into** use up large quantities of stores or resources.
[from *in* (adverb) + an old sense of *road* = riding]

inrush *NOUN* **inrushes** a sudden rushing in.

insane *ADJECTIVE* not sane; mad.
▷ **insanely** *adverb* **insanity** *noun*

insanitary *ADJECTIVE* unclean and likely to be harmful to health.

insatiable (*say* in-say-sha-bul) *ADJECTIVE* impossible to satisfy • *an insatiable appetite.*
[from *in-* + Latin *satiare* = satiate]

inscribe *VERB* **inscribes, inscribing, inscribed** write or carve words etc. on something.
[from *in-* + Latin *scribere* = write]

inscription *NOUN* **inscriptions** words written or carved on a monument, coin, stone, etc. or written in the front of a book.

inscrutable *ADJECTIVE* mysterious; impossible to interpret • *an inscrutable smile.*
[from *in-* + Latin *scrutari* = to search]

insect *NOUN* **insects** a small animal with six legs, no backbone, and a body divided into three parts (head, thorax, abdomen).
[from Latin *insectum* = cut up]

insecticide *NOUN* **insecticides** a substance for killing insects.
[from *insect* + *-cide*]

insectivorous *ADJECTIVE* feeding on insects and other small invertebrate creatures.
▷ **insectivore** *noun*

insecure *ADJECTIVE* **1** not secure or safe. **2** lacking confidence about yourself.
▷ **insecurely** *adverb* **insecurity** *noun*

inseminate *VERB* **inseminates, inseminating, inseminated** insert semen into the womb.
▷ **insemination** *noun*
[from *in-* + Latin *seminare* = to sow]

insensible *ADJECTIVE* **1** unconscious. **2** unaware of something • *He was insensible of her needs.*

insensitive *ADJECTIVE* not sensitive or thinking about other people's feelings.
▷ **insensitively** *adverb* **insensitivity** *noun*

a b c d e f g h i j k l m n o p q r s t u v w x y z

inseparable *ADJECTIVE* **1** not able to be separated. **2** liking to be constantly together • *inseparable friends.*
▷ **inseparably** *adverb*

insert *VERB* **inserts, inserting, inserted** put a thing into something else.
▷ **insert** *noun* **insertion** *noun*
[from *in-* + Latin *serere* = to plant]

inshore *ADVERB & ADJECTIVE* near or nearer to the shore.

inside *NOUN* **insides** the inner side, surface, or part.
- **inside out** with the inside turned to face outwards.
- **insides** (*informal*) the organs in the abdomen; the stomach and bowels.

inside *ADJECTIVE* on or coming from the inside; in or nearest to the middle.

inside *ADVERB & PREPOSITION* on or to the inside of something; in • *Come inside. It's inside that box.*

insider *NOUN* **insiders** a member of a certain group, especially someone with access to private information.

insidious *ADJECTIVE* causing harm gradually, without being noticed.
▷ **insidiously** *adverb*
[from Latin *insidiae* = an ambush]

insight *NOUN* **insights 1** being able to perceive the truth about things. **2** an understanding of something.

insignia *SINGULAR & PLURAL NOUN* a badge or symbol that shows that you belong to something or hold a particular office.
[from Latin; related to *sign*]

insignificant *ADJECTIVE* not important or influential.
▷ **insignificance** *noun*

insincere *ADJECTIVE* not sincere.
▷ **insincerely** *adverb* **insincerity** *noun*

insinuate *VERB* **insinuates, insinuating, insinuated 1** hint something unpleasant. **2** introduce a thing or yourself gradually or craftily into a place.
▷ **insinuation** *noun*
[from *in-* + Latin *sinuare* = to curve]

insipid *ADJECTIVE* **1** lacking flavour. **2** not lively or interesting.
▷ **insipidity** *noun*
[from *in-* + Latin *sapidus* = having flavour]

insist *VERB* **insists, insisting, insisted** be very firm in saying or asking for something • *I insist on seeing the manager.*
▷ **insistent** *adjective* **insistence** *noun*
[from *in-* + Latin *sistere* = to stand]

in situ (*say* in **sit**-yoo) *ADVERB* in its original place.
[Latin]

insolent *ADJECTIVE* very rude and insulting.
▷ **insolently** *adverb* **insolence** *noun*
[from Latin *insolentia* = pride]

insoluble *ADJECTIVE* **1** impossible to solve • *an insoluble problem.* **2** impossible to dissolve.
▷ **insolubility** *noun*
[from *in-* + Latin *solubilis* = soluble]

insolvent *ADJECTIVE* unable to pay your debts.
▷ **insolvency** *noun*

insomnia *NOUN* being unable to sleep.
▷ **insomniac** *noun*
[from *in-* + Latin *somnus* = sleep]

inspect *VERB* **inspects, inspecting, inspected** examine something carefully and critically.
▷ **inspection** *noun*
[from *in-* + Latin *specere* = to look]

inspector *NOUN* **inspectors 1** a person whose job is to inspect or supervise things. **2** a police officer ranking next above a sergeant.

inspiration *NOUN* **inspirations 1** a sudden brilliant idea. **2** inspiring; an inspiring influence.

inspire *VERB* **inspires, inspiring, inspired** fill a person with ideas or enthusiasm or creative feeling • *The applause inspired us with confidence.*
[from *in-* + Latin *spirare* = breathe]

instability *NOUN* lack of stability.

install *VERB* **installs, installing, installed 1** put something in position and ready to use • *They installed central heating.* **2** put a person into an important position with a ceremony • *He was installed as pope.*
▷ **installation** *noun*
[from *in-* + Latin *stallum* = a place or position]

instalment *NOUN* **instalments** each of the parts in which something is given or paid for over a period of time • *an instalment of a serial; You can pay by instalments.*
[from old French]

instance *NOUN* **instances** an example.
- **for instance** for example.
[from Latin]

instant *ADJECTIVE* **1** happening immediately • *an instant success.* **2** (said about food) designed to be prepared quickly and easily • *instant coffee.*
▷ **instantly** *adverb*

instant *NOUN* **instants** a moment • *not an instant too soon.*
[from Latin *instans* = urgent]

instantaneous *ADJECTIVE* happening immediately.
▷ **instantaneously** *adverb*

instead *ADVERB* in place of something else.
[from *in-* + *stead* = a place]

instep *NOUN* **insteps** the top of the foot between the toes and the ankle.
[origin unknown]

instigate *VERB* **instigates, instigating, instigated** stir up; cause something to be done • *instigate a rebellion.*
▷ **instigation** *noun* **instigator** *noun*
[same origin as *instinct*]

instil *VERB* **instils, instilling, instilled** put ideas into a person's mind gradually.
[from *in-* + Latin *stilla* = a drop]

instinct *NOUN* **instincts** a natural tendency or ability • *Birds fly by instinct.*
▷ **instinctive** *adjective* **instinctively** *adverb*
[from Latin *instinguere* = urge on]

institute *NOUN* **institutes** a society or organization; the building used by this.

institute *VERB* **institutes, instituting, instituted** establish or found something; start an inquiry or custom etc.
[from *in-* + Latin *statuere* = set up]

institution *NOUN* **institutions 1** an institute; a public organization, e.g. a hospital or university. **2** a habit or custom. **3** instituting something.
▷ **institutional** *adjective*

instruct *VERB* **instructs, instructing, instructed 1** teach a person a subject or skill. **2** inform. **3** tell a person what he or she must do.
▷ **instructor** *noun*
[from Latin *instruere* = to build up or prepare]

instruction *NOUN* **instructions 1** teaching a subject or skill. **2** an order or piece of information • *Follow the instructions carefully.*
▷ **instructional** *adjective*

instructive *ADJECTIVE* giving knowledge.

instrument *NOUN* **instruments 1** a device for producing musical sounds. **2** a tool used for delicate or scientific work. **3** a measuring device.
[same origin as *instruct*]

instrumental *ADJECTIVE* **1** performed on musical instruments, without singing. **2** being the means of doing something • *She was instrumental in getting me a job.*

instrumentalist *NOUN* **instrumentalists** a person who plays a musical instrument.

insubordinate *ADJECTIVE* disobedient or rebellious.
▷ **insubordination** *noun*

insufferable *ADJECTIVE* unbearable.

insufficient *ADJECTIVE* not sufficient.

insular *ADJECTIVE* **1** to do with or like an island. **2** narrow-minded.
[same origin as *insulate*]

insulate *VERB* **insulates, insulating, insulated** cover or protect something to prevent heat, cold, or electricity etc. from passing in or out.
▷ **insulation** *noun* **insulator** *noun*
[from Latin *insula* = island]

insulin *NOUN* a substance that controls the amount of sugar in the blood. The lack of insulin causes diabetes.
[from Latin]

insult (*say* in-**sult**) *VERB* **insults, insulting, insulted** hurt a person's feelings or pride.

insult (*say* **in**-sult) *NOUN* **insults** an insulting remark or action.
[from Latin]

insuperable *ADJECTIVE* unable to be overcome • *an insuperable difficulty.*
[from *in-* + Latin *superare* = to overcome]

insurance *NOUN* an agreement to compensate someone for a loss, damage, or injury etc., in return for a payment (called a *premium*) made in advance.

insure *VERB* **insures, insuring, insured** protect with insurance • *Is your jewellery insured?*
[a different spelling of *ensure*]
USAGE Do not confuse with **ensure**.

insurgent *NOUN* **insurgents** a rebel.
▷ **insurgent** *adjective*
[from *in-* = against + Latin *surgere* = to rise]

insurmountable *ADJECTIVE* unable to be overcome.

insurrection *NOUN* **insurrections** a rebellion.
[same origin as *insurgent*]

intact *ADJECTIVE* not damaged; complete.
[from *in-* + Latin *tactum* = touched]

intake *NOUN* **intakes 1** taking something in. **2** the number of people or things taken in • *We have a high intake of students this year.*

intangible *ADJECTIVE* not able to be touched; not solid.

integer *NOUN* **integers** a whole number (e.g. 0, 3, 19), not a fraction.
[Latin, = whole]

integral (*say* **in**-tig-ral) *ADJECTIVE* **1** being an essential part of a whole thing • *An engine is an integral part of a car.* **2** whole or complete.
[same origin as *integer*]

integrate *VERB* **integrates, integrating, integrated 1** make parts into a whole; combine. **2** bring people together harmoniously into a single community.
▷ **integration** *noun*
[from Latin *integrare* = make whole]

integrity (*say* in-**teg**-rit-ee) *NOUN* honesty.
[from Latin *integritas* = wholeness or purity]

intellect *NOUN* **intellects** the ability to think and work things out with the mind.
[same origin as *intelligent*]

intellectual *ADJECTIVE* **1** to do with or using the intellect. **2** having a good intellect and a liking for knowledge.
▷ **intellectually** *adverb*

intellectual *NOUN* **intellectuals** an intellectual person.

intelligence *NOUN* **1** being intelligent. **2** information, especially of military value; the people who collect and study this information.

intelligent *ADJECTIVE* able to learn and understand things; having great mental ability.
▷ **intelligently** *adverb*
[from Latin *intelligere* = understand]

intelligentsia *NOUN* intellectual people regarded as a group.
[via Russian and Polish from Latin]

intelligible *ADJECTIVE* able to be understood.
▷ **intelligibly** *adverb* **intelligibility** *noun*
[same origin as *intelligent*]

intend *VERB* **intends, intending, intended 1** have something in mind as what you want to do. **2** plan that something should be used or understood in a particular way.
[from Latin *intendere* = stretch, aim]

intense *ADJECTIVE* **1** very strong or great. **2** feeling things very strongly and seriously • *He's a very intense young man.*
▷ **intensely** *adverb* **intensity** *noun*
[from Latin *intensus* = stretched tight]

intensify *VERB* **intensifies, intensifying, intensified** make or become more intense.
▷ **intensification** *noun*

intensive *ADJECTIVE* concentrated; using a lot of effort over a short time.
▷ **intensively** *adverb*

intensive care *NOUN* medical treatment of a patient who is dangerously ill, with constant supervision.

intent *NOUN* **intents** intention.

intent *ADJECTIVE* with concentrated attention; very interested.
▷ **intently** *adverb*
- **intent on** eager or determined.
[same origin as *intend*]

intention *NOUN* **intentions** what a person intends; a purpose or plan.

intentional *ADJECTIVE* deliberate, not accidental.
▷ **intentionally** *adverb*

inter *VERB* **inters, interring, interred** bury.
[from *in-* + Latin *terra* = earth]

inter- *PREFIX* between; among.
[from Latin]

interact *VERB* **interacts, interacting, interacted** have an effect upon one another.
▷ **interaction** *noun*

interactive *ADJECTIVE* (*in computing*) allowing information to be sent immediately in either direction between a computer system and its user.

interbreed *VERB* **interbreeds, interbreeding, interbred** breed with each other; cross-breed.

intercede *VERB* **intercedes, interceding, interceded** intervene on behalf of another person or as a peacemaker.
▷ **intercession** *noun*
[from *inter-* + Latin *cedere* = go]

intercept *VERB* **intercepts, intercepting, intercepted** stop or catch a person or thing that is going from one place to another.
▷ **interception** *noun*
[from *inter-* + Latin *captum* = seized]

interchange *VERB* **interchanges, interchanging, interchanged** **1** put each of two things into the other's place. **2** exchange things. **3** alternate.
▷ **interchangeable** *adjective*

interchange *NOUN* **interchanges** **1** interchanging. **2** a road junction where vehicles can move from one motorway etc. to another.

intercom *NOUN* **intercoms** (*informal*) a system of communication between rooms or compartments, operating rather like a telephone.
[short for *intercommunication*]

intercourse *NOUN* **1** communication or dealings between people. **2** sexual intercourse.
[from Latin *intercursus* = running between]

interdependent *ADJECTIVE* dependent upon each other.

interest *NOUN* **interests** **1** a feeling of wanting to know about or help with something. **2** a thing that interests somebody • *Science fiction is one of my interests.* **3** an advantage or benefit • *She looks after her own interests.* **4** money paid regularly in return for money lent or deposited.

interest *VERB* **interests, interesting, interested** attract a person's interest.
▷ **interested** *adjective* **interesting** *adjective* **interestingly** *adverb*
[Latin, = it matters]

interface *NOUN* **interfaces** a connection between two parts of a computer system.

interfere *VERB* **interferes, interfering, interfered** **1** take part in something that has nothing to do with you. **2** get in the way; obstruct.
[from *inter-* + Latin *ferire* = to strike]

interference *NOUN* **1** interfering. **2** a crackling or distorting of a radio or television signal.

interim *NOUN* an interval of time between two events.

interim *ADJECTIVE* in the interim; temporary • *an interim arrangement.*
[Latin, = meanwhile]

interior *ADJECTIVE* inner.

interior *NOUN* **interiors** the inside of something; the central or inland part of a country.
[Latin, = further in]

interject *VERB* **interjects, interjecting, interjected** break in with a remark while someone is speaking.
[from *inter-* + Latin *jactum* = thrown]

interjection *NOUN* **interjections** a word or words exclaimed expressing joy or pain or surprise, such as *oh!* or *wow!* or *good heavens!*

interlock *VERB* **interlocks, interlocking, interlocked** fit into each other.
[from *inter-* + *lock*[1]]

interloper *NOUN* **interlopers** an intruder.
[from *inter-* + Dutch = runner]

interlude *NOUN* **interludes** **1** an interval. **2** something happening in an interval or between other events.
[from *inter-* + Latin *ludus* = game]

intermediary *NOUN* **intermediaries** someone who tries to settle a dispute by negotiating with both sides; a mediator.
[from French; related to *intermediate*]

intermediate *ADJECTIVE* coming between two things in time, place, or order.
[from *inter-* + Latin *medius* = middle]

A B C D E F G H I J K L M N O P Q R S T U V W X Y Z

interment *NOUN* **interments** burial.
USAGE Do not confuse with **internment**.

interminable *ADJECTIVE* seeming to be endless; long and boring.
▷ **interminably** *adverb*
[from *in-* + Latin *terminare* = to limit or end]

intermission *NOUN* **intermissions** an interval, especially between parts of a film.
[same origin as *intermittent*]

intermittent *ADJECTIVE* happening at intervals; not continuous.
▷ **intermittently** *adverb*
[from *inter-* + Latin *mittere* = to let go]

intern *VERB* **interns, interning, interned** imprison in a special camp or area, usually in wartime.
[from French]

internal *ADJECTIVE* inside.
▷ **internally** *adverb*
[from Latin]

internal-combustion engine *NOUN* **internal-combustion engines** an engine that produces power by burning fuel inside the engine itself.

international *ADJECTIVE* to do with or belonging to more than one country; agreed between nations.
▷ **internationally** *adverb*

international *NOUN* **internationals 1** a sports contest between teams representing different countries. **2** a sports player who plays for his or her country.

Internet *NOUN* an international computer network that allows users all over the world to communicate and exchange information.

internment *NOUN* being interned.
USAGE Do not confuse with **interment**.

interplanetary *ADJECTIVE* between planets.

interplay *NOUN* the way two things have an effect on each other.

interpolate *VERB* **interpolates, interpolating, interpolated 1** interject a remark in a conversation. **2** insert words; put terms into a mathematical series.
▷ **interpolation** *noun*
[from Latin *interpolare* = redecorate or smarten up]

interpose *VERB* **interposes, interposing, interposed** place something between two things.
[from *inter-* + Latin *positum* = put]

interpret *VERB* **interprets, interpreting, interpreted 1** explain what something means. **2** translate what someone says into another language orally. **3** perform music etc. in a way that shows your feelings about its meaning.
▷ **interpretation** *noun* **interpreter** *noun*
[from Latin]

interregnum *NOUN* **interregnums** or **interregna** an interval between the reign of one ruler and that of his or her successor.
[from *inter-* + Latin *regnum* = reign]

interrogate *VERB* **interrogates, interrogating, interrogated** question someone closely or formally.
▷ **interrogation** *noun* **interrogator** *noun*
[from *inter-* + Latin *rogare* = ask]

interrogative *ADJECTIVE* questioning; expressing a question.
▷ **interrogatory** *adjective*

interrupt *VERB* **interrupts, interrupting, interrupted 1** break in on what someone is saying by inserting a remark. **2** prevent something from continuing.
▷ **interruption** *noun*
[from *inter-* + Latin *ruptum* = broken]

intersect *VERB* **intersects, intersecting, intersected 1** divide a thing by passing or lying across it. **2** (said about lines or roads etc.) cross each other.
▷ **intersection** *noun*
[from *inter-* + Latin *sectum* = cut]

intersperse *VERB* **intersperses, interspersing, interspersed** insert things here and there in something.
[from *inter-* + Latin *sparsum* = scattered]

interval *NOUN* **intervals 1** a time between two events or parts of a play etc. **2** a space between two things. **3** (*in music*) the musical difference between the pitches of two notes.
- **at intervals** with some time or distance between each one.
[from Latin *intervallum* = space between ramparts]

intervene *VERB* **intervenes, intervening, intervened** 1 come between two events • *in the intervening years.* 2 interrupt a discussion or fight etc. to try and stop it or change its result.
▷ **intervention** *noun*
[from *inter-* + Latin *venire* = come]

interview *NOUN* **interviews** a formal meeting with someone to ask him or her questions or to obtain information.

interview *VERB* **interviews, interviewing, interviewed** hold an interview with someone.
▷ **interviewer** *noun*
[from *inter-* + French *voir* = see]

intestine *NOUN* **intestines** the long tube along which food passes while being absorbed by the body, between the stomach and the anus.
▷ **intestinal** *adjective*
[from Latin *intestinus* = internal]

intimate (*say* in-tim-at) *ADJECTIVE* 1 very friendly with someone. 2 private and personal • *intimate thoughts.* 3 detailed • *an intimate knowledge of the country.*
▷ **intimately** *adverb* **intimacy** *noun*

intimate (*say* in-tim-ayt) *VERB* **intimates, intimating, intimated** hint at something.
▷ **intimation** *noun*
[from Latin *intimus* = close friend]

intimidate *VERB* **intimidates, intimidating, intimidated** frighten a person by threats into doing something.
▷ **intimidation** *noun*
[from *in-* + Latin *timidus* = timid]

into *PREPOSITION* used to express 1 movement to the inside (*Go into the house*), 2 change of condition or occupation etc. (*It broke into pieces. She went into politics*), 3 (in division) *4 into 20* = 20 divided by 4.

intolerable *ADJECTIVE* unbearable.
▷ **intolerably** *adverb*

intolerant *ADJECTIVE* not tolerant.
▷ **intolerantly** *adverb* **intolerance** *noun*

intonation *NOUN* **intonations** 1 the tone or pitch of the voice in speaking. 2 intoning.

intone *VERB* **intones, intoning, intoned** recite in a chanting voice.
[from *in-* + Latin *tonus* = tone]

intoxicate *VERB* **intoxicates, intoxicating, intoxicated** make a person drunk or very excited.
▷ **intoxication** *noun*
[from *in-* + Latin *toxicum* = poison]

intra- *PREFIX* within.
[from Latin]

intractable *ADJECTIVE* unmanageable; difficult to deal with or control.
▷ **intractability** *noun*
[from *in-* + Latin *tractare* = to handle]

intransigent *ADJECTIVE* stubborn.
▷ **intransigence** *noun*
[from *in-* + Latin *transigere* = come to an understanding]

intransitive *ADJECTIVE* (said about a verb) used without a direct object after it, e.g. *hear* in *we can hear* (but not in *we can hear you*). (COMPARE **transitive**)
▷ **intransitively** *adverb*
[from *in-* + Latin *transitivus* = passing over]

intravenous (*say* in-tra-veen-us) *ADJECTIVE* directly into a vein.
[from *intra-* + Latin *vena* = vein]

intrepid *ADJECTIVE* fearless and brave.
▷ **intrepidly** *adverb* **intrepidity** *noun*
[from *in-* + Latin *trepidus* = alarmed]

intricate *ADJECTIVE* very complicated.
▷ **intricately** *adverb* **intricacy** *noun*
[from Latin *intricatus* = entangled]

intrigue (*say* in-treeg) *VERB* **intrigues, intriguing, intrigued** 1 interest someone very much • *The subject intrigues me.* 2 plot with someone in an underhand way.

intrigue *NOUN* **intrigues** 1 plotting; an underhand plot. 2 (*old use*) a secret love affair.
[from Italian; related to *intricate*]

intrinsic *ADJECTIVE* being part of the essential nature or character of something • *The coin has little intrinsic value.*
▷ **intrinsically** *adverb*
[from Latin *intrinsecus* = inwardly or inwards]

intro- *PREFIX* into; inwards.
[from Latin]

introduce *VERB* **introduces, introducing, introduced** **1** bring an idea or practice into use. **2** make a person known to other people. **3** announce a broadcast, speaker, etc.
[from *intro-* + Latin *ducere* = to lead]

introduction *NOUN* **introductions** **1** introducing somebody or something. **2** an explanation put at the beginning of a book or speech etc.
▷ **introductory** *adjective*

introspective *ADJECTIVE* examining your own thoughts and feelings.
▷ **introspection** *noun*
[from *intro-* + Latin *specere* = to look]

introvert *NOUN* **introverts** a shy person who does not like to talk about his or her own thoughts and feelings with other people. (The opposite is **extrovert**)
▷ **introverted** *adjective*
[from *intro-* + Latin *vertere* = to turn]

intrude *VERB* **intrudes, intruding, intruded** come in or join in without being wanted.
▷ **intrusion** *noun* **intrusive** *adjective*
[from *in-* + Latin *trudere* = to push]

intruder *NOUN* **intruders 1** someone who intrudes. **2** a burglar.

intuition *NOUN* the power to know or understand things without having to think hard or without being taught.
▷ **intuitive** *adjective* **intuitively** *adverb*
[from *in-* + Latin *tueri* = to look]

Inuit (*say* in-yoo-it) *NOUN* **Inuit 1** a member of a people living in northern Canada and Greenland; an Eskimo. **2** the language of the Inuit.
[Inuit, = people]
USAGE See note at **Eskimo**.

inundate *VERB* **inundates, inundating, inundated** flood or overwhelm a place • *We've been inundated with letters about the programme.*
▷ **inundation** *noun*
[from *in-* + Latin *unda* = a wave]

inure (*say* in-yoor) *VERB* **inures, inuring, inured** accustom someone to something unpleasant • *I've become inured to criticism by now.*
[from old French]

invade *VERB* **invades, invading, invaded** **1** attack and enter a country etc. **2** crowd into a place • *Tourists invade Oxford in summer.*
▷ **invader** *noun*
[from *in-* + Latin *vadere* = go]

invalid (*say* in-va-leed) *NOUN* **invalids** a person who is ill or who is weakened by illness.

invalid (*say* in-val-id) *ADJECTIVE* not valid • *This passport is invalid.*
▷ **invalidity** *noun*
[from *in-* + Latin *validus* = strong or powerful]

invalidate *VERB* **invalidates, invalidating, invalidated** make a thing invalid.
▷ **invalidation** *noun*

invaluable *ADJECTIVE* having a value that is too great to be measured; extremely valuable.
[from *in-* + *value* + *-able*]

invariable *ADJECTIVE* not variable; never changing.

invariably *ADVERB* without exception; always.

invasion *NOUN* **invasions** attacking and entering a country etc.
[same origin as *invade*]

invective *NOUN* abusive words.
[from Latin *invehere* = attack in words]

inveigle (*say* in-vay-gul) *VERB* **inveigles, inveigling, inveigled** entice.
▷ **inveiglement** *noun*
[from old French *aveugler* = to blind]

invent *VERB* **invents, inventing, invented** **1** be the first person to make or think of a particular thing. **2** make up a false story • *She had to invent an excuse.*
▷ **invention** *noun* **inventor** *noun* **inventive** *adjective*
[from *in-* + Latin *venire* = come]

inventory (*say* in-ven-ter-ee) *NOUN* **inventories** a detailed list of goods or furniture.
[from Latin *inventarium* = list of things found]

inverse *ADJECTIVE* opposite or reverse.
▷ **inversely** *adverb*
[same origin as *invert*]

invert *VERB* **inverts, inverting, inverted** turn something upside down.
▷ **inversion** *noun*
[from *in-* + Latin *vertere* = to turn]

invertebrate *NOUN* **invertebrates** an animal without a backbone.
▷ **invertebrate** *adjective*

inverted commas *PLURAL NOUN* punctuation marks " " or ' ' put round quotations and spoken words.

invest *VERB* **invests, investing, invested**
1 use money to make a profit, e.g. by lending it in return for interest to be paid, or by buying stocks and shares or property.
2 give somebody an honour, medal, or special title in a formal ceremony.
▷ **investor** *noun*
[from Latin *investire* = to clothe]

investigate *VERB* **investigates, investigating, investigated** find out as much as you can about something; make a systematic inquiry.
▷ **investigation** *noun* **investigator** *noun* **investigative** *adjective*
[from Latin]

investiture *NOUN* **investitures** the process or ceremony of investing someone with an honour etc.

investment *NOUN* **investments 1** an amount of money invested. **2** something in which money is invested • *Property is a good investment.*

inveterate *ADJECTIVE* firmly established; habitual • *an inveterate gambler.*
[from Latin *inveterare* = to make old]

invidious *ADJECTIVE* causing resentment because of unfairness.
[from Latin *invidia* = bad feeling or envy]

invigilate *VERB* **invigilates, invigilating, invigilated** supervise candidates at an examination.
▷ **invigilation** *noun* **invigilator** *noun*
[from *in-* + Latin *vigilare* = to watch]

invigorate *VERB* **invigorates, invigorating, invigorated** give a person strength or courage. (COMPARE **vigour**)
[from *in-* + Latin *vigor* = vigour]

invincible *ADJECTIVE* not able to be defeated.
▷ **invincibly** *adverb* **invincibility** *noun*
[from *in-* + Latin *vincere* = conquer]

invisible *ADJECTIVE* not visible; not able to be seen.
▷ **invisibly** *adverb* **invisibility** *noun*

invite *VERB* **invites, inviting, invited 1** ask a person to come or do something. **2** be likely to cause something to happen • *You are inviting disaster.*
▷ **invitation** *noun*
[from Latin]

inviting *ADJECTIVE* attractive or tempting.
▷ **invitingly** *adverb*

invoice *NOUN* **invoices** a list of goods sent or work done, with the prices charged.
[from French *envoyer* = send]

invoke *VERB* **invokes, invoking, invoked**
1 appeal to a law or someone's authority for help or protection. **2** call upon a god in prayer asking for help etc.
▷ **invocation** *noun*
[from *in-* + Latin *vocare* = to call]

involuntary *ADJECTIVE* not deliberate; unintentional.
▷ **involuntarily** *adverb*

involve *VERB* **involves, involving, involved 1** have as a part; make a thing necessary • *The job involves hard work.*
2 make someone share or take part in something • *They involved us in their charity work.*
▷ **involvement** *noun*
[from *in-* + Latin *volvere* = to roll]

involved *ADJECTIVE* **1** complicated.
2 concerned; sharing in something.

invulnerable *ADJECTIVE* not vulnerable.

inward *ADJECTIVE* **1** on the inside. **2** going or facing inwards.

inward *ADVERB* inwards.
[from Old English]

inwardly *ADVERB* in your thoughts; privately.

inwards *ADVERB* towards the inside.

iodine *NOUN* a chemical substance used as an antiseptic.
[from Greek *iodes* = violet-coloured (because it gives off violet-coloured vapour)]

ion *NOUN* **ions** an electrically charged particle.
[from Greek]

-ion or **-sion** or **-tion** or **-xion** *SUFFIXES* form nouns meaning 'condition or action' (e.g. *dominion, dimension, attraction, pollution, inflexion*).

ionosphere (*say* I-on-os-feer) *NOUN* a region of the upper atmosphere, containing ions.

iota *NOUN* **iotas** a tiny amount of something • *There's not an iota of truth in what she says.*
[the name of *i*, the ninth and smallest letter of the Greek alphabet]

IOU *NOUN* **IOUs** a signed note acknowledging that you owe someone some money.
[short for 'I owe you']

IQ *ABBREVIATION* intelligence quotient; a number showing how a person's intelligence compares with that of an average person.

ir- *PREFIX* **1** in; into. **2** on; towards. **3** not. SEE **in-**.

IRA *ABBREVIATION* Irish Republican Army.

irascible (*say* ir-as-ib-ul) *ADJECTIVE* easily becoming angry; irritable.
[from Latin *irasci* = become angry]

irate (*say* I-rayt) *ADJECTIVE* angry.
[from Latin *ira* = anger]

iridescent *ADJECTIVE* showing rainbow-like colours.
▷ **iridescence** *noun*
[from Greek *iris* = iris or rainbow]

iris *NOUN* **irises 1** the coloured part of the eyeball. **2** a plant with long pointed leaves and large flowers.
[from Greek]

irk *VERB* **irks, irking, irked** annoy.
[probably from a Scandinavian language]

irksome *ADJECTIVE* annoying or tiresome.

iron *NOUN* **irons 1** a hard grey metal. **2** a device with a flat base that is heated for smoothing clothes or cloth. **3** a tool made of iron • *a branding iron.*
▷ **iron** *adjective*

iron *VERB* **irons, ironing, ironed** smooth clothes or cloth with an iron.
- **iron out** sort out a difficulty or problem.
[from Old English]

Iron Age *NOUN* the time when tools and weapons were made of iron.

ironic (*say* I-ron-ik) *ADJECTIVE* using irony; full of irony.
▷ **ironical** *adjective* **ironically** *adverb*

ironmonger *NOUN* **ironmongers** a shopkeeper who sells tools and other metal objects.
▷ **ironmongery** *noun*
[from *iron* + an old word *monger* = trader]

irons *PLURAL NOUN* shackles or fetters.

irony (*say* I-ron-ee) *NOUN* **ironies 1** saying the opposite of what you mean in order to emphasize it, e.g. saying 'What a lovely day' when it is pouring with rain. **2** an oddly contradictory situation • *The irony of it is that I tripped while telling someone else to be careful.*
[from Greek *eiron* = someone who pretends not to know]

irrational *ADJECTIVE* not rational; illogical.
▷ **irrationally** *adverb*

irreducible *ADJECTIVE* unable to be reduced • *an irreducible minimum.*

irrefutable (*say* ir-ef-yoo-ta-bul) *ADJECTIVE* unable to be refuted.

irregular *ADJECTIVE* **1** not regular; uneven. **2** against the rules or usual custom. **3** (said about troops) not in the regular armed forces.
▷ **irregularly** *adverb* **irregularity** *noun*

irrelevant (*say* ir-el-iv-ant) *ADJECTIVE* not relevant.
▷ **irrelevantly** *adverb* **irrelevance** *noun*

irreparable (*say* ir-ep-er-a-bul) *ADJECTIVE* unable to be repaired or replaced.
▷ **irreparably** *adverb*
[from *ir-* + Latin *reparare* = repair]

irreplaceable *ADJECTIVE* unable to be replaced.

irrepressible *ADJECTIVE* unable to be repressed; always lively and cheerful.
▷ **irrepressibly** *adverb*

irreproachable *ADJECTIVE* blameless or faultless.
▷ **irreproachably** *adverb*
[from *ir-* + French *reprocher* = reproach]

irresistible *ADJECTIVE* too strong or attractive to be resisted.
▷ **irresistibly** *adverb*

irresolute *ADJECTIVE* feeling uncertain; hesitant.
▷ **irresolutely** *adverb*

irrespective *ADJECTIVE* not taking something into account • *Prizes are awarded to winners, irrespective of age.*

irresponsible *ADJECTIVE* not showing a proper sense of responsibility.
▷ **irresponsibly** *adverb* **irresponsibility** *noun*

irretrievable *ADJECTIVE* not able to be retrieved.
▷ **irretrievably** *adverb*

irreverent *ADJECTIVE* not reverent or respectful.
▷ **irreverently** *adverb* **irreverence** *noun*

irrevocable (*say* ir-ev-ok-a-bul) *ADJECTIVE* unable to be revoked or altered.
▷ **irrevocably** *adverb*

irrigate *VERB* **irrigates, irrigating, irrigated** supply land with water so that crops can grow.
▷ **irrigation** *noun*
[from *ir-* + Latin *rigare* = to water]

irritable *ADJECTIVE* easily annoyed; bad-tempered.
▷ **irritably** *adverb* **irritability** *noun*

irritate *VERB* **irritates, irritating, irritated** **1** annoy. **2** cause itching.
▷ **irritation** *noun* **irritant** *adjective* & *noun*
[from Latin]

irrupt *VERB* **irrupts, irrupting, irrupted** enter forcibly or violently.
▷ **irruption** *noun*
[from *ir-* + Latin *ruptum* = burst]
USAGE Do not confuse with **erupt**.

-ise *SUFFIX*, SEE **-ize**.

-ish *SUFFIX* forms nouns meaning **1** 'of a certain nature' (e.g. *foolish*), **2** 'rather' (e.g. *greenish, yellowish*).

Islam *NOUN* the religion of Muslims.
▷ **Islamic** *adjective*
[Arabic, = submission to God]

island *NOUN* **islands 1** a piece of land surrounded by water. **2** something that resembles an island because it is isolated or detached • *a traffic island.*
[from Old English]

islander *NOUN* **islanders** an inhabitant of an island.

isle (*say as* I'll) *NOUN* **isles** (*poetic & in names*) an island.
[from Latin *insula* = island]

-ism *SUFFIX* forms nouns showing action from verbs ending in *-ize* (e.g. *baptism, criticism*), or condition (e.g. *heroism*).

isn't (*mainly spoken*) is not.

iso- *PREFIX* equal (as in *isobar*).
[from Greek]

isobar (*say* I-so-bar) *NOUN* **isobars** a line on a map connecting places that have the same atmospheric pressure.
[from *iso-* + Greek *baros* = weight]

isolate *VERB* **isolates, isolating, isolated** place a person or thing apart or alone; separate.
▷ **isolation** *noun*
[from Latin *insulatus* = made into an island]

isosceles (*say* I-soss-il-eez) *ADJECTIVE* an isosceles triangle has two sides of equal length.
[from *iso-* + Greek *skelos* = leg]

isotope *NOUN* **isotopes** (*in science*) a form of an element that differs from other forms in the structure of its nucleus but has the same chemical properties as the other forms.
[from *iso-* + Greek *topos* = place (because they appear in the same place in the table of chemical elements)]

ISP *ABBREVIATION* Internet service provider, a company providing individual users with a connection to the Internet.

issue *VERB* **issues, issuing, issued 1** supply; give out • *We issued one blanket to each refugee.* **2** send out • *They issued a gale warning.* **3** put out for sale; publish. **4** come or go out; flow out.

issue *NOUN* **issues 1** a subject for discussion or concern • *What are the real issues?* **2** a particular edition of a newspaper or magazine • *the Christmas issue of Radio Times.* **3** issuing something • *The issue of passports has been held up.* **4** (*formal*) children • *He died without issue.*

- **take issue with** disagree with.
[from old French; related to *exit*]

-ist *SUFFIX* forms nouns meaning 'person who does something or believes in or supports something' (e.g. *cyclist, Communist*).

isthmus (*say* iss-mus) *NOUN* **isthmuses** a narrow strip of land connecting two larger pieces of land.
[from Greek]

IT *ABBREVIATION* information technology.

it *PRONOUN* **1** the thing being talked about. **2** the player who has to catch others in a game. **3** used in statements about the weather or about circumstances etc. • *It is raining. It is six miles to York.* **4** used as an indefinite object • *Run for it!* **5** used to refer to a phrase • *It is unlikely that she will fail.*
[from Old English]

italic (*say* it-al-ik) *ADJECTIVE* printed with sloping letters (called - **italics**) *like this.*
[because this style was first used in Italy]

itch *VERB* **itches, itching, itched** **1** have or feel a tickling sensation in the skin that makes you want to scratch it. **2** long to do something.

itch *NOUN* **itches** **1** an itching feeling. **2** a longing.
▷ **itchy** *adjective* **itchiness** *noun*
[from Old English]

-ite *SUFFIX* (in scientific use) forms names of minerals (e.g. *anthracite*), explosives (e.g. *dynamite*), and salts of certain acids (e.g. *nitrite*; compare **-ate**).

item *NOUN* **items** **1** one thing in a list or group of things. **2** one piece of news, article etc. in a newspaper or bulletin.
[Latin, = just so, similarly (used to introduce each item on a list)]

itinerant (*say* it-**in**-er-ant) *ADJECTIVE* travelling from place to place • *an itinerant preacher.*
[same origin as *itinerary*]

itinerary (*say* I-**tin**-er-er-ee) *NOUN* **itineraries** a list of places to be visited on a journey; a route.
[from Latin *itinerari* = travel from place to place]

-itis *SUFFIX* forms nouns meaning inflammation of part of the body (as in *bronchitis*).
[Greek]

its *POSSESSIVE PRONOUN* belonging to it • *The cat hurt its paw.*
USAGE Do not put an apostrophe into *its* unless you mean 'it is' or 'it has' (see the next entry).

it's (*mainly spoken*) **1** it is • *It's very hot.* **2** it has • *It's broken all records.*
USAGE Do not confuse with **its**.

itself *PRONOUN* it and nothing else. (COMPARE **herself**)

- **by itself** on its own; alone.

ITV *ABBREVIATION* Independent Television.

-ive *SUFFIX* forms adjectives, chiefly from verbs (e.g. *active, explosive*).

ivory *NOUN* **1** the hard creamy-white substance that forms elephants' tusks. **2** a creamy-white colour.
[from Latin]

ivy *NOUN* **ivies** a climbing evergreen plant with shiny leaves.
[from Old English]

-ize or **-ise** *SUFFIX* forms verbs meaning 'bring or come into a certain condition' (e.g. *civilize*), or 'treat in a certain way' (e.g. *pasteurize*), or 'have a certain feeling' (e.g. *sympathize*).
[from the Greek verb- ending *-izein*, or French *-iser*]

Jj

jab *VERB* **jabs, jabbing, jabbed** poke roughly; push a thing into something.

jab *NOUN* **jabs** **1** a jabbing movement. **2** (*informal*) an injection.
[originally Scots]

jabber *VERB* **jabbers, jabbering, jabbered** speak quickly and not clearly; chatter.
▷ **jabber** *noun*
[imitating the sound]

jack *NOUN* **jacks 1** a device for lifting something heavy off the ground. **2** a playing card with a picture of a young man. **3** a small white ball aimed at in bowls.
- **jack of all trades** someone who can do many different kinds of work.

jack *VERB* **jacks, jacking, jacked** lift something with a jack.
- **jack it in** (*slang*) give up or abandon an attempt etc.
[the name *Jack*, used for various sorts of tool (as though it was a person helping you)]

jackal *NOUN* **jackals** a wild animal rather like a dog.
[from Persian]

jackass *NOUN* **jackasses 1** a male donkey. **2** a stupid person.
[from the name *Jack* + *ass*]

jackdaw *NOUN* **jackdaws** a kind of small crow.
[from the name *Jack* + Middle English *dawe* = jackdaw]

jackeroo *NOUN* **jackaroos** (*informal*) (*Australian*) a young male trainee worker on a sheep or cattle station.

jacket *NOUN* **jackets 1** a short coat, usually reaching to the hips. **2** a cover to keep the heat in a water tank etc. **3** a paper wrapper for a book. **4** the skin of a potato that is baked without being peeled.
[from old French]

jack-in-the-box *NOUN* **jack-in-the-boxes** a toy figure that springs out of a box when the lid is lifted.

jackknife *VERB* **jackknifes, jackknifing, jackknifed** if an articulated lorry jackknifes, it folds against itself in an accidental skidding movement.
[from *jackknife*, a folding knife]

jackpot *NOUN* **jackpots** an amount of prize money that increases until someone wins it.
- **hit the jackpot 1** win a large prize. **2** have remarkable luck or success.
[originally = a kitty which could be won only by playing a pair of jacks or cards of higher value: from *jack* + *pot*[1]]

Jacobean *ADJECTIVE* from the reign of James I of England (1603-25).
[from Latin *Jacobus* = James]

Jacobite *NOUN* **Jacobites** a supporter of the exiled Stuarts after the abdication of James II (1688).
[same origin as *Jacobean*]

Jacuzzi (*say* ja-koo-zi) *NOUN* **Jacuzzis** (*trademark*) a large bath in which underwater jets of water massage the body.
[named after its inventor C. *Jacuzzi*]

jade *NOUN* a green stone that is carved to make ornaments.
[from Spanish *piedra de ijada* = colic stone (because it was believed to cure diseases of the stomach)]

jaded *ADJECTIVE* tired and bored.
[from an old word *jade* = a worn-out horse]

jagged (*say* jag-id) *ADJECTIVE* having an uneven edge with sharp points.
[from Scots *jag* = stab]

jaguar *NOUN* **jaguars** a large fierce South American animal rather like a leopard.
[via Portuguese from a South American language]

jail *NOUN* **jails** a prison.

jail *VERB* **jails, jailing, jailed** put into prison.
▷ **jailer** *noun*
[from old French *jaiole* = cage or prison]

Jain (*say as* Jane) *NOUN* **Jains** a believer in an Indian religion rather like Buddhism.
[from Sanskrit]

jam *NOUN* **jams 1** a sweet food made of fruit boiled with sugar until it is thick. **2** a lot of people, cars, or logs etc. crowded together so that movement is difficult.
- **in a jam** in a difficult situation.

jam *VERB* **jams, jamming, jammed 1** make or become fixed and difficult to move • *The window has jammed.* **2** crowd or squeeze into a space. **3** push something forcibly • *I jammed the brakes on.* **4** block a broadcast by causing interference with the transmission.
[origin unknown]

jamb (*say* jam) *NOUN* **jambs** a side post of a doorway or window frame.
[from French *jambe* = leg]

jamboree *NOUN* **jamborees** a large party or celebration.
[origin unknown]

jangle *VERB* **jangles, jangling, jangled** make a loud harsh ringing sound.
▷ **jangle** *noun*
[from old French]

janitor *NOUN* **janitors** a caretaker.
[originally = doorkeeper: from Latin *janua* = door]

January *NOUN* the first month of the year.
[named after *Janus*, a Roman god of gates and beginnings, usually shown with two faces that look in opposite directions]

jar¹ *NOUN* **jars** a container made of glass or pottery.
[via French from Arabic]

jar² *VERB* **jars, jarring, jarred 1** cause an unpleasant jolt or shock. **2** sound harshly, especially in an annoying way • *Her voice really jars on me.*

jar *NOUN* **jars** a jarring effect.
[imitating the sound]

jargon *NOUN* words or expressions used by a profession or group that are difficult for other people to understand • *scientists' jargon.*
[from French]

jasmine *NOUN* a shrub with yellow or white flowers.
[via French from Arabic]

jaundice *NOUN* a disease in which the skin becomes yellow.
[from French *jaune* = yellow]

jaunt *NOUN* **jaunts** a short trip.
[origin unknown]

jaunty *ADJECTIVE* **jauntier, jauntiest** lively and cheerful.
▷ **jauntily** *adverb* **jauntiness** *noun*
[originally = stylish, elegant: from French, related to *gentle*]

javelin *NOUN* **javelins** a lightweight spear.
[from French]

jaw *NOUN* **jaws 1** either of the two bones that form the framework of the mouth. **2** the lower part of the face. **3** something shaped like the jaws or used for gripping things.
[from old French]

jay *NOUN* **jays** a noisy brightly-coloured bird.
[from French]

jaywalker *NOUN* **jaywalkers** a person who dangerously walks across a road without looking out for traffic.
▷ **jaywalking** *noun*
[from an American meaning of *jay* = fool]

jazz *NOUN* a kind of music with strong rhythm, often improvised.
▷ **jazzy** *adjective*
- **jazz up** make more lively or interesting.
[probably a black American word]

jealous *ADJECTIVE* **1** unhappy or resentful because you feel that someone is your rival or is better or luckier than yourself. **2** careful in keeping something • *He is very jealous of his own rights.*
▷ **jealously** *adverb* **jealousy** *noun*
[from French]

jeans *PLURAL NOUN* trousers made of strong cotton fabric.
[from *Genoa*, a city in Italy, where such a cloth was once made]

Jeep *NOUN* **Jeeps** (*trademark*) a small sturdy motor vehicle with four-wheel drive, especially one used in the army.
[from *G.P.*, short for 'general purpose']

jeer *VERB* **jeers, jeering, jeered** laugh or shout at somebody rudely or scornfully.
▷ **jeer** *noun*
[origin unknown]

jelly *NOUN* **jellies 1** a soft transparent food. **2** any soft slippery substance.
▷ **jellied** *adjective*
[from Latin *gelare* = freeze]

jellyfish *NOUN* **jellyfish** a sea animal with a body like jelly.

jemmy *NOUN* **jemmies** a burglar's crowbar.
[from the name *Jimmy* (compare *jack*)]

jeopardize (*say* jep-er-dyz) *VERB* **jeopardizes, jeopardizing, jeopardized** put someone in danger; put something at risk.

jeopardy (*say* jep-er-dee) *NOUN* danger of harm or failure.
[from old French]

jerk *VERB* **jerks, jerking, jerked 1** make a sudden sharp movement. **2** pull something suddenly.

jerk *NOUN* **jerks 1** a sudden sharp movement. **2** (*slang*) a stupid person.
▷ **jerky** *adjective* **jerkily** *adverb*
[origin unknown]

jerkin *NOUN* **jerkins** a sleeveless jacket.
[origin unknown]

jerry-built *ADJECTIVE* built badly and with poor materials.
[origin unknown]

jersey *NOUN* **jerseys 1** a pullover with sleeves. **2** a plain machine-knitted material used for making clothes.
[originally = a woollen cloth made in *Jersey*, one of the Channel Islands]

jest *NOUN* **jests** a joke.

jest *VERB* **jests, jesting, jested** make jokes.
[from Middle English *gest* = a story]

jester *NOUN* **jesters** a professional entertainer at a royal court in the Middle Ages.

jet[1] *NOUN* **jets 1** a stream of water, gas, flame, etc. shot out from a narrow opening. **2** a spout or nozzle from which a jet comes. **3** an aircraft driven by engines that send out a high-speed jet of hot gases at the back.

jet *VERB* **jets, jetting, jetted 1** come or send out in a strong stream. **2** (*informal*) travel in a jet aircraft.
[from French *jeter* = to throw]

jet[2] *NOUN* **1** a hard black mineral substance. **2** a deep glossy black colour.
[from old French]

jet lag *NOUN* extreme tiredness that a person feels after a long flight between different time zones.

jetsam *NOUN* goods thrown overboard and washed ashore from a ship in distress.
[from *jettison*]

jettison *VERB* **jettisons, jettisoning, jettisoned 1** throw something overboard. **2** get rid of something that is no longer wanted. **3** release or drop something from an aircraft or spacecraft in flight.
[same origin as *jet*[1]]

jetty *NOUN* **jetties** a small landing stage.
[same origin as *jet*[1]]

Jew *NOUN* **Jews 1** a member of a people descended from the ancient tribes of Israel. **2** someone who believes in Judaism.
▷ **Jewish** *adjective*
[from Hebrew *yehudi* = belonging to the tribe of Judah (the founder of one of the ten tribes of ancient Israel)]

jewel *NOUN* **jewels 1** a precious stone. **2** an ornament containing precious stones.
▷ **jewelled** *adjective*
[from old French]

jeweller *NOUN* **jewellers** a person who sells or makes jewellery.

jewellery *NOUN* jewels and similar ornaments for wearing.

jib[1] *NOUN* **jibs 1** a triangular sail stretching forward from a ship's front mast. **2** the arm of a crane.
[origin unknown]

jib[2] *VERB* **jibs, jibbing, jibbed** be reluctant or unwilling to do something.
[origin unknown]

jiffy *NOUN* (*informal*) a moment.
[origin unknown]

jig *NOUN* **jigs 1** a lively jumping dance. **2** a device that holds something in place while you work on it with tools.

jig *VERB* **jigs, jigging, jigged** move up and down quickly and jerkily.
[origin unknown]

jiggle *VERB* **jiggles, jiggling, jiggled** rock or jerk something lightly.
[from *jig*]

jigsaw *NOUN* **jigsaws 1** a picture cut into irregular pieces which are then shuffled and fitted together again for amusement. **2** a saw that can cut curved shapes.

jihad *NOUN* **jihads** (in Islam) a holy war.
[Arabic]

jilt *VERB* **jilts, jilting, jilted** abandon a boyfriend or girlfriend, especially after promising to marry him or her.
[origin unknown]

jingle *VERB* **jingles, jingling, jingled** make or cause to make a tinkling sound.

jingle *NOUN* **jingles 1** a jingling sound. **2** a very simple verse or tune, especially one used in advertising.
[imitating the sound]

jingoism *NOUN* an extremely strong and unreasonable belief that your country is superior to others.
▷ **jingoistic** *adjective*
[from the saying *by jingo!*, used in a warlike popular song in the 19th century]

jinx *NOUN* **jinxes** a person or thing that is thought to bring bad luck.
[probably a variation of *jynx* = wryneck, a bird used in witchcraft]

jitters *PLURAL NOUN* (*informal*) a feeling of extreme nervousness.
▷ **jittery** *adjective*
[origin unknown]

job *NOUN* **jobs 1** work that someone does regularly to earn a living. **2** a piece of work to be done. **3** (*informal*) a difficult task • *You'll have a job to lift that box.* **4** (*informal*) a thing; a state of affairs • *It's a good job you're here.*
- **just the job** (*informal*) exactly what you want.
[origin unknown]

jobcentre *NOUN* **jobcentres** a government office with information about available jobs.

jockey *NOUN* **jockeys** a person who rides horses in races.
[pet form of the name *Jock*]

jocular *ADJECTIVE* joking.
▷ **jocularly** *adverb* **jocularity** *noun*
[from Latin *jocus* = a joke]

jodhpurs (*say* **jod**-perz) *PLURAL NOUN* trousers for horse riding, fitting closely from the knee to the ankle.
[named after *Jodhpur*, a city in India, where similar trousers are worn]

joey *NOUN* **joeys** (*Australian*) a young animal, especially a kangaroo, still young enough to be carried in its mother's pouch.
[from Aboriginal]

jog *VERB* **jogs, jogging, jogged 1** run or trot slowly, especially for exercise. **2** give something a slight push.
▷ **jogger** *noun*
- **jog someone's memory** help him or her to remember something.

jog *NOUN* **jogs 1** a slow run or trot. **2** a slight knock or push.
[same origin as *jagged*]

joggle *VERB* **joggles, joggling, joggled** shake slightly or move jerkily.
▷ **joggle** *noun*
[from *jog*]

jogtrot *NOUN* a slow steady trot.

joie de vivre (*say zh*wah der **veevr**) *NOUN* a feeling of great enjoyment of life.
[French, = joy of life]

join *VERB* **joins, joining, joined 1** put or come together; fasten or connect. **2** take part with others in doing something • *We all joined in the chorus.* **3** become a member of a group or organization etc. • *Join the Navy.*
- **join up** enlist in the armed forces.

join *NOUN* **joins** a place where things join.
[from French]

joiner *NOUN* **joiners** a person whose job is to make doors, window frames, etc. and furniture out of wood.
▷ **joinery** *noun*

joint *NOUN* **joints 1** a place where two things are joined. **2** the place where two bones fit together. **3** a large piece of meat cut ready for cooking. **4** (*informal*) a cannabis cigarette.

joint *ADJECTIVE* shared or done by two or more people, nations, etc. • *a joint project.*
▷ **jointly** *adverb*
[from French]

joist *NOUN* **joists** any of the long beams supporting a floor or ceiling.
[from old French]

joke *NOUN* **jokes** something said or done to make people laugh.

joke *VERB* **jokes, joking, joked 1** make jokes. **2** tease someone or not be serious • *I'm only joking.*
[originally slang: probably from Latin]

joker *NOUN* **jokers 1** someone who jokes. **2** an extra playing card with a jester on it.

jolly *ADJECTIVE* **jollier, jolliest** cheerful and good-humoured.
▷ **jollity** *noun*

jolly *ADVERB* (*informal*) very • *jolly good.*

jolly *VERB* **jollies, jollying, jollied** (*informal*)
- **jolly along** keep someone in a cheerful mood.
[from old French]

jolt *VERB* **jolts, jolting, jolted 1** shake or dislodge something with a sudden sharp movement. **2** move along jerkily, e.g. on a rough road. **3** give someone a shock.

jolt *NOUN* **jolts 1** a jolting movement. **2** a shock.
[origin unknown]

jostle *VERB* **jostles, jostling, jostled** push roughly, especially in a crowd.
[from *joust*]

jot *VERB* **jots, jotting, jotted** write something quickly • *Let me jot down that phone number.*
[from Greek]

jotter *NOUN* **jotters** a notepad or notebook.

joule (*say* jool) *NOUN* **joules** (*in science*) a unit of work or energy.
[named after an English scientist, James *Joule*]

journal *NOUN* **journals 1** a newspaper or magazine. **2** a diary.
[from Latin, = by day]

journalist *NOUN* **journalists** a person who writes for a newspaper or magazine.
▷ **journalism** *noun* **journalistic** *adjective*

journey *NOUN* **journeys 1** going from one place to another. **2** the distance or time taken to travel somewhere • *two days' journey.*

journey *VERB* **journeys, journeying, journeyed** make a journey.
[from French *journée* = a day's travel, from *jour* = day]

joust (*say* jowst) *VERB* **jousts, jousting, jousted** fight on horseback with lances, as knights did in medieval times.
▷ **joust** *noun*
[from old French *juster* = bring together]

jovial *ADJECTIVE* cheerful and good-humoured.
▷ **jovially** *adverb* **joviality** *noun*
[from Latin *jovialis* = to do with Jupiter (because people born under its influence were said to be cheerful)]

jowl *NOUN* **jowls 1** the jaw or cheek. **2** loose skin on the neck.
[from Old English]

joy *NOUN* **joys 1** a feeling of great pleasure or happiness. **2** a thing that causes joy. **3** satisfaction or success • *Any joy with the crossword?*
[from old French]

joyful *ADJECTIVE* very happy.
▷ **joyfully** *adverb* **joyfulness** *noun*

joyous *ADJECTIVE* full of joy; causing joy.
▷ **joyously** *adverb*

joyride *NOUN* **joyrides** a drive in a stolen car for amusement.
▷ **joyrider** *noun* **joyriding** *noun*

joystick *NOUN* **joysticks 1** the control lever of an aircraft. **2** a device for moving a cursor or image on a VDU screen, especially in computer games.

JP *ABBREVIATION* Justice of the Peace.

jubilant *ADJECTIVE* rejoicing or triumphant.
▷ **jubilantly** *adverb* **jubilation** *noun*
[from Latin *jubilans* = shouting for joy]

jubilee (*say* joo-bil-ee) *NOUN* **jubilees** a special anniversary *silver* (25th), *golden* (50th), *and diamond* (60th) *jubilee.*
[from Hebrew *yobel* = a year when slaves were freed and property returned to its owners, held in ancient Israel every 50 years]

Judaism (*say* joo-day-izm) *NOUN* the religion of the Jewish people.
[from Greek *Ioudaios* = Jew]

judder *VERB* **judders, juddering, juddered** shake noisily or violently.
[imitating the sound]

judge *NOUN* **judges 1** a person appointed to hear cases in a lawcourt and decide what should be done. **2** a person deciding who has won a contest or competition. **3** someone who is good at forming opinions or making decisions about things • *She's a good judge of character.*

judge *VERB* **judges, judging, judged 1** act as a judge. **2** form and give an opinion. **3** estimate • *He judged the distance carefully.*
[from Latin *judex* = a judge, from *jus* = law + *-dicus* = saying]

judgement *NOUN* **judgements 1** judging. **2** the decision made by a lawcourt. **3** someone's opinion. **4** the ability to judge wisely. **5** something considered as a punishment from God • *It's a judgement on you!*

judicial *ADJECTIVE* to do with lawcourts, judges, or judgements • *the British judicial system.*
▷ **judicially** *adverb*
USAGE Do not confuse with **judicious**.

judiciary (*say* joo-**dish**-er-ee) *NOUN* **judiciaries** all the judges in a country.

judicious (*say* joo-**dish**-us) *ADJECTIVE* having or showing good sense or good judgement.
▷ **judiciously** *adverb*
[same origin as *judge*]
USAGE Do not confuse with **judicial**.

judo *NOUN* a Japanese method of self-defence without using weapons.
[from Japanese *ju* = gentle + *do* = way]

jug *NOUN* **jugs** a container for holding and pouring liquids, with a handle and a lip.
[pet form of *Joan* or *Jenny*]

juggernaut *NOUN* **juggernauts** a huge lorry.
[named after a Hindu god whose image was dragged in procession on a huge wheeled vehicle]

juggle *VERB* **juggles, juggling, juggled** **1** toss and catch a number of objects skilfully for entertainment, keeping one or more in the air at any time. **2** rearrange or alter things skilfully or in order to deceive people.
▷ **juggler** *noun*
[from old French]

jugular *ADJECTIVE* to do with the throat or neck • *the jugular veins.*
[from Latin *jugulum* = throat]

juice *NOUN* **juices 1** the liquid from fruit, vegetables, or other food. **2** a liquid produced by the body • *the digestive juices.*
▷ **juicy** *adjective*
[from Latin]

jukebox *NOUN* **jukeboxes** a machine that automatically plays a record you have selected when you put a coin in.
[probably from a West African word]

July *NOUN* the seventh month of the year.
[named after Julius Caesar, who was born in this month]

jumble *VERB* **jumbles, jumbling, jumbled** mix things up into a confused mass.

jumble *NOUN* a confused mixture of things; a muddle.
[origin unknown]

jumble sale *NOUN* **jumble sales** a sale of second-hand goods.

jumbo *NOUN* **jumbos 1** something very large; a jumbo jet. **2** an elephant.
[the name of a very large elephant in London Zoo]

jumbo jet *NOUN* **jumbo jets** a very large jet aircraft.

jump *VERB* **jumps, jumping, jumped** **1** move up suddenly from the ground into the air. **2** go over something by jumping • *The horse jumped the fence.* **3** pass over something; miss out part of a book etc. **4** move suddenly in surprise. **5** pass quickly to a different place or level.
- **jump at** accept something eagerly.
- **jump on** start criticizing someone.
- **jump the gun** start before you should.
- **jump the queue** not wait your turn.

jump *NOUN* **jumps 1** a jumping movement. **2** an obstacle to jump over. **3** a sudden rise or change.
[origin unknown]

jumper *NOUN* **jumpers** a jersey.
[from French *jupe* = tunic]

jumpy *ADJECTIVE* nervous and edgy.

junction *NOUN* **junctions 1** a join. **2** a place where roads or railway lines meet.
[from Latin *junctum* = joined]

juncture *NOUN* **junctures 1** a point of time, especially in a crisis. **2** a place where things join.
[from Latin *junctura* = joint]

June *NOUN* the sixth month of the year.
[named after the Roman goddess Juno]

jungle *NOUN* **jungles** a thick tangled forest, especially in the tropics.
▷ **jungly** *adjective*
[from Hindi]

junior *ADJECTIVE* **1** younger. **2** for young children • *a junior school.* **3** lower in rank or importance • *junior officers.*

junior *NOUN* **juniors** a junior person.
[Latin, = younger]

juniper *NOUN* **junipers** an evergreen shrub.
[from Latin]

junk[1] *NOUN* rubbish; things of no value.
[origin unknown]

junk[2] *NOUN* **junks** a Chinese sailing boat.
[via Portuguese or French from Malay (a language spoken in Malaysia)]

junk food *NOUN* food that is not nourishing.

junkie *NOUN* **junkies** (*slang*) a drug addict.
[from an American meaning of *junk*[1] = heroin]

junk mail *NOUN* unwanted advertising material sent by post.

jurisdiction *NOUN* authority; official power, especially to interpret and apply the law.
[from old French; related to *judge*]

juror *NOUN* **jurors** a member of a jury.

jury *NOUN* **juries** a group of people (usually twelve) appointed to give a verdict about a case in a lawcourt.
▷ **juryman** *noun* **jurywoman** *noun*
[from Latin *jurare* = take an oath]

just *ADJECTIVE* **1** giving proper consideration to everyone's claims. **2** deserved; right in amount etc. • *a just reward.*
▷ **justly** *adverb* **justness** *noun*

just *ADVERB* **1** exactly • *It's just what I wanted.* **2** only; simply • *I just wanted to see him.* **3** barely; by only a small amount • *just below the knee.* **4** at this moment or only a little while ago • *She has just gone.*
[from Latin *justus* = rightful]

justice *NOUN* **justices 1** being just; fair treatment. **2** legal proceedings • *a court of justice.* **3** a judge or magistrate.

justify *VERB* **justifies, justifying, justified 1** show that something is fair, just, or reasonable. **2** arrange lines of printed text so that one or both edges are straight.
▷ **justifiable** *adjective* **justification** *noun*

jut *VERB* **juts, jutting, jutted** stick out.
[a different spelling of *jet*[1]]

jute *NOUN* fibre from tropical plants, used for making sacks etc.
[from Bengali (a language spoken in Bangladesh and West Bengal)]

juvenile *ADJECTIVE* **1** to do with or for young people. **2** childish.

juvenile *NOUN* **juveniles** a young person, not old enough to be legally considered an adult.
[from Latin *juvenis* = young person]

juvenile delinquent *NOUN* **juvenile delinquents** a young person who has broken the law.

juxtapose *VERB* **juxtaposes, juxtaposing, juxtaposed** put things side by side.
▷ **juxtaposition** *noun*
[from Latin *juxta* = next + *positum* = put]

Kk

kale *NOUN* a kind of cabbage.
[from Old English]

kaleidoscope (*say* kal-I-dos-kohp) *NOUN* **kaleidoscopes** a tube that you look through to see brightly coloured patterns which change as you turn the end of the tube.
▷ **kaleidoscopic** *adjective*
[from Greek *kalos* = beautiful + *eidos* = form + *skopein* = look at]

kangaroo *NOUN* **kangaroos** an Australian animal that jumps along on its strong hind legs. (See *marsupial*.)
[an Australian Aboriginal word]

kaolin *NOUN* fine white clay used in making porcelain and in medicine.
[from Chinese *gao ling* = high hill (because it was first found on a hill in northern China)]

karaoke *NOUN* a form of entertainment in which people sing well-known songs against a pre-recorded backing.
[Japanese = empty orchestra]

karate (*say* ka-**rah**-tee) *NOUN* a Japanese method of self-defence in which the hands and feet are used as weapons.
[from Japanese *kara* = empty + *te* = hand]

karoo *NOUN* **karoos** (*S. African*) a dry plateau in southern Africa.

kayak *NOUN* **kayaks** a small canoe with a covering that fits round the canoeist's waist.
[an Inuit word]

KB or **Kb** *ABBREVIATION* kilobytes.

kebab *NOUN* **kebabs** small pieces of meat or vegetables cooked on a skewer.
[from Arabic]

keel *NOUN* **keels** the long piece of wood or metal along the bottom of a boat.
- **on an even keel** steady.

keel *VERB* **keels, keeling, keeled**
- **keel over** fall down or overturn • *The ship keeled over.*
[from Old Norse]

keen[1] *ADJECTIVE* **1** enthusiastic; very interested in or eager to do something • *a keen swimmer.* **2** sharp • *a keen edge.* **3** piercingly cold • *a keen wind.*
▷ **keenly** *adverb* **keenness** *noun*
[from Old English]

keen[2] *VERB* **keens, keening, keened** wail, especially in mourning.
[from Irish]

keep *VERB* **keeps, keeping, kept** **1** have something and look after it or not get rid of it. **2** stay or cause to stay in the same condition etc. • *Keep still; I'll keep it hot.* **3** do something continually • *She keeps laughing.* **4** last without going bad • *How long will this milk keep?* **5** respect and not break • *keep a promise.* **6** make entries in • *keep a diary.*
- **keep up** **1** make the same progress as others. **2** continue something.

keep *NOUN* **keeps** **1** maintenance; the food etc. that you need to live • *She earns her keep.* **2** a strong tower in a castle.
- **for keeps** (*informal*) permanently; to keep • *Is this football mine for keeps?*
[origin unknown]

keeper *NOUN* **keepers** **1** a person who looks after an animal, building, etc. • *the park keeper.* **2** a goalkeeper or wicketkeeper.

keeping *NOUN* care; looking after something • *in safe keeping.*
- **in keeping with** conforming to; suiting • *Modern furniture is not in keeping with an old house.*

keepsake *NOUN* **keepsakes** a gift to be kept in memory of the person who gave it.

keg *NOUN* **kegs** a small barrel.
[from Old Norse]

kelp *NOUN* a large seaweed.
[origin unknown]

kelvin *NOUN* **kelvins** the SI unit of thermodynamic temperature.
[named after a British scientist, Lord *Kelvin*, who invented it]

kennel *NOUN* **kennels** a shelter for a dog.
[from Latin *canis* = dog]

kennels *NOUN* a place where dogs are bred or where they can be looked after while their owners are away.

kerb *NOUN* **kerbs** the edge of a pavement.
[a different spelling of *curb*]

kerchief *NOUN* **kerchiefs** (*old use*) **1** a square scarf worn on the head. **2** a handkerchief.
[from old French *couvre* = cover + *chief* = head]

kernel *NOUN* **kernels** the part inside the shell of a nut etc.
[from Old English]

kerosene (*say* ke-ro-seen) *NOUN* paraffin.
[from Greek *keros* = wax]

kestrel *NOUN* **kestrels** a small falcon.
[probably from French]

ketchup *NOUN* a thick sauce made from tomatoes and vinegar etc.
[probably from Chinese *k'e chap* = tomato juice]

kettle *NOUN* **kettles** a container with a spout and handle, for boiling water in.
[from Old English]

kettledrum *NOUN* **kettledrums** a drum consisting of a large metal bowl with skin or plastic over the top.

key *NOUN* **keys** **1** a piece of metal shaped so that it will open a lock. **2** a device for winding up a clock or clockwork toy etc. **3** a small lever to be pressed by a finger, e.g. on a piano, typewriter, or computer. **4** a system of notes in music • *the key of C major.* **5** a fact or clue that explains or solves something • *the key to the mystery.* **6** a list of symbols used in a map or table.

key *VERB* **keys, keying, keyed**
- **key in** type information into a computer using a keyboard.
[from Old English]

keyboard *NOUN* **keyboards** the set of keys on a piano, typewriter, computer, etc.

keyhole *NOUN* **keyholes** the hole through which a key is put into a lock.

keyhole surgery *NOUN* surgery carried out through a very small cut in the patient's body, using special instruments.

keynote *NOUN* **keynotes 1** the note on which a key in music is based • *The keynote of C major is C.* **2** the main idea in something said, written, or done; a theme.

keypad *NOUN* **keypads** a small keyboard or set of buttons used to operate a telephone, television, etc.

keystone *NOUN* **keystones** the central wedge-shaped stone in an arch, locking the others together.

keyword *NOUN* **keywords** a word that you type into a computer search engine so that it will search for that word on the Internet.

kg *ABBREVIATION* kilogram.

khaki *NOUN* a dull yellowish-brown colour, used for military uniforms.
[from Urdu *khaki* = dust-coloured]

kibbutz *NOUN* **kibbutzim** a commune in Israel, especially for farming.
[from Hebrew *qibbus* = gathering]

kick *VERB* **kicks**, **kicking**, **kicked 1** hit or move a person or thing with your foot. **2** move your legs about vigorously. **3** (said about a gun) recoil when fired.
- **kick off 1** start a football match. **2** (*informal*) start doing something.
- **kick out** get rid of; dismiss.
- **kick up** (*informal*) make a noise or fuss.

kick *NOUN* **kicks 1** a kicking movement. **2** the recoiling movement of a gun. **3** (*informal*) a thrill. **4** (*informal*) an interest or activity • *He's on a health kick.*
[origin unknown]

kick-off *NOUN* **kick-offs** the start of a football match.

kid *NOUN* **kids 1** (*informal*) a child. **2** a young goat. **3** fine leather made from goatskin.

kid *VERB* **kids**, **kidding**, **kidded** (*informal*) deceive someone in fun.
[from Old Norse]

kiddie *NOUN* **kiddies** (*informal*) a child.

kidnap *VERB* **kidnaps**, **kidnapping**, **kidnapped** take someone away by force, especially in order to obtain a ransom.
▷ **kidnapper** *noun*
[from *kid* + an old word *napper* = thief]

kidney *NOUN* **kidneys** either of the two organs in the body that remove waste products from the blood and excrete urine into the bladder.
[origin unknown]

kidney bean *NOUN* **kidney beans** a dark red bean with a curved shape like a kidney.

kill *VERB* **kills**, **killing**, **killed 1** make a person or thing die. **2** destroy or put an end to something. **3** (*informal*) cause a person pain or mental suffering • *My feet are killing me.*
▷ **killer** *noun*
- **kill time** occupy time idly while waiting.

kill *NOUN* **kills 1** killing an animal. **2** the animal or animals killed by a hunter.
[probably from Old English]

killing *NOUN* **killings** an act causing death.
- **make a killing** make a lot of money.

kiln *NOUN* **kilns** an oven for hardening pottery or bricks, for drying hops, or for burning lime.
[from Latin *culina* = cooking-stove]

kilo *NOUN* **kilos** a kilogram.

kilo- *PREFIX* one thousand (as in *kilolitre* = 1,000 litres, *kilohertz* = 1,000 hertz).
[from Greek *chilioi* = thousand]

kilogram *NOUN* **kilograms** a unit of mass or weight equal to 1,000 grams (about 2.2 pounds).

kilometre (*say* kil-o-meet-er or kil-om-it-er) *NOUN* **kilometres** a unit of length equal to 1,000 metres (about $\frac{3}{4}$ of a mile).

kilowatt *NOUN* **kilowatts** a unit of electrical power equal to 1,000 watts.

kilt *NOUN* **kilts** a kind of pleated skirt worn especially by Scotsmen.
▷ **kilted** *adjective*
[probably from a Scandinavian language]

kimono *NOUN* **kimonos** a long loose Japanese robe.
[from Japanese *ki* = wearing + *mono* = thing]

kin *NOUN* a person's relatives.
▷ **kinsman** *noun* **kinswoman** *noun*
- **next of kin** a person's closest relative.
[from Old English]

-kin *SUFFIX* forms diminutives (e.g. *lambkin* = little lamb).
[from old Dutch]

kind[1] *NOUN* **kinds** a class of similar things or animals; a sort or type.
- **in kind** **1** in the same way • *She repaid his insults in kind.* **2** (said about payment) in goods or services, not in money.
- **kind of** (*informal*) in a way, to some extent • *I felt kind of sorry for him.*
[from Old English *cynd* = nature]
USAGE Correct use is *this kind of thing* or *these kinds of things* (not 'these kind of things').

kind[2] *ADJECTIVE* friendly and helpful; considerate.
▷ **kind-hearted** *adjective* **kindness** *noun*
[from Old English *gecynd* = natural or proper]

kindergarten *NOUN* **kindergartens** a school or class for very young children.
[from German *Kinder* = children + *Garten* = garden]

kindle *VERB* **kindles, kindling, kindled** **1** start a flame; set light to something. **2** begin burning.
[from Old Norse]

kindling *NOUN* small pieces of wood used for lighting fires.

kindly *ADJECTIVE* **kindlier, kindliest** kind • *a kindly smile.*
▷ **kindliness** *noun*

kindred *NOUN* kin.

kindred *ADJECTIVE* related or similar • *chemistry and kindred subjects.*

kinetic *ADJECTIVE* to do with or produced by movement • *kinetic energy.*
[from Greek *kinetikos* = moving]

king *NOUN* **kings** **1** a man who is the ruler of a country through inheriting the position. **2** a person or thing regarded as supreme • *The lion is the king of beasts.* **3** the most important piece in chess. **4** a playing card with a picture of a king.
▷ **kingly** *adjective* **kingship** *noun*
[from Old English]

kingdom *NOUN* **kingdoms** **1** a country ruled by a king or queen. **2** a division of the natural world • *the animal kingdom.*

kingfisher *NOUN* **kingfishers** a small bird with blue feathers that dives to catch fish.

king-size or **king-sized** *ADJECTIVE* extra large.

kink *NOUN* **kinks** **1** a short twist in a rope, wire, piece of hair, etc. **2** a peculiarity.
[from old German]

kinky *ADJECTIVE* involving peculiar sexual behaviour.

kiosk *NOUN* **kiosks** **1** a telephone box. **2** a small hut or stall where newspapers, sweets, etc. are sold.
[via French and Turkish from Persian]

kip *NOUN* **kips** (*informal*) a sleep.
▷ **kip** *verb*
[perhaps from Danish]

kipper *NOUN* **kippers** a smoked herring.
[from Old English]

kirk *NOUN* **kirks** (*Scottish*) a church.
[from Old Norse]

kiss *NOUN* **kisses** touching somebody with your lips as a sign of affection.

kiss *VERB* **kisses, kissing, kissed** give somebody a kiss.
[from Old English]

kiss of life *NOUN* blowing air from your mouth into another person's to help the other person to start breathing again, especially after an accident.

kit *NOUN* **kits** **1** equipment or clothes for a particular occupation. **2** a set of parts sold ready to be fitted together.
[from old Dutch]

kitchen *NOUN* **kitchens** a room in which meals are prepared and cooked.
[from Old English]

kitchenette *NOUN* **kitchenettes** a small kitchen.

kite *NOUN* **kites** **1** a light framework covered with cloth, paper, etc. and flown in the wind on the end of a long piece of string. **2** a large hawk.
[from Old English]

kith and kin friends and relatives.
[from Old English *cyth* = what or who you know, + *kin*]

kitten *NOUN* **kittens** a very young cat.
[from old French *chitoun* = small cat]

kitty *NOUN* **kitties 1** a fund of money for use by several people. **2** an amount of money that you can win in a card game.
[origin unknown]

kiwi (*say* kee-wee) *NOUN* **kiwis 1** a New Zealand bird that cannot fly. **2** (*informal*) (**Kiwi**) **3** someone who comes from or lives in New Zealand.
[a Maori word]

kiwi fruit *NOUN* **kiwi fruits** a fruit with thin hairy skin, green flesh, and black seeds.
[named after the kiwi, because the fruit was exported from New Zealand]

kleptomania *NOUN* an uncontrollable urge to steal things.
▷ **kleptomaniac** *noun*
[from Greek *kleptes* = thief, + *mania*]

kloof *NOUN* **kloofs** (*S. African*) a narrow valley or mountain pass, usually wooded.
[via Afrikaans from Dutch *clove*]

km *ABBREVIATION* kilometre.

knack *NOUN* a special skill • *There's a knack to putting up a deckchair.*
[origin unknown]

knacker *NOUN* a person who buys and slaughters horses and sells the meat and hides.
[origin unknown]

knapsack *NOUN* **knapsacks** a bag carried on the back by soldiers, hikers, etc.
[from Dutch]

knave *NOUN* **knaves 1** (*old use*) a dishonest man; a rogue. **2** a jack in playing cards.
[from Old English *cnafa* = a boy or male servant]

knead *VERB* **kneads, kneading, kneaded** press and stretch something soft (especially dough) with your hands.
[from Old English]

knee *NOUN* **knees** the joint in the middle of the leg.
[from Old English]

kneecap *NOUN* **kneecaps** the small bone covering the front of the knee joint.

kneel *VERB* **kneels, kneeling, knelt** be or get yourself in a position on your knees.
[from Old English]

knell *NOUN* **knells** the sound of a bell rung solemnly after a death or at a funeral.
[from Old English]

knickerbockers *PLURAL NOUN* loose-fitting short trousers gathered in at the knees.
[from D. *Knickerbocker*, the imaginary author of a book in which people were shown wearing knickerbockers]

knickers *PLURAL NOUN* underpants worn by women and girls.
[from *knickerbockers*]

knick-knack *NOUN* **knick-knacks** a small ornament.
[probably from old Dutch]

knife *NOUN* **knives** a cutting instrument consisting of a sharp blade set in a handle.

knife *VERB* **knifes, knifing, knifed** stab with a knife.
[from Old English]

knight *NOUN* **knights 1** a man who has been given the rank that allows him to put 'Sir' before his name. **2** (in the Middle Ages) a warrior of high social rank, usually mounted and in armour. **3** a piece in chess, with a horse's head.
▷ **knighthood** *noun*

knight *VERB* **knights, knighting, knighted** make someone a knight.
[from Old English *cniht* = young man]

knit *VERB* **knits, knitting, knitted** or **knit** make something by looping together wool or other yarn, using long needles or a machine.
▷ **knitter** *noun* **knitting needle** *noun*
- **knit your brow** frown.
[from Old English *cnyttan* = tie in knots]

knob *NOUN* **knobs 1** the round handle of a door, drawer, etc. **2** a round lump on something. **3** a round button or switch on a dial or machine. **4** a small round piece of something • *a knob of butter.*
▷ **knobbly** *adjective* **knobby** *adjective*
[from old German]

knock *VERB* **knocks, knocking, knocked** **1** hit a thing hard so as to make a noise. **2** produce by hitting • *We need to knock a hole in the wall.* **3** (*slang*) criticize unfavourably • *People are always knocking this country.*
- **knock off** **1** (*informal*) stop working. **2** deduct something from a price. **3** (*slang*) steal.
- **knock out** make a person unconscious, especially by a blow to the head.

knock *NOUN* **knocks** the act or sound of knocking.
[from Old English]

knocker *NOUN* **knockers** a hinged metal device for knocking on a door.

knockout *NOUN* **knockouts** **1** knocking somebody out. **2** a contest in which the loser in each round has to drop out. **3** (*slang*) an extremely attractive or outstanding person or thing.

knoll *NOUN* **knolls** a small round hill; a mound.
[from Old English]

knot *NOUN* **knots** **1** a place where a piece of string, rope, or ribbon etc. is twisted round itself or another piece. **2** a tangle; a lump. **3** a round spot on a piece of wood where a branch joined it. **4** a cluster of people or things. **5** a unit for measuring the speed of ships and aircraft, equal to 2,025 yards (1,852 metres or 1 nautical mile) per hour.

knot *VERB* **knots, knotting, knotted** **1** tie or fasten with a knot. **2** entangle.
[from Old English]

knotty *ADJECTIVE* **knottier, knottiest** **1** full of knots. **2** difficult or puzzling • *a knotty problem.*

know *VERB* **knows, knowing, knew, known** **1** have something in your mind that you have learned or discovered. **2** recognize or be familiar with a person or place • *I've known him for years.* **3** understand • *She knows how to please people.*
[from Old English]

know-all *NOUN* **know-alls** a person who behaves as if he or she knows everything.

know-how *NOUN* practical knowledge or skill for a particular job.

knowing *ADJECTIVE* showing that you know something • *a knowing look.*

knowingly *ADVERB* **1** in a knowing way. **2** deliberately.

knowledge *NOUN* **1** knowing. **2** all that a person knows. **3** all that is known.
- **to my knowledge** as far as I know.
[from *know* + Old English *lac* = practice]

knowledgeable *ADJECTIVE* well-informed.
▷ **knowledgeably** *adverb*

knuckle *NOUN* **knuckles** a joint in the finger.

knuckle *VERB* **knuckles, knuckling, knuckled**
- **knuckle down** begin to work hard.
- **knuckle under** yield or submit.
[from old German]

koala (*say* koh-**ah**-la) *NOUN* **koalas** an Australian animal that looks like a small bear.
[an Australian Aboriginal word]

koppie (*say* **kop**-i) *NOUN* **koppies** (*S. African*) a small hill.
[via Afrikaans from Dutch *kop* = head]

Koran (*say* kor-**ahn**) *NOUN* the sacred book of Islam, written in Arabic, believed by Muslims to contain the words of Allah revealed to the prophet Muhammad.
[from Arabic *kur'an* = reading]

kosher *ADJECTIVE* keeping to Jewish laws about the preparation of food • *kosher meat.*
[from Hebrew *kasher* = suitable or proper]

kraal (*say* krahl) *NOUN* **kraals** (*S. African*) **1** a traditional African village of huts. **2** an enclosure for sheep and cattle.
[from Dutch]

kremlin *NOUN* **kremlins** a citadel in a Russian city.
- **the Kremlin** the citadel in Moscow, housing the Russian government.
[from Russian]

krill *NOUN* a mass of tiny shrimp-like creatures, the chief food of certain whales.
[from Norwegian *kril* = fish fry]

krypton *NOUN* an inert gas that is present in the earth's atmosphere and is used in fluorescent lamps.
[from Greek *kryptos* = hidden]

kudos (*say* kew-doss) *NOUN* honour and glory.
[Greek, = praise]

kung fu *NOUN* a Chinese method of self-defence, rather like karate.
[from Chinese *kung* = merit + *fu* = master]

kw *ABBREVIATION* kilowatt.

Ll

L *ABBREVIATION* learner, a person learning to drive a car.

lab *NOUN* **labs** (*informal*) a laboratory.

label *NOUN* **labels** a small piece of paper, cloth, or metal etc. fixed on or beside something to show what it is or what it costs, or its owner or destination, etc.

label *VERB* **labels, labelling, labelled** put a label on something.
[from old French]

labial (*say* lay-bee-al) *ADJECTIVE* to do with the lips.
[from Latin *labia* = lips]

laboratory *NOUN* **laboratories** a room or building equipped for scientific experiments.
[from Latin *laboratorium* = workplace]

laborious *ADJECTIVE* **1** needing or using a lot of hard work. **2** explaining something at great length and with obvious effort.
▷ **laboriously** *adverb*

Labour *NOUN* the Labour Party, a British political party formed to represent the interests of working people and believing in social equality and socialism.

labour *NOUN* **labours 1** hard work. **2** a task. **3** workers. **4** the contractions of the womb when a baby is being born.

labour *VERB* **labours, labouring, laboured 1** work hard. **2** explain or discuss something at great length and with obvious effort • *I will not labour the point.*
[from Latin *labor* = work, trouble, or suffering]

labourer *NOUN* **labourers** a person who does hard manual work, especially outdoors.

Labrador *NOUN* **Labradors** a large black or light-brown dog.
[named after Labrador, a district in Canada, where it was bred]

laburnum *NOUN* **laburnums** a tree with hanging yellow flowers.
[Latin]

labyrinth *NOUN* **labyrinths** a complicated arrangement of passages or paths; a maze.
[from Greek, originally referring to the maze in Greek mythology that the Minotaur lived in]

lace *NOUN* **laces 1** net-like material with decorative patterns of holes in it. **2** a piece of thin cord or leather for fastening a shoe, etc.

lace *VERB* **laces, lacing, laced 1** fasten with a lace. **2** thread a cord etc. through something. **3** add spirits to a drink.
[from old French]

lacerate *VERB* **lacerates, lacerating, lacerated** injure flesh by cutting or tearing it.
▷ **laceration** *noun*
[from Latin]

lachrymal (*say* lak-rim-al) *ADJECTIVE* to do with tears; producing tears • *lachrymal ducts.*
[from Latin *lacrima* = a tear]

lachrymose *ADJECTIVE* (*formal*) tearful.

lack *NOUN* being without something.

lack *VERB* **lacks, lacking, lacked** be without something • *He lacks courage.*
[probably from Old English]

lackadaisical *ADJECTIVE* lacking energy or determination; careless.
[from *lack-a-day*, an old phrase expressing grief or surprise]

lackey *NOUN* **lackeys** a servant; a person who behaves or is treated like a servant.
[from French]

lacking *ADJECTIVE* absent or deficient • *The story is lacking in humour.*

laconic *ADJECTIVE* using few words; terse • *a laconic reply.*
▷ **laconically** *adverb*
[from Greek *Lakon* = a native of Laconia, an area in Greece (because the Laconians were famous for their terse speech)]

lacquer *NOUN* a hard glossy varnish.
▷ **lacquered** *adjective*
[via French from Portuguese]

lacrosse *NOUN* a game using a stick with a net on it (a *crosse*) to catch and throw a ball.
[from French *la crosse* = the crosse]

lactate *VERB* **lactates, lactating, lactated** (said about mammals) produce milk.
[from Latin *lac* = milk]

lacy *ADJECTIVE* made of lace or like lace.

lad *NOUN* **lads** a boy or youth.
[origin unknown]

ladder *NOUN* **ladders** **1** two upright pieces of wood or metal etc. and crosspieces (*rungs*), used for climbing up or down. **2** a vertical ladder-like flaw in a pair of tights or stockings where a stitch has become undone.

ladder *VERB* **ladders, laddering, laddered** get a ladder in a pair of tights or stockings.
[from Old English]

laden *ADJECTIVE* carrying a heavy load.
[from Old English *hladan* = load a ship]

ladle *NOUN* **ladles** a large deep spoon with a long handle, used for lifting and pouring liquids.

ladle *VERB* **ladles, ladling, ladled** lift and pour a liquid with a ladle.
[from Old English]

lady *NOUN* **ladies** **1** a well-mannered woman. **2** a woman of good social position. **3** (in polite use) a woman.
▷ **ladylike** *adjective* **ladyship** *noun*
- **Lady** *noun* the title of a noblewoman.
[from Old English *hlaefdige* = person who makes the bread (compare *lord*)]

ladybird *NOUN* **ladybirds** a small flying beetle, usually red with black spots.

lady-in-waiting *NOUN* **ladies-in-waiting** a woman of good social position who attends a queen or princess.

lag[1] *VERB* **lags, lagging, lagged** go too slowly and fail to keep up with others.

lag *NOUN* **lags** a delay.
[origin unknown]

lag[2] *VERB* **lags, lagging, lagged** wrap pipes or boilers etc. in insulating material (*lagging*) to prevent loss of heat.
[probably from a Scandinavian language]

lager (*say* lah-ger) *NOUN* **lagers** a light beer.
[from German *Lager* = storehouse (because the beer was kept to mature)]

laggard *NOUN* **laggards** a person who lags behind.

lagoon *NOUN* **lagoons** a salt-water lake separated from the sea by sandbanks or reefs.
[from Latin *lacuna* = pool]

laid *past tense* of **lay**.

laid-back *ADJECTIVE* (*informal*) relaxed and easy-going.

lain *past participle* of **lie**[2].

lair *NOUN* **lairs** a sheltered place where a wild animal lives.
[from Old English]

laissez-faire (*say* lay-say-fair) *NOUN* a government's policy of not interfering.
[French, = let (them) act]

laity (*say* lay-it-ee) *NOUN* lay people, not the clergy.

lake *NOUN* **lakes** a large area of water entirely surrounded by land.
[from Latin]

lakh (*say* lak) *NOUN* **lakh** (*Indian*) a hundred thousand (rupees etc.).
[from Hindi]

lama *NOUN* **lamas** a Buddhist priest or monk in Tibet and Mongolia.
[from Tibetan]

lamb *NOUN* **lambs** **1** a young sheep. **2** meat from a lamb.
▷ **lambswool** *noun*
[from Old English]

lame *ADJECTIVE* **1** unable to walk normally. **2** weak; not convincing • *a lame excuse.*
▷ **lamely** *adverb* **lameness** *noun*
[from Old English]

lament *NOUN* **laments** a statement, song, or poem expressing grief or regret.

lament *VERB* **laments, lamenting, lamented** express grief or regret about something.
▷ **lamentation** *noun*
[from Latin *lamentari* = weep]

lamentable (*say* lam-in-ta-bul) *ADJECTIVE* regrettable or deplorable.

laminated *ADJECTIVE* made of thin layers or sheets joined one upon the other • *laminated plastic.*
[from Latin *lamina* = layer]

lamp *NOUN* **lamps** a device for producing light from electricity, gas, or oil.
▷ **lamplight** *noun* **lampshade** *noun*
[from Greek *lampas* = torch]

lamppost *NOUN* **lampposts** a tall post in a street etc., with a lamp at the top.

lamprey *NOUN* **lampreys** a small eel-like water animal.
[from Latin]

lance *NOUN* **lances** a long spear.

lance *VERB* **lances, lancing, lanced** cut open a boil etc. with a surgeon's lancet.
[from Latin]

lance corporal *NOUN* **lance corporals** a soldier ranking between a private and a corporal.
[origin unknown]

lancet *NOUN* **lancets** **1** a pointed two-edged knife used by surgeons. **2** a tall narrow pointed window or arch.
[from French *lancette* = small lance]

land *NOUN* **lands** **1** the part of the earth's surface not covered by sea. **2** the ground or soil; an area of country • *forest land.* **3** the area occupied by a nation; a country.

land *VERB* **lands, landing, landed** **1** arrive or put on land from a ship or aircraft.
2 reach the ground after jumping or falling.
3 bring a fish out of the water. **4** obtain • *She landed an excellent job.* **5** arrive or cause to arrive at a certain place or position etc. • *They landed up in jail.* **6** present with a problem • *He landed me with this task.*
[from Old English]

landed *ADJECTIVE* **1** owning land.
2 consisting of land • *landed estates.*

landing *NOUN* **landings** **1** the level area at the top of a flight of stairs. **2** bringing or coming to land • *The pilot made a smooth landing.* **3** a place where people can get on and off a boat.

landing stage *NOUN* **landing stages** a platform on which people and goods are taken on and off a boat.

landlady *NOUN* **landladies** **1** a woman who lets rooms to lodgers. **2** a woman who runs a pub.

landlocked *ADJECTIVE* almost or entirely surrounded by land.

landlord *NOUN* **landlords** **1** a person who lets a house, room, or land to a tenant. **2** a person who runs a pub.

landlubber *NOUN* **landlubbers** (*informal*) a person who is not used to the sea.
[from *land* + an old word *lubber* = an awkward, clumsy person]

landmark *NOUN* **landmarks** **1** an object that is easily seen in a landscape. **2** an important event in the history or development of something.

landmine *NOUN* **landmines** an explosive mine laid on or just under the surface of the ground.

landowner *NOUN* **landowners** a person who owns a large amount of land.

landscape *NOUN* **landscapes** **1** a view of a particular area of countryside or town. **2** a picture of the countryside.
[from Dutch]

landscape gardening *NOUN* laying out a garden to imitate natural scenery.

landslide *NOUN* **landslides** **1** a landslip.
2 an overwhelming victory in an election • *She won the General Election by a landslide.*

landslip *NOUN* **landslips** a huge mass of soil and rocks sliding down a slope.

landward *ADJECTIVE & ADVERB* towards the land.
▷ **landwards** *adverb*

lane *NOUN* **lanes** **1** a narrow road, especially in the country. **2** a strip of road for a single line of traffic. **3** a strip of track or water for one runner, swimmer, etc. in a race.
[from Old English]

language *NOUN* **languages** **1** words and their use. **2** the words used in a particular country or by a particular group of people. **3** a system of signs or symbols giving information, especially in computing. [from Latin *lingua* = tongue]

language laboratory *NOUN* **language laboratories** a room equipped with audio equipment for learning a foreign language.

languid *ADJECTIVE* slow and lacking energy because of tiredness, weakness, or laziness.
▷ **languidly** *adverb* **languor** *noun*
[same origin as *languish*]

languish *VERB* **languishes, languishing, languished** **1** live in miserable conditions; be neglected • *He has been languishing in prison for three years.* **2** become weak or listless.
[from Latin *languere* = be faint or weak]

lank *ADJECTIVE* (said about hair) long and limp.
[from Old English]

lanky *ADJECTIVE* **lankier, lankiest** awkwardly thin and tall.
▷ **lankiness** *noun*

lanolin *NOUN* a kind of ointment, made of fat from sheep's wool.
[from Latin *lana* = wool + *oleum* = oil]

lantern *NOUN* **lanterns** a transparent case for holding a light and shielding it from the wind.
[from Latin; related to *lamp*]

lanyard *NOUN* **lanyards** a short cord for fastening or holding something.
[from old French]

lap[1] *NOUN* **laps** **1** the level place formed by the front of the legs above the knees when a person is sitting down. **2** going once round a racetrack. **3** one section of a journey • *the last lap.*

lap *VERB* **laps, lapping, lapped** overtake another competitor in a race to become one or more laps ahead.
[from Old English *laeppa*]

lap[2] *VERB* **laps, lapping, lapped** **1** take up liquid by moving the tongue, as a cat does. **2** make a gentle splash against something • *Waves lapped the shore.*
[from Old English *lapian*]

lapel (*say* la-**pel**) *NOUN* **lapels** a flap folded back at the front edge of a coat or jacket.
[from *lap*[1]]

lapse *NOUN* **lapses** **1** a slight mistake or failure • *a lapse of memory.* **2** an amount of time elapsed • *after a lapse of six months.*

lapse *VERB* **lapses, lapsing, lapsed** **1** pass or slip gradually • *He lapsed into unconsciousness.* **2** be no longer valid, through not being renewed • *My insurance policy has lapsed.*
[from Latin *lapsus* = sliding]

laptop *NOUN* **laptops** a portable computer for use while travelling.

lapwing *NOUN* **lapwings** a black and white bird with a crested head and a shrill cry.
[from Old English]

larceny *NOUN* stealing possessions.
[from Latin *latro* = robber]

larch *NOUN* **larches** a tall deciduous tree that bears small cones.
[via old German from Latin]

lard *NOUN* a white greasy substance prepared from pig fat and used in cooking.
[French, = bacon]

larder *NOUN* **larders** a cupboard or small room for storing food.
[from Latin]

large *ADJECTIVE* of more than the ordinary or average size; big.
▷ **largeness** *noun*
- **at large** **1** free to roam about, not captured • *The escaped prisoners are still at large.* **2** in general, as a whole • *She is respected by the country at large.*
[from Latin *largus* = abundant or generous]

largely *ADVERB* to a great extent • *You are largely responsible for the accident.*

largesse (*say* lar-**jess**) *NOUN* money or gifts generously given.
[French, related to *large*]

lark[1] *NOUN* **larks** a small sandy-brown bird; the skylark.
[from Old English]

lark[2] *NOUN* **larks** (*informal*) something amusing; a bit of fun • *We did it for a lark.*

lark *VERB* **larks, larking, larked**
- **lark about** have fun; play tricks.
[origin unknown]

larrikin *NOUN* **larrikins** (*Australian/NZ*) a young person who behaves in a wild and mischievous way.
[origin unknown]

larva *NOUN* **larvae** an insect in the first stage of its life, after it comes out of the egg.
▷ **larval** *adjective*
[Latin, = ghost or mask]

laryngitis *NOUN* inflammation of the larynx, causing hoarseness.

larynx (*say* la-rinks) *NOUN* **larynxes** the part of the throat that contains the vocal cords.
[from Greek]

lasagne (*say* laz-**an**-ya) *NOUN* pasta in the form of sheets, usually cooked with minced meat and cheese sauce.
[Italian]

laser *NOUN* **lasers** a device that makes a very strong narrow beam of light or other electromagnetic radiation.
[from the initials of 'light amplification (by) stimulated emission (of) radiation']

lash *NOUN* **lashes** **1** a stroke with a whip or stick. **2** the cord or cord-like part of a whip. **3** an eyelash.

lash *VERB* **lashes, lashing, lashed** **1** strike with a whip; beat violently. **2** tie with cord etc. • *Lash the sticks together.*
- **lash down** (said about rain or wind) pour or beat down forcefully.
- **lash out** **1** speak or hit out angrily. **2** spend money extravagantly.
[origin unknown]

lashings *PLURAL NOUN* plenty • *lashings of custard.*

lass *NOUN* **lasses** a girl or young woman.
▷ **lassie** *noun*
[from Old Norse]

lassitude *NOUN* tiredness; lack of energy.
[from Latin *lassus* = weary]

lasso *NOUN* **lassoes** or **lassos** a rope with a sliding noose at the end, used for catching cattle etc.

lasso *VERB* **lassoes, lassoing, lassoed** catch an animal with a lasso.
[from Spanish]

last[1] *ADJECTIVE & ADVERB* **1** coming after all others; final. **2** latest; most recent • *last night.* **3** least likely • *She is the last person I'd have chosen.*
- **the last straw** a final thing that makes a problem unbearable.

last *NOUN* **1** a person or thing that is last. **2** the end • *He was brave to the last.*
- **at last** or **at long last** finally; after much delay.
[from Old English *latost*]

last[2] *VERB* **lasts, lasting, lasted** **1** continue; go on existing or living or being usable. **2** be enough for • *The food will last us for three days.*
[from Old English *laestan*]

last[3] *NOUN* **lasts** a block of wood or metal shaped like a foot, used in making and repairing shoes.
[from Old English *laeste*]

lasting *ADJECTIVE* able to last for a long time • *a lasting peace.*

lastly *ADVERB* in the last place; finally.

last post *NOUN* a military bugle call sounded at sunset and at military funerals etc.

last rites *PLURAL NOUN* (in the Christian Church) the ceremony given to a person who is close to death.

latch *NOUN* **latches** a small bar fastening a door or gate, lifted by a lever or spring.
▷ **latchkey** *noun*

latch *VERB* **latches, latching, latched** fasten with a latch.
- **latch onto** **1** meet someone and follow them around all the time. **2** understand something.
[from Old English]

late *ADJECTIVE & ADVERB* **1** after the usual or expected time. **2** near the end • *late in the afternoon.* **3** recent • *the latest news.* **4** who has died recently • *the late king.*
- **of late** recently.
[from Old English]

lately *ADVERB* recently.

latent (*say* **lay**-tent) *ADJECTIVE* existing but not yet developed, active, or visible • *her latent talent.*
[from Latin *latens* = lying hidden]

latent heat *NOUN* the heat needed to change a solid into a liquid or vapour, or a liquid into a vapour, without a change in temperature.

lateral *ADJECTIVE* **1** to do with the side or sides. **2** sideways • *lateral movement.*
▷ **laterally** *adverb*
[from Latin *lateris* = of a side]

lateral thinking *NOUN* solving problems by thinking about them in an unusual and creative (and apparently illogical) way.

latex *NOUN* the milky juice of various plants and trees, especially the rubber tree.

lath *NOUN* **laths** a narrow thin strip of wood.
[from Old English]

lathe (*say* layth) *NOUN* **lathes** a machine for holding and turning pieces of wood while they are being shaped.
[from Old English]

lather *NOUN* a mass of froth.

lather *VERB* **lathers, lathering, lathered** **1** cover with lather. **2** form a lather.
[from Old English]

Latin *NOUN* the language of the ancient Romans.
[from *Latium*, an ancient district of Italy including Rome]

Latin America *NOUN* the parts of Central and South America where the main language is Spanish or Portuguese.
[because these languages developed from Latin]

latitude *NOUN* **latitudes** **1** the distance of a place from the equator, measured in degrees. **2** freedom from restrictions on what people can do or believe.
[from Latin *latitudo* = breadth]

latrine (*say* la-treen) *NOUN* **latrines** a toilet in a camp or barracks.
[French, related to *lavatory*]

latter *ADJECTIVE* later • *the latter part of the year.* (COMPARE **former**)
- **the latter** the second of two people or things just mentioned.
[from Old English]

latterly *ADVERB* recently.

lattice *NOUN* **lattices** a framework of crossed strips or bars with spaces between.
[from French]

laud *VERB* **lauds, lauding, lauded** (*formal*) praise.
▷ **laudatory** (*say* law-dat-er-ee) *adjective*
[from Latin]

laudable *ADJECTIVE* deserving praise.
▷ **laudably** *adverb*

laugh *VERB* **laughs, laughing, laughed** make the sounds that show you are happy or think something is funny.

laugh *NOUN* **laughs** the sound of laughing.
[from Old English]

laughable *ADJECTIVE* deserving to be laughed at.

laughing stock *NOUN* **laughing stocks** a person or thing that is the object of ridicule and scorn.

laughter *NOUN* the act, sound, or manner of laughing.
[from Old English]

launch[1] *VERB* **launches, launching, launched** **1** send a ship from the land into the water. **2** send a rocket etc. into space. **3** set a thing moving by throwing or pushing it. **4** make a new product available for the first time • *Our new model will be launched in April.* **5** start something off • *launch an attack.*

launch *NOUN* **launches** the launching of a ship or spacecraft.
[from old French]

launch[2] *NOUN* **launches** a large motor boat.
[from Spanish]

launch pad *NOUN* **launch pads** a platform from which a rocket is launched.

launder *VERB* **launders, laundering, laundered** wash and iron clothes etc.
[same origin as *laundry*]

launderette *NOUN* **launderettes** a place fitted with washing machines that people pay to use.
[from *laundry* + *-ette*]

laundry *NOUN* **laundries** **1** a place where clothes etc. are washed and ironed for customers. **2** clothes etc. sent to or from a laundry.
[from Latin *lavandaria* = things to be washed]

laureate (*say* lorri-at) *ADJECTIVE*
- **Poet Laureate** a person appointed to write poems for national occasions.
[from *laurel*, because a laurel wreath was worn in ancient times as a sign of victory]

laurel *NOUN* **laurels** an evergreen shrub with smooth shiny leaves.
[from Latin]

lava *NOUN* molten rock that flows from a volcano; the solid rock formed when it cools.
[from Latin *lavare* = to wash]

lavatory *NOUN* **lavatories** **1** a toilet. **2** a room containing a toilet.
[from Latin *lavatorium* = a basin or bath for washing]

lavender *NOUN* **1** a shrub with sweet-smelling purple flowers. **2** a light-purple colour.
[from Latin]

lavish *ADJECTIVE* **1** generous. **2** plentiful.
▷ **lavishly** *adverb* **lavishness** *noun*

lavish *VERB* **lavishes, lavishing, lavished** give generously • *They lavished praise upon him.*
[from Old French *lavasse* = heavy rain]

law *NOUN* **laws** **1** a rule or set of rules that everyone must obey. **2** the profession of being a lawyer. **3** (*informal*) the police. **4** a scientific statement of something that always happens • *the law of gravity.*
[via Old English from Old Norse]

law-abiding *ADJECTIVE* obeying the law.

lawcourt *NOUN* **lawcourts** a room or building in which a judge or magistrate hears evidence and decides whether someone has broken the law.

lawful *ADJECTIVE* allowed or accepted by the law.
▷ **lawfully** *adverb*

lawless *ADJECTIVE* **1** not obeying the law. **2** without proper laws • *a lawless country.*
▷ **lawlessly** *adverb* **lawlessness** *noun*

lawn[1] *NOUN* **lawns** an area of closely-cut grass in a garden or park.
[from old French]

lawn[2] *NOUN* very fine cotton material.
[probably from *Laon*, a town in France where cloth was made]

lawnmower *NOUN* **lawnmowers** a machine for cutting the grass of lawns.

lawn tennis *NOUN* tennis played on an outdoor grass or hard court.

lawsuit *NOUN* **lawsuits** a dispute or claim that is brought to a lawcourt to be settled.

lawyer *NOUN* **lawyers** a person who is qualified to give advice in matters of law.

lax *ADJECTIVE* slack; not strict • *Discipline was lax.*
▷ **laxly** *adverb* **laxity** *noun*
[from Latin *laxus* = loose]

laxative *NOUN* **laxatives** a medicine that stimulates the bowels to empty.
[from Latin *laxare* = loosen]

lay[1] *VERB* **lays, laying, laid** **1** put something down in a particular place or way. **2** arrange things, especially for a meal • *Can you lay the table?* **3** place • *He laid the blame on his sister.* **4** form or prepare • *We laid our plans.* **5** produce an egg.
- **lay off** **1** stop employing somebody for a while. **2** (*informal*) stop doing something.
- **lay on** supply or provide.
- **lay out** **1** arrange or prepare. **2** knock a person unconscious. **3** prepare a corpse for burial.
[from Old English]
USAGE Do not confuse **lay/laid/laying** = 'put down', with *lie/lay/lain/lying* = 'be in a flat position'. Correct uses are as follows: *Go and lie down; she went and lay down; please lay it on the floor.* 'Go and lay down' is incorrect.

lay[2] *past tense* of **lie**[2].

lay[3] *NOUN* **lays** (*old use*) a poem meant to be sung; a ballad.
[from old French]

lay[4] *ADJECTIVE* **1** not belonging to the clergy • *a lay preacher.* **2** not professionally qualified • *lay opinion.*
[from Greek *laos* = people]

layabout *NOUN* **layabouts** a person who lazily avoids working for a living.

lay-by *NOUN* **lay-bys** a place where vehicles can stop beside a main road.

layer *NOUN* **layers** a single thickness or coating.
[from *lay*[1]]

A B C D E F G H I J K L M N O P Q R S T U V W X Y Z

layman or **layperson** *NOUN* **laymen** or **laypeople** **1** a person who does not have specialized knowledge or training (e.g. as a doctor or lawyer). **2** a person who is not ordained as a member of the clergy.
[from *lay*[4] + *man*]

layout *NOUN* **layouts** an arrangement of parts of something according to a plan.

laywoman *NOUN* **laywomen** **1** a woman who does not have specialized knowledge or training (e.g. as a doctor or lawyer). **2** a woman who is not ordained as a member of the clergy.

laze *VERB* **lazes, lazing, lazed** spend time in a lazy way.
[from *lazy*]

lazy *ADJECTIVE* **lazier, laziest** not wanting to work; doing little work.
▷ **lazily** *adverb* **laziness** *noun*
[probably from old Dutch]

lea *NOUN* **leas** (*poetical use*) a meadow.
[from Old English]

leach *VERB* **leaches, leaching, leached** remove a soluble substance from soil or rock by making water percolate through it.
[from Old English *leccan* = water]

lead[1] (*say* leed) *VERB* **leads, leading, led** **1** take or guide someone, especially by going in front. **2** be winning in a race or contest etc.; be ahead. **3** be in charge of a group of people. **4** be a way or route • *This path leads to the beach.* **5** play the first card in a card game. **6** live or experience • *He leads a dull life.*
- **lead to** result in; cause.

lead (*say* leed) *NOUN* **leads** **1** a leading place or part or position • *She took the lead on the final bend.* **2** guidance or example • *We should be taking a lead on this issue.* **3** a clue to be followed. **4** a strap or cord for leading a dog or other animal. **5** an electrical wire attached to something.
[from Old English *laedan*]

lead[2] (*say* led) *NOUN* **leads** **1** a soft heavy grey metal. **2** the writing substance (graphite) in a pencil.
▷ **lead** *adjective*
[from Old English *lead*]

leaden (*say* **led**-en) *ADJECTIVE* **1** made of lead. **2** heavy and slow. **3** lead-coloured; dark grey • *leaden skies.*

leader *NOUN* **leaders** **1** the person in charge of a group of people; a chief. **2** the person who is winning. **3** a newspaper article giving the editor's opinion.
▷ **leadership** *noun*

leaf *NOUN* **leaves** **1** a flat usually green part of a plant, growing out from its stem, branch, or root. **2** the paper forming one page of a book. **3** a very thin sheet of metal • *gold leaf.* **4** a flap that makes a table larger.
▷ **leafy** *adjective* **leafless** *adjective*
- **turn over a new leaf** make a fresh start and improve your behaviour.
[from Old English]

leaflet *NOUN* **leaflets** a piece of paper printed with information.

league[1] *NOUN* **leagues** **1** a group of teams who compete against each other for a championship. **2** a group of people or nations who agree to work together.
- **in league with** working or plotting together.
[from Latin *legare* = bind]

league[2] *NOUN* **leagues** an old measure of distance, about 3 miles.
[from Greek]

leak *NOUN* **leaks** **1** a hole or crack etc. through which liquid or gas accidentally escapes. **2** the revealing of secret information.
▷ **leaky** *adjective*

leak *VERB* **leaks, leaking, leaked** **1** get out or let out through a leak. **2** reveal secret information.
▷ **leakage** *noun*
[probably from old German or Dutch]

lean[1] *ADJECTIVE* **1** with little or no fat • *lean meat.* **2** thin • *a lean body.*
[from Old English *hlaene*]

lean[2] *VERB* **leans, leaning, leaned** or **leant** **1** bend your body towards or over something. **2** put or be in a sloping position. **3** rest against something. **4** rely or depend on someone for help.
[from Old English *hleonian*]

leaning *NOUN* **leanings** a tendency or preference.

leap *VERB* **leaps, leaping, leaped** or **leapt** jump vigorously.
▷ **leap** *noun*
[from Old English]

leapfrog *NOUN* a game in which each player jumps with legs apart over another who is bending down.

leap year *NOUN* **leap years** a year with an extra day in it (29 February).
[probably because the dates from March onwards 'leap' a day of the week; a date which would fall on a Monday in an ordinary year will be on Tuesday in a leap year]

learn *VERB* **learns, learning, learned** or **learnt** **1** get knowledge or skill through study or training. **2** find out about something.
[from Old English]
USAGE It is not acceptable in standard English to use *learn* to mean 'to teach'.

learned (*say* ler-nid) *ADJECTIVE* having much knowledge obtained by study.

learner *NOUN* **learners** a person who is learning something, especially to drive a car.

learning *NOUN* knowledge obtained by study.

lease *NOUN* **leases** an agreement to allow someone to use a building or land etc. for a fixed period in return for payment.
▷ **leaseholder** *noun*
- **a new lease of life** a chance to be healthy, active, or usable again.

lease *VERB* **leases, leasing, leased** allow or obtain the use of something by lease.
[from old French]

leash *NOUN* **leashes** a dog's lead.
[from old French]

least *ADJECTIVE* & *ADVERB* very small in amount etc. • *the least bit; the least expensive bike.*
- **at least** **1** not less than what is mentioned • *It will cost at least £40.* **2** anyway • *He's at home, or at least I think he is.*

least *NOUN* the smallest amount or degree.
[from Old English]

leather *NOUN* material made from animal skins.
▷ **leathery** *adjective*
[from Old English]

leave *VERB* **leaves, leaving, left** **1** go away from a person or place. **2** stop belonging to a group or working somewhere. **3** cause or allow something to stay where it is or as it is • *You left the door open.* **4** go away without taking something • *I left my book at home.* **5** let someone deal with something • *Leave the washing-up to me.* **6** put something to be collected or passed on • *Would you like to leave a message?*
- **leave off** stop.
- **leave out** omit; not include.

leave *NOUN* **1** permission. **2** official permission to be away from work; the time for which this permission lasts • *three days' leave.*
[from Old English]

leaven (*say* lev-en) *NOUN* a substance (e.g. yeast) used to make dough rise.

leaven *VERB* **leavens, leavening, leavened** add leaven to dough.
[from Latin *levare* = to lighten or raise]

lechery *NOUN* excessive sexual lust.
▷ **lecherous** *adjective*
[via old French from Germanic]

lectern *NOUN* **lecterns** a stand to hold a Bible or other large book or notes for reading.
[same origin as *lecture*]

lecture *NOUN* **lectures** **1** a talk about a subject to an audience or a class. **2** a long serious warning or reprimand given to someone.

lecture *VERB* **lectures, lecturing, lectured** give a lecture.
▷ **lecturer** *noun*
[from Latin *lectura* = reading, or something to be read]

led *past tense* of **lead**[1].

ledge *NOUN* **ledges** a narrow shelf • *a window ledge; a mountain ledge.*
[origin unknown]

ledger *NOUN* **ledgers** an account book.
[probably from Dutch]

lee *NOUN* **lees** the sheltered side or part of something, away from the wind.
[from Old English]

leech *NOUN* **leeches** a small blood-sucking worm that lives in water.
[from Old English]

a b c d e f g h i j k l m n o p q r s t u v w x y z

A B C D E F G H I J K L M N O P Q R S T U V W X Y Z

leek *NOUN* **leeks** a long green and white vegetable of the onion family.
[from Old English]

leer *VERB* **leers, leering, leered** look at someone in a lustful or unpleasant way.
▷ **leer** *noun*
[origin unknown]

leeward *ADJECTIVE* on the lee side.

leeway *NOUN* **1** extra space or time available. **2** a drift to leeward or off course.
- **make up leeway** make up lost time; regain a lost position.

left[1] *ADJECTIVE & ADVERB* **1** on or towards the west if you think of yourself as facing north. **2** (said about political groups) in favour of socialist or radical views.
▷ **left-hand** *adjective*

left *NOUN* the left-hand side or part etc.
[from Old English *lyft* = weak]

left[2] *past tense* of **leave**.

left-handed *ADJECTIVE* using the left hand in preference to the right hand.
[same origin as *left*[1]]

leftovers *PLURAL NOUN* food not eaten at a meal.

leg *NOUN* **legs** **1** one of the limbs on a person's or animal's body, on which it stands or moves. **2** the part of a piece of clothing covering a leg. **3** each of the supports of a chair or other piece of furniture. **4** one part of a journey. **5** one of a pair of matches between the same teams.
[from Old Norse]

legacy *NOUN* **legacies** **1** something left to a person in a will. **2** a thing received from someone who did something before you or because of earlier events • *a legacy of distrust.*
[from Latin]

legal *ADJECTIVE* **1** lawful. **2** to do with the law or lawyers.
▷ **legally** *adverb* **legality** *noun*
[from Latin]

legalize *VERB* **legalizes, legalizing, legalized** make a thing legal.
▷ **legalization** *noun*

legate *NOUN* **legates** an official representative, especially of the Pope.
[from Latin]

legend *NOUN* **legends** **1** an old story handed down from the past, which may or may not be true. (COMPARE **myth**) **2** a very famous person.
▷ **legendary** *adjective*
[from Latin *legenda* = things to be read]

leggings *PLURAL NOUN* **1** tight-fitting stretchy trousers, worn by women. **2** protective outer coverings for each leg from knee to ankle.

legible *ADJECTIVE* clear enough to read.
▷ **legibly** *adverb* **legibility** *noun*
[from Latin *legere* = to read]

legion *NOUN* **legions** **1** a division of the ancient Roman army. **2** a group of soldiers or former soldiers.
[from Latin]

legionnaire *NOUN* **legionnaires** a member of an association of former soldiers.

legionnaires' disease *NOUN* a serious form of pneumonia caused by bacteria.
[so-called because of an outbreak at a meeting of the American Legion of ex-servicemen in 1976]

legislate *VERB* **legislates, legislating, legislated** make laws.
▷ **legislation** *noun* **legislator** *noun*
[from Latin *legis* = of a law + *latio* = proposing]

legislative *ADJECTIVE* making laws • *a legislative assembly.*

legislature *NOUN* **legislatures** a country's parliament or law-making assembly.

legitimate *ADJECTIVE* **1** lawful. **2** born of parents who are married to each other.
▷ **legitimately** *adverb* **legitimacy** *noun*
[from Latin *legitimare* = make something lawful]

leisure *NOUN* time that is free from work, when you can do what you like.
▷ **leisured** *adjective*
- **at leisure** having leisure; not hurried.
- **at your leisure** when you have time.
[from old French]

leisurely *ADJECTIVE* done with plenty of time; unhurried • *a leisurely stroll.*

lemming *NOUN* **lemmings** a small mouse-like animal of Arctic regions that

migrates in large numbers and is said to run headlong into the sea and drown.
[from Norwegian or Danish]

lemon *NOUN* **lemons** **1** an oval yellow citrus fruit with a sour taste. **2** a pale-yellow colour.
[same origin as *lime*²]

lemonade *NOUN* a lemon-flavoured drink.

lemur (*say* lee-mer) *NOUN* **lemurs** a monkey-like animal.
[from Latin]

lend *VERB* **lends, lending, lent** **1** allow a person to use something of yours for a short time. **2** provide someone with money that they must repay, usually in return for payments (called *interest*). **3** give or add a quality • *She lent dignity to the occasion.*
▷ **lender** *noun*
- **lend a hand** help somebody.
[from Old English]
USAGE Do not confuse **lend** with **borrow**, which means just the opposite.

length *NOUN* **lengths** **1** how long something is. **2** a piece of cloth, rope, wire, etc. cut from a larger piece. **3** the distance of a swimming pool from one end to the other. **4** the amount of thoroughness in an action • *They went to great lengths to make us comfortable.*
- **at length** **1** after a long time. **2** taking a long time; in detail.
[from Old English]

lengthen *VERB* **lengthens, lengthening, lengthened** make or become longer.

lengthways
or **lengthwise** *ADVERB* from end to end; along the longest part.

lengthy *ADJECTIVE* going on for a long time.
▷ **lengthily** *adverb*

lenient (*say* lee-nee-ent) *ADJECTIVE* merciful; not severe.
▷ **leniently** *adverb* **lenience** *noun*
[from Latin *lenis* = gentle]

lens *NOUN* **lenses** **1** a curved piece of glass or plastic used to focus things. **2** the transparent part of the eye, immediately behind the pupil.
[Latin, = lentil (because of its shape)]

Lent *NOUN* a time of fasting and penitence observed by Christians for about six weeks before Easter.
▷ **Lenten** *adjective*
[from Old English *lencten* = the spring]

lent *past tense* of **lend**.

lentil *NOUN* **lentils** a kind of small bean.
[from old French; related to *lens*]

leopard (*say* lep-erd) *NOUN* **leopards** a large spotted mammal of the cat family, also called a panther.
▷ **leopardess** *noun*
[from Greek]

leotard (*say* lee-o-tard) *NOUN* **leotards** a close-fitting piece of clothing worn for dance, exercise, and gymnastics.
[named after a French trapeze artist, J. *Leotard*, who designed it]

leper *NOUN* **lepers** a person who has leprosy.

lepidopterous *ADJECTIVE* to do with the group of insects that includes butterflies and moths.
[from Greek *lepis* = *scale*² + *pteron* = wing]

leprechaun (*say* lep-rek-awn) *NOUN* **leprechauns** (in Irish folklore) an elf who looks like a little old man.
[from Irish, = a small body]

leprosy *NOUN* an infectious disease that makes parts of the body waste away.
▷ **leprous** *adjective*
[from Greek *lepros* = scaly (because white scales form on the skin)]

lesbian *NOUN* **lesbians** a homosexual woman.
[named after the Greek island of Lesbos (because Sappho, a poetess who lived there about 600 BC, was said to be homosexual)]

less *ADJECTIVE* & *ADVERB* smaller in amount; not so much • *Make less noise. It is less important.*
USAGE Do not use *less* when you mean *fewer*. You should use *fewer* when you are talking about a number of individual things, and *less* when you are talking about a quantity or mass of something: • *The less batter you make, the fewer pancakes you'll get.*

less *NOUN* a smaller amount.

less *PREPOSITION* minus; deducting • *She earned £100, less tax.*
[from Old English]

-less *SUFFIX* forms adjectives meaning 'without' (e.g. *colourless*) or 'unable to be ' (e.g. *countless*).
[from Old English]

lessen *VERB* **lessens, lessening, lessened** make or become less.

lesser *ADJECTIVE* not so great as the other • *the lesser evil.*

lesson *NOUN* **lessons** **1** an amount of teaching given at one time. **2** something to be learnt by a pupil or student. **3** an example or experience from which you should learn • *Let this be a lesson to you!* **4** a passage from the Bible read aloud as part of a church service.
[from old French; related to *lecture*]

lest *CONJUNCTION* (*old use*) so that something should not happen • *Remind us, lest we forget.*
[from Old English]

let *VERB* **lets, letting, let** **1** allow somebody or something to do something; not prevent or forbid • *Let me see it.* **2** cause to • *Let us know what happens.* **3** allow or cause to come or go or pass • *Let me out!* **4** allow someone to use a house or building etc. in return for payment (*rent*). **5** leave • *Let it alone.*
- **let down** **1** disappoint somebody. **2** deflate.
- **let off** **1** excuse somebody from a duty or punishment etc. **2** make something explode.
- **let on** (*informal*) reveal a secret.
- **let up** (*informal*) **1** relax or do less work. **2** become less intense.

▷ **let-up** *noun*
[from Old English]

lethal (*say* lee-thal) *ADJECTIVE* deadly; causing death.
▷ **lethally** *adverb*
[from Latin *letum* = death]

lethargy (*say* leth-er-jee) *NOUN* extreme lack of energy or vitality.
▷ **lethargic** (*say* lith-ar-jik) *adjective*
[from Greek *lethargos* = forgetful]

letter *NOUN* **letters** **1** a symbol representing a sound used in speech. **2** a written message, usually sent by post.
- **to the letter** paying strict attention to every detail.

[from Latin]

letter box *NOUN* **letter boxes** **1** a slot in a door, through which letters are delivered. **2** a postbox.

lettering *NOUN* letters drawn or painted.

lettuce *NOUN* **lettuces** a garden plant with broad crisp leaves used in salads.
[from Latin]

leukaemia (*say* lew-kee-mee-a) *NOUN* a disease in which there are too many white corpuscles in the blood.
[from Greek *leukos* = white + *haima* = blood]

level *ADJECTIVE* **1** flat or horizontal. **2** at the same height or position as something else.

level *NOUN* **levels** **1** height, depth, position, or value etc. • *Fix the shelves at eye level.* **2** a level surface. **3** a device that shows whether something is level.
- **on the level** (*informal*) honest.

level *VERB* **levels, levelling, levelled** **1** make or become level. **2** aim a gun or missile. **3** direct an accusation at a person.
[from Latin *libra* = balance]

level crossing *NOUN* **level crossings** a place where a road crosses a railway at the same level.

lever *NOUN* **levers** **1** a bar that turns on a fixed point (the *fulcrum*) in order to lift something or force something open. **2** a bar used as a handle to operate machinery etc. • *a gear lever.*

lever *VERB* **levers, levering, levered** lift or move something by means of a lever.
[from Latin *levare* = raise]

leverage *NOUN* **1** the force you need when you use a lever. **2** influence.

leveret *NOUN* **leverets** a young hare.
[from French *lièvre* = hare]

levitation *NOUN* rising into the air and floating there.
▷ **levitate** *verb*
[same origin as *levity*]

levity *NOUN* being humorous, especially at an unsuitable time.
[from Latin *levis* = lightweight]

levy *VERB* **levies, levying, levied** impose or collect a tax or other payment by the use of authority or force.

levy *NOUN* **levies** an amount of money paid in tax.
[same origin as *lever*]

lewd *ADJECTIVE* indecent or crude.
▷ **lewdly** *adverb* **lewdness** *noun*
[origin unknown]

lexicography *NOUN* the writing of dictionaries.
▷ **lexicographer** *noun*
[from Greek *lexis* = word, + *-graphy*]

liability *NOUN* **liabilities** **1** being legally responsible for something. **2** a debt or obligation. **3** a disadvantage or handicap.

liable *ADJECTIVE* **1** likely to do or suffer something • *She is liable to colds. The cliff is liable to crumble*. **2** legally responsible for something.
[probably from old French]

liaise (*say* lee-ayz) *VERB* **liaises, liaising, liaised** (*informal*) act as a liaison or go-between.
[from *liaison*]

liaison (*say* lee-ay-zon) *NOUN* **liaisons** **1** communication and cooperation between people or groups. **2** a person who is a link or go-between. **3** a sexual affair.
[from French *lier* = bind]

liar *NOUN* **liars** a person who tells lies.
[from Old English]

libel (*say* ly-bel) *NOUN* **libels** an untrue written, printed, or broadcast statement that damages a person's reputation. (COMPARE **slander**)
▷ **libellous** *adjective*

libel *VERB* **libels, libelling, libelled** make a libel against someone.
[from Latin *libellus* = little book]

liberal *ADJECTIVE* **1** giving generously. **2** given in large amounts. **3** not strict; tolerant.
▷ **liberally** *adverb* **liberality** *noun*
[same origin as *liberty*]

Liberal Democrat *NOUN* **Liberal Democrats** a member of the Liberal Democrat party, a political party favouring moderate reforms.

liberalize *VERB* **liberalizes, liberalizing, liberalized** make less strict.
▷ **liberalization** *noun*

liberate *VERB* **liberates, liberating, liberated** set free.
▷ **liberation** *noun* **liberator** *noun*
[same origin as *liberty*]

liberty *NOUN* **liberties** freedom.
- **take liberties** behave too casually or in too familiar a way.
[from Latin *liber* = free]

librarian *NOUN* **librarians** a person in charge of or working in a library.
▷ **librarianship** *noun*

library (*say* ly-bra-ree) *NOUN* **libraries** **1** a place where books are kept for people to use or borrow. **2** a collection of books, records, films, etc.
[from Latin *libraria* = bookshop]

libretto *NOUN* **librettos** the words of an opera or other long musical work.
[Italian, = little book]

lice *plural* of **louse**

licence *NOUN* **licences** **1** an official permit to do or use or own something • *a driving licence.* **2** special freedom to avoid the usual rules or customs.
[from Latin *licere* = be allowed]

license *VERB* **licenses, licensing, licensed** give a licence to a person; authorize • *We are not licensed to sell alcohol.*

licensee *NOUN* **licensees** a person who holds a licence, especially to sell alcohol.

licentious (*say* ly-sen-shus) *ADJECTIVE* breaking the rules of conduct; immoral.
▷ **licentiousness** *noun*
[from Latin *licentiosus* = not restrained]

lichen (*say* ly-ken) *NOUN* **lichens** a dry-looking plant that grows on rocks, walls, trees, etc.
[from Greek]

lick *VERB* **licks, licking, licked** **1** move your tongue over something. **2** (said about a wave or flame) move like a tongue; touch lightly. **3** (*slang*) defeat.

lick *NOUN* **licks** **1** licking. **2** a slight application of paint etc.
- **at a lick** (*informal*) at a fast pace.
[from Old English]

lid *NOUN* **lids** **1** a cover for a box or pot etc. **2** an eyelid.
[from Old English]

lido (*say* leed-oh) *NOUN* **lidos** a public open-air swimming pool or pleasure beach.
[from Lido, the name of a beach near Venice]

lie[1] *NOUN* **lies** a statement that the person who makes it knows to be untrue.

lie *VERB* **lies, lying, lied** tell a lie or lies; be deceptive.
[from Old English *leogan*]

lie[2] *VERB* **lies, lying, lay, lain** **1** be or get in a flat or resting position • *He lay on the grass.* • *The cat has lain here all night.* **2** be or remain • *The island lies near the coast.* • *The machinery lay idle.*
- **lie low** keep yourself hidden.

lie *NOUN* **lies** the way something lies • *the lie of the land.*
[from Old English *licgan*]
USAGE See the note at **lay**[1].

liege (*say* leej) *NOUN* **lieges** (*old use*) a person who is entitled to receive feudal service or allegiance (*a liege lord*) or bound to give it
(*a liege man*).
[from old French]

lieu (*say* lew) *NOUN*
- **in lieu** instead • *He accepted a cheque in lieu of cash.*
[French, = place]

lieutenant (*say* lef-ten-ant) *NOUN* **lieutenants** **1** an officer in the army or navy. **2** a deputy or chief assistant.
[from French *lieu* = place + *tenant* = holding]

life *NOUN* **lives** **1** the period between birth and death. **2** being alive and able to function and grow. **3** living things • *Is there life on Mars?* **4** liveliness • *She is full of life.* **5** a biography. **6** the length of time that something exists or functions • *The battery has a life of two years.*
[from Old English]

lifebelt *NOUN* **lifebelts** a ring of material that will float, used to support someone's body in water.

lifeboat *NOUN* **lifeboats** a boat for rescuing people at sea.

lifebuoy *NOUN* **lifebuoys** a device to support someone's body in water.

life cycle *NOUN* **life cycles** the series of changes in the life of a living thing.

lifeguard *NOUN* **lifeguards** someone whose job is to rescue swimmers who are in difficulty.

life jacket *NOUN* **life jackets** a jacket of material that will float, used to support someone's body in water.

lifeless *ADJECTIVE* **1** without life.
2 unconscious.
▷ **lifelessly** *adverb*

lifelike *ADJECTIVE* looking exactly like a real person or thing.

lifelong *ADJECTIVE* continuing for the whole of someone's life.

lifespan *NOUN* **lifespans** the length of someone's life.

lifestyle *NOUN* **lifestyles** the way of life of a person or a group of people.

lifetime *NOUN* **lifetimes** the time for which someone is alive.

lift *VERB* **lifts, lifting, lifted** **1** raise or pick up something. **2** rise or go upwards.
3 remove or abolish something • *The ban has been lifted.* **4** (*informal*) steal.

lift *NOUN* **lifts** **1** lifting. **2** a device for taking people or goods from one floor or level to another in a building. **3** a ride in somebody else's vehicle • *Can you give me a lift to the station?*
[from Old Norse]

lift-off *NOUN* **lift-offs** the vertical take-off of a rocket or spacecraft.

ligament *NOUN* **ligaments** a piece of the tough flexible tissue that holds your bones together.
[from Latin *ligare* = bind]

ligature *NOUN* **ligatures** a thing used in tying something, especially in surgical operations.
[same origin as *ligament*]

light[1] *NOUN* **lights** **1** radiation that stimulates the sense of sight and makes things visible. **2** something that provides light, especially an electric lamp. **3** a flame.
- **bring** or **come to light** make or become known.
- **in the light of** taking into consideration.

light *ADJECTIVE* **1** full of light; not dark. **2** pale • *light blue.*

light *VERB* **lights, lighting, lit** or **lighted**
1 start a thing burning; begin to burn.
2 provide light for something.
- **light up** **1** put lights on, especially at dusk.
2 make or become light or bright.
[from Old English *leoht*]

USAGE Say *He lit the lamps; the lamps were lit* (not 'lighted'), but *She carried a lighted torch* (not 'a lit torch').

light² *ADJECTIVE* **1** having little weight; not heavy. **2** small in amount or force etc. • *light rain; a light punishment*. **3** needing little effort • *light work*. **4** cheerful, not sad • *with a light heart*. **5** not serious or profound • *light music*.
▷ **lightly** *adverb* **lightness** *noun*

light *ADVERB* lightly; with only a small load • *We were travelling light.*
[from Old English *liht*]

lighten¹ *VERB* **lightens, lightening, lightened** make or become lighter or brighter.

lighten² *VERB* **lightens, lightening, lightened** make or become lighter or less heavy.

lighter *NOUN* **lighters** a device for lighting cigarettes etc.

light-hearted *ADJECTIVE* **1** cheerful and free from worry. **2** not serious.

lighthouse *NOUN* **lighthouses** a tower with a bright light at the top to guide or warn ships.

light industry *NOUN* **light industries** an industry producing small or light articles.

lighting *NOUN* lamps, or the light they provide.

lightning *NOUN* a flash of bright light produced by natural electricity during a thunderstorm.
- **like lightning** with very great speed.

lightning conductor *NOUN* **lightning conductors** a metal rod or wire fixed on a building to divert lightning into the earth.

lightweight *NOUN* **lightweights** **1** a person who is not heavy. **2** a boxer weighing between 57.1 and 59 kg.
▷ **lightweight** *adjective*

light year *NOUN* **light years** a unit of distance equal to the distance that light travels in one year (about 9.5 million million km).

like¹ *VERB* **likes, liking, liked** **1** think a person or thing is pleasant or satisfactory.
2 wish • *I'd like to come.*
[from Old English]

like² *PREPOSITION* **1** similar to; in the manner of • *He swims like a fish.* **2** in a suitable state for • *It looks like rain.* • *I feel like a cup of tea.*
3 such as • *She's good at things like art and music.*

like *ADJECTIVE* similar; having some or all of the qualities of another person or thing • *They are as like as two peas.*

like *NOUN* a similar person or thing • *We shall not see his like again.*
[from Old Norse]

likeable *ADJECTIVE* easy to like; pleasant.

likelihood *NOUN* being likely; probability.

likely *ADJECTIVE* **likelier, likeliest**
1 probable; expected to happen or be true etc. • *Rain is likely.* **2** expected to be suitable or successful • *a likely spot.*
[from *like*²]

liken *VERB* **likens, likening, likened**
compare • *He likened the human heart to a pump.*

likeness *NOUN* **likenesses** **1** a similarity in appearance; a resemblance. **2** a portrait.

likewise *ADVERB* similarly; in the same way.

liking *NOUN* a feeling that you like something • *She has a liking for ice cream.*

lilac *NOUN* **1** a bush with fragrant purple or white flowers. **2** pale purple.
[from Persian *lilak* = bluish]

lilt *NOUN* **lilts** a light pleasant rhythm in a voice or tune.
▷ **lilting** *adjective*
[from old German or Dutch]

lily *NOUN* **lilies** a garden plant with trumpet-shaped flowers, growing from a bulb.
[from Greek]

limb *NOUN* **limbs** **1** a leg, arm, or wing. **2** a large branch of a tree.
- **out on a limb** isolated; without any support.
[from Old English]

limber *VERB* **limbers, limbering, limbered**
- **limber up** do exercises in preparation for a sport or athletic activity.
[origin unknown]

limbo[1] *NOUN*
- **in limbo** in an uncertain situation where you are waiting for something to happen • *Lack of money has left our plans in limbo.*
[the name of a place formerly believed by Christians to exist on the borders of hell, where the souls of people who were not baptized waited for God's judgement]

limbo[2] *NOUN* a West Indian dance in which you bend backwards to pass under a low bar.

lime[1] *NOUN* a white chalky substance (calcium oxide) used in making cement and as a fertilizer.
[from Old English *lim*]

lime[2] *NOUN* **limes** **1** a green fruit like a small round lemon. **2** a drink made from lime juice.
[from Arabic *lima* = citrus fruit]

lime[3] *NOUN* **limes** a tree with yellow flowers.
[from Old English *lind*]

limelight *NOUN*
- **in the limelight** receiving a lot of publicity and attention.
[from *lime*[1] which gives a bright light when heated, formerly used to light up the stage of a theatre]

limerick *NOUN* **limericks** a type of amusing poem with five lines.
[named after Limerick, a town in Ireland]

limestone *NOUN* a kind of rock from which lime (calcium oxide) is obtained.

limit *NOUN* **limits** **1** a line, point, or level where something ends. **2** the greatest amount allowed • *the speed limit.*

limit *VERB* **limits, limiting, limited** **1** keep something within certain limits. **2** be a limit to something.
▷ **limitation** *noun*
[from Latin *limes* = boundary]

limited *ADJECTIVE* kept within limits; not great • *a limited choice; limited experience.*

limited company *NOUN* **limited companies** a business company whose shareholders would have to pay only some of its debts.

limousine (*say* lim-oo-zeen) *NOUN* **limousines** a large luxurious car.
[originally, a hooded cape worn in *Limousin*, a district in France; the name given to the cars because early ones had a canvas roof to shelter the driver]

limp[1] *VERB* **limps, limping, limped** walk lamely.

limp *NOUN* **limps** a limping walk.
[origin unknown]

limp[2] *ADJECTIVE* **1** not stiff or firm. **2** without strength or energy.
▷ **limply** *adverb* **limpness** *noun*
[origin unknown]

limpet *NOUN* **limpets** a small shellfish that attaches itself firmly to rocks.
[via Old English from Latin]

limpid *ADJECTIVE* (said about liquids) clear; transparent.
▷ **limpidity** *noun*
[from Latin]

linchpin *NOUN* **linchpins** **1** a pin passed through the end of an axle to keep a wheel in position. **2** the person or thing that is vital to the success of something.
[from Old English]

line[1] *NOUN* **lines** **1** a long thin mark. **2** a row or series of people or things; a row of words. **3** a length of rope, string, wire, etc. used for a special purpose • *a fishing line.* **4** a railway; a line of railway track. **5** a company operating a transport service of ships, aircraft, or buses. **6** a way of doing things or behaving; a type of business. **7** a telephone connection.
- **in line** **1** forming a straight line. **2** conforming.

line *VERB* **lines, lining, lined** **1** mark something with lines • *Use lined paper.* **2** form something into a line or lines • *Line them up.*
[from Old English]

line[2] *VERB* **lines, lining, lined** cover the inside of something.
[from *linen* (used for linings)]

lineage (*say* lin-ee-ij) *NOUN* **lineages** ancestry; a line of descendants from an ancestor.

lineal (*say* lin-ee-al) *ADJECTIVE* in the direct line of descent or ancestry.

linear (*say* lin-ee-er) *ADJECTIVE* **1** arranged in a line. **2** to do with a line or length.

linen *NOUN* **1** cloth made from flax. **2** shirts, sheets, and tablecloths etc. (which were formerly made of linen).
[from Latin *linum* = flax]

liner *NOUN* **liners** a large passenger ship.
[from *line*[1]]

linesman *NOUN* **linesmen** an official in football or tennis etc. who decides whether the ball has crossed a line.

-ling *SUFFIX* forms nouns meaning 'having a certain quality' (e.g. *weakling*) or diminutives meaning 'little' (e.g. *duckling*).
[from Old English]

linger *VERB* **lingers, lingering, lingered** stay for a long time, as if unwilling to leave; be slow to leave.
[from Old English]

lingerie (*say* lan-zher-ee) *NOUN* women's underwear.
[French, from *linge* = linen]

lingo *NOUN* **lingos** or **lingoes** (*informal*) a foreign langauage.
[via Portuguese from Latin *lingua* = tongue]

linguist *NOUN* **linguists** an expert in languages.
[same origin as *language*]

linguistics *NOUN* the study of languages.
▷ **linguistic** *adjective*

liniment *NOUN* a lotion for rubbing on parts of the body that ache; embrocation.
[from Latin *linire* = to smear]

lining *NOUN* **linings** a layer that covers the inside of something.
[from *line*[2]]

link *NOUN* **links** **1** one of the rings or loops of a chain. **2** a connection or relationship.

link *VERB* **links, linking, linked** join things together; connect.
▷ **linkage** *noun*
[from Old Norse]

links *NOUN* & *PLURAL NOUN* a golf course, especially one near the sea.
[from Old English *hlinc* = sandy ground near the seashore]

linnet *NOUN* **linnets** a kind of finch.
[from old French (named because the bird feeds on linseed)]

lino *NOUN* linoleum.

linocut *NOUN* **linocuts** a print made from a design cut into a block of thick linoleum.

linoleum *NOUN* a stiff shiny floor covering.
[from Latin *linum* = flax + *oleum* = oil (because linseed oil is used to make linoleum)]

linseed *NOUN* the seed of flax, from which oil is obtained.
[from Latin *linum* = flax, + *seed*]

lint *NOUN* a soft material for covering wounds.
[probably from old French *lin* = flax (from which lint was originally made)]

lintel *NOUN* **lintels** a horizontal piece of wood or stone etc. above a door or other opening.
[from old French]

lion *NOUN* **lions** a large strong flesh-eating animal of the cat family found in Africa and India.
▷ **lioness** *noun*
[from Greek]

lip *NOUN* **lips** **1** either of the two fleshy edges of the mouth. **2** the edge of something hollow, such as a cup or crater. **3** the pointed part at the top of a jug etc., from which you pour things.
[from Old English]

lip-read *VERB* **lip-reads, lip-reading, lip-read** understand what a person says by watching the movements of his or her lips, not by hearing.

lip-service *NOUN*
- **pay lip-service to something** say that you approve of it but do nothing to support it.

lipstick *NOUN* **lipsticks** a stick of a waxy substance for colouring the lips.

liquefy *VERB* **liquefies, liquefying, liquefied** make or become liquid.
▷ **liquefaction** *noun*

liqueur (*say* lik-yoor) *NOUN* **liqueurs** a strong sweet alcoholic drink.
[French, = liquor]

liquid *NOUN* **liquids** a substance like water or oil that flows freely but (unlike a gas) has a constant volume.

liquid *ADJECTIVE* **1** in the form of a liquid; flowing freely. **2** easily converted into cash • *the firm's liquid assets.*
▷ **liquidity** *noun*
[from Latin *liquidus* = flowing]

liquidate *VERB* **liquidates, liquidating, liquidated** **1** pay off or settle a debt. **2** close down a business and divide its value between its creditors. **3** get rid of someone, especially by killing them.
▷ **liquidation** *noun* **liquidator** *noun*

liquidize *VERB* **liquidizes, liquidizing, liquidized** make something, especially food, into a liquid or pulp.
▷ **liquidizer** *noun*

liquor *NOUN* **1** alcoholic drink. **2** juice produced in cooking; liquid in which food has been cooked.
[from Latin]

liquorice (*say* lick-er-iss) *NOUN* **1** a black substance used in medicine and as a sweet. **2** the plant from whose root this substance is obtained.
[from Greek *glykys* = sweet + *rhiza* = root]

lisp *NOUN* **lisps** a fault in speech in which *s* and *z* are pronounced like *th*.
▷ **lisp** *verb*
[from Old English]

list[1] *NOUN* **lists** a number of names, items, or figures etc. written or printed one after another.

list *VERB* **lists, listing, listed** make a list of people or things.
[from old French]

list[2] *VERB* **lists, listing, listed** (said about a ship) lean over to one side.
▷ **list** *noun*
[origin unknown]

listed *ADJECTIVE* (said about a building) protected from being demolished or altered because of its historical importance.

listen *VERB* **listens, listening, listened** pay attention in order to hear something.
▷ **listener** *noun*
[from Old English]

listless *ADJECTIVE* too tired to be active or enthusiastic.
▷ **listlessly** *adverb* **listlessness** *noun*
[from an old word *list* = desire, + *-less*]

lit *past tense* of **light**[1].

litany *NOUN* **litanies** a formal prayer with fixed responses.
[from Greek *litaneia* = prayer]

literacy *NOUN* the ability to read and write.

literal *ADJECTIVE* **1** meaning exactly what is said, not metaphorical or exaggerated. **2** word for word • *a literal translation.*
[from Latin *littera* = letter]

literally *ADVERB* really; exactly as stated • *The noise made me literally jump out of my seat.*

literary (*say* **lit**-er-er-i) *ADJECTIVE* to do with literature; interested in literature.
[same origin as *literal*]

literate *ADJECTIVE* able to read and write.
[same origin as *literal*]

literature *NOUN* books and other writings, especially those considered to have been written well.
[same origin as *literal*]

lithe *ADJECTIVE* flexible and supple.
[from Old English]

litigant *NOUN* **litigants** a person who is involved in a lawsuit.
[from Latin *litigare* = start a lawsuit]

litigation *NOUN* **litigations** a lawsuit; the process of carrying on a lawsuit.
[same origin as *litigant*]

litmus *NOUN* a blue substance that is turned red by acids and can be turned back to blue by alkalis.
[from Old Norse *litr* = dye + *mosi* = moss (because litmus is obtained from some kinds of moss)]

litmus paper *NOUN* paper stained with litmus.

litre *NOUN* **litres** a measure of liquid, about 13/4 pints.
[French]

litter *NOUN* **litters** **1** rubbish or untidy things left lying about. **2** the young animals born to one mother at one time. **3** absorbent material put down on a tray for a cat to urinate and defecate in indoors. **4** a kind of stretcher.

litter *VERB* **litters, littering, littered** make a place untidy with litter.
[from old French *litière* = bed]

little *ADJECTIVE* **less, least** small in amount or size or intensity etc.; not great or big or much.
- **a little** **1** a small amount • *Have a little sugar.* **2** slightly • *I'm a little tired.*
- **little by little** gradually; by a small amount at a time.

little *ADVERB* not much • *I eat very little.*
[from Old English]

liturgy *NOUN* **liturgies** a fixed form of public worship used in churches.
▷ **liturgical** *adjective*
[from Greek *leitourgia* = worship]

live[1] *(rhymes with* **give***)* *VERB* **lives, living, lived** **1** have life; be alive. **2** have your home • *She lives in Glasgow.* **3** pass your life in a certain way • *He lived as a hermit.*
- **live down** if you cannot live down a mistake or embarrassment, you cannot make people forget it.
- **live on** use something as food; depend on for your living.
[from Old English]

live[2] *(rhymes with* **hive***)* *ADJECTIVE* **1** alive. **2** connected to a source of electric current. **3** broadcast while it is actually happening, not from a recording. **4** burning • *live coals.*
[from *alive*]

livelihood *NOUN* **livelihoods** a way of earning money or providing enough food to support yourself.
[from Old English *lif* = life + *lad* = course or way]

lively *ADJECTIVE* **livelier, liveliest** full of life or action; vigorous and cheerful.
▷ **liveliness** *noun*

liven *VERB* **livens, livening, livened** make or become lively • *The match livened up in the second half.*

liver *NOUN* **livers** **1** a large organ of the body, found in the abdomen, that processes digested food and purifies the blood. **2** an animal's liver used as food.
[from Old English]

livery *NOUN* **liveries** **1** a uniform worn by male servants in a household. **2** the distinctive colours used by a railway, bus company, or airline.
[originally = the giving of food or clothing: from Latin *librare* = to set free or hand over]

livery stable *NOUN* **livery stables** a place where horses are kept for their owner or where horses may be hired.

livestock *NOUN* farm animals.

live wire *NOUN* **live wires** a forceful energetic person.

livid *ADJECTIVE* **1** bluish-grey • *a livid bruise.* **2** furiously angry.
[from Latin]

living *NOUN* **1** being alive. **2** the way that a person lives • *a good standard of living.* **3** a way of earning money or providing enough food to support yourself.

living room *NOUN* **living rooms** a room for general use during the day.

lizard *NOUN* **lizards** a reptile with a rough or scaly skin, four legs, and a long tail.
[from Latin]

llama (*say* **lah**-ma) *NOUN* **llamas** a South American animal with woolly fur, like a camel but with no hump.
[via Spanish from Quechua (a South American language)]

lo *INTERJECTION* (*old use*) see, behold.
[from Old English]

load *NOUN* **loads** **1** something carried; a burden. **2** the quantity that can be carried. **3** the total amount of electric current supplied. **4** (*informal*) a large amount • *It's a load of nonsense.*
- **loads** (*informal*) plenty • *We've got loads of time.*

load *VERB* **loads, loading, loaded** **1** put a load in or on something. **2** fill heavily. **3** weight with something heavy • *loaded dice.* **4** put a bullet or shell into a gun; put a film into a camera. **5** enter programs or data into a computer.
[from Old English]

loaf[1] *NOUN* **loaves** a shaped mass of bread baked in one piece.
- **use your loaf** think; use common sense.
[from Old English]

loaf[2] *VERB* **loafs, loafing, loafed** spend time idly; loiter or stand about.
▷ **loafer** *noun*
[probably from German *Landläufer* = a tramp]

loam *NOUN* rich soil containing clay, sand, and decayed leaves etc.
▷ **loamy** *adjective*
[from Old English]

loan *NOUN* **loans** something lent, especially money.
- **on loan** being lent • *These books are on loan from the library.*

loan *VERB* **loans, loaning, loaned** lend.
[from Old Norse]
USAGE Some people dislike the use of this verb except when it means to lend money, but it is now well established in standard English.

loath (*rhymes with* **both**) *ADJECTIVE* unwilling • *I was loath to go.*
[from Old English *lath* = angry or repulsive]

loathe (*rhymes with* **clothe**) *VERB* **loathes, loathing, loathed** feel great hatred and disgust for something.
▷ **loathing** *noun*
[same origin as *loath*]

loathsome *ADJECTIVE* making you feel great hatred and disgust; repulsive.

lob *VERB* **lobs, lobbing, lobbed** throw, hit, or kick a ball etc. high into the air, especially in a high arc.

lob *NOUN* **lobs** a lobbed ball.
[probably from Dutch]

lobby *NOUN* **lobbies 1** an entrance hall. **2** a group who lobby MPs etc. • *the anti-hunting lobby.*

lobby *VERB* **lobbies, lobbying, lobbied** try to persuade an MP or other person to support your cause, by speaking to them in person or writing letters.
[same origin as *lodge*: the lobby of the Houses of Parliament is where members of the public can meet MPs]

lobe *NOUN* **lobes 1** a rounded fairly flat part of a leaf or an organ of the body. **2** the rounded soft part at the bottom of an ear.
▷ **lobed** *adjective*
[from Greek]

lobster *NOUN* **lobsters** a large shellfish with eight legs and two long claws.
[via Old English from Latin]

lobster pot *NOUN* **lobster pots** a basket for catching lobsters.

local *ADJECTIVE* belonging to a particular place or a small area.
▷ **locally** *adverb*

local *NOUN* **locals** (*informal*) **1** someone who lives in a particular district. **2** a pub near a person's home.
[from Latin *locus* = a place]

local anaesthetic *NOUN* **local anaesthetics** an anaesthetic affecting only the part of the body where it is applied.

local government *NOUN* the system of administration of a town or county etc. by people elected by those who live there.

locality *NOUN* **localities** a district or location.

localized *ADJECTIVE* restricted to a particular place • *localized showers.*

locate *VERB* **locates, locating, located** discover where something is • *I have located the fault.*
- **be located** be situated in a particular place • *The cinema is located in the High Street.*
[from Latin *locare* = to place]

location *NOUN* **locations 1** the place where something is situated. **2** discovering where something is; locating.
- **on location** filmed in natural surroundings, not in a studio.

loch *NOUN* **lochs** a lake in Scotland.
[Scottish Gaelic]

lock[1] *NOUN* **locks 1** a fastening that is opened with a key or other device. **2** a section of a canal or river fitted with gates and sluices so that boats can be raised or lowered to the level beyond each gate. **3** the distance that a vehicle's front wheels can turn. **4** a wrestling hold that keeps an opponent's arm or leg from moving.
- **lock, stock, and barrel** completely.

lock *VERB* **locks, locking, locked** **1** fasten or secure something by means of a lock.
2 store something away securely. **3** become fixed in one place; jam.
[from Old English *loc*]

lock² *NOUN* **locks** a clump of hair.
[from Old English *locc*]

locker *NOUN* **lockers** a small cupboard or compartment where things can be stowed safely.

locket *NOUN* **lockets** a small ornamental case for holding a portrait or lock of hair etc., worn on a chain round the neck.
[from old French *locquet* = small latch or lock]

locks *PLURAL NOUN* the hair of the head.

locksmith *NOUN* **locksmiths** a person whose job is to make and mend locks.

locomotive *NOUN* **locomotives** a railway engine.

locomotive *ADJECTIVE* to do with movement or the ability to move
• *locomotive power.*
▷ **locomotion** *noun*
[from Latin *locus* = place + *motivus* = moving]

locum *NOUN* **locums** a doctor or member of the clergy who takes the place of another who is temporarily away.
[short for Latin *locum tenens* = person holding the place]

locus (*say* **loh**-kus) *NOUN* **loci** (*say* **loh**-ky)
1 (*in mathematics*) the path traced by a moving point, or made by points placed in a certain way. **2** the exact place of something.
[Latin, = place]

locust *NOUN* **locusts** a kind of grasshopper that travels in large swarms which eat all the plants in an area.
[from Latin]

lodestone *NOUN* **lodestones** a kind of stone that can be used as a magnet.
[from Old English *lad* = way (because it was used in compasses to guide travellers)]

lodge *NOUN* **lodges** **1** a small house, especially at the gates of a park. **2** a porter's room at the entrance to a college, factory, etc. **3** a beaver's or otter's lair.

lodge *VERB* **lodges, lodging, lodged** **1** stay somewhere as a lodger. **2** provide a person with somewhere to live temporarily.
3 become stuck or caught somewhere
• *The ball lodged in the tree.*
- **lodge a complaint** make an official complaint.
[from old French *loge* = hut, from Germanic]

lodger *NOUN* **lodgers** a person who pays to live in another person's house.

lodgings *PLURAL NOUN* a room or rooms, not in a hotel, rented for living in.

loft *NOUN* **lofts** a room or storage space under the roof of a house or barn etc.
[from Old Norse]

lofty *ADJECTIVE* **1** tall. **2** noble. **3** haughty.
▷ **loftily** *adverb* **loftiness** *noun*
[from an old sense of *loft* = sky]

log¹ *NOUN* **logs** **1** a large piece of a tree that has fallen or been cut down; a piece cut off this. **2** a detailed record kept of a voyage or flight.

log *VERB* **logs, logging, logged** enter facts in a log.
- **log in** (or **on**) gain access to a computer.
- **log out** (or **off**) finish using a computer.
[origin unknown]

log² *NOUN* **logs** a logarithm • *log tables.*

loganberry *NOUN* **loganberries** a dark-red fruit like a blackberry.
[named after an American lawyer H. R. *Logan*, who first grew it]

logarithm *NOUN* **logarithms** one of a series of numbers set out in tables which make it possible to do sums by adding and subtracting instead of multiplying and dividing.
[from Greek *logos* = reckoning + *arithmos* = number]

logbook *NOUN* **logbooks** **1** a book in which a log of a voyage is kept. **2** the registration document of a motor vehicle.

log cabin *NOUN* **log cabins** a hut built of logs.

loggerheads *PLURAL NOUN*
- **at loggerheads** disagreeing or quarrelling.
[from an old word *loggerhead* = a stupid person]

logic *NOUN* **1** reasoning; a system or method of reasoning. **2** the principles used in designing a computer; the circuits involved in this.
[from Greek *logos* = word, reason]

logical *ADJECTIVE* using logic; reasoning or reasoned correctly.
▷ **logically** *adverb* **logicality** *noun*

-logical *SUFFIX* forms adjectives (e.g. *biological*) from nouns ending in *-logy*.

-logist *SUFFIX* forms nouns meaning 'an expert in or student of something' (e.g. *biologist*).
[same origin as *-logy*]

logo (*say* **loh**-goh or **log**-oh) *NOUN* **logos** a printed symbol used by a business company etc. as its emblem.
[short for *logograph*, from Greek *logos* = word, + *-graph*]
WORD FAMILY There are a number of English words that are related to *logo* because part of their original meaning comes from the Greek word *logos* meaning 'speech, word, or reason'. These include *dialogue*, *epilogue*, *logic*, *monologue*, and *prologue*.

-logy or **-ology** *SUFFIXES* form nouns meaning a subject of study (e.g. *biology*).
[from Greek *-logia* = study]

loin *NOUN* **loins** the side and back of the body between the ribs and the hip bone.
[from old French; related to *lumbar*]

loincloth *NOUN* **loincloths** a piece of cloth wrapped round the hips, worn by men in some hot countries as their only piece of clothing.

loiter *VERB* **loiters, loitering, loitered** linger or stand about idly.
▷ **loiterer** *noun*
[probably from old Dutch]

loll *VERB* **lolls, lolling, lolled** **1** lean lazily against something. **2** hang loosely.
[origin unknown]

lollipop *NOUN* **lollipops** a large round hard sweet on a stick.
[origin unknown]

lollipop woman or **lollipop man** *NOUN* **lollipop women, lollipop men** an official who uses a circular sign on a stick to signal traffic to stop so that children can cross a road.

lolly *NOUN* **lollies** (*informal*) **1** a lollipop or an ice lolly. **2** (*slang*) money.
[short for *lollipop*]

lone *ADJECTIVE* solitary.
[from *alone*]

lonely *ADJECTIVE* **lonelier, loneliest** **1** sad because you are on your own. **2** solitary. **3** far from inhabited places; not often visited or used • *a lonely road.*
▷ **loneliness** *noun*
[from *lone*]

lonesome *ADJECTIVE* lonely.

long[1] *ADJECTIVE* **1** measuring a lot from one end to the other. **2** taking a lot of time • *a long holiday.* **3** having a certain length • *The river is 10 miles long.*

long *ADVERB* **1** for a long time • *Have you been waiting long?* **2** at a long time before or after • *They left long ago.* **3** throughout a time • *all night long.*
- **as long as** or **so long as** provided that; on condition that.
- **before long** soon.
- **no longer** not any more.
[from Old English *lang*]

long[2] *VERB* **longs, longing, longed** feel a strong desire.
[from Old English *langian*]

long division *NOUN* dividing one number by another and writing down all the calculations.

longevity (*say* lon-**jev**-it-ee) *NOUN* long life.
[from Latin *longus* = long + *aevum* = age]

longhand *NOUN* ordinary writing, contrasted with shorthand or typing.

longing *NOUN* **longings** a strong desire.

longitude *NOUN* **longitudes** the distance east or west, measured in degrees, from the Greenwich meridian.
[from Latin *longitudo* = length]

longitudinal *ADJECTIVE* **1** to do with longitude. **2** to do with length; measured lengthways.

long jump *NOUN* an athletic contest in which competitors jump as far as possible along the ground in one leap.

long-range *ADJECTIVE* covering a long distance or period of time • *a long-range missile.*

longship *NOUN* **longships** a long narrow warship, with oars and a sail, used by the Vikings.

long-sighted *ADJECTIVE* able to see distant things clearly but not things close to you.

long-suffering *ADJECTIVE* putting up with things patiently.

long-term *ADJECTIVE* to do with a long period of time.

long wave *NOUN* a radio wave of a wavelength above one kilometre and a frequency less than 300 kilohertz.

long-winded *ADJECTIVE* talking or writing at great length.

loo *NOUN* **loos** (*informal*) a toilet.
[origin unknown]

loofah *NOUN* **loofahs** a rough sponge made from a dried gourd.
[from Arabic]

look *VERB* **looks, looking, looked** **1** use your eyes; turn your eyes in a particular direction. **2** face in a particular direction. **3** have a certain appearance; seem • *You look sad.*
- **look after** **1** protect or take care of someone. **2** be in charge of something.
- **look down on** regard with contempt.
- **look for** try to find.
- **look forward to** be waiting eagerly for something you expect.
- **look into** investigate.
- **look out** be careful.
- **look up** **1** search for information about something. **2** improve in prospects • *Things are looking up.*
- **look up to** admire or respect.

look *NOUN* **looks** **1** the act of looking; a gaze or glance. **2** appearance • *I don't like the look of this place.*
[from Old English]

look-alike *NOUN* **look-alikes** someone who looks very like a famous person.

looking glass *NOUN* **looking glasses** (*old use*) a glass mirror.

lookout *NOUN* **lookouts** **1** looking out or watching for something • *Keep a lookout for snakes.* **2** a place from which you can keep watch. **3** a person whose job is to keep watch. **4** (*informal*) a person's own fault or concern • *If he wastes his money, that's his lookout.*

loom[1] *NOUN* **looms** a machine for weaving cloth.
[from Old English]

loom[2] *VERB* **looms, looming, loomed** appear suddenly; seem large or close and threatening • *An iceberg loomed up through the fog.*
[probably from old Dutch]

loony *ADJECTIVE* **loonier, looniest** (*slang*) crazy.
[short for *lunatic*]

loop *NOUN* **loops** the shape made by a curve crossing itself; a piece of string, ribbon, wire, etc. made into this shape.

loop *VERB* **loops, looping, looped** **1** make string etc. into a loop. **2** enclose something in a loop.
[origin unknown]

loophole *NOUN* **loopholes** **1** a way of avoiding a law or rule or promise etc. without actually breaking it. **2** a narrow opening in the wall of a fort etc.

loose *ADJECTIVE* **1** not tight; not firmly fixed • *a loose tooth.* **2** not tied up or shut in • *There's a lion loose!* **3** not packed in a box or packet etc. **4** not exact • *a loose translation.*
▷ **loosely** *adverb* **looseness** *noun*
- **at a loose end** with nothing to do.
- **on the loose** escaped or free.

loose *VERB* **looses, loosing, loosed** **1** loosen. **2** untie or release.
[from Old Norse]

loose-leaf *ADJECTIVE* with each sheet of paper separate and able to be removed • *a loose-leaf folder.*

loosen *VERB* **loosens, loosening, loosened** make or become loose or looser.

loot *NOUN* stolen things; goods taken from an enemy.

A B C D E F G H I J K L M N O P Q R S T U V W X Y Z

loot *VERB* **loots, looting, looted** **1** rob a place or an enemy, especially in a time of war or disorder. **2** take something as loot.
▷ **looter** *noun*
[from Hindi]

lop *VERB* **lops, lopping, lopped** cut away branches or twigs; cut off.
[origin unknown]

lope *VERB* **lopes, loping, loped** run with a long jumping stride.
▷ **lope** *noun*
[from Old Norse *hlaupa* = to leap]

lop-eared *ADJECTIVE* with drooping ears.
[from an old word *lop* = droop]

lopsided *ADJECTIVE* with one side lower or smaller than the other.
[same origin as *lop-eared*]

loquacious (*say* lok-way-shus) *ADJECTIVE* talkative.
▷ **loquacity** (*say* lok-wass-it-ee) *noun*
[from Latin *loqui* = speak]

lord *NOUN* **lords** **1** a nobleman, especially one who is allowed to use the title 'Lord' in front of his name. **2** a master or ruler.
- **Our Lord** Jesus Christ.
- **the Lord** God.

lord *VERB* **lords, lording, lorded**
- **lord it over** behave in a superior or domineering way • *At school Liam always used to lord it over the rest of us.*
[from Old English *hlaford* = person who keeps the bread (compare *lady*)]

lordly *ADJECTIVE* **lordlier, lordliest** **1** to do with a lord. **2** proud or haughty.

Lord Mayor *NOUN* **Lord Mayors** the title of the mayor of some large cities.

lordship *NOUN* a title used in speaking to or about a man of the rank of 'Lord'.

lore *NOUN* a set of traditional facts or beliefs • *gypsy lore.*
[from Old English]

lorgnette (*say* lorn-yet) *NOUN* **lorgnettes** a pair of spectacles held on a long handle.
[French, from *lorgner* = to squint]

lorry *NOUN* **lorries** a large strong motor vehicle for carrying heavy goods or troops.
[origin unknown]

lose *VERB* **loses, losing, lost** **1** be without something that you once had, especially because you cannot find it. **2** fail to keep or obtain something • *We lost control.* **3** be defeated in a contest or argument etc.
4 cause the loss of • *That one mistake lost us the game.* **5** (said about a clock or watch) become behind the correct time.
▷ **loser** *noun*
- **lose your life** be killed.
- **lose your way** not know where you are or which is the right path.
[from Old English]

loss *NOUN* **losses** **1** losing something.
2 something lost.
- **be at a loss** not know what to do or say.
[from Old English]

lost *past tense and past participle* of **lose**.

lost *ADJECTIVE* **1** not knowing where you are or not able to find your way • *I think we're lost.* **2** missing or strayed • *a lost dog.*
- **lost cause** an idea or policy etc. that is failing.
- **lost in** engrossed • *She was lost in thought.*

lot *NOUN* **lots** **1** a large number or amount • *You have a lot of friends.* • *There's lots of time.*
2 one of a set of objects used in choosing or deciding something by chance • *We drew lots to see who should go first.* **3** a person's share or fate. **4** something for sale at an auction. **5** a piece of land.
- **a lot** very much • *I feel a lot better.*
- **the lot** or **the whole lot** everything; all.
[from Old English]

loth *ADJECTIVE* a different spelling of *loath*.

lotion *NOUN* **lotions** a liquid for putting on the skin.
[from Latin *lotio* = washing]

lottery *NOUN* **lotteries** a way of raising money by selling numbered tickets and giving prizes to people who hold winning numbers, which are chosen by a method depending on chance. (COMPARE **lot** 2)
[probably from Dutch]

lotto *NOUN* a game like bingo.
[Italian]

lotus *NOUN* **lotuses** a kind of tropical water lily.
[from Greek]

loud *ADJECTIVE* **1** easily heard; producing much noise. **2** unpleasantly bright; gaudy • *loud colours.*
▷ **loudly** *adverb* **loudness** *noun*
[from Old English]

loudspeaker *NOUN* **loudspeakers** a device that changes electrical signals into sound, for reproducing music or voices.

lounge *NOUN* **lounges** a sitting room.

lounge *VERB* **lounges, lounging, lounged** sit or stand in a lazy and relaxed way.
[originally Scots; origin unknown]

louring (*rhymes with* **flowering**) *ADJECTIVE* looking dark and threatening • *a louring sky.*
[origin unknown]

louse *NOUN* **lice** a small insect that lives as a parasite on animals or plants.
[from Old English]

lousy *ADJECTIVE* **lousier, lousiest 1** full of lice. **2** (*slang*) very bad or unpleasant.

lout *NOUN* **louts** a bad-mannered man.
[origin unknown]

lovable *ADJECTIVE* easy to love.

love *NOUN* **loves 1** great liking or affection. **2** sexual affection or passion. **3** a loved person; a sweetheart. **4** (in tennis) no score; nil.
- **in love** feeling strong love.
- **make love** have sexual intercourse.

love *VERB* **loves, loving, loved** feel love for a person or thing.
▷ **lovingly** *adverb*
[from Old English]

love affair *NOUN* **love affairs** a romantic or sexual relationship between two people in love.

loveless *ADJECTIVE* without love.

lovelorn *ADJECTIVE* pining with love, especially when abandoned by a lover.
[from *love* + an old word *lorn* = abandoned]

lovely *ADJECTIVE* **lovelier, loveliest**
1 beautiful. **2** very pleasant or enjoyable.
▷ **loveliness** *noun*

lover *NOUN* **lovers 1** someone who loves something • *an art lover.* **2** a person who someone is having a sexual relationship with but is not married to.

lovesick *ADJECTIVE* longing for someone you love, especially someone who does not love you.

low[1] *ADJECTIVE* **1** only reaching a short way up; not high. **2** below average in importance, quality, amount, etc. • *low prices; of low rank.* **3** unhappy • *I'm feeling low.* **4** not high-pitched; not loud • *low notes; a low voice.*
▷ **lowness** *noun*

low *ADVERB* at or to a low level or position etc. • *The plane was flying low.*
[from Old Norse]

low[2] *VERB* **lows, lowing, lowed** moo like a cow.
[from Old English]

lower *ADJECTIVE & ADVERB* less high.

lower *VERB* **lowers, lowering, lowered** make or become lower.

lower case *NOUN* small letters, not capitals.

lowlands *PLURAL NOUN* low-lying country.
▷ **lowland** *adjective* **lowlander** *noun*

lowly *ADJECTIVE* **lowlier, lowliest** humble.
▷ **lowliness** *noun*

loyal *ADJECTIVE* always firmly supporting your friends or group or country etc.
▷ **loyally** *adverb* **loyalty** *noun*
[from old French]

Loyalist *NOUN* **Loyalists** (in Northern Ireland) a person who is in favour of keeping Northern Ireland's link with Britain.

loyalist *NOUN* **loyalists** a person who is loyal to the government during a revolt.

lozenge *NOUN* **lozenges 1** a small flavoured tablet, especially one containing medicine. **2** a diamond shape.
[from old French]

Ltd. *ABBREVIATION* (in names of companies) limited.

lubricant *NOUN* **lubricants** a lubricating substance.

lubricate *VERB* **lubricates, lubricating, lubricated** oil or grease something so that it moves smoothly.
▷ **lubrication** *noun*
[from Latin *lubricus* = slippery]

lucid *ADJECTIVE* **1** clear and easy to understand. **2** thinking clearly; not confused in your mind.
▷ **lucidly** *adverb* **lucidity** *noun*
[from Latin *lucidus* = bright]

luck *NOUN* **1** the way things happen without being planned; chance. **2** good fortune • *It will bring you luck.*
[from old German]

luckless *ADJECTIVE* unlucky.

lucky *ADJECTIVE* **luckier, luckiest** having or bringing or resulting from good luck.
▷ **luckily** *adverb*

lucrative (*say* loo-kra-tiv) *ADJECTIVE* profitable; earning you a lot of money.
[same origin as *lucre*]

lucre (*say* loo-ker) *NOUN* (*contemptuous*) money.
[from Latin *lucrum* = profit]

Luddite *NOUN* **Luddites** a person who opposes the introduction of new technology or methods, like the English workers who in 1811-16 destroyed the new machinery because they thought it would take their jobs.
[probably named after one of them, Ned *Lud*]

ludicrous *ADJECTIVE* ridiculous or laughable.
▷ **ludicrously** *adverb*
[from Latin *ludere* = play or have fun]

ludo *NOUN* a game played with dice and counters on a board.
[Latin, = I play]

lug *VERB* **lugs, lugging, lugged** drag or carry something heavy.

lug *NOUN* **lugs 1** an ear-like part on an object, by which it may be carried or fixed. **2** (*slang*) an ear.
[probably from a Scandinavian language]

luggage *NOUN* suitcases and bags etc. holding things for taking on a journey.
[from *lug*]

lugubrious (*say* lug-oo-bree-us) *ADJECTIVE* gloomy or mournful.
▷ **lugubriously** *adverb*
[from Latin *lugubris* = mourning]

lukewarm *ADJECTIVE* **1** only slightly warm; tepid. **2** not very enthusiastic • *lukewarm applause.*
[from an old word *luke* = tepid, + *warm*]

lull *VERB* **lulls, lulling, lulled 1** soothe or calm; send someone to sleep. **2** give someone a false feeling of being safe.

lull *NOUN* **lulls** a short period of quiet or inactivity.
[imitating the sounds you make to soothe a child]

lullaby *NOUN* **lullabies** a song that is sung to send a baby to sleep.
[from *lull* + *bye* as in *bye-byes*, a child's word for bed or sleep]

lumbago *NOUN* pain in the muscles of the lower back.
[same origin as *lumbar*]

lumbar *ADJECTIVE* to do with the lower back area.
[from Latin *lumbus* = loin]

lumber *NOUN* **1** unwanted furniture etc.; junk. **2** (*American*) timber.

lumber *VERB* **lumbers, lumbering, lumbered 1** leave someone with an unwanted or unpleasant task. **2** move in a heavy clumsy way.
[origin unknown]

lumberjack *NOUN* **lumberjacks** (*American*)
a person whose job is to cut or carry timber.

luminescent *ADJECTIVE* giving out light.
▷ **luminescence** *noun*
[from Latin *lumen* = light]

luminous *ADJECTIVE* glowing in the dark.
▷ **luminosity** *noun*
[same origin as *luminescent*]

lump[1] *NOUN* **lumps 1** a solid piece of something. **2** a swelling.
▷ **lumpy** *adjective*

lump *VERB* **lumps, lumping, lumped** put or treat things together in a group because you regard them as alike in some way.
[origin unknown]

lump[2] *VERB* **lumps, lumping, lumped**
- **lump it** (*informal*) put up with something you dislike.
[from an old word *lump* = look sulky]

lump sum *NOUN* **lump sums** a single payment, especially one covering a number of items.

lunacy *NOUN* **lunacies** insanity or great foolishness.
[from *lunatic*]

lunar *ADJECTIVE* to do with the moon.
[from Latin *luna* = moon]

lunar month *NOUN* **lunar months** the period between new moons; four weeks.

lunatic *NOUN* **lunatics** an insane person.
▷ **lunatic** *adjective*
[from Latin *luna* = moon (because formerly people were thought to be affected by changes of the moon)]

lunch *NOUN* **lunches** a meal eaten in the middle of the day.
▷ **lunch** *verb*
[short for *luncheon*]

luncheon *NOUN* **luncheons** (*formal*) lunch.
[origin unknown]

lung *NOUN* **lungs** either of the two parts of the body, in the chest, used in breathing.
[from Old English]

lunge *VERB* **lunges, lunging, lunged** thrust the body forward suddenly.
▷ **lunge** *noun*
[from French *allonger* = lengthen]

lupin *NOUN* **lupins** a garden plant with tall spikes of flowers.
[from Latin]

lurch[1] *VERB* **lurches, lurching, lurched** stagger; lean suddenly to one side.
▷ **lurch** *noun*
[originally a sailor's word: origin unknown]

lurch[2] *NOUN*
- **leave somebody in the lurch** leave somebody in difficulties.
[from old French]

lure *VERB* **lures, luring, lured** tempt a person or animal into a trap; entice.
▷ **lure** *noun*
[via old French from Germanic]

lurid (*say* lewr-id) *ADJECTIVE* **1** in very bright colours; gaudy. **2** sensational and shocking • *the lurid details of the murder.*
▷ **luridly** *adverb* **luridness** *noun*
[from Latin]

lurk *VERB* **lurks, lurking, lurked** wait where you cannot be seen.
[origin unknown]

luscious (*say* lush-us) *ADJECTIVE* delicious.
▷ **lusciously** *adverb* **lusciousness** *noun*
[origin unknown]

lush *ADJECTIVE* **1** growing thickly and strongly • *lush grass.* **2** luxurious.
▷ **lushly** *adverb* **lushness** *noun*
[origin unknown]

lust *NOUN* **lusts** powerful desire, especially sexual desire.
▷ **lustful** *adjective*

lust *VERB* **lusts, lusting, lusted** have a powerful desire for a person or thing • *people who lust after power.*
[Old English, = pleasure]

lustre *NOUN* brightness or brilliance.
▷ **lustrous** *adjective*
[from Latin *lustrare* = illuminate]

lusty *ADJECTIVE* **lustier, lustiest** strong and vigorous.
▷ **lustily** *adverb* **lustiness** *noun*
[originally = lively and cheerful: same origin as *lust*]

lute *NOUN* **lutes** a stringed musical instrument with a pear-shaped body, popular in the 14th-17th centuries.
[via French from Arabic]

luxuriant *ADJECTIVE* growing abundantly.
[same origin as *luxury*]
USAGE Do not confuse with **luxurious**.

luxuriate *VERB* **luxuriates, luxuriating, luxuriated** enjoy something as a luxury • *We've been luxuriating in the warm sunshine.*

luxury *NOUN* **luxuries** **1** something expensive that you enjoy but do not really need. **2** expensive and comfortable surroundings • *a life of luxury.*
▷ **luxurious** *adjective* **luxuriously** *adverb*
[from Latin *luxus* = plenty]

-ly *SUFFIX* forms **1** adjectives (e.g. *friendly, heavenly, sickly*), **2** adverbs from adjectives (e.g. *boldly, sweetly, thoroughly*).
[from Old English]

lychgate *NOUN* **lychgates** a churchyard gate with a roof over it.
[from Old English *lic* = corpse (because the coffin-bearers would shelter there until it was time to enter the church)]

Lycra *NOUN* (*trademark*) a thin stretchy material used especially for sports clothing.
[origin unknown]

lying *present participle* of **lie**[1] and **lie**[2].

lymph (*say* limf) *NOUN* a colourless fluid from the flesh or organs of the body, containing white blood cells.
▷ **lymphatic** *adjective*
[from Latin]

lynch *VERB* **lynches, lynching, lynched** join together to execute someone without a proper trial, especially by hanging them.
[named after William *Lynch*, an American judge who allowed this kind of punishment in about 1780]

lynx *NOUN* **lynxes** a wild animal like a very large cat with thick fur and very sharp sight.
[from Greek]

lyre *NOUN* **lyres** an ancient musical instrument like a small harp.
[from Greek]

lyric (*say* **li**-rik) *NOUN* **lyrics 1** a short poem that expresses the poet's feelings. **2** the words of a popular song.
[from Greek *lyrikos* = to be sung to the lyre]

lyrical *ADJECTIVE* **1** like a song. **2** expressing poetic feelings. **3** expressing yourself enthusiastically.
▷ **lyrically** *adverb*

Mm

MA *ABBREVIATION* Master of Arts.

ma *NOUN* (*informal*) mother.
[short for *mama*]

ma'am (*say* mam) *NOUN* madam.

mac *NOUN* **macs** (*informal*) a mackintosh.

macabre (*say* mak-**ahbr**) *ADJECTIVE* gruesome; strange and horrible.
[from French]

macadam *NOUN* layers of broken stone rolled flat to make a firm road surface.
▷ **macadamized** *adjective*
[named after a Scottish engineer, J. *McAdam*, who first laid such roads]

macaroni *NOUN* pasta in the form of short tubes.
[via Italian from Greek]

macaroon *NOUN* **macaroons** a small sweet cake or biscuit made with ground almonds.

macaw (*say* ma-**kaw**) *NOUN* **macaws** a brightly coloured parrot from Central and South America.
[from Portuguese]

mace *NOUN* **maces** an ornamental staff carried or placed in front of an official.
[from old French]

mach (*say* mahk) *NOUN*
- **mach number** the ratio of the speed of a moving object to the speed of sound. Mach one is the speed of sound, mach two is twice the speed of sound, and so on.
[named after the Austrian scientist Ernst *Mach* (1838-1916)]

machete (*say* mash-**et**-ee) *NOUN* **machetes** a broad heavy knife used as a tool or weapon.
[from Spanish]

machiavellian (*say* mak-ee-a-**vel**-ee-an) *ADJECTIVE* very cunning or deceitful in your dealings.
[named after an unscrupulous Italian statesman, Niccolo dei *Machiavelli* (1469-1527)]

machinations (*say* mash-in-**ay**-shonz) *PLURAL NOUN* clever schemes or plots.
[from Latin *machinare* = devise or plot; related to *machine*]

machine *NOUN* **machines** something with parts that work together to do a job.

machine *VERB* **machines, machining, machined** make something with a machine.
[from Greek *mechane* = device]

machine gun *NOUN* **machine guns** a gun that can keep firing bullets quickly one after another.

machine-readable *ADJECTIVE* (said about data) in a form that a computer can process.

machinery *NOUN* **1** machines. **2** the moving parts of a machine. **3** an organized system for doing something • *the machinery of local government.*

macho (*say* mach-oh) *ADJECTIVE* showing off masculine strength.
[Spanish, = male]

mackerel *NOUN* **mackerel** a sea fish used as food.
[from old French]

mackintosh *NOUN* **mackintoshes** a raincoat.
[named after the Scottish inventor of a waterproof material, C. *Macintosh*]

mad *ADJECTIVE* **madder, maddest** **1** having something wrong with the mind; insane. **2** extremely foolish. **3** very keen • *He is mad about football.* **4** (*informal*) very excited or annoyed.
▷ **madly** *adverb* **madness** *noun* **madman** *noun*
- **like mad** (*informal*) with great speed, energy, or enthusiasm.
[from Old English]

madam *NOUN* a word used when speaking politely to a woman • *Can I help you, madam?*
[from French *ma dame* = my lady]

madcap *ADJECTIVE* foolish and rash • *a madcap scheme.*

mad cow disease *NOUN* BSE.

madden *VERB* **maddens, maddening, maddened** make a person mad or angry.
▷ **maddening** *adjective*

madly *ADVERB* extremely; very much • *They are madly in love.*

madonna *NOUN* **madonnas** a picture or statue of the Virgin Mary.
[from old Italian *ma donna* = my lady]

madrigal *NOUN* **madrigals** a song for several voices singing different parts together.
[from Italian]

maelstrom (*say* mayl-strom) *NOUN* **maelstroms** **1** a great whirlpool. **2** a state of great confusion.
[originally the name of a whirlpool off the Norwegian coast: from Dutch *malen* = whirl + *stroom* = stream]

maestro (*say* my-stroh) *NOUN* **maestros** a master, especially a musician.
[Italian, = master]

mafia *NOUN* **1** a large organization of criminals in Italy, Sicily, and the United States of America. **2** any group of people believed to act together in a sinister way.
[Italian, = bragging]

magazine *NOUN* **magazines** **1** a paper-covered publication that comes out regularly, with articles, stories, or features by several writers. **2** the part of a gun that holds the cartridges. **3** a store for weapons and ammunition or for explosives. **4** a device that holds film for a camera or slides for a projector.
[from Arabic *makhazin* = storehouses]

magenta (*say* ma-**jen**-ta) *NOUN* a colour between bright red and purple.
[named after *Magenta*, a town in north Italy, where Napoleon III won a battle in the year when the dye was discovered (1859)]

maggot *NOUN* **maggots** the larva of some kinds of fly.
▷ **maggoty** *adjective*
[origin unknown]

Magi (*say* mayj-I) *PLURAL NOUN* the 'wise men' from the East who brought offerings to the infant Jesus at Bethlehem.
[from old Persian *magus* = priest; later = astrologer or wizard]

magic *NOUN* **1** the art of making impossible things happen by a mysterious or supernatural power. **2** mysterious tricks performed for entertainment. **3** a mysterious and enchanting quality • *the magic of Greece.*
▷ **magic** *adjective*
[same origin as *Magi*]

magical **1** to do with magic, or using magic. **2** wonderful or marvellous • *a magical evening.*
▷ **magically** *adverb*

magician *NOUN* **magicians** **1** a person who does magic tricks. **2** a wizard.

magisterial *ADJECTIVE* **1** to do with a magistrate. **2** masterful or imperious.
[same origin as *magistrate*]

magistrate *NOUN* **magistrates** an official who hears and judges minor cases in a local court.
▷ **magistracy** *noun*
[from Latin *magister* = master]

magma *NOUN* a molten substance beneath the earth's crust.
[from Greek]

magnanimous (*say* mag-**nan**-im-us) *ADJECTIVE* generous and forgiving, not petty-minded.
▷ **magnanimously** *adverb* **magnanimity** *noun*
[from Latin *magnus* = great + *animus* = mind]

magnate *NOUN* **magnates** a wealthy influential person, especially in business.
[from Latin *magnus* = great]

magnesia *NOUN* a white powder that is a compound of magnesium, used in medicine.
[from Greek *Magnesia lithos* = stone from Magnesia (now part of Turkey)]

magnesium *NOUN* a silvery-white metal that burns with a very bright flame.
[from *magnesia*]

magnet *NOUN* **magnets** a piece of iron or steel that can attract iron and that points north and south when it is hung up.
[same origin as *magnesia*]

magnetic *ADJECTIVE* **1** having or using the powers of a magnet. **2** having the power to attract people • *a magnetic personality.*
▷ **magnetically** *adverb*

magnetic tape *NOUN* **magnetic tapes** a plastic strip coated with a magnetic substance for recording sound or pictures or storing computer data.

magnetism *NOUN* **1** the properties and effects of magnetic substances. **2** great personal charm and attraction.

magnetize *VERB* **magnetizes, magnetizing, magnetized 1** make into a magnet. **2** attract strongly like a magnet.
▷ **magnetization** *noun*

magneto (*say* mag-**neet**-oh) *NOUN* **magnetos** a small electric generator using magnets.

magnificent *ADJECTIVE* **1** grand or splendid in appearance etc. **2** excellent.
▷ **magnificently** *adverb* **magnificence** *noun*
[from Latin *magnificus* = splendid]

magnify *VERB* **magnifies, magnifying, magnified 1** make something look bigger than it really is, as a lens or microscope does. **2** exaggerate.
▷ **magnification** *noun* **magnifier** *noun*
[from Latin *magnus* = great + *facere* = make]

magnifying glass *NOUN* **magnifying glasses** a lens that magnifies things.

magnitude *NOUN* **magnitudes 1** size or extent. **2** importance.
[from Latin *magnus* = great]

magnolia *NOUN* **magnolias** a tree with large white or pale-pink flowers.
[named after a French botanist, P. Magnol]

magnum *NOUN* **magnums** a large wine bottle of about twice the standard size (about 1.5 litres).
[Latin, = large thing]

magpie *NOUN* **magpies** a noisy bird with black and white feathers, related to the crow.
[from *Mag* (short for Margaret) + an old word *pie* = magpie]

maharajah *NOUN* **maharajahs** the title of certain Indian princes.
[from Sanskrit *maha* = great + *raja* = rajah]

mah-jong *NOUN* a Chinese game for four people, played with pieces called tiles.
[from Chinese]

mahogany *NOUN* a hard brown wood.
[origin unknown]

maid *NOUN* **maids 1** a female servant. **2** (*old use*) a girl.
▷ **maidservant** *noun*
[short for *maiden*]

maiden *NOUN* **maidens** (*old use*) a girl.
▷ **maidenhood** *noun*

maiden *ADJECTIVE* **1** not married • *a maiden aunt.* **2** first • *a maiden voyage.*
[from Old English]

maiden name *NOUN* **maiden names** a woman's family name before she marries.

maiden over *NOUN* **maiden overs** a cricket over in which no runs are scored.

mail[1] *NOUN* letters and parcels sent by post.

mail *VERB* **mails, mailing, mailed** send by post.
[from old French *male* = a bag]

mail[2] *NOUN* armour made of metal rings joined together • *a suit of chain mail.*
[from Latin *macula* = mesh]

mailing list *NOUN* **mailing lists** a list of names and addresses of people to whom an organization sends information from time to time.

mail order *NOUN* a system for buying and selling goods by post.

maim *VERB* **maims, maiming, maimed** injure a person so that part of his or her body is made useless.
[from old French]

main *ADJECTIVE* largest or most important.

main *NOUN* **1** the main pipe or cable in a public system carrying water, gas, or (usually called **mains**) **1** electricity to a building. **2** (*old use*) the seas • *Drake sailed the Spanish main.*
- **in the main** for the most part; on the whole.
[from Old English]

main clause *NOUN* **main clauses** a clause that can be used as a complete sentence. (COMPARE **subordinate clause**)

mainframe *NOUN* **mainframes** a large powerful computer that a lot of people can use at the same time.

mainland *NOUN* the main part of a country or continent, not the islands round it.

mainly *ADVERB* **1** chiefly. **2** almost completely. **3** usually.

mainmast *NOUN* **mainmasts** the tallest and most important mast on a ship.

mainstay *NOUN* the chief support or main part.
[from *main* + *stay*[2]]

mainstream *NOUN* the most widely accepted ideas or opinions about something • *Fascism is not in the mainstream of British politics.*

maintain *VERB* **maintains, maintaining, maintained** **1** cause something to continue; keep in existence. **2** keep a thing in good condition. **3** provide money for a person to live on. **4** state that something is true.
[from Latin *manu* = by hand + *tenere* = to hold]

maintenance *NOUN* **1** maintaining or keeping something in good condition. **2** money for food and clothing. **3** money to be paid by a husband or wife to the other partner after a divorce.

maisonette *NOUN* **maisonettes** **1** a small house. **2** part of a house used as a separate dwelling.
[from French]

maître d'hôtel (*say* metr doh-**tel**) *NOUN* **maîtres d'hôtel** a head waiter.
[French, = master of house]

maize *NOUN* a tall kind of corn with large seeds on cobs.
[via French and Spanish from Taino (a South American language)]

majestic *ADJECTIVE* **1** stately and dignified. **2** imposing.
▷ **majestically** *adverb*

majesty *NOUN* **majesties** **1** the title of a king or queen • *Her Majesty the Queen.* **2** being majestic.
[from old French; related to *major*]

major *ADJECTIVE* **1** greater; very important • *major roads.* **2** of the musical scale that has a semitone after the 3rd and 7th notes. (COMPARE **minor**)

major *NOUN* **majors** an army officer ranking next above a captain.
[Latin, = larger, greater]

major *VERB* **majors, majoring, majored** (*American & Australian/NZ*) specialize in a particular subject at college or university. • *He's majoring in psychology.*

majority *NOUN* **majorities** **1** the greatest part of a group of people or things. (COMPARE **minority**) **2** the amount by which the winner in an election beats the loser • *She had a majority of 25 over her opponent.* **3** the age at which a person becomes an adult according to the law, now usually 18 • *He attained his majority.*
[same origin as *major*]

A B C D E F G H I J K L M N O P Q R S T U V W X Y Z

make *VERB* **makes, making, made 1** bring something into existence, especially by putting things together. **2** cause or compel • *You made me jump! Make him repeat it.* **3** gain or earn • *She makes £15,000 a year.* **4** achieve or reach • *He made 25 runs. The swimmer just made the shore.* **5** reckon • *What do you make the time?* **6** result in or add up to • *4 and 6 make 10.* **7** perform an action etc. • *make an effort.* **8** arrange for use • *make the beds.* **9** cause to be successful or happy • *Her visit made my day.*

- **make do** manage with something that is not what you really want.
- **make for** go towards.
- **make love 1** have sexual intercourse. **2** (*old use*) try to win someone's love.
- **make off** go away quickly.
- **make out 1** manage to see, hear, or understand something. **2** claim or pretend that something is true.
- **make up 1** build or put together. **2** invent a story or excuse. **3** be friendly again after a disagreement. **4** compensate for something. **5** put on make-up.
- **make up your mind** decide.

make *NOUN* **makes 1** making; how something is made. **2** a brand of goods; something made by a particular firm.
[from Old English]

make-believe *NOUN* pretending or imagining things.

make-over *NOUN* **make-overs** changes in your make-up, hairstyle, and the way you dress to make you look and feel more attractive.

maker *NOUN* **makers** the person or firm that has made something.

makeshift *ADJECTIVE* improvised or used because you have nothing better • *We used a box as a makeshift table.*
[from an old phrase *make shift* = manage somehow, put up with]

make-up *NOUN* **1** cosmetics. **2** the way something is made up. **3** a person's character.

mal- *PREFIX* **1** bad. **2** badly (as in *malnourished*).
[from Latin *male* = badly]

maladjusted *ADJECTIVE* unable to fit in or cope with other people or your own circumstances.
[from *mal-* + *adjust*]

maladministration *NOUN* (*formal*) bad administration, especially of business affairs.

malady *NOUN* **maladies** an illness or disease.
[from French *malade* = ill]

malapropism *NOUN* **malapropisms** a comical confusion of words, e.g. using *hooligan* instead of *hurricane*.
[named after Mrs *Malaprop* in Sheridan's play *The Rivals*, who made mistakes of this kind]

malaria *NOUN* a feverish disease spread by mosquitoes.
▷ **malarial** *adjective*
[from Italian *mala aria* = bad air, which was once thought to cause the disease]

malcontent *NOUN* **malcontents** a discontented person who is likely to make trouble.

male *ADJECTIVE* **1** belonging to the sex that reproduces by fertilizing egg cells produced by the female. **2** of men • *a male voice choir.*

male *NOUN* **males** a male person, animal, or plant.
[from old French; related to *masculine*]

male chauvinist *NOUN* **male chauvinists** a man who thinks that women are not as good as men.

malefactor (*say* mal-if-ak-ter) *NOUN* **malefactors** a criminal or wrongdoer.
[from *mal-* + Latin *factor* = doer]

malevolent (*say* ma-lev-ol-ent) *ADJECTIVE* wishing to harm people.
▷ **malevolently** *adverb* **malevolence** *noun*
[from *mal-* + Latin *volens* = wishing]

malformed *ADJECTIVE* faultily formed.

malfunction *NOUN* **malfunctions** faulty functioning • *a malfunction in the computer.*

malfunction *VERB* **malfunctions, malfunctioning, malfunctioned** fail to work properly.

malice *NOUN* a desire to harm other people; spite.
▷ **malicious** *adjective* **maliciously** *adverb*
[from Latin *malus* = evil]

malign (*say* mal-I'n) ADJECTIVE **1** harmful • *a malign influence.* **2** showing malice.
▷ **malignity** (*say* mal-ig-nit-ee) *noun*

malign VERB **maligns, maligning, maligned** say unpleasant and untrue things about somebody.
[from Latin *malignare* = plot wickedly]

malignant ADJECTIVE **1** (said about a tumour) growing uncontrollably. **2** full of malice.
▷ **malignantly** *adverb* **malignancy** *noun*
[same origin as *malign*]

malinger VERB **malingers, malingering, malingered** pretend to be ill in order to avoid work.
▷ **malingerer** *noun*
[from old French]

mall (*say* mal or mawl) NOUN **malls** a shopping area closed to traffic.
[from the name of The *Mall*, a street in London]

mallard NOUN **mallard** or **mallards** a kind of wild duck of North America, Europe, and parts of Asia.
[from old French]

malleable ADJECTIVE **1** able to be pressed or hammered into shape. **2** easy to influence; adaptable.
▷ **malleability** *noun*
[from Latin *malleare* = to hammer]

mallet NOUN **mallets 1** a large hammer, usually made of wood. **2** an implement with a long handle, used in croquet or polo for striking the ball.
[from Latin *malleus* = a hammer]

malnutrition NOUN bad health because you do not have enough food or the right kind of food.
▷ **malnourished** *adjective*

malpractice NOUN wrongdoing by a professional person such as a doctor or lawyer.

malt NOUN dried barley used in brewing, making vinegar, etc.
▷ **malted** *adjective*
[from Old English]

maltreat VERB **maltreats, maltreating, maltreated** ill-treat.
▷ **maltreatment** *noun*

mama or **mamma** NOUN (*old use*) mother.
[imitating the sounds a child makes when it first tries to speak]

mammal NOUN **mammals** any animal of which the female gives birth to live babies which are fed with milk from her own body.
▷ **mammalian** (*say* mam-ay-lee-an) *adjective*
[from Latin *mamma* = breast]

mammoth NOUN **mammoths** an extinct elephant with a hairy skin and curved tusks.

mammoth ADJECTIVE huge.
[from Russian]

man NOUN **men 1** a grown-up male human being. **2** an individual person. **3** mankind. **4** a piece used in chess or some other board game.

man VERB **mans, manning, manned** supply with people to work something • *Man the pumps!*
[from Old English]

manacle NOUN **manacles** a fetter or handcuff.

manacle VERB **manacles, manacling, manacled** fasten with manacles.
[from Latin *manus* = hand]

manage VERB **manages, managing, managed 1** be able to cope with something difficult. **2** be in charge of a business or part of it, or a group of people.
▷ **manageable** *adjective*
[from Italian *maneggiare* = to handle]

management NOUN **1** managing. **2** managers; the people in charge.

manager NOUN **managers** a person who manages something.
▷ **managerial** (*say* man-a-jeer-ee-al) *adjective*

manageress NOUN **manageresses** a woman manager, especially of a shop or hotel.

mandarin NOUN **mandarins 1** an important official. **2** a kind of small orange.
[via Portuguese and Malay (a language spoken in Malaysia) from Sanskrit]

mandate NOUN **mandates** authority given to someone to carry out a certain task or policy • *An elected government has a mandate to govern the country.*
[from Latin *mandatum* = commanded]

mandatory *ADJECTIVE* obligatory or compulsory.
[same origin as *mandate*]

mandible *NOUN* **mandibles** **1** a jaw, especially the lower one. **2** either part of a bird's beak or the similar part in insects etc. (COMPARE **maxilla**)
[from Latin *mandere* = chew]

mandolin *NOUN* **mandolins** a musical instrument rather like a guitar.
[via French from Italian]

mane *NOUN* **manes** the long hair on a horse's or lion's neck.
[from Old English]

manful *ADJECTIVE* brave or determined.
▷ **manfully** *adverb*

manganese *NOUN* a hard brittle metal.
[via French from Italian; related to *magnesia*]

mange *NOUN* a skin disease of dogs etc.
[from old French]

manger *NOUN* **mangers** a trough in a stable for horses or cattle to feed from.
[from French *manger* = eat]

mangle *VERB* **mangles**, **mangling**, **mangled** damage something by crushing or cutting it roughly.
[from old French]

mango *NOUN* **mangoes** a tropical fruit with yellow pulp.
[via Portuguese and Malay (a language spoken in Malaysia) from Tamil]

mangold *NOUN* **mangolds** a large beet used as cattle food.
[from German]

mangrove *NOUN* **mangroves** a tropical tree growing in mud and swamps, with many tangled roots above the ground.
[probably from a South American language]

mangy *ADJECTIVE* **1** having mange. **2** scruffy or dirty.

manhandle *VERB* **manhandles**, **manhandling**, **manhandled** treat or push roughly.

manhole *NOUN* **manholes** a space or opening, usually with a cover, by which a person can get into a sewer or boiler etc. to inspect or repair it.

manhood *NOUN* **1** the condition of being a man. **2** manly qualities.

mania *NOUN* **manias** **1** violent madness. **2** great enthusiasm • *a mania for sport.*
[Greek, = madness]

maniac *NOUN* **maniacs** a person with mania.

manic *ADJECTIVE* suffering from mania.

manicure *NOUN* **manicures** care and treatment of the hands and nails.
▷ **manicure** *verb* **manicurist** *noun*
[from Latin *manus* = hand + *cura* = care]

manifest *ADJECTIVE* clear and obvious.
▷ **manifestly** *adverb*

manifest *VERB* **manifests**, **manifesting**, **manifested** show a thing clearly.
▷ **manifestation** *noun*
[from Latin]

manifesto *NOUN* **manifestos** a public statement of a group's or person's policy or principles.
[Italian; related to *manifest*]

manifold *ADJECTIVE* of many kinds; very varied.
[from *many* + *-fold*]

manipulate *VERB* **manipulates**, **manipulating**, **manipulated** **1** handle or arrange something skilfully. **2** get someone to do what you want by treating them cleverly.
▷ **manipulation** *noun* **manipulator** *noun*
[from Latin *manus* = hand]

mankind *NOUN* human beings in general.

manly *ADJECTIVE* **1** suitable for a man. **2** brave and strong.
▷ **manliness** *noun*

manner *NOUN* **1** the way something happens or is done. **2** a person's way of behaving. **3** sort • *all manner of things.*
[from old French]

mannerism *NOUN* **mannerisms** a person's own particular gesture or way of speaking.

manners *PLURAL NOUN* how a person behaves with other people; politeness.

mannish *ADJECTIVE* (said about a woman) like a man.

manoeuvre (*say* man-oo-ver) *NOUN* **manoeuvres** a difficult or skilful or cunning action.

manoeuvre *VERB* **manoeuvres, manoeuvring, manoeuvred** move carefully and skilfully.
▷ **manoeuvrable** *adjective*
[via French from Latin *manu operari* = work by hand]

man-of-war *NOUN* **men-of-war** a warship.

manor *NOUN* **manors 1** a manor house. **2** the land belonging to a manor house.
▷ **manorial** *adjective*
[from old French; related to *mansion*]

manor house *NOUN* **manor houses** a large important house in the country.

manpower *NOUN* the number of people who are working or needed or available for work on something.

manse *NOUN* **manses** a church minister's house, especially in Scotland.
[same origin as *mansion*]

mansion *NOUN* **mansions** a large stately house.
[from Latin *mansio* = a place to stay, a dwelling]

manslaughter *NOUN* killing a person unlawfully but without meaning to.

mantelpiece *NOUN* **mantelpieces** a shelf above a fireplace.
[same origin as *mantle* (because it goes over the fireplace)]

mantilla *NOUN* **mantillas** a lace veil worn by Spanish women over the hair and shoulders.
[Spanish, = little mantle]

mantle *NOUN* **mantles 1** a cloak. **2** a covering • *a mantle of snow.*
[from Latin]

mantra *NOUN* **mantras** a word or phrase that is constantly repeated to help people meditate, originally in Hinduism and Buddhism.
[Sanskrit, = thought]

manual *ADJECTIVE* worked by or done with the hands • *a manual typewriter; manual work.*
▷ **manually** *adverb*

manual *NOUN* **manuals** a handbook.
[from Latin *manus* = hand]

manufacture *VERB* **manufactures, manufacturing, manufactured** make things.
▷ **manufacture** *noun* **manufacturer** *noun*
[from Latin *manu* = by hand + *facere* = make]

manure *NOUN* fertilizer, especially dung.
[from old French]

manuscript *NOUN* **manuscripts** something written or typed but not printed.
[from Latin *manu* = by hand + *scriptum* = written]

Manx *ADJECTIVE* to do with the Isle of Man.

many *ADJECTIVE* **more, most** great in number; numerous • *many people.*

many *NOUN* many people or things • *Many were found.*
[from Old English]

Maori (*rhymes with* **flowery**) *NOUN* **Maoris 1** a member of the aboriginal people of New Zealand. **2** their language.

map *NOUN* **maps** a diagram of part or all of the earth's surface or of the sky.

map *VERB* **maps, mapping, mapped** make a map of an area.
- **map out** plan the details of something.
[from Latin *mappa mundi* = sheet of the world]

maple *NOUN* **maples** a tree with broad leaves.
[from Old English]

maple syrup *NOUN* a sweet substance made from the sap of some kinds of maple.

mar *VERB* **mars, marring, marred** spoil.
[from Old English]

marathon *NOUN* **marathons** a long-distance running race, especially one covering 26 miles 385 yards (42.195 km).
[named after *Marathon* in Greece, from which a messenger is said to have run to Athens (about 40 kilometres) to announce that the Greeks had defeated the Persian army]

marauding *ADJECTIVE* going about in search of plunder or prey.
▷ **marauder** *noun*
[from French *maraud* = rogue]

marble *NOUN* **marbles 1** a small glass ball used in games. **2** a kind of limestone polished and used in sculpture or building.
[from Greek *marmaros* = shining stone]

March *NOUN* the third month of the year.
[named after Mars, the Roman god of war]

march *VERB* **marches, marching, marched** **1** walk with regular steps. **2** make somebody walk somewhere • *He marched them up the hill.*
▷ **marcher** *noun*

march *NOUN* **marches** **1** marching. **2** music suitable for marching to.
[from old French]

marchioness *NOUN* **marchionesses** the wife or widow of a marquis.
[from Latin]

mare *NOUN* **mares** a female horse or donkey.
[from Old English]

margarine (*say* mar-ja-**reen** or mar-ga-**reen**) *NOUN* a substance used like butter, made from animal or vegetable fats.
[from French]

marge *NOUN* (*informal*) margarine.

margin *NOUN* **margins** **1** an edge or border. **2** the blank space between the edge of a page and the writing or pictures on it. **3** the difference between two scores or prices etc. • *She won by a narrow margin.*
[from Latin]

marginal *ADJECTIVE* **1** in a margin • *marginal notes.* **2** very slight • *a marginal difference.*
▷ **marginally** *adverb*

marginal seat *NOUN* **marginal seats** a constituency where an MP was elected with only a small majority and may be defeated in the next election.

marigold *NOUN* **marigolds** a yellow or orange garden flower.
[from the name *Mary* + *gold*]

marijuana (*say* ma-ri-**hwah**-na) *NOUN* a drug made from hemp.
[an American Spanish word]

marina *NOUN* **marinas** a harbour for yachts, motor boats, etc.
[same origin as *marine*]

marinade *NOUN* **marinades** a flavoured liquid in which meat or fish is soaked before being cooked.
▷ **marinade** *verb*
[via French from Spanish]

marinate *VERB* **marinates, marinating, marinated** soak in a marinade.
[via French from Italian]

marine (*say* ma-**reen**) *ADJECTIVE* to do with the sea; living in the sea.

marine *NOUN* **marines** a member of the troops who are trained to serve at sea as well as on land.
[from Latin *mare* = sea]

mariner (*say* ma-rin-er) *NOUN* **mariners** a sailor.

marionette *NOUN* **marionettes** a puppet worked by strings or wires.
[French, = little Mary]

marital *ADJECTIVE* to do with marriage.
[from Latin *maritus* = husband]

maritime *ADJECTIVE* **1** to do with the sea or ships. **2** found near the sea.
[same origin as *marine*]

marjoram *NOUN* a herb with a mild flavour, used in cooking.
[from old French]

mark[1] *NOUN* **marks** **1** a spot, dot, line, or stain etc. on something. **2** a number or letter put on a piece of work to show how good it is. **3** a distinguishing feature. **4** a sign or symbol • *They all stood as a mark of respect.* **5** a target.
- **on your marks!** a command to runners to get ready to begin a race.
- **up to the mark** of the normal or expected standard.

mark *VERB* **marks, marking, marked** **1** put a mark on something. **2** give a mark to a piece of work. **3** pay attention to something • *Mark my words!* **4** keep close to an opposing player in football etc.
▷ **marker** *noun*
- **mark time** **1** march on the spot without moving forward. **2** occupy your time without making any progress.
[from Old English *merc*]

mark[2] *NOUN* **marks** a unit of money used in Germany before the introduction of the euro.

marked *ADJECTIVE* noticeable • *a marked improvement.*
▷ **markedly** *adverb*

market *NOUN* **markets** **1** a place where things are bought and sold, usually from stalls in the open air. **2** demand for things • *Is there a market for typewriters now?*
▷ **marketplace** *noun*
- **on the market** offered for sale.

market *VERB* **markets, marketing, marketed** offer things for sale.
▷ **marketable** *adjective*
[via Old English from Latin *merx* = goods, merchandise]

marketing *NOUN* the branch of business concerned with advertising and selling the product.

market research *NOUN* the study of what people need or want to buy.

marksman *NOUN* **marksmen** an expert in shooting at a target.
▷ **marksmanship** *noun*

marmalade *NOUN* jam made from oranges, lemons, or other citrus fruit.
[via French from Portuguese *marmelo* = quince (from which marmalade was first made)]

marmoset *NOUN* **marmosets** a kind of small monkey.
[from French]

maroon[1] *VERB* **maroons, marooning, marooned** abandon or isolate somebody in a deserted place; strand.
[via French from Spanish *cimarrón* = runaway slave]

maroon[2] *NOUN* dark red.
[from French *marron* = chestnut]

marquee (*say* mar-**kee**) *NOUN* **marquees** a large tent used for a party or exhibition etc.
[from French; related to *marquis*]

marquis *NOUN* **marquises** a nobleman ranking next above an earl.
[from old French]

marriage *NOUN* **marriages** **1** the state of being married. **2** a wedding.

marrow *NOUN* **marrows** **1** a large gourd eaten as a vegetable. **2** the soft substance inside bones.
[from Old English]

marry *VERB* **marries, marrying, married** **1** become a person's husband or wife. **2** join two people as husband and wife; be in charge of a marriage ceremony.
[from Latin *maritus* = husband]

marsh *NOUN* **marshes** a low-lying area of very wet ground.
▷ **marshy** *adjective*
[from Old English]

marshal *NOUN* **marshals** **1** an official who supervises a contest or ceremony etc. **2** an officer of very high rank • *a Field Marshal.*

marshal *VERB* **marshals, marshalling, marshalled** **1** arrange neatly. **2** usher or escort.
[via old French from Germanic]

marshmallow *NOUN* **marshmallows** a soft spongy sweet, usually pink or white.
[originally made from the root of the marshmallow, a pink flower that grows in marshes]

marsupial (*say* mar-**soo**-pee-al) *NOUN* **marsupials** an animal such as a kangaroo or wallaby. The female has a pouch on the front of its body in which its babies are carried.
[from Greek *marsypion* = pouch]

martial *ADJECTIVE* to do with war; warlike.
[Latin, = belonging to Mars, the Roman god of war]

martial arts *PLURAL NOUN* fighting sports, such as judo and karate.

martial law *NOUN* government of a country by the armed forces during a crisis.

martin *NOUN* **martins** a bird rather like a swallow.
[probably after St Martin of Tours, who gave half his cloak to a beggar (because of the bird's markings, which look like a torn cloak)]

martinet *NOUN* **martinets** a very strict person.
[named after a French army officer, J. *Martinet*, who imposed harsh discipline on his troops]

martyr *NOUN* **martyrs** a person who is killed or made to suffer because of his or her beliefs.
▷ **martyrdom** *noun*

martyr *VERB* **martyrs, martyring, martyred** kill or torment someone as a martyr.
[via Old English from Greek]

marvel *NOUN* **marvels** a wonderful thing.

marvel *VERB* **marvels, marvelling, marvelled** be filled with wonder.
[from old French; related to *miracle*]

marvellous *ADJECTIVE* wonderful.

Marxism *NOUN* the Communist theories of the German writer Karl Marx (1818-83).
▷ **Marxist** *noun & adjective*

marzipan *NOUN* a soft sweet food made of ground almonds, eggs, and sugar.
[via German from Italian]

mascara *NOUN* a cosmetic for darkening the eyelashes.
[Italian, = mask]

mascot *NOUN* **mascots** a person, animal, or thing that is believed to bring good luck.
[from French]

masculine *ADJECTIVE* **1** to do with men. **2** typical of or suitable for men. **3** (in some languages) belonging to the class of words which includes the words referring to men, such as *garçon* and *livre* in French.
▷ **masculinity** *noun*
[from Latin *masculus* = male]

mash *VERB* **mashes, mashing, mashed** crush into a soft mass.

mash *NOUN* **mashes** **1** a soft mixture of cooked grain or bran etc. **2** (*informal*) mashed potatoes.
[from Old English]

mask *NOUN* **masks** a covering worn over the face to disguise or protect it.

mask *VERB* **masks, masking, masked** **1** cover with a mask. **2** disguise or conceal.
[via French from Italian]

masochist (*say* mas-ok-ist) *NOUN* **masochists** a person who enjoys things that seem painful or tiresome.
▷ **masochistic** *adjective* **masochism** *noun*
[named after an Austrian novelist, L. von *Sacher-Masoch*, who wrote about masochism]

Mason *NOUN* **Masons** a Freemason.
▷ **Masonic** (*say* ma-sonn-ik) *adjective*

mason *NOUN* **masons** a person who builds or works with stone.
[from old French]

masonry *NOUN* **1** the stone parts of a building; stonework. **2** a mason's work.

masquerade *NOUN* **masquerades** a pretence.

masquerade *VERB* **masquerades, masquerading, masqueraded** pretend to be something • *He masqueraded as a policeman.*
[via French from Italian *mascara* = mask]

Mass *NOUN* **Masses** the Communion service in a Roman Catholic church.
[via Old English from Latin]

mass *NOUN* **masses** **1** a large amount. **2** a heap or other collection of matter. **3** (*in science*) the quantity of physical matter that a thing contains.
- **the masses** the ordinary people.

mass *ADJECTIVE* involving a large number of people • *mass murder.*

mass *VERB* **masses, massing, massed** collect into a mass.
[from Greek]

massacre *NOUN* **massacres** the killing of a large number of people.
▷ **massacre** *verb*
[from French, = butchery]

massage (*say* mas-ahzh) *VERB* **massages, massaging, massaged** rub and press the body to make it less stiff or less painful.
▷ **massage** *noun* **masseur** *noun* **masseuse** *noun*
[from French]

massive *ADJECTIVE* large and heavy; huge.
[from French; related to *mass*]

mass media *PLURAL NOUN* the main media of news information, especially newspapers and broadcasting.

mass production *NOUN* manufacturing goods in large quantities.
▷ **mass-produced** *adjective*

mast *NOUN* **masts** a tall pole that holds up a ship's sails or a flag or an aerial.
[from Old English]

master *NOUN* **masters** **1** a man who is in charge of something. **2** a male teacher. **3** a great artist, composer, sportsman, etc. **4** something from which copies are made. **5** (*old use*) a title put before a boy's name.

master *VERB* **masters, mastering, mastered** **1** learn a subject or a skill thoroughly. **2** overcome; bring under control.
[same origin as *magistrate*]

masterful *ADJECTIVE* **1** domineering. **2** very skilful.
▷ **masterfully** *adverb*

master key *NOUN* **master keys** a key that will open several different locks.

masterly *ADJECTIVE* very skilful.

mastermind *NOUN* **masterminds** **1** a very clever person. **2** the person who plans and organizes a scheme or crime.

mastermind *VERB* **masterminds, masterminding, masterminded** plan and organize a scheme or crime.

Master of Arts *NOUN* **Masters of Arts** a person who has taken the next degree after Bachelor of Arts.

master of ceremonies *NOUN* **masters of ceremonies** a person who introduces the speakers at a formal event, or the entertainers at a variety show.

Master of Science *NOUN* **Masters of Science** a person who has taken the next degree after Bachelor of Science.

masterpiece *NOUN* **masterpieces** **1** an excellent piece of work. **2** a person's best piece of work.

mastery *NOUN* complete control or thorough knowledge or skill in something.

masticate *VERB* **masticates, masticating, masticated** (*formal*) chew food.
▷ **mastication** *noun*
[from Greek *mastichan* = gnash the teeth]

mastiff *NOUN* **mastiffs** a large kind of dog.
[from old French]

masturbate *VERB* **masturbates, masturbating, masturbated** get sexual pleasure by rubbing your genitals.
▷ **masturbation** *noun*
[from Latin]

mat *NOUN* **mats** **1** a small carpet. **2** a doormat. **3** a small piece of material put on a table to protect the surface.
[from Old English]

matador *NOUN* **matadors** a bullfighter who fights on foot.
[Spanish, from *matar* = kill]

match[1] *NOUN* **matches** a small thin stick with a head made of a substance that gives a flame when rubbed on something rough.
▷ **matchbox** *noun* **matchstick** *noun*
[from old French]

match[2] *NOUN* **matches** **1** a game or contest between two teams or players. **2** one person or thing that matches another. **3** a marriage.

match *VERB* **matches, matching, matched** **1** be equal or similar to another person or thing. **2** put teams or players to compete against each other. **3** find something that is similar or corresponding.
[from Old English]

matchboard *NOUN* **matchboards** a piece of board that fits into a groove in a similar piece.

mate[1] *NOUN* **mates** **1** a companion or friend. **2** each of a mated pair of birds or animals. **3** an officer on a merchant ship.

mate *VERB* **mates, mating, mated** **1** come together or bring two together in order to breed. **2** put things together as a pair or because they correspond.
[from old German]

mate[2] *NOUN & VERB* (in chess) checkmate.

material *NOUN* **materials** **1** anything used for making something else. **2** cloth or fabric.

material *ADJECTIVE* **1** to do with possessions, money, etc. • *material comforts.* **2** important • *a material difference.*
[from Latin *materia* = matter]

materialism *NOUN* the belief that possessions are very important.
▷ **materialist** *noun* **materialistic** *adjective*
[same origin as *material*]

materialize *VERB* **materializes, materializing, materialized 1** become visible; appear • *The ghost didn't materialize.* **2** become a fact; happen • *The trip did not materialize.*
▷ **materialization** *noun*
[same origin as *material*]

maternal *ADJECTIVE* **1** to do with a mother. **2** motherly.
▷ **maternally** *adverb*
[from Latin *mater* = mother]

maternity *NOUN* motherhood.

maternity *ADJECTIVE* to do with having a baby • *maternity ward.*
[same origin as *maternal*]

matey *ADJECTIVE* friendly and sociable.

mathematics *NOUN* the study of numbers, measurements, and shapes.
▷ **mathematical** *adjective* **mathematically** *adverb* **mathematician** *noun*
[from Greek *mathema* = science]

maths *NOUN* (*informal*) mathematics.

matinée *NOUN* **matinées** an afternoon performance at a theatre or cinema.
[French, literally = morning]

matins *NOUN* the church service of morning prayer.
[from Latin *matutinus* = belonging to the morning]

matriarch (*say* may-tree-ark) *NOUN* **matriarchs** a woman who is head of a family or tribe. (COMPARE **patriarch**)
▷ **matriarchal** *adjective* **matriarchy** *noun*
[from Latin *mater* = mother, + *-arch*]

matrimony *NOUN* marriage.
▷ **matrimonial** *adjective*
[from Latin *mater* = mother]

matrix (*say* may-triks) *NOUN* **matrices**, (*say* may-tri-seez) **1** (*in mathematics*) a set of quantities arranged in rows and columns. **2** a mould or framework in which something is made or allowed to develop.
[from Latin]

matron *NOUN* **matrons 1** a mature married woman. **2** a woman in charge of nursing in a school etc. or (formerly) of the nursing staff in a hospital.
▷ **matronly** *adjective*
[same origin as *matrimony*]

matt *ADJECTIVE* not shiny • *matt paint.*
[from French]

matted *ADJECTIVE* tangled into a mass.
[from *mat*]

matter *NOUN* **matters 1** something you can touch or see, not spirit or mind or qualities etc. **2** a substance • *Peat consists mainly of vegetable matter.* **3** things of a certain kind • *printed matter.* **4** something to be thought about or done • *It's a serious matter.* **5** a quantity • *in a matter of minutes.*
- **a matter of course** the natural or expected thing • *I always lock my bike up, as a matter of course.*
- **as a matter of fact** in fact.
- **no matter** it does not matter.
- **what is the matter?** what is wrong?

matter *VERB* **matters, mattering, mattered** be important.
[same origin as *material*]

matter-of-fact *ADJECTIVE* keeping to facts; not imaginative or emotional • *She talked about death in a very matter-of-fact way.*

matting *NOUN* rough material for covering floors.

mattress *NOUN* **mattresses** soft or springy material in a fabric covering, used on or as a bed.
[via French from Arabic]

mature *ADJECTIVE* **1** fully grown or developed. **2** grown-up.
▷ **maturely** *adverb* **maturity** *noun*

mature *VERB* **matures, maturing, matured** make or become mature.
[from Latin *maturus* = ripe]

maudlin *ADJECTIVE* sentimental in a silly or tearful way.
[from an old pronunciation of St Mary Magdalen (because pictures usually show her weeping)]

maul *VERB* **mauls, mauling, mauled** injure by handling or clawing • *He was mauled by a lion.*
[originally = knock down: from Latin *malleus* = a hammer]

mausoleum (*say* maw-sol-ee-um) *NOUN* **mausoleums** a magnificent tomb.
[named after the tomb of *Mausolus*, a king in the 4th century BC in what is now Turkey]

mauve (*say* mohv) *NOUN* pale purple.
[from Latin *malva* = a plant with mauve flowers]

maverick *NOUN* **mavericks** a person who belongs to a group but often disagrees with its beliefs or acts on his or her own.
[originally = an unbranded calf: named after an American rancher, S. A. *Maverick*, who did not brand his cattle]

maw *NOUN* **maws** the jaws, mouth, or stomach of a hungry or fierce animal.
[from Old English]

maxilla *NOUN* **maxillae**, (*say* mak-si-lee) the upper jaw; a similar part in a bird or insect etc. (COMPARE **mandible**)
[Latin, = jaw]

maxim *NOUN* **maxims** a short saying giving a general truth or rule of behaviour, e.g. 'Waste not, want not'.
[from Latin *maxima propositio* = greatest statement]

maximize *VERB* **maximizes, maximizing, maximized** make something as great, large, or effective as possible.

maximum *NOUN* **maxima** or **maximums** the greatest possible number or amount. (The opposite is **minimum**.)

maximum *ADJECTIVE* greatest or most.
[Latin, = greatest thing]

May *NOUN* the fifth month of the year.
[named after Maia, a Roman goddess]

may[1] *AUXILIARY VERB* **may, might**
used to express **1** permission (*You may go now*), **2** possibility (*It may be true*), **3** wish (*Long may she reign*), **4** uncertainty (*whoever it may be*).
[from Old English]
USAGE See note at **can**.

may[2] *NOUN* hawthorn blossom.
[because the hawthorn blooms in the month of May]

maybe *ADVERB* perhaps; possibly.

mayday *NOUN* **maydays** an international radio signal calling for help.
[from French *m'aider* = help me]

mayfly *NOUN* **mayflies** an insect that lives for only a short time, in spring.

mayhem *NOUN* violent confusion or damage • *The mob caused mayhem.*
[from old French; related to *maim*]

mayonnaise *NOUN* a creamy sauce made from eggs, oil, vinegar, etc., eaten with salad.
[French, named after Mahón on Minorca, which the French had just captured when mayonnaise was invented]

mayor *NOUN* **mayors** the person in charge of the council in a town or city.
▷ **mayoral** *adjective* **mayoress** *noun*
[from old French; related to *major*]

maypole *NOUN* **maypoles** a decorated pole round which people dance on 1 May.

maze *NOUN* **mazes** a network of paths, especially one designed as a puzzle in which to try and find your way.
[from *amaze*]

Mb *ABBREVIATION* megabyte(s).

MC *ABBREVIATION* master of ceremonies.

MD *ABBREVIATION* Doctor of Medicine.

ME *NOUN* long-lasting fever, weakness, and pain in the muscles following a viral infection.
[abbreviation of the scientific name, *myalgic encephalomyelitis*]

me *PRONOUN* the form of *I* used as the object of a verb or after a preposition.
[from Old English]

mead *NOUN* an alcoholic drink made from honey and water.
[from Old English]

meadow (*say* med-oh) *NOUN* **meadows** a field of grass.
[from Old English]

meagre *ADJECTIVE* scanty in amount; barely enough • *a meagre diet.*
[from French]

meal[1] *NOUN* **meals** food served and eaten at one sitting.
[from Old English *mael*]

meal[2] *NOUN* coarsely-ground grain.
▷ **mealy** *adjective*
[from Old English *melu*]

mealie *NOUN* **mealies** (*S. African*) maize or an ear of maize.
[via Afrikaans from Latin *milium*]

mealtime *NOUN* **mealtimes** a regular time for having a meal.

mealy-mouthed *ADJECTIVE* too polite or timid to say what you really mean.
[from *meal*[2] (because of the softness of meal)]

mean[1] *VERB* **means, meaning, meant** (*say* ment) **1** have as an equivalent or explanation • *'Maybe' means 'perhaps'.* **2** have as a purpose; intend • *I meant to tell you, but I forgot.* **3** indicate • *Dark clouds mean rain.* **4** have as a result • *It means I'll have to get the early train.*
[from Old English *maenan*]

mean[2] *ADJECTIVE* **meaner, meanest 1** not generous; miserly. **2** unkind or spiteful • *a mean trick.* **3** poor in quality or appearance • *a mean little house.*
▹ **meanly** *adverb* **meanness** *noun*
[from Old English *maene*]

mean[3] *NOUN* **means** a point or number midway between two extremes; the average of a set of numbers.

mean *ADJECTIVE* midway between two points; average.
[from old French; related to *medial*]

meander (*say* mee-an-der) *VERB* **meanders, meandering, meandered** take a winding course; wander.
▹ **meander** *noun*
[named after the *Meander*, a river in Turkey (now Mendere or Menderes)]

meaning *NOUN* **meanings** what something means.
▹ **meaningful** *adjective* **meaningless** *adjective*

means *NOUN* a way of achieving something or producing a result • *a means of transport.*
- **by all means** certainly.
- **by means of** by this method; using this.
- **by no means** not at all.

means *PLURAL NOUN* money or other wealth.
- **live beyond your means** spend more than you can afford.
[from *mean*[3], in an old sense = someone in the middle, a go- between]

means test *NOUN* **means tests** an inquiry into how much money or income a person has, in order to decide whether he or she is entitled to get help from public funds.

meantime *NOUN*
- **in the meantime** the time between two events or while something else is happening.
[from *mean*[3] + *time*]

meanwhile *ADVERB* in the time between two events or while something else is happening.
[from *mean*[3] + *while*]

measles *NOUN* an infectious disease that causes small red spots on the skin.
[probably from old German *masele* = pimple]

measly *ADJECTIVE* (*informal*) not adequate or generous • *He paid me a measly £50 for a whole day's work.*
[originally = infected with measles; later = blotchy, marked, of poor quality]

measure *VERB* **measures, measuring, measured 1** find the size, amount, or extent of something by comparing it with a fixed unit or with an object of known size. **2** be a certain size • *The room measures 3.4 metres.*
▹ **measurable** *adjective*

measure *NOUN* **measures 1** a unit used for measuring • *A kilometre is a measure of length.* **2** a device used in measuring. **3** the size or quantity of something. **4** something done for a particular purpose • *We took measures to stop vandalism.*
[from Latin]

measurement *NOUN* **measurements 1** the process of measuring something. **2** a size or amount found by measuring.

meat *NOUN* animal flesh used as food.
▹ **meaty** *adjective*
[from Old English *mete* = food]

mecca *NOUN* a place which attracts people with a particular interest • *Wimbledon is a mecca for tennis fans.*
[from *Mecca* in Saudi Arabia, a holy city and place of pilgrimage for Muslims]

mechanic *NOUN* **mechanics** a person who maintains or repairs machinery.

mechanical *ADJECTIVE* **1** to do with machines. **2** produced or worked by machines. **3** done or doing things without thought.
▹ **mechanically** *adverb*
[from Greek *mechane* = machine]

mechanics *NOUN* **1** the study of movement and force. **2** the study or use of machines.

mechanism *NOUN* **mechanisms** **1** the moving parts of a machine. **2** the way a machine works. **3** the process by which something is done.

mechanized *ADJECTIVE* equipped with machines.
▷ **mechanization** *noun*

medal *NOUN* **medals** a piece of metal shaped like a coin, star, or cross, given to a person for bravery or for achieving something.
[from French]

medallion *NOUN* **medallions** a large medal, usually worn round the neck as an ornament.
[via French from Italian]

medallist *NOUN* **medallists** a winner of a medal.

meddle *VERB* **meddles, meddling, meddled** **1** interfere. **2** tinker • *Don't meddle with it.*
▷ **meddler** *noun* **meddlesome** *adjective*
[from old French; related to *mix*]

media *plural* of **medium**
noun
- **the media** newspapers, radio, and television, which convey information and ideas to the public. (SEE *medium*)
USAGE This word is a plural and should have a plural verb. Although it is commonly used with a singular verb, this is not generally approved of. Say *The media are* (not 'is') *very influential.* It is incorrect to speak of one of them (e.g. television) as *a media* or *this media.*

medial *ADJECTIVE* **1** in the middle. **2** average.
[from Latin *medius* = middle]

median *ADJECTIVE* in the middle.

median *NOUN* **medians** **1** a median point or line. **2** (*in mathematics*) the middle number in a set of numbers that have been arranged in order. The median of 2, 3, 5, 8, 9, 14, and 15 is 8. **3** a straight line passing from a point of a triangle to the centre of the opposite side.
[same origin as *medial*]

mediate *VERB* **mediates, mediating, mediated** negotiate between the opposing sides in a dispute.
▷ **mediation** *noun* **mediator** *noun*
[same origin as *medial*]

medical *ADJECTIVE* to do with the treatment of disease.
▷ **medically** *adverb*
[from Latin *medicus* = doctor]

medicated *ADJECTIVE* treated with a medicinal substance.
[from Latin *medicare* = give medicine]

medication *NOUN* **1** a medicine. **2** treatment using medicine.

medicine *NOUN* **medicines** **1** a substance, usually swallowed, used to try to cure a disease. **2** the study and treatment of diseases.
▷ **medicinal** (*say* med-**iss**-in-al) *adjective* **medicinally** *adverb*
[same origin as *medical*]

medieval (*say* med-ee-**ee**-val) *ADJECTIVE* belonging to or to do with the Middle Ages.
[from Latin *medius* = middle + *aevum* = age]

mediocre (*say* mee-dee-**oh**-ker) *ADJECTIVE* not very good; of only medium quality.
▷ **mediocrity** *noun*
[from Latin *mediocris* = of medium height]

meditate *VERB* **meditates, meditating, meditated** think deeply and quietly.
▷ **meditation** *noun* **meditative** *adjective*
[from Latin]

Mediterranean *ADJECTIVE* to do with the Mediterranean Sea (which lies between Europe and Africa) or the countries round it.
[from Latin *Mare Mediterraneum* = sea in the middle of land, from *medius* = middle + *terra* = land]

medium *ADJECTIVE* neither large nor small; moderate.

medium *NOUN* **media** **1** a thing in which something exists, moves, or is expressed • *Air is the medium in which sound travels.* • *Television is used as a medium for advertising.* (SEE *media*) **mediums** **2** a person who claims to be able to communicate with the dead.
[Latin, = middle thing]

A B C D E F G H I J K L M N O P Q R S T U V W X Y Z

medium wave *NOUN* a radio wave of a frequency between 300 kilohertz and 3 megahertz.

medley *NOUN* **medleys** **1** an assortment or mixture of things. **2** a collection of songs or tunes played as a continuous piece.
[from old French]

meek *ADJECTIVE* **meeker**, **meekest** quiet and obedient.
▷ **meekly** *adverb* **meekness** *noun*
[from Old Norse]

meet[1] *VERB* **meets**, **meeting**, **met** **1** come together from different places • *We all met in London.* **2** get to know someone • *We met at a party.* **3** come into contact; touch. **4** go to receive an arrival • *I'll meet your train.* **5** pay a bill or the cost of something. **6** satisfy or fulfil • *I hope this meets your needs.*

meet *NOUN* **meets** a gathering of riders and hounds for a hunt.
[from Old English *metan*]

meet[2] *ADJECTIVE* (*old use*) proper or suitable.
[from Old English *gemaete*]

meeting *NOUN* **meetings** **1** coming together. **2** a number of people who have come together for a discussion, contest, etc.

mega- *PREFIX* **1** large or great (as in *megaphone*). **2** one million (as in *megahertz* = one million hertz).
[from Greek *megas* = great]

megabyte *NOUN* **megabytes** (*in computing*) a unit of information roughly equal to one million bytes.
[from *mega-* + *byte*]

megalomania *NOUN* an exaggerated idea of your own importance.
▷ **megalomaniac** *noun*
[from *mega-* + *mania*]

megaphone *NOUN* **megaphones** a funnel-shaped device for amplifying a person's voice.
[from *mega-* + Greek *phone* = voice]

melamine *NOUN* a strong kind of plastic.
[from *melam*, a chemical used to make melamine]

melancholy *ADJECTIVE* sad; gloomy.

melancholy *NOUN* sadness or depression.
[from Greek *melas* = black + *chole* = bile (because black bile in the body was once thought to cause melancholy)]

mêlée (*say* mel-ay) *NOUN* **mêlées** **1** a confused fight. **2** a muddle.
[French, = medley]

mellow *ADJECTIVE* **mellower**, **mellowest** **1** not harsh; soft and rich in flavour, colour, or sound. **2** having become more kindly and sympathetic with age.
▷ **mellowness** *noun*

mellow *VERB* **mellows**, **mellowing**, **mellowed** make or become mellow.
[origin unknown]

melodic *ADJECTIVE* to do with melody.

melodious *ADJECTIVE* like a melody; pleasant to listen to.

melodrama *NOUN* **melodramas** a play full of dramatic excitement and strong emotion.
▷ **melodramatic** *adjective*
[from Greek *melos* = music + French *drame* = drama (because melodramas were originally musicals)]

melody *NOUN* **melodies** a tune, especially a pleasing tune.
[from Greek *melos* = music + *oide* = song]

melon *NOUN* **melons** a large sweet fruit with a yellow or green skin.
[from French]

melt *VERB* **melts**, **melting**, **melted** **1** make or become liquid by heating. **2** disappear slowly • *The crowd just melted away.* **3** soften • *a pudding that melts in the mouth.*
[from Old English]

melting pot *NOUN* **melting pots** a place where people of many different races and cultures live and influence each other.

member *NOUN* **members** **1** a person or thing that belongs to a particular society or group. **2** a part of something.
▷ **membership** *noun*
[from Latin *membrum* = limb]

Member of Parliament *NOUN* **Members of Parliament** a person elected to represent the people of an area in Parliament.

membrane *NOUN* **membranes** a thin skin or similar covering.
▷ **membranous** *adjective*
[from Latin]

memento *NOUN* **mementoes** a souvenir.
[Latin, = remember]

memo (*say* mem-oh) *NOUN* **memos** (*informal*) a memorandum.

memoir (*say* mem-wahr) *NOUN* **memoirs** a biography, especially one written by someone who knew the person.
[from French *mémoire* = memory]

memoirs *PLURAL NOUN* an autobiography.

memorable *ADJECTIVE* **1** worth remembering. **2** easy to remember.
▷ **memorably** *adverb*

memorandum *NOUN* **memoranda** or **memorandums** **1** a note to remind yourself of something. **2** a note from one person to another in the same firm.
[Latin, = thing to be remembered]

memorial *NOUN* **memorials** something to remind people of a person or event • *a war memorial.*
▷ **memorial** *adjective*
[from Latin *memoria* = memory]

memorize *VERB* **memorizes, memorizing, memorized** get something into your memory.
[from *memory*]

memory *NOUN* **memories** **1** the ability to remember things. **2** something that you remember. **3** the part of a computer where information is stored.
- **in memory of** in honour of a person or event remembered.
[from Latin *memor* = remembering]

menace *NOUN* **menaces** **1** a threat or danger. **2** a troublesome person or thing.

menace *VERB* **menaces, menacing, menaced** threaten with harm or danger.
[from Latin *minax* = threatening]

menagerie *NOUN* **menageries** a small zoo.
[from French]

mend *VERB* **mends, mending, mended** **1** repair. **2** make or become better; improve.
▷ **mender** *noun*

mend *NOUN* **mends** a repair.
- **on the mend** getting better after an illness.
[from *amend*]

mendacious (*say* men-day-shus) *ADJECTIVE* (*formal*) untruthful; telling lies.
▷ **mendaciously** *adverb* **mendacity** *noun*
[from Latin]

meneer *NOUN* (*S. African*) a title in Afrikaans meaning 'Mr' or 'sir'.
[via Afrikaans from Dutch *mijnheer* = my lord]

menial (*say* meen-ee-al) *ADJECTIVE* needing little or no skill or thought • *menial tasks.*
▷ **menially** *adverb*

menial *NOUN* **menials** a person who does menial work; a servant.
[from old French]

meningitis *NOUN* a disease causing inflammation of the membranes (*meninges*) round the brain and spinal cord.

menopause *NOUN* the time of life when a woman gradually stops menstruating.
[from Greek *menos* = of a month + *pausis* = stopping]

menstruate *VERB* **menstruates, menstruating, menstruated** bleed from the womb about once a month, as girls and women normally do from their teens until middle age.
▷ **menstruation** *noun* **menstrual** *adjective*
[from Latin *menstruus* = monthly]

mental *ADJECTIVE* **1** to do with or in the mind. **2** (*informal*) mad.
▷ **mentally** *adverb*
[from Latin *mentis* = of the mind]

mentality *NOUN* **mentalities** a person's mental ability or attitude.

menthol *NOUN* a solid white peppermint-flavoured substance.
[from Latin *mentha* = *mint*^{1}]

mention *VERB* **mentions, mentioning, mentioned** speak or write about a person or thing briefly; refer to.

mention *NOUN* **mentions** an example of mentioning something • *Our school got a mention in the local paper.*
[from Latin]

mentor *NOUN* **mentors** an experienced and trusted adviser.
[named after *Mentor* in Greek legend, who advised Odysseus' son]

menu (*say* men-yoo) *NOUN* **menus** **1** a list of the food available in a restaurant or served at a meal. **2** (*in computing*) a list of possible actions, shown on a screen, from which you decide what you want a computer to do.
[from French]

MEP *ABBREVIATION* Member of the European Parliament.

mercantile *ADJECTIVE* to do with trade or trading.
[from Italian *mercante* = merchant]

mercenary *ADJECTIVE* working only for money or some other reward.

mercenary *NOUN* **mercenaries** a soldier hired to serve in a foreign army.
[from Latin *merces* = wages]

merchandise *NOUN* goods for sale.
[from French *marchand* = merchant]

merchant *NOUN* **merchants** a person involved in trade.
[from Latin *mercari* = to trade]

merchant bank *NOUN* **merchant banks** a bank that gives loans and advice to businesses.

merchant navy *NOUN* the ships and sailors that carry goods for trade.

merciful *ADJECTIVE* showing mercy.
▷ **mercifully** *adverb*

merciless *ADJECTIVE* showing no mercy; cruel.
▷ **mercilessly** *adverb*

mercurial *ADJECTIVE* **1** having sudden changes of mood. **2** to do with mercury.

mercury *NOUN* a heavy silvery metal that is usually liquid, used in thermometers.
▷ **mercuric** *adjective*
[from the name of the planet *Mercury*]

mercy *NOUN* **mercies** **1** kindness or pity shown in not punishing a wrongdoer severely or not harming a defeated enemy etc. **2** something to be thankful for.
- **at the mercy of** completely in the power of.
[from old French]

mere[1] *ADJECTIVE* not more than • *He's a mere child.*
[from old French]

mere[2] *NOUN* **meres** (*poetical use*) a lake.
[from Old English]

merely *ADVERB* only; simply.

merest *ADJECTIVE* very small • *the merest trace of colour.*

merge *VERB* **merges, merging, merged** combine or blend.
[from Latin *mergere* = dip]

merger *NOUN* **mergers** the combining of two business companies into one.

meridian *NOUN* **meridians** a line on a map or globe from the North Pole to the South Pole. The meridian that passes through Greenwich is shown on maps as 0° longitude.
[from Latin]

meringue (*say* mer-ang) *NOUN* **meringues** a crisp cake made from egg white and sugar.
[French]

merino *NOUN* **merinos** a kind of sheep with fine soft wool.
[Spanish]

merit *NOUN* **merits** **1** a quality that deserves praise. **2** excellence.
▷ **meritorious** *adjective*

merit *VERB* **merits, meriting, merited** deserve.
[from Latin *meritum* = value]

mermaid *NOUN* **mermaids** a mythical sea creature with a woman's body but with a fish's tail instead of legs.
▷ **merman** *noun*
[from Old English *mere* = sea, + *maid*]

merry *ADJECTIVE* **merrier, merriest** cheerful and lively.
▷ **merrily** *adverb* **merriment** *noun*
[from Old English]

merry-go-round *NOUN* **merry-go-rounds** a roundabout at a fair.

mesh *NOUN* **meshes** **1** the open spaces in a net, sieve, or other criss-cross structure. **2** material made like a net; network.

mesh *VERB* **meshes, meshing, meshed** (said about gears) engage.
[probably from old Dutch]

mesmerize *VERB* **mesmerizes, mesmerizing, mesmerized** **1** (*old use*) hypnotize. **2** fascinate or hold a person's attention completely.
▷ **mesmerism** *noun* **mesmeric** *adjective*
[named after an Austrian doctor, F. A. *Mesmer*, who made hypnosis famous]

mess *NOUN* **messes** **1** a dirty or untidy condition or thing. **2** a difficult or confused situation. **3** (in the armed forces) a dining room.
- **make a mess of** bungle.

mess *VERB* **messes, messing, messed**
- **mess about** behave stupidly or idly.
- **mess up** **1** make a thing dirty or untidy. **2** bungle or spoil • *They messed up our plans.*
- **mess with** interfere or tinker with.
[from old French *mes* = a portion of food]

message *NOUN* **messages** **1** a piece of information etc. sent from one person to another. **2** the main theme or moral of a book, film, etc.
[from old French; related to *missile*]

messenger *NOUN* **messengers** a person who carries a message.

Messiah (*say* mis-I-a) *NOUN* **Messiahs** **1** the saviour expected by the Jews. **2** Jesus Christ, who Christians believe was this saviour.
▷ **Messianic** *adjective*
[from Hebrew *mashiah* = anointed]

Messrs (plural of **Mr**) [abbreviation of French *messieurs* = gentlemen]

messy *ADJECTIVE* **messier, messiest** dirty and untidy.
▷ **messily** *adverb* **messiness** *noun*

metabolism (*say* mit-ab-ol-izm) *NOUN* the process by which food is built up into living material in a plant or animal, or used to supply it with energy.
▷ **metabolic** *adjective* **metabolize** *verb*
[from Greek *metabole* = change]

metal *NOUN* **metals** a chemical substance, usually hard, that conducts heat and electricity and melts when it is heated. Gold, silver, copper, iron, and uranium are metals.
▷ **metallic** *adjective*
[from Latin]

metallurgy (*say* mit-al-er-jee) *NOUN* **1** the study of metals. **2** the craft of making and using metals.
▷ **metallurgical** *adjective* **metallurgist** *noun*
[from *metal* + Greek *-ourgia* = working]

metamorphic *ADJECTIVE* formed or changed by heat or pressure • *Marble is a metamorphic rock.*
[from Greek *meta-* = change + *morphe* = form]

metamorphosis (*say* met-a-mor-fo-sis) *NOUN* **metamorphoses** (*say* met-a-mor-fo-seez) **1** a complete change made by some living things, such as a caterpillar changing into a butterfly. **2** a change of form or character.
▷ **metamorphose** *verb*
[same origin as *metamorphic*]

metaphor *NOUN* **metaphors** using a word or phrase in a way that is not literal, e.g. 'The pictures of starving people • *touched our hearts*'.
▷ **metaphorical** *adjective*
metaphorically *adverb*
[from Greek *metapherein* = transfer]

mete *VERB* **metes, meting, meted**
- **mete out** deal out or allot, usually something unpleasant • *mete out punishment.*
[from Old English]

meteor (*say* meet-ee-er) *NOUN* **meteors** a piece of rock or metal that moves through space and burns up when it enters the earth's atmosphere.
[from Greek *meteoros* = high in the air]

meteoric (*say* meet-ee-o-rik) *ADJECTIVE* **1** to do with meteors. **2** like a meteor in brilliance or sudden appearance • *a meteoric career.*

meteorite *NOUN* **meteorites** the remains of a meteor that has landed on the earth.

meteorology *NOUN* the study of the conditions of the atmosphere, especially in order to forecast the weather.
▷ **meteorological** *adjective*
meteorologist *noun*
[from Greek *meteoros* = high in the air, + *-logy*]

meter *NOUN* **meters** a device for measuring something, e.g. the amount supplied • *a gas meter.*
▷ **meter** *verb*
[from *mete*]
USAGE Do not confuse with **metre**.

methane (*say* mee-thayn) *NOUN* an inflammable gas produced by decaying matter.
[from *methyl*, a chemical which methane contains]

method *NOUN* **methods** **1** a procedure or way of doing something. **2** methodical behaviour; orderliness.
[from Greek *methodos* = pursuit of knowledge]

methodical *ADJECTIVE* doing things in an orderly or systematic way.
▷ **methodically** *adverb*

Methodist *NOUN* **Methodists** a member of a Christian religious group started by John and Charles Wesley in the 18th century.
▷ **Methodism** *noun*

methodology *NOUN* **methodologies** the methods and main principles that you use when you are studying a particular subject or doing a particular kind of work.
▷ **methodological** *adjective*

meths *NOUN* (*informal*) methylated spirit.

methylated spirit or **spirits** *NOUN* a liquid fuel made from alcohol.
[from *methyl*, a chemical added to make alcohol nasty to drink]

meticulous *ADJECTIVE* very careful and precise.
▷ **meticulously** *adverb*
[from Latin]

metre *NOUN* **metres** **1** a unit of length in the metric system, about 39½ inches. **2** rhythm in poetry.
[from Greek *metron* = a measure]
USAGE Do not confuse with **meter**.

metric *ADJECTIVE* **1** to do with the metric system. **2** to do with metre in poetry.
▷ **metrically** *adverb*

metrical *ADJECTIVE* in, or to do with, rhythmic metre, not prose • *metrical psalms.*

metrication *NOUN* changing to the metric system.

metric system *NOUN* a measuring system based on decimal units (the metre, litre, and gram).

metric ton *NOUN* **metric tons** 1,000 kilograms.

metronome *NOUN* **metronomes** a device that makes a regular clicking noise to help a person keep in time when practising music.
[from Greek *metron* = measure + *nomos* = law]

metropolis *NOUN* **metropolises** the chief city of a country or region.
[from Greek *meter* = mother + *polis* = city]

metropolitan *ADJECTIVE* **1** to do with a metropolis. **2** to do with a city and its suburbs.

mettle *NOUN* courage or strength of character.
▷ **mettlesome** *adjective*
- **be on your mettle** be determined to show your courage or ability.
[a different spelling of *metal*]

mew *VERB* **mews, mewing, mewed** make a cat's cry.
▷ **mew** *noun*
[imitating the sound]

mews *NOUN* **mews** a row of houses in a small street or square, converted from former stables.
[first used of royal stables in London, built on the site of hawks' cages (called *mews*)]

miaow (*say* mee-ow) *VERB* & *NOUN* mew.
[imitating the sound]

miasma (*say* mee-az-ma) *NOUN* **miasmas** unpleasant or unhealthy air.
[Greek, = pollution]

mica *NOUN* a mineral substance used to make electrical insulators.
[Latin]

mice plural of **mouse**.

micro- *PREFIX* very small (as in *microfilm*).
[from Greek *mikros* = small]

microbe *NOUN* **microbes** a micro-organism.
[from *micro-* + Greek *bios* = life]

microchip *NOUN* **microchips** a very small piece of silicon etc. made to work like a complex wired electric circuit.

microcomputer *NOUN* **microcomputers** a small computer with a microprocessor as its central processing unit.

microcosm *NOUN* **microcosms** a world in miniature; something regarded as resembling something else on a very small scale.
[from Greek *mikros kosmos* = little world]

microfiche *NOUN* **microfiches** a piece of film on which pages of information are photographed in greatly reduced size.
[from *micro-* + French *fiche* = slip of paper]

microfilm *NOUN* a length of film on which written or printed material is photographed in greatly reduced size.

micron *NOUN* **microns** a unit of measurement equal to one millionth of a metre.
[same origin as *micro-*]

micro-organism *NOUN* **micro-organisms** a microscopic creature, e.g. a bacterium or virus.

microphone *NOUN* **microphones** an electrical device that picks up sound waves for recording, amplifying, or broadcasting.
[from *micro-* + Greek *phone* = sound]

microprocessor *NOUN* **microprocessors** the central processing unit of a computer, consisting of one or more microchips.

microscope *NOUN* **microscopes** an instrument with lenses that magnify tiny objects or details.
[from *micro-* + Greek *skopein* = look at]

microscopic *ADJECTIVE* **1** extremely small; too small to be seen without the aid of a microscope. **2** to do with a microscope.

microwave *NOUN* **microwaves** **1** a very short electromagnetic wave. **2** a microwave oven.

microwave *VERB* **microwaves, microwaving, microwaved** cook in a microwave oven.

microwave oven *NOUN* **microwave ovens** an oven that uses microwaves to heat or cook food very quickly.

mid *ADJECTIVE* **1** in the middle of • *mid-July.* **2** middle • *He's in his mid thirties.*
[from Old English]

midday *NOUN* the middle of the day; noon.

middle *NOUN* **middles** **1** the place or part of something that is at the same distance from all its sides or edges or from both its ends. **2** someone's waist.
- **in the middle of** during or halfway through a process or activity • *I'm just in the middle of cooking.*

middle *ADJECTIVE* **1** placed or happening in the middle. **2** moderate in size or rank etc.
[from Old English]

middle-aged *ADJECTIVE* aged between about 40 and 60.
▷ **middle age** *noun*

Middle Ages *NOUN* the period in history from about AD1000 to 1400.

middle class or **classes** *NOUN* the class of people between the upper class and the working class, including business and professional people such as teachers, doctors, and lawyers.
▷ **middle-class** *adjective*

Middle East *NOUN* the countries from Egypt to Iran inclusive.

Middle English *NOUN* the English language from about 1150 to 1500.

middleman *NOUN* **middlemen** **1** a trader who buys from a producer and sells to a consumer. **2** a go-between or intermediary.

middle school *NOUN* **middle schools** a school for children aged from about 9 to 13.

middling *ADJECTIVE* of medium size or quality.

midge *NOUN* **midges** a small insect like a gnat.
[from Old English]

midget *NOUN* **midgets** an extremely small person or thing.
▷ **midget** *adjective*
[from *midge*]

midland *ADJECTIVE* **1** to do with the middle part of a country. **2** to do with the Midlands.

Midlands *PLURAL NOUN* the central part of England.

midnight *NOUN* twelve o'clock at night.

midriff *NOUN* **midriffs** the front part of the body just above the waist.
[from *mid* + Old English *hrif* = stomach]

midshipman *NOUN* **midshipmen** a sailor ranking next above a cadet.
[because they were stationed in the middle part of the ship]

midst *NOUN*
- **in the midst of** in the middle of or surrounded by.
- **in our midst** among us.

A B C D E F G H I J K L M N O P Q R S T U V W X Y Z

midsummer *NOUN* the middle of summer, about 21 June in the northern hemisphere.

Midsummer's Day *NOUN* 24 June.

midway *ADVERB* halfway.

midwife *NOUN* **midwives** a person trained to look after a woman who is giving birth to a baby.
▷ **midwifery** (*say* **mid**-wif-ri) *noun*
[from Old English *mid* = with + *wif* = woman]

midwinter *NOUN* the middle of winter, about 21 December in the northern hemisphere.

mien (*say* meen) *NOUN* a person's manner and expression.
[origin unknown]

might[1] *NOUN* great strength or power.
- **with all your might** using all your strength and determination.
[from Old English]

might[2] *AUXILIARY VERB* used **1** as the past tense of *may*[1] (*We told her she might go*), **2** to express possibility (*It might be true*).

mighty *ADJECTIVE* very strong or powerful.
▷ **mightily** *adverb* **mightiness** *noun*

migraine (*say* **mee**-grayn or **my**-grayn) *NOUN* **migraines** a severe kind of headache.
[French]

migrant *NOUN* **migrants** a person or animal that migrates or has migrated.

migrate *VERB* **migrates, migrating, migrated** **1** leave one place or country and settle in another. **2** (said about birds or animals) move periodically from one area to another.
▷ **migration** *noun* **migratory** *adjective*
[from Latin]

mike *NOUN* **mikes** (*informal*) a microphone.

mild *ADJECTIVE* **milder, mildest** **1** not harsh or severe. **2** gentle and kind. **3** not strongly flavoured. **4** (said about weather) quite warm and pleasant.
▷ **mildly** *adverb* **mildness** *noun*
[from Old English]

mildew *NOUN* a tiny fungus that forms a white coating on things kept in damp conditions.
▷ **mildewed** *adjective*
[from Old English]

mile *NOUN* **miles** a measure of distance equal to 1,760 yards (about 1.6 kilometres).
[from Latin *mille* = thousand (paces)]

mileage *NOUN* **mileages** **1** the number of miles travelled. **2** (*informal*) benefit or advantage.

milestone *NOUN* **milestones** **1** a stone of a kind that used to be fixed beside a road to mark the distance between towns. **2** an important event in life or history.

milieu (*say* **meel**-yer) *NOUN* **milieus** or **milieux** environment or surroundings.
[French, from *mi* = mid + *lieu* = place]

militant *ADJECTIVE* **1** eager to fight. **2** forceful or aggressive • *a militant protest.*
▷ **militant** *noun* **militancy** *noun*
[same origin as *militate*]

militarism *NOUN* belief in the use of military strength and methods.
▷ **militarist** *noun* **militaristic** *adjective*

military *ADJECTIVE* to do with soldiers or the armed forces.
- **the military** a country's armed forces.
[from Latin *miles* = soldier]

militate *VERB* **militates, militating, militated** be a strong influence against; make something difficult or unlikely • *The weather militated against the success of our plans.*
[from Latin *militare* = be a soldier]
USAGE Do not confuse with **mitigate**.

militia (*say* mil-**ish**-a) *NOUN* **militias** a military force, especially one raised from civilians.
[Latin, = military service]

milk *NOUN* **1** a white liquid that female mammals produce in their bodies to feed their babies. **2** the milk of cows, used as food by human beings. **3** a milky liquid, e.g. that in a coconut.

milk *VERB* **milks, milking, milked** get the milk from a cow or other animal.
[from Old English]

milkman *NOUN* **milkmen** a man who delivers milk to customers' houses.

milkshake *NOUN* **milkshakes** a cold frothy drink made from milk whisked with sweet fruit flavouring.

milk tooth *NOUN* **milk teeth** one of the first set of teeth of a child or animal, which will be replaced by adult teeth.

milky *ADJECTIVE* **milkier, milkiest 1** like milk. **2** white.

Milky Way *NOUN* the broad band of stars formed by our galaxy.

mill *NOUN* **mills 1** machinery for grinding corn to make flour; a building containing this machinery. **2** a grinding machine • *a coffee mill.* **3** a factory for processing certain materials • *a paper mill.*

mill *VERB* **mills, milling, milled 1** grind or crush in a mill. **2** cut markings round the edge of a coin. **3** move in a confused crowd • *The animals were milling around.*

▷ **miller** *noun*

[via Old English from Latin *molere* = grind]

millennium *NOUN* **millenniums** a period of 1,000 years.
[from Latin *mille* = thousand + *annus* = year]

millet *NOUN* a kind of cereal with tiny seeds.
[from Latin]

milli- *PREFIX* **1** one-thousandth (as in *milligram*, *millilitre*, *millimetre*). **2** one thousand (as in *millipede*).
[from Latin *mille* = thousand]

milliner *NOUN* **milliners** a person who makes or sells women's hats.

▷ **millinery** *noun*

[originally = a person from Milan, an Italian city where fashionable accessories and hats were made]

million *NOUN* **millions** one thousand thousand (1,000,000).

▷ **millionth** *adjective & noun*

[French, related to *milli-*]

USAGE Say *a few million*, not 'a few millions'.

millionaire *NOUN* **millionaires** a person who has at least a million pounds or dollars; an extremely rich person.

millipede *NOUN* **millipedes** a small crawling creature like a centipede, with many legs.
[from Latin *mille* = thousand + *pedes* = feet]

millstone *NOUN* **millstones** either of a pair of large circular stones between which corn is ground.

- **a millstone around someone's neck** a heavy responsibility or burden.

milometer *NOUN* **milometers** an instrument for measuring how far a vehicle has travelled.
[from *mile* + *meter*]

mime *NOUN* **mimes** acting with movements of the body, not using words.

▷ **mime** *verb*

[from Greek *mimos* = a mimic]

mimic *VERB* **mimics, mimicking, mimicked** imitate someone, especially to amuse people.

▷ **mimicry** *noun*

mimic *NOUN* **mimics** a person who mimics others.

[same origin as *mime*]

mimosa *NOUN* **mimosas** a tropical tree or shrub with small ball-shaped flowers.
[from Latin]

minaret *NOUN* **minarets** the tall tower of a mosque.
[from Arabic *manara* = lighthouse]

mince *VERB* **minces, mincing, minced**

1 cut into very small pieces in a machine.

2 walk in an affected way with short quick steps.

▷ **mincer** *noun*

- **not to mince words** or **matters** speak bluntly.

mince *NOUN* minced meat.

[from French; related to *minute*[2]]

mincemeat *NOUN* a sweet mixture of currants, raisins, apple, etc. used in pies.
[from *mince* + an old sense of *meat* = food]

mince pie *NOUN* **mince pies** a pie containing mincemeat.

mind *NOUN* **minds 1** the ability to think, feel, understand, and remember, originating in the brain. **2** a person's thoughts, opinion, or intention • *Have you made your mind up? I changed my mind.*

- **in two minds** not able to decide.
- **out of your mind** insane.

mind *VERB* **minds, minding, minded** **1** look after • *He was minding the baby.* **2** be careful about • *Mind the step.* **3** be sad or upset about something; object to • *We don't mind waiting.*
▷ **minder** *noun*
[from Old English]

mindful *ADJECTIVE* taking thought or care • *He was mindful of his reputation.*

mindless *ADJECTIVE* done without thinking; stupid or pointless.

mine[1] *POSSESSIVE PRONOUN* belonging to me.
[from Old English]

mine[2] *NOUN* **mines** **1** a place where coal, metal, precious stones, etc. are dug out of the ground. **2** an explosive placed in or on the ground or in the sea etc. to destroy people or things that come close to it.

mine *VERB* **mines, mining, mined** **1** dig from a mine. **2** lay explosive mines in a place.
[from old French]

minefield *NOUN* **minefields** **1** an area where explosive mines have been laid. **2** something with hidden dangers or problems.

miner *NOUN* **miners** a person who works in a mine.

mineral *NOUN* **minerals** **1** a hard inorganic substance found in the ground. **2** a cold fizzy non-alcoholic drink.
[from Latin *minera* = ore]

mineralogy (*say* min-er-**al**-o-jee) *NOUN* the study of minerals.
▷ **mineralogist** *noun*
[from *mineral* + *-logy*]

mineral water *NOUN* water from a natural spring, containing mineral salts or gases.

minestrone (*say* mini-**stroh**-nee) *NOUN* an Italian soup containing vegetables and pasta.
[Italian, from *ministrare* = to serve up a dish]

mingle *VERB* **mingles, mingling, mingled** mix or blend.
[from Old English]

mingy *ADJECTIVE* **mingier, mingiest** (*informal*) not generous; mean.
[probably from *mean*[2] + *stingy*]

mini- *PREFIX* miniature; very small.
[short for *miniature*]

miniature *ADJECTIVE* **1** very small. **2** copying something on a very small scale • *a miniature railway.*

miniature *NOUN* **miniatures** **1** a very small portrait. **2** a small-scale model.
[from Italian]

minibus *NOUN* **minibuses** a small bus, seating about ten people.

minim *NOUN* **minims** a note in music, lasting twice as long as a crotchet (written 𝅗𝅥).
[same origin as *minimum*]

minimal *ADJECTIVE* very little; as little as possible.

minimize *VERB* **minimizes, minimizing, minimized** make something as small as possible.

minimum *NOUN* **minima** or **minimums** the lowest possible number or amount.
(COMPARE **maximum**)

minimum *ADJECTIVE* least or smallest.
[Latin, = least thing]

minion *NOUN* **minions** a very humble or obedient assistant or servant.
[from French]

minister *NOUN* **ministers** **1** a person in charge of a government department. **2** a member of the clergy.
▷ **ministerial** *adjective*

minister *VERB* **ministers, ministering, ministered** attend to people's needs.
[Latin, = servant]

ministry *NOUN* **ministries** **1** a government department • *the Ministry of Defence.* **2** the work of the clergy.
[same origin as *minister*]

mink *NOUN* **mink** or **minks** **1** an animal rather like a stoat. **2** this animal's valuable brown fur, or a coat made from it.
[origin unknown]

minnow *NOUN* **minnows** a tiny freshwater fish.
[probably from Old English]

minor *ADJECTIVE* **1** not very important, especially when compared to something else. **2** to do with the musical scale that has a semitone after the second note. (COMPARE **major**)

minor *NOUN* **minors** a person under the age of legal responsibility.
[Latin, = smaller, lesser]

minority *NOUN* **minorities 1** the smallest part of a group of people or things. **2** a small group that is different from others. (COMPARE **majority**)
[same origin as *minor*]

minstrel *NOUN* **minstrels** a travelling singer and musician in the Middle Ages.
[from old French; related to *minister*]

mint[1] *NOUN* **mints 1** a plant with fragrant leaves that are used for flavouring things. **2** peppermint or a sweet flavoured with this.
[from Latin *mentha* = mint]

mint[2] *NOUN* **mints** the place where a country's coins are made.
- **in mint condition** in perfect condition, as though it had never been used.

mint *VERB* **mints, minting, minted** make coins.
[from Latin *moneta* = coins; a mint]

minuet *NOUN* **minuets** a slow stately dance.
[from French *menuet* = small or delicate]

minus *PREPOSITION* with the next number or thing subtracted • *Ten minus four equals six* (10 - 4 = 6).

minus *ADJECTIVE* less than zero • *temperatures of minus ten degrees* (-10°).
[Latin, = less]

minuscule *ADJECTIVE* extremely small.

minute[1] (*say* min-it) *NOUN* **minutes 1** one-sixtieth of an hour. **2** a very short time; a moment. **3** a particular time • *Come here this minute!* **4** one-sixtieth of a degree (used in measuring angles).
[from Latin *pars minuta prima* = first little part]

minute[2] (*say* my-**newt**) *ADJECTIVE* **1** very small • *a minute insect.* **2** very detailed • *a minute examination.*
▷ **minutely** *adverb*
[from Latin *minutus* = little]

minutes *PLURAL NOUN* a written summary of what was said at a meeting.
[probably from Latin *minuta scriptura* = small writing]

minx *NOUN* **minxes** (*old use*) a cheeky or mischievous girl.
[origin unknown]

miracle *NOUN* **miracles** something wonderful and good that happens, especially something believed to have a supernatural or divine cause.
▷ **miraculous** *adjective* **miraculously** *adverb*
[same origin as *mirror*]

mirage (*say* mi-**rahzh**) *NOUN* **mirages** an illusion; something that seems to be there but is not, especially when a lake seems to appear in a desert.
[French, from *se mirer* = be reflected or mirrored]

mire *NOUN* **1** a swamp. **2** deep mud.
[from Old Norse]

mirror *NOUN* **mirrors** a device or surface of reflecting material, usually glass.

mirror *VERB* **mirrors, mirroring, mirrored** reflect in or like a mirror.
[from Latin *mirari* = to look at or wonder at]

mirth *NOUN* merriment or laughter.
▷ **mirthful** *adjective* **mirthless** *adjective*
[from Old English]

mis- *PREFIX* badly or wrongly. (COMPARE **amiss**)
[from Old English *mis-* (related to *amiss*), or old French *mes-* (related to *minus*)]

misadventure *NOUN* **misadventures** a piece of bad luck.
[from old French *mesavenir* = to turn out badly]

misanthropy *NOUN* dislike of people in general.
▷ **misanthropist** *noun*
misanthropic *adjective*
[from Greek *misos* = hatred + *anthropos* = human being]

misapprehend *VERB* **misapprehends, misapprehending, misapprehended** misunderstand something.
▷ **misapprehension** *noun*

misappropriate *VERB* **misappropriates, misappropriating, misappropriated** take something dishonestly.
▷ **misappropriation** *noun*

misbehave *VERB* **misbehaves, misbehaving, misbehaved** behave badly.
▷ **misbehaviour** *noun*

miscalculate *VERB* **miscalculates, miscalculating, miscalculated** calculate incorrectly.
▷ **miscalculation** *noun*

miscarriage *NOUN* **miscarriages 1** the birth of a baby before it has developed enough to live. **2** failure to achieve the right result • *a miscarriage of justice.*
▷ **miscarry** *verb*
[from *miscarry* = to be lost, destroyed, or badly managed]

miscellaneous (*say* mis-el-ay-nee-us) *ADJECTIVE* of various kinds; mixed.
[from Latin *miscellus* = mixed]

miscellany (*say* mis-**el**-an-ee) *NOUN* **miscellanies** a collection or mixture of different things.

mischance *NOUN* misfortune.

mischief *NOUN* **1** naughty or troublesome behaviour. **2** trouble caused by this.
▷ **mischievous** *adjective* **mischievously** *adverb*
[from old French *meschever* = come to a bad end]

misconception *NOUN* **misconceptions** a mistaken idea.

misconduct *NOUN* bad behaviour by someone in a responsible position • *professional misconduct.*

misconstrue *VERB* **misconstrues, misconstruing, misconstrued** understand or interpret something wrongly.
▷ **misconstruction** *noun*

miscreant (*say* mis-kree-ant) *NOUN* **miscreants** a wrongdoer or criminal.
[originally = heretic: from old French *mescreance* = false belief]

misdeed *NOUN* **misdeeds** a wrong or improper action.

misdemeanour *NOUN* **misdemeanours** an action which is wrong or illegal, but not very serious; a petty crime.

miser *NOUN* **misers** a person who hoards money and spends as little as possible.
▷ **miserly** *adjective* **miserliness** *noun*
[same origin as *misery*]

miserable *ADJECTIVE* **1** full of misery; very unhappy, poor, or uncomfortable. **2** disagreeable or unpleasant • *miserable weather.*
▷ **miserably** *adverb*
[same origin as *misery*]

misery *NOUN* **miseries 1** great unhappiness or discomfort or suffering, especially lasting for a long time. **2** (*informal*) a person who is always unhappy or complaining.
[from Latin *miser* = wretched]

misfire *VERB* **misfires, misfiring, misfired 1** fail to fire. **2** fail to function correctly or to have the required effect • *The joke misfired.*

misfit *NOUN* **misfits** a person who does not fit in well with other people or who is not well suited to his or her work.

misfortune *NOUN* **misfortunes 1** bad luck. **2** an unlucky event or accident.

misgiving *NOUN* **misgivings** a feeling of doubt or slight fear or mistrust.
[from an old word *misgive* = give someone bad feelings about something]

misguided *ADJECTIVE* guided by mistaken ideas or beliefs.

mishap (*say* mis-hap) *NOUN* **mishaps** an unlucky accident.
[from *mis-* + Middle English *hap* = luck]

misinterpret *VERB* **misinterprets, misinterpreting, misinterpreted** interpret incorrectly.
▷ **misinterpretation** *noun*

misjudge *VERB* **misjudges, misjudging, misjudged** judge wrongly; form a wrong opinion or estimate.
▷ **misjudgement** *noun*

mislay *VERB* **mislays, mislaying, mislaid** lose something for a short time because you cannot remember where you put it.

mislead *VERB* **misleads, misleading, misled** give somebody a wrong idea or impression deliberately.

mismanagement *NOUN* bad management.

misnomer *NOUN* **misnomers** an unsuitable name for something.
[from *mis-* + Latin *nomen* = name]

misogynist (*say* mis-**oj**-in-ist) *NOUN* **misogynists** a person who hates women.
▷ **misogyny** *noun*
[from Greek *misos* = hatred + *gyne* = woman]

misplaced *ADJECTIVE* **1** placed wrongly. **2** inappropriate • *misplaced loyalty.*
▷ **misplacement** *noun*

misprint *NOUN* **misprints** a mistake in printing.

mispronounce *VERB* **mispronounces, mispronouncing, mispronounced** pronounce incorrectly.
▷ **mispronunciation** *noun*

misquote *VERB* **misquotes, misquoting, misquoted** quote incorrectly.
▷ **misquotation** *noun*

misread *VERB* **misreads, misreading, misread** (*say* mis-**red**) read or interpret incorrectly.

misrepresent *VERB* **misrepresents, misrepresenting, misrepresented** represent in a false or misleading way.
▷ **misrepresentation** *noun*

misrule *NOUN* bad government.

Miss *NOUN* **Misses** a title put before a girl's or unmarried woman's name.
[short for *mistress*]

miss *VERB* **misses, missing, missed 1** fail to hit, reach, catch, see, hear, or find something. **2** be sad because someone or something is not with you. **3** notice that something has gone.
- **miss out** leave out.
- **miss out on** not get the benefit or enjoyment from something that others have had.

miss *NOUN* **misses** missing something • *Was that shot a hit or a miss?*
[from Old English]

misshapen *ADJECTIVE* badly shaped.
[from *mis-* + *shapen*, the old past participle of *shape*]

missile *NOUN* **missiles** a weapon or other object for firing or throwing at a target.
[from Latin *missum* = sent]
WORD FAMILY There are a number of English words that are related to *missile* because part of their original meaning comes from the Latin words *mittere* meaning 'to send' or *missum* meaning 'sent'. These include *admit, commit, dismiss, emit, mission, permit, remit, submit,* and *transmit.*

missing *ADJECTIVE* **1** lost; not in the proper place. **2** absent.

mission *NOUN* **missions 1** an important job that somebody is sent to do or feels he or she must do. **2** a place or building where missionaries work. **3** a military or scientific expedition.
[from Latin *missio* = sending someone out]

missionary *NOUN* **missionaries** a person who is sent to another country to spread a religious faith.

misspell *VERB* **misspells, misspelling, misspelt** or **misspelled** spell a word wrongly.

mist *NOUN* **mists 1** damp cloudy air near the ground. **2** condensed water vapour on a window, mirror, etc.
▷ **mist** *verb*
[from Old English]

mistake *NOUN* **mistakes 1** something done wrongly. **2** an incorrect opinion.

mistake *VERB* **mistakes, mistaking, mistook, mistaken 1** misunderstand • *Don't mistake my meaning.* **2** choose or identify wrongly • *We mistook her for her sister.*
[from *mis-* + Old Norse *taka* = take]

mistaken *ADJECTIVE* **1** incorrect. **2** having an incorrect opinion.

mister *NOUN* (*informal*) a form of address to a man.

mistime *VERB* **mistimes, mistiming, mistimed** do or say something at a wrong time.

mistletoe *NOUN* a plant with white berries that grows as a parasite on trees.
[from Old English]

mistreat *VERB* **mistreats, mistreating, mistreated** treat badly.

mistress *NOUN* **mistresses** **1** a woman who is in charge of something. **2** a woman teacher. **3** the woman owner of a dog or other animal. **4** a woman who is a man's lover but not his wife.
[from old French *maistresse*, feminine form of *maistre* = master]

mistrust *VERB* **mistrusts, mistrusting, mistrusted** feel no trust in somebody or something.
▷ **mistrust** *noun*

misty *ADJECTIVE* **mistier, mistiest** **1** full of mist. **2** not clear or distinct.
▷ **mistily** *adverb* **mistiness** *noun*

misunderstand *VERB* **misunderstands, misunderstanding, misunderstood** get a wrong idea or impression of something.
▷ **misunderstanding** *noun*

misuse (*say* mis-yooz) *VERB* **misuses, misusing, misused** **1** use incorrectly. **2** treat badly.
▷ **misuse** (*say* mis-yooss) *noun*

mite *NOUN* **mites** **1** a tiny spider-like creature that lives on plants, animals, carpets, etc. **2** a small child.
[from Old English]

mitigate *VERB* **mitigates, mitigating, mitigated** make a thing less intense or less severe • *These measures are designed to mitigate pollution.*
▷ **mitigation** *noun*
[from Latin *mitigare* = make mild]
USAGE Do not confuse with **militate**.

mitigating circumstances *PLURAL NOUN* facts that may partially excuse wrongdoing.

mitre *NOUN* **mitres** **1** the tall tapering hat worn by a bishop. **2** a joint of two pieces of wood or cloth with their ends tapered so that together they form a right angle.

mitre *VERB* **mitres, mitring, mitred** join pieces of wood or cloth with a mitre.
[from Greek *mitra* = turban]

mitten *NOUN* **mittens** a kind of glove without separate parts for the fingers.
[from French]

mix *VERB* **mixes, mixing, mixed** **1** put different things together so that the substances etc. are no longer distinct; blend or combine. **2** (said about a person) get together with others.
▷ **mixer** *noun*
- **mix up** **1** mix thoroughly. **2** confuse.

mix *NOUN* **mixes** a mixture.
[from *mixed*]

mixed *ADJECTIVE* **1** containing two or more kinds of things or people. **2** for both sexes • *mixed doubles.*
[from Latin *mixtus* = mingled]

mixed farming *NOUN* farming of both crops and animals.

mixture *NOUN* **mixtures** something made of different things mixed together.

mix-up *NOUN* a confusion or misunderstanding.

mnemonic (*say* nim-on-ik) *NOUN* **mnemonics** a verse or saying that helps you to remember something.
[from Greek *mnemonikos* = for the memory]

moan *VERB* **moans, moaning, moaned** **1** make a long low sound of pain or suffering. **2** grumble.
▷ **moan** *noun*
[probably from Old English]

moat *NOUN* **moats** a deep wide ditch round a castle, usually filled with water.
[from old French]

mob *NOUN* **mobs** a large disorderly crowd.

mob *VERB* **mobs, mobbing, mobbed** crowd round somebody.
[from Latin *mobile vulgus* = excitable crowd]

mobile *ADJECTIVE* able to move or be moved or carried easily.
▷ **mobility** *noun*

mobile *NOUN* **mobiles** **1** a decoration for hanging up so that its parts move in currents of air. **2** a mobile phone.
[from Latin *movere* = move]

mobile phone *NOUN* **mobile phones** a phone you can carry about that uses a cellular radio system.

mobilize *VERB* **mobilizes, mobilizing, mobilized** assemble people or things for a particular purpose, especially for war.
▷ **mobilization** *noun*

moccasin *NOUN* **moccasins** a soft leather shoe.
[a Native American word]

mock *VERB* **mocks, mocking, mocked** **1** make fun of a person or thing. **2** imitate someone or something to make people laugh.

mock *ADJECTIVE* **1** imitation, not real • *mock horror.* **2** (said about an exam) done as a practice before the real one.
[from old French]

mockery *NOUN* **1** ridicule or contempt. **2** a ridiculous imitation.

mock-up *NOUN* **mock-ups** a model of something, made in order to test or study it.

modal verb *NOUN* a verb such as *can, may,* or *will* that is used with another verb to express possibility, permission, intention, etc.

mode *NOUN* **modes** **1** the way a thing is done. **2** what is fashionable.
[from Latin]

model *NOUN* **models** **1** a copy of an object, usually on a smaller scale. **2** a particular design. **3** a person who poses for an artist or displays clothes by wearing them. **4** a person or thing that is worth copying.

model *VERB* **models, modelling, modelled** **1** make a model of something; make something out of wood or clay. **2** design or plan something using another thing as an example. **3** work as an artist's model or a fashion model.
[from Latin *modulus* = a small measure]

modem (*say* moh-dem) *NOUN* **modems** a device that links a computer to a telephone line for transmitting data.
[from *mo*dulator + *dem*odulator]

moderate (*say* mod-er-at) *ADJECTIVE* **1** medium; not extremely small or great or hot etc. • *a moderate climate.* **2** not extreme or unreasonable • *moderate opinions.*
▷ **moderately** *adverb*

moderate (*say* mod-er-ayt) *VERB* **moderates, moderating, moderated** make or become moderate.
[from Latin *moderari* = restrain]

moderation *NOUN* being moderate.
- **in moderation** in moderate amounts.

modern *ADJECTIVE* **1** belonging to the present or recent times. **2** in fashion now.
▷ **modernity** *noun*
[from Latin *modo* = just now]

modernize *VERB* **modernizes, modernizing, modernized** make a thing more modern.
▷ **modernization** *noun*

modest *ADJECTIVE* **1** not vain or boastful. **2** moderate in size or amount • *a modest income.* **3** not showy or splendid. **4** behaving or dressing decently or decorously.
▷ **modestly** *adverb* **modesty** *noun*
[from Latin, = keeping the proper measure]

modicum *NOUN* a small amount.
[Latin, from *modicus* = moderate]

modify *VERB* **modifies, modifying, modified** **1** change something slightly. **2** describe a word or limit its meaning • *Adjectives modify nouns.*
▷ **modification** *noun*
[from Latin *modificare* = to limit]

modulate *VERB* **modulates, modulating, modulated** **1** adjust or regulate. **2** vary in pitch or tone etc. **3** alter an electronic wave to allow signals to be sent.
▷ **modulation** *noun*
[same origin as *model*]

module *NOUN* **modules** **1** an independent part of a spacecraft, building, etc. **2** a unit; a section of a course of study. **3** (*in computing*) a unit of a computer system or program that has a particular function • *software modules*
▷ **modular** *adjective*
[same origin as *model*]

modus operandi (*say* moh-dus op-er-and-ee) *NOUN* a particular method of working.
[Latin, = way of working]

mogul (*say* moh-gul) *NOUN* **moguls** (*informal*) an important or influential person.
[the Moguls were the ruling family in northern India in the 16th-19th centuries]

mohair *NOUN* fine silky wool from an angora goat.
[from Arabic]

moist *ADJECTIVE* slightly wet.
▷ **moistness** *noun*
[from old French]

A B C D E F G H I J K L M N O P Q R S T U V W X Y Z

moisten *VERB* **moistens, moistening, moistened** make something moist.

moisture *NOUN* water in tiny drops in the air or on a surface.

moisturizer *NOUN* a cream used to make the skin less dry.

molar *NOUN* **molars** any of the wide teeth at the back of the jaw, used in chewing.
[from Latin *mola* = millstone]

molasses *NOUN* dark syrup from raw sugar.
[from Latin *mellaceus* = like honey]

mole[1] *NOUN* **moles** **1** a small furry animal that burrows under the ground. **2** a spy working within an organization and passing information to another organization or country.
[probably from old Dutch]

mole[2] *NOUN* **moles** a small dark spot on skin.
[from Old English]

molecule *NOUN* **molecules** the smallest part into which a substance can be divided without changing its chemical nature; a group of atoms.
▷ **molecular** (*say* mo-**lek**-yoo-ler) *adjective*
[from Latin *molecula* = little mass]

molehill *NOUN* **molehills** a small pile of earth thrown up by a burrowing mole.

molest *VERB* **molests, molesting, molested** **1** annoy or pester. **2** attack or abuse someone sexually.
▷ **molestation** *noun*
[from Latin *molestus* = troublesome]

mollify *VERB* **mollifies, mollifying, mollified** make a person less angry.
[from Latin *mollificare* = soften]

mollusc *NOUN* **molluscs** any of a group of animals including snails, slugs, and mussels, with soft bodies, no backbones, and, in some cases, external shells.
[from Latin *molluscus* = soft thing]

molten *ADJECTIVE* melted; made liquid by great heat.
[the old past participle of *melt*]

moment *NOUN* **moments** **1** a very short time. **2** a particular time • *Call me the moment she arrives.*
[from Latin *movere* = move]

momentary *ADJECTIVE* lasting for only a moment.
▷ **momentarily** *adverb*

momentous (*say* mo-**ment**-us) *ADJECTIVE* very important.
[from an old sense of *moment* = importance]

momentum *NOUN* **1** the ability something has to keep developing or increasing. **2** the ability an object has to keep moving as a result of the speed it already has • *The stone gathered momentum as it rolled downhill.* **3** (*in science*) the quantity of motion of a moving object, measured as its mass multiplied by its velocity.
[Latin, = movement]

monarch *NOUN* **monarchs** a king, queen, emperor, or empress ruling a country.
[from Greek *monos* = alone + *archein* = to rule]

monarchy *NOUN* **monarchies** **1** a country ruled by a monarch. **2** government by a monarch.
▷ **monarchist** *noun*

monastery *NOUN* **monasteries** a building where monks live and work.
▷ **monastic** *adjective*
[from Greek *monazein* = live alone]

Monday *NOUN* the day of the week following Sunday.
[from Old English *monandaeg* = day of the moon]

monetary *ADJECTIVE* to do with money.

money *NOUN* **1** coins and banknotes. **2** wealth.
[same origin as *mint*[2]]

mongoose *NOUN* **mongooses** a small tropical animal rather like a stoat, that can kill snakes.
[from a southern Indian language]

mongrel (*say* **mung**-rel) *NOUN* **mongrels** a dog of mixed breeds.
[related to *mingle*]

monitor *NOUN* **monitors** **1** a device for watching or testing how something is working. **2** a screen that displays data and images produced by a computer. **3** a pupil who is given a special responsibility in a school.

monitor *VERB* **monitors, monitoring, monitored** watch or test how something is working.
[from Latin *monere* = warn]

monk *NOUN* **monks** a member of a community of men who live according to the rules of a religious organization.
(COMPARE **nun**)
[via Old English from Greek *monachos* = single or solitary]

monkey *NOUN* **monkeys** **1** an animal with long arms, hands with thumbs, and often a tail. **2** a mischievous person, especially a child.
[origin unknown]

mono- *PREFIX* one; single • *monorail.*
[from Greek *monos* = alone]

monochrome *ADJECTIVE* done in one colour or in black and white.
[from *mono-* + Greek *chroma* = colour]

monocle *NOUN* **monocles** a lens worn over one eye, like half of a pair of spectacles.
[from *mono-* + Latin *oculus* = eye]

monogamy *NOUN* the custom of being married to only one person at a time.
(COMPARE **polygamy**)
▷ **monogamous** *adjective*
[from *mono-* + Greek *gamos* = marriage]

monogram *NOUN* **monograms** a design made up of a letter or letters, especially a person's initials.
▷ **monogrammed** *adjective*
[from *mono-* + *-gram*]

monograph *NOUN* **monographs** a scholarly book or article on one particular subject.
[from *mono-* + *-graph*]

monolith *NOUN* **monoliths** a large single upright block of stone.
[from *mono-* + Greek *lithos* = stone]

monolithic *ADJECTIVE* **1** to do with or like a monolith. **2** huge and difficult to move or change.

monologue *NOUN* **monologues** a long speech by one person.
[from *mono-* + Greek *logos* = word]

monoplane *NOUN* **monoplanes** a type of aeroplane with only one set of wings.

monopolize *VERB* **monopolizes, monopolizing, monopolized** take the whole of something for yourself • *One girl monopolized my attention.*
▷ **monopolization** *noun*
[from *monopoly*]

monopoly *NOUN* **monopolies** **1** the exclusive right or opportunity to sell a commodity or supply a service. **2** complete possession, control, or use of something by one group.
[from *mono-* + Greek *polein* = sell]

monorail *NOUN* **monorails** a railway that uses a single rail, not a pair of rails.

monosyllable *NOUN* **monosyllables** a word with only one syllable.
▷ **monosyllabic** *adjective*

monotone *NOUN* a level unchanging tone of voice in speaking or singing.

monotonous *ADJECTIVE* boring because it does not change • *monotonous work.*
▷ **monotonously** *adverb* **monotony** *noun*
[from *mono-* + Greek *tonos* = tone]

monoxide *NOUN* **monoxides** an oxide with one atom of oxygen.

monsoon *NOUN* **monsoons** **1** a strong wind in and near the Indian Ocean, bringing heavy rain in summer. **2** the rainy season brought by this wind.
[via Dutch from Arabic *mawsim* = a season]

monster *NOUN* **monsters** **1** a large frightening creature. **2** a huge thing. **3** a wicked or cruel person.

monster *ADJECTIVE* huge.
[from Latin *monstrum* = marvel]

monstrosity *NOUN* **monstrosities** a monstrous thing.

monstrous *ADJECTIVE* **1** like a monster; huge. **2** very shocking or outrageous.

montage (*say* mon-ta*hzh*) *NOUN* a picture, film, or other work of art made by putting together separate pieces or pieces from other works.
[a French word]

month *NOUN* **months** each of the twelve parts into which a year is divided.
[from Old English; related to *moon* (because time was measured by the changes in the moon's appearance)]

a b c d e f g h i j k l m n o p q r s t u v w x y z

A B C D E F G H I J K L M N O P Q R S T U V W X Y Z

monthly *ADJECTIVE & ADVERB* happening or done once a month.

monument *NOUN* **monuments** a statue, building, or column etc. put up as a memorial of some person or event.
[from Latin *monumentum* = a memorial]

monumental *ADJECTIVE* **1** built as a monument. **2** very large or important.

moo *VERB* **moos, mooing, mooed** make the low deep sound of a cow.
▷ **moo** *noun*
[imitating the sound]

mood *NOUN* **moods** the way someone feels • *She is in a cheerful mood.*
[from Old English]

moody *ADJECTIVE* **moodier, moodiest**
1 gloomy or sullen. **2** having sudden changes of mood for no apparent reason.
▷ **moodily** *adverb* **moodiness** *noun*

moon *NOUN* **moons** **1** the natural satellite of the earth that can be seen in the sky at night. **2** a satellite of any planet.
▷ **moonbeam** *noun* **moonlight** *noun* **moonlit** *adjective*

moon *VERB* **moons, mooning, mooned** go about in a dreamy or listless way.
[from Old English]

Moor *NOUN* **Moors** a member of a Muslim people of north-west Africa.
▷ **Moorish** *adjective*
[from Greek]

moor[1] *NOUN* **moors** an area of rough land covered with heather, bracken, and bushes.
▷ **moorland** *noun*
[from Old English]

moor[2] *VERB* **moors, mooring, moored** fasten a boat to a fixed object by means of a cable.
[probably from old German]

moorhen *NOUN* **moorhens** a small waterbird.
[from an old sense of *moor*[1] = fen]

mooring *NOUN* **moorings** a place where a boat can be moored.

moose *NOUN* **moose** a North American elk.
[from Abnaki, a Native American language]

moot *ADJECTIVE*
- **a moot point** a question that is undecided or debatable.
[from Old English *mot* = a meeting]

mop *NOUN* **mops** **1** a bunch or pad of soft material fastened on the end of a stick, used for cleaning floors etc. **2** a thick mass of hair.

mop *VERB* **mops, mopping, mopped** clean or wipe with a mop etc.
- **mop up** **1** wipe or soak up liquid. **2** deal with the last parts of something • *The army is mopping up the last of the rebels.*
[origin unknown]

mope *VERB* **mopes, moping, moped** be sad.
[probably from a Scandinavian language]

moped (*say* moh-ped) *NOUN* **mopeds** a kind of small motorcycle that can be pedalled.
[from *motor* + *pedal*]

moraine *NOUN* **moraines** a mass of stones and earth etc. carried down by a glacier.
[from French]

moral *ADJECTIVE* **1** connected with what is right and wrong in behaviour. **2** good or virtuous.
▷ **morally** *adverb* **morality** *noun*
- **moral support** help in the form of encouragement.

moral *NOUN* **morals** a lesson in right behaviour taught by a story or event.
[from Latin *mores* = customs]
USAGE Do not confuse with **morale**.

morale (*say* mor-**ahl**) *NOUN* the level of confidence and good spirits in a person or group of people • *Morale was high after the victory.*
[same origin as *moral*]
USAGE Do not confuse with **moral**.

moralize *VERB* **moralizes, moralizing, moralized** talk or write about right and wrong behaviour.
▷ **moralist** *noun*

morals *PLURAL NOUN* standards of behaviour.

morass (*say* mo-rass) *NOUN* **morasses** **1** a marsh or bog. **2** a confused mass.
[via Dutch from French *marais* = marsh]

moratorium *NOUN* **moratoriums** a temporary ban.
[from Latin *morari* = to delay]

morbid *ADJECTIVE* **1** thinking about gloomy or unpleasant things. **2** (*in medicine*) unhealthy • *a morbid growth.*
▷ **morbidly** *adverb* **morbidity** *noun*
[from Latin *morbus* = disease]

more *ADJECTIVE* (comparative of **much** and **many**) greater in amount or degree.

more *NOUN* a greater amount.

more *ADVERB* **1** to a greater extent • *more beautiful.* **2** again • *once more.*
- **more or less** **1** approximately. **2** nearly or practically.
[from Old English]

moreover *ADVERB* besides; in addition to what has been said.

Mormon *NOUN* **Mormons** a member of a religious group founded in the USA.
[the name of a prophet who they believe wrote their sacred book]

morn *NOUN* (*poetical use*) morning.
[from Old English]

morning *NOUN* **mornings** the early part of the day, before noon or before lunchtime.
[from *morn*]

morocco *NOUN* a kind of leather originally made in Morocco from goatskins.

moron *NOUN* **morons** (*informal*) a very stupid person.
▷ **moronic** *adjective*
[from Greek *moros* = foolish]

morose (*say* mo-rohss) *ADJECTIVE* bad-tempered and miserable.
▷ **morosely** *adverb* **moroseness** *noun*
[from Latin]

morphine (*say* mor-feen) *NOUN* a drug made from opium, used to lessen pain.
[named after *Morpheus*, the Roman god of dreams]

morris dance *NOUN* **morris dances** a traditional English dance performed in costume by men with ribbons and bells.
[originally *Moorish dance* (because it was thought to have come from the Moors)]

morrow *NOUN* (*poetical use*) the following day.
[same origin as *morn*]

Morse code *NOUN* a signalling code using short and long sounds or flashes of light (dots and dashes) to represent letters.
[named after its American inventor, S. F. B. *Morse*]

morsel *NOUN* **morsels** a small piece of food.
[from old French]

mortal *ADJECTIVE* **1** not living for ever • *All of us are mortal.* **2** causing death; fatal • *a mortal wound.* **3** deadly • *mortal enemies.*
▷ **mortally** *adverb*

mortal *NOUN* **mortals** a human being, as compared to a god or immortal spirit.
[from Latin *mortis* = of death]

mortality *NOUN* **mortals** **1** the state of being mortal and bound to die. **2** the number of people who die over a period of time • *a low rate of infant mortality.*

mortar *NOUN* **mortars** **1** a mixture of sand, cement, and water used in building to stick bricks together. **2** a hard bowl in which substances are pounded with a pestle. **3** a short cannon for firing shells at a high angle.
[from old French]

mortarboard *NOUN* **mortarboards** an academic cap with a stiff square top.
[because it looks like the board used by workmen to hold mortar]

mortgage (*say* mor-gij) *NOUN* **mortgages** an arrangement to borrow money to buy a house, with the house as security for the loan.

mortgage *VERB* **mortgages, mortgaging, mortgaged** offer a house etc. as security in return for a loan.
[from old French]

mortify *VERB* **mortifies, mortifying, mortified** humiliate someone or make them feel very ashamed.
▷ **mortification** *noun*
[originally = kill or destroy: from Latin *mors* = death]

mortise *NOUN* **mortises** a hole made in a piece of wood for another piece to be joined to it. (COMPARE **tenon**)
[from old French]

mortise lock *NOUN* **mortise locks** a lock set into a door.

mortuary *NOUN* **mortuaries** a place where dead bodies are kept before being buried or cremated.
[from Latin *mortuus* = dead]

mosaic (*say* mo-zay-ik) *NOUN* **mosaics** a picture or design made from small coloured pieces of stone or glass.
[via old French from Italian]

mosque (*say* mosk) *NOUN* **mosques** a building where Muslims worship.
[via French and Italian from Arabic]

mosquito *NOUN* **mosquitoes** a kind of gnat that sucks blood.
[Spanish or Portuguese, = little fly]

moss *NOUN* **mosses** a plant that grows in damp places and has no flowers.
▷ **mossy** *adjective*
[from Old English]

most *ADJECTIVE* (superlative of **much** and **many**)
greatest in amount or degree • *Most people came by bus.*

most *NOUN* the greatest amount • *Most of the food was eaten.*

most *ADVERB* **1** to the greatest extent; more than any other • *most beautiful.* **2** very or extremely • *most impressive.*
[from Old English]

-most *SUFFIX* forms superlative adjectives (e.g. *hindmost*, *uppermost*).
[from Old English *-mest*]

mostly *ADVERB* mainly.

MOT *ABBREVIATION* a compulsory annual test of motor vehicles of more than a specified age.
[from the initial letters of *Ministry of Transport*, the government department that introduced it]

motel *NOUN* **motels** a hotel providing accommodation for motorists and their cars.
[from *motor* + *hotel*]

moth *NOUN* **moths** an insect rather like a butterfly, that usually flies at night.
[from Old English]

mother *NOUN* **mothers** a female parent.
▷ **motherhood** *noun*

mother *VERB* **mothers**, **mothering**, **mothered** look after someone in a motherly way.
[from Old English]

Mothering Sunday *NOUN* Mother's Day.

mother-in-law *NOUN* **mothers-in-law** the mother of a married person's husband or wife.

motherly *ADJECTIVE* kind and gentle like a mother.
▷ **motherliness** *noun*

mother-of-pearl *NOUN* a pearly substance lining the shells of mussels etc.

Mother's Day *NOUN* the fourth Sunday in Lent, when many people give cards or presents to their mothers.

motif (*say* moh-teef) *NOUN* **motifs** a repeated design or theme.
[French]

motion *NOUN* **motions** **1** a way of moving; movement. **2** a formal statement to be discussed and voted on at a meeting.

motion *VERB* **motions**, **motioning**, **motioned** signal by a gesture • *She motioned him to sit beside her.*
[from Latin *motio* = movement]

motionless *ADJECTIVE* not moving.

motivate *VERB* **motivates**, **motivating**, **motivated** **1** give a person a motive or reason to do something • *She seems to be motivated by a sense of duty.* **2** make a person determined to achieve something • *He is good at motivating his players.*
▷ **motivation** *noun*

motive *NOUN* **motives** what makes a person do something • *a motive for murder.*

motive *ADJECTIVE* producing movement • *The engine provides motive power.*
[from Latin *motivus* = moving]

motley *ADJECTIVE* **1** multicoloured. **2** made up of various sorts of things.
[origin unknown]

motor *NOUN* **motors** a machine providing power to drive machinery etc.; an engine.

motor *VERB* **motors**, **motoring**, **motored** go or take someone in a car.
[Latin, = mover]

motorbike *NOUN* **motorbikes** (*informal*) a motorcycle.

motorcade *NOUN* **motorcades** a procession of cars.
[from *motor* + *cavalcade*]

motorcycle *NOUN* **motorcycles** a two-wheeled road vehicle with an engine.
▷ **motorcyclist** *noun*

motorist *NOUN* **motorists** a person who drives a car.

motorized *ADJECTIVE* equipped with a motor or with motor vehicles.

motor neuron disease *NOUN* a disease of the nerves that control movement, so that the muscles get weaker and weaker until the person dies.

motorway *NOUN* **motorways** a wide road for fast long-distance traffic.

mottled *ADJECTIVE* marked with spots or patches of colour.
[probably from *motley*]

motto *NOUN* **mottoes** **1** a short saying used as a guide for behaviour • *Their motto is 'Who dares, wins'.* **2** a short verse or riddle etc. found inside a cracker.
[Italian]

mould[1] *NOUN* **moulds** a hollow container of a particular shape, in which a liquid or soft substance is put to set into this shape.

mould *VERB* **moulds, moulding, moulded** make something have a particular shape or character.
[from Latin *modulus* = little measure]

mould[2] *NOUN* a fine furry growth of very small fungi.
▷ **mouldy** *adjective*
[from Old Norse]

moulder *VERB* **moulders, mouldering, mouldered** rot away or decay into dust.
[origin unknown]

moult *VERB* **moults, moulting, moulted** shed feathers, hair, or skin etc. while a new growth forms.
[from Latin *mutari* = to change, probably via Old English]

mound *NOUN* **mounds** **1** a pile of earth or stones etc. **2** a small hill.
[origin unknown]

mount *VERB* **mounts, mounting, mounted** **1** climb or go up; ascend. **2** get on a horse or bicycle etc. **3** increase in amount • *Our costs are mounting.* **4** place or fix in position for use or display • *Mount your photos in an album.* **5** organize • *The gallery is to mount an exhibition of young British artists.*

mount *NOUN* **mounts** **1** a mountain • *Mount Everest.* **2** something on which an object is mounted. **3** a horse for riding.
[from Latin *mons* = mountain]

mountain *NOUN* **mountains** **1** a very high hill. **2** a large heap or pile or quantity.
▷ **mountainous** *adjective*
[from old French; related to *mount*]

mountaineer *NOUN* **mountaineers** a person who climbs mountains.
▷ **mountaineering** *noun*

mounted *ADJECTIVE* serving on horseback • *mounted police.*

mourn *VERB* **mourns, mourning, mourned** be sad, especially because someone has died.
▷ **mourner** *noun*
[from Old English]

mournful *ADJECTIVE* sad and sorrowful.
▷ **mournfully** *adverb*

mouse *NOUN* **mice** **1** a small animal with a long thin tail and a pointed nose. **2** (*in computing*)
mouses or **mice** **3** a small device which you move around on a mat to control the movements of a cursor on a VDU screen.
▷ **mousetrap** *noun* **mousy** *adjective*
[from Old English]

moussaka *NOUN* a dish of minced meat, aubergine, etc., with a cheese sauce.
[from Arabic]

mousse (*say* mooss) *NOUN* **mousses** **1** a creamy pudding flavoured with fruit or chocolate. **2** a frothy creamy substance put on the hair so that it can be styled more easily.
[French, = froth]

moustache (*say* mus-**tahsh**) *NOUN* **moustaches** hair allowed to grow on a man's upper lip.
[via French from Italian]

A B C D E F G H I J K L M N O P Q R S T U V W X Y Z

mouth *NOUN* **mouths** **1** the opening through which food is taken into the body. **2** the place where a river enters the sea. **3** an opening or outlet.
▷ **mouthful** *noun*

mouth *VERB* **mouths**, **mouthing**, **mouthed** form words carefully with your lips, especially without saying them aloud.
[from Old English]

mouth organ *NOUN* **mouth organs** a small musical instrument that you play by blowing and sucking while passing it along your lips.

mouthpiece *NOUN* **mouthpieces** the part of a musical instrument or other device that you put to your mouth.

movable *ADJECTIVE* able to be moved.

move *VERB* **moves**, **moving**, **moved** **1** take or go from one place to another; change a person's or thing's position. **2** affect a person's feelings • *Their sad story moved us deeply.* **3** put forward a formal statement (a *motion*) to be discussed and voted on at a meeting.
▷ **mover** *noun*

move *NOUN* **moves** **1** a movement or action. **2** a player's turn to move a piece in a game such as chess.
- **get a move on** (*informal*) hurry up.
- **on the move** moving or making progress.
[from Latin]

movement *NOUN* **movements** **1** moving or being moved. **2** a group of people working together to achieve something. **3** (*in music*) one of the main divisions of a symphony or other long musical work.

movie *NOUN* **movies** (*American*) (*informal*) a cinema film.
[short for *moving picture*]

moving *ADJECTIVE* making someone feel strong emotion, especially sorrow or pity • *It was a very moving story.*

mow *VERB* **mows**, **mowing**, **mowed**, **mown** cut down grass etc.
▷ **mower** *noun*
- **mow down** knock down and kill.
[from Old English]

mozzarella *NOUN* a kind of Italian cheese used in cooking, originally made from buffalo's milk.

MP *ABBREVIATION* Member of Parliament.

Mr (*say* **mist**-er) *NOUN* **Messrs** a title put before a man's name.
[short for *mister*]

Mrs (*say* **mis**-iz) *NOUN* **Mrs** a title put before a married woman's name.
[short for *mistress*]

MS *ABBREVIATION* multiple sclerosis.

Ms (*say* miz) *NOUN* a title put before a woman's name.
[from *Mrs* and *Miss*]

USAGE You put *Ms* before the name of a woman if she does not wish to be called 'Miss' or 'Mrs', or if you do not know whether she is married.

M.Sc. *ABBREVIATION* Master of Science.

MSP *ABBREVIATION* Member of the Scottish Parliament.

Mt *ABBREVIATION* mount or mountain.

much *ADJECTIVE* **more**, **most** existing in a large amount • *much noise.*

much *NOUN* a large amount of something.

much *ADVERB* **1** greatly or considerably • *much to my surprise.* **2** approximately • *It is much the same.*
[from Old English]

muck *NOUN* **1** farmyard manure. **2** (*informal*) dirt or filth. **3** (*informal*) a mess.
▷ **mucky** *adjective*

muck *VERB*
- **muck about** (*informal*) mess about.
- **muck out** clean out the place where an animal is kept.
- **muck up** (*informal*) **1** make dirty. **2** make a mess of; spoil.
[probably from a Scandinavian language]

mucous (*say* **mew**-kus) *ADJECTIVE* **1** like mucus. **2** covered with mucus • *a mucous membrane.*

mucus (*say* **mew**-kus) *NOUN* the moist sticky substance on the inner surface of the throat etc.
[Latin]

mud *NOUN* wet soft earth.
▷ **muddy** *adjective* **muddiness** *noun*
[probably from old German]

muddle *VERB* **muddles, muddling, muddled 1** jumble or mix things up. **2** confuse.
▷ **muddler** *noun*

muddle *NOUN* **muddles** a muddled condition or thing; confusion or disorder.
[origin unknown]

mudguard *NOUN* **mudguards** a curved cover over the top part of the wheel of a bicycle etc. to protect the rider from the mud and water thrown up by the wheel.

muesli (*say* mooz-lee) *NOUN* a breakfast food made of mixed cereals, dried fruit, and nuts.
[Swiss German]

muezzin (*say* moo-ez-in) *NOUN* **muezzins** a Muslim crier who calls the hours of prayer from a minaret.
[from Arabic *mu'addin* = calling to prayer]

muff[1] *NOUN* **muffs** a short tube-shaped piece of warm material into which the hands are pushed from opposite ends.
[from Dutch]

muff[2] *VERB* **muffs, muffing, muffed** (*informal*) bungle.
[origin unknown]

muffin *NOUN* **muffins 1** a flat bun eaten toasted and buttered. **2** a small sponge cake, usually containing fruit, chocolate chips, etc.
[origin unknown]

muffle *VERB* **muffles, muffling, muffled 1** cover or wrap something to protect it or keep it warm. **2** deaden the sound of something • *a muffled scream.*
[probably from old French]

muffler *NOUN* **mufflers** a warm scarf.
[from *muffle*]

mufti *NOUN* ordinary clothes worn by someone who usually wears a uniform.
[probably from Arabic]

mug *NOUN* **mugs 1** a kind of large straight-sided cup. **2** (*slang*) a fool; a person who is easily deceived. **3** (*slang*) a person's face.

mug *VERB* **mugs, mugging, mugged** attack and rob somebody in the street.
▷ **mugger** *noun*
[probably from a Scandinavian language]

muggy *ADJECTIVE* **muggier, muggiest** (said about the weather) unpleasantly warm and damp.
▷ **mugginess** *noun*
[probably from a Scandinavian language]

mulberry *NOUN* **mulberries** a purple or white fruit rather like a blackberry.
[from Old English]

mule *NOUN* **mules** an animal that is the offspring of a donkey and a mare, known for being stubborn.
▷ **mulish** *adjective*
[from Old English]

mull *VERB* **mulls, mulling, mulled**
- **mull something over** think about something carefully; ponder.
[probably related to *mill*]

mulled *ADJECTIVE* (said about wine or beer) heated with sugar and spices.
[origin unknown]

mullet *NOUN* **mullet** a kind of fish used as food.
[from Greek]

multi- *PREFIX* many (as in *multicoloured* = with many colours).
[from Latin *multus* = many]

multicultural *ADJECTIVE* made up of people of many different races, religions, and cultures.

multifarious (*say* multi-**fair**-ee-us) *ADJECTIVE* of many kinds; very varied.
[from Latin]

multilateral *ADJECTIVE* (said about an agreement or treaty) made between three or more people or countries etc.
[from Latin *multilaterus* = many sided]

multimedia *ADJECTIVE* using more than one medium • *a multimedia show with pictures, lights, and music.*

multimedia *NOUN* a computer program with sound and still and moving pictures linked to the text.

multimillionaire *NOUN* **multimillionaires** a person with a fortune of several million pounds or dollars.

multinational *NOUN* **multinationals** a large business company which works in several countries.

multiple *ADJECTIVE* having many parts or elements.

multiple *NOUN* **multiples** a number that contains another number (a *factor*) an exact amount of times with no remainder • *8 and 12 are multiples of 4.*
[same origin as *multiply*]

multiple sclerosis *NOUN* a disease of the nervous system which makes a person unable to control their movements, and may affect their sight.

multiplex *NOUN* **multiplexes** a large cinema complex that has many screens.
[from *multi-* + Latin *plex* = fold]

multiplicity *NOUN* a great variety or large number.

multiply *VERB* **multiplies, multiplying, multiplied 1** take a number a given quantity of times • *Five multiplied by four equals twenty* (5 x 4 = 20). **2** make or become many; increase.
▷ **multiplication** *noun* **multiplier** *noun*
[from Latin *multiplex* = many- sided]

multiracial *ADJECTIVE* consisting of people of many different races.

multitude *NOUN* **multitudes** a great number of people or things.
▷ **multitudinous** *adjective*
[from Latin *multus* = many]

mum[1] *NOUN* **mums** (*informal*) mother.
[short for *mummy*[1]]

mum[2] *ADJECTIVE* (*informal*) silent • *keep mum.*
[imitating a sound made with closed lips]

mumble *VERB* **mumbles, mumbling, mumbled** speak indistinctly so that you are not easy to hear.
▷ **mumble** *noun* **mumbler** *noun*
[from *mum*[2]]

mumbo-jumbo *NOUN* talk or ceremony that has no real meaning.
[probably from a West African language]

mummy[1] *NOUN* **mummies** (*informal*) mother.
[from *mama*]

mummy[2] *NOUN* **mummies** a corpse wrapped in cloth and treated with oils etc. before being buried so that it does not decay, as was the custom in ancient Egypt.
▷ **mummify** *verb*
[from Arabic]

mumps *NOUN* an infectious disease that makes the neck swell painfully.
[from an old word *mump* = pull a face (because the glands in the face sometimes swell)]

munch *VERB* **munches, munching, munched** chew vigorously.
[imitating the sound]

mundane *ADJECTIVE* **1** ordinary, not exciting. **2** concerned with practical matters, not ideals.
[from Latin *mundus* = world]

municipal (*say* mew-**nis**-ip-al) *ADJECTIVE* to do with a town or city.
[from Latin *municipium* = a town whose citizens had the same privileges as Roman citizens]

municipality *NOUN* **municipalities** a town or city that has its own local government.

munificent *ADJECTIVE* (*formal*) extremely generous.
▷ **munificently** *adverb* **munificence** *noun*
[from Latin *munus* = gift]

munitions *PLURAL NOUN* military weapons, ammunition, and equipment.
[from Latin *munitum* = fortified]

mural *NOUN* **murals** a picture painted on a wall.

mural *ADJECTIVE* on or to do with a wall.
[from Latin *murus* = wall]

murder *VERB* **murders, murdering, murdered** kill a person unlawfully and deliberately.
▷ **murderer** *noun* **murderess** *noun*

murder *NOUN* **murders** the murdering of somebody.
▷ **murderous** *adjective*
[from Old English]

murky *ADJECTIVE* **murkier, murkiest** dark and gloomy.
▷ **murk** *noun* **murkiness** *noun*
[from Old English]

murmur *VERB* **murmurs, murmuring, murmured 1** make a low continuous sound. **2** speak in a soft voice.
▷ **murmur** *noun*
[from Latin]

muscle *NOUN* **muscles** **1** a band or bundle of fibrous tissue that can contract and relax and so produce movement in parts of the body. **2** the power of muscles; strength.
[from Latin]

muscular *ADJECTIVE* **1** to do with the muscles. **2** having well-developed muscles.
▷ **muscularity** *noun*

muse *VERB* **muses, musing, mused** think deeply about something; ponder or meditate.
[from old French]

museum *NOUN* **museums** a place where interesting, old, or valuable objects are displayed for people to see.
[from Greek *mouseion* = place of Muses (goddesses of the arts and sciences)]

mush *NOUN* soft pulp.
▷ **mushy** *adjective*
[different spelling of *mash*]

mushroom *NOUN* **mushrooms** an edible fungus with a stem and a dome-shaped top.

mushroom *VERB* **mushrooms, mushrooming, mushroomed** grow or appear suddenly in large numbers • *Blocks of flats mushroomed in the city.*
[from old French]

music *NOUN* **1** a pattern of pleasant or interesting sounds made by instruments or by the voice. **2** printed or written symbols which stand for musical sounds.
[from Greek *mousike* = of the Muses (SEE **museum**)]

musical *ADJECTIVE* **1** to do with music. **2** producing music. **3** good at music or interested in it.
▷ **musically** *adverb*

musical *NOUN* **musicals** a play or film containing a lot of songs.

musician *NOUN* **musicians** someone who plays a musical instrument.

musk *NOUN* a strong-smelling substance used in perfumes.
▷ **musky** *adjective*
[from Persian]

musket *NOUN* **muskets** a kind of gun with a long barrel, formerly used by soldiers.
[via French from Italian]

musketeer *NOUN* **musketeers** a soldier armed with a musket.

Muslim *NOUN* **Muslims** a person who follows the religious teachings of Muhammad (who lived in about 570-632), set out in the Koran.
[Arabic, = someone who submits to God]

muslin *NOUN* very thin cotton cloth.
[named after Mosul, a city in Iraq, where it was first made]

mussel *NOUN* **mussels** a black shellfish.
[from Old English]

must *AUXILIARY VERB* used to express **1** necessity or obligation (*You must go*), **2** certainty (*You must be joking!*)
[from Old English]

mustang *NOUN* **mustangs** a wild horse of the United States of America and Mexico.
[from Spanish]

mustard *NOUN* a yellow paste or powde r used to give food a hot taste.
[from old French]

muster *VERB* **musters, mustering, mustered** assemble or gather together.

muster *NOUN* **musters** an assembly of people or things.
- **pass muster** be up to the required standard.
[from Latin *monstrare* = to show]

mustn't (*mainly spoken*) must not.

musty *ADJECTIVE* **mustier, mustiest** smelling or tasting mouldy or stale.
▷ **mustiness** *noun*
[probably from *moist*]

mutable (*say* mew-ta-bul) *ADJECTIVE* able or likely to change.
▷ **mutability** *noun*
[from Latin *mutare* = to change]

mutation *NOUN* **mutations** a change in the form of a living creature because of changes in its genes.
▷ **mutate** *verb* **mutant** *noun*
[same origin as *mutable*]

mute *ADJECTIVE* **1** silent; not speaking or able to speak. **2** not pronounced • *The g in 'gnat' is mute.*
▷ **mutely** *adverb* **muteness** *noun*

mute *NOUN* **mutes** **1** a person who cannot speak. **2** a device fitted to a musical instrument to deaden its sound.

mute *VERB* **mutes, muting, muted** make a thing quieter or less intense.
▷ **muted** *adjective*
[from Latin]

mutilate *VERB* **mutilates, mutilating, mutilated** damage something by breaking or cutting off part of it.
▷ **mutilation** *noun*
[from Latin *mutilus* = maimed]

mutineer *NOUN* **mutineers** a person who mutinies.

mutiny *NOUN* **mutinies** rebellion against authority, especially refusal by members of the armed forces to obey orders.
▷ **mutinous** *adjective* **mutinously** *adverb*

mutiny *VERB* **mutinies, mutinying, mutinied** take part in a mutiny.
[from old French]

mutter *VERB* **mutters, muttering, muttered** **1** speak in a low voice. **2** grumble.
▷ **mutter** *noun*
[related to *mute*]

mutton *NOUN* meat from a sheep.
[from old French]

mutual (*say* mew-tew-al) *ADJECTIVE* **1** given or done to each other • *mutual destruction.* **2** shared by two or more people • *a mutual friend.*
▷ **mutually** *adverb*
[from Latin]

muzzle *NOUN* **muzzles** **1** an animal's nose and mouth. **2** a cover put over an animal's nose and mouth so that it cannot bite. **3** the open end of a gun.

muzzle *VERB* **muzzles, muzzling, muzzled** **1** put a muzzle on an animal. **2** silence; prevent a person from expressing opinions.
[from old French]

my *ADJECTIVE* belonging to me.
[originally, the form of *mine*[1] used before consonants]

myriad (*say* mirri-ad) *ADJECTIVE* very many; countless.
▷ **myriad** *noun*
[from Greek *myrioi* = 10,000]

myrrh (*say* mer) *NOUN* a substance used in perfumes and incense and medicine.
[from Old English]

myrtle *NOUN* **myrtles** an evergreen shrub with dark leaves and white flowers.
[from Greek]

myself *PRONOUN* I or me and nobody else. (COMPARE **herself**)

mysterious *ADJECTIVE* full of mystery; puzzling.
▷ **mysteriously** *adverb*

mystery *NOUN* **mysteries** something that cannot be explained or understood; something puzzling.
[from Greek *mysterion* = a secret thing or ceremony]

mystic *ADJECTIVE* **1** having a spiritual meaning. **2** mysterious and filling people with wonder.
▷ **mystical** *adjective* **mystically** *adverb* **mysticism** *noun*

mystic *NOUN* **mystics** a person who seeks to obtain spiritual contact with God by deep religious meditation.
[from Greek *mystikos* = secret]

mystify *VERB* **mystifies, mystifying, mystified** puzzle or bewilder.
▷ **mystification** *noun*
[from French]

mystique (*say* mis-**teek**) *NOUN* an air of mystery or secret power.
[French, = mystic]

myth (*say* mith) *NOUN* **myths** **1** an old story containing ideas about ancient times or about supernatural beings. (COMPARE **legend**) **2** an untrue story or belief.
[from Greek *mythos* = story]

mythical *ADJECTIVE* **1** imaginary; found only in myths • *a mythical animal.* **2** to do with myths.

mythology *NOUN* myths or the study of myths.
▷ **mythological** *adjective*

myxomatosis (*say* miks-om-at-**oh**-sis) *NOUN* a disease that kills rabbits.
[from Greek *myxa* = mucus (because the mucous membranes swell up)]

Supplement

Grammar

Grammar is the set of rules that governs how words change and how they can be put together in sentences. We only know what a word is when it is in a sentence. For instance, the word *place* has several meanings and could be a noun, a verb, or an adjective. Only when we put it into a sentence such as *They visited some interesting places* do we know which meaning is given and which grammatical rules (like adding an '- s' for the plural) apply to it.

The grammar rules that cover words are called 'morphology'. This simply means how words change. If a word is a noun, for instance, it usually changes in its plural form. But, if it is a verb, a different set of changes apply. Words also change if they are used as different parts of speech.

Parts of speech

In English, parts of speech, or word classes, change in only a few circumstances: nouns change into plural and possessive forms; verbs change according to person and tense; and adverbs and adjectives have comparative forms.

Nouns

The vast majority of English nouns form their plurals by adding '- s':

hat – hats   cathedral – cathedrals   toy – toys

Some nouns add '- es' to make an 'es' sound:

lash – lashes   wish – wishes   fox – foxes

Nouns that end in 'o' also add '- es':

echo – echoes   hero – heroes

Nouns ending in 'y' when there is a consonant before the 'y', change '- y' to '- ies':

baby – babies   lady – ladies

Unfortunately some very common words have irregular plurals such as nouns that swap 'f' or 'fe' for '- ves':

loaf – loaves   leaf – leaves   calf – calves   life – lives

Nouns that have a different form in the plural:

mouse – mice   goose – geese   child – children   woman – women

Nouns that have the same singular and plural form:

sheep   fish   aircraft

Nouns that are always plural:

shorts   scissors

Words of foreign origin:

gateau – gateaux (French)   cactus – cacti (Latin)
crisis – crises (Greek)

⊙ **Activity** Use the dictionary to find an example of each of the five types of irregular plural.

Possessives

When we want to show possession or function, we add an apostrophe and an '- s' to a word, e.g. the girl's room, the children's library.

If the word is plural, the apostrophe is added after the '- s', e.g. the girls' room (more than one girl), the elephants' enclosure (several elephants).

If the word is not plural but ends in '- s', the second '- s' is optional, e.g. Keats' poetry or Keats's poetry.

⊙ **Activity** Write a sentence using two apostrophes to describe the single house that belongs to the cousin of several friends.

Verbs

Verbs change forms because of person or tense.

1st person singular	I eat	I walk	I listen
2nd person singular	you eat	you walk	you listen
3rd person singular	he/she/it eats	you walk	he/she/it listens
1st person plural	we eat	we walk	we listen
2nd person plural	you eat	you walk	you walk
3rd person plural	they eat	they walk	they walk

You can see that with most verbs, the third person singular form only is changed by adding an '- s'

The suffixes '- ing' and '- ed' are used to show different tenses:

I walk   I am walking   I walked   I have walked

But some common verbs do not follow this pattern. For example:

I *am* you *are* he/she/it *is* I am *being* I *was* I have *been* I will *be*

I *do* he/she/it *does* I am *doing* I did I have *done*

I *think* he/she/it *thinks* I am *thinking* I *thought* I have *thought*

I *freeze* he/she/it *freezes* I am *frozen* I *froze* I have *frozen*

⊙ **Activity** Use the dictionary to find two further examples of verbs like *freeze* that have four forms.

Adjectives and adverbs

Adjectives only change when they are being compared:

green, greener, greenest

The same goes for adverbs:

late, later, latest

The general rule is that single and double syllable words have these forms. Words with more than two syllables use *more* and *most*. For example:

beautiful, more beautiful, most beautiful (*adjectives*)

quietly, more quietly, most quietly (*adverbs*)

As usual, exceptions occur amongst common words:

good, better, best little, less, least bad, worse, worst (*adjectives*)

far, further/farther, furthest/farthest well, better, best badly, worse, worst (*adverbs*)

⊙ **Activity** Use the dictionary to find four examples of an irregular comparative adverb or adjective.

Changing parts of speech

English is a very flexible language because most words can be used as different parts of speech. Almost any noun or verb can be used as an adjective. To do this, simply place it in front of a noun, e.g. the *house* wine; a *running* joke; a *car* pool; a *talking* shop.

Some nouns can be used as verbs with no change at all. For instance, 'table', 'chair', and 'floor' can also be used as verbs without any change:

I *tabled* a motion at the meeting which you *chaired*. We were both *floored* when it did not pass.

Nouns and adjectives into verbs

Some nouns can be used as verbs with no change at all. For instance, 'table', 'chair', and 'floor' can be used as verbs without any change:

I *tabled* a motion at the meeting which you *chaired*. We were both *floored* when it did not pass.

However, most nouns and adjectives take on a suffix such as '- ate', '- en', '- ify', '- ise' or '- ize' when they are used as verbs, e.g.

just	justify	solid	solidify
bright	brighten	dark	darken
alien	alienate	pollen	pollinate
priority	prioritize	critic	criticise

⊙ **Activity** Both '- ize' and '- ise' are used in the above list. Find out, using the dictionary, where in the world the '- ize' spelling is more common.

Adjectives, nouns, and adverbs

Adjectives can be formed into nouns by adding '- ness'.

Nouns can be formed into adjectives by adding '- ic', '- ual' or changing '- ence' to '- ent'.

Adjectives can be formed into adverbs by adding '- ly'. The list below shows some common transformations.

Noun	**Adjective**	**Adverb**
habit	habitual	habitually
shoddiness	shoddy	shoddily
insolence	insolent	insolently
ecstasy	ecstatic	ecstatically
patriot	patriotic	patriotically
rite	ritual	ritually
bleakness	bleak	bleakly
magnificence	magnificent	magnificently
stealthiness	stealthy	stealthily
rowdiness	rowdy	rowdily

⊙ **Activity** Imagine that there was an adjective 'volicent'. What would its noun and adverbial forms be?

Verbs into nouns

The suffixes '- ation', '- tion', and '- ment' are often used when a verb is being transformed into a noun. For example:

Verb	Noun
distribute	distribution
commence	commencement
damn	damnation
quote	quotation
establish	establishment
legalise	legalisation
appoint	appointment
nourishment	nourishment

The person or thing that does an action is often shown by the addition of the suffixes –er/- or and –ee. As in:

Verb	Noun
walk	walker
collect	collector
detain	detainee
pay	payer / payee
employ	employer/ employee
licence	licensor / licensee

⊙ **Activity** Look up some of the - er/- ee pairs and write down a general statement that describes the difference between these two suffixes.

Different meanings for different parts of speech

In all of the transformations we have looked at so far, the basic meaning of the word has not changed. However, many words have different meanings according to if they are acting as a different part of speech or word class. For instance, the verb *excise* means 'to remove by cutting' but the noun *excise* can mean either 'a tax' or 'a tax gathering organisation'. It is possible to see how the meaning of these words are related; tax representing a 'cut' from the cost of something but the words are now so far apart that they have separate entries in the dictionary.

Other examples include:

green *noun* a grassy area
green *adjective* inexperienced

career *verb* move quickly in an uncontrolled way
career *noun* a series of jobs

spirit *verb* to carry off quickly and secretly
spirit *noun* ghost or supernatural being

⊙ **Activity** The distance in meaning from *excise* as a noun to *excise* as a verb is not very far. Your challenge is to find a word with what you think has the greatest difference between the meaning of the different parts of speech.

Prefixes and suffixes

In English, most, but not all, suffixes affect the grammatical function of a word. For example, the suffixes '- ist' and '- ism' make nouns out of verbs but can also be added to nouns to give a different meaning, For example:

Marx	Marxism	Marxist
Capital	Capitalism	Capitalist

Most prefixes also affect a word's meaning rather than its grammatical function. Let's start off with the word *act.*

act means to do something.

react means to do something in response.

overreact means to something excessive in response.

The noun form would be: **overreaction**.

Or, as a plural, **overreactions**.

And a possible adjectival form would be: **overreactional**.

This makes a total of four prefixes and suffixes that can be added to the word *act.* A fifth (not very likely) affix could be 'semi- ' as in the sentence:

He used to start getting *over-excited* and then stop; he was *semi-overreactional.*

⊙ **Activity** Can you find fit more than four suffixes and prefixes to a single word?

Prefixes

There is a great variety of prefixes, some of which do the same job. A word can be made negative by adding 'in-', 'un-', 'im-', 'a-', 'ir', and so on. The idea of going beyond the ordinary can be conveyed by adding 'over-', extra-', 'super-', and 'hyper-'. As we have already seen, prefixes can be combined together as in *hemisemidemiquaver.*

Prefixes allow single words to take on a whole range of meanings. For example:

do	redo	undo	overdo	
take	retake	undertake	overtake	mistake
market	supermarket	hypermarket	mini-market	
mount	dismount	remount	unmount	surmount
sold	resold	unsold	oversold	undersold
fast	extra-fast	super-fast	ultra-fast	

Note that some prefixes are attached with a hyphen; this usually disappears when a combination becomes familiar.

⊙ **Activity** Use the dictionary to find a single word that can take on more than four prefixes.

Prefixes

a-	ar-	counter-	extra-	ir-
ab-	arch-	cross-	for-	iso-
abs-	as-	de-	fore-	kilo-
ac-	at-	deca-	geo-	mal-
ad-	aut-	deci-	hecto-	mega-
aero-	auto-	demi-	hepta-	micro-
af-	be-	di-	hetero-	milli-
Afro-	bene-	dia-	hexa-	mini-
ag-	bi-	dif-	homo-	mis-
al-	bio-	dis-	hydr-	mono-
ambi-	cata-	dys-	hydro-	multi-
amphi-	cath-	e-	hyper-	neo-
an-	centi-	ef-	hypo-	non-
ana-	circum-	electro-	il-	ob-
Anglo-	co-	em-	im-	oc-
ant-	col-	en-	in-	octa-
ante-	com-	epi-	infra-	octo-
anti-	con-	equi-	inter-	of-
ap-	contra-	eu-	intra-	omni-
apo-	cor-	ex-	intro-	op-

ortho-	photo-	radio-	sum-	thermo-
out-	poly-	re-	sup-	trans-
over-	post-	retro-	super-	tri-
pan-	pre-	se-	sur-	ultra-
para-	pro-	self-	sus-	un-
penta-	proto-	semi-	syl-	under-
per-	pseudo-	step-	sym-	uni-
peri-	psycho-	sub-	syn-	vice-
phil-	quadri-	suc-	tele-	
philo-	quasi-	suf-	tetra-	

Suffixes

- able	- ee	- ible	- ite	- phobia
- arch	- er	- ic	- itis	- ship
- archy	- esque	- ical	- ive	- sion
- arian	- ess	- ician	- ize	- some
- ary	- est	- icity	- kin	- teen
- ate	- ette	- ics	- less	- tion
- ation	- faction	- ie	- ling	- tude
- bility	- ferous	- ier	- logical	- uble
- ble	- fold	- iest	- logist	- vore
- cide	- ful	- iferous	- logy	- vorous
- cle	- fy	- ification	- ly	- ward
- cracy	- gen	- ing	- most	- wards
- crat	- gon	- ion	- ness	- ways
- cule	- gram	- ise	- oid	- wise
- cy	- graph	- ish	- ology	- xion
- dom	- graphy	- ism	- or	- y
- ed	- hood	- ist	- pathy	

Root words

Suffixes and prefixes show how English makes new words or new meanings, by combining known elements. This process also occurs with word elements from other languages known as root words. Most root words are ancient Latin or Greek in origin and but they are still being used to describe modern ideas. For example:

tele – from the Greek for 'far" as in *telephone, television, teletext*
geo – from the Greek for 'earth' as in *geology, geophysics, geography*
dict – from the Latin for 'to say" as in *dictate, dictionary, predict*

An understanding of root words can help you to understand new and unfamiliar words. The Greek word for 'footed' *podos*, for instance, crops up in a number of words. For example:

bi-pod	two footed
tripod	three footed
octopod	eight footed
pseudopod	false foot

It is not difficult to guess that 'mono- pod' means 'one- footed'. The related Latin word *pedalis* has given us the English word 'pedal' and can be seen in words such as:

quadruped	four footed
centipede	hundred footed
millipede	thousand footed

Other useful roots include:

anima	having life
aqua	water
audio	hearing
bio-	to do with life
cosmo-	to do with the world or universe
eco	to do with the house
graph or **-graphy**	writing
mono	one
-metry	measuring
-mobile	moving
-nomy	governing
phil-	love of
phobia	fear of
photo	to do with light
poly	many
video	to see
xeno	strange or foreign

⊙ **Activity** If it existed, what would the science of 'autobiometry' consist of?

Sentence grammar

Although dictionaries are concerned with individual words, they give help with sentence grammar through information on parts of speech, example sentences, and in usage notes. Sentences contain a complete idea or action and make sense on their own. There are three main types of sentences: simple, compound, and complex.

simple sentences must have a subject (either a noun or a noun phrase) and a verb, e.g. *Mary disappeared.*

compound sentences consist of simple sentences joined by conjunctions such as 'and' or 'but', e.g. *Mary disappeared and we all went off to search for the missing girl.*

complex sentences consist of a main clause and at least one other clause that is subordinated to it.

The two clauses are joined by conjunctions such as 'although', 'because' and 'in order to', e.g. *Mary disappeared so we all went out to look for her.*

A fourth type of sentence is called a **minor sentence**. This type of sentence usually lacks a subject for its verb and is often used in commands or exclamations, e.g. *No smoking. Listen!*

Spelling

One of the main difficulties with English spelling is that there are about 44 sounds in English and only 26 letters in the alphabet. Even worse than this, is the fact that some consonants do not have sounds of their own and that many vowels aren't clearly sounded at all.

Consonants

'C' has either a 'k' sound as in 'cat' or an 's' sound as in 'cease'.

'Qu' can usually be replaced by a 'kw' sound as in 'quick'.

'X' has either a 'z' sound as in ''xylophone' or an 'eks' sound as in 'X-ray'.

'Ph' always has an 'f' sound.

'Ch' can be pronounced as 'ch' in church or 'k' as in chemist or 'sh' as in champagne.

'Wh' at the beginning of words has a 'w' sound.

Using spelling patterns

The majority of English spellings follow recognisable patterns which a dictionary can help you to identify. For instance, the odd silent 'p' at the beginning of words like 'psychology' and 'psychiatry' is because both words refer to Psyche; the embodiment of the mind or soul in Greek mythology.

Another pattern helps to explain the behaviour of 'ch':

'Ch- ' words pronounced 'ch' tend to be English in origin.

'Ch- ' words pronounced 'sh' tend to be from French.

'Ch- ' words pronounced 'k' tend to be from Greek.

'Ph- ' words also tend to be derived from Greek and are an interesting example of 'tidying up' by early dictionary makers - several 'ph' words were spelt with an 'f' when they were first used in English, as in 'fantosme' (for phantasm) and 'fesan' (for pheasant). The word 'fantasy' escaped this process but it is spelled 'phantasy' in some old books.

The etymology of many 'wh- ' words shows that they derive from Old English words that had a voiced 'h' sound at the beginning. For example:

whale - hwæl   what - hwæt   when - hwanne

The 'w' and 'h' seem to have been reversed over time and the 'h' sound lost.

When you look up a word in the dictionary, it is always a good idea to look at the words around it. You may find similar spelling patterns.

⊙ **Activity** Use the dictionary to find a pattern that helps with the spelling of a group of words.

Unstressed vowels

The commonest vowel sound in English is the unstressed vowel. This is a sort of 'uh' sound. This makes spelling words like 'definite' difficult because sounding out the word does not help.

There are a number of ways to deal with this problem.

Vowels that are unstressed in some words are stressed in others:

Unstressed	**Stressed**
definite	infinity
infinite	infinity
competition	compete

Unstressed	**Stressed**
grammar	grammatical
hypocrite	hypodermic

Another way is to find words within words, for example:

'get' in vegetable

'our' in favourite

'sin' in business

'a rat' in separate

'wed' in Wednesday

Deliberately sounding out a word can also be useful; say the 'ah' sound separately.

Usage

Most modern rules are based on the language found in formal writing. As what is acceptable in formal writing changes, so the rules change. For instance, you will find a usage note in this dictionary about not using 'disinterested'' to mean 'uninterested' but even writers in newspapers sometimes fail to make a distinction between these two words. It is likely that this usage note will disappear in a few years' time.

Comparisons

The comparative endings '- er' and '- est' are added to single and two syllable adjectives and adverbs. For example:

green – greenest

Longer adjectives and adverbs use *more* and *most* or *less* and *least* to make their comparative form. For example

plentiful	more plentiful	most plentiful
abruptly	less abruptly	least abruptly

It is not acceptable to use these two ways at the same time, for example, in 'most hungriest'.

Comparisons with absolute terms such as 'empty', 'dead', 'unique', and 'perfect' can also cause problems. Logically a thing can be alive or dead so it cannot be deader than anything else. Nor can one empty cup be emptier than another.

The word 'unique' seems to annoy some readers more than others and there are frequent objections to phrases such as 'very unique' and 'most unique'. Oddly, the same objections are not made to phrases like 'very dead' or 'most perfect'.

Collective nouns

Collective nouns like 'committee' or 'team' cause problems because they refer to more than one thing but they take singular verbs. For example:

The committee is sitting.

They can take plural verbs if the focus is on the members of the group rather than the group itself.

The team is practising this afternoon.

This refers to the whole team but:

The team are taking this very seriously

shows that each member of the team is involved.

I and me

'I' and 'me' are usually confused when used with other pronouns. It is polite to mention others before yourself in sentences like:

My friends and I went to the cinema.

But in spoken English 'me' is often used in a sentence like this:

My friends and me went to the cinema.

Or even:

Me and my friends went to the cinema.

If you remove 'my friends' from the sentences above it is easy to see which is correct.

Another problem with 'I and me' probably comes about because people remember being told about 'me and my friends'. They therefore write:

The tickets were given to my friends and I.

If 'my friends' is removed, the correct version of the above sentence is clear:

The tickets were given to me.

In grammatical terms 'I' is used as the subject of a sentence whereas 'me' is used as the object.

Lay and lie

Many people find 'lie, lay, lain' and 'lay' confusing. The verb 'lie' has the following forms:

I lie   you lie   he/she/it lies
we lie   you lie   they lie
he is lying   he lay   he has lain

The verb 'lay' has:

I lay   you lay   he/she/it lays
we lay   you lay   they lay
he is laying   he has laid

The confusion arises because 'lay' can be the past tense 'lie':

I lay in bed all day (past tense) is correct.

He lays in bed all day (present tense) is not correct.

Past and passed

The confusion between these two words comes from their sound but if you remember that 'passed' is a verb, you should able to distinguish them. The rule is that 'passed' can stand on its own as in the sentence,

The car passed dangerously close.

However, 'past' always needs a verb to go with it. For instance,

We walked past the incident without noticing anything.

Who and whom

The problem with 'who' and 'whom' is similar to the one with 'I' and 'me'. 'Who' is used as the subject of a sentence and 'whom' is used as the object, or after a preposition.

Is that the woman who gave you the letter?

That is the woman to whom I gave the letter.

This is the letter from the woman whom you met?

'Whom' is only ever used in very formal English.

Some highly formal rules

Modern dictionaries and most books on language tell you how language *is* used rather than how it *ought* to be used. This was not always the case and there are many highly formal grammatical 'rules' that were invented by grammarians which still trouble writers and readers.

These highly formal rules include such advice as not splitting infinitives, not ending sentences with prepositions, and not using double negatives.

Split infinitives

The infinitive form of a verb is 'to' plus the verb as in 'to go' or 'to listen'. Old fashioned grammarians based the grammar of English on Latin and, as the infinitive was never split in Latin (it is always one word) they decreed that it should not be split in English. This rule is largely ignored nowadays.

Ending sentences with a preposition

Old fashioned grammarians also noticed that Latin sentences never ended with prepositions like 'up' or "with'. Again this rule is largely ignored. Sir Winston Churchill once remarked about this rule, *This is the kind of nonsense up with which I will not put.*

Double negatives

The double negative rule is one case where the grammarians seem to have won. In speech it is natural to use multiple negative terms for emphasis – there are many double negatives in Shakespeare for instance – but the grammarians decided to use mathematical logic in writing. One negative term cancels out the other in a sentence such as:

I haven't got no money.

Logically the speaker must have some money.

In formal writing the *I don't know nothing* kind of double negative is unacceptable although you can use the mathematically correct *not un-* sort of double negative as in:

The chair was not uncomfortable

The task was not impossible.

Nn

N. *ABBREVIATION* **1** north. **2** northern.

nab *VERB* **nabs, nabbing, nabbed** (*informal*) catch or arrest someone; seize or grab something.
[origin unknown]

nag[1] *VERB* **nags, nagging, nagged** **1** pester a person by keeping on criticizing, complaining, or asking for things. **2** keep on hurting or bothering you • *a nagging pain.*
[origin unknown]

nag[2] *NOUN* **nags** (*informal*) a horse.
[origin unknown]

nail *NOUN* **nails** **1** the hard covering over the end of a finger or toe. **2** a small sharp piece of metal hammered in to fasten pieces of wood etc. together.

nail *VERB* **nails, nailing, nailed** **1** fasten with a nail or nails. **2** catch or arrest someone.
[from Old English]

naive or **naïve** (*say* nah-**eev**) *ADJECTIVE* showing a lack of experience or good judgement; innocent and trusting.
▷ **naively** *adverb* **naivety** *noun*
[French; related to *native*]

naked *ADJECTIVE* **1** without any clothes or coverings on. **2** obvious; not hidden • *the naked truth.*
▷ **nakedly** *adverb* **nakedness** *noun*
[from Old English]

naked eye *NOUN* the eye when it is not helped by a telescope or microscope etc.

name *NOUN* **names** **1** the word or words by which a person, animal, place, or thing is known. **2** a person's reputation.

name *VERB* **names, naming, named** **1** give a name to. **2** state the name or names of. **3** say what you want something to be • *Name your price.*
- **name the day** decide when something, especially a wedding, is to take place or happen • *Have you two named the day yet?*
[from Old English]

nameless *ADJECTIVE* without a name.

namely *ADVERB* that is to say • *My two favourite subjects are sciences, namely chemistry and biology.*

namesake *NOUN* **namesakes** a person or thing with the same name as another.

nanny *NOUN* **nannies** **1** a nurse who looks after young children. **2** (*informal*) grandmother.
[pet form of *Ann*]

nanny goat *NOUN* **nanny goats** a female goat. (COMPARE **billy goat**)

nap[1] *NOUN* **naps** a short sleep.
- **catch a person napping** catch a person unprepared for something or not alert.
[from Old English]

nap[2] *NOUN* short raised fibres on the surface of cloth or leather.
[from old German or Dutch]

napalm (*say* nay-pahm) *NOUN* a substance made of petrol, used in some incendiary bombs.
[from *naphtha* and *palmitic acid* (two chemicals from which it is made)]

nape *NOUN* **napes** the back part of the neck.
[origin unknown]

napkin *NOUN* **napkins** **1** a piece of cloth or paper used at meals to protect your clothes or for wiping your lips or fingers. **2** (*old use*) a nappy.
[from French *nappe* = tablecloth, + *-kin*]

nappy *NOUN* **nappies** a piece of cloth or other fabric put round a baby's bottom.

narcissistic *ADJECTIVE* extremely vain.
[from *Narcissus*, a youth in Greek legend who fell in love with his own reflection and was turned into a flower]

narcissus *NOUN* **narcissi** a garden flower like a daffodil.
[same origin as *narcissistic*]

narcotic *NOUN* **narcotics** a drug that makes a person sleepy or unconscious.
▷ **narcotic** *adjective*
[from Greek *narke* = numbness]

narrate *VERB* **narrates, narrating, narrated** tell a story or give an account of something.
▷ **narration** *noun* **narrator** *noun*
[from Latin]

narrative *NOUN* **narratives** a spoken or written account of something.

narrow *ADJECTIVE* **1** not wide or broad. **2** uncomfortably close; with only a small margin of error or safety • *a narrow escape.*
▷ **narrowly** *adverb*

narrow *VERB* **narrows, narrowing, narrowed** make or become narrower. [from Old English]

narrow-minded *ADJECTIVE* not tolerant of other people's beliefs and ways.

nasal *ADJECTIVE* **1** to do with the nose. **2** sounding as if the breath comes out through the nose • *a nasal voice.*
▷ **nasally** *adverb*
[from Latin *nasus* = nose]

nasturtium (*say* na-**ster**-shum) *NOUN* **nasturtiums** a garden plant with round leaves and red, yellow, or orange flowers. [from Latin *nasus* = nose + *torquere* = to twist (because of its sharp smell)]

nasty *ADJECTIVE* **nastier, nastiest** **1** unpleasant. **2** unkind.
▷ **nastily** *adverb* **nastiness** *noun*
[origin unknown]

N

natal (*say* **nay**-tal) *ADJECTIVE* **1** to do with birth. **2** from or since birth. [from Latin *natus* = born]

nation *NOUN* **nations** a large community of people most of whom have the same ancestors, language, history, and customs, and who usually live in the same part of the world under one government. [from Latin *natio* = birth or race]

national *ADJECTIVE* to do with or belonging to a nation or country • *national dress; a national newspaper.*
▷ **nationally** *adverb*

national *NOUN* **nationals** a citizen of a particular country.

national anthem *NOUN* **national anthems** a nation's official song, which is played or sung on important occasions.

national curriculum *NOUN* the subjects that must be taught by state schools in England and Wales.

nationalist *NOUN* **nationalists** **1** a person who is very patriotic. **2** a person who wants his or her country to be independent and not to form part of another country • *Scottish Nationalists.*
▷ **nationalism** *noun* **nationalistic** *adjective*

nationality *NOUN* **nationalities** the condition of belonging to a particular nation • *What is his nationality?*

nationalize *VERB* **nationalizes, nationalizing, nationalized** put an industry or business under state ownership or control.
▷ **nationalization** *noun*

national park *NOUN* **national parks** an area of natural beauty which is protected by the government and which the public may visit.

nationwide *ADJECTIVE & ADVERB* over the whole of a country.

native *NOUN* **natives** a person born in a particular place • *He is a native of Sweden.*

native *ADJECTIVE* **1** belonging to a person because of the place of his or her birth • *my native country.* **2** grown or originating in a particular place • *a plant native to China.* **3** natural; belonging to a person by nature • *native ability.*
[from Latin *nativus* = natural or innate]

Native American *NOUN* **Native Americans** one of the original inhabitants of North and South America.
USAGE See note at **Indian**.

nativity *NOUN* **nativities** a person's birth.
- **the Nativity** the birth of Jesus Christ.

natty *ADJECTIVE* **nattier, nattiest** (*informal*) neat and trim; dapper.
▷ **nattily** *adverb*
[probably from *neat*]

natural *ADJECTIVE* **1** produced or done by nature, not by people or machines. **2** normal; not surprising. **3** having a quality or ability that you were born with • *a natural leader.* **4** (said about a note in music) neither sharp nor flat.
▷ **naturally** *adverb* **naturalness** *noun*

natural *NOUN* **naturals** **1** a person who is naturally good at something. **2** a natural note in music; a sign (♮) that shows this.

natural gas *NOUN* gas found underground or under the sea, not made from coal.

natural history *NOUN* the study of plants and animals.

naturalist *NOUN* **naturalists** an expert in natural history.

naturalize *VERB* **naturalizes, naturalizing, naturalized** **1** give a person full rights as a citizen of a country although they were not born there. **2** cause a plant or animal to grow or live naturally in a country that is not its own.
▷ **naturalization** *noun*

natural science *NOUN* the study of physics, chemistry, and biology.

natural selection *NOUN* Charles Darwin's theory that only the plants and animals best suited to their surroundings will survive and breed.

nature *NOUN* **natures** **1** everything in the world that was not made by people. **2** the qualities and characteristics of a person or thing • *She has a loving nature.* **3** a kind or sort of thing • *He likes things of that nature.*
[from Latin]

nature reserve *NOUN* **nature reserves** an area of land which is managed so as to preserve the wild animals and plants that live there.

nature trail *NOUN* **nature trails** a path in a country area with signs telling you about the plants and animals that live there.

naturist *NOUN* **naturists** a nudist.
▷ **naturism** *noun*

naught *NOUN* (*old use*) nothing.
[from Old English]

naughty *ADJECTIVE* **naughtier, naughtiest** **1** badly behaved or disobedient. **2** slightly rude or indecent • *naughty pictures.*
▷ **naughtily** *adverb* **naughtiness** *noun*
[originally = poor: from *naught*]

nausea (*say* naw-zee-a) *NOUN* a feeling of sickness or disgust.
▷ **nauseous** *adjective* **nauseating** *adjective*
[from Greek *nausia* = seasickness]

nautical *ADJECTIVE* to do with ships or sailors.
[from Greek *nautes* = sailor]

nautical mile *NOUN* **nautical miles** a measure of distance used at sea, equal to 2,025 yards (1.852 kilometres).

naval *ADJECTIVE* to do with a navy.
[from Latin *navis* = ship]

nave *NOUN* **naves** the main central part of a church (the other parts are the chancel, aisles, and transepts).
[from Latin]

navel *NOUN* **navels** the small hollow in the centre of the abdomen, where the umbilical cord was attached.
[from Old English]

navigable *ADJECTIVE* suitable for ships to sail in • *a navigable river.*
▷ **navigability** *noun*

navigate *VERB* **navigates, navigating, navigated** **1** sail in or through a river or sea etc. • *The ship navigated the Suez Canal.* **2** make sure that a ship, aircraft, or vehicle is going in the right direction.
▷ **navigation** *noun* **navigator** *noun*
[from Latin *navis* = ship + *agere* = to drive]

navvy *NOUN* **navvies** a labourer digging a road, railway, canal, etc.
[short for 'navigator', = person who constructs a 'navigation' (= canal)]

navy *NOUN* **navies** **1** a country's warships and the people trained to use them. (also **navy blue**) **2** a very dark blue, the colour of naval uniform.
[from old French *navie* = a ship or fleet; related to *naval*]

nay *ADVERB* (*old use*) no.
[from Old Norse]

Nazi (*say* nah-tsee) *NOUN* **Nazis** a member of the National Socialist Party in Germany in Hitler's time, with Fascist beliefs.
▷ **Nazism** *noun*
[from the German pronunciation of *Nationalsozialist*]

NB *ABBREVIATION* take note that.
[Latin *nota bene* = note well]

NCO *ABBREVIATION* non-commissioned officer.

NE *ABBREVIATION* **1** north-east. **2** north-eastern.

Neanderthal (*say* nee-an-der-tahl) *NOUN* an early type of human who lived in Europe during the Stone Age.
[named after *Neanderthal*, an area in Germany where fossil remains have been found]

near *ADVERB* & *ADJECTIVE* not far away.
- **near by** not far away • *They live near by.*

near *PREPOSITION* not far away from • *near the shops.*

near *VERB* **nears, nearing, neared** come near to • *The ship neared the harbour.* [from Old Norse]

nearby *ADJECTIVE* near • *a nearby house.*

nearly *ADVERB* almost • *We have nearly finished.*

neat *ADJECTIVE* **neater, neatest** **1** simple and clean and tidy. **2** skilful. **3** undiluted • *neat whisky.* **4** (*American*) (*informal*) excellent.
▷ **neatly** *adverb* **neatness** *noun*
[from Latin *nitidus* = clean, shining]

neaten *VERB* **neatens, neatening, neatened** make something neat.

nebula *NOUN* **nebulae** a bright or dark patch in the sky, caused by a distant galaxy or a cloud of dust or gas.
[Latin, = mist]

nebulous *ADJECTIVE* indistinct or vague • *nebulous ideas.*
[same origin as *nebula*]

necessary *ADJECTIVE* not able to be done without; essential.
▷ **necessarily** *adverb*
[from Latin]

necessitate *VERB* **necessitates, necessitating, necessitated** make a thing necessary.

necessity *NOUN* **necessities** **1** need • *the necessity of buying food and clothing.* **2** something necessary.

neck *NOUN* **necks** **1** the part of the body that joins the head to the shoulders. **2** the part of a piece of clothing round the neck. **3** a narrow part of something, especially of a bottle.
- **neck and neck** almost exactly together in a race or contest.
[from Old English]

necklace or **necklet** *NOUN* **necklaces** or **necklets** an ornament worn round the neck.

necktie *NOUN* **neckties** a strip of material worn passing under the collar of a shirt and knotted in front.

nectar *NOUN* **1** a sweet liquid collected by bees from flowers. **2** a delicious drink.
[from Greek *nektar* = the drink of the gods]

nectarine *NOUN* **nectarines** a kind of peach with a thin, smooth skin.

nectary *NOUN* **nectaries** the nectar-producing part of a plant.

née (*say* nay) *ADJECTIVE* born (used in giving a married woman's maiden name) • *Mrs Smith, née Jones.*
[French]

need *VERB* **needs, needing, needed** **1** be without something you should have; require • *We need two more chairs.* **2** (as an *auxiliary verb*) have to do something • *You need not answer.*

need *NOUN* **needs** **1** something needed; a necessary thing. **2** a situation where something is necessary • *There is no need to cry.* **3** great poverty or hardship.
▷ **needless** *adjective* **needlessly** *adverb*
[from Old English]

needle *NOUN* **needles** **1** a very thin pointed piece of steel used in sewing. **2** something long and thin and sharp • *a knitting needle; pine needles.* **3** the pointer of a meter or compass.
[from Old English]

needlework *NOUN* sewing or embroidery.

needy *ADJECTIVE* **needier, neediest** very poor; lacking things necessary for life.
▷ **neediness** *noun*

ne'er *ADVERB* (*poetical use*) never.

nefarious (*say* nif-air-ee-us) *ADJECTIVE* wicked.
[from Latin *nefas* = wickedness]

negate *VERB* **negates, negating, negated** **1** make a thing ineffective. **2** disprove or deny.
▷ **negation** *noun*
[from Latin *negare* = deny]

negative *ADJECTIVE* **1** that says 'no' • *a negative answer.* **2** looking only at the bad aspects of a situation • *Don't be so negative.* **3** showing no sign of what is being tested for • *Her pregnancy test was negative.* **4** less than nought; minus. **5** to do with the kind of electric charge carried by electrons.
▷ **negatively** *adverb*
USAGE The opposite of sense 1 is *affirmative*; the opposite of the other senses is *positive*.

negative *NOUN* **negatives** **1** a negative statement. **2** a photograph on film with the dark parts light and the light parts dark, from which a positive print (with the dark and light or colours correct) can be made.
[same origin as *negate*]

neglect *VERB* **neglects, neglecting, neglected** **1** not look after or pay attention to a person or thing. **2** not do something; forget • *He neglected to shut the door.*

neglect *NOUN* neglecting or being neglected.
▷ **neglectful** *adjective*
[from Latin *nec* = not + *legere* = choose]

negligence *NOUN* lack of proper care or attention; carelessness.
▷ **negligent** *adjective* **negligently** *adverb*
[same origin as *neglect*]

negligible *ADJECTIVE* not big enough or important enough to be worth bothering about.
[from French *négliger* = neglect]

negotiable *ADJECTIVE* able to be changed after being discussed • *The salary is negotiable.*
[from *negotiate*]

negotiate *VERB* **negotiates, negotiating, negotiated** **1** bargain or discuss with others in order to reach an agreement. **2** arrange after discussion • *They negotiated a treaty.* **3** get over an obstacle or difficulty.
▷ **negotiation** *noun* **negotiator** *noun*
[from Latin *negotium* = business]

Negro *NOUN* **Negroes** a member of a dark-skinned people originating in Africa.
[from Latin *niger* = black]
USAGE This word is usually considered to be offensive. *Black* is the term that is generally preferred.

neigh *VERB* **neighs, neighing, neighed** make the high-pitched cry of a horse.
▷ **neigh** *noun*
[from Old English; imitating the sound]

neighbour *NOUN* **neighbours** a person who lives next door or near to another.
▷ **neighbouring** *adjective*
[from Old English *neahgebur* = near dweller]

neighbourhood *NOUN* **neighbourhoods** **1** the surrounding district or area. **2** a part of a town where people live • *a quiet neighbourhood.*

neighbourly *ADVERB* friendly and helpful to people who live near you.

neither (*say* **ny**-ther or **nee**-ther) *ADJECTIVE & PRONOUN* not either.
USAGE Correct use is *Neither of them likes it. Neither he nor his children like it.* Use a singular verb (e.g. *likes*) unless one of its subjects is plural (e.g. *children*).

neither *ADVERB & CONJUNCTION*
- **neither ... nor** not one thing and not the other • *She neither knew nor cared.*
[from Old English]
USAGE Say *I don't know that either* (not 'neither').

nemesis (*say* **nem**-i-sis) *NOUN* deserved punishment that comes upon somebody who hoped to escape it.
[named after *Nemesis*, goddess of retribution in Greek mythology]

neo- *PREFIX* new.
[from Greek]

neolithic (*say* nee-o-**lith**-ik) *ADJECTIVE* belonging to the later part of the Stone Age.
[from *neo-* + Greek *lithos* = stone]

neon *NOUN* a gas that glows when electricity passes through it, used in glass tubes to make illuminated signs.
[from Greek *neos* = new]

nephew *NOUN* **nephews** the son of a person's brother or sister.
[same origin as *nepotism*]

nepotism (*say* **nep**-ot-izm) *NOUN* showing favouritism to relatives in appointing them to jobs.
[from Latin *nepos* = nephew]

nerve *NOUN* **nerves** **1** any of the fibres in the body that carry messages to and from the brain, so that parts of the body can feel and move. **2** courage; calmness in a dangerous situation • *Don't lose your nerve.* **3** impudence • *You've got a nerve!*
- **get on someone's nerves** irritate someone.
- **nerves** nervousness • *I suffer from nerves before exams.*

nerve *VERB* **nerves, nerving, nerved** give strength or courage to someone.
[from Latin *nervus* = sinew]

nerve centre *NOUN* **nerve centres** **1** a cluster of neurons. **2** the place from which a system or organization is controlled.

nerve-racking *ADJECTIVE* making you feel anxious or stressed.

nervous *ADJECTIVE* **1** easily upset or agitated; excitable. **2** slightly afraid; timid. **3** to do with the nerves • *a nervous illness.*
▷ **nervously** *adverb* **nervousness** *noun*

nervous breakdown *NOUN* **nervous breakdowns** a state of severe depression and anxiety, so that the person cannot cope with life.

nervous system *NOUN* **nervous systems** the system, consisting of the brain, spinal cord, and nerves, which sends electrical messages from one part of the body to another.

nervy *ADJECTIVE* **nervier, nerviest** nervous.

-ness *SUFFIX* forming nouns from adjectives (e.g. *kindness*, *sadness*).
[from Old English]

nest *NOUN* **nests** **1** a structure or place in which a bird lays its eggs and feeds its young. **2** a place where some small creatures (e.g. mice, wasps) live. **3** a set of similar things that fit inside each other • *a nest of tables.*

nest *VERB* **nests, nesting, nested** **1** have or make a nest. **2** fit inside something.
[from Old English]

nest egg *NOUN* **nest eggs** a sum of money saved up for future use.
[originally = an egg left in the nest to encourage a hen to lay more]

nestle *VERB* **nestles, nestling, nestled** curl up comfortably.
[from Old English *nestlian* = to nest]

nestling *NOUN* **nestlings** a bird that is too young to leave the nest.

net[1] *NOUN* **nets** **1** material made of pieces of thread, cord, or wire etc. joined together in a criss-cross pattern with holes between. **2** something made of this.
- **the Net** the Internet.

net *VERB* **nets, netting, netted** cover or catch with a net.
[from Old English]

net[2] *ADJECTIVE* remaining when nothing more is to be deducted • *The net weight, without the box, is 100 grams.* (COMPARE **gross**)

net *VERB* **nets, netting, netted** obtain or produce as net profit.
[from French *net* = neat]

netball *NOUN* a game in which two teams try to throw a ball into a high net hanging from a ring.

nether *ADJECTIVE* lower • *the nether regions.*
[from Old English]

netting *NOUN* a piece of net.

nettle *NOUN* **nettles** a wild plant with leaves that sting when they are touched.

nettle *VERB* **nettles, nettling, nettled** annoy or provoke someone.
[from Old English]

network *NOUN* **networks** **1** a net-like arrangement or pattern of intersecting lines or parts • *the railway network.* **2** an organization with many connecting parts that work together • *a spy network.* **3** a group of radio or television stations which broadcast the same programmes. **4** a set of computers which are linked to each other.

neuralgia (*say* newr-**al**-ja) *NOUN* pain along a nerve, especially in your face or head.
[from Greek *neuron* = nerve + *algos* = pain]

neurology *NOUN* the study of nerves and their diseases.
▷ **neurological** *adjective* **neurologist** *noun*
[from Greek *neuron* = nerve, + *-logy*]

neuron or **neurone** *NOUN* **neurons** or **neurones** a cell that is part of the nervous system and sends impulses to and from the brain.

neurotic (*say* newr-**ot**-ik) *ADJECTIVE* always very worried about something.
[from Greek *neuron* = nerve]

neuter *ADJECTIVE* **1** neither masculine nor feminine. **2** (in some languages) belonging to the class of words which are neither masculine nor feminine, such as *Fenster* in German.

neuter *VERB* **neuters, neutering, neutered** remove an animal's sex organs so that it cannot breed.
[Latin, = neither]

neutral *ADJECTIVE* **1** not supporting either side in a war or quarrel. **2** not very distinctive • *a neutral colour such as grey.* **3** neither acid nor alkaline.
▷ **neutrally** *adverb* **neutrality** *noun*

neutral *NOUN* **neutrals** **1** a neutral person or country. **2** a gear that is not connected to the driving parts of an engine.
[same origin as *neuter*]

neutralize *VERB* **neutralizes, neutralizing, neutralized** **1** stop something from having any effect. **2** make a substance chemically neutral.
▷ **neutralization** *noun*

neutron *NOUN* **neutrons** a particle of matter with no electric charge.
[from *neutral*]

never *ADVERB* **1** at no time; not ever. **2** not at all.
[from Old English *naefre* = not ever]

nevertheless *ADVERB & CONJUNCTION* in spite of this; although this is a fact.

new *ADJECTIVE* not existing before; just made, invented, discovered, or received etc.
▷ **newly** *adverb* **newness** *noun*

new *ADVERB* newly • *newborn; new-laid.*
[from Old English]

New Age *ADJECTIVE* to do with a way of living and thinking that includes belief in astrology and alternative medicine, and concern for environmental and spiritual matters rather than possessions.

newcomer *NOUN* **newcomers** a person who has arrived recently.

newel *NOUN* **newels** the upright post to which the handrail of a stair is fixed, or that forms the centre pillar of a winding stair.
[from old French]

newfangled *ADJECTIVE* disliked because it is new in method or style.
[from *new* + Middle English *fang* = seize]

newly *ADVERB* **1** recently. **2** in a new way.

new moon *NOUN* **new moons** the moon at the beginning of its cycle, when only a thin crescent can be seen.

news *NOUN* **1** information about recent events or a broadcast report of this. **2** a piece of new information • *That's news to me.*

newsagent *NOUN* **newsagents** a shopkeeper who sells newspapers.

newsflash *NOUN* **newsflashes** a short news broadcast which interrupts a programme because something important has happened.

newsgroup *NOUN* **newsgroups** a place on the Internet where people discuss a particular subject and exchange information about it.

newsletter *NOUN* **newsletters** a short, informal report sent regularly to members of an organization.

newspaper *NOUN* **newspapers** **1** a daily or weekly publication on large sheets of paper, containing news reports, articles, etc. **2** the sheets of paper forming a newspaper
• *Wrap it in newspaper.*

newsy *ADJECTIVE* (*informal*) full of news.

newt *NOUN* **newts** a small animal rather like a lizard, that lives near or in water.
[from Old English: originally *an ewt*]

newton *NOUN* **newtons** a unit for measuring force.
[named after an English scientist, Isaac *Newton*]

New Year's Day *NOUN* 1 January.

next *ADJECTIVE* nearest; coming immediately after • *on the next day.*

next *ADVERB* **1** in the next place. **2** on the next occasion • *What happens next?*
[from Old English]

next door *ADVERB & ADJECTIVE* in the next house or room.

nib *NOUN* **nibs** the pointed metal part of a pen.
[from old German or old Dutch]

nibble *VERB* **nibbles, nibbling, nibbled** take small, quick, or gentle bites.
[probably from old Dutch]

nice *ADJECTIVE* **nicer, nicest** **1** pleasant or kind. **2** precise or careful • *Dictionaries make nice distinctions between meanings of words.*
▷ **nicely** *adverb* **niceness** *noun*
[originally = stupid: from Latin *nescius* = ignorant]

nicety (*say* ny-sit-ee) *NOUN* **niceties** **1** precision. **2** a small detail or difference pointed out.
[from *nice*]

niche (*say* nich or neesh) NOUN **niches** **1** a small recess, especially in a wall • *The vase stood in a niche.* **2** a suitable place or position • *She found her niche in the drama club.*
[old French, from *nichier* = make a nest]

nick NOUN **nicks** **1** a small cut or notch. **2** (*slang*) a police station or prison.
- **in good nick** (*informal*) in good condition.
- **in the nick of time** only just in time.

nick VERB **nicks, nicking, nicked** **1** make a nick in something. **2** (*slang*) steal. **3** (*slang*) arrest.
[origin unknown]

nickel NOUN **nickels** **1** a silvery-white metal. **2** (*American*) a 5-cent coin.
[from German]

nickname NOUN **nicknames** a name given to a person instead of his or her real name.
[originally *an eke-name*: from Middle English *eke* = addition, + *name*]

nicotine NOUN a poisonous substance found in tobacco.
[from the name of J. *Nicot*, who introduced tobacco into France in 1560]

niece NOUN **nieces** the daughter of a person's brother or sister.
[from French; related to *nephew*]

niggardly ADJECTIVE mean or stingy.
▷ **niggardliness** *noun*
[from Middle English *nig* = a mean person]

niggle VERB **niggles, niggling, niggled** **1** fuss over details or very small faults. **2** be a small but constant worry.
▷ **niggling** *adjective*
[probably from a Scandinavian language]

nigh ADVERB & PREPOSITION (*poetical use*) near.
[from Old English]

night NOUN **nights** **1** the dark hours between sunset and sunrise. **2** a particular night or evening • *the first night of the play.*
[from Old English]

nightcap NOUN **nightcaps** **1** (*old use*) a knitted cap worn in bed. **2** a drink, especially an alcoholic one, which you have before going to bed.

nightclub NOUN **nightclubs** a place that is open at night where people go to drink and dance.

nightdress NOUN **nightdresses** a loose dress that girls or women wear in bed.

nightfall NOUN the coming of darkness at the end of the day.

nightie NOUN **nighties** (*informal*) a nightdress.

nightingale NOUN **nightingales** a small brown bird that sings sweetly.
[from Old English *nihtegala* = night- singer (because it often sings until late in the evening)]

nightlife NOUN the places of entertainment that you can go to at night • *a popular resort with plenty of nightlife.*

nightly ADJECTIVE & ADVERB happening every night.

nightmare NOUN **nightmares** **1** a frightening dream. **2** an unpleasant experience • *the journey was a nightmare.*
▷ **nightmarish** *adjective*
[from *night* + Middle English *mare* = an evil spirit]

nil NOUN nothing or nought.
[from Latin *nihil* = nothing]

nimble ADJECTIVE able to move quickly; agile.
▷ **nimbly** *adverb*
[from Old English]

nine NOUN & ADJECTIVE **nines** the number 9.
▷ **ninth** *adjective* & *noun*
[from Old English]

ninepins NOUN the game of skittles played with nine objects.

nineteen NOUN & ADJECTIVE the number 19.
▷ **nineteenth** *adjective* & *noun*
[from Old English]

ninety NOUN & ADJECTIVE **nineties** the number 90.
▷ **ninetieth** *adjective* & *noun*
[from Old English]

nip VERB **nips, nipping, nipped** **1** pinch or bite quickly. **2** (*informal*) go quickly.

nip NOUN **nips** **1** a quick pinch or bite. **2** sharp coldness • *There's a nip in the air.* **3** a small drink of a spirit • *a nip of brandy.*
[probably from old Dutch]

nipper NOUN **nippers** (*informal*) a young child.

nippers PLURAL NOUN pincers.

nipple *NOUN* **nipples** the small part that sticks out at the front of a person's breast, from which babies suck milk.
[origin unknown]

nippy *ADJECTIVE* **nippier**, **nippiest** (*informal*) **1** quick or nimble. **2** cold.

nirvana *NOUN* (in Buddhism and Hinduism) the highest state of knowledge and understanding, achieved by meditation.
[Sanskrit]

nit *NOUN* **nits** a parasitic insect or its egg, found in people's hair.
[from Old English]

nit-picking *NOUN* pointing out very small faults.

nitrate *NOUN* **nitrates 1** a chemical compound containing nitrogen.
2 potassium or sodium nitrate, used as a fertilizer.

nitric acid (*say* ny-trik) *NOUN* a very strong colourless acid containing nitrogen.

nitrogen (*say* ny-tro-jen) *NOUN* a gas that makes up about four-fifths of the air.
[from *nitre* = a substance once thought to be a vital part of the air]

nitwit *NOUN* **nitwits** (*informal*) a stupid person.
▷ **nitwitted** *adjective*
[origin unknown]

no *ADJECTIVE* not any • *We have no money.*

no *ADVERB* **1** used to deny or refuse something • *Will you come? No.* **2** not at all • *She is no better.*
[from *none*]

No. or **no.** *ABBREVIATION* **Nos.** or **nos.** number.
[from Latin *numero* = by number]

nobility *NOUN* **1** being noble. **2** the aristocracy.

noble *ADJECTIVE* **nobler**, **noblest 1** of high social rank; aristocratic. **2** having a very good character or qualities • *a noble king.*
3 stately or impressive • *a noble building.*
▷ **nobly** *adverb*

noble *NOUN* **nobles** a person of high social rank.
▷ **nobleman** *noun* **noblewoman** *noun*
[from Latin]

nobody *PRONOUN* no person; no one.

nobody *NOUN* **nobodies** (*informal*) an unimportant person.

nocturnal *ADJECTIVE* **1** happening at night.
2 active at night • *Badgers are nocturnal animals.*
[from Latin *noctis* = of night]

nocturne *NOUN* **nocturnes** a piece of music with the quiet dreamy feeling of night.
[French; related to *nocturnal*]

nod *VERB* **nods, nodding, nodded 1** move the head up and down, especially as a way of agreeing with somebody or as a greeting.
2 be drowsy.
▷ **nod** *noun*
[origin unknown]

node *NOUN* **nodes** a swelling like a small knob.
[from Latin *nodus* = knot]

nodule *NOUN* **nodules** a small node.

noise *NOUN* **noises** a sound, especially one that is loud or unpleasant.
▷ **noisy** *adjective* **noisily** *adverb*
noiseless *adjective*
[from French]

noisome (*say* noi-sum) *ADJECTIVE* smelling unpleasant; harmful.
[from *annoy* + *-some*]

nomad *NOUN* **nomads** a member of a tribe that moves from place to place looking for pasture for their animals.
▷ **nomadic** *adjective*
[from Greek *nomas* = roaming]

no man's land *NOUN* an area that does not belong to anybody, especially the land between opposing armies.

nom de plume *NOUN* **noms de plume** a writer's pseudonym.
[French, = pen-name (this phrase is not used in French)]

nominal *ADJECTIVE* **1** in name • *He is the nominal ruler, but the real power is held by the generals.* **2** small • *We charged them only a nominal fee.*
▷ **nominally** *adverb*
[from Latin *nomen* = name]

nominate *VERB* **nominates, nominating, nominated** propose that someone should be a candidate in an election or appointed to a post.
▷ **nomination** *noun* **nominator** *noun*
[from Latin *nominare* = to name]

nominee *NOUN* **nominees** a person who is nominated.

non- *PREFIX* not.
[from Latin]

nonagenarian *NOUN* **nonagenarians** a person aged between 90 and 99.
[from Latin *nonageni* = 90 each]

nonchalant (*say* **non**-shal-ant) *ADJECTIVE* calm and casual; showing no anxiety or excitement.
▷ **nonchalantly** *adverb* **nonchalance** *noun*
[from *non-* + French *chalant* = being concerned]

non-commissioned officer *NOUN* **non-commissioned officers** a member of the armed forces, such as a corporal or sergeant, who has not been commissioned as an officer but has been promoted from the ranks of ordinary soldiers.

non-committal *ADJECTIVE* not committing yourself; not showing what you think.

Nonconformist *NOUN* **Nonconformists** a member of a Protestant Church (e.g. Baptist, Methodist) that does not conform to all the customs of the Church of England.

nondescript *ADJECTIVE* having no special or distinctive qualities and therefore difficult to describe.

none *PRONOUN* **1** not any. **2** no one • *None can tell.*
USAGE It is better to use a singular verb (e.g. *None of them is here*), but the plural is not incorrect (e.g. *None of them are here*).

none *ADVERB* not at all • *He is none too bright.*
[from Old English *nan* = not one]

nonentity (*say* non-en-tit-ee) *NOUN* **nonentities** an unimportant person.
[from *non-* + *entity*]

non-existent *ADJECTIVE* not existing or unreal.

non-fiction *NOUN* writings that are not fiction; books about real people and things and true events.

non-flammable *ADJECTIVE* not able to be set on fire.
USAGE See note at **inflammable**.

nonplussed *ADJECTIVE* puzzled or confused.
[from Latin *non plus* = not further]

nonsense *NOUN* **1** words put together in a way that does not mean anything. **2** stupid ideas or behaviour.
▷ **nonsensical** (*say* non-**sens**-ik-al) *adjective*
[from *non-* + *sense*]

non sequitur (*say* non **sek**-wit-er) *NOUN* **non sequiturs** a conclusion that does not follow from the evidence given.
[Latin, = it does not follow]

non-stop *ADJECTIVE* & *ADVERB* **1** not stopping • *They talked non-stop for hours.* **2** not stopping between two main stations • *a non-stop train.*

noodles *PLURAL NOUN* pasta made in narrow strips, used in soups etc.
[from German]

nook *NOUN* **nooks** a sheltered corner; a recess.
[origin unknown]

noon *NOUN* twelve o'clock midday.
[via Old English from Latin]

no one *NOUN* no person; nobody.

noose *NOUN* **nooses** a loop in a rope that gets smaller when the rope is pulled.
[origin unknown]

nor *CONJUNCTION* and not • *She cannot do it; nor can I.*
[from Old English]

norm *NOUN* **norms** **1** a standard or average type, amount, level, etc. **2** normal or expected behaviour • *social norms.*
[from Latin *norma* = a pattern or rule]

normal *ADJECTIVE* **1** usual or ordinary. **2** natural and healthy; not suffering from an illness.
▷ **normally** *adverb* **normality** *noun*
[same origin as *norm*]

Norman *NOUN* **Normans** a member of the people of Normandy in northern France, who conquered England in 1066.
▷ **Norman** *adjective*
[from Old Norse *northmathr* = man from the north (because the Normans were partly descended from the Vikings)]

north *NOUN* **1** the direction to the left of a person who faces east. **2** the northern part of a country, city, etc.

north *ADJECTIVE* & *ADVERB* towards or in the north.
▷ **northerly** *adjective* **northern** *adjective* **northerner** *noun* **northernmost** *adjective*
[from Old English]

north-east *NOUN, ADJECTIVE,* & *ADVERB* midway between north and east.
▷ **north-easterly** *adjective* **north-eastern** *adjective*

northward *ADJECTIVE* & *ADVERB* towards the north.
▷ **northwards** *adverb*

north-west *NOUN, ADJECTIVE,* & *ADVERB* midway between north and west.
▷ **north-westerly** *adjective* **north-western** *adjective*

Nos. or **nos.** *plural* of **No.** or **no.**

nose *NOUN* **noses** **1** the part of the face that is used for breathing and for smelling things. **2** the front end or part.

nose *VERB* **noses**, **nosing**, **nosed** **1** push the nose into or near something. **2** go forward cautiously • *Ships nosed through the ice.*
[from Old English]

nosebag *NOUN* **nosebags** a bag containing fodder, for hanging on a horse's head.

nosedive *NOUN* **nosedives** a steep downward dive, especially of an aircraft.
▷ **nosedive** *verb*

nosegay *NOUN* **nosegays** a small bunch of flowers.
[from *nose* + Middle English *gay* = an ornament]

nostalgia (*say* nos-tal-ja) *NOUN* sentimental remembering or longing for the past.
▷ **nostalgic** *adjective* **nostalgically** *adverb*
[originally = homesickness: from Greek *nostos* = return home + *algos* = pain]

nostril *NOUN* **nostrils** either of the two openings in the nose.
[from Old English *nosthryl* = nose-hole]

nosy *ADJECTIVE* **nosier**, **nosiest** (*informal*) inquisitive.
▷ **nosily** *adverb* **nosiness** *noun*
[from *sticking your nose in* = being inquisitive]

not *ADVERB* used to change the meaning of something to its opposite or absence.
[from *nought*]

notable *ADJECTIVE* worth noticing; remarkable or famous.
▷ **notably** *adverb* **notability** *noun*

notation *NOUN* **notations** a system of symbols representing numbers, quantities, musical notes, etc.

notch *NOUN* **notches** a small V-shape cut into a surface.

notch *VERB* **notches**, **notching**, **notched** cut a notch or notches in.
- **notch up** score.
[from old French]

note *NOUN* **notes** **1** something written down as a reminder or as a comment or explanation. **2** a short letter. **3** a banknote • *a £5 note.* **4** a single sound in music. **5** any of the keys on a piano or other keyboard instrument. **6** a sound or quality that indicates something • *a note of warning.* **7** notice or attention • *Take note.*

note *VERB* **notes**, **noting**, **noted** **1** make a note about something; write down. **2** notice or pay attention to • *Note what we say.*
[from Latin *nota* = a mark]

notebook *NOUN* **notebooks** a book with blank pages on which to write notes.

noted *ADJECTIVE* famous, especially for a particular reason • *an area noted for its mild climate.*

notepaper *NOUN* paper for writing letters.

nothing *NOUN* **1** no thing; not anything. **2** no amount; nought.
- **for nothing** **1** without payment, free. **2** without a result.

nothing *ADVERB* **1** not at all. **2** in no way • *It's nothing like as good.*
[from *no thing*]

notice *NOUN* **notices** **1** something written or printed and displayed for people to see. **2** attention • *It escaped my notice.* **3** warning that something is going to happen. **4** a formal announcement that you are about to end an agreement or leave a job at a specified time • *You will need to give a month's notice.*

notice *VERB* **notices, noticing, noticed** see or become aware of something.
[from Latin *notus* = known]

noticeable *ADJECTIVE* easily seen or noticed.
▷ **noticeably** *adverb*

noticeboard *NOUN* **noticeboards** a board on which notices may be displayed.

notifiable *ADJECTIVE* that must be reported • *Cholera is a notifiable disease.*

notify *VERB* **notifies, notifying, notified** tell someone formally or officially • *Notify the police.*
▷ **notification** *noun*
[from Latin *notificare* = make known]

notion *NOUN* **notions** an idea, especially one that is vague or incorrect.
[from Latin *notio* = getting to know]

notional *ADJECTIVE* guessed and not definite.
▷ **notionally** *adverb*

notorious *ADJECTIVE* well-known for something bad.
▷ **notoriously** *adverb* **notoriety** (*say* noh-ter-I-it-ee) *noun*
[same origin as *notice*]

notwithstanding *PREPOSITION* in spite of.

nougat (*say* noo-gah) *NOUN* a chewy sweet made from nuts, sugar or honey, and egg white.
[French]

nought (*say* nawt) *NOUN* **1** the figure 0. **2** nothing.
[from Old English *nowiht* = not anything]

noun *NOUN* **nouns** a word that stands for a person, place, or thing. *Common nouns* are words such as *boy*, *dog*, *river*, *sport*, *table*, which are used of a whole kind of people or things; *proper nouns* are words such as *Charles*, *Thames*, and *London* which name a particular person or thing.
[from Latin *nomen* = name]

nourish *VERB* **nourishes, nourishing, nourished** keep a person, animal, or plant alive and well by means of food.
▷ **nourishing** *adjective* **nourishment** *noun*
[from old French; related to *nutrient*]

nouveau riche (*say* noo-voh reesh) *NOUN* **nouveaux riches** a person who has only recently become rich.
[French, = new rich]

nova (*say* noh-va) *NOUN* **novae** or **novas** a star that suddenly becomes much brighter for a short time.
[Latin, = new]
USAGE The plural form *novae* is pronounced '**noh**- vee'.

novel *NOUN* **novels** a story that fills a whole book.

novel *ADJECTIVE* of a new and unusual kind • *a novel experience.*
[from Latin *novus* = new]

novelist *NOUN* **novelists** a person who writes novels.

novelty *NOUN* **novelties** **1** newness and originality. **2** something new and unusual. **3** a cheap toy or ornament.

November *NOUN* the eleventh month of the year.
[from Latin *novem* = nine, because it was the ninth month of the ancient Roman calendar]

novice *NOUN* **novices** **1** a beginner. **2** a person preparing to be a monk or nun.
[from French; related to *novel*]

now *ADVERB* **1** at this time. **2** by this time. **3** immediately • *You must go now.* **4** I wonder, or I am telling you • *Now why didn't I think of that?*
- **now and again** or **now and then** sometimes; occasionally.

now *CONJUNCTION* as a result of or at the same time as something • *Now that you have come, we'll start.*

now *NOUN* this moment • *They will be at home by now.*
[from Old English]

nowadays *ADVERB* at the present time, as contrasted with years ago.

nowhere *ADVERB* not anywhere.

nowhere *NOUN* no place • *Nowhere is as beautiful as Scotland.*

noxious *ADJECTIVE* unpleasant and harmful.
[from Latin]

nozzle *NOUN* **nozzles** the spout of a hose, pipe, or tube.
[= little nose]

nuance (*say* new-ahns) *NOUN* **nuances** a slight difference or shade of meaning.
[from French]

nub *NOUN* **nubs** **1** a small knob or lump. **2** the central point of a problem. [from old German]

nuclear *ADJECTIVE* **1** to do with a nucleus, especially of an atom. **2** using the energy that is created by reactions in the nuclei of atoms • *nuclear power; nuclear weapons.*

nucleus *NOUN* **nuclei** **1** the part in the centre of something, round which other things are grouped. **2** the central part of an atom or of a seed or a biological cell. [Latin, = kernel]

nude *ADJECTIVE* not wearing any clothes; naked.
▷ **nudity** *noun*

nude *NOUN* **nudes** a painting, sculpture, etc. of a naked human figure.
- **in the nude** not wearing any clothes. [from Latin *nudus* = bare]

nudge *VERB* **nudges, nudging, nudged** **1** poke a person gently with your elbow. **2** push slightly or gradually.
▷ **nudge** *noun*
[origin unknown]

nudist *NOUN* **nudists** a person who believes that going naked is enjoyable and good for the health.
▷ **nudism** *noun*

nugget *NOUN* **nuggets** **1** a rough lump of gold or platinum found in the earth. **2** a small but valuable fact. [origin unknown]

nuisance *NOUN* **nuisances** an annoying person or thing. [from French *nuire* = to hurt someone]

null *ADJECTIVE*
- **null and void** not legally valid • *The agreement is null and void.* [from Latin *nullus* = none]

nullify *VERB* **nullifies, nullifying, nullified** make a thing null.
▷ **nullification** *noun*

numb *ADJECTIVE* unable to feel or move.
▷ **numbly** *adverb* **numbness** *noun*

numb *VERB* **numbs, numbing, numbed** make numb. [from Old English]

number *NOUN* **numbers** **1** a symbol or word indicating how many; a numeral or figure. **2** a numeral given to a thing to identify it • *a telephone number.* **3** a quantity of people or things • *the number of people present.* **4** one issue of a magazine or newspaper. **5** a song or piece of music.
USAGE Note that *a number of*, meaning 'several', should be followed by a plural verb: • *A number of problems remain.*

number *VERB* **numbers, numbering, numbered** **1** mark with numbers. **2** count. **3** amount to • *The crowd numbered 10,000.* [from old French; related to *numeral*]

numberless *ADJECTIVE* too many to count.

numeral *NOUN* **numerals** a symbol that represents a certain number; a figure. [from Latin *numerus* = number]

numerate (*say* new-mer-at) *ADJECTIVE* having a good basic knowledge of mathematics.
▷ **numeracy** *noun*
[same origin as *numeral*]

numerator *NOUN* **numerators** the number above the line in a fraction, showing how many parts are to be taken, e.g. 2 in $\frac{2}{3}$. (COMPARE **denominator**) [from Latin *numerare* = to number]

numerical (*say* new-merri-kal) *ADJECTIVE* to do with or consisting of numbers • *in numerical order.*
▷ **numerically** *adverb*
[same origin as *numeral*]

numerous *ADJECTIVE* many. [same origin as *numeral*]

numismatics (*say* new-miz-mat-iks) *NOUN* the study of coins.
▷ **numismatist** *noun*
[from Greek *nomisma* = coin]

nun *NOUN* **nuns** a member of a community of women who live according to the rules of a religious organization. (COMPARE **monk**) [via Old English from Latin *nonna*, feminine of *nonnus* = monk]

nunnery *NOUN* **nunneries** a convent.

nuptial *ADJECTIVE* to do with marriage or a wedding. [from Latin *nuptiae* = a wedding]

nuptials *PLURAL NOUN* a wedding.

A B C D E F G H I J K L M N O P Q R S T U V W X Y Z

nurse *NOUN* **nurses** **1** a person trained to look after people who are ill or injured. **2** a woman employed to look after young children.

nurse *VERB* **nurses, nursing, nursed** **1** look after someone who is ill or injured. **2** feed a baby at the breast. **3** have a feeling for a long time • *She's been nursing a grudge against him for years.* **4** hold carefully.
[from *nourish*]

nursemaid *NOUN* **nursemaids** a young woman employed to look after young children.

nursery *NOUN* **nurseries** **1** a place where young children are looked after or play. **2** a place where young plants are grown and usually for sale.

nursery rhyme *NOUN* **nursery rhymes** a simple rhyme or song of the kind that young children like.

nursery school *NOUN* **nursery schools** a school for children below primary school age.

nursing home *NOUN* **nursing homes** a small hospital or home for invalids.

nurture *VERB* **nurtures, nurturing, nurtured** **1** train and educate; bring up. **2** nourish.

nurture *NOUN* **1** upbringing and education. **2** nourishment.
[from old French *nourture* = nourishment]

nut *NOUN* **nuts** **1** a fruit with a hard shell. **2** a kernel. **3** a small piece of metal with a hole in the middle, for screwing onto a bolt. **4** (*slang*) the head. **5** (*slang*) a mad or eccentric person.
▷ **nutty** *adjective*
[from Old English]

nutcrackers *PLURAL NOUN* pincers for cracking nuts.

nutmeg *NOUN* the hard seed of a tropical tree, grated and used in cooking.
[from Latin *nux muscata* = spicy nut]

nutrient (*say* new-tree-ent) *NOUN* **nutrients** a nourishing substance.
▷ **nutrient** *adjective*
[from Latin *nutrire* = nourish]

nutriment (*say* new-trim-ent) *NOUN* nourishing food.
[same origin as *nutrient*]

nutrition (*say* new-trish-on) *NOUN* **1** nourishment. **2** the study of what nourishes people.
▷ **nutritional** *adjective* **nutritionally** *adverb*
[same origin as *nutrient*]

nutritious (*say* new-**trish**-us) *ADJECTIVE* nourishing; giving good nourishment.
▷ **nutritiousness** *noun*
[same origin as *nutrient*]

nutshell *NOUN* **nutshells** the shell of a nut.
- **in a nutshell** stated very briefly.

nuzzle *VERB* **nuzzles, nuzzling, nuzzled** rub gently with the nose.
[from *nose*]

NVQ *ABBREVIATION* National Vocational Qualification.

NW *ABBREVIATION* **1** north-west. **2** north-western.

nylon *NOUN* a synthetic, strong, lightweight cloth or fibre.
[invented to go with *rayon* and *cotton*]

nymph (*say* nimf) *NOUN* **nymphs** **1** (in myths) a young goddess living in the sea or woods etc. **2** the immature form of insects such as the dragonfly.
[from Greek]

NZ *ABBREVIATION* New Zealand.

Oo

O *INTERJECTION* oh.

oaf *NOUN* **oafs** a stupid lout.
[from Old Norse]

oak *NOUN* **oaks** a large deciduous tree with seeds called acorns.
▷ **oaken** *adjective*
[from Old English]

OAP *ABBREVIATION* old-age pensioner.

oar *NOUN* **oars** a pole with a flat blade at one end, used for rowing a boat.
▷ **oarsman** *noun* **oarsmanship** *noun*
[from Old English]

oasis (*say* oh-ay-sis) *NOUN* **oases** a fertile place in a desert, with a spring or well of water.
[from Greek]

oath *NOUN* **oaths** **1** a solemn promise to do something or that something is true, sometimes appealing to God as witness. **2** a swear word.
- **on** or **under oath** having sworn to tell the truth in a lawcourt.
[from Old English]

oatmeal *NOUN* ground oats.

oats *PLURAL NOUN* a cereal used to make food (*oats* for horses, *oatmeal* for people).
[from Old English]

ob- *PREFIX* (changing to **oc-** before *c*, **of-** before *f*, **op-** before *p*) **1** to; towards (as in *observe*). **2** against (as in *opponent*). **3** in the way; blocking (as in *obstruct*).
[from Latin *ob* = towards, against]

obedient *ADJECTIVE* doing what you are told; willing to obey.
▷ **obediently** *adverb* **obedience** *noun*
[from Latin]

obeisance (*say* o-bay-sans) *NOUN* **obeisances** a deep bow or curtsy showing respect.
[French, from *obéissant* = obeying]

obelisk *NOUN* **obelisks** a tall pillar set up as a monument.
[from Greek *obeliskos* = small pillar]

obese (*say* o-beess) *ADJECTIVE* very fat.
▷ **obesity** (*say* o-beess-it-ee) *noun*
[from Latin *obesus* = having overeaten]

obey *VERB* **obeys**, **obeying**, **obeyed** do what you are told to do by a person, law, etc.
[from *ob-* + Latin *audire* = listen or hear]

obituary *NOUN* **obituaries** an announcement in a newspaper of a person's death, often with a short account of his or her life.
[from Latin *obitus* = death]

object (*say* ob-jikt) *NOUN* **objects** **1** something that can be seen or touched. **2** a purpose or intention. **3** a person or thing to which some action or feeling is directed • *She has become an object of pity.* **4** (*in grammar*) the word or words naming who or what is acted upon by a verb or by a preposition, e.g. *him* in *the dog bit him* and *against him*.

object (*say* ob-jekt) *VERB* **objects**, **objecting**, **objected** say that you are not in favour of something or do not agree.
▷ **objector** *noun*
[from *ob-* + Latin *-jectum* = thrown]

objection *NOUN* **objections** **1** objecting to something. **2** a reason for objecting.

objectionable *ADJECTIVE* unpleasant or nasty.
▷ **objectionably** *adverb*

objective *NOUN* **objectives** what you are trying to reach or do; an aim.

objective *ADJECTIVE* **1** real or actual • *Is there any objective evidence to prove his claims?* **2** not influenced by personal feelings or opinions • *an objective account of the quarrel.* (COMPARE **subjective**)
▷ **objectively** *adverb* **objectivity** *noun*

objet d'art (*say* ob-zhay dar) *NOUN* **objets d'art** a small artistic object.
[French, = object of art]

obligation *NOUN* **obligations** **1** being obliged to do something. **2** what you are obliged to do; a duty.
- **under an obligation** owing gratitude to someone who has helped you.

obligatory (*say* ob-lig-a-ter-ee) *ADJECTIVE* compulsory, not optional.

oblige *VERB* **obliges**, **obliging**, **obliged** **1** force or compel. **2** help and please someone • *Can you oblige me with a loan?*
- **be obliged to someone** feel gratitude to a person who has helped you.
[from *ob-* + Latin *ligare* = bind]

obliging *ADJECTIVE* polite and helpful.

oblique (*say* ob-leek) *ADJECTIVE* **1** slanting. **2** not saying something straightforwardly • *an oblique reply.*
▷ **obliquely** *adverb*
[from Latin]

obliterate *VERB* **obliterates**, **obliterating**, **obliterated** blot out; destroy and remove all traces of something.
▷ **obliteration** *noun*
[from Latin *obliterare* = cross out, from *ob-* + *littera* = letter]

oblivion *NOUN* **1** being forgotten. **2** being unconscious.

oblivious *ADJECTIVE* completely unaware of something • *She seemed oblivious to the danger.*
[from Latin *oblivisci* = forget]

oblong *ADJECTIVE* rectangular in shape and longer than it is wide.
▷ **oblong** *noun*
[from Latin]

obnoxious *ADJECTIVE* very unpleasant; objectionable.
[from *ob-* + Latin *noxa* = harm]

oboe *NOUN* **oboes** a high-pitched woodwind instrument.
▷ **oboist** *noun*
[from French *haut* = high + *bois* = wood]

obscene (*say* ob-seen) *ADJECTIVE* indecent in a very offensive way.
▷ **obscenely** *adverb* **obscenity** *noun*
[from Latin]

obscure *ADJECTIVE* **1** difficult to see or to understand; not clear. **2** not well-known.
▷ **obscurely** *adverb* **obscurity** *noun*

obscure *VERB* **obscures, obscuring, obscured** make a thing obscure; darken or conceal • *Clouds obscured the sun.*
[from Latin *obscurus* = dark]

obsequious (*say* ob-seek-wee-us) *ADJECTIVE* showing too much respect or too willing to obey or serve someone; servile.
▷ **obsequiously** *adverb* **obsequiousness** *noun*
[from *ob-* + Latin *sequi* = follow]

observance *NOUN* obeying or keeping a law, custom, religious festival, etc.

observant *ADJECTIVE* quick at observing or noticing things.
▷ **observantly** *adverb*

observation *NOUN* **observations** **1** observing or watching. **2** a comment or remark.

observatory *NOUN* **observatories** a building with telescopes etc. for observing the stars or weather.

observe *VERB* **observes, observing, observed** **1** see and notice; watch carefully. **2** obey a law. **3** keep or celebrate a custom or religious festival etc. **4** make a remark.
▷ **observer** *noun*
[from *ob-* + Latin *servare* = to watch or keep]

obsess *VERB* **obsesses, obsessing, obsessed** occupy a person's thoughts continually.
▷ **obsession** *noun* **obsessive** *adjective*
[from Latin *obsessum* = haunted or besieged]

obsolescent *ADJECTIVE* becoming obsolete; going out of use or fashion.
▷ **obsolescence** *noun*

obsolete *ADJECTIVE* not used any more; out of date.
[from Latin *obsoletus* = worn out]

obstacle *NOUN* **obstacles** something that stands in the way or obstructs progress.
[from *ob-* + Latin *stare* = to stand]

obstetrics *NOUN* the branch of medicine and surgery that deals with the birth of babies.
[from Latin *obstetrix* = midwife]

obstinate *ADJECTIVE* **1** keeping firmly to your own ideas or ways, even though they may be wrong. **2** difficult to overcome or remove • *an obstinate problem.*
▷ **obstinately** *adverb* **obstinacy** *noun*
[from Latin *obstinare* = keep on, persist]

obstreperous (*say* ob-strep-er-us) *ADJECTIVE* noisy and unruly.
[from *ob-* + Latin *strepere* = make a noise]

obstruct *VERB* **obstructs, obstructing, obstructed** stop a person or thing from getting past; hinder.
▷ **obstruction** *noun* **obstructive** *adjective*
[from *ob-* + Latin *structum* = built]

obtain *VERB* **obtains, obtaining, obtained** get or be given something.
▷ **obtainable** *adjective*
[from *ob-* + Latin *tenere* = to hold]

obtrude *VERB* **obtrudes, obtruding, obtruded** force yourself or your ideas on someone; be obtrusive.
▷ **obtrusion** *noun*
[from *ob-* + Latin *trudere* = to push]

obtrusive *ADJECTIVE* unpleasantly noticeable.
▷ **obtrusiveness** *noun*
[same origin as *obtrude*]

obtuse *ADJECTIVE* slow to understand.
▷ **obtusely** *adverb* **obtuseness** *noun*
[from *ob-* + Latin *tusum* = blunted]

obtuse angle *NOUN* **obtuse angles** an angle of more than 90° but less than 180°. (COMPARE **acute angle**)

obverse *NOUN* the side of a coin or medal showing the head or chief design (the other side is the *reverse*).
[from *ob-* + Latin *versum* = turned]

obvious *ADJECTIVE* easy to see or understand.
▷ **obviously** *adverb*
[from Latin *ob viam* = in the way]

oc- *PREFIX* **1** to; towards. **2** against. **3** in the way; blocking. SEE **ob-**.

occasion *NOUN* **occasions** **1** the time when something happens. **2** a special event. **3** a suitable time; an opportunity.
- **on occasion** from time to time.

occasion *VERB* **occasions**, **occasioning**, **occasioned** (*formal*) cause.
[from Latin]

occasional *ADJECTIVE* **1** happening from time to time but not regularly or frequently. **2** for special occasions • *occasional music.*
▷ **occasionally** *adverb*

Occident (*say* **ok**-sid-ent) *NOUN* (*formal*) the West as opposed to the Orient.
▷ **occidental** *adjective*
[from Latin, = sunset]

occult *ADJECTIVE* to do with the supernatural or magic • *occult powers.*
[from Latin *occultum* = hidden]

occupant *NOUN* **occupants** someone who occupies a place.
▷ **occupancy** *noun*

occupation *NOUN* **occupations** **1** a person's job or profession. **2** something you do to pass your time. **3** capturing a country etc. by military force.

occupational *ADJECTIVE* caused by an occupation • *an occupational disease.*

occupational therapy *NOUN* creative work designed to help people to recover from certain illnesses.

occupy *VERB* **occupies**, **occupying**, **occupied** **1** live in a place; inhabit. **2** fill a space or position. **3** capture a country etc. and place troops there. **4** keep somebody busy.
▷ **occupier** *noun*
[from Latin]

occur *VERB* **occurs**, **occurring**, **occurred** **1** happen or exist. **2** be found; appear • *These plants occur in ponds.* **3** come into a person's mind • *An idea occurred to me.*
[from Latin]

occurrence *NOUN* **occurrences** **1** occurring. **2** an incident or event; a happening.

ocean *NOUN* **oceans** the seas that surround the continents of the earth, especially one of the large named areas of this • *the Pacific Ocean.*
▷ **oceanic** *adjective*
[from Oceanus, the river that the ancient Greeks thought surrounded the world]

ocelot (*say* **oss**-il-ot) *NOUN* **ocelots** a leopard-like animal of Central and South America.
[via French from Nahuatl (a Central American language)]

ochre (*say* **oh**-ker) *NOUN* **1** a mineral used as a pigment. **2** pale brownish-yellow.
[via French from Greek *ochros* = pale yellow]

o'clock *ADVERB* by the clock • *Lunch is at one o'clock.*
[short for *of the clock*]

octa- or **octo-** *PREFIX* eight.
[from Greek]

octagon *NOUN* **octagons** a flat shape with eight sides and eight angles.
▷ **octagonal** *adjective*
[from *octa-* + Greek *gonia* = angle]

octave *NOUN* **octaves** the interval of eight steps between one musical note and the next note of the same name above or below it.
[from Latin *octavus* = eighth]

octet *NOUN* **octets** a group of eight instruments or singers.
[from *octo-*]

octo- *PREFIX* eight. SEE **octa-**.

October *NOUN* the tenth month of the year.
[from Latin *octo* = eight, because it was the eighth month of the ancient Roman calendar]

octogenarian *NOUN* **octogenarians** a person aged between 80 and 89.
[from Latin *octogeni* = 80 each]

octopus *NOUN* **octopuses** a sea creature with eight long tentacles.
[from *octo-* + Greek *pous* = foot]

ocular *ADJECTIVE* to do with or for the eyes.
[from Latin *oculus* = eye]

oculist *NOUN* **oculists** a doctor who treats diseases of the eye.
[same origin as *ocular*]

odd *ADJECTIVE* **1** strange or unusual. **2** (said about a number) not able to be divided exactly by 2; not even. **3** left over from a pair or set • *I've got one odd sock.* **4** of various kinds; not regular • *odd jobs.*
▷ **oddly** *adverb* **oddness** *noun*
[from Old Norse]

oddity *NOUN* **oddities** a strange person or thing.

oddments *PLURAL NOUN* scraps or pieces left over from a larger piece or set.

odds *PLURAL NOUN* **1** the chances that a certain thing will happen. **2** the proportion of money that you will win if a bet is successful • *When the odds are 10 to 1, you will win £10 if you bet £1.*
- **at odds with** in conflict with; quarrelling.
- **odds and ends** small things of various kinds.

ode *NOUN* **odes** a poem addressed to a person or thing.
[from Greek *oide* = song]

odious (*say* oh-dee-us) *ADJECTIVE* extremely unpleasant; hateful.
▷ **odiously** *adverb* **odiousness** *noun*
[same origin as *odium*]

odium (*say* oh-dee-um) *NOUN* general hatred or disgust felt towards a person or actions.
[Latin, = hatred]

odour *NOUN* **odours** a smell, especially an unpleasant one.
▷ **odorous** *adjective* **odourless** *adjective*
[Latin *odor* = smell]

odyssey (*say* od-iss-ee) *NOUN* **odysseys** a long adventurous journey.
[named after the *Odyssey*, a Greek poem telling of the wanderings of Odysseus]

o'er *PREPOSITION* & *ADVERB* (*poetical use*) over.

oesophagus (*say* ee-sof-a-gus) *NOUN* **oesophagi** the tube leading from the throat to the stomach; the gullet.
[from Greek]

oestrogen (*say* ees-tro-jen) *NOUN* a hormone which develops and maintains female sexual and physical characteristics.
[from Greek]

of *PREPOSITION* (used to indicate relationships) **1** belonging to • *the mother of the child.* **2** concerning; about • *news of the disaster.* **3** made from • *built of stone.* **4** from • *north of the town.*
[from Old English]

of- *PREFIX* **1** to; towards. **2** against. **3** in the way; blocking. SEE **ob-**.

off *PREPOSITION* **1** not on; away or down from • *He fell off the ladder.* **2** not taking or wanting • *She is off her food.* **3** deducted from • *£5 off the price.*

off *ADVERB* **1** away or down from something • *His hat blew off.* **2** not working or happening • *The heating is off. The match is off because of snow.* **3** to the end; completely • *Finish it off.* **4** as regards money or supplies • *How are you off for cash?* **5** behind or at the side of a stage • *There were noises off.* **6** (said about food) beginning to go bad.
[from Old English]

offal *NOUN* the organs of an animal (e.g. liver, kidneys) sold as food.
[originally = waste products: from *off* + *fall*]

off-colour *ADJECTIVE* slightly unwell.

offence *NOUN* **offences** **1** an illegal action. **2** a feeling of annoyance or resentment.
- **give offence** hurt someone's feelings.
- **take offence** be upset by something said or done.

offend *VERB* **offends, offending, offended** **1** cause offence to someone; hurt a person's feelings. **2** do wrong or commit a crime.
▷ **offender** *noun*
[from *ob-* + Latin *fendere* = to strike]

offensive *ADJECTIVE* **1** causing offence; insulting. **2** disgusting • *an offensive smell.* **3** used in attacking • *offensive weapons.*
▷ **offensively** *adverb* **offensiveness** *noun*

offensive *NOUN* **offensives** an attack.
- **take the offensive** be the first to attack.

offer *VERB* **offers, offering, offered**
1 present something so that people can accept it if they want to. **2** say that you are willing to do or give something or to pay a certain amount.

offer *NOUN* **offers** **1** offering something. **2** an amount of money offered. **3** a specially reduced price.
[from Old English]

offering *NOUN* **offerings** what is offered.

offhand *ADJECTIVE* **1** said or done without preparation. **2** rather casual and rude; curt.
▷ **offhanded** *adjective*

office *NOUN* **offices** **1** a room or building used for business, especially for clerical work; the people who work there. **2** a government department • *the Foreign and Commonwealth Office.* **3** an important job or position.
- **be in office** hold an official position.
[from Latin *officium* = a service or duty]

officer *NOUN* **officers** **1** a person who is in charge of others, especially in the armed forces. **2** an official. **3** a member of the police force.

official *ADJECTIVE* **1** done or said by someone with authority. **2** done as part of your job or position • *official duties.*
▷ **officially** *adverb*
USAGE Do not confuse with **officious**.

official *NOUN* **officials** a person who holds a position of authority.
[from Latin]

officiate *VERB* **officiates, officiating, officiated** be in charge of a meeting, event, etc.
[from Latin *officiare* = hold a service]

officious *ADJECTIVE* too ready to give orders; bossy.
▷ **officiously** *adverb*
[from Latin *officiosus* = ready to do your duty]
USAGE Do not confuse with **official**.

offing *NOUN*
- **in the offing** likely to happen soon.

off-licence *NOUN* **off-licences** a shop with a licence to sell alcoholic drinks to be drunk away from the shop.

off-putting *ADJECTIVE* making you less keen on something; disconcerting.

offset *VERB* **offsets, offsetting, offset** cancel out or make up for something
• *Defeats are offset by successes.*

offshoot *NOUN* **offshoots** **1** a side shoot on a plant. **2** a by-product.

offshore *ADJECTIVE* **1** from the land towards the sea • *an offshore breeze.* **2** in the sea some distance from the shore • *an offshore island.*

offside *ADJECTIVE & ADVERB* (said about a player in football etc.) in a position where the rules do not allow him or her to play the ball.

offspring *NOUN* **offspring** a person's child or children; the young of an animal.

oft *ADVERB* (*old use*) often.
[from Old English]

often *ADVERB* many times; in many cases.
[from *oft*]

ogle *VERB* **ogles, ogling, ogled** stare at someone whom you find attractive.
[probably from old Dutch]

ogre *NOUN* **ogres** **1** a cruel giant in fairy tales. **2** a terrifying person.
[French]

oh *INTERJECTION* an exclamation of pain, surprise, delight, etc., or used for emphasis
• *Oh yes I will!.*

ohm *NOUN* **ohms** a unit of electrical resistance.
[named after a German scientist, G. S. *Ohm*, who studied electric currents]

OHMS *ABBREVIATION* On Her (or His) Majesty's Service.

oil *NOUN* **oils** **1** a thick slippery liquid that will not dissolve in water. **2** a kind of petroleum used as fuel. **3** oil paint.

oil *VERB* **oils, oiling, oiled** put oil on something, especially to make it work smoothly.
[from Latin]

oilfield *NOUN* **oilfields** an area where oil is found in the ground or under the sea.

oil paint *NOUN* **oil paints** paint made with oil.

oil painting *NOUN* **oil paintings** a painting done with oil paints.

A B C D E F G H I J K L M N **O** P Q R S T U V W X Y Z

oil rig *NOUN* **oil rigs** a structure with equipment for drilling for oil.

oilskin *NOUN* **oilskins** cloth made waterproof by treatment with oil.

oil well *NOUN* **oil wells** a hole drilled in the ground or under the sea to get oil.

oily *ADJECTIVE* **1** containing or like oil; covered or soaked with oil. **2** behaving in an insincerely polite way.
▷ **oiliness** *noun*

ointment *NOUN* **ointments** a cream or slippery paste for putting on sore skin and cuts.
[from old French]

OK or **okay** *ADVERB* & *ADJECTIVE* (*informal*) all right.
[perhaps from the initials of *oll* (or *orl*) *korrect*, a humorous spelling of *all correct*, first used in the USA in 1839]

old *ADJECTIVE* **1** not new; born or made or existing from a long time ago. **2** of a particular age • *I'm ten years old.* **3** former or original • *Put it back in its old place.*
▷ **oldness** *noun*
- **of old** long ago; in the distant past.
[from Old English]

old age *NOUN* the time when a person is old.

olden *ADJECTIVE* of former times.

Old English *NOUN* the English language from about 700 to 1150, also called *Anglo-Saxon*.

old-fashioned *ADJECTIVE* of the kind that was usual a long time ago; no longer fashionable.

Old Norse *NOUN* the language spoken by the Vikings, the ancestor of modern Scandinavian languages.

olfactory *ADJECTIVE* to do with the sense of smell.
[from Latin *olfacere* = to smell]

oligarchy *NOUN* **oligarchies** a country ruled by a small group of people.
▷ **oligarch** *noun* **oligarchic** *adjective*
[from Greek *oligoi* = few, + *-archy*]

olive *NOUN* **olives** **1** an evergreen tree with a small bitter fruit. **2** this fruit, from which an oil (*olive oil*) is made. **3** a shade of green like an unripe olive.
[from Greek]

olive branch *NOUN* **olive branches** something you do or offer that shows you want to make peace.
[from a story in the Bible, where the dove brings Noah an olive branch as a sign that God is no longer angry with mankind]

-ology *SUFFIX*, SEE **-logy**.

Olympic Games or **Olympics** *PLURAL NOUN* a series of international sports contests held every four years in a different part of the world.
▷ **Olympic** *adjective*
[from the name of *Olympia*, a city in Greece where they were held in ancient times]

ombudsman *NOUN* **ombudsmen** an official whose job is to investigate complaints against government organizations etc.
[from Swedish *ombud* = legal representative]

omega (*say* **oh**-meg-a) *NOUN* the last letter of the Greek alphabet, equivalent to Roman *o*.
[from Greek *o mega* = big O]

omelette *NOUN* **omelettes** eggs beaten together and cooked in a pan, often with a filling.
[French]

omen *NOUN* **omens** an event regarded as a sign of what is going to happen.
[Latin]

ominous *ADJECTIVE* suggesting that trouble is coming.
▷ **ominously** *adverb*
[from Latin *ominosus* = acting as an omen]

omission *NOUN* **omissions** **1** omitting. **2** something that has been omitted or not done.

omit *VERB* **omits, omitting, omitted** **1** miss something out. **2** fail to do something.
[from Latin]

omni- *PREFIX* all.
[from Latin]

omnibus *NOUN* **omnibuses** **1** a book containing several stories or books that were previously published separately. **2** a single edition of several radio or television programmes previously broadcast separately. **3** (*old use*) a bus.
[Latin, = for everybody]

omnipotent *ADJECTIVE* having unlimited power or very great power.
[from *omni-* + Latin *potens* = potent, able]

omniscient (*say* om-**niss**-ee-ent) *ADJECTIVE* knowing everything.
▷ **omniscience** *noun*
[from *omni-* + Latin *sciens* = knowing]

omnivorous (*say* om-**niv**-er-us) *ADJECTIVE* feeding on all kinds of food. (COMPARE **carnivorous, herbivorous**)
[from *omni-* + Latin *vorare* = devour]

on *PREPOSITION* **1** supported by; covering; added or attached to • *the sign on the door.* **2** close to; towards • *The army advanced on Paris.* **3** during; at the time of • *on my birthday.* **4** by reason of • *Arrest him on suspicion.* **5** concerning • *a book on butterflies.* **6** in a state of; using or showing • *The house was on fire.*

on *ADVERB* **1** so as to be on something • *Put it on.* **2** further forward • *Move on.* **3** working; in action • *Is the heater on?*
- **on and off** not continually.
[from Old English]

once *ADVERB* **1** for one time or on one occasion only • *They came only once.* **2** formerly • *They once lived here.*

once *NOUN* one time • *Once is enough.*

once *CONJUNCTION* as soon as • *You can go once I have taken your names.*
[from *one*]

oncoming *ADJECTIVE* approaching; coming towards you • *oncoming traffic.*

one *ADJECTIVE* **1** single. **2** individual or united.

one *NOUN* **1** the smallest whole number, 1. **2** a person or thing alone.
- **one another** each other.

one *PRONOUN* **1** a person or thing previously mentioned • *There are lots of films on but I can't find one I want to see.* **2** a person; any person • *One likes to help.*
▷ **oneself** *pronoun*
[from Old English]

onerous (*say* **ohn**-er-us or **on**-er-us) *ADJECTIVE* difficult to bear or do • *an onerous task.*
[from Latin *onus* = burden]

one-sided *ADJECTIVE* **1** with one side or person in a contest, conversation etc. being much stronger or doing a lot more than the other • *a one-sided match.* **2** showing only one point of view in an unfair way • *This is a very one-sided account of the conflict.*

one-way *ADJECTIVE* where traffic is allowed to travel in one direction only.

ongoing *ADJECTIVE* continuing to exist or be in progress • *an ongoing project.*

onion *NOUN* **onions** a round vegetable with a strong flavour.
▷ **oniony** *adjective*
[from old French]

online *ADJECTIVE* & *ADVERB* connected to a computer, the Internet, etc.

onlooker *NOUN* **onlookers** a spectator.

only *ADJECTIVE* being the one person or thing of a kind; sole • *my only wish.*
- **only child** a child who has no brothers or sisters.

only *ADVERB* no more than; and that is all • *There are only three cakes left.*

only *CONJUNCTION* but then; however • *He makes promises, only he never keeps them.*
[from Old English]

onomatopoeia (*say* on-om-at-o-**pee**-a) *NOUN* the formation of words that imitate what they stand for, e.g. *cuckoo, plop.*
▷ **onomatopoeic** *adjective*
[from Greek *onoma* = name + *poiein* = make]

onrush *NOUN* an onward rush.

onset *NOUN* **1** a beginning • *the onset of winter.* **2** an attack.

onshore *ADJECTIVE* from the sea towards the land • *an onshore breeze.*

onslaught *NOUN* **onslaughts** a fierce attack.
[from old Dutch *aan* = on + *slag* = a blow]

onto *PREPOSITION* to a position on.

onus (*say* **oh**-nus) *NOUN* the duty or responsibility of doing something • *The onus is on the prosecution to prove he did it.*
[Latin, = burden]

onward *ADVERB* & *ADJECTIVE* going forward; further on.
▷ **onwards** *adverb*

onyx *NOUN* a stone rather like marble, with different colours in layers.
[from Greek]

ooze *VERB* **oozes, oozing, oozed** **1** flow out slowly; trickle. **2** allow something to flow out slowly • *The wound oozed blood.*

ooze *NOUN* mud at the bottom of a river or sea.
[from Old English]

op- *PREFIX* **1** to; towards. **2** against. **3** in the way; blocking. SEE **ob-**.

opal *NOUN* **opals** a kind of stone with a rainbow sheen.
▷ **opalescent** *adjective*
[via French or Latin from Sanskrit]

opaque (*say* o-**payk**) *ADJECTIVE* not able to be seen through; not transparent or translucent.
[from Latin *opacus* = shady or dark]

OPEC *ABBREVIATION* Organization of Petroleum Exporting Countries.

open *ADJECTIVE* **1** allowing people or things to go in and out; not closed or fastened. **2** not covered or blocked up. **3** spread out; unfolded. **4** not limited or restricted • *an open championship.* **5** letting in visitors or customers. **6** with wide empty spaces • *open country.* **7** honest and frank; not secret or secretive • *Be open about the danger.* **8** not decided • *an open mind.* **9** willing or likely to receive • *I'm open to suggestions.*
▷ **openness** *noun*
- **in the open** **1** outside. **2** not secret.
- **in the open air** not inside a house or building.
- **open-air** *adjective*

open *VERB* **opens, opening, opened** **1** make or become open or more open. **2** begin.
▷ **opener** *noun*
[from Old English]

opencast *ADJECTIVE* (said about a mine) worked by removing layers of earth from the surface, not underground.

opening *NOUN* **openings** **1** a space or gap; a place where something opens. **2** the beginning of something. **3** an opportunity.

openly *ADVERB* without secrecy.

open-minded *ADJECTIVE* ready to listen to other people's ideas and opinions; not having fixed ideas.

opera[1] *NOUN* **operas** a play in which all or most of the words are sung.
▷ **operatic** *adjective*
[Latin, = work]

opera[2] *plural* of **opus**.

operate *VERB* **operates, operating, operated** **1** make a machine work. **2** be in action; work. **3** perform a surgical operation on somebody.
▷ **operable** *adjective*
[from Latin *operari* = to work]

operation *NOUN* **operations** **1** a piece of work or method of working. **2** something done to the body to take away or repair a part of it. **3** a planned military activity.
- **in operation** working or in use • *When does the new system come into operation?*
▷ **operational** *adjective*

operating system *NOUN* **operating systems** the software that controls a computer's basic functions.

operative *ADJECTIVE* **1** working or functioning. **2** to do with surgical operations.

operator *NOUN* **operators** a person who works something, especially a telephone switchboard or exchange.

operetta *NOUN* **operettas** a short light opera.
[Italian, = little opera]

ophthalmic (*say* off-**thal**-mik) *ADJECTIVE* to do with or for the eyes.
[from Greek *ophthalmos* = eye]

ophthalmic optician *NOUN* **ophthalmic opticians** a person who is qualified to test people's eyesight and prescribe spectacles etc.

opinion *NOUN* **opinions** what you think of something; a belief or judgement.
[from Latin *opinari* = believe]

opinionated *ADJECTIVE* having strong opinions and holding them whatever anybody says.

opinion poll *NOUN* **opinion polls** an estimate of what people think, made by questioning a sample of them.

opium *NOUN* a drug made from the juice of certain poppies, used in medicine.
[from Greek *opion* = poppy juice]

opossum *NOUN* **opossums** a small furry marsupial that lives in trees, with different kinds in America and Australia.
[from a Native American language]

opponent *NOUN* **opponents** a person or group opposing another in a contest or war.
[from Latin *opponere* = to set against]

opportune *ADJECTIVE* **1** (said about time) suitable for a purpose. **2** done or happening at a suitable time.
▷ **opportunely** *adverb*
[from *op-* + Latin *portus* = harbour (originally used of wind blowing a ship towards a harbour)]

opportunist *NOUN* **opportunists** a person who is quick to seize opportunities.
▷ **opportunism** *noun*

opportunity *NOUN* **opportunities** a good chance to do a particular thing.
[same origin as *opportune*]

oppose *VERB* **opposes, opposing, opposed** **1** argue or fight against; resist. **2** contrast • *'Soft' is opposed to 'hard'.*
- **as opposed to** in contrast with.
- **be opposed to** be strongly against • *We are opposed to parking in the town centre.*
[from French; related to *opponent*]

opposite *ADJECTIVE* **1** placed on the other or further side; facing • *on the opposite side of the road.* **2** moving away from or towards each other • *The trains were travelling in opposite directions.* **3** completely different • *opposite characters.*

opposite *NOUN* **opposites** an opposite person or thing.

opposite *ADVERB* in an opposite position or direction • *I'll sit opposite.*

opposite *PREPOSITION* opposite to • *They live opposite the school.*
[from Latin *oppositus* = set or placed against]

opposition *NOUN* **1** opposing something; resistance. **2** the people who oppose something.
- **the Opposition** the chief political party opposing the one that is in power.

oppress *VERB* **oppresses, oppressing, oppressed** **1** govern or treat somebody cruelly or unjustly. **2** weigh somebody down with worry or sadness.
▷ **oppression** *noun* **oppressor** *noun*
[from *op-* + Latin *pressus* = pressed]

oppressive *ADJECTIVE* **1** cruel or harsh • *an oppressive regime.* **2** worrying and difficult to bear. **3** (said about weather) unpleasantly hot and humid.

opt *VERB* **opts, opting, opted** choose.
- **opt out** decide not to take part in something.
[from Latin *optare* = wish for]

optic *ADJECTIVE* to do with the eye or sight.
[from Greek *optos* = seen]

optical *ADJECTIVE* to do with sight; aiding sight • *optical instruments.*
▷ **optically** *adverb*
[from *optic*]

optical illusion *NOUN* **optical illusions** a deceptive appearance that makes you think you see something that is not really there.

optician *NOUN* **opticians** a person who tests people's eyesight and makes or sells glasses and contact lenses.
[from French, related to *optic*]

optics *NOUN* the study of sight and of light as connected with this.

optimist *NOUN* **optimists** a person who expects that things will turn out well.
(COMPARE **pessimist**)
▷ **optimism** *noun* **optimistic** *adjective* **optimistically** *adverb*
[from French, related to *optimum*]

optimum *ADJECTIVE* best; most favourable.
▷ **optimum** *noun* **optimal** *adjective*
[Latin, = best thing]

option *NOUN* **options** **1** the right or power to choose something. **2** something chosen or that may be chosen.
[same origin as *opt*]

optional *ADJECTIVE* that you can choose, not compulsory.
▷ **optionally** *adverb*

opulent *ADJECTIVE* **1** wealthy or luxurious. **2** plentiful.
▷ **opulently** *adverb* **opulence** *noun*
[from Latin *opes* = wealth]

opus (*say* oh-pus) *NOUN* **opuses** or **opera** a numbered musical composition • *Beethoven opus 15.*
[Latin, = work]

or *CONJUNCTION* used to show that there is a choice or an alternative • *Do you want a cake or a biscuit?*
[from *other*]

-or *SUFFIX* forms nouns meaning 'a person or thing that does something' (e.g. *tailor*, *refrigerator*).
[from Latin or old French]

oracle *NOUN* **oracles** **1** a shrine where the ancient Greeks consulted one of their gods for advice or a prophecy. **2** a wise or knowledgeable adviser.
▷ **oracular** (*say* or-**ak**-yoo-ler) *adjective*
[from Latin *orare* = speak]

oracy (*say* **or**-a-see) *NOUN* the ability to express yourself well in speaking.
[same origin as *oral*]

oral *ADJECTIVE* **1** spoken, not written. **2** to do with or using the mouth.
▷ **orally** *adverb*

oral *NOUN* **orals** a spoken examination or test.
[from Latin *oris* = of the mouth]
USAGE Do not confuse with **aural**.

orange *NOUN* **oranges** **1** a round juicy citrus fruit with reddish-yellow peel. **2** a reddish-yellow colour.
[via French, Arabic, and Persian from Sanskrit]

orangeade *NOUN* an orange-flavoured drink.

orang-utan *NOUN* **orang-utans** a large ape of Borneo and Sumatra.
[from Malay *orang hutan* = man of the forest (Malay is spoken in Malaysia)]

oration *NOUN* **orations** a long formal speech.
[from Latin *orare* = speak]
WORD FAMILY There are a number of English words that are related to *oration* because part of their original meaning comes from the Latin words *orare* meaning 'to speak' or *oratio* meaning 'speech'. These include *oracle*, *oracy*, *oral*, *orator*, and *peroration*.

orator *NOUN* **orators** a person who is good at making speeches in public.
▷ **oratorical** *adjective*

oratorio *NOUN* **oratorios** a piece of music for voices and an orchestra, usually on a religious subject.
[Italian, related to *oration*]

oratory *NOUN* **1** the art of making speeches in public. **2** eloquent speech.

orb *NOUN* **orbs** a sphere or globe.
[from Latin *orbis* = circle]

orbit *NOUN* **orbits** **1** the curved path taken by something moving round a planet, moon, or star. **2** the range of someone's influence or control.
▷ **orbital** *adjective*

orbit *VERB* **orbits**, **orbiting**, **orbited** move in an orbit round something • *The satellite has been orbiting the earth since 1986.*
[same origin as *orb*]

orchard *NOUN* **orchards** a piece of ground planted with fruit trees.
[from Old English]

orchestra *NOUN* **orchestras** a large group of people playing various musical instruments together.
▷ **orchestral** *adjective*
[Greek, = the space where the chorus danced during a play]

orchestrate *VERB* **orchestrates**, **orchestrating**, **orchestrated** **1** compose or arrange music for an orchestra. **2** coordinate things deliberately • *We need to orchestrate our campaigns.*
▷ **orchestration** *noun*
[from *orchestra*]

orchid *NOUN* **orchids** a kind of plant with brightly coloured, often unevenly shaped, flowers.
[from Latin]

ordain *VERB* **ordains**, **ordaining**, **ordained** **1** make a person a member of the clergy in the Christian Church • *He was ordained in 1981.* **2** declare or order something by law.
[from old French; related to *order*]

ordeal *NOUN* **ordeals** a difficult or horrific experience.
[from Old English]

order *NOUN* **orders** **1** a command. **2** a request for something to be supplied. **3** the way things are arranged • *in alphabetical order.* **4** a neat arrangement; a proper arrangement or condition • *in working order.* **5** obedience to rules or laws • *law and order.* **6** a kind or sort • *She showed courage of the highest order.* **7** a group of monks or nuns who live by certain religious rules.
- **in order that** or **in order to** for the purpose of.

order *VERB* **orders, ordering, ordered** **1** command. **2** ask for something to be supplied. **3** put something into order; arrange neatly.
[from Latin *ordo* = a row, series, or arrangement]

orderly *ADJECTIVE* **1** arranged neatly or well; methodical. **2** well-behaved and obedient.
▷ **orderliness** *noun*

orderly *NOUN* **orderlies** **1** a soldier whose job is to assist an officer. **2** an assistant in a hospital.

ordinal number *NOUN* **ordinal numbers** a number that shows a thing's position in a series, e.g. first, fifth, twentieth, etc. (COMPARE **cardinal number**)
[from Latin *ordinalis* = showing the order]

ordinance *NOUN* **ordinances** a command or decree.
[from Latin *ordinare* = put in order]

ordinary *ADJECTIVE* normal or usual; not special.
▷ **ordinarily** *adverb*
- **out of the ordinary** unusual.
[from Latin *ordinarius* = orderly or usual]

ordination *NOUN* **ordinations** ordaining or being ordained as a member of the clergy.

ordnance *NOUN* weapons and other military equipment.
[from old French *ordenance* = ordinance]

Ordnance Survey *NOUN* an official survey organization that makes detailed maps of the British Isles.
[because the maps were originally made for the army]

ore *NOUN* **ores** rock with metal or other useful substances in it • *iron ore.*
[from Old English]

oregano (*say* o-ri-**gah**-noh) *NOUN* the dried leaves of wild marjoram used as a herb in cooking.
[via Spanish from Greek]

organ *NOUN* **organs** **1** a musical instrument from which sounds are produced by air forced through pipes, played by keys and pedals. **2** a part of the body with a particular function • *the digestive organs.*
[from Greek *organon* = tool]

organdie *NOUN* a kind of thin fabric, usually stiffened.
[from French]

organic *ADJECTIVE* **1** to do with the organs of the body • *organic diseases.* **2** to do with or formed from living things • *organic matter.* **3** organic food is grown or produced without the use of chemical fertilizers, pesticides, etc. • *organic farming.*
▷ **organically** *adverb*

organism *NOUN* **organisms** a living thing; an individual animal or plant.
[from Greek]

organist *NOUN* **organists** a person who plays the organ.

organization *NOUN* **organizations** **1** an organized group of people, such as a business, charity, government department, etc. **2** the organizing of something.
▷ **organizational** *adjective*

organize *VERB* **organizes, organizing, organized** **1** plan and prepare something • *We organized a picnic.* **2** form people into a group to work together. **3** put things in order.
▷ **organizer** *noun*
[same origin as *organ*]

orgasm *NOUN* **orgasms** the climax of sexual excitement.
[from Greek]

orgy *NOUN* **orgies** **1** a wild party that involves a lot of drinking and sex. **2** an extravagant activity • *an orgy of spending.*
[from Latin *orgia* = secret rites (held in honour of Bacchus, the Greek and Roman god of wine)]

Orient *NOUN* the East; oriental countries. (COMPARE **Occident**)
[from Latin, = sunrise]

orient *VERB* **orients, orienting, oriented** orientate.

oriental *ADJECTIVE* to do with the countries east of the Mediterranean Sea, especially China and Japan.

orientate *VERB* **orientates, orientating, orientated** **1** place something or face in a certain direction. **2** get your bearings • *I'm just trying to orientate myself.*
▷ **orientation** *noun*
[originally = turn to face the east: same origin as *Orient*]

orienteering *NOUN* the sport of finding your way across rough country with a map and compass.
[from Swedish *orientering* = orientating]

orifice (*say* o-rif-iss) *NOUN* **orifices** an opening in your body.
[from Latin *oris* = of the mouth]

origami (*say* o-rig-**ah**-mee) *NOUN* folding paper into decorative shapes.
[from Japanese *ori* = fold + *kami* = paper]

origin *NOUN* **origins** **1** the start of something; the point or cause from which something began. **2** a person's family background • *a man of humble origins.* **3** the point where two or more axes on a graph meet.
[from Latin *oriri* = to rise]

original *ADJECTIVE* **1** existing from the start; earliest • *the original inhabitants.* **2** new in its design etc.; not a copy. **3** producing new ideas; inventive.
▷ **originally** *adverb* **originality** *noun*

original *NOUN* **originals** a document, painting etc. which was the first one made and is not a copy.

originate *VERB* **originates, originating, originated** **1** cause something to begin; create. **2** have its origin • *The quarrel originated in rivalry.*
▷ **origination** *noun* **originator** *noun*

ornament *NOUN* **ornaments** an object displayed or worn as a decoration.

ornament *VERB* **ornaments, ornamenting, ornamented** decorate something with beautiful things.
▷ **ornamentation** *noun*
[from Latin *ornare* = adorn]

ornamental *ADJECTIVE* used as an ornament; decorative rather than useful.

ornate *ADJECTIVE* elaborately decorated.
▷ **ornately** *adverb*
[from Latin *ornatum* = adorned]

ornithology *NOUN* the study of birds.
▷ **ornithologist** *noun*
ornithological *adjective*
[from Greek *ornithos* = of a bird, + *-logy*]

orphan *NOUN* **orphans** a child whose parents are dead.
▷ **orphaned** *adjective*
[from Greek]

orphanage *NOUN* **orphanages** a home for orphans.

ortho- *PREFIX* right; straight; correct.
[from Greek *orthos* = straight]

orthodox *ADJECTIVE* **1** holding beliefs that are correct or generally accepted.
2 conventional or normal.
▷ **orthodoxy** *noun*
[from *ortho-* + Greek *doxa* = opinion]

Orthodox Church *NOUN* the Christian Churches of eastern Europe.

orthopaedics (*say* orth-o-**pee**-diks) *NOUN* the treatment of deformities and injuries to bones and muscles.
▷ **orthopaedic** *adjective*
[from *ortho-* + Greek *paideia* = rearing of children (because the treatment was originally of children)]

oscillate *VERB* **oscillates, oscillating, oscillated** **1** move to and fro like a pendulum; vibrate. **2** waver or vary.
▷ **oscillation** *noun* **oscillator** *noun*
[from Latin *oscillare* = to swing]

osier (*say* **oh**-zee-er) *NOUN* **osiers** a willow with flexible twigs used in making baskets.
[from old French]

-osis *SUFFIX* **1** a diseased condition (as in *tuberculosis*). **2** an action or process (as in *metamorphosis*).
[from Latin or Greek]

osmosis *NOUN* the passing of fluid through a porous partition into another more concentrated fluid.
[from Greek *osmos* = a push]

ostensible *ADJECTIVE* apparent, but actually concealing the true reason • *Their ostensible reason for travelling was to visit friends.*
▷ **ostensibly** *adverb*
[from Latin *ostendere* = to show]

ostentatious *ADJECTIVE* making a showy display of something to impress people.
▷ **ostentatiously** *adverb* **ostentation** *noun*
[same origin as *ostensible*]

osteopath *NOUN* **osteopaths** a person who treats certain diseases etc. by manipulating a patient's bones and muscles.
▷ **osteopathy** *noun* **osteopathic** *adjective*
[from Greek *osteon* = bone + *-patheia* = suffering]

ostinato (*say* ost-i-**nah**-toh) *NOUN* **ostinatos** (*in music*) a continually repeated phrase or rhythm.
[Italian, = obstinate]

ostracize *VERB* **ostracizes, ostracizing, ostracized** exclude someone from your group and completely ignore them.
▷ **ostracism** *noun*
[from Greek *ostrakon* = piece of pottery (because people voted to banish someone by writing his name on this)]

ostrich *NOUN* **ostriches** a large long-legged African bird that can run very fast but cannot fly. It is said to bury its head in the sand when pursued, in the belief that it then cannot be seen.
[from old French]

other *ADJECTIVE* **1** different • *some other tune.* **2** remaining • *Try the other shoe.* **3** additional • *my other friends.* **4** just recent or past • *I saw him the other day.*

other *NOUN & PRONOUN* **others** the other person or thing • *Where are the others?*
[from Old English]

otherwise *ADVERB* **1** if things happen differently; if you do not • *Write it down, otherwise you'll forget.* **2** in other ways • *It rained, but otherwise the holiday was good.* **3** differently • *We could not do otherwise.*
[from *other* + *-wise*]

otter *NOUN* **otters** a fish-eating animal with webbed feet, a flat tail, and thick brown fur, living near water.
[from Old English]

ottoman *NOUN* **ottomans** **1** a long padded seat. **2** a storage box with a padded top.
[from *Ottomanus*, the Latin name of the family who ruled Turkey from the 14th to the 20th century (because the ottoman originated in Turkey)]

ought *AUXILIARY VERB* expressing duty (*We ought to feed them*), rightness or advisability (*You ought to take more exercise*), or probability (*At this speed, we ought to be there by noon*).
[from Old English *ahte* = owed]

oughtn't (*mainly spoken*) ought not.

ounce *NOUN* **ounces** a unit of weight equal to 1/16 of a pound (about 28 grams).
[from Latin]

our *ADJECTIVE* belonging to us.
[from Old English]

ours *POSSESSIVE PRONOUN* belonging to us • *These seats are ours.*
[from *our*]
USAGE It is incorrect to write *our's*.

ourselves *PRONOUN* we or us and nobody else. (COMPARE **herself**)

oust *VERB* **ousts, ousting, ousted** drive a person out from a position or office.
[from old French]

out *ADVERB* **1** away from or not in a particular place or position or state etc.; not at home. **2** into the open; into existence or sight etc. • *The sun came out.* **3** no longer burning or shining. **4** in error • *Your estimate was 10% out.* **5** to or at an end; completely • *sold out; tired out.* **6** without restraint; boldly or loudly • *Speak out!* **7** (in cricket) no longer batting.
- **be out for** or **out to** be seeking or wanting • *They are out to make trouble.*
- **be out of** have no more of something left.
- **out of date** **1** old-fashioned. **2** no longer valid.
- **out of doors** in the open air.
- **out of the way** remote.
[from Old English]

out- *PREFIX* **1** out of; away from (as in *outcast*). **2** external; separate (as in *outhouse*). **3** more than; so as to defeat or exceed (as in *outdo*).

out and out *ADJECTIVE* thorough or complete • *an out and out villain.*

outback *NOUN* the remote inland districts of Australia.

outboard motor *NOUN* **outboard motors** a motor fitted to the outside of a boat's stern.

outbreak *NOUN* **outbreaks** the start of a disease or war or anger etc.

outburst *NOUN* **outbursts** a sudden bursting out of anger or laughter etc.

outcast *NOUN* **outcasts** a person who has been rejected by family, friends, or society.

outcome *NOUN* **outcomes** the result of what happens or has happened.

outcrop *NOUN* **outcrops** a piece of rock from a lower level that sticks out on the surface of the ground.
[from *out* + *crop* = outcrop]

outcry *NOUN* **outcries** a strong protest.

outdated *ADJECTIVE* out of date.

outdistance *VERB* **outdistances, outdistancing, outdistanced** get far ahead of someone in a race etc.

outdo *VERB* **outdoes, outdoing, outdid, outdone** do better than another person.

outdoor *ADJECTIVE* done or used outdoors.

outdoors *ADVERB* in the open air.

outer *ADJECTIVE* outside or external; nearer to the outside.
▷ **outermost** *adjective*

outer space *NOUN* the universe beyond the earth's atmosphere.

outfit *NOUN* **outfits 1** a set of clothes worn together. **2** a set of equipment. **3** (*informal*) a team or organization.

outflow *NOUN* **outflows 1** flowing out; what flows out. **2** a pipe for liquid flowing out.

outgoing *ADJECTIVE* **1** going out; retiring from office • *the outgoing chairman.* **2** sociable and friendly.

outgoings *PLURAL NOUN* expenditure.

outgrow *VERB* **outgrows, outgrowing, outgrew, outgrown 1** grow out of clothes or habits etc. **2** grow faster or larger than another person or thing.

outgrowth *NOUN* **outgrowths** something that grows out of another thing • *Feathers are outgrowths on a bird's skin.*

outhouse *NOUN* **outhouses** a small building (e.g. a shed or barn) that belongs to a house but is separate from it.

outing *NOUN* **outings** a journey for pleasure.

outlandish *ADJECTIVE* looking or sounding strange or foreign.
[from Old English *utland* = a foreign land]

outlast *VERB* **outlasts, outlasting, outlasted** last longer than something else.

outlaw *NOUN* **outlaws** a person who is punished by being excluded from legal rights and the protection of the law, especially a robber or bandit.

outlaw *VERB* **outlaws, outlawing, outlawed 1** make a person an outlaw. **2** declare something to be illegal; forbid.

outlay *NOUN* **outlays** what is spent on something.

outlet *NOUN* **outlets 1** a way for something to get out. **2** a way of expressing strong feelings. **3** a place from which goods are sold or distributed.

outline *NOUN* **outlines 1** a line round the outside of something, showing its boundary or shape. **2** a summary.

outline *VERB* **outlines, outlining, outlined 1** make an outline of something. **2** summarize.

outlive *VERB* **outlives, outliving, outlived** live or last longer than another person etc.

outlook *NOUN* **outlooks 1** a view on which people look out. **2** a person's mental attitude to something. **3** future prospects • *The outlook is bleak.*

outlying *ADJECTIVE* far from the centre; remote • *the outlying districts.*

outmanoeuvre *VERB* **outmanoeuvres, outmanoeuvring, outmanoeuvred** use skill or cunning to gain an advantage over someone.

outmoded *ADJECTIVE* out of date.

outnumber *VERB* **outnumbers, outnumbering, outnumbered** be more numerous than another group.

outpatient *NOUN* **outpatients** a person who visits a hospital for treatment but does not stay there.

outpost *NOUN* **outposts** a distant settlement.
[from *out* + *post*³]

output *NOUN* **outputs** **1** the amount produced. **2** the information or results produced by a computer.

outrage *NOUN* **outrages** **1** something that shocks people by being very wicked or cruel. **2** great anger.
▷ **outrageous** *adjective* **outrageously** *adverb*

outrage *VERB* **outrages**, **outraging**, **outraged** shock and anger people greatly.
[from old French *outrer* = go beyond, exaggerate, influenced by *rage*]

outrider *NOUN* **outriders** a person riding on a motorcycle as an escort or guard.

outrigger *NOUN* **outriggers** a framework attached to the side of a boat, e.g. to prevent a canoe from capsizing.
[origin unknown]

outright *ADVERB* **1** completely; not gradually • *This drug should be banned outright.* **2** frankly • *We told him this outright.*

outright *ADJECTIVE* thorough or complete • *an outright fraud.*

outrun *VERB* **outruns**, **outrunning**, **outran**, **outrun** run faster or further than another.

outset *NOUN* the beginning of something • *from the outset of his career.*

outside *NOUN* **outsides** the outer side, surface, or part.
- **at the outside** at the most • *a mile at the outside.*

outside *ADJECTIVE* **1** on or coming from the outside • *the outside edge.* **2** greatest possible • *the outside price.* **3** remote or slight • *an outside chance.*

outside *ADVERB* on or to the outside; outdoors • *Leave it outside. It's cold outside.*

outside *PREPOSITION* on or to the outside of • *Leave it outside the door.*

outside broadcast *NOUN* **outside broadcasts** a broadcast made on location and not in a studio.

outsider *NOUN* **outsiders** **1** a person who does not belong to a certain group. **2** a horse or person thought to have no chance of winning a race or competition.

outsize *ADJECTIVE* much larger than average.

outskirts *PLURAL NOUN* the outer parts or districts, especially of a town.

outspoken *ADJECTIVE* speaking or spoken very frankly.

outspread *ADJECTIVE* spread out.

outstanding *ADJECTIVE* **1** extremely good or distinguished. **2** not yet paid or dealt with.

outstretched *ADJECTIVE* stretched out.

outstrip *VERB* **outstrips**, **outstripping**, **outstripped** **1** run faster or further than another. **2** surpass in achievement or success.
[from *out-* + Middle English *strypen* = move quickly]

outvote *VERB* **outvotes**, **outvoting**, **outvoted** defeat someone by a majority of votes.

outward *ADJECTIVE* **1** going outwards. **2** on the outside.
▷ **outwardly** *adverb* **outwards** *adverb*

outweigh *VERB* **outweighs**, **outweighing**, **outweighed** be greater in weight or importance than something else.

outwit *VERB* **outwits**, **outwitting**, **outwitted** deceive somebody by being crafty.

ova *plural* of **ovum**.

oval *ADJECTIVE* shaped like an 0, rounded and longer than it is broad.
▷ **oval** *noun*
[from Latin *ovum* = egg]

ovary *NOUN* **ovaries** **1** either of the two organs in which ova or egg-cells are produced in a woman's or female animal's body. **2** part of the pistil in a plant, from which fruit is formed.
[from Latin *ovum* = egg]

ovation *NOUN* **ovations** enthusiastic applause.
[from Latin *ovare* = rejoice]

oven *NOUN* **ovens** a closed space in which things are cooked or heated.
[from Old English]

over *PREPOSITION* **1** above. **2** more than • *It's over a mile away.* **3** concerning • *They quarrelled over money.* **4** across the top of; on or to the other side of • *They rowed the boat over the lake.* **5** during • *We can talk over dinner.* **6** in superiority or preference to • *their victory over United.*

over *ADVERB* **1** out and down from the top or edge; from an upright position • *He fell over.* **2** so that a different side shows • *Turn it over.* **3** at or to a place; across • *Walk over to our house.* **4** remaining • *There is nothing left over.* **5** all through; thoroughly • *Think it over.* **6** at an end • *The lesson is over.*

- **over and over** many times; repeatedly.

over *NOUN* **overs** a series of six balls bowled in cricket.
[from Old English]

over- *PREFIX* **1** over (as in *overturn*). **2** too much; too (as in *over-anxious*).

overact *VERB* **overacts, overacting, overacted** (said about an actor) act in an exaggerated manner.

overall *ADJECTIVE* including everything; total • *the overall cost.*

overall *NOUN* **overalls** a type of coat worn over other clothes to protect them when working.

overalls *PLURAL NOUN* a piece of clothing, like a shirt and trousers combined, worn over other clothes to protect them.

overarm *ADJECTIVE & ADVERB* with the arm lifted above shoulder level and coming down in front of the body • *bowling overarm.*

overawe *VERB* **overawes, overawing, overawed** overcome a person with awe.

overbalance *VERB* **overbalances, overbalancing, overbalanced** lose balance and fall over.

overbearing *ADJECTIVE* domineering.

overblown *ADJECTIVE* **1** exaggerated or pretentious. **2** (said about a flower) too fully open; past its best.

overboard *ADVERB* from in or on a ship into the water • *She jumped overboard.*

overcast *ADJECTIVE* covered with cloud.

overcoat *NOUN* **overcoats** a warm outdoor coat.

overcome *VERB* **overcomes, overcoming, overcame, overcome** **1** win a victory over somebody; defeat. **2** have a strong physical or emotional effect on someone and make them helpless • *He was overcome by the fumes.* **3** find a way of dealing with a problem etc.

▷ **overcome** *adjective*

overcrowd *VERB* **overcrowds, overcrowding, overcrowded** crowd too many people into a place or vehicle.

▷ **overcrowded** *adjective*

overdo *VERB* **overdoes, overdoing, overdid, overdone** **1** do something too much. **2** cook food for too long.

overdose *NOUN* **overdoses** too large a dose of a drug.

▷ **overdose** *verb*

overdraft *NOUN* **overdrafts** the amount by which a bank account is overdrawn.

overdraw *VERB* **overdraws, overdrawing, overdrew, overdrawn** draw more money from a bank account than the amount you have in it.

▷ **overdrawn** *adjective*

overdue *ADJECTIVE* late; not paid or arrived etc. by the proper time.

overestimate *VERB* **overestimates, overestimating, overestimated** estimate something too highly.

overflow *VERB* **overflows, overflowing, overflowed** flow over the edge or limits of something.

▷ **overflow** *noun*

overgrown *ADJECTIVE* covered with weeds or unwanted plants.

overhang *VERB* **overhangs, overhanging, overhung** jut out over something.

▷ **overhang** *noun*

overhaul *VERB* **overhauls, overhauling, overhauled** **1** examine something thoroughly and repair it if necessary. **2** overtake.

▷ **overhaul** *noun*

overhead *ADJECTIVE & ADVERB* **1** above the level of your head. **2** in the sky.

overheads *PLURAL NOUN* the expenses of running a business.

overhear *VERB* **overhears, overhearing, overheard** hear something accidentally or without the speaker intending you to hear it.

overjoyed *ADJECTIVE* filled with great joy.

overland *ADJECTIVE & ADVERB* travelling over the land, not by sea or air.

overlap *VERB* **overlaps, overlapping, overlapped** **1** lie across part of something. **2** happen partly at the same time.
▷ **overlap** *noun*
[from *over* + *lap*¹]

overlay *VERB* **overlays, overlaying, overlaid** cover with a layer; lie on top of something.

overlay *NOUN* **overlays** a thing laid over another.

overleaf *ADVERB* on the other side of the page.

overlie *VERB* **overlies, overlying, overlay, overlain** lie over something.

overload *VERB* **overloads, overloading, overloaded** put too great a load on someone or something.

overlook *VERB* **overlooks, overlooking, overlooked** **1** not notice or consider something. **2** deliberately ignore; not punish an offence. **3** have a view over something.

overlord *NOUN* **overlords** a supreme lord.

overnight *ADJECTIVE & ADVERB* of or during a night • *an overnight stop in Rome.*

overpower *VERB* **overpowers, overpowering, overpowered** defeat someone by greater strength or numbers.

overpowering *ADJECTIVE* very strong.

overrate *VERB* **overrates, overrating, overrated** have too high an opinion of something.

overreach *VERB* **overreaches, overreaching, overreached**
- **overreach yourself** fail through being too ambitious.

override *VERB* **overrides, overriding, overrode, overridden** **1** overrule. **2** be more important than • *Safety overrides all other considerations.*
▷ **overriding** *adjective*

overripe *ADJECTIVE* too ripe.

overrule *VERB* **overrules, overruling, overruled** reject a suggestion etc. by using your authority • *We voted for having a disco but the headteacher overruled the idea.*

overrun *VERB* **overruns, overrunning, overran, overrun** **1** spread over and occupy or harm something • *Mice overran the place.* **2** go on for longer than it should • *The programme overran by ten minutes.*

overseas *ADVERB* across or beyond the sea; abroad.

oversee *VERB* **oversees, overseeing, oversaw, overseen** watch over or supervise people working.
▷ **overseer** *noun*

overshadow *VERB* **overshadows, overshadowing, overshadowed** **1** cast a shadow over something. **2** make a person or thing seem unimportant in comparison.

overshoot *VERB* **overshoots, overshooting, overshot** go beyond a target or limit • *The plane overshot the runway.*

oversight *NOUN* **oversights** a mistake made by not noticing something.

oversleep *VERB* **oversleeps, oversleeping, overslept** sleep for longer than you intended.

overspill *NOUN* **1** what spills over. **2** the extra population of a town, who take homes in nearby districts.

overstate *VERB* **overstates, overstating, overstated** exaggerate how important something is.

overstep *VERB* **oversteps, overstepping, overstepped** go beyond a limit.

overt *ADJECTIVE* done or shown openly • *overt hostility.*
▷ **overtly** *adverb*
[from old French, = open]

overtake *VERB* **overtakes, overtaking, overtook, overtaken** **1** pass a moving vehicle or person etc. **2** catch up with someone.

overtax *VERB* **overtaxes, overtaxing, overtaxed** **1** tax too heavily. **2** put too heavy a burden or strain on someone.

A B C D E F G H I J K L M N O P Q R S T U V W X Y Z

overthrow VERB **overthrows**, **overthrowing**, **overthrew**, **overthrown** remove someone from power by force • *They overthrew the king.*

overthrow NOUN **overthrows** **1** overthrowing. **2** throwing a ball too far.

overtime NOUN time spent working outside the normal hours; payment for this.

overtone NOUN **overtones** a feeling or quality that is suggested but not expressed directly • *There were overtones of envy in his speech.*

overture NOUN **overtures** **1** a piece of music written as an introduction to an opera, ballet, etc. **2** a friendly attempt to start a discussion • *They made overtures of peace.*
[from old French, = opening]

overturn VERB **overturns**, **overturning**, **overturned** **1** turn over or upside down. **2** reverse a legal decision.

overview NOUN **overviews** a general outline of a subject or situation that gives the main ideas without explaining all the details • *He gave me a quick overview of the company.*

overweight ADJECTIVE too heavy.

overwhelm VERB **overwhelms**, **overwhelming**, **overwhelmed** **1** bury or drown beneath a huge mass. **2** overcome completely.
▷ **overwhelming** *adjective*
[from *over* + Middle English *whelm* = turn upside down]

overwork VERB **overworks**, **overworking**, **overworked** **1** work or make someone work too hard. **2** use something too often • *'Nice' is an overworked word.*
▷ **overwork** *noun*

overwrought ADJECTIVE very upset and nervous or worried.

ovoid ADJECTIVE egg-shaped.
[from French, related to *ovum*]

ovulate VERB **ovulates**, **ovulating**, **ovulated** produce an ovum from an ovary.
[from French, related to *ovum*]

ovum (*say* oh-vum) NOUN **ova** a female cell that can develop into a new individual when it is fertilized.
[Latin, = egg]

owe VERB **owes**, **owing**, **owed** **1** have a duty to pay or give something to someone, especially money. **2** have something because of the action of another person or thing • *They owed their lives to the pilot's skill.*
- **owing to** because of; caused by.
[from Old English]
USAGE The use of *owing to* as a preposition meaning 'because of' is entirely acceptable, unlike this use of *due to*, which some people object to. See note at **due**.

owl NOUN **owls** a bird of prey with large eyes, usually flying at night.
[from Old English]

own ADJECTIVE belonging to yourself or itself.
- **get your own back** get revenge.
- **on your own** alone.

own VERB **owns**, **owning**, **owned** **1** possess; have something as your property. **2** acknowledge or admit something • *I own that I made a mistake.*
- **own up** confess; admit guilt.
[from Old English]

owner NOUN **owners** the person who owns something.
▷ **ownership** *noun*

own goal NOUN **own goals** a goal scored by a member of a team against his or her own side.

ox NOUN **oxen** a large animal kept for its meat and for pulling carts.
[from Old English]

oxide NOUN **oxides** a compound of oxygen and one other element.
[from French]

oxidize VERB **oxidizes**, **oxidizing**, **oxidized** **1** combine or cause to combine with oxygen. **2** coat with an oxide.
▷ **oxidation** *noun*

oxtail NOUN **oxtails** the tail of an ox, used to make soup or stew.

oxygen NOUN a colourless odourless tasteless gas that exists in the air and is essential for living things.
[from French]

oxymoron (*say* oksi-**mor**-on) NOUN **oxymorons** putting together words which seem to contradict one another, e.g. *bitter-sweet, living death.*
[from Greek *oxumoros* = pointedly foolish]

oyster *NOUN* **oysters** a kind of shellfish whose shell sometimes contains a pearl.
[from Greek]

ozone *NOUN* a form of oxygen with a sharp smell.
[from Greek *ozein* = to smell]

ozone layer *NOUN* a layer of ozone high in the atmosphere, protecting the earth from harmful amounts of the sun's radiation.

Pp

p *ABBREVIATION* penny or pence.

p. *ABBREVIATION* **pp.** page.

pa *NOUN* (*informal*) father.
[short for *papa*]

pace *NOUN* **paces** **1** one step in walking, marching, or running. **2** speed • *He set a fast pace.*

pace *VERB* **paces, pacing, paced** **1** walk with slow or regular steps. **2** measure a distance in paces • *We paced out the length of a cricket pitch.*
[from Latin *passus*, literally = a stretch of the leg]

pacemaker *NOUN* **pacemakers** **1** a person who sets the pace for another in a race. **2** an electrical device to keep the heart beating.

pacific (*say* pa-**sif**-ik) *ADJECTIVE* peaceful; making or loving peace.
▷ **pacifically** *adverb*

pacifist (*say* pas-if-ist) *NOUN* **pacifists** a person who believes that war is always wrong.
▷ **pacifism** *noun*

pacify *VERB* **pacifies, pacifying, pacified** **1** calm a person down. **2** bring peace to a country or warring sides.
▷ **pacification** *noun*
[from Latin *pacis* = of peace]

pack *NOUN* **packs** **1** a bundle or collection of things wrapped or tied together. **2** a set of playing cards (usually 52). **3** a bag carried on your back. **4** a large amount • *a pack of lies.* **5** a group of hounds or wolves etc. **6** a group of people; a group of Brownies or Cub Scouts.

pack *VERB* **packs, packing, packed** **1** put things into a suitcase, bag, or box etc. in order to move or store them. **2** crowd together; fill tightly • *The hall was packed.*
- **pack off** send a person away.
- **send a person packing** dismiss him or her.
[from old German or Dutch]

package *NOUN* **packages** **1** a parcel or packet. **2** a number of things offered or accepted together.
▷ **packaging** *noun*
[from *pack*]

package holiday *NOUN* **package holidays** a holiday with all the travel and accommodation arranged and included in the price.

packet *NOUN* **packets** a small parcel.
[from *pack*]

pack ice *NOUN* a mass of pieces of ice floating in the sea.

pact *NOUN* **pacts** an agreement or treaty.
[from Latin]

pad[1] *NOUN* **pads** **1** a soft thick mass of material, used e.g. to protect or stuff something. **2** a piece of soft material worn to protect your leg in cricket and other games. **3** a set of sheets of paper fastened together at one edge. **4** the soft fleshy part under an animal's foot or the end of a finger or toe. **5** a flat surface from which rockets are launched or where helicopters take off and land.

pad *VERB* **pads, padding, padded** put a pad on or in something.
- **pad out** make a book, speech, etc. longer than it needs to be.
[probably from old Dutch]

pad[2] *VERB* **pads, padding, padded** walk softly.
[from Dutch *pad* = path]

padding *NOUN* material used to pad things.

paddle[1] *VERB* **paddles, paddling, paddled** walk about in shallow water.
▷ **paddle** *noun*
[probably from old Dutch]

paddle[2] *NOUN* **paddles** a short oar with a broad blade; something shaped like this.

paddle *VERB* **paddles, paddling, paddled** move a boat along with a paddle or paddles; row gently.
[origin unknown]

paddock *NOUN* **paddocks** a small field where horses are kept.
[from Old English]

paddy *NOUN* **paddies** a field where rice is grown.
▷ **paddy field** *noun*
[from Malay *padi* = rice (Malay is spoken in Malaysia)]

padkos *NOUN* (*S.African*) food that is packed for and eaten on a journey.
[from Afrikaans *pad* = road, + *kos* = food]

padlock *NOUN* **padlocks** a detachable lock with a metal loop that passes through a ring or chain etc.
▷ **padlock** *verb*
[origin unknown]

padre (*say* pah-dray) *NOUN* **padres** (*informal*) a chaplain in the armed forces.
[Italian, Spanish, and Portuguese, = father]

paean (*say* pee-an) *NOUN* **paeans** a song of praise or triumph.
[from Greek, = hymn]

paediatrics (*say* peed-ee-at-riks) *NOUN* the study of children's diseases.
▷ **paediatric** *adjective* **paediatrician** *noun*
[from Greek *paidos* = of a child + *iatros* = doctor]

pagan (*say* pay-gan) *NOUN* **pagans** a person who does not believe in one of the chief religions; a heathen.
▷ **pagan** *adjective*
[same origin as *peasant*]

page[1] *NOUN* **pages** a piece of paper that is part of a book or newspaper etc.; one side of this.
[from Latin]

page[2] *NOUN* **pages** **1** a boy or man employed to go on errands or be an attendant. **2** a young boy attending a bride at a wedding.
[from Greek *paidion* = small boy]

pageant *NOUN* **pageants** **1** a play or entertainment about historical events and people. **2** a procession of people in costume as an entertainment.
▷ **pageantry** *noun*
[origin unknown]

pagoda (*say* pag-oh-da) *NOUN* **pagodas** a Buddhist tower, or a Hindu temple shaped like a pyramid, in India and the Far East.
[via Portuguese from Persian]

paid *past tense* of **pay**.
- **put paid to** (*informal*) put an end to someone's activity or hope etc.

pail *NOUN* **pails** a bucket.
[from Old English]

pain *NOUN* **pains** **1** an unpleasant feeling caused by injury or disease. **2** suffering in the mind.
▷ **painful** *adjective* **painfully** *adverb* **painless** *adjective*
- **on** or **under pain of** with the threat of.
- **take pains** make a careful effort or take trouble over something.

pain *VERB* **pains, paining, pained** cause suffering or distress to someone.
[from Latin *poena* = punishment]

painkiller *NOUN* **painkillers** a medicine or drug that relieves pain.

painstaking *ADJECTIVE* very careful and thorough.

paint *NOUN* **paints** a liquid substance put on something to colour it.
▷ **paintbox** *noun* **paintbrush** *noun*

paint *VERB* **paints, painting, painted** **1** put paint on something. **2** make a picture with paints.
[from Latin]

painter[1] *NOUN* **painters** a person who paints.

painter[2] *NOUN* **painters** a rope used to tie up a boat.
[from old French *penteur* = rope]

painting *NOUN* **paintings** **1** a painted picture. **2** using paints to make a picture.

pair *NOUN* **pairs** **1** a set of two things or people; a couple. **2** something made of two joined parts • *a pair of scissors.*

pair *VERB* **pairs**, **pairing**, **paired** put two things together as a pair.
- **pair off** or **up** form a couple.
[from Latin *paria* = equal things]

pal *NOUN* **pals** (*informal*) a friend.
[Romany, = brother]

palace *NOUN* **palaces** a mansion where a king, queen, or other important person lives.
[from *Palatium*, the name of a hill on which the house of the emperor Augustus stood in ancient Rome]

palaeolithic (*say* pal-ee-o-**lith**-ik) *ADJECTIVE* belonging to the early part of the Stone Age.
[from Greek *palaios* = old + *lithos* = stone]

palaeontology (*say* pal-ee-on-**tol**-o-jee) *NOUN* the study of fossils.
[from Greek *palaios* = ancient + *onta* = beings, + *-ology*]

palatable *ADJECTIVE* tasting pleasant.

palate *NOUN* **palates** **1** the roof of your mouth. **2** a person's sense of taste.
[from Latin]
USAGE Do not confuse with **palette** and **pallet**.

palatial (*say* pa-**lay**-shal) *ADJECTIVE* like a palace; large and splendid.
[same origin as *palace*]

pale[1] *ADJECTIVE* **1** almost white • *a pale face.* **2** not bright in colour or light • *pale green; the pale moonlight.*
▷ **palely** *adverb* **paleness** *noun*
[from Latin *pallidus* = pallid]

pale[2] *NOUN* **pales** a boundary.
- **beyond the pale** beyond the limits of acceptable behaviour.
[from Latin *palus* = a stake or fence post]

palette *NOUN* **palettes** a board on which an artist mixes colours ready for use.
[French]
USAGE Do not confuse with **palate** and **pallet**.

palindrome *NOUN* **palindromes** a word or phrase that reads the same backwards as forwards, e.g. *radar* or *Madam, I'm Adam.*
[from Greek *palindromos* = running back again]

paling *NOUN* **palings** a fence made of wooden posts or railings; one of its posts.
[from *pale*[2]]

palisade *NOUN* **palisades** a fence of pointed sticks or boards.
[French, related to *pale*[2]]

pall[1] (*say* pawl) *NOUN* **palls** **1** a cloth spread over a coffin. **2** a dark covering • *A pall of smoke lay over the town.*
[from Latin *pallium* = cloak]

pall[2] (*say* pawl) *VERB* **palls**, **palling**, **palled** become uninteresting or boring to someone • *The novelty of the new computer game soon began to pall.*
[from *appal*]

pallbearer *NOUN* **pallbearers** a person helping to carry the coffin at a funeral.

pallet *NOUN* **pallets** **1** a mattress stuffed with straw. **2** a hard narrow bed. **3** a large platform for carrying goods that are being stacked, especially one that can be lifted by a forklift truck.
[from old French *paille* = straw]
USAGE Do not confuse with **palate** and **palette**.

palliate *VERB* **palliates**, **palliating**, **palliated** make a thing less serious or less severe.
▷ **palliation** *noun*
[same origin as *pall*[1]]

palliative *NOUN* **palliatives** something that lessens pain or suffering.
▷ **palliative** *adjective*

pallid *ADJECTIVE* pale, especially because of illness.
[from Latin]

pallor *NOUN* paleness in a person's face, especially because of illness.

palm *NOUN* **palms** **1** the inner part of the hand, between the fingers and the wrist. **2** a palm tree.

palm *VERB* **palms, palming, palmed** pick up something secretly and hide it in the palm of your hand.
- **palm off** deceive a person into accepting something.
[from Latin]

palmistry *NOUN* fortune-telling by looking at the creases in the palm of a person's hand.
▷ **palmist** *noun*

Palm Sunday *NOUN* the Sunday before Easter, when Christians commemorate Jesus Christ's entry into Jerusalem when the people spread palm leaves in his path.

palm tree *NOUN* **palm trees** a tropical tree with large leaves and no branches.

palpable *ADJECTIVE* **1** able to be touched or felt. **2** obvious • *a palpable lie.*
▷ **palpably** *adverb*
[from Latin *palpare* = to touch]

palpitate *VERB* **palpitates, palpitating, palpitated** **1** (said about the heart) beat hard and quickly. **2** (said about a person) quiver with fear or excitement.
▷ **palpitation** *noun*
[from Latin]

palsy (*say* pawl-zee) *NOUN* (*old use*) paralysis.
[same origin as *paralysis*]

paltry (*say* pol-tree) *ADJECTIVE* very small and almost worthless • *a paltry amount.*
[origin unknown]

pampas *NOUN* wide grassy plains in South America.
[via Spanish from Quechua (a South American language)]

pampas grass *NOUN* a tall grass with long feathery flowers.

pamper *VERB* **pampers, pampering, pampered** treat or look after someone very kindly and indulgently.
[probably from old German or old Dutch]

pamphlet *NOUN* **pamphlets** a leaflet or booklet giving information on a subject.
[from *Pamphilet*, the name of a long 12th- century poem in Latin]

pan *NOUN* **pans** **1** a wide container with a flat base, used for cooking. **2** something shaped like this. **3** the bowl of a lavatory.
[from Old English]

pan- *PREFIX* **1** all (as in *panorama*). **2** to do with the whole of a continent or group etc. (as in *pan-African*).
[from Greek]

panacea (*say* pan-a-see-a) *NOUN* **panaceas** a cure for all kinds of diseases or troubles.
[from *pan-* + Greek *akos* = remedy]

panache (*say* pan-**ash**) *NOUN* a confident stylish manner.
[originally referring to a plume of feathers on a helmet or headdress, via French and Italian from Latin *pinnaculum* = little feather]

panama *NOUN* **panamas** a hat made of a fine straw-like material.
[from *Panama* in Central America (because the hats were originally made from the leaves of a plant which grows there)]

pancake *NOUN* **pancakes** a thin round cake of batter fried on both sides.
[from *pan* + *cake*]

Pancake Day *NOUN* Shrove Tuesday, when people often eat pancakes.

pancreas (*say* **pan**-kree-as) *NOUN* a gland near the stomach, producing insulin and digestive juices.
[from Greek]

panda *NOUN* **pandas** a large bear-like black-and-white animal found in China.
[from the name given to a related animal in Nepal]

panda car *NOUN* **panda cars** a police patrol car, originally white with black stripes on the doors.

pandemonium *NOUN* uproar and complete confusion.
[from *Pandemonium*, John Milton's name for the capital of hell in his poem Paradise Lost, from *pan-* + *demon*]

pander *VERB* **panders, pandering, pandered**
- **pander to** indulge someone by giving them whatever they want • *Don't pander to his taste for sweet things!*
[from *Pandare*, a character in an old poem who acted as go- between for two lovers]

pane *NOUN* **panes** a sheet of glass in a window.
[from Latin]

panegyric (*say* pan-i-jirrik) NOUN **panegyrics** a speech or piece of writing praising a person or thing.
[from Greek]

panel NOUN **panels** **1** a long flat piece of wood, metal, etc. that is part of a door, wall, piece of furniture, etc. **2** a flat board with controls or instruments on it. **3** a group of people chosen to discuss or decide something.
▷ **panelled** *adjective* **panelling** *noun*
[from old French, related to *pane*]

pang NOUN **pangs** a sudden sharp pain.
[from *prong*]

panic NOUN sudden uncontrollable fear.
▷ **panic-stricken** *adjective* **panicky** *adjective*

panic VERB **panics, panicking, panicked** fill or be filled with panic.
[from the name of *Pan*, an ancient Greek god thought to be able to cause sudden fear]

pannier NOUN **panniers** a large bag or basket hung on one side of a bicycle, motorcycle, or horse.
[from Latin *panarium* = breadbasket]

panoply NOUN **panoplies** a splendid display or collection of things.
[from *pan-* + Greek *hopla* = weapons]

panorama NOUN **panoramas** a view or picture of a wide area.
▷ **panoramic** *adjective*
[from *pan-* + Greek *horama* = view]

pansy NOUN **pansies** a small brightly coloured garden flower with velvety petals.
[from French *pensée* = thought]

pant VERB **pants, panting, panted** take short quick breaths, usually after running or working hard.
[from old French]

pantaloons PLURAL NOUN wide trousers, gathered at the ankle.
[from *Pantalone*, a character in old Italian comedies who wore these]

pantechnicon NOUN **pantechnicons** a kind of large lorry, used for carrying furniture.
[originally the name of a large art and craft gallery in London, which was later used for storing furniture: from *pan-* + Greek *techne* = art]

panther NOUN **panthers** a leopard, especially a black one.
[from Greek]

panties PLURAL NOUN (*informal*) short knickers.
[from *pants*]

pantile NOUN **pantiles** a curved tile for a roof.
[because the curved shape reminded people of a pan]

pantomime NOUN **pantomimes** **1** a Christmas entertainment, usually based on a fairy tale. **2** mime.
[from *pan-* + *mime* (because in its most ancient form an actor mimed the different parts)]

pantry NOUN **pantries** a small room for storing food; a larder.
[from old French *paneterie*, literally = bread- store]

pants PLURAL NOUN (*informal*) **1** trousers. **2** underpants or knickers.
[short for *pantaloons*]

pantyhose PLURAL NOUN (*American*) women's nylon tights.

pap NOUN **1** soft food suitable for babies. **2** trivial entertainment; nonsense.
[probably via old German from Latin *pappare* = eat]

papa NOUN (*old use*) father.
[from Greek *pappas* = father]

papacy (*say* pay-pa-see) NOUN **papacies** the position of pope.
[from Latin *papa* = pope]

papal (*say* pay-pal) ADJECTIVE to do with the pope.

paparazzo (*say* pap-a-rat-so) NOUN **paparazzi** (*say* pap-a-rat-si) a photographer who follows famous people in order to get interesting photographs of them to sell to a newspaper or magazine.
[from Italian]

paper NOUN **papers** **1** a substance made in thin sheets from wood, rags, etc. and used for writing or printing or drawing on or for wrapping things. **2** a newspaper. **3** wallpaper. **4** a document. **5** a set of examination questions • *the history paper.*

paper *VERB* **papers, papering, papered** cover a wall or room with wallpaper.
[from old French, related to *papyrus*]

paperback *NOUN* **paperbacks** a book with a thin flexible cover.

paperweight *NOUN* **paperweights** a small heavy object used for holding down loose papers.

paperwork *NOUN* all the writing of reports, keeping of records etc. that someone has to do as part of their job.

papier mâché (*say* pap-yay **mash**-ay) *NOUN* paper made into pulp and moulded to make models, ornaments, etc.
[French, = chewed paper]

paprika (*say* **pap**-rik-a) *NOUN* a powdered spice made from red pepper.
[Hungarian]

papyrus (*say* pap-I-rus) *NOUN* **papyri** **1** a kind of paper made from the stems of a plant like a reed, used in ancient Egypt. **2** a document written on this paper.
[Greek, = paper- reed]

par *NOUN* **1** an average or normal amount or condition • *I'm feeling below par today.* **2** (in golf) the number of strokes that a good player should normally take for a particular hole or course.
- **on a par with** equal to in amount or quality.
[Latin, = equal]

para-[1] *PREFIX* **1** beside (as in *parallel*). **2** beyond (as in *paradox*).
[from Greek]

para-[2] *PREFIX* protecting from (as in *parasol*).
[from Italian]

parable *NOUN* **parables** a story told to teach people something, especially one of those told by Jesus Christ.
[from Greek *paraballein* = put beside or compare: related to *parabola*]

parabola (*say* pa-**rab**-ol-a) *NOUN* **parabolas** a curve like the path of an object thrown into the air and falling down again.
▷ **parabolic** *adjective*
[from *para-*[1] + Greek *bole* = a throw]

parachute *NOUN* **parachutes** an umbrella-like device on which people or things can float slowly to the ground from an aircraft.
▷ **parachute** *verb* **parachutist** *noun*
[from *para-*[2] + French *chute* = a fall]

parade *NOUN* **parades** **1** a procession that displays people or things. **2** an assembly of troops for inspection, drill, etc.; a ground for this. **3** a public square, promenade, or row of shops.

parade *VERB* **parades, parading, paraded** **1** move in a parade. **2** assemble for a parade.
[from Spanish or Italian, = display]

paradigm (*say* pa-ra-diym) *NOUN* **paradigms** **1** a very clear and typical example of something. **2** a model or example that shows how something works.
▷ **paradigmatic** *adjective*

paradise *NOUN* **1** heaven; a heavenly place. **2** the Garden of Eden.
[from ancient Persian *pairidaeza* = garden]

paradox *NOUN* **paradoxes** a statement that seems to contradict itself but which contains a truth, e.g. 'More haste, less speed'.
▷ **paradoxical** *adjective* **paradoxically** *adverb*
[from *para-*[1] + Greek *doxa* = opinion]

paraffin *NOUN* a kind of oil used as fuel.
[via German from Latin *parum* = hardly + *affinis* = related (because paraffin does not combine readily with other substances)]

paragliding *NOUN* the sport of being towed through the air while being supported by a kind of parachute.

paragon *NOUN* **paragons** a person or thing that seems to be perfect.
[from Italian *paragone* = touchstone]

paragraph *NOUN* **paragraphs** one or more sentences on a single subject, forming a section of a piece of writing and beginning on a new line, usually slightly in from the margin of the page.
[from *para-*[1] + *-graph*]

parakeet *NOUN* **parakeets** a kind of small parrot.
[from old French]

parallax *NOUN* what seems to be a change in the position of something when you look at it from a different place.
[from *para-*[1] + Greek *allassein* = to change]

parallel *ADJECTIVE* **1** (said about lines etc.) side by side and the same distance apart from each other for their whole length, like railway lines. **2** similar or corresponding • *When petrol prices rise there is a parallel rise in bus fares.*
▷ **parallelism** *noun*

parallel *NOUN* **parallels** **1** something similar or corresponding. **2** a comparison • *You can draw a parallel between the two situations.* **3** a line that is parallel to another. **4** a line of latitude.

parallel *VERB* **parallels, paralleling, paralleled** find or be a parallel to something.
[from *para-*[1] + Greek *allelos* = one another]
USAGE Take care with the spelling of this word: one 'r', two 'l's, then one 'l'.

parallelogram *NOUN* **parallelograms** a quadrilateral with its opposite sides equal and parallel.
[from *parallel* + *-gram*]

paralyse *VERB* **paralyses, paralysing, paralysed** **1** cause paralysis in a person etc. **2** make something be unable to move • *She was paralysed with fear.*
[from French, related to *paralysis*]

paralysis *NOUN* being unable to move, especially because of a disease or an injury to the nerves.
▷ **paralytic** (*say* pa-ra-**lit**-ik) *adjective*
[from Greek *para* = on one side + *lysis* = loosening]

paramedic *NOUN* **paramedics** a person who is trained to do medical work, especially emergency first aid, but is not a fully qualified doctor.
[from *para-*[1] + *medical*]

parameter (*say* pa-**ram**-it-er) *NOUN* **parameters** a quantity, quality, or factor that is variable and affects other things by its changes.
[from *para-*[1] + Greek *metron* = measure]
USAGE Do not confuse with **perimeter**.

paramilitary *ADJECTIVE* organized like a military force but not part of the armed services.
[from *para-*[1] + *military*]

paramount *ADJECTIVE* more important than anything else • *Secrecy is paramount.*
[from old French *paramont* = above]

paranoia *NOUN* **1** a mental illness in which a person has delusions or suspects and distrusts people. **2** an unjustified suspicion and mistrust of others.
▷ **paranoid** *adjective*
[from *para-*[1] + Greek *noos* = the mind]

paranormal *ADJECTIVE* beyond what is normal and can be rationally explained; supernatural.

parapet *NOUN* **parapets** a low wall along the edge of a balcony, bridge, roof, etc.
[via French from Italian]

paraphernalia *NOUN* numerous pieces of equipment, belongings, etc.
[originally = the personal belongings a woman could keep after her marriage (as opposed to her dowry, which went to her husband): from *para-*[1] + Greek *pherne* = dowry]

paraphrase *VERB* **paraphrases, paraphrasing, paraphrased** give the meaning of something by using different words.
▷ **paraphrase** *noun*
[from *para-*[1] + *phrase*]

paraplegia *NOUN* paralysis of the lower half of the body.
▷ **paraplegic** *noun* & *adjective*
[from *para-*[1] + Greek *plessein* = strike]

parasite *NOUN* **parasites** an animal or plant that lives in or on another, from which it gets its food.
▷ **parasitic** *adjective*
[from Greek *parasitos* = guest at a meal]

parasol *NOUN* **parasols** a lightweight umbrella used to shade yourself from the sun.
[from *para-*[2] + Italian *sole* = sun]

paratroops *PLURAL NOUN* troops trained to be dropped from aircraft by parachute.
▷ **paratrooper** *noun*
[from *parachute* + *troops*]

parboil *VERB* **parboils, parboiling, parboiled** boil food until it is partly cooked.
[from Latin *per-* = thoroughly + *bullire* = to boil (*per-* was later confused with *part*)]

parcel *NOUN* **parcels** something wrapped up to be sent by post or carried.

parcel *VERB* **parcels, parcelling, parcelled** **1** wrap something up as a parcel. **2** divide something into portions • *We'll need to parcel out the work.*
[from old French, related to *particle*]

parched *ADJECTIVE* very dry or thirsty.
[origin unknown]

parchment *NOUN* **parchments** a kind of heavy paper, originally made from animal skins.
[from the city of Pergamum, now in Turkey, where parchment was made in ancient times]

pardon *NOUN* **1** forgiveness. **2** the cancelling of a punishment • *a free pardon.*

pardon *VERB* **pardons, pardoning, pardoned** **1** forgive or excuse somebody. **2** cancel a person's punishment.
▷ **pardonable** *adjective* **pardonably** *adverb*

pardon *INTERJECTION* (also **I beg your pardon** or **pardon me**) used to mean 'I didn't hear or understand what you said' or 'I apologize'.
[from old French]

pare (*say as* *pair*) *VERB* **pares, paring, pared** **1** trim something by cutting away the edges. **2** reduce something gradually • *We had to pare down our expenses.*
[from Latin *parare* = prepare]

parent *NOUN* **parents** **1** a father or mother; a living thing that has produced others of its kind. **2** a source from which others are derived • *the parent company.*
▷ **parenthood** *noun* **parenting** *noun* **parental** (*say* pa-**rent**-al) *adjective*
[from Latin *parens* = producing offspring]

parentage *NOUN* who your parents are.

parenthesis (*say* pa-**ren**-thi-sis) *NOUN* **parentheses** **1** something extra that is inserted in a sentence, usually between brackets or dashes. **2** either of the pair of brackets (like these) used to mark off words from the rest of a sentence.
▷ **parenthetical** *adjective*
[Greek, = putting in besides]

par excellence (*say* par eks-el-**ahns**) *ADVERB* more than all the others; to the greatest degree.
[French, = because of special excellence]

pariah (*say* pa-**ry**-a) *NOUN* **pariahs** an outcast.
[from Tamil]

parish *NOUN* **parishes** a district with its own church.
▷ **parishioner** *noun*
[from Greek *paroikia* = neighbourhood, from *para-*[1] = beside + *oikos* = house]

parity *NOUN* equality.
[same origin as *par*]

park *NOUN* **parks** **1** a large garden or recreation ground for public use. **2** an area of grassland or woodland belonging to a country house.

park *VERB* **parks, parking, parked** leave a vehicle somewhere for a time.
[from French]

parka *NOUN* **parkas** a warm jacket with a hood attached.
[via an Eskimo language from Russian]

Parkinson's disease *NOUN* a disease that makes a person's arms and legs shake and the muscles become stiff.
[named after an English doctor, James *Parkinson*]

parley *VERB* **parleys, parleying, parleyed** hold a discussion with someone.
▷ **parley** *noun*
[from French *parler* = speak]

parliament *NOUN* **parliaments** the assembly that makes a country's laws.
▷ **parliamentary** *adjective*
[same origin as *parley*]

parliamentarian *NOUN* **parliamentarians** a person who is good at debating things in parliament.

parlour *NOUN* **parlours** (*old use*) a sitting room.
[originally = a room in a monastery where the monks were allowed to talk: from French *parler* = speak]

parochial (*say* per-oh-kee-al) *ADJECTIVE* **1** to do with a church parish. **2** local; interested only in your own area • *a narrow parochial attitude.*

parody *NOUN* **parodies** an amusing imitation of the style of a writer, composer, literary work, etc.

parody *VERB* **parodies, parodying, parodied** make or be a parody of a person or thing.
[from *para-*[1] + Greek *oide* = song]

parole *NOUN* the release of a prisoner before the end of his or her sentence on condition of good behaviour • *He was on parole.*
▷ **parole** *verb*
[French, = word of honour]

paroxysm (*say* pa-roks-izm) *NOUN* **paroxysms** a sudden outburst of rage, jealousy, laughter, etc.
[from Greek *paroxynein* = to annoy or exasperate]

parquet (*say* par-kay) *NOUN* wooden blocks arranged in a pattern to make a floor.
[French]

parrot *NOUN* **parrots** a brightly-coloured tropical bird that can learn to repeat words etc.
[from French]

parry *VERB* **parries, parrying, parried** **1** turn aside an opponent's weapon or blow by using your own to block it. **2** avoid an awkward question skilfully.
[from Italian *parare* = defend]

parse *VERB* **parses, parsing, parsed** state what is the grammatical form and function of a word or words in a sentence.
[origin unknown]

parsimonious *ADJECTIVE* stingy; very sparing in the use of something.
▷ **parsimony** *noun*
[from Latin]

parsley *NOUN* a plant with crinkled green leaves used to flavour and decorate food.
[via Old English from Latin]

parsnip *NOUN* **parsnips** a plant with a pointed pale-yellow root used as a vegetable.
[from old French]

parson *NOUN* **parsons** a member of the clergy, especially a rector or vicar.
[from old French *persone* = person]

parsonage *NOUN* **parsonages** a rectory or vicarage.

part *NOUN* **parts** **1** some but not all of a thing or number of things; anything that belongs to something bigger. **2** the character played by an actor or actress. **3** the words spoken by a character in a play. **4** how much a person or thing is involved in something • *She played a huge part in her daughter's success.* **5** one side in an agreement or in a dispute or quarrel.
- **take in good part** not be offended at something.
- **take part** join in an activity.

part *VERB* **parts, parting, parted** separate or divide.
- **part with** give away or get rid of something.
[from Latin]

partake *VERB* **partakes, partaking, partook, partaken** **1** eat or drink something • *We all partook of the food.* **2** take part in something.
[from *part* + *take*]

part exchange *NOUN* giving something that you own, as part of the price of what you are buying.

Parthian shot *NOUN* **Parthian shots** a sharp remark made by a person who is just leaving.
[named after the horsemen of Parthia (an ancient kingdom in what is now Iran), who were famous for shooting arrows at the enemy while retreating]

partial *ADJECTIVE* **1** not complete or total • *a partial eclipse.* **2** favouring one side more than the other; biased or unfair.
▷ **partially** *adverb* **partiality** *noun*
- **be partial to** be fond of something.

A B C D E F G H I J K L M N O **P** Q R S T U V W X Y Z

participate *VERB* **participates, participating, participated** take part or have a share in something.
▷ **participant** *noun* **participation** *noun* **participator** *noun*
[from Latin *pars* = part + *capere* = take]

participle *NOUN* **participles** a word formed from a verb (e.g. *gone, going; guided, guiding*) and used with an auxiliary verb to form certain tenses (e.g. *It has gone. It is going*) or the passive (e.g. *We were guided to our seats*), or as an adjective (e.g. *a guided missile; a guiding light*). The **past participle** (e.g. *gone, guided*) describes a completed action or past condition. The **present participle** (which ends in *-ing*) describes a continuing action or condition.
[from Latin *particeps* = taking part]

particle *NOUN* **particles** a very small piece or amount.
[from Latin, = little part]

particoloured *ADJECTIVE* partly of one colour and partly of another; variegated.

particular *ADJECTIVE* **1** of this one and no other; individual • *This particular stamp is very rare.* **2** special • *Take particular care of it.* **3** giving something close attention; choosing carefully • *He is very particular about his clothes.*
▷ **particularly** *adverb* **particularity** *noun*

particular *NOUN* **particulars** a detail or single fact • *Can you give me the particulars of the case?*
- **in particular 1** especially • *We liked this one in particular.* **2** special • *We did nothing in particular.*
[same origin as *particle*]

parting *NOUN* **partings 1** leaving or separation. **2** a line where hair is combed away in different directions.

partisan *NOUN* **partisans 1** a strong supporter of a party or group etc. **2** a member of an organization resisting the authorities in a conquered country.

partisan *ADJECTIVE* strongly supporting a particular cause.
[via French from Italian]

partition *NOUN* **partitions 1** a thin wall that divides a room or space. **2** dividing something, especially a country, into separate parts.

partition *VERB* **partitions, partitioning, partitioned 1** divide something into separate parts. **2** divide a room or space by means of a partition.
[from Latin *partitio* = division]

partly *ADVERB* to some extent but not completely.

partner *NOUN* **partners 1** one of a pair of people who do something together, such as dancing or playing a game. **2** a person who jointly owns a business with one or more other people. **3** the person that someone is married to or is having a sexual relationship with.
▷ **partnership** *noun*

partner *VERB* **partners, partnering, partnered** be a person's partner.
[from Latin *partiri* = to divide or share]

part of speech *NOUN* **parts of speech** any of the groups into which words are divided in grammar (noun, pronoun, adjective, verb, adverb, preposition, conjunction, interjection).

partook *past tense* of **partake**.

partridge *NOUN* **partridges** a game bird with brown feathers.
[from old French]

part-time *ADJECTIVE* & *ADVERB* working for only some of the normal hours.
▷ **part-timer** *noun*

party *NOUN* **parties 1** a gathering of people to enjoy themselves • *a birthday party.* **2** a group working or travelling together. **3** an organized group of people with similar political beliefs • *the Labour Party.* **4** a person who is involved in an action or lawsuit etc. • *the guilty party.*
[from old French; related to *part*]

pas de deux (*say* pah der **der**) *NOUN* **pas de deux** a dance (e.g in a ballet) for two people.
[French, = step of two]

pass *VERB* **passes, passing, passed** **1** go past something; go or move in a certain direction. **2** move something in a certain direction • *Pass the cord through the ring.* **3** give or transfer something to another person • *Could you pass the butter?* **4** (in ball games) to kick or throw the ball to another player of your own side. **5** be successful in a test or examination. **6** approve or accept • *They passed a law.* **7** occupy time. **8** happen • *We heard what passed when they met.* **9** come to an end. **10** utter • *Pass a remark.* **11** (in a game, quiz, etc.) let your turn go by or choose not to answer.
- **pass out** **1** complete your military training. **2** faint.

pass *NOUN* **passes** **1** passing something. **2** a success in an examination. **3** (in ball games) kicking or throwing the ball to another player of your own side. **4** a permit to go in or out of a place. **5** a route through a gap in a range of mountains. **6** a critical state of affairs • *Things have come to a pretty pass!*
[from Latin *passus* = pace]

passable *ADJECTIVE* **1** able to be passed. **2** satisfactory but not especially good.
▷ **passably** *adverb*

passage *NOUN* **passages** **1** a way through something; a corridor. **2** a journey by sea or air. **3** a section of a piece of writing or music. **4** passing • *the passage of time.*
▷ **passageway** *noun*
[old French, = passing]

passé (*say* pas-say) *ADJECTIVE* no longer fashionable.
[French, = passed]

passenger *NOUN* **passengers** a person who is driven or carried in a car, train, ship, or aircraft etc.
[same origin as *passage*]

passer-by *NOUN* **passers-by** a person who happens to be going past something.

passion *NOUN* **passions** **1** strong emotion. **2** great enthusiasm.
- **the Passion** the sufferings of Jesus Christ at the Crucifixion.
[from Latin *passio* = suffering]

passionate *ADJECTIVE* full of passion.
▷ **passionately** *adverb*

passive *ADJECTIVE* **1** not resisting or fighting against something. **2** acted upon and not active. **3** (said about a form of a verb) used when the subject of the sentence receives the action, e.g. *was hit* in 'She was hit on the head'. (COMPARE **active**)
▷ **passively** *adverb* **passiveness** *noun* **passivity** *noun*
[from Latin *passivus* = capable of suffering]

passive smoking *NOUN* breathing in other people's cigarette smoke, thought of as a health risk.

Passover *NOUN* a Jewish religious festival commemorating the freeing of the Jews from slavery in Egypt.
[from *pass over*, because God spared the Jews from the fate which affected the Egyptians]

passport *NOUN* **passports** an official document that entitles the person holding it to travel abroad.
[from *pass* + *port*[1]]

password *NOUN* **passwords** **1** a secret word or phrase used to distinguish friends from enemies. **2** a word you need to key in to gain access to certain computer files.

past *ADJECTIVE* of the time gone by • *during the past week.*

past *NOUN* the time gone by.

past *PREPOSITION* **1** beyond • *Walk past the school.* **2** after • *It is past midnight.*
- **past it** (*slang*) too old to be able to do something.
[the old past participle of *pass*]

pasta *NOUN* an Italian food consisting of a dried paste made from flour and shaped into macaroni, spaghetti, etc.
[Italian, = paste]

paste *NOUN* **pastes** **1** a soft, moist, and sticky substance. **2** a glue, especially for paper. **3** a soft edible mixture • *tomato paste.* **4** a hard glassy substance used to make imitation jewellery.

paste *VERB* **pastes, pasting, pasted** **1** stick something onto a surface by using paste. **2** coat something with paste. **3** (*slang*) beat or thrash someone.
[from Greek]

pastel *NOUN* **pastels** **1** a crayon that is like chalk. **2** a light delicate colour.
[from Latin *pastellus* = woad]

pastern *NOUN* **pasterns** the part of a horse's foot between the fetlock and the hoof.
[from old French]

pasteurize *VERB* **pasteurizes, pasteurizing, pasteurized** purify milk by heating and then cooling it.
[named after a French scientist, Louis *Pasteur*, who invented the process]

pastille *NOUN* **pastilles** a small flavoured sweet for sucking.
[from Latin *pastillus* = lozenge]

pastime *NOUN* **pastimes** something you do to make time pass pleasantly; a hobby or game.

pastor *NOUN* **pastors** a member of the clergy who is in charge of a church or congregation.
[Latin, = shepherd]

pastoral *ADJECTIVE* **1** to do with country life • *a pastoral scene.* **2** to do with a pastor or a pastor's duties.

pastry *NOUN* **pastries** **1** dough made with flour, fat, and water, rolled flat and baked. **2** something made of pastry.
[from *paste*]

pasture *NOUN* **pastures** land covered with grass etc. that cattle, sheep, or horses can eat.

pasture *VERB* **pastures, pasturing, pastured** put animals to graze in a pasture.
[from Latin *pastum* = fed]

pasty[1] (*say* pas-tee) *NOUN* **pasties** pastry with a filling of meat and vegetables, baked without a dish to shape it.
[from old French *pasté* = paste or pastry]

pasty[2] (*say* pay-stee) *ADJECTIVE* looking pale and unhealthy.
[from *paste*]

pat *VERB* **pats, patting, patted** tap gently with the open hand or with something flat.

pat *NOUN* **pats** **1** a patting movement or sound. **2** a small piece of butter or other soft substance.
- **a pat on the back** praise.
[probably from the sound]

patch *NOUN* **patches** **1** a piece of material or metal etc. put over a hole or damaged place. **2** an area that is different from its surroundings. **3** a piece of ground • *the cabbage patch.* **4** a small area or piece of something • *There are patches of fog.*
- **not a patch on** (*informal*) not nearly as good as.

patch *VERB* **patches, patching, patched** put a patch on something.
- **patch up** **1** repair something roughly. **2** settle a quarrel.
[probably from old French *pieche* = piece]

patchwork *NOUN* needlework in which small pieces of different cloth are sewn edge to edge.

patchy *ADJECTIVE* occurring in patches; uneven.
▷ **patchily** *adverb* **patchiness** *noun*

pate *NOUN* **pates** (*old use*) the top of a person's head • *his bald pate.*
[origin unknown]

pâté (*say* pat-ay) *NOUN* **pâtés** paste made of meat or fish.
[French]

pâté de foie gras (*say* pat-ay der fwah grah) *NOUN* a paste or pie of goose liver.
[French, = paste of fat liver]

patent (*say* pat-ent or pay-tent) *NOUN* **patents** the official right given to an inventor to make or sell his or her invention and to prevent other people from copying it.

patent (*say* pay-tent) *ADJECTIVE* **1** protected by a patent • *patent medicines.* **2** obvious.

patent *VERB* **patents, patenting, patented** get a patent for something.
[originally, in *letters patent*, an open letter from a monarch or government recording a contract or granting a right: from Latin *patens* = lying open]

patentee (*say* pay-ten-tee or pat-en-tee) *NOUN* **patentees** a person who holds a patent.

patent leather *NOUN* glossy leather.

patently *ADVERB* clearly or obviously • *They were patently lying.*

paternal *ADJECTIVE* **1** to do with a father. **2** fatherly.
▷ **paternally** *adverb*
[from Latin *pater* = father]

paternalistic *ADJECTIVE* treating people in a paternal way, providing for their needs but giving them no responsibility.
▷ **paternalism** *noun*

paternity *NOUN* **1** fatherhood. **2** being the father of a particular baby.
[same origin as *paternal*]

path *NOUN* **paths** **1** a narrow way along which people or animals can walk. **2** a line along which a person or thing moves. **3** a course of action.
[from Old English]

pathetic *ADJECTIVE* **1** making you feel pity or sympathy. **2** miserably inadequate or useless • *a pathetic attempt.*
▷ **pathetically** *adverb*
[same origin as *pathos*]

pathological *ADJECTIVE* **1** to do with pathology or disease. **2** (*informal*) compulsive • *a pathological liar.*

pathology *NOUN* the study of diseases of the body.
▷ **pathologist** *noun*
[from Greek *pathos* = suffering, + *-logy*]

pathos (*say* pay-thoss) *NOUN* a quality of making people feel pity or sympathy.
[Greek, = feeling or suffering]
WORD FAMILY There are a number of English words that are related to *pathos* because part of their original meaning comes from the Greek word *pathos* meaning 'suffering or feeling'. These include *antipathy*, *apathy*, *empathy*, *homeopathy*, *osteopathy*, *pathetic*, *pathology*, *sympathy*, and *telepathy*.

-pathy *SUFFIX* forms nouns meaning 'feeling or suffering something' (e.g. *sympathy*, *telepathy*).
[from Greek *patheia* = feeling or suffering]

patience *NOUN* **1** being patient. **2** a card game for one person.

patient *ADJECTIVE* able to wait for a long time or put up with trouble or inconvenience without getting anxious or angry.
▷ **patiently** *adverb*

patient *NOUN* **patients** a person who is receiving treatment from a doctor or dentist.
[from Latin *patiens* = suffering]

patio *NOUN* **patios** a paved area beside a house.
[Spanish, = courtyard]

patriarch (*say* pay-tree-ark) *NOUN* **patriarchs** **1** the male who is head of a family or tribe. **2** a bishop of high rank in the Orthodox Christian churches.
▷ **patriarchal** *adjective*
[from Greek *patria* = family + *archein* = to rule]

patrician *NOUN* **patricians** an ancient Roman noble. (COMPARE **plebeian**)

patrician *ADJECTIVE* from a noble family; aristocratic.
[from Latin *patricius* = having a noble father]

patriot (*say* pay-tree-ot or pat-ree-ot) *NOUN* **patriots** a person who loves his or her country and supports it loyally.
▷ **patriotic** *adjective* **patriotically** *adverb* **patriotism** *noun*
[from Greek *patris* = fatherland]

patrol *VERB* **patrols, patrolling, patrolled** walk or travel regularly over an area in order to guard it and see that all is well.

patrol *NOUN* **patrols** **1** a patrolling group of people, ships, aircraft, etc. **2** a group of Scouts or Guides.
- **on patrol** patrolling.
[from French *patrouiller* = paddle in mud]

patron (*say* pay-tron) *NOUN* **patrons** **1** someone who supports a person or cause with money or encouragement. **2** a regular customer.
▷ **patronage** (*say* pat-ron-ij) *noun*
[from Latin *patronus* = protector]

patronize (*say* pat-ron-I'z) *VERB* **patronizes, patronizing, patronized** **1** be a regular customer of a particular shop, restaurant, etc. **2** talk to someone in a way that shows you think they are stupid or inferior to you.

patron saint *NOUN* **patron saints** a saint who is thought to protect a particular place or activity.

patter[1] *NOUN* a series of light tapping sounds.

patter *VERB* **patters, pattering, pattered** make light tapping sounds • *Rain pattered on the window panes.*
[from *pat*]

patter[2] *NOUN* the quick talk of a comedian, conjuror, salesperson, etc.
[originally = recite a prayer: from Latin *pater noster* = Our Father, the first words of a Christian prayer]

pattern *NOUN* **patterns** **1** a repeated arrangement of lines, shapes, or colours etc. **2** a thing to be copied in order to make something • *a dress pattern.* **3** the regular way in which something happens • *James Bond films follow a set pattern.* **4** an excellent example or model.
▷ **patterned** *adjective*
[same origin as *patron*]

patty *NOUN* **patties** a small pie or pasty.
[from *pâté*]

paucity *NOUN* (*formal*) smallness of number or quantity; scarcity.
[from Latin *pauci* = few]

paunch *NOUN* **paunches** a large belly.
[from old French]

pauper *NOUN* **paupers** a person who is very poor.
[Latin, = poor]

pause *NOUN* **pauses** a temporary stop in speaking or doing something.

pause *VERB* **pauses, pausing, paused** **1** stop speaking or doing something for a short time. **2** temporarily interrupt the playing of a CD, video tape, etc.
[from Greek *pauein* = to stop]

pave *VERB* **paves, paving, paved** lay a hard surface on a road or path etc.
▷ **paving-stone** *noun*
- **pave the way** prepare for something.
[from Latin *pavire* = ram down]

pavement *NOUN* **pavements** a paved path along the side of a street.

pavilion *NOUN* **pavilions** **1** a building for use by players and spectators etc., especially at a cricket ground. **2** an ornamental building or shelter used for dances, concerts, exhibitions, etc.
[from French *pavillon* = tent]

paw *NOUN* **paws** the foot of an animal that has claws.

paw *VERB* **paws, pawing, pawed** touch or scrape something with a hand or foot.
[from old French]

pawl *NOUN* **pawls** a bar with a catch that fits into the notches of a ratchet.
[origin unknown]

pawn[1] *NOUN* **pawns** **1** the least valuable piece in chess. **2** a person whose actions are controlled by somebody else.
[from Latin *pedo* = foot-soldier]

pawn[2] *VERB* **pawns, pawning, pawned** leave something with a pawnbroker as security for a loan.
[from old French *pan* = pledge]

pawnbroker *NOUN* **pawnbrokers** a shopkeeper who lends money to people in return for objects that they leave as security.
▷ **pawnshop** *noun*

pawpaw *NOUN* **pawpaws** an orange-coloured tropical fruit used as food.
[via Spanish and Portuguese from a South American language]

pay *VERB* **pays, paying, paid** **1** give money in return for goods or services. **2** give what is owed • *pay your debts; pay the rent.* **3** be profitable or worthwhile • *It pays to advertise.* **4** give or express • *Now pay attention. It's time we paid them a visit. He doesn't often pay her compliments.* **5** suffer a penalty. **6** let out a rope by loosening it gradually.
▷ **payer** *noun*
- **pay off** **1** pay in full what you owe. **2** be worthwhile or have good results • *All the preparation she did really paid off.*
- **pay up** pay the full amount you owe.

pay *NOUN* salary or wages.
[from Latin *pacare* = appease]

payable *ADJECTIVE* that must be paid.

PAYE *ABBREVIATION* pay-as-you-earn; a method of collecting income tax by deducting it from wages before these are paid to people who earn them.

payee *NOUN* **payees** a person to whom money is paid or is to be paid.

paymaster *NOUN* **paymasters** an official who pays troops or workmen etc.

payment *NOUN* **payments** **1** paying. **2** money paid.

payola *NOUN* (*American*) bribery in return for the promotion of a commercial product.
[an invented word]

payphone *NOUN* **payphones** a public telephone operated by coins or a card.

PC *ABBREVIATION* **1** personal computer. **2** police constable.

PE *ABBREVIATION* physical education.

pea *NOUN* **peas** the small round green seed of a climbing plant, growing inside a pod and used as a vegetable; the plant bearing these pods.
[via Old English from Greek]

peace *NOUN* **1** a time when there is no war, violence, or disorder. **2** quietness and calm.
[from Latin]

peaceable *ADJECTIVE* fond of peace; not quarrelsome or warlike.
▷ **peaceably** *adverb*

peaceful *ADJECTIVE* quiet and calm.
▷ **peacefully** *adverb* **peacefulness** *noun*

peach *NOUN* **peaches** **1** a round soft juicy fruit with a pinkish or yellowish skin and a large stone. **2** (*informal*) a thing of great quality • *a peach of a shot.*
[from old French]

peacock *NOUN* **peacocks** a large male bird with a long brightly-coloured tail that it can spread out like a fan.
▷ **peahen** *noun*
[via Old English from Latin]

peak *NOUN* **peaks** **1** a pointed top, especially of a mountain. **2** the highest or most intense part of something • *Traffic reaches its peak at 5 p.m.* **3** the part of a cap that sticks out in front.
▷ **peaked** *adjective*

peak *VERB* **peaks, peaking, peaked** reach its highest point or value.
[origin unknown]

peaky *ADJECTIVE* looking pale and ill.
[from Middle English *peak* = mope]

peal *NOUN* **peals** **1** the loud ringing of a bell or set of bells. **2** a loud burst of thunder or laughter.

peal *VERB* **peals, pealing, pealed** (said about bells) ring loudly.
[from *appeal*]

peanut *NOUN* **peanuts** a small round nut that grows in a pod in the ground.

peanut butter *NOUN* roasted peanuts crushed into a paste.

pear *NOUN* **pears** a juicy fruit that gets narrower near the stalk.
[via Old English from Latin]

pearl *NOUN* **pearls** a small shiny white ball found in the shells of some oysters and used as a jewel.
▷ **pearly** *adjective*
[from French]

pearl barley *NOUN* grains of barley made small by grinding.

peasant *NOUN* **peasants** a person who belongs to a farming community, especially in poor areas of the world.
▷ **peasantry** *noun*
[from Latin *paganus* = villager]

peat *NOUN* rotted plant material that can be dug out of the ground and used as fuel or in gardening.
▷ **peaty** *adjective*
[from Latin *peta*, probably from a Celtic word]

pebble *NOUN* **pebbles** a small round stone.
▷ **pebbly** *adjective*
[origin unknown]

peccadillo *NOUN* **peccadilloes** a small and unimportant fault or offence.
[Spanish, = little sin]

peck[1] *VERB* **pecks, pecking, pecked** **1** bite at something quickly with the beak. **2** kiss someone lightly on the cheek.

peck *NOUN* **pecks** **1** a quick bite by a bird. **2** a light kiss on the cheek.
[probably from old German]

peck[2] *NOUN* **pecks** a measure of grain or fruit etc. • *4 pecks = 1 bushel.*
[from old French]

peckish *ADJECTIVE* (*informal*) hungry.
[from *peck*[1] + *-ish*]

pectin *NOUN* a substance found in ripe fruits, causing jam to set firmly.
[from Greek *pektos* = fixed or set]

pectoral *ADJECTIVE* to do with the chest or breast • *pectoral muscles.*
[from Latin *pectus* = breast]

peculiar *ADJECTIVE* **1** strange or unusual. **2** belonging to a particular person, place, or thing; restricted • *The custom is peculiar to this tribe.* **3** special • *This point is of peculiar interest.*
▷ **peculiarly** *adverb* **peculiarity** *noun*
[from Latin *peculium* = private property]

pecuniary *ADJECTIVE* (*formal*) to do with money • *pecuniary aid.*
[from Latin *pecunia* = money (from *pecu* = cattle, because in early times wealth consisted in cattle and sheep)]

pedagogue (*say* ped-a-gog) *NOUN* **pedagogues** a teacher, especially one who teaches in a pedantic way.
[from Greek *paidagogos* = a slave who took a boy to school]

pedal *NOUN* **pedals** a lever pressed by the foot to operate a bicycle, car, machine, etc. or in certain musical instruments.

pedal *VERB* **pedals, pedalling, pedalled** use a pedal; move or work something, especially a bicycle, by means of pedals.
[from Latin *pedis* = of a foot]
WORD FAMILY There are a number of English words that are related to *pedal* because part of their original meaning comes from the Latin words *pedes* meaning 'feet' or *pedis* meaning 'of a foot'. These include *biped*, *centipede*, *millepede*, *pedestrian*, and *quadruped*. The word *expedite* derives from a Latin word meaning 'to free someone's feet', while the word *impede* comes from a Latin word meaning 'to shackle someone's feet'.

pedant *NOUN* **pedants** a pedantic person.
[from French *pédant* = schoolteacher]

pedantic *ADJECTIVE* too concerned with minor details or with sticking strictly to formal rules.
▷ **pedantically** *adverb*

peddle *VERB* **peddles, peddling, peddled** **1** go from house to house selling goods. **2** sell illegal drugs. **3** try to get people to accept an idea, way of life, etc.
[from *pedlar*]

pedestal *NOUN* **pedestals** the raised base on which a statue or pillar etc. stands.
- **put someone on a pedestal** admire him or her greatly.
[from Italian *piede* = foot, + *stall*[1]]

pedestrian *NOUN* **pedestrians** a person who is walking.

pedestrian *ADJECTIVE* ordinary and dull.
[same origin as *pedal*]

pedestrian crossing *NOUN* **pedestrian crossings** a place where pedestrians can cross the road safely.

pedigree *NOUN* **pedigrees** a list of a person's or animal's ancestors, especially to show how well an animal has been bred.
[from old French *pé de grue* = crane's foot (from the shape made by the lines on a family tree)]

pediment *NOUN* **pediments** a wide triangular part decorating the top of a building.
[origin unknown]

pedlar *NOUN* **pedlars** a person who goes from house to house selling small things.
[from Middle English *ped* = a hamper or basket (in which a pedlar carried his goods)]

peek *VERB* **peeks, peeking, peeked** have a quick or sly look at something.
▷ **peek** *noun*
[origin unknown]

peel *NOUN* **peels** the skin of certain fruits and vegetables.

peel *VERB* **peels, peeling, peeled** **1** remove the peel or covering from something. **2** come off in strips or layers. **3** lose a covering or skin.
[Middle English; related to Latin *pilare* = cut off the hair]

peelings *PLURAL NOUN* strips of skin peeled from potatoes etc.

peep *VERB* **peeps, peeping, peeped** **1** look quickly or secretly. **2** look through a narrow opening. **3** come slowly or briefly into view • *The moon peeped out from behind the clouds.*
▷ **peep** *noun* **peephole** *noun*
[origin unknown]

peer[1] *VERB* **peers, peering, peered** look at something closely or with difficulty.
[perhaps from *appear*]

peer[2] *NOUN* **peers** **1** a noble. **2** someone who is equal to another in rank, merit, or age etc. • *She had no peer.*
▷ **peeress** *noun*
[from Latin *par* = equal]

peerage *NOUN* **peerages** **1** peers. **2** the rank of peer • *He was raised to the peerage.*

peer group *NOUN* **peer groups** a group of people of roughly the same age or status.

peerless *ADJECTIVE* without an equal; better than the others.

peer pressure *NOUN* the pressure to do what others in your peer group do.

peeved *ADJECTIVE* (*informal*) annoyed. [from *peevish*]

peevish *ADJECTIVE* irritable. [origin unknown]

peewit *NOUN* **peewits** a lapwing. [imitating its call]

peg *NOUN* **pegs** a piece of wood or metal or plastic for fastening things together or for hanging things on.

peg *VERB* **pegs, pegging, pegged** **1** fix something with pegs. **2** keep wages or prices at a fixed level.
- **peg away** work diligently; persevere.
- **peg out** (*slang*) die.

[probably from old Dutch]

pejorative (*say* pij-orra-tiv) *ADJECTIVE* showing disapproval; insulting or derogatory. [from Latin *pejor* = worse]

peke *NOUN* **pekes** (*informal*) a Pekingese.

Pekinese or **Pekingese** *NOUN* **Pekinese** or **Pekingese** a small kind of dog with short legs, a flat face, and long silky hair. [from *Peking*, the old name of Beijing, the capital of China (where the breed came from)]

pelican *NOUN* **pelicans** a large bird with a pouch in its long beak for storing fish. [from Greek]

pelican crossing *NOUN* **pelican crossings** a place where pedestrians can cross a street safely by operating lights that signal traffic to stop. [from *pe(destrian) li(ght) con(trolled)*]

pellet *NOUN* **pellets** a tiny ball of metal, food, paper, etc. [from Latin *pila* = ball]

pell-mell *ADVERB* & *ADJECTIVE* in a hasty untidy way. [from old French]

pelmet *NOUN* **pelmets** an ornamental strip of wood or material etc. above a window, used to conceal a curtain rail. [probably from French]

pelt[1] *VERB* **pelts, pelting, pelted** **1** throw a lot of things at someone. **2** run fast. **3** rain very hard.
- **at full pelt** as fast as possible.

[origin unknown]

pelt[2] *NOUN* **pelts** an animal skin, especially with the fur still on it. [from Latin *pellis* = skin or leather]

pelvis *NOUN* **pelvises** the round framework of bones at the lower end of the spine.
▷ **pelvic** *adjective*

[Latin, = basin (because of its shape)]

pen[1] *NOUN* **pens** an instrument with a point for writing with ink. [from Latin *penna* = feather (because a pen was originally a sharpened quill)]

pen[2] *NOUN* **pens** an enclosure for cattle, sheep, hens, or other animals.

pen *VERB* **pens, penning, penned** shut animals etc. into a pen or other enclosed space. [from Old English]

pen[3] *NOUN* **pens** a female swan. (COMPARE **cob**) [origin unknown]

penal (*say* peen-al) *ADJECTIVE* to do with the punishment of criminals, especially in prisons. [from Latin *poena* = punishment]

penalize *VERB* **penalizes, penalizing, penalized** punish; put a penalty on someone.
▷ **penalization** *noun*

penalty *NOUN* **penalties** **1** a punishment. **2** a point or advantage given to one side in a game when a member of the other side has broken a rule, e.g. a free kick at goal in football.

penance *NOUN* a punishment that you willingly suffer to show that you regret something wrong that you have done. [from Latin *poenitentia* = penitence]

pence *PLURAL NOUN*, SEE **penny**. [from *pennies*]

a b c d e f g h i j k l m n o p q r s t u v w x y z

penchant (*say* pahn-shahn) *NOUN* a liking or inclination • *She has a penchant for old films.*
[French]

pencil *NOUN* **pencils** an instrument for drawing or writing, made of a thin stick of graphite or coloured chalk etc. enclosed in a cylinder of wood or metal.

pencil *VERB* **pencils, pencilling, pencilled** write, draw, or mark with a pencil.
[from Latin *penicillum* = paintbrush]

pendant *NOUN* **pendants** an ornament worn hanging on a cord or chain round the neck.
[from Latin *pendens* = hanging]
WORD FAMILY There are a number of English words that are related to *pendant* because part of their original meaning comes from the Latin words *pendere* meaning 'to hang' or *pendens* meaning 'hanging'. These include *append, depend, impending, pendent, pending, pendulous, pendulum, propensity,* and *suspend.*

pendent *ADJECTIVE* hanging down.
[same origin as *pendant*]

pending *ADJECTIVE* **1** waiting to be decided or settled. **2** about to happen.

pending *PREPOSITION* while waiting for; until • *Please take charge, pending his return.*
[same origin as *pendant*]

pendulous *ADJECTIVE* hanging down.
[from Latin]

pendulum *NOUN* **pendulums** a weight hung so that it can swing to and fro, especially in the works of a clock.
[from Latin, = something hanging down]

penetrable *ADJECTIVE* able to be penetrated.

penetrate *VERB* **penetrates, penetrating, penetrated** make or find a way through or into something; pierce.
▷ **penetration** *noun* **penetrative** *adjective*
[from Latin *penitus* = inside]

penetrating *ADJECTIVE* **1** showing great insight. **2** clearly heard above other sounds.

penfriend *NOUN* **penfriends** a friend who you write to without meeting.

penguin *NOUN* **penguins** an Antarctic seabird that cannot fly but uses its wings as flippers for swimming.
[origin unknown]

penicillin *NOUN* an antibiotic obtained from mould.
[from the Latin name of the mould used]

peninsula *NOUN* **peninsulas** a piece of land that is almost surrounded by water.
▷ **peninsular** *adjective*
[from Latin *paene* = almost + *insula* = island]

penis (*say* peen-iss) *NOUN* **penises** the part of the body with which a male urinates and has sexual intercourse.
[Latin, = tail]

penitence *NOUN* regret for having done wrong.
▷ **penitent** *adjective* **penitently** *adverb*
[from Latin *paenitere* = to make someone sorry]

penknife *NOUN* **penknives** a small folding knife.
[originally used for sharpening quill pens]

pen-name *NOUN* **pen-names** a name used by an author instead of his or her real name.

pennant *NOUN* **pennants** a long pointed flag.
[a mixture of *pendant* and *pennon* = the flag on a knight's lance]

penniless *ADJECTIVE* having no money; very poor.

penny *NOUN* **pennies** for separate coins, **pence** for a sum of money) **1** a British coin worth $\frac{1}{100}$ of a pound. **2** a former coin worth $\frac{1}{12}$ of a shilling.
[from Old English]

pension *NOUN* **pensions** an income consisting of regular payments made to someone who is retired, widowed, or disabled.

pension *VERB* **pensions, pensioning, pensioned** pay a pension to someone.
[from Latin *pensio* = payment]

pensioner *NOUN* **pensioners** a person who receives a pension.

pensive *ADJECTIVE* deep in thought.
▷ **pensively** *adverb*
[from Latin *pensare* = consider]

penta- *PREFIX* five.
[from Greek]

pentagon *NOUN* **pentagons** a flat shape with five sides and five angles.
▷ **pentagonal** (*say* pent-ag-on-al) *adjective*
- **the Pentagon** a five-sided building in Washington, headquarters of the leaders of the American armed forces.
[from *penta-* + Greek *gonia* = angle]

pentameter *NOUN* **pentameters** a line of verse with five rhythmic beats.
[from *penta-* + Greek *metron* = measure]

pentathlon *NOUN* **pentathlons** an athletic contest consisting of five events.
[from *penta-* + Greek *athlon* = contest]

Pentecost *NOUN* **1** the Jewish harvest festival, fifty days after Passover. **2** Whit Sunday.
[from Greek *pentekoste* = fiftieth (day)]

penthouse *NOUN* **penthouses** a flat at the top of a tall building.
[from Latin *appendicium* = something added on, later confused with French *pente* = slope and with *house*]

pent-up *ADJECTIVE* shut in • *pent-up feelings.*
[old past participle of *pen*[2]]

penultimate *ADJECTIVE* last but one.
[from Latin *paene* = almost, + *ultimate*]

penumbra *NOUN* **penumbras** or **penumbrae** an area that is partly but not fully shaded, e.g. during an eclipse.
[from Latin *paene* = almost + *umbra* = shade]

penurious (*say* pin-yoor-ee-us) *ADJECTIVE* (*formal*) **1** in great poverty. **2** mean or stingy.
[from Latin *penuria* = poverty]

penury (*say* pen-yoor-ee) *NOUN* (*formal*) great poverty.

peony *NOUN* **peonies** a plant with large round red, pink, or white flowers.
[named after *Paion*, physician of the Greek gods (because the plant was once used in medicines)]

people *PLURAL NOUN* human beings; persons, especially those belonging to a particular country, area, or group etc.

people *NOUN* **peoples** a community or nation • *a warlike people; the English-speaking peoples.*

people *VERB* **peoples, peopling, peopled** fill a place with people; populate.
[from Latin]

people carrier *NOUN* **people carriers** a large car which carries up to eight people.

pep *NOUN* (*slang*) vigour or energy.
[from *pepper*]

pepper *NOUN* **peppers** **1** a hot-tasting powder used to flavour food. **2** a bright green, red, or yellow vegetable.
▷ **peppery** *adjective*

pepper *VERB* **peppers, peppering, peppered** **1** sprinkle with pepper. **2** pelt with many small objects.
[from Old English]

peppercorn *NOUN* **peppercorns** the dried black berry from which pepper is made.

peppermint *NOUN* **peppermints** **1** a kind of mint used for flavouring. **2** a sweet flavoured with this mint.
[because of its sharp taste]

pepperoni *NOUN* beef and pork sausage seasoned with pepper.
[from Italian *peperone* = chilli]

pep talk *NOUN* **pep talks** (*informal*) a talk given to someone to encourage them.

per *PREPOSITION* for each • *The charge is £2 per person.*
[from Latin, = through]

per- *PREFIX* **1** through (as in *perforate*). **2** thoroughly (as in *perturb*). **3** away entirely; towards badness (as in *pervert*).
[from Latin]

perambulate *VERB* **perambulates, perambulating, perambulated** (*formal*) walk through or round an area.
▷ **perambulation** *noun*
[from *per-* + Latin *ambulare* = to walk]

perambulator *NOUN* **perambulators** (*formal*) a baby's pram.

per annum *ADVERB* for each year; yearly.
[from *per* + Latin *annus* = year]

per capita (*say* kap-it-a) *ADVERB* & *ADJECTIVE* for each person.
[Latin, = for heads]

perceive *VERB* **perceives, perceiving, perceived** see, notice, or understand something.
[from Latin *percipere* = seize, understand]

per cent *ADVERB* for or in every hundred • *three per cent* (3%).
[from *per* + Latin *centum* = hundred]

percentage *NOUN* **percentages** an amount or rate expressed as a proportion of 100.

perceptible *ADJECTIVE* able to be seen or noticed.
▷ **perceptibly** *adverb* **perceptibility** *noun*

perception *NOUN* **perceptions** **1** the ability to notice or understand something. **2** receiving information through the senses, especially the sense of sight.
[same origin as *perceive*]

perceptive *ADJECTIVE* quick to notice or understand things.

perch[1] *NOUN* **perches** **1** a place where a bird sits or rests. **2** a seat high up.

perch *VERB* **perches**, **perching**, **perched** rest or place on a perch.
[from Latin *pertica* = pole]

perch[2] *NOUN* **perch** an edible freshwater fish.
[from Greek]

percipient *ADJECTIVE* (*formal*) quick to notice or understand things; perceptive.
▷ **percipience** *noun*
[same origin as *perceive*]

percolate *VERB* **percolates**, **percolating**, **percolated** flow through small holes or spaces.
▷ **percolation** *noun*
[from *per-* + Latin *colum* = strainer]

percolator *NOUN* **percolators** a pot for making coffee, in which boiling water percolates through coffee grounds.

percussion *NOUN* **1** musical instruments (e.g. drums, cymbals) played by being struck or shaken. **2** the striking of one thing against another.
▷ **percussive** *adjective*
[from Latin *percussum* = hit]

peregrine *NOUN* **peregrines** a kind of falcon.
[from Latin *peregrinus* = travelling (because it migrates)]

peremptory *ADJECTIVE* giving commands and expecting to be obeyed at once.
[from Latin *peremptorius* = final, decisive]

perennial *ADJECTIVE* lasting for many years; keeping on recurring.
▷ **perennially** *adverb*

perennial *NOUN* **perennials** a plant that lives for many years.
[from *per-* + Latin *annus* = year]

perestroika (*say* peri-**stroik**-a) *NOUN* restructuring a system, especially the political and economic system of the former Soviet Union.
[Russian, = restructuring]

perfect (*say* **per**-fikt) *ADJECTIVE* **1** so good that it cannot be made any better. **2** complete • *a perfect stranger.* **3** (said about a tense of a verb) showing a completed action, e.g. *He has arrived.*
▷ **perfectly** *adverb*

perfect (*say* per-**fekt**) *VERB* **perfects**, **perfecting**, **perfected** make a thing perfect.
▷ **perfection** *noun*
- **to perfection** perfectly.
[from Latin *perfectum* = completed]

perfectionist *NOUN* **perfectionists** a person who is only satisfied if something is done perfectly.

perfidious *ADJECTIVE* treacherous or disloyal.
▷ **perfidiously** *adverb* **perfidy** *noun*
[from *per-* = becoming bad + Latin *fides* = faith]

perforate *VERB* **perforates**, **perforating**, **perforated** **1** make tiny holes in something, especially so that it can be torn off easily. **2** pierce.
▷ **perforated** *adjective* **perforation** *noun*
[from *per-* + Latin *forare* = bore through]

perforce *ADVERB* (*old use*) by necessity; unavoidably.
[from old French *par force* = by force]

perform *VERB* **performs**, **performing**, **performed** **1** do something in front of an audience • *They performed the play in the school hall.* **2** do or carry out something • *Surgeons had to perform an emergency operation.*
▷ **performance** *noun* **performer** *noun*
[from old French]

perfume *NOUN* **perfumes** **1** a pleasant smell. **2** a liquid for giving something a pleasant smell; scent.
▷ **perfume** *verb* **perfumery** *noun*
[originally used of smoke from something burning: via French from old Italian *parfumare* = to smoke through]

perfunctory *ADJECTIVE* done without much care or interest • *a perfunctory glance.*
▷ **perfunctorily** *adverb*
[from Latin]

pergola *NOUN* **pergolas** an arch formed by climbing plants growing over trellis-work.
[Italian]

perhaps *ADVERB* it may be; possibly.
[from *per* + Middle English *hap* = luck]

peri- *PREFIX* around (as in *perimeter*).
[from Greek]

peril *NOUN* **perils** danger.
▷ **perilous** *adjective* **perilously** *adverb*
- **at your peril** at your own risk.
[from Latin *periculum* = danger]

perimeter *NOUN* **perimeters** **1** the outer edge or boundary of something. **2** the distance round the edge.
[from *peri-* + Greek *metron* = measure]
USAGE Do not confuse with **parameter**.

period *NOUN* **periods** **1** a length of time. **2** the time allowed for a lesson in school. **3** the time when a woman menstruates. **4** (in punctuation) a full stop.
[from Greek *periodos* = course or cycle (of events)]

periodic *ADJECTIVE* occurring at regular intervals.
▷ **periodically** *adverb*

periodical *NOUN* **periodicals** a magazine published at regular intervals (e.g. monthly).

periodic table *NOUN* a table in which the chemical elements are arranged in order of increasing atomic number.

peripatetic *ADJECTIVE* going from place to place.
[from *peri-* + Greek *patein* = to walk]

peripheral *ADJECTIVE* **1** of minor importance. **2** at the edge or boundary.

periphery (*say* per-**if**-er-ee) *NOUN* **peripheries** the part at the edge or boundary.
[from Greek, = circumference]

periphrasis (*say* per-**if**-ra-sis) *NOUN* **periphrases** a roundabout way of saying something; a circumlocution.
[from *peri-* + Greek *phrasis* = speech]

periscope *NOUN* **periscopes** a device with a tube and mirrors with which a person in a trench or submarine etc. can see things that are otherwise out of sight.
[from *peri-* + Greek *skopein* = look at]

perish *VERB* **perishes, perishing, perished** **1** die; be destroyed. **2** rot • *The rubber ring has perished.*
▷ **perishable** *adjective*
[from *per-* + Latin *ire* = go]

perished *ADJECTIVE* (*informal*) feeling very cold.

perishing *ADJECTIVE* (*informal*) freezing cold • *It's perishing outside!*

periwinkle[1] *NOUN* **periwinkles** a trailing plant with blue or white flowers.
[from Latin]

periwinkle[2] *NOUN* **periwinkles** a winkle.
[origin unknown]

perjure *VERB* **perjures, perjuring, perjured**
- **perjure yourself** commit perjury.

perjury *NOUN* telling a lie while you are on oath to speak the truth.
[from Latin *perjurare* = break an oath]

perk[1] *VERB* **perks, perking, perked**
- **perk up** make or become more cheerful.
[from *perch*[1]]

perk[2] *NOUN* **perks** (*informal*) something extra given to a worker • *Free bus travel is one of the perks of the job.*
[from *perquisite*]

perky *ADJECTIVE* lively and cheerful.
▷ **perkily** *adverb*
[from *perk*[1]]

perm *NOUN* **perms** treatment of the hair to give it long-lasting waves or curls.
▷ **perm** *verb*
[short for *permanent wave*]

permafrost *NOUN* a permanently frozen layer of soil in polar regions.
[from *permanent* + *frost*]

permanent *ADJECTIVE* lasting for always or for a very long time.
▷ **permanently** *adverb* **permanence** *noun*
[from *per-* + Latin *manens* = remaining]

permeable *ADJECTIVE* able to be permeated by fluids etc.
▷ **permeability** *noun*

permeate *VERB* **permeates, permeating, permeated** spread into every part of something; pervade • *Smoke had permeated the hall.*
▷ **permeation** *noun*
[from *per-* + Latin *meare* = to pass]

permissible *ADJECTIVE* permitted or allowable.

permission *NOUN* the right to do something, given by someone in authority; authorization.
[same origin as *permit*]

permissive *ADJECTIVE* letting people do what they wish; tolerant or liberal.

permit (*say* per-**mit**) *VERB* **permits, permitting, permitted** give permission or consent or a chance to do something; allow.

permit (*say* **per**-mit) *NOUN* **permits** written or printed permission to do something or go somewhere.
[from *per-* + Latin *mittere* = send or let go]

permutation *NOUN* **permutations**
1 changing the order of a set of things. **2** a changed order • *3, 1, 2 is a permutation of 1, 2, 3.*
[from *per-* + Latin *mutare* = to change]

pernicious *ADJECTIVE* very harmful.
[from Latin *pernicies* = destruction]

peroration *NOUN* **perorations** an elaborate ending to a speech.
[from *per-* + Latin *oratio* = speech, oration]

peroxide *NOUN* a chemical used for bleaching hair.
[from *per-* + *oxide*]

perpendicular *ADJECTIVE* upright; at a right angle (90°) to a line or surface.
[from Latin *perpendiculum* = plumb line]

perpetrate *VERB* **perpetrates, perpetrating, perpetrated** commit or be guilty of a crime, error, etc.
▷ **perpetration** *noun* **perpetrator** *noun*
[from *per-* + Latin *patrare* = make something happen]

perpetual *ADJECTIVE* lasting for a long time; continual.
▷ **perpetually** *adverb*
[from Latin *perpes* = uninterrupted]

perpetuate *VERB* **perpetuates, perpetuating, perpetuated** cause to continue or be remembered for a long time • *The statue will perpetuate his memory.*
▷ **perpetuation** *noun*

perpetuity *NOUN* being perpetual.
- **in perpetuity** for ever.

perplex *VERB* **perplexes, perplexing, perplexed** bewilder or puzzle somebody.
▷ **perplexity** *noun*
[from *per-* + Latin *plexus* = twisted together]

perquisite (*say* **per**-kwiz-it) *NOUN* **perquisites** (*formal*) something extra given to a worker; a perk • *Use of the firm's car is a perquisite of this job.*
[originally = property that you got yourself, as opposed to property left to you: from *per-* + Latin *quaerere* = seek]

perry *NOUN* a drink rather like cider, made from pears.
[from old French; related to *pear*]

persecute *VERB* **persecutes, persecuting, persecuted** be continually cruel to somebody, especially because you disagree with his or her beliefs.
▷ **persecution** *noun* **persecutor** *noun*
[from Latin *persecutum* = pursued]

persevere *VERB* **perseveres, persevering, persevered** go on doing something even though it is difficult.
▷ **perseverance** *noun*
[from *per-* + Latin *severus* = strict]

Persian *ADJECTIVE* to do with Persia, a country in the Middle East now called Iran, or its people or language.

Persian *NOUN* the language of Persia.

persist *VERB* **persists, persisting, persisted** **1** continue firmly or obstinately • *She persists in breaking the rules.* **2** continue to exist • *The custom persists in some countries.*
▷ **persistent** *adjective* **persistently** *adverb* **persistence** *noun* **persistency** *noun*
[from *per-* + Latin *sistere* = to stand]

person *NOUN* **people** or **persons** **1** a human being; a man, woman, or child. **2** (*in grammar*) any of the three groups of personal pronouns and forms taken by verbs. The **first person** (= *I*, *me*, *we*, *us*) refers to the person(s) speaking; the **second person** (= *you*) refers to the person(s) spoken to; the **third person** (= *he*, *him*, *she*, *her*, *it*, *they*, *them*) refers to the person(s) spoken about.
- **in person** being actually present oneself • *She hopes to be there in person.*
[from Latin *persona* = mask used by an actor]

personable *ADJECTIVE* pleasing in appearance and behaviour.

personage *NOUN* **personages** an important or well-known person.

personal *ADJECTIVE* **1** belonging to, done by, or concerning a particular person • *personal belongings.* **2** private • *We have personal business to discuss.* **3** criticizing a person's appearance, character, or private affairs • *making personal remarks.*
USAGE Do not confuse with **personnel**.

personal computer *NOUN* **personal computers** a small computer designed to be used by one person at a time.

personality *NOUN* **personalities** **1** a person's character • *She has a cheerful personality.* **2** a well-known person • *a TV personality.*

personally *ADVERB* **1** in person; being actually there • *The head thanked me personally.* **2** as far as I am concerned • *Personally, I'd rather stay here.*

personal stereo *NOUN* **personal stereos** a small portable cassette player with headphones.

personify *VERB* **personifies**, **personifying**, **personified** represent a quality or idea etc. as a person.
▷ **personification** *noun*

personnel *NOUN* the people employed by a firm or other large organization.
[French, = personal]
USAGE Do not confuse with **personal**.

perspective *NOUN* **perspectives** **1** the impression of depth and space in a picture or scene. **2** a person's point of view.
- **in perspective** giving a well-balanced view of things • *Try to see the problem in perspective.*
[from Latin *perspicere* = look at closely]

Perspex *NOUN* (*trademark*) a tough transparent plastic used instead of glass.
[from Latin *perspectum* = looked through]

perspicacious *ADJECTIVE* quick to notice or understand things.
▷ **perspicacity** *noun*
[same origin as *perspective*]

perspire *VERB* **perspires**, **perspiring**, **perspired** sweat.
▷ **perspiration** *noun*
[from *per-* + Latin *spirare* = breathe]

persuade *VERB* **persuades**, **persuading**, **persuaded** make someone believe or agree to do something.
▷ **persuasion** *noun* **persuasive** *adjective*
[from *per-* + Latin *suadere* = advise or induce]

pert *ADJECTIVE* cheeky.
▷ **pertly** *adverb* **pertness** *noun*
[from old French]

pertain *VERB* **pertains**, **pertaining**, **pertained** be relevant to something • *evidence pertaining to the crime.*
[from Latin *pertinere* = belong]

pertinacious *ADJECTIVE* (*formal*) persistent and determined.
▷ **pertinaciously** *adverb* **pertinacity** *noun*
[from *per-* + Latin *tenax* = holding fast, tenacious]

pertinent *ADJECTIVE* relevant to what you are talking about.
▷ **pertinently** *adverb* **pertinence** *noun*

perturb *VERB* **perturbs**, **perturbing**, **perturbed** worry someone.
▷ **perturbation** *noun*
[from *per-* + Latin *turbare* = disturb]

peruse (*say* per-ooz) *VERB* **peruses**, **perusing**, **perused** read something carefully.
▷ **perusal** *noun*
[from *per-* + Latin *usitari* = use often]

pervade *VERB* **pervades, pervading, pervaded** spread all through something.
▷ **pervasion** *noun* **pervasive** *adjective*
[from *per-* + Latin *vadere* = go]

perverse *ADJECTIVE* obstinately doing something different from what is reasonable or required.
▷ **perversely** *adverb* **perversity** *noun*
[same origin as *pervert*]

pervert (*say* per-**vert**) *VERB* **perverts, perverting, perverted 1** turn something from the right course of action • *By false evidence they perverted the course of justice.* **2** make a person behave wickedly or abnormally.
▷ **perversion** *noun*

pervert (*say* **per**-vert) *NOUN* **perverts** a person whose sexual behaviour is thought to be unnatural or disgusting.
[from *per-* + Latin *vertere* = to turn]

Pesach *NOUN* the Passover festival.
[Hebrew]

pessimist *NOUN* **pessimists** a person who expects that things will turn out badly. (COMPARE **optimist**)
▷ **pessimism** *noun* **pessimistic** *adjective* **pessimistically** *adverb*
[from Latin *pessimus* = worst]

pest *NOUN* **pests 1** a destructive insect or animal, such as a locust or a mouse. **2** a nuisance.
[from Latin *pestis* = plague]

pester *VERB* **pesters, pestering, pestered** keep annoying someone by frequent questions or requests.
[from French *empestrer* = infect with plague]

pesticide *NOUN* **pesticides** a substance for killing harmful insects and other pests.
[from *pest* + *-cide*]

pestilence *NOUN* **pestilences** a deadly epidemic.
[same origin as *pest*]

pestilential *ADJECTIVE* troublesome or harmful.
[same origin as *pest*]

pestle *NOUN* **pestles** a tool with a heavy rounded end for pounding substances in a mortar.
[from Latin]

pet *NOUN* **pets 1** a tame animal kept for companionship and pleasure. **2** a person treated as a favourite • *teacher's pet.*

pet *ADJECTIVE* favourite or particular • *Natural history is my pet subject.*

pet *VERB* **pets, petting, petted** treat or fondle someone affectionately.
[origin unknown]

petal *NOUN* **petals** one of the separate coloured outer parts of a flower.
[from Greek *petalos* = spread out, unfolded]

peter *VERB* **peters, petering, petered**
- **peter out** become gradually less and cease to exist.
[origin unknown]

petition *NOUN* **petitions** a formal request for something, especially a written one signed by many people.

petition *VERB* **petitions, petitioning, petitioned** request something by a petition.
▷ **petitioner** *noun*
[from Latin *petere* = claim or ask for]

petrel *NOUN* **petrels** a kind of seabird.
[perhaps named after St Peter, who tried to walk on the water (because the bird flies just over the waves with its legs dangling)]

petrify *VERB* **petrifies, petrifying, petrified 1** make someone so terrified that he or she cannot move. **2** turn to stone.
▷ **petrifaction** *noun*
[from Greek *petra* = rock]

petrochemical *NOUN* **petrochemicals** a chemical substance obtained from petroleum or natural gas.

petrol *NOUN* a liquid made from petroleum, used as fuel for engines.

petroleum *NOUN* an oil found underground that is refined to make fuel (e.g. petrol, paraffin) or for use in dry-cleaning etc.
[from Greek *petra* = rock + Latin *oleum* = oil]

petticoat *NOUN* **petticoats** a woman's or girl's dress-length piece of underwear worn under a skirt or dress.
[from *petty* = little, + *coat*]

pettifogging *ADJECTIVE* paying too much attention to unimportant details.
[from an old slang word *pettifogger* = a lawyer who dealt with trivial cases]

petting *NOUN* affectionate touching or fondling.

pettish *ADJECTIVE* irritable or bad-tempered; peevish.

petty *ADJECTIVE* **pettier, pettiest**
1 unimportant or trivial • *petty regulations.*
2 mean and small-minded.
▷ **pettily** *adverb* **pettiness** *noun*
[from French *petit* = small]

petty cash *NOUN* cash kept by an office for small payments.

petty officer *NOUN* **petty officers** an NCO in the navy.

petulant *ADJECTIVE* irritable or bad-tempered, especially in a childish way; peevish.
▷ **petulantly** *adverb* **petulance** *noun*
[from old French]

petunia *NOUN* **petunias** a garden plant with funnel-shaped flowers.
[from *petun*, an old word for tobacco (because it is related to the tobacco plant)]

pew *NOUN* **pews** a long wooden seat, usually fixed in rows, in a church.
[from old French; related to *podium*]

pewter *NOUN* a grey alloy of tin and lead.
[from old French]

pH *NOUN* a measure of the acidity or alkalinity of a solution. Pure water has a pH of 7, acids have a pH between 0 and 7, and alkalis have a pH between 7 and 14.
[from the initial letter of German *Potenz* = power, + H, the symbol for hydrogen]

phalanx *NOUN* **phalanxes** a number of people or soldiers in a close formation.
[from Greek]

phantasm *NOUN* **phantasms** a phantom.
[from Greek *phantasma* = a vision, a ghost]

phantom *NOUN* **phantoms** **1** a ghost.
2 something that does not really exist.
[from old French; related to *phantasm*]

Pharaoh (*say* fair-oh) *NOUN* **Pharaohs** the title of the king of ancient Egypt.
[from ancient Egyptian *pr-'o* = great house]

pharmaceutical (*say* farm-as-yoot-ik-al) *ADJECTIVE* to do with medicinal drugs or with pharmacy • *the pharmaceutical industry.*
[from Greek *pharmakeutes* = pharmacist]

pharmacist *NOUN* **pharmacists** a person who is trained to prepare and sell medicines.
[from *pharmacy*]

pharmacology *NOUN* the study of medicinal drugs.
▷ **pharmacological** *adjective*
pharmacologist *noun*
[from Greek *pharmakon* = drug, + *-logy*]

pharmacy *NOUN* **pharmacies** **1** a shop selling medicines; a dispensary. **2** the job of preparing medicines.
[from Greek *pharmakon* = drug]

pharynx (*say* fa-rinks) *NOUN* **pharynges** the cavity at the back of the mouth and nose.
[Greek, = throat]

phase *NOUN* **phases** a stage in the progress or development of something.

phase *VERB* **phases, phasing, phased** do something in stages, not all at once • *a phased withdrawal.*
[from Latin]

Ph.D. *ABBREVIATION* Doctor of Philosophy; a university degree awarded to someone who has done advanced research in their subject.

pheasant (*say* fez-ant) *NOUN* **pheasants** a game bird with a long tail.
[from Greek]

phenomenal *ADJECTIVE* amazing or remarkable.
▷ **phenomenally** *adverb*

phenomenon *NOUN* **phenomena** an event or fact, especially one that is remarkable.
[from Greek *phainomenon* = something appearing]
USAGE Note that *phenomena* is a plural. It is incorrect to say 'this phenomena' or 'these phenomenas'.

phial *NOUN* **phials** a small glass bottle.
[from Greek]

phil- *PREFIX* **1** fond of. **2** a lover of. SEE **philo-**.

A B C D E F G H I J K L M N O P Q R S T U V W X Y Z

philander *VERB* **philanders, philandering, philandered** (said about a man) have casual affairs with women.
▷ **philanderer** *noun*
[from Greek]

philanthropy *NOUN* concern for your fellow human beings, especially as shown by kind and generous acts that benefit large numbers of people.
▷ **philanthropist** *noun*
philanthropic *adjective*
[from *phil-* + Greek *anthropos* = mankind]

philately (*say* fil-at-il-ee) *NOUN* stamp-collecting.
▷ **philatelist** *noun*
[from *phil-* + Greek *ateleia* = not needing to pay (because postage has been paid for by buying a stamp)]

philharmonic *ADJECTIVE* (in names of orchestras etc.) devoted to music.
[from *phil-* + French *harmonique* = harmonic]

philistine (*say* fil-ist-l'n) *NOUN* **philistines** a person who dislikes art, poetry, etc.
[from the Philistines in the Bible, who were enemies of the Israelites]

philo- *PREFIX* **1** fond of. **2** a lover of.
[from Greek *philein* = to love]

philology *NOUN* the study of words and their history.
▷ **philological** *adjective* **philologist** *noun*
[from *philo-* + Greek *logos* = word]

philosopher *NOUN* **philosophers** an expert in philosophy.

philosophical *ADJECTIVE* **1** to do with philosophy. **2** calm and not upset after a misfortune or disappointment • *Be philosophical about losing.*
▷ **philosophically** *adverb*

philosophy *NOUN* **philosophies** **1** the study of truths about life, morals, etc. **2** a set of ideas or principles or beliefs.
[from *philo-* + Greek *sophia* = wisdom]

philtre (*say* fil-ter) *NOUN* **philtres** a magic drink, especially a love potion.
[from Greek *philein* = to love]

phlegm (*say* flem) *NOUN* thick mucus that forms in the throat and lungs when you have a bad cold.
[from Greek]

phlegmatic (*say* fleg-mat-ik) *ADJECTIVE* not easily excited or worried.
▷ **phlegmatically** *adverb*
[same origin as *phlegm* (because too much phlegm in the body was believed to make you sluggish)]

phobia (*say* foh-bee-a) *NOUN* **phobias** great or abnormal fear of something.
[from Greek *phobos* = fear]

-phobia *SUFFIX* forms nouns meaning 'fear or great dislike of something' (e.g. *hydrophobia*).

phoenix (*say* feen-iks) *NOUN* **phoenixes** a mythical bird that was said to burn itself to death in a fire and be born again from the ashes.
[from Greek]

phone *NOUN* **phones** a telephone.

phone *VERB* **phones, phoning, phoned** telephone.
[short for *telephone*]

phonecard *NOUN* **phonecards** a plastic card that you can use to work some public telephones instead of money.

phone-in *NOUN* **phone-ins** a radio or television programme in which people telephone the studio and take part in a discussion.

phonetic (*say* fon-et-ik) *ADJECTIVE* **1** to do with speech sounds. **2** representing speech sounds.
▷ **phonetically** *adverb*
[from Greek *phonein* = speak]

phoney *ADJECTIVE* (*informal*) sham; not genuine.
[origin unknown]

phosphate *NOUN* **phosphates** a substance containing phosphorus, especially an artificial fertilizer.

phosphorescent (*say* fos-fer-ess-ent) *ADJECTIVE* glowing in the dark; luminous.
▷ **phosphorescence** *noun*
[from *phosphorus*]

phosphorus *NOUN* a chemical substance that glows in the dark.
[from Greek *phos* = light + *-phoros* = bringing]

photo *NOUN* **photos** (*informal*) a photograph.

photo- *PREFIX* light (as in *photograph*). [from Greek]

photocopy *NOUN* **photocopies** a copy of a document or page etc. made by photographing it on special paper.
▷ **photocopy** *verb* **photocopier** *noun*

photoelectric *ADJECTIVE* using the electrical effects of light.

photogenic *ADJECTIVE* looking attractive in photographs.
[from *photo-* + *-genic* = producing]

photograph *NOUN* **photographs** a picture made by the effect of light or other radiation on film or special paper, using a camera.

photograph *VERB* **photographs, photographing, photographed** take a photograph of a person or thing.
▷ **photographer** *noun*

photography *NOUN* taking photographs.
▷ **photographic** *adjective*

photosynthesis *NOUN* the process by which green plants use sunlight to turn carbon dioxide and water into complex substances, giving off oxygen.

phrase *NOUN* **phrases 1** a group of words that form a unit in a sentence or clause, e.g. *in the garden* in 'The Queen was in the garden'. **2** a short section of a tune.

phrase *VERB* **phrases, phrasing, phrased 1** put something into words. **2** divide music into phrases.
[from Greek *phrazein* = declare]

phrase book *NOUN* **phrase books** a book which lists useful words and expressions in a foreign language, with their translations.

phraseology (*say* fray-zee-**ol**-o-jee) *NOUN* **phraseologies** wording; the way something is worded.
[from *phrase* + *-ology*]

physical *ADJECTIVE* **1** to do with the body rather than the mind or feelings. **2** to do with things that you can touch or see. **3** to do with physics. **4** physical geography is the study of natural features of the Earth's surface, such as mountains and volcanoes.
▷ **physically** *adverb*
[same origin as *physics*]

physical education or **physical training** *NOUN* exercises and sports done to keep the body healthy.

physician *NOUN* **physicians** a doctor, especially one who is not a surgeon.
[from old French *fisicien* = physicist]

physicist (*say* **fiz**-i-sist) *NOUN* **physicists** an expert in physics.

physics (*say* **fiz**-iks) *NOUN* the study of the properties of matter and energy (e.g. heat, light, sound, movement).
[from Greek *physikos* = natural]

physiognomy (*say* fiz-ee-**on**-o-mee) *NOUN* **physiognomies** the features of a person's face.
[from Greek *physis* = nature + *gnomon* = indicator]

physiology (*say* fiz-ee-**ol**-o-jee) *NOUN* the study of the body and its parts and how they function.
▷ **physiological** *adjective* **physiologist** *noun*
[from Greek *physis* = nature, + *-ology*]

physiotherapy (*say* fiz-ee-o-**th'erra**-pee) *NOUN* the treatment of a disease or weakness by massage, exercises, etc.
▷ **physiotherapist** *noun*
[from Greek *physis* = nature, + *therapy*]

physique (*say* fiz-**eek**) *NOUN* **physiques** a person's build.
[French, = physical]

pi *NOUN* the symbol (π) of the ratio of the circumference of a circle to its diameter. The value of pi is approximately 3.14159.
[the name of the sixteenth letter (π) of the Greek alphabet]

pianist *NOUN* **pianists** a person who plays the piano.

piano *NOUN* **pianos** a large musical instrument with a keyboard.
[short for *pianoforte*, from Italian *piano* = soft + *forte* = loud (because it can produce soft notes and loud notes)]

piccolo *NOUN* **piccolos** a small high-pitched flute.
[Italian, = small]

A B C D E F G H I J K L M N O **P** Q R S T U V W X Y Z

pick[1] *VERB* **picks, picking, picked**
1 separate a flower or fruit from its plant • *We picked apples.* **2** choose; select carefully. **3** pull bits off or out of something. **4** open a lock by using something pointed, not with a key.
- **pick a quarrel** deliberately provoke a quarrel with somebody.
- **pick holes in** find fault with.
- **pick on** single someone out for criticism or unkind treatment.
- **pick someone's pocket** steal from it.
- **pick up** **1** lift or take up. **2** collect. **3** take someone into a vehicle. **4** learn or acquire something. **5** manage to hear something. **6** get better or recover.

pick *NOUN* **1** choice • *Take your pick.* **2** the best of a group.
[origin unknown]

pick[2] *NOUN* **picks** **1** a pickaxe. **2** a plectrum.
[a different spelling of *pike*]

pickaxe *NOUN* **pickaxes** a heavy pointed tool with a long handle, used for breaking up hard ground etc.
[from old French *picois*, later confused with *axe*]

picket *NOUN* **pickets** **1** a striker or group of strikers who try to persuade other people not to go into a place of work during a strike. **2** a pointed post as part of a fence.

picket *VERB* **pickets, picketing, picketed** stand outside a place of work to try to persuade other people not to go in during a strike.
[from French *picquet* = small pike]

pickle *NOUN* **pickles** **1** a strong-tasting food made of pickled vegetables. **2** (*informal*) a mess.

pickle *VERB* **pickles, pickling, pickled** preserve food in vinegar or salt water.
[from old German or old Dutch]

pickpocket *NOUN* **pickpockets** a thief who steals from people's pockets or bags.

pick-up *NOUN* **pick-ups** **1** an open truck for carrying small loads. **2** the part of a record player that holds the stylus.

picnic *NOUN* **picnics** a meal eaten in the open air away from home.

picnic *VERB* **picnics, picnicking, picnicked** have a picnic.
▷ **picnicker** *noun*
[from French]

Pict *NOUN* **Picts** a member of an ancient people of north Britain.
▷ **Pictish** *adjective*
[from Latin *Picti* = painted or tattooed people]

pictorial *ADJECTIVE* with or using pictures.
▷ **pictorially** *adverb*

picture *NOUN* **pictures** **1** a representation of a person or thing made by painting, drawing, or photography. **2** a film at the cinema. **3** how something seems; an impression.
- **in the picture** fully informed about something.

picture *VERB* **pictures, picturing, pictured** **1** show in a picture. **2** imagine.
[from Latin *pictum* = painted]

picturesque *ADJECTIVE* **1** forming an attractive scene • *a picturesque village.* **2** vividly described; expressive • *picturesque language.*
▷ **picturesquely** *adverb*

pidgin *NOUN* **pidgins** a simplified form of a language used by people who do not speak the same language.
[from the Chinese pronunciation of *business* (because it was used by traders)]

pie *NOUN* **pies** a baked dish of meat, fish, or fruit covered with pastry.
[perhaps from *magpie* (because the contents of a pie look like the bits and pieces a magpie collects in its nest)]

piebald *ADJECTIVE* with patches of black and white • *a piebald donkey.*
[from *pie* = magpie, + *bald*]

piece *NOUN* **pieces** **1** a part or portion of something; a fragment. **2** a separate thing or example • *a fine piece of work.* **3** something written, composed, or painted etc. • *a piece of music.* **4** one of the objects used to play a game on a board • *a chess piece.* **5** a coin • *a 50p piece.*
- **in one piece** not harmed or damaged.
- **piece by piece** gradually; one bit at a time.

piece *VERB* **pieces, piecing, pieced** put pieces together to make something.
[from old French]

pièce de résistance (*say* pee-ess der ray-zees-tahns) *NOUN* **pièces de résistance** the most important item.
[French]

piecemeal *ADJECTIVE* & *ADVERB* done or made one piece at a time.
[from *piece* + Old English *mael* = a measure]

pie chart *NOUN* **pie charts** a circle divided into sectors to represent the way in which a quantity is divided up.

pier *NOUN* **piers** **1** a long structure built out into the sea for people to walk on. **2** a pillar supporting a bridge or arch.
[from Latin]

pierce *VERB* **pierces, piercing, pierced** make a hole through something; penetrate.
[from old French]

piercing *ADJECTIVE* **1** very loud and high-pitched. **2** penetrating; very strong • *a piercing wind.*

piety *NOUN* being very religious and devout; piousness.
[from Latin *pietas* = dutiful behaviour]

piffle *NOUN* (*slang*) nonsense.
[originally a dialect word]

pig *NOUN* **pigs** **1** a fat animal with short legs and a blunt snout, kept for its meat. **2** (*informal*) someone greedy, dirty, or unpleasant.
▷ **piggy** *adjective* & *noun*
[origin unknown]

pigeon[1] *NOUN* **pigeons** a bird with a fat body and a small head.
[from old French *pijon* = young bird]

pigeon[2] *NOUN* (*informal*) a person's business or responsibility • *That's your pigeon.*
[same origin as *pidgin*]

pigeon-hole *NOUN* **pigeon-holes** a small compartment for holding letters, messages, or papers, for someone to collect.

pigeon-hole *VERB* **pigeon-holes, pigeon-holing, pigeon-holed** decide that a person belongs to a particular category • *She doesn't want to be pigeon-holed simply as a pop singer.*

piggery *NOUN* **piggeries** a place where pigs are bred or kept.

piggyback *ADVERB* carried on somebody else's back or shoulders.
▷ **piggyback** *noun*
[from *pick-a-back*]

piggy bank *NOUN* **piggy banks** a money box made in the shape of a hollow pig.

pig-headed *ADJECTIVE* obstinate.

pig iron *NOUN* iron that has been processed in a smelting furnace.
[because the blocks of iron reminded people of pigs]

piglet *NOUN* **piglets** a young pig.

pigment *NOUN* **pigments** **1** a substance that colours skin or other tissue in animals and plants. **2** a substance that gives colour to paint, inks, dyes, etc.
▷ **pigmented** *adjective* **pigmentation** *noun*
[from Latin *pingere* = to paint]

pigsty *NOUN* **pigsties** **1** a partly-covered pen for pigs. **2** a filthy room or house.

pigtail *NOUN* **pigtails** a plait of hair worn hanging at the back of the head.

pike *NOUN* **pikes** **1** a heavy spear. **pike** **2** a large freshwater fish.
[origin unknown]

pilau (*say* pi-low) *NOUN* an Indian dish of spiced rice with meat and vegetables.
[from Turkish]

pilchard *NOUN* **pilchards** a small sea fish.
[origin unknown]

pile[1] *NOUN* **piles** **1** a number of things on top of one another. **2** (*informal*) a large quantity; a lot of money. **3** a large impressive building.

pile *VERB* **piles, piling, piled** put things into a pile; make a pile.
[from Latin *pila* = pillar]

pile[2] *NOUN* **piles** a heavy beam made of metal, concrete, or timber driven into the ground to support something.
[from Old English]

pile[3] *NOUN* a raised surface on fabric, made of upright threads • *a carpet with a thick pile.*
[from Latin *pilus* = hair]

pile-up *NOUN* **pile-ups** a road accident that involves a number of vehicles.

pilfer *VERB* **pilfers, pilfering, pilfered** steal small things.
▷ **pilferer** *noun* **pilferage** *noun*
[from old French]

pilgrim *NOUN* **pilgrims** a person who travels to a holy place for religious reasons.
▷ **pilgrimage** *noun*
[same origin as *peregrine*]

pill *NOUN* **pills** a small solid piece of medicine for swallowing.
- **the pill** a contraceptive pill.
[from Latin *pila* = ball]

pillage *VERB* **pillages, pillaging, pillaged** carry off goods using force, especially in a war; plunder.
▷ **pillage** *noun*
[from Latin *pilare* = cut the hair from]

pillar *NOUN* **pillars** a tall stone or wooden post.
[same origin as *pile*¹]

pillar box *NOUN* **pillar boxes** a postbox standing in a street.
[because many of them are shaped like a short pillar]

pillion *NOUN* **pillions** a seat behind the driver on a motorcycle.
[from Scottish Gaelic *pillean* = cushion]

pillory *NOUN* **pillories** a wooden framework with holes for a person's head and hands, in which offenders were formerly made to stand and be ridiculed by the public as a punishment.

pillory *VERB* **pillories, pillorying, pilloried** expose a person to public ridicule and scorn • *Football managers get used to being pilloried in the newpapers.*
[from old French]

pillow *NOUN* **pillows** a cushion for a person's head to rest on, especially in bed.

pillow *VERB* **pillows, pillowing, pillowed** rest the head on a pillow or something soft • *He pillowed his head on his arms.*
[from Old English]

pillowcase or **pillowslip** *NOUN* **pillowcases, pillowslips** a cloth cover for a pillow.

pilot *NOUN* **pilots** **1** a person who works the controls for flying an aircraft. **2** a person qualified to steer a ship in and out of a port or through a difficult stretch of water. **3** a guide.

pilot *VERB* **pilots, piloting, piloted** **1** be pilot of an aircraft or ship. **2** guide or steer.

pilot *ADJECTIVE* testing on a small scale how something will work • *a pilot scheme.*
[from Greek *pedon* = oar or rudder]

pilot light *NOUN* **pilot lights** **1** a small flame that lights a larger burner on a gas cooker etc. **2** an electric indicator light.

pimp *NOUN* **pimps** a man who gets clients for prostitutes and lives off their earnings.
[origin unknown]

pimpernel (*say* pimp-er-nel) *NOUN* **pimpernels** a plant with small red, blue, or white flowers that close in cloudy weather.
[from old French]

pimple *NOUN* **pimples** a small round raised spot on the skin.
▷ **pimply** *adjective*
[via Old English from Latin]

PIN *ABBREVIATION* personal identification number; a number used as a person's password so that he or she can use a cash dispenser, computer, etc.

pin *NOUN* **pins** **1** a short thin piece of metal with a sharp point and a rounded head, used to fasten pieces of cloth or paper etc. together. **2** a pointed device for fixing or marking something.
- **pins and needles** a tingling feeling in the skin.

pin *VERB* **pins, pinning, pinned** **1** fasten something with a pin or pins. **2** hold someone firmly so that they cannot move • *He was pinned under the wreckage.* **3** fix blame or responsibility on someone • *They pinned the blame for the mix-up on her.*
[via Old English from Latin]

pinafore *NOUN* **pinafores** an apron.
[from *pin* + *afore* = in front (because originally the bib of the apron was pinned to the front of the dress)]

pinball *NOUN* **pinballs** a game in which you shoot small metal balls across a special table and score points when they strike pins with lights etc.

pincer *NOUN* **pincers** the claw of a shellfish such as a lobster.
[from old French *pincier* = to pinch]

pincers *PLURAL NOUN* a tool with two parts that are pressed together for gripping and holding things.

pinch *VERB* **pinches, pinching, pinched** **1** squeeze something tightly or painfully between two things, especially between the finger and thumb. **2** (*informal*) steal.

pinch *NOUN* **pinches** **1** a pinching movement. **2** the amount that can be held between the tips of the thumb and forefinger • *a pinch of salt.*
- **at a pinch** in time of difficulty; if necessary.
- **feel the pinch** suffer from lack of money.
[same origin as *pincer*]

pincushion *NOUN* **pincushions** a small pad into which pins are stuck to keep them ready for use.

pine[1] *NOUN* **pines** an evergreen tree with needle-shaped leaves.
[from Latin]

pine[2] *VERB* **pines, pining, pined** **1** feel an intense longing for somebody or something. **2** become weak through longing for somebody or something.
[from Old English]

pineapple *NOUN* **pineapples** a large tropical fruit with a tough prickly skin and yellow flesh.
[from *pine*[1] + *apple* (because it looks like a pine cone)]

ping *NOUN* **pings** a short sharp ringing sound.
▷ **ping** *verb*
[imitating the sound]

ping-pong *NOUN* table tennis.
[from the sound of the bats hitting the ball]

pinion[1] *NOUN* **pinions** a bird's wing, especially the outer end.

pinion *VERB* **pinions, pinioning, pinioned** **1** clip a bird's wings to prevent it from flying. **2** hold or fasten someone's arms or legs in order to prevent them from moving.
[from Latin *pinna* = pin, arrow, or feather]

pinion[2] *NOUN* **pinions** a small cogwheel that fits into another or into a rod (called a *rack*).
[from Latin *pinus* = pine tree (because the wheel's teeth reminded people of a pine cone)]

pink[1] *ADJECTIVE* pale red.
▷ **pinkness** *noun*

pink *NOUN* **pinks** **1** a pink colour. **2** a garden plant with fragrant flowers, often pink or white.
[origin unknown]

pink[2] *VERB* **pinks, pinking, pinked** **1** pierce slightly. **2** cut a zigzag edge on cloth.
[probably from old Dutch]

pinnacle *NOUN* **pinnacles** **1** a pointed ornament on a roof. **2** a high pointed piece of rock. **3** the highest point of something • *It was the pinnacle of her career.*
[from old French]

pinpoint *ADJECTIVE* exact or precise • *with pinpoint accuracy.*

pinpoint *VERB* **pinpoints, pinpointing, pinpointed** find or identify something precisely.

pinprick *NOUN* **pinpricks** a small annoyance.

pinstripe *NOUN* **pinstripes** one of the very narrow stripes that form a pattern in cloth.
▷ **pinstriped** *adjective*

pint *NOUN* **pints** a measure for liquids, equal to one-eighth of a gallon.
[from old French]

pin-up *NOUN* **pin-ups** (*informal*) a picture of an attractive or famous person for pinning on a wall.

pioneer *NOUN* **pioneers** one of the first people to go to a place or do or investigate something.
▷ **pioneer** *verb*
[from French *pionnier* = foot soldier, later = one of the troops who went ahead of the army to prepare roads etc.]

pious *ADJECTIVE* very religious; devout.
▷ **piously** *adverb* **piousness** *noun*
[from Latin *pius* = dutiful]

A B C D E F G H I J K L M N O **P** Q R S T U V W X Y Z

pip *NOUN* **pips** **1** a small hard seed of an apple, pear, orange, etc. **2** one of the stars on the shoulder of an army officer's uniform. **3** a short high-pitched sound • *She heard the six pips of the time signal on the radio.*

pip *VERB* **pips, pipping, pipped** (*informal*) defeat someone by a small amount.
[short for *pippin*]

pipe *NOUN* **pipes** **1** a tube through which water or gas etc. can flow from one place to another. **2** a short narrow tube with a bowl at one end in which tobacco can burn for smoking. **3** a tube forming a musical instrument or part of one.
- **the pipes** bagpipes.

pipe *VERB* **pipes, piping, piped** **1** send something along pipes. **2** transmit music or other sound by wire or cable. **3** play music on a pipe or the bagpipes. **4** decorate a cake with thin lines of icing, cream, etc.
- **pipe down** (*informal*) be quiet.
- **pipe up** begin to say something.
[from Old English]

pipe dream *NOUN* **pipe dreams** an impossible wish.
[perhaps from dreams produced by smoking opium]

pipeline *NOUN* **pipelines** a pipe for carrying oil or water etc. a long distance.
- **in the pipeline** in the process of being made or organized.

piper *NOUN* **pipers** a person who plays a pipe or bagpipes.

pipette *NOUN* **pipettes** a small glass tube used in a laboratory, usually filled by suction.
[French, = little pipe]

piping *NOUN* **1** pipes; a length of pipe. **2** a decorative line of icing, cream, etc. on a cake or other dish. **3** a long narrow pipe-like fold decorating clothing, upholstery, etc.

piping *ADJECTIVE* shrill • *a piping voice.*
- **piping hot** very hot.

pipit *NOUN* **pipits** a small songbird.
[imitating its call]

pippin *NOUN* **pippins** a kind of apple.
[from French]

piquant (*say* pee-kant) *ADJECTIVE* **1** pleasantly sharp and appetizing • *a piquant smell.* **2** pleasantly stimulating.
▷ **piquancy** *noun*
[same origin as *pique*]

pique (*say* peek) *NOUN* a feeling of hurt pride.
▷ **pique** *verb*
[from French *piquer* = to prick]

piranha *NOUN* **piranhas** a South American freshwater fish that has sharp teeth and eats flesh.
[via Portuguese from Tupi (a South American language)]

pirate *NOUN* **pirates** **1** a person on a ship who attacks and robs other ships at sea. **2** someone who produces or publishes something or broadcasts without authorization • *a pirate radio station; pirate videos.*
▷ **piratical** *adjective* **piracy** *noun*
[from Greek *peiraein* = to attack]

pirouette (*say* pir-oo-et) *NOUN* **pirouettes** a spinning movement of the body made while balanced on the point of the toe or on one foot.
▷ **pirouette** *verb*
[French, = spinning top]

pistachio *NOUN* **pistachios** a nut with an edible green kernel.
[from Greek]

pistil *NOUN* **pistils** the part of a flower that produces the seed, consisting of the ovary, style, and stigma.
[from Latin *pistillum* = pestle (because of its shape)]

pistol *NOUN* **pistols** a small handgun.
[via French and German from Czech]

piston *NOUN* **pistons** a disc or cylinder that fits inside a tube in which it moves up and down as part of an engine or pump etc.
[via French from Italian *pestone* = pestle]

pit *NOUN* **pits** **1** a deep hole. **2** a hollow. **3** a coal mine. **4** the part of a race circuit where racing cars are refuelled and repaired during a race.

pit *VERB* **pits, pitting, pitted** **1** make holes or hollows in something • *The ground was pitted with craters.* **2** put somebody in competition with somebody else • *He was pitted against the champion in the final.*
▷ **pitted** *adjective*
[from Old English]

pit bull terrier *NOUN* **pit bull terriers** a small strong and fierce breed of dog.

pitch[1] *NOUN* **pitches** **1** a piece of ground marked out for cricket, football, or another game. **2** the highness or lowness of a voice or a musical note. **3** intensity or strength • *Excitement was at fever pitch.* **4** the steepness of a slope • *the pitch of the roof.*

pitch *VERB* **pitches, pitching, pitched** **1** throw or fling. **2** set up a tent or camp. **3** fall heavily • *He pitched forward as the bus braked suddenly.* **4** move up and down on a rough sea. **5** set something at a particular level • *We are pitching our hopes high.* **6** (said about a bowled ball in cricket) strike the ground.
- **pitch in** (*informal*) start working or doing something vigorously.
[origin unknown]

pitch[2] *NOUN* a black sticky substance rather like tar.
[from Old English]

pitch-black or **pitch-dark** *NOUN* completely black or dark.

pitchblende *NOUN* a mineral ore (uranium oxide) from which radium is obtained.
[from *pitch*² + German *blenden* = deceive (because it looks like pitch)]

pitched battle *NOUN* **pitched battles** a battle between armies in prepared positions.

pitcher *NOUN* **pitchers** a large jug.
[from old French *pichier* = pot]

pitchfork *NOUN* **pitchforks** a large fork with two prongs, used for lifting hay.

pitchfork *VERB* **pitchforks, pitchforking, pitchforked** **1** lift something with a pitchfork. **2** put a person somewhere suddenly.
[originally *pickfork*: from *pick*¹]

piteous *ADJECTIVE* making you feel pity.
▷ **piteously** *adverb*

pitfall *NOUN* **pitfalls** an unsuspected danger or difficulty.

pith *NOUN* the spongy substance in the stems of certain plants or lining the rind of oranges etc.
[from Old English]

pithy *ADJECTIVE* **1** like pith; containing much pith. **2** short and full of meaning • *pithy comments.*

pitiable *ADJECTIVE* making you feel pity; pitiful.

pitiful *ADJECTIVE* making you feel pity; pathetic.
▷ **pitifully** *adverb*

pitiless *ADJECTIVE* showing no pity.
▷ **pitilessly** *adverb*

pittance *NOUN* a very small allowance of money.
[originally = a 'pious gift' (one given to a church): same origin as *piety*]

pity *NOUN* **1** the feeling of being sorry because someone is in pain or trouble. **2** a cause for regret • *It's a pity that you can't come.*
- **take pity on** feel sorry for someone and help them.

pity *VERB* **pities, pitying, pitied** feel pity for someone.
[same origin as *piety*]

pivot *NOUN* **pivots** a point or part on which something turns or balances.
▷ **pivotal** *adjective*

pivot *VERB* **pivots, pivoting, pivoted** turn or place something to turn on a pivot.
[from French]

pixel (*say* **piks**-el) *NOUN* **pixels** one of the tiny dots on a computer display screen from which the image is formed.
[short for *picture element*]

pixie *NOUN* **pixies** a small fairy; an elf.
[origin unknown]

pizza (*say* **peets**-a) *NOUN* **pizzas** an Italian food that consists of a layer of dough baked with a savoury topping.
[Italian, = pie]

pizzicato (*say* pits-i-**kah**-toh) *ADJECTIVE & ADVERB* (*in music*) plucking the strings of a musical instrument.
[Italian, = pinched or twitched]

A B C D E F G H I J K L M N O **P** Q R S T U V W X Y Z

placard *NOUN* **placards** a poster or notice, especially one carried at a demonstration.
[from old French *plaquier* = to lay flat]

placate *VERB* **placates, placating, placated** make someone feel calmer and less angry.
▷ **placatory** *adjective*
[from Latin *placare* = please or appease]

place *NOUN* **places 1** a particular part of space, especially where something belongs; an area or position. **2** a seat • *Save me a place.* **3** a job; employment. **4** a building; a home • *Come round to our place.* **5** a duty or function • *It's not my place to interfere.* **6** a point in a series of things • *In the first place, the date is wrong.*
- **in place** in the proper position.
- **in place of** instead of.
- **out of place 1** in the wrong position. **2** unsuitable.
- **take place** happen.

place *VERB* **places, placing, placed** put something in a particular place.
▷ **placement** *noun*
[from Greek *plateia* = broad way]

placebo (*say* plas-ee-boh) *NOUN* **placebos** a harmless substance given as if it were a medicine, usually to reassure a patient.
[Latin, = I shall be pleasing]

placenta *NOUN* a piece of body tissue that forms in the womb during pregnancy and supplies the foetus with nourishment.
[from Greek *plakous* = flat cake (because of its shape)]

placid *ADJECTIVE* calm and peaceful; not easily made anxious or upset.
▷ **placidly** *adverb* **placidity** *noun*
[from Latin *placidus* = gentle]

placket *NOUN* **plackets** an opening in a skirt to make it easy to put on and take off.
[same origin as *placard*]

plagiarize (*say* play-jee-er-I'z) *VERB* **plagiarizes, plagiarizing, plagiarized** take someone else's writings or ideas and use them as if they were your own.
▷ **plagiarism** *noun* **plagiarist** *noun*
[from Latin *plagiarius* = kidnapper]

plague *NOUN* **plagues 1** a dangerous illness that spreads very quickly. **2** a large number of pests • *a plague of locusts.*

plague *VERB* **plagues, plaguing, plagued** pester or annoy • *We've been plagued by wasps all afternoon.*
[from Latin]

plaice *NOUN* **plaice** a flat edible sea fish.
[from Greek *platys* = broad]

plaid (*say* plad) *NOUN* cloth with a tartan or similar pattern.
[from Scottish Gaelic]

plain *ADJECTIVE* **1** simple; not decorated or elaborate. **2** not beautiful. **3** easy to see or hear or understand. **4** frank and straightforward.
▷ **plainly** *adverb* **plainness** *noun*

plain *NOUN* **plains** a large area of flat country.
[from Latin *planus* = flat]
USAGE Do not confuse with **plane**.

plain clothes *NOUN* civilian clothes worn instead of a uniform, e.g. by police.

plaintiff *NOUN* **plaintiffs** the person who brings a complaint against somebody else to a lawcourt. (COMPARE **defendant**)
[same origin as *plaintive*]

plaintive *ADJECTIVE* sounding sad • *a plaintive cry.*
[from French *plaintif* = grieving or complaining]

plait (*say* plat) *VERB* **plaits, plaiting, plaited** weave three or more strands of hair or rope to form one length.

plait *NOUN* **plaits** a length of hair or rope that has been plaited.
[from Latin *plicatum* = folded]

plan *NOUN* **plans 1** a way of doing something thought out in advance. **2** a drawing showing the arrangement of parts of something. **3** a map of a town or district.

plan *VERB* **plans, planning, planned** make a plan for something.
▷ **planner** *noun*
[French, = flat surface, plan of a building: related to *plain*]

plane[1] *NOUN* **planes 1** an aeroplane. **2** a tool for making wood smooth by scraping its surface. **3** a flat or level surface.

plane *VERB* **planes, planing, planed** smooth wood with a plane.

plane *ADJECTIVE* flat or level • *a plane surface.*
[same origin as *plain*]
USAGE Do not confuse with **plain**.

plane[2] *NOUN* **planes** a tall tree with broad leaves.
[from Greek]

planet *NOUN* **planets** one of the bodies that move in an orbit round the sun. The main planets of the solar system are Mercury, Venus, Earth, Mars, Jupiter, Saturn, Uranus, Neptune, and Pluto.
▷ **planetary** *adjective*
[from Greek *planetes* = wanderer (because planets seem to move in relation to the stars)]

plank *NOUN* **planks** a long flat piece of wood.
[from Latin]

plankton *NOUN* microscopic plants and animals that float in the sea, lakes, etc.
[Greek, = wandering or drifting]

plant *NOUN* **plants** **1** a living thing that cannot move, makes its food from chemical substances, and usually has a stem, leaves, and roots. Flowers, trees, and shrubs are plants. **2** a small plant, not a tree or shrub. **3** a factory or its equipment. **4** (*informal*) something deliberately placed for other people to find, usually to mislead people or cause trouble.

plant *VERB* **plants, planting, planted** **1** put something in soil for growing. **2** fix something firmly in place. **3** place something where it will be found, usually to mislead people or cause trouble.
▷ **planter** *noun*
[from Latin]

plantain[1] (*say* plan-tin) *NOUN* **plantains** a wild plant with broad flat leaves, bearing seeds that are used as food for cage birds.
[from a Latin word *planta* meaning 'sole of the foot' (because of the shape of its leaves)]

plantain[2] (*say* plan-tin) *NOUN* **plantain** a tropical tree and fruit resembling the banana.
[probably from a Spanish word *plantano* meaning 'plane tree']

plantation *NOUN* **plantations** **1** a large area of land where cotton, tobacco, or tea etc. is planted. **2** a group of planted trees.

plaque (*say* plak) *NOUN* **plaques** **1** a flat piece of metal or porcelain fixed on a wall as an ornament or memorial. **2** a filmy substance that forms on teeth and gums, where bacteria can live.
[via French from Dutch]

plasma *NOUN* the colourless liquid part of blood, carrying the corpuscles.
[from Greek]

plaster *NOUN* **plasters** **1** a small covering put over the skin around a cut or wound to protect it. **2** a mixture of lime, sand, and water etc. for covering walls and ceilings. **3** plaster of Paris, or a cast made of this to hold broken bones in place.

plaster *VERB* **plasters, plastering, plastered** **1** cover a wall etc. with plaster. **2** cover something thickly.
[via Old English from Latin]

plaster of Paris *NOUN* a white paste used for making moulds or for casts round a broken leg or arm.

plastic *NOUN* **plastics** a strong light synthetic substance that can be moulded into a permanent shape.

plastic *ADJECTIVE* **1** made of plastic. **2** soft and easy to mould • *Clay is a plastic substance.*
▷ **plasticity** *noun*
[from Greek *plastos* = moulded or formed]

plastic surgery *NOUN* surgery to repair deformed or injured parts of the body.
▷ **plastic surgeon** *noun*

plate *NOUN* **plates** **1** an almost flat usually circular object from which food is eaten or served. **2** a thin flat sheet of metal, glass, or other hard material. **3** an illustration on special paper in a book.
▷ **plateful** *noun*

plate *VERB* **plates, plating, plated** **1** coat metal with a thin layer of gold, silver, tin, etc. **2** cover something with sheets of metal.
[from Latin *platus* = broad or flat]

plateau (*say* plat-oh) *NOUN* **plateaux** or **plateaus** (*say* plat-ohz) a flat area of high land.
[French, related to *plate*]

platform *NOUN* **platforms** **1** a flat raised area along the side of a line at a railway station. **2** a flat surface that is above the level of the ground or floor, especially one from which someone speaks to an audience. **3** the policies that a political party puts forward when there is an election.
[from French *plateforme* = a flat surface]

platinum *NOUN* a valuable silver-coloured metal that does not tarnish.
[from Spanish *plata* = silver]

platitude *NOUN* **platitudes** a trite or hackneyed remark.
▷ **platitudinous** *adjective*
[French, from *plat* = flat]

platoon *NOUN* **platoons** a small group of soldiers.
[from French *peloton* = little ball]

platter *NOUN* **platters** a flat dish or plate.
[from old French; related to *plate*]

platypus *NOUN* **platypuses** an Australian animal with a beak like that of a duck, that lays eggs like a bird but is a mammal and suckles its young.
[from Greek *platys* = broad + *pous* = foot]

plaudits *PLURAL NOUN* applause; expressions of approval.
[from Latin *plaudere* = to clap]

plausible *ADJECTIVE* seeming to be honest or worth believing but perhaps deceptive • *a plausible excuse.*
▷ **plausibly** *adverb* **plausibility** *noun*
[from Latin *plausibilis* = deserving applause]

play *VERB* **plays, playing, played** **1** take part in a game, sport, or other amusement. **2** make music or sound with a musical instrument, record player, etc. **3** perform a part in a play or film.
▷ **player** *noun*
- **play about** or **play around** have fun or be mischievous.
- **play down** give people the impression that something is not important.
- **play up** (*informal*) tease or annoy someone.

play *NOUN* **plays** **1** a story acted on a stage or on radio or television. **2** playing or having fun.
- **a play on words** a pun.
[from Old English]

playback *NOUN* **playbacks** playing back something that has been recorded.

playful *ADJECTIVE* **1** wanting to play; full of fun. **2** done in fun; not serious.
▷ **playfully** *adverb* **playfulness** *noun*

playground *NOUN* **playgrounds** a piece of ground for children to play on.

playgroup *NOUN* **playgroups** a group of very young children who play together regularly, supervised by adults.

playing card *NOUN* **playing cards** each of a set of cards (usually 52) used for playing games.

playing field *NOUN* **playing fields** a field used for outdoor games.

playmate *NOUN* **playmates** a person you play games with.

play-off *NOUN* **play-offs** an extra match that is played to decide a draw or tie.

plaything *NOUN* **playthings** a toy.

playtime *NOUN* the time when young schoolchildren go out to play.

playwright *NOUN* **playwrights** a person who writes plays; a dramatist.
[from *play* + *wright* = maker]

PLC or **plc** *ABBREVIATION* public limited company.

plea *NOUN* **pleas** **1** a request or appeal • *a plea for mercy.* **2** an excuse • *He stayed at home on the plea of a headache.* **3** a formal statement of 'guilty' or 'not guilty' made in a lawcourt by someone accused of a crime.
[from old French]

plead *VERB* **pleads, pleading, pleaded** **1** beg someone to do something. **2** state formally in a lawcourt that you are guilty or not guilty of a crime. **3** give something as an excuse • *She didn't come on holiday with us, pleading poverty.*

pleasant *ADJECTIVE* pleasing; giving pleasure.
▷ **pleasantly** *adverb* **pleasantness** *noun*
[from French *plaisant* = pleasing]

pleasantry *NOUN* **pleasantries** a friendly or good-humoured remark.

please *VERB* **pleases, pleasing, pleased** **1** make a person feel satisfied or glad. **2** used to make a request or an order polite • *Please ring the bell.* **3** like; think suitable • *Do as you please.*
[from Latin *placere* = satisfy]

pleasurable *ADJECTIVE* causing pleasure.

pleasure *NOUN* **pleasures** **1** a feeling of satisfaction or gladness; enjoyment. **2** something that pleases you.
[from French *plaisir* = to please]

pleat *NOUN* **pleats** a flat fold made by doubling cloth upon itself.
▷ **pleated** *adjective*
[from *plait*]

plebeian (*say* plib-ee-an) *NOUN* **plebeians** a member of the common people in ancient Rome. (COMPARE **patrician**)
▷ **plebeian** *adjective*
[from Latin *plebs* = the common people]

plebiscite (*say* **pleb**-iss-it) *NOUN* **plebiscites** a referendum.
[from Latin *plebs* = the common people + *scitum* = decree]

plectrum *NOUN* **plectra** a small piece of metal or bone etc. for plucking the strings of a musical instrument.
[from Greek *plektron* = something to strike with]

pledge *NOUN* **pledges** **1** a solemn promise. **2** a thing handed over as security for a loan or contract.

pledge *VERB* **pledges, pledging, pledged** **1** promise solemnly to do or give something. **2** hand something over as security.
[from old French]

plenary (*say* **pleen**-er-ee) *ADJECTIVE* attended by all members • *a plenary session of the council.*
[from Latin *plenus* = full]

plenipotentiary (*say* plen-i-pot-**en**-sher-ee) *ADJECTIVE* having full authority to make decisions on behalf of a government • *Our ambassador has plenipotentiary power.*
▷ **plenipotentiary** *noun*
[from Latin *plenus* = full + *potentia* = power]

plentiful *ADJECTIVE* quite enough in amount; abundant.
▷ **plentifully** *adverb*

plenty *NOUN* quite enough; as much as is needed or wanted.

plenty *ADVERB* (*informal*) quite or fully • *It's plenty big enough.*
[from Latin *plenitas* = fullness]

plethora *NOUN* too large a quantity of something.
[from Greek]

pleurisy (*say* **ploor**-i-see) *NOUN* inflammation of the membrane round the lungs.
[from Greek *pleura* = ribs]

pliable *ADJECTIVE* **1** easy to bend; flexible. **2** easy to influence or control.
▷ **pliability** *noun*
[French, from *plier* = to bend]

pliant *ADJECTIVE* pliable.
[French, = bending]

pliers *PLURAL NOUN* pincers that have jaws with flat surfaces for gripping things.
[from *ply*²]

plight¹ *NOUN* **plights** a difficult situation.
[from old French]

plight² *VERB* **plights, plighting, plighted** (*old use*) pledge devotion or loyalty.
[from Old English]

plimsoll *NOUN* **plimsolls** a canvas sports shoe with a rubber sole.
[same origin as *Plimsoll line* (because the thin sole reminded people of a Plimsoll line)]

Plimsoll line *NOUN* **Plimsoll lines** a mark on a ship's side showing how deeply it may legally go down in the water when loaded.
[named after an English politician, S. *Plimsoll*, who in the 1870s protested about ships being overloaded]

plinth *NOUN* **plinths** a block or slab forming the base of a column or a support for a statue or vase etc.
[from Greek]

PLO *ABBREVIATION* Palestine Liberation Organization.

plod *VERB* **plods, plodding, plodded** **1** walk slowly and heavily. **2** work slowly but steadily.
▷ **plodder** *noun*
[origin unknown]

plonk *NOUN* (*informal*) cheap wine.

plonk *VERB* **plonks, plonking, plonked** (*informal*) put something down clumsily or heavily.
[originally Australian; probably from French *blanc* = white, in *vin blanc* = white wine]

plop *NOUN* **plops** the sound of something dropping into water.
▷ **plop** *verb*
[imitating the sound]

plot *NOUN* **plots 1** a secret plan. **2** the story in a play, novel, or film. **3** a small piece of land.

plot *VERB* **plots, plotting, plotted 1** make a secret plan. **2** make a chart or graph of something • *We plotted the ship's route on our map.*
[origin unknown]

plough *NOUN* **ploughs** a farming implement for turning the soil over, in preparation for planting seeds.

plough *VERB* **ploughs, ploughing, ploughed 1** turn over soil with a plough. **2** go through something with great effort or difficulty • *He ploughed through the book.*
▷ **ploughman** *noun*
- **plough back** reinvest profits in the business that produced them.
[from Old Norse]

ploughshare *NOUN* **ploughshares** the cutting blade of a plough.
[from *plough* + Old English *scaer* = blade]

plover (*say* pluv-er) *NOUN* **plovers** a kind of wading bird.
[from Latin *pluvia* = rain]

ploy *NOUN* **ploys** a cunning manoeuvre to gain an advantage; a ruse.
[originally Scots: origin unknown]

pluck *VERB* **plucks, plucking, plucked 1** pick a flower or fruit. **2** pull the feathers off a bird. **3** pull something up or out. **4** pull a string (e.g. on a guitar) and let it go again.
- **pluck up courage** summon up courage and overcome fear.

pluck *NOUN* courage or spirit.
[from Old English]

plucky *ADJECTIVE* **pluckier, pluckiest** brave or spirited.
▷ **pluckily** *adverb*

plug *NOUN* **plugs 1** something used to stop up a hole • *a bath plug.* **2** a device that fits into a socket to connect wires to a supply of electricity. **3** (*informal*) a piece of publicity for something.

plug *VERB* **plugs, plugging, plugged 1** stop up a hole. **2** (*informal*) publicize something.
- **plug in** put a plug into an electrical socket.
[from old German or old Dutch]

plum *NOUN* **plums 1** a soft juicy fruit with a pointed stone in the middle.
2 reddish-purple colour. **3** (*informal*) the best of its kind • *a plum job.*
[via Old English from Latin]

plumage (*say* ploom-ij) *NOUN* **plumages** a bird's feathers.
[same origin as *plume*]

plumb *VERB* **plumbs, plumbing, plumbed**
1 measure how deep something is. **2** get to the bottom of a matter • *We could not plumb the mystery.* **3** fit a room or building with a plumbing system.

plumb *ADJECTIVE* exactly upright; vertical • *The wall was plumb.*

plumb *ADVERB* (*informal*) exactly • *It fell plumb in the middle.*
[from Latin *plumbum* = *lead*² (originally *plumb* = the lead weight on a plumb line)]

plumber *NOUN* **plumbers** a person who fits and mends plumbing.

plumbing *NOUN* **1** the water pipes, water tanks, and drainage pipes in a building.
2 the work of a plumber.
[from *plumb* (because water pipes used to be made of lead)]

plumb line *NOUN* **plumb lines** a cord with a weight on the end, used to find how deep something is or whether a wall etc. is vertical.

plume *NOUN* **plumes 1** a large feather.
2 something shaped like a feather • *a plume of smoke.*
[from Latin *pluma* = feather]

plumed *ADJECTIVE* decorated with plumes • *a plumed helmet.*

plummet *NOUN* **plummets** a plumb line or the weight on its end.

plummet *VERB* **plummets, plummeting, plummeted** **1** drop downwards quickly. **2** decrease rapidly in value • *Prices have plummeted.*
[from old French; related to *plumb*]

plump[1] *ADJECTIVE* slightly fat; rounded.
▷ **plumpness** *noun*

plump *VERB* **plumps, plumping, plumped** make something rounded • *plump up a cushion.*
[from old German *plumpich* = bulky]

plump[2] *VERB* **plumps, plumping, plumped**
- **plump for** (*informal*) choose.
[from old German *plompen* = to plop]

plunder *VERB* **plunders, plundering, plundered** rob a person or place using force, especially during a war or riot.
▷ **plunderer** *noun*

plunder *NOUN* **1** plundering. **2** goods that have been plundered.
[from old German]

plunge *VERB* **plunges, plunging, plunged** **1** go or push forcefully into something; dive. **2** fall or go downwards suddenly. **3** go or force into action etc. • *They plunged the world into war.*

plunge *NOUN* **plunges** a sudden fall or dive.
- **take the plunge** start a bold course of action.
[from old French; related to *plumb*]

plunger *NOUN* **plungers** a rubber cup on a handle used for clearing blocked pipes.

plural *NOUN* **plurals** the form of a noun or verb used when it stands for more than one person or thing • *The plural of 'child' is 'children'.* (COMPARE **singular**)
▷ **plural** *adjective* **plurality** *noun*
[from Latin *pluralis* = of many]

plus *PREPOSITION* with the next number or thing added • *2 plus 2 equals four* (2 + 2 = 4).

plus *ADJECTIVE* **1** being a grade slightly higher • *B plus.* **2** more than zero • *a temperature between minus ten and plus ten degrees.*
[Latin, = more]

plush *NOUN* a thick velvety cloth used in furnishings.
▷ **plushy** *adjective*
[from Latin *pilus* = hair]

plutocrat *NOUN* **plutocrats** a person who is powerful because of his or her wealth.
[from Greek *ploutos* = wealth, + *-crat*]

plutonium *NOUN* a radioactive substance used in nuclear weapons and reactors.
[named after the planet *Pluto*]

ply[1] *NOUN* **plies** **1** a thickness or layer of wood or cloth etc. **2** a strand in yarn • *4-ply wool.*
[from French *pli* = a fold]

ply[2] *VERB* **plies, plying, plied** **1** use or wield a tool or weapon. **2** work at • *Tailors plied their trade.* **3** keep offering • *They plied her with food.* **4** go regularly • *The boat plies between the two harbours.* **5** drive or wait about looking for custom • *Taxis are allowed to ply for hire.*
[from *apply*]

plywood *NOUN* strong thin board made of layers of wood glued together.

PM *ABBREVIATION* Prime Minister.

p.m. *ABBREVIATION* after noon.
[short for Latin *post meridiem* = after noon]

pneumatic (*say* new-**mat**-ik) *ADJECTIVE* filled with or worked by compressed air • *a pneumatic drill.*
▷ **pneumatically** *adverb*
[from Greek *pneuma* = wind]

pneumonia (*say* new-**moh**-nee-a) *NOUN* a serious illness caused by inflammation of one or both lungs.
[from Greek *pneumon* = lung]

PO *ABBREVIATION* **1** Post Office. **2** postal order.

poach *VERB* **poaches, poaching, poached** **1** cook an egg (removed from its shell) in or over boiling water. **2** cook fish or fruit in a small amount of liquid. **3** steal game or fish from someone else's land or water. **4** take something unfairly • *One club was poaching members from another.*
▷ **poacher** *noun*
[same origin as *pouch*]

pocket *NOUN* **pockets** **1** a small bag-shaped part, especially in a piece of clothing. **2** a person's supply of money • *The expense is beyond my pocket.* **3** an isolated part or area • *small pockets of rain.*
▷ **pocketful** *noun*
- **be out of pocket** have spent more money than you have gained.

pocket *ADJECTIVE* small enough to carry in a pocket • *a pocket calculator.*

pocket *VERB* **pockets, pocketing, pocketed** put something into a pocket.
[from Old French *pochet* = little pouch]

pocket money *NOUN* money given to a child to spend as he or she likes.

pockmark *NOUN* **pockmarks** a scar or mark left on the skin by a disease.
▷ **pockmarked** *adjective*
[from Old English *poc* = pustule]

pod *NOUN* **pods** a long seed-container of the kind found on a pea or bean plant.
[origin unknown]

podgy *ADJECTIVE* **podgier, podgiest** short and fat.
[origin unknown]

podium (*say* poh-dee-um) *NOUN* **podiums** or **podia** a small platform on which a music conductor or someone making a speech stands.
[from Greek *podion* = little foot]

poem *NOUN* **poems** a piece of poetry.
[from Greek *poiema* = thing made]

poet *NOUN* **poets** a person who writes poetry.
▷ **poetess** *noun*
[from Greek *poietes* = maker]

poetry *NOUN* writing arranged in short lines, usually with a particular rhythm and sometimes with rhymes.
▷ **poetic** *adjective* **poetical** *adjective* **poetically** *adverb*

pogrom *NOUN* **pogroms** an organized massacre.
[Russian, = destruction]

poignant (*say* poin-yant) *ADJECTIVE* very distressing; affecting the feelings • *poignant memories.*
▷ **poignancy** *noun*
[from French, = pricking]

point *NOUN* **points** **1** the narrow or sharp end of something. **2** a dot • *the decimal point.* **3** a particular place or time • *At this point she was winning.* **4** a detail or characteristic • *He has his good points.* **5** the important or essential idea • *Keep to the point!* **6** purpose or value • *There is no point in hurrying.* **7** an electrical socket. **8** a device for changing a train from one track to another.

point *VERB* **points, pointing, pointed** **1** show where something is, especially by holding out a finger etc. towards it. **2** aim or direct • *She pointed a gun at me.* **3** fill in the parts between bricks with mortar or cement.
- **point out** draw attention to something.
[from Latin *punctum* = pricked]

point-blank *ADJECTIVE* **1** aimed or fired from close to the target. **2** direct and straightforward • *a point-blank refusal.*

point-blank *ADVERB* in a point-blank manner • *He refused point-blank.*
[from to *point* + *blank* = the white centre of a target]

point duty *NOUN* being stationed at a road junction to control the movement of traffic.
[because the person stays at one point, rather than patrolling]

pointed *ADJECTIVE* **1** with a point at the end. **2** clearly directed at a person • *a pointed remark.*
▷ **pointedly** *adverb*

pointer *NOUN* **pointers** **1** a stick, rod, or mark etc. used to point at something. **2** a dog that points with its muzzle towards birds that it scents. **3** an indication or hint.

pointless *ADJECTIVE* without a point; with no purpose.
▷ **pointlessly** *adverb*

point of view *NOUN* **points of view** a way of looking or thinking of something.

poise *NOUN* **1** a dignified self-confident manner. **2** balance.

poise *VERB* **poises, poising, poised** balance.
[from old French]

poised *ADJECTIVE* dignified and self-confident.
- **be poised to** be ready to do something.

poison *NOUN* **poisons** a substance that can harm or kill a living thing if swallowed or absorbed into the body.
▷ **poisonous** *adjective*

poison *VERB* **poisons, poisoning, poisoned** **1** give poison to; kill somebody with poison. **2** put poison in something. **3** corrupt or spoil something • *He poisoned their minds.*
▷ **poisoner** *noun*
[same origin as *potion*]

poke[1] *VERB* **pokes, poking, poked** **1** prod or jab. **2** push out or forward; stick out. **3** search • *I was poking about in the attic.*
- **poke fun at** ridicule.

poke *NOUN* **pokes** a poking movement; a prod.
[from old German or old Dutch]

poke[2] *NOUN*
- **buy a pig in a poke** buy something without seeing it.
[same origin as *pouch*]

poker[1] *NOUN* **pokers** a stiff metal rod for poking a fire.

poker[2] *NOUN* a card game in which players bet on who has the best cards.
[probably from German *pochen* = to brag]

poky *ADJECTIVE* **pokier, pokiest** small and cramped • *poky little rooms.*
[from *poke*[1]]

polar *ADJECTIVE* **1** to do with or near the North Pole or South Pole. **2** to do with either pole of a magnet.
▷ **polarity** *noun*

polar bear *NOUN* **polar bears** a white bear living in Arctic regions.

polarize *VERB* **polarizes, polarizing, polarized** **1** (*in science*) keep vibrations of light waves etc. to a single direction. **2** divide into two groups of completely opposite extremes of feeling or opinion • *Opinions had polarized.*
▷ **polarization** *noun*
[from *pole*[2]]

Polaroid *NOUN* (*trademark*) a type of plastic, used in sunglasses, which reduces the brightness of light passing through it.
[originally = a material which polarizes light passing through it: from *polarize* + *-oid*]

Polaroid camera *NOUN* **Polaroid cameras** (*trademark*) a camera that takes a picture and produces the finished photograph a few seconds later.

pole[1] *NOUN* **poles** a long slender rounded piece of wood or metal.
[same origin as *pale*[2]]

pole[2] *NOUN* **poles** **1** a point on the earth's surface that is as far north (**North Pole**) or as far south (**South Pole**) as possible. **2** either of the ends of a magnet. **3** either terminal of an electric cell or battery.
[from Greek *polos* = axis]

polecat *NOUN* **polecats** an animal of the weasel family with an unpleasant smell.
[origin unknown]

polemic (*say* pol-em-ik) *NOUN* **polemics** an attack in words against someone's opinion or actions.
▷ **polemical** *adjective*
[from Greek *polemos* = war]

pole star *NOUN* the star above the North Pole.

pole vault *NOUN* an athletic contest in which competitors jump over a high bar with the help of a long flexible pole.

police *NOUN* the people whose job is to catch criminals and make sure that the law is kept.
▷ **policeman** *noun* **policewoman** *noun*

police *VERB* **polices, policing, policed** keep order in a place by means of police.
[same origin as *political*]

police officer *NOUN* **police officers** a member of the police.

policy[1] *NOUN* **policies** the aims or plan of action of a person or group.
[same origin as *political*]

policy[2] *NOUN* **policies** a document stating the terms of a contract of insurance.
[from Greek *apodeixis* = evidence]

polio *NOUN* poliomyelitis.

poliomyelitis (*say* poh-lee-oh-my-il-**I**-tiss) *NOUN* a disease that can cause paralysis.
[from Greek]

polish *VERB* **polishes, polishing, polished** **1** make a thing smooth and shiny by rubbing. **2** make a thing better by making corrections and alterations.
▷ **polisher** *noun*
- **polish off** finish off.

polish *NOUN* **polishes** **1** a substance used in polishing. **2** a shine. **3** elegance of manner.
[from Latin]

polite *ADJECTIVE* having good manners.
▷ **politely** *adverb* **politeness** *noun*
[from Latin *politus* = polished]

politic (*say* pol-it-ik) *ADJECTIVE* prudent or wise.
[same origin as *political*]

political *ADJECTIVE* connected with the governing of a country or region.
▷ **politically** *adverb*
[from Greek *politeia* = citizenship or government]

politician *NOUN* **politicians** a person who is involved in politics.

politics *NOUN* political matters; the business of governing a country or region.

polka *NOUN* **polkas** a lively dance for couples.
[via German and French from Czech]

poll (*say as* *pole*) *NOUN* **polls** **1** voting or votes at an election. **2** an opinion poll. **3** (*old use*) the head.

poll *VERB* **polls, polling, polled** **1** vote at an election. **2** receive a stated number of votes in an election.
▷ **polling booth** *noun* **polling station** *noun*
[probably from old Dutch word *polle* = head. In some polls those voting yes stand apart from those voting no, and the decision is reached by counting the heads in the two groups]

pollarded *ADJECTIVE* (said about trees) with the tops trimmed so that young shoots start to grow thickly there.
[from *poll* **3**]

polled *ADJECTIVE* (said about cattle) with the horns trimmed.
[from *poll* **3**]

pollen *NOUN* powder produced by the anthers of flowers, containing male cells for fertilizing other flowers.
[Latin, = fine flour]

pollen count *NOUN* **pollen counts** a measurement of the amount of pollen in the air, given as a warning for people who are allergic to pollen.

pollinate *VERB* **pollinates, pollinating, pollinated** fertilize a plant with pollen.
▷ **pollination** *noun*

pollster *NOUN* **pollsters** a person who conducts an opinion poll.

poll tax *NOUN* **poll taxes** a tax that every adult has to pay regardless of income.

pollutant *NOUN* **pollutants** something that pollutes.

pollute *VERB* **pollutes, polluting, polluted** make the air, water, etc. dirty or impure.
▷ **pollution** *noun*
[from Latin]

polo *NOUN* a game rather like hockey, with players on horseback.
[from Tibetan]

polo neck *NOUN* **polo necks** a high round turned-over collar.
▷ **polo-necked** *adjective*

poltergeist *NOUN* **poltergeists** a ghost or spirit that throws things about noisily.
[from German *poltern* = make a disturbance + *Geist* = ghost]

poly *NOUN* **polys** (*informal*) a polytechnic.

poly- *PREFIX* many (as in *polygon*).
[from Greek]

polyanthus *NOUN* **polyanthuses** a kind of cultivated primrose.
[from *poly-* + Greek *anthos* = flower]

polychromatic or **polychrome** *ADJECTIVE* having many colours.
[from *poly-* + Greek *chroma* = colour]

polyester *NOUN* a synthetic material, often used to make clothing.
[from *polymer* + *ester*]

polygamy (*say* pol-**ig**-a-mee) *NOUN* having more than one wife at a time.
▷ **polygamous** *adjective* **polygamist** *noun*
[from *poly-* + Greek *gamos* = marriage]

polyglot *ADJECTIVE* knowing or using several languages.
[from *poly-* + Greek *glotta* = language]

polygon *NOUN* **polygons** a shape with many sides. Hexagons and octagons are polygons.
▷ **polygonal** *adjective*
[from *poly-* + Greek *gonia* = corner]

polyhedron *NOUN* **polyhedrons** a solid shape with many sides.
[from *poly-* + Greek *hedra* = base]

polymer *NOUN* **polymers** a substance whose molecule is formed from a large number of simple molecules combined.
[from *poly-* + Greek *meros* = part]

polyp (*say* pol-ip) *NOUN* **polyps** **1** a tiny creature with a tube-shaped body. **2** a small abnormal growth.
[from Latin]

polystyrene *NOUN* a kind of plastic used for insulating or packing things.
[from *polymer* + *styrene*, the name of a resin]

polytechnic *NOUN* **polytechnics** a college giving instruction in many subjects at degree level or below. In 1992 the British polytechnics were able to change their names and call themselves universities.
[from *poly-* + Greek *techne* = skill]

polytheism (*say* pol-ith-ee-izm) *NOUN* belief in more than one god.
▷ **polytheist** *noun*
[from *poly-* + Greek *theos* = god]

polythene *NOUN* a lightweight plastic used to make bags, wrappings, etc.
[from *polyethylene*, a polymer from which it is made]

pomegranate *NOUN* **pomegranates** a tropical fruit with many seeds.
[from Latin *pomum* = apple + *granatum* = having many seeds]

pommel *NOUN* **pommels** **1** a knob on the handle of a sword. **2** the raised part at the front of a saddle.
[from Latin *pomum* = apple]

pomp *NOUN* the ceremonial splendour that is traditional on important public occasions.
[from Greek *pompe* = solemn procession]

pompom or **pompon** *NOUN* **pompoms, pompons** a ball of coloured threads used as a decoration.
[French]

pompous *ADJECTIVE* full of excessive dignity and self-importance.
▷ **pompously** *adverb* **pomposity** *noun*
[from *pomp*]

pond *NOUN* **ponds** a small lake.
[from *pound*²]

ponder *VERB* **ponders, pondering, pondered** think deeply and seriously.
[from Latin *ponderare* = weigh]

ponderous *ADJECTIVE* **1** heavy and awkward. **2** laborious and dull • *He writes in a ponderous style.*
▷ **ponderously** *adverb*
[from Latin *ponderis* = of weight]

pong *NOUN* (*informal*) an unpleasant smell.
▷ **pong** *verb*
[origin unknown]

pontiff *NOUN* **pontiffs** the Pope.
[from Latin *pontifex* = chief priest]

pontifical *ADJECTIVE* **1** to do with a pontiff. **2** speaking or writing pompously.
▷ **pontifically** *adverb*

pontificate *VERB* **pontificates, pontificating, pontificated** give your opinions in a pompous way.
▷ **pontification** *noun*
[literally = behave like a pontiff]

pontoon¹ *NOUN* **pontoons** a boat or float used to support a bridge (a **pontoon bridge**) over a river.
[from Latin *pontis* = of a bridge]

pontoon² *NOUN* **1** a card game in which players try to get cards whose value totals 21. **2** a score of 21 from two cards in this game.
[from a bad English pronunciation of French *vingt-et-un* = 21]

pony *NOUN* **ponies** a small horse.
[from French *poulenet* = small foal]

ponytail *NOUN* **ponytails** a bunch of long hair tied at the back of the head.

pony-trekking *NOUN* travelling across country on a pony for pleasure.
▷ **pony-trekker** *noun*

poodle *NOUN* **poodles** a dog with thick curly hair.
[from German *Pudelhund* = water- dog]

pooh *INTERJECTION* an exclamation of disgust or contempt.

pool[1] *NOUN* **pools** **1** a pond. **2** a puddle. **3** a swimming pool.
[from Old English]

pool[2] *NOUN* **pools** **1** the fund of money staked in a gambling game. **2** a group of things shared by several people. **3** a game resembling billiards.
- **the pools** gambling based on the results of football matches.

pool *VERB* **pools, pooling, pooled** put money or things together for sharing.
[from French]

poop *NOUN* **poops** the stern of a ship.
[from Latin]

poor *ADJECTIVE* **1** with very little money or other resources. **2** not good; inadequate • *a poor piece of work.* **3** unfortunate; deserving pity • *Poor fellow!*
▷ **poorness** *noun*
[from old French; related to *pauper*]

poorly *ADVERB* **1** in a poor way • *We've played poorly this season.* **2** rather ill.

pop[1] *NOUN* **pops** **1** a small explosive sound. **2** a fizzy drink.

pop *VERB* **pops, popping, popped** **1** make a pop. **2** (*informal*) go or put quickly • *Can you pop down to the shop for me? I'll just pop this pie into the microwave.*
[imitating the sound]

pop[2] *NOUN* modern popular music.
[short for *popular*]

popcorn *NOUN* maize heated to burst and form fluffy balls.

Pope *NOUN* **Popes** the leader of the Roman Catholic Church.
[from Greek *papas* = father]

pop-eyed *ADJECTIVE* with bulging eyes.

popgun *NOUN* **popguns** a toy gun that shoots a cork etc. with a popping sound.

poplar *NOUN* **poplars** a tall slender tree.
[from Latin]

poplin *NOUN* a plain woven cotton material.
[from old French]

poppadam or **poppadom** *NOUN* **poppadams** or **poppadoms** a thin crisp biscuit made of lentil flour, eaten with Indian food.
[from Tamil]

poppy *NOUN* **poppies** a plant with large red flowers.
[via Old English from Latin]

populace *NOUN* the general public.
[same origin as *popular*]

popular *ADJECTIVE* **1** liked or enjoyed by many people. **2** held or believed by many people • *popular superstitions.* **3** intended for the general public.
▷ **popularly** *adverb* **popularity** *noun*
[from Latin *populus* = people]

popularize *VERB* **popularizes, popularizing, popularized** make a thing generally liked or known.
▷ **popularization** *noun*

populate *VERB* **populates, populating, populated** supply with a population; inhabit.
[same origin as *popular*]

population *NOUN* **populations** the people who live in a district or country; the total number of these people.

porcelain *NOUN* the finest kind of china.
[from French]

porch *NOUN* **porches** a shelter outside the entrance to a building.
[same origin as *portico*]

porcupine *NOUN* **porcupines** a small animal covered with long prickles.
[from old French *porc espin* = spiny pig]

pore[1] *NOUN* **pores** a tiny opening on the skin through which moisture can pass in or out.
[from Greek *poros* = passage]

pore[2] *VERB* **pores, poring, pored**
- **pore over** study with close attention • *He was poring over his books.*
[origin unknown]
USAGE Do not confuse with **pour**.

pork *NOUN* meat from a pig.
[from Latin *porcus* = pig]

pornography (*say* porn-og-ra-fee) *NOUN* obscene pictures or writings.
▷ **pornographic** *adjective*
[from Greek *porne* = prostitute, + *-graphy*]

porous *ADJECTIVE* allowing liquid or air to pass through.
▷ **porosity** *noun*
[same origin as *pore*[1]]

porphyry (*say* por-fir-ee) *NOUN* a kind of rock containing crystals of minerals.
[from Greek *porphyrites* = purple stone]

porpoise (*say* por-pus) *NOUN* **porpoises** a sea animal rather like a small whale.
[from Latin *porcus* = pig + *piscis* = fish]

porridge *NOUN* a food made by boiling oatmeal to a thick paste.
[from an old word *pottage* = soup]

port[1] *NOUN* **ports 1** a harbour. **2** a city or town with a harbour. **3** the left-hand side of a ship or aircraft when you are facing forward. (COMPARE **starboard**)
[from Latin *portus* = harbour]

port[2] *NOUN* a strong red Portuguese wine.
[from the city of *Oporto* in Portugal]

portable *ADJECTIVE* able to be carried.
[from Latin *portare* = carry]
WORD FAMILY There are a number of English words that are related to *portable* because part of their original meaning comes from the Latin word *portare* meaning 'to carry'. These include *deport*, *export*, *import*, *porter*, *report*, *support*, and *transport*.

portal *NOUN* **portals** a doorway or gateway.
[from Latin *porta* = gate]

portcullis *NOUN* **portcullises** a strong heavy vertical grating that can be lowered in grooves to block the gateway to a castle.
[from old French *porte coleice* = sliding door]

portend *VERB* **portends, portending, portended** be a sign or warning that something will happen • *Dark clouds portend a storm.*
[from Latin *pro-* = forwards + *tendere* = stretch]

portent *NOUN* **portents** an omen; a sign that something will happen.
▷ **portentous** *adjective*
[same origin as *portend*]

porter[1] *NOUN* **porters** a person whose job is to carry luggage or other goods.
[from Latin *portare* = carry]

porter[2] *NOUN* **porters** a person whose job is to look after the entrance to a large building.
[from Latin *porta* = gate]

portfolio *NOUN* **portfolios 1** a case for holding documents or drawings. **2** a government minister's special responsibility.
[from Italian *portare* = carry + *foglio* = sheet of paper]

porthole *NOUN* **portholes** a small window in the side of a ship or aircraft.
[from Latin *porta* = gate, + *hole*]

portico *NOUN* **porticoes** a roof supported on columns, usually forming a porch to a building.
[from Latin *porticus* = porch]

portion *NOUN* **portions** a part or share given to somebody.

portion *VERB* **portions, portioning, portioned** divide something into portions • *Portion it out.*
[from Latin]

portly *ADJECTIVE* **portlier, portliest** rather fat.
▷ **portliness** *noun*
[originally = dignified: from Middle English *port* = bearing, deportment]

portmanteau (*say* port-**mant**-oh) *NOUN* **portmanteaus** a trunk that opens into two equal parts for holding clothes etc.
[from French *porter* = carry + *manteau* = coat]

portmanteau word *NOUN* **portmanteau words** a word made from the sounds and meanings of two others, e.g. *motel* (from *motor* + *hotel*).

portrait *NOUN* **portraits 1** a picture of a person or animal. **2** a description in words.

portray *VERB* **portrays, portraying, portrayed 1** make a picture of a person or scene etc. **2** describe or show • *The play portrays the king as a kindly man.*
▷ **portrayal** *noun*
[from old French]

pose *NOUN* **poses 1** a position or posture of the body, e.g. for a portrait or photograph. **2** a way of behaving that someone adopts to give a particular impression.

pose *VERB* **poses, posing, posed 1** take up a pose. **2** put someone into a pose. **3** pretend. **4** put forward or present • *It poses several problems for us.*
[from French]

a b c d e f g h i j k l m n o p q r s t u v w x y z

poser *NOUN* **posers 1** a puzzling question or problem. **2** a person who behaves in an affected way in order to impress other people.

posh *ADJECTIVE* (*informal*) **1** very smart; high-class • *a posh restaurant.* **2** upper-class • *a posh accent.*
[origin unknown]

position *NOUN* **positions 1** the place where something is or should be. **2** the way a person or thing is placed or arranged • *in a sitting position.* **3** a situation or condition • *I am in no position to help you.* **4** paid employment; a job.
▷ **positional** *adjective*

position *VERB* **positions, positioning, positioned** place a person or thing in a certain position.
[from Latin *positio* = placing]

positive *ADJECTIVE* **1** definite or certain • *Are you positive you saw him? We have positive proof that he is guilty*. **2** agreeing; saying 'yes' • *We received a positive reply.* **3** confident and hopeful. **4** showing signs of what is being tested for • *Her pregnancy test was positive.* **5** greater than nought. **6** to do with the kind of electric charge that lacks electrons. **7** (said about an adjective or adverb) in the simple form, not comparative or superlative • *The positive form is 'big', the comparative is 'bigger', the superlative is 'biggest'.*
▷ **positively** *adverb*
USAGE The opposite of senses 2-6 is *negative.*

positive *NOUN* **positives** a photograph with the light and dark parts or colours as in the thing photographed. (COMPARE **negative**)
[from Latin *positivus* = settled]

positron *NOUN* **positrons** a particle of matter with a positive electric charge.
[from *positive* + *electron*]

posse (*say* poss-ee) *NOUN* **posses** a group of people, especially one that helps a sheriff.
[from Latin *posse comitatus* = force of the county]

possess *VERB* **possesses, possessing, possessed 1** have or own something. **2** control someone's thoughts or behaviour • *I don't know what possessed you to do such a thing!*
▷ **possessor** *noun*
[from Latin]

possessed *ADJECTIVE* seeming to be controlled by strong emotion or an evil spirit • *He fought like a man possessed.*

possession *NOUN* **possessions 1** something you possess or own. **2** owning something.

possessive *ADJECTIVE* **1** wanting to possess and keep things for yourself. **2** (*in grammar*) showing that somebody owns something • *a possessive pronoun* (see *pronoun*).

possibility *NOUN* **possibilities 1** being possible. **2** something that may exist or happen etc.

possible *ADJECTIVE* able to exist, happen, be done, or be used.
[from Latin *posse* = be able]

possibly *ADVERB* **1** in any way • *I can't possibly do it.* **2** perhaps.

possum *NOUN* **possums** an opossum.

post[1] *NOUN* **posts 1** an upright piece of wood, concrete, or metal etc. set in the ground. **2** the starting point or finishing point of a race • *He was left at the post.*

post *VERB* **posts, posting, posted 1** put up a notice or poster etc. to announce something. **2** send a message to an Internet site; display information online.
[from Latin *postis* = post]

post[2] *NOUN* **1** the collecting and delivering of letters, parcels, etc. **2** these letters and parcels etc.

post *VERB* **posts, posting, posted** put a letter or parcel etc. into a postbox for collection.
- **keep me posted** keep me informed.
[from French; related to *post*[3] (because originally mail was carried in relays by riders posted along the route)]

post[3] *NOUN* **posts 1** a position of paid employment; a job. **2** the place where someone is on duty • *a sentry post.* **3** a place occupied by soldiers, traders, etc.

post *VERB* **posts, posting, posted** place someone on duty • *We posted sentries.*
[from Latin *positum* = placed]

post- *PREFIX* after (as in *post-war*).
[from Latin]

postage *NOUN* the charge for sending something by post.

postage stamp *NOUN* **postage stamps** a stamp for sticking on things to be posted, showing the amount paid.

postal *ADJECTIVE* to do with or by the post.

postal order *NOUN* **postal orders** a document bought from a post office for sending money by post.

postbox *NOUN* **postboxes** a box into which letters are put for collection.

postcard *NOUN* **postcards** a card for sending messages by post without an envelope.

postcode *NOUN* **postcodes** a group of letters and numbers included in an address to help in sorting the post.

poster *NOUN* **posters** a large sheet of paper announcing or advertising something, for display in a public place.
[from *post*[1]]

poste restante (*say* rest-**ahnt**) *NOUN* a part of a post office where letters etc. are kept until called for.
[French, = letters remaining]

posterior *ADJECTIVE* situated at the back of something. (The opposite is **anterior**)

posterior *NOUN* **posteriors** the buttocks.
[Latin, = further back]

posterity *NOUN* future generations of people • *These letters and diaries should be preserved for posterity.*
[from Latin *posterus* = following, future]

postern *NOUN* **posterns** a small entrance at the back or side of a fortress etc.
[from old French; related to *posterior*]

postgraduate *ADJECTIVE* to do with studies carried on after taking a first university degree.

postgraduate *NOUN* **postgraduates** a person who continues studying or doing research after taking a first university degree.

post-haste *ADVERB* with great speed or haste.
[from *post*[2] + *haste* (because post was the quickest way of communication)]

posthumous (*say* **poss**-tew-mus) *ADJECTIVE* coming or happening after a person's death • *a posthumous award for bravery.*
▷ **posthumously** *adverb*
[from Latin *postumus* = last]

postilion (*say* poss-**til**-yon) *NOUN* **postilions** a person riding one of the horses pulling a carriage.
[from Italian *postiglione* = post-boy]

postman *NOUN* **postmen** a person who delivers or collects letters etc.

postmark *NOUN* **postmarks** an official mark put on something sent by post to show where and when it was posted.

post-mortem *NOUN* **post-mortems** an examination of a dead body to discover the cause of death.
[Latin, = after death]

post office *NOUN* **post offices** **1** a building or room where postal business is carried on. **2** the national organization responsible for postal services.

postpone *VERB* **postpones, postponing, postponed** fix a later time for something • *They postponed the meeting for a fortnight.*
▷ **postponement** *noun*
[from *post-* + Latin *ponere* = to place]

postscript *NOUN* **postscripts** something extra added at the end of a letter (after the writer's signature) or at the end of a book.
[from *post-* + Latin *scriptum* = written]

postulant *NOUN* **postulants** a person who applies to be admitted to an order of monks or nuns.
[from Latin, = claiming]

postulate *VERB* **postulates, postulating, postulated** assume that something is true and use it in reasoning.
▷ **postulation** *noun*

postulate *NOUN* **postulates** something postulated.
[from Latin *postulare* = to claim]

posture *NOUN* **postures** a particular position of the body, or the way in which a person stands, sits, or walks.
[from Latin *positura* = position or situation]

post-war *ADJECTIVE* happening during the time after a war.

posy *NOUN* **posies** a small bunch of flowers.
[from French *poésie* = poetry]

pot[1] *NOUN* **pots** **1** a deep usually round container. **2** (*informal*) a lot of something • *He has got pots of money.*
- **go to pot** (*informal*) lose quality; be ruined.
- **take pot luck** (*informal*) take whatever is available.

pot *VERB* **pots, potting, potted** put into a pot.
[from Old English]

pot[2] *NOUN* (*slang*) cannabis.
[short for Spanish *potiguaya* = drink of grief]

potash *NOUN* potassium carbonate.
[from Dutch *potasch* = pot ash (because it was first obtained from vegetable ashes washed in a pot)]

potassium *NOUN* a soft silvery-white metal substance that is essential for living things.
[from *potash*]

potato *NOUN* **potatoes** a starchy white tuber growing underground, used as a vegetable.
[via Spanish from Taino (a South American language)]

potent (*say* poh-tent) *ADJECTIVE* powerful.
▷ **potency** *noun*
[from Latin *potens* = able]

potentate (*say* poh-ten-tayt) *NOUN* **potentates** a powerful monarch or ruler.
[from Latin *potentatus* = power or rule]

potential (*say* po-ten-shal) *ADJECTIVE* capable of happening or being used or developed • *a potential winner.*
▷ **potentially** *adverb* **potentiality** *noun*

potential *NOUN* **1** the ability of a person or thing to develop in the future. **2** the voltage between two points.
[from Latin *potentia* = power]

pothole *NOUN* **potholes** **1** a deep natural hole in the ground. **2** a hole in a road.

potholing *NOUN* exploring underground potholes.
▷ **potholer** *noun*

potion *NOUN* **potions** a liquid for drinking as a medicine etc.
[from Latin *potio* = a drink]

pot-pourri (*say* poh-poor-ee) *NOUN* **pot-pourris** a scented mixture of dried petals and spices.
[French, = rotten pot]

pot shot *NOUN* **pot shots** a shot aimed casually at something.

potted *ADJECTIVE* **1** shortened or abridged • *a potted account of the story.* **2** preserved in a pot • *potted shrimps.*

potter[1] *NOUN* **potters** a person who makes pottery.

potter[2] *VERB* **potters, pottering, pottered** work or move about in a leisurely way • *I spent the afternoon pottering around in the garden.*
[from an old word *pote* = push or poke]

pottery *NOUN* **potteries** **1** cups, plates, ornaments, etc. made of baked clay. **2** the craft of making these things. **3** a place where a potter works.

potty[1] *ADJECTIVE* (*slang*) mad or foolish.
[origin unknown]

potty[2] *NOUN* **potties** (*informal*) a small bowl used by a young child instead of a toilet.
[from *pot*[1]]

pouch *NOUN* **pouches** **1** a small bag. **2** a fold of skin in which a kangaroo etc. keeps its young. **3** something shaped like a bag.
[from French *poche* = bag or pocket]

pouffe (*say* poof) *NOUN* **pouffes** a low padded stool.
[French]

poultice *NOUN* **poultices** a soft hot dressing put on a sore or inflamed place.
[from Latin *pultes* = soft food, pap]

poultry *NOUN* birds (e.g. chickens, geese, turkeys) kept for their eggs and meat.
[from old French *poulet* = pullet]

pounce *VERB* **pounces, pouncing, pounced** jump or swoop down quickly on something.
▷ **pounce** *noun*
[from old French]

pound[1] *NOUN* **pounds 1** a unit of money (in Britain = 100 pence). **2** a unit of weight equal to 16 ounces or about 454 grams.
[from Old English *pund*]

pound[2] *NOUN* **pounds 1** a place where stray animals are taken. **2** a public enclosure for vehicles officially removed.
[origin unknown]

pound[3] *VERB* **pounds, pounding, pounded 1** hit something often, especially in order to crush it. **2** run or go heavily • *He pounded down the stairs.* **3** thump • *My heart was pounding.*
[from Old English *punian*]

poundage *NOUN* a payment or charge of so much for each pound.

pour *VERB* **pours, pouring, poured 1** flow or make something flow. **2** rain heavily • *It poured all day.* **3** come or go in large amounts • *Letters poured in.*
▷ **pourer** *noun*
[origin unknown]
USAGE Do not confuse with **pore**.

pout *VERB* **pouts, pouting, pouted** push out your lips when you are annoyed or sulking.
▷ **pout** *noun*
[probably from a Scandinavian language]

poverty *NOUN* **1** being poor. **2** a lack or scarcity • *a poverty of ideas.*
[from old French; related to *pauper*]

POW *ABBREVIATION* prisoner of war.

powder *NOUN* **powders 1** a mass of fine dry particles of something. **2** a medicine or cosmetic etc. made as a powder.
3 gunpowder • *Keep your powder dry.*
▷ **powdery** *adjective*

powder *VERB* **powders, powdering, powdered 1** put powder on something.
2 make something into powder.
[from old French; related to *pulverize*]

powder room *NOUN* **powder rooms** a women's toilet in a public building.

power *NOUN* **powers 1** strength or energy. **2** the ability to do something • *the power of speech.* **3** political authority or control. **4** a powerful country, person, or organization. **5** mechanical or electrical energy; the electricity supply • *There was a power failure after the storm.* **6** (*in science*) the rate of doing work, measured in watts or horsepower.
7 (*in mathematics*) the product of a number multiplied by itself a given number of times • *The third power of 2 = 2 x 2 x 2 = 8.*
▷ **powered** *adjective* **powerless** *adjective*
[from old French]

powerboat *NOUN* **powerboats** a powerful motor boat.

powerful *ADJECTIVE* having great power, strength, or influence.
▷ **powerfully** *adverb*

powerhouse *NOUN* **powerhouses 1** a person with great strength and energy. **2** a power station.

power station *NOUN* **power stations** a building where electricity is produced.

pp. *ABBREVIATION* pages.

practicable *ADJECTIVE* able to be done.
[French, from *pratiquer* = put into practice]
USAGE Do not confuse with **practical**.

practical *ADJECTIVE* **1** able to do or make useful things • *a practical person.* **2** likely to be useful • *a very practical invention.*
3 actually doing something, rather than just learning or thinking about it • *She has had practical experience.*
▷ **practicality** *noun*
USAGE Do not confuse with **practicable**.

practical *NOUN* **practicals** a lesson or examination in which you actually do or make something rather than reading or writing about it • *a chemistry practical.*
[from Greek *prattein* = do]

practical joke *NOUN* **practical jokes** a trick played on somebody.

practically *ADVERB* **1** in a practical way.
2 almost • *I've practically finished.*

A B C D E F G H I J K L M N O P Q R S T U V W X Y Z

practice *NOUN* **practices** **1** doing something repeatedly in order to become better at it • *Have you done your piano practice?* **2** actually doing something; action, not theory • *It works well in practice.* **3** the professional business of a doctor, dentist, lawyer, etc. **4** a habit or custom • *It is his practice to work until midnight.*
- **out of practice** no longer skilful because you have not practised recently.
[from *practise*]
USAGE See the note on **practise**.

practise *VERB* **practises, practising, practised** **1** do something repeatedly in order to become better at it. **2** do something actively or habitually • *Practise what you preach.* **3** work as a doctor, lawyer, or other professional person.
[from Latin *practicare* = carry out, perform]
USAGE Note the spelling: *practice* is a noun, *practise* is a verb.

practised *ADJECTIVE* experienced or expert.

practitioner *NOUN* **practitioners** a professional worker, especially a doctor.
[from old French]

pragmatic *ADJECTIVE* treating things in a practical way • *We need to take a pragmatic approach to the problem.*
▷ **pragmatically** *adverb* **pragmatism** *noun* **pragmatist** *noun*
[from Greek *pragmatikos* = businesslike]

prairie *NOUN* **prairies** a large area of flat grass-covered land in North America.
[French, from Latin *pratum* = meadow]

praise *VERB* **praises, praising, praised** **1** say that somebody or something is very good. **2** honour God in words.

praise *NOUN* words that praise somebody or something.
▷ **praiseworthy** *adjective*
[from Latin *pretium* = value]

pram *NOUN* **prams** a four-wheeled carriage for a baby, pushed by a person walking.
[short for *perambulator*]

prance *VERB* **prances, prancing, pranced** move about in a lively or happy way.
[origin unknown]

prank *NOUN* **pranks** a trick played for mischief; a practical joke.
▷ **prankster** *noun*
[probably from German or Dutch]

prattle *VERB* **prattles, prattling, prattled** chatter like a young child.
▷ **prattle** *noun*
[from old German]

prawn *NOUN* **prawns** an edible shellfish like a large shrimp.
[origin unknown]

pray *VERB* **prays, praying, prayed** **1** talk to God. **2** ask earnestly for something. **3** (*formal*) please • *Pray be seated.*
[from old French]

prayer *NOUN* **prayers** praying; words used in praying.

pre- *PREFIX* before (as in *prehistoric*).
[from Latin]

preach *VERB* **preaches, preaching, preached** give a religious or moral talk.
▷ **preacher** *noun*
[from old French]

preamble *NOUN* **preambles** the introduction to a speech or book or document etc.
[from *pre-* + Latin *ambulare* = go]

pre-arranged *ADJECTIVE* arranged beforehand.
▷ **pre-arrangement** *noun*

precarious (*say* pri-kair-ee-us) *ADJECTIVE* not very safe or secure.
▷ **precariously** *adverb*
[from Latin *precarius* = uncertain]

precaution *NOUN* **precautions** something done to prevent future trouble or danger.
▷ **precautionary** *adjective*
[from *pre-* + Latin *cavere* = take care]

precede *VERB* **precedes, preceding, preceded** come or go before something else.
[from *pre-* + Latin *cedere* = go]
USAGE Do not confuse with **proceed**.

precedence (*say* press-i-dens) *NOUN* the right of something to be put first because it is more important.
- **take precedence** have priority.

precedent (*say* press-i-dent) *NOUN* **precedents** a previous case that is taken as an example to be followed.

precept (*say* pree-sept) *NOUN* **precepts** a rule for action or conduct; an instruction.
[from *pre-* + Latin *-ceptum* = taken]

precinct (*say* pree-sinkt) *NOUN* **precincts** **1** a part of a town where traffic is not allowed • *a shopping precinct.* **2** the area round a place, especially round a cathedral. **3** (*American*) one of the districts into which a city or town is divided for elections or policing purposes.
[from *pre-* + Latin *cinctum* = surrounded]

precious *ADJECTIVE* **1** very valuable. **2** greatly loved.
▷ **preciousness** *noun*

precious *ADVERB* (*informal*) very • *We have precious little time.*
[from Latin *pretium* = value]

precipice *NOUN* **precipices** a very steep place, such as the face of a cliff.
[from Latin *praeceps* = headlong]

precipitate *VERB* **precipitates, precipitating, precipitated** **1** make something happen suddenly or soon • *The insult precipitated a quarrel.* **2** throw or send something down; make something fall • *The push precipitated him through the window.* **3** cause a solid substance to separate chemically from a solution.

precipitate *NOUN* **precipitates** a substance precipitated from a solution.

precipitate *ADJECTIVE* hurried or hasty • *a precipitate departure.*
[same origin as *precipice*]

precipitation *NOUN* the amount of rain, snow, or hail that falls during a period of time.

precipitous *ADJECTIVE* like a precipice; steep.
▷ **precipitously** *adverb*

précis (*say* pray-see) *NOUN* **précis** (*say* pray-seez) a summary.
[French, = precise]

precise *ADJECTIVE* exact; clearly stated.
▷ **precisely** *adverb* **precision** *noun*
[from Latin *praecisum* = cut short]

preclude *VERB* **precludes, precluding, precluded** prevent something from happening.
[from *pre-* + Latin *claudere* = shut]

precocious (*say* prik-oh-shus) *ADJECTIVE* (said about a child) very advanced or developed for his or her age.
▷ **precociously** *adverb* **precocity** *noun*
[from Latin *praecox* = ripe very early]

preconceived *ADJECTIVE* (said about an idea) formed in advance, before full information is available.
▷ **preconception** *noun*
[from *pre-* + *conceive*]

precursor *NOUN* **precursors** something that was an earlier form of something that came later; a forerunner.
[from *pre-* + Latin *cursor* = runner]

predator (*say* pred-a-ter) *NOUN* **predators** an animal that hunts or preys upon others.
▷ **predatory** *adjective*
[from Latin *praedator* = plunderer]

predecessor (*say* pree-dis-ess-er) *NOUN* **predecessors** an earlier person or thing, e.g. an ancestor or the former holder of a job.
[from *pre-* + Latin *decessor* = person departed]

predestine *VERB* **predestines, predestining, predestined** determine something beforehand.
▷ **predestination** *noun*

predicament (*say* prid-ik-a-ment) *NOUN* **predicaments** a difficult or unpleasant situation.
[from Latin]

predicate *NOUN* **predicates** the part of a sentence that says something about the subject, e.g. 'is short' in *Life is short.*
[from Latin *praedicare* = proclaim]

predicative (*say* prid-ik-a-tiv) *ADJECTIVE* (*in grammar*) forming part of the predicate, e.g. 'old' in *The dog is old.* (COMPARE **attributive**)
▷ **predicatively** *adverb*

predict *VERB* **predicts, predicting, predicted** say what will happen in the future; foretell or prophesy.
▷ **predictable** *adjective* **prediction** *noun* **predictor** *noun*
[from *pre-* + Latin *dicere* = say]

predispose *VERB* **predisposes, predisposing, predisposed** influence you in advance so that you are likely to do or be in favour of something • *We were predisposed to help them.*
▷ **predisposition** *noun*

predominate *VERB* **predominates, predominating, predominated** be the largest or most important or most powerful.
▷ **predominant** *adjective* **predominance** *noun* **predominantly** *adverb*
[from *pre-* + Latin *dominari* = rule, dominate]

pre-eminent *ADJECTIVE* excelling others; outstanding.
▷ **pre-eminently** *adverb* **pre-eminence** *noun*

pre-empt *VERB* **pre-empts, pre-empting, pre-empted** take action to prevent or block something; forestall.
▷ **pre-emptive** *adjective*

preen *VERB* **preens, preening, preened** (said about a bird) smooth its feathers with its beak.
- **preen yourself 1** smarten your appearance. **2** congratulate yourself.
[origin unknown]

prefab *NOUN* **prefabs** (*informal*) a prefabricated building.

prefabricated *ADJECTIVE* made in sections ready to be assembled on a site.
▷ **prefabrication** *noun*
[from *pre-* + *fabricate*]

preface (*say* pref-as) *NOUN* **prefaces** an introduction at the beginning of a book or speech.
▷ **preface** *verb*
[from Latin *praefatio* = something said beforehand]

prefect *NOUN* **prefects 1** a senior pupil in a school, given authority to help to keep order. **2** a regional official in France, Japan, and other countries.
[from Latin *praefectus* = overseer]

prefer *VERB* **prefers, preferring, preferred 1** like one person or thing more than another. **2** (*formal*) put forward • *They preferred charges of forgery against him.*
▷ **preference** *noun*
[from *pre-* + Latin *ferre* = carry]
WORD FAMILY There are a number of English words that are related to *prefer* because part of their original meaning comes from the Latin word *ferre* meaning 'to bear, carry, or bring'. These include *carboniferous*, *confer*, *coniferous*, *differ*, *infer*, *refer*, *transfer*, and *vociferous*.

preferable (*say* pref-er-a-bul) *ADJECTIVE* liked better; more desirable.
▷ **preferably** *adverb*

preferential (*say* pref-er-en-shal) *ADJECTIVE* being favoured above others • *preferential treatment.*

preferment *NOUN* promotion.

prefix *NOUN* **prefixes** a word or syllable joined to the front of a word to change or add to its meaning, as in *dis*order, *out*stretched, *un*happy.
[from Latin]

pregnant *ADJECTIVE* **1** having a baby developing in the womb. **2** full of meaning or significance • *There was a pregnant pause.*
▷ **pregnancy** *noun*
[from *pre-* + Latin *gnasci* = be born]

prehensile *ADJECTIVE* (said about an animal's foot or tail etc.) able to grasp things.
[from Latin *prehendere* = seize]

prehistoric *ADJECTIVE* belonging to very ancient times, before written records of events were made.
▷ **prehistory** *noun*

prejudice *NOUN* **prejudices** an unfavourable opinion or dislike formed without examining the facts fairly.
▷ **prejudiced** *adjective*
[from *pre-* + Latin *judicium* = judgement]

prelate (*say* prel-at) *NOUN* **prelates** an important member of the clergy.
[from Latin *praelatus* = preferred]

preliminary *ADJECTIVE* coming before an important action or event and preparing for it.
[from *pre-* + Latin *limen* = threshold]

prelude *NOUN* **preludes** **1** a thing that introduces or leads up to something else. **2** a short piece of music, especially one that introduces a longer piece.
[from *pre-* + Latin *ludere* = to play]

premature *ADJECTIVE* too early; coming before the usual or proper time.
▷ **prematurely** *adverb*
[from *pre-* + Latin *maturus* = mature]

premeditated *ADJECTIVE* planned beforehand • *a premeditated crime.*
[from *pre-* + Latin *meditare* = meditate]

premier (*say* **prem**-ee-er) *ADJECTIVE* first in importance, order, or time.

premier *NOUN* **premiers** a prime minister or other head of government.
[French, = first]

première (*say* prem-**yair**) *NOUN* **premières** the first public performance of a play or film.
[French, feminine of *premier* = first]

premises *PLURAL NOUN* a building and its grounds.
[originally, the buildings etc. previously mentioned on a deed: from Latin *praemittere* = put before]

premiss (*say* **prem**-iss) *NOUN* **premisses** a statement used as the basis for a piece of reasoning.
[same origin as *premises*]

premium *NOUN* **premiums** **1** an amount or instalment paid to an insurance company. **2** an extra charge or payment.
- **at a premium** **1** above the normal price. **2** in demand but scarce.
[from Latin *praemium* = reward]

Premium Bond *NOUN* **Premium Bonds** a savings certificate that gives the person who holds it a chance to win a prize of money.

premonition *NOUN* **premonitions** a feeling that something is about to happen, especially something bad.
[from *pre-* + Latin *monere* = warn]

preoccupied *ADJECTIVE* having your thoughts completely busy with something.
▷ **preoccupation** *noun*

prep *NOUN* (*informal*) homework.
[short for *preparation*]

preparation *NOUN* **preparations** **1** getting something ready. **2** something done in order to get ready for an event or activity • *We were making last-minute preparations.* **3** something prepared, especially medicine or food.

preparatory *ADJECTIVE* preparing for something.

preparatory school *NOUN* **preparatory schools** a school that prepares pupils for a higher school.

prepare *VERB* **prepares, preparing, prepared** get ready; make something ready.
- **be prepared to** be ready and willing to do something.
[from *pre-* + Latin *parare* = get something ready]

preponderate *VERB* **preponderates, preponderating, preponderated** be greater than others in number or importance.
▷ **preponderance** *noun*
preponderant *adjective*
[from Latin *praeponderare* = outweigh]

preposition *NOUN* **prepositions** a word used with a noun or pronoun to show place, position, time, or means, e.g. *at* home, *in* the hall, *on* Sunday, *by* train.
[from *pre-* + Latin *positio* = placing]

prepossessing *ADJECTIVE* attractive • *Its appearance is not very prepossessing.*
[from *pre-* + *possess*]

preposterous *ADJECTIVE* completely absurd or ridiculous.
[from Latin *praeposterus* = back to front, from *prae* = before + *posterus* = behind]

prep school *NOUN* **prep schools** a preparatory school.

prerequisite *NOUN* **prerequisites** something required as a condition or in preparation for something else • *The ability to swim is a prerequisite for learning to sail.*
▷ **prerequisite** *adjective*

prerogative *NOUN* **prerogatives** a right or privilege that belongs to one person or group.
[from Latin *praerogativa* = the people who vote first]

Presbyterian (*say* prez-bit-eer-ee-an) *NOUN* **Presbyterians** a member of a Christian Church governed by elders who are all of equal rank, especially the national Church of Scotland.
[from Greek *presbyteros* = elder]

presbytery *NOUN* **presbyteries** the house of a Roman Catholic priest.

pre-school *ADJECTIVE* to do with the time before a child is old enough to attend school.

prescribe *VERB* **prescribes, prescribing, prescribed** **1** advise a person to use a particular medicine or treatment etc. **2** say what should be done.
[from *pre-* + Latin *scribere* = write]
USAGE Do not confuse with **proscribe**.

prescription *NOUN* **prescriptions** **1** a doctor's written order for a medicine. **2** the medicine prescribed. **3** prescribing.

prescriptive *ADJECTIVE* laying down rules.

presence *NOUN* **1** being present in a place • *Your presence is required.* **2** a person's impressive appearance or manner.

presence of mind *NOUN* the ability to act quickly and sensibly in an emergency.

present[1] *ADJECTIVE* **1** in a particular place • *No one else was present.* **2** belonging or referring to what is happening now; existing now • *the present Queen.*

present *NOUN* present times or events; the time now • *The head is away at present.*
[from Latin *praesens* = being at hand]

present[2] *NOUN* **presents** something given or received as a gift.

present (*say* priz-ent) *VERB* **presents, presenting, presented** **1** give something, especially with a ceremony • *Who is to present the prizes?* **2** introduce someone to another person; introduce a radio or television programme to an audience. **3** put on a play or other entertainment. **4** show. **5** cause or provide something • *Translating a poem presents a number of problems.*
▷ **presentation** *noun* **presenter** *noun*
[from Latin *praesentare* = place before someone]

presentable *ADJECTIVE* fit to be presented to other people; looking good.

presentiment *NOUN* **presentiments** a feeling that something bad is about to happen; a foreboding.
[from *pre-* + old French *sentement* = feeling]

presently *ADVERB* **1** soon • *I shall be with you presently.* **2** now • *the person who is presently in charge.*
[from *present*[1]]

preservative *NOUN* **preservatives** a substance added to food to preserve it.

preserve *VERB* **preserves, preserving, preserved** keep something safe or in good condition.
▷ **preserver** *noun* **preservation** *noun*

preserve *NOUN* **preserves** **1** jam made with preserved fruit. **2** an activity that belongs to a particular person or group.
[from *pre-* + Latin *servare* = keep]

preside *VERB* **presides, presiding, presided** be in charge of a meeting etc.
[from *pre-* + Latin *-sidere* = sit]

president *NOUN* **presidents** **1** the person in charge of a club, society, or council etc. **2** the head of a republic.
▷ **presidency** *noun* **presidential** *adjective*
[from Latin *praesidens* = sitting in front]

press *VERB* **presses, pressing, pressed** **1** put weight or force steadily on something; squeeze. **2** make something by pressing. **3** make clothes smooth by ironing them. **4** urge; make demands • *They pressed for an increase in wages.*

press *NOUN* **presses** **1** a device for pressing things • *a trouser press.* **2** a machine for printing things. **3** a firm that prints or publishes books etc. • *Oxford University Press.* **4** newspapers; journalists.
[from Latin *pressum* = squeezed]

press conference *NOUN* **press conferences** an interview with a group of journalists.

press-gang *NOUN* **press-gangs** (*historical*) a group of men whose job was to force people to serve in the army or navy.

pressing *ADJECTIVE* needing immediate action; urgent • *a pressing need.*

press-up *NOUN* **press-ups** an exercise in which you lie face downwards and press down with your hands to lift your body.

pressure *NOUN* **pressures** **1** continuous pressing. **2** the force with which something presses. **3** the force of the atmosphere on the earth's surface • *a band of high pressure.* **4** an influence that persuades or compels you to do something.
[from Latin]

pressure cooker *NOUN* **pressure cookers** a large air-tight pan used for cooking food quickly under steam pressure.

pressure group *NOUN* **pressure groups** an organized group that tries to influence public policy on a particular issue.

pressurize *VERB* **pressurizes, pressurizing, pressurized** **1** keep a compartment at the same air pressure all the time. **2** try to force a person to do something.
▷ **pressurization** *noun*

prestige (*say* pres-teej) *NOUN* good reputation.
▷ **prestigious** *adjective*
[from Latin *praestigium* = an illusion]

presumably *ADVERB* according to what you may presume.

presume *VERB* **presumes, presuming, presumed** **1** suppose; assume something to be true • *I presumed that she was dead.* **2** take the liberty of doing something; venture • *I wouldn't presume to advise you.*
▷ **presumption** *noun*
[from *pre-* + Latin *sumere* = take]

presumptive *ADJECTIVE* presuming something.

presumptuous *ADJECTIVE* too bold or confident.
▷ **presumptuously** *adverb*

presuppose *VERB* **presupposes, presupposing, presupposed** suppose or assume something beforehand.
▷ **presupposition** *noun*
[from French]

pretence *NOUN* **pretences** an attempt to pretend that something is true.
- **false pretences** pretending to be something that you are not, in order to deceive people • *You've invited me here under false pretences.*

pretend *VERB* **pretends, pretending, pretended** **1** behave as if something is true or real when you know that it is not, either in play or so as to deceive people. **2** put forward a claim • *The son of King James II pretended to the British throne.*
[from Latin *praetendere* = put forward or claim]

pretender *NOUN* **pretenders** a person who claims a throne or title • *The son of King James II was known as the Old Pretender .*

pretension *NOUN* **pretensions** **1** a doubtful claim. **2** pretentious or showy behaviour.

pretentious *ADJECTIVE* **1** trying to impress by claiming greater importance or merit than is actually the case. **2** showy or ostentatious.
▷ **pretentiously** *adverb*
pretentiousness *noun*
[from French; related to *pretend*]

pretext *NOUN* **pretexts** a reason put forward to conceal the true reason.
[from Latin *praetextus* = an outward display]

pretty *ADJECTIVE* **prettier, prettiest** attractive in a delicate way.
▷ **prettily** *adverb* **prettiness** *noun*

pretty *ADVERB* quite • *It's pretty cold.*
[from Old English]

prevail *VERB* **prevails, prevailing, prevailed** **1** be the most frequent or general • *The prevailing wind is from the south-west.* **2** be victorious.
[from *pre-* + Latin *valere* = have power]

prevalent (*say* prev-a-lent) *ADJECTIVE* most frequent or common; widespread.
▷ **prevalence** *noun*
[same origin as *prevail*]

prevaricate *VERB* **prevaricates, prevaricating, prevaricated** say something that is not actually a lie but is evasive or misleading.
▷ **prevarication** *noun*
[from Latin *praevaricari* = go crookedly]

prevent *VERB* **prevents, preventing, prevented** 1 stop something from happening. 2 stop a person from doing something.
▷ **preventable** *adjective* **prevention** *noun* **preventive** or **preventative** *adjective*
[from Latin *praevenire* = come first, anticipate]

preview *NOUN* **previews** a showing of a film or play etc. before it is shown to the general public.

previous *ADJECTIVE* coming before this; preceding.
▷ **previously** *adverb*
[from *pre-* + Latin *via* = way]

prey (*say as* pray) *NOUN* an animal that is hunted or killed by another for food.

prey *VERB* **preys, preying, preyed**
- **prey on** 1 hunt or take as prey. 2 cause to worry • *The problem preyed on his mind.*
[from old French]

price *NOUN* **prices** 1 the amount of money for which something is bought or sold. 2 what must be given or done in order to achieve something.

price *VERB* **prices, pricing, priced** decide the price of something.
[from old French: related to *praise*]

priceless *ADJECTIVE* 1 very valuable. 2 (*informal*) very amusing.

prick *VERB* **pricks, pricking, pricked** 1 make a tiny hole in something. 2 hurt somebody with a pin or needle etc.
▷ **prick** *noun*
- **prick up your ears** start listening suddenly.
[from Old English]

prickle *NOUN* **prickles** 1 a small thorn. 2 a sharp spine on a hedgehog or cactus etc. 3 a feeling that something is pricking you.
▷ **prickly** *adjective*

prickle *VERB* **prickles, prickling, prickled** feel or cause a pricking feeling.
[from Old English]

pride *NOUN* **prides** 1 a feeling of deep pleasure or satisfaction when you have done something well. 2 something that makes you feel proud. 3 dignity or self-respect. 4 too high an opinion of yourself. 5 a group of lions.
- **pride of place** the most important or most honoured position.

pride *VERB* **prides, priding, prided**
- **pride yourself on** be proud of.
[from *proud*]

priest *NOUN* **priests** 1 a member of the clergy in certain Christian Churches. 2 a person who conducts religious ceremonies in a non-Christian religion.
▷ **priesthood** *noun* **priestly** *adjective*
[via Old English from Latin]

priestess *NOUN* **priestesses** a female priest in a non-Christian religion.

prig *NOUN* **prigs** a self-righteous person.
▷ **priggish** *adjective*
[origin unknown]

prim *ADJECTIVE* **primmer, primmest** formal and correct in manner; disliking anything rough or rude.
▷ **primly** *adverb* **primness** *noun*
[origin unknown]

primacy (*say* pry-ma-see) *NOUN* being the first or most important.

prima donna (*say* preem-a) *NOUN* **prima donnas** the chief female singer in an opera.
[Italian, = first lady]

prima facie (*say* pry-ma fay-shee) *ADVERB & ADJECTIVE* at first sight; judging by the first impression.
[Latin, = on first appearance]

primary *ADJECTIVE* first; most important. (COMPARE **secondary**)
▷ **primarily** (*say* pry-mer-il-ee) *adverb*
[same origin as *prime*]

primary colour *NOUN* **primary colours** one of the colours from which all others can be made by mixing (red, yellow, and blue for paint; red, green, and violet for light).

primary school *NOUN* **primary schools** a school for the first stage of a child's education.

primate (*say* pry-mat) *NOUN* **primates** **1** an animal of the group that includes human beings, apes, and monkeys. **2** an archbishop.
[from Latin *primas* = of the first rank]

prime *ADJECTIVE* **1** chief; most important • *the prime cause.* **2** excellent; first-rate • *prime beef.*

prime *NOUN* the best time or stage of something • *in the prime of life.*

prime *VERB* **primes, priming, primed** **1** prepare something for use or action. **2** put a coat of liquid on something to prepare it for painting. **3** equip a person with information.
[from Latin *primus* = first]

prime minister *NOUN* **prime ministers** the leader of a government.

prime number *NOUN* **prime numbers** a number (e.g. 2, 3, 5, 7, 11) that can be divided exactly only by itself and one.

primer *NOUN* **primers** **1** a liquid for priming a surface. **2** an elementary textbook.

primeval (*say* pry-mee-val) *ADJECTIVE* belonging to the earliest times of the world.
[from Latin *primus* = first + *aevum* = age]

primitive *ADJECTIVE* **1** at an early stage of civilization. **2** at an early stage of development; not complicated or sophisticated • *primitive technology.*

primogeniture *NOUN* being a first-born child; the custom by which an eldest son inherits all his parents' property.
[from Latin *primo* = first + *genitus* = born]

primordial *ADJECTIVE* belonging to the earliest times of the world; primeval.
[from Latin *primus* = first + *ordiri* = begin]

primrose *NOUN* **primroses** a pale-yellow flower that blooms in spring.
[from Latin *prima rosa* = first rose]

prince *NOUN* **princes** **1** the son of a king or queen. **2** a man or boy in a royal family.
▷ **princely** *adjective*
[from Latin *princeps* = chieftain]

princess *NOUN* **princesses** **1** the daughter of a king or queen. **2** a woman or girl in a royal family. **3** the wife of a prince.
[from French]

principal *ADJECTIVE* chief; most important.
▷ **principally** *adverb*

principal *NOUN* **principals** the head of a college or school.
[from Latin *principalis* = first or chief]
USAGE Do not confuse with **principle**.

principality *NOUN* **principalities** a country ruled by a prince.
- **the Principality** Wales.

principle *NOUN* **principles** **1** a general truth, belief, or rule • *She taught me the principles of geometry.* **2** a rule of conduct • *Cheating is against his principles.*
- **in principle** in general, not in details.
- **on principle** because of your principles of behaviour.
[from Latin *principium* = source]
USAGE Do not confuse with **principal**.

print *VERB* **prints, printing, printed** **1** put words or pictures on paper by using a machine. **2** write with letters that are not joined together. **3** press a mark or design etc. on a surface. **4** make a picture from the negative of a photograph.

print *NOUN* **prints** **1** printed lettering or words. **2** a mark made by something pressing on a surface. **3** a printed picture, photograph, or design.
- **in print** available from a publisher.
- **out of print** no longer available from a publisher.
[from old French *priente* = pressed]

printed circuit *NOUN* **printed circuits** an electric circuit made by pressing thin metal strips on to a board.

printer *NOUN* **printers** **1** someone who prints books or newspapers. **2** a machine that prints on paper from data in a computer.

printout *NOUN* **printouts** information produced in printed form by a computer.

prior *ADJECTIVE* earlier or more important than something else • *a prior engagement.*

prior *NOUN* **priors** a monk who is the head of a religious house or order.
▷ **prioress** *noun*
[Latin, = former, more important]

prioritize *VERB* **prioritizes, prioritizing, prioritized** put tasks in order of importance, so that you can deal with the most important first.
[from *priority*]

priority *NOUN* **priorities** **1** being earlier or more important than something else; precedence. **2** something considered more important than other things • *Safety is a priority.*
[from French; related to *prior*]

priory *NOUN* **priories** a religious house governed by a prior or prioress.

prise *VERB* **prises, prising, prised** lever something out or open • *Prise the lid off the crate.*
[French, = seized]

prism (*say* prizm) *NOUN* **prisms** **1** (*in mathematics*) a solid shape with ends that are triangles or polygons which are equal and parallel. **2** a glass prism that breaks up light into the colours of the rainbow.
▷ **prismatic** *adjective*
[from Greek]

prison *NOUN* **prisons** a place where criminals are kept as a punishment.
[from old French]

prisoner *NOUN* **prisoners** **1** a person kept in prison. **2** a captive.

prisoner of war *NOUN* **prisoners of war** a person captured and imprisoned by the enemy in a war.

pristine *ADJECTIVE* in its original condition; unspoilt.
[from Latin *pristinus* = former]

private *ADJECTIVE* **1** belonging to a particular person or group • *private property.* **2** confidential • *private talks.* **3** quiet and secluded. **4** not holding public office • *a private citizen.* **5** independent or commercial; not run by the government • *private medicine; a private detective.*
▷ **privately** *adverb* **privacy** (*say* priv-a-see) *noun*
- **in private** where only particular people can see or hear; not in public.

private *NOUN* **privates** a soldier of the lowest rank.
[from Latin *privus* = single or individual]

privation *NOUN* **privations** loss or lack of something; lack of necessities.
[from Latin *privatus* = deprived]

privatize *VERB* **privatizes, privatizing, privatized** transfer the running of a business or industry from the state to private owners.
▷ **privatization** *noun*

privet *NOUN* **privets** an evergreen shrub with small leaves, used to make hedges.
[origin unknown]

privilege *NOUN* **privileges** a special right or advantage given to one person or group.
▷ **privileged** *adjective*
[from Latin *privus* = an individual + *legis* = of law]

privy *ADJECTIVE* (*old use*) secret and private.
- **be privy to** be sharing in the secret of someone's plans etc.

privy *NOUN* **privies** (*old use*) an outside toilet.
[from Latin *privatus* = private]

Privy Council *NOUN* a group of distinguished people who advise the sovereign.

privy purse *NOUN* an allowance made to the sovereign from public funds.

prize *NOUN* **prizes** **1** an award given to the winner of a game or competition etc. **2** something taken from an enemy.

prize *VERB* **prizes, prizing, prized** value something greatly.
[a different spelling of *price*]

pro[1] *NOUN* **pros** (*informal*) a professional.

pro[2] *NOUN* **pros** - **pros and cons** reasons for and against something.
[from Latin *pro* = for + *contra* = against]

pro- *PREFIX* **1** favouring or supporting (as in *pro-British*). **2** deputizing or substituted for (as in *pronoun*). **3** onwards; forwards (as in *proceed*).
[from Latin *pro* = for; in front of]

probability *NOUN* **probabilities** **1** likelihood. **2** something that is probable.

probable *ADJECTIVE* likely to happen or be true.
▷ **probably** *adverb*
[from Latin *probare* = prove]

probate *NOUN* the official process of proving that a person's will is valid.
[from Latin *probatum* = tested, proved]

probation *NOUN* the testing of a person's character and abilities, e.g. to see whether they are suitable for a job they have recently started.
▷ **probationary** *adjective*
- **on probation** being supervised by a probation officer instead of being sent to prison.
[same origin as *prove*]

probationer *NOUN* **probationers** a person at an early stage of training, e.g. as a nurse.

probation officer *NOUN* **probation officers** an official who supervises the behaviour of a convicted criminal who is not in prison.

probe *NOUN* **probes 1** a long thin instrument used to look closely at something such as a wound. **2** an unmanned spacecraft used for exploring. **3** an investigation.

probe *VERB* **probes, probing, probed**
1 explore or look at something with a probe.
2 investigate.
[from Latin *proba* = proof]
WORD FAMILY There are a number of English words that are related to *propel* because part of their original meaning comes from the Latin word *pellere* meaning 'to drive'. These include *compel*, *dispel*, *expel*, *impel*, and *repel*.

probity (*say* **proh**-bit-ee) *NOUN* honesty or integrity.
[from Latin *probus* = good, honest]

problem *NOUN* **problems 1** something difficult to deal with or understand.
2 something that has to be done or answered.
▷ **problematic** or **problematical** *adjective*
[from Greek]

proboscis (*say* pro-**boss**-iss) *NOUN* **proboscises 1** a long flexible snout. **2** an insect's long mouthpart.
[from Greek]

procedure *NOUN* **procedures** an orderly way of doing something.
[French, from *procéder* = proceed]

proceed *VERB* **proceeds, proceeding, proceeded 1** go forward or onward.
2 continue; go on to do something • *She proceeded to explain the plan.*
[from *pro-* + Latin *cedere* = go]
USAGE Do not confuse with **precede**.

proceedings *PLURAL NOUN* **1** things that happen; activities. **2** a lawsuit.

proceeds *PLURAL NOUN* the money made from a sale or event.

process[1] (*say* **proh**-sess) *NOUN* **processes** a series of actions for making or doing something.
- **in the process of** in the course of doing something.

process *VERB* **processes, processing, processed** put something through a manufacturing or other process • *processed cheese.*
[same origin as *proceed*]

process[2] (*say* pro-**sess**) *VERB* **processes, processing, processed** go in procession.
[from *procession*]

procession *NOUN* **processions** a number of people or vehicles etc. moving steadily forward following each other.
[from Latin *processio* = an advance]

processor *NOUN* **processors 1** a machine that processes things. **2** the part of a computer that controls all its operations.

proclaim *VERB* **proclaims, proclaiming, proclaimed** announce something officially or publicly.
▷ **proclamation** *noun*
[from *pro-* + Latin *clamare* = to shout]

procrastinate *VERB* **procrastinates, procrastinating, procrastinated** put off doing something.
▷ **procrastination** *noun* **procrastinator** *noun*
[from *pro-* + Latin *crastinus* = of tomorrow]

procreate *VERB* **procreates, procreating, procreated** produce offspring by the natural process of reproduction.
▷ **procreation** *noun*
[from *pro-* + Latin *creare* = to produce]

procure *VERB* **procures, procuring, procured** obtain or acquire something.
▷ **procurement** *noun*
[from *pro-* + Latin *curare* = look after]

prod *VERB* **prods, prodding, prodded**
1 poke. **2** stimulate someone into action.
▷ **prod** *noun*
[origin unknown]

prodigal *ADJECTIVE* wasteful or extravagant.
▷ **prodigally** *adverb* **prodigality** *noun*
[from Latin *prodigus* = lavish, generous]

prodigious *ADJECTIVE* wonderful or enormous.
▷ **prodigiously** *adverb*
[same origin as *prodigy*]

prodigy *NOUN* **prodigies** **1** a person, especially a child or young person, with wonderful abilities. **2** a wonderful thing.
[from Latin *prodigium* = good omen]

produce *VERB* **produces, producing, produced** **1** make or create something; bring something into existence. **2** bring something out so that it can be seen.
3 organize the performance of a play, making of a film, etc. **4** extend a line further • *Produce the base of the triangle.*
▷ **producer** *noun*

produce (*say* **prod**-yooss) *NOUN* things produced, especially by farmers.
[from *pro-* + Latin *ducere* = to lead]

product *NOUN* **products** **1** something produced. **2** the result of multiplying two numbers. (COMPARE **quotient**)
[from Latin *productum* = produced]

production *NOUN* **productions** **1** the process of making or creating something.
2 the amount produced • *Oil production increased last year.* **3** a version of a play, opera, etc.

productive *ADJECTIVE* **1** producing a lot of things. **2** producing good results; useful.
▷ **productivity** *noun*

profane *ADJECTIVE* showing disrespect for religion; blasphemous.
▷ **profanely** *adverb*

profane *VERB* **profanes, profaning, profaned** treat something, especially religion, with disrespect.
[from Latin *profanus* = outside the temple]

profanity *NOUN* **profanities** words or language that show disrespect for religion.

profess *VERB* **professes, professing, professed** **1** declare or express something.
2 claim to have something • *She professed interest in our work.*
▷ **professedly** *adverb*
[from Latin *professus* = declared publicly]

profession *NOUN* **professions** **1** an occupation that needs special education and training, such as medicine or law. **2** a declaration • *They made professions of loyalty.*
[from Latin *professio* = public declaration]

professional *ADJECTIVE* **1** to do with a profession. **2** doing a certain kind of work as a full-time job for payment, not as an amateur • *a professional footballer.* **3** done with a high standard of skill.
▷ **professional** *noun* **professionally** *adverb*

professor *NOUN* **professors** a university teacher of the highest rank.
▷ **professorship** *noun*
[same origin as *profess*]

proffer *VERB* **proffers, proffering, proffered** offer.
[from *pro-* + French *offrir* = to offer]

proficient *ADJECTIVE* doing something properly because of training or practice; skilled.
▷ **proficiency** *noun*
[from Latin *proficiens* = making progress]

profile *NOUN* **profiles** **1** a side view of a person's face. **2** a short description of a person's character or career.
- **keep a low profile** not make yourself noticeable.
[from old Italian *profilare* = draw in outline]

profit *NOUN* **profits** **1** the extra money obtained by selling something for more than it cost to buy or make. **2** an advantage gained by doing something.
▷ **profitable** *adjective* **profitably** *noun*

profit *VERB* **profits, profiting, profited** gain an advantage or benefit from something.
[from old French]

profiteer *NOUN* **profiteers** a person who makes a great profit unfairly.
▷ **profiteering** *noun*

profligate *ADJECTIVE* wasteful and extravagant.
▷ **profligacy** *noun*
[from Latin *profligare* = to ruin]

profound *ADJECTIVE* **1** very deep or intense • *We take a profound interest in it.* **2** showing or needing great knowledge, understanding, or thought • *a profound statement.*
▷ **profoundly** *adverb* **profundity** *noun*
[from *pro-* + Latin *fundus* = bottom]

profuse *ADJECTIVE* lavish or plentiful.
▷ **profusely** *adverb* **profuseness** *noun* **profusion** *noun*
[from Latin *profusus* = poured out]

progenitor *NOUN* **progenitors** an ancestor.
[same origin as *progeny*]

progeny (*say* proj-in-ee) *NOUN* offspring or descendants.
[from *pro-* + Latin *gignere* = create, father]

prognosis (*say* prog-**noh**-sis) *NOUN* **prognoses** a forecast or prediction, especially about a disease.
▷ **prognostication** *noun*
[from Greek *pro-* = before + *gnosis* = knowing]

program *NOUN* **programs** a series of coded instructions for a computer to carry out.

program *VERB* **programs**, **programming**, **programmed** put instructions into a computer by means of a program.
▷ **programmer** *noun*
[the American spelling of *programme*]

programme *NOUN* **programmes** **1** a list of planned events. **2** a leaflet or pamphlet giving details of a play, concert, football match, etc. **3** a show, play or talk etc. on radio or television.
[from Greek *programma* = public notice]

progress (*say* **proh**-gress) *NOUN* **1** forward movement; an advance. **2** a development or improvement.
- **in progress** taking place.

progress (*say* pro-**gress**) *VERB* **progresses**, **progressing**, **progressed** **1** move forward. **2** develop or improve.
▷ **progression** *noun*
[from *pro-* + Latin *gressus* = going]

progressive *ADJECTIVE* **1** moving forward or developing. **2** in favour of political or social reforms. **3** (said about a disease) becoming gradually more severe.

prohibit *VERB* **prohibits**, **prohibiting**, **prohibited** forbid or ban • *Smoking is prohibited.*
▷ **prohibition** *noun*
[from Latin]

prohibitive *ADJECTIVE* **1** prohibiting. **2** (said about prices) so high that people will not buy things.

project (*say* **proj**-ekt) *NOUN* **projects** **1** a plan or scheme. **2** the task of finding out as much as you can about something and writing about it.

project (*say* pro-**jekt**) *VERB* **projects**, **projecting**, **projected** **1** stick out. **2** show a picture on a screen. **3** give people a particular impression • *He likes to project an image of absent-minded brilliance.*
▷ **projection** *noun*
[from *pro-* + Latin *-jectum* = thrown]

projectile *NOUN* **projectiles** a missile.

projectionist *NOUN* **projectionists** a person who works a projector.

projector *NOUN* **projectors** a machine for showing films or photographs on a screen.

proletariat (*say* proh-lit-**air**-ee-at) *NOUN* working people.
[from Latin]

proliferate *VERB* **proliferates**, **proliferating**, **proliferated** increase rapidly in numbers.
▷ **proliferation** *noun*
[from Latin *proles* = offspring + *ferre* = to bear]

prolific *ADJECTIVE* producing a lot • *a prolific author.*
▷ **prolifically** *adverb*
[same origin as *proliferate*]

prologue (*say* **proh**-log) *NOUN* **prologues** an introduction to a poem or play etc.
[from Greek *pro-* = before + *logos* = speech]

prolong *VERB* **prolongs**, **prolonging**, **prolonged** make a thing longer or make it last for a long time.
▷ **prolongation** *noun*
[from *pro-* + Latin *longus* = long]

prom *NOUN* **proms** (*informal*) **1** a promenade. **2** a promenade concert.

promenade (*say* prom-in-**ahd**) *NOUN* **promenades 1** a place suitable for walking, especially beside the seashore. **2** a leisurely walk.
▷ **promenade** *verb*
[French, from *se promener* = to walk]

promenade concert **promenade concerts** a concert where part of the audience may stand or walk about.

prominent *ADJECTIVE* **1** easily seen; conspicuous • *The house stood in a prominent position.* **2** sticking out. **3** important.
▷ **prominently** *adverb* **prominence** *noun*
[from Latin]

promiscuous *ADJECTIVE* **1** having many casual sexual relationships.
2 indiscriminate.
▷ **promiscuously** *adverb* **promiscuity** *noun*
[from Latin]

promise *NOUN* **promises 1** a statement that you will definitely do or not do something. **2** an indication of future success or good results • *His work shows promise.*

promise *VERB* **promises, promising, promised** make a promise.
[from Latin]

promising *ADJECTIVE* likely to be good or successful • *a promising pianist.*

promontory *NOUN* **promontories** a piece of high land that sticks out into a sea or lake.
[from Latin]

promote *VERB* **promotes, promoting, promoted 1** move a person to a higher rank or position. **2** help the progress of something • *He has done much to promote the cause of peace.* **3** publicize or advertise a product in order to sell it.
▷ **promoter** *noun* **promotion** *noun*
[from *pro-* + Latin *motum* = moved]

prompt *ADJECTIVE* **1** without delay • *a prompt reply.* **2** punctual.
▷ **promptly** *adverb* **promptness** *noun*

prompt *ADVERB* exactly at that time • *I'll pick you up at 7.20 prompt.*

prompt *VERB* **prompts, prompting, prompted 1** cause or encourage a person to do something. **2** remind an actor or speaker of words when he or she has forgotten them.
▷ **prompter** *noun*
[from Latin *promptum* = produced]

promulgate *VERB* **promulgates, promulgating, promulgated** make something known to the public; proclaim.
▷ **promulgation** *noun*
[from Latin]

prone *ADJECTIVE* lying face downwards. (The opposite is **supine**)
- **be prone to** be likely to do or suffer from something • *He is prone to jealousy.*
[from Latin *pro* = forwards]

prong *NOUN* **prongs** one of the spikes on a fork.
▷ **pronged** *adjective*
[origin unknown]

pronoun *NOUN* **pronouns** a word used instead of a noun: **demonstrative pronouns** are *this, that, these, those*; **interrogative pronouns** are *who?*, *what?*, *which?*, etc.; **personal pronouns** are *I, me, we, us, thou, thee, you, ye, he, him, she, her, it, they, them*; **possessive pronouns** are *mine, yours, theirs*, etc.; **reflexive pronouns** are *myself, yourself*, etc.; **relative pronouns** are *who, what, which, that.*
[from *pro-* = in place of + *noun*]

pronounce *VERB* **pronounces, pronouncing, pronounced 1** say a sound or word in a particular way • *'Two' and 'too' are pronounced the same.* **2** declare something formally • *I now pronounce you man and wife.*
[from *pro-* + Latin *nuntiare* = announce]

pronounced *ADJECTIVE* noticeable • *This street has a pronounced slope.*

pronouncement *NOUN* **pronouncements** a declaration.

pronunciation *NOUN* **pronunciations** the way a word is pronounced.
USAGE Note the spelling; this word should not be written or spoken as 'pronounciation'.

proof *NOUN* **proofs 1** a fact or thing that shows something is true. **2** a printed copy of a book or photograph etc. made for checking before other copies are printed.

proof *ADJECTIVE* able to resist something or not be penetrated • *a bullet-proof jacket.*
[from old French; related to *prove*]

prop[1] *NOUN* **props** a support, especially one made of a long piece of wood or metal.

prop *VERB* **props, propping, propped** support something by leaning it against something else.
[probably from old Dutch]

prop[2] *NOUN* **props** an object or piece of furniture used on a theatre stage or in a film.
[from *property*]

propaganda *NOUN* biased or misleading publicity intended to make people believe something.
[Italian, = propagating, spreading]

propagate *VERB* **propagates, propagating, propagated 1** breed or reproduce. **2** spread an idea or belief to a lot of people.
▷ **propagation** *noun* **propagator** *noun*
[from Latin]

propel *VERB* **propels, propelling, propelled** push something forward.
[from *pro-* + Latin *pellere* = to drive]

propellant *NOUN* **propellants** a substance that propels things • *Liquid fuel is the propellant used in these rockets.*

propeller *NOUN* **propellers** a device with blades that spin round to drive an aircraft or ship.

propensity *NOUN* **propensities** a tendency.
[from Latin *propendere* = lean forward or hang down]

proper *ADJECTIVE* **1** suitable or right • *the proper way to hold a bat.* **2** respectable • *prim and proper.* **3** (*informal*) complete or thorough • *You're a proper nuisance!*
▷ **properly** *adverb*
[from Latin *proprius* = your own, special]

proper fraction *NOUN* **proper fractions** a fraction that is less than 1, with the numerator less than the denominator, e.g. $\frac{3}{5}$.

proper noun *NOUN* **proper nouns** the name of an individual person or thing, e.g. *Mary, London, Spain*, usually written with a capital first letter.

property *NOUN* **properties 1** a thing or things that belong to somebody. **2** a building or someone's land. **3** a quality or characteristic • *It has the property of becoming soft when heated.*
[same origin as *proper*]

prophecy *NOUN* **prophecies 1** a statement that prophesies something. **2** the action of prophesying.

prophesy *VERB* **prophesies, prophesying, prophesied** say what will happen in the future; foretell.
[from Greek *pro* = before + *phanai* = speak]

prophet *NOUN* **prophets 1** a person who makes prophecies. **2** a religious teacher who is believed to be inspired by God.
▷ **prophetess** *noun*
- **the Prophet** a name for Muhammad, the founder of the Muslim faith.
[from Greek *prophetes* = someone who speaks for a god]

prophetic *ADJECTIVE* saying or showing what will happen in the future.

propinquity *NOUN* (*formal*) nearness.
[from Latin *propinquus* = neighbouring]

propitiate (*say* pro-**pish**-ee-ayt) *VERB* **propitiates, propitiating, propitiated** win a person's favour or forgiveness.
▷ **propitiation** *noun* **propitiatory** *adjective*
[same origin as *propitious*]

propitious (*say* pro-**pish**-us) *ADJECTIVE* favourable.
[from Latin *propitius*]

proponent (*say* prop-**oh**-nent) *NOUN* **proponents** the person who puts forward a proposal.
[from *pro-* + Latin *ponere* = to place]

proportion *NOUN* **proportions 1** a part or share of a whole thing. **2** a ratio. **3** the correct relationship in size, amount, or importance between two things • *You've drawn his head out of proportion.*
- **proportions** *plural noun* size or scale • *a ship of large proportions.*
[from *pro-* + Latin *portio* = portion or share]

proportional or **proportionate** *ADJECTIVE* in proportion; according to a ratio.
▷ **proportionally** *adverb* **proportionately** *adverb*

proportional representation *NOUN* a system in which each political party has a number of Members of Parliament in proportion to the number of votes for all its candidates.

propose *VERB* **proposes, proposing, proposed** **1** suggest an idea or plan etc. **2** plan or intend to do something. **3** ask a person to marry you.
▷ **proposal** *noun*
[from old French; related to *proponent*]

proposition *NOUN* **propositions** **1** a suggestion or offer. **2** a statement. **3** (*informal*) an undertaking or problem • *a difficult proposition.*
[same origin as *proponent*]

propound *VERB* **propounds, propounding, propounded** put forward an idea for consideration.
[same origin as *proponent*]

proprietary (*say* pro-**pry**-it-er-ee) *ADJECTIVE* **1** made or sold by one firm; branded • *proprietary medicines.* **2** to do with an owner or ownership.
[same origin as *proper*]

proprietor *NOUN* **proprietors** the owner of a shop or business.
▷ **proprietress** *noun*
[from *proprietary*]

propriety (*say* pro-**pry**-it-ee) *NOUN* **proprieties** **1** being proper. **2** correct behaviour.
[same origin as *proper*]

propulsion *NOUN* propelling something.

prorogue (*say* pro-**rohg**) *VERB* **prorogues, proroguing, prorogued** stop the meetings of a parliament temporarily without dissolving it.
▷ **prorogation** *noun*
[from Latin *prorogare* = prolong]

prosaic *ADJECTIVE* plain or dull and ordinary.
▷ **prosaically** *adverb*
[from *prose*]

proscribe *VERB* **proscribes, proscribing, proscribed** forbid by law.
[from Latin *proscribere* = to outlaw]
USAGE Do not confuse with **prescribe**.

prose *NOUN* writing or speech that is not in verse.
[from Latin *prosa* = straightforward, plain]

prosecute *VERB* **prosecutes, prosecuting, prosecuted** **1** make someone go to a lawcourt to be tried for a crime. **2** continue with something; pursue • *prosecuting their trade.*
▷ **prosecution** *noun* **prosecutor** *noun*
[from Latin *prosecutus* = pursued]

proselyte *NOUN* **proselytes** a person who has been converted from one religion, opinion, etc. to another, especially to Judaism.
[from Greek *proselythos* = stranger]

proselytize *VERB* **proselytizes, proselytizing, proselytized** convert people from one religion, opinion, etc. to another.

prosody (*say* **pross**-od-ee) *NOUN* the study of verse and its structure.
[from Greek *prosodia* = song]

prospect *NOUN* **prospects** **1** a possibility or expectation of something • *There is no prospect of success.* **2** a wide view.

prospect (*say* pro-**spekt**) *VERB* **prospects, prospecting, prospected** explore in search of gold or some other mineral.
▷ **prospector** *noun*
[from *pro-* + Latin *-spicere* = to look]

prospective *ADJECTIVE* expected to be or to happen; possible • *prospective customers.*

prospectus *NOUN* **prospectuses** a booklet describing and advertising a school, business company, etc.
[Latin, = view or prospect]

prosper *VERB* **prospers, prospering, prospered** be successful.
[from Latin]

prosperous *ADJECTIVE* successful or rich.
▷ **prosperity** *noun*

prostitute *NOUN* **prostitutes** a person who takes part in sexual acts for payment.
▷ **prostitution** *noun*
[from Latin *prostitutus* = for sale]

prostrate *ADJECTIVE* lying face downwards.

prostrate *VERB* **prostrates, prostrating, prostrated**
- **prostrate yourself** throw yourself flat on the ground, usually in submission.
▷ **prostration** *noun*
[from Latin *prostratum* = laid flat]

protagonist *NOUN* **protagonists** 1 the main character in a play. 2 a person competing against another.
[from *proto-* + Greek *agonistes* = actor]

protect *VERB* **protects, protecting, protected** keep safe from harm or injury.
▷ **protection** *noun* **protective** *adjective* **protector** *noun*
[from *pro-* + Latin *tectum* = covered]

protectorate *NOUN* **protectorates** a country that is under the official protection of a stronger country.

protégé (*say* prot-ezh-ay) *NOUN* **protégés** someone who is helped and supported by an older or more experienced person.
[French, = protected]

protein *NOUN* **proteins** a substance that is found in all living things and is an essential part of the food of animals.
[from Greek *proteios* = primary, most important]

protest (*say* proh-test) *NOUN* **protests** a statement or action showing that you disapprove of something.

protest (*say* pro-test) *VERB* **protests, protesting, protested** 1 make a protest. 2 declare firmly • *They protested their innocence.*
▷ **protestation** *noun* **protester** *noun*
[from *pro-* + Latin *testari* = say on oath]

Protestant *NOUN* **Protestants** a member of any of the western Christian Churches separated from the Roman Catholic Church.
[because in the 16th century many people protested (= declared firmly) their opposition to the Catholic Church]

proto- *PREFIX* 1 first. 2 at an early stage of development.
[from Greek *protos* = first or earliest]

protocol *NOUN* the correct or official procedure for behaving in certain formal situations.
[from Greek]

proton *NOUN* **protons** a particle of matter with a positive electric charge.
[same origin as *proto-*]

prototype *NOUN* **prototypes** the first model of something, from which others are copied or developed.

protract *VERB* **protracts, protracting, protracted** make something last longer than usual; prolong.
▷ **protracted** *adjective* **protraction** *noun*
[from *pro-* + Latin *tractum* = drawn out]

protractor *NOUN* **protractors** a device for measuring angles, usually a semicircle marked off in degrees.

protrude *VERB* **protrudes, protruding, protruded** stick out from a surface.
▷ **protrusion** *noun*
[from *pro-* + Latin *trudere* = push]

protuberance *NOUN* **protuberances** a part that bulges out from a surface.

protuberant *ADJECTIVE* bulging out from a surface.
[from *pro-* + Latin *tuber* = a swelling]

proud *ADJECTIVE* 1 very pleased with yourself or with someone else who has done well • *I am so proud of my sister.* 2 causing pride • *This is a proud moment for us.* 3 full of self-respect and independence • *They were too proud to ask for help.* 4 having too high an opinion of yourself.
▷ **proudly** *adverb*
[via Old English from old French *prud* = brave]

prove *VERB* **proves, proving, proved** 1 show that something is true. 2 turn out • *The forecast proved to be correct.*
▷ **provable** *adjective*
[from Latin *probare* = to test]

proven (*say* proh-ven) *ADJECTIVE* proved • *a man of proven ability.*

provender *NOUN* food, especially for animals.
[from old French *provendre* = provide]

proverb *NOUN* **proverbs** a short well-known saying that states a truth, e.g. 'Many hands make light work'.
[from *pro-* + Latin *verbum* = word]

proverbial *ADJECTIVE* 1 referred to in a proverb. 2 well-known.

provide *VERB* **provides, providing, provided** 1 make something available; supply. 2 prepare for something • *Try to provide for emergencies.*
▷ **provider** *noun*
[from Latin *providere* = foresee]

provided *CONJUNCTION* on condition • *You can stay provided that you help.*

providence *NOUN* **1** being provident. **2** God's or nature's care and protection.

provident *ADJECTIVE* wisely providing for the future; thrifty.
[same origin as *provide*]

providential *ADJECTIVE* happening very luckily.
▷ **providentially** *adverb*
[from *providence*]

providing *CONJUNCTION* provided.

province *NOUN* **provinces 1** a section of a country. **2** the area of a person's special knowledge or responsibility • *I'm afraid carpentry is not my province.*
- **the provinces** the parts of a country outside its capital city.
[from Latin]

provincial (*say* pro-**vin**-shul) *ADJECTIVE* **1** to do with the provinces. **2** culturally limited or narrow-minded.

provision *NOUN* **provisions 1** providing something. **2** a statement in a document • *the provisions of the treaty.*
[from Latin *provisum* = provided]

provisional *ADJECTIVE* arranged or agreed upon temporarily but possibly to be altered later.
▷ **provisionally** *adverb*

provisions *PLURAL NOUN* supplies of food and drink.

proviso (*say* prov-**I**-zoh) *NOUN* **provisos** a condition inisisted on in advance.
[from Latin *proviso quod* = provided that]

provocative *ADJECTIVE* **1** likely to make someone angry • *a provocative remark.* **2** intended to arouse sexual desire.
▷ **provocatively** *adverb*

provoke *VERB* **provokes, provoking, provoked 1** make a person angry. **2** cause or give rise to something • *The joke provoked laughter.*
▷ **provocation** *noun*
[from *pro-* + Latin *vocare* = summon]

provost *NOUN* **provosts** a Scottish official with authority similar to a mayor in England and Wales.
[from Old English]

prow *NOUN* **prows** the front end of a ship.
[from French]

prowess *NOUN* great ability or daring.
[from old French; related to *proud*]

prowl *VERB* **prowls, prowling, prowled** move about quietly or cautiously, like a hunter.
▷ **prowl** *noun* **prowler** *noun*
[origin unknown]

proximity *NOUN* nearness.
[from Latin *proximus* = nearest]

proxy *NOUN* **proxies** a person authorized to represent or act for another person • *I will be abroad, so I have arranged to vote by proxy.*
[from Latin]

prude *NOUN* **prudes** a person who is easily shocked.
▷ **prudish** *adjective* **prudery** *noun*
[from old French]

prudent *ADJECTIVE* careful, not rash or reckless.
▷ **prudently** *adverb* **prudence** *noun* **prudential** *adjective*
[from French; related to *provide*]

prune[1] *NOUN* **prunes** a dried plum.
[from Greek]

prune[2] *VERB* **prunes, pruning, pruned** cut off unwanted parts of a tree or bush etc.
[from old French]

pry *VERB* **pries, prying, pried** look into or ask about someone else's private business.
[origin unknown]

PS *ABBREVIATION* postscript.

psalm (*say* sahm) *NOUN* **psalms** a religious song, especially one from the Book of Psalms in the Bible.
▷ **psalmist** *noun*
[via Old English from Greek *psalmos* = song sung to the harp]

pseudo- (*say* s'**yood**-oh) *PREFIX* false; pretended.
[from Greek]

pseudonym *NOUN* **pseudonyms** a false name used by an author.
[from *pseudo-* + Greek *onyma* = name]

PSHE *ABBREVIATION* personal, social, and health education.

psychedelic *ADJECTIVE* having vivid colours and patterns • *a psychedelic design.*
[from Greek *psyche* = life, soul + *deloun* = reveal]

psychiatrist (*say* sy-ky-a-trist) *NOUN* **psychiatrists** a doctor who treats mental illnesses.
▷ **psychiatry** *noun* **psychiatric** *adjective*
[from *psycho-* + Greek *iatreia* = healing]

psychic (*say* sy-kik) *ADJECTIVE*
1 supernatural. **2** having supernatural powers, especially being able to predict the future. **3** to do with the mind or soul.
▷ **psychical** *adjective*
[same origin as *psycho-*]

psycho- *PREFIX* to do with the mind.
[from Greek *psyche* = life or soul]

psychoanalysis *NOUN* investigation of a person's mental processes, especially in psychotherapy.
▷ **psychoanalyst** *noun*

psychology *NOUN* the study of the mind and how it works.
▷ **psychological** *adjective* **psychologist** *noun*
[from *psycho-* + *-logy*]

psychotherapy *NOUN* treatment of mental illness by psychological methods.
▷ **psychotherapist** *noun*

PT *ABBREVIATION* physical training.

PTA *ABBREVIATION* parent-teacher association; an organization that arranges discussions between teachers and parents about school business, and raises money for the school.

ptarmigan (*say* tar-mig-an) *NOUN* **ptarmigans** a bird of the grouse family.
[from Scottish Gaelic]

pterodactyl (*say* te-ro-dak-til) *NOUN* **pterodactyls** an extinct flying reptile.
[from Greek *pteron* = wing + *daktylos* = finger (because one of the 'fingers' on its front leg was enlarged to support its wing)]

PTO *ABBREVIATION* please turn over.

pub *NOUN* **pubs** a building licensed to serve alcoholic drinks to the public.
[short for *public house*]

puberty (*say* pew-ber-tee) *NOUN* the time when a young person is developing physically into an adult.
[same origin as *pubic*]

pubic (*say* pew-bik) *ADJECTIVE* to do with the lower front part of the abdomen.
[from Latin *pubes* = an adult, the genitals]

public *ADJECTIVE* belonging to or known by everyone, not private.
▷ **publicly** *adverb*

public *NOUN* people in general.
- **in public** openly, not in private.
[from Latin *publicus* = of the people]

publican *NOUN* **publicans** the person in charge of a pub.

publication *NOUN* **publications**
1 publishing. **2** a published book or newspaper etc.

public house *NOUN* **public houses** a pub.

publicity *NOUN* public attention; doing things (e.g. advertising) to draw people's attention to something.

publicize *VERB* **publicizes, publicizing, publicized** bring something to people's attention; advertise.
[from *public*]

public school *NOUN* **public schools** **1** a secondary school that charges fees. **2** (in Scotland and the USA) a school run by a local authority or by the state.

publish *VERB* **publishes, publishing, published** **1** have something printed and sold to the public. **2** announce something in public.
▷ **publisher** *noun*
[from Latin *publicare* = make public]

puce *NOUN* brownish-purple colour.
[from French *couleur puce* = the colour of a flea]

puck *NOUN* **pucks** a hard rubber disc used in ice hockey.
[origin unknown]

pucker *VERB* **puckers, puckering, puckered** wrinkle.
[origin unknown]

pudding *NOUN* **puddings** **1** a food made in a soft mass, especially in a mixture of flour and other ingredients. **2** the sweet course of a meal.
[from French]

puddle *NOUN* **puddles** a shallow patch of liquid, especially of rainwater on a road.
[from Old English]

pudgy *ADJECTIVE* short and fat • *pudgy fingers.*
[origin unknown]

puerile (*say* pew-er-I'll) *ADJECTIVE* silly and childish.
▷ **puerility** *noun*
[from Latin *puer* = boy]

puff *NOUN* **puffs** **1** a short blowing of breath, wind, or smoke etc. **2** a soft pad for putting powder on the skin. **3** a cake of very light pastry filled with cream.

puff *VERB* **puffs, puffing, puffed** **1** blow out puffs of smoke etc. **2** breathe with difficulty; pant. **3** inflate or swell something • *He puffed out his chest.*
[imitating the sound]

puffin *NOUN* **puffins** a seabird with a large striped beak.
[origin unknown]

puffy *ADJECTIVE* puffed out; swollen.
▷ **puffiness** *noun*

pug *NOUN* **pugs** a small dog with a flat face like a bulldog.
[probably from old Dutch]

pugilist (*say* pew-jil-ist) *NOUN* **pugilists** a boxer.
[from Latin]

pugnacious *ADJECTIVE* wanting to fight; aggressive.
▷ **pugnaciously** *adverb* **pugnacity** *noun*
[from Latin *pugnare* = to fight]

puke *VERB* **pukes, puking, puked** (*informal*) vomit.
[origin unknown]

pull *VERB* **pulls, pulling, pulled** **1** make a thing come towards or after you by using force on it. **2** move by a driving force • *The car pulled out into the road.*
▷ **pull** *noun*
- **pull a face** make a strange face.
- **pull in** **1** (said about a vehicle) move to the side of the road and stop. **2** (said about a train) come to a station and stop.
- **pull somebody's leg** tease him or her.
- **pull off** achieve something.
- **pull through** recover from an illness.
- **pull up** (said about a vehicle) stop abruptly.
- **pull yourself together** become calm or sensible.

[from Old English]

pullet *NOUN* **pullets** a young hen.
[from French]

pulley *NOUN* **pulleys** a wheel with a rope, chain, or belt over it, used for lifting or moving heavy things.
[from old French]

pullover *NOUN* **pullovers** a knitted piece of clothing for the top half of the body.

pulmonary (*say* pul-mon-er-ee) *ADJECTIVE* to do with the lungs.
[from Latin *pulmo* = lung]

pulp *NOUN* **1** the soft moist part of fruit. **2** any soft moist mass.
▷ **pulpy** *adjective*
[from Latin]

pulpit *NOUN* **pulpits** a small enclosed platform for the preacher in a church or chapel.
[from Latin *pulpitum* = a platform, stage, or scaffold]

pulsate *VERB* **pulsates, pulsating, pulsated** expand and contract rhythmically; vibrate.
▷ **pulsation** *noun*
[from Latin]

pulse[1] *NOUN* **pulses** **1** the rhythmical movement of the arteries as blood is pumped through them by the beating of the heart • *The pulse can be felt in a person's wrists.* **2** a throb.

pulse *VERB* **pulses, pulsing, pulsed** throb or pulsate.
[from Latin *pulsum* = driven, beaten]

pulse[2] *NOUN* **pulses** the edible seed of peas, beans, lentils, etc.
[from Latin]

pulverize *VERB* **pulverizes, pulverizing, pulverized** crush something into powder.
▷ **pulverization** *noun*
[from Latin *pulveris* = of dust]

puma (*say* pew-ma) *NOUN* **pumas** a large brown cat of western America, also called a cougar or mountain lion.
[via Spanish from Quechua (a South American language)]

pumice *NOUN* a kind of porous stone used for rubbing stains from the skin or as powder for polishing things.
[from Latin]

pummel *VERB* **pummels, pummelling, pummelled** keep on hitting something.
[a different spelling of *pommel*]

pump[1] *NOUN* **pumps** a device that pushes air or liquid into or out of something, or along pipes.

pump *VERB* **pumps, pumping, pumped**
1 move air or liquid with a pump.
2 (*informal*) question a person to obtain information.
- **pump up** inflate.
[originally a sailors' word: origin unknown]

pump[2] *NOUN* **pumps** a canvas sports shoe with a rubber sole.
[origin unknown]

pumpkin *NOUN* **pumpkins** a very large round fruit with a hard orange skin.
[from Greek *pepon*, a kind of large melon]

pun *NOUN* **puns** a joking use of a word sounding the same as another, e.g. 'Deciding where to bury him was a *grave* decision'.
[origin unknown]

punch[1] *VERB* **punches, punching, punched** **1** hit someone with your fist.
2 make a hole in something.

punch *NOUN* **punches** **1** a hit with a fist. **2** a device for making holes in paper, metal, leather, etc. **3** vigour.
[same origin as *puncture*]

punch[2] *NOUN* a drink made by mixing wine or spirits and fruit juice in a bowl.
[from Sanskrit *pañca* = five (the number of ingredients in the traditional recipe: spirits, fruit juice, water, sugar, and spice)]

punchline *NOUN* **punchlines** words that give the climax of a joke or story.

punch-up *NOUN* **punch-ups** (*informal*) a fight.

punctilious *ADJECTIVE* very careful about correct behaviour and detail.
▷ **punctiliously** *adverb* **punctiliousness** *noun*
[from Latin *punctillum* = little point]

punctual *ADJECTIVE* doing things exactly at the time arranged; not late.
▷ **punctually** *adverb* **punctuality** *noun*
[from Latin *punctum* = a point]

punctuate *VERB* **punctuates, punctuating, punctuated** **1** put punctuation marks into something. **2** put something in at intervals • *His speech was punctuated with cheers.*
[from Latin *punctuare* = mark with points or dots]

punctuation *NOUN* marks such as commas, full stops, and brackets put into a piece of writing to make it easier to read.

puncture *NOUN* **punctures** a small hole made by something sharp, especially in a tyre.

puncture *VERB* **punctures, puncturing, punctured** make a puncture in something.
[from Latin]

pundit *NOUN* **pundits** a person who is an authority on something.
[from Sanskrit *pandita* = learned]

pungent (*say* **pun**-jent) *ADJECTIVE* **1** having a strong taste or smell. **2** (said about remarks) sharp.
▷ **pungently** *adverb* **pungency** *noun*
[from Latin *pungere* = to prick]

punish *VERB* **punishes, punishing, punished** make a person suffer because he or she has done something wrong.
▷ **punishable** *adjective* **punishment** *noun*
[same origin as *pain*]

punitive (*say* **pew**-nit-iv) *ADJECTIVE* inflicting or intended as a punishment.

punk *NOUN* **punks** (also **punk rock**) **1** a loud aggressive style of rock music. **2** a person who likes this music.
[origin unknown]

punnet *NOUN* **punnets** a small container for soft fruit such as strawberries.
[origin unknown]

punt[1] *NOUN* **punts** a flat-bottomed boat, usually moved by pushing a pole against the bottom of a river while standing in the punt.

punt *VERB* **punts, punting, punted** move a punt with a pole.
[from Latin *ponto* = *pontoon*[1]]

punt[2] *VERB* **punts, punting, punted** kick a football after dropping it from your hands and before it touches the ground.
[origin unknown]

a b c d e f g h i j k l m n o p q r s t u v w x y z

punt[3] *VERB* **punts, punting, punted** (*informal*) gamble; bet on a horse race.
▷ **punt** *noun*
[from French]

punter *NOUN* **punters** **1** a person who lays a bet. **2** (*informal*) a customer.

puny (*say* pew-nee) *ADJECTIVE* small or undersized; feeble.
[from old French *puisne* = a younger or inferior person]

pup *NOUN* **pups** **1** a puppy. **2** a young seal.
[from *puppy*]

pupa (*say* pew-pa) *NOUN* **pupae** a chrysalis.
[from Latin; related to *pupil*]

pupate (*say* pew-payt) *VERB* **pupates, pupating, pupated** become a pupa.
▷ **pupation** *noun*

pupil *NOUN* **pupils** **1** someone who is being taught by a teacher, especially at school. **2** the opening in the centre of the eye.
[from Latin *pupilla* = little girl or doll (the use in sense 2 refers to the tiny images of people and things that can be seen in the eye)]

puppet *NOUN* **puppets** **1** a kind of doll that can be made to move by fitting it over your hand or working it by strings or wires. **2** a person whose actions are controlled by someone else.
▷ **puppetry** *noun*
[probably related to *pupil*]

puppy *NOUN* **puppies** a young dog.
[from old French; related to *pupil*]

purchase *VERB* **purchases, purchasing, purchased** buy.
▷ **purchaser** *noun*

purchase *NOUN* **purchases** **1** something bought. **2** buying. **3** a firm hold or grip.
[from old French]

purdah *NOUN* the Muslim or Hindu custom of keeping women from the sight of men or strangers.
[from Persian or Urdu *parda* = veil or curtain]

pure *ADJECTIVE* **1** not mixed with anything else • *pure olive oil.* **2** clean or clear • *pure spring water.* **3** free from evil or sin. **4** mere; nothing but • *pure nonsense.*
▷ **purely** *adverb* **pureness** *noun*
[from Latin]

purée (*say* pewr-ay) *NOUN* **purées** fruit or vegetables made into pulp.
[French, = squeezed]

purgative *NOUN* **purgatives** a strong laxative.
[same origin as *purge*]

purgatory *NOUN* **1** a state of temporary suffering. **2** (in Roman Catholic belief) a place in which souls are purified by punishment before they can enter heaven.
[same origin as *purge*]

purge *VERB* **purges, purging, purged** get rid of unwanted people or things.

purge *NOUN* **purges** **1** purging. **2** a purgative.
[from Latin *purgare* = make pure]

purify *VERB* **purifies, purifying, purified** make a thing pure.
▷ **purification** *noun* **purifier** *noun*

purist *NOUN* **purists** a person who likes things to be exactly right, especially in people's use of words.

Puritan *NOUN* **Puritans** a Protestant in the 16th and 17th centuries who wanted simpler religious ceremonies and strictly moral behaviour.

puritan *NOUN* **puritans** a person with very strict morals.
▷ **puritanical** *adjective*
[from Latin *puritas* = purity]

purity *NOUN* pureness.

purl[1] *NOUN* **purls** a knitting stitch that makes a ridge towards the knitter.
▷ **purl** *verb*
[from Scottish *pirl* = twist]

purl[2] *VERB* **purls, purling, purled** (*poetical use*) (said about a stream) ripple with a murmuring sound.
[probably from a Scandinavian language]

purloin *VERB* **purloins, purloining, purloined** (*formal*) take something without permission.
[from old French]

purple *NOUN* deep reddish-blue colour.
[via Old English from Latin]

purport (*say* per-port) *VERB* **purports, purporting, purported** claim • *The letter purports to be from the council.*
▷ **purportedly** *adverb*

purport (*say* per-port) *NOUN* meaning • *The purport of the letter could not be clearer.* [from old French]

purpose *NOUN* **purposes** **1** what you intend to do; a plan or aim. **2** determination.
▷ **purposeful** *adjective* **purposefully** *adverb*
- **on purpose** by intention, not by accident. [from old French; related to *propose*]

purposely *ADVERB* on purpose.

purr *VERB* **purrs, purring, purred** make the low murmuring sound that a cat does when it is pleased.
▷ **purr** *noun*
[imitating the sound]

purse *NOUN* **purses** **1** a small pouch for carrying money. **2** (*American*) a handbag

purse *VERB* **purses, pursing, pursed** draw your lips tightly together • *She pursed up her lips.*
[from Latin *bursa* = a bag]

purser *NOUN* **pursers** a ship's officer in charge of accounts.
[from *purse*]

pursuance *NOUN* (*formal*) the performance or carrying out of something • *in pursuance of my duties.*

pursue *VERB* **pursues, pursuing, pursued** **1** chase someone in order to catch them. **2** continue with something; work at • *We are pursuing our enquiries.*
▷ **pursuer** *noun*
[from old French; related to *prosecute*]

pursuit *NOUN* **pursuits** **1** pursuing. **2** a regular activity.

purvey *VERB* **purveys, purveying, purveyed** supply food etc. as a trade.
▷ **purveyor** *noun*
[from old French; related to *provide*]

pus *NOUN* a thick yellowish substance produced in inflamed or infected tissue, e.g. in an abscess or boil.
[Latin]

push *VERB* **pushes, pushing, pushed** **1** make a thing go away from you by using force on it. **2** move yourself by using force • *He pushed in front of me.* **3** try to force someone to do or use something; urge.
- **push off** (*slang*) go away.

push *NOUN* **pushes** a pushing movement or effort.
- **at a push** if necessary but only with difficulty.
- **get the push** (*informal*) be dismissed from a job.
[from French; related to *pulse*[1]]

pushchair *NOUN* **pushchairs** a folding chair on wheels, in which a child can be pushed along.

pusher *NOUN* **pushers** a person who sells illegal drugs.

pushy *ADJECTIVE* unpleasantly self-confident and eager to do things.

pusillanimous (*say* pew-zil-an-im-us) *ADJECTIVE* timid or cowardly.
[from Latin *pusillus* = small + *animus* = mind]

puss *NOUN* (*informal*) a cat.
[probably from old German or old Dutch]

pussy *NOUN* **pussies** (*informal*) a cat.

pussyfoot *VERB* **pussyfoots, pussyfooting, pussyfooted** act too cautiously and timidly.

pussy willow *NOUN* **pussy willows** a willow with furry catkins.

pustule *NOUN* **pustules** a pimple containing pus.
[from Latin]

put *VERB* **puts, putting, put**
This word has many uses, including **1** move a person or thing to a place or position • *Put the lamp on the table.* **2** make a person or thing do or experience something or be in a certain condition • *Put the light on; That put me in a good mood.* **3** express in words • *She put it tactfully.*
- **be hard put** have difficulty in doing something.
- **put off** **1** postpone. **2** dissuade. **3** stop someone wanting something • *The smell puts me off.*
- **put out** **1** stop a fire from burning or a light from shining. **2** annoy or inconvenience • *Our lateness has put her out.*
- **put up** **1** construct or build. **2** raise. **3** give someone a place to sleep • *Can you put me up for the night?* **4** provide • *Who will put up the money?*
- **put up with** endure or tolerate.
[from Old English]

A B C D E F G H I J K L M N O P Q R S T U V W X Y Z

putrefy (*say* pew-trif-I) *VERB* **putrefies, putrefying, putrefied** decay or rot.
▷ **putrefaction** *noun*
[from Latin *puter* = rotten]

putrid (*say* pew-trid) *ADJECTIVE* **1** rotting. **2** smelling bad.
[same origin as *putrefy*]

putt *VERB* **putts, putting, putted** hit a golf ball gently towards the hole.
▷ **putt** *noun* **putter** *noun* **putting green** *noun*
[a different spelling of *put*]

putty *NOUN* a soft paste that sets hard, used for fitting the glass into a window frame.
[from French]

puzzle *NOUN* **puzzles** **1** a difficult question or problem. **2** a game or toy that sets a problem to solve or a difficult task to complete.

puzzle *VERB* **puzzles, puzzling, puzzled** **1** give someone a problem so that they have to think hard. **2** think patiently about how to solve something.
▷ **puzzlement** *noun*
[origin unknown]

PVC *ABBREVIATION* polyvinyl chloride, a plastic used to make clothing, pipes, flooring, etc.
[the initial letters of *polyvinyl chloride*, a polymer of vinyl, from which it is made]

pygmy (*say* pig-mee) *NOUN* **pygmies** **1** a very small person or thing. **2** a member of certain unusually short peoples of equatorial Africa.
[from Greek]

pyjamas *PLURAL NOUN* a loose jacket and trousers worn in bed.
[from Persian or Urdu *pay* = leg + *jamah* = clothing]

pylon *NOUN* **pylons** a tall framework made of strips of steel, supporting electric cables.
[from Greek]

pyramid *NOUN* **pyramids** **1** a structure with a square base and with sloping sides that meet in a point at the top. **2** an ancient Egyptian tomb shaped like this.
▷ **pyramidal** (*say* pir-am-id-al) *adjective*
[from Greek]

pyre *NOUN* **pyres** a pile of wood etc. for burning a dead body as part of a funeral ceremony.
[from Greek *pyr* = fire]

python *NOUN* **pythons** a large snake that kills its prey by coiling round and crushing it.
[the name of a large serpent or monster in Greek legend, killed by Apollo]

Qq

QC *ABBREVIATION* Queen's Counsel.

QED *ABBREVIATION* quod erat demonstrandum (Latin, = which was the thing that had to be proved).

quack[1] *VERB* **quacks, quacking, quacked** make the harsh cry of a duck.
▷ **quack** *noun*
[imitating the sound]

quack[2] *NOUN* **quacks** a person who falsely claims to have medical skill or have remedies to cure diseases.
[from Dutch *quacken* = to boast]

quad (*say* kwod) *NOUN* **quads** **1** a quadrangle. **2** a quadruplet.

quadrangle *NOUN* **quadrangles** a rectangular courtyard with large buildings round it.
[from *quadri-* + *angle*]

quadrant *NOUN* **quadrants** a quarter of a circle.
[from Latin *quadrare* = to make square]

quadratic equation *NOUN* **quadratic equations** an equation that involves quantities or variables raised to the power of two, but no higher than two.
[from Latin *quadrare* = to square]

quadri- *PREFIX* four.
[from Latin]

quadriceps *NOUN* **quadriceps** the large muscle at the front of the thigh.
[Latin, = four- headed (because the muscle is attached at four points)]

quadrilateral *NOUN* **quadrilaterals** a flat geometric shape with four sides.

quadruped *NOUN* **quadrupeds** an animal with four feet.
[from *quadri-* + Latin *pedis* = of a foot]

quadruple *ADJECTIVE* **1** four times as much or as many. **2** having four parts.

quadruple *VERB* **quadruples, quadrupling, quadrupled** make or become four times as much or as many.
[from Latin]

quadruplet *NOUN* **quadruplets** each of four children born to the same mother at one time.
[from *quadruple*]

quadruplicate *NOUN* **quadruplicates** each of four things that are exactly alike.
[from Latin]

quaff (*say* kwof) *VERB* **quaffs, quaffing, quaffed** drink.
[probably from old German]

quagmire *NOUN* **quagmires** a bog or marsh.
[from an old word *quag* = marsh, + *mire*]

quail[1] *NOUN* **quail** or **quails** a bird related to the partridge.
[from old French]

quail[2] *VERB* **quails, quailing, quailed** feel or show fear.
[origin unknown]

quaint *ADJECTIVE* attractively odd or old-fashioned.
▷ **quaintly** *adverb* **quaintness** *noun*
[from old French]

quake *VERB* **quakes, quaking, quaked** tremble; shake with fear.
[from Old English]

Quaker *NOUN* **Quakers** a member of a religious group called the Society of Friends, founded by George Fox in the 17th century.
[originally an insult, probably from George Fox's saying that people should 'tremble at the name of the Lord']

qualification *NOUN* **qualifications 1** a skill or ability that makes someone suitable for a job. **2** an exam that you have passed or a course of study that you have completed.
3 something that qualifies a remark or statement.

qualify *VERB* **qualifies, qualifying, qualified 1** make or become able to do something through having certain qualities or training, or by passing an exam. **2** make a remark or statement less extreme; limit its meaning. **3** (said about an adjective) add meaning to a noun.
▷ **qualified** *adjective*
[from Latin *qualis* = of what kind?, of a particular kind]

qualitative *ADJECTIVE* to do with qualities and characteristics of something rather than its size or amount • *a qualitative approach to the issues.*
▷ **qualitatively** *adverb*
[from Latin qualitas]

quality *NOUN* **qualities 1** how good or bad something is. **2** a characteristic; something that is special in a person or thing.
[same origin as *qualify*]

qualm (*say* kwahm) *NOUN* **qualms** a misgiving or scruple.
[origin unknown]

quandary *NOUN* **quandaries** a difficult situation where you are uncertain what to do.
[origin unknown]

quantify *VERB* **quantifies, quantifying, quantified** describe or express something as an amount or a number • *The risks to health are impossible to quantify.*
[from Latin *quantitas*]

quantitative *ADJECTIVE* to do with the size and amount of something rather than the qualities and characteristics • *quantitative analysis of the data.*
▷ **quantitatively** *adverb*
[from Latin *quantitas*]

quantity *NOUN* **quantities 1** how much there is of something; how many things there are of one sort. **2** a large amount.
[from Latin *quantus* = how big?, how much?]

quantum *NOUN* **quanta** a quantity or amount.
[same origin as *quantity*]

quantum leap or **quantum jump** *NOUN* **quantum leaps** or **quantum jumps** a sudden large increase or advance.

quarantine *NOUN* keeping a person or animal isolated in case they have a disease which could spread to others.
[from Italian *quaranta* = forty (the original period of isolation was 40 days)]

quarrel *NOUN* **quarrels** an angry disagreement.

quarrel *VERB* **quarrels, quarrelling, quarrelled** have a quarrel.
▷ **quarrelsome** *adjective*
[from Latin *querela* = complaint]

quarry[1] *NOUN* **quarries** an open place where stone or slate is dug or cut out of the ground.

quarry *VERB* **quarries, quarrying, quarried** dig or cut from a quarry.
[from Latin]

quarry[2] *NOUN* **quarries** an animal etc. being hunted or pursued.
[from old French]

quart *NOUN* **quarts** two pints, a quarter of a gallon.
[from old French; related to *quarter*]

quarter *NOUN* **quarters** **1** each of four equal parts into which a thing is or can be divided. **2** three months, one-fourth of a year. **3** a district or region • *People came from every quarter.*
- **at close quarters** very close together.
- **give no quarter** show no mercy.

quarter *VERB* **quarters, quartering, quartered** **1** divide something into quarters. **2** put soldiers etc. into lodgings.
[from Latin *quartus* = fourth]

quarterdeck *NOUN* **quarterdecks** the part of a ship's upper deck nearest the stern, usually reserved for the officers.

quarter-final *NOUN* **quarter-finals** each of the matches or rounds before a semi-final, in which there are eight contestants or teams.
▷ **quarter-finalist** *noun*

quarterly *ADJECTIVE* & *ADVERB* happening or produced once in every three months.

quarterly *NOUN* **quarterlies** a quarterly magazine.

quarters *PLURAL NOUN* lodgings.

quartet *NOUN* **quartets** **1** a group of four musicians. **2** a piece of music for four musicians. **3** a set of four people or things.
[via French from Italian *quarto* = fourth]

quartz *NOUN* a hard mineral, often in crystal form.
[via German from Polish]

quash *VERB* **quashes, quashing, quashed** cancel or annul something • *The judges quashed his conviction.*
[from Latin *cassus* = null, not valid]

quasi- (*say* kwayz-I) *PREFIX* seeming to be something but not really so • *a quasi-scientific explanation.*
[from Latin *quasi* = as if]

quatrain *NOUN* **quatrains** a stanza with four lines.
[French, from *quatre* = four]

quaver *VERB* **quavers, quavering, quavered** tremble or quiver.

quaver *NOUN* **quavers** **1** a quavering sound. **2** a note in music (♪) lasting half as long as a crotchet.
[from Old English]

quay (*say* kee) *NOUN* **quays** a landing place where ships can be tied up for loading and unloading; a wharf.
▷ **quayside** *noun*
[from old French]

queasy *ADJECTIVE* feeling slightly sick.
▷ **queasily** *adverb* **queasiness** *noun*
[origin unknown]

queen *NOUN* **queens** **1** a woman who is the ruler of a country through inheriting the position. **2** the wife of a king. **3** a female bee or ant that produces eggs. **4** an important piece in chess. **5** a playing card with a picture of a queen on it.
▷ **queenly** *adjective*
[from Old English]

queen mother *NOUN* **queen mothers** a king's widow who is the mother of the present king or queen.

Queen's Counsel *NOUN* **Queen's Counsels** a senior barrister.

queer *ADJECTIVE* **1** strange or eccentric. **2** slightly ill or faint.
▷ **queerly** *adverb* **queerness** *noun*

queer *VERB* **queers, queering, queered**
- **queer a person's pitch** spoil his or her chances beforehand.
[origin unknown]

quell *VERB* **quells, quelling, quelled**
1 crush a rebellion. **2** stop yourself from feeling fear, anger etc.; suppress.
[from Old English]

quench *VERB* **quenches, quenching, quenched** **1** satisfy your thirst by drinking. **2** put out a fire or flame.
[from Old English]

querulous (*say* kwe-rew-lus) *ADJECTIVE* complaining all the time.
▷ **querulously** *adverb*
[same origin as *quarrel*]

query (*say* kweer-ee) *NOUN* **queries 1** a question. **2** a question mark.

query *VERB* **queries, querying, queried** question whether something is true or correct.
[from Latin *quaere* = ask!]

quest *NOUN* **quests** a long search for something • *the quest for gold.*
[same origin as *question*]

question *NOUN* **questions 1** a sentence asking something. **2** a problem to be discussed or solved • *Parliament debated the question of education.* **3** doubt • *Whether we shall win is open to question.*
- **in question** being discussed or disputed • *His honesty is not in question.*
- **out of the question** impossible.

question *VERB* **questions, questioning, questioned** **1** ask someone questions. **2** say that you are doubtful about something.
▷ **questioner** *noun*
[from Latin *quaesitum* = sought for]

questionable *ADJECTIVE* causing doubt; not certainly true or honest or advisable.

question mark *NOUN* **question marks** the punctuation mark ? placed after a question.

questionnaire *NOUN* **questionnaires** a written set of questions asked to provide information for a survey.

queue (*say* kew) *NOUN* **queues** a line of people or vehicles waiting for something.

queue *VERB* **queues, queueing, queued** wait in a queue.
[French]

quibble *NOUN* **quibbles** a trivial complaint or objection.

quibble *VERB* **quibbles, quibbling, quibbled** make trivial complaints or objections.
[probably from Latin *quibus* = what?, for which, for whom (because *quibus* often appeared in legal documents)]

quiche (*say* keesh) *NOUN* **quiches** an open tart with a savoury filling.
[French]

quick *ADJECTIVE* **1** taking only a short time to do something. **2** done in a short time. **3** able to notice or learn or think quickly. **4** (*old use*) alive • *the quick and the dead.*
▷ **quickly** *adverb* **quickness** *noun*
[from Old English]

quicken *VERB* **quickens, quickening, quickened** **1** make or become quicker. **2** stimulate; make or become livelier.

quicksand *NOUN* **quicksands** an area of loose wet deep sand that sucks in anything resting or falling on top of it.
[from *quick* in sense 4 (because the sand moves as if it were alive and 'eats' things)]

quicksilver *NOUN* mercury.

quid *NOUN* **quid** (*slang*) £1.
[origin unknown]

quid pro quo (*say* kwoh) *NOUN* **quid pro quos** something given or done in return for something.
[Latin, = something for something]

quiescent (*say* kwee-ess-ent) *ADJECTIVE* inactive or quiet.
▷ **quiescence** *noun*
[from Latin *quiescens* = becoming quiet]

quiet *ADJECTIVE* **1** silent • *Be quiet!* **2** with little sound; not loud or noisy. **3** calm and peaceful; without disturbance • *a quiet life.* **4** (said about colours) not bright.
▷ **quietly** *adverb* **quietness** *noun*

quiet *NOUN* quietness.
[from Latin *quietus* = calm]

quieten *VERB* **quietens, quietening, quietened** make or become quiet.

quiff *NOUN* **quiffs** an upright tuft of hair.
[origin unknown]

quill *NOUN* **quills 1** a large feather. **2** a pen made from a large feather. **3** one of the spines on a hedgehog.
[probably from old German]

quilt *NOUN* **quilts** a padded bedcover.

quilt *VERB* **quilts, quilting, quilted** line material with padding and fix it with lines of stitching.
[from Latin *culcita* = mattress or cushion]

quin *NOUN* **quins** a quintuplet.

quince *NOUN* **quinces** a hard pear-shaped fruit used for making jam.
[from Latin]

quincentenary *NOUN* **quincentenaries** the 500th anniversary of something.
[from Latin *quinque* = five, + *centenary*]

quinine (*say* kwin-een) *NOUN* a bitter-tasting medicine used to cure malaria.
[via Spanish from Quechua (a South American language)]

quintessence *NOUN* **1** the most essential part of something. **2** a perfect example of a quality.
▷ **quintessential** *adjective*
[from Latin *quinta essentia* = the fifth essence (after earth, air, fire, and water, which the alchemists thought everything contained)]

quintet *NOUN* **quintets 1** a group of five musicians. **2** a piece of music for five musicians.
[from Italian *quinto* = fifth]

quintuplet *NOUN* **quintuplets** each of five children born to the same mother at one time.
[from Latin *quintus* = fifth]

quip *NOUN* **quips** a witty remark.
[origin unknown]

quirk *NOUN* **quirks 1** a peculiarity of a person's behaviour. **2** a trick of fate.
▷ **quirky** *adjective*
[origin unknown]

quit *VERB* **quits, quitting, quitted** or **quit 1** leave or abandon. **2** (*informal*) stop doing something.
▷ **quitter** *noun*
[same origin as *quiet*]

quite *ADVERB* **1** completely or entirely • *I am quite all right*. **2** somewhat; to some extent • *She is quite a good swimmer*. **3** really • *It's quite a change*.
[same origin as *quiet*]

quits *ADJECTIVE* even or equal after retaliating or paying someone back • *I think you and I are quits now.*

quiver[1] *NOUN* **quivers** a container for arrows.
[via old French from Germanic]

quiver[2] *VERB* **quivers, quivering, quivered** tremble.
▷ **quiver** *noun*
[from Old English]

quixotic (*say* kwiks-ot-ik) *ADJECTIVE* having imaginative or idealistic ideas that are not practical.
▷ **quixotically** *adverb*
[named after Don *Quixote*, hero of a Spanish story]

quiz *NOUN* **quizzes** a series of questions, especially as an entertainment or competition.

quiz *VERB* **quizzes, quizzing, quizzed** question someone closely.
[origin unknown]

quizzical *ADJECTIVE* **1** in a questioning way. **2** gently amused.
▷ **quizzically** *adverb*
[from *quiz*]

quoit (*say* koit) *NOUN* **quoits** a ring thrown at a peg in the game of **quoits**.
[origin unknown]

quorum *NOUN* the smallest number of people needed to make a meeting of a committee etc. valid.
[Latin, = of which people]

quota *NOUN* **quotas 1** a fixed share that must be given or received or done. **2** a limited amount.
[from Latin *quot* = how many?]

quotation *NOUN* **quotations 1** quoting. **2** something quoted. **3** a statement of the price.

quotation marks *PLURAL NOUN* inverted commas, used to mark a quotation.

quote *VERB* **quotes, quoting, quoted** **1** repeat words that were first written or spoken by someone else. **2** mention something as proof. **3** state the price of goods or services that you can supply.

quote *NOUN* **quotes** a quotation.
[from Latin *quotare* = to number]

quoth *VERB* (*old use*) said.
[from Old English]

quotient (*say* kwoh-shent) *NOUN* **quotients** the result of dividing one number by another. (COMPARE **product**)
[from Latin *quotiens* = how many times?]

Rr

rabbi (*say* rab-I) *NOUN* **rabbis** a Jewish religious leader.
[Hebrew, = my master]

rabbit *NOUN* **rabbits** a furry animal with long ears that digs burrows.
[origin unknown]

rabble *NOUN* **rabbles** a disorderly crowd or mob.
[probably from old German or old Dutch]

rabid (*say* rab-id) *ADJECTIVE* **1** fanatical • *a rabid tennis fan.* **2** suffering from rabies.

rabies (*say* ray-beez) *NOUN* a fatal disease that affects dogs, cats, etc. and can be passed to humans by the bite of an infected animal.
[Latin, from *rabere* = to be mad]

raccoon *NOUN* **raccoons** or **raccoon** a North American animal with a bushy, striped tail.
[from a Native American language]

race[1] *NOUN* **races 1** a competition to be the first to reach a particular place or to do something. **2** a strong fast current of water • *the tidal race.*

race *VERB* **races, racing, raced 1** compete in a race. **2** move very fast.
▷ **racer** *noun*
[from Old Norse]

race[2] *NOUN* **races 1** a very large group of people thought to have the same ancestors and with physical characteristics (e.g. colour of skin and hair, shape of eyes and nose) that differ from those of other groups. **2** racial origin • *discrimination on grounds of race.*
[via French from Italian]

racecourse *NOUN* **racecourses** a place where horse races are run.

racehorse *NOUN* **racehorses** a horse bred or kept for racing.

race relations *NOUN* relationships between people of different races in the same country.

racetrack *NOUN* **racetracks** a track for horse or vehicle races.

racial (*say* ray-shul) *ADJECTIVE* to do with a particular race or based on race.
▷ **racially** *adverb*

racialism (*say* ray-shal-izm) *NOUN* racism.
▷ **racialist** *noun*

racism (*say* ray-sizm) *NOUN* **1** belief that a particular race of people is better than others. **2** discrimination against or hostility towards people of other races.
▷ **racist** *noun*

rack[1] *NOUN* **racks 1** a framework used as a shelf or container. **2** a bar or rail with cogs into which the cogs of a gear or wheel etc. fit. **3** an ancient device for torturing people by stretching them.

rack *VERB* **racks, racking, racked** torment • *He was racked with guilt.*
- **rack your brains** think hard in trying to solve a problem.
[from old German or old Dutch]

rack[2] *NOUN*
- **go to rack and ruin** gradually become worse in condition due to neglect.
[a different spelling of *wreck*]

racket[1] *NOUN* **rackets** a bat with strings stretched across a frame, used in tennis, badminton, and squash.
[from Arabic *rahat* = palm of the hand]

racket[2] *NOUN* **rackets 1** a loud noise; a din. **2** a dishonest or illegal business • *a drugs racket.*
[origin unknown]

racketeer *NOUN* **racketeers** a person involved in a dishonest or illegal business.
▷ **racketeering** *noun*

A B C D E F G H I J K L M N O P Q **R** S T U V W X Y Z

racoon *NOUN* **racoons** or **racoon** a different spelling of *raccoon*.

racquet *NOUN* **racquets** a different spelling of *racket*[1].

racy *ADJECTIVE* **racier**, **raciest** lively and slightly shocking in style • *She gave a racy account of her travels.*
[originally = having a particular quality: from *race*[2]]

radar *NOUN* a system or apparatus that uses radio waves to show on a screen etc. the position of objects that cannot be seen because of darkness, fog, distance, etc.
[from the initial letters of *radio detection and ranging*]

radar trap *NOUN* **radar traps** a system using radar that the police use to catch drivers who are going too fast.

radial *ADJECTIVE* **1** to do with rays or radii. **2** having spokes or lines that radiate from a central point.
▷ **radially** *adverb*

radiant *ADJECTIVE* **1** radiating light or heat etc. **2** radiated • *radiant heat*. **3** looking very bright and happy.
▷ **radiantly** *adverb* **radiance** *noun*

radiate *VERB* **radiates**, **radiating**, **radiated** **1** send out light, heat, or other energy in rays. **2** give out a strong feeling or quality • *She radiated confidence*. **3** spread out from a central point like the spokes of a wheel.
[same origin as *radium*]

radiation *NOUN* **1** light, heat, or other energy radiated. **2** the energy or particles sent out by a radioactive substance. **3** the process of radiating.

radiator *NOUN* **radiators** **1** a device that gives out heat, especially a metal case that is heated electrically or through which steam or hot water flows. **2** a device that cools the engine of a motor vehicle.
[from *radiate*]

radical *ADJECTIVE* **1** basic and thorough • *radical changes*. **2** wanting to make great reforms • *a radical politician*.
▷ **radically** *adverb*

radical *NOUN* **radicals** a person who wants to make great reforms.
[from Latin *radicis* = of a root]

radicchio (*say* ra-dee-ki-oh) *NOUN* a kind of chicory with dark red leaves.
[Italian, = chicory]

radicle *NOUN* **radicles** a root that forms in the seed of a plant.
[from Latin *radicula* = little root]

radio *NOUN* **radios** **1** the process of sending and receiving sound or pictures by means of electromagnetic waves. **2** an apparatus for receiving sound (a *receiver*) or sending it out (a *transmitter*) in this way. **3** sound broadcasting.

radio *VERB* **radios**, **radioing**, **radioed** send a message to someone by radio.
[same origin as *radium*]

radio- *PREFIX* **1** to do with rays or radiation. **2** to do with radio.

radioactive *ADJECTIVE* having atoms that break up spontaneously and send out radiation which produces electrical and chemical effects and penetrates things.
▷ **radioactivity** *noun*

radio beacon *NOUN* **radio beacons** an instrument that sends out radio signals, which aircraft use to find their way.

radiocarbon dating *NOUN* the use of a kind of radioactive carbon that decays at a steady rate, to find out how old something is.

radiography *NOUN* the production of X-ray photographs.
▷ **radiographer** *noun*

radiology *NOUN* the study of X-rays and similar radiation, especially in treating diseases.
▷ **radiologist** *noun*

radio telescope *NOUN* **radio telescopes** an instrument that can detect radio waves from space.

radiotherapy *NOUN* the use of radioactive substances in treating diseases such as cancer.

radish *NOUN* **radishes** a small hard round red vegetable, eaten raw in salads.
[from Latin *radix* = root]

radium *NOUN* a radioactive substance found in pitchblende, often used in radiotherapy.
[from Latin *radius* = a spoke or ray]

radius *NOUN* **radii** or **radiuses 1** a straight line from the centre of a circle or sphere to the circumference; the length of this line. **2** a range or distance from a central point • *The school takes pupils living within a radius of ten kilometres.*
[Latin, = a spoke or ray]

radon *NOUN* a radioactive gas used in radiotherapy.
[from *radium*]

RAF *ABBREVIATION* Royal Air Force.

raffia *NOUN* soft fibre from the leaves of a kind of palm tree.
[from Malagasy (the language of Madagascar)]

raffish *ADJECTIVE* cheerfully disreputable.
[from *riff-raff*]

raffle *NOUN* **raffles** a kind of lottery, usually to raise money for a charity.

raffle *VERB* **raffles, raffling, raffled** offer something as a prize in a raffle.
[probably from French]

raft[1] *NOUN* **rafts** a flat floating structure made of wood etc., used as a boat.
[from Old Norse]

raft[2] *NOUN* **rafts** a large number or amount of things • *a raft of new proposals.*
[perhaps from Scandinavian]

rafter *NOUN* **rafters** any of the long sloping pieces of wood that hold up a roof.
[from Old English]

rag[1] *NOUN* **rags 1** an old or torn piece of cloth. **2** a piece of ragtime music.
- **dressed in rags** wearing old and torn clothes.
[from *ragged*]

rag[2] *NOUN* **rags** a series of entertainments and activities held by students to collect money for charity.

rag *VERB* **rags, ragging, ragged** (*informal*) tease.
[origin unknown]

rage *NOUN* **rages** great or violent anger.
- **all the rage** very popular or fashionable for a time.

rage *VERB* **rages, raging, raged 1** be very angry. **2** continue violently or with great force • *A storm was raging.*
[from old French; related to *rabies*]

ragged *ADJECTIVE* **1** torn or frayed. **2** wearing torn clothes. **3** irregular or uneven • *a ragged performance.*
[from Old Norse *roggvathr* = tufted]

raglan *ADJECTIVE* (said about a sleeve) joined to a piece of clothing by sloping seams.
[named after Lord *Raglan*, British military commander (died 1855), who wore a coat with raglan sleeves]

ragtime *NOUN* a kind of jazz music.
[perhaps from *ragged time*]

raid *NOUN* **raids 1** a sudden attack. **2** a surprise visit by police etc. to arrest people or seize illegal goods.

raid *VERB* **raids, raiding, raided** make a raid on a place.
▷ **raider** *noun*
[from Old English]

rail[1] *NOUN* **rails 1** a level or sloping bar for hanging things on or forming part of a fence, banisters, etc. **2** a long metal bar forming part of a railway track.
- **by rail** on a train.
[from old French; related to *rule*]

rail[2] *VERB* **rails, railing, railed** protest angrily or bitterly.
[via French from Portuguese]

railings *PLURAL NOUN* a fence made of metal bars.

railroad *NOUN* **railroads** (*American*) a railway.

railway *NOUN* **1** the parallel metal bars that trains travel on. **2** a system of transport using rails.

raiment *NOUN* (*old use*) clothing.
[from *array*]

rain *NOUN* drops of water that fall from the sky.
▷ **rainy** *adjective*

rain *VERB* **rains, raining, rained 1** fall as rain or like rain. **2** send down like rain • *They rained blows on him.*
[from Old English]

rainbow *NOUN* **rainbows** an arch of all the colours of the spectrum formed in the sky when the sun shines through rain.

raincoat *NOUN* **raincoats** a waterproof coat.

raindrop *NOUN* **raindrops** a single drop of rain.

rainfall *NOUN* the amount of rain that falls in a particular place or time.

rainforest *NOUN* **rainforests** a dense tropical forest in an area of very heavy rainfall.

raise *VERB* **raises, raising, raised 1** move something to a higher place or an upright position. **2** increase the amount or level of something • *We are trying to raise standards.* **3** collect; manage to obtain • *They raised £100 for Oxfam.* **4** bring up young children or animals • *She had to raise her family alone.* **5** rouse or cause • *He raised a laugh with his elephant joke.* **6** put forward • *We raised objections.* **7** end a siege.
[from Old Norse]

raisin *NOUN* **raisins** a dried grape.
[French, = grape]

raison d'être (*say* ray-zawn **detr**) *NOUN* **raisons d'être** the purpose of a thing's existence.
[French, = reason for being]

raj (*say* rahj) *NOUN* the period of Indian history when the country was ruled by Britain.
[Hindi, = reign]

rajah *NOUN* **rajahs** an Indian king or prince. (COMPARE **ranee**)
[from Sanskrit]

rake[1] *NOUN* **rakes** a gardening tool with a row of short spikes fixed to a long handle.

rake *VERB* **rakes, raking, raked 1** gather or smooth with a rake. **2** search.
- **rake it in** (*informal*) make a lot of money.
- **rake up 1** collect. **2** remind people of an old quarrel, scandal, etc. that is best forgotten • *Don't rake that up again.*
[from Old English]

rake[2] *NOUN* **rakes** a man who lives an irresponsible and immoral life.
[from an old word *rakehell*]

rakish (*say* ray-kish) *ADJECTIVE* jaunty and dashing.
[from *rake*[2]]

rally *NOUN* **rallies 1** a large meeting to support something or share an interest. **2** a competition to test skill in driving • *the Monte Carlo Rally.* **3** a series of strokes in tennis before a point is scored. **4** a recovery.

rally *VERB* **rallies, rallying, rallied 1** bring or come together for a united effort • *They rallied support.* • *People rallied round.* **2** revive; recover strength.
[from French]

RAM *ABBREVIATION* (*in computing*) random-access memory, with contents that can be retrieved or stored directly without having to read through items already stored.

ram *NOUN* **rams 1** a male sheep. **2** a device for ramming things.

ram *VERB* **rams, ramming, rammed** push one thing hard against another.
[from Old English]

Ramadan *NOUN* the ninth month of the Muslim year, when Muslims do not eat or drink between sunrise and sunset.
[Arabic, from *ramida* = to be parched]

ramble *NOUN* **rambles** a long walk in the country.

ramble *VERB* **rambles, rambling, rambled 1** go for a ramble; wander. **2** talk or write a lot without keeping to the subject.
▷ **rambler** *noun*
[origin unknown]

ramifications *PLURAL NOUN* **1** the branches of a structure. **2** the many effects of a plan or action.
[from Latin *ramificare* = to branch out]

ramp *NOUN* **ramps** a slope joining two different levels.
[from French *ramper* = to climb]

rampage *VERB* **rampages, rampaging, rampaged** rush about wildly or destructively.
- **on the rampage** rampaging.
[origin unknown]

rampant *ADJECTIVE* **1** growing or spreading uncontrollably • *Disease was rampant in the poorer districts.* **2** (said about an animal on coats of arms) standing upright on a hind leg • *a lion rampant.*
[same origin as *ramp*]

rampart *NOUN* **ramparts** a wide bank of earth built as a fortification or a wall on top of this.
[from French *remparer* = fortify]

ramrod *NOUN* **ramrods** a straight rod formerly used for ramming an explosive into a gun.
- **like a ramrod** very stiff and straight.

ramshackle *ADJECTIVE* badly made and rickety • *a ramshackle hut*.
[from *ransack*]

ranch *NOUN* **ranches** a large cattle farm in America.
[from Spanish]

rancid *ADJECTIVE* smelling or tasting unpleasant like stale fat.
[from Latin]

rancour (*say* rank-er) *NOUN* bitter resentment or ill will.
▷ **rancorous** *adjective*
[from old French; related to *rancid*]

random *NOUN*
- **at random** using no particular order or method • *numbers chosen at random*.

random *ADJECTIVE* done or taken at random • *a random sample*.
▷ **randomly** *adverb*
[via old French from Germanic]

ranee (*say* rah-nee) *NOUN* **ranees** a rajah's wife or widow.
[from Sanskrit]

range *NOUN* **ranges 1** a set of different things of the same type • *a wide range of backgrounds; a lovely range of colours*. **2** the limits between which something varies • *the age range 15 to 18*. **3** the distance that a gun can shoot, an aircraft can travel, a sound can be heard, etc. **4** a place with targets for shooting practice. **5** a line or series of mountains or hills. **6** a large open area of grazing land or hunting ground. **7** a kitchen fireplace with ovens.

range *VERB* **ranges, ranging, ranged** **1** exist between two limits; extend • *Prices ranged from £1 to £50*. **2** arrange. **3** move over a wide area; wander.
[from old French; related to *rank*[1]]

Ranger *NOUN* **Rangers** a senior Guide.

ranger *NOUN* **rangers** someone who looks after or patrols a park, forest, etc.
[from *range*]

rank[1] *NOUN* **ranks 1** a line of people or things. **2** a place where taxis stand to await customers. **3** a position in a series of different levels • *He holds the rank of sergeant*.

rank *VERB* **ranks, ranking, ranked 1** put things in order according to their rank. **2** have a certain rank or place • *She ranks among the greatest novelists*.
[via old French from Germanic]

rank[2] *ADJECTIVE* **ranker, rankest 1** growing too thickly and coarsely. **2** smelling very unpleasant. **3** unmistakably bad • *rank injustice*.
▷ **rankly** *adverb* **rankness** *noun*
[from Old English]

rank and file *NOUN* the ordinary people or soldiers, not the leaders.

rankle *VERB* **rankles, rankling, rankled** cause lasting annoyance or resentment.
[from old French]

ransack *VERB* **ransacks, ransacking, ransacked 1** search thoroughly or roughly. **2** rob or pillage a place.
[from Old Norse]

ransom *NOUN* **ransoms** money that has to be paid for a prisoner to be set free.
- **hold to ransom** hold someone captive or in your power and demand ransom.

ransom *VERB* **ransoms, ransoming, ransomed 1** free someone by paying a ransom. **2** get a ransom for someone.
[from old French; related to *redeem*]

rant *VERB* **rants, ranting, ranted** speak loudly and violently.
[from Dutch]

rap *VERB* **raps, rapping, rapped 1** knock loudly. **2** (*informal*) reprimand. **3** (*informal*) chat. **4** speak rhymes with a backing of rock music.

rap *NOUN* **raps 1** a rapping movement or sound. **2** (*informal*) blame or punishment • *take the rap*. **3** (*informal*) a chat. **4** rhymes spoken with a backing of rock music.
[imitating the sound]

rapacious (*say* ra-pay-shus) *ADJECTIVE* **1** greedy. **2** using threats or force to get everything you can.
▷ **rapaciously** *adverb* **rapacity** *noun*
[from Latin *rapax* = grasping]

rape[1] *NOUN* **rapes** the act of having sexual intercourse with a person without her or his consent.

rape *VERB* **rapes, raping, raped** force someone to have sexual intercourse.
▷ **rapist** *noun*
[from Latin *rapere* = take by force]

rape[2] *NOUN* a plant with bright yellow flowers, grown as food for sheep and for its seed from which oil is obtained.
[from Latin *rapum* = turnip (to which it is related)]

rapid *ADJECTIVE* moving very quickly; swift.
▷ **rapidly** *adverb* **rapidity** *noun*
[from Latin]

rapids *PLURAL NOUN* part of a river where the water flows very quickly.

rapier *NOUN* **rapiers** a thin lightweight sword.
[probably from Dutch]

rapport (*say* rap-**or**) *NOUN* a friendly and understanding relationship between people.
[French]

rapt *ADJECTIVE* very intent and absorbed; enraptured.
▷ **raptly** *adverb*
[from Latin *raptum* = seized]

rapture *NOUN* very great delight.
▷ **rapturous** *adjective* **rapturously** *adverb*
[from old French; related to *rapt*]

rare[1] *ADJECTIVE* **rarer, rarest** **1** unusual; not often found or happening. **2** (said about air) thin; below normal pressure.
▷ **rarely** *adverb* **rareness** *noun*
[from Latin]

rare[2] *ADJECTIVE* (said about meat) only lightly cooked; undercooked.
[from Old English]

rarefied *ADJECTIVE* **1** (said about air) rare. **2** remote from everyday life • *the rarefied atmosphere of the university*.

rarity *NOUN* **rarities** **1** rareness. **2** something uncommon; a thing valued because it is rare.

rascal *NOUN* **rascals** a dishonest or mischievous person; a rogue.
▷ **rascally** *adjective*
[from old French]

rash[1] *ADJECTIVE* doing something or done without thinking of the possible risks or effects.
▷ **rashly** *adverb* **rashness** *noun*
[probably from Old English]

rash[2] *NOUN* **rashes** **1** an outbreak of spots or patches on the skin. **2** a number of (usually unwelcome) events happening in a short time • *a rash of accidents*.
[probably from old French]

rasher *NOUN* **rashers** a slice of bacon.
[origin unknown]

rasp *NOUN* **rasps** **1** a file with sharp points on its surface. **2** a rough grating sound.

rasp *VERB* **rasps, rasping, rasped** **1** scrape roughly. **2** make a rough grating sound or effect.
[via old French from Germanic]

raspberry *NOUN* **raspberries** a small soft red fruit.
[origin unknown]

Rastafarian *NOUN* **Rastafarians** a member of a religious group that started in Jamaica.
[from *Ras Tafari* (*ras* = chief), the title of a former Ethiopian king whom the group reveres]

rat *NOUN* **rats** **1** an animal like a large mouse. **2** an unpleasant or treacherous person.
[from Old English]

ratchet *NOUN* **ratchets** a row of notches on a bar or wheel in which a device (a *pawl*) catches to prevent it running backwards.
[from French]

rate *NOUN* **rates** **1** speed • *The train travelled at a great rate*. **2** a measure of cost, value, etc. • *Postage rates went up*. **3** quality or standard • *first-rate*.
- **at any rate** anyway.

rate *VERB* **rates, rating, rated** **1** put a value on something. **2** regard as • *He rated me among his friends*.
[from Latin *ratum* = reckoned]

rates *PLURAL NOUN* a local tax paid by owners of commercial land and buildings.

rather *ADVERB* **1** slightly or somewhat • *It's rather dark.* **2** preferably or more willingly • *I would rather not go.* **3** more exactly; instead of • *He is lazy rather than stupid.* **4** (*informal*) definitely, yes • *'Will you come?' 'Rather!'*
[from Old English]

ratify *VERB* **ratifies, ratifying, ratified** confirm or agree to something officially • *They ratified the treaty.*
▷ **ratification** *noun*
[from Latin *ratus* = fixed or established]

rating *NOUN* **ratings 1** the way something is rated. **2** a sailor who is not an officer.
[from *rate*]

ratio (*say* ray-shee-oh) *NOUN* **ratios 1** the relationship between two numbers, given by the quotient • *The ratio of 2 to 10 = 2:10 =* $\frac{5}{10} = \frac{1}{5}$. **2** proportion • *Mix flour and butter in the ratio of two to one* (= two measures of flour to one measure of butter).
[Latin, = reasoning, reckoning]

ration *NOUN* **rations** an amount allowed to one person.

ration *VERB* **rations, rationing, rationed** share something out in fixed amounts.
[French; related to *ratio*]

rational *ADJECTIVE* **1** reasonable or sane. **2** able to reason • *Plants are not rational.*
▷ **rationally** *adverb* **rationality** *noun*
[same origin as *ratio*]

rationale (*say* rash-un-**ahl**) *NOUN* **rationales** the reasons which explain a particular decision, course of action, belief • *the rationale behind my decision.*
[from Latin *rationalis*]

rationalize *VERB* **rationalizes, rationalizing, rationalized 1** make a thing logical and consistent • *Attempts to rationalize English spelling have failed.* **2** justify something by inventing a reasonable explanation for it • *She rationalized her meanness by calling it economy.* **3** make a company or industry more efficient by reorganizing it.
▷ **rationalization** *noun*

rations *PLURAL NOUN* a fixed daily amount of food issued to a soldier etc.

rat race *NOUN* a continuous struggle for success in a career, business, etc.

rattle *VERB* **rattles, rattling, rattled** **1** make a series of short sharp hard sounds. **2** make a person nervous or flustered.
- **rattle off** say or recite rapidly.

rattle *NOUN* **rattles 1** a rattling sound. **2** a device or baby's toy that rattles.
[imitating the sound]

rattlesnake *NOUN* **rattlesnakes** a poisonous American snake with a tail that rattles.

rattling *ADJECTIVE* **1** that rattles. **2** vigorous or brisk • *a rattling pace.*

ratty *ADJECTIVE* **rattier, rattiest** (*informal*) angry or irritable.
[from *rat*]

raucous (*say* raw-kus) *ADJECTIVE* loud and harsh • *a raucous voice.*
[from Latin *raucus* = hoarse]

ravage *VERB* **ravages, ravaging, ravaged** do great damage to something; devastate.

ravages *PLURAL NOUN* damaging effects • *the ravages of war.*
[same origin as *ravine*]

rave *VERB* **raves, raving, raved 1** talk wildly or angrily or madly. **2** talk enthusiastically about something.

rave *NOUN* **raves** (*informal*) **1** a large party or event with dancing to loud fast electronic music. **2** a very enthusiastic review.
[from old French]

raven *NOUN* **ravens** a large black bird, related to the crow.
[from Old English]

ravenous *ADJECTIVE* very hungry.
▷ **ravenously** *adverb*
[from French *raviner* = rush, ravage]

ravine (*say* ra-veen) *NOUN* **ravines** a deep narrow gorge or valley.
[French, = a rush of water (because a ravine is cut by rushing water)]

ravings *PLURAL NOUN* wild talk that makes no sense.
[from *rave*]

ravish *VERB* **ravishes, ravishing, ravished** **1** rape. **2** enrapture.
[from old French; related to *rape*[1]]

ravishing *ADJECTIVE* very beautiful.

raw *ADJECTIVE* **1** not cooked. **2** in the natural state; not yet processed • *raw materials.* **3** without experience • *raw recruits.* **4** with the skin removed • *a raw wound.* **5** cold and damp • *a raw morning.*
▷ **rawness** *noun*
[from Old English]

raw deal *NOUN* unfair treatment.

raw material *NOUN* **raw materials** natural substances used in industry • *rich in iron ore, coal, and other raw materials.*

ray[1] *NOUN* **rays 1** a thin line of light, heat, or other radiation. **2** each of a set of lines or parts extending from a centre. **3** a trace of something • *a ray of hope.*
[from Latin *radius*]

ray[2] *NOUN* **ray** or **rays** a large sea fish with a flat body and a long tail.
[from Latin *raia*]

rayon *NOUN* a synthetic fibre or cloth made from cellulose.
[a made-up word, probably based on French *rayon* = a ray of light (because of its shiny surface)]

raze *VERB* **razes, razing, razed** destroy a building or town completely • *The fort was razed to the ground.*
[from Latin *rasum* = scraped]

razor *NOUN* **razors** a device with a very sharp blade, especially one used for shaving.
▷ **razor blade** *noun*
[same origin as *raze*]

razzmatazz *NOUN* (*informal*) showy publicity.
[origin unknown]

RC *ABBREVIATION* Roman Catholic.

re- *PREFIX* **1** again (as in *rebuild*). **2** back again, to an earlier condition (as in *reopen*). **3** in return; to each other (as in *react*). **4** against (as in *rebel*). **5** away or down (as in *recede*).
[from Latin]

reach *VERB* **reaches, reaching, reached** **1** go as far as; arrive at a place or thing. **2** stretch out your hand to get or touch something. **3** succeed in achieving something • *The cheetah can reach a speed of 70 m.p.h. Have you reached a decision?*
▷ **reachable** *adjective*

reach *NOUN* **reaches 1** the distance a person or thing can reach. **2** a distance you can easily travel • *We live within reach of the sea.* **3** a straight stretch of a river or canal.
[from Old English]

react *VERB* **reacts, reacting, reacted** **1** respond to something; have a reaction. **2** undergo a chemical change.
[from *re-* + Latin *agere* = act or do]

reaction *NOUN* **reactions 1** an effect or feeling etc. produced in one person or thing by another. **2** a chemical change caused when substances act upon each other.
- **reactions** your ability to move quickly in response to something • *Racing drivers need to have quick reactions.*

reactionary *ADJECTIVE* opposed to progress or reform.
▷ **reactionary** *noun*

reactor *NOUN* **reactors** an apparatus for producing nuclear power in a controlled way.

read (*say as* red) *VERB* **reads, reading, read** **1** look at something written or printed and understand it or say it aloud. **2** (said about a computer) copy, search, or extract data. **3** indicate or register • *The thermometer reads 20° Celsius.* **4** study a subject at university.
▷ **readable** *adjective*
[from Old English]

reader *NOUN* **readers 1** a person who reads. **2** a book that helps you learn to read.

readership *NOUN* **readerships** the readers of a newspaper or magazine; the number of these.

readily (*say* red-il-ee) *ADVERB* **1** willingly. **2** easily; without any difficulty.

reading *NOUN* **readings 1** reading books. **2** the figure shown on a meter, gauge, or other instrument. **3** a gathering of people at which something is read aloud • *a poetry reading.*

ready *ADJECTIVE* **readier, readiest 1** fully prepared to do something; completed and able to be used • *Are you ready to go? The meal's ready.* **2** willing to do something. **3** quick or prompt • *a ready wit.*
▷ **readiness** *noun*
- **at the ready** ready for use or action.

ready *ADVERB* beforehand • *This meat is ready cooked.*
▷ **ready-made** *adjective*
[from Old English]

reagent *NOUN* **reagents** a substance used in a chemical reaction, especially to detect another substance.
[from *re-* + *agent*]

real *ADJECTIVE* **1** existing or true; not imaginary. **2** genuine; not an imitation • *real pearls*. **3** (said about food) regarded as superior because it is produced by traditional methods • *real ale*.
[from Latin]

real estate *NOUN* (*American*) property consisting of land and buildings.

realism *NOUN* seeing or showing things as they really are.
▷ **realist** *noun*

realistic *ADJECTIVE* **1** true to life. **2** seeing things as they really are.
▷ **realistically** *adverb*

reality *NOUN* **realities 1** what is real • *You must face reality*. **2** something real • *Her worst fears had become a reality*.

realize *VERB* **realizes, realizing, realized**
1 be fully aware of something; accept something as true. **2** make a hope or plan etc. happen • *She realized her ambition to become a racing driver*. **3** obtain money in exchange for something by selling it.
▷ **realization** *noun*
[from *real* + *-ize*]

really *ADVERB* **1** truly or in fact. **2** very • *She's really clever*.

realm (*say* relm) *NOUN* **realms 1** a kingdom.
2 an area of knowledge, interest, etc. • *the realms of science*.
[from old French; related to *regiment*]

ream *NOUN* **reams** 500 (originally 480) sheets of paper.
[via French from Arabic *rizma* = bundle]

reams *PLURAL NOUN* a large quantity of writing.

reap *VERB* **reaps, reaping, reaped 1** cut down and gather corn when it is ripe.
2 obtain as the result of something done • *They reaped great benefit from their training*.
▷ **reaper** *noun*
[from Old English]

reappear *VERB* **reappears, reappearing, reappeared** appear again.

reappraise *VERB* **reappraises, reappraising, reappraised** think about or examine something again.
▷ **reappraisal** *noun*
[from *re-* + *appraise*]

rear[1] *NOUN* the back part.

rear *ADJECTIVE* placed at the rear.
[from Latin *retro-* = back]

rear[2] *VERB* **rears, rearing, reared 1** bring up young children or animals. **2** rise up; raise itself on hind legs • *The horse reared up in fright*. **3** build or set up a monument etc.
[from Old English]

rearguard *NOUN* **rearguards** troops protecting the rear of an army.
- **fight a rearguard action** go on defending or resisting something even though you are losing.

rearrange *VERB* **rearranges, rearranging, rearranged** arrange in a different way or order.
▷ **rearrangement** *noun*

reason *NOUN* **reasons 1** a cause or explanation of something. **2** reasoning; common sense • *You must listen to reason*.
USAGE Do not use the phrase *the reason is* with the word *because* (which means the same thing). Correct usage is *We cannot come. The reason is that we both have flu* (not 'The reason is because ...').

reason *VERB* **reasons, reasoning, reasoned 1** use your ability to think and draw conclusions. **2** try to persuade someone by giving reasons • *We reasoned with the rebels*.
[from old French; related to *ratio*]

reasonable *ADJECTIVE* **1** ready to use or listen to reason; sensible or logical. **2** fair or moderate; not expensive • *reasonable prices*.
3 acceptable or fairly good • *a reasonable standard of living*.
▷ **reasonably** *adverb*

reassure *VERB* **reassures, reassuring, reassured** restore someone's confidence by removing doubts and fears.
▷ **reassurance** *noun*

rebate *NOUN* **rebates** a reduction in the amount to be paid; a partial refund.
[from *re-* + French *abattre* = abate]

rebel (*say* rib-el) *VERB* **rebels, rebelling, rebelled** refuse to obey someone in authority, especially the government; fight against the rulers of your own country.

rebel (*say* reb-el) *NOUN* **rebels** someone who rebels against the government, or against accepted standards of behaviour. [from *re-* + Latin *bellum* = war (originally referring to a defeated enemy who began to fight again)]

rebellion *NOUN* **rebellions 1** rebelling against authority. **2** organized armed resistance to the government; a revolt.

rebellious *ADJECTIVE* often refusing to obey authority; likely to rebel • *a rebellious child*.

rebirth *NOUN* a return to life or activity; a revival of something.

rebound *VERB* **rebounds, rebounding, rebounded** bounce back after hitting something.
▷ **rebound** *noun*

rebuff *NOUN* **rebuffs** an unkind refusal; a snub.
▷ **rebuff** *verb*
[from *re-* + Italian *buffo* = a gust]

rebuild *VERB* **rebuilds, rebuilding, rebuilt** build something again after it has been destroyed.

rebuke *VERB* **rebukes, rebuking, rebuked** speak severely to a person who has done wrong.
▷ **rebuke** *noun*
[originally = to force back: from *re-* + old French *buker* = to hit]

rebut *VERB* **rebuts, rebutting, rebutted** prove that something said about you is not true.
▷ **rebuttal** *noun*
[from *re-* + French *boter* = to butt]

recalcitrant *ADJECTIVE* disobedient or uncooperative.
▷ **recalcitrance** *noun*
[from Latin *recalcitrare* = to kick back]

recall *VERB* **recalls, recalling, recalled** **1** bring back into the mind; remember. **2** ask a person to come back. **3** ask for something to be returned.

recall *NOUN* **1** the ability to remember; remembering. **2** an order to return.

recant *VERB* **recants, recanting, recanted** state formally and publicly that you no longer believe something.
▷ **recantation** *noun*
[from *re-* + Latin *cantare* = sing]

recap *VERB* **recaps, recapping, recapped** (*informal*) recapitulate.
▷ **recap** *noun*

recapitulate *VERB* **recapitulates, recapitulating, recapitulated** state again the main points of what has been said.
▷ **recapitulation** *noun*
[from *re-* + Latin *capitulare* = arrange under headings]

recapture *VERB* **recaptures, recapturing, recaptured** **1** capture again. **2** bring or get back a mood or feeling.
▷ **recapture** *noun*

recede *VERB* **recedes, receding, receded** **1** go back from a certain point • *The floods have receded*. **2** (said about a man's hair) stop growing at the front of the head.
[from *re-* + Latin *cedere* = go]

receipt (*say* ris-eet) *NOUN* **receipts 1** a written statement that money has been paid or something has been received. **2** receiving something.

receive *VERB* **receives, receiving, received** **1** take or get something that is given or sent to you. **2** experience something • *He received injuries to his face and hands.* **3** greet someone who comes.
[from *re-* + Latin *capere* = take]

receiver *NOUN* **receivers 1** a person or thing that receives something. **2** a person who buys and sells stolen goods. **3** an official who takes charge of a bankrupt person's property. **4** a radio or television set that receives broadcasts. **5** the part of a telephone that receives the sound and is held to a person's ear.

recent *ADJECTIVE* happening or made or done a short time ago.
▷ **recently** *adverb*
[from Latin]

receptacle *NOUN* **receptacles** something for holding or containing what is put into it.
[same origin as *receive*]

reception *NOUN* **receptions 1** the way a person or thing is received. **2** a formal party to receive guests • *a wedding reception.* **3** a place in a hotel or office where visitors are greeted and registered. **4** the first class in an infant school. **5** the quality of television or radio signals.

receptionist *NOUN* **receptionists** a person whose job is to greet and deal with visitors, clients, patients, etc.

receptive *ADJECTIVE* quick or willing to receive ideas etc.

recess (*say* ris-ess) *NOUN* **recesses 1** an alcove. **2** a time when work or business is stopped for a while.
[same origin as *recede*]

recession *NOUN* **recessions 1** a reduction in a country's trade or prosperity. **2** receding from a point.

recharge *VERB* **recharges, recharging, recharged 1** reload or refill. **2** put an electric charge in a used battery so that it will work again.
▷ **rechargeable** *adjective*

recipe (*say* ress-ip-ee) *NOUN* **recipes** instructions for preparing or cooking food.
[Latin, = take (used at the beginning of a list of ingredients)]

recipient *NOUN* **recipients** a person who receives something.

reciprocal (*say* ris-ip-rok-al) *ADJECTIVE* given and received; mutual • *reciprocal help.*
▷ **reciprocally** *adverb* **reciprocity** *noun*

reciprocal *NOUN* **reciprocals** a reversed fraction, • $\frac{3}{2}$ *is the reciprocal of* $\frac{2}{3}$.
[from Latin *reciprocus* = moving backwards and forwards]

reciprocate *VERB* **reciprocates, reciprocating, reciprocated** give and receive; do the same thing in return • *She did not reciprocate his love.*
▷ **reciprocation** *noun*
[same origin as *reciprocal*]

recital *NOUN* **recitals 1** reciting something. **2** a musical entertainment given by one performer or group.

recite *VERB* **recites, reciting, recited** say a poem etc. aloud from memory.
▷ **recitation** *noun*
[from Latin *recitare* = to read aloud]

reckless *ADJECTIVE* rash; ignoring risk or danger.
▷ **recklessly** *adverb* **recklessness** *noun*
[from an old word *reck* = heed, + *-less*]

reckon *VERB* **reckons, reckoning, reckoned 1** calculate or count up. **2** have as an opinion; feel confident • *I reckon we shall win.*
- **reckon with** think about or deal with • *We didn't reckon with the rail strike when we planned our journey.*
[from Old English]

reclaim *VERB* **reclaims, reclaiming, reclaimed 1** claim or get something back. **2** make a thing usable again • *reclaimed land.*
▷ **reclamation** *noun*

recline *VERB* **reclines, reclining, reclined** lean or lie back.
[from *re-* + Latin *-clinare* = to lean]

recluse *NOUN* **recluses** a person who lives alone and avoids mixing with people.
▷ **reclusive** *adjective*
[from *re-* + Latin *clausum* = shut]

recognize *VERB* **recognizes, recognizing, recognized 1** know who someone is or what something is because you have seen that person or thing before. **2** realize • *She recognized the truth of what he was saying.* **3** accept something as genuine, welcome, or lawful etc. • *Nine countries recognized the island's new government.*
▷ **recognition** *noun* **recognizable** *adjective*
[from *re-* + Latin *cognoscere* = know]

recoil *VERB* **recoils, recoiling, recoiled 1** move back suddenly in shock or disgust. **2** (said about a gun) jerk backwards when it is fired.
[from French]

recollect *VERB* **recollects, recollecting, recollected** remember.
▷ **recollection** *noun*
[from *re-* + Latin *colligere* = collect]

recommend *VERB* **recommends, recommending, recommended 1** say that a person or thing would be a good one to do a job or achieve something. **2** advise someone to do something.
▷ **recommendation** *noun*
[from *re-* + Latin *commendare* = commend]

recompense *VERB* **recompenses, recompensing, recompensed** repay or reward someone; compensate.
▷ **recompense** *noun*
[from *re-* + Latin *compensare* = compensate]

reconcile *VERB* **reconciles, reconciling, reconciled** 1 make people who have quarrelled become friendly again. 2 persuade a person to put up with something • *He soon became reconciled to wearing glasses.* 3 make things agree • *I cannot reconcile what you say with what you do.*
▷ **reconciliation** *noun*
[from *re-* + Latin *conciliare* = conciliate]

recondition *VERB* **reconditions, reconditioning, reconditioned** overhaul and repair.

reconnaissance (*say* rik-on-i-sans) *NOUN* an exploration of an area, especially in order to gather information about it for military purposes.
[French, = recognition]

reconnoitre *VERB* **reconnoitres, reconnoitring, reconnoitred** make a reconnaissance of an area.
[old French, = recognize]

reconsider *VERB* **reconsiders, reconsidering, reconsidered** consider something again and perhaps change an earlier decision.
▷ **reconsideration** *noun*

reconstitute *VERB* **reconstitutes, reconstituting, reconstituted** 1 form something again, especially in a different way. 2 make dried food edible again by adding water.

reconstruct *VERB* **reconstructs, reconstructing, reconstructed**
1 construct or build something again.
2 create or act out past events again • *Police reconstructed the robbery.*
▷ **reconstruction** *noun*

record (*say* rek-ord) *NOUN* **records**
1 information kept in a permanent form, e.g. written or printed. 2 a disc on which sound has been recorded. 3 the best performance in a sport etc., or the most remarkable event of its kind • *He holds the record for the high jump.* 4 facts known about a person's past life or career etc. • *She has a good school record.*

record (*say* rik-ord) *VERB* **records, recording, recorded** 1 put something down in writing or other permanent form.
2 store sounds or scenes (e.g. television pictures) on a disc or magnetic tape etc. so that you can play or show them later.
[from French]

recorder *NOUN* **recorders** 1 a kind of flute held downwards from the player's mouth.
2 a person or thing that records something.

record player *NOUN* **record players** a device for reproducing sound from records.

recount[1] (*say* ri-kownt) *VERB* **recounts, recounting, recounted** give an account of • *We recounted our adventures.*
[from old French *reconter* = tell]

recount[2] (*say* ree-kownt) *VERB* **recounts, recounting, recounted** count something again.
▷ **recount** *noun*

recoup (*say* ri-koop) *VERB* **recoups, recouping, recouped** recover the cost of an investment etc. or of a loss.
[from old French]
USAGE Note that this word does not mean *recuperate*.

recourse *NOUN* a source of help.
- **have recourse to** go to a person or thing for help.
[from old French]

recover *VERB* **recovers, recovering, recovered** 1 get something back again after losing it; regain. 2 get well again after being ill or weak.
▷ **recovery** *noun*
[from old French; related to *recuperate*]

re-cover *VERB* **re-covers, re-covering, re-covered** put a new cover on something.

recreation *NOUN* **recreations** 1 refreshing or entertaining yourself after work by some enjoyable activity. 2 a game or hobby etc. that is an enjoyable activity.
▷ **recreational** *adjective*
[from *re-* + Latin *creatio* = creation]

recrimination *NOUN* **recriminations** an accusation made against a person who has criticized or blamed you.
[from *re-* + Latin *criminare* = accuse]

recrudescence (*say* rek-roo-dess-ens) *NOUN* (*formal*) a fresh outbreak of a disease or trouble etc.
[from *re-* + Latin *crudescens* = becoming raw]

recruit *NOUN* **recruits 1** a person who has just joined the armed forces. **2** a new member of a society, company, or other group.

recruit *VERB* **recruits, recruiting, recruited** enlist recruits.
▷ **recruitment** *noun*
[from French *recroître* = to increase again]

rectangle *NOUN* **rectangles** a shape with four sides and four right angles.
▷ **rectangular** *adjective*
[from Latin *rectus* = straight or right, + *angle*]
WORD FAMILY There are a number of English words that are related to *rectangle* because part of their original meaning comes from the Latin word *rectus* meaning 'straight or right'. These include *correct*, *direct*, *erect*, *rectify*, *rectitude*, and *rectum*.

rectify *VERB* **rectifies, rectifying, rectified** correct or put something right.
▷ **rectification** *noun*
[from Latin *rectus* = right]

rectilinear *ADJECTIVE* with straight lines • *Squares and triangles are rectilinear figures.*
[from Latin *rectus* = straight, + *linear*]

rectitude *NOUN* moral goodness; honest or straightforward behaviour.
[same origin as *rectify*]

rector *NOUN* **rectors** a member of the Church of England clergy in charge of a parish.
[Latin = ruler]

rectum *NOUN* **rectums** or **recta** the last part of the large intestine, ending at the anus.
[Latin, = straight (intestine)]

recumbent *ADJECTIVE* lying down.
[from *re-* + Latin *cumbens* = lying]

recuperate *VERB* **recuperates, recuperating, recuperated** get better after an illness.
▷ **recuperation** *noun*
[from Latin]

recur *VERB* **recurs, recurring, recurred** happen again; keep on happening.
▷ **recurrent** *adjective* **recurrence** *noun*
[from *re-* + Latin *currere* = to run]

recurring decimal *NOUN* **recurring decimals** (*in mathematics*) a decimal fraction in which a digit or group of digits is repeated indefinitely, e.g. 0.666 ...

recycle *VERB* **recycles, recycling, recycled** convert waste material into a form in which it can be used again.

red *ADJECTIVE* **redder, reddest 1** of the colour of blood or a colour rather like this. **2** to do with Communists; favouring Communism.
▷ **redness** *noun*

red *NOUN* **1** a red colour. **2** a Communist.
- **in the red** in debt.
- **see red** become suddenly angry.
[from Old English]

red deer *NOUN* **red deer** a kind of large deer with a reddish-brown coat, found in Europe and Asia.

redden *VERB* **reddens, reddening, reddened** make or become red.

reddish *ADJECTIVE* rather red.

redeem *VERB* **redeems, redeeming, redeemed 1** make up for faults • *His one redeeming feature is his generosity.* **2** buy something back or pay off a debt. **3** save a person from damnation, as in some religions.
▷ **redeemer** *noun* **redemption** *noun*
- **redeem yourself** make up for doing badly in the past.
[from *re-* + Latin *emere* = buy]

redevelop *VERB* **redevelops, redeveloping, redeveloped** develop land etc. in a different way.
▷ **redevelopment** *noun*

red-handed *ADJECTIVE*
- **catch red-handed** catch while actually committing a crime.

redhead *NOUN* **redheads** a person with reddish hair.

red herring *NOUN* **red herrings** something that draws attention away from the main subject; a misleading clue.
[because a red herring (= a kipper) drawn across a fox's path put hounds off the scent]

red-hot *ADJECTIVE* very hot; so hot that it has turned red.

Red Indian *NOUN* **Red Indians** (*old use*) a Native American from North America.
USAGE See note at **Indian**.

red-light district *NOUN* **red-light districts** an area in a city where there are many prostitutes, strip clubs, etc.

red meat *NOUN* meat, such as beef, lamb, or mutton, which is red when raw.

redolent (*say* red-ol-ent) *ADJECTIVE* **1** having a strong smell • *redolent of onions*.
2 strongly suggesting or reminding you of something • *a castle redolent of romance*.
[from *re-* + Latin *olens* = giving off a smell]

redoubtable *ADJECTIVE* formidable.
[from French *redouter* = to fear]

redound *VERB* **redounds, redounding, redounded** (*formal*) come back as an advantage • *This will redound to our credit*.
[from Latin *redundare* = overflow]

redress *VERB* **redresses, redressing, redressed** set right or rectify • *redress the balance*.

redress *NOUN* **1** redressing.
2 compensation • *You should seek redress for this damage*.
[from French]

red tape *NOUN* use of too many rules and forms in official business.
[because bundles of official papers are tied up with red or pink tape]

reduce *VERB* **reduces, reducing, reduced** **1** make or become smaller or less. **2** force someone into a condition or situation • *He was reduced to borrowing the money*.
▷ **reduction** *noun*
[from *re-* + Latin *ducere* = bring]

redundant *ADJECTIVE* not needed, especially for a particular job.
▷ **redundancy** *noun*
[same origin as *redound*]

reed *NOUN* **reeds** **1** a tall plant that grows in water or marshy ground. **2** a thin strip that vibrates to make the sound in a clarinet, saxophone, oboe, etc.
[from Old English]

reedy *ADJECTIVE* **reedier, reediest** **1** full of reeds. **2** (said about a voice) having a thin high tone like a reed instrument.
▷ **reediness** *noun*

reef[1] *NOUN* **reefs** a ridge of rock, coral, or sand, especially one near the surface of the sea.
[via old German or old Dutch from Old Norse]

reef[2] *VERB* **reefs, reefing, reefed** shorten a sail by drawing in a strip (called a *reef*) at the top or bottom to reduce the area exposed to the wind.
[via Dutch from Old Norse]

reef knot *NOUN* a symmetrical double knot that is very secure.
[from *reef*[2]]

reek *VERB* **reeks, reeking, reeked** smell strongly or unpleasantly.
▷ **reek** *noun*
[from Old English]

reel *NOUN* **reels** **1** a round device on which cotton, thread, film, etc. is wound. **2** a lively Scottish dance.

reel *VERB* **reels, reeling, reeled** **1** wind something onto or off a reel. **2** stagger.
3 feel giddy or confused • *I am still reeling from the shock*.
- **reel off** say something quickly.
[from Old English]

re-elect *VERB* **re-elects, re-electing, re-elected** elect again.

re-enter *VERB* **re-enters, re-entering, re-entered** enter again.
▷ **re-entry** *noun*

re-examine *VERB* **re-examines, re-examining, re-examined** examine again.

ref *NOUN* **refs** (*informal*) a referee.

refectory *NOUN* **refectories** the dining room of a college or monastery etc.
[from Latin *refectum* = refreshed]

refer *VERB* **refers, referring, referred** pass a problem etc. to someone else • *My doctor referred me to a specialist*.
▷ **referral** *noun*
- **refer to** **1** mention or speak about • *I wasn't referring to you*. **2** look in a book etc. for information • *We referred to our dictionary*.
[from *re-* + Latin *ferre* = bring]

referee *NOUN* **referees** someone appointed to see that people keep to the rules of a game.

referee *VERB* **referees, refereeing, refereed** act as a referee; umpire.
[literally = someone who is referred to]

reference *NOUN* **references 1** referring to something • *There was no reference to recent events.* **2** a direction to a book or page or file etc. where information can be found. **3** a letter from a previous employer describing someone's abilities and qualities.
- **in with reference to** concerning or about.

reference book *NOUN* **reference books** a book (such as a dictionary or encyclopedia) that gives information systematically.

reference library *NOUN* **reference libraries** a library where books can be used but not taken away.

referendum *NOUN* **referendums** or **referenda** a vote on a particular question by all the people of a country.
[Latin, = referring]

refill *VERB* **refills, refilling, refilled** fill again.

refill *NOUN* **refills** a container holding a substance which is used to refill something • *My pen needs a refill.*

refine *VERB* **refines, refining, refined 1** purify. **2** improve something, especially by making small changes.
[from *re-* + Middle English *fine* = make pure]

refined *ADJECTIVE* **1** purified. **2** cultured; having good taste or good manners.

refinement *NOUN* **refinements 1** the action of refining. **2** being refined. **3** something added to improve a thing.

refinery *NOUN* **refineries** a factory for refining something • *an oil refinery.*

reflect *VERB* **reflects, reflecting, reflected 1** send back light, heat, or sound etc. from a surface. **2** form an image of something as a mirror does. **3** think something over; consider. **4** be a sign of something; be influenced by something • *Her hard work was reflected in her exam results.*
▷ **reflection** *noun* **reflective** *adjective* **reflector** *noun*
[from *re-* + Latin *flectere* = to bend]

reflex *NOUN* **reflexes** a movement or action done without any conscious thought.
[same origin as *reflect*]

reflex angle *NOUN* **reflex angles** an angle of more than 180°.

reflexive pronoun *NOUN* **reflexive pronouns** (*in grammar*) any of the pronouns *myself, herself, himself*, etc. (as in 'She cut *herself*'), which refer back to the subject of the verb.

reflexive verb *NOUN* **reflexive verbs** a verb where the subject and the object are the same person or thing, as in 'She *cut herself*', 'The cat *washed itself*'.

reform *VERB* **reforms, reforming, reformed 1** make changes in something in order to improve it. **2** give up a criminal or immoral lifestyle, or make someone do this.
▷ **reformer** *noun* **reformative** *adjective* **reformatory** *adjective*

reform *NOUN* **reforms 1** reforming. **2** a change made in order to improve something.
[from *re-* + Latin *formare* = to form]

reformation *NOUN* reforming.
- **the Reformation** a religious movement in Europe in the 16th century intended to reform certain teachings and practices of the Roman Catholic Church, which resulted in the establishment of the Reformed or Protestant Churches.

refract *VERB* **refracts, refracting, refracted** bend a ray of light at the point where it enters water or glass etc. at an angle.
▷ **refraction** *noun* **refractor** *noun* **refractive** *adjective*
[from *re-* + Latin *fractum* = broken]

refractory *ADJECTIVE* **1** difficult to control; stubborn. **2** (said about substances) resistant to heat.
[from *re-* + Latin *frangere* = break]

refrain[1] *VERB* **refrains, refraining, refrained** stop yourself from doing something • *Please refrain from talking.*
[from Latin *refrenare* = to bridle]

refrain[2] *NOUN* **refrains** the chorus of a song.
[from French]

refresh *VERB* **refreshes, refreshing, refreshed** make a tired person etc. feel fresh and strong again.
- **refresh someone's memory** remind someone of something by going over previous information.

refresher course *NOUN* **refresher courses** a training course to bring people's knowledge up to date.

refreshing *ADJECTIVE* **1** producing new strength • *a refreshing sleep*. **2** pleasantly different or unusual • *refreshing honesty*.

refreshment *NOUN* **refreshments 1** being refreshed. **2** food and drink.

refreshments *PLURAL NOUN* drinks and snacks provided at an event.

refrigerate *VERB* **refrigerates, refrigerating, refrigerated** make a thing extremely cold, especially in order to preserve it and keep it fresh.
▷ **refrigeration** *noun*
[from *re-* + Latin *frigus* = cold]

refrigerator *NOUN* **refrigerators** a cabinet in which food is stored at a very low temperature.

refuel *VERB* **refuels, refuelling, refuelled** supply a ship or aircraft with more fuel.

refuge *NOUN* **refuges** a place where a person is safe from pursuit or danger.
- **take refuge** go somewhere or do something so that you are protected.
[from *re-* + Latin *fugere* = flee]

refugee *NOUN* **refugees** someone who has had to leave their home or country and seek refuge elsewhere, e.g. because of war or persecution or famine.

refund *VERB* **refunds, refunding, refunded** pay money back.

refund *NOUN* **refunds** money paid back.
[from Latin *refundere* = pour back]

refurbish *VERB* **refurbishes, refurbishing, refurbished** freshen something up; redecorate and repair.

refuse (*say* ri-fewz) *VERB* **refuses, refusing, refused** say that you are unwilling to do or give or accept something.
▷ **refusal** *noun*

refuse (*say* ref-yooss) *NOUN* waste material • *Lorries collected the refuse*.
[from French]

refute *VERB* **refutes, refuting, refuted** prove that a person or statement etc. is wrong.
▷ **refutation** *noun*
[from Latin *refutare* = repel]
USAGE This word is sometimes used as if it meant 'deny', but this meaning is not fully accepted as part of standard English and should be avoided.

regain *VERB* **regains, regaining, regained** **1** get something back after losing it. **2** reach a place again.

regal (*say* ree-gal) *ADJECTIVE* **1** by or to do with a monarch. **2** dignified and splendid; fit for a king or queen.
[from Latin *regis* = of a king]

regale (*say* rig-ayl) *VERB* **regales, regaling, regaled** amuse or entertain someone with conversation • *She regaled us with stories of her life in the theatre*.
[from French]

regalia (*say* rig-ayl-i-a) *PLURAL NOUN* the emblems of royalty or rank • *The royal regalia include the crown, sceptre, and orb*.

regard *VERB* **regards, regarding, regarded** **1** think of in a certain way; consider to be • *We regard the matter as serious*. **2** look or gaze at.

regard *NOUN* **1** consideration or heed • *You acted without regard to people's safety*. **2** respect • *We have a great regard for her*. **3** a gaze.
- **as regards** concerning • *He is innocent as regards the first charge*.
- **with /in regard to** concerning.
[from *re-* + French *garder* = to guard]

regarding *PREPOSITION* concerning • *There are laws regarding drugs*.

regardless *ADVERB* without considering something • *Do it, regardless of the cost*.

regards *PLURAL NOUN* kind wishes sent in a message • *Give him my regards*.

regatta *NOUN* **regattas** a meeting for boat or yacht races.
[from Italian]

regency *NOUN* **regencies 1** being a regent. **2** a period when a country is ruled by a regent.

regenerate *VERB* **regenerates, regenerating, regenerated** give new life or strength to something.
▷ **regeneration** *noun*

regent *NOUN* **regents** a person appointed to rule a country while the monarch is too young or unable to rule.
[from Latin *regens* = ruling]

reggae (*say* reg-ay) *NOUN* a West Indian style of music with a strong beat.
[origin unknown]

regime (*say* ray-*zh*eem) *NOUN* **regimes** a system of government or organization • *a Fascist regime.*
[French; related to *regiment*]

regiment *NOUN* **regiments** an army unit, usually divided into battalions or companies.
▷ **regimental** *adjective*
[from Latin *regimentum* = rule, governing]

region *NOUN* **regions** an area; a part of a country or of the world • *in tropical regions.*
▷ **regional** *adjective* **regionally** *adverb*
- **in the region of** near • *The cost will be in the region of £100.*
[from Latin *regio* = boundary]

register *NOUN* **registers 1** an official list of things or names etc. **2** a book in which information about school attendances is recorded. **3** the range of a voice or musical instrument.

register *VERB* **registers, registering, registered 1** list something in a register. **2** indicate; show • *The thermometer registered 100°.* **3** make an impression on someone's mind. **4** pay extra for a letter or parcel to be sent with special care.
▷ **registration** *noun*
[from Latin]

register office *NOUN* **register offices** an office where marriages are performed and records of births, marriages, and deaths are kept.

registrar *NOUN* **registrars** an official whose job is to keep written records or registers.

registration number *NOUN* **registration numbers** a series of letters and numbers identifying a motor vehicle.

registry *NOUN* **registries** a place where registers are kept.

registry office *NOUN* **registry offices** (*informal*) a register office.

regress *VERB* **regresses, regressing, regressed** return to an earlier condition or way of behaving, especially a worse one.
▷ **regression** *noun* **regressive** *adjective*
[from *re-* + Latin *gressus* = gone]

regret *NOUN* **regrets** a feeling of sorrow or disappointment about something that has happened or been done.
▷ **regretful** *adjective* **regretfully** *adverb*

regret *VERB* **regrets, regretting, regretted** feel regret about something.
▷ **regrettable** *adjective* **regrettably** *adverb*
[from old French *regreter* = mourn for the dead]

regular *ADJECTIVE* **1** always happening or doing something at certain times • *Try to eat regular meals.* **2** even or symmetrical • *regular teeth.* **3** normal, standard, or correct • *the regular procedure.* **4** belonging to a country's permanent armed forces • *a regular soldier.*
▷ **regularly** *adverb* **regularity** *noun*
[from Latin *regula* = a rule]

regulate *VERB* **regulates, regulating, regulated 1** control, especially by rules. **2** make a machine work at a certain speed.
▷ **regulator** *noun* **regulatory** *adjective*
[same origin as *regular*]

regulation *NOUN* **1** regulating. **2** a rule or law.

regurgitate *VERB* **regurgitates, regurgitating, regurgitated** bring swallowed food up again into the mouth.
▷ **regurgitation** *noun*
[from *re-* + Latin *gurgitare* = to swallow]

rehabilitation *NOUN* restoring a person to a normal life after being in prison, ill, etc.
▷ **rehabilitate** *verb*
[from *re-* + Latin *habilitare* = enable]

rehash *VERB* **rehashes, rehashing, rehashed** (*informal*) repeat something without changing it very much.
[from *re-* + *hash* = to make into hash]

rehearse *VERB* **rehearses, rehearsing, rehearsed** practise something before performing to an audience.
▷ **rehearsal** *noun*
[from old French]

reign *VERB* **reigns, reigning, reigned** **1** rule a country as king or queen. **2** be supreme; be the strongest influence • *Silence reigned.*

reign *NOUN* the time when someone reigns.
[from Latin *regnum* = royal authority]

reimburse *VERB* **reimburses, reimbursing, reimbursed** repay money that has been spent • *Your travelling expenses will be reimbursed.*
▷ **reimbursement** *noun*
[from *re-* + an old word *imburse* = pay]

rein *NOUN* **reins 1** a strap used to guide a horse. **2** a similar device used to restrain a young child.
[from old French; related to *retain*]

reincarnation *NOUN* being born again into a new body.
[from *re-* + *incarnation* (SEE **incarnate**)]

reindeer *NOUN* **reindeer** a kind of deer that lives in Arctic regions.
[from Old Norse]

reinforce *VERB* **reinforces, reinforcing, reinforced** strengthen by adding extra people or supports etc.
[from *re-* + old French *enforcer* = enforce]

reinforced concrete *NOUN* concrete containing metal bars or wires to strengthen it.

reinforcement *NOUN* **reinforcements** **1** reinforcing. **2** something that reinforces.

reinforcements *PLURAL NOUN* extra troops or ships etc. sent to strengthen a force.

reinstate *VERB* **reinstates, reinstating, reinstated** put a person or thing back into a former position.
▷ **reinstatement** *noun*
[from *re-* + *in-* + *state*]

reiterate *VERB* **reiterates, reiterating, reiterated** say something again or repeatedly.
▷ **reiteration** *noun*
[from *re-* + Latin *iterare* = repeat]

reject (*say* ri-jekt) *VERB* **rejects, rejecting, rejected** **1** refuse to accept a person or thing. **2** throw away or discard.
▷ **rejection** *noun*

reject (*say* ree-jekt) *NOUN* **rejects** a person or thing that is rejected, especially because of being faulty or poorly made.
[from *re-* + Latin *-jectum* = thrown]

rejoice *VERB* **rejoices, rejoicing, rejoiced** feel or show great joy.
[from old French]

rejoin *VERB* **rejoins, rejoining, rejoined** join again.

rejoinder *NOUN* **rejoinders** an answer or retort.
[old French, = rejoin]

rejuvenate *VERB* **rejuvenates, rejuvenating, rejuvenated** make a person seem young again.
▷ **rejuvenation** *noun*
[from *re-* + Latin *juvenis* = young]

relapse *VERB* **relapses, relapsing, relapsed** return to a previous condition; become worse after improving.
▷ **relapse** *noun*
[from *re-* + Latin *lapsum* = slipped]

relate *VERB* **relates, relating, related** **1** narrate. **2** connect or compare one thing with another. **3** understand and get on well with • *Some people cannot relate to animals.*
[from Latin]

related *ADJECTIVE* belonging to the same family.

relation *NOUN* **relations 1** a relative. **2** the way one thing is related to another.

relationship *NOUN* **relationships 1** how people or things are related. **2** how people get on with each other. **3** an emotional or sexual association between two people.

relative *NOUN* **relatives** a person who is related to another.

relative *ADJECTIVE* connected or compared with something; compared with the average • *They live in relative comfort.*
▷ **relatively** *adverb*
- **relative pronoun** see *pronoun*.

relative density *NOUN* **relative densities** the ratio of the density of a substance to that of a standard substance (usually water for liquids and solids and air for gases).

relax *VERB* **relaxes**, **relaxing**, **relaxed** **1** stop working; rest. **2** become less anxious or worried. **3** make a rule etc. less strict or severe. **4** make a limb or muscle less stiff or tense.
▷ **relaxed** *adjective* **relaxation** *noun*
[from *re-* + Latin *laxus* = loose]

relay (*say* ri-lay) *VERB* **relays**, **relaying**, **relayed** pass on a message or broadcast.

relay (*say* re-lay) *NOUN* **relays 1** a fresh group taking the place of another • *The firemen worked in relays.* **2** a relay race. **3** a device for relaying a broadcast.
[from old French]

relay race *NOUN* **relay races** a race between teams in which each person covers part of the distance.

release *VERB* **releases**, **releasing**, **released** **1** set free or unfasten. **2** let a thing fall or fly or go out. **3** make a film or record etc. available to the public.

release *NOUN* **releases 1** being released. **2** something released, such as a new film or record. **3** a device that unfastens something.
[from old French; related to *relax*]

relegate *VERB* **relegates**, **relegating**, **relegated** **1** put into a less important place. **2** put a sports team into a lower division of a league.
▷ **relegation** *noun*
[from *re-* + Latin *legatum* = sent]

relent *VERB* **relents**, **relenting**, **relented** become less severe or more merciful.
[from *re-* + Latin *lentare* = bend, soften]

relentless *ADJECTIVE* not stopping or relenting; pitiless.
▷ **relentlessly** *adverb*

relevant *ADJECTIVE* connected with what is being discussed or dealt with. (The opposite is **irrelevant**.)
▷ **relevance** *noun*
[from Latin]

reliable *ADJECTIVE* able to be relied on; trustworthy.
▷ **reliably** *adverb* **reliability** *noun*

reliance *NOUN* **1** relying or depending. **2** trust.
▷ **reliant** *adjective*

relic *NOUN* **relics** something that has survived from an earlier time.
[from Latin *reliquus* = remaining]

relief *NOUN* **reliefs 1** the ending or lessening of pain, trouble, boredom, etc. **2** something that gives relief or help. **3** help given to people in need • *a relief fund for the earthquake victims.* **4** a person who takes over a turn of duty when another finishes. **5** a method of making a map or design that stands out from a flat surface.

relief map *NOUN* **relief maps** a map that shows hills and valleys by shading or moulding.

relieve *VERB* **relieves**, **relieving**, **relieved** give relief to a person or thing.
- **relieve of** take something from a person • *The thief relieved him of his wallet.*
[from *re-* + Latin *levare* = raise, lighten]

religion *NOUN* **religions 1** what people believe about God or gods, and how they worship. **2** a particular system of beliefs and worship.
[from Latin *religio* = reverence]

religious *ADJECTIVE* **1** to do with religion. **2** believing firmly in a religion and taking part in its customs.
▷ **religiously** *adverb*

relinquish *VERB* **relinquishes**, **relinquishing**, **relinquished** give something up; let go.
▷ **relinquishment** *noun*
[from *re-* + Latin *linquere* = to leave]

relish *NOUN* **relishes 1** great enjoyment. **2** a tasty sauce or pickle that adds flavour to plainer food.

relish *VERB* **relishes**, **relishing**, **relished** enjoy greatly.
[from old French]

relive *VERB* **relives**, **reliving**, **relived** remember something that happened very vividly, as though it was happening again.

relocate *VERB* **relocates**, **relocating**, **relocated** move or be moved to a new place.

reluctant *ADJECTIVE* unwilling or not keen.
▷ **reluctantly** *adverb* **reluctance** *noun*
[from *re-* + Latin *luctatus* = struggling]

rely *VERB* **relies, relying, relied**
- **rely on** **1** trust a person or thing to help or support you. **2** be dependent on something • *Many people rely on this local bus service.*
[from old French *relier* = bind together]

remain *VERB* **remains, remaining, remained** **1** be there after other parts have gone or been dealt with; be left over. **2** continue to be in the same place or condition; stay.
[from *re-* + Latin *manere* = to stay]

remainder *NOUN* **1** the remaining part of people or things. **2** the number left after subtraction or division.

remains *PLURAL NOUN* **1** all that is left over after other parts have been removed or destroyed. **2** ancient ruins or objects; relics. **3** a dead body.

remand *VERB* **remands, remanding, remanded** send a prisoner back into custody while further evidence is being gathered.
▷ **remand** *noun*
- **on remand** in prison while waiting for a trial.
[from *re-* + Latin *mandare* = entrust]

remark *NOUN* **remarks** something said; a comment.

remark *VERB* **remarks, remarking, remarked** **1** make a remark; say. **2** notice.
[from French]

remarkable *ADJECTIVE* unusual or extraordinary.
▷ **remarkably** *adverb*
[from *remark*]

remedial *ADJECTIVE* **1** helping to cure an illness or deficiency. **2** helping children who learn slowly.
[same origin as *remedy*]

remedy *NOUN* **remedies** something that cures or relieves a disease etc. or that puts a matter right.

remedy *VERB* **remedies, remedying, remedied** be a remedy for something; put right.
[from *re-* + Latin *mederi* = heal]

remember *VERB* **remembers, remembering, remembered** **1** keep something in your mind. **2** bring something back into your mind.
▷ **remembrance** *noun*
[from *re-* + Latin *memor* = mindful, remembering]

remind *VERB* **reminds, reminding, reminded** **1** help or make a person remember something • *Remind me to buy some stamps.* **2** make a person think of something because of being similar • *She reminds me of my history teacher.*
▷ **reminder** *noun*
[from *re-* + an old sense of *mind* = put into someone's mind, mention]

reminisce (*say* rem-in-iss) *VERB* **reminisces, reminiscing, reminisced** think or talk about things that you remember.
▷ **reminiscence** *noun* **reminiscent** *adjective*
[from Latin *reminisci* = remember]

remiss *ADJECTIVE* negligent; careless about doing what you ought to do.
[same origin as *remit*]

remission *NOUN* **1** a period during which a serious illness improves for a time. **2** reduction of a prison sentence, especially for good behaviour while in prison. **3** remitting.

remit *VERB* **remits, remitting, remitted** **1** forgive; reduce or cancel a punishment or debt. **2** send money in payment. **3** make or become less intense; slacken • *We must not remit our efforts.*
[from *re-* + Latin *mittere* = send]

remittance *NOUN* **remittances** **1** sending money. **2** the money sent.

remnant *NOUN* **remnants** a part or piece left over from something.
[from old French; related to *remain*]

remonstrate *VERB* **remonstrates, remonstrating, remonstrated** make a protest • *We remonstrated with him about his behaviour.*
[from *re-* + Latin *monstrare* = to show]

remorse *NOUN* deep regret for having done wrong.
▷ **remorseful** *adjective* **remorsefully** *adverb*
[from *re-* + Latin *morsum* = bitten]

remorseless *ADJECTIVE* relentless.

remote *ADJECTIVE* **1** far away in place or time. **2** isolated. **3** unlikely or slight • *a remote chance.*
▷ **remotely** *adverb* **remoteness** *noun*
[from Latin *remotum* = removed]

remote control *NOUN* **remote controls** **1** controlling something from a distance, usually by electricity or radio. **2** a device for doing this.

remould *NOUN* **remoulds** a worn tyre that has been given a new tread.

removable *ADJECTIVE* able to be removed.

removal *NOUN* removing or moving something.

remove *VERB* **removes, removing, removed** **1** take something away or off. **2** get rid of • *This should remove all doubts.*

remove *NOUN* **removes** a distance or degree away from something • *That is several removes from the truth.*
[from *re-* + Latin *movere* = move]

remunerate *VERB* **remunerates, remunerating, remunerated** pay or reward someone.
▷ **remuneration** *noun* **remunerative** *adjective*
[from *re-* + Latin *muneris* = of a gift]

Renaissance (*say* ren-ay-sans) *NOUN* the revival of classical styles of art and literature in Europe in the 14th-16th centuries.
[French, = rebirth]

renal (*say* reen-al) *ADJECTIVE* to do with the kidneys.
[from Latin]

rename *VERB* **renames, renaming, renamed** give a new name to a person or thing.

rend *VERB* **rends, rending, rent** (*poetical use*) rip or tear.
[from Old English]

render *VERB* **renders, rendering, rendered** **1** cause to become • *This news rendered us speechless.* **2** give or perform something • *The local community was quick to render help to the victims.*
[from French]

rendezvous (*say* rond-ay-voo) *NOUN* **rendezvous**, (*say* rond-ay-vooz) **1** a meeting with somebody. **2** a place arranged for this.
[French, = present yourselves]

rendition *NOUN* **renditions** the way a piece of music, a poem, or a dramatic role is performed.
[same origin as *render*]

renegade (*say* ren-ig-ayd) *NOUN* **renegades** a person who deserts a group or religion etc.
[from *re-* + Latin *negare* = deny]

renege (*say* re-nayg) *VERB* **reneges, reneging, reneged** break your word or an agreement.

renew *VERB* **renews, renewing, renewed** **1** restore something to its original condition or replace it with something new. **2** begin or make or give again • *We renewed our request.*
▷ **renewal** *noun*

renewable *ADJECTIVE* able to be renewed.

renewable resource *NOUN* **renewable resources** a resource (such as power from the sun, wind, or waves) that can never be used up, or which can be renewed.

rennet *NOUN* a substance used to curdle milk in making cheese.
[probably from Old English]

renounce *VERB* **renounces, renouncing, renounced** give up or reject.
▷ **renunciation** *noun*
[from *re-* + Latin *nuntiare* = announce]

renovate *VERB* **renovates, renovating, renovated** repair a thing and make it look new.
▷ **renovation** *noun*
[from *re-* + Latin *novus* = new]

renowned *ADJECTIVE* famous.
▷ **renown** *noun*
[from *re-* + French *nomer* = to name]

rent[1] *NOUN* **rents** a regular payment for the use of something, especially a house that belongs to another person.

rent *VERB* **rents, renting, rented** have or allow the use of something in return for rent.
[from French]

rent[2] *past tense* of **rend**.

rent[3] *NOUN* **rents** a torn place; a split.
[from *rend*]

rental *NOUN* **1** the amount paid as rent. **2** renting something.

renunciation *NOUN* renouncing something.

reorganize *VERB* **reorganizes, reorganizing, reorganized** change the way in which something is organized.
▷ **reorganization** *noun*

repair[1] *VERB* **repairs, repairing, repaired** put something into good condition after it has been damaged or broken etc.
▷ **repairable** *adjective*

repair *NOUN* **repairs 1** repairing • *closed for repair.* **2** a mended place • *The repair is hardly visible.*
- **in good repair** in good condition; well maintained.
[from *re-* + Latin *parare* = get something ready]

repair[2] *VERB* **repairs, repairing, repaired** (*formal*) go • *The guests repaired to the dining room.*
[from old French; related to *repatriate*]

reparation *NOUN* **reparations** (*formal*) compensate; pay for damage or loss.
- **make reparations** compensate.
[same origin as *repair*[1]]

reparations *PLURAL NOUN* compensation for war damage paid by the defeated nation.

repartee *NOUN* witty replies and remarks.
[from French *repartir* = answer back]

repast *NOUN* **repasts** (*formal*) a meal.
[from *re-* + Latin *pascere* = to feed]

repatriate *VERB* **repatriates, repatriating, repatriated** send a person back to his or her own country.
▷ **repatriation** *noun*
[from *re-* + Latin *patria* = native country]

repay *VERB* **repays, repaying, repaid** pay back, especially money.
▷ **repayable** *adjective* **repayment** *noun*
[from old French]

repeal *VERB* **repeals, repealing, repealed** cancel a law officially.
▷ **repeal** *noun*
[from *re-* + French *appeler* = to appeal]

repeat *VERB* **repeats, repeating, repeated** **1** say or do the same thing again. **2** tell another person about something told to you.
▷ **repeatedly** *adverb*

repeat *NOUN* **repeats 1** the action of repeating. **2** something that is repeated • *There are too many repeats on television.*
[from *re-* + Latin *petere* = seek]

repel *VERB* **repels, repelling, repelled** **1** drive back or away • *They fought bravely and repelled the attackers.* **2** push something away from itself by means of a physical force • *One north magnetic pole repels another.* **3** disgust somebody.
▷ **repellent** *adjective* & *noun*
[from *re-* + Latin *pellere* = to drive]

repent *VERB* **repents, repenting, repented** be sorry for what you have done.
▷ **repentance** *noun* **repentant** *adjective*
[from old French; related to *penitent*]

repercussion *NOUN* **repercussions** a result or reaction produced indirectly by something.
[from *re-* + Latin *percutere* = to strike]

repertoire (*say* rep-er-twahr) *NOUN* a stock of songs or plays etc. that a person or company knows and can perform.
[French; related to *repertory*]

repertory *NOUN* **repertories** a repertoire.
[from Latin *repertorium* = a list or catalogue]

repertory company *NOUN* **repertory companies** a theatre company giving performances of various plays for short periods.

repetition *NOUN* **repetitions 1** repeating. **2** something repeated.
▷ **repetitious** *adjective*

repetitive *ADJECTIVE* full of repetitions.
▷ **repetitively** *adverb*

replace *VERB* **replaces, replacing, replaced** **1** put a thing back in its place. **2** take the place of another person or thing. **3** put a new or different thing in place of something.
▷ **replacement** *noun*

replay *NOUN* **replays 1** a sports match played again after a draw. **2** the playing or showing again of a recording.
▷ **replay** *verb*

replenish *VERB* **replenishes, replenishing, replenished** **1** fill again. **2** add a new supply of something.
▷ **replenishment** *noun*
[from *re-* + Latin *plenus* = full]

replete *ADJECTIVE* **1** well supplied. **2** feeling full after eating.
[from *re-* + Latin *-pletum* = filled]

replica *NOUN* **replicas** an exact copy.
▷ **replicate** *verb*
[from Italian]

reply *NOUN* **replies** something said or written to deal with a question, letter, etc.; an answer.

reply *VERB* **replies, replying, replied** give a reply to; answer.
[from old French]

report *VERB* **reports, reporting, reported** **1** describe something that has happened or that you have done or studied. **2** make a complaint or accusation against somebody. **3** go and tell somebody that you have arrived or are ready for work.

report *NOUN* **reports** **1** a description or account of something. **2** a regular statement of how someone has worked or behaved, e.g. at school. **3** an explosive sound.
[from *re-* + Latin *portare* = carry]

reported speech *NOUN* indirect speech.

reporter *NOUN* **reporters** a person whose job is to collect and report news for a newspaper, radio or television programme, etc.

repose *NOUN* calm, rest, or sleep.

repose *VERB* **reposes, reposing, reposed** rest or lie somewhere.
[from *re-* + Latin *pausare* = to pause]

repository *NOUN* **repositories** a place where things are stored.
[from Latin]

repossess *VERB* **repossesses, repossessing, repossessed** take something back because it has not been paid for.

reprehensible *ADJECTIVE* extremely bad and deserving blame or rebuke.
[from Latin *reprehendere* = blame, rebuke]

represent *VERB* **represents, representing, represented** **1** help someone by speaking or doing something on their behalf. **2** symbolize or stand for • *In Roman numerals, V represents 5.* **3** be an example or equivalent of something. **4** show a person or thing in a picture or play etc. **5** describe a person or thing in a particular way.
▷ **representation** *noun*
[from *re-* + Latin *praesentare* = to present]

representative *NOUN* **representatives** a person or thing that represents another or others.

representative *ADJECTIVE* **1** representing others. **2** typical of a group.

repress *VERB* **represses, repressing, repressed** **1** keep down; control by force. **2** restrain or suppress.
▷ **repression** *noun* **repressive** *adjective*
[from Latin]

reprieve *NOUN* **reprieves** postponement or cancellation of a punishment etc., especially the death penalty.

reprieve *VERB* **reprieves, reprieving, reprieved** give a reprieve to.
[from old French]

reprimand *NOUN* **reprimands** a rebuke, especially a formal or official one.

reprimand *VERB* **reprimands, reprimanding, reprimanded** give someone a reprimand.
[from French; related to *repress*]

reprisal *NOUN* **reprisals** an act of revenge.
[from old French]

reproach *VERB* **reproaches, reproaching, reproached** tell someone you are upset and disappointed by something he or she has done.
▷ **reproach** *noun* **reproachful** *adjective* **reproachfully** *adverb*
[from old French]

reproduce *VERB* **reproduces, reproducing, reproduced** **1** cause to be seen or heard or happen again. **2** make a copy of something. **3** produce offspring.

reproduction *NOUN* **1** a copy of something, especially a work of art. **2** the process of producing offspring.

reproductive *ADJECTIVE* to do with reproduction • *the reproductive system.*

reprove *VERB* **reproves, reproving, reproved** rebuke or reproach.
▷ **reproof** *noun*
[from Latin *reprobare* = disapprove]

reptile *NOUN* **reptiles** a cold-blooded animal that has a backbone and very short legs or no legs at all, e.g. a snake, lizard, crocodile, or tortoise.
[from Latin *reptilis* = crawling]

republic *NOUN* **republics** a country that has a president, especially one who is elected. (COMPARE **monarchy**)
▷ **republican** *adjective*
[from Latin *res publica* = public affairs]

Republican *NOUN* **Republicans** a supporter of the Republican Party in the USA.

repudiate *VERB* **repudiates, repudiating, repudiated** reject or deny.
▷ **repudiation** *noun*
[from Latin *repudiare* = to divorce]

repugnant *ADJECTIVE* distasteful; very unpleasant or disgusting.
▷ **repugnance** *noun*
[from *re-* + Latin *pugnans* = fighting]

repulse *VERB* **repulses, repulsing, repulsed** **1** drive away or repel. **2** reject an offer etc.; rebuff.
[same origin as *repel*]

repulsion *NOUN* **1** repelling or repulsing. **2** a feeling of disgust. (The opposite is **attraction**.)

repulsive *ADJECTIVE* **1** disgusting. **2** repelling things. (The opposite is **attractive**.)
▷ **repulsively** *adverb* **repulsiveness** *noun*

reputable (*say* rep-yoo-ta-bul) *ADJECTIVE* having a good reputation; respected.
▷ **reputably** *adverb*

reputation *NOUN* **reputations** what people say about a person or thing.
[from Latin *reputare* = consider]

repute *NOUN* reputation.

reputed *ADJECTIVE* said or thought to be something • *This is reputed to be the best hotel.*
▷ **reputedly** *adverb*

request *VERB* **requests, requesting, requested** **1** ask for a thing. **2** ask a person to do something.

request *NOUN* **requests** **1** asking for something. **2** a thing asked for.
[from old French; related to *require*]

requiem (*say* rek-wee-em) *NOUN* **requiems** **1** a special Mass for someone who has died. **2** music for the words of this.
[Latin, = rest]

require *VERB* **requires, requiring, required** **1** need. **2** make somebody do something; oblige • *Drivers are required to pass a test.*
[from *re-* + Latin *quaerere* = seek]

requirement *NOUN* **requirements** what is required; a need.

requisite (*say* rek-wiz-it) *ADJECTIVE* required or needed.

requisite *NOUN* **requisites** a thing needed for something.
[same origin as *require*]

requisition *VERB* **requisitions, requisitioning, requisitioned** take something over for official use.
[same origin as *require*]

rescue *VERB* **rescues, rescuing, rescued** save from danger, harm, etc.; free from captivity.
▷ **rescuer** *noun*

rescue *NOUN* **rescues** the action of rescuing.
[from old French]

research *NOUN* careful study or investigation to discover facts or information.

research (*say* ri-serch) *VERB* **researches, researching, researched** do research into something.
▷ **researcher** *noun*
[from old French *recherche* = careful search]

resemblance *NOUN* **resemblances** likeness or similarity.

resemble *VERB* **resembles, resembling, resembled** be like another person or thing.
[from old French; related to *similar*]

resent *VERB* **resents, resenting, resented** feel indignant about or insulted by something.
▷ **resentful** *adjective* **resentfully** *adverb* **resentment** *noun*
[from *re-* + Latin *sentire* = feel]

reservation *NOUN* **reservations**
1 reserving. **2** something reserved • *a hotel reservation*. **3** an area of land kept for a special purpose. **4** a doubt or feeling of unease. **5** a limit on how far you agree with something; a doubt or condition • *I accept the plan in principle but have certain reservations*.

reserve *VERB* **reserves, reserving, reserved** **1** keep or order something for a particular person or a special use.
2 postpone • *reserve judgement*.

reserve *NOUN* **reserves** **1** a person or thing kept ready to be used if necessary. **2** an extra player chosen in case a substitute is needed in a team. **3** an area of land kept for a special purpose • *a nature reserve*.
4 shyness; being reserved.
[from *re-* + Latin *servare* = keep]

reserved *ADJECTIVE* **1** kept for someone's use • *reserved seats*. **2** shy or unwilling to show your feelings.

reservoir (*say* rez-er-vwar) *NOUN* **reservoirs** a place where water is stored, especially an artificial lake.
[from French *réservoir*; related to *reserve*]

reshuffle *NOUN* **reshuffles** a rearrangement, especially an exchange of jobs between members of a group • *a Cabinet reshuffle*.
▷ **reshuffle** *verb*

reside *VERB* **resides, residing, resided** live in a particular place; dwell.
[from *re-* + Latin *-sidere* = sit]

residence *NOUN* **residences** **1** a place where a person lives. **2** residing.

resident *NOUN* **residents** a person living or residing in a particular place.
▷ **resident** *adjective*
[from *re-* + Latin *-sidens* = sitting]

residential *ADJECTIVE* **1** containing people's homes • *a residential area*. **2** providing accommodation • *a residential course*.

residue *NOUN* **residues** what is left over.
▷ **residual** *adjective*
[from Latin *residuus* = remaining]

resign *VERB* **resigns, resigning, resigned** give up your job or position.
– **be resigned /resign yourself to something** accept that you must put up with it.
[from Latin *resignare* = unseal]

resignation *NOUN* **resignations**
1 accepting a difficulty without complaining. **2** resigning a job or position; a letter saying you wish to do this.

resilient *ADJECTIVE* **1** springy. **2** recovering quickly from illness or trouble.
▷ **resilience** *noun*
[from Latin *resilire* = jump back]

resin *NOUN* **resins** a sticky substance that comes from plants or is manufactured, used in varnish, plastics, etc.
▷ **resinous** *adjective*
[from Latin]

resist *VERB* **resists, resisting, resisted** oppose; fight or act against something.
[from *re-* + Latin *sistere* = stand firmly]

resistance *NOUN* **1** resisting • *The troops came up against armed resistance*. **2** the ability of a substance to hinder the flow of electricity.
▷ **resistant** *adjective*

resistor *NOUN* **resistors** a device that increases the resistance to an electric current.

resit *VERB* **resits, resitting, resat** to sit an examination again because you did not do well enough the first time.
▷ **resit** *noun*

resolute *ADJECTIVE* showing great determination.
▷ **resolutely** *adverb*
[same origin as *resolve*]

resolution *NOUN* **resolutions** **1** being resolute. **2** something you have resolved to do • *New Year resolutions*. **3** a formal decision made by a committee etc. **4** the solving of a problem etc. **5** the point in a story where conflict is resolved.

resolve *VERB* **resolves, resolving, resolved** **1** decide firmly or formally.
2 solve a problem etc. **3** overcome doubts or disagreements.

resolve *NOUN* **1** something you have decided to do; a resolution. **2** great determination.
[from *re-* + Latin *solvere* = loosen]

resonant *ADJECTIVE* **1** resounding or echoing. **2** suggesting or bringing to mind a feeling, memory, etc.
▷ **resonance** *noun* **resonate** *verb*
[from *re-* + Latin *sonans* = sounding]

resort *VERB* **resorts, resorting, resorted** turn to or make use of something • *They resorted to violence.*

resort *NOUN* **resorts 1** a place where people go for relaxation or holidays. **2** resorting • *without resort to cheating.*
- **the last resort** something to be tried when everything else has failed.
[from *re-* + French *sortir* = go out]

resound *VERB* **resounds, resounding, resounded** fill a place with sound; echo.
[from *re-* + Latin *sonare* = to sound]

resounding *ADJECTIVE* **1** loud and echoing. **2** very great; outstanding • *a resounding victory.*

resource *NOUN* **resources 1** something that can be used; an asset • *The country's natural resources include coal and oil.* **2** an ability; ingenuity.

resource *VERB* **resources, resourcing, resourced** provide money or other resources for.
[from old French; related to *resurgence*]

resourceful *ADJECTIVE* clever at finding ways of doing things.
▷ **resourcefully** *adverb*
resourcefulness *noun*

respect *NOUN* **respects 1** admiration for a person's or thing's good qualities.
2 politeness or consideration • *Have respect for people's feelings.* **3** a detail or aspect • *In this respect he is like his sister.* **4** reference • *The rules with respect to bullying are quite clear.*

respect *VERB* **respects, respecting, respected** have respect for a person or thing.
[from Latin *respicere* = look back at, consider]

respectable *ADJECTIVE* **1** having good manners and character etc. **2** fairly good • *a respectable score.*
▷ **respectably** *adverb* **respectability** *noun*

respectful *ADJECTIVE* showing respect.
▷ **respectfully** *adverb*

respecting *PREPOSITION* concerning.

respective *ADJECTIVE* belonging to each one of several • *We went to our respective rooms.*

respectively *ADVERB* in the same order as the people or things already mentioned • *Ruth and Emma finished first and second respectively.*

respiration *NOUN* breathing.
▷ **respiratory** *adjective*

respirator *NOUN* **respirators 1** a device that fits over a person's nose and mouth to purify air before it is breathed. **2** an apparatus for giving artificial respiration.

respire *VERB* **respires, respiring, respired** breathe.
[from *re-* + Latin *spirare* = breathe]

respite *NOUN* **respites** an interval of rest, relief, or delay.
[from old French]

resplendent *ADJECTIVE* brilliant with colour or decorations.
[from *re-* + Latin *splendens* = glittering]

respond *VERB* **responds, responding, responded 1** reply. **2** act in answer to, or because of, something; react.
[from *re-* + Latin *spondere* = to promise]

respondent *NOUN* **respondents** the person answering.

response *NOUN* **responses 1** a reply. **2** a reaction.

responsibility *NOUN* **responsibilities 1** being responsible. **2** something for which a person is responsible.

responsible *ADJECTIVE* **1** looking after a person or thing and having to take the blame if something goes wrong. **2** reliable and trustworthy. **3** with important duties • *a responsible job.* **4** causing something • *His carelessness was responsible for their deaths.*
▷ **responsibly** *adverb*
[same origin as *respond*]

responsive *ADJECTIVE* responding well.

rest[1] *NOUN* **rests 1** a time of sleep or freedom from work as a way of regaining strength. **2** a support • *an armrest.* **3** an interval of silence between notes in music.

rest *VERB* **rests, resting, rested 1** have a rest; be still. **2** allow to rest • *Sit down and rest your feet.* **3** lean or place something so it is supported; be supported • *Rest the ladder against the wall.* **4** be left without further investigation etc. • *And there the matter rests.*
[from Old English]

rest[2] *NOUN*
- **the rest** the remaining part; the others.

rest *VERB* **rests, resting, rested** remain • *Rest assured, it will be a success.*
- **rest with** be left to someone to deal with • *It rests with you to suggest a date.*
[from Latin *restare* = stay behind]

restaurant *NOUN* **restaurants** a place where you can buy a meal and eat it.
[French, literally = restoring]

restaurateur (*say* rest-er-a-**tur**) *NOUN* **restaurateurs** a person who owns or manages a restaurant.
USAGE Note the spelling of this word. Unlike 'restaurant' there is no 'n' in it.

restful *ADJECTIVE* giving rest or a feeling of rest.

restitution *NOUN* **1** restoring something. **2** compensation.
[from *re-* + Latin *statutum* = established]

restive *ADJECTIVE* restless or impatient because of delay, boredom, etc.
[earlier (said about a horse) = refusing to move: from *rest*[1]]

restless *ADJECTIVE* unable to rest or keep still.
▷ **restlessly** *adverb*

restore *VERB* **restores, restoring, restored 1** put something back to its original place or condition. **2** clean and repair a work of art or building etc. so that it looks as good as it did originally.
▷ **restoration** *noun*
[from Latin]

restrain *VERB* **restrains, restraining, restrained** hold a person or thing back; keep under control.
▷ **restraint** *noun*
[from Latin *restringere* = tie up firmly, confine]

restrict *VERB* **restricts, restricting, restricted** keep within certain limits.
▷ **restriction** *noun* **restrictive** *adjective*
[from Latin *restrictus* = restrained]

restroom *NOUN* **restrooms** (*American*) a toilet in a public building.

result *NOUN* **results 1** something produced by an action or condition etc.; an effect or consequence. **2** the score or situation at the end of a game, competition, or race etc. **3** the answer to a sum or calculation.

result *VERB* **results, resulting, resulted 1** happen as a result. **2** have a particular result • *The match resulted in a draw.*
▷ **resultant** *adjective*
[from Latin]

resume *VERB* **resumes, resuming, resumed 1** begin again after stopping for a while. **2** take or occupy again • *After the interval we resumed our seats.*
▷ **resumption** *noun*
[from *re-* + Latin *sumere* = take up]

résumé (*say* rez-yoo-may) *NOUN* **résumés** a summary.
[French, = summed up]

resurgence *NOUN* **resurgences** a rise or revival of something • *a resurgence of interest in Latin.*
[from *re-* + Latin *surgens* = rising]

resurrect *VERB* **resurrects, resurrecting, resurrected** bring back into use or existence • *It may be time to resurrect this old custom.*
[from *resurrection*]

resurrection *NOUN* **1** coming back to life after being dead. **2** the revival of something.
- **the Resurrection** in the Christian religion, the resurrection of Jesus Christ three days after his death.
[same origin as *resurgence*]

resuscitate *VERB* **resuscitates, resuscitating, resuscitated** revive a person from unconsciousness or apparent death.
▷ **resuscitation** *noun*
[from *re-* + Latin *suscitare* = revive]

retail *VERB* **retails, retailing, retailed 1** sell goods to the general public. **2** tell what happened; recount or relate.
▷ **retailer** *noun*

retail *NOUN* selling to the general public. (COMPARE **wholesale**)
[from old French *retaille* = a piece cut off]

retain *VERB* **retains, retaining, retained 1** continue to have something; keep in your possession or memory etc. **2** hold something in place.
[from *re-* + Latin *tenere* = to hold]

retainer *NOUN* **retainers 1** a sum of money regularly paid to someone so that he or she will work for you when needed. **2** a servant who has worked for a person or family for a long time.

retake *VERB* **retakes, retaking, retook, retaken** take a test or examination again.

retake *NOUN* **retakes 1** a test or examination taken again. **2** a scene filmed again.

retaliate *VERB* **retaliates, retaliating, retaliated** repay an injury or insult etc. with a similar one; attack someone in return for a similar attack.
▷ **retaliation** *noun*
[from *re-* + Latin *talis* = the same kind]

retard *VERB* **retards, retarding, retarded** slow down or delay the progress or development of something.
▷ **retarded** *adjective* **retardation** *noun*
[from *re-* + Latin *tardus* = slow]

retch *VERB* **retches, retching, retched** strain your throat as if being sick.
[from Old English]
USAGE Do not confuse with **wretch**.

retention *NOUN* retaining or keeping.

retentive *ADJECTIVE* able to retain things • *a retentive memory*.

reticent (*say* ret-i-sent) *ADJECTIVE* not telling people what you feel or think; discreet.
▷ **reticence** *noun*
[from Latin *reticere* = keep silent]

retina *NOUN* **retinas** a layer of membrane at the back of the eyeball, sensitive to light.
[from Latin]

retinue *NOUN* **retinues** a group of people accompanying an important person.
[from old French *retenue* = restrained, in someone's service]

retire *VERB* **retires, retiring, retired 1** give up your regular work because you are getting old. **2** retreat or withdraw. **3** go to bed or to your private room.
▷ **retirement** *noun*
[from *re-* + French *tirer* = to draw]

retiring *ADJECTIVE* shy; avoiding company.

retort *NOUN* **retorts 1** a quick, witty, or angry reply. **2** a glass bottle with a long downward-bent neck, used in distilling liquids. **3** a receptacle used in making steel etc.

retort *VERB* **retorts, retorting, retorted** make a quick, witty, or angry reply.
[from *re-* + Latin *tortum* = twisted]

retrace *VERB* **retraces, retracing, retraced** go back over the route that you have just taken • *We retraced our steps and returned to the ferry*.
[from French]

retract *VERB* **retracts, retracting, retracted 1** pull back or in • *The snail retracts its horns*. **2** withdraw an offer or statement.
▷ **retraction** *noun* **retractable** *adjective* **retractile** *adjective*
[from *re-* + Latin *tractum* = pulled]

retread *NOUN* **retreads** a remould.

retreat *VERB* **retreats, retreating, retreated** go back after being defeated or to avoid danger or difficulty etc.; withdraw.

retreat *NOUN* **retreats 1** retreating. **2** a quiet place to which someone can withdraw.
[from old French; related to *retract*]

retrench *VERB* **retrenches, retrenching, retrenched** reduce costs or economize.
▷ **retrenchment** *noun*
[from French; related to *truncate*]

retribution *NOUN* **retributions** a deserved punishment.
[from *re-* + Latin *tributum* = assigned]

retrieve *VERB* **retrieves, retrieving, retrieved** 1 bring or get something back. 2 rescue.
▷ **retrievable** *adjective* **retrieval** *noun*
[from Old French *retrover* = find again]

retriever *NOUN* **retrievers** a kind of dog that is often trained to retrieve game.

retro- *PREFIX* 1 back. 2 backward (as in *retrograde*).
[from Latin]

retrograde *ADJECTIVE* 1 going backwards. 2 becoming less good.
[from *retro-* + Latin *gradus* = a step]

retrogress *VERB* **retrogresses, retrogressing, retrogressed** go back to an earlier and less good condition.
▷ **retrogression** *noun* **retrogressive** *adjective*
[from *retro-* + *progress*]

retrospect *NOUN*
- **in retrospect** when you look back at what has happened.
[from *retro-* + *prospect*]

retrospective *ADJECTIVE* 1 looking back on the past. 2 applying to the past as well as the future • *The law could not be made retrospective.*
▷ **retrospection** *noun*

return *VERB* **returns, returning, returned** 1 come back or go back. 2 bring, give, put, or send back. 3 elect to parliament.

return *NOUN* **returns** 1 returning. 2 something returned. 3 profit • *He gets a good return on his savings.* 4 a return ticket.
[from *re-* + Latin *tornare* = to turn]

return match *NOUN* **return matches** a second match played between the same teams.

return ticket *NOUN* **return tickets** a ticket for a journey to a place and back again.

reunify *VERB* **reunifies, reunifying, reunified** make a divided country into one again • *How long has Germany been reunified?*
▷ **reunification** *noun*

reunion *NOUN* **reunions** 1 reuniting. 2 a meeting of people who have not met for some time.

reunite *VERB* **reunites, reuniting, reunited** unite again after being separated.

reuse (*say* ree-yooz) *VERB* **reuses, reusing, reused** use again.
▷ **reusable** *adjective*

reuse (*say* ree-yooss) *NOUN* using again.

Rev. *ABBREVIATION* Reverend.

rev *VERB* **revs, revving, revved** (*informal*) make an engine run quickly, especially when starting.

rev *NOUN* **revs** (*informal*) a revolution of an engine.
[short for *revolution*]

reveal *VERB* **reveals, revealing, revealed** let something be seen or known.
[from Latin *revelare* = unveil]

reveille (*say* riv-al-ee) *NOUN* **reveilles** a military waking signal sounded on a bugle or drums.
[from French *réveillez* = wake up!]

revel *VERB* **revels, revelling, revelled** 1 take great delight in something. 2 hold revels.
▷ **reveller** *noun*
[from old French; related to *rebel*]

revelation *NOUN* **revelations** 1 revealing. 2 something revealed, especially something surprising.

revelry *NOUN* 1 revelling. 2 revels.

revels *PLURAL NOUN* lively and noisy festivities.

revenge *NOUN* harming somebody in return for harm that they have done to you.

revenge *VERB* **revenges, revenging, revenged** avenge; take vengeance.
[from old French; related to *vindicate*]

revenue *NOUN* **revenues** 1 a country's income from taxes etc., used for paying public expenses. 2 a company's income.
[French, = returned]

reverberate *VERB* **reverberates, reverberating, reverberated** be repeated as an echo; resound.
▷ **reverberation** *noun*
[from *re-* + Latin *verberare* = to beat]

revere (*say* riv-eer) *VERB* **reveres, revering, revered** respect deeply or with reverence.
[from Latin]

reverence *NOUN* a feeling of awe and deep or religious respect.

Reverend *NOUN* the title of a member of the clergy • *the Reverend John Smith.*
[from Latin *reverendus* = someone to be revered]
USAGE Do not confuse with **reverent**.

reverent *ADJECTIVE* feeling or showing reverence.
▷ **reverently** *adverb* **reverential** *adjective*
USAGE Do not confuse with **Reverend**.

reverie (*say* rev-er-ee) *NOUN* **reveries** a daydream.
[from French]

reversal *NOUN* **reversals 1** reversing or being reversed. **2** a piece of bad luck; a reverse.

reverse *ADJECTIVE* opposite in direction, order, or manner etc.

reverse *NOUN* **reverses 1** the reverse side, order, manner, etc. **2** a piece of misfortune • *They suffered several reverses.*
- **in reverse** the opposite way round.

reverse *VERB* **reverses, reversing, reversed 1** turn in the opposite direction or order etc.; turn something inside out or upside down. **2** move backwards. **3** cancel a decision or decree.
▷ **reversible** *adjective*
[same origin as *revert*]

reverse gear *NOUN* a gear that allows a vehicle to be driven backwards.

revert *VERB* **reverts, reverting, reverted** return to a former condition, habit, or subject etc.
▷ **reversion** *noun*
[from *re-* + Latin *vertere* = to turn]

review *NOUN* **reviews 1** an inspection or survey. **2** a published description and opinion of a book, film, play, etc.

review *VERB* **reviews, reviewing, reviewed 1** write a review of a book, film, play, etc. **2** reconsider. **3** inspect or survey.
▷ **reviewer** *noun*
USAGE Do not confuse with **revue**.

revile *VERB* **reviles, reviling, reviled** criticize angrily; abuse.
▷ **revilement** *noun*
[from *re-* + old French *vil* = vile]

revise *VERB* **revises, revising, revised 1** go over work that you have already done, especially in preparing for an examination. **2** alter or correct something.
▷ **revision** *noun*
[from *re-* + Latin *visere* = examine]

revitalize *VERB* **revitalizes, revitalizing, revitalized** put new strength or vitality into something.
[from *re-* + *vital* + *-ize*]

revive *VERB* **revives, reviving, revived** come or bring back to life, strength, activity, or use etc.
▷ **revival** *noun*
[from *re-* + Latin *vivere* = to live]

revoke *VERB* **revokes, revoking, revoked** withdraw or cancel a decree or licence etc.
[from *re-* + Latin *vocare* = to call]

revolt *VERB* **revolts, revolting, revolted 1** rebel. **2** disgust somebody.

revolt *NOUN* **revolts 1** a rebellion. **2** a feeling of disgust.
[same origin as *revolve*]

revolting *ADJECTIVE* disgusting.

revolution *NOUN* **revolutions 1** a rebellion that overthrows the government. **2** a complete change. **3** revolving or rotation; one complete turn of a wheel, engine, etc.

revolutionary *ADJECTIVE* **1** involving a great change. **2** to do with a political revolution.

revolutionize *VERB* **revolutionizes, revolutionizing, revolutionized** make a great change in something.

revolve *VERB* **revolves, revolving, revolved 1** turn in a circle round a central point. **2** have something as the most important element • *Her life revolves around her work.*
[from *re-* + Latin *volvere* = to roll]

revolver *NOUN* **revolvers** a pistol with a revolving mechanism that makes it possible to fire it a number of times without reloading.

revue *NOUN* **revues** an entertainment consisting of songs, sketches, etc., often about current events.
[French, = review]
USAGE Do not confuse with **review**.

revulsion *NOUN* **1** strong disgust. **2** a sudden violent change of feeling.
[from *re-* + Latin *vulsus* = pulled]

reward *NOUN* **rewards 1** something given in return for something good you have done. **2** a sum of money offered for help in catching a criminal or finding lost property.

reward *VERB* **rewards, rewarding, rewarded** give a reward to someone.
[originally = consider, take notice: related to *regard*]

rewarding *ADJECTIVE* giving satisfaction and a feeling of achievement • *a rewarding job.*

rewind *VERB* **rewinds, rewinding, rewound** wind a cassette or videotape back to or towards the beginning.

rewrite *VERB* **rewrites, rewriting, rewrote, rewritten** write something again or differently.

rhapsody (*say* rap-so-dee) *NOUN* **rhapsodies 1** a statement of great delight about something. **2** a romantic piece of music.
▷ **rhapsodize** *verb*
[from Greek *rhapsoidos* = someone who stitches songs together]

rhesus monkey *NOUN* **rhesus monkeys** a kind of small monkey from Northern India.
[from Latin]

rhesus positive *ADJECTIVE* having a substance (*rhesus factor*) found in the red blood cells of many humans and some other primates, first found in the rhesus monkey.
- **rhesus negative** *adjective* without rhesus factor.

rhetoric (*say* ret-er-ik) *NOUN* **1** the act of using words impressively, especially in public speaking. **2** affected or exaggerated expressions used because they sound impressive.
▷ **rhetorical** *adjective* **rhetorically** *adverb*
[from Greek *rhetor* = orator]

rhetorical question *NOUN* **rhetorical questions** a question asked for dramatic effect and not intended to get an answer, e.g. 'Who cares?'
(= nobody cares).

rheumatism *NOUN* a disease that causes pain and stiffness in joints and muscles.
▷ **rheumatic** *adjective* **rheumatoid** *adjective*
[from Greek *rheuma*, a substance in the body which was once believed to cause rheumatism]

rhino *NOUN* **rhino** or **rhinos** (*informal*) a rhinoceros.

rhinoceros *NOUN* **rhinoceros** or **rhinoceroses** a large heavy animal with a horn or two horns on its nose.
[from Greek *rhinos* = of the nose + *keras* = horn]

rhizome *NOUN* **rhizomes** a thick underground stem which produces roots and new plants.
[from Greek]

rhododendron *NOUN* **rhododendrons** an evergreen shrub with large trumpet-shaped flowers.
[from Greek *rhodon* = rose + *dendron* = tree]

rhombus *NOUN* **rhombuses** a shape with four equal sides but no right angles, like the diamond on playing cards.
[from Greek]

rhubarb *NOUN* a plant with thick reddish stalks that are used as fruit.
[from Latin]

rhyme *NOUN* **rhymes 1** a similar sound in the endings of words, e.g. *bat/fat/mat, batter/fatter/matter*. **2** a poem with rhymes. **3** a word that rhymes with another.

rhyme *VERB* **rhymes, rhyming, rhymed**
1 form a rhyme. **2** have rhymes.
[from old French; related to *rhythm* (originally used of a kind of rhythmic verse which also usually rhymed)]

rhythm *NOUN* **rhythms** a regular pattern of beats, sounds, or movements.
▷ **rhythmic** *adjective* **rhythmical** *adjective* **rhythmically** *adverb*
[from Greek]

rib *NOUN* **ribs 1** each of the curved bones round the chest. **2** a curved part that looks like a rib or supports something • *the ribs of an umbrella.*
▷ **ribbed** *adjective*
[from Old English]

ribald (*say* rib-ald) *ADJECTIVE* funny in a rude or disrespectful way.
▷ **ribaldry** *noun*
[via old French from Germanic]

riband *NOUN* **ribands** a ribbon.
[from old French]

ribbon *NOUN* **ribbons 1** a narrow strip of silk or nylon etc. used for decoration or for tying something. **2** a long narrow strip of inked material used in a typewriter etc.
[a different spelling of *riband*]

rice *NOUN* a cereal plant grown in flooded fields in hot countries, or its seeds.
[from Greek]

rich *ADJECTIVE* **1** having a lot of money or property; wealthy. **2** having a large supply of something • *The country is rich in natural resources*. **3** (said about colour, sound, or smell) pleasantly deep or strong. **4** (said about food) containing a lot of fat, butter, eggs, etc. **5** expensive or luxurious.
▷ **richness** *noun*
[from Old English]

riches *PLURAL NOUN* wealth.

richly *ADVERB* **1** in a rich or luxurious way. **2** fully or thoroughly • *This award is richly deserved*.

Richter scale *NOUN* a scale (from 0-10) used to show the force of an earthquake.
[named after an American scientist, C. F. Richter, who studied earthquakes]

rick[1] *NOUN* **ricks** a large neat stack of hay or straw.
[from Old English]

rick[2] *VERB* **ricks, ricking, ricked** sprain or wrench.
[origin unknown]

rickets *NOUN* a disease caused by lack of vitamin D, causing deformed bones.
[origin unknown]

rickety *ADJECTIVE* shaky; likely to break or fall down.
[from *rickets*]

rickshaw *NOUN* **rickshaws** a two-wheeled carriage pulled by one or more people, used in the Far East.
[from Japanese *jin-riki-sha* = person- power- vehicle]

ricochet (*say* rik-osh-ay) *VERB* **ricochets, ricocheting, ricocheted** bounce off something; rebound • *The bullets ricocheted off the wall*.
▷ **ricochet** *noun*
[French, = the skipping of a flat stone on water]

ricotta *NOUN* a kind of soft Italian cheese made from sheep's milk.
[Italian]

rid *VERB* **rids, ridding, rid** make a person or place free from something unwanted • *He rid the town of rats*.
- **get rid of** remove something or throw it away.
[from Old Norse]

riddle[1] *NOUN* **riddles** a puzzling question, especially as a joke.
[from Old English *raedels*]

riddle[2] *NOUN* **riddles** a coarse sieve.

riddle *VERB* **riddles, riddling, riddled** **1** pass gravel etc. through a riddle. **2** pierce with many holes • *The car was riddled with bullets*.
[from Old English *hridder*]

ride *VERB* **rides, riding, rode, ridden 1** sit on a horse, bicycle, etc. and be carried along on it. **2** travel in a car, bus, train, etc. **3** float or be supported on something • *The ship rode the waves*.

ride *NOUN* **rides 1** a journey on a horse, bicycle, etc. or in a vehicle. **2** a roundabout etc. that you ride on at a fair or amusement park.
[from Old English]

rider *NOUN* **riders 1** someone who rides. **2** an extra comment or statement.

ridge *NOUN* **ridges 1** a long narrow part higher than the rest of something. **2** a long narrow range of hills or mountains.
▷ **ridged** *adjective*
[from Old English]

ridicule *VERB* **ridicules, ridiculing, ridiculed** make fun of a person or thing.
▷ **ridicule** *noun*
[from Latin *ridere* = to laugh]

ridiculous *ADJECTIVE* so silly that it makes people laugh or despise it.
▷ **ridiculously** *adverb*

rife *ADJECTIVE* widespread; happening frequently • *Crime was rife in the town.*
[probably from Old Norse]

riff-raff *NOUN* the rabble; disreputable people.
[from old French *rif et raf* = everybody and everything]

rifle *NOUN* **rifles** a long gun with spiral grooves (called *rifling*) inside the barrel that make the bullet spin and so travel more accurately.

rifle *VERB* **rifles, rifling, rifled** search and rob • *They rifled his desk.*
[from French]

rift *NOUN* **rifts 1** a crack or split. **2** a disagreement that separates friends.
[a Scandinavian word]

rift valley *NOUN* **rift valleys** a steep-sided valley formed where the land has sunk.

rig[1] *VERB* **rigs, rigging, rigged 1** provide a ship with ropes, spars, sails, etc. **2** set something up quickly or out of makeshift materials • *We managed to rig up a shelter for the night.*
- **rig out** provide with clothes or equipment.
▷ **rig-out** *noun*

rig *NOUN* **rigs 1** a framework supporting the machinery for drilling an oil well. **2** the way a ship's masts and sails etc. are arranged. **3** (*informal*) an outfit of clothes.
[probably from a Scandinavian language]

rig[2] *VERB* **rigs, rigging, rigged** arrange the result of an election or contest dishonestly.
[origin unknown]

rigging *NOUN* the ropes etc. that support a ship's mast and sails.

right *ADJECTIVE* **1** on or towards the east if you think of yourself as facing north. **2** correct; true • *the right answer*. **3** morally good; fair or just • *It's not right to cheat.* **4** (said about political groups) conservative; not in favour of socialist reforms.
▷ **right-hand** *adjective* **rightness** *noun*

right *ADVERB* **1** on or towards the right • *Turn right here.* **2** straight • *Go right on.* **3** completely • *Turn right round.* **4** exactly • *right in the middle.* **5** correctly or appropriately • *Did I do that right?*
- **right away** immediately.

right *NOUN* **rights 1** the right-hand side or part etc. **2** what is morally good or fair or just. **3** something that people are allowed to do or have • *People over 18 have the right to vote in elections.*

right *VERB* **rights, righting, righted** **1** make a thing upright • *The crew righted the boat.* **2** put right • *The fault might right itself.*
[from Old English]

right angle *NOUN* an angle of 90°.

righteous *ADJECTIVE* doing what is right; virtuous.
▷ **righteously** *adverb* **righteousness** *noun*

rightful *ADJECTIVE* deserved or proper • *in her rightful place.*
▷ **rightfully** *adverb*

right-handed *ADJECTIVE* using the right hand in preference to the left hand.

right-hand man *NOUN* **right-hand men** a trusted and impartial assistant.

rightly *ADVERB* correctly or justifiably.

right-minded *ADJECTIVE* having ideas and opinions which are sensible and morally good.

right of way *NOUN* **rights of way 1** a public path across private land. **2** the right of one vehicle to pass or cross a junction etc. before another.

rigid *ADJECTIVE* **1** stiff or firm; not bending • *a rigid support*. **2** strict • *rigid rules.*
▷ **rigidly** *adverb* **rigidity** *noun*
[from Latin]

rigmarole *NOUN* **rigmaroles 1** a long rambling statement. **2** a complicated procedure.
[from Middle English *ragman* = a legal document]

rigor mortis (*say* ri-ger **mor**-tis) *NOUN* stiffening of the body after death.
[Latin, = stiffness of death]

rigorous *ADJECTIVE* **1** strict or severe. **2** careful and thorough.
▷ **rigorously** *adverb*

rigour *NOUN* **rigours 1** strictness or severity. **2** harshness of weather or conditions • *the rigours of winter.*
[from Latin *rigor* = stiffness]

rile *VERB* **riles, riling, riled** (*informal*) annoy.
[probably from old French]

rill *NOUN* **rills** a very small stream.
[probably from old Dutch]

rim *NOUN* **rims** the outer edge of a cup, wheel, or other round object.
[from Old English]

rimmed *ADJECTIVE* edged.

rind *NOUN* the tough skin on bacon, cheese, or fruit.
[from Old English]

ring[1] *NOUN* **rings 1** a circle. **2** a thin circular piece of metal worn on a finger. **3** the space where a circus performs. **4** a square area in which a boxing match or wrestling match takes place.

ring *VERB* **rings, ringing, ringed** put a ring round something; encircle.
[from Old English *hring*]

ring[2] *VERB* **rings, ringing, rang, rung** **1** cause a bell to sound. **2** make a loud clear sound like that of a bell. **3** be filled with sound • *The hall rang with cheers.* **4** telephone • *Please ring me tomorrow.*
▷ **ringer** *noun*

ring *NOUN* **rings** the act or sound of ringing.
- **give someone a ring** (*informal*) telephone someone.
[from Old English *hringan*]

ringleader *NOUN* **ringleaders** a person who leads others in rebellion, mischief, crime, etc.
[from *ring*[1]]

ringlet *NOUN* **ringlets** a tube-shaped curl of hair.

ringmaster *NOUN* **ringmasters** the person in charge of a performance in a circus ring.

ring road *NOUN* **ring roads** a road that runs around the edge of a town so that traffic does not have to go through the centre.

ringworm *NOUN* a fungal skin infection that causes itchy circular patches, especially on the scalp.

rink *NOUN* **rinks** a place made for skating.
[origin unknown]

rinse *VERB* **rinses, rinsing, rinsed** **1** wash something lightly. **2** wash in clean water to remove soap.

rinse *NOUN* **rinses 1** rinsing. **2** a liquid for colouring the hair.
[from French]

riot *NOUN* **riots** wild or violent behaviour by a crowd of people.
- **run riot** behave or spread in an unruly or uncontrolled way.

riot *VERB* **riots, rioting, rioted** take part in a riot.
[from old French *rihoter* = to quarrel]

riot gear *NOUN* protective clothing, helmets, shields, etc. worn or carried by the police or army if rioting is expected.

riotous *ADJECTIVE* **1** disorderly or unruly. **2** boisterous • *riotous laughter.*

RIP *ABBREVIATION* may he or she (or they) rest in peace.
[short for Latin *requiescat* (or *requiescant*) *in pace*]

rip *VERB* **rips, ripping, ripped** **1** tear roughly. **2** rush.
- **rip off** (*informal*) swindle or charge too much.

rip *NOUN* a torn place.
[origin unknown]

ripe *ADJECTIVE* **riper, ripest** **1** ready to be harvested or eaten. **2** ready and suitable • *The time is ripe for revolution.*
▷ **ripeness** *noun*
- **a ripe old age** a great age.
[from Old English]

ripen *VERB* **ripens, ripening, ripened** make or become ripe.

rip-off *NOUN* **rip-offs** (*informal*) a fraud or swindle.

riposte (*say* rip-ost) *NOUN* **ripostes 1** a quick clever reply. **2** a quick return thrust in fencing.
[from Italian; related to *respond*]

ripple *NOUN* **ripples** a small wave or series of waves.

ripple *VERB* **ripples, rippling, rippled** form ripples.
[origin unknown]

rise *VERB* **rise, rising, rose, risen** **1** go upwards. **2** increase • *Prices are expected to rise*. **3** get up from lying, sitting, or kneeling. **4** get out of bed. **5** rebel • *They rose in revolt against the tyrant*. **6** (said about bread or cake etc.) swell up by the action of yeast. **7** (said about a river) begin its course. **8** (said about the wind) begin to blow more strongly.

rise *NOUN* **rises** **1** the action of rising; an upward movement. **2** an increase in amount etc. or in wages. **3** an upward slope.
- **give rise to** cause.
[from Old English]

rising *NOUN* **risings** a revolt.

risk *NOUN* **risks** a chance of danger or loss.

risk *VERB* **risks, risking, risked** **1** take the chance of damaging or losing something • *They risked their lives to rescue the children*. **2** accept the risk of something unpleasant happening • *He risks injury each time he climbs*.
[via French from Italian]

risky *ADJECTIVE* **riskier, riskiest** full of risk.

risotto *NOUN* an Italian dish of rice cooked with vegetables and, usually, meat.
[Italian, from *riso* = rice]

rissole *NOUN* **rissoles** a fried cake of minced meat or fish.
[French]

rite *NOUN* **rites** a religious ceremony; a solemn ritual.
[from Latin]

ritual *NOUN* **rituals** the series of actions used in a religious or other ceremony.
▷ **ritual** *adjective* **ritually** *adverb*
[from Latin *ritus* = rite]

rival *NOUN* **rivals** a person or thing that competes with another or tries to do the same thing.
▷ **rivalry** *noun*

rival *VERB* **rivals, rivalling, rivalled** be a rival of a person or thing.
[from Latin *rivalis* = someone using the same stream (from *rivus* = stream)]

river *NOUN* **rivers** a large stream of water flowing in a natural channel.
[from Latin *ripa* = bank]

rivet *NOUN* **rivets** a strong nail or bolt for holding pieces of metal together. The end opposite the head is flattened to form another head when it is in place.

rivet *VERB* **rivets, riveting, riveted** **1** fasten with rivets. **2** hold firmly • *He stood riveted to the spot*. **3** fascinate • *The concert was riveting*.
▷ **riveter** *noun*
[from old French]

rivulet *NOUN* **rivulets** a small stream.
[from Latin *rivus* = stream]

RN *ABBREVIATION* Royal Navy.

roach[1] *NOUN* **roach** a small freshwater fish.
[from old French]

roach[2] *NOUN* **roaches** (*informal*) (*American*) a cockroach.

road *NOUN* **roads** **1** a level way with a hard surface made for traffic to travel on. **2** a way or course • *the road to success*.
[from Old English]

roadblock *NOUN* **roadblocks** a barrier across a road, set up by the police or army to stop and check vehicles.

road-holding *ADJECTIVE* the ability of a vehicle to remain stable and under control when cornering, especially when travelling fast.

road rage *NOUN* abuse, violence, or aggressive behaviour by a driver towards other drivers.

roadway *NOUN* the middle part of the road, used by traffic.

roadworthy *ADJECTIVE* safe to be used on roads.

roam *VERB* **roams, roaming, roamed** wander.
▷ **roam** *noun*
[origin unknown]

roan *ADJECTIVE* (said about a horse) brown or black with many white hairs.
[from old French]

roar *NOUN* **roars** a loud deep sound like that made by a lion.

roar *VERB* **roars, roaring, roared** **1** make a roar. **2** laugh loudly.
- **do a roaring trade** do very good business.
[from Old English]

roast *VERB* **roasts, roasting, roasted**
1 cook meat etc. in an oven or by exposing it to heat. **2** make or be very hot.

roast *ADJECTIVE* roasted • *roast beef.*

roast *NOUN* **roasts 1** meat for roasting.
2 roast meat.
[via old French from Germanic]

rob *VERB* **robs, robbing, robbed** take or steal from somebody • *He robbed me of my watch.*
▷ **robber** *noun* **robbery** *noun*
[via old French from Germanic]

robe *NOUN* **robes** a long loose piece of clothing, especially one worn in ceremonies.

robe *VERB* **robes, robing, robed** dress in a robe or ceremonial robes.
[via old French from Germanic]

robin *NOUN* **robins** a small brown bird with a red breast.
[from old French, = Robert]

robot *NOUN* **robots 1** a machine that looks or acts like a person. **2** a machine operated by remote control. **3** (*S. African*) a set of tra ffic lights.
▷ **robotic** *adjective*
[from Czech *robota* = forced labour]

robust *ADJECTIVE* strong and vigorous.
▷ **robustly** *adverb* **robustness** *noun*
[from Latin *robur* = strength, an oak tree]

rock[1] *NOUN* **rocks 1** a large stone or boulder. **2** the hard part of the earth's crust, under the soil. **3** a hard sweet usually shaped like a stick and sold at the seaside.
[from old French]

rock[2] *VERB* **rocks, rocking, rocked** **1** move gently backwards and forwards while supported on something. **2** shake violently
• *The earthquake rocked the city.*

rock *NOUN* **1** a rocking movement. **2** rock music.
[from Old English]

rock and roll or **rock 'n' roll** *NOUN* a kind of popular dance music with a strong beat, originating in the 1950s.

rock-bottom *ADJECTIVE* at the lowest level
• *rock-bottom prices.*

rocker *NOUN* **rockers 1** a thing that rocks something or is rocked. **2** a rocking chair.
- **off your rocker** (*slang*) mad.

rockery *NOUN* **rockeries** a mound or bank in a garden, where plants are made to grow between large rocks.

rocket *NOUN* **rockets 1** a firework that shoots high into the air. **2** a structure that is propelled into the air by burning gases, used to send up a missile or a spacecraft.
▷ **rocketry** *noun*

rocket *VERB* **rockets, rocketing, rocketed** move quickly upwards or away.
[from Italian *rocchetto* = small distaff (because of the shape)]

rocking chair *NOUN* **rocking chairs** a chair that can be rocked by a person sitting in it.

rocking horse *NOUN* **rocking horses** a model of a horse that can be rocked by a child sitting on it.

rock music *NOUN* popular music with a heavy beat.

rocky[1] *ADJECTIVE* **rockier, rockiest** **1** like rock. **2** full of rocks.

rocky[2] *ADJECTIVE* **rockier, rockiest** unsteady.
▷ **rockiness** *noun*

rod *NOUN* **rods 1** a long thin stick or bar. **2** a stick with a line attached for fishing.
[from Old English]

rodent *NOUN* **rodents** an animal that has large front teeth for gnawing things. Rats, mice, and squirrels are rodents.
[from Latin *rodens* = gnawing]

rodeo (*say* roh-day-oh) *NOUN* **rodeos** a display of cowboys' skill in riding, controlling horses, etc.
[Spanish, from *rodear* = go round]

roe[1] *NOUN* a mass of eggs or reproductive cells in a fish's body.
[from old German or old Dutch]

roe[2] *NOUN* **roes** or **roe** a kind of small deer of Europe and Asia. The male is called a **roebuck**.
[from Old English]

rogue *NOUN* **rogues 1** a dishonest person. **2** a mischievous person.
▷ **roguery** *noun*
[origin unknown]

roguish *ADJECTIVE* playful and mischievous.

roister *VERB* **roisters, roistering, roistered** make merry noisily.
[from old French *rustre* = ruffian]

role *NOUN* **roles 1** a performer's part in a play or film etc. **2** someone's or something's purpose or function • *the role of computers in education.*
[from French *rôle* = roll (originally the roll of paper on which an actor's part was written)]

role model *NOUN* **role models** a person looked to by others as an example of how to behave.

roll *VERB* **rolls, rolling, rolled 1** move along by turning over and over, like a ball or wheel. **2** form something into the shape of a cylinder or ball. **3** flatten something by rolling a rounded object over it. **4** rock from side to side. **5** pass steadily • *The years rolled on.* **6** make a long vibrating sound • *The thunder rolled.*

roll *NOUN* **rolls 1** a cylinder made by rolling something up. **2** a small individual portion of bread baked in a rounded shape. **3** an official list of names. **4** a long vibrating sound • *a drum roll.*
[from Latin *rotula* = little wheel]

roll-call *NOUN* **roll-calls** the calling of a list of names to check that everyone is present.

roller *NOUN* **rollers 1** a cylinder used for flattening or spreading things, or on which something is wound. **2** a long swelling sea wave.

rollerball *NOUN* **rollerballs** a ballpoint pen using a smaller ball and thinner ink so that it writes very smoothly.

Rollerblade *NOUN* **Rollerblades** (*trademark*) a boot like an ice-skating boot, with a line of wheels in place of the skate, for rolling smoothly on hard ground.
▷ **rollerblading** *noun*

roller coaster *NOUN* **roller coasters** a type of railway used for amusement at fairgrounds etc. with a series of alternate steep descents and ascents.

roller skate *NOUN* **roller skates** a framework with wheels, fitted under a shoe so that the wearer can roll smoothly over the ground.
▷ **roller-skating** *noun*

rollicking *ADJECTIVE* boisterous and full of fun.
[from *romp* + *frolic*]

rolling pin *NOUN* a heavy cylinder for rolling over pastry to flatten it.

rolling stock *NOUN* railway engines and carriages and wagons etc.

roly-poly *NOUN* **roly-polies** a pudding of paste covered with jam, rolled up and boiled.
[a nonsense word based on *roll*]

ROM *ABBREVIATION* read-only memory, a type of computer memory with contents that can be searched or copied but not changed.

Roman *ADJECTIVE* to do with ancient or modern Rome or its people.
▷ **Roman** *noun*

Roman alphabet *NOUN* this alphabet, in which most European languages are written.

Roman candle *NOUN* **Roman candles** a tubular firework that sends out coloured fireballs.

Roman Catholic *ADJECTIVE* belonging to or to do with the Christian Church that has the Pope (bishop of Rome) as its leader.
▷ **Roman Catholicism** *noun*

Roman Catholic *NOUN* **Roman Catholics** a member of this Church.

romance (*say* ro-manss) *NOUN* **romances 1** tender feelings, experiences, and qualities connected with love. **2** a love story. **3** a love affair. **4** an imaginative story about the adventures of heroes • *a romance of King Arthur's court.*
[from old French]

Roman numerals *PLURAL NOUN* letters that represent numbers (I = 1, V = 5, X = 10, etc.), used by the ancient Romans. (COMPARE **arabic numerals**)

romantic *ADJECTIVE* **1** to do with love or romance. **2** sentimental or idealistic; not realistic or practical.
▷ **romantically** *adverb*

Romany *NOUN* **Romanies 1** a gypsy. **2** the language of gypsies.
[from a Romany word *rom* = man]

romp *VERB* **romps, romping, romped** play in a lively way.
▷ **romp** *noun*
[origin unknown]

rompers *PLURAL NOUN* a piece of clothing for a baby or young child, covering the body and legs.

rondo *NOUN* **rondos** a piece of music whose first part recurs several times.
[Italian, from French *rondeau* = circle]

roof *NOUN* **roofs 1** the part that covers the top of a building, shelter, or vehicle. **2** the top inside surface of something • *the roof of the mouth*.
[from Old English]

roof rack *NOUN* **roof racks** a framework for carrying luggage on top of a vehicle.

rook[1] *NOUN* **rooks** a black crow that nests in large groups.

rook *VERB* **rooks, rooking, rooked** (*informal*) swindle; charge people an unnecessarily high price.
[from Old English]

rook[2] *NOUN* **rooks** a chess piece shaped like a castle.
[from Arabic]

rookery *NOUN* **rookeries 1** a place where many rooks nest. **2** a breeding place of penguins or seals.

room *NOUN* **rooms 1** a part of a building with its own walls and ceiling. **2** enough space • *Is there room for me?*
▷ **roomful** *noun*

room *VERB* **rooms, rooming, roomed** (*American*) to share lodgings • *I roomed with him during my freshman year.*

roomy *ADJECTIVE* **roomier, roomiest** containing plenty of room; spacious.

roost *VERB* **roosts, roosting, roosted** (said about birds) perch or settle for sleep.

roost *NOUN* **roosts** a place where birds roost.
[from Old English]

rooster *NOUN* **roosters** (*American*) a cockerel.

root[1] *NOUN* **roots 1** that part of a plant that grows under the ground and absorbs water and nourishment from the soil. **2** a source or basis • *The love of money is the root of all evil.* **3** a number in relation to the number it produces when multiplied by itself • *9 is the square root of 81* (9 x 9 = 81).
- **take root 1** grow roots. **2** become established.

root *VERB* **roots, rooting, rooted 1** take root; cause something to take root. **2** fix firmly • *Fear rooted us to the spot.*
- **root out** get rid of something.
[from Old Norse]

root[2] *VERB* **roots, rooting, rooted 1** (said about an animal) turn up ground in search of food. **2** rummage; find something by doing this • *I've managed to root out some facts and figures.*
[from Old English]

rope *NOUN* **ropes** a strong thick cord made of twisted strands of fibre.
- **show someone the ropes** show him or her how to do something.

rope *VERB* **ropes, roping, roped** fasten with a rope.
- **rope in** persuade a person to take part in something.
[from Old English]

rosary *NOUN* **rosaries** a string of beads for keeping count of a set of prayers as they are said.
[from Latin]

rose[1] *NOUN* **roses 1** a shrub that has showy flowers often with thorny stems. **2** a deep pink colour. **3** a sprinkling nozzle with many holes, e.g. on a watering can or hosepipe.
[via Old English from Greek]

rose[2] *past tense* of **rise**.

rosemary *NOUN* an evergreen shrub with fragrant leaves, used in cooking.
[from Latin]

rosette *NOUN* **rosettes** a large circular badge or ornament, made of ribbon.
[French, = little rose]

Rosh Hashanah or **Rosh Hashana** *NOUN* the Jewish New Year.
[Hebrew, = head of the year]

roster *NOUN* **rosters** a list showing people's turns to be on duty etc.

roster *VERB* **rosters**, **rostering**, **rostered** place on a roster.
[from Dutch]

rostrum *NOUN* **rostra** a platform for one person.
[Latin, = beak, prow of a warship (because a rostrum in ancient Rome was decorated with the prows of captured enemy ships)]

rosy *ADJECTIVE* **rosier**, **rosiest** **1** deep pink. **2** hopeful or cheerful • *a rosy future.*
▷ **rosiness** *noun*

rot *VERB* **rots**, **rotting**, **rotted** go soft or bad and become useless; decay.

rot *NOUN* **1** rotting or decay. **2** (*informal*) nonsense.
[from Old English]

rota (*say* roh-ta) *NOUN* **rotas** a list of people to do things or of things to be done in turn.
[Latin, = wheel]

rotate *VERB* **rotates**, **rotating**, **rotated** **1** go round like a wheel; revolve. **2** arrange or happen in a series; take turns at doing something.
▷ **rotation** *noun* **rotary** *adjective* **rotatory** *adjective*
[same origin as *rota*]

rote *NOUN*
- **by rote** from memory or by routine, without full understanding of the meaning • *We used to learn French songs by rote.*
[origin unknown]

rotor *NOUN* **rotors** a rotating part of a machine or helicopter.
[from *rotate*]

rotten *ADJECTIVE* **1** rotted • *rotten apples.* **2** (*informal*) very bad or unpleasant • *rotten weather.*
▷ **rottenness** *noun*

rottweiler *NOUN* **rottweilers** a German breed of powerful black-and-tan working dog, sometimes used as guard dogs.
[German, from *Rottweil*, a town in Germany where the dog was bred]

rotund *ADJECTIVE* rounded or plump.
▷ **rotundity** *noun*
[from Latin *rotundus* = round]

rouble (*say* roo-bul) *NOUN* **roubles** the unit of money in Russia.
[via French from Russian]

rouge (*say* roozh) *NOUN* a reddish cosmetic for colouring the cheeks.
▷ **rouge** *verb*
[French, = red]

rough *ADJECTIVE* **rougher**, **roughest** **1** not smooth; uneven. **2** not gentle or careful; violent • *a rough push.* **3** not exact • *a rough guess.* **4** (said about weather or the sea) wild and stormy.
▷ **roughly** *adverb* **roughness** *noun*

rough *VERB* **roughs**, **roughing**, **roughed**
- **rough it** do without ordinary comforts.
- **rough out** draw or plan something roughly.
- **rough up** (*slang*) treat a person violently.
[from Old English]

roughage *NOUN* fibre in food, which helps digestion.

roughen *VERB* **roughens**, **roughening**, **roughened** make or become rough.

roulette (*say* roo-let) *NOUN* a gambling game where players bet on where the ball in a rotating disc will come to rest.
[French, = little wheel]

round *ADJECTIVE* **1** shaped like a circle or ball or cylinder; curved. **2** full or complete • *a round dozen.* **3** returning to the start • *a round trip.*
▷ **roundness** *noun*
- **in round figures** approximately, without giving exact units.

round *ADVERB* **1** in a circle or curve; round something • *Go round to the back of the house.* **2** in every direction or to every person • *Hand the cakes round.* **3** in a new direction • *Turn your chair round.* **4** to someone's house or place of work • *Come round after lunch.*
- **come round** become conscious again.
- **round about** **1** near by. **2** approximately.

round *PREPOSITION* **1** on all sides of • *Put a fence round the field*. **2** in a curve or circle at an even distance from • *The earth moves round the sun*. **3** to all parts of • *Show them round the house*. **4** on the further side of • *The shop is round the corner*.

round *NOUN* **rounds 1** a series of visits made by a doctor, postman, etc. **2** one section or stage in a competition • *Winners go on to the next round*. **3** a shot or volley of shots from a gun; ammunition for this. **4** a whole slice of bread; a sandwich made with two slices of bread. **5** a song in which people sing the same words but start at different times. **6** a set of drinks bought for all the members of a group.

round *VERB* **rounds, rounding, rounded**
1 make or become round. **2** travel round • *The car rounded the corner*.
- **round off** finish something.
- **round up** gather people or animals together.

[from old French; related to *rotund*]

roundabout *NOUN* **roundabouts 1** a road junction where traffic has to pass round a circular structure in the road. **2** a circular revolving ride at a fair.

roundabout *ADJECTIVE* indirect; not using the shortest way of going or of saying or doing something • *I heard the news in a roundabout way*.

rounders *NOUN* a game in which players try to hit a ball and run round a circuit.

Roundhead *NOUN* **Roundheads** an opponent of King Charles I in the English Civil War (1642-9).
[so called because many of them wore their hair cut short at a time when long hair was in fashion for men]

roundly *ADVERB* **1** thoroughly or severely • *We were roundly told off for being late*. **2** in a rounded shape.

round-shouldered *ADJECTIVE* with the shoulders bent forward, so that the back is rounded.

round-the-clock *ADJECTIVE* lasting or happening all day and all night.

round trip *NOUN* **round trips** a trip to one or more places and back to where you started.

round-up *NOUN* **round-ups 1** a gathering up of cattle or people • *a police round-up of suspects*. **2** a summary • *a round-up of the news*.

roundworm *NOUN* **roundworms** a kind of worm that lives as a parasite in the intestines of animals and birds.

rouse *VERB* **rouses, rousing, roused**
1 make or become awake. **2** cause to become active or excited.
[probably from old French]

rousing *ADJECTIVE* loud or exciting • *three rousing cheers*.

rout *VERB* **routs, routing, routed** defeat an enemy completely and force them to retreat.
▷ **rout** *noun*
[from old French]

route (*say as* root) *NOUN* **routes** the way taken to get to a place.
[from old French]

routine (*say* roo-teen) *NOUN* **routines** a regular way of doing things.
▷ **routinely** *adverb*
[French; related to *route*]

rove *VERB* **roves, roving, roved** roam or wander.
▷ **rover** *noun*
[probably from a Scandinavian language]

row[1] (*rhymes with* **go**) *NOUN* **rows** a line of people or things.
[from Old English *raw*]

row[2] (*rhymes with* **go**) *VERB* **rows, rowing, rowed** make a boat move by using oars.
▷ **rower** *noun* **rowing boat** *noun*
[from Old English *rowan*]

row[3] (*rhymes with* **cow**) *NOUN* **rows 1** a loud noise. **2** a quarrel. **3** a scolding.
[origin unknown]

rowan (*say* roh-an) *NOUN* **rowans** a tree that bears hanging bunches of red berries.
[a Scandinavian word]

rowdy ADJECTIVE **rowdier**, **rowdiest** noisy and disorderly.
▷ **rowdiness** *noun*
[originally American; origin unknown]

rowlock (*say* rol-ok) NOUN **rowlocks** a device on the side of a boat, keeping an oar in place.
[from an earlier word *oarlock*, with *row*[2] in place of *oar*]

royal ADJECTIVE to do with a king or queen.
▷ **royally** *adverb*
[from old French; related to *regal*]

royalty NOUN **1** being royal. **2** a royal person or persons • *in the presence of royalty*. **3** (*plural* **royalties**) a payment made to an author or composer etc. for each copy of a work sold or for each performance.

RSVP ABBREVIATION répondez s'il vous plaît (French, = please reply).

rub VERB **rubs**, **rubbing**, **rubbed** move something backwards and forwards while pressing it on something else.
▷ **rub** *noun*
- **rub out** remove something by rubbing.
[origin unknown]

rubber NOUN **rubbers 1** a strong elastic substance used for making tyres, balls, hoses, etc. **2** a piece of rubber for rubbing out pencil or ink marks.
▷ **rubbery** *adjective*

rubber plant NOUN **rubber plants 1** a tall evergreen plant with tough shiny leaves, often grown as a house plant. **2** a rubber tree.

rubber stamp NOUN **rubber stamps** a small device with lettering or a design on it, which is inked and used to mark paper etc.

rubber-stamp VERB **rubber-stamps**, **rubber-stamping**, **rubber-stamped** give official approval to a decision without thinking about it.

rubber tree NOUN **rubber trees** a tropical tree from which rubber is obtained.

rubbish NOUN **1** things that are worthless or not wanted. **2** nonsense.
[from old French]

rubble NOUN broken pieces of brick or stone.
[from old French]

rubella NOUN an infectious disease which causes a red rash, and which can damage a baby if the mother catches it early in pregnancy.
[from Latin *rubellus* = reddish]

rubric NOUN a set of instructions at the beginning of an official document or an examination paper.
[from Latin *rubeus* = red (because rubrics used to be written in red)]

ruby NOUN **rubies** a red jewel.
[from Latin *rubeus* = red]

ruby wedding NOUN a couple's fortieth wedding anniversary.

ruck NOUN **rucks** a dense crowd.
[probably from a Scandinavian language]

rucksack NOUN **rucksacks** a bag on straps for carrying on the back.
[from German *Rücken* = back + *Sack* = *sack*[1]]

ructions PLURAL NOUN (*informal*) protests and noisy argument.
[origin unknown]

rudder NOUN **rudders** a hinged upright piece at the back of a ship or aircraft, used for steering.
[from Old English]

ruddy ADJECTIVE **ruddier**, **ruddiest** red and healthy-looking • *a ruddy complexion*.
[from Old English]

rude ADJECTIVE **ruder**, **rudest 1** impolite. **2** indecent or improper. **3** roughly made; crude • *a rude shelter*. **4** vigorous and hearty • *in rude health*.
▷ **rudely** *adverb* **rudeness** *noun*
[from Latin *rudis* = raw, wild]

rudimentary ADJECTIVE **1** to do with rudiments; elementary. **2** not fully developed • *Penguins have rudimentary wings*.

rudiments (*say* rood-i-ments) PLURAL NOUN the elementary principles of a subject • *She taught me the rudiments of chemistry*.
[same origin as *rude*]

rueful ADJECTIVE regretful.
▷ **ruefully** *adverb*
[from Old English]

ruff *NOUN* **ruffs 1** a starched pleated frill worn round the neck in the 16th century. **2** a collar-like ring of feathers or fur round a bird's or animal's neck.
[a different spelling of *rough*]

ruffian *NOUN* **ruffians** a violent lawless person.
▷ **ruffianly** *adjective*
[via French and Italian from Germanic]

ruffle *VERB* **ruffles, ruffling, ruffled 1** disturb the smoothness of a thing. **2** upset or annoy someone.

ruffle *NOUN* **ruffles** a gathered ornamental frill.
[origin unknown]

rug *NOUN* **rugs 1** a thick mat for the floor. **2** a piece of thick fabric used as a blanket.
[probably from a Scandinavian language]

rugby or **rugby football** *NOUN* a kind of football game using an oval ball that players may carry or kick.
[named after *Rugby* School in Warwickshire, where it was first played]

rugged *ADJECTIVE* **1** having an uneven surface or outline; craggy. **2** sturdy.
[probably from a Scandinavian language]

rugger *NOUN* rugby football.

ruin *NOUN* **ruins 1** severe damage or destruction to something. **2** a building that has fallen down.

ruin *VERB* **ruins, ruining, ruined** damage or spoil a thing so severely that it is useless.
▷ **ruination** *noun*
[from Latin *ruere* = to fall]

ruinous *ADJECTIVE* **1** causing ruin. **2** in ruins; ruined.

rule *NOUN* **rules 1** something that people have to obey. **2** ruling; governing • *under French rule*. **3** a carpenter's ruler.
- **as a rule** usually; more often than not.

rule *VERB* **rules, ruling, ruled 1** govern or reign. **2** make a decision • *The referee ruled that it was a foul*. **3** draw a straight line with a ruler or other straight edge.
[from old French; related to *regulate*]

ruler *NOUN* **rulers 1** a person who governs. **2** a strip of wood, metal, or plastic with straight edges, used for measuring and drawing straight lines.

ruling *NOUN* **rulings** a judgement.

rum *NOUN* a strong alcoholic drink made from sugar or molasses.
[origin unknown]

rumble *VERB* **rumbles, rumbling, rumbled** make a deep heavy continuous sound like thunder.
▷ **rumble** *noun*
[probably from old Dutch]

rumble strip *NOUN* **rumble strips** a series of raised strips on a road that warns drivers of the edge of the roadway, or tells them to slow down, by making vehicles vibrate.

ruminant *ADJECTIVE* ruminating.

ruminant *NOUN* **ruminants** an animal that chews the cud (see *cud*).

ruminate *VERB* **ruminates, ruminating, ruminated 1** chew the cud. **2** meditate or ponder.
▷ **rumination** *noun* **ruminative** *adjective*
[from Latin]

rummage *VERB* **rummages, rummaging, rummaged** turn things over or move them about while looking for something.
▷ **rummage** *noun*
[from old French]

rummy *NOUN* a card game in which players try to form sets or sequences of cards.
[originally American: origin unknown]

rumour *NOUN* **rumours** information that spreads to a lot of people but may not be true.

rumour *VERB*
- **be rumoured** be spread as a rumour.
[from Latin *rumor* = noise]

rump *NOUN* **rumps** the hind part of an animal.
[probably from a Scandinavian language]

rumple *VERB* **rumples, rumpling, rumpled** crumple; make a thing untidy.
[from Dutch]

rump steak *NOUN* **rump steaks** a piece of meat from the rump of a cow.

rumpus *NOUN* **rumpuses** (*informal*) an uproar; an angry protest.
[origin unknown]

run *VERB* **runs, running, ran, run** **1** move with quick steps so that both or all feet leave the ground at each stride. **2** go or travel; flow • *Tears ran down his cheeks.* **3** produce a flow of liquid • *Run some water into it.* **4** work or function • *The engine was running smoothly.* **5** manage or organize • *She runs a corner shop.* **6** compete in a contest • *He ran for President.* **7** extend • *A fence runs round the estate.* **8** go or take in a vehicle • *I'll run you to the station.*
- **run a risk** take a chance.
- **run away** leave a place secretly or quickly.
- **run down** **1** run over. **2** stop gradually; decline. **3** (*informal*) say unkind or unfair things about someone.
- **run into** **1** collide with. **2** happen to meet.
- **run out** **1** have used up your stock of something. **2** knock over the wicket of a running batsman.
- **run over** knock down or crush with a moving vehicle.
- **run through** examine or rehearse.

run *NOUN* **runs** **1** the action of running; a time spent running • *Go for a run.* **2** a point scored in cricket or baseball. **3** a continuous series of events, etc. • *She had a run of good luck.* **4** an enclosure for animals • *a chicken run.* **5** a series of damaged stitches in a pair of tights or stockings. **6** a track • *a ski run.*
- **on the run** running away, especially from the police.

[from Old English]

runaway *NOUN* **runaways** someone who has run away.

runaway *ADJECTIVE* **1** having run away or out of control. **2** won easily • *a runaway victory.*

rundown *ADJECTIVE* **1** tired and in bad health. **2** in bad condition; dilapidated.

rung[1] *NOUN* **rungs** one of the crossbars on a ladder.
[from Old English]

rung[2] *past participle* of **ring**[2].

runner *NOUN* **runners** **1** a person or animal that runs, especially in a race. **2** a stem that grows away from a plant and roots itself. **3** a groove, rod, or roller for a thing to move on; each of the long strips under a sledge. **4** a long narrow strip of carpet or covering.

runner bean *NOUN* **runner beans** a kind of climbing bean with long green pods which are eaten.

runner-up *NOUN* **runners-up** someone who comes second in a competition.

running *present participle* of **run**.
- **in the running** competing and with a chance of winning.

running *ADJECTIVE* continuous or consecutive; without an interval • *It rained for four days running.*

runny *ADJECTIVE* **runnier, runniest**
1 flowing like liquid • *runny honey.*
2 producing a flow of liquid • *a runny nose.*

run-of-the-mill *ADJECTIVE* ordinary, not special.

runway *NOUN* **runways** a long hard surface on which aircraft take off and land.

rupee *NOUN* **rupees** the unit of money in India and Pakistan.
[from Sanskrit *rupya* = wrought silver]

rupture *VERB* **ruptures, rupturing, ruptured** break or burst.
▷ **rupture** *noun*
[from Latin *ruptum* = broken]
WORD FAMILY There are a number of English words that are related to *rupture* because part of their original meaning comes from the Latin word *ruptum* meaning 'broken or burst'. These include *corrupt, disrupt, erupt, irrupt,* and *interrupt.*

rural *ADJECTIVE* to do with or belonging to the countryside.
[from Latin *ruris* = of the country]

ruse *NOUN* **ruses** a deception or trick.
[from French]

rush[1] *VERB* **rushes, rushing, rushed**
1 move or do something quickly. **2** make someone hurry. **3** attack or capture by dashing forward suddenly.

rush *NOUN* **rushes** **1** a hurry. **2** a sudden movement towards something. **3** a sudden great demand for something.
[from old French]

rush[2] *NOUN* **rushes** a plant with a thin stem that grows in marshy places.
[from Old English]

rush hour *NOUN* **rush hours** the time when traffic is busiest.

rusk *NOUN* **rusks** a kind of hard, dry biscuit, especially for feeding babies.
[from Spanish or Portuguese]

russet *NOUN* reddish-brown colour.
[from Latin *russus* = red]

rust *NOUN* **1** a red or brown substance that forms on iron or steel exposed to damp and corrodes it. **2** a reddish-brown colour.

rust *VERB* **rusts, rusting, rusted** make or become rusty.
[from Old English]

rustic *ADJECTIVE* **1** rural. **2** made of rough timber or branches • *a rustic bridge.*
[same origin as *rural*]

rustle *VERB* **rustles, rustling, rustled** **1** make a sound like paper being crumpled. **2** (*American*) steal horses or cattle • *cattle rustling.*
▷ **rustle** *noun* **rustler** *noun*
- **rustle up** (*informal*) produce • *rustle up a meal.*
[imitating the sound]

rusty *ADJECTIVE* **rustier, rustiest** **1** coated with rust. **2** weakened by lack of use or practice • *My French is a bit rusty.*
▷ **rustiness** *noun*

rut *NOUN* **ruts** **1** a deep track made by wheels in soft ground. **2** a settled and usually dull way of life • *We are getting into a rut.*
▷ **rutted** *adjective*
[probably related to *route*]

ruthless *ADJECTIVE* pitiless, merciless, or cruel.
▷ **ruthlessly** *adverb* **ruthlessness** *noun*
[from Middle English *ruth* = pity]

rye *NOUN* a cereal used to make bread, biscuits, etc.
[from Old English]

Ss

S. *ABBREVIATION* **1** south. **2** southern.

sabbath *NOUN* **sabbaths** a weekly day for rest and prayer, Saturday for Jews, Sunday for Christians.
[from Hebrew *shabat* = rest]

sabbatical (*say* sa-bat-ikal) *NOUN* **sabbaticals** a period of paid leave granted to a university teacher for study or travel.
[from Greek *sabbatikos* = of the sabbath]

sable *NOUN* **1** a kind of dark fur. **2** (*poetical use*) black.
[via old French and Latin from a Slavonic language]

sabotage *NOUN* deliberate damage or disruption to hinder an enemy, employer, etc.
▷ **sabotage** *verb* **saboteur** *noun*
[from French *saboter* = make a noise with *sabots* (= wooden clogs)]

sabre *NOUN* **sabres** **1** a heavy sword with a curved blade. **2** a light fencing sword.
[from Hungarian]

sac *NOUN* **sacs** a bag-shaped part in an animal or plant.
[French, from Latin *saccus* = *sack*[1]]

saccharin (*say* sak-er-in) *NOUN* a very sweet substance used as a substitute for sugar.
[from Greek *saccharon* = sugar]

saccharine (*say* sak-er-een) *ADJECTIVE* unpleasantly sweet • *a saccharine smile.*

sachet (*say* sash-ay) *NOUN* **sachets** a small sealed packet or bag containing a small amount of shampoo, sugar, etc.
[French, = little sack]

sack[1] *NOUN* **sacks** a large bag made of strong material.
▷ **sacking** *noun*
- **the sack** (*informal*) dismissal from a job • *He got the sack.*

sack *VERB* **sacks, sacking, sacked** (*informal*) dismiss someone from a job.
[via Old English from Latin]

sack[2] *VERB* **sacks, sacking, sacked** (*old use*) plunder a captured town in a violent destructive way.
▷ **sack** *noun*
[from French *mettre à sac* = put in a sack]

sacrament *NOUN* **sacraments** an important Christian religious ceremony such as baptism or Holy Communion.
[same origin as *sacred*]

sacred *ADJECTIVE* holy; to do with God or a god.
[from Latin]

sacrifice *NOUN* **sacrifices 1** giving something that you think will please a god, e.g. an offering of a killed animal. **2** giving up a thing you value, so that something good may happen. **3** a thing sacrificed.
▷ **sacrificial** *adjective*

sacrifice *VERB* **sacrifices, sacrificing, sacrificed** offer something or give it up as a sacrifice.
[from Latin *sacrificare* = make something holy]

sacrilege (*say* sak-ril-ij) *NOUN* disrespect or damage to something people regard as sacred.
▷ **sacrilegious** *adjective*
[from Latin *sacer* = sacred + *legere* = take away]

sacrosanct *ADJECTIVE* sacred or respected and therefore not to be harmed.
[from Latin *sacro* = by a sacred rite + *sanctus* = holy]

sad *ADJECTIVE* **sadder, saddest** unhappy; showing or causing sorrow.
▷ **sadly** *adverb* **sadness** *noun*
[from Old English]

sadden *VERB* **saddens, saddening, saddened** make a person sad.

saddle *NOUN* **saddles 1** a seat for putting on the back of a horse or other animal. **2** the seat of a bicycle. **3** a ridge of high land between two peaks.

saddle *VERB* **saddles, saddling, saddled** put a saddle on a horse etc.
- **saddle someone with** burden someone with a task or problem.
[from Old English]

sadist (*say* say-dist) *NOUN* **sadists** a person who enjoys hurting or humiliating other people.
▷ **sadism** *noun* **sadistic** *adjective*
[named after a French novelist, the Marquis de *Sade*, noted for the cruelties in his stories]

s.a.e. *ABBREVIATION* stamped addressed envelope.

safari *NOUN* **safaris** an expedition to see or hunt wild animals.
[from Arabic *safar* = a journey]

safari park *NOUN* **safari parks** a park where wild animals are kept in large enclosures to be seen by visitors.

safe *ADJECTIVE* **1** not in danger. **2** not dangerous • *Drive at a safe speed.*
▷ **safely** *adverb* **safeness** *noun* **safety** *noun*

safe *NOUN* **safes** a strong cupboard or box in which valuables can be locked safely.
[from old French; related to *save*]

safeguard *NOUN* **safeguards** a protection.

safeguard *VERB* **safeguards, safeguarding, safeguarded** protect.

safe sex *NOUN* sexual activity in which precautions, such as using a condom, are taken to prevent the spread of Aids or other infections.

safety pin *NOUN* **safety pins** a U-shaped pin with a clip fastening over the point.

saffron *NOUN* **1** deep yellow colour. **2** a kind of crocus with orange-coloured stigmas. **3** these stigmas dried and used to colour or flavour food.
[from Arabic]

sag *VERB* **sags, sagging, sagged 1** go down in the middle because something heavy is pressing on it. **2** hang down loosely; droop.
▷ **sag** *noun*
[from old German]

saga (*say* sah-ga) *NOUN* **sagas** a long story with many episodes or adventures.
[from Old Norse]

sagacious (*say* sa-gay-shus) *ADJECTIVE* shrewd and wise.
▷ **sagaciously** *adverb* **sagacity** *noun*
[from Latin]

sage[1] *NOUN* a kind of herb used in cooking and formerly used in medicine.
[from Latin *salvia* = healing plant]

sage[2] *ADJECTIVE* wise.
▷ **sagely** *adverb*

sage *NOUN* **sages** a wise and respected person.
[from Latin *sapere* = to be wise]

sago *NOUN* a starchy white food used to make puddings.
[from Malay (a language spoken in Malaysia)]

said *past tense of* **say**.

sail *NOUN* **sails 1** a large piece of strong cloth attached to a mast etc. to catch the wind and make a ship or boat move. **2** a short voyage. **3** an arm of a windmill.
- **set sail** start on a voyage in a ship.

sail *VERB* **sails, sailing, sailed 1** travel in a ship or boat. **2** start a voyage • *We sail at noon.* **3** control a ship or boat. **4** move quickly and smoothly.
▷ **sailing ship** *noun*
[from Old English]

sailboard *NOUN* **sailboards** a flat board with a mast and sail, used in windsurfing.

sailor *NOUN* **sailors** a person who sails; a member of a ship's crew or of a navy.

saint *NOUN* **saints** a holy or very good person.
▷ **saintly** *adverb* **saintliness** *noun*
[via Old English from Latin *sanctus* = holy]

sake *NOUN*
- **for the sake of** in order to get or achieve something • *He'll do anything for the sake of money.*
- **for someone's sake** so as to help or please them • *Don't go to any trouble for my sake.*
[from Old English]

salad *NOUN* **salads** a mixture of vegetables eaten raw or cold.
[from French]

salamander *NOUN* **salamanders** a lizard-like amphibian formerly thought to live in fire.
[from Greek]

salami *NOUN* a spiced sausage, originally made in Italy.
[Italian]

salary *NOUN* **salaries** a regular wage, usually for a year's work, paid in monthly instalments.
▷ **salaried** *adjective*
[from Latin *salarium* = salt-money, money given to Roman soldiers to buy salt]

sale *NOUN* **sales 1** selling. **2** a time when things are sold at reduced prices.
- **for sale** or **on sale** available to be bought.
[from Old Norse]

salesperson *NOUN* **salespersons** a person employed to sell goods.
▷ **salesman** *noun* **salesmen**
saleswoman *noun* **saleswomen**

salient (*say* say-lee-ent) *ADJECTIVE* **1** most noticeable or important • *the salient features of the plan.* **2** jutting out; projecting.
[from Latin *saliens* = leaping]

saline *ADJECTIVE* containing salt.
[from Latin *sal* = salt]

saliva *NOUN* the natural liquid in a person's or animal's mouth.
▷ **salivary** *adjective*
[Latin]

salivate (*say* sal-iv-ayt) *VERB* **salivates, salivating, salivated** form saliva, especially a large amount.
▷ **salivation** *noun*

sallow *ADJECTIVE* (said about the skin) slightly yellow.
▷ **sallowness** *noun*
[from Old English]

sally *NOUN* **sallies 1** a sudden rush forward. **2** an excursion. **3** a lively or witty remark.

sally *VERB* **sallies, sallying, sallied** make a sudden attack or an excursion.
[same origin as *salient*]

salmon (*say* sam-on) *NOUN* **salmon** a large edible fish with pink flesh.
[from Latin]

salmonella (*say* sal-mon-el-a) *NOUN* a bacterium that can cause food poisoning.
[named after an American scientist, Elmer *Salmon*, who studied the causes of disease]

salon *NOUN* **salons 1** a large elegant room. **2** a room or shop where a hairdresser etc. receives customers.
[French]

saloon *NOUN* **saloons 1** a car with a hard roof and a separate boot. **2** a place where alcoholic drinks are bought and drunk, especially a comfortable bar in a pub.
[from French *salon*]

salsa *NOUN* **1** a hot spicy sauce. **2** a kind of modern Latin American dance music; a dance to this.
[Spanish, = sauce]

salt *NOUN* **salts 1** sodium chloride, the white substance that gives sea water its taste and is used for flavouring food. **2** a chemical compound of a metal and an acid.
▷ **salty** *adjective*

salt *VERB* **salts, salting, salted** flavour or preserve food with salt.
[from Old English]

salt cellar *NOUN* **salt cellars** a small dish or perforated pot holding salt for use at meals.
[*cellar* from old French *salier* = salt- box]

salts *PLURAL NOUN* a substance that looks like salt, especially a laxative.

salubrious *ADJECTIVE* good for people's health.
▷ **salubrity** *noun*
[from Latin *salus* = health]

salutary *ADJECTIVE* beneficial; having a good effect • *She gave us some salutary advice.*
[same origin as *salubrious*]

salutation *NOUN* **salutations** a greeting.

salute *VERB* **salutes, saluting, saluted** **1** raise your right hand to your forehead as a sign of respect. **2** greet. **3** say that you respect or admire something • *We salute this achievement.*

salute *NOUN* **salutes 1** the act of saluting. **2** the firing of guns as a sign of greeting or respect.
[same origin as *salubrious*]

salvage *VERB* **salvages, salvaging, salvaged** save or rescue something such as a damaged ship's cargo so that it can be used again.
▷ **salvage** *noun*
[from Latin *salvare* = save]

salvation *NOUN* **1** saving from loss or damage etc. **2** (in Christian teaching) saving the soul from sin and its consequences.
[same origin as *salvage*]

salve *NOUN* **salves 1** a soothing ointment. **2** something that soothes.

salve *VERB* **salves, salving, salved** soothe a person's conscience or wounded pride.
[from Old English]

salver *NOUN* **salvers** a small tray, usually of metal.
[via French from Spanish]

salvo *NOUN* **salvoes** or **salvos** a volley of shots or of applause.
[from Italian *salva* = salutation]

same *ADJECTIVE* **1** of one kind, exactly alike or equal. **2** not changing; not different.
▷ **sameness** *noun*
[from Old Norse]

samosa *NOUN* **samosas** a triangular, thin pastry case filled with spicy meat or vegetables, fried and eaten as a snack.
[from Urdu]

samovar *NOUN* **samovars** a Russian tea urn.
[Russian, = self- boiler]

sampan *NOUN* **sampans** a small flat-bottomed boat used in China.
[from Chinese *sanpan* (*san* = three, *pan* = boards)]

sample *NOUN* **samples** a small amount that shows what something is like; a specimen.

sample *VERB* **samples, sampling, sampled** **1** take a sample of something. **2** try part of something.
[from old French *essample* = example]

sampler *NOUN* **samplers** a piece of embroidery worked in various stitches to show skill in needlework.
[same origin as *sample*]

samurai (*say* **sam**-oor-eye or **sam**-yoor-eye) *NOUN* **samurai** a member of an ancient Japanese warrior caste.
[Japanese]

sanatorium *NOUN* **sanatoriums** or **sanatoria** a hospital for treating chronic diseases or convalescents.
[from Latin *sanare* = heal]

sanctify *VERB* **sanctifies, sanctifying, sanctified** make holy or sacred.
▷ **sanctification** *noun*
[from Latin *sanctus* = holy]

sanctimonious *ADJECTIVE* making a show of being virtuous or pious.
[from Latin *sanctimonia* = holiness, piety]

sanction *NOUN* **sanctions 1** action taken against a nation that is considered to have broken an international law etc. • *Sanctions against that country include refusing to trade with it.* **2** a penalty for disobeying a law. **3** permission or authorization.

sanction *VERB* **sanctions, sanctioning, sanctioned** permit or authorize.
[from Latin *sancire* = make holy]

sanctity *NOUN* being sacred; holiness.
[same origin as *sanctify*]

sanctuary *NOUN* **sanctuaries 1** a safe place; a refuge. **2** an area where wildlife is protected • *a bird sanctuary*. **3** a sacred place; the part of a church where the altar stands.
[same origin as *sanctify*]

sanctum *NOUN* **sanctums** a person's private room.
[Latin, = holy thing]

sand *NOUN* the tiny particles that cover the ground in deserts, seashores, etc.

sand *VERB* **sands, sanding, sanded** smooth or polish with sandpaper or some other rough material.
▷ **sander** *noun*
[from Old English]

sandal *NOUN* **sandals** a lightweight shoe with straps over the foot.
▷ **sandalled** *adjective*
[from Greek *sandalon* = wooden shoe]

sandalwood *NOUN* a scented wood from a tropical tree.
[via Latin, Greek, and Persian from Sanskrit]

sandbag *NOUN* **sandbags** a bag filled with sand, used to build defences.

sandbank *NOUN* **sandbanks** a bank of sand under water.

sandpaper *NOUN* strong paper coated with sand or a similar substance, rubbed on rough surfaces to make them smooth.

sands *PLURAL NOUN* a beach or sandy area.

sandstone *NOUN* rock made of compressed sand.

sandwich *NOUN* **sandwiches** two or more slices of bread with jam, meat, or cheese etc. between them.

sandwich *VERB* **sandwiches, sandwiching, sandwiched** put a thing between two other things.
[invented by the Earl of *Sandwich* (1718-92) so that he could eat while gambling]

sandwich course *NOUN* **sandwich courses** a college or university course which includes periods in industry or business.

sandy *ADJECTIVE* **1** like sand. **2** covered with sand. **3** yellowish-red • *sandy hair*.
▷ **sandiness** *noun*

sane *ADJECTIVE* **1** having a healthy mind; not mad. **2** sensible.
▷ **sanely** *adverb* **sanity** *noun*
[from Latin *sanus* = healthy]

sang-froid (*say* sahn-**frwah**) *NOUN* calmness in danger or difficulty.
[French, = cold blood]

sanguinary *ADJECTIVE* **1** bloodthirsty. **2** involving much violence and slaughter.
[from Latin *sanguis* = blood]

sanguine (*say* sang-gwin) *ADJECTIVE* hopeful; cheerful and optimistic.
[same origin as *sanguinary* (because good blood was believed to be the cause of cheerfulness)]

sanitary *ADJECTIVE* **1** free from germs and dirt; hygienic. **2** to do with sanitation.
[from Latin *sanitas* = health]

sanitary towel *NOUN* **sanitary towels** an absorbent pad worn by women during menstruation.

sanitation *NOUN* arrangements for drainage and the disposal of sewage.
[from *sanitary*]

sanitize *VERB* **sanitizes, sanitizing, sanitized 1** make sanitary; clean and disinfect. **2** make less unpleasant by taking out anything that might shock or offend • *sanitized stories of 'the good old days'*.

sanity *NOUN* being sane.

Sanskrit *NOUN* the ancient and sacred language of the Hindus in India.

sap *NOUN* the liquid inside a plant, carrying food to all its parts.

sap *VERB* **saps, sapping, sapped** take away a person's strength gradually.
[from Old English]

sapling *NOUN* **saplings** a young tree.
[from *sap*]

sapphire *NOUN* **sapphires** a bright-blue jewel.
[from Latin]

Saracen *NOUN* **Saracens** an Arab or Muslim of the time of the Crusades.

sarcastic *ADJECTIVE* saying amusing or contemptuous things that hurt someone's feelings.
▷ **sarcastically** *adverb* **sarcasm** *noun*
[from Greek *sarkazein* = tear the flesh]

sarcophagus *NOUN* **sarcophagi** a stone coffin, often decorated with carvings.
[from Greek *sarkos* = of flesh + *-phagos* = eating]

sardine *NOUN* **sardines** a small sea fish, usually sold in tins, packed tightly in oil.
[from French]

sardonic *ADJECTIVE* funny in a grim or sarcastic way.
▷ **sardonically** *adverb*
[from French]

sari *NOUN* **saris** a length of cloth worn wrapped round the body as a dress, especially by Indian women and girls.
[from Hindi]

sarong *NOUN* **sarongs** a strip of cloth worn like a kilt by men and women of Malaya and Java.
[from Malay (a language spoken in Malaysia)]

sartorial *ADJECTIVE* to do with clothes.
[from Latin *sartor* = tailor]

sash *NOUN* **sashes** a strip of cloth worn round the waist or over one shoulder.
[from Arabic *shash* = turban]

sash window *NOUN* **sash windows** a window that slides up and down.
[from *chassis*]

SAT *ABBREVIATION* standard assessment task.

satanic (*say* sa-tan-ik) *ADJECTIVE* to do with or like Satan, the Devil in Jewish and Christian teaching.

satchel *NOUN* **satchels** a bag worn on the shoulder or the back, especially for carrying books to and from school.
[from Latin *saccellus* = little sack]

sate *VERB* **sates, sating, sated** satisfy fully; satiate.
[from Old English]

satellite *NOUN* **satellites 1** a spacecraft put in orbit round a planet to collect information or transmit communications signals. **2** a moon moving in an orbit round a planet. **3** a country that is under the influence of a more powerful neighbouring country.
[from Latin *satelles* = a guard]

satellite dish *NOUN* **satellite dishes** a bowl-shaped aerial for receiving broadcasting signals transmitted by satellite.

satellite television *NOUN* television broadcasting in which the signals are transmitted by means of a communications satellite.

satiate (*say* say-shee-ayt) *VERB* **satiates, satiating, satiated** satisfy an appetite or desire etc. fully.
[from Latin *satis* = enough]

satiety (*say* sat-I-it-ee) *NOUN* being or feeling satiated.

satin *NOUN* a silky material that is shiny on one side.
▷ **satiny** *adjective*
[via old French from Arabic]

satire *NOUN* **satires 1** using humour or exaggeration to show what is bad or weak about a person or thing, especially the government. **2** a play or poem etc. that does this.
▷ **satirical** *adjective* **satirically** *adverb*
satirist *noun* **satirize** *verb*
[from Latin]
USAGE Do not confuse with **satyr**.

satisfaction *NOUN* **1** satisfying. **2** being satisfied and pleased because of this. **3** something that satisfies a desire etc.
[from Latin *satis* = enough + *facere* = make]

satisfactory *ADJECTIVE* good enough; sufficient.
▷ **satisfactorily** *adverb*

satisfy *VERB* **satisfies, satisfying, satisfied** **1** give someone what they need or want. **2** make someone feel certain; convince • *The police are satisfied that the death was accidental.* **3** fulfil • *You have satisfied all our requirements.*
[same origin as *satisfaction*]

satsuma *NOUN* **satsumas** a kind of mandarin orange originally grown in Japan.
[named after *Satsuma*, a province of Japan]

saturate *VERB* **saturates, saturating, saturated** **1** make a thing very wet. **2** make something take in as much as possible of a substance or goods etc.
▷ **saturation** *noun*
[from Latin *satur* = full, satiated]

Saturday *NOUN* the day of the week following Friday.
[from Old English *Saeternesdaeg* = day of Saturn, a Roman god]

A B C D E F G H I J K L M N O P Q R S T U V W X Y Z

saturnine *ADJECTIVE* looking gloomy and forbidding • *a saturnine face.*
[because people born under the influence of the planet Saturn were believed to be gloomy]

satyr (*say* sat-er) *NOUN* **satyrs** (in Greek myths) a woodland god with a man's body and a goat's ears, tail, and legs.
USAGE Do not confuse with **satire**.

sauce *NOUN* **sauces 1** a thick liquid served with food to add flavour. **2** (*informal*) being cheeky; impudence.
[from Latin *salsus* = salted]

saucepan *NOUN* **saucepans** a metal cooking pan with a handle at the side.

saucer *NOUN* **saucers** a small shallow object on which a cup etc. is placed.
[from old French *saussier* = container for sauce]

saucy *ADJECTIVE* **saucier**, **sauciest** cheeky or impudent.
▷ **saucily** *adverb* **sauciness** *noun*

sauerkraut (*say* sour-krowt) *NOUN* chopped and pickled cabbage, originally made in Germany.
[from German *sauer* = sour + *Kraut* = cabbage]

sauna *NOUN* **saunas** a room or compartment filled with steam, used as a kind of bath.
[Finnish]

saunter *VERB* **saunters**, **sauntering**, **sauntered** walk slowly and casually.
▷ **saunter** *noun*
[origin unknown]

sausage *NOUN* **sausages** a tube of skin or plastic stuffed with minced meat and other filling.
[from old French; related to *sauce*]

savage *ADJECTIVE* wild and fierce; cruel.
▷ **savagely** *adverb* **savageness** *noun* **savagery** *noun*

savage *NOUN* **savages 1** a savage person. **2** (*old use*) a member of a people thought of as primitive or uncivilized.

savage *VERB* **savages**, **savaging**, **savaged** attack fiercely by biting or scratching • *The sheep was savaged by a dog.*
[from Latin *silvaticus* = of the woods, wild]

savannah or **savanna** *NOUN* **savannahs** or **savannas** a grassy plain in a hot country, with few or no trees.
[via Spanish from Taino (a South American language)]

save *VERB* **saves**, **saving**, **saved 1** keep safe; free a person or thing from danger or harm. **2** keep something, especially money, so that it can be used later. **3** avoid wasting something • *This will save time.* **4** (*in computing*) keep data by storing it in the computer's memory or on a disk. **5** (in sports) prevent an opponent from scoring.
▷ **save** *noun* **saver** *noun*

save *PREPOSITION* except • *All the trains save one were late.*
[from old French; related to *salvage*]

savings *PLURAL NOUN* money saved.

saviour *NOUN* **saviours** a person who saves someone.
- **the our Saviour** (in Christianity) Jesus Christ.

savoir faire (*say* sav-wahr **fair**) *NOUN* knowledge of how to behave socially.
[French, = knowing how to do]

savour *NOUN* **savours** the taste or smell of something.

savour *VERB* **savours**, **savouring**, **savoured 1** enjoy the taste or smell of something. **2** have a certain taste or smell.
[from Latin *sapor* = flavour]

savoury *ADJECTIVE* **1** tasty but not sweet. **2** having an appetizing taste or smell.

savoury *NOUN* **savouries** a savoury dish.

savoy *NOUN* **savoys** a kind of cabbage with wrinkled leaves.
[named after *Savoie*, a region in France]

saw[1] *NOUN* **saws** a tool with a zigzag edge for cutting wood or metal etc.

saw *VERB* **saws**, **sawing**, **sawed**, **sawn** **1** cut something with a saw. **2** move to and fro as a saw does.
[from Old English]

saw[2] *past tense* of **see**[1].

sawdust *NOUN* powder that comes from wood cut by a saw.

sawmill *NOUN* **sawmills** a mill where timber is cut into planks etc. by machinery.

Saxon *NOUN* **Saxons 1** a member of a people who came from Europe and occupied parts of England in the 5th-6th centuries. **2** an Anglo-Saxon.

saxophone *NOUN* **saxophones** a brass wind instrument with a reed in the mouthpiece.
▷ **saxophonist** *noun*
[named after a Belgian instrument maker, Adolphe *Sax*, who invented it]

say *VERB* **says, saying, said 1** speak or express something in words. **2** give an opinion.

say *NOUN* the power to decide something • *I have no say in the matter.*
[from Old English]

saying *NOUN* **sayings** a well-known phrase or proverb or other statement.

scab *NOUN* **scabs 1** a hard crust that forms over a cut or graze while it is healing. **2** (*offensive*) a blackleg.
▷ **scabby** *adjective*
[from Old Norse]

scabbard *NOUN* **scabbards** the sheath of a sword or dagger.
[from old French]

scabies (*say* skay-beez) *NOUN* a contagious skin disease with severe itching, caused by a parasite.
[Latin, from *scabere* = to scratch]

scaffold *NOUN* **scaffolds** a platform on which criminals are executed.
[from old French; related to *catafalque*]

scaffolding *NOUN* a structure of poles or tubes and planks making platforms for workers to stand on while building or repairing a house etc.

scald *VERB* **scalds, scalding, scalded 1** burn yourself with very hot liquid or steam. **2** heat milk until it is nearly boiling. **3** clean pans etc. with boiling water.
▷ **scald** *noun*
[from Latin *excaldare* = wash in hot water]

scale[1] *NOUN* **scales 1** a series of units, degrees, or qualities etc. for measuring something. **2** a series of musical notes going up or down in a fixed pattern. **3** proportion or ratio • *The scale of this map is one centimetre to the kilometre.* **4** the relative size or importance of something • *They organize parties on a large scale.*
- **to scale** with the parts in the same proportions as those of an original • *The architect's plans were drawn to scale.*

scale *VERB* **scales, scaling, scaled** climb • *She scaled the ladder.*
- **scale down** or **up** reduce or increase at a fixed rate, or in proportion to something else.
[from Latin *scala* = ladder]

scale[2] *NOUN* **scales 1** each of the thin overlapping parts on the outside of fish, snakes, etc.; a thin flake or part like this. **2** a hard substance formed in a kettle or boiler by hard water, or on teeth.

scale *VERB* **scales, scaling, scaled** remove scales or scale from something.
[from old French; related to *scales*]

scale model *NOUN* **scale models** a model of something, made to scale.

scalene (*say* skay-leen) *ADJECTIVE* (said about a triangle) having unequal sides.
[from Greek *skalenos* = unequal]

scales *PLURAL NOUN* a device for weighing things.
[from Old Norse *skal* = bowl]

scallop *NOUN* **scallops 1** a shellfish with two hinged fan-shaped shells. **2** each curve in an ornamental wavy border.
▷ **scalloped** *adjective*
[from old French]

scalp *NOUN* **scalps** the skin on the top of the head.

scalp *VERB* **scalps, scalping, scalped** cut or tear the scalp from.
[probably from a Scandinavian language]

scalpel *NOUN* **scalpels** a small knife with a thin, sharp blade, used by a surgeon or artist.
[from Latin]

scaly *ADJECTIVE* **scalier, scaliest** covered in scales or scale.

A B C D E F G H I J K L M N O P Q R **S** T U V W X Y

scam *NOUN* **scams** (*slang*) a dishonest scheme; a swindle.
[originally American; origin unknown]

scamp *NOUN* **scamps** a rascal.
[same origin as *scamper*]

scamper *VERB* **scampers, scampering, scampered** run quickly, lightly, or playfully.
▷ **scamper** *noun*
[originally = run away, decamp; probably via old Dutch from Latin *ex-* = away + *campus* = field]

scampi *PLURAL NOUN* large prawns.
[Italian]

scan *VERB* **scans, scanning, scanned 1** look at every part of something. **2** glance at something. **3** count the beats of a line of poetry; be correct in rhythm • *This line doesn't scan.* **4** sweep a radar or electronic beam over an area to examine it or in search of something.

scan *NOUN* **scans 1** scanning. **2** an examination using a scanner • *a brain scan.*
[from Latin]

scandal *NOUN* **scandals 1** something shameful or disgraceful. **2** gossip about people's faults and wrongdoing.
▷ **scandalous** *adjective*
[from Greek *skandalon* = stumbling block]

scandalize *VERB* **scandalizes, scandalizing, scandalized** shock a person by something considered shameful or disgraceful.

scandalmonger *NOUN* **scandalmongers** a person who invents or spreads scandal.
[from *scandal* + an old word *monger* = trader]

Scandinavian *ADJECTIVE* from or to do with Scandinavia (= Norway, Sweden, and Denmark; sometimes also Finland and Iceland).
▷ **Scandinavian** *noun*

scanner *NOUN* **scanners 1** a machine that examines things by means of light or other rays. **2** a machine that converts printed text, pictures, etc. into chine-readable form.

nsion *NOUN* the scanning of verse.

scant *ADJECTIVE* barely enough or adequate • *We paid scant attention.*

scanty *ADJECTIVE* **scantier, scantiest** small in amount or extent; meagre • *a scanty harvest.*
▷ **scantily** *adverb* **scantiness** *noun*
[from Old Norse]

scapegoat *NOUN* **scapegoats** a person who is made to bear the blame or punishment for what others have done.
[named after the *goat* which the ancient Jews allowed to *escape* into the desert after the priest had symbolically laid the people's sins upon it]

scar[1] *NOUN* **scars 1** the mark left by a cut or burn etc. after it has healed. **2** a lasting effect left by an unpleasant experience.

scar *VERB* **scars, scarring, scarred** make a scar or scars on skin.
[from Latin]

scar[2] *NOUN* **scars** a steep craggy place.
[from Old Norse]

scarab *NOUN* **scarabs** an ancient Egyptian ornament or symbol carved in the shape of a beetle.
[from Latin *scarabaeus* = beetle]

scarce *ADJECTIVE* **scarcer, scarcest 1** not enough to supply people. **2** rare.
▷ **scarcity** *noun*
- **make yourself scarce** (*informal*) go away; keep out of the way.
[from old French]

scarcely *ADVERB* only just; only with difficulty • *She could scarcely walk.*

scare *VERB* **scares, scaring, scared** frighten.

scare *NOUN* **scares 1** a fright. **2** a sudden widespread sense of alarm about something • *a bomb scare.*
[from Old Norse]

scarecrow *NOUN* **scarecrows** a figure of a person dressed in old clothes, set up to frighten birds away from crops.

scaremonger *NOUN* **scaremongers** a person who spreads scare stories.
[from *scare* + an old word *monger* = trader]

scare story *NOUN* **scare stories** an inaccurate or exaggerated account of something which makes people worry unnecessarily.

scarf *NOUN* **scarves** a strip of material worn round the neck or head.
[from old French]

scarlet *ADJECTIVE* & *NOUN* bright red.
[via old French and Arabic from Latin]

scarlet fever *NOUN* an infectious fever producing a scarlet rash.

scarp *NOUN* **scarps** a steep slope on a hill.
[from Italian]

scarper *VERB* **scarpers, scarpering, scarpered** (*informal*) run away.
[probably from Italian *scappare* = escape]

scary *ADJECTIVE* (*informal*) frightening.

scathing (*say* skayth-ing) *ADJECTIVE* severely criticizing a person or thing.
[from Old Norse *skatha* = injure or damage]

scatter *VERB* **scatters, scattering, scattered** **1** throw or send things in all directions. **2** run or leave quickly in all directions.
[a different spelling of *shatter*]

scatterbrain *NOUN* **scatterbrains** a careless forgetful person.
▷ **scatterbrained** *adjective*

scavenge *VERB* **scavenges, scavenging, scavenged** **1** search for useful things amongst rubbish. **2** (said about a bird or animal) search for decaying flesh as food.
▷ **scavenger** *noun*
[from old French]

scenario *NOUN* **scenarios** **1** a summary of the plot of a play etc. **2** an imagined series of events or set of circumstances.
[Italian]
USAGE Note that this word does not mean the same as *scene*.

scene *NOUN* **scenes** **1** the place where something has happened • *the scene of the crime*. **2** a part of a play or film. **3** a view as seen by a spectator. **4** an angry or noisy outburst • *He made a scene about the money*. **5** stage scenery. **6** an area of activity • *the local music scene*.
[from Greek *skene* = stage]

scenery *NOUN* **1** the natural features of a landscape. **2** things put on a stage to make it look like a place.

scenic *ADJECTIVE* having fine natural scenery • *a scenic road along the coast*.

scent *NOUN* **scents** **1** a pleasant smell. **2** a liquid perfume. **3** an animal's smell that other animals can detect.

scent *VERB* **scents, scenting, scented**
1 discover something by its scent; detect.
2 put scent on or in something; make fragrant • *scented soap*.
▷ **scented** *adjective*
[from Latin]

sceptic (*say* skep-tik) *NOUN* **sceptics** a sceptical person.

sceptical (*say* skep-tik-al) *ADJECTIVE* inclined to question things; not believing easily.
▷ **sceptically** *adverb* **scepticism** *noun*
[from Greek *skeptikos* = thoughtful]

sceptre *NOUN* **sceptres** a rod carried by a king or queen as a symbol of power.
[from old French]

schedule (*say* shed-yool) *NOUN* **schedules** a programme or timetable of planned events or work.
- **on schedule** on time according to a schedule.

schedule *VERB* **schedules, scheduling, scheduled** **1** put into a schedule. **2** arrange something for a certain time.
[from Latin *scedula* = little piece of paper]

schematic (*say* skee-mat-ik) *ADJECTIVE* in the form of a diagram or chart.
[same origin as *scheme*]

scheme *NOUN* **schemes** a plan of action.

scheme *VERB* **schemes, scheming, schemed** make plans; plot.
▷ **schemer** *noun*
[from Greek *schema* = form]

scherzo (*say* skairts-oh) *NOUN* **scherzos** a lively piece of music.
[Italian, = joke]

schism (*say* sizm) *NOUN* **schisms** the splitting of a group into two opposing sections because they disagree about something important.
[from Greek *schisma* = a split]

schizophrenia (*say* skid-zo-free-nee-a) *NOUN* a kind of mental illness in which people cannot relate their thoughts and feelings to reality.
▷ **schizophrenic** *adjective* & *noun*
[from Greek *schizein* = to split + *phren* = mind]

scholar *NOUN* **scholars 1** a person who has studied a subject thoroughly. **2** a person who has been awarded a scholarship.
▷ **scholarly** *adjective*
[from Latin *scholaris* = to do with a school]

scholarship *NOUN* **scholarships 1** a grant of money given to someone to help to pay for his or her education. **2** scholars' knowledge or methods; advanced study.

scholastic *ADJECTIVE* to do with schools or education; academic.
[from Greek *scholastikos* = studious]

school[1] *NOUN* **schools 1** a place where teaching is done, especially of pupils aged 5-18. **2** the pupils in a school. **3** the time when teaching takes place in a school • *School ends at 4.30 p.m.* **4** a group of people who have the same beliefs or style of work etc.

school *VERB* **schools, schooling, schooled** teach or train • *She was schooling her horse for the competition.*
[from Greek]

school[2] *NOUN* **schools** a shoal of fish or whales etc.
[from old German or old Dutch *schole* = a troop]

schoolchild *NOUN* **schoolchildren** a child who goes to school.
▷ **schoolboy** *noun* **schoolgirl** *noun*

schooling *NOUN* **1** training. **2** education, especially in a school.

schoolteacher *NOUN* **schoolteachers** a person who teaches in a school.
▷ **schoolmaster** *noun* **schoolmistress** *noun*

schooner (*say* skoon-er) *NOUN* **schooners 1** a sailing ship with two or more masts. **2** a tall glass for serving sherry.
[origin unknown]

sciatica (*say* sy-at-ik-a) *NOUN* pain in the sciatic nerve (a large nerve in the hip and ...gh).
...tin]

science *NOUN* **1** the study of the physical world by means of observation and experiment. **2** a branch of this, such as chemistry, physics, or biology.
[from Latin *scientia* = knowledge]

science fiction *NOUN* stories about imaginary scientific discoveries or space travel and life on other planets.

science park *NOUN* **science parks** an area set up for industries using science or for organizations doing scientific research.

scientific *ADJECTIVE* **1** to do with science or scientists. **2** studying things systematically and testing ideas carefully.
▷ **scientifically** *adverb*

scientist *NOUN* **scientists 1** an expert in science. **2** someone who uses scientific methods.

scimitar (*say* sim-it-ar) *NOUN* **scimitars** a curved oriental sword.
[from French or Italian]

scintillate *VERB* **scintillates, scintillating, scintillated 1** sparkle. **2** be lively and witty • *The conversation was scintillating.*
▷ **scintillation** *noun*
[from Latin *scintilla* = spark]

scion (*say* sy-on) *NOUN* **scions** a descendant, especially of a noble family.
[from Old French *cion* = a twig or shoot]

scissors *PLURAL NOUN* a cutting instrument used with one hand, with two blades pivoted so that they can close against each other.
[from Latin *scissum* = cut]

scoff[1] *VERB* **scoffs, scoffing, scoffed** jeer; speak contemptuously.
▷ **scoffer** *noun*
[probably from a Scandinavian language]

scoff[2] *VERB* **scoffs, scoffing, scoffed** (*informal*) eat greedily; eat up.
[from a dialect word *scaff* = food]

scold *VERB* **scolds, scolding, scolded** speak angrily; tell someone off.
▷ **scolding** *noun*
[probably from Old Norse]

scone (*say* skon or skohn) *NOUN* **scones** a soft flat cake, usually eaten with butter.
[origin unknown]

scoop *NOUN* **scoops 1** a kind of deep spoon for serving ice cream etc. **2** a deep shovel for lifting grain, sugar, etc. **3** a scooping movement. **4** an important piece of news published by only one newspaper.

scoop *VERB* **scoops, scooping, scooped** lift or hollow something out with a scoop.
[from old German or old Dutch]

scoot *VERB* **scoots, scooting, scooted**
1 propel a bicycle or scooter by sitting or standing on it and pushing it along with one foot. **2** run or go away quickly.
[origin unknown]

scooter *NOUN* **scooters 1** a kind of motorcycle with small wheels. **2** a board with wheels and a long handle, which you ride on by scooting.
[from *scoot*]

scope *NOUN* **1** opportunity or possibility for something • *There is scope for improvement.*
2 the range or extent of a subject.
[from Greek *skopos* = target]

scorch *VERB* **scorches, scorching, scorched** make something go brown by burning it slightly.
[origin unknown]

scorching *ADJECTIVE* (*informal*) very hot.

score *NOUN* **scores** or, in sense 2, **score 1** the number of points or goals made in a game; a result. **2** (*old use*) twenty • *'Three score years and ten' means 3 x 20 + 10 = 70 years.*
3 written or printed music.
- **on that score** for that reason, because of that • *You needn't worry on that score.*

score *VERB* **scores, scoring, scored 1** get a point or goal in a game. **2** keep a count of the score. **3** mark with lines or cuts. **4** write out a musical score.
▷ **scorer** *noun*
[from Old Norse]

scores *PLURAL NOUN* many; a large number.

scorn *NOUN* contempt.
▷ **scornful** *adjective* **scornfully** *adverb*

scorn *VERB* **scorns, scorning, scorned**
1 treat someone with contempt. **2** refuse something scornfully.
[via old French from Germanic]

scorpion *NOUN* **scorpions** an animal that looks like a tiny lobster, with a poisonous sting.
[from Greek]

Scot *NOUN* **Scots** a person who comes from Scotland.

scotch[1] *NOUN* whisky made in Scotland.
[from *Scottish*]

scotch[2] *VERB* **scotches, scotching, scotched** put an end to an idea or rumour etc.
[origin unknown]

Scotch egg *NOUN* **Scotch eggs** a hard-boiled egg enclosed in sausage meat and fried.

Scotch terrier *NOUN* **Scotch terriers** a breed of terrier with rough hair.

scot-free *ADJECTIVE* without harm or punishment.
[from *scot* = a form of tax + *free*]

Scots *ADJECTIVE* from or belonging to Scotland.
USAGE See note at **Scottish**.

Scottish *ADJECTIVE* to do with or belonging to Scotland.
USAGE *Scottish* is the most widely used word for describing things to do with Scotland: *Scottish education, Scottish mountains. Scots* is less common and is mainly used to describe people: *a Scots girl. Scotch* is only used in fixed expressions like *Scotch egg* and *Scotch terrier.*

scoundrel *NOUN* **scoundrels** a wicked or dishonest person.
[origin unknown]

scour[1] *VERB* **scours, scouring, scoured**
1 rub something until it is clean and bright.
2 clear a channel or pipe by the force of water flowing through it.
▷ **scourer** *noun*
[from *ex-* + *curare* = take care of, clean]

scour[2] *VERB* **scours, scouring, scoured** search thoroughly.
[origin unknown]

scourge (*say* skerj) *NOUN* **scourges 1** a whip for flogging people. **2** something that inflicts suffering or punishment.
[from *ex-* + Latin *corrigia* = whip]

Scout *NOUN* **Scouts** a member of the Scout Association, an organization for boys.

scout *NOUN* **scouts** someone sent out to collect information.

scout *VERB* **scouts, scouting, scouted** **1** act as a scout. **2** search an area thoroughly.
[from Latin *auscultare* = listen]

scowl *NOUN* **scowls** a bad-tempered frown.

scowl *VERB* **scowls, scowling, scowled** make a scowl.
[probably from a Scandinavian language]

Scrabble *NOUN* (*trademark*) a game played on a board, in which words are built up from single letters.

scrabble *VERB* **scrabbles, scrabbling, scrabbled** **1** scratch or claw at something with the hands or feet. **2** grope or struggle to get something.
[from old Dutch]

scraggy *ADJECTIVE* thin and bony.
[origin unknown]

scram *VERB* (*slang*) go away!
[probably from *scramble*]

scramble *VERB* **scrambles, scrambling, scrambled** **1** move quickly and awkwardly. **2** struggle to do or get something. **3** (said about aircraft or their crew) hurry and take off quickly. **4** cook eggs by mixing them up and heating them in a pan. **5** mix things together. **6** alter a radio or telephone signal so that it cannot be used without a decoding device.
▷ **scrambler** *noun*

scramble *NOUN* **scrambles** **1** a climb or walk over rough ground. **2** a struggle to do or get something. **3** a motorcycle race over rough country.
[origin unknown]

scrap[1] *NOUN* **scraps** **1** a small piece. **2** rubbish; waste material, especially metal that is suitable for reprocessing.

scrap *VERB* **scraps, scrapping, scrapped** get rid of something that is useless or unwanted.
[from Old Norse]

scrap[2] *NOUN* **scraps** (*informal*) a fight.

scrap *VERB* **scraps, scrapping, scrapped** (*informal*) fight.
[probably from *scrape*]

scrape *VERB* **scrapes, scraping, scraped** **1** clean or smooth or damage something by passing something hard over it. **2** make a harsh sound by rubbing against a rough or hard surface. **3** remove by scraping • *Scrape the mud off your shoes*. **4** get something by great effort or care • *They scraped together enough money for a holiday*.
▷ **scraper** *noun*
- **scrape through** succeed or pass an examination by only a small margin.

scrape *NOUN* **scrapes** **1** a scraping movement or sound. **2** a mark etc. made by scraping. **3** an awkward situation caused by mischief or foolishness.
[from Old English]

scrappy *ADJECTIVE* **1** made of scraps or bits or disconnected things. **2** carelessly done.
▷ **scrappiness** *noun*

scratch *VERB* **scratches, scratching, scratched** **1** mark or cut the surface of a thing with something sharp. **2** rub the skin with fingernails or claws because it itches. **3** withdraw from a race or competition.

scratch *NOUN* **scratches** **1** a mark made by scratching. **2** the action of scratching.
▷ **scratchy** *adjective*
- **start from scratch** start from the beginning or with nothing prepared.
- **up to scratch** up to the proper standard.
[origin unknown]

scratch card *NOUN* **scratch cards** a card you buy as part of a lottery; you scratch off part of the surface to see whether you have won a prize.

scrawl *NOUN* **scrawls** untidy handwriting.

scrawl *VERB* **scrawls, scrawling, scrawled** write in a scrawl.
[origin unknown]

scrawny *ADJECTIVE* scraggy.
[originally American; origin unknown]

scream *NOUN* **screams** **1** a loud cry of pain, fear, anger, or excitement. **2** a loud piercing sound. **3** (*informal*) a very amusing person or thing.

scream *VERB* **screams, screaming, screamed** make a scream.
[origin unknown]

scree *NOUN* a mass of loose stones on the side of a mountain.
[from Old Norse]

screech *NOUN* **screeches** a harsh high-pitched scream or sound.
▷ **screech** *verb*
[imitating the sound]

screed *NOUN* **screeds** a very long piece of writing.
[probably from Old English]

screen *NOUN* **screens 1** a movable panel used to hide, protect, or divide something. **2** a surface on which films or television pictures or computer data are shown. **3** a windscreen.

screen *VERB* **screens, screening, screened 1** protect, hide, or divide with a screen. **2** show a film or television pictures on a screen. **3** carry out tests on someone to find out if they have a disease. **4** check whether a person is suitable for a job.
[from old French]

screenplay *NOUN* **screenplays** the script of a film, with instructions to the actors etc.

screw *NOUN* **screws 1** a metal pin with a spiral ridge (the *thread*) round it, holding things together by being twisted in. **2** a twisting movement. **3** something twisted. **4** a propeller, especially for a ship or motor boat.

screw *VERB* **screws, screwing, screwed 1** fasten with a screw or screws. **2** fit ot turn something by twisting.
[from old French]

screwdriver *NOUN* **screwdrivers** a tool for turning screws.

scribble *VERB* **scribbles, scribbling, scribbled 1** write quickly or untidily or carelessly. **2** make meaningless marks.
▷ **scribble** *noun*
[same origin as *scribe*]

WORD FAMILY There are a number of English words that are related to *scribble* because part of their original meaning comes from the Latin words *scribere* meaning 'to write' or *scriptum* meaning 'written'. These include *ascribe*, *conscript*, *describe*, *inscribe*, *prescribe*, *proscribe*, *postscript*, *scribe*, *script*, *scripture*, *subscribe*, *superscript*, and *transcribe*.

scribe *NOUN* **scribes 1** a person who made copies of writings before printing was invented. **2** (in biblical times) a professional religious scholar.
▷ **scribal** *adjective*
[from Latin *scribere* = write]

scrimmage *NOUN* **scrimmages** a confused struggle.
[from *skirmish*]

scrimp *VERB* **scrimps, scrimping, scrimped** skimp • *scrimp and save.*
[origin unknown]

script *NOUN* **scripts 1** handwriting. **2** the text of a play, film, broadcast talk, etc.
[from Latin *scriptum* = written]

scripture *NOUN* **scriptures 1** sacred writings. **2** (in Christianity) the Bible.
[same origin as *script*]

scroll *NOUN* **scrolls 1** a roll of paper or parchment used for writing on. **2** a spiral design.

scroll *VERB* **scrolls, scrolling, scrolled** move the display on a computer screen up or down to see what comes before or after it.
[from old French]

scrotum (*say* skroh-tum) *NOUN* **scrota** or **scrotums** the pouch of skin behind the penis, containing the testicles.
▷ **scrotal** *adjective*
[Latin]

scrounge *VERB* **scrounges, scrounging, scrounged** get something without paying for it.
▷ **scrounger** *noun*
[from an old word *scringe* = squeeze roughly]

scrub[1] *VERB* **scrubs, scrubbing, scrubbed 1** rub with a hard brush, especially to clean something. **2** (*informal*) cancel.
▷ **scrub** *noun*
[probably from old German or old Dutch]

scrub[2] *NOUN* **1** low trees and bushes. **2** land covered with these.
[from *shrub*]

scrubby *ADJECTIVE* small and shabby.
[from *scrub*[2]]

scruff *NOUN* the back of the neck.
[from Old Norse]

scruffy *ADJECTIVE* shabby and untidy.
▷ **scruffily** *adverb* **scruffiness** *noun*
[a different spelling of *scurfy*]

scrum *NOUN* **scrums** (also **scrummage**) **1** a group of players from each side in rugby football who push against each other and try to heel out the ball which is thrown between them. **2** a crowd pushing against each other.
[a different spelling of *scrimmage*]

scrumptious *ADJECTIVE* (*informal*) delicious.
[origin unknown]

scrunch *VERB* **scrunches, scrunching, scrunched 1** crunch. **2** crush or crumple.
[imitating the sound]

scrunchy or **scrunchie** *NOUN* **scrunchies** a band of elastic covered in fabric, used to tie up your hair.
[from *scrunch*]

scruple *NOUN* **scruples** a feeling of doubt or hesitation when your conscience tells you that an action would be wrong.

scruple *VERB* **scruples, scrupling, scrupled** have scruples • *He would not scruple to betray us.*
[from Latin]

scrupulous *ADJECTIVE* **1** very careful and conscientious. **2** strictly honest or honourable.
▷ **scrupulously** *adverb*
[from *scruple*]

scrutinize *VERB* **scrutinizes, scrutinizing, scrutinized** look at or examine something carefully.
[from *scrutiny*]

scrutiny *NOUN* a careful look at or examination of something.
[from Latin *scrutari* = examine, (originally) = sort rags]

scuba diving *NOUN* swimming underwater using a tank of air strapped to your back.
[from the initials of *self-contained underwater breathing apparatus*]

scud *VERB* **scuds, scudding, scudded** move quickly and lightly; skim along • *Clouds scudded across the sky.*
[origin unknown]

scuff *VERB* **scuffs, scuffing, scuffed 1** drag your feet while walking. **2** scrape with your foot; mark or damage something by doing this.
[origin unknown]

scuffle *NOUN* **scuffles** a confused fight or struggle.

scuffle *VERB* **scuffles, scuffling, scuffled** take part in a scuffle.
[probably from a Scandinavian language]

scull *NOUN* **sculls** a small or lightweight oar.

scull *VERB* **sculls, sculling, sculled** row with sculls.
[origin unknown]

scullery *NOUN* **sculleries** a room where dishes etc. are washed up.
[from Latin *scutella* = small dish]

sculpt *VERB* **sculpts, sculpting, sculpted** sculpture; make sculptures.

sculptor *NOUN* **sculptors** a person who makes sculptures.

sculpture *NOUN* **sculptures 1** making shapes by carving wood or stone or casting metal. **2** a shape made in this way.
▷ **sculpture** *verb*
[from Latin *sculpere* = carve]

scum *NOUN* **1** froth or dirt on top of a liquid. **2** worthless people.
[from old German or old Dutch]

scupper *NOUN* **scuppers** an opening in a ship's side to let water drain away.

scupper *VERB* **scuppers, scuppering, scuppered 1** sink a ship deliberately. **2** (*informal*) wreck • *It scuppered our plans.*
[probably from old French]

scurf *NOUN* flakes of dry skin.
▷ **scurfy** *adjective*
[from Old English]

scurrilous *ADJECTIVE* rude, insulting, and probably untrue • *scurrilous attacks in the newspapers.*
▷ **scurrilously** *adverb*
[from Latin]

scurry *VERB* **scurries, scurrying, scurried** run with short steps; hurry.
[origin unknown]

scurvy *NOUN* a disease caused by lack of vitamin C in food.
[a different spelling of *scurfy*]

scut *NOUN* **scuts** the short tail of a rabbit, hare, or deer.
[origin unknown]

scutter *VERB* **scutters, scuttering, scuttered** scurry.
[probably from *scuttle*[2]]

scuttle[1] *NOUN* **scuttles** a bucket or container for coal in a house.
[via Old Norse from Latin *scutella* = dish]

scuttle[2] *VERB* **scuttles, scuttling, scuttled** scurry; hurry away.
[from *scud*]

scuttle[3] *NOUN* **scuttles** a small opening with a lid in a ship's deck or side.

scuttle *VERB* **scuttles, scuttling, scuttled** sink a ship deliberately by letting water into it.
[probably from Spanish *escotar* = cut out]

scythe *NOUN* **scythes** a tool with a long curved blade for cutting grass or corn.

scythe *VERB* **scythes, scything, scythed** cut with a scythe.
[from Old English]

SE *ABBREVIATION* **1** south-east. **2** south-eastern.

se- *PREFIX* **1** apart or aside (as in *secluded*). **2** without (as in *secure*).
[Latin]

sea *NOUN* **seas 1** the salt water that covers most of the earth's surface; a part of this. **2** a large lake • *the Sea of Galilee*. **3** a large area of something • *a sea of faces*.
- **at sea 1** on the sea. **2** not knowing what to do.
[from Old English]

sea anemone *NOUN* **sea anemones** a sea creature with short tentacles round its mouth.

seaboard *NOUN* **seaboards** a coastline or coastal region.

sea breeze *NOUN* **sea breezes** a breeze blowing from the sea onto the land.

sea change *NOUN* **sea changes** a dramatic change.

seafaring *ADJECTIVE* & *NOUN* working or travelling on the sea.
▷ **seafarer** *noun*

seafood *NOUN* fish or shellfish from the sea eaten as food.

seagull *NOUN* **seagulls** a seabird with long wings.

sea horse *NOUN* **sea horses** a small fish that swims upright, with a head rather like a horse's head.

seal[1] *NOUN* **seals** a sea mammal with thick fur or bristles, that breeds on land.
[from Old English]

seal[2] *NOUN* **seals 1** a piece of metal with an engraved design for pressing on a soft substance to leave an impression. **2** this impression, especially one made on a piece of wax . **3** something designed to close an opening and prevent air or liquid etc. from getting in or out. **4** a small decorative sticker • *Christmas seals*.

seal *VERB* **seals, sealing, sealed 1** close something by sticking two parts together • *Now seal the envelope*. **2** close securely; stop up. **3** press a seal on something. **4** settle or decide • *His fate was sealed*.
- **seal off** prevent people getting to an area.
[from old French; related to *sign*]

sea level *NOUN* the level of the sea halfway between high and low tide.

sealing wax *NOUN* a substance that is soft when heated but hardens when cooled, used for sealing documents or for marking with a seal.

sea lion *NOUN* **sea lions** a kind of large seal that lives in the Pacific Ocean.

seam *NOUN* **seams 1** the line where two edges of cloth or wood etc. join. **2** a layer of coal in the ground.
[from Old English]

seaman *NOUN* **seamen** a sailor.

seamanship *NOUN* skill in seafaring.

seamy *ADJECTIVE*
- **seamy side** the less attractive side or part • *Police see a lot of the seamy side of life*.
[originally, the 'wrong' side of a piece of sewing, where the rough edges of the seams show]

seance (*say* say-ahns) *NOUN* **seances** a meeting at which people try to make contact with the spirits of dead people.
[French, = a sitting]

seaplane *NOUN* **seaplanes** an aeroplane that can land on and take off from water.

seaport *NOUN* **seaports** a port on the coast.

sear *VERB* **sears, searing, seared** scorch or burn the surface of something.
[from Old English]

search *VERB* **searches, searching, searched** **1** look very carefully in a place in order to find something. **2** examine the clothes and body of a person to see if something is hidden there.
▷ **search** *noun* **searcher** *noun*
[from old French]

search engine *NOUN* **search engines** (*in computing*) a computer program that allows you to enter keywords and then searches the Internet for all the documents containing these keywords.

searching *ADJECTIVE* examining closely and thoroughly • *searching questions.*

searchlight *NOUN* **searchlights** a light with a strong beam that can be turned in any direction.

search party *NOUN* **search parties** a group of people organized to search for a missing person or thing.

search warrant *NOUN* **search warrants** an official document giving the police permission to search private property.

searing *ADJECTIVE* (said about a pain) sharp and burning.

seascape *NOUN* **seascapes** a picture or view of the sea.
[from *sea* + *-scape* as in *landscape*]

seasick *ADJECTIVE* sick because of the movement of a ship.
▷ **seasickness** *noun*

seaside *NOUN* a place by the sea where people go for holidays.

season *NOUN* **seasons** **1** each of the four main parts of the year (spring, summer, autumn, winter). **2** the time of year when something happens • *the football season.*
- **in season** available and ready for eating • *Strawberries are in season in the summer.*

season *VERB* **seasons, seasoning, seasoned** **1** give extra flavour to food by adding salt, pepper, or other strong-tasting substances. **2** dry and treat timber etc. to make it ready for use.
[from Latin *satio* = time for sowing seed]

seasonable *ADJECTIVE* suitable for the season • *Hot weather is seasonable in summer.*
▷ **seasonably** *adverb*
USAGE Do not confuse with **seasonal**.

seasonal *ADJECTIVE* **1** for or to do with a season. **2** happening in a particular season • *Fruit-picking is seasonal work.*
▷ **seasonally** *adverb*
USAGE Do not confuse with **seasonable**.

seasoning *NOUN* **seasonings** a substance used to season food.

season ticket *NOUN* **season tickets** a ticket that can be used as often as you like throughout a period of time.

seat *NOUN* **seats** **1** a thing made or used for sitting on. **2** the right to be a member of a council, committee, parliament, etc. • *She won the seat ten years ago.* **3** the buttocks; the part of a skirt or trousers covering these. **4** the place where something is based or located • *London is the seat of our government.*

seat *VERB* **seats, seating, seated** **1** place in or on a seat. **2** have seats for • *The theatre seats 3,000 people.*
[from Old Norse]

seat belt *NOUN* **seat belts** a strap to hold a person securely in a seat.

seating *NOUN* **1** the seats in a place • *seating for 400.* **2** the arrangement of seats • *a seating plan.*

sea urchin *NOUN* **sea urchins** a sea animal with a spherical shell covered in sharp spikes.
[from an old meaning of *urchin* = hedgehog]

seaward *ADJECTIVE & ADVERB* towards the sea.
▷ **seawards** *adverb*

seaweed *NOUN* a plant or plants that grow in the sea.

seaworthy *ADJECTIVE* (said about a ship) fit for a sea voyage.
▷ **seaworthiness** *noun*

sebum *NOUN* the natural oil produced by glands (*sebaceous glands*) in the skin to lubricate the skin and hair.
[Latin, = grease or tallow]

secateurs *PLURAL NOUN* clippers held in the hand for pruning plants.
[French, from Latin *secare* = to cut]

secede (*say* sis-seed) VERB **secedes, seceding, seceded** withdraw from being a member of a political or religious organization.
▷ **secession** *noun*
[from *se-* + Latin *cedere* = go]

secluded ADJECTIVE quiet and sheltered from view • *a secluded beach.*
▷ **seclusion** *noun*
[from *se-* + Latin *claudere* = shut]

second[1] ADJECTIVE **1** next after the first. **2** another • *a second chance.* **3** less good • *second quality.*
- **have second thoughts** wonder whether a decision you have made was the right one.

second NOUN **seconds 1** a person or thing that is second. **2** an attendant of a fighter in a boxing match, duel, etc. **3** one-sixtieth of a minute of time or of a degree used in measuring angles. **4** (*informal*) a short time • *Wait a second.*

second VERB **seconds, seconding, seconded 1** assist someone. **2** support a proposal, motion, etc.
▷ **seconder** *noun*
[from Latin *secundus* = next]

second[2] (*say* sik-ond) VERB **seconds, seconding, seconded** transfer a person temporarily to another job or department etc.
▷ **secondment** *noun*
[from French *en second* = in the second rank (because officers seconded to another company served under officers who belonged to that company)]

secondary ADJECTIVE **1** coming after or from something. **2** less important. **3** (said about education etc.) for children of more than about 11 years old. (COMPARE **primary**)

secondary colour NOUN **secondary colours** a colour made by mixing two primary colours.

secondary school NOUN **secondary schools** a school for children of more than about 11 years old.

second-hand ADJECTIVE **1** bought or used after someone else has owned it. **2** selling used goods • *a second-hand shop.*

secondly ADVERB in the second place; as the second one.

second nature NOUN behaviour that has become automatic or a habit • *Lying is second nature to him.*

second-rate ADJECTIVE inferior; not very good.

seconds PLURAL NOUN **1** goods that are not of the best quality, sold at a reduced price. **2** a second helping of food at a meal.

second sight NOUN the ability to foresee the future.

secrecy NOUN being secret; keeping things secret.

secret ADJECTIVE **1** that must not be told or shown to other people. **2** not known by everybody. **3** working secretly.
▷ **secretly** *adverb*

secret NOUN **secrets** something secret.
[from Latin *secretum* = set apart]

secretariat NOUN **secretariats** an administrative department of a large organization such as the United Nations.
[same origin as *secretary*]

secretary (*say* sek-rit-ree) NOUN **secretaries 1** a person whose job is to help with letters, answer the telephone, and make business arrangements for a person or organization. **2** the chief assistant of a government minister or ambassador.
▷ **secretarial** *adjective*
[from Latin *secretarius* = an officer or servant allowed to know your secrets]

secrete (*say* sik-reet) VERB **secretes, secreting, secreted 1** hide something. **2** produce a substance in the body • *Saliva is secreted in the mouth.*
▷ **secretion** *noun*
[same origin as *secret*]

secretive (*say* seek-rit-iv) ADJECTIVE liking or trying to keep things secret.
▷ **secretively** *adverb* **secretiveness** *noun*

secret police NOUN a police force which works in secret for political purposes, not to deal with crime.

secret service NOUN a government department responsible for espionage.

A B C D E F G H I J K L M N O P Q R S T U V W X Y Z

sect *NOUN* **sects** a group of people whose beliefs differ from those of others in the same religion.
[from Latin]
WORD FAMILY There are a number of English words that are related to *sect* because part of their original meaning comes from the Latin words *secare* meaning 'to cut' or *sectum* meaning 'a cut'. These include *bisect, dissect, intersect, secateurs, section,* and *sector.*

sectarian (*say* sekt-air-ee-an) *ADJECTIVE* belonging to or supporting a sect.

section *NOUN* **sections 1** a part of something. **2** a cross-section.
[from Latin *sectum* = cut]

sectional *ADJECTIVE* **1** made in sections that can be put together and taken apart.
2 concerned with only one group within a community.

sector *NOUN* **sectors 1** one part of an area.
2 a part of something • *the private sector of industry.* **3** (*in mathematics*) a section of a circle between two lines drawn from its centre to its circumference.
[from Latin *secare* = to cut]

secular *ADJECTIVE* to do with worldly affairs, not spiritual or religious matters.
[from Latin *saecularis* = worldly]

secure *ADJECTIVE* **1** safe, especially against attack. **2** certain not to slip or fail. **3** reliable.
▷ **securely** *adverb*

secure *VERB* **secures, securing, secured**
1 make a thing secure. **2** fasten something firmly. **3** obtain • *We secured two tickets for the show.*
[from *se-* + Latin *cura* = care]

security *NOUN* **securities 1** being secure; safety. **2** precautions against theft or spying etc. **3** something given as a guarantee that a promise will be kept or a debt repaid.
4 investments such as stocks and shares.

security guard *NOUN* **security guards** a person employed to guard a building or its contents against theft and vandalism.

security risk *NOUN* **security risks** a person or situation thought likely to threaten the security of a country.

sedan chair *NOUN* **sedan chairs** an enclosed chair for one person, mounted on two horizontal poles and carried by two men, used in the 17th-18th centuries.
[origin unknown]

sedate *ADJECTIVE* calm and dignified.
▷ **sedately** *adverb* **sedateness** *noun*

sedate *VERB* **sedates, sedating, sedated** give a sedative to.
▷ **sedation** *noun*
[from Latin *sedatum* = made calm]

sedative (*say* sed-a-tiv) *NOUN* **sedatives** a medicine that makes a person calm.
[from Latin *sedare* = settle]

sedentary (*say* sed-en-ter-ee) *ADJECTIVE* done sitting down • *sedentary work.*
[from Latin *sedens* = sitting]

Seder *NOUN* **Seders** (in Judaism) a ritual and a ceremonial meal to mark the beginning of Passover.
[Hebrew, = order, procedure]

sedge *NOUN* a grass-like plant growing in marshes or near water.
[from Old English]

sediment *NOUN* fine particles of solid matter that float in liquid or sink to the bottom of it.
[from Latin *sedere* = sit]

sedimentary *ADJECTIVE* formed from particles that have settled on a surface
• *sedimentary rocks.*

sedition *NOUN* speeches or actions intended to make people rebel against the authority of the state.
▷ **seditious** *adjective*
[from *se-* + Latin *itio* = going]

seduce *VERB* **seduces, seducing, seduced**
1 persuade a person to have sexual intercourse. **2** attract or lead astray by offering temptations.
▷ **seducer** *noun* **seduction** *noun*
[from *se-* + Latin *ducere* = to lead]

seductive *ADJECTIVE* **1** sexually attractive.
2 temptingly attractive.

sedulous *ADJECTIVE* diligent and persevering.
▷ **sedulously** *adverb*
[from Latin]

see[1] *VERB* **sees, seeing, saw, seen**
1 perceive with the eyes. **2** meet or visit somebody • *See a doctor about your cough.* **3** understand • *She saw what I meant.* **4** imagine • *Can you see yourself as a teacher?* **5** consider • *I will see what can be done.* **6** make sure • *See that the windows are shut.* **7** discover • *See who is at the door.* **8** escort • *I'll see you to the door.*
- **see through** not be deceived by something.
- **see to** attend to.
[from Old English]

see[2] *NOUN* **sees** the district of which a bishop or archbishop is in charge • *the see of Canterbury.*
[from Latin *sedes* = seat]

seed *NOUN* **seeds** or **seed 1** a fertilized part of a plant, capable of growing into a new plant. **2** (*old use*) descendants. **3** a seeded player.

seed *VERB* **seeds, seeding, seeded 1** plant or sprinkle seeds in something. **2** name the best players and arrange for them not to play against each other in the early rounds of a tournament.
[from Old English]

seedling *NOUN* **seedlings** a very young plant growing from a seed.

seedy *ADJECTIVE* **seedier, seediest 1** full of seeds. **2** shabby and disreputable.
▷ **seediness** *noun*

seeing *CONJUNCTION* considering • *Seeing that we have all finished, let's go.*

seek *VERB* **seeks, seeking, sought 1** search for. **2** try to do or obtain something • *She is seeking fame.*
[from Old English]

seem *VERB* **seems, seeming, seemed** give the impression of being something • *She seems worried about her work.*
▷ **seemingly** *adverb*
[from Old Norse]

seemly *ADJECTIVE* (*old use*) (said about behaviour etc.) proper or suitable.
▷ **seemliness** *noun*
[from an old sense of *seem* = be suitable]

seep *VERB* **seeps, seeping, seeped** ooze slowly out or through something.
▷ **seepage** *noun*
[probably from Old English]

seer *NOUN* **seers** a prophet.
[from *see*[1] + *-er*[2]]

seersucker *NOUN* fabric woven with a puckered surface.
[from Persian *shir o shakar*, literally = milk and sugar, also = striped cloth]

see-saw *NOUN* **see-saws** a plank balanced in the middle so that two people can sit, one on each end, and make it go up and down.
[from an old rhyme which imitated the rhythm of a saw going to and fro, later used by children on a see-saw]

seethe *VERB* **seethes, seething, seethed**
1 bubble and surge like water boiling. **2** be very angry or excited.
[from Old English]

segment *NOUN* **segments** a part that is cut off or separates naturally from other parts • *the segments of an orange.*
▷ **segmented** *adjective*
[from Latin]

segregate *VERB* **segregates, segregating, segregated 1** separate people of different religions, races, etc. **2** isolate a person or thing.
▷ **segregation** *noun*
[from *se-* + Latin *gregis* = from a flock]

seismic (*say* sy-zmik) *ADJECTIVE* to do with earthquakes or other vibrations of the earth.
[from Greek *seismos* = earthquake]

seismograph (*say* sy-zmo-grahf) *NOUN* **seismographs** an instrument for measuring the strength of earthquakes.
[from Greek *seismos* = earthquake, + *-graph*]

seize *VERB* **seizes, seizing, seized 1** take hold of a person or thing suddenly or forcibly. **2** take possession of something by force or by legal authority • *Customs officers seized the smuggled goods.* **3** take eagerly • *Seize your chance!* **4** have a sudden effect on • *Panic seized us.*
- **seize up** become jammed, especially because of friction or overheating.
[via old French from Germanic]

seizure *NOUN* **seizures 1** seizing. **2** a sudden fit, as in epilepsy or a heart attack.

seldom *ADVERB* rarely; not often.
[from Old English]

select *VERB* **selects, selecting, selected** choose a person or thing.
▷ **selector** *noun*

select *ADJECTIVE* **1** carefully chosen • *a select group of pupils*. **2** (said about a club etc.) choosing its members carefully; exclusive. [from *se-* + Latin *lectus* = collected]

selection *NOUN* **selections 1** selecting; being selected. **2** a person or thing selected. **3** a group selected from a larger group. **4** a range of goods from which to choose.

selective *ADJECTIVE* choosing or chosen carefully.
▷ **selectively** *adverb* **selectivity** *noun*

self *NOUN* **selves 1** a person as an individual. **2** a person's particular nature • *She has recovered and is her old self again*. **3** a person's own advantage • *He always puts self first*. [from Old English]

self- *PREFIX* **1** of or to or done by yourself or itself. **2** automatic (as in *self-loading*).

self-addressed *ADJECTIVE* addressed to yourself.

self-assured *ADJECTIVE* confident.

self-catering *NOUN* catering for yourself (instead of having meals provided).

self-centred *ADJECTIVE* selfish.

self-confident *ADJECTIVE* confident of your own abilities.

self-conscious *ADJECTIVE* embarrassed or unnatural because you know that people are watching you.

self-contained *ADJECTIVE* (said about accommodation) complete in itself; containing all the necessary facilities.

self-control *NOUN* the ability to control your own behaviour.
▷ **self-controlled** *adjective*

self-defence *NOUN* **1** defending yourself. **2** techniques for doing this.

self-denial *NOUN* deliberately going without things you would like to have.

self-determination *NOUN* a country's right to rule itself and choose its own government.

self-employed *ADJECTIVE* working independently, not for an employer.

self-esteem *NOUN* your own opinion of yourself and your own worth.

self-evident *ADJECTIVE* obvious and not needing proof or explanation.

self-help group *NOUN* **self-help groups** a group of people with similar problems who help each other.

self-image *NOUN* **self-images** your own idea of your appearance, personality, and abilities.

self-important *ADJECTIVE* pompous.

self-interest *NOUN* your own advantage.

selfish *ADJECTIVE* doing what you want and not thinking of other people; keeping things for yourself.
▷ **selfishly** *adverb* **selfishness** *noun*

selfless *ADJECTIVE* unselfish.

self-made *ADJECTIVE* rich or successful because of your own efforts.

self-pity *NOUN* too much sorrow and pity for yourself and your own problems.

self-possessed *ADJECTIVE* calm and dignified.

self-raising *ADJECTIVE* (said about flour) making cakes rise without needing to have baking powder etc. added.

self-respect *NOUN* your own proper respect for yourself.

self-righteous *ADJECTIVE* smugly sure that you are behaving virtuously.

selfsame *ADJECTIVE* the very same.

self-satisfied *ADJECTIVE* very pleased with yourself.

self-seeking *ADJECTIVE* selfishly trying to benefit yourself.

self-service *ADJECTIVE* where customers help themselves to things and pay a cashier for what they have taken.

self-sufficient *ADJECTIVE* able to produce or provide what you need without help from others.

self-supporting *ADJECTIVE* earning enough to keep yourself without needing money from others.

self-willed *ADJECTIVE* obstinately doing what you want; stubborn.

sell *VERB* **sells, selling, sold** **1** exchange something for money. **2** have something available for people to buy • *Do you sell stamps?* **3** be on sale at a certain price • *It sells for £5.99.*
▷ **seller** *noun*
- **sell out** **1** sell all your stock of something. **2** (*informal*) betray someone.

sell *NOUN* the manner of selling something.
- **hard sell** *noun* forceful selling; putting pressure on someone to buy.
- **soft sell** selling by suggestion or gentle persuasion.

[from Old English]

sell-by date *NOUN* **sell-by dates** a date marked on the packaging of food etc. by which it must be sold.

sell-out *NOUN* **sell-outs** an entertainment, sporting event, etc. for which all the tickets have been sold.

selvage *NOUN* **selvages** an edge of cloth woven so that it does not unravel.
[from *self* + *edge*]

selves *plural* of **self**.

semantic (*say* sim-an-tik) *ADJECTIVE* to do with the meanings of words.
▷ **semantically** *adverb*
[from Greek *semantikos* = significant]

semaphore *NOUN* a system of signalling by holding flags out with your arms in positions that indicate letters of the alphabet.
[from Greek *sema* = sign + *-phoros* = carrying]

semblance *NOUN* an outward appearance or apparent likeness.
[from old French; related to *similar*]

semen (*say* seem-en) *NOUN* a white liquid produced by males and containing sperm.
[Latin, from *semere* = to sow]

semi *NOUN* **semis** (*informal*) a semi-detached house.

semi- *PREFIX* **1** half. **2** partly.
[from Latin]

semibreve *NOUN* **semibreves** the longest musical note normally used (𝅝), lasting four times as long as a crotchet.

semicircle *NOUN* **semicircles** half a circle.
▷ **semicircular** *adjective*

semicolon *NOUN* **semicolons** a punctuation mark (;) used to mark a break that is more than that marked by a comma.

semiconductor *NOUN* **semiconductors** a substance that can conduct electricity but not as well as most metals do.

semi-detached *ADJECTIVE* (said about a house) joined to another house on one side only.

semifinal *NOUN* **semifinals** a match or round whose winner will take part in the final.

seminar *NOUN* **seminars** a meeting for advanced discussion and research on a subject.
[German; related to *seminary*]

seminary *NOUN* **seminaries** a training college for priests or rabbis.
[from Latin *seminarium* = seedbed]

semiquaver *NOUN* **semiquavers** a note in music (𝅘𝅥𝅯), equal in length to one quarter of a crotchet.

semi-skimmed *ADJECTIVE* (said about milk) having had some of the cream taken out.

Semitic (*say* sim-it-ik) *ADJECTIVE* to do with the Semites, the group of people that includes the Jews and Arabs.
▷ **Semite** (*say* see-my't) *noun*

semitone *NOUN* **semitones** half a tone in music.

semolina *NOUN* hard round grains of wheat used to make milk puddings and pasta.
[from Italian *semola* = bran]

senate *NOUN* **senates** **1** the governing council in ancient Rome. **2** the upper house of the parliament of the United States, France, and certain other countries.
▷ **senator** *noun*
[from Latin *senatus* = council of elders]

send *VERB* **sends, sending, sent** **1** make a person or thing go or be taken somewhere. **2** cause to become • *The noise is sending me crazy.*
▷ **sender** *noun*
- **send for** order a person or thing to come or be brought to you.
- **send up** (*informal*) make fun of something by imitating it.

[from Old English]

senile (*say* seen-I'll) *ADJECTIVE* weak or confused and forgetful because of old age.
▷ **senility** *noun*
[from Latin *senilis* = old]

a b c d e f g h i j k l m n o p q r **s** t u v w x y z

senior *ADJECTIVE* **1** older than someone else. **2** higher in rank. **3** for older children • *a senior school.*
▷ **seniority** *noun*

senior *NOUN* **seniors 1** a person who is older or higher in rank than you are • *He is my senior.* **2** a member of a senior school.
[Latin, = older]

senior citizen *NOUN* **senior citizens** an elderly person, especially a pensioner.

senna *NOUN* the dried pods or leaves of a tropical tree, used as a laxative.
[via Latin from Arabic]

sensation *NOUN* **sensations 1** a feeling • *a sensation of warmth.* **2** a very excited condition; something causing this • *The news caused a great sensation.*
[from Latin *sensus* = sense]

sensational *ADJECTIVE* **1** causing great excitement, interest, or shock. **2** (*informal*) very good; wonderful.
▷ **sensationally** *adverb*

sensationalism *NOUN* deliberate use of dramatic words or style etc. to arouse excitement.
▷ **sensationalist** *noun*

sense *NOUN* **senses 1** the ability to see, hear, smell, touch, or taste things. **2** the ability to feel or appreciate something • *a sense of guilt; a sense of humour.* **3** the power to think or make wise decisions • *He hasn't got the sense to come in out of the rain.* **4** meaning • *The word 'run' has many senses.*
- **make sense 1** have a meaning you can understand. **2** be a sensible idea.

sense *VERB* **senses, sensing, sensed 1** feel; get an impression • *I sensed that she did not like me.* **2** detect something • *This device senses radioactivity.*
[from Latin]

senseless *ADJECTIVE* **1** stupid; not showing good sense. **2** unconscious.

senses *PLURAL NOUN* sanity • *He is out of his senses.*

sensibility *NOUN* **sensibilities** sensitiveness or delicate feeling • *The criticism hurt the artist's sensibilities.*
USAGE Note that this word does not mean 'being sensible' or 'having good sense'.

sensible *ADJECTIVE* wise; having or showing good sense.
▷ **sensibly** *adverb*

sensitive *ADJECTIVE* **1** affected by something • *Photographic paper is sensitive to light.* **2** receiving impressions quickly and easily • *sensitive fingers.* **3** easily hurt or offended • *She is very sensitive about her age.* **4** considerate about other people's feelings. **5** needing to be deal with tactfully • *a sensitive subject.*
▷ **sensitively** *adverb* **sensitivity** *noun*

sensitize *VERB* **sensitizes, sensitizing, sensitized** make a thing sensitive to something.

sensor *NOUN* **sensors** a device or instrument for detecting a physical property such as light, heat, or sound.

sensory *ADJECTIVE* **1** to do with the senses. **2** receiving sensations • *sensory nerves.*

sensual *ADJECTIVE* **1** to do with physical pleasure. **2** liking or suggesting physical or sexual pleasures.

sensuous *ADJECTIVE* giving pleasure to the senses, especially by being beautiful or delicate.

sentence *NOUN* **sentences 1** a group of words that express a complete thought and form a statement, question, exclamation, or command. **2** the punishment announced to a convicted person in a lawcourt.

sentence *VERB* **sentences, sentencing, sentenced** give someone a sentence in a lawcourt • *The judge sentenced him to a year in prison.*
[from Latin *sententia* = opinion]

sententious *ADJECTIVE* giving moral advice in a pompous way.
[same origin as *sentence*]

sentient *ADJECTIVE* capable of feeling and perceiving things • *sentient beings.*
[from Latin *sentiens* = feeling]

sentiment *NOUN* **sentiments 1** an opinion. **2** sentimentality.
[from Latin *sentire* = feel]
WORD FAMILY There are a number of English words that are related to *sentiment* because part of their original meaning comes from the Latin words *sentire*

meaning 'to feel' or *sensus* meaning 'sense'. These include *assent*, *consent*, *dissent*, *resent*, *sensation*, *sense*, *sensitive*, and *sentient*.

sentimental *ADJECTIVE* showing or arousing tenderness or romantic feeling or foolish emotion.
▷ **sentimentally** *adverb* **sentimentality** *noun*

sentinel *NOUN* **sentinels** a guard or sentry. [via French from Italian]

sentry *NOUN* **sentries** a soldier guarding something.
[origin unknown]

sepal *NOUN* **sepals** each of the leaves forming the calyx of a bud.
[from French]

separable *ADJECTIVE* able to be separated.

separate (*say* sep-er-at) *ADJECTIVE* **1** not joined to anything. **2** not shared.
▷ **separately** *adverb*

separate (*say* sep-er-ayt) *VERB* **separates, separating, separated** **1** make or keep separate; divide. **2** become separate. **3** stop living together as a couple.
▷ **separation** *noun* **separator** *noun*
[from *se-* + Latin *parare* = prepare]

sepia *NOUN* reddish-brown, like the colour of early photographs.
[Greek, = cuttlefish (from which the dye was originally obtained)]

sepsis *NOUN* a septic condition.

September *NOUN* the ninth month of the year.
[from Latin *septem* = seven, because it was the seventh month of the ancient Roman calendar]

septet *NOUN* **septets** **1** a group of seven musicians. **2** a piece of music for seven musicians.
[from Latin *septem* = seven]

septic *ADJECTIVE* infected with harmful bacteria that cause pus to form.
[from Greek *septikos* = made rotten]

sepulchral (*say* sep-**ul**-kral) *ADJECTIVE* **1** to do with a sepulchre. **2** (said about a voice) sounding deep and hollow.

sepulchre (*say* sep-ul-ker) *NOUN* **sepulchres** a tomb.
[from Latin *sepultum* = buried]

sequel *NOUN* **sequels** **1** a book or film etc. that continues the story of an earlier one. **2** something that follows or results from an earlier event.
[from Latin *sequi* = follow]

sequence *NOUN* **sequences** **1** the following of one thing after another; the order in which things happen. **2** a series of things.
[from Latin *sequens* = following]

sequestrate *VERB* **sequestrates, sequestrating, sequestrated** confiscate property until the owner pays a debt or obeys a court order.
▷ **sequestration** *noun*
[from Latin]

sequin *NOUN* **sequins** a tiny bright disc sewn on clothes etc. to decorate them.
▷ **sequinned** *adjective*
[via French and Italian from Arabic *sikka* = a coin]

seraph *NOUN* **seraphim** or **seraphs** a kind of angel.
[from Hebrew]

seraphic (*say* ser-af-ik) *ADJECTIVE* angelic
• *a seraphic smile*.
▷ **seraphically** *adverb*

serenade *NOUN* **serenades** a song or tune of a kind played by a man under his lover's window.

serenade *VERB* **serenades, serenading, serenaded** sing or play a serenade to someone.
[via French from Italian *sereno* = serene]

serendipity *NOUN* the ability to make pleasant or interesting discoveries by accident.
▷ **serendipitous** *adjective*.
[made up by an 18th-century writer, Horace Walpole, from the title of a story *The Three Princes of Serendip* (who had this ability)]

serene *ADJECTIVE* calm and peaceful.
▷ **serenely** *adverb* **serenity** (*say* ser-en-iti) *noun*
[from Latin]

serf *NOUN* **serfs** a farm labourer who worked for a landowner in the Middle Ages, and who was not allowed to leave.
▷ **serfdom** *noun*
[same origin as *servant*]

serge *NOUN* a kind of strong woven fabric.
[from old French]

sergeant (*say* sar-jent) *NOUN* **sergeants** a soldier or policeman who is in charge of others.
[from old French; related to *serve*]

sergeant major *NOUN* **sergeant majors** a soldier who is one rank higher than a sergeant.
[from *sergeant* + *major* = greater]

serial *NOUN* **serials** a story or film etc. that is presented in separate parts.
[from *series*]
USAGE Do not confuse with **cereal**.

serialize *VERB* **serializes, serializing, serialized** produce a story or film etc. as a serial.
▷ **serialization** *noun*

serial killer *NOUN* **serial killers** a person who commits a series of murders.

serial number *NOUN* **serial numbers** a number put onto an object, usually by the manufacturers, to distinguish it from other identical objects.

series *NOUN* **series 1** a number of things following or connected with each other. **2** a number of games or matches between the same competitors. **3** a number of separate radio or television programmes with the same characters or on the same subject.
[Latin, = row or chain]

serious *ADJECTIVE* **1** solemn and thoughtful; not smiling. **2** needing careful thought; important • *We need a serious talk.* **3** sincere; not casual or light-hearted • *a serious attempt.* **4** causing anxiety, not trivial • *a serious accident.*
▷ **seriously** *adverb* **seriousness** *noun*
[from Latin]

sermon *NOUN* **sermons** a talk given by a preacher, especially as part of a religious service.
[from Latin *sermo* = talk, conversation]

serpent *NOUN* **serpents** a snake.
[from Latin *serpens* = creeping]

serpentine *ADJECTIVE* twisting and curving like a snake • *a serpentine road.*

serrated *ADJECTIVE* having a notched edge.
[from Latin *serratum* = sawn]

serried *ADJECTIVE* arranged in rows close together • *serried ranks of troops.*
[from Latin *serere* = join together]

serum (*say* seer-um) *NOUN* **sera** or **serums** **1** the thin pale-yellow liquid that remains from blood when the rest has clotted. **2** this fluid used medically, usually for the antibodies it contains.
[Latin, = whey]

servant *NOUN* **servants** a person whose job is to work or serve in someone else's house.
[from Latin *servus* = slave]

serve *VERB* **serves, serving, served 1** work for a person or organization or country etc. **2** sell things to people in a shop. **3** give out food to people at a meal. **4** spend time doing something; undergo • *He served a prison sentence.* **5** be suitable for something • *This will serve our purpose.* **6** start play in tennis etc. by hitting the ball.
- **it serves you right** you deserve it.

serve *NOUN* **serves** a service in tennis etc.
[same origin as *servant*]

server *NOUN* **servers 1** a person or thing that serves. **2** (*in computing*) a computer or program that controls or supplies information to several computers connected to a network.

service *NOUN* **services 1** working for a person or organization or country etc. **2** something that helps people or supplies what they want • *a bus service.* **3** the army, navy, or air force • *the armed services.* **4** a religious ceremony. **5** providing people with goods, food, etc. • *The service at the restaurant was slow.* **6** a set of dishes and plates etc. for a meal • *a dinner service.* **7** the servicing of a vehicle or machine etc. **8** the action of serving in tennis etc.

service *VERB* **services, servicing, serviced** **1** repair or keep a vehicle or machine etc. in working order. **2** supply with services.
[from Latin *servitium* = slavery]

serviceable *ADJECTIVE* usable; suitable for ordinary use or wear.

service charge *NOUN* **service charges** **1** an amount added to a restaurant or hotel bill to reward the waiters and waitresses for their service. **2** money paid to the landlord of a block of flats for services used by all the flats, e.g. central heating or cleaning the stairs.

service industry *NOUN* **service industries** an industry which sells service, not goods.

serviceman *NOUN* **servicemen** a man serving in the armed forces.

service road *NOUN* **service roads** a road beside a main road, for use by vehicles going to the houses or shops etc.

services *PLURAL NOUN* an area beside a motorway with a garage, shop, restaurant, lavatories, etc. for travellers to use.

service station *NOUN* **service stations** a place beside a road, where petrol and other services are available.

servicewoman *NOUN* **servicewomen** a woman serving in the armed forces.

serviette *NOUN* **serviettes** a piece of cloth or paper used to keep your clothes or hands clean at a meal.
[French, from *servir* = to serve]

servile *ADJECTIVE* like a slave; too willing to serve or obey others.
▷ **servility** *noun*
[same origin as *servant*]

serving *NOUN* **servings** a helping of food.

servitude *NOUN* the condition of being obliged to work for someone else and having no independence; slavery.
[same origin as *servant*]

sesame *NOUN* an African plant whose seeds can be eaten or used to make an edible oil.
[from Greek]

session *NOUN* **sessions** **1** a meeting or series of meetings • *The Queen will open the next session of Parliament.* **2** a time spent doing one thing • *a recording session.*
[from Latin *sessio* = sitting]

set *VERB* **sets, setting, set**
This word has many uses, including **1** put or fix • *Set the vase on the table. Set a date for the wedding.* **2** make ready to work • *I'd better set the alarm.* **3** make or become firm or hard • *Leave the jelly to set.* **4** give someone a task • *This sets us a problem.* **5** put into a condition • *Set them free.* **6** go down below the horizon • *The sun was setting.*
- **set about** **1** start doing something. **2** (*informal*) attack somebody.
- **set off** **1** begin a journey. **2** start something happening. **3** cause something to explode.
- **set out** **1** begin a journey. **2** display or make known.
- **set to** **1** begin doing something vigorously. **2** begin fighting or arguing.
- **set up** **1** place in position. **2** arrange or establish • *We want to set up a playgroup.*

set *NOUN* **sets** **1** a group of people or things that belong together. **2** a radio or television receiver. **3** (*in mathematics*) a collection of things that have a common property. **4** the way something is placed • *the set of his jaw.* **5** the scenery or stage for a play or film. **6** a group of games in a tennis match. **7** a badger's burrow.

set *ADJECTIVE* **1** fixed or arranged in advance • *a set time.* **2** ready or prepared to do something.
- **set on** determined about doing something.
[from Old English]

set-aside *NOUN* the policy of paying farmers not to use some of their land because too much food is being produced.

setback *NOUN* **setbacks** something that stops progress or slows it down.

set book *NOUN* **set books** a book that must be studied for a literature examination.

set square *NOUN* **set squares** a device shaped like a right-angled triangle, used in drawing lines parallel to each other etc.

settee *NOUN* **settees** a long soft seat with a back and arms.
[probably from *settle*[2]]

setter *NOUN* **setters** a dog of a long-haired breed that can be trained to stand rigid when it scents game.

set theory *NOUN* the branch of mathematics that deals with sets and the relations between them.

setting *NOUN* **settings 1** the way or place in which something is set. **2** music for the words of a song etc. **3** a set of cutlery or crockery for one person at a meal.

settle[1] *VERB* **settles, settling, settled 1** arrange; decide or solve something • *That settles the problem.* **2** make or become calm or comfortable or orderly; stop being restless • *Stop chattering and settle down!* **3** go and live somewhere • *They settled in Canada.* **4** sink; come to rest on something • *Dust had settled on his books.* **5** pay a bill or debt.
[from Old English *setlan*; related to *settle*[2]]

settle[2] *NOUN* **settles** a long wooden seat with a high back and arms.
[from Old English *setl* = a place to sit]

settlement *NOUN* **settlements 1** settling something. **2** the way something is settled. **3** a small number of people or houses established in a new area.

settler *NOUN* **settlers** one of the first people to settle in a new country; a pioneer or colonist.

set-up *NOUN* (*informal*) the way something is organized or arranged.

seven *NOUN* & *ADJECTIVE* **sevens** the number 7.
▷ **seventh** *adjective* & *noun*
[from Old English]

seventeen *NOUN* & *ADJECTIVE* the number 17.
▷ **seventeenth** *adjective* & *noun*
[from Old English]

seventy *NOUN* & *ADJECTIVE* **seventies** the number 70.
▷ **seventieth** *adjective* & *noun*
[from Old English]

sever *VERB* **severs, severing, severed** cut or break off.
▷ **severance** *noun*
[from old French; related to *separate*]

several *ADJECTIVE* & *NOUN* more than two but not many.
[from *sever*]

severally *ADVERB* separately.
[from *several*]

severance pay *NOUN* money paid to a worker who is no longer needed by his or her employer.
[from *sever*]

severe *ADJECTIVE* **1** strict; not gentle or kind. **2** intense or forceful • *severe gales.* **3** very plain • *a severe style of dress.*
▷ **severely** *adverb* **severity** *noun*
[from Latin]

sew *VERB* **sews, sewing, sewed, sewn** or **sewed 1** join things together by using a needle and thread. **2** work with a needle and thread or with a sewing machine.
[from Old English]
USAGE Do not confuse with **sow**.

sewage (*say* soo-ij) *NOUN* liquid waste matter carried away in drains.

sewer (*say* soo-er) *NOUN* **sewers** a large underground drain for carrying away sewage.
[from old French]

sewing machine *NOUN* **sewing machines** a machine for sewing things.

sex *NOUN* **sexes 1** each of the two groups (*male*, and *female*) into which living things are placed according to their functions in the process of reproduction. **2** the instinct that causes members of the two sexes to be attracted to one another. **3** sexual intercourse.
[from Latin]

sexism *NOUN* discrimination against people of a particular sex, especially women.
▷ **sexist** *adjective* & *noun*

sextant *NOUN* **sextants** an instrument for measuring the angle of the sun and stars, used for finding your position when navigating.
[from Latin *sextus* = sixth (because early sextants consisted of an arc of one- sixth of a circle)]

sextet *NOUN* **sextets 1** a group of six musicians. **2** a piece of music for six musicians.
[from Latin *sextus* = sixth]

sexton *NOUN* **sextons** a person whose job is to take care of a church and churchyard.
[from old French]

sextuplet *NOUN* **sextuplets** each of six children born to the same mother at one time.
[same origin as *sextet*]

sexual *ADJECTIVE* **1** to do with sex or the sexes. **2** (said about reproduction) happening by the fusion of male and female cells.
▷ **sexually** *adverb* **sexuality** *noun*

sexual harassment *NOUN* annoying or upsetting someone, especially a woman, by touching her or making obscene remarks or gestures.

sexual intercourse *NOUN* an intimate act between two people, in which the man puts his penis into the woman's vagina, to express love, for pleasure, or to conceive a child.

sexy *ADJECTIVE* **sexier, sexiest** (*informal*) **1** sexually attractive. **2** concerned with sex.

SF *ABBREVIATION* science fiction.

shabby *ADJECTIVE* **shabbier, shabbiest 1** in a poor or worn-out condition; dilapidated. **2** poorly dressed. **3** unfair or dishonourable • *a shabby trick.*
▷ **shabbily** *adverb* **shabbiness** *noun*
[from Old English *sceabb* = scab]

shack *NOUN* **shacks** a roughly-built hut.
[probably from a Mexican word]

shackle *NOUN* **shackles** an iron ring for fastening a prisoner's wrist or ankle to something.

shackle *VERB* **shackles, shackling, shackled 1** put shackles on a prisoner. **2** restrict or limit someone • *They felt shackled by tradition.*
[from Old English]

shade *NOUN* **shades 1** slight darkness produced where something blocks the sun's light. **2** a device that reduces or shuts out bright light. **3** a colour; how light or dark a colour is. **4** a slight difference • *The word had several shades of meaning.* **5** (*poetical use*) a ghost.

shade *VERB* **shades, shading, shaded 1** shelter something from bright light. **2** make part of a drawing darker than the rest. **3** move gradually from one state or quality to another • *evening shading into night.*
▷ **shading** *noun*
[from Old English *sceadu*]

shadow *NOUN* **shadows 1** the dark shape that falls on a surface when something is between the surface and a light. **2** an area of shade. **3** a slight trace • *a shadow of doubt.*
▷ **shadowy** *adjective*

shadow *VERB* **shadows, shadowing, shadowed 1** cast a shadow on something. **2** follow a person secretly.
[same origin as *shade*]

Shadow Cabinet *NOUN* members of the Opposition in Parliament who each have responsibility for a particular area of policy.

shady *ADJECTIVE* **shadier, shadiest 1** giving shade • *a shady tree.* **2** in the shade • *a shady place.* **3** not completely honest; disreputable • *a shady deal.*

shaft *NOUN* **shafts 1** a long slender rod or straight part • *the shaft of an arrow.* **2** a ray of light. **3** a deep narrow hole • *a mine shaft.*
[from Old English]

shaggy *ADJECTIVE* **shaggier, shaggiest 1** having long rough hair or fibre. **2** rough, thick, and untidy • *shaggy hair.*
[from Old English]

shah *NOUN* **shahs** the title of the former ruler of Iran.
[from Persian *shah* = king]

shake *VERB* **shakes, shaking, shook, shaken 1** move quickly up and down or from side to side. **2** shock or upset • *The news shook us.* **3** tremble; be unsteady • *His voice was shaking.*
▷ **shaker** *noun*
- **shake hands** clasp a person's right hand with yours in greeting or parting or as a sign of agreement.

shake *NOUN* **shakes 1** shaking; a shaking movement. **2** (*informal*) a milkshake.
▷ **shaky** *adjective* **shakily** *adverb*
- **in two shakes** very soon.
[from Old English]

shale *NOUN* a kind of stone that splits easily into layers.
[probably from German]

shall *AUXILIARY VERB* **1** used with *I* and *we* to refer to the future • *I shall arrive tomorrow.* **2** used with *I* and *we* in questions when making a suggestion or offer or asking for advice • *Shall I shut the door?* **3** (*old-fashioned use*) used with words other than *I* and *we* in promises or to express determination • *Trust me, you shall have a party.*
[from Old English]

shallot *NOUN* **shallots** a kind of small onion.
[from French]

shallow *ADJECTIVE* **shallower, shallowest** **1** not deep • *shallow water.* **2** not capable of deep feelings • *a shallow character.*
▷ **shallowness** *noun*
[origin unknown]

shallows *PLURAL NOUN* a shallow part of a stretch of water.

sham *NOUN* **shams** something that is not genuine; a pretence.
▷ **sham** *adjective*

sham *VERB* **shams, shamming, shammed** pretend.
[probably from *shame*]

shamble *VERB* **shambles, shambling, shambled** walk or run in a lazy or awkward way.
[origin unknown]

shambles *NOUN* a scene of great disorder or bloodshed.
[from an old word *shamble* = a slaughter- house or meat- market]

shambolic (*say* sham-**bol**-ik) *ADJECTIVE* (*informal*) chaotic or disorganized.
[from *shambles*]

shame *NOUN* **1** a feeling of great sorrow or guilt because you have done wrong. **2** dishonour or disgrace. **3** something you regret; a pity • *It's a shame that it rained.*
▷ **shameful** *adjective* **shamefully** *adverb*

shame *VERB* **shames, shaming, shamed** make a person feel ashamed.
[from Old English]

shamefaced *ADJECTIVE* looking ashamed.

shameless *ADJECTIVE* not feeling or looking ashamed.
▷ **shamelessly** *adverb*

shampoo *NOUN* **shampoos** **1** a liquid substance for washing the hair. **2** a substance for cleaning a carpet etc. or washing a car. **3** a wash with shampoo • *a shampoo and set.*

shampoo *VERB* **shampoos, shampooing, shampooed** wash or clean with a shampoo.
[originally = to massage: from Hindi *champo* = press]

shamrock *NOUN* **shamrocks** a plant rather like clover, the national emblem of Ireland.
[Irish]

shandy *NOUN* **shandies** a mixture of beer and lemonade or some other soft drink.
[origin unknown]

shank *NOUN* **shanks** **1** the leg, especially the part from knee to ankle. **2** a long narrow part • *the shank of a pin.*
[from Old English]

shan't (*mainly spoken*) shall not.

shanty[1] *NOUN* **shanties** a shack.
[from Canadian French]

shanty[2] *NOUN* **shanties** a sailors' song with a chorus.
[probably from French *chanter* = sing]

shanty town *NOUN* **shanty towns** a settlement consisting of shanties.

shape *NOUN* **shapes** **1** a thing's outline; the appearance an outline produces. **2** proper form or condition • *Get it into shape.* **3** the general form or condition of something • *the shape of British industry.*

shape *VERB* **shapes, shaping, shaped** **1** make into a particular shape. **2** develop • *The plan is shaping up nicely.*
[from Old English]

shapeless *ADJECTIVE* having no definite shape.

shapely *ADJECTIVE* **shapelier, shapeliest** having an attractive shape.

share *NOUN* **shares** **1** a part given to one person or thing out of something that is being divided. **2** each of the equal parts forming a business company's capital, giving the person who holds it the right to receive a portion (a *dividend*) of the company's profits.

share *VERB* **shares, sharing, shared** **1** give portions of something to two or more people. **2** have or use or experience something jointly with others • *She shared a room with me.*
[from Old English]

shareholder *NOUN* **shareholders** a person who owns shares in a company.

shareware *NOUN* computer software which is given away or which you can use free of charge.

shark[1] *NOUN* **sharks** a large sea fish with sharp teeth.
[origin unknown]

shark[2] *NOUN* **sharks** a person who exploits or cheats people.
[same origin as *shirk*]

sharp *ADJECTIVE* **1** with an edge or point that can cut or make holes. **2** quick at noticing or learning things • *sharp eyes.* **3** steep or pointed; not gradual • *a sharp bend.*
4 forceful or severe • *a sharp frost.*
5 distinct; loud and shrill • *a sharp cry.*
6 slightly sour. **7** (*in music*) one semitone higher than the natural note • *C sharp.*
▷ **sharply** *adverb* **sharpness** *noun*

sharp *ADVERB* **1** sharply • *Turn sharp right.* **2** punctually or precisely • *I'll see you at six o'clock sharp.* **3** (*in music*) above the correct pitch • *You were singing sharp.*

sharp *NOUN* **sharps** (*in music*) a note one semitone higher than the natural note; the sign (#) that indicates this.
[from Old English]

sharpen *VERB* **sharpens, sharpening, sharpened** make or become sharp.
▷ **sharpener** *noun*

sharp practice *NOUN* dishonest or barely honest dealings in business.

sharpshooter *NOUN* **sharpshooters** a skilled marksman.

shatter *VERB* **shatters, shattering, shattered** **1** break violently into small pieces. **2** destroy • *It shattered our hopes.*
3 upset greatly • *We were shattered by the news.*
[origin unknown]

shave *VERB* **shaves, shaving, shaved** **1** scrape growing hair off the skin. **2** cut or scrape a thin slice off something.
▷ **shaver** *noun*

shave *NOUN* **shaves** the act of shaving the face.
- **close shave** (*informal*) a narrow escape.
[from Old English]

shaven *ADJECTIVE* shaved • *a shaven head.*

shavings *PLURAL NOUN* thin strips shaved off a piece of wood or metal.

shawl *NOUN* **shawls** a large piece of material worn round the shoulders or head or wrapped round a baby.
[from Persian or Urdu]

she *PRONOUN* the female person or animal being talked about.
[Middle English; related to *he*]

sheaf *NOUN* **sheaves** **1** a bundle of cornstalks tied together. **2** a bundle of arrows, papers, etc. held together.
[from Old English]

shear *VERB* **shears, shearing, sheared, sheared** or, in sense 1, **shorn** **1** cut or trim; cut the wool off a sheep. **2** break because of a sideways or twisting force • *One of the bolts sheared off.*
▷ **shearer** *noun*
[from Old English]
USAGE Do not confuse with **sheer**.

shears *PLURAL NOUN* a cutting tool shaped like a very large pair of scissors and worked with both hands.
[from Old English]

sheath *NOUN* **sheaths** **1** a cover for the blade of a knife or sword etc. **2** a close-fitting cover. **3** a condom.
[from Old English]

sheathe *VERB* **sheathes, sheathing, sheathed** **1** put into a sheath • *He sheathed his sword.* **2** put a close covering on something.
[from *sheath*]

shed[1] *NOUN* **sheds** a simply-made building used for storing things or sheltering animals, or as a workshop.
[from *shade*]

A B C D E F G H I J K L M N O P Q R S T U V W X Y Z

shed[2] *VERB* **sheds, shedding, shed 1** let something fall or flow • *The tree shed its leaves.* • *We shed tears.* **2** give off • *A heater sheds warmth.* **3** get rid of • *The company has shed 200 workers.*
[from Old English]

sheen *NOUN* a shine or gloss.
[from Old English *sciene* = beautiful]

sheep *NOUN* **sheep** an animal that eats grass and has a thick fleecy coat, kept in flocks for its wool and its meat.
[from Old English]

sheepdog *NOUN* **sheepdogs** a dog trained to guard and herd sheep.

sheepish *ADJECTIVE* **1** bashful.
2 embarrassed or shamefaced.
▷ **sheepishly** *adverb* **sheepishness** *noun*
[originally = innocent or silly: from *sheep* + *-ish*]

sheepshank *NOUN* **sheepshanks** a knot used to shorten a rope.

sheer[1] *ADJECTIVE* **1** complete or thorough • *sheer stupidity*. **2** vertical, with almost no slope • *a sheer drop*. **3** (said about material) very thin; transparent.
[from Old English *scir* = shining, noble, or pure]

sheer[2] *VERB* **sheers, sheering, sheered** swerve; move sharply away.
[probably from old German]
USAGE Do not confuse with **shear**.

sheet[1] *NOUN* **sheets 1** a large piece of lightweight material used on a bed in pairs for a person to sleep between. **2** a whole flat piece of paper, glass, or metal. **3** a wide area of water, ice, flame, etc.
[from Old English *scete*]

sheet[2] *NOUN* **sheets** a rope or chain fastening a sail.
[from Old English *sceata*]

sheikh (*say* shayk or sheek) *NOUN* **sheikhs** the leader of an Arab tribe or village.
[from Arabic *shaykh* = elder, old man]

sheila *NOUN* **sheilas** (*informal*) (*Australian/NZ*) a girl or woman.
[origin unknown]

shelf *NOUN* **shelves 1** a flat piece of wood, metal, or glass etc. fixed to a wall or in a piece of furniture so that things can be placed on it. **2** a flat level surface that sticks out; a ledge.
[from old German]

shelf life *NOUN* **shelf lives** the length of time something can be kept in a shop before it becomes too old to sell • *Newspapers have a shelf life of only a day.*

shell *NOUN* **shells 1** the hard outer covering of an egg, nut, etc., or of an animal such as a snail, crab, or tortoise. **2** the walls or framework of a building, ship, etc. **3** a metal case filled with explosive, fired from a large gun.

shell *VERB* **shells, shelling, shelled 1** take something out of its shell. **2** fire explosive shells at something.
- **shell out** (*informal*) pay out money.
[from Old English]

shellfish *NOUN* **shellfish** a sea animal that has a shell.

shelter *NOUN* **shelters 1** something that protects people from rain, wind, danger, etc. **2** protection • *We took shelter from the rain.*

shelter *VERB* **shelters, sheltering, sheltered 1** provide with shelter. **2** protect. **3** find a shelter • *They sheltered under the trees.*
[origin unknown]

shelve *VERB* **shelves, shelving, shelved 1** put things on a shelf or shelves. **2** fit a wall or cupboard etc. with shelves. **3** postpone or reject a plan etc. **4** slope • *The bed of the river shelves steeply.*
[from *shelf*]

shepherd *NOUN* **shepherds** a person whose job is to look after sheep.

shepherd *VERB* **shepherds, shepherding, shepherded** guide or direct people.
[from *sheep* + *herd*]

shepherdess *NOUN* **shepherdesses** (*now usually poetical*) a woman whose job is to look after sheep.

shepherd's pie *NOUN* a dish of minced beef or lamb under a layer of mashed potato.

sherbet *NOUN* a fizzy sweet powder or drink.
[from Arabic *sharbat* = a drink]

sheriff *NOUN* **sheriffs** the chief law officer of a county, whose duties vary in different countries.
[from Old English *scir* = shire + *refa* = officer]

sherry *NOUN* **sherries** a kind of strong wine.
[named after Jerez de la Frontera, a town in Spain, where it was first made]

Shetland pony *NOUN* **Shetland ponies** a kind of small, strong, shaggy pony, originally from the Shetland Isles.

shield *NOUN* **shields 1** a large piece of metal, wood, etc. carried to protect the body in fighting. **2** a model of a triangular shield used as a trophy. **3** a protection.

shield *VERB* **shields, shielding, shielded** protect from harm or from being discovered.
[from Old English]

shift *VERB* **shifts, shifting, shifted 1** move or cause to move. **2** (said about an opinion or situation) change slightly.
- **shift for yourself** manage without help from other people.

shift *NOUN* **shifts 1** a change of position or condition etc. **2** a group of workers who start work as another group finishes; the time when they work • *the night shift*. **3** a straight dress with no waist.
[from Old English]

shifty *ADJECTIVE* evasive, not straightforward; untrustworthy.
▷ **shiftily** *adverb* **shiftiness** *noun*

Shi'ite (*say* shee-eyt) *NOUN* **Shi'ites** a member of one of the two main branches of Islam, based on the teachings of Muhammad and his son-in-law, Ali. (COMPARE **Sunni**)
[from Arabic *shia* = the party of Ali]

shilling *NOUN* **shillings** a former British coin, equal to 5p.
[from Old English]

shilly-shally *VERB* **shilly-shallies, shilly-shallying, shilly-shallied** be unable to make up your mind.
[from *shall I? shall I?*]

shimmer *VERB* **shimmers, shimmering, shimmered** shine with a quivering light • *The sea shimmered in the moonlight.*
▷ **shimmer** *noun*
[from Old English]

shin *NOUN* **shins** the front of the leg between the knee and the ankle.

shin *VERB* **shins, shinning, shinned** climb by using the arms and legs, not on a ladder.
[from Old English]

shindig *NOUN* **shindigs** (*informal*) a noisy party.
[origin unknown]

shine *VERB* **shines, shining, shone** in sense 4 **shined 1** give out or reflect light; be bright. **2** be excellent • *He doesn't shine in maths.* **3** aim a light • *Shine your torch on it*. **4** polish • *Have you shined your shoes?*

shine *NOUN* **1** brightness. **2** a polish.
[from Old English]

shingle *NOUN* pebbles on a beach.
[origin unknown]

shingles *NOUN* a disease caused by the chicken pox virus, producing a painful rash.

Shinto *NOUN* a Japanese religion which includes worship of ancestors and nature.

shiny *ADJECTIVE* **shinier, shiniest** shining or glossy.

ship *NOUN* **ships** a large boat, especially one that goes to sea.

ship *VERB* **ships, shipping, shipped** transport goods etc., especially by ship.
[from Old English]

-ship *SUFFIX* forms nouns meaning 'condition' (e.g. *friendship*, *hardship*), position (e.g. *chairmanship*), or skill (e.g. *seamanship*).
[from Old English]

shipment *NOUN* **shipments 1** the process of shipping goods. **2** the amount shipped.

shipping *NOUN* **1** ships • *Britain's shipping*. **2** transporting goods by ship.

shipshape *ADJECTIVE* in good order; tidy.

shipwreck *NOUN* **shipwrecks 1** the wrecking of a ship by storm or accident. **2** a wrecked ship.
▷ **shipwrecked** *adjective*

shipyard *NOUN* **shipyards** a place where ships are built or repaired.

shire *NOUN* **shires** a county.
- **the Shires** the country areas of (especially central) England, away from the cities.
[from Old English]

shire horse *NOUN* **shire horses** a kind of large, strong horse used for ploughing or pulling carts.

shirk *VERB* **shirks, shirking, shirked** avoid a duty or work etc. selfishly or unfairly.
▷ **shirker** *noun*
[probably from German *Schurke* = scoundrel]

shirt *NOUN* **shirts** a piece of clothing for the top half of the body, made of light material and with a collar and sleeves.
- **in your shirtsleeves** not wearing a jacket over your shirt.
[from Old English]

shirty *ADJECTIVE* (*informal*) annoyed.
[perhaps from *Keep your shirt on!* = calm down, don't be angry]

shiver *VERB* **shivers, shivering, shivered** tremble with cold or fear.
▷ **shiver** *noun* **shivery** *adjective*
[origin unknown]

shoal[1] *NOUN* **shoals** a large number of fish swimming together.
[same origin as *school*[2]]

shoal[2] *NOUN* **shoals 1** a shallow place. **2** an underwater sandbank.
[from Old English]

shock[1] *NOUN* **shocks 1** a sudden unpleasant surprise. **2** great weakness caused by pain or injury etc. **3** the effect of a violent shake or knock. **4** an effect caused by electric current passing through the body.

shock *VERB* **shocks, shocking, shocked 1** give someone a shock; surprise or upset a person greatly. **2** seem very improper or scandalous to a person.
[from French]

shock[2] *NOUN* **shocks** a bushy mass of hair.
[origin unknown]

shocking *ADJECTIVE* **1** causing indignation or disgust. **2** (*informal*) very bad • *shocking weather.*

shock wave *NOUN* **shock waves** a sharp change in pressure in the air around an explosion or an object moving very quickly.

shod *past tense* of **shoe**.

shoddy *ADJECTIVE* **shoddier, shoddiest** of poor quality; badly made or done • *shoddy work.*
▷ **shoddily** *adverb* **shoddiness** *noun*
[origin unknown]

shoe *NOUN* **shoes 1** a strong covering for the foot. **2** a horseshoe. **3** something shaped or used like a shoe.
- **be in somebody's shoes** be in his or her situation.

shoe *VERB* **shoes, shoeing, shod** fit with a shoe or shoes.
[from Old English]

shoehorn *NOUN* **shoehorns** a curved piece of stiff material for easing your heel into the back of a shoe.
[originally made from a cow's horn]

shoelace *NOUN* **shoelaces** a cord for lacing up and fastening a shoe.

shoestring *NOUN*
- **on a shoestring** using only a small amount of money • *travel the world on a shoestring.*

shoo *INTERJECTION* a word used to frighten animals away.
▷ **shoo** *verb*

shoot *VERB* **shoots, shooting, shot 1** fire a gun or missile etc. **2** hurt or kill by shooting. **3** move or send very quickly • *The car shot past us.* **4** kick or hit a ball at a goal. **5** (said about a plant) put out buds or shoots. **6** slide the bolt of a door into or out of its fastening. **7** film or photograph something • *The film was shot in Africa.*

shoot *NOUN* **shoots 1** a young branch or new growth of a plant. **2** an expedition for shooting animals.
[from Old English]

shooting star *NOUN* **shooting stars** a meteor.

shop *NOUN* **shops 1** a building or room where goods or services are on sale to the public. **2** a workshop. **3** talk that is about your own work or job • *She is always talking shop.*

shop *VERB* **shops, shopping, shopped** go and buy things at shops.
▷ **shopper** *noun*
- **shop around** compare goods and prices in several shops before buying.
[from old French]

shopfitter *NOUN* **shopfitters** a person whose job is to make or fit counters, shelves, display stands, etc. in shops.

shop floor *NOUN* **1** the workers in a factory, not the managers. **2** the place where they work.

shopkeeper *NOUN* **shopkeepers** a person who owns or manages a shop.

shoplifter *NOUN* **shoplifters** a person who steals goods from a shop after entering as a customer.
▷ **shoplifting** *noun*

shopping *NOUN* **1** buying goods in shops. **2** the goods bought.

shop-soiled *ADJECTIVE* dirty, faded, or slightly damaged through being displayed in a shop.

shop steward *NOUN* **shop stewards** a trade-union official who represents his or her fellow workers.

shop window *NOUN* **shop windows 1** a window in a shop where goods are displayed. **2** an opportunity to show off your abilities • *The exhibition will be a shop window for British industry.*

shore[1] *NOUN* **shores** the land along the edge of a sea or of a lake.
[from old German or old Dutch *schore*]

shore[2] *VERB* **shores, shoring, shored** prop something up with a piece of wood etc.
[from old German or old Dutch *schoren*]

shorn *past participle* of **shear**.

short *ADJECTIVE* **1** not long; occupying a small distance or time • *a short walk.* **2** not tall • *a short person.* **3** not enough; not having enough of something • *Water is short. We are short of water.* **4** bad-tempered; curt. **5** (said about pastry) rich and crumbly because it contains a lot of fat.
▷ **shortness** *noun*
- **for short** as an abbreviation • *Raymond is called Ray for short.*
- **in short** in a few words.
- **short for** an abbreviation of • *Ray is short for Raymond.*
- **short of** without going to the length of • *I'll do anything to help, short of robbing a bank.*

short *ADVERB* suddenly • *She stopped short.*
[from Old English]

shortage *NOUN* **shortages** lack or scarcity of something; insufficiency.

shortbread *NOUN* a rich sweet biscuit, made with butter.

shortcake *NOUN* shortbread.

short circuit *NOUN* **short circuits** a fault in an electrical circuit in which current flows along a shorter route than the normal one.

short-circuit *VERB* **short-circuits, short-circuiting, short-circuited** cause a short circuit.

shortcoming *NOUN* **shortcomings** a fault or failure to reach a good standard.

short cut *NOUN* **short cuts** a route or method that is quicker than the usual one.

shorten *VERB* **shortens, shortening, shortened** make or become shorter.

shortfall *NOUN* **shortfalls** a shortage; an amount lower than needed or expected.

shorthand *NOUN* a set of special signs for writing words down as quickly as people say them.

short-handed *ADJECTIVE* not having enough workers or helpers.

shortlist *NOUN* **shortlists** a list of the most suitable people or things, from which a final choice will be made.

shortlist *VERB* **shortlists, shortlisting, shortlisted** put on a shortlist.

shortly *ADVERB* **1** in a short time; soon • *They will arrive shortly.* **2** in a few words. **3** curtly.

shorts *PLURAL NOUN* trousers with legs that do not reach to the knee.

short-sighted *ADJECTIVE* **1** unable to see things clearly when they are further away. **2** lacking imagination or foresight.

short-staffed *ADJECTIVE* not having enough workers or staff.

short-tempered *ADJECTIVE* easily becoming angry.

short-term *ADJECTIVE* to do with a short period of time.

short wave *NOUN* a radio wave of a wavelength between 10 and 100 metres and a frequency of about 3 to 30 megahertz.

shot[1] *past tense* of **shoot**.

shot[2] *NOUN* **shots 1** the firing of a gun or missile etc.; the sound of this. **2** something fired from a gun; lead pellets for firing from small guns. **3** a person judged by skill in shooting • *He's a good shot*. **4** a heavy metal ball thrown as a sport. **5** a stroke in tennis, cricket, billiards, etc. **6** a photograph; a filmed scene. **7** an attempt • *Have a shot at the crossword*. **8** an injection of a drug or vaccine.

shot *ADJECTIVE* (said about fabric) woven so that different colours show at different angles • *shot silk*.
[from Old English]

shotgun *NOUN* **shotguns** a gun for firing small shot at close range.

shot put *NOUN* an athletic contest in which competitors throw a heavy metal ball.
▷ **shot putter** *noun*

should *AUXILIARY VERB* used **1** to say what someone ought to do • *You should have told me*. **2** to say what someone expects • *They should be here by ten o'clock*. **3** to say what might happen • *If you should happen to see him, tell him to come*. **4** with *I* and *we* to make a polite statement (*I should like to come*) or in a conditional clause (*If they had supported us we should have won*).
[past tense of *shall*]
USAGE In sense 4, although *should* is strictly correct, many people nowadays use *would* and this is not regarded as wrong.

shoulder *NOUN* **shoulders 1** the part of the body between the neck and the arm, foreleg, or wing. **2** a side that juts out • *the shoulder of the bottle*.

shoulder *VERB* **shoulders, shouldering, shouldered 1** take something on your shoulder or shoulders. **2** push with your shoulder. **3** accept responsibility or blame.
[from Old English]

shoulder blade *NOUN* **shoulder blades** either of the two large flat bones at the top of your back.

shouldn't (*mainly spoken*) should not.

shout *NOUN* **shouts** a loud cry or call.
[origin unknown]

shout *VERB* **shouts, shouting, shouted** give a shout; speak or call loudly.
[origin unknown]

shove *VERB* **shoves, shoving, shoved** push roughly.
▷ **shove** *noun*
- **shove off** (*informal*) go away.
[from Old English]

shovel *NOUN* **shovels** a tool like a spade with the sides turned up, used for lifting coal, earth, snow, etc.

shovel *VERB* **shovels, shovelling, shovelled 1** move or clear with a shovel. **2** scoop or push roughly • *He was shovelling food into his mouth*.
[from Old English]

show *VERB* **shows, showing, showed, shown 1** allow or cause something to be seen • *Show me your new bike*. **2** make a person understand; demonstrate • *Show me how to use it*. **3** guide • *Show him in*. **4** treat in a certain way • *She showed us much kindness*. **5** be visible • *That scratch won't show*. **6** prove your ability to someone • *We'll show them!*
- **show off 1** show something proudly. **2** try to impress people.
- **show up 1** make or be clearly visible; reveal a fault etc. **2** (*informal*) arrive.

show *NOUN* **shows 1** a display or exhibition • *a flower show*. **2** an entertainment. **3** (*informal*) something that happens or is done • *He runs the whole show*.
[from Old English]

show business *NOUN* the entertainment industry; the theatre, films, radio, and television.

showcase *NOUN* **showcases 1** a glass case for displaying something in a shop, museum, etc. **2** a situation or setting in which something can be presented attractively • *The programme is a showcase for new acts*.

showdown *NOUN* **showdowns** a final test or confrontation.

shower *NOUN* **showers 1** a brief fall of rain or snow. **2** a lot of small things coming or falling like rain • *a shower of stones*. **3** a device or cabinet for spraying water to wash a person's body; a wash in this.

shower *VERB* **showers, showering, showered 1** fall or send things in a shower. **2** wash under a shower.
[from Old English]

showery *ADJECTIVE* (said about weather) with many showers.

show house *NOUN* **show houses** a furnished and decorated house on a new estate that can be shown to people who are thinking of buying a house there.

showjumping *NOUN* a competition in which riders make their horses jump over fences and other obstacles, with penalty points for errors.
▷ **showjumper** *noun*

showman *NOUN* **showmen 1** a person who presents entertainments. **2** someone who is good at entertaining.
▷ **showmanship** *noun*

show-off *NOUN* **show-offs** (*informal*) a person who tries to impress people boastfully.

showpiece *NOUN* **showpieces** a fine example of something for people to see and admire.

showroom *NOUN* **showrooms** a large room where goods are displayed for people to look at.

showy *ADJECTIVE* **showier, showiest** likely to attract attention; brightly or highly decorated.
▷ **showily** *adverb* **showiness** *noun*

shrapnel *NOUN* pieces of metal scattered from an exploding shell.
[named after H. *Shrapnel*, a British officer who invented it in about 1806]

shred *NOUN* **shreds 1** a tiny piece torn or cut off something. **2** a small amount • *There is not a shred of evidence.*

shred *VERB* **shreds, shredding, shredded** cut into shreds.
▷ **shredder** *noun*
[from Old English]

shrew *NOUN* **shrews 1** a small mouse-like animal. **2** (*old use*) a bad-tempered woman who is constantly scolding people.
▷ **shrewish** *adjective*
[from Old English]

shrewd *ADJECTIVE* having common sense and good judgement; clever.
▷ **shrewdly** *adverb* **shrewdness** *noun*
[from old sense of *shrew* = spiteful or cunning person]

shriek *NOUN* **shrieks** a shrill cry or scream.

shriek *VERB* **shrieks, shrieking, shrieked** give a shriek.
[imitating the sound]

shrift *NOUN*
- **short shrift** curt treatment.
[originally = a short time allowed for someone to confess to a priest before being executed: from *shrive*]

shrill *ADJECTIVE* sounding very high and piercing.
▷ **shrilly** *adverb* **shrillness** *noun*
[probably from Old English]

shrimp *NOUN* **shrimps** a small shellfish, pink when boiled.
[origin unknown]

shrimping *NOUN* fishing for shrimps.

shrine *NOUN* **shrines** an altar, chapel, or other sacred place.
[originally = a container for holy relics: via Old English from Latin *scrinium* = a case or chest]

shrink *VERB* **shrinks, shrinking, shrank, shrunk 1** make or become smaller. **2** move back to avoid something. **3** avoid doing something because of fear, conscience, embarrassment, etc.
▷ **shrinkage** *noun*
[from Old English]

shrive *VERB* **shrives, shriving, shrove, shriven** (*old use*) (said about a priest) hear a person's confession and give absolution.
[from Old English]

shrivel *VERB* **shrivels, shrivelling, shrivelled** make or become dry and wrinkled.
[probably from Old Norse]

shroud *NOUN* **shrouds 1** a cloth in which a dead body is wrapped. **2** each of a set of ropes supporting a ship's mast.

shroud *VERB* **shrouds, shrouding, shrouded 1** wrap in a shroud. **2** cover or conceal • *The town was shrouded in mist.*
[from Old English]

shrove *past tense* of **shrive**.

Shrove Tuesday *NOUN* the day before Lent, when pancakes are eaten, originally to use up fat before the fast.
[from the past tense of *shrive*, because it was the custom to be shriven on this day]

a b c d e f g h i j k l m n o p q r s t u v w x y z

shrub *NOUN* **shrubs** a woody plant smaller than a tree; a bush.
▷ **shrubby** *adjective*
[from Old English]

shrubbery *NOUN* **shrubberies** an area planted with shrubs.

shrug *VERB* **shrugs, shrugging, shrugged** raise your shoulders as a sign that you do not care, do not know, etc.
▷ **shrug** *noun*
- **shrug something off** treat it as unimportant.
[origin unknown]

shrunken *ADJECTIVE* having shrunk.

shudder *VERB* **shudders, shuddering, shuddered** **1** shiver violently with horror, fear, or cold. **2** make a strong shaking movement.
▷ **shudder** *noun*
[from old German or old Dutch]

shuffle *VERB* **shuffles, shuffling, shuffled** **1** walk without lifting the feet from the ground. **2** slide playing cards over each other to get them into random order. **3** shift or rearrange.
▷ **shuffle** *noun*
[probably from old German]

shun *VERB* **shuns, shunning, shunned** avoid; deliberately keep away from something.
[from Old English]

shunt *VERB* **shunts, shunting, shunted** **1** move a train or wagons on to another track. **2** divert to a less important place or position.
▷ **shunt** *noun* **shunter** *noun*
[origin unknown]

shut *VERB* **shuts, shutting, shut** **1** move a door, lid, or cover etc. so that it blocks an opening; make or become closed. **2** bring or fold parts together • *Shut the book.*
- **shut down** **1** stop something working. **2** stop business.
- **shut up** **1** shut securely. **2** (*informal*) stop talking or making a noise.
[from Old English]

shutter *NOUN* **shutters** **1** a panel or screen that can be closed over a window. **2** the device in a camera that opens and closes to let light fall on the film.
▷ **shuttered** *adjective*
[from *shut*]

shuttle *NOUN* **shuttles** **1** a holder carrying the weft thread across a loom in weaving. **2** a train, bus, or aircraft that makes frequent short journeys between two points. **3** a space shuttle.

shuttle *VERB* **shuttles, shuttling, shuttled** move, travel, or send backwards and forwards.
[from Old English]

shuttlecock *NOUN* **shuttlecocks** a small rounded piece of cork or plastic with a crown of feathers, struck to and fro by players in badminton etc.
[from *shuttle* and *cock*]

shy[1] *ADJECTIVE* **shyer, shyest** afraid to meet or talk to other people; timid.
▷ **shyly** *adverb* **shyness** *noun*

shy *VERB* **shies, shying, shied** jump or move suddenly in alarm.
[from Old English]

shy[2] *VERB* **shies, shying, shied** throw a stone etc.

shy *NOUN* **shies** a throw.
[origin unknown]

SI *NOUN* an internationally recognized system of metric units of measurement, including the metre and kilogram.
[short for French *Système International d'Unités* = International System of Units]

Siamese *ADJECTIVE* to do with or belonging to Siam (now called Thailand) or its people.
▷ **Siamese** *noun*

Siamese cat *NOUN* **Siamese cats** a cat with short pale fur with darker face, ears, tail, and feet.

Siamese twins *PLURAL NOUN* twins who are born with their bodies joined together.
[after two famous twins born in Siam (now called Thailand), who were joined near the waist]

sibilant *ADJECTIVE* having a hissing sound • *a sibilant whisper.*

sibilant *NOUN* **sibilants** a speech sound that sounds like hissing, e.g. *s, sh*.
[from Latin *sibilans* = hissing]

sibling *NOUN* **siblings** a brother or sister.
[from Old English *sib* = related by birth, a blood relative, + *-ling*]

sibyl *NOUN* **sibyls** a prophetess in ancient Greece or Rome.

sick *ADJECTIVE* **1** ill; physically or mentally unwell. **2** vomiting or likely to vomit • *I feel sick.* **3** distressed or disgusted. **4** making fun of death, disability, or misfortune in an unpleasant way.
- **sick of** tired of.
[from Old English]

sicken *VERB* **sickens, sickening, sickened**
1 begin to be ill. **2** make or become distressed or disgusted • *Vandalism sickens us all.*
▷ **sickening** *adjective*

sickle *NOUN* **sickles** a tool with a narrow curved blade, used for cutting corn etc.
[from Old English]

sickle-cell anaemia *NOUN* a severe form of anaemia which is passed on in the genes, and which causes pain in the joints, fever, jaundice, and sometimes death.
[so called because the red blood cells become sickle-shaped]

sickly *ADJECTIVE* **1** often ill; unhealthy.
2 making people feel sick • *a sickly smell.*
3 weak • *a sickly smile.*

sickness *NOUN* **sicknesses 1** illness. **2** a disease. **3** vomiting.

side *NOUN* **sides 1** a surface, especially one joining the top and bottom of something.
2 a line that forms part of the boundary of a triangle, square, etc. **3** either of the two halves into which something can be divided by a line down its centre. **4** the part near the edge and away from the centre. **5** the place or region next to a person or thing • *He stood at my side.* **6** one aspect or view of something • *Study all sides of the problem.*
7 one of two groups or teams etc. who oppose each other.
- **on the side** as a sideline.
- **side by side** next to each other.
- **take sides** support one person or group in a dispute or disagreement and not the other.

side *ADJECTIVE* at or on a side • *the side door.*

side *VERB* **sides, siding, sided**
- **side with** take a person's side in an argument.
[from Old English]

sideboard *NOUN* **sideboards** a long piece of furniture with drawers and cupboards for china etc. and a flat top.

sideburns *PLURAL NOUN* the strips of hair growing on each side of a man's face in front of his ears.

sidecar *NOUN* **sidecars** a small compartment for a passenger, fixed to the side of a motorcycle.

side effect *NOUN* **side effects** an effect, especially an unpleasant one, that a medicine has on you as well as the effect intended.

sidelight *NOUN* **sidelights 1** a light at the side of a vehicle or ship. **2** light from one side.

sideline *NOUN* **sidelines 1** something done in addition to your main work or activity.
2 each of the lines on the two long sides of a sports pitch.

sidelong *ADJECTIVE* towards one side; sideways • *a sidelong glance.*
[from *side* + Old English *-ling* = extending in a certain direction]

sidereal (*say* sid-eer-ee-al) *ADJECTIVE* to do with or measured by the stars.
[from Latin *sideris* = of a star]

sideshow *NOUN* **sideshows** a small entertainment forming part of a large one, e.g. at a fair.

sidetrack *VERB* **sidetracks, sidetracking, sidetracked** take someone's attention away from the main subject or problem.

sidewalk *NOUN* **sidewalks** (*American*) a pavement.

sideways *ADVERB* & *ADJECTIVE* **1** to or from one side • *Move it sideways.* **2** with one side facing forwards • *We sat sideways in the bus.*

siding *NOUN* **sidings** a short railway line by the side of a main line.

sidle *VERB* **sidles, sidling, sidled** walk in a shy or nervous manner.
[from *sidelong*]

A B C D E F G H I J K L M N O P Q R S T U V W X Y Z

siege *NOUN* **sieges** the surrounding of a place in order to capture it or force someone to surrender.
- **lay siege to** begin a siege of a place.
[from old French]

sienna *NOUN* a kind of clay used in making brownish paints.
[from *Siena*, a town in Italy]

sierra *NOUN* **sierras** a range of mountains with sharp peaks, in Spain or parts of America.
[Spanish, from Latin *serra* = a saw]

siesta (*say* see-est-a) *NOUN* **siestas** an afternoon rest.
[from Latin *sexta hora* = sixth hour, midday]

sieve (*say* siv) *NOUN* **sieves** a device made of mesh or perforated metal or plastic, used to separate the smaller or soft parts of something from the larger or hard parts.

sieve *VERB* **sieves, sieving, sieved** put something through a sieve.
[from Old English]

sift *VERB* **sifts, sifting, sifted 1** sieve. **2** examine and analyse facts or evidence etc. carefully.
▷ **sifter** *noun*
[from Old English]

sigh *NOUN* **sighs** a sound made by breathing out heavily when you are sad, tired, relieved, etc.

sigh *VERB* **sighs, sighing, sighed** make a sigh.
[probably from Old English]

sight *NOUN* **sights 1** the ability to see. **2** a view or glimpse • *I caught sight of her in the crowd*. **3** a thing that can be seen or is worth seeing • *Our garden is a lovely sight*. **4** an unsightly thing • *You do look a sight in those clothes!* **5** a device looked through to help aim a gun or telescope etc.
- **at sight** or **on sight** as soon as a person or thing has been seen.
- **in sight 1** visible. **2** clearly near • *Victory was in sight.*
USAGE Do not confuse with **site**.

sight *VERB* **sights, sighting, sighted 1** see or observe something. **2** aim a gun or telescope etc.
[from Old English]

sighted *ADJECTIVE* able to see; not blind.

sightless *ADJECTIVE* blind.

sight-reading *NOUN* playing or singing music at sight, without preparation.

sightseeing *NOUN* visiting interesting places in a town etc.
▷ **sightseer** *noun*

sign *NOUN* **signs 1** something that shows that a thing exists • *There are signs of decay*. **2** a mark, device, or notice etc. that gives a special meaning • *a road sign*. **3** an action or movement giving information or a command etc. **4** any of the twelve divisions of the zodiac, represented by a symbol.

sign *VERB* **signs, signing, signed 1** make a sign or signal. **2** write your signature on something; accept a contract etc. by doing this. **3** use signing.
- **sign on 1** accept a job etc. by signing a contract. **2** sign a form to say that you are unemployed and want to claim benefit.
[same origin as *signify*]

signal *NOUN* **signals 1** a device, gesture, or sound etc. that gives information or a command. **2** a message made up of such things. **3** a sequence of electrical impulses or radio waves.

signal *VERB* **signals, signalling, signalled** make a signal to somebody.
▷ **signaller** *noun*
USAGE Do not use this word in mistake for *single* in the phrase *to single out*.

signal *ADJECTIVE* remarkable • *a signal success*.
▷ **signally** *adverb*
[same origin as *signify*]

signal box *NOUN* **signal boxes** a building from which railway signals, points, etc. are controlled.

signalman *NOUN* **signalmen** a person who controls railway signals.

signatory *NOUN* **signatories** a person who signs an agreement etc.

signature *NOUN* **signatures 1** a person's name written by himself or herself. **2** (*in music*) a set of sharps and flats after the clef in a score, showing the key the music is written in (the *key signature*), or the sign, often a fraction such as ¾, (the *time signature*), showing the number of beats in the bar and their rhythm
[from Latin *signare* = make a mark]

signature tune *NOUN* **signature tunes** a special tune always used to announce a particular programme, performer, etc.

signet ring *NOUN* **signet rings** a ring with a person's initials or a design engraved on it.
[same origin as *signify*]

significant *ADJECTIVE* **1** having a meaning; full of meaning. **2** important • *a significant event.*
▷ **significantly** *adverb* **significance** *noun*

signification *NOUN* meaning.

signify *VERB* **signifies, signifying, signified 1** be a sign or symbol of; mean. **2** indicate • *She signified her approval.* **3** be important; matter.
[from Latin *signum* = sign]

signing or **sign language** *NOUN* a way of communicating by using gestures etc. instead of sounds, used mainly by deaf people.

signpost *NOUN* **signposts** a sign at a road junction etc. showing the names and distances of places down each road.

Sikh (*say* seek) *NOUN* **Sikhs** a member of a religion founded in northern India, believing in one God and accepting some Hindu and some Islamic beliefs.
▷ **Sikhism** *noun*
[from Sanskrit *sisya* = disciple]

silage *NOUN* fodder made from green crops stored in a silo.

silence *NOUN* **silences 1** absence of sound. **2** not speaking.
- **in silence** without speaking or making a sound.

silence *VERB* **silences, silencing, silenced** make a person or thing silent.

silencer *NOUN* **silencers** a device for reducing the sound made by a gun or a vehicle's exhaust system etc.

silent *ADJECTIVE* **1** without any sound. **2** not speaking.
▷ **silently** *adverb*
[from Latin *silere* = to be silent]

silhouette (*say* sil-oo-et) *NOUN* **silhouettes 1** a dark shadow seen against a light background. **2** a portrait of a person in profile, showing the shape and outline only in solid black.
▷ **silhouette** *verb*
[named after a French author, É. de *Silhouette*, who made paper cut- outs of people's profiles from their shadows]

silica *NOUN* a hard white mineral that is a compound of silicon, used to make glass.

silicon *NOUN* a substance found in many rocks, used in making transistors, chips for microprocessors, etc.
[from Latin *silex* = flint or quartz]

silicone *NOUN* a compound of silicon used in paints, varnish, and lubricants.

silk *NOUN* **silks 1** a fine soft thread or cloth made from the fibre produced by silkworms for making their cocoons. **2** a length of silk thread used for embroidery.
▷ **silken** *adjective* **silky** *adjective*
[from Old English, probably from Latin]

silkworm *NOUN* **silkworms** the caterpillar of a kind of moth, which feeds on mulberry leaves and spins itself a cocoon.

sill *NOUN* **sills** a strip of stone, wood, or metal underneath a window or door.
[from Old English]

silly *ADJECTIVE* **sillier, silliest** foolish or unwise.
▷ **silliness** *noun*
[from Old English *saelig* = happy, blessed by God, later = innocent, helpless]

silo (*say* sy-loh) *NOUN* **silos 1** a pit or tower for storing green crops (see *silage*) or corn or cement etc. **2** an underground place for storing a missile ready for firing.
[Spanish]

silt *NOUN* sediment laid down by a river or sea etc.

silt *VERB* **silts, silting, silted**
- **silt up** block or clog or become blocked with silt.
[origin unknown]

silver *NOUN* **1** a shiny white precious metal. **2** the colour of silver. **3** coins or objects made of silver or silver-coloured metal. **4** a silver medal, usually given as second prize.
▷ **silvery** *adjective*

silver *ADJECTIVE* **1** made of silver. **2** coloured like silver.

silver *VERB* **silvers, silvering, silvered** make or become silvery.
[from Old English]

silver wedding *NOUN* **silver weddings** a couple's 25th wedding anniversary.

simian *ADJECTIVE* like a monkey.
[from Latin *simia* = monkey]

similar *ADJECTIVE* **1** nearly the same as another person or thing; of the same kind. **2** (*in mathematics*) having the same shape but not the same size • *similar triangles.*
▷ **similarly** *adverb* **similarity** *noun*
[from Latin *similis* = like]

simile (*say* sim-il-ee) *NOUN* **similes** a comparison of one thing with another, e.g. *He is as strong as a horse. We ran like the wind.*
[same origin as *similar*]

simmer *VERB* **simmers, simmering, simmered** boil very gently.
- **simmer down** calm down.
[origin unknown]

simper *VERB* **simpers, simpering, simpered** smile in a silly affected way.
▷ **simper** *noun*
[origin unknown]

simple *ADJECTIVE* **simpler, simplest** **1** easy • *a simple question.* **2** not complicated or elaborate. **3** plain, not showy • *a simple cottage.* **4** without much sense or intelligence. **5** not of high rank; ordinary • *a simple countryman.*
▷ **simplicity** *noun*
[from Latin]

simple-minded *ADJECTIVE* naive or foolish.

simpleton *NOUN* **simpletons** (*old use*) a foolish person.

simplify *VERB* **simplifies, simplifying, simplified** make a thing simple or easy to understand.
▷ **simplification** *noun*

simply *ADVERB* **1** in a simple way • *Explain it simply.* **2** without doubt; completely • *It's simply marvellous.* **3** only or merely • *It's simply a question of time.*

simulate *VERB* **simulates, simulating, simulated** **1** reproduce the appearance or conditions of something; imitate • *This device simulates a space flight.* **2** pretend • *They simulated fear.*
▷ **simulation** *noun*
[same origin as *similar*]

simulator *NOUN* **simulators** a machine or device for simulating actual conditions or events, often used for training • *a flight simulator.*

simultaneous (*say* sim-ul-tay-nee-us) *ADJECTIVE* happening at the same time.
▷ **simultaneously** *adverb*
[from Latin]

sin *NOUN* **sins** **1** the breaking of a religious or moral law. **2** a very bad action.

sin *VERB* **sins, sinning, sinned** commit a sin.
▷ **sinner** *noun*
[from Old English]

since *CONJUNCTION* **1** from the time when • *Where have you been since I last saw you?* **2** because • *Since we have missed the bus we must walk home.*

since *PREPOSITION* from a certain time • *She has been here since Christmas.*

since *ADVERB* between then and now • *He ran away and hasn't been seen since.*
[from Old English *sithon* = then]

sincere *ADJECTIVE* without pretence; truly felt or meant • *my sincere thanks.*
▷ **sincerely** *adverb* **sincerity** *noun*
- **Yours sincerely** see *yours.*
[from Latin *sincerus* = clean or pure]

sine *NOUN* **sines** (in a right-angled triangle) the ratio of the length of a side opposite one of the acute angles to the length of the hypotenuse. (COMPARE **cosine**)
[same origin as *sinus*]

sinecure (*say* sy-nik-yoor) *NOUN* **sinecures** a paid job that requires no work.
[from Latin *sine cura* = without care]

sinew *NOUN* **sinews** strong tissue that connects a muscle to a bone.
[from Old English]

sinewy *ADJECTIVE* slim, muscular, and strong.

sinful *ADJECTIVE* **1** guilty of sin. **2** wicked.
▷ **sinfully** *adverb* **sinfulness** *noun*

sing *VERB* **sings, singing, sang, sung**
1 make musical sounds with the voice.
2 perform a song.
▷ **singer** *noun*
[from Old English]

singe (*say* sinj) *VERB* **singes, singeing, singed** burn something slightly.
[from Old English]

single *ADJECTIVE* **1** one only; not double or multiple. **2** suitable for one person • *single beds*. **3** separate • *We sold every single thing*. **4** not married. **5** for the journey to a place but not back again • *a single ticket*.

single *NOUN* **singles 1** a single person or thing. **2** a single ticket. **3** a record with one short piece of music on each side.
- **singles** a game of tennis etc. between two players.

single *VERB* **singles, singling, singled**
- **single out** pick out or distinguish from other people or things.
[from Latin]

single file *NOUN*
- **in single file** in a line, one behind the other.

single-handed *ADJECTIVE* without help.

single-minded *ADJECTIVE* with your mind set on one purpose only.

single parent *NOUN* **single parents** a person bringing up a child or children without a partner.

singles bar *NOUN* **singles bars** a bar where unmarried people go to drink and meet each other.

singlet *NOUN* **singlets** a man's vest or similar piece of clothing worn under or instead of a shirt.
[originally = a jacket something like a doublet: from *single* with a pun on *double* and *doublet*]

singly *ADVERB* in ones; one by one.

singsong *ADJECTIVE* having a monotonous tone or rhythm • *a singsong voice*.

singsong *NOUN* **singsongs 1** informal singing by a gathering of people. **2** a singsong tone.

singular *NOUN* **singulars** the form of a noun or verb used when it stands for only one person or thing • *The singular is 'man', the plural is 'men'*.

singular *ADJECTIVE* **1** to do with the singular. **2** uncommon or extraordinary • *a woman of singular courage*.
▷ **singularly** *adverb* **singularity** *noun*
[from Latin *singulus* = single]

sinister *ADJECTIVE* **1** looking evil or harmful. **2** wicked • *a sinister motive*.
[from Latin, = on the left (which was thought to be unlucky)]

sink *VERB* **sinks, sinking, sank, sunk 1** go or cause to go under the surface or to the bottom of the sea etc. • *The ship sank*. • *They sank the ship*. **2** go or fall slowly downwards • *He sank to his knees*. **3** push something sharp deeply into something • *The dog sank its teeth into my leg*. **4** dig or drill • *They sank a well*. **5** invest money in something.
- **sink in** become understood.

sink *NOUN* **sinks** a fixed basin with a drainpipe and usually a tap or taps to supply water.
[from Old English]

sinuous *ADJECTIVE* with many bends or curves.
[same origin as *sinus*]

sinus (*say* sy-nus) *NOUN* **sinuses** a hollow part in the bones of the skull, connected with the nose • *My sinuses are blocked*.
[Latin, = curve]

-sion *SUFFIX*, SEE **-ion**.

sip *VERB* **sips, sipping, sipped** drink in small mouthfuls.
▷ **sip** *noun*
[probably from *sup*]

siphon *NOUN* **siphons 1** a pipe or tube in the form of an upside-down U, arranged so that liquid is forced up it and down to a lower level. **2** a bottle containing soda water which is released through a tube.

siphon *VERB* **siphons, siphoning, siphoned** flow or draw out through a siphon.
[Greek, = pipe]

sir *NOUN* **1** a word used when speaking politely to a man • *Please sir, may I go?* **2 Sir** the title given to a knight or baronet • *Sir John Moore*.
[from *sire*]

sire *NOUN* **sires 1** the male parent of a horse or dog etc. (COMPARE **dam**²) **2** a word formerly used when speaking to a king.

sire *VERB* **sires, siring, sired** be the sire of • *This stallion has sired several winners.*
[from French; related to *senior*]

siren *NOUN* **sirens 1** a device that makes a long loud sound as a signal. **2** a dangerously attractive woman.
[named after the *Sirens* in Greek legend, women who by their sweet singing lured seafarers to shipwreck on the rocks]

sirloin *NOUN* beef from the upper part of the loin.
[from *sur-*² + old French *loigne* = loin]

sirocco *NOUN* **siroccos** a hot dry wind that reaches Italy from Africa.
[from Arabic *sharuk* = east wind]

sisal (*say* sy-sal) *NOUN* fibre from a tropical plant, used for making ropes.
[named after *Sisal*, a port in Mexico from which it was exported]

sissy *NOUN* **sissies** a timid or cowardly person.
[from *sis* = sister]

sister *NOUN* **sisters 1** a daughter of the same parents as another person. **2** a woman who is a fellow member of an association etc. **3** a nun. **4** a senior hospital nurse, especially one in charge of a ward.
▷ **sisterly** *adjective*
[from Old English]

sisterhood *NOUN* **sisterhoods 1** being sisters. **2** companionship and mutual support between women. **3** a society or association of women.

sister-in-law *NOUN* **sisters-in-law 1** the sister of a married person's husband or wife. **2** the wife of a person's brother.

sit *VERB* **sits, sitting, sat 1** rest with your body supported on the buttocks; occupy a seat • *We were sitting in the front row.*
2 seat; cause someone to sit. **3** (said about birds) perch; stay on the nest to hatch eggs. **4** be a candidate for an examination. **5** be situated; stay. **6** (said about Parliament or a lawcourt etc.) be assembled for business.
[from Old English]

sitar *NOUN* **sitars** an Indian musical instrument that is like a guitar.
[Hindi, from Persian and Urdu *sih* = three + *tar* = string]

sitcom *NOUN* **sitcoms** (*informal*) a situation comedy.

site *NOUN* **sites** the place where something happens or happened or is built etc. • *a camping site.*
USAGE Do not confuse with **sight**.

site *VERB* **sites, siting, sited** provide with a site; locate.
[from Latin *situs* = position]

sit-in *NOUN* **sit-ins** a protest in which people sit down or occupy a public place and refuse to move.

sitter *NOUN* **sitters 1** a person who poses for a portrait. **2** a person who looks after children, pets, or a house while the owners are away.

sitting *NOUN* **sittings 1** the time when people are served a meal. **2** the time when a parliament or committee is conducting business.

sitting room *NOUN* **sitting rooms** a room with comfortable chairs for sitting in.

sitting tenant *NOUN* **sitting tenants** a tenant who is entitled to stay if the place he or she rents is bought by someone else.

situated *ADJECTIVE* in a particular place or situation.

situation *NOUN* **situations 1** a position, with its surroundings. **2** a state of affairs at a certain time • *The police faced a difficult situation.* **3** a job.
[same origin as *site*]

situation comedy *NOUN* **situation comedies** a comedy series on radio or television, based on how characters react to unusual or comic situations.

six *NOUN* & *ADJECTIVE* **sixes** the number 6.
▷ **sixth** *adjective* & *noun*
- **at sixes and sevens** in disorder or disagreement.
[from Old English]

sixth form *NOUN* **sixth forms** a form for students aged 16-18 in a secondary school.

sixth sense *NOUN* the ability to know something by instinct rather than by using any of the five senses; intuition.

sixteen *NOUN* & *ADJECTIVE* the number 16.
▷ **sixteenth** *adjective* & *noun*
[from Old English]

sixty *NOUN* & *ADJECTIVE* **sixties** the number 60.
▷ **sixtieth** *adjective* & *noun*
[from Old English]

size[1] *NOUN* **sizes 1** the measurements or extent of something. **2** any of the series of standard measurements in which certain things are made • *a size eight shoe.*

size *VERB* **sizes, sizing, sized** arrange things according to their size.
- **size up 1** estimate the size of something. **2** form an opinion or judgement about a person or thing.
[originally, a law fixing the amount of a tax: from old French *assise* = law, court session]

size[2] *NOUN* a gluey substance used to glaze paper or stiffen cloth etc.

size *VERB* **sizes, sizing, sized** treat with size.
[origin unknown]

sizeable *ADJECTIVE* large or fairly large.

sizzle *VERB* **sizzles, sizzling, sizzled** make a crackling or hissing sound.
[imitating the sound]

sjambok (*say* sham-bok) *NOUN* **sjamboks** (*S. African*) a strong whip originally made from the skin of a rhinoceros.
[via Afrikaans from Persian *chabuk* = whip]

skate[1] *NOUN* **skates 1** a boot with a steel blade attached to the sole, used for sliding smoothly over ice. **2** a roller skate.

skate *VERB* **skates, skating, skated** move on skates.
▷ **skater** *noun*
[from Dutch]

skate[2] *NOUN* **skate** a large flat edible sea fish.
[from Old Norse]

skateboard *NOUN* **skateboards** a small board with wheels, used for standing and riding on as a sport.
▷ **skateboarder, skateboarding** *nouns*

skein *NOUN* **skeins** a coil of yarn or thread.
[from old French]

skeleton *NOUN* **skeletons 1** the framework of bones of the body. **2** the shell or other hard part of a crab etc. **3** a framework, e.g. of a building.
▷ **skeletal** *adjective*
[from Greek *skeletos* = dried-up]

sketch *NOUN* **sketches 1** a rough drawing or painting. **2** a short account of something. **3** a short amusing play.

sketch *VERB* **sketches, sketching, sketched** make a sketch.
[from Greek *schedios* = done without practice or preparation]

sketchy *ADJECTIVE* rough and not detailed or careful.

skew *ADJECTIVE* askew or slanting.

skew *VERB* **skews, skewing, skewed** make a thing askew.
[from old French]

skewer *NOUN* **skewers** a long pin pushed through meat to hold it together while it is being cooked.
▷ **skewer** *verb*
[origin unknown]

ski (*say* skee) *NOUN* **skis** each of a pair of long narrow strips of wood, metal, or plastic fixed under the feet for moving quickly over snow.

ski *VERB* **skies, skiing, skied** travel on skis.
▷ **skier** *noun*
[Norwegian]

skid *VERB* **skids, skidding, skidded** slide accidentally.

skid *NOUN* **skids 1** a skidding movement. **2** a runner on a helicopter, for use in landing.
[probably from Old Norse *skith* = ski]

ski jump *NOUN* **ski jumps** a steep slope with a sharp drop where it levels out at the bottom, for skiers to jump off as a sport.

skilful *ADJECTIVE* having or showing great skill.
▷ **skilfully** *adverb*

skill *NOUN* **skills** the ability to do something well.
▷ **skilled** *adjective*
[from Old Norse]

skilled *ADJECTIVE* **1** skilful; highly trained or experienced. **2** (said about work) needing skill or special training.

a b c d e f g h i j k l m n o p q r s t u v w x y z

skim *VERB* **skims, skimming, skimmed** **1** remove something from the surface of a liquid; take the cream off milk. **2** move quickly over a surface or through the air. **3** read something quickly.
[from old French *escume* = scum]

skimp *VERB* **skimps, skimping, skimped** supply or use less than is needed • *Don't skimp on the food.*
[origin unknown]

skimpy *ADJECTIVE* **skimpier, skimpiest** scanty or too small.

skin *NOUN* **skins 1** the flexible outer covering of a person's or animal's body. **2** an outer layer or covering, e.g. of a fruit. **3** a skin-like film formed on the surface of a liquid.

skin *VERB* **skins, skinning, skinned** take the skin off something.
[from Old Norse]

skin diving *NOUN* swimming under water with flippers and breathing apparatus but without a diving suit.
▷ **skin diver** *noun*

skinflint *NOUN* **skinflints** a miserly person.

skinhead *NOUN* **skinheads** a youth with very closely cropped hair.

skinny *ADJECTIVE* **skinnier, skinniest** very thin.

skip[1] *VERB* **skips, skipping, skipped** **1** move along lightly, especially by hopping on each foot in turn. **2** jump with a skipping rope. **3** go quickly from one subject to another. **4** miss something out • *You can skip chapter six.*

skip *NOUN* **skips** a skipping movement.
[probably from a Scandinavian language]

skip[2] *NOUN* **skips** a large metal container for taking away builders' rubbish etc.
[from Old Norse *skeppa* = basket]

skipper *NOUN* **skippers** (*informal*) a captain.
[from old German or old Dutch *schip* = ship]

skipping rope *NOUN* **skipping ropes** a rope, usually with a handle at each end, that is swung over your head and under your feet as you jump.

skirmish *NOUN* **skirmishes** (*informal*) a small fight or conflict.
▷ **skirmish** *verb*
[from old French]

skirt *NOUN* **skirts 1** a piece of clothing for a woman or girl that hangs down from the waist. **2** the part of a dress below the waist.

skirt *VERB* **skirts, skirting, skirted** go round the edge of something.
[from Old Norse]

skirting or **skirting board** *NOUN* **skirtings, skirting boards** a narrow board round the wall of a room, close to the floor.

skit *NOUN* **skits** a satirical sketch or parody • *He wrote a skit on 'Hamlet'.*
[origin unknown]

skittish *ADJECTIVE* frisky; lively and excitable.
[origin unknown]

skittle *NOUN* **skittles** a wooden bottle-shaped object that people try to knock down by bowling a ball in the game of **skittles**.
[origin unknown]

skive *VERB* **skives, skiving, skived** (*informal*) dodge work.
▷ **skiver** *noun*
[probably from French *esquiver* = dodge]

skulk *VERB* **skulks, skulking, skulked** loiter stealthily.
[probably from a Scandinavian language]

skull *NOUN* **skulls** the framework of bones of the head.
[probably from a Scandinavian language]

skullcap *NOUN* **skullcaps** a small close-fitting cap worn on the top of the head.

skunk *NOUN* **skunks** a North American animal with black and white fur that can spray a bad-smelling fluid.
[a Native American word]

sky *NOUN* **skies** the space above the earth, appearing blue in daylight on fine days.
[from Old Norse]

skydiving *NOUN* the sport of jumping from an aeroplane and performing manoeuvres before opening your parachute.
▷ **skydiver** *noun*

skylark *NOUN* **skylarks** a lark that sings while it hovers high in the air.

skylight *NOUN* **skylights** a window in a roof.

skyline *NOUN* **skylines** the outline of land or buildings seen against the sky • *the Manhattan skyline.*

skyscraper *NOUN* **skyscrapers** a very tall building.

slab *NOUN* **slabs** a thick flat piece.
[origin unknown]

slack *ADJECTIVE* **1** not pulled tight. **2** not busy; not working hard.
▷ **slackly** *adverb* **slackness** *noun*

slack *NOUN* the slack part of a rope etc.

slack *VERB* **slacks, slacking, slacked** avoid work; be lazy.
▷ **slacker** *noun*
[from Old English]

slacken *VERB* **slackens, slackening, slackened** make or become slack.

slacks *PLURAL NOUN* trousers for informal occasions.

slag *NOUN* waste material separated from metal in smelting.
[from old German]

slag heap *NOUN* **slag heaps** a mound of waste matter from a mine etc.

slain *past participle* of **slay**.

slake *VERB* **slakes, slaking, slaked** quench • *slake your thirst.*
[from Old English]

slalom *NOUN* **slaloms** a ski race down a zigzag course.
[Norwegian *sla* = sloping + *låm* = track]

slam *VERB* **slams, slamming, slammed** **1** shut loudly. **2** hit violently.
▷ **slam** *noun*
[probably from a Scandinavian language]

slander *NOUN* **slanders** a spoken statement that damages a person's reputation and is untrue. (COMPARE **libel**)
▷ **slanderous** *adjective*

slander *VERB* **slanders, slandering, slandered** make a slander against someone.
▷ **slanderer** *noun*
[from old French; related to *scandal*]

slang *NOUN* words that are used very informally to add vividness or humour to what is said, especially those used only by a particular group of people • *teenage slang.*
▷ **slangy** *adjective*
[origin unknown]

slanging match *NOUN* **slanging matches** a noisy quarrel, with people shouting insults at each other.

slant *VERB* **slants, slanting, slanted** **1** slope. **2** present news or information etc. from a particular point of view.
[probably from a Scandinavian language]

slap *VERB* **slaps, slapping, slapped** **1** hit with the palm of the hand or with something flat. **2** put forcefully or carelessly • *We slapped paint on the walls.*
▷ **slap** *noun*
[imitating the sound]

slapdash *ADJECTIVE* hasty and careless.

slapstick *NOUN* comedy with people hitting each other, falling over, etc.
[from *slap* + *stick*[1]]

slash *VERB* **slashes, slashing, slashed** **1** make large cuts in something. **2** cut or strike with a long sweeping movement. **3** reduce greatly • *Prices were slashed.*

slash *NOUN* **slashes** **1** a slashing cut. **2** a slanting line (/) used in writing and printing.
[probably from old French]

slat *NOUN* **slats** each of the thin strips of wood or metal or plastic arranged so that they overlap and form a screen, e.g. in a venetian blind.
[from old French *esclat* = piece, splinter]

slate *NOUN* **slates** **1** a kind of grey rock that is easily split into flat plates. **2** a piece of this rock used in covering a roof or (formerly) for writing on.
▷ **slaty** *adjective*

slate *VERB* **slates, slating, slated** **1** cover a roof with slates. **2** (*informal*) criticize severely.
[same origin as *slat*]

slattern *NOUN* **slatterns** (*old use*) a slovenly woman.
▷ **slatternly** *adjective*
[origin unknown]

slaughter *VERB* **slaughters, slaughtering, slaughtered** **1** kill an animal for food. **2** kill people or animals ruthlessly or in great numbers.
▷ **slaughter** *noun*
[from Old Norse]

slaughterhouse *NOUN* **slaughterhouses** a place where animals are killed for food.

slave *NOUN* **slaves** a person who is owned by another and obliged to work for him or her without being paid.
▷ **slavery** *noun*

slave *VERB* **slaves, slaving, slaved** work very hard.
[from Latin *sclavus* = captive]

slave-driver *NOUN* **slave-drivers** a person who makes others work very hard.

slaver (*say* slav-er or slay-ver) *VERB* **slavers, slavering, slavered** have saliva flowing from the mouth • *a slavering dog.*
[origin unknown]

slavish *ADJECTIVE* **1** like a slave. **2** showing no independence or originality.

slay *VERB* **slays, slaying, slew, slain** (*old or poetical use*) kill.
[from Old English]

sled *NOUN* **sleds** (*now mainly American*) a sledge.
[from old German; related to *sledge*]

sledge *NOUN* **sledges** a vehicle for travelling over snow, with strips of metal or wood instead of wheels.
▷ **sledging** *noun*
[from old Dutch; related to *sled*]

sledgehammer *NOUN* **sledgehammers** a very large heavy hammer.
[from Old English *slecg* = sledgehammer, + *hammer*]

sleek *ADJECTIVE* smooth and shiny.
[a different spelling of *slick*]

sleep *NOUN* the condition or time of rest in which the eyes are closed, the body relaxed, and the mind unconscious.
- **go to sleep** (said about part of the body) become numb.
- **put to sleep** kill an animal painlessly, e.g. with an injection of a drug.

sleep *VERB* **sleeps, sleeping, slept** have a sleep.
- **sleep with** have sexual intercourse with.
[from Old English]

sleeper *NOUN* **sleepers** **1** someone who is asleep. **2** each of the wooden or concrete beams on which the rails of a railway rest. **3** a railway carriage with beds or berths for passengers to sleep in; a place in this.

sleeping bag *NOUN* **sleeping bags** a padded bag to sleep in, especially when camping.

sleepless *ADJECTIVE* unable to sleep.

sleepwalker *NOUN* **sleepwalkers** a person who walks about while asleep.
▷ **sleepwalking** *noun*

sleepy *ADJECTIVE* **1** feeling a need or wish to sleep. **2** quiet and lacking activity • *a sleepy little town.*
▷ **sleepily** *adverb* **sleepiness** *noun*

sleet *NOUN* a mixture of rain and snow or hail.
[probably from Old English]

sleeve *NOUN* **sleeves** **1** the part of a piece of clothing that covers the arm. **2** the cover of a record.
- **up your sleeve** hidden but ready for you to use.
[from Old English]

sleeveless *ADJECTIVE* without sleeves.

sleigh (*say as* slay) *NOUN* **sleighs** a sledge, especially a large one pulled by horses.
▷ **sleighing** *noun*
[originally American, from Dutch; related to *sled*]

sleight (*say as* slight) *NOUN*
- **sleight of hand** skill in using the hands to do conjuring tricks etc.
[from Old Norse]

slender *ADJECTIVE* **1** slim and graceful. **2** slight or small • *a slender chance*
▷ **slenderness** *noun*
[origin unknown]

sleuth (*say* slooth) *NOUN* **sleuths** a detective.
[from Old Norse *sloth* = a track or trail]

slew *past tense* of **slay**.

slice *NOUN* **slices 1** a thin piece cut off something. **2** a portion.

slice *VERB* **slices, slicing, sliced 1** cut into slices. **2** cut from a larger piece • *Slice the top off the egg.* **3** cut cleanly • *The knife sliced through the apple.*
[from old French]

slick *ADJECTIVE* **1** done or doing things quickly and cleverly. **2** slippery.

slick *NOUN* **slicks 1** a large patch of oil floating on water. **2** a slippery place.
[from Old English]

slide *VERB* **slides, sliding, slid 1** move or cause to move smoothly on a surface.
2 move quietly or secretly • *The thief slid behind a bush.*

slide *NOUN* **slides 1** a sliding movement. **2** a smooth surface or structure on which people or things can slide. **3** a photograph that can be projected on a screen. **4** a small glass plate on which things are placed to be examined under a microscope. **5** a fastener to keep hair tidy.
[from Old English]

slight *ADJECTIVE* very small; not serious or important.
▷ **slightly** *adverb* **slightness** *noun*

slight *VERB* **slights, slighting, slighted** insult a person by treating him or her without respect.
▷ **slight** *noun*
[from Old Norse]

slim *ADJECTIVE* **slimmer, slimmest 1** thin and graceful. **2** small; hardly enough • *a slim chance.*
▷ **slimness** *noun*

slim *VERB* **slims, slimming, slimmed** try to make yourself thinner, especially by dieting.
▷ **slimmer** *noun*
[from old German or old Dutch]

slime *NOUN* unpleasant wet slippery stuff.
▷ **slimy** *adjective* **sliminess** *noun*
[from Old English]

sling *NOUN* **slings 1** a loop or band placed round something to support or lift it • *He had his arm in a sling.* **2** a looped strap used to throw a stone etc.

sling *VERB* **slings, slinging, slung 1** hang something up or support it with a sling or so that it hangs loosely. **2** (*informal*) throw forcefully or carelessly.
[from old Dutch or Old Norse]

slink *VERB* **slinks, slinking, slunk** move in a stealthy or guilty way.
▷ **slinky** *adjective*
[from Old English]

slip *VERB* **slips, slipping, slipped 1** slide accidentally; lose your balance by sliding.
2 move or put quickly and quietly • *Slip it in your pocket. We slipped away from the party.*
3 escape from • *The dog slipped its leash. It slipped my memory.*
- **slip up** make a mistake.

slip *NOUN* **slips 1** an accidental slide or fall.
2 a mistake. **3** a small piece of paper. **4** a petticoat. **5** a pillowcase.
- **give someone the slip** escape or avoid him or her skilfully.
[probably from old German or old Dutch]

slipper *NOUN* **slippers** a soft comfortable shoe to wear indoors.

slippery *ADJECTIVE* smooth or wet so that it is difficult to stand on or hold.
▷ **slipperiness** *noun*

slip road *NOUN* **slip roads** a road by which you enter or leave a motorway.

slipshod *ADJECTIVE* careless; not systematic.
[originally = wearing slippers or badly fitting shoes; from *slip* + *shod*]

slipstream *NOUN* **slipstreams** a current of air driven backward as an aircraft or vehicle is propelled forward.

slit *NOUN* **slits** a narrow straight cut or opening.

slit *VERB* **slits, slitting, slit** make a slit or slits in something.
[from Old English]

slither *VERB* **slithers, slithering, slithered** slip or slide unsteadily.
[from Old English]

sliver (*say* sliv-er) *NOUN* **slivers** a thin strip of wood or glass etc.
[from Middle English *slive* = to split or to cut a piece off]

slob *NOUN* **slobs** (*informal*) a careless, untidy, lazy person.
[from an old word *slab* = mud or slime, + *slobber*]

slobber *VERB* **slobbers, slobbering, slobbered** slaver or dribble.
[probably from old Dutch *slobberen* = paddle in mud]

sloe *NOUN* **sloes** the small dark plum-like fruit of blackthorn.
[from Old English]

slog *VERB* **slogs, slogging, slogged 1** hit hard. **2** work or walk hard and steadily.
▷ **slog** *noun* **slogger** *noun*
[origin unknown]

slogan *NOUN* **slogans** a phrase used to advertise something or to sum up the aims of a campaign etc. • *Their slogan was 'Ban the bomb!'*
[from Scottish Gaelic *sluagh-ghairm* = battle-cry]

sloop *NOUN* **sloops** a small sailing ship with one mast.
[from Dutch]

slop *VERB* **slops, slopping, slopped** spill liquid over the edge of its container.
[probably from Old English]

slope *VERB* **slopes, sloping, sloped** lie or turn at an angle; slant.
- **slope off** (*informal*) go away.

slope *NOUN* **slopes 1** a sloping surface. **2** the amount by which something slopes.
[origin unknown]

sloppy *ADJECTIVE* **sloppier, sloppiest 1** liquid and splashing easily. **2** careless or slipshod • *sloppy work*. **3** weakly sentimental • *a sloppy story*.
▷ **sloppily** *adverb* **sloppiness** *noun*
[from *slop*]

slops *PLURAL NOUN* **1** slopped liquid. **2** liquid waste matter.

slosh *VERB* **sloshes, sloshing, sloshed** (*informal*) **1** splash or slop. **2** pour liquid carelessly. **3** hit.
[a different spelling of *slush*]

slot *NOUN* **slots** a narrow opening to put things in.
▷ **slotted** *adjective*

slot *VERB* **slots, slotting, slotted** put something into a place where it fits.
[from old French]

sloth (*rhymes with* **both**) *NOUN* **sloths 1** laziness. **2** a South American animal that lives in trees and moves very slowly.
▷ **slothful** *adjective*
[from *slow*]

slot machine *NOUN* **slot machines** a machine worked by putting a coin in the slot.

slouch *VERB* **slouches, slouching, slouched** stand, sit, or move in a lazy awkward way, not with an upright posture.
▷ **slouch** *noun*
[origin unknown]

slough[1] (*rhymes with* **cow**) *NOUN* **sloughs** a swamp or marshy place.
[origin unknown]

slough[2] (*say* sluf) *VERB* **sloughs, sloughing, sloughed** shed • *A snake sloughs its skin periodically*.
[probably from old German]

slovenly (*say* **sluv**-en-lee) *ADJECTIVE* careless or untidy.
▷ **slovenliness** *noun*
[probably from Dutch]

slow *ADJECTIVE* **1** not quick; taking more time than is usual. **2** showing a time earlier than the correct time • *Your watch is slow*. **3** not clever; not able to understand quickly or easily.
▷ **slowly** *adverb* **slowness** *noun*

slow *ADVERB* slowly • *Go slow*.

slow *VERB* **slows, slowing, slowed** go more slowly; cause to go more slowly • *The storm slowed us down*.
[from Old English]

slow motion *NOUN* movement in a film or on television which has been slowed down.

slow-worm *NOUN* **slow-worms** a small European legless lizard that looks like a snake, and gives birth to live young.

sludge *NOUN* thick mud.
[origin unknown]

slug *NOUN* **slugs 1** a small slimy animal like a snail without a shell. **2** a pellet for firing from a gun.
[probably from a Scandinavian language]

sluggard *NOUN* **sluggards** a slow or lazy person.
[from *slug*]

sluggish *ADJECTIVE* slow-moving; not alert or lively.
[from *slug*]

sluice (*say* slooss) *NOUN* **sluices 1** a sluice gate. **2** a channel carrying off water.

sluice *VERB* **sluices, sluicing, sluiced** wash with a flow of water.
[from old French]

sluice gate *NOUN* **sluice gates** a sliding barrier for controlling a flow of water.

slum *NOUN* **slums** an area of dirty overcrowded houses.
[origin unknown]

slumber *VERB* **slumbers, slumbering, slumbered** sleep.
▷ **slumber** *noun* **slumberer** *noun* **slumberous** or **slumbrous** *adjective*
[from Old English]

slump *VERB* **slumps, slumping, slumped** fall heavily or suddenly.

slump *NOUN* **slumps** a sudden great fall in prices or trade.
[origin unknown]

slur *VERB* **slurs, slurring, slurred** **1** pronounce words indistinctly by running the sounds together. **2** mark with a slur in music.

slur *NOUN* **slurs 1** a slurred sound. **2** something that harms a person's reputation. **3** a curved line placed over notes in music to show that they are to be sung or played smoothly without a break.
[probably from old German or old Dutch]

slurp *VERB* **slurps, slurping, slurped** eat or drink with a loud sucking sound.
▷ **slurp** *noun*
[from Dutch]

slurry *NOUN* a semi-liquid mixture of water and cement, clay, or manure etc.
[origin unknown]

slush *NOUN* **1** partly melted snow on the ground. **2** very sentimental talk or writing.
▷ **slushy** *adjective*
[imitating the sound when you walk in it]

sly *ADJECTIVE* **slyer, slyest 1** unpleasantly cunning or secret. **2** mischievous and knowing • *a sly smile*.
▷ **slyly** *adverb* **slyness** *noun*
[from Old Norse]

smack[1] *NOUN* **smacks 1** a slap. **2** a loud sharp sound • *It hit the wall with a smack*. **3** a loud kiss. **4** (*informal*) a hard hit or blow.

smack *VERB* **smacks, smacking, smacked** **1** slap. **2** hit hard.
- **smack your lips** close and then part them noisily in enjoyment.

smack *ADVERB* (*informal*) forcefully or directly • *The ball went smack through the window*.
[from old German or old Dutch]

smack[2] *NOUN* **smacks** a slight flavour of something; a trace.

smack *VERB* **smacks, smacking, smacked** have a slight flavour or trace • *His manner smacks of conceit*.
[from Old English]

smack[3] *NOUN* **smacks** a small sailing boat used for fishing etc.
[from Dutch]

small *ADJECTIVE* **1** not large; less than the usual size. **2** not important or significant.
▷ **smallness** *noun*
- **the small of the back** the smallest part of the back, at the waist.
[from Old English]

smallholding *NOUN* **smallholdings** a small area of land used for farming.
▷ **smallholder** *noun*

small hours *PLURAL NOUN* the early hours of the morning, after midnight.

small-minded *ADJECTIVE* selfish; petty.

smallpox *NOUN* a serious contagious disease that causes a fever and produces spots that leave permanent scars on the skin.

small print *NOUN* the details of a contract, especially if in very small letters or difficult to understand.

small talk *NOUN* conversation about unimportant things.

smarmy *ADJECTIVE* (*informal*) trying to win someone's favour by flattering them or being polite in an exaggerated way.
[origin unknown]

smart *ADJECTIVE* **1** neat and elegant; dressed well. **2** clever. **3** forceful; brisk • *She ran at a smart pace.*
▷ **smartly** *adverb* **smartness** *noun*

smart *VERB* **smarts, smarting, smarted** feel a stinging pain.
▷ **smart** *noun*
[from Old English]

smart card *NOUN* **smart cards** a card like a credit card with a microprocessor built in, which stores information or enables you to draw or spend money from your bank account.

smarten *VERB* **smartens, smartening, smartened** make or become smarter.

smash *VERB* **smashes, smashing, smashed** **1** break noisily into pieces. **2** hit or move with great force. **3** (in tennis etc.) strike the ball forcefully downwards. **4** destroy or defeat completely.

smash *NOUN* **smashes 1** the action or sound of smashing. **2** a collision between vehicles. **3** (*informal*) a smash hit.
[imitating the sound]

smash hit *NOUN* **smash hits** (*informal*) a very successful song, show, etc.

smashing *ADJECTIVE* (*informal*) excellent or beautiful.
▷ **smasher** *noun*
[from *smash*]

smattering *NOUN* a slight knowledge of a subject or a foreign language.
[origin unknown]

smear *VERB* **smears, smearing, smeared** **1** rub something greasy or sticky or dirty on a surface. **2** try to damage someone's reputation.
▷ **smeary** *adjective*

smear *NOUN* **smears 1** smearing; something smeared. **2** material smeared on a slide to be examined under a microscope. **3** a smear test.
[from Old English]

smear campaign *NOUN* **smear campaigns** an organized attempt to ruin someone's reputation by spreading rumours about him or her.

smear test *NOUN* **smear tests** the taking and examination of a sample of the cervix lining, to check for faulty cells which may cause cancer.

smell *VERB* **smells, smelling, smelt** or **smelled** **1** be aware of something by means of the sense organs of the nose • *I can smell smoke.* **2** give out a smell.

smell *NOUN* **smells 1** something you can smell; a quality in something that makes people able to smell it. **2** an unpleasant quality of this kind. **3** the ability to smell things.
▷ **smelly** *adjective*
[origin unknown]

smelt *VERB* **smelts, smelting, smelted** melt ore to get the metal it contains.
[from old German or old Dutch]

smile *NOUN* **smiles** an expression on the face that shows pleasure or amusement, with the lips stretched and turning upwards at the ends.

smile *VERB* **smiles, smiling, smiled** give a smile.
[probably from a Scandinavian language]

smirch *VERB* **smirches, smirching, smirched** **1** soil. **2** disgrace or dishonour a reputation.
▷ **smirch** *noun*
[origin unknown]

smirk *NOUN* **smirks** a self-satisfied smile.

smirk *VERB* **smirks, smirking, smirked** give a smirk.
[from Old English]

smite *VERB* **smites, smiting, smote, smitten** (*old use*) hit hard.
[from Old English]

smith *NOUN* **smiths 1** a person who makes things out of metal. **2** a blacksmith.
[from Old English]

smithereens *PLURAL NOUN* small fragments.
[from Irish]

smithy *NOUN* **smithies** a blacksmith's workshop.

smitten *past participle* of **smite**.
- **be smitten with** be suddenly affected by a disease or desire or fascination etc.

smock *NOUN* **smocks 1** an overall shaped like a long loose shirt. **2** a loose top worn by a pregnant woman.

smock *VERB* **smocks, smocking, smocked** stitch into close gathers with embroidery.
▷ **smocking** *noun*
[from Old English]

smog *NOUN* a mixture of smoke and fog.
[from *smoke* + *fog*]

smoke *NOUN* **1** the mixture of gas and solid particles given off by a burning substance. **2** a period of smoking tobacco • *He wanted a smoke.*
▷ **smoky** *adjective*

smoke *VERB* **smokes, smoking, smoked** **1** give out smoke. **2** have a lighted cigarette, cigar, or pipe between your lips and draw its smoke into your mouth; do this as a habit. **3** preserve meat or fish by treating it with smoke • *smoked haddock.*
▷ **smoker** *noun*
[from Old English]

smokeless *ADJECTIVE* without producing smoke.

smokescreen *NOUN* **smokescreens 1** a mass of smoke used to hide the movement of troops. **2** something that conceals what is happening.

smooth *ADJECTIVE* **1** having a surface without any lumps, wrinkles, roughness, etc. **2** moving without bumps or jolts etc. **3** not harsh • *a smooth flavour.* **4** without problems or difficulties.
▷ **smoothly** *adverb* **smoothness** *noun*

smooth *VERB* **smooths, smoothing, smoothed** make a thing smooth.
[from Old English]

smote *past tense* of **smite.**

smother *VERB* **smothers, smothering, smothered** **1** suffocate. **2** put out a fire by covering it. **3** cover thickly • *The chips were smothered in ketchup.* **4** restrain or conceal • *She smothered a smile.*
[from Old English]

smoulder *VERB* **smoulders, smouldering, smouldered** **1** burn slowly without a flame. **2** feel an emotion strongly without showing it • *He was smouldering with jealousy.*
[origin unknown]

smudge *NOUN* **smudges** a dirty mark made by rubbing something.
▷ **smudgy** *adjective*

smudge *VERB* **smudges, smudging, smudged** make a smudge on something; become smudged.
[origin unknown]

smug *ADJECTIVE* self-satisfied; too pleased with your own good fortune or abilities.
▷ **smugly** *adverb* **smugness** *noun*
[from old German *smuk* = pretty]

smuggle *VERB* **smuggles, smuggling, smuggled** bring something into a country etc. secretly or illegally.
▷ **smuggler** *noun*
[from old German or old Dutch]

smut *NOUN* **smuts 1** a small piece of soot or dirt. **2** indecent talk or pictures etc.
▷ **smutty** *adjective*
[origin unknown]

snack *NOUN* **snacks 1** a small meal. **2** food eaten between meals.
[from old Dutch]

snack bar *NOUN* **snack bars** a small cafe where snacks are sold.

snack food *NOUN* **snack foods** food such as peanuts, crisps, popcorn, etc. sold to be eaten between meals.

snag *NOUN* **snags 1** an unexpected difficulty. **2** a sharp or jagged part sticking out from something. **3** a tear in material that has been caught on something sharp.
[probably from a Scandinavian language]

snail *NOUN* **snails** a small animal with a soft body and a shell.
[from Old English]

snail's pace *NOUN* a very slow pace.

snake *NOUN* **snakes** a reptile with a long narrow body and no legs.
▷ **snaky** *adjective*
[from Old English]

snap *VERB* **snaps, snapping, snapped** **1** break suddenly or with a sharp sound. **2** bite suddenly or quickly. **3** say something quickly and angrily. **4** take something or move quickly. **5** take a snapshot of something.
- **snap your fingers** make a sharp snapping sound with your thumb and a finger.

snap *NOUN* **snaps 1** the action or sound of snapping. **2** a snapshot. **3 Snap** a card game in which players shout 'Snap!' when they see two similar cards.

snap *ADJECTIVE* sudden • *a snap decision.*
[probably from old German or old Dutch]

snapdragon *NOUN* **snapdragons** a plant with flowers that have a mouth-like opening.

snappy *ADJECTIVE* **1** snapping at people. **2** quick and lively.
▷ **snappily** *adverb*

snapshot *NOUN* **snapshots** an informal photograph.

snare *NOUN* **snares 1** a trap for catching birds or animals. **2** something that attracts someone but is a trap or a danger.

snare *VERB* **snares, snaring, snared** catch in a snare.
[from Old English]

snarl[1] *VERB* **snarls, snarling, snarled**
1 growl angrily. **2** speak in a bad-tempered way.
▷ **snarl** *noun*
[imitating the sound]

snarl[2] *VERB* **snarls, snarling, snarled** make or become tangled or jammed • *Traffic was snarled up.*
[from *snare*]

snatch *VERB* **snatches, snatching, snatched** seize; take quickly, eagerly, or by force.

snatch *NOUN* **snatches 1** snatching. **2** a short and incomplete part of a song, conversation, etc.
[origin unknown]

sneak *VERB* **sneaks, sneaking, sneaked**
1 move quietly and secretly. **2** (*informal*) take secretly • *He sneaked a biscuit from the tin.* **3** (*informal*) tell tales.

sneak *NOUN* **sneaks** a telltale.
[probably from Old English]

sneakers *PLURAL NOUN* (*American*) soft-soled shoes.

sneaky *ADJECTIVE* dishonest or deceitful.
▷ **sneakily** *adverb*

sneer *VERB* **sneers, sneering, sneered** speak or behave in a scornful way.
▷ **sneer** *noun*
[probably from Old English]

sneeze *VERB* **sneezes, sneezing, sneezed** send out air suddenly and uncontrollably through the nose and mouth in order to get rid of something irritating the nostrils.
▷ **sneeze** *noun*
- **not to be sneezed at** (*informal*) worth having.
[from Old English *fneosan*, imitating the sound]

snide *ADJECTIVE* sneering in a sly way • *a snide remark.*

sniff *VERB* **sniffs, sniffing, sniffed 1** make a sound by drawing in air through the nose. **2** smell something.
▷ **sniff** *noun* **sniffer** *noun*
[imitating the sound]

sniffer dog *NOUN* **sniffer dogs** a dog trained to find drugs, explosives, etc. by smell.

sniffle *VERB* **sniffles, sniffling, sniffled**
1 sniff slightly. **2** keep on sniffing.
▷ **sniffle** *noun*
[imitating the sound]

snigger *VERB* **sniggers, sniggering, sniggered** giggle slyly.
▷ **snigger** *noun*
[imitating the sound]

snip *VERB* **snips, snipping, snipped** cut with scissors or shears in small quick cuts.
▷ **snip** *noun*
[from old German or old Dutch]

snipe *NOUN* **snipe** a marsh bird with a long beak.

snipe *VERB* **snipes, sniping, sniped 1** shoot at people from a hiding place. **2** attack someone with sly critical remarks.
▷ **sniper** *noun*
[probably from a Scandinavian language; the verb because the birds are shot from a hiding place]

snippet *NOUN* **snippets** a small piece of news, information, etc.
[from *snip*]

snivel *VERB* **snivels, snivelling, snivelled** cry or complain in a whining way.
[from Old English]

snob *NOUN* **snobs** a person who despises those who have not got wealth, power, or particular tastes or interests.
▷ **snobbery** *noun* **snobbish** *adjective*
[origin unknown]

snooker *NOUN* a game played with cues and 21 balls on a special cloth-covered table.
[origin unknown]

snoop *VERB* **snoops, snooping, snooped** pry; ask or look around secretly.
▷ **snooper** *noun*
[from Dutch]

snooty *ADJECTIVE* (*informal*) haughty and contemptuous.
[from *snout*]

snooze *NOUN* **snoozes** (*informal*) a nap.
▷ **snooze** *verb*
[origin unknown]

snore *VERB* **snores, snoring, snored** breathe very noisily while sleeping.
▷ **snore** *noun*
[imitating the sound]

snorkel *NOUN* **snorkels** a tube through which a person swimming under water can take in air.
▷ **snorkelling** *noun*
[from German]

snort *VERB* **snorts, snorting, snorted** make a rough sound by breathing forcefully through the nose.
▷ **snort** *noun*
[imitating the sound]

snout *NOUN* **snouts** an animal's projecting nose and jaws.
[from old German or old Dutch]

snow *NOUN* frozen drops of water that fall from the sky in small white flakes.

snow *VERB* **snows, snowing, snowed** come down as snow.
- **be snowed under** be overwhelmed with a mass of letters or work etc.
[from Old English]

snowball *NOUN* **snowballs** snow pressed into a ball for throwing.
▷ **snowballing** *noun*

snowball *VERB* **snowballs, snowballing, snowballed** grow quickly in size or intensity.

snow-blindness *NOUN* temporary blindness caused by the glare of light reflected by snow.

snowdrift *NOUN* **snowdrifts** a large heap or bank of snow piled up by the wind.

snowdrop *NOUN* **snowdrops** a small white flower that blooms in early spring.

snowflake *NOUN* **snowflakes** a flake of snow.

snowline *NOUN* the level above which snow never melts.

snowman *NOUN* **snowmen** a figure made of snow.

snowplough *NOUN* **snowploughs** a vehicle or device for clearing a road or railway tract etc. by pushing snow aside.

snowshoe *NOUN* **snowshoes** a frame rather like a tennis racket for walking on soft snow.

snowstorm *NOUN* **snowstorms** a storm in which snow falls.

snow white *ADJECTIVE* pure white.

snowy *ADJECTIVE* **1** with snow falling • *snowy weather*. **2** covered with snow • *snowy roofs*. **3** pure white.

snub *VERB* **snubs, snubbing, snubbed** treat in a scornful or unfriendly way.

snub *NOUN* **snubs** scornful or unfriendly treatment.
[from Old Norse]

snub-nosed *ADJECTIVE* having a short turned-up nose.

snuff[1] *NOUN* powdered tobacco for taking into the nose by sniffing.
[from old Dutch *snuffen* = snuffle]

snuff[2] *VERB* **snuffs, snuffing, snuffed** put out a candle by covering or pinching the flame.
▷ **snuffer** *noun*
[origin unknown]

snuffle *VERB* **snuffles, snuffling, snuffled** sniff in a noisy way.
▷ **snuffle** *noun*
[same origin as *snuff*[1]]

snug *ADJECTIVE* **snugger, snuggest 1** cosy. **2** fitting closely.
▷ **snugly** *adverb* **snugness** *noun*
[probably from Dutch]

snuggle *VERB* **snuggles, snuggling, snuggled** curl up in a warm comfortable place.
[from *snug*]

so *ADVERB* **1** in this way; to such an extent • *Why are you so cross?* **2** very • *Cricket is so boring*. **3** also • *I was wrong but so were you.*
- **and so on** and other similar things.
- **or so** or about that number.
- **so as to** in order to.
- **so far** up to now.
- **so long!** (*informal*) goodbye.
- **so what?** (*informal*) that is not important.

so *CONJUNCTION* for that reason • *They threw me out, so I came here.*
[from Old English]

soak *VERB* **soaks, soaking, soaked** make a person or thing very wet.
▷ **soak** *noun*
- **soak up** take in a liquid in the way that a sponge does.

[from Old English]

so-and-so *NOUN* **so-and-sos** a person or thing that need not be named.

soap *NOUN* **soaps 1** a substance used with water for washing and cleaning things. **2** a soap opera.
▷ **soapy** *adjective*

soap *VERB* **soaps, soaping, soaped** put soap on something.
[from Old English]

soap opera *NOUN* **soap operas** a television serial about the everyday lives of a group of people.
[originally American, where they were sponsored by soap manufacturers]

soar *VERB* **soars, soaring, soared 1** rise high in the air. **2** rise very high • *Prices were soaring.*
[from old French; related to *aura*]

sob *VERB* **sobs, sobbing, sobbed** make a gasping sound when crying.
▷ **sob** *noun*
[probably from old Dutch]

sober *ADJECTIVE* **1** not drunk. **2** serious and calm. **3** (said about colour) not bright or showy.
▷ **soberly** *adverb* **sobriety** (*say* so-**bry**-it-ee) *noun*

sober *VERB* **sobers, sobering, sobered** make or become sober.
[from Latin]

sob story *NOUN* **sob stories** an account of someone's experiences, told to get your help or sympathy • *She gave me some sob story about having her purse stolen.*

so-called *ADJECTIVE* named in what may be the wrong way • *This so-called gentleman slammed the door.*

soccer *NOUN* Association Football.
[short for *Association*]

sociable *ADJECTIVE* liking to be with other people; friendly.
▷ **sociably** *adverb* **sociability** *noun*
[same origin as *social*]

social *ADJECTIVE* **1** living in a community, not alone • *Bees are social insects*. **2** to do with life in a community • *social science*. **3** concerned with people's welfare • *a social worker*. **4** helping people to meet each other • *a social club*. **5** sociable.
▷ **socially** *adverb*
[from Latin *sociare* = unite, associate]

socialism *NOUN* a political system where wealth is shared equally between people, and the main industries and trade etc. are controlled by the government. (COMPARE **capitalism**)
[from French; related to *social*]

socialist *NOUN* **socialists** a person who believes in socialism.

socialize *VERB* **socializes, socializing, socialized** meet other people socially.

social security *NOUN* money and other assistance provided by the government for those in need through being unemployed, ill, or disabled.

social services *PLURAL NOUN* welfare services provided by the government, including schools, hospitals, and pensions.

society *NOUN* **societies 1** a community; people living together in a group or nation • *We live in a multiracial society*. **2** a group of people organized for a particular purpose • *the school dramatic society*. **3** company or companionship • *We enjoy the society of our friends.*
[same origin as *social*]

sociology (*say* soh-see-ol-o-jee) *NOUN* the study of human society and social behaviour.
▷ **sociological** *adjective* **sociologist** *noun*
[from Latin *socius* = companion, ally, + *-logy*]

sock[1] *NOUN* **socks** a piece of clothing that covers your foot and the lower part of your leg.
[from Old English]

sock[2] *VERB* **socks, socking, socked** (*slang*) hit hard; punch • *He socked me on the jaw.*
▷ **sock** *noun*
[origin unknown]

socket *NOUN* **sockets 1** a hollow into which something fits • *a tooth socket.* **2** a device into which an electric plug or bulb is put to make a connection.
[from old French]

sod *NOUN* **sods** a piece of turf.
[from old German or old Dutch]

soda *NOUN* **1** a substance made from sodium, such as baking soda. **2** soda water. **3** (*American*) a sweet fizzy drink.
[probably from Persian]

soda water *NOUN* water made fizzy with carbon dioxide, used in drinks.
[because originally it was made with *soda*]

sodden *ADJECTIVE* made very wet.
[the old past participle of *seethe*]

sodium *NOUN* a soft white metal.
[from *soda*, to which it is related]

sodium bicarbonate *NOUN* a soluble white powder used in fire extinguishers and fizzy drinks, and to make cakes rise; baking soda.

sodium carbonate *NOUN* white powder or crystals used to clean things; washing soda.

sofa *NOUN* **sofas** a long soft seat with a back and arms.
[from Arabic *suffa* = long stone bench]

soft *ADJECTIVE* **1** not hard or firm; easily pressed. **2** smooth, not rough or stiff. **3** gentle; not loud. **4** (said about drugs) not likely to be addictive.
▷ **softly** *adverb* **softness** *noun*
[from Old English]

soft drink *NOUN* **soft drinks** a cold drink that is not alcoholic.

soften *VERB* **softens, softening, softened** make or become soft or softer.
▷ **softener** *noun*

soft furnishings *PLURAL NOUN* cushions, curtains, rugs, loose covers for chairs, etc.

soft-hearted *ADJECTIVE* sympathetic and easily moved.

software *NOUN* computer programs and data, which are not part of the machinery of a computer. (COMPARE **hardware**)

soft water *NOUN* water that is free of minerals that prevent soap from making much lather.

softwood *NOUN* **softwoods** wood from pine trees or other conifers, which is easy to saw.

soggy *ADJECTIVE* **soggier, soggiest** very wet and heavy • *soggy ground.*
[from dialect *sog* = swamp]

soil[1] *NOUN* **soils 1** the loose earth in which plants grow. **2** territory • *on British soil.*
[old French *soil*]

soil[2] *VERB* **soils, soiling, soiled** make a thing dirty.
[from old French *suillier*]

sojourn (*say* soj-ern) *VERB* **sojourns, sojourning, sojourned** stay at a place temporarily.

sojourn *NOUN* **sojourns** a temporary stay.
[from old French]

solace (*say* sol-as) *VERB* **solaces, solacing, solaced** comfort someone who is unhappy or disappointed.
▷ **solace** *noun*
[from Latin *solari* = to console]

solar *ADJECTIVE* from or to do with the sun.
[from Latin *sol* = sun]

solar panel *NOUN* **solar panels** a panel designed to catch the sun's rays and use their energy for heating or to make electricity.

solar power *NOUN* electricity or other forms of power derived from the sun's rays.

solar system *NOUN* the sun and the planets that revolve round it.

solder *NOUN* a soft alloy that is melted to join pieces of metal together.
▷ **solder** *verb*
[from Latin *solidare* = make firm or solid]

soldier *NOUN* **soldiers** a member of an army.
[from old French]

sole[1] *NOUN* **soles 1** the bottom surface of a foot or shoe. **2** a flat edible sea fish.

sole *VERB* **soles, soling, soled** put a sole on a shoe.
[from Latin *solum*]

sole[2] *ADJECTIVE* single; only • *She was the sole survivor.*
▷ **solely** *adverb*
[from Latin *solus*]

solemn *ADJECTIVE* **1** not smiling or cheerful. **2** dignified or formal.
▷ **solemnly** *adverb* **solemnity** *noun*
[from Latin]

solemnize *VERB* **solemnizes, solemnizing, solemnized 1** celebrate a festival. **2** perform a marriage ceremony.
▷ **solemnization** *noun*

solenoid *NOUN* **solenoids** a coil of wire that becomes magnetic when an electric current is passed through it.
[from Greek *solen* = channel]

sol-fa *NOUN* a system of syllables (*doh, ray, me fah, so, la, te*) used to represent the notes of the musical scale.
[*sol* was an earlier spelling of *soh*; the names of the notes came from syllables of a Latin hymn]

solicit *VERB* **solicits, soliciting, solicited 1** ask for or try to obtain • *I've been soliciting opinions from rail users. All the candidates are busy soliciting for votes*. **2** approach someone as a prostitute.
▷ **solicitation** *noun*
[same origin as *solicitous*]

solicitor *NOUN* **solicitors** a lawyer who advises clients, prepares legal documents, etc.
[old French; related to *solicit*]

solicitous *ADJECTIVE* anxious and concerned about a person's comfort, welfare, etc.
▷ **solicitously** *adverb* **solicitude** *noun*
[from Latin *sollicitus* = worrying]

solid *ADJECTIVE* **1** not hollow; with no space inside. **2** keeping its shape; not liquid or gas. **3** continuous • *for two solid hours*. **4** firm or strongly made; not flimsy • *a solid foundation*. **5** showing solidarity; unanimous.
▷ **solidly** *adverb* **solidity** *noun*

solid *NOUN* **solids 1** a solid thing. **2** a shape that has three dimensions (length, width, and height or depth).
[from Latin]

solidarity *NOUN* **1** being solid. **2** unity and support for each other because of agreement in opinions, interests, etc.

solidify *VERB* **solidifies, solidifying, solidified** make or become solid.

solids *PLURAL NOUN* solid food; food that is not liquid • *Is your baby eating solids yet?*

soliloquy (*say* sol-il-ok-wee) *NOUN* **soliloquies** a speech in which a person speaks his or her thoughts aloud when alone or without addressing anyone.
▷ **soliloquize** *verb*
[from Latin *solus* = alone + *loqui* = speak]

solitaire *NOUN* **solitaires 1** a game for one person, in which marbles are moved on a special board until only one is left. **2** a diamond or other precious stone set by itself.
[French; related to *solitary*]

solitary *ADJECTIVE* **1** alone, without companions. **2** single • *a solitary example*.
[from Latin *solus* = alone]

solitary confinement *NOUN* a form of punishment in which a prisoner is kept alone in a cell and not allowed to talk to others.

solitude *NOUN* being solitary.

solo *NOUN* **solos** something sung, played, danced, or done by one person.
▷ **solo** *adjective* & *adverb* **soloist** *noun*
[Italian, = alone]

solstice (*say* sol-stiss) *NOUN* **solstices** either of the two times in each year when the sun is at its furthest point north or south of the equator.
- **summer solstice** about 21 June.
- **winter solstice** about 22 December.
[from Latin *sol* = sun + *sistere* = stand still]

soluble *ADJECTIVE* **1** able to be dissolved. **2** able to be solved.
▷ **solubility** *noun*
[same origin as *solve*]

solution *NOUN* **solutions 1** a liquid in which something is dissolved. **2** the answer to a problem or puzzle.
[same origin as *solve*]

solve *VERB* **solves, solving, solved** find the answer to a problem or puzzle.
[from Latin *solvere* = unfasten]

solvent *ADJECTIVE* **1** having enough money to pay all your debts. **2** able to dissolve another substance.
▷ **solvency** *noun*

solvent *NOUN* **solvents** a liquid used for dissolving something.

sombre *ADJECTIVE* dark and gloomy.
[from *sub-* + Latin *umbra* = shade]

sombrero (*say* som-**brair**-oh) *NOUN* **sombreros** a hat with a very wide brim.
[Spanish; related to *sombre*]

some *ADJECTIVE* **1** a few; a little • *some apples; some sugar*. **2** an unknown person or thing • *Some fool left the door open*. **3** about • *We waited some 20 minutes*.
- **some time 1** quite a long time • *I've been wondering about it for some time*. **2** at some point in time • *You must come round for a meal some time*.

some *PRONOUN* a certain number or amount that is less than the whole • *Some of them were late*.
[from Old English]

-some *SUFFIX* forms **1** adjectives meaning 'quality or manner' (e.g. *handsome, quarrelsome*), **2** nouns from numbers, meaning 'a group of this many' (e.g. *foursome*).
[from Old English]

somebody *PRONOUN* **1** some person. **2** an important or impressive person.

somehow *ADVERB* in some way.

someone *PRONOUN* somebody.

somersault *NOUN* **somersaults** a movement in which you turn head over heels before landing on your feet.
▷ **somersault** *verb*
[from Latin *supra* = above + *saltus* = a leap]

something *NOUN* some thing; a thing which you cannot or do not want to name.
- **something like 1** rather like • *It's something like a rabbit*. **2** approximately • *It cost something like £10*.

sometime *ADVERB* at some point in time • *You must come round for a meal sometime*.

sometime *ADJECTIVE* former • *her sometime friend*.

sometimes *ADVERB* at some times but not always • *We sometimes walk to school*.

somewhat *ADVERB* to some extent • *He was somewhat annoyed*.

somewhere *ADVERB* in or to some place.

somnambulist *NOUN* **somnambulists** a sleepwalker.
[from Latin *somnus* = sleep + *ambulare* = to walk]

somnolent *ADJECTIVE* sleepy or drowsy.
▷ **somnolence** *noun*
[from Latin *somnus* = sleep]

son *NOUN* **sons** a boy or man who is someone's child.
[from Old English]

sonar *NOUN* a device for finding objects under water by the reflection of sound waves.
[from *sound navigation and ranging*]

sonata *NOUN* **sonatas** a piece of music for one instrument or two, in several movements.
[from Italian *sonare* = to sound]

song *NOUN* **songs 1** a tune for singing. **2** singing • *He burst into song*.
- **a song and dance** (*informal*) a great fuss.
- **for a song** bought or sold very cheaply.
[from Old English]

songbird *NOUN* **songbirds** a bird that sings sweetly.

sonic *ADJECTIVE* to do with sound or sound waves.
[from Latin *sonus* = sound]

sonic boom *NOUN* **sonic booms** a loud noise caused by the shock wave of an aircraft travelling faster than the speed of sound.

son-in-law *NOUN* **sons-in-law** a daughter's husband.

sonnet *NOUN* **sonnets** a kind of poem with 14 lines.
[from Italian *sonetto* = a little sound]

sonny *NOUN* (*informal*) boy or young man
• *Come on, sonny!*

sonorous (*say* sonn-er-us) *ADJECTIVE* giving a loud deep sound; resonant.
[from Latin *sonor* = sound]

soon *ADVERB* **1** in a short time from now. **2** not long after something.
- **as soon** as willingly • *I'd just as soon stay here.*
- **as soon as** at the moment that.
- **sooner or later** at some time in the future.
[from Old English]

soot *NOUN* the black powder left by smoke in a chimney or on a building etc.
▷ **sooty** *adjective*
[from Old English]

soothe *VERB* **soothes, soothing, soothed** **1** calm or comfort. **2** ease pain or distress.
▷ **soothing** *adjective* **soothingly** *adverb*
[from Old English]

soothsayer *NOUN* **soothsayers** a prophet.
[from an old word *sooth* = truth, + *say*]

sop *NOUN* **sops 1** a piece of bread dipped in liquid before being eaten or cooked. **2** something unimportant given to pacify or bribe a troublesome person.

sop *VERB* **sops, sopping, sopped**
- **sop up** soak up liquid like a sponge.
[from Old English]

sophisticated *ADJECTIVE* **1** having refined or cultured tastes or experienced about the world. **2** complicated • *a sophisticated machine.*
▷ **sophistication** *noun*
[from Latin *sophisticare* = tamper with, mix with something]

sophistry (*say* sof-ist-ree) *NOUN* **sophistries** a piece of reasoning that is clever but false or misleading.
[from Greek *sophos* = wise]

sophomore (*say* sof-o-mor) *NOUN* **sophomores** (*American*) a second-year university or high-school student.

soporific *ADJECTIVE* causing sleep or drowsiness.
[from Latin *sopor* = sleep + *facere* = make]

sopping *ADJECTIVE* very wet; drenched.
[from *sop*]

soppy *ADJECTIVE* **1** very wet. **2** (*informal*) sentimental in a silly way.
[from *sop*]

soprano *NOUN* **sopranos** a woman, girl, or boy with a high singing voice.
[Italian, from *sopra* = above]

sorcerer *NOUN* **sorcerers** a person who can perform magic.
▷ **sorceress** *noun*
[from old French]

sorcery *NOUN* magic or witchcraft.

sordid *ADJECTIVE* **1** dirty and nasty. **2** dishonourable; selfish and mercenary • *sordid motives.*
▷ **sordidly** *adverb* **sordidness** *noun*
[from Latin]

sore *ADJECTIVE* **1** painful or smarting. **2** (*informal*) annoyed or offended. **3** serious or distressing • *in sore need.*
▷ **soreness** *noun*

sore *NOUN* **sores** a sore place.
[from Old English]

sorely *ADVERB* seriously; very • *I was sorely tempted to run away.*

sorrel[1] *NOUN* a herb with sharp-tasting leaves.
[from old French *sur* = sour]

sorrel[2] *NOUN* **sorrels** a reddish-brown horse.
[from old French *sor* = yellowish]

sorrow *NOUN* **sorrows 1** unhappiness or regret caused by loss or disappointment. **2** something that causes this.
▷ **sorrowful** *adjective* **sorrowfully** *adverb*

sorrow *VERB* **sorrows, sorrowing, sorrowed** feel sorrow; grieve.
[from Old English]

sorry *ADJECTIVE* **sorrier, sorriest 1** feeling regret • *I'm sorry I forgot your birthday.* **2** feeling pity or sympathy. **3** wretched • *His clothes were in a sorry state.*
[from Old English]

sort *NOUN* **sorts** a group of things or people that are similar; a kind or variety.
- **out of sorts** slightly unwell or depressed.
- **sort of** (*informal*) rather; to some extent • *I sort of expected it.*

USAGE Correct use is *this sort of thing* or *these sorts of things* (not 'these sort of things').

sort *VERB* **sorts, sorting, sorted** arrange things in groups according to their size, kind, etc.
▷ **sorter** *noun*
- **sort out** **1** deal with and solve a problem or difficulty. **2** (*informal*) deal with and punish someone.

[from Latin]

sortie *NOUN* **sorties** **1** an attack by troops coming out of a besieged place. **2** an attacking expedition by a military aircraft.
[from French *sortir* = go out]

SOS *NOUN* **SOSs** an urgent appeal for help.
[the international Morse code signal of extreme distress, chosen because it is easy to recognize, but often said to stand for Save Our Souls]

sosatie *NOUN* **sosaties** (*S. African*) a number of meat pieces that have been spiced and placed on a skewer for grilling.
[from Javanese]

sotto voce (*say* sot-oh **voh**-chee) *ADVERB* in a very quiet voice.
[Italian, = under the voice]

sought *past tense* of **seek**.

soul *NOUN* **souls** **1** the invisible part of a person that is believed to go on living after the body has died. **2** a person's mind and emotions etc. **3** a person • *There isn't a soul about.* **4** a kind of popular music that originated in gospel music.
[from Old English]

soulful *ADJECTIVE* having or showing deep feeling.
▷ **soulfully** *adverb*

sound[1] *NOUN* **sounds** **1** vibrations that travel through the air and can be detected by the ear; the sensation they produce. **2** sound reproduced in a film etc. **3** a mental impression • *We don't like the sound of his plans.*

sound *VERB* **sounds, sounding, sounded** **1** produce or cause to produce a sound. **2** give an impression when heard • *He sounds angry.* **3** test by noting the sounds heard • *A doctor sounds a patient's lungs with a stethoscope.*
[from Latin]

sound[2] *VERB* **sounds, sounding, sounded** test the depth of water beneath a ship.
- **sound out** try to find out what a person thinks or feels about something.

[from *sub-* + Latin *unda* = a wave]

sound[3] *ADJECTIVE* **1** in good condition; not damaged. **2** healthy; not diseased. **3** reasonable or correct • *His ideas are sound.* **4** reliable or secure • *a sound investment.* **5** thorough or deep • *a sound sleep.*
▷ **soundly** *adverb* **soundness** *noun*
[from Old English *gesund* = healthy]

sound[4] *NOUN* **sounds** a strait • *Plymouth Sound.*
[from Old English *sund* = swimming or sea]

sound barrier *NOUN* the resistance of the air to objects moving at speeds near the speed of sound.

sound bite *NOUN* **sound bites** a very short part of a speech or statement broadcast on radio or television because it seems to sum up the person's opinion in a few words.

sound effects *PLURAL NOUN* sounds produced artificially to make a play, film, etc. seem more realistic.

soundtrack *NOUN* **soundtracks** the sound that goes with a cinema film.

soup *NOUN* **soups** liquid food made from stewed bones, meat, fish, vegetables, etc.
- **in the soup** (*informal*) in trouble.

[from old French]

sour *ADJECTIVE* **1** tasting sharp like unripe fruit. **2** stale and unpleasant, not fresh • *sour milk.* **3** bad-tempered.
▷ **sourly** *adverb* **sourness** *noun*

sour *VERB* **sours, souring, soured** make or become sour.
[from Old English]

source *NOUN* **sources** **1** the place from which something comes. **2** the starting point of a river.
[from old French; related to *surge*]

A B C D E F G H I J K L M N O P Q R S T U V W X Y Z

sour grapes *PLURAL NOUN* pretending that something you want is no good because you know you cannot have it.
[from a fable in which a fox says that the grapes he cannot reach are probably sour]

souse *VERB* **souses, sousing, soused** **1** soak or drench. **2** soak fish in pickle.
[from old French]

south *NOUN* **1** the direction to the right of a person who faces east. **2** the southern part of a country, city, etc.

south *ADJECTIVE & ADVERB* towards or in the south.
▷ **southerly** (*say* suth-er-lee) *adjective*
southern *adjective* **southerner** *noun*
southernmost *adjective*
[from Old English]

south-east *NOUN, ADJECTIVE, & ADVERB* midway between south and east.
▷ **south-easterly** *adjective*
south-eastern *adjective*

southward *ADJECTIVE & ADVERB* towards the south.
▷ **southwards** *adverb*

south-west *NOUN, ADJECTIVE, & ADVERB* midway between south and west.
▷ **south-westerly** *adjective*
south-western *adjective*

souvenir (*say* soo-ven-eer) *NOUN* **souvenirs** something that you keep to remind you of a person, place, or event.
[from French *se souvenir* = remember]

sou'wester *NOUN* **sou'westers** a waterproof hat with a wide flap at the back.
[from *south-wester*, a wind from the south-west, often bringing rain]

sovereign *NOUN* **sovereigns** **1** a king or queen who is the ruler of a country; a monarch. **2** an old British gold coin, originally worth £1.

sovereign *ADJECTIVE* **1** supreme • *sovereign power*. **2** having sovereignty; independent • *sovereign states*.
[from old French; related to *super-*]

sovereignty *NOUN* the power a country has to govern itself and make its own laws.

sow[1] (*rhymes with* **go**) *VERB* **sows, sowing, sowed, sown** or **sowed** **1** put seeds into the ground so that they will grow into plants. **2** cause feelings or ideas to develop • *Her words sowed doubt in my mind.*
▷ **sower** *noun*
[from Old English *sawan*]
USAGE Do not confuse with **sew**.

sow[2] (*rhymes with* **cow**) *NOUN* **sows** a female pig.
[from Old English *sugu*]

soya bean *NOUN* **soya beans** a kind of bean from which edible oil and flour are made.
[via Dutch from Japanese]

soy sauce or **soya sauce** *NOUN* a Chinese or Japanese sauce made from fermented soya beans.

spa *NOUN* **spas** a health resort where there is a spring of water containing mineral salts.
[from *Spa*, a town in Belgium with a mineral spring]

space *NOUN* **spaces** **1** the whole area outside the earth, where the stars and planets are. **2** an area or volume • *This table takes too much space*. **3** an empty area; a gap. **4** an interval of time • *within the space of an hour*.

space *VERB* **spaces, spacing, spaced** arrange things with spaces between • *Space them out.*
[from Latin *spatium* = a space]

spacecraft *NOUN* **spacecraft** a vehicle for travelling in outer space.

spaceman *NOUN* **spacemen** an astronaut.

spaceship *NOUN* **spaceships** a spacecraft, especially one carrying people.

space shuttle *NOUN* **space shuttles** a spacecraft for repeated use to and from outer space.

space station *NOUN* **space stations** a satellite which orbits the earth and is used as a base by scientists and astronauts.

space suit *NOUN* **space suits** a protective suit which enables an astronaut to survive in space.

space walk *NOUN* **space walks** moving about or walking by an astronaut outside the spacecraft.

spacewoman *NOUN* **spacewomen** a female astronaut.

spacious *ADJECTIVE* providing a lot of space; roomy.
▷ **spaciousness** *noun*

spade[1] *NOUN* **spades** a tool with a long handle and a wide blade for digging.
[from Old English *spadu*]

spade[2] *NOUN* **spades** a playing card with black shapes like upside-down hearts on it, each with a short stem.
[from Italian *spada* = sword]

spadework *NOUN* hard or uninteresting work done to prepare for an activity or project.

spaghetti *NOUN* pasta made in long thin sticks.
[Italian, = little strings]

span *NOUN* **spans 1** the length from end to end or across something. **2** the part between two uprights of an arch or bridge. **3** the length of a period of time. **4** the distance from the tip of the thumb to the tip of the little finger when the hand is spread out.

span *VERB* **spans, spanning, spanned**
reach from one side or end to the other • *A bridge spans the river.*
[from Old English]

spangle *NOUN* **spangles** a small piece of glittering material.
▷ **spangled** *adjective*
[from old Dutch]

spaniel *NOUN* **spaniels** a kind of dog with long ears and silky fur.
[from old French *espaigneul* = Spanish (because it originated in Spain)]

spank *VERB* **spanks, spanking, spanked**
smack a person on the bottom as a punishment.
[imitating the sound]

spanking *ADJECTIVE* brisk and lively • *at a spanking pace.*
[from *spank*]

spanner *NOUN* **spanners** a tool for gripping and turning the nut on a bolt etc.
[German, from *spannen* = tighten]

spar[1] *NOUN* **spars** a strong pole used for a mast or boom etc. on a ship.
[from Old Norse]

spar[2] *VERB* **spars, sparring, sparred**
1 practise boxing. **2** quarrel or argue.
[from Old English]

spare *VERB* **spares, sparing, spared**
1 afford to give or do without something • *Can you spare a moment?* **2** be merciful towards someone; not hurt or harm a person or thing. **3** avoid making a person suffer something • *Spare me the details.* **4** use or treat economically • *No expense will be spared.*
- **to spare** left over without being needed • *We arrived with five minutes to spare.*

spare *ADJECTIVE* **1** not used but kept ready in case it is needed; extra • *a spare wheel.* **2** thin or lean.
▷ **sparely** *adverb* **spareness** *noun*
- **go spare** (*slang*) become very annoyed.
[from Old English]

spare time *NOUN* time not needed for work.

sparing (*say* spair-ing) *ADJECTIVE* careful or economical; not wasteful.
▷ **sparingly** *adverb*
[from *spare*]

spark *NOUN* **sparks 1** a tiny glowing particle. **2** a flash produced electrically. **3** a trace • *a spark of hope.*

spark *VERB* **sparks, sparking, sparked**
give off a spark or sparks.
[from Old English]

sparking plug *NOUN* **sparking plugs** a spark plug.

sparkle *VERB* **sparkles, sparkling, sparkled 1** shine with tiny flashes of light. **2** show brilliant wit or liveliness.
▷ **sparkle** *noun*
[from *spark*]

sparkler *NOUN* **sparklers** a hand-held firework that gives off sparks.

sparkling wine *NOUN* **sparkling wines** a bubbly wine.

spark plug *NOUN* **spark plugs** a device that makes a spark to ignite the fuel in an engine.

sparrow *NOUN* **sparrows** a small brown bird.
[from Old English]

sparse *ADJECTIVE* thinly scattered; not numerous • *a sparse population.*
▷ **sparsely** *adverb* **sparseness** *noun*
[from Latin *sparsum* = scattered]

spartan *ADJECTIVE* simple and without comfort or luxuries.
[named after the people of *Sparta* in ancient Greece, famous for their hardiness]

spasm *NOUN* **spasms 1** a sudden involuntary movement of a muscle. **2** a sudden brief spell of activity etc.
[from Greek]

spasmodic *ADJECTIVE* **1** happening or done at irregular intervals. **2** to do with or caused by a spasm.
▷ **spasmodically** *adverb*

spastic *NOUN* **spastics** a person suffering from spasms of the muscles and jerky movements, especially caused by cerebral palsy.
▷ **spastic** *adjective*

spat[1] *past tense* of **spit**[1].

spat[2] *NOUN* **spats** a short gaiter.
[from *spatter*]

spate *NOUN* **spates** a sudden flood or rush.
[origin unknown]

spathe (*rhymes with* **bathe**) *NOUN* **spathes** a large petal-like part of a flower, round a central spike.
[from Greek]

spatial *ADJECTIVE* to do with space.
[same origin as *space*]

spatter *VERB* **spatters, spattering, spattered 1** scatter in small drops. **2** splash • *spattered with mud.*
▷ **spatter** *noun*
[origin unknown]

spatula *NOUN* **spatulas** a tool like a knife with a broad blunt flexible blade, used for spreading or mixing things.
[from Latin *spathula* = small spear]

spawn *NOUN* **1** the eggs of fish, frogs, toads, or shellfish. **2** the thread-like matter from which fungi grow.

spawn *VERB* **spawns, spawning, spawned 1** produce spawn. **2** be produced from spawn. **3** produce something in great quantities.
[from old French]

spay *VERB* **spays, spaying, spayed** sterilize a female animal by removing the ovaries.
[from old French]

speak *VERB* **speaks, speaking, spoke, spoken 1** say something; talk. **2** talk or be able to talk in a foreign language • *Do you speak French?*
- **speak up 1** speak more loudly. **2** give your opinion.
[from Old English]

speaker *NOUN* **speakers 1** a person who is speaking. **2** someone who makes a speech. **3** a loudspeaker.
- **the Speaker** the person who controls the debates in the House of Commons or a similar assembly.

spear *NOUN* **spears** a weapon for throwing or stabbing, with a long shaft and a pointed tip.

spear *VERB* **spears, spearing, speared** pierce with a spear or with something pointed.
[from Old English]

spearhead *VERB* **spearheads, spearheading, spearheaded** lead an attacking or advancing force.

spearmint *NOUN* mint used in cookery and for flavouring chewing gum.
[from *spear* + *mint*[1] (probably because the leaves are shaped like spearheads)]

special *ADJECTIVE* **1** not ordinary or usual; exceptional • *a special occasion; Take special care of it.* **2** meant for a particular person or purpose • *You need a special tool for this job.*
[same origin as *species*]

special effects *PLURAL NOUN* illusions created for films or television by using props, trick photography, or computer images.

specialist *NOUN* **specialists** an expert in one subject • *a skin specialist.*

speciality *NOUN* **specialities 1** something in which a person specializes. **2** a special product, especially a food.

specialize *VERB* **specializes, specializing, specialized** give particular attention or study to one subject or thing • *She specialized in biology.*
▷ **specialization** *noun*

specially *ADVERB* **1** in a special way. **2** for a special purpose.

special needs *PLURAL NOUN* educational requirements resulting from learning difficulties, physical disability, or emotional and behavioural difficulties • *children with special needs.*

species (*say* spee-shiz) *NOUN* **species 1** a group of animals or plants that are very similar. **2** a kind or sort • *a species of sledge.* [Latin, = appearance, form, or kind]

specific *ADJECTIVE* definite or precise; of or for a particular thing • *The money was given for a specific purpose.*
▷ **specifically** *adverb*
[same origin as *species*]

specification *NOUN* **specifications** a detailed description of how to make or do something.

specific gravity *NOUN* **specific gravities** relative density.

specify *VERB* **specifies, specifying, specified** name or list things precisely • *The recipe specified cream, not milk.*
▷ **specification** *noun*
[same origin as *species*]

specimen *NOUN* **specimens 1** a sample. **2** an example • *a fine specimen of an oak tree.* [Latin, from *specere* = to look]

specious (*say* spee-shus) *ADJECTIVE* seeming good but lacking real merit • *specious reasoning.*
[same origin as *species*]

speck *NOUN* **specks** a small spot or particle. [from Old English]

speckle *NOUN* **speckles** a small spot or mark.
▷ **speckled** *adjective*
[from old Dutch]

specs *PLURAL NOUN* (*informal*) spectacles.

spectacle *NOUN* **spectacles 1** an impressive sight or display. **2** a ridiculous sight. [from Latin *spectaculum* = a public show]

spectacles *PLURAL NOUN* a pair of glasses.
▷ **spectacled** *adjective*

spectacular *ADJECTIVE* impressive or striking.
[same origin as *spectacle*]

spectator *NOUN* **spectators** a person who watches a game, show, incident, etc. [from Latin *spectare* = to look at]
WORD FAMILY There are a number of English words that are related to *spectator* because part of their original meaning comes from the Latin word *spectare* meaning 'to look at'. These include *aspect, expect, inspect, introspective, prospect, spectacle,* and *suspect.*

spectre *NOUN* **spectres** a ghost.
▷ **spectral** *adjective*
[same origin as *spectrum*]

spectrum *NOUN* **spectra 1** the bands of colours seen in a rainbow. **2** a wide range of things, ideas, etc.
[Latin, = image]

speculate *VERB* **speculates, speculating, speculated 1** form opinions without having any definite evidence. **2** invest in stocks, property, etc. in the hope of making a profit but with the risk of loss.
▷ **speculation** *noun* **speculator** *noun* **speculative** *adjective*
[from Latin *speculari* = spy out]

sped *past tense* of **speed**.

speech *NOUN* **speeches 1** the action or power of speaking. **2** a talk to an audience. **3** a group of lines spoken by a character in a play.
[from Old English]

speechless *ADJECTIVE* unable to speak because of great emotion.

speed *NOUN* **speeds 1** a measure of the time in which something moves or happens. **2** quickness or swiftness.
- **at speed** quickly.

speed *VERB* **speeds, speeding, sped** (in senses 2 and 3 **speeded**)
1 go quickly • *The train sped by.* **2** make or become quicker • *This will speed things up.* **3** drive faster than the legal limit.
▷ **speeding** *noun*
[from Old English]

speedboat *NOUN* **speedboats** a fast motor boat.

speed camera *NOUN* **speed cameras** a camera by the side of a road which automatically photographs any vehicle which is going too fast.

speed hump *NOUN* **speed humps** a ridge built across a road to make vehicles slow down.

speed limit *NOUN* **speed limits** the maximum speed at which vehicles may legally travel on a particular road.

speedometer *NOUN* **speedometers** a device in a vehicle, showing its speed.
[from *speed* + *meter*]

speedway *NOUN* **speedways** a track for motorcycle racing.

speedwell *NOUN* **speedwells** a wild plant with small blue flowers.
[from *speed* + *well*^{2} (perhaps because the plant often grows by the roadside)]

speedy *ADJECTIVE* **speedier**, **speediest** quick or swift.
▷ **speedily** *adverb*

speleology (*say* spel-ee-ol-o-jee) *NOUN* the exploration and study of caves.
[from Greek *spelaion* = cave, + *-logy*]

spell^1 *NOUN* **spells** a saying or action etc. supposed to have magical power.
[from Old English *spel* = speech, story]

spell^2 *NOUN* **spells 1** a period of time. **2** a period of a certain work or activity etc.
[from Old English *spelian* = take someone's place, take over a task]

spell^3 *VERB* **spells**, **spelling**, **spelled** or **spelt 1** put letters in the right order to make a word or words. **2** (said about letters) form a word • *C-A-T spells 'cat'.* **3** have as a result • *Wet weather spells ruin for crops.*
▷ **speller** *noun* **spelling** *noun*
[via old French from Germanic]

spellbound *ADJECTIVE* entranced as if by a magic spell.

spend *VERB* **spends**, **spending**, **spent 1** use money to pay for things. **2** use up • *Don't spend too much time on it.* **3** pass time • *We spent a holiday in Spain.*
[from Old English]

spendthrift *NOUN* **spendthrifts** a person who spends money extravagantly and wastefully.
[from *spend* + an old sense of *thrift* = prosperity, earnings]

sperm *NOUN* **sperms** or **sperm** the male cell that fuses with an ovum to produce offspring.
[from Greek *sperma* = seed]

spermatozoon (*say* sper-ma-toe-zoe-on) *NOUN* **spermatozoa** a sperm.
[from *sperm* + Greek *zoion* = animal]

spew *VERB* **spews**, **spewing**, **spewed 1** vomit. **2** cast out in a stream • *The volcano spewed out lava.*
[from Old English]

sphere *NOUN* **spheres 1** a perfectly round solid shape; the shape of a ball. **2** a field of action or interest etc. • *That country is in Russia's sphere of influence.*
▷ **spherical** *adjective*
[from Greek *sphaira* = ball]

spheroid *NOUN* **spheroids** a solid which is sphere-like but not perfectly spherical.

sphinx *NOUN* **sphinxes** a stone statue with the body of a lion and a human head, especially the huge one (almost 5,000 years old) in Egypt.
[from the *Sphinx* in Greek mythology, a winged creature with a woman's head and a lion's body]

spice *NOUN* **spices 1** a strong-tasting substance used to flavour food, often made from dried parts of plants. **2** something that adds interest or excitement • *Variety is the spice of life.*
▷ **spice** *verb* **spicy** *adjective*
[from old French]

spick and span *ADJECTIVE* neat and clean.
[*span* is from Old Norse; *spick* is probably from old Dutch]

spider *NOUN* **spiders** a small animal with eight legs that spins webs to catch insects on which it feeds.
[from Old English *spithra* = spinner]

spidery *ADJECTIVE* (said about handwriting) having long thin lines and sharp angles, like a spider's legs.

spike *NOUN* **spikes** a pointed piece of metal; a sharp point.
▷ **spiky** *adjective*

spike *VERB* **spikes, spiking, spiked 1** put spikes on something • *spiked running shoes.* **2** pierce with a spike.
- **spike a person's guns** spoil his or her plans.
[origin unknown]

spill *VERB* **spills, spilling, spilt** or **spilled 1** let something fall out of a container • *Try not to spill your drink.* **2** become spilt • *The coins came spilling out.*
▷ **spillage** *noun*

spill *NOUN* **spills 1** spilling; something spilt. **2** a fall from a horse, bicycle, etc.
[from Old English]

spin *VERB* **spins, spinning, spun 1** turn round and round quickly. **2** make raw wool or cotton into threads by pulling and twisting its fibres. **3** (said about a spider or silkworm) make a web or cocoon out of threads from its body.
- **spin a yarn** tell a story.
- **spin out** make something last as long as possible.

spin *NOUN* **spins 1** a spinning movement. **2** a short outing in a car.
[from Old English]

spinach *NOUN* a vegetable with dark green leaves.
[via Spanish and Arabic from Persian]

spinal *ADJECTIVE* to do with the spine.

spinal cord *NOUN* **spinal cords** the thick cord of nerves enclosed in the spine, that carries impulses to and from the brain.

spindle *NOUN* **spindles 1** a thin rod on which thread is wound. **2** a pin or bar that turns round or on which something turns.
[from Old English]

spindly *ADJECTIVE* thin and long or tall.
[from *spindle*]

spin doctor *NOUN* **spin doctors** a person whose job is to make information or events seem favourable to his or her employer, usually a politician or political party.

spin-drier *NOUN* **spin-driers** a machine in which washed clothes are spun round and round to dry them.

spindrift *NOUN* spray blown along the surface of the sea.
[from an old word *spoon* = be blown by the wind, + *drift*]

spine *NOUN* **spines 1** the line of bones down the middle of the back. **2** a thorn or prickle. **3** the back part of a book where the pages are joined together.
[from Latin]

spine-chilling *ADJECTIVE* frightening and exciting • *a spine-chilling horror film.*

spineless *ADJECTIVE* **1** without a backbone. **2** lacking in determination or strength of character.

spinet *NOUN* **spinets** a small harpsichord.
[from old French]

spinney *NOUN* **spinneys** a small wood or thicket.
[from old French]

spinning wheel *NOUN* **spinning wheels** a household device for spinning fibre into thread.

spin-off *NOUN* **spin-offs** something extra produced while making something else.

spinster *NOUN* **spinsters** a woman who has not married.
[the original meaning was 'one who spins' (because many unmarried women used to earn their living by spinning, which could be done at home)]

spiny *ADJECTIVE* covered with spines; prickly.

spiral *ADJECTIVE* going round and round a central point and becoming gradually closer to it or further from it; twisting continually round a central line or cylinder etc.
▷ **spirally** *adverb*

spiral *NOUN* **spirals** a spiral line or course.

spiral *VERB* **spirals, spiralling, spiralled 1** move in a spiral. **2** increase or decrease continuously and quickly • *Prices were spiralling.*
[from Greek *speira* = winding]

spire *NOUN* **spires** a tall pointed part on top of a church tower.
[from Old English]

spirit *NOUN* **spirits 1** the soul. **2** a person's mood or mind and feelings • *He was in good spirits.* **3** a ghost or a supernatural being. **4** courage or liveliness • *She answered with spirit.* **5** a kind of quality in something • *the romantic spirit of the book.* **6** a strong distilled alcoholic drink.

spirit *VERB* **spirits, spiriting, spirited** carry off quickly and secretly • *They spirited her away.*
[from Latin *spiritus* = breath]

spirited *ADJECTIVE* brave; self-confident and lively.

spirit level *NOUN* **spirit levels** a device consisting of a tube of liquid with an air bubble in it, used to find out whether something is level.

spiritual *ADJECTIVE* **1** to do with the human soul; not physical. **2** to do with religion.
▷ **spiritually** *adverb* **spirituality** *noun*

spiritual *NOUN* **spirituals** a religious folk song, originally sung by black Christians in America.

spiritualism *NOUN* the belief that the spirits of dead people communicate with living people.
▷ **spiritualist** *noun*

spit[1] *VERB* **spits, spitting, spat** or **spit** **1** send out drops of liquid etc. forcibly from the mouth • *He spat at me.* **2** fall lightly • *It's spitting with rain.*

spit *NOUN* saliva or spittle.
[from Old English *spittan*]

spit[2] *NOUN* **spits 1** a long thin metal spike put through meat to hold it while it is being roasted. **2** a narrow strip of land sticking out into the sea.
[from Old English *spitu*]

spite *NOUN* a desire to hurt or annoy somebody.
▷ **spiteful** *adjective* **spitefully** *adverb* **spitefulness** *noun*
- **in spite of** not being prevented by • *We went out in spite of the rain.*

spite *VERB* **spites, spiting, spited** hurt or annoy somebody from spite.
[same origin as *despite*]

spitfire *NOUN* **spitfires** a fiery-tempered person.

spitting image *NOUN* an exact likeness.

spittle *NOUN* saliva, especially when it is spat out.
[from Old English]

spittoon *NOUN* **spittoons** a receptacle for people to spit into.

splash *VERB* **splashes, splashing, splashed 1** make liquid fly about in drops. **2** (said about liquid) fly about in drops. **3** wet by splashing • *The bus splashed us.*

splash *NOUN* **splashes 1** the action or sound or mark of splashing. **2** a bright patch of colour or light.
- **make a splash** attract a lot of attention.
[imitating the sound]

splatter *VERB* **splatters, splattering, splattered** splash noisily.
[imitating the sound]

splay *VERB* **splays, splaying, splayed** spread or slope apart.
[from *display*]

spleen *NOUN* **spleens 1** an organ of the body, close to the stomach, that helps to keep the blood in good condition. **2** bad temper or spite • *He vented his spleen on us.*
[from Latin]

splendid *ADJECTIVE* **1** magnificent; full of splendour. **2** excellent.
▷ **splendidly** *adverb*
[from Latin *splendidus* = shining]

splendour *NOUN* a brilliant display or appearance.
[from Latin *splendere* = shine brightly]

splice *VERB* **splices, splicing, spliced 1** join pieces of rope etc. by twisting their strands together. **2** join pieces of film or wood etc. by overlapping the ends.
[probably from old Dutch]

splint *NOUN* **splints** a straight piece of wood or metal etc. tied to a broken arm or leg to hold it firm.

splint *VERB* **splints, splinting, splinted** hold with a splint.
[from old German or old Dutch]

splinter *NOUN* **splinters** a thin sharp piece of wood, glass, stone, etc. broken off a larger piece.

splinter *VERB* **splinters, splintering, splintered** break into splinters.
[from old German or old Dutch]

splinter group *NOUN* **splinter groups** a group of people that has broken away from a larger group or movement.

split *VERB* **splits, splitting, split 1** break apart, especially along the length of something. **2** divide something into parts. **3** divide something among people • *I'll split the cost with you.*
- **split up 1** end a marriage or other relationship. **2** go in different directions.

split *NOUN* **splits 1** the splitting or dividing of something. **2** a place where something has split.
- **the splits** an acrobatic position in which the legs are stretched widely in opposite directions.

[from Dutch]

split second *NOUN* a very brief moment of time; an instant.

split-second *ADJECTIVE* **1** very quick. **2** (said about timing) very precise.

splodge *NOUN* **splodges** a dirty mark or stain.
[origin unknown]

splurge *VERB* **splurges, splurging, splurged** (*informal*) to spend a lot of money on something, especially a luxury • *She splurged her first week's wages on a make-over.*
[originally American; origin unknown]

splutter *VERB* **splutters, spluttering, spluttered 1** make a quick series of spitting sounds. **2** speak quickly but not clearly.
▷ **splutter** *noun*
[imitating the sound]

spoil *VERB* **spoils, spoiling, spoilt** or **spoiled 1** damage something and make it useless or unsatisfactory. **2** make someone selfish by always letting them have what they want. **3** treat someone kindly • *Go on, spoil yourself!*
[from Latin]

spoils *PLURAL NOUN* plunder or other things gained by a victor • *the spoils of war.*

spoilsport *NOUN* **spoilsports** a person who spoils other people's enjoyment of things.

spoke[1] *NOUN* **spokes** each of the bars or rods that go from the centre of a wheel to its rim.
[from Old English]

spoke[2] *past tense* of **speak**.

spokesman *NOUN* **spokesmen** a spokesperson, especially a man.
[from *spoke*[2]]

spokesperson *NOUN* **spokespersons** a person who speaks on behalf of a group of people.

spokeswoman *NOUN* **spokeswomen** a female spokesperson.

spoliation *NOUN* pillaging.
[from Latin]

sponge *NOUN* **sponges 1** a sea creature with a soft porous body. **2** the skeleton of this creature, or a piece of a similar substance, used for washing or padding things. **3** a soft lightweight cake or pudding.
▷ **spongy** *adjective*

sponge *VERB* **sponges, sponging, sponged 1** wipe or wash something with a sponge. **2** get money or food off other people without giving anything in return • *He's always sponging off his friends.*
▷ **sponger** *noun*
[via Old English from Greek]

sponsor *NOUN* **sponsors 1** a person or organization that provides money for an arts or sports event or for a broadcast in return for advertising. **2** someone who gives money to a charity in return for something achieved by another person.
▷ **sponsorship** *noun*

sponsor *VERB* **sponsors, sponsoring, sponsored** be a sponsor for a person or thing.
[from Latin *sponsum* = promised]

spontaneous (*say* spon-tay-nee-us) *ADJECTIVE* happening or done naturally; not forced or suggested by someone else.
▷ **spontaneously** *adverb* **spontaneity** *noun*
[from Latin *sponte* = of your own accord]

spoof *NOUN* **spoofs 1** a hoax. **2** a parody.
[originally = a card game invented and named by an English comedian, Arthur Roberts (1852-1933)]

spook *NOUN* **spooks** (*informal*) a ghost.
▷ **spooky** *adjective* **spookiness** *noun*
[Dutch]

spool *NOUN* **spools** a rod or cylinder on which something is wound.
[via old French from Germanic]

a b c d e f g h i j k l m n o p q r s t u v w x y z

spoon *NOUN* **spoons** a small device with a rounded bowl on a handle, used for lifting things to the mouth or for stirring or measuring things.
▷ **spoonful** *noun*
spoonfuls **spoon** *VERB* **spoons, spooning, spooned** take or lift something with a spoon.
[from Old English]

spoonerism *NOUN* **spoonerisms** an accidental exchange of the initial letters of two words, e.g. by saying *a boiled sprat* instead of *a spoiled brat*.
[named after Canon *Spooner* (1844-1930), who made mistakes of this kind]

spoon-feed *VERB* **spoon-feeds, spoon-feeding, spoon-fed** **1** feed a baby or invalid with a spoon. **2** provide someone with so much help or information that he or she does not have to make any effort.

spoor *NOUN* the track left by an animal.
[Afrikaans]

sporadic *ADJECTIVE* happening or found at irregular intervals; scattered.
▷ **sporadically** *adverb*
[from Greek *sporas* = sown, scattered]

spore *NOUN* **spores** a tiny reproductive cell of a plant such as a fungus or fern.
[from Greek *spora* = seed]

sporran *NOUN* **sporrans** a pouch worn in front of a kilt.
[via Scottish Gaelic from Latin *bursa* = purse]

sport *NOUN* **sports** **1** an athletic activity; a game or pastime, especially outdoors. **2** games of this kind • *Are you keen on sport?* **3** (*informal*) a person who behaves well in response to teasing or defeat • *Thanks for being such a good sport.*

sport *VERB* **sports, sporting, sported** **1** play; amuse yourself. **2** wear • *He sported a gold tiepin.*
[from old French]

sporting *ADJECTIVE* **1** connected with sport; interested in sport. **2** behaving fairly and generously.

sporting chance *NOUN* a reasonable chance of success.

sports car *NOUN* **sports cars** an open low-built fast car.

sports jacket *NOUN* **sports jackets** a man's jacket for informal wear (not part of a suit).

sportsman *NOUN* **sportsmen** **1** a man who takes part in sport. **2** a person who shows sportsmanship.

sportsmanship *NOUN* sporting behaviour; behaving fairly and generously to rivals.

sportswoman *NOUN* **sportswomen** **1** a woman who takes part in sport. **2** a woman who shows sportsmanship.

spot *NOUN* **spots** **1** a small round mark. **2** a pimple. **3** a small amount • *We had a spot of trouble*. **4** a place. **5** a drop • *a few spots of rain*.
- **on the spot** **1** without delay or change of place. **2** under pressure to take action • *This really puts him on the spot!*
- **spot on** (*informal*) exactly right or accurate.

spot *VERB* **spots, spotting, spotted** **1** mark with spots. **2** notice or recognize • *We spotted her in the crowd*. **3** watch for and take note of • *train-spotting*.
▷ **spotter** *noun*
[probably from old German or old Dutch]

spot check *NOUN* **spot checks** a check, usually without warning, on one of a group of people or things.

spotless *ADJECTIVE* perfectly clean.

spotlight *NOUN* **spotlights** **1** a strong light that can shine on one small area. **2** public attention • *The Royal Family are used to being in the spotlight*.

spotty *ADJECTIVE* marked with spots.

spouse *NOUN* **spouses** a person's husband or wife.
[from old French; related to *sponsor*]

spout *NOUN* **spouts** **1** a pipe or similar opening from which liquid can pour. **2** a jet of liquid.

spout *VERB* **spouts, spouting, spouted** **1** come or send out as a jet of liquid. **2** (*informal*) speak for a long time.
[from old Dutch]

sprain *VERB* **sprains, spraining, sprained** injure a joint by twisting it.
▷ **sprain** *noun*
[origin unknown]

sprat *NOUN* **sprats** a small edible fish.
[from Old English]

sprawl *VERB* **sprawls, sprawling, sprawled** **1** sit or lie with the arms and legs spread out loosely. **2** spread out loosely or untidily.
▷ **sprawl** *noun*
[from Old English]

spray[1] *VERB* **sprays, spraying, sprayed** scatter tiny drops of liquid over something.

spray *NOUN* **sprays 1** tiny drops of liquid sent through the air. **2** a device for spraying liquid. **3** a liquid for spraying • *fly spray*.
[origin unknown]

spray[2] *NOUN* **sprays 1** a single shoot with its leaves and flowers. **2** a small bunch of flowers.
[from Old English]

spread *VERB* **spreads, spreading, spread** **1** open or stretch something out to its full size • *The bird spread its wings*. **2** make something cover a surface • *We spread jam on the bread*. **3** become longer or wider • *The stain was spreading*. **4** make or become more widely known or felt or distributed etc. • *We spread the news. The story quickly spread round the village*.

spread *NOUN* **spreads 1** the action or result of spreading. **2** a thing's breadth or extent. **3** a paste for spreading on bread. **4** (*informal*) a large or grand meal.
[from Old English]

spreadeagled *ADJECTIVE* with arms and legs stretched out • *He lay spreadeagled on the bed*.
[originally = a picture of an eagle with legs and wings stretched out, used as an emblem on a knight's shield, inn sign, etc.]

spreadsheet *NOUN* **spreadsheets** a computer program for handling information, especially figures, displayed in a table.

spree *NOUN* **sprees** a period in which you do something freely • *a shopping spree*.
[origin unknown]

sprig *NOUN* **sprigs** a small branch; a shoot.
[from old German]

sprightly *ADJECTIVE* **sprightlier, sprightliest** lively and full of energy.
[from *sprite*]

spring *VERB* **springs, springing, sprang, sprung** **1** jump; move quickly or suddenly • *He sprang to his feet*. **2** originate, arise, or grow • *The trouble has sprung from carelessness. Weeds have started to spring up*. **3** present or produce suddenly • *They sprang a surprise on us*.

spring *NOUN* **springs 1** a springy coil or bent piece of metal. **2** a springing movement. **3** a place where water comes up naturally from the ground. **4** the season when most plants begin to grow.
[from Old English]

springboard *NOUN* **springboards** a springy board from which people jump in diving and gymnastics.

springbok *NOUN* **springboks** or **springbok** a South African gazelle.
[Afrikaans, from Dutch *springen* = to spring + *bok* = buck, antelope]

spring-clean *VERB* **spring-cleans, spring-cleaning, spring-cleaned** clean a house thoroughly in springtime.

spring onion *NOUN* **spring onions** a small onion with a long green stem, eaten raw in salads.

spring roll *NOUN* **spring rolls** a Chinese pancake filled with vegetables and (sometimes) meat, and fried until crisp.

springtime *NOUN* the season of spring.

springy *ADJECTIVE* **springier, springiest** able to spring back easily after being bent or squeezed.
▷ **springiness** *noun*

sprinkle *VERB* **sprinkles, sprinkling, sprinkled** make tiny drops or pieces fall on something.
▷ **sprinkler** *noun*
[probably from old Dutch]

sprinkling *NOUN* **sprinklings** a few here and there; a small amount.

sprint *VERB* **sprints, sprinting, sprinted** run very fast for a short distance.
▷ **sprint** *noun* **sprinter** *noun*
[from Old Norse]

sprite *NOUN* **sprites** an elf, fairy, or goblin.
[from *spirit*]

A B C D E F G H I J K L M N O P Q R S T U V W X Y Z

sprocket *NOUN* **sprockets** each of the row of teeth round a wheel, fitting into links on a chain.
[origin unknown]

sprout *VERB* **sprouts, sprouting, sprouted** start to grow; put out shoots.

sprout *NOUN* **sprouts 1** a shoot of a plant. **2** a Brussels sprout.
[probably from Old English]

spruce[1] *NOUN* **spruces** a kind of fir tree.
[from *Pruce*, the old name of Prussia, an area in central Europe, where it was grown]

spruce[2] *ADJECTIVE* neat and trim; smart.

spruce *VERB* **spruces, sprucing, spruced** smarten • *Spruce yourself up*.
[probably from *spruce jerkin*, made of leather from Prussia (see *spruce*[1])]

spry *ADJECTIVE* **spryer, spryest** active, nimble, and lively.
[origin unknown]

spud *NOUN* **spuds** (*informal*) a potato.
[origin unknown]

spume *NOUN* froth or foam.
[from Latin]

spur *NOUN* **spurs 1** a sharp device worn on the heel of a rider's boot to urge a horse to go faster. **2** something shaped like a spur, such as a hard spike on the back of a cock's leg. **3** a stimulus or incentive. **4** a ridge that sticks out from a mountain.
- **on the spur of the moment** on an impulse; without planning.

spur *VERB* **spurs, spurring, spurred** urge on; encourage.
[from Old English]

spurious *ADJECTIVE* not genuine.
[from Latin]

spurn *VERB* **spurns, spurning, spurned** reject scornfully.
[from Old English]

spurt *VERB* **spurts, spurting, spurted 1** gush out. **2** increase your speed suddenly.

spurt *NOUN* **spurts 1** a sudden gush. **2** a sudden increase in speed or effort.
[origin unknown]

sputter *VERB* **sputters, sputtering, sputtered** splutter.
▷ **sputter** *noun*
[from Dutch]

sputum *NOUN* saliva or phlegm.
[Latin]

spy *NOUN* **spies** someone who works secretly for one country, person, etc. to find out things about another.

spy *VERB* **spies, spying, spied 1** be a spy. **2** keep watch secretly • *Have you been spying on me?* **3** see or notice • *She spied a house in the distance*.
[from old French *espier* = espy]

squabble *VERB* **squabbles, squabbling, squabbled** quarrel or bicker.
▷ **squabble** *noun*
[origin unknown]

squad *NOUN* **squads** a small group of people working or being trained together.
[from old French; related to *squadron*]

squadron *NOUN* **squadrons** part of an army, navy, or air force.
[from Italian; related to *squad*]

squalid *ADJECTIVE* dirty and unpleasant.
▷ **squalidly** *adverb*
[from Latin *squalidus* = rough, dirty]

squall *NOUN* **squalls 1** a sudden storm or gust of wind. **2** a baby's loud cry.
▷ **squally** *adverb*

squall *VERB* **squalls, squalling, squalled** (said about a baby) cry loudly.
[probably from *squeal* and *bawl*]

squalor *NOUN* dirty and unpleasant conditions • *Some families were living in squalor*.

squander *VERB* **squanders, squandering, squandered** spend money or time etc. wastefully.
[origin unknown]

square *NOUN* **squares 1** a flat shape with four equal sides and four right angles. **2** an area surrounded by buildings • *Leicester Square*. **3** the result of multiplying a number by itself • *9 is the square of 3* (9 = 3 x 3).

square *ADJECTIVE* **1** having the shape of a square. **2** forming a right angle • *The desk has square corners*. **3** equal or even • *The teams are all square with six points each*. **4** used to give the length of each side of a square shape or object • *The carpet is four metres square*. **5** used to give a measurement of an area • *an area of 25 square metres*.
▷ **squareness** *noun*

square *VERB* **squares, squaring, squared** **1** make a thing square. **2** multiply a number by itself • *5 squared is 25.* **3** match; make or be consistent • *His story doesn't square with yours.* **4** settle or pay.
[from old French; related to *quadrant*]

square deal *NOUN* **square deals** a deal that is honest and fair.

squarely *ADVERB* directly or exactly • *The ball hit him squarely in the mouth.*

square meal *NOUN* **square meals** a good satisfying meal.

square root *NOUN* **square roots** the number that gives a particular number if it is multiplied by itself • *3 is the square root of 9* (3 x 3 = 9).

squash[1] *VERB* **squashes, squashing, squashed** **1** press something so that it becomes flat or out of shape. **2** force into a small space; pack tightly. **3** suppress or quash.

squash *NOUN* **squashes** **1** a crowded condition. **2** a fruit-flavoured soft drink. **3** a game played with rackets and a soft ball in a special indoor court.
[a different spelling of *quash*]

squash[2] *NOUN* **squashes** a kind of gourd used as a vegetable.
[from a Native American word]

squat *VERB* **squats, squatting, squatted** **1** sit on your heels; crouch. **2** live in an unoccupied building without permission.
▷ **squat** *noun* **squatter** *noun*

squat *ADJECTIVE* short and fat.
[from *ex-* + old French *quatir* = press down, crouch]

squaw *NOUN* **squaws** a North American Indian woman or wife.
[a Native American word]
USAGE This word is now considered to be offensive.

squawk *VERB* **squawks, squawking, squawked** make a loud harsh cry.
▷ **squawk** *noun*
[imitating the sound]

squeak *VERB* **squeaks, squeaking, squeaked** make a short high-pitched cry or sound.
▷ **squeak** *noun* **squeaky** *adjective* **squeakily** *adverb*
[imitating the sound]

squeal *VERB* **squeals, squealing, squealed** make a long shrill cry or sound.
▷ **squeal** *noun*
[imitating the sound]

squeamish *ADJECTIVE* easily disgusted or shocked.
▷ **squeamishness** *noun*
[from old French]

squeeze *VERB* **squeezes, squeezing, squeezed** **1** press something from opposite sides, especially to get liquid out of it. **2** force into or through a place • *We squeezed through a gap in the hedge.*
▷ **squeezer** *noun*

squeeze *NOUN* **squeezes** **1** the action of squeezing. **2** a drop of liquid squeezed out • *Add a squeeze of lemon.* **3** a time when money is difficult to get or borrow.
[origin unknown]

squelch *VERB* **squelches, squelching, squelched** make a sound like someone treading in thick mud.
▷ **squelch** *noun*
[imitating the sound]

squib *NOUN* **squibs** a small firework that hisses and then explodes.
[origin unknown]

squid *NOUN* **squids** a sea animal with eight short tentacles and two long ones.
[origin unknown]

squiggle *NOUN* **squiggles** a short curly line.
[probably from *squirm* + *wriggle*]

squint *VERB* **squints, squinting, squinted** **1** be cross-eyed. **2** peer; look with half-shut eyes at something.
▷ **squint** *noun*
[origin unknown]

squire *NOUN* **squires** **1** the man who owns most of the land in a country parish or district. **2** a young nobleman in the Middle Ages who served a knight.
[from *esquire*]

squirm *VERB* **squirms, squirming, squirmed** wriggle about, especially when you feel embarrassed or awkward.
[origin unknown]

squirrel *NOUN* **squirrels** a small animal with a bushy tail and red or grey fur, living in trees.
[from Greek]

squirt *VERB* **squirts, squirting, squirted** send or come out in a jet of liquid.
▷ **squirt** *noun*
[imitating the sound]

St. or **St** *ABBREVIATION* **1** Saint. **2** Street.

stab *VERB* **stabs, stabbing, stabbed** pierce or wound with something sharp.

stab *NOUN* **stabs 1** the action of stabbing. **2** a sudden sharp pain • *She felt a stab of fear.* **3** (*informal*) an attempt • *I'll have a stab at it.*
[origin unknown]

stability *NOUN* being stable.

stabilize *VERB* **stabilizes, stabilizing, stabilized** make or become stable.
▷ **stabilization** *noun*

stabilizer *NOUN* **stabilizers** a device for keeping a vehicle or ship steady.

stable[1] *ADJECTIVE* **1** steady and firmly fixed or balanced. **2** not likely to change or end suddenly • *a stable relationship.* **3** sensible and dependable.
▷ **stably** *adverb*
[from Latin *stare* = to stand]

stable[2] *NOUN* **stables** a building where horses are kept.

stable *VERB* **stables, stabling, stabled** put or keep in a stable.
[from old French; related to *stable*[1]]

staccato *ADVERB* & *ADJECTIVE* (*in music*) played with each note short and separate.
[Italian, from *distaccare* = detach]

stack *NOUN* **stacks 1** a neat pile. **2** a haystack. **3** (*informal*) a large amount • *I have a stack of work to get through.* • *There's stacks to do.* **4** a single tall chimney; a group of small chimneys.

stack *VERB* **stacks, stacking, stacked** pile things up.
[from Old Norse]

stadium *NOUN* **stadiums** a sports ground surrounded by seats for spectators.
[Latin]

staff *NOUN* **staffs** or, in sense 4, **staves 1** the people who work in an office, shop, etc. **2** the teachers in a school or college. **3** a stick or pole used as a weapon or support or as a symbol of authority. **4** a set of five horizontal lines on which music is written.

staff *VERB* **staffs, staffing, staffed** provide with a staff of people • *The centre is staffed by volunteers.*
[from Old English]

stag *NOUN* **stags** a male deer.
[probably from Old English]

stage *NOUN* **stages 1** a platform for performances in a theatre or hall. **2** a point or part of a process, journey, etc. • *Now for the final stage.*
- **the stage** the profession of acting or working in the theatre.

stage *VERB* **stages, staging, staged** **1** present a performance on a stage. **2** organize • *We decided to stage a protest.*
[from old French]

stagecoach *NOUN* **stagecoaches** a horse-drawn coach that formerly ran regularly from one point to another along the same route.
[so called because it ran in stages, picking up passengers at points along the route]

stage fright *NOUN* fear or nervousness before or while performing to an audience.

stage-manage *VERB* **stage-manages, stage-managing, stage-managed 1** be stage manager. **2** organize and control an event so that it has a particular effect.

stage manager *NOUN* **stage managers** the person in charge of the scenery, lighting, sound, etc. during a performance.

stage-struck *ADJECTIVE* fascinated by the theatre and longing to be an actor.

stagger *VERB* **staggers, staggering, staggered** **1** walk unsteadily. **2** shock deeply; amaze • *We were staggered at the price.* **3** arrange things so that they do not all happen at the same time • *Please stagger your holidays so that there is always someone here.*
▷ **stagger** *noun* **staggering** *adjective*
[from Old Norse]

stagnant *ADJECTIVE* **1** not flowing. **2** not active or developing • *Business is stagnant.*
[from Latin *stagnum* = a pool]

stagnate *VERB* **stagnates, stagnating, stagnated** **1** be stagnant. **2** be dull through lack of activity or variety.
▷ **stagnation** *noun*

staid *ADJECTIVE* steady and serious in manner; sedate.
[old past participle of *stay*]

stain *NOUN* **stains** **1** a dirty mark on something. **2** a blemish on someone's character or past record. **3** a liquid used for staining things.

stain *VERB* **stains, staining, stained** **1** make a stain on something. **2** colour with a liquid that sinks into the surface.
[from an old word *distain* = dye]

stained glass *NOUN* pieces of coloured glass held together in a lead framework to make a picture or pattern.

stainless *ADJECTIVE* without a stain.

stainless steel *NOUN* steel that does not rust easily.

stair *NOUN* **stairs** each of the fixed steps in a series that lead from one level or floor to another in a building.
[from Old English]

staircase *NOUN* **staircases** a set of stairs.

stairway *NOUN* **stairways** a staircase.

stairwell *NOUN* **stairwells** the space going up through a building, which contains the stairs.

stake *NOUN* **stakes** **1** a thick pointed stick to be driven into the ground. **2** the post to which people used to be tied for execution by being burnt alive. **3** an amount of money bet on something. **4** an investment that gives a person a share or interest in a business etc.
- **at stake** being risked.

stake *VERB* **stakes, staking, staked** **1** fasten, support, or mark out with stakes. **2** bet or risk money etc. on an event.
- **stake a claim** claim or obtain a right to something.
[from Old English]

stalactite *NOUN* **stalactites** a stony spike hanging like an icicle from the roof of a cave.
[from Greek *stalaktos* = dripping]
USAGE See note at **stalagmite**.

stalagmite *NOUN* **stalagmites** a stony spike standing like a pillar on the floor of a cave.
[from Greek *stalagma* = a drop]
USAGE Remember that a *stala***g***mite* stands up from the ground, while a *stala***c***tite* hangs down from the ceiling.

stale *ADJECTIVE* **1** not fresh. **2** bored and lacking new ideas because you have been doing something for too long.
▷ **staleness** *noun*
[old French, = at a standstill]

stalemate *NOUN* **1** a drawn position in chess when a player cannot make a move without putting his or her king in check. **2** a deadlock; a situation in which neither side in an argument will give way.
[from old French *stale* = at a standstill, + *mate*²]

stalk¹ *NOUN* **stalks** a stem of a plant etc.
[from Old English *stalu*]

stalk² *VERB* **stalks, stalking, stalked** **1** track or hunt stealthily. **2** walk in a stiff or dignified way.
[from Old English *stealcian*]

stall¹ *NOUN* **stalls** **1** a table or counter from which things are sold. **2** a place for one animal in a stable or shed.

stall *VERB* **stalls, stalling, stalled** stop suddenly because of lack of power • *The car engine stalled.*
[from Old English]

stall² *VERB* **stalls, stalling, stalled** delay things or avoid giving an answer to give yourself more time.
[from an old word *stall* = a decoy or a pickpocket's helper]

stallion *NOUN* **stallions** a male horse.
[from old French]

stalls *PLURAL NOUN* the seats in the lowest level of a theatre.

stalwart *ADJECTIVE* strong and faithful • *my stalwart supporters.*
[from Old English]

stamen *NOUN* **stamens** the part of a flower bearing pollen.
[Latin, = thread]

stamina *NOUN* strength and ability to endure pain or hard effort over a long time.
[Latin, plural of *stamen* (referring to the threads of life spun by the fates)]

stammer *VERB* **stammers, stammering, stammered** keep repeating the same syllables when you speak.
▷ **stammer** *noun*
[from Old English]

stamp *NOUN* **stamps 1** a small piece of gummed paper with a special design on it; a postage stamp. **2** a small device for pressing words or marks on something; the words or marks made by this. **3** a distinctive characteristic • *His story bears the stamp of truth.*

stamp *VERB* **stamps, stamping, stamped 1** bang your foot heavily on the ground. **2** walk with loud heavy steps. **3** stick a postage stamp on something. **4** press a mark or design etc. on something.
- **stamp out 1** put out a fire by stamping. **2** put an end to • *We have stamped out vandalism in the area.*
[probably from Old English]

stampede *NOUN* **stampedes** a sudden rush by animals or people.
▷ **stampede** *verb*
[from Spanish *estampida* = crash, uproar]

stance *NOUN* **stances 1** the way a person or animal stands. **2** a person's attitude to something.
[French, related to *stable*[1]]

stanchion *NOUN* **stanchions** an upright bar or post forming a support.
[from old French]

stand *VERB* **stands, standing, stood 1** be on your feet without moving; rise to your feet • *We were standing at the back of the hall. Please stand up.* **2** set or be upright; place • *We stood the vase on the table.* **3** stay the same • *My offer still stands.* **4** be a candidate for election • *She stood for Parliament.* **5** tolerate or endure • *I can't stand that noise.* **6** provide and pay for • *I'll stand you a drink.*
- **it stands to reason** it is reasonable or obvious.
- **stand by** be ready for action.
- **stand for 1** represent • *'US' stands for 'United States'.* **2** tolerate.
- **stand in for** take someone's place.
- **stand out** be clear or obvious.
- **stand up for** support or defend.
- **stand up to 1** resist bravely. **2** stay in good condition in hard use.

stand *NOUN* **stands 1** something made for putting things on • *a music stand.* **2** a stall where things are sold or displayed. **3** a grandstand. **4** a stationary condition or position • *He took his stand near the door.* **5** resistance to attack • *The time has come to make a stand.*
[from Old English]

standard *NOUN* **standards 1** how good something is • *a high standard of work.* **2** a thing used to measure or judge something else. **3** a special flag • *the royal standard.* **4** an upright support.

standard *ADJECTIVE* **1** of the usual or average quality or kind. **2** regarded as the best and widely used • *the standard book on spiders.*
[from old French]

standard assessment task *NOUN* **standard assessment tasks** a standard test given to schoolchildren to assess their progress in one of the subjects of the national curriculum.

Standard English *NOUN* the form of English widely accepted as the normal and correct form. It is taught in schools and spoken and written by educated people.

standardize *VERB* **standardizes, standardizing, standardized** make things be of a standard size, quality, etc.
▷ **standardization** *noun*

standard lamp *NOUN* **standard lamps** a lamp on an upright pole that stands on the floor.

standard of living *NOUN* the level of comfort and wealth that a country or a person has.

standby *NOUN* **standbys 1** something or someone kept to be used if needed. **2** a system by which tickets for a play or an air flight can be bought cheaply at the last minute if there are any seats left.
- **on standby** ready to be used if needed • *Troops were on standby during the crisis.*

stand-in *NOUN* **stand-ins** a deputy or substitute.

standing *NOUN* **1** a person's status or reputation. **2** the period for which something has existed • *a contract of five years' standing.*

standing order *NOUN* **standing orders** an instruction to a bank to make regular payments, or to a trader to supply something regularly.

stand-offish *ADJECTIVE* cold and formal; not friendly.

standpipe *NOUN* **standpipes** a pipe connected directly to a water supply, especially one set up in the street to provide water in an emergency.

standpoint *NOUN* **standpoints** a point of view.

standstill *NOUN* a stop; an end to movement or activity.

stanza *NOUN* **stanzas** a verse of poetry. [Italian]

staple[1] *NOUN* **staples 1** a small piece of metal pushed through papers and clenched to fasten them together. **2** a U-shaped nail.
▷ **staple** *verb* **stapler** *noun*
[from Old English]

staple[2] *ADJECTIVE* main or usual • *Rice is their staple food.*

staple *NOUN* **staples** a staple food or product.
[from old French]

star *NOUN* **stars 1** a large mass of burning gas that is seen as a bright speck of light in the sky at night. **2** a shape with a number of points or rays sticking out from it; an asterisk. **3** an object or mark of this shape showing rank or quality • *a five-star hotel.* **4** a famous performer; one of the chief performers in a play, film, or show.

star *VERB* **stars, starring, starred 1** be one of the main performers in a film or show. **2** have someone as a main performer. **3** mark with an asterisk or star symbol.
[from Old English]

starboard *NOUN* the right-hand side of a ship or aircraft when you are facing forward. (COMPARE *port*[1])
[from Old English *steor* = paddle for steering (usually mounted on the right- hand side), + *board*]

starch *NOUN* **starches 1** a white carbohydrate in bread, potatoes, etc. **2** this or a similar substance used to stiffen clothes.
▷ **starchy** *adjective*

starch *VERB* **starches, starching, starched** stiffen with starch.
[from Old English]

stardom *NOUN* being a star performer.

stare *VERB* **stares, staring, stared** look at something intensely.
▷ **stare** *noun*
[from Old English]

starfish *NOUN* **starfish** or **starfishes** a sea animal shaped like a star with five points.

stark *ADJECTIVE* **1** complete or unmistakable • *stark nonsense.* **2** desolate and bare • *the stark lunar landscape.*
▷ **starkly** *adverb* **starkness** *noun*

stark *ADVERB* completely • *stark naked.*
[from Old English]

starlight *NOUN* light from the stars.

starling *NOUN* **starlings** a noisy black bird with speckled feathers.
[from Old English]

starry *ADJECTIVE* full of stars.

starry-eyed *ADJECTIVE* made happy by foolish dreams or unrealistic hopes.

start *VERB* **starts, starting, started 1** begin or cause to begin. **2** make an engine or machine begin running • *I'll start the car.* **3** begin a journey. **4** make a sudden movement because of pain or surprise.
▹ **starter** *noun*

start *NOUN* **starts 1** the beginning; the place where a race starts. **2** an advantage that someone starts with • *We gave the young ones ten minutes' start.* **3** a sudden movement.
[from Old English]

startle *VERB* **startles, startling, startled** surprise or alarm someone.
[from Old English]

starve *VERB* **starves, starving, starved 1** suffer or die from lack of food; cause to do this. **2** deprive someone of something they need • *She was starved of love.*
▹ **starvation** *noun*
[from Old English]

starving *ADJECTIVE* (*informal*) very hungry.

stash *VERB* **stashes, stashing, stashed** (*informal*) store something safely in a secret place.
[origin unknown]

state *NOUN* **states 1** the quality of a person's or thing's characteristics or circumstances; condition. **2** an organized community under one government (*the State of Israel*) or forming part of a republic (*the 50 States of the USA*). **3** a country's government • *Help for the earthquake victims was provided by the state.* **4** a grand style • *She arrived in state.* **5** (*informal*) an excited or upset condition • *Don't get into a state about the robbery.*

state *VERB* **states, stating, stated** express something in spoken or written words.
[from Latin *status* = standing, condition]

stately *ADJECTIVE* **statelier, stateliest** dignified, imposing, or grand.
▹ **stateliness** *noun*
[from *state*]

stately home *NOUN* **stately homes** a large and magnificent house belonging to an aristocratic family.

statement *NOUN* **statements 1** words stating something. **2** a formal account of facts • *The witness made a statement to the police.* **3** a written report of a financial account • *a bank statement.*

state school *NOUN* **state schools** a school which is funded by the government and which does not charge fees to pupils.

statesman *NOUN* **statesmen** a person, especially a man, who is important or skilled in governing a country.
▹ **statesmanship** *noun*

stateswoman *NOUN* **stateswomen** a woman who is important or skilled in governing a country.

static *ADJECTIVE* not moving or changing.
[from Greek]

static electricity *NOUN* electricity that is present in something, not flowing as current.

station *NOUN* **stations 1** a stopping place for trains, buses, etc. with platforms and buildings for passengers and goods. **2** a building equipped for people who serve the public or for certain activities • *the police station.* **3** a broadcasting company with its own frequency. **4** a place where a person or thing stands or is stationed; a position. **5** (*Australian/NZ*) a large sheep or cattle farm.

station *VERB* **stations, stationing, stationed** put someone in a certain place for a purpose • *He was stationed at the door to take the tickets.*
[from Latin *statio* = a stand, standing]

stationary *ADJECTIVE* not moving • *The car was stationary when the van hit it.*
USAGE Do not confuse with **stationery**.

stationer *NOUN* **stationers** a shopkeeper who sells stationery.
[from Latin *stationarius* = a tradesman (usually a bookseller) who had a shop or stand (as opposed to one who sold goods wherever he could)]

stationery *NOUN* paper, envelopes, and other articles used in writing or typing.
USAGE Do not confuse with **stationary**.

station wagon *NOUN* **station wagons** (*American & Australian/NZ*) a car with a large area behind the rear seats that can be used for extra seating or for carrying things.

statistic *NOUN* **statistics** a piece of information expressed as a number • *These statistics show that the population has doubled.*
▷ **statistical** *adjective* **statistically** *adverb*
[from German]

statistician (*say* stat-is-**tish**-an) *NOUN* **statisticians** an expert in statistics.

statistics *NOUN* the study of information based on the numbers of things.

statuary *NOUN* statues.

statue *NOUN* **statues** a model made of stone or metal etc. to look like a person or animal.
[from Latin *stare* = to stand]

statuesque (*say* stat-yoo-**esk**) *ADJECTIVE* like a statue in stillness or dignity.

statuette *NOUN* **statuettes** a small statue.

stature *NOUN* **1** the natural height of the body. **2** greatness gained by ability or achievement.
[from Latin *stare* = to stand]

status (*say* stay-tus) *NOUN* **statuses 1** a person's or thing's position or rank in relation to others. **2** high rank or prestige.
[from Latin *status* = standing]

status quo (*say* stay-tus **kwoh**) *NOUN* the state of affairs as it was before a change.
[Latin, = the state in which]

status symbol *NOUN* **status symbols** something that you own because it shows off your wealth or position in society, rather than because you like it or need it.

statute *NOUN* **statutes** a law passed by a parliament.
▷ **statutory** *adjective*
[from Latin *statuere* = set up, decree]

staunch *ADJECTIVE* firm and loyal • *our staunch supporters.*
▷ **staunchly** *adverb*
[from old French]

stave *NOUN* **staves 1** each of the curved strips of wood forming the side of a cask or tub. **2** a set of five horizontal lines on which music is written.

stave *VERB* **staves, staving, staved** or **stove** dent or break a hole in something • *The collision stove in the front of the ship.*
- **stave off** keep something away • *We staved off the disaster.*
[from *staves* (SEE *staff*)]

stay[1] *VERB* **stays, staying, stayed**
1 continue to be in the same place or condition; remain. **2** spend time in a place as a visitor. **3** satisfy temporarily • *We stayed our hunger with a sandwich.* **4** pause. **5** show endurance in a race or task.
- **stay put** (*informal*) remain in place.

stay *NOUN* **stays 1** a time spent somewhere • *We made a short stay in Rome.* **2** a postponement • *a stay of execution.*
[same origin as *stable*[1]]

stay[2] *NOUN* **stays** a support, especially a rope or wire holding up a mast etc.
[via old French from Germanic]

stead *NOUN*
- **in a person's** or **thing's stead** instead of this person or thing.
- **stand a person in good stead** be very useful to him or her.
[from Old English]

steadfast *ADJECTIVE* firm and not changing • *a steadfast refusal.*

steady *ADJECTIVE* **steadier, steadiest 1** not shaking or moving; firm. **2** regular; continuing the same • *a steady pace.*
▷ **steadily** *adverb* **steadiness** *noun*

steady *VERB* **steadies, steadying, steadied** make or become steady.
[from *stead*]

steak *NOUN* **steaks** a thick slice of meat (especially beef) or fish.
[from Old Norse]

steal *VERB* **steals, stealing, stole, stolen**
1 take and keep something that does not belong to you; take secretly or dishonestly.
2 move secretly or without being noticed • *He stole out of the room.*
[from Old English]

stealthy (*say* stelth-ee) *ADJECTIVE* **stealthier, stealthiest** quiet and secret, so as not to be noticed.
▷ **stealth** *noun* **stealthily** *adverb* **stealthiness** *noun*
[probably from Old English and related to *steal*]

A B C D E F G H I J K L M N O P Q R S T U V W X Y Z

steam *NOUN* **1** the gas or vapour that comes from boiling water; this used to drive machinery. **2** energy • *He ran out of steam.*
▷ **steamy** *adjective*

steam *VERB* **steams, steaming, steamed**
1 give off steam. **2** move by the power of steam • *The ship steamed down the river.*
3 cook or treat by steam • *a steamed pudding.*
- **steam up** be covered with mist or condensation.
[from Old English]

steam engine *NOUN* **steam engines** an engine driven by steam.

steamer *NOUN* **steamers 1** a steamship. **2** a container in which things are steamed.

steamroller *NOUN* **steamrollers** a heavy vehicle with a large roller used to flatten surfaces when making roads.
[because the first ones were powered by steam]

steamship *NOUN* **steamships** a ship driven by steam.

steed *NOUN* **steeds** (*old or poetical use*) a horse.
[from Old English]

steel *NOUN* **steels 1** a strong metal made from iron and carbon. **2** a steel rod for sharpening knives.

steel *VERB* **steels, steeling, steeled**
- **steel yourself** find courage to face something difficult.
[from Old English]

steel band *NOUN* **steel bands** a West Indian band of musicians with instruments usually made from oil drums.

steel wool *NOUN* a mass of fine, sharp steel threads used for cleaning a surface or rubbing it smooth.

steely *ADJECTIVE* **1** like or to do with steel. **2** cold, hard, and severe • *a steely glare.*

steep[1] *ADJECTIVE* **1** sloping very sharply, not gradually. **2** (*informal*) unreasonably high • *a steep price.*
▷ **steeply** *adverb* **steepness** *noun*
[from Old English]

steep[2] *VERB* **steeps, steeping, steeped** soak thoroughly; saturate.
- **be steeped in** be completely filled or familiar with something • *The story is steeped in mystery.*
[probably from a Scandinavian language]

steepen *VERB* **steepens, steepening, steepened** make or become steeper.

steeple *NOUN* **steeples** a church tower with a spire on top.
[from Old English]

steeplechase *NOUN* **steeplechases** a race across country or over hedges or fences.
[so called because the race originally had a distant church steeple in view as its goal]

steeplejack *NOUN* **steeplejacks** a person who climbs tall chimneys or steeples to do repairs.

steer[1] *VERB* **steers, steering, steered** make a car, ship, or bicycle etc. go in the direction you want; guide.
▷ **steersman** *noun*
- **steer clear of** take care to avoid.
[from Old English *stieran*]

steer[2] *NOUN* **steers** a young castrated bull kept for its beef.
[from Old English *steor*]

steering wheel *NOUN* **steering wheels** a wheel for steering a car, boat, etc.

stellar *ADJECTIVE* to do with a star or stars.
[from Latin *stella* = star]

stem[1] *NOUN* **stems 1** the main central part of a tree, shrub, or plant. **2** a thin part on which a leaf, flower, or fruit is supported. **3** a thin upright part, e.g. the thin part of a wine glass between the bowl and the foot. **4** (*in grammar*) the main part of a verb or other word, to which endings are attached. **5** the front part of a ship • *from stem to stern.*

stem *VERB* **stems, stemming, stemmed**
- **stem from** arise from; have as its source.
[from Old English]

stem[2] *VERB* **stems, stemming, stemmed** stop the flow of something.
[from Old Norse]

stench *NOUN* **stenches** a very unpleasant smell.
[from Old English]

stencil *NOUN* **stencils** a piece of card, metal, or plastic with pieces cut out of it, used to produce a picture, design, etc.

stencil *VERB* **stencils**, **stencilling**, **stencilled** produce or decorate with a stencil.
[from old French]

stentorian *ADJECTIVE* very loud • *a stentorian voice.*
[from the name of *Stentor*, a herald in ancient Greek legend]

step *NOUN* **steps 1** a movement made by lifting the foot and setting it down. **2** the sound of a person putting down their foot when walking or running. **3** a level surface for placing the foot on in climbing up or down. **4** each of a series of things done in some process or action • *The first step is to find somewhere to practise.*
- **in step 1** stepping in time with others in marching or dancing. **2** in agreement.
- **watch your step** be careful.

step *VERB* **steps**, **stepping**, **stepped** tread or walk.
- **step in** intervene.
- **step on it** (*informal*) hurry.
- **step up** increase something.
[from Old English *steppan*]

step- *PREFIX* related through remarriage of one parent.
[from Old English *steop-*]

stepbrother *NOUN* **stepbrothers** the son of one of your parents from an earlier or later marriage.

stepchild *NOUN* **stepchildren** a child that a person's husband or wife has from an earlier marriage.
▷ **stepdaughter,stepson** *nouns*

stepfather *NOUN* **stepfathers** a man who is married to your mother but was not your natural father.

stepladder *NOUN* **stepladders** a folding ladder with flat treads.

stepmother *NOUN* **stepmothers** a woman who is married to your father but was not your natural mother.

steppe *NOUN* **steppes** a grassy plain with few trees, especially in Russia.
[from Russian]

stepping stone *NOUN* **stepping stones 1** each of a line of stones put into a shallow stream so that people can walk across. **2** a way of achieving something, or a stage in achieving it • *Good exam results can be a stepping stone to a career.*

steps *PLURAL NOUN* a stepladder.

stepsister *NOUN* **stepsisters** the daughter of one of your parents from an earlier or later marriage.

stereo *ADJECTIVE* stereophonic.

stereo *NOUN* **stereos 1** stereophonic sound or recording. **2** a stereophonic CD player, record player, etc.
[from *stereophonic*]

stereophonic *ADJECTIVE* using sound that comes from two different directions to give a natural effect.
[from Greek *stereos* = solid, three- dimensional + *phone* = sound]

stereoscopic *ADJECTIVE* giving the effect of being three-dimensional, e.g. in photographs.
[from Greek *stereos* = solid, three- dimensional + *skopein* = look at]

stereotype *NOUN* **stereotypes** a fixed image or idea of a type of person or thing that is widely held • *The stereotype of a hero is one who is tall, strong, brave, and good-looking.*
[originally = a kind of printing which appeared three- dimensional: from Greek *stereos* = solid, three- dimensional, + *type*]

sterile *ADJECTIVE* **1** not fertile; barren. **2** free from germs.
▷ **sterility** *noun*
[from Latin]

sterilize *VERB* **sterilizes**, **sterilizing**, **sterilized 1** make a thing free from germs, e.g. by heating it. **2** make a person or animal unable to reproduce.
▷ **sterilization** *noun* **sterilizer** *noun*

sterling *NOUN* British money.

sterling *ADJECTIVE* **1** genuine • *sterling silver.* **2** excellent; of great worth • *her sterling qualities.*
[probably from Old English *steorra* = star + *-ling* (because some early coins had a star on them)]

stern[1] *ADJECTIVE* strict and severe, not lenient or kindly.
▷ **sternly** *adverb* **sternness** *noun*
[from Old English]

stern[2] *NOUN* **sterns** the back part of a ship.
[from Old Norse]

steroid *NOUN* **steroids** a substance of a kind that includes certain hormones and other natural secretions.
[from Greek]

stethoscope *NOUN* **stethoscopes** a device used for listening to sounds in a person's body, e.g. heartbeats and breathing.
[from Greek *stethos* = breast + *skopein* = look at]

stew *VERB* **stews, stewing, stewed** cook slowly in liquid.

stew *NOUN* **stews** a dish of stewed food, especially meat and vegetables.
- **in a stew** (*informal*) very worried or agitated.
[from old French]

steward *NOUN* **stewards 1** a man whose job is to look after the passengers on a ship or aircraft. **2** an official who keeps order or looks after the arrangements at a large public event.
[from Old English *stig* = house or hall, + *ward*]

stewardess *NOUN* **stewardesses** a woman whose job is to look after the passengers on a ship or aircraft.

stick[1] *NOUN* **sticks 1** a long thin piece of wood. **2** a walking stick. **3** the implement used to hit the ball in hockey, polo, etc. **4** a long thin piece of something • *a stick of celery.*
[from Old English *sticca*]

stick[2] *VERB* **sticks, sticking, stuck 1** push a thing into something • *Stick a pin in it.* **2** fix or be fixed by glue or as if by this • *Stick stamps on the parcel.* **3** become fixed and unable to move • *The drawer keeps sticking.* **4** (*informal*) endure or tolerate • *I can't stick that noise!*
- **stick out 1** come or push out from a surface; stand out from the surrounding area. **2** be very noticeable.
- **stick to 1** remain faithful to a friend or promise etc. **2** keep to and not alter • *He stuck to his story.*
- **stick together 1** stay together. **2** support each other.
- **stick up for** (*informal*) support or defend.
- **be stuck with** (*informal*) be unable to avoid something unwelcome.
[from Old English *stician*]

sticker *NOUN* **stickers** an adhesive label or sign for sticking to something.

sticking plaster *NOUN* **sticking plasters** a strip of adhesive material for covering cuts.

stick insect *NOUN* **stick insects** an insect with a long thin body and legs, which looks like a twig.

stickleback *NOUN* **sticklebacks** a small fish with sharp spines on its back.
[from Old English *sticel* = thorn]

stickler *NOUN* **sticklers** a person who insists on something • *a stickler for punctuality.*
[from Old English *stihtan* = put in order]

sticky *ADJECTIVE* **stickier, stickiest 1** able or likely to stick to things. **2** (said about weather) hot and humid, causing perspiration. **3** (*informal*) difficult or awkward • *a sticky situation.*
▷ **stickily** *adverb* **stickiness** *noun*
- **come to a sticky end** die or end in a painful or unpleasant way.

stiff *ADJECTIVE* **1** not bending or moving or changing its shape easily. **2** not fluid; hard to stir • *a stiff dough.* **3** difficult • *a stiff examination.* **4** formal in manner; not friendly. **5** severe or strong • *a stiff breeze.*
▷ **stiffly** *adverb* **stiffness** *noun*
[from Old English]

stiffen *VERB* **stiffens, stiffening, stiffened** make or become stiff.
▷ **stiffener** *noun*

stifle *VERB* **stifles, stifling, stifled** **1** suffocate. **2** suppress • *She stifled a yawn.* [from old French]

stigma *NOUN* **stigmas 1** a mark of disgrace; a stain on a reputation. **2** the part of a pistil that receives the pollen in pollination. [from Greek]

stigmatize *VERB* **stigmatizes, stigmatizing, stigmatized** brand as something disgraceful • *He was stigmatized as a coward.*

stile *NOUN* **stiles** an arrangement of steps or bars for people to climb over a fence. [from Old English]

stiletto *NOUN* **stilettos** a dagger with a narrow blade. [Italian, = little dagger]

stiletto heel *NOUN* **stiletto heels** a high pointed shoe heel.

still[1] *ADJECTIVE* **1** not moving • *still water.* **2** silent. **3** not fizzy.
▷ **stillness** *noun*

still *ADVERB* **1** without moving • *Stand still.* **2** up to this or that time • *He was still there.* **3** in a greater amount or degree • *You can do still better.* **4** nevertheless • *They've lost. Still, they tried, and that was good.*

still *VERB* **stills, stilling, stilled** make or become still.

still *NOUN* **stills** a photograph of a scene from a cinema film. [from Old English]

still[2] *NOUN* **stills** an apparatus for distilling alcohol or other liquid. [from *distil*]

stillborn *ADJECTIVE* born dead. [from *still*[1] + *born*]

still life *NOUN* **still lifes** a painting of lifeless things such as ornaments and fruit.

stilted *ADJECTIVE* stiffly formal. [originally = raised on stilts]

stilts *PLURAL NOUN* **1** a pair of poles with supports for the feet so that the user can walk high above the ground. **2** posts for supporting a house etc. above marshy ground. [Middle English, from a Germanic language]

stimulant *NOUN* **stimulants** something that stimulates.

stimulate *VERB* **stimulates, stimulating, stimulated 1** make someone excited or enthusiastic. **2** make more lively or active • *The programme has stimulated a lot of interest in her work.*
▷ **stimulation** *noun*

stimulus *NOUN* **stimuli** something that stimulates or produces a reaction. [Latin, = goad]

sting *NOUN* **stings 1** a sharp-pointed part of an animal or plant, often containing a poison, that can cause a wound. **2** a painful wound caused by this part.

sting *VERB* **stings, stinging, stung** **1** wound or hurt with a sting. **2** feel a sharp pain. **3** make someone feel upset or hurt • *I was stung by this criticism.* **4** (*slang*) cheat someone by charging them too much; swindle. [from Old English]

stingray *NOUN* **stingrays** a fish with a flat body, fins like wings, and a poisonous spine in its tail.

stingy (*say* stin-jee) *ADJECTIVE* **stingier, stingiest** mean, not generous; giving or given in small amounts.
▷ **stingily** *adverb* **stinginess** *noun* [from *sting*]

stink *NOUN* **stinks 1** an unpleasant smell. **2** (*informal*) an unpleasant fuss or protest.

stink *VERB* **stinks, stinking, stank** or **stunk** have an unpleasant smell. [from Old English]

stint *NOUN* **stints 1** a fixed amount of work to be done. **2** limitation of a supply or effort • *They gave help without stint.*

stint *VERB* **stints, stinting, stinted** be sparing; restrict to a small amount • *Don't stint on the cream.* [from Old English]

stipend (*say* sty-pend) *NOUN* **stipends** a salary, especially one paid to a clergyman. [from Latin *stips* = wages + *pendere* = to pay]

stipple *VERB* **stipples, stippling, stippled** paint, draw, or engrave in small dots. [from Dutch]

stipulate *VERB* **stipulates, stipulating, stipulated** insist on something as part of an agreement.
▷ **stipulation** *noun*
[from Latin]

stir *VERB* **stirs, stirring, stirred** **1** mix a liquid or soft mixture by moving a spoon etc. round and round in it. **2** move slightly; start to move. **3** excite or stimulate • *They stirred up trouble.*
▷ **stirring** *adjective*

stir *NOUN* **1** the action of stirring. **2** a disturbance; excitement • *The news caused a stir.*
[from Old English]

stir-fry *VERB* **stir-fries, stir-frying, stir-fried** to cook by frying quickly over a high heat while stirring and tossing.
▷ **stir-fry** *noun*

stirrup *NOUN* **stirrups** a metal part that hangs from each side of a horse's saddle, for a rider to put his or her foot in.
[from Old English]

stitch *NOUN* **stitches** **1** a loop of thread made in sewing or knitting. **2** a method of arranging the threads • *cross stitch.* **3** a sudden sharp pain in the side of the body, caused by running.

stitch *VERB* **stitches, stitching, stitched** sew or fasten with stitches.
[from Old English]

stoat *NOUN* **stoats** a kind of weasel also called an ermine.
[origin unknown]

stock *NOUN* **stocks** **1** a number of things kept ready to be sold or used. **2** livestock. **3** a line of ancestors • *a man of Irish stock.* **4** a number of shares in a company's capital. **5** liquid made by stewing meat, fish, or vegetables, used for making soup etc. **6** the main stem of a tree or plant. **7** the base, holder, or handle of an implement, weapon, etc. **8** a garden flower with a sweet smell.
- **take stock** make an overall assessment of a situation.

stock *VERB* **stocks, stocking, stocked** **1** keep goods in stock. **2** provide a place with a stock of something.
- **stock up** buy a supply of goods etc.
[from Old English]

stockade *NOUN* **stockades** a fence made of stakes.
[from Spanish]

stockbroker *NOUN* **stockbrokers** a broker who deals in stocks and shares.

stock car *NOUN* **stock cars** an ordinary car strengthened for use in races where deliberate bumping is allowed.

stock exchange *NOUN* **stock exchanges** a country's central place for buying and selling stocks and shares.

stocking *NOUN* **stockings** a piece of clothing covering the foot and part or all of the leg.
[from *stock*]

stockist *NOUN* **stockists** a shopkeeper who stocks a certain kind of goods.

stock market *NOUN* **stock markets** **1** a stock exchange. **2** the buying and selling of stocks and shares.

stockpile *NOUN* **stockpiles** a large stock of things kept in reserve.
▷ **stockpile** *verb*

stocks *PLURAL NOUN* a wooden framework with holes for a seated person's legs, used like the pillory.
[from *stock*]

stock-still *ADJECTIVE* quite still.

stocktaking *NOUN* the counting, listing, and checking of the amount of stock held by a shop or business.

stocky *ADJECTIVE* **stockier, stockiest** short and solidly built • *a stocky man.*
[from *stock*]

stodge *NOUN* stodgy food.
[probably from *stuff* and *podgy*]

stodgy *ADJECTIVE* **stodgier, stodgiest** **1** (said about food) heavy and filling. **2** dull and boring • *a stodgy book.*
▷ **stodginess** *noun*

stoical (*say* **stoh-ik-al**) *ADJECTIVE* bearing pain or difficulties etc. calmly without complaining.
▷ **stoically** *adverb* **stoicism** *noun*
[named after ancient Greek philosophers called *Stoics*]

stoke *VERB* **stokes, stoking, stoked** put fuel in a furnace or on a fire.
▷ **stoker** *noun*
[from Dutch]

stole[1] *NOUN* **stoles** a wide piece of material worn round the shoulders by women.
[from Old English]

stole[2] *past tense* of **steal**.

stolid *ADJECTIVE* not showing much emotion or excitement.
▷ **stolidly** *adverb* **stolidity** *noun*
[from Latin]

stomach *NOUN* **stomachs 1** the part of the body where food starts to be digested. **2** the abdomen.

stomach *VERB* **stomachs, stomaching, stomached** endure or tolerate.
[from Greek]

stone *NOUN* **stones 1** a piece of rock. **2** stones or rock as material, e.g. for building. **3** a jewel. **4** the hard case round the kernel of plums, cherries, etc. **5** a unit of weight equal to 14 pounds (6.35 kg) • *She weighs 8 stone.*

stone *VERB* **stones, stoning, stoned 1** throw stones at somebody. **2** remove the stones from fruit.
[from Old English]

Stone Age *NOUN* the earliest period of human history, when tools and weapons were made of stone.

stone circle *NOUN* **stone circles** a circle of large stones or boulders, put up in prehistoric times.

stone-cold *ADJECTIVE* extremely cold.

stoned *ADJECTIVE* (*informal*) under the influence of drugs or alcohol.

stone-deaf *ADJECTIVE* completely deaf.

stoneware *NOUN* a kind of pottery with a hard shiny surface.

stony *ADJECTIVE* **1** full of stones. **2** like stone; hard. **3** unfriendly and not answering • *a stony silence.*

stooge *NOUN* **stooges** (*informal*) **1** a comedian's assistant, used as a target for jokes. **2** an assistant who does dull or routine work.
[originally American; origin unknown]

stool *NOUN* **stools 1** a movable seat without arms or a back. **2** a footstool. **3** a lump of faeces.
[from Old English]

stoop[1] *VERB* **stoops, stooping, stooped 1** bend your body forwards and down. **2** lower yourself • *He would not stoop to cheating.*
▷ **stoop** *noun*
[from Old English]

stoop[2] *NOUN* **stoops** (*American & S. African*) a porch, small verandah, or set of steps in front of a house.
[from Dutch *stoep*]

stop *VERB* **stops, stopping, stopped 1** bring or come to an end; no longer do something. **2** be no longer moving or working • *A car stopped in front of us.* **3** prevent or obstruct something. **4** stay for a short time. **5** fill a hole, especially in a tooth.

stop *NOUN* **stops 1** stopping; a pause or end. **2** a place where a bus or train etc. regularly stops. **3** a punctuation mark, especially a full stop. **4** a lever or knob that controls pitch in a wind instrument or allows organ pipes to sound.
[from Old English]

stopcock *NOUN* **stopcocks** a valve controlling the flow of liquid or gas in a pipe.

stopgap *NOUN* **stopgaps** a temporary substitute.

stoppage *NOUN* **stoppages 1** an interruption in the work of a factory etc. **2** a blockage. **3** an amount taken off someone's wages.

stopper *NOUN* **stoppers** a plug for closing a bottle etc.

stop press *NOUN* late news put into a newspaper after printing has started.
[because the printing presses are stopped to allow the late news to be added]

stopwatch *NOUN* **stopwatches** a watch that can be started and stopped when you wish, used for timing races etc.

storage *NOUN* the storing of things.

storage heater *NOUN* **storage heaters** an electric heater that gives out heat that it has stored.

store *NOUN* **stores 1** a supply of things kept for future use. **2** a place where things are kept until they are needed. **3** a shop, especially a large one. **4** (*American*) any shop.
- **in store 1** being stored. **2** going to happen • *There's a surprise in store for you.*
- **set store by something** value it greatly.

store *VERB* **stores, storing, stored** keep things until they are needed.
[from old French]

storey *NOUN* **storeys** one whole floor of a building.
[from Latin]
USAGE Do not confuse with **story**.

stork *NOUN* **storks** a large bird with long legs and a long beak.
[from Old English]

storm *NOUN* **storms 1** a very strong wind usually with rain, snow, etc. **2** a violent attack or outburst • *a storm of protest.*
▷ **stormy** *adjective*
- **a storm in a teacup** a great fuss over something unimportant.

storm *VERB* **storms, storming, stormed 1** move or behave violently or angrily • *He stormed out of the room.* **2** suddenly attack and capture a place • *They stormed the castle.*
[from Old English]

story *NOUN* **stories 1** an account of a real or imaginary event. **2** the plot of a play or novel etc. **3** (*informal*) a lie • *Don't tell stories!*
[from Latin *historia* = history]
USAGE Do not confuse with **storey**.

stout *ADJECTIVE* **1** rather fat. **2** thick and strong. **3** brave and determined • *a stout defender of human rights.*
▷ **stoutly** *adverb* **stoutness** *noun*

stout *NOUN* a kind of dark beer.
[from old French]

stove[1] *NOUN* **stoves 1** a device containing an oven or ovens. **2** a device for heating a room.
[from old German or old Dutch]

stove[2] *past tense* of **stave**.

stow *VERB* **stows, stowing, stowed** pack or store something away.
▷ **stowage** *noun*
- **stow away** hide on a ship or aircraft so as to travel without paying.
[from *bestow*]

stowaway *NOUN* **stowaways** someone who stows away on a ship or aircraft.

straddle *VERB* **straddles, straddling, straddled 1** sit or stand astride something. **2** be built across something • *A long bridge straddles the river.*
[from Old English]

straggle *VERB* **straggles, straggling, straggled 1** grow or spread in an untidy way. **2** lag behind; wander on your own.
▷ **straggler** *noun* **straggly** *adjective*
[origin unknown]

straight *ADJECTIVE* **1** going continuously in one direction; not curving or bending. **2** level, horizontal, or upright • *Is the picture straight?* **3** tidy; in proper order. **4** honest and frank • *a straight answer.*
▷ **straightness** *noun*

straight *ADVERB* **1** in a straight line or manner. **2** directly; without delay • *Go straight home.*
[old past participle of *stretch*]
USAGE Do not confuse with **strait**.

straightaway or **straight away** *ADVERB* immediately.

straighten *VERB* **straightens, straightening, straightened** make or become straight.

straightforward *ADJECTIVE* **1** easy, not complicated. **2** honest and frank.

strain[1] *VERB* **strains, straining, strained 1** injure or weaken something by stretching or working it too hard. **2** stretch tightly. **3** make a great effort. **4** put something through a sieve or filter to separate liquid from solid matter.

strain *NOUN* **strains 1** straining; the force of straining. **2** an injury caused by straining. **3** something that uses up strength, patience, resources, etc. **4** exhaustion. **5** a part of a tune.
[from old French]

strain[2] *NOUN* **strains 1** a breed or variety of animals, plants, etc.; a line of descent. **2** an inherited characteristic • *There's an artistic strain in the family.*
[from Old English]

strainer *NOUN* **strainers** a device for straining liquids • *a tea strainer.*

strait *ADJECTIVE* (*old use*) narrow or restricted.

strait *NOUN* **straits** a narrow stretch of water connecting two seas.
[from Latin *strictus* = tightened]
USAGE Do not confuse with **straight**.

straitened *ADJECTIVE*
- **in straitened circumstances** short of money.
[from *strait*]

straitjacket *NOUN* **straitjackets** a strong jacket-like piece of clothing put round a violent person to restrain his or her arms.

strait-laced *ADJECTIVE* very prim and proper.

straits *PLURAL NOUN* **1** a strait • *the Straits of Dover.* **2** a difficult condition • *We were in dire straits when we lost our money.*

strand[1] *NOUN* **strands 1** each of the threads or wires etc. twisted together to form a rope, yarn, or cable. **2** a single thread or hair. **3** an idea, theme, story, etc. that forms part of a whole • *a novel with several strands.*
[origin unknown]

strand[2] *NOUN* **strands** a shore.
[from Old English]

stranded *ADJECTIVE* **1** left on sand or rocks in shallow water • *a stranded ship.* **2** left in a difficult or helpless position • *We were stranded when our car broke down.*
[from *strand*[2]]

strange *ADJECTIVE* **1** unusual or surprising. **2** not known or seen or experienced before.
▷ **strangely** *adverb* **strangeness** *noun*
[from Latin *extraneus* = extraneous]

stranger *NOUN* **strangers 1** a person you do not know. **2** a person who is in a place that he or she does not know.

strangle *VERB* **strangles, strangling, strangled 1** kill by squeezing the throat to prevent breathing. **2** restrict something so that it does not develop.
▷ **strangler** *noun*
[from Greek]

strangulate *VERB* **strangulates, strangulating, strangulated** squeeze so that nothing can pass through.
▷ **strangulation** *noun*
[from Latin *strangulare* = strangle]

strap *NOUN* **straps** a flat strip of leather or cloth etc. for fastening things or holding them in place.

strap *VERB* **straps, strapping, strapped** fasten with a strap or straps; bind.
[via old German or old Dutch from Latin]

strapping *ADJECTIVE* tall and healthy-looking • *a strapping lad.*

strata *plural* of **stratum**.

stratagem *NOUN* **stratagems** a cunning method of achieving something; a plan or trick.
[same origin as *strategy*]

strategic *ADJECTIVE* **1** to do with strategy. **2** giving an advantage • *a strategic move.*
▷ **strategical** *adjective* **strategically** *adverb*

strategist *NOUN* **strategists** an expert in strategy.

strategy *NOUN* **strategies 1** a plan or policy to achieve something • *our economic strategy.* **2** the planning of a war or campaign. (COMPARE **tactics**)
[from Greek *strategos* = a general]

stratified *ADJECTIVE* arranged in strata.
▷ **stratification** *noun*

stratosphere *NOUN* a layer of the atmosphere between about 10 and 60 kilometres above the earth's surface.
[from *stratum* + *sphere*]

stratum (*say* **strah**-tum or **stray**-tum) *NOUN* **strata** a layer or level • *strata of rock.*
[Latin, = something spread]
USAGE The word *strata* is a plural. It is incorrect to say 'a strata' or 'this strata'; correct use is *this stratum* or *these strata.*

straw *NOUN* **straws 1** dry cut stalks of corn. **2** a narrow tube for drinking through.
[from Old English]

strawberry *NOUN* **strawberries** a small red juicy fruit, with its seeds on the outside.
[probably because straw is put around the plants to keep slugs away]

stray *VERB* **strays, straying, strayed** leave a group or proper place and wander; get lost.

stray *ADJECTIVE* **1** that has strayed; wandering around lost • *a stray cat.* **2** found on its own, separated from the others • *a stray sock.*
▷ **stray** *noun*
[from old French]

A B C D E F G H I J K L M N O P Q R S T U V W X Y Z

streak *NOUN* **streaks 1** a long thin line or mark. **2** a trace • *a streak of cruelty.* **3** a spell of success, luck, etc. • *on a winning streak .*
▷ **streaky** *adjective*

streak *VERB* **streaks, streaking, streaked** **1** mark with streaks. **2** move very quickly. **3** run naked in a public place for fun or to get attention.
▷ **streaker** *noun*
[from Old English]

streaky bacon *NOUN* bacon with alternate strips of lean and fat.
[from *streak*]

stream *NOUN* **streams 1** water flowing in a channel; a brook or small river. **2** a flow of liquid or of things or people. **3** a group in which children of similar ability are placed in a school.

stream *VERB* **streams, streaming, streamed** **1** move in or like a stream. **2** produce a stream of liquid. **3** arrange schoolchildren in streams according to their ability.
[from Old English]

streamer *NOUN* **streamers** a long narrow ribbon or strip of paper etc.

streamline *VERB* **streamlines, streamlining, streamlined** **1** give something a smooth shape that helps it to move easily through air or water. **2** organize something so that it works more efficiently.
▷ **streamlined** *adjective*

street *NOUN* **streets** a road with houses beside it in a city or village.
[via Old English from Latin *strata via* = paved way]

streetcar *NOUN* **streetcars** (*American*) a tram.

strength *NOUN* **strengths 1** how strong a person or thing is; being strong. **2** an ability or good quality • *Patience is your great strength.*
[from Old English]

strengthen *VERB* **strengthens, strengthening, strengthened** make or become stronger.

strenuous *ADJECTIVE* needing or using great effort.
▷ **strenuously** *adverb*
[from Latin *strenuus* = brave, energetic]

stress *NOUN* **stresses 1** a force that acts on something, e.g. by pressing, pulling, or twisting it; strain. **2** emphasis, especially the extra force with which you pronounce part of a word or phrase. **3** distress caused by having too many problems or too much to do.

stress *VERB* **stresses, stressing, stressed** **1** pronounce part of a word or phrase with extra emphasis. **2** emphasize a point or idea • *I must stress the importance of arriving on time.* **3** cause stress to someone.
[from *distress*]

stretch *VERB* **stretches, stretching, stretched** **1** pull something or be pulled so that it becomes longer or wider or larger. **2** extend or be continuous • *The wall stretches right round the estate.* **3** push out your arms and legs etc. as far as you can. **4** make use of all your ability or intelligence • *This course should really stretch you.*
- **stretch out** lie down with your arms and legs at full length.

stretch *NOUN* **stretches 1** the action of stretching. **2** a continuous period of time or area of land or water.
[from Old English]

stretcher *NOUN* **stretchers** a framework for carrying a sick or injured person.

strew *VERB* **strews, strewing, strewed, strewn** or **strewed** scatter things over a surface • *Paper cups were strewn over the floor.*
[from Old English]

striated (*say* stry-ay-tid) *ADJECTIVE* marked with lines or ridges.
▷ **striation** *noun*
[from Latin *stria* = a groove or furrow]

stricken *ADJECTIVE* overcome or strongly affected by an illness, grief, fear, etc.
[past participle of *strike*]

strict *ADJECTIVE* **1** demanding obedience and good behaviour • *a strict teacher.* **2** complete or exact • *in strict confidence; the strict truth.*
▷ **strictly** *adverb* **strictness** *noun*
[same origin as *strait*]

stricture *NOUN* **strictures 1** criticism. **2** constriction.
[from Latin]

stride *VERB* **strides, striding, strode, stridden** walk with long steps.

stride *NOUN* **strides 1** a long step when walking or running. **2** progress.
- **get into your stride** settle into a fast and steady pace of working.
- **take something in your stride** cope with something without difficulty.
[from Old English]

strident (*say* stry-dent) *ADJECTIVE* loud and harsh.
▷ **stridently** *adverb* **stridency** *noun*
[from Latin]

strife *NOUN* conflict; fighting or quarrelling.
[from old French]

strike *VERB* **strikes, striking, struck 1** hit. **2** attack or afflict suddenly • *Plague struck the village.* **3** make an impression on someone's mind • *She strikes me as being lazy.* **4** light a match by rubbing it against a rough surface. **5** refuse to work as a protest against pay or conditions. **6** produce by pressing or stamping something • *They are striking some special coins.* **7** sound • *The clock struck ten.* **8** find gold or oil etc. by digging or drilling. **9** go in a certain direction • *We struck north through the forest.*
- **strike off** or **out** cross out.
- **strike up 1** begin playing or singing. **2** start a friendship or conversation.

strike *NOUN* **strikes 1** a hit. **2** an attack • *an air strike.* **3** refusing to work as a way of making a protest. **4** a sudden discovery of gold or oil etc.
- **on strike** (said about workers) striking.
[from Old English]

striker *NOUN* **strikers 1** a person or thing that strikes something. **2** a worker who is on strike. **3** a football player whose function is to try to score goals.

striking *ADJECTIVE* **1** impressive or attractive. **2** noticeable.
▷ **strikingly** *adverb*

string *NOUN* **strings 1** thin cord made of twisted threads, used to fasten or tie things; a piece of this or similar material. **2** a piece of wire or cord etc. stretched and vibrated to produce sounds in a musical instrument. **3** a line or series of things • *a string of buses.*

string *VERB* **strings, stringing, strung 1** fit or fasten with string. **2** thread on a string. **3** remove the tough fibre from beans.
- **string along** mislead someone over a period of time.
- **string out 1** spread out in a line. **2** make something last a long time.
[from Old English]

stringed *ADJECTIVE* (said about musical instruments) having strings.

stringent (*say* strin-jent) *ADJECTIVE* strict • *There are stringent rules.*
▷ **stringently** *adverb* **stringency** *noun*
[from Latin *stringere* = to bind]

strings *PLURAL NOUN* stringed instruments.

stringy *ADJECTIVE* **1** like string. **2** containing tough fibres.

strip[1] *VERB* **strips, stripping, stripped 1** take a covering or layer off something. **2** undress. **3** deprive a person of something.

strip *NOUN* the distinctive clothes worn by a sports team while playing.
[probably from Old English]

strip[2] *NOUN* **strips** a long narrow piece or area.
[from old German]

strip cartoon *NOUN* **strip cartoons** a series of drawings telling a story.

stripe *NOUN* **stripes 1** a long narrow band of colour. **2** a strip of cloth worn on the sleeve of a uniform to show the wearer's rank.
▷ **striped** *adjective* **stripy** *adjective*
[probably from old German and related to *strip*[2]]

strip light *NOUN* **strip lights** a fluorescent lamp in the form of a tube.

stripling *NOUN* **striplings** a youth.
[from *strip*[2] + *-ling*]

stripper *NOUN* **strippers 1** something that strips • *paint stripper.* **2** a person who performs striptease.

striptease *NOUN* **stripteases** an entertainment in which a person slowly undresses.

strive *VERB* **strives, striving, strove, striven 1** try hard to do something. **2** carry on a conflict.
[from old French]

strobe *NOUN* **strobes** (short for **stroboscope**) a light that flashes on and off continuously.
[from Greek *strobos* = whirling]

stroke[1] *NOUN* **strokes 1** a hit. **2** a movement; a style of swimming. **3** an action or effort • *a stroke of genius.* **4** the sound made by a clock striking. **5** a sudden illness that often causes paralysis.
[from *strike*]

stroke[2] *VERB* **strokes, stroking, stroked** move your hand gently along something.
▷ **stroke** *noun*
[from Old English]

stroll *VERB* **strolls, strolling, strolled** walk in a leisurely way.
▷ **stroll** *noun* **stroller** *noun*
[from German]

strong *ADJECTIVE* **1** having great power, energy, or effect. **2** not easy to break, damage, or defeat. **3** great in intensity • *strong feelings.* **4** having a lot of flavour or smell. **5** having a certain number of members • *an army 5,000 strong.*
▷ **strongly** *adverb*

strong *ADVERB*
- **be going strong** be making good progress.
[from Old English]

stronghold *NOUN* **strongholds 1** a fortified place. **2** an area where many people live or think in a particular way • *a Tory stronghold.*

strong point *NOUN* **strong points** a strength; something that you are very good at • *Maths is her strong point.*

strongroom *NOUN* **strongrooms** a room designed to protect valuable things from fire and theft.

strontium *NOUN* a soft silvery metal.
[named after *Strontia* in the Scottish highlands, where it was discovered]

strove *past tense* of **strive**.

structure *NOUN* **structures 1** something that has been constructed or built. **2** the way something is constructed or organized.
▷ **structural** *adjective* **structurally** *adverb*

structure *VERB* **structures, structuring, structured** organize or arrange something into a system or pattern • *You need to structure your arguments with more care.*
[from Latin *struere* = build]

struggle *VERB* **struggles, struggling, struggled 1** move your arms, legs, etc. in trying to get free. **2** make strong efforts to do something. **3** try to overcome an opponent or a problem etc.

struggle *NOUN* **struggles** the action of struggling; a hard fight or great effort.
[origin unknown]

strum *VERB* **strums, strumming, strummed** sound a guitar by running your fingers across its strings.
[imitating the sound]

strut *VERB* **struts, strutting, strutted** walk proudly or stiffly.

strut *NOUN* **struts 1** a bar of wood or metal strengthening a framework. **2** a strutting walk.
[probably from old German]

strychnine (*say* strik-neen) *NOUN* a bitter poisonous substance.
[from Greek]

stub *NOUN* **stubs 1** a short stump left when the rest has been used or worn down. **2** a counterfoil of a cheque, ticket, etc.

stub *VERB* **stubs, stubbing, stubbed** bump your toe painfully.
- **stub out** put out a cigarette by pressing it against something hard.
[from Old English]

stubble *NOUN* **1** the short stalks of corn left in the ground after the harvest is cut. **2** short hairs growing after shaving.
[from old French]

stubborn *ADJECTIVE* **1** determined not to change your ideas or ways; obstinate. **2** difficult to remove or deal with • *stubborn stains.*
▷ **stubbornly** *adverb* **stubbornness** *noun*
[origin unknown]

stubby *ADJECTIVE* short and thick.

stucco *NOUN* plaster or cement used for coating walls and ceilings, often moulded into decorations.
▷ **stuccoed** *adjective*
[Italian]

stuck *past tense and past participle* of **stick**.

stuck ADJECTIVE unable to move or make progress • *I'm stuck.*

stuck-up ADJECTIVE (*informal*) conceited or snobbish.

stud[1] NOUN **studs 1** a small curved lump or knob. **2** a device like a button on a stalk, used to fasten a detachable collar to a shirt.

stud VERB **studs, studding, studded 1** set or decorate with studs etc. • *The necklace was studded with jewels.* **2** scatter or sprinkle • *The sky was studded with stars.*
[from Old English *studu*]

stud[2] NOUN **studs 1** a number of horses kept for breeding; the place where they are kept. **2** a stallion.
[from Old English *stod*]

student NOUN **students** a person who studies a subject, especially at a college or university.
[from Latin *studere* = to study]

studied ADJECTIVE not natural but done with deliberate effort • *She answered with studied indifference.*

studio NOUN **studios 1** the room where a painter or photographer etc. works. **2** a place where cinema films are made. **3** a room from which radio or television broadcasts are made or recorded.
[Italian; related to *study*]

studious ADJECTIVE **1** keen on studying; studying hard. **2** deliberate • *with studious politeness.*
▷ **studiously** *adverb* **studiousness** *noun*

study VERB **studies, studying, studied**
1 spend time learning about something.
2 look at something carefully.

study NOUN **studies 1** the process of studying. **2** a subject studied; a piece of research. **3** a room used for studying or writing. **4** a piece of music for playing as an exercise. **5** a drawing done for practice or in preparation for another work.
[from Latin *studium* = zeal]

stuff NOUN **1** a substance or material. **2** things • *Leave your stuff outside.*

stuff VERB **stuffs, stuffing, stuffed 1** fill tightly. **2** fill with stuffing. **3** push a thing into something • *He stuffed the notebook into his pocket.* **4** (*informal*) eat greedily.
[from old French]

stuffing NOUN **1** material used to fill the inside of something; padding. **2** a savoury mixture put into meat or poultry etc. before cooking.

stuffy ADJECTIVE **stuffier, stuffiest 1** badly ventilated; without fresh air. **2** with blocked breathing passages • *a stuffy nose.* **3** formal and boring.
▷ **stuffily** *adverb* **stuffiness** *noun*

stultify VERB **stultifies, stultifying, stultified** prevent from being effective • *Their stubbornness stultified the discussions.*
▷ **stultification** *noun*
[from Latin *stultus* = foolish]

stumble VERB **stumbles, stumbling, stumbled 1** trip and lose your balance. **2** speak or do something hesitantly or uncertainly.
▷ **stumble** *noun*
- **stumble across** or **on** find accidentally.
[from Old Norse]

stumbling block NOUN **stumbling blocks** an obstacle; something that causes difficulty.

stump NOUN **stumps 1** the bottom of a tree trunk left in the ground when the rest has fallen or been cut down. **2** something left when the main part is cut off or worn down. **3** each of the three upright sticks of a wicket in cricket.

stump VERB **stumps, stumping, stumped**
1 put a batsman out by knocking the bails off the stumps while he or she is out of the crease. **2** be too difficult or puzzling for somebody • *The last question stumped everyone.* **3** walk stiffly or noisily.
- **stump up** (*informal*) produce the money to pay for something.
[from old German or old Dutch]

stumpy ADJECTIVE short and thick.
▷ **stumpiness** *noun*

stun VERB **stuns, stunning, stunned**
1 knock a person unconscious. **2** daze or shock • *She was stunned by the news.*
[from old French]

stunt[1] *VERB* prevent a thing from growing or developing normally • *a stunted tree.*
[probably from Old English]

stunt[2] *NOUN* **stunts 1** something daring done as a performance or as part of the action of a film. **2** something unusual done to attract attention • *a publicity stunt.*
[originally American: origin unknown]

stupefy *VERB* **stupefies, stupefying, stupefied** make a person dazed.
▷ **stupefaction** *noun*
[from Latin *stupere* = be amazed]

stupendous *ADJECTIVE* amazing or tremendous.
▷ **stupendously** *adverb*
[same origin as *stupefy*]

stupid *ADJECTIVE* **1** not clever or thoughtful. **2** without reason or common sense.
▷ **stupidly** *adverb* **stupidity** *noun*
[from Latin *stupidus* = dazed]

stupor (*say* stew-per) *NOUN* **stupors** a dazed condition.
[same origin as *stupefy*]

sturdy *ADJECTIVE* **sturdier, sturdiest** strong and vigorous or solid.
▷ **sturdily** *adverb* **sturdiness** *noun*
[from old French]

sturgeon *NOUN* **sturgeon** a large edible fish.
[via old French from Germanic]

stutter *VERB* **stutters, stuttering, stuttered** stammer.
▷ **stutter** *noun*
[imitating the sound]

sty[1] *NOUN* **sties** a pigsty.
[from Old English *sti*]

sty[2] or **stye** *NOUN* **sties** or **styes** a sore swelling on an eyelid.
[from Old English *stigend* = rising, swelling]

style *NOUN* **styles 1** the way something is done, made, said, or written. **2** fashion or elegance. **3** the part of a pistil that supports the stigma in a plant.
▷ **stylistic** *adjective*

style *VERB* **styles, styling, styled** design or arrange something, especially in a fashionable style.
▷ **stylist** *noun*
[from old French; related to *stylus*]

stylish *ADJECTIVE* in a fashionable style.

stylus *NOUN* **styluses** or **styli** the device like a needle that travels in the grooves of a record to produce the sound.
[from Latin *stilus* = pointed writing instrument]

suave (*say* swahv) *ADJECTIVE* smoothly polite.
▷ **suavely** *adverb* **suavity** *noun*
[from Latin *suavis* = sweet, pleasant]

sub *NOUN* **subs** (*informal*) **1** a submarine. **2** a subscription. **3** a substitute.

sub- *PREFIX* (often changing to **suc-, suf-, sum-, sup-, sur-, sus-** before certain consonants) **1** under (as in *submarine*). **2** subordinate, secondary (as in *subsection*).
[from Latin *sub* = under]

subaltern *NOUN* **subalterns** an army officer ranking below a captain.
[from Latin *subalternus* = inferior, lower in rank]

subaqua *ADJECTIVE* to do with underwater sports, such as diving.
[from *sub-* + Latin *aqua* = water]

subatomic *ADJECTIVE* **1** smaller than an atom. **2** forming part of an atom.

subconscious *ADJECTIVE* to do with mental processes of which we are not fully aware but which influence our actions.
▷ **subconscious** *noun*

subcontinent *NOUN* **subcontinents** a large mass of land not large enough to be called a continent • *the Indian subcontinent.*

subcontractor *NOUN* **subcontractors** a person or company hired by another company to do a particular part of their work.
▷ **subcontract** *verb*

subdivide *VERB* **subdivides, subdividing, subdivided** divide again or into smaller parts.
▷ **subdivision** *noun*

subdue *VERB* **subdues, subduing, subdued 1** overcome or bring under control. **2** make quieter or gentler.
▷ **subdued** *adjective*
[from old French]

subject *NOUN* **subjects 1** the person or thing being talked or written about or dealt with. **2** something that is studied. **3** (*in grammar*) the word or words naming who or what does the action of a verb, e.g. '*the book*' in *the book fell off the table*. **4** someone who is ruled by a monarch or government.

subject *ADJECTIVE* ruled by a monarch or government; not independent.
- **subject to 1** having to obey. **2** liable to • *Trains are subject to delays because of flooding.* **3** depending upon • *Our decision is subject to your approval.*

subject (*say* sub-**jekt**) *VERB* **subjects, subjecting, subjected 1** make a person or thing undergo something • *They subjected him to torture.* **2** bring a country under your control.
▷ **subjection** *noun*
[from *sub-* + Latin *-jectum* = thrown]

subjective *ADJECTIVE* **1** existing in a person's mind and not produced by things outside it. **2** depending on a person's own taste or opinions etc. (COMPARE **objective**)

sub judice (*say* joo-dis-ee) *ADJECTIVE* being decided by a judge or lawcourt and therefore not able to be discussed publicly. [Latin, = under a judge]

subjugate *VERB* **subjugates, subjugating, subjugated** bring under your control; conquer.
▷ **subjugation** *noun*
[from *sub-* + Latin *jugum* = a yoke]

subjunctive *NOUN* **subjunctives** the form of a verb used to indicate what is imagined or wished or possible. There are only a few cases where it is commonly used in English, e.g. '*were*' in *if I were you* and '*save*' in *God save the Queen*.
[from *sub-* + Latin *junctum* = joined]

sublet *VERB* **sublets, subletting, sublet** let to another person a house etc. that is let to you by a landlord.

sublime *ADJECTIVE* **1** noble or impressive. **2** extreme; not caring about the consequences • *with sublime carelessness.* [from Latin]

submarine *ADJECTIVE* under the sea • *We laid a submarine cable.*

submarine *NOUN* **submarines** a ship that can travel under water.

submerge *VERB* **submerges, submerging, submerged** go under or put under water.
▷ **submergence** *noun* **submersion** *noun*
[from *sub-* + Latin *mergere* = dip]

submission *NOUN* **submissions 1** submitting to someone. **2** something submitted or offered for consideration.

submissive *ADJECTIVE* willing to obey. [from *submission*]

submit *VERB* **submits, submitting, submitted 1** let someone have authority over you; surrender. **2** put forward for consideration, testing, etc. • *Submit your plans to the committee.*
[from *sub-* + Latin *mittere* = send]

subnormal *ADJECTIVE* below normal.

subordinate *ADJECTIVE* **1** less important. **2** lower in rank.

subordinate *NOUN* **subordinates** a person working under someone's authority or control.

subordinate *VERB* **subordinates, subordinating, subordinated** treat as being less important than another person or thing.
▷ **subordination** *noun*
[from *sub-* + Latin *ordinare* = arrange]

subordinate clause *NOUN* **subordinate clauses** a clause which adds details to the main clause of the sentence, but cannot be used as a sentence by itself.

suborn *VERB* **suborns, suborning, suborned** bribe or incite someone secretly. [from *sub-* + Latin *ornare* = equip]

sub-plot *NOUN* **sub-plots** a secondary plot in a play etc.

subpoena (*say* sub-**peen**-a) *NOUN* **subpoenas** an official document ordering a person to appear in a lawcourt.

subpoena *VERB* **subpoenas, subpoenaing, subpoenaed** summon by a subpoena.
[from Latin *sub poena* = under a penalty (because there is a punishment for not obeying)]

sub-post office *NOUN* **sub-post offices** a small local post office, often in a shop, which offers fewer services than a main post office.

subscribe *VERB* **subscribes, subscribing, subscribed** **1** pay regularly in order to be a member of a society, receive a periodical, have the use of a telephone, etc. **2** apply to take part in something • *The course is already fully subscribed.* **3** contribute money to a project or charity etc. **4** say that you agree • *We cannot subscribe to this theory.*
▷ **subscriber** *noun*
[from *sub-* + Latin *scribere* = write]

subscription *NOUN* **subscriptions** money paid to subscribe to something.

subsequent *ADJECTIVE* coming after in time or order; later.
▷ **subsequently** *adverb*
[from *sub-* + Latin *sequens* = following]

subservient *ADJECTIVE* prepared to obey others without question.
▷ **subservience** *noun*
[from *sub-* + Latin *serviens* = serving]

subset *NOUN* **subsets** a group or set forming part of a larger group or set.

subside *VERB* **subsides, subsiding, subsided** **1** sink • *The house has subsided over the years.* **2** become less intense or quieter • *Her fear subsided.*
[from *sub-* + Latin *sidere* = settle]

subsidence (*say* sub-sy-dens or sub-sid-ens) *NOUN* the gradual sinking or caving in of an area of land.

subsidiary *ADJECTIVE* **1** less important; secondary. **2** (said about a business) controlled by another • *a subsidiary company.*
▷ **subsidiary** *noun*
[same origin as *subsidy*]

subsidize *VERB* **subsidizes, subsidizing, subsidized** pay a subsidy to a person or firm etc.

subsidy *NOUN* **subsidies** money paid to an industry etc. that needs help, or to keep down the price at which its goods etc. are sold to the public.
[from Latin *subsidium* = assistance]

subsist *VERB* **subsists, subsisting, subsisted** exist; keep yourself alive • *We subsisted on nuts.*
▷ **subsistence** *noun*
[from Latin *subsistere* = stand firm]

subsoil *NOUN* soil lying just below the surface layer.

subsonic *ADJECTIVE* not as fast as the speed of sound. (COMPARE **supersonic**)

substance *NOUN* **substances** **1** matter of a particular kind. **2** the main or essential part of something • *We agree with the substance of your report but not with its details.*
[from Latin *substantia* = essence]

sub-standard *ADJECTIVE* below the normal or required standard.

substantial *ADJECTIVE* **1** of great size, value, or importance • *a substantial fee.* **2** solidly built • *substantial houses.*
[same origin as *substance*]

substantially *ADVERB* mostly • *The two books are substantially the same.*

substantiate *VERB* **substantiates, substantiating, substantiated** produce evidence to prove something.
▷ **substantiation** *noun*
[same origin as *substance*]

substation *NOUN* **substations** a subsidiary station for distributing electric current.

substitute *NOUN* **substitutes** a person or thing that acts or is used instead of another.

substitute *VERB* **substitutes, substituting, substituted** put or use a person or thing as a substitute.
▷ **substitution** *noun*
[from *sub-* + Latin *statuere* = to set up]

subterfuge *NOUN* **subterfuges** a deception.
[from Latin *subterfugere* = escape secretly]

subterranean *ADJECTIVE* underground.
[from *sub-* + Latin *terra* = ground]

subtitle *NOUN* **subtitles** **1** a secondary or additional title. **2** words shown on the screen during a film, e.g. to translate a foreign language.

subtle (*say* sut-el) *ADJECTIVE* **1** faint or delicate • *a subtle perfume.* **2** slight and difficult to detect or describe • *a subtle distinction.* **3** ingenious but not immediately obvious • *a subtle joke.*
▷ **subtly** *adverb* **subtlety** *noun*
[from Latin]

subtotal *NOUN* **subtotals** the total of part of a group of figures.

subtract *VERB* **subtracts, subtracting, subtracted** deduct; take away a part, quantity, or number from a greater one.
▷ **subtraction** *noun*
[from *sub-* + Latin *tractum* = pulled]

subtropical *ADJECTIVE* of regions that border on the tropics.

suburb *NOUN* **suburbs** a district with houses that is outside the central part of a city.
▷ **suburban** *adjective*
[from *sub-* + Latin *urbs* = city]

suburbia *NOUN* **1** suburbs. **2** the way people in the suburbs live and think.

subvert *VERB* **subverts, subverting, subverted** **1** get someone to be disloyal to their government, religion, standards of behaviour, etc. **2** overthrow a government etc. in this way.
▷ **subversion** *noun* **subversive** *adjective*
[from *sub-* + Latin *vertere* = to turn]

subway *NOUN* **subways 1** an underground passage for pedestrians. **2** (*American*) an underground railway.

suc- *PREFIX* **1** under. **2** subordinate, secondary. SEE **sub-**.

succeed *VERB* **succeeds, succeeding, succeeded** **1** do or get what you wanted or intended. **2** come after another person or thing. **3** become the next holder of an office, especially the monarchy • *She succeeded to the throne. Edward VII succeeded Queen Victoria.*
[from *suc-* + Latin *cedere* = go]

success *NOUN* **successes 1** doing or getting what you wanted or intended. **2** a person or thing that does well • *The show was a great success.*
[same origin as *succeed*]

successful *ADJECTIVE* having success; being a success.
▷ **successfully** *adverb*

succession *NOUN* **successions 1** a series of people or things. **2** the process of following in order. **3** succeeding to the throne; the right of doing this.
- **in succession** one after another.
[same origin as *succeed*]

successive *ADJECTIVE* following one after another • *on five successive days.*
▷ **successively** *adverb*

successor *NOUN* **successors** a person or thing that succeeds another.

succinct (*say* suk-**sinkt**) *ADJECTIVE* concise; expressed briefly.
▷ **succinctly** *adverb*
[originally = encircled: from *suc-* + Latin *cingere* = gird]

succour (*say* **suk**-er) *NOUN* help given in time of need.
▷ **succour** *verb*
[from old French]

succulent *ADJECTIVE* **1** juicy and tasty. **2** (said about plants) having thick juicy leaves or stems.
[from Latin *succus* = juice]

succumb (*say* suk-**um**) *VERB* **succumbs, succumbing, succumbed** give way to something overpowering.
[from *suc-* + Latin *cumbere* = to lie]

such *ADJECTIVE* **1** of the same kind; similar • *Cakes, biscuits, and all such foods are fattening.* **2** of the kind described • *There's no such person.* **3** so great or intense • *It gave me such a fright!*
- **such as** for example.
[from Old English]

such-and-such *ADJECTIVE* particular but not now named • *He promises to come at such-and-such a time but is always late.*

suchlike *ADJECTIVE* of that kind.

suck *VERB* **sucks, sucking, sucked** **1** take in liquid or air through almost-closed lips. **2** squeeze something in your mouth by using your tongue • *She was sucking a toffee.* **3** draw in • *The canoe was sucked into the whirlpool.*
▷ **suck** *noun*
- **suck up to** (*informal*) flatter someone in the hope of winning their favour.
[from Old English]

sucker *NOUN* **suckers 1** an organ of certain animals, or a device of rubber etc., that can stick to a surface by suction. **2** a shoot coming up from a root or underground stem. **3** (*informal*) a person who is easily deceived.

suckle *VERB* **suckles, suckling, suckled** feed on milk at the mother's breast or udder.

sucrose *NOUN* the form of sugar that is obtained from sugar cane and sugar beet.
[from French *sucre* = sugar]

suction *NOUN* **1** sucking. **2** producing a vacuum so that things are sucked into the empty space • *Vacuum cleaners work by suction.*
[from Latin]

sudden *ADJECTIVE* happening or done quickly or without warning.
▷ **suddenly** *adverb* **suddenness** *noun*
[from old French]

suds *PLURAL NOUN* froth on soapy water.
[probably from old German or old Dutch]

sue *VERB* **sues, suing, sued** start a lawsuit to claim money from somebody.
[from old French]

suede (*say* swayd) *NOUN* leather with one side rubbed to make it velvety.
[from French *gants de Suède* = gloves from Sweden]

suet *NOUN* hard fat from cattle and sheep, used in cooking.
[from old French; related to *sebum*]

suf- *PREFIX* **1** under. **2** subordinate, secondary. SEE **sub-**.

suffer *VERB* **suffers, suffering, suffered** **1** feel pain or sadness. **2** experience something bad • *The house suffered some damage. She suffers from hay fever*. **3** become worse or be badly affected • *She's not sleeping and her work is suffering.* **4** (*old use*) allow or tolerate.
▷ **sufferer** *noun* **suffering** *noun*
[from *suf-* + Latin *ferre* = to bear]

sufferance *NOUN*
- **on sufferance** allowed but only reluctantly.
[from Latin *sufferentia* = suffering]

suffice *VERB* **suffices, sufficing, sufficed** be enough for someone's needs.
[from *suf-* + Latin *facere* = make or do]

sufficient *ADJECTIVE* enough.
▷ **sufficiently** *adverb* **sufficiency** *noun*
[same origin as *suffice*]

suffix *NOUN* **suffixes** a letter or set of letters joined to the end of a word to make another word (e.g. in forget*ful*, lion*ess*, rust*y*) or a form of a verb (e.g. sing*ing*, wait*ed*).
[from *suf-* + Latin *figere* = fix]

suffocate *VERB* **suffocates, suffocating, suffocated** **1** make it difficult or impossible for someone to breathe. **2** suffer or die because breathing is prevented.
▷ **suffocation** *noun*
[from *suf-* + Latin *fauces* = throat]

suffrage *NOUN* the right to vote in political elections.
[from Latin]

suffragette *NOUN* **suffragettes** a woman who campaigned in the early 20th century for women to have the right to vote.

suffuse *VERB* **suffuses, suffusing, suffused** spread through or over something • *A blush suffused her cheeks.*
[from *suf-* + Latin *fusum* = poured]

sugar *NOUN* a sweet food obtained from the juices of various plants, such as sugar cane or sugar beet.
▷ **sugar** *verb* **sugary** *adjective*
[via old French, Italian, Latin, Arabic, and Persian from Sanskrit]

suggest *VERB* **suggests, suggesting, suggested** **1** put forward an idea or plan for someone to consider. **2** cause an idea or possibility to come into the mind.
▷ **suggestion** *noun* **suggestive** *adjective*
[from Latin]

suggestible *ADJECTIVE* easily influenced by people's suggestions.

suicide *NOUN* **suicides** **1** killing yourself deliberately • *He committed suicide.* **2** a person who deliberately kills himself or herself.
▷ **suicidal** *adjective*
[from Latin *sui* = of yourself, + *-cide*]

suit *NOUN* **suits** **1** a matching jacket and trousers, or a jacket and skirt, that are meant to be worn together. **2** a set of clothing for a particular activity • *a diving suit.* **3** any of the four sets of cards (clubs, hearts, diamonds, spades) in a pack of playing cards. **4** a lawsuit.
USAGE Do not confuse with **suite**.

suit *VERB* **suits, suiting, suited** **1** be suitable or convenient for a person or thing. **2** make a person look attractive.
[from Latin *sequi* = to go together or follow]

suitable *ADJECTIVE* satisfactory or right for a particular person, purpose, or occasion.
▷ **suitably** *adverb* **suitability** *noun*

suitcase *NOUN* **suitcases** a rectangular container for carrying clothes, usually with a hinged lid and a handle.

suite (*say as* sweet) *NOUN* **suites 1** a set of furniture. **2** a set of rooms. **3** a set of short pieces of music.
[French; related to *suit*]
USAGE Do not confuse with **suit**.

suitor *NOUN* **suitors** a man who is courting a woman.
[from Latin *secutor* = follower]

sulk *VERB* **sulks, sulking, sulked** be silent and bad-tempered because you are not pleased.
▷ **sulks** *plural noun* **sulky** *adjective* **sulkily** *adverb* **sulkiness** *noun*
[origin unknown]

sullen *ADJECTIVE* sulking and gloomy.
▷ **sullenly** *adverb* **sullenness** *noun*
[from old French; related to *sole*[2]]

sully *VERB* **sullies, sullying, sullied** soil or stain something; blemish • *The scandal sullied his reputation.*
[same origin as *soil*[2]]

sulphur *NOUN* a yellow chemical used in industry and in medicine.
▷ **sulphurous** *adjective*
[from Latin]

sulphuric acid *NOUN* a strong colourless acid containing sulphur.

sultan *NOUN* **sultans** the ruler of certain Muslim countries.
[Arabic, = ruler]

sultana *NOUN* **sultanas** a raisin without seeds.
[Italian, literally = sultan's wife]

sultry *ADJECTIVE* **1** hot and humid • *sultry weather.* **2** suggesting passion or sexual desire • *her sultry smile.*
▷ **sultriness** *noun*
[origin unknown]

sum *NOUN* **sums 1** a total. **2** a problem in arithmetic. **3** an amount of money.

sum *VERB* **sums, summing, summed**
- **sum up** give a summary at the end of a talk etc.
[from Latin *summa* = main thing]

sum- *PREFIX* **1** under. **2** subordinate, secondary. SEE **sub-**.

summarize *VERB* **summarizes, summarizing, summarized** make or give a summary of something.

summary *NOUN* **summaries** a statement of the main points of something said or written.

summary *ADJECTIVE* **1** brief. **2** done or given hastily, without delay • *summary punishment.*
▷ **summarily** *adverb*
[same origin as *sum*]

summer *NOUN* **summers** the warm season between spring and autumn.
▷ **summery** *adjective*
[from Old English]

summer house *NOUN* **summer houses** a small building providing shade in a garden or park.

summit *NOUN* **summits 1** the top of a mountain or hill. **2** a meeting between the leaders of powerful countries • *a summit conference.*
[from Latin *summus* = highest]

summon *VERB* **summons, summoning, summoned 1** order someone to come or appear. **2** call people together • *A meeting of the governors was quickly summoned.*
- **summon up** gather together your strength or courage in order to do something • *I couldn't even summon up the energy to get out of bed.*
[from *sum-* + Latin *monere* = warn]

summons *NOUN* **summonses** a command to appear in a lawcourt.

sump *NOUN* **sumps** a metal case that holds oil round an engine.
[from old German or old Dutch]

sumptuous *ADJECTIVE* splendid and expensive-looking.
▷ **sumptuously** *adverb*
[from Latin *sumptus* = cost, expense]

sun *NOUN* **suns 1** the star round which the earth travels. **2** light and warmth from the sun • *Let's sit in the sun.* **3** any star in the universe round which planets travel.

sun *VERB* **suns, sunning, sunned**
- **sun yourself** sit or lie in the sunshine.
[from Old English]

a b c d e f g h i j k l m n o p q r **s** t u v w x y z

A B C D E F G H I J K L M N O P Q R S T U V W X Y Z

sunbathe *VERB* **sunbathes, sunbathing, sunbathed** expose your body to the sun, especially to get a tan.

sunbeam *NOUN* **sunbeams** a ray of sun.

sunbed *NOUN* **sunbeds** a bench that you lie on under a sunlamp.

sunblock *NOUN* sunscreen.

sunburn *NOUN* redness of the skin caused by the sun.
▷ **sunburnt** *adjective*

sundae (*say* sun-day) *NOUN* **sundaes** a mixture of ice cream and fruit, nuts, cream, etc.
[from *Sunday* (because sundaes were originally sold then, possibly to use up ice cream not sold during the week)]

Sunday *NOUN* the first day of the week, observed by Christians as a day of rest and worship.
[from Old English *sunnandaeg* = day of the sun]

sunder *VERB* **sunders, sundering, sundered** (*poetical use*) break or tear apart.
[from Old English]

sundial *NOUN* **sundials** a device that shows the time by a shadow on a dial.

sundown *NOUN* sunset.

sundries *PLURAL NOUN* various small things.
[from *sundry*]

sundry *ADJECTIVE* various or several.
- **all and sundry** everyone.
[from Old English]

sunflower *NOUN* **sunflowers** a very tall flower with golden petals round a dark centre.
[so called because the flower head turns to follow the sun]

sunglasses *PLURAL NOUN* dark glasses to protect your eyes from strong sunlight.

sunken *ADJECTIVE* sunk deeply into a surface
• *Their cheeks were pale and sunken.*

sunlamp *NOUN* **sunlamps** a lamp which uses ultraviolet light to give people an artificial tan.

sunlight *NOUN* light from the sun.
▷ **sunlit** *adjective*

Sunni *NOUN* **Sunnis** a member of one of the two main branches of Islam; about 80% of Muslims are Sunnis. (COMPARE **Shi'ite**)
[from Arabic *sunna* = law or custom]

sunny *ADJECTIVE* **sunnier, sunniest** **1** full of sunshine. **2** cheerful • *She was in a sunny mood.*
▷ **sunnily** *adverb*

sunrise *NOUN* **sunrises** the rising of the sun; dawn.

sunscreen *NOUN* an oil or lotion that you put on your skin to protect it from the sun's harmful rays.

sunset *NOUN* **sunsets** the setting of the sun.

sunshade *NOUN* **sunshades** a parasol or other device to protect people from the sun.

sunshine *NOUN* sunlight with no cloud between the sun and the earth.

sunspot *NOUN* **sunspots** **1** a dark place on the sun's surface. **2** a sunny place.

sunstroke *NOUN* illness caused by being in the sun too long.

suntan *NOUN* **suntans** a brown colour of the skin caused by the sun.
▷ **suntanned** *adjective*

sun visor *NOUN* **sun visors** a flap at the top of a vehicle's windscreen that shields your eyes from the sun.

sup *VERB* **sups, supping, supped** drink liquid in sips or spoonfuls.
[from Old English]

sup- *PREFIX* **1** under. **2** subordinate, secondary. SEE **sub-**.

super *ADJECTIVE* (*informal*) excellent or superb.
[from *super-*]

super- *PREFIX* **1** over or on top (as in *superstructure*). **2** of greater size or quality etc. (as in *supermarket*). **3** extremely (as in *superabundant*). **4** beyond (as in *supernatural*).
[from Latin *super* = over]

superannuation *NOUN* regular payments made by an employee towards his or her pension.
[from *super-* + Latin *annus* = a year]

superb *ADJECTIVE* magnificent or excellent.
▷ **superbly** *adverb*
[from Latin *superbus* = proud]

supercilious *ADJECTIVE* haughty and scornful.
▷ **superciliously** *adverb*
[from Latin *supercilium* = eyebrow]

superficial *ADJECTIVE* **1** on the surface • *a superficial cut.* **2** not deep or thorough • *a superficial knowledge of French.*
▷ **superficially** *adverb* **superficiality** *noun*
[from *super-* + Latin *facies* = face]

superfluous *ADJECTIVE* more than is needed.
▷ **superfluity** *noun*
[from *super-* + Latin *fluere* = flow]

superglue *NOUN* a kind of strong glue that sticks very quickly.

superhuman *ADJECTIVE* **1** beyond ordinary human ability • *superhuman strength.* **2** higher than human; divine.

superimpose *VERB* **superimposes, superimposing, superimposed** place a thing on top of something else.
▷ **superimposition** *noun*

superintend *VERB* **superintends, superintending, superintended** supervise.
[from *super-* + Latin *intendere* = direct, intend]

superintendent *NOUN* **superintendents** **1** a supervisor. **2** a police officer above the rank of inspector.

superior *ADJECTIVE* **1** higher in position or rank • *She is your superior officer.* **2** better than another person or thing. **3** showing conceit.
▷ **superiority** *noun*

superior *NOUN* **superiors** a person or thing that is superior to another.
[Latin, = higher]

superlative *ADJECTIVE* of the highest degree or quality • *superlative skill.*
▷ **superlatively** *adverb*

superlative *NOUN* **superlatives** the form of an adjective or adverb that expresses 'most' • *The superlative of 'great' is 'greatest'.* (COMPARE **positive and comparative**)
[from Latin *superlatum* = carried above]

superman *NOUN* **supermen** a man with superhuman powers.

supermarket *NOUN* **supermarkets** a large self-service shop that sells food and other goods.

supernatural *ADJECTIVE* not belonging to the natural world or having a natural explanation • *supernatural beings such as ghosts.*
▷ **supernatural** *noun*

superpower *NOUN* **superpowers** one of the most powerful nations of the world, such as the USA.

supersede *VERB* **supersedes, superseding, superseded** take the place of something • *Cars superseded horse-drawn carriages.*
[from *super-* + Latin *sedere* = sit]
USAGE Note that this word ends '-sede' and not '-cede'.

supersonic *ADJECTIVE* faster than the speed of sound. (COMPARE **subsonic**)

superstition *NOUN* **superstitions** a belief or action that is not based on reason or evidence, e.g. the belief that it is unlucky to walk under a ladder.
▷ **superstitious** *adjective*
[from Latin *superstare* = stand over]

superstore *NOUN* **superstores** a very large supermarket selling a wide range of goods.

superstructure *NOUN* **superstructures** **1** a structure that rests on something else. **2** a building as distinct from its foundations.

supertanker *NOUN* **supertankers** a very large tanker.

supervise *VERB* **supervises, supervising, supervised** be in charge of a person or thing and inspect what is done.
▷ **supervision** *noun* **supervisor** *noun* **supervisory** *adjective*
[from *super-* + Latin *visum* = seen]

superwoman *NOUN* **superwomen** a woman with superhuman powers.

supine (*say* soop-I'n) *ADJECTIVE* **1** lying face upwards. (The opposite is **prone**) **2** not taking action.
[from Latin]

supper *NOUN* **suppers** a meal eaten in the evening.
[from old French *soper* = sup]

supplant *VERB* **supplants, supplanting, supplanted** take the place of a person or thing that has been ousted.
[from Latin *supplantare* = to trip someone up]

supple *ADJECTIVE* bending easily; flexible.
▷ **supplely** *adverb* **suppleness** *noun*
[from *sup-* + Latin *plicare* = to fold, bend]

supplement *NOUN* **supplements**
1 something added as an extra. **2** an extra section added to a book or newspaper • *the colour supplement.*
▷ **supplementary** *adjective*

supplement *VERB* **supplements, supplementing, supplemented** add to something • *She supplements her pocket money by working on Saturdays.*
[same origin as *supply*]

suppliant (*say* sup-lee-ant) or **supplicant** *NOUN* **suppliants, supplicants** a person who asks humbly for something.
[from old French; related to *supplicate*]

supplicate *VERB* **supplicates, supplicating, supplicated** ask or beg humbly for something.
▷ **supplication** *noun*
[from Latin *supplicare* = kneel]

supply *VERB* **supplies, supplying, supplied** give or sell or provide what is needed or wanted.
▷ **supplier** *noun*

supply *NOUN* **supplies 1** an amount of something that is available for use when needed. **2** the action of supplying something.
[from *sup-* + Latin *-plere* = fill]

supply teacher *NOUN* **supply teachers** a teacher who takes the place of a regular teacher when he or she is away.

support *VERB* **supports, supporting, supported 1** keep something from falling or sinking; hold something up. **2** give strength, help, or encouragement to someone • *Support your local team.*
3 provide with the necessities of life • *She has two children to support.*
▷ **supporter** *noun* **supportive** *adjective*

support *NOUN* **supports 1** the action of supporting. **2** a person or thing that supports.
[from *sup-* + Latin *portare* = carry]

suppose *VERB* **supposes, supposing, supposed 1** think that something is likely to happen or be true. **2** assume; consider as a suggestion • *Suppose the world were flat.*
▷ **supposition** *noun*
- **be supposed to** be expected to do something; have as a duty.
[from old French]

supposedly *ADVERB* so people suppose or think • *They are supposedly the best team in the world.*

suppress *VERB* **suppresses, suppressing, suppressed 1** put an end to something forcibly or by authority • *Troops suppressed the rebellion.* **2** keep something from being known or seen • *They suppressed the truth.*
▷ **suppression** *noun* **suppressor** *noun*
[from *sup-* + Latin *pressus* = pressed]

supremacy (*say* soo-prem-asi) *NOUN* highest authority or power.

supreme *ADJECTIVE* **1** most important or highest in rank. **2** greatest • *supreme courage.*
▷ **supremely** *adverb*
[from Latin *supremus* = highest]

sur-[1] *PREFIX* **1** under. **2** subordinate, secondary. SEE **sub-**.

sur-[2] *PREFIX* = super- (as in *surcharge*, *surface*).
[from old French]

surcharge *NOUN* **surcharges** an extra charge.

sure *ADJECTIVE* **1** completely confident that you are right; feeling no doubt. **2** certain to happen or do something • *Our team is sure to win.* **3** reliable; undoubtedly true.
▷ **sureness** *noun*
- **for sure** definitely.
- **make sure 1** find out exactly. **2** make something happen or be true • *Make sure the door is locked.*

sure *ADVERB* (*informal*) surely.
- **sure enough** certainly; in fact.
[from old French; related to *secure*]

surely *ADVERB* **1** in a sure way; certainly or securely. **2** it must be true; I feel sure • *Surely I met you last year.*

surety *NOUN* **sureties 1** a guarantee. **2** a person who promises to pay a debt or fulfil a contract etc. if another person fails to do so.
[from old French; related to *security*]

surf *NOUN* the white foam of waves breaking on a rock or shore.

surf *VERB* **surfs, surfing, surfed 1** go surfing. **2** browse through the Internet.
[origin unknown]

surface *NOUN* **surfaces 1** the outside of something. **2** any of the sides of an object, especially the top part. **3** an outward appearance • *On the surface he was a kindly man.*

surface *VERB* **surfaces, surfacing, surfaced 1** put a surface on a road, path, etc. **2** come up to the surface from under water.
[French]

surface mail *NOUN* letters and parcels etc. carried by sea or over land, not by air.

surfboard *NOUN* **surfboards** a board used in surfing.

surfeit (*say* ser-fit) *NOUN* too much of something.
▷ **surfeited** *adjective*
[from *sur-*² + Latin *facere* = do]

surfing *NOUN* balancing yourself on a board that is carried to the shore on the waves.
▷ **surfer** *noun*

surge *VERB* **surges, surging, surged 1** move forwards or upwards like waves. **2** increase suddenly and powerfully.
▷ **surge** *noun*
[from Latin *surgere* = rise]

surgeon *NOUN* **surgeons** a doctor who treats disease or injury by cutting or repairing the affected parts of the body.

surgery *NOUN* **surgeries 1** the work of a surgeon. **2** the place where a doctor or dentist regularly gives advice and treatment to patients. **3** the time when patients can visit a doctor or dentist.
▷ **surgical** *adjective* **surgically** *adverb*
[from Greek *cheirourgia* = handiwork]

surly *ADJECTIVE* **surlier, surliest** bad-tempered and unfriendly.
▷ **surliness** *noun*
[originally = majestic, haughty: from *sir* + *-ly*]

surmise *VERB* **surmises, surmising, surmised** guess or suspect.
▷ **surmise** *noun*
[from old French *surmettre* = accuse]

surmount *VERB* **surmounts, surmounting, surmounted 1** overcome a difficulty. **2** get over an obstacle. **3** be on top of something • *The church tower is surmounted by a steeple.*
[from French]

surname *NOUN* **surnames** the name held by all members of a family.
[from French]

surpass *VERB* **surpasses, surpassing, surpassed** do or be better than all others; excel.
[from French]

surplus *NOUN* **surpluses** an amount left over after spending or using all that was needed.
▷ **surplus** *adjective*
[from *sur-*² + Latin *plus* = more]

surprise *NOUN* **surprises 1** something unexpected. **2** the feeling caused by something that was not expected.
- **take someone by surprise** happen to someone unexpectedly.

surprise *VERB* **surprises, surprising, surprised 1** be a surprise; make someone feel surprise. **2** come upon or attack somebody unexpectedly.
▷ **surprised** *adjective* **surprising** *adjective* **surprisingly** *adverb*

surrealism *NOUN* a style of painting etc. that shows strange objects and scenes like those seen in dreams and fantasies.
▷ **surrealist** *noun* **surrealistic** *adjective*
[from *sur-*² + French *réalisme* = realism]

surrender *VERB* **surrenders, surrendering, surrendered 1** stop fighting and give yourself up to an enemy. **2** hand something over to another person, especially when compelled to do so.
▷ **surrender** *noun*
[from *sur-*² + French *rendre* = give, deliver]

surreptitious (*say* su-rep-tish-us) *ADJECTIVE* stealthy.
▷ **surreptitiously** *adverb*
[from Latin *surrepticius* = stolen, taken secretly]

surrogate (*say* su-rog-at) *NOUN* **surrogates** a deputy or substitute.
▷ **surrogacy** *noun*
[from Latin]

surrogate mother *NOUN* **surrogate mothers** a woman who agrees to conceive and give birth to a baby for a woman who cannot do so herself, using a fertilized egg of the other woman or sperm from the other woman's partner.

surround *VERB* **surrounds**, **surrounding**, **surrounded** come or be all round a person or thing • *Police surrounded the building.* [from *sur-*[2] + Latin *undare* = rise in waves]

surroundings *PLURAL NOUN* the conditions or area around a person or thing.

surveillance (*say* ser-vay-lans) *NOUN* a close watch kept on a person or thing • *Police kept him under surveillance.* [from *sur-*[2] + French *veiller* = to watch]

survey (*say* ser-vay) *NOUN* **surveys 1** a general look at something. **2** an inspection of an area, building, etc.

survey (*say* ser-vay) *VERB* **surveys**, **surveying**, **surveyed** make a survey of something; inspect.
▷ **surveyor** *noun*
[from *sur-*[2] + Latin *videre* = see]

survival *NOUN* **survivals 1** surviving; the likelihood of surviving. **2** something that has survived from an earlier time.

survive *VERB* **survives**, **surviving**, **survived 1** stay alive; continue to exist. **2** remain alive after an accident or disaster • *Only two people survived the crash.* **3** continue living after someone has died.
▷ **survivor** *noun*
[from *sur-*[2] + Latin *vivere* = to live]

sus- *PREFIX* **1** under. **2** subordinate, secondary. SEE **sub-**.

susceptible (*say* sus-ept-ib-ul) *ADJECTIVE* likely to be affected by something • *She is susceptible to colds.*
▷ **susceptibility** *noun*
[from Latin *susceptum* = caught up]

suspect (*say* sus-pekt) *VERB* **suspects**, **suspecting**, **suspected 1** think that a person is not to be trusted or has committed a crime; distrust. **2** have a feeling that something is likely or possible.

suspect (*say* sus-pekt) *NOUN* **suspects** a person who is suspected of a crime etc.
▷ **suspect** *adjective*
[from *sus-* + Latin *specere* = to look]

suspend *VERB* **suspends**, **suspending**, **suspended 1** hang something up. **2** postpone; stop something temporarily. **3** remove a person from a job or position for a time. **4** keep something from falling or sinking in air or liquid • *Particles are suspended in the fluid.*
[from *sus-* + Latin *pendere* = hang]

suspender *NOUN* **suspenders** a fastener to hold up a sock or stocking by its top.

suspense *NOUN* an anxious or uncertain feeling while waiting for something to happen or become known.
[same origin as *suspend*]

suspension *NOUN* **1** suspending. **2** the springs etc. in a vehicle that lessen the effect of rough road surfaces. **3** a liquid containing small pieces of solid material which do not dissolve.

suspension bridge *NOUN* **suspension bridges** a bridge supported by cables.

suspicion *NOUN* **suspicions 1** suspecting or being suspected; distrust. **2** a slight belief.
[same origin as *suspect*]

suspicious *ADJECTIVE* feeling or causing suspicion.
▷ **suspiciously** *adverb*

sustain *VERB* **sustains**, **sustaining**, **sustained 1** keep someone alive. **2** keep something happening. **3** undergo or suffer • *He sustained serious injuries.* **4** support or uphold.
▷ **sustainable** *adjective*
[from *sus-* + Latin *tenere* = hold, keep]

sustenance *NOUN* food and drink; nourishment.
[same origin as *sustain*]

suture (*say* soo-cher) *NOUN* **sutures** surgical stitching of a cut.
[from Latin *suere* = sew]

suzerainty (*say* soo-zer-en-tee) *NOUN* **1** the partial control of a weaker country by a stronger one. **2** the power of an overlord in feudal times.
[from old French]

svelte *ADJECTIVE* slim and graceful.
[via French from Italian]

SW *ABBREVIATION* **1** south-west. **2** south-western.

swab (*say* swob) *NOUN* **swabs 1** a mop or pad for cleaning or wiping something; a small pad for cleaning a wound. **2** a specimen of fluid from the body taken on a swab for testing.

swab *VERB* **swabs, swabbing, swabbed** clean or wipe with a swab.
[from Dutch]

swagger *VERB* **swaggers, swaggering, swaggered** walk or behave in a conceited way; strut.
▷ **swagger** *noun*
[probably from a Scandinavian language]

swain *NOUN* **swains** (*old use*) **1** a country lad. **2** a suitor.
[from Old Norse]

swallow[1] *VERB* **swallows, swallowing, swallowed 1** make something go down your throat. **2** believe something that ought not to be believed.
▷ **swallow** *noun*
- **swallow up** take in and cover; engulf • *She was swallowed up in the crowd.*
[from Old English *swelgan*]

swallow[2] *NOUN* **swallows** a small bird with a forked tail and pointed wings.
[from Old English *swealwe*]

swamp *NOUN* **swamps** a marsh.
▷ **swampy** *adjective*

swamp *VERB* **swamps, swamping, swamped 1** flood. **2** overwhelm with a great mass or number of things.
[origin unknown]

swan *NOUN* **swans** a large usually white swimming bird with a long neck.
[from Old English]

swank *VERB* **swanks, swanking, swanked** (*informal*) boast or swagger; show off.

swank *NOUN* (*informal*) showing yourself or your possessions off in a conceited way.
[origin unknown]

swansong *NOUN* **swansongs** a person's last performance or work.
[from the old belief that a swan sang sweetly when about to die]

swap *VERB* **swaps, swapping, swapped** (*informal*) exchange one thing for another.
▷ **swap** *noun*
[formerly = seal a bargain by slapping each other's hands; imitating the sound]

swarm *NOUN* **swarms** a large number of insects or birds etc. flying or moving about together.

swarm *VERB* **swarms, swarming, swarmed 1** gather or move in a swarm. **2** be crowded with people etc. • *The town is swarming with tourists in the summer.*
[from Old English]

swarthy *ADJECTIVE* having a dark complexion.
▷ **swarthiness** *noun*
[from Old English]

swashbuckling *ADJECTIVE* **1** daring; loving adventure and fighting. **2** (said about a film etc.) showing daring adventures set in the past.
[from an old word *swash* = hit, + *buckler*]

swastika *NOUN* **swastikas** an ancient symbol formed by a cross with its ends bent at right angles, adopted by the Nazis as their sign.
[from Sanskrit *svasti* = well- being, luck]

swat *VERB* **swats, swatting, swatted** hit or crush a fly etc.
▷ **swatter** *noun*
[originally American, a different spelling of *squat*]

swathe[1] (*say* swawth) *NOUN* **swathes 1** a broad strip or area • *vast swathes of countryside.* **2** a line of cut corn or grass.
- **cut a swathe through** pass through an area causing destruction.
[from Old English]

swathe[2] (*say* swayth) *VERB* **swathes, swathing, swathed** wrap in layers of bandages, paper, or clothes etc.
[from Old English]

sway *VERB* **sways, swaying, swayed 1** move or swing gently from side to side. **2** influence • *His speech swayed the crowd.*
▷ **sway** *noun*
[origin unknown]

swear *VERB* **swears, swearing, swore, sworn 1** make a solemn promise • *She swore to tell the truth.* **2** make a person take an oath • *We swore him to secrecy.* **3** use curses or coarse words in anger or surprise etc.
- **swear by** have great confidence in something.
[from Old English]

swear word *NOUN* **swear words** a word considered rude or shocking, often used by someone who is angry.

sweat (*say* swet) *NOUN* moisture given off by the body through the pores of the skin; perspiration.
▷ **sweaty** *adjective*

sweat *VERB* **sweats, sweating, sweated** give off sweat; perspire.
[from Old English]

sweater *NOUN* **sweaters** a jersey or pullover.

sweatshirt *NOUN* **sweatshirts** a thick cotton jersey worn for sports or casual wear.

swede *NOUN* **swedes** a large kind of turnip with purple skin and yellow flesh.
[short for *Swedish turnip* (because it originally came from Sweden)]

sweep *VERB* **sweeps, sweeping, swept** **1** clean or clear with a broom or brush etc. **2** move or remove quickly • *The floods swept away the bridge.* **3** go smoothly and quickly • *She swept out of the room.* **4** travel quickly over an area • *A new craze is sweeping the country.*
▷ **sweeper** *noun*

sweep *NOUN* **sweeps 1** the process of sweeping • *Give this room a good sweep.* **2** a sweeping movement. **3** a chimney sweep. **4** a sweepstake.
[from Old English]

sweeping *ADJECTIVE* general or wide-ranging • *He made sweeping changes.*

sweepstake *NOUN* **sweepstakes** a form of gambling on sporting events in which all the money staked is divided among the winners.
[so called because the winner 'sweeps up' all the other players' stakes]

sweet *ADJECTIVE* **1** tasting as if it contains sugar; not bitter. **2** very pleasant • *a sweet smell.* **3** charming or delightful.
▷ **sweetly** *adverb* **sweetness** *noun*
- **a sweet tooth** a liking for sweet things.

sweet *NOUN* **sweets 1** a small shaped piece of sweet food made with sugar, chocolate, etc. **2** a pudding; the sweet course in a meal. **3** a beloved person.
[from Old English]

sweetbread *NOUN* **sweetbreads** an animal's pancreas used as food.

sweetcorn *NOUN* the juicy yellow seeds of maize.

sweeten *VERB* **sweetens, sweetening, sweetened** make or become sweet.
▷ **sweetener** *noun*

sweetheart *NOUN* **sweethearts** a person you love very much.

sweetmeat *NOUN* **sweetmeats** (*old use*) a sweet.
[from an old sense of *meat* = food]

sweet pea *NOUN* **sweet peas** a climbing plant with fragrant flowers.

sweet potato *NOUN* **sweet potatoes** a root vegetable with reddish skin and sweet yellow flesh.

swell *VERB* **swells, swelling, swelled, swollen** or **swelled** **1** make or become larger • *My ankle was starting to swell.* **2** increase in amount, volume, or force.

swell *NOUN* **swells 1** the process of swelling. **2** the rise and fall of the sea's surface.

swell *ADJECTIVE* (*informal*) (*American*) very good.
[from Old English]

swelling *NOUN* **swellings** a swollen place.

swelter *VERB* **swelters, sweltering, sweltered** feel uncomfortably hot.
▷ **sweltering** *adjective*
[from Old English]

swerve *VERB* **swerves, swerving, swerved** turn to one side suddenly.
▷ **swerve** *noun*
[from Old English]

swift *ADJECTIVE* quick or rapid.
▷ **swiftly** *adverb* **swiftness** *noun*

swift *NOUN* **swifts** a small bird rather like a swallow.
[from Old English]

swig *VERB* **swigs, swigging, swigged** (*informal*) drink quickly, taking large mouthfuls.
▷ **swig** *noun*
[origin unknown]

swill *VERB* **swills, swilling, swilled** pour water over or through something; wash or rinse.

swill *NOUN* **1** the process of swilling • *Give it a swill.* **2** a sloppy mixture of waste food given to pigs.
[from Old English]

swim *VERB* **swims, swimming, swam, swum** **1** move the body through the water; be in the water for pleasure. **2** cross by swimming • *She swam the Channel.* **3** float. **4** be covered with or full of liquid • *Our eyes were swimming in tears.* **5** feel dizzy • *His head swam.*
▷ **swimmer** *noun*

swim *NOUN* **swims** the action of swimming • *We went for a swim.*
[from Old English]

swimming bath *NOUN* **swimming baths** a public swimming pool.

swimming costume *NOUN* **swimming costumes** the clothing a woman wears to go swimming; a bikini or swimsuit.

swimming pool *NOUN* **swimming pools** an artificial pool for swimming in.

swimming trunks *PLURAL NOUN* shorts which a man wears to go swimming.

swimsuit *NOUN* **swimsuits** a one-piece swimming costume.

swindle *VERB* **swindles, swindling, swindled** cheat a person in business etc.
▷ **swindle** *noun* **swindler** *noun*
[from German *Schwindler* = a fool, a cheat]

swine *NOUN* **swine** **1** a pig. **2** a very unpleasant person. **3** (*informal*) a difficult thing • *This crossword's a real swine!*
[from Old English]

swing *VERB* **swings, swinging, swung** **1** move back and forth while hanging. **2** move or turn in a curve • *The door swung open.* **3** change from one opinion or mood etc. to another.

swing *NOUN* **swings** **1** a swinging movement. **2** a seat hung on chains or ropes etc. so that it can be moved backwards and forwards. **3** the amount by which votes or opinions etc. change from one side to another. **4** a kind of jazz music.
- **in full swing** full of activity; working fully.
[from Old English]

swingeing (*say* swin-jing) *ADJECTIVE* **1** (said about a blow) very powerful. **2** huge in amount • *a swingeing increase in taxes.*
[from Old English]

swipe *VERB* **swipes, swiping, swiped** **1** hit with a swinging blow. **2** (*informal*) steal something. **3** pass a credit card through an electronic reading device when making a payment.
▷ **swipe** *noun*
[a different spelling of *sweep*]

swirl *VERB* **swirls, swirling, swirled** move round quickly in circles.
▷ **swirl** *noun*
[probably from old Dutch]

swish *VERB* **swishes, swishing, swished** move with a hissing sound.
▷ **swish** *noun*

swish *ADJECTIVE* (*informal*) smart and fashionable.
[imitating the sound]

Swiss roll *NOUN* **Swiss rolls** a thin sponge cake spread with jam or cream and rolled up.

switch *NOUN* **switches** **1** a device that is pressed or turned to start or stop something working, especially by electricity. **2** a change of opinion, policy, or methods. **3** a mechanism for moving the points on a railway track. **4** a flexible rod or whip.

switch *VERB* **switches, switching, switched** **1** turn something on or off by means of a switch. **2** change something suddenly. **3** replace a thing with something else.
[probably from old German]

switchback *NOUN* **switchbacks** a railway at a fair, with steep slopes up and down alternately.

switchboard *NOUN* **switchboards** a panel with switches etc. for making telephone connections or operating electric circuits.

swivel *VERB* **swivels, swivelling, swivelled** turn round.

swivel *NOUN* **swivels** a device joining two things so that one can revolve without turning the other.
[from Old English]

swollen *past participle* of **swell**.

swoon *VERB* **swoons, swooning, swooned** (*old use*) faint.
▷ **swoon** *noun*
[from Old English]

swoop *VERB* **swoops, swooping, swooped 1** dive or come down with a rushing movement. **2** make a sudden attack or raid.
▷ **swoop** *noun*
[probably from *sweep*]

swop *VERB* **swops, swopping, swopped** swap.

sword (*say* sord) *NOUN* **swords** a weapon with a long pointed blade fixed in a handle or hilt.
▷ **swordsman** *noun*
[from Old English]

swordfish *NOUN* **swordfish** a large sea fish with a long sword-like upper jaw.

sworn *ADJECTIVE* **1** given under oath • *sworn testimony.* **2** determined to remain so • *They are sworn enemies.*

swot *VERB* **swots, swotting, swotted** (*informal*) study hard.
▷ **swot** *noun*
[a dialect word for *sweat*]

sycamore *NOUN* **sycamores** a tall tree with winged seeds, often grown for its timber.
[from Greek]

sycophant (*say* sik-o-fant) *NOUN* **sycophants** a person who tries to win people's favour by flattering them.
▷ **sycophantic** *adjective*
sycophantically *adverb* **sycophancy** *noun*
[from Greek]

syl- *PREFIX* **1** with, together. **2** alike. SEE **syn-**.

syllable *NOUN* **syllables** a word or part of a word that has one vowel sound when you say it • *'Cat' has one syllable, 'el-e-phant' has three syllables.*
▷ **syllabic** *adjective*
[from *syl-* + Greek *lambanein* = take]

syllabus *NOUN* **syllabuses** a summary of the things to be studied by a class or for an examination etc.
[from Greek]

sylph *NOUN* **sylphs** a slender girl or woman.
[probably from Latin *sylvestris nympha* = nymph of the woods]

sym- *PREFIX* **1** with, together. **2** alike. SEE **syn-**.

symbol *NOUN* **symbols 1** a thing used as a sign • *The crescent is a symbol of Islam.* **2** a mark or sign with a special meaning (e.g. +, -, and x, in mathematics).
[from Greek *symbolon* = token]
USAGE Do not confuse with **cymbal**.

symbolic *ADJECTIVE* acting as a symbol of something.
▷ **symbolical** *adjective* **symbolically** *adverb*

symbolism *NOUN* the use of symbols to represent things.

symbolize *VERB* **symbolizes, symbolizing, symbolized** make or be a symbol of something.

symmetrical *ADJECTIVE* able to be divided into two halves which are exactly the same but the opposite way round • *Wheels and butterflies are symmetrical.*
▷ **symmetrically** *adverb*
[from *sym-* + Greek *metron* = a measure]

symmetry *NOUN* the quality of being symmetrical or well-proportioned.

sympathize *VERB* **sympathizes, sympathizing, sympathized** show or feel sympathy.
▷ **sympathizer** *noun*

sympathy *NOUN* **sympathies 1** the sharing or understanding of other people's feelings, opinions, etc. **2** a feeling of pity or tenderness towards someone who is hurt, sad, or in trouble.
▷ **sympathetic** *adjective*
sympathetically *adverb*
[from *sym-* + Greek *pathos* = feeling]

symphony *NOUN* **symphonies** a long piece of music for an orchestra.
▷ **symphonic** *adjective*
[from *sym-* + Greek *phone* = sound]

symptom *NOUN* **symptoms** a sign that a disease or condition exists • *Red spots are a symptom of measles.*
▷ **symptomatic** *adjective*
[from Greek *symptoma* = chance, accident]

syn- *PREFIX* (changing to **syl-** or **sym-** before certain consonants) **1** with, together (as in *synchronize*). **2** alike (as in *synonym*).
[from Greek]

synagogue (*say* sin-a-gog) *NOUN* **synagogues** a place where Jews meet for worship.
[from Greek *synagoge* = assembly]

synchronize (*say* sink-ron-I'z) *VERB* **synchronizes, synchronizing, synchronized 1** make things happen at the same time. **2** make watches or clocks show the same time. **3** happen at the same time.
▷ **synchronization** *noun*
[from *syn-* + Greek *chronos* = time]

syncopate (*say* sink-o-payt) *VERB* **syncopates, syncopating, syncopated** change the strength of beats in a piece of music.
▷ **syncopation** *noun*
[from Latin]

syndicate *NOUN* **syndicates 1** a group of people or firms who work together in business. **2** a group of people who buy something together, or who gamble together, sharing the cost and any gains.
[from *syn-* + Greek *dike* = judgement]

syndrome *NOUN* **syndromes 1** a set of symptoms. **2** a set of opinions, behaviour, etc. that are characteristic of a particular condition.
[from *syn-* + Greek *dramein* = to run]

synod (*say* sin-od) *NOUN* **synods** a council of senior members of the clergy.
[from Greek *synodos* = meeting]

synonym (*say* sin-o-nim) *NOUN* **synonyms** a word that means the same or almost the same as another word • *'Large' and 'great' are synonyms of 'big'.*
▷ **synonymous** (*say* sin-on-im-us) *adjective*
[from *syn-* + Greek *onyma* = name]

synopsis (*say* sin-op-sis) *NOUN* **synopses** a summary.
[from *syn-* + Greek *opsis* = view, seeing]

syntax (*say* sin-taks) *NOUN* the way words are arranged to make phrases or sentences.
▷ **syntactic** *adjective* **syntactically** *adverb*
[from *syn-* + Greek *taxis* = arrangement]

synthesis (*say* sin-thi-sis) *NOUN* **syntheses** combining different things to make something.
[from *syn-* + Greek *thesis* = placing]

synthesize (*say* sin-thi-syz) *VERB* **synthesizes, synthesizing, synthesized** make something by combining parts.

synthesizer *NOUN* **synthesizers** an electronic musical instrument that can make a large variety of sounds.

synthetic *ADJECTIVE* artificially made; not natural.
▷ **synthetically** *adverb*
[same origin as *synthesis*]

syringe *NOUN* **syringes** a device for sucking in a liquid and squirting it out.
[from Greek *syrinx* = pipe, tube]

syrup *NOUN* a thick sweet liquid.
▷ **syrupy** *adjective*
[from Arabic *sharab* = a drink]

system *NOUN* **systems 1** a set of parts, things, or ideas that are organized to work together. **2** a way of doing something • *a new system of training motorcyclists.*
[from Greek]

systematic *ADJECTIVE* methodical; carefully planned.
▷ **systematically** *adverb*

Tt

tab *NOUN* **tabs** a small flap or strip that sticks out.
[origin unknown]

tabard *NOUN* **tabards** a kind of tunic decorated with a coat of arms.
[from old French]

tabby *NOUN* **tabbies** a grey or brown cat with dark stripes.
[originally = a kind of striped silk material: named after al-Attabiyya, a district of Baghdad where it was made]

tabernacle *NOUN* **tabernacles** (in the Bible) the portable shrine used by the ancient Jews during their wanderings in the desert.
[from Latin *tabernaculum* = tent or shed]

table *NOUN* **tables 1** a piece of furniture with a flat top supported on legs. **2** a list of facts or figures arranged in order. **3** a list of the results of multiplying a number by other numbers • *multiplication tables.*

table *VERB* **tables, tabling, tabled** put forward a proposal etc. for discussion at a meeting.
[from Latin *tabula* = plank, tablet, or list]

tableau (*say* tab-loh) *NOUN* **tableaux** (*say* tab-lohz) a dramatic or attractive scene, especially one posed on a stage by a group of people who do not speak or move.
[French; related to *table*]

tablecloth *NOUN* **tablecloths** a cloth for covering a table, especially at meals.

table d'hôte (*say* tahbl **doht**) *NOUN* a restaurant meal served at a fixed price. (COMPARE **à la carte**)
[French, = host's table]

tablespoon *NOUN* **tablespoons** a large spoon for serving food.
▷ **tablespoonful** *noun*

tablet *NOUN* **tablets 1** a pill. **2** a solid piece of soap. **3** a flat piece of stone or wood etc. with words carved or written on it.
[from old French *tablete* = small table or slab]

table tennis *NOUN* a game played on a table divided by a net, over which you hit a small ball with bats.

tabloid *NOUN* **tabloids** a newspaper with pages that are half the size of larger newspapers.
[originally, the trade mark of a kind of pill, later = something in a smaller form than usual]

taboo *ADJECTIVE* not to be done or used or talked about.
▷ **taboo** *noun*
[from Tongan *tabu* = sacred]

tabor (*say* tay-ber) *NOUN* **tabors** a small drum.
[from old French]

tabular *ADJECTIVE* arranged in a table or in columns.

tabulate *VERB* **tabulates, tabulating, tabulated** arrange information or figures in a table or list.
▷ **tabulation** *noun*

tabulator *NOUN* **tabulators** a device on a typewriter or computer that automatically sets the positions for columns.

tachograph (*say* tak-o-grahf) *NOUN* **tachographs** a device that automatically records the speed and travelling time of a motor vehicle in which it is fitted.
[from Greek *tachos* = speed, + *-graph*]

tacit (*say* tas-it) *ADJECTIVE* implied or understood without being put into words • *tacit approval.*
[from Latin *tacitus* = not speaking]

taciturn (*say* tas-i-tern) *ADJECTIVE* saying very little.
▷ **taciturnity** *noun*
[same origin as *tacit*]

tack[1] *NOUN* **tacks 1** a short nail with a flat top. **2** a tacking stitch. **3** (in sailing) the direction taken when tacking. **4** a course of action or policy • *I think we need to change tack.*

tack *VERB* **tacks, tacking, tacked 1** nail something down with tacks. **2** fasten material together with long stitches. **3** sail a zigzag course to take advantage of what wind there is.
- **tack on** add an extra thing.
[from old French]

tack[2] *NOUN* harness, saddles, etc.
[from *tackle* = equipment]

tackle *VERB* **tackles, tackling, tackled 1** try to do something that needs doing. **2** try to get the ball from someone else in a game of football or hockey. **3** talk to someone about a difficult or awkward matter.

tackle *NOUN* **tackles 1** equipment, especially for fishing. **2** a set of ropes and pulleys. **3** tackling someone in football or hockey.
[probably from old German]

tacky[1] *ADJECTIVE* sticky, not quite dry • *The paint is still tacky.*
▷ **tackiness** *noun*
[from *tack*[1] = a fastening]

tacky[2] *ADJECTIVE* (*informal*) showing poor taste or style.
[origin unknown]

tact *NOUN* skill in not offending people.
▷ **tactful** *adjective* **tactfully** *adverb*
tactless *adjective* **tactlessly** *adverb*
[from Latin *tactus* = sense of touch]

tactics *NOUN* **1** the method of arranging troops etc. skilfully for a battle. **2** the methods you use to achieve something or gain an advantage.
▷ **tactical** *adjective* **tactically** *adverb*
tactician *noun*
[from Greek *taktika* = things arranged]
USAGE *Strategy* is a general plan for a whole campaign, *tactics* refers to one part of this.

tactile *ADJECTIVE* to do with the sense of touch.
[same origin as *tact*]

tadpole *NOUN* **tadpoles** a young frog or toad that has developed from the egg and lives entirely in water.
[from *toad* + *poll* = head]

taffeta *NOUN* a stiff silky material.
[from Persian *taftan* = to shine]

tag[1] *NOUN* **tags 1** a label tied on or stuck into something. **2** a metal or plastic point at the end of a shoelace.

tag *VERB* **tags, tagging, tagged 1** label something with a tag. **2** add as an extra thing • *A postscript was tagged on to her letter.* **3** (*informal*) go with other people • *Her sister tagged along.*
[origin unknown]

tag[2] *NOUN* a game in which one person chases the others.
[origin unknown]

tail *NOUN* **tails 1** the part that sticks out from the rear end of the body of a bird, fish, or animal. **2** the part at the end or rear of something. **3** the side of a coin opposite the head • *Heads or tails?*

tail *VERB* **tails, tailing, tailed 1** remove stalks etc. from fruit • *top and tail gooseberries.* **2** (*informal*) follow someone closely.
- **tail off** become fewer, smaller, or slighter etc.; cease gradually.
[from Old English]

tailback *NOUN* **tailbacks** a long line of traffic stretching back from an obstruction.

tailless *ADJECTIVE* without a tail.

tailor *NOUN* **tailors** a person who makes men's clothes.

tailor *VERB* **tailors, tailoring, tailored 1** make or fit clothes. **2** adapt or make something for a special purpose.
[from old French]

tailor-made *ADJECTIVE* specially made or suited for a purpose.

tails *PLURAL NOUN* a man's formal jacket with two long pieces hanging down at the back.

taint *NOUN* **taints** a small amount of decay, pollution, or a bad quality that spoils something.

taint *VERB* **taints, tainting, tainted** give something a taint.
[from old French; related to *tint*]

take *VERB* **takes, taking, took, taken** This word has many uses, including **1** get something into your hands or possession or control etc. • *Take this cup; We took many prisoners.* **2** carry or convey • *Take this parcel to the post.* **3** make use of • *Let's take a taxi.* **4** indulge in or undertake • *You need to take a holiday.* **5** perform or deal with • *When do you take your music exam?* **6** study or teach a subject • *Who takes you for maths?* **7** make an effort • *Thanks for taking the trouble to see me.* **8** experience a feeling • *Don't take offence.* **9** accept; endure • *I'll take a risk.* **10** require • *It takes a strong man to lift this.* **11** write down • *I'd better take notes.* **12** make a photograph. **13** subtract • *Take 4 from 10.* **14** assume • *I take it that you agree.*
▷ **taker** *noun*
- **take after** be like a parent etc.
- **take in** deceive somebody.
- **take leave of** say goodbye to.
- **take off** (said about an aircraft) leave the ground and become airborne.
- **take on 1** begin to employ someone. **2** play or fight against someone. **3** (*informal*) show that you are upset.
- **take over** take control of a business or activity.
- **take place** happen or occur.
- **take to** develop a liking or ability for something.
- **take up 1** start something. **2** occupy space or time etc. **3** accept an offer.
[from Old Norse]

takeaway *NOUN* **takeaways 1** a place that sells cooked meals for customers to take away. **2** a meal from this.

take-off *NOUN* **take-offs** the act of an aircraft leaving the ground and becoming airborne.

takeover *NOUN* **takeovers** the taking control of one business company by another.

takings *PLURAL NOUN* money received.

talcum powder *NOUN* a scented powder put on the skin to make it feel smooth and dry.
[from *talc*, the substance from which it is made]

tale *NOUN* **tales** a story.
[from Old English]

talent *NOUN* **talents** a special or very great ability.
▷ **talented** *adjective*
[from Greek *talanton* = sum of money]

talisman *NOUN* **talismans** an object that is supposed to bring good luck.
[from Greek *telesma* = consecrated object]

talk *VERB* **talks, talking, talked** speak; have a conversation.
▷ **talker** *noun*
- **talk down to** speak to someone using simple language in a condescending way.

talk *NOUN* **talks 1** a conversation or discussion. **2** an informal lecture.
[from Middle English; related to *tale*]

talkative *ADJECTIVE* talking a lot.

tall *ADJECTIVE* **1** higher than the average • *a tall tree.* **2** measured from the bottom to the top • *It is 10 metres tall.*
▷ **tallness** *noun*
[from Old English]

tallow *NOUN* animal fat used to make candles, soap, lubricants, etc.
[from old German]

tall story *NOUN* **tall stories** (*informal*) a story that is hard to believe.

tally *NOUN* **tallies** the total amount of a debt or score.

tally *VERB* **tallies, tallying, tallied** correspond or agree with something else • *Does your list tally with mine?*
[from Latin]

Talmud *NOUN* the collection of writings that contain Jewish religious law.
[Hebrew, = instruction]

talon *NOUN* **talons** a strong claw.
[from Latin]

tambourine *NOUN* **tambourines** a circular musical instrument with metal discs round it, tapped or shaken to make it jingle.
[from French]

tame *ADJECTIVE* **1** (said about animals) gentle and not afraid of people; not wild or dangerous. **2** not exciting; dull.
▷ **tamely** *adverb* **tameness** *noun*

tame *VERB* **tames, taming, tamed** make an animal become tame.
▷ **tamer** *noun*
[from Old English]

Tamil *NOUN* **Tamils 1** a member of a people of southern India and Sri Lanka. **2** their language.

tam-o'-shanter *NOUN* **tam-o'-shanters** a beret with a wide top.
[named after *Tam o' Shanter*, hero of a poem by the Scottish poet Robert Burns]

tamp *VERB* **tamps, tamping, tamped** pack or ram down tightly.
[from French]

tamper *VERB* **tampers, tampering, tampered** meddle or interfere with something.
[from *temper*]

tampon *NOUN* **tampons** a plug of soft material that a woman puts into her vagina to absorb the blood during her period.
[French]

tan *NOUN* **tans 1** a light brown colour. **2** brown colour in skin that has been exposed to sun.

tan *VERB* **tans, tanning, tanned 1** make or become brown by exposing skin to the sun. **2** make an animal's skin into leather by treating it with chemicals.
[probably from Latin]

tandem *NOUN* **tandems** a bicycle for two riders, one behind the other.
- **in tandem** one behind another; together.
[Latin, = at length]

tandoori *NOUN* a style of Indian cooking in which food is cooked in a clay oven (a **tandoor**).
[from Persian or Urdu]

tang *NOUN* **tangs** a strong flavour or smell.
[from Old Norse]

tangent *NOUN* **tangents** a straight line that touches the outside of a curve or circle.
- **go off at a tangent** move away suddenly from a subject or line of thought being considered.
[from Latin *tangens* = touching]

tangerine *NOUN* **tangerines** a kind of small orange.
[named after *Tangier* in Morocco, where the fruit originally came from]

tangible *ADJECTIVE* **1** able to be touched. **2** real or definite • *tangible benefits.*
▷ **tangibly** *adverb* **tangibility** *noun*
[from Latin *tangere* = to touch]

tangle *VERB* **tangles, tangling, tangled** make or become twisted into a confused mass.
▷ **tangle** *noun*
[probably from a Scandinavian language]

tango *NOUN* **tangos** a ballroom dance with gliding steps.
[American Spanish, perhaps from an African language]

tank *NOUN* **tanks 1** a large container for a liquid or gas. **2** a heavy armoured vehicle used in war.
[from Gujarati or Marathi, languages spoken in India]

tankard *NOUN* **tankards** a large mug for drinking beer from, usually made of silver or pewter.
[origin unknown]

tanker *NOUN* **tankers 1** a large ship for carrying oil. **2** a large lorry for carrying a liquid.
[from *tank*]

tanner *NOUN* **tanners** a person who tans animal skins into leather.
▷ **tannery** *noun*

tannin *NOUN* a substance obtained from the bark or fruit of various trees (also found in tea), used in tanning and dyeing things.
[from French; related to *tan*]

tantalize *VERB* **tantalizes, tantalizing, tantalized** tease or torment a person by showing him or her something good but keeping it out of reach.
[from the name of *Tantalus* in Greek mythology, who was punished by being made to stand near water and fruit which moved away when he tried to reach them]

tantamount *ADJECTIVE* equivalent • *The Queen's request was tantamount to a command.*
[from Italian *tanto montare* = amount to so much]

tantrum *NOUN* **tantrums** an outburst of bad temper.
[origin unknown]

tap[1] *NOUN* **taps** a device for letting out liquid or gas in a controlled flow.

tap *VERB* **taps, tapping, tapped 1** take liquid out of something, especially through a tap. **2** obtain supplies or information etc. from a source. **3** fix a device to a telephone line so that you can overhear conversations on it.
[from Old English]

tap[2] *NOUN* **taps 1** a quick light hit; the sound of this. **2** tap-dancing.

tap *VERB* **taps, tapping, tapped** hit a person or thing quickly and lightly.
[from French]

tap-dance *NOUN* a dance with shoes that make elaborate tapping sounds on the floor.
▷ **tap-dancer** *noun*

tape *NOUN* **tapes 1** a narrow strip of cloth, paper, plastic, etc. **2** a narrow plastic strip coated with a magnetic substance and used for making recordings. **3** a tape recording. **4** a tape measure.

tape *VERB* **tapes, taping, taped 1** fix, cover, or surround something with tape. **2** record something on magnetic tape.
- **have something taped** (*informal*) understand it or be able to deal with it.
[from Old English]

tape deck *NOUN* **tape decks** the part of a stereo system on which you can play cassette tapes.

tape measure *NOUN* **tape measures** a long strip marked in centimetres or inches for measuring things.

taper *VERB* **tapers, tapering, tapered** **1** make or become thinner towards one end. **2** make or become gradually less.

taper *NOUN* **tapers** a very thin candle. [via Old English from Latin]

tape recorder *NOUN* **tape recorders** a machine for recording music or sound on magnetic tape and playing it back.
▷ **tape recording** *noun*

tapestry *NOUN* **tapestries** a piece of strong cloth with pictures or patterns woven or embroidered on it.
[from French *tapis* = carpet]

tapeworm *NOUN* **tapeworms** a long flat worm that can live as a parasite in the intestines of people and animals.

tapioca *NOUN* a starchy substance in hard white grains obtained from cassava, used for making puddings.
[from Tupi (a South American language)]

tapir (*say* tay-per) *NOUN* **tapirs** a pig-like animal with a long flexible snout.
[via Spanish or Portuguese from Tupi (a South American language)]

tar *NOUN* a thick black liquid made from coal or wood etc. and used in making roads.

tar *VERB* **tars, tarring, tarred** coat something with tar.
[from Old English]

tarantula *NOUN* **tarantulas** a large kind of spider found in southern Europe and in tropical countries.
[from Italian]

tardy *ADJECTIVE* **tardier, tardiest** slow or late.
▷ **tardily** *adverb* **tardiness** *noun*
[from Latin *tardus* = slow]

target *NOUN* **targets** something aimed at; a thing that someone tries to hit or reach.

target *VERB* **targets, targeting, targeted** aim at or have as a target.
[from Old English]

tariff *NOUN* **tariffs** a list of prices or charges.
[via French and Italian from Arabic]

tarmac *NOUN* an area surfaced with tarmacadam, especially on an airfield.
[*Tarmac* is a trade mark]

tarmacadam *NOUN* a mixture of tar and broken stone, used for making a hard surface on roads, paths, playgrounds, etc.
[from *tar* and *macadam*]

tarnish *VERB* **tarnishes, tarnishing, tarnished** **1** make or become less shiny • *The silver has tarnished.* **2** spoil or blemish • *The scandal tarnished his reputation.*
▷ **tarnish** *noun*
[from French *terne* = dark, dull]

tarot cards (*rhymes with* **barrow**) *PLURAL NOUN* a special pack of cards used for fortune-telling.
[via French from Italian]

tarpaulin *NOUN* **tarpaulins** a large sheet of waterproof canvas.
[from *tar* + *pall*[1]]

tarragon *NOUN* a plant with leaves that are used to flavour salads etc.
[from Latin]

tarry[1] (*say* tar-ee) *ADJECTIVE* covered with or like tar.

tarry[2] (*say* ta-ree) *VERB* **tarries, tarrying, tarried** (*old use*) stay for a while longer; linger.
[origin unknown]

tart[1] *NOUN* **tarts** **1** a pie containing fruit or sweet filling. **2** a piece of pastry with jam etc. on top.
[from Latin]

tart[2] *ADJECTIVE* **1** sour. **2** sharp in manner • *a tart reply.*
▷ **tartly** *adverb* **tartness** *noun*
[origin unknown]

tartan *NOUN* a pattern with coloured stripes crossing each other, especially one that is used by a Scottish clan.
[probably from old French *tiretaine*, a kind of material]

tartar[1] *NOUN* **tartars** a person who is fierce or difficult to deal with.
[named after the *Tartars*, warriors from central Asia in the 13th century]

tartar[2] *NOUN* **tartars** a hard chalky deposit that forms on teeth.
[from Latin]

tartlet *NOUN* **tartlets** a small pastry tart.

task *NOUN* **tasks** a piece of work to be done.
- **take a person to task** rebuke him or her.
[from old French; related to *tax*]

task force *NOUN* **task forces** a group specially organized for a particular task.

taskmaster *NOUN* **taskmasters** a person who sets a lot of difficult tasks for other people to do • *a hard taskmaster.*

tassel *NOUN* **tassels** a bundle of threads tied together at the top and used to decorate something.
▷ **tasselled** *adjective*
[from old French]

taste *VERB* **tastes, tasting, tasted** **1** take a small amount of food or drink to try its flavour. **2** be able to perceive flavours. **3** have a certain flavour.

taste *NOUN* **tastes** **1** the feeling caused in the tongue by something placed on it. **2** the ability to taste things. **3** the ability to enjoy beautiful things or to choose what is suitable • *She shows good taste in her choice of clothes.* **4** a liking • *I've developed quite a taste for skiing.* **5** a very small amount of food or drink.
[from old French]

tasteful *ADJECTIVE* showing good taste.
▷ **tastefully** *adverb* **tastefulness** *noun*

tasteless *ADJECTIVE* **1** having no flavour. **2** showing poor taste.
▷ **tastelessly** *adverb* **tastelessness** *noun*

tasty *ADJECTIVE* **tastier, tastiest** having a strong pleasant taste.

tattered *ADJECTIVE* badly torn; ragged.
[from *tatters*]

tatters *PLURAL NOUN* rags; badly torn pieces.
- **in tatters** torn to pieces • *My coat was in tatters.*
[from Old Norse]

tatting *NOUN* a kind of handmade lace.
[origin unknown]

tattle *VERB* **tattles, tattling, tattled** gossip.
▷ **tattle** *noun*
[from old Flemish]

tattoo[1] *VERB* **tattoos, tattooing, tattooed** mark a person's skin with a picture or pattern by using a needle and some dye.

tattoo *NOUN* **tattoos** a tattooed picture or pattern.
[from a Polynesian language]

tattoo[2] *NOUN* **tattoos** **1** a drumming or tapping sound. **2** an entertainment consisting of military music, marching, etc.
[from Dutch]

tatty *ADJECTIVE* **1** ragged; shabby and untidy. **2** cheap and gaudy.
▷ **tattily** *adverb* **tattiness** *noun*
[from Old English *taettec* = rag]

taunt *VERB* **taunts, taunting, taunted** jeer at or insult someone.
▷ **taunt** *noun*
[from French *tant pour tant* = tit for tat]

taut *ADJECTIVE* stretched tightly.
▷ **tautly** *adverb* **tautness** *noun*
[probably from *tough*]

tauten *VERB* **tautens, tautening, tautened** make or become taut.

tautology *NOUN* **tautologies** saying the same thing again in different words, e.g. *You can get the book free for nothing* (where *free* and *for nothing* mean the same).
[from Greek *tauto* = the same + *logos* = word]

tavern *NOUN* **taverns** (*old use*) an inn or public house.
[from Latin]

tawdry *ADJECTIVE* cheap and gaudy.
▷ **tawdriness** *noun*
[from *St Audrey's lace* (cheap finery formerly sold at St Audrey's fair at Ely)]

tawny *ADJECTIVE* brownish-yellow.
[from old French; related to *tan*]

tax *NOUN* **taxes** **1** money that people or business firms have to pay to the government, to be used for public purposes. **2** a strain or burden • *The long walk was a tax on his strength.*

tax *VERB* **taxes, taxing, taxed** **1** put a tax on something. **2** charge someone a tax. **3** pay the tax on something • *I have taxed the car up to June.* **4** put a strain or burden on a person or thing • *This will tax your strength.* **5** accuse • *I taxed him with leaving the door open.*
▷ **taxable** *adjective* **taxation** *noun*
[from Latin *taxare* = calculate]

taxi *NOUN* **taxis** a car that carries passengers for payment, usually with a meter to record the fare to be paid.
▷ **taxicab** *noun*

taxi *VERB* **taxies, taxiing, taxied** (said about an aircraft) move along the ground or water, especially before or after flying.
[short for *taximeter cab*, from French *taxe* = tariff, charge + *mètre* = meter]

taxidermist *NOUN* **taxidermists** a person who prepares and stuffs the skins of animals in a lifelike form.
▷ **taxidermy** *noun*
[from Greek *taxis* = arrangement + *derma* = skin]

taxpayer *NOUN* **taxpayers** a person who pays tax.

TB *ABBREVIATION* tuberculosis.

tea *NOUN* **teas 1** a drink made by pouring hot water on the dried leaves of an evergreen shrub (the *tea plant*). **2** these dried leaves. **3** a drink made with the leaves of other plants *camomile tea*. **4** a meal in the afternoon or early evening.
▷ **teacup** *noun* **tea leaf** *noun* **teatime** *noun*
[via Dutch from Chinese]

tea bag *NOUN* **tea bags** a small bag holding about a teaspoonful of tea.

teacake *NOUN* **teacakes** a kind of bun usually served toasted and buttered.

teach *VERB* **teaches, teaching, taught** **1** give a person knowledge or skill; train. **2** give lessons, especially in a particular subject. **3** show someone what to do or avoid • *That will teach you not to meddle!*
[from Old English]

teachable *ADJECTIVE* able to be taught.

teacher *NOUN* **teachers** a person who teaches others, especially in a school.

teaching *NOUN* **teachings** things that are taught • *the teachings of Plato.*

tea cloth *NOUN* **tea cloths** a tea towel.

teak *NOUN* the hard strong wood of an evergreen Asian tree.
[via Portuguese from a south Indian language]

teal *NOUN* **teal** a kind of duck.
[origin unknown]

team *NOUN* **teams 1** a set of players forming one side in certain games and sports. **2** a set of people working together. **3** two or more animals harnessed to pull a vehicle or a plough etc.

team *VERB* **teams, teaming, teamed** put or join together in a team.
[from Old English]

teamwork *NOUN* the ability of a team or group to work well together.

teapot *NOUN* **teapots** a pot with a lid and a handle, for making and pouring tea.

tear[1] (*say* teer) *NOUN* **tears** a drop of the water that comes from the eyes when a person cries.
▷ **teardrop** *noun*
- **in tears** crying.
[from Old English *taeher*]

tear[2] (*say* tair) *VERB* **tears, tearing, tore, torn** **1** pull something apart, away, or into pieces. **2** become torn • *Newspaper tears easily.* **3** run or travel hurriedly.

tear *NOUN* **tears** a split made by tearing.
[from Old English *teran*]

tearful *ADJECTIVE* in tears; crying easily.
▷ **tearfully** *adverb*

tear gas *NOUN* a gas that makes people's eyes water painfully.

tease *VERB* **teases, teasing, teased** **1** amuse yourself by deliberately annoying or making fun of someone. **2** pick threads apart into separate strands.

tease *NOUN* **teases** a person who often teases others.
[from Old English]

teasel *NOUN* **teasels** a plant with bristly heads formerly used to brush up the surface of cloth.
[from *tease***2**]

teaser *NOUN* **teasers** a difficult problem or puzzle.

teaspoon *NOUN* **teaspoons** a small spoon for stirring tea etc.
▷ **teaspoonful** *noun*

teat *NOUN* **teats 1** a nipple through which a baby sucks milk. **2** the cap of a baby's feeding bottle.
[from old French]

tea towel *NOUN* **tea towels** a cloth for drying washed dishes, cutlery, etc.

tech (*say* tek) *NOUN* **techs** (*informal*) a technical college.

technical *ADJECTIVE* **1** to do with technology. **2** to do with a particular subject and its methods • *the technical terms of chemistry.* **3** using language that only experts can understand.
[from Greek *technikos* = skilled in an art or craft]

technical college *NOUN* **technical colleges** a college where technical subjects are taught.

technicality *NOUN* **technicalities 1** being technical. **2** a technical word, phrase, or detail.

technically *ADVERB* according to the strict facts, rules, etc.

technician *NOUN* **technicians** a person whose job is to look after scientific equipment and do practical work in a laboratory.

technique *NOUN* **techniques** the method of doing something skilfully.
[French, related to *technical*]

technology *NOUN* **technologies** the study of machinery, engineering, and how things work.
▷ **technological** *adjective* **technologist** *noun*
[from Greek *techne* = craft, skill, + *-ology*]

teddy bear *NOUN* **teddy bears** a soft furry toy bear.
[named after US President Theodore ('*Teddy*') Roosevelt, who liked hunting bears]

tedious *ADJECTIVE* annoyingly slow or long; boring.
▷ **tediously** *adverb* **tediousness** *noun*
[from Latin *taedium* = tiredness]

tedium *NOUN* a dull or boring time or experience.

tee *NOUN* **tees 1** the flat area from which golfers strike the ball at the start of play for each hole. **2** a small piece of wood or plastic on which a golf ball is placed for being struck.
[origin unknown]

teem[1] *VERB* **teems, teeming, teemed** be full of something • *The river was teeming with fish.*
[from Old English]

teem[2] *VERB* **teems, teeming, teemed** rain very hard; pour.
[from Old Norse]

-teen *SUFFIX* a form of 'ten' added to numbers from *three* to *nine* to form *thirteen* to *nineteen*.

teen *ADJECTIVE* & *NOUN* **teens** (*informal*) a teenager.

teenage *ADJECTIVE* to do with teenagers.

teenaged *ADJECTIVE* in your teens.

teenager *NOUN* **teenagers** a person in his or her teens.

teens *PLURAL NOUN* the time of life between 13 and 19 years of age.

teeny *ADJECTIVE* **teenier, teeniest** (*informal*) tiny.
[a different spelling of *tiny*]

tee-shirt *NOUN* **tee-shirts** a T-shirt.

teeter *VERB* **teeters, teetering, teetered** stand or move unsteadily.
[from Old Norse]

teethe *VERB* **teethes, teething, teethed** (said about a baby) have its first teeth beginning to grow through the gums.

teetotal *ADJECTIVE* never drinking alcohol.
▷ **teetotaller** *noun*
[from *total* with *tee* added for emphasis]

Teflon *NOUN* (*trademark*) a type of plastic used as a non-stick coating for pans.
[from poly*tetrafluoroethylene*, its scientific name]

tele- *PREFIX* far; at a distance (as in *telescope*).
[from Greek]

telecommunications *PLURAL NOUN* communications over a long distance, e.g. by telephone, telegraph, radio, or television.

telegram *NOUN* **telegrams** a message sent by telegraph.

telegraph *NOUN* a way of sending messages by using electric current along wires or by radio.
▷ **telegraphic** *adjective* **telegraphy** *noun*

telepathy (*say* til-ep-ath-ee) *NOUN* communication of thoughts from one person's mind to another without speaking, writing, or gestures.
▷ **telepathic** *adjective*
[from *tele-* + Greek *pathos* = feeling]

telephone *NOUN* **telephones** a device or system using electric wires or radio etc. to enable one person to speak to another who is some distance away.

telephone *VERB* **telephones**, **telephoning**, **telephoned** speak to a person on the telephone.
[from *tele-* + Greek *phone* = sound, voice]

telephonist (*say* til-ef-on-ist) *NOUN* **telephonists** a person who operates a telephone switchboard.

telescope *NOUN* **telescopes** an instrument using lenses to magnify distant objects.
▷ **telescopic** *adjective*

telescope *VERB* **telescopes**, **telescoping**, **telescoped** **1** make or become shorter by sliding overlapping sections into each other. **2** compress or condense something so that it takes less space or time.
[from *tele-* + Greek *skopein* = look at]

teletext *NOUN* a system for displaying news and information on a television screen.

televise *VERB* **televises**, **televising**, **televised** broadcast something by television.
[from *television*]

television *NOUN* **televisions** **1** a system using radio waves to reproduce a view of scenes, events, or plays etc. on a screen. **2** an apparatus for receiving these pictures. **3** televised programmes.

telex *NOUN* **telexes** a system for sending printed messages by telegraphy; a message sent by this system.
▷ **telex** *verb*
[from *teleprinter* (the machine used) + *exchange*]

tell *VERB* **tells**, **telling**, **told** **1** make a thing known to someone, especially by words. **2** speak • *Tell the truth.* **3** order • *Tell them to wait.* **4** reveal a secret • *Promise you won't tell.* **5** decide or distinguish • *Can you tell the difference between butter and margarine?* **6** produce an effect • *The strain was beginning to tell on him.*
- **all told** in all, all together • *There are ten of them, all told.*
- **tell off** (*informal*) reprimand.
- **tell tales** report something naughty or bad that someone else has done.
[from Old English]

telling *ADJECTIVE* having a strong effect or meaning • *It was a telling reply.*

tell-tale *NOUN* **tell-tales** a person who tells tales.

tell-tale *ADJECTIVE* revealing or indicating something • *There was a tell-tale spot of jam on his chin.*

telly *NOUN* **tellies** (*informal*) **1** television. **2** a television set.

temerity (*say* tim-erri-tee) *NOUN* rashness or boldness.
[from Latin]

temp *NOUN* **temps** (*informal*) a secretary or other worker who works for short periods of time in different companies.
[from *temporary*]

temper *NOUN* **tempers** **1** a person's mood • *He is in a good temper.* **2** an angry mood • *She was in a temper.*
- **lose your temper** lose your calmness and become angry.

temper *VERB* **tempers**, **tempering**, **tempered** **1** harden or strengthen metal etc. by heating and cooling it. **2** moderate or soften the effects of something • *Justice needs to be tempered with mercy.*
[via Old English from Latin *temperare* = mix]

temperament *NOUN* **temperaments** a person's nature as shown in the way he or she usually behaves • *a nervous temperament.*
[same origin as *temper*]

temperamental *ADJECTIVE* **1** likely to become excitable or moody suddenly. **2** to do with a person's temperament.
▷ **temperamentally** *adverb*

temperance *NOUN* **1** moderation or self-restraint. **2** drinking little or no alcohol.
[from Latin *temperantia* = moderation]

temperate *ADJECTIVE* neither extremely hot nor extremely cold • *Britain has a temperate climate.*
[originally = not affected by strong emotions: same origin as *temper*]

temperature *NOUN* **temperatures 1** how hot or cold a person or thing is. **2** an abnormally high temperature of the body.
[from Latin *temperatus* = tempered]

tempest *NOUN* **tempests** a violent storm.
[from Latin *tempestas* = weather]

tempestuous *ADJECTIVE* stormy; full of commotion.

template *NOUN* **templates** a thin sheet of shaped metal, plastic, etc. used as a guide for cutting or shaping things.
[from an earlier spelling *templet*, from *temple*, a device in a loom for keeping the cloth stretched]

temple[1] *NOUN* **temples** a building where a god is worshipped.
[from Latin *templum* = consecrated place]

temple[2] *NOUN* **temples** the part of the head between the forehead and the ear.
[from Latin *tempora* = sides of the head]

tempo *NOUN* **tempos** or **tempi** the speed or rhythm of something, especially of a piece of music.
[Italian, from Latin *tempus* = time]

temporary *ADJECTIVE* lasting for a limited time only; not permanent.
▷ **temporarily** (*say* tem-per-er-il-ee) *adverb*
[from Latin *temporis* = of a time]

temporize *VERB* **temporizes, temporizing, temporized** avoid giving a definite answer, in order to postpone something.
[from Latin *tempus* = time]

tempt *VERB* **tempts, tempting, tempted** try to persuade or attract someone, especially into doing something wrong or unwise.
▷ **temptation** *noun* **tempter** *noun* **temptress** *noun*
[from Latin *temptare* = test]

ten *NOUN* **tens** *ADJECTIVE* the number 10.
[from Old English]

tenable *ADJECTIVE* able to be held or defended • *a tenable theory; the job is tenable for one year only.*
[French, from *tenir* = to hold]

tenacious (*say* ten-ay-shus) *ADJECTIVE* **1** holding or clinging firmly to something. **2** obstinate and persistent.
▷ **tenaciously** *adverb* **tenacity** *noun*
[from Latin *tenere* = to hold]
WORD FAMILY There are a number of English words that are related to *tenacious* because part of their original meaning comes from the Latin word *tenere* meaning 'to hold'. These include *contain, detain, maintain, retain, sustain, tenant,* and *tenet.*

tenant *NOUN* **tenants** a person who rents a house, building, or land etc. from a landlord.
▷ **tenancy** *noun*
[French, = holding]

tend[1] *VERB* **tends, tending, tended** be inclined or likely to do something • *Prices tend to rise.*
[same origin as *tender*[2]]

tend[2] *VERB* **tends, tending, tended** look after • *Shepherds were tending their sheep.*
[from *attend*]

tendency *NOUN* **tendencies** the way a person or thing is likely to behave • *She has a tendency to be lazy.*

tender[1] *ADJECTIVE* **1** easy to chew; not tough or hard. **2** easily hurt or damaged; sensitive or delicate • *tender plants.* **3** (said about a part of the body) painful when touched. **4** gentle and loving • *a tender smile.*
▷ **tenderly** *adverb* **tenderness** *noun*
[from Latin *tener* = soft]

tender[2] *VERB* **tenders, tendering, tendered** offer something formally • *He tendered his resignation.*

tender *NOUN* **tenders** a formal offer to supply goods or carry out work at a stated price • *The council asked for tenders to build a school.*
- **legal tender** kinds of money that are legal for making payments • *Are pound notes still legal tender?*
[from Latin *tendere* = stretch, hold out]
WORD FAMILY There are a number of English words that are related to *tender* because part of their original meaning comes from the Latin word *tendere* meaning

'to stretch, hold out, or strive'. These include *attend*, *contend*, *distend*, *extend*, *tendon*, *tense*, *tensile*, and *tension*.

tender[3] *NOUN* **tenders 1** a truck attached to a steam locomotive to carry its coal and water. **2** a small boat carrying stores or passengers to and from a larger one.
[from *tend*[2]]

tendon *NOUN* **tendons** a strong strip of tissue that joins muscle to bone.
[same origin as *tender*[2]]

tendril *NOUN* **tendrils 1** a thread-like part by which a climbing plant clings to a support. **2** a thin curl of hair etc.
[from French; related to *tender*[1]]

tenement *NOUN* **tenements** a large house or building divided into flats or rooms that are let to separate tenants.
[from Latin *tenementum* = holding]

tenet (*say* ten-it) *NOUN* **tenets** a firm belief held by a person or group.
[Latin, = he or she holds]

tenner *NOUN* **tenners** (*informal*) a ten-pound note; £10.

tennis *NOUN* a game played with rackets and a ball on a court with a net across the middle.
[from old French]

tenon *NOUN* **tenons** a piece of wood etc. shaped to fit into a mortise.
[French, from *tenir* = to hold]

tenor *NOUN* **tenors 1** a male singer with a high voice. **2** the general meaning or drift • *What was the tenor of her speech?*
[from Latin]

tenpin bowling *NOUN* a game in which players try to knock over ten skittles set up at the end of a track by rolling hard balls down it.

tense[1] *NOUN* **tenses** the form of a verb that shows when something happens, e.g. he *came* (**past tense**), he *comes* or *is coming* (**present tense**), he *will come* (**future tense**).
[from Latin *tempus* = time]

tense[2] *ADJECTIVE* **1** tightly stretched. **2** nervous or worried and unable to relax. **3** making people tense • *a tense moment.*
▷ **tensely** *adverb* **tenseness** *noun*

tense *VERB* **tenses, tensing, tensed** make or become tense.
[from Latin *tensus* = stretched]

tensile *ADJECTIVE* **1** to do with tension. **2** able to be stretched.

tension *NOUN* **tensions 1** how tightly stretched a rope or wire is. **2** a feeling of anxiety or nervousness about something that is just about to happen. **3** voltage • *high-tension cables.*
[from Latin *tensio* = stretching]

tent *NOUN* **tents** a shelter made of canvas or other material.
[from French; related to *tense*[2]]

tentacle *NOUN* **tentacles** a long flexible part of the body of certain animals (e.g. snails, octopuses), used for feeling or grasping things or for moving.
[from Latin]

tentative *ADJECTIVE* cautious; trying something out • *a tentative suggestion.*
▷ **tentatively** *adverb*
[same origin as *tempt*]

tenterhooks *PLURAL NOUN*
- on tenterhooks tense and anxious.
[from *tenter* = a machine with hooks for stretching cloth to dry]

tenth *ADJECTIVE & NOUN* next after the ninth.
[from Old English]

tenuous *ADJECTIVE* very slight or thin • *tenuous threads; a tenuous connection.*
[from Latin *tenuis* = thin]

tenure (*say* ten-yoor) *NOUN* **tenures** the holding of a position of employment, or of land, accommodation, etc.
[old French, from *tenir* = to hold]

tepee (*say* tee-pee) *NOUN* **tepees** a tent formerly used by Native Americans, made by fastening skins or mats over poles.
[a Native American word]

tepid *ADJECTIVE* only slightly warm; lukewarm • *tepid water.*
[from Latin *tepere* = to be warm]

term *NOUN* **terms 1** the period of weeks when a school or college is open. **2** a definite period • *a term of imprisonment.* **3** a word or expression • *technical terms.*

term *VERB* **terms, terming, termed** name; call something by a certain term • *This music is termed jazz.*
[from French; related to *terminus*]

termagant *NOUN* **termagants** a bad-tempered bullying woman.
[named after *Tervagant*, a fierce god in medieval plays]

terminable *ADJECTIVE* able to be terminated.

terminal *NOUN* **terminals 1** the place where something ends; a terminus. **2** a building where air passengers arrive or depart. **3** a place where a wire is connected in an electric circuit or battery etc. **4** a monitor and keyboard used for putting data into a computer, or for receiving it.

terminal *ADJECTIVE* **1** to do with or at the end or boundary of something. **2** in the last stage of a fatal disease • *terminal cancer.*
▷ **terminally** *adverb*
[same origin as *terminus*]

terminate *VERB* **terminates, terminating, terminated** end; stop finally.
▷ **termination** *noun*
[same origin as *terminus*]

terminology *NOUN* **terminologies** the technical terms of a subject.
▷ **terminological** *adjective*
[via German from Latin]

terminus *NOUN* **termini 1** the end of something. **2** the last station on a railway or bus route.
[Latin, = end, limit, or boundary]

termite *NOUN* **termites** a small insect that is very destructive to timber.
[from Latin]

terms *PLURAL NOUN* **1** a relationship between people • *They ended up on friendly terms.* **2** conditions offered or accepted • *peace terms.*
- **come to terms with** become reconciled to a difficulty or unwelcome situation.

tern *NOUN* **terns** a seabird with long wings.
[probably from a Scandinavian language]

ternary *ADJECTIVE* consisting of three parts.
[from Latin *terni* = three each]

terrace *NOUN* **terraces 1** a level area on a slope or hillside. **2** a paved area beside a house. **3** a row of houses joined together.
▷ **terraced** *adjective*
[from French; related to *terrain*]

terracotta *NOUN* **1** a kind of pottery. **2** the brownish-red colour of flowerpots.
[Italian, = baked earth]

terra firma *NOUN* dry land; the ground.
[Latin, = firm land]

terrain *NOUN* **terrains** a stretch of land • *hilly terrain.*
[from Latin *terra* = earth]
WORD FAMILY There are a number of English words that are related to *terrain* because part of their original meaning comes from the Latin word *terra* meaning 'earth'. These include *inter*, *subterranean*, *terrestrial*, and *territory*.

terrapin *NOUN* **terrapins** an edible freshwater turtle of North America.
[a Native American word]

terrestrial *ADJECTIVE* to do with the earth or land.
[same origin as *terrain*]

terrible *ADJECTIVE* very bad; awful.
▷ **terribly** *adverb*
[same origin as *terror*]

terrier *NOUN* **terriers** a kind of small lively dog.
[from old French *chien terrier* = earth-dog (because they were used to dig out foxes from their earths)]

terrific *ADJECTIVE* (*informal*) **1** very great • *a terrific storm.* **2** excellent.
▷ **terrifically** *adverb*
[from Latin *terrificus* = frightening]

terrify *VERB* **terrifies, terrifying, terrified** fill someone with terror.
[same origin as *terrific*]

territorial *ADJECTIVE* **1** to do with or belonging to a country's territory • *a territorial dispute.* **2** (said about an animal or bird) guarding and defending an area of land it believes to be its own • *Cats are very territorial.*

territory *NOUN* **territories** an area of land, especially one that belongs to a country or person.
[same origin as *terrain*]

terror *NOUN* **terrors 1** very great fear. **2** a terrifying person or thing.
[from Latin *terrere* = frighten]

terrorist *NOUN* **terrorists** a person who uses violence for political purposes.
▷ **terrorism** *noun*

terrorize *VERB* **terrorizes, terrorizing, terrorized** fill someone with terror; frighten someone by threatening them.
▷ **terrorization** *noun*

terse *ADJECTIVE* using few words; concise or curt.
▷ **tersely** *adverb* **terseness** *noun*
[from Latin *tersum* = polished]

tertiary (*say* ter-sher-ee) *ADJECTIVE* to do with the third stage of something; coming after secondary.
[from Latin *tertius* = third]

tessellate *VERB* **tessellates, tessellating, tessellated** fit shapes into a pattern without overlapping or leaving gaps.
▷ **tessellated** *adjective* **tessellation** *noun*
[from Latin *tessella* = a small piece of wood, bone, or glass, used as a token or in a mosaic]

test *NOUN* **tests 1** a short examination. **2** a way of discovering the qualities, abilities, or presence of a person or thing • *a test for radioactivity.* **3** a test match.

test *VERB* **tests, testing, tested** carry out a test on a person or thing.
▷ **tester** *noun*
[from Latin]

testament *NOUN* **testaments 1** a written statement. **2** either of the two main parts of the Bible, the Old Testament or the New Testament.
[from Latin *testari* = act as a witness, make a will]

testator *NOUN* **testators** a person who has made a will.
[same origin as *testament*]

testicle *NOUN* **testicles** either of the two glands in the scrotum where semen is produced.
[from Latin]

testify *VERB* **testifies, testifying, testified 1** give evidence; swear that something is true. **2** be evidence or proof of something.
[from Latin *testis* = witness]

testimonial *NOUN* **testimonials 1** a letter describing someone's abilities, character, etc. **2** a gift presented to someone as a mark of respect.
[same origin as *testify*]

testimony *NOUN* **testimonies** evidence; what someone testifies.

test match *NOUN* **test matches** a cricket or rugby match between teams from different countries.

testosterone (*say* test-ost-er-ohn) *NOUN* a male sex hormone.

test tube *NOUN* **test tubes** a tube of thin glass with one end closed, used for experiments in chemistry etc.

test-tube baby *NOUN* **test-tube babies** a baby that develops from an egg that has been fertilized outside the mother's body and then placed back in the womb.

testy *ADJECTIVE* easily annoyed; irritable.
[from old French *testif* = headstrong]

tetanus *NOUN* a disease that makes the muscles become stiff, caused by bacteria.
[from Greek *tetanos* = a spasm]

tetchy *ADJECTIVE* easily annoyed; irritable.
[probably from Scots *tache* = blotch or fault]

tête-à-tête (*say* tayt-ah-**tayt**) *NOUN* **tête-à-têtes** a private conversation, especially between two people.
[French, = head to head]

tether *VERB* **tethers, tethering, tethered** tie an animal so that it cannot move far.

tether *NOUN* **tethers** a rope for tethering an animal.
- **at the end of your tether** unable to endure something any more.
[from Old Norse]

tetra- *PREFIX* four.
[from Greek]

tetrahedron *NOUN* **tetrahedrons** a solid with four sides (i.e. a pyramid with a triangular base).
[from *tetra-* + Greek *hedra* = base]

text *NOUN* **texts 1** the words of something written or printed. **2** a message sent from one mobile phone to another. **3** a sentence from the Bible used as the subject of a sermon etc.
[from Latin *textus* = literary style]

text *VERB* **texts, texting, texted** send a text message to someone on a mobile phone • *He texted me to tell me when the train would arrive.*

textbook *NOUN* **textbooks** a book that teaches you about a subject.

textiles *PLURAL NOUN* kinds of cloth; fabrics. [from Latin *textum* = woven]

text message *NOUN* **text messages** a written message sent on a mobile phone.

texture *NOUN* **textures** the way that the surface of something feels. [from Latin *textura* = weaving]

thalidomide *NOUN* a medicinal drug that was found (in 1961) to cause babies to be born with deformed arms and legs. [from its chemical name]

than *CONJUNCTION* compared with another person or thing • *His brother is taller than he is* or *taller than him.* [from Old English]

thank *VERB* **thanks, thanking, thanked** tell someone that you are grateful to him or her.
- **thank you** an expression of thanks. [from Old English]

thankful *ADJECTIVE* grateful.

thankfully *ADVERB* **1** in a grateful way. **2** fortunately • *Thankfully, it has stopped raining.*

thankless *ADJECTIVE* not likely to win thanks from people • *a thankless task.*

thanks *PLURAL NOUN* **1** statements of gratitude. **2** (*informal*) thank you.
- **thanks to** as a result of; because of • *Thanks to you, we succeeded.*

thanksgiving *NOUN* an expression of gratitude, especially to God.

that *ADJECTIVE & PRONOUN* **those** the one there • *That book is mine. Whose is that?*

that *ADVERB* to such an extent • *I'll come that far but no further.*

that *RELATIVE PRONOUN* which, who, or whom • *This is the record that I wanted. We liked the people that we met on holiday.*

that *CONJUNCTION* used to introduce a wish, reason, result, etc. • *I hope that you are well. The puzzle was so hard that no one could solve it.* [from Old English]

thatch *NOUN* straw or reeds used to make a roof.

thatch *VERB* **thatches, thatching, thatched** make a roof with thatch.
▷ **thatcher** *noun*
[from Old English]

thaw *VERB* **thaws, thawing, thawed** melt; stop being frozen.

thaw *NOUN* **thaws** a period of warm weather that thaws ice and snow. [from Old English]

the *ADJECTIVE* (called the *definite article*) a particular one; that or those. [from Old English]

theatre *NOUN* **theatres 1** a building where plays etc. are performed to an audience. **2** the writing, acting, and producing of plays. **3** a special room where surgical operations are done • *the operating theatre.* [from Greek *theatron* = place for seeing things]

theatrical *ADJECTIVE* **1** to do with plays or acting. **2** (said about a person's behaviour) exaggerated and done for showy effect.
▷ **theatrically** *adverb*

theatricals *PLURAL NOUN* performances of plays etc.

thee *PRONOUN* (*old use*) you (referring to one person and used as the object of a verb or after a preposition). [from Old English]

theft *NOUN* **thefts** stealing. [from Old English]

their *ADJECTIVE* **1** belonging to them • *Their coats are over there.* **2** (*informal*) belonging to a person • *Somebody has left their coat on the bus.* [from Old Norse]
USAGE Do not confuse with **there**.

theirs *POSSESSIVE PRONOUN* belonging to them • *These coats are theirs.*
USAGE It is incorrect to write *their's*.

them *PRONOUN* the form of *they* used as the object of a verb or after a preposition • *We saw them.* [from Old Norse]

theme *NOUN* **themes 1** the subject about which a person speaks, writes, or thinks. **2** a melody.
[from Greek]

theme park *NOUN* **theme parks** an amusement park where the rides and attractions are based on a particular subject.

theme tune *NOUN* **theme tunes** a special tune always used to announce a particular programme, performer, etc.

themselves *PRONOUN* they or them and nobody else. (COMPARE **herself**)

then *ADVERB* **1** at that time • *We were younger then.* **2** after that; next • *Make the tea, then pour it out.* **3** in that case • *If this is yours, then this must be mine.*
[from Old English]

thence *ADVERB* from that place.
[from Old English]

theology *NOUN* the study of religion.
▷ **theological** *adjective* **theologian** *noun*
[from Greek *theos* = a god, + *-logy*]

theorem *NOUN* **theorems** a mathematical statement that can be proved by reasoning.
[from Greek *theorema* = theory]

theoretical *ADJECTIVE* based on theory not on practice or experience.
▷ **theoretically** *adverb*

theorize *VERB* **theorizes**, **theorizing**, **theorized** form a theory or theories.

theory *NOUN* **theories 1** an idea or set of ideas put forward to explain something • *Darwin's theory of evolution.* **2** the principles of a subject rather than its practice.
- **in theory** according to what should happen rather than what may in fact happen.
▷ **theorist** *noun*
[from Greek *theoria* = thinking about, considering]

therapeutic (*say* therra-pew-tik) *ADJECTIVE* treating or curing a disease etc. • *Sunshine can have a therapeutic effect.*

therapy *NOUN* **therapies** a way of treating a physical or mental illness, especially without using surgery or artificial medicines.
▷ **therapist** *noun*
[from Greek *therapeia* = healing]

there *ADVERB* **1** in or to that place etc. **2** used to call attention to something (*There's a good boy!*) or to introduce a sentence where the verb comes before its subject (*There was plenty to eat*).
[from Old English]
USAGE Do not confuse with **their**.

thereabouts *ADVERB* near there.

thereafter *ADVERB* from then or there onwards.

thereby *ADVERB* by that means; because of that.

therefore *ADVERB* for that reason.
[from *there* + *fore*]

therm *NOUN* **therms** a unit for measuring heat, especially from gas.
[from Greek *therme* = heat]

thermal *ADJECTIVE* **1** to do with heat; worked by heat. **2** hot • *thermal springs.*
[same origin as *therm*]

thermo- *PREFIX* heat.
[same origin as *therm*]

thermodynamics *NOUN* the science dealing with the relation between heat and other forms of energy.

thermometer *NOUN* **thermometers** a device for measuring temperature.

Thermos *NOUN* **Thermoses** (*trademark*) a kind of vacuum flask.
[from Greek *thermos* = hot]

thermostat *NOUN* **thermostats** a piece of equipment that automatically keeps the temperature of a room or piece of equipment steady.
▷ **thermostatic** *adjective* **thermostatically** *adverb*
[from *thermo-* + Greek *statos* = standing]

thesaurus (*say* thi-sor-us) *NOUN* **thesauruses** or **thesauri** a kind of dictionary containing sets of words grouped according to their meaning.
[from Greek *thesauros* = storehouse, treasury]

these *plural* of **this**.

thesis *NOUN* **theses 1** a theory put forward. **2** a long essay written by a candidate for a university degree.
[Greek, = placing]

thews *PLURAL NOUN* (*literary*) muscles; muscular strength.
[from Old English]

they *PRONOUN* **1** the people or things being talked about. **2** people in general • *They say the show is a great success.* **3** (*informal*) he or she; a person • *I am never angry with anyone unless they deserve it.*
[from Old Norse]

they're (*mainly spoken*) they are.
USAGE Do not confuse with **their** and **there**.

thick *ADJECTIVE* **1** measuring a lot between its opposite surfaces. **2** measuring from one side to the other • *The wall is ten centimetres thick.* **3** (said about a line) broad, not fine. **4** crowded with things; dense • *a thick forest; thick fog.* **5** fairly stiff, not flowing easily • *thick cream.* **6** (*informal*) stupid.
▷ **thickly** *adverb* **thickness** *noun*
[from Old English]

thicken *VERB* **thickens, thickening, thickened** make or become thicker.

thicket *NOUN* **thickets** a number of shrubs and small trees etc. growing close together.
[from Old English]

thickset *ADJECTIVE* **1** having a stocky or burly body. **2** with parts placed or growing close together.

thief *NOUN* **thieves** a person who steals things.
▷ **thievish** *adjective* **thievery** *noun* **thieving** *noun*
[from Old English]

thigh *NOUN* **thighs** the part of the leg between the hip and the knee.
[from Old English]

thimble *NOUN* **thimbles** a small metal or plastic cap worn on the end of the finger to push the needle in sewing.
[from Old English]

thin *ADJECTIVE* **thinner, thinnest 1** not thick; not fat. **2** feeble • *a thin excuse.*
▷ **thinly** *adverb* **thinness** *noun*

thin *VERB* **thins, thinning, thinned** make or become less thick.
▷ **thinner** *noun*
thin out make or become less dense or crowded.
[from Old English]

thine *ADJECTIVE & POSSESSIVE PRONOUN* (*old use*) yours (referring to one person).
[from Old English]

thing *NOUN* **things** an object; something which can be seen, touched, thought about, etc.
[from Old English]

things *PLURAL NOUN* **1** personal belongings • *Can I leave my things here?*
2 circumstances • *Things are looking good.*

think *VERB* **thinks, thinking, thought**
1 use your mind; form connected ideas.
2 have as an idea or opinion • *Do you think we have enough time?* **3** intend or plan • *I'm thinking of buying a guitar.*
▷ **think** *noun* **thinker** *noun*
[from Old English]

third *ADJECTIVE* next after the second.
▷ **thirdly** *adverb*

third *NOUN* **thirds 1** the third person or thing. **2** one of three equal parts of something.
[from Old English]

Third World *NOUN* the poorest and underdeveloped countries of Asia, Africa, and South America.
[originally called 'third' because they were not considered to be politically connected with the USA and its allies (the *First World*) or with the Communist countries led by Russia (the *Second World*)]

thirst *NOUN* **1** a feeling of dryness in the mouth and throat, causing a desire to drink.
2 a strong desire • *a thirst for adventure.*
▷ **thirsty** *adjective* **thirstily** *adverb*

thirst *VERB* **thirsts, thirsting, thirsted** have a strong desire for something.
[from Old English]

thirteen *NOUN & ADJECTIVE* the number 13.
▷ **thirteenth** *adjective & noun*
[from Old English]

thirty *NOUN* **thirties** *ADJECTIVE* the number 30.
▷ **thirtieth** *adjective & noun*
[from Old English]

this *ADJECTIVE & PRONOUN* **these** the one here • *This house is ours. Whose is this?*

this *ADVERB* to such an extent • *I'm surprised he got this far.*
[from Old English]

thistle *NOUN* **thistles** a prickly wild plant with purple, white, or yellow flowers.
[from Old English]

thistledown *NOUN* the very light fluff on thistle seeds.

thither *ADVERB* (*old use*) to that place.
[from Old English]

thong *NOUN* **thongs** a narrow strip of leather etc. used for fastening things.
[from Old English]

thorax *NOUN* **thoraxes** the part of the body between the head or neck and the abdomen.
▷ **thoracic** *adjective*
[Greek, = breastplate]

thorn *NOUN* **thorns 1** a small pointed growth on the stem of a plant. **2** a thorny tree or shrub.
[from Old English]

thorny *ADJECTIVE* **thornier, thorniest**
1 having many thorns; prickly. **2** difficult • *a thorny problem.*

thorough *ADJECTIVE* **1** done or doing things carefully and in detail. **2** complete in every way • *a thorough mess.*
▷ **thoroughly** *adverb* **thoroughness** *noun*
[a different spelling of *through*]

thoroughbred *ADJECTIVE* bred of pure or pedigree stock.
▷ **thoroughbred** *noun*

thoroughfare *NOUN* **thoroughfares** a public road or path that is open at both ends.
[from an old sense of *thorough* = through, + *fare* = to progress]

those *plural* of **that**.

thou *PRONOUN* (*old use*) you (referring to one person).
[from Old English]

though *CONJUNCTION* in spite of the fact that; even if • *We can try phoning her, though she may already have left.*

though *ADVERB* however • *She's right, though.*
[from Old English]

thought[1] *NOUN* **thoughts 1** something that you think; an idea or opinion. **2** the process of thinking • *She was deep in thought.*
[from Old English; related to *think*]

thought[2] *past tense* of **think**.

thoughtful *ADJECTIVE* **1** thinking a lot.
2 showing thought for other people's needs; considerate.
▷ **thoughtfully** *adverb* **thoughtfulness** *noun*

thoughtless *ADJECTIVE* **1** careless; not thinking of what may happen.
2 inconsiderate.
▷ **thoughtlessly** *adverb*
thoughtlessness *noun*

thousand *NOUN* **thousands** *ADJECTIVE* the number 1,000.
▷ **thousandth** *adjective & noun*
[from Old English]
USAGE Say *a few thousand* (not 'a few thousands').

thrall *NOUN*
- **in thrall to somebody** in his or her power; in a state of slavery.
[from Old Norse]

thrash *VERB* **thrashes, thrashing, thrashed 1** beat someone with a stick or whip; keep hitting very hard. **2** defeat someone thoroughly. **3** move violently • *The crocodile thrashed its tail.*
- **thrash something out** discuss a matter thoroughly.
[a different spelling of *thresh*]

thread *NOUN* **threads 1** a thin length of any substance. **2** a length of spun cotton, wool, or nylon etc. used for making cloth or in sewing or knitting. **3** the spiral ridge round a screw. **4** a theme or idea running through a story, argument, etc. • *I'm afraid I've lost the thread.*

thread *VERB* **threads, threading, threaded 1** put a thread through the eye of a needle. **2** pass a strip of film etc. through or round something. **3** put beads on a thread.
[from Old English]

threadbare *ADJECTIVE* (said about cloth) with the surface worn away so that the threads show.

threat *NOUN* **threats 1** a warning that you will punish, hurt, or harm a person or thing. **2** a sign of something undesirable. **3** a person or thing causing danger.
[from Old English]

threaten *VERB* **threatens, threatening, threatened 1** make threats against someone. **2** be a threat or danger to a person or thing.

three *NOUN* **threes** *ADJECTIVE* the number 3.
[from Old English]

three-dimensional *ADJECTIVE* having three dimensions (length, width, and height or depth).

thresh *VERB* **threshes, threshing, threshed** beat corn in order to separate the grain from the husks.
[from Old English]

threshold *NOUN* **thresholds 1** a slab of stone or board etc. forming the bottom of a doorway; the entrance. **2** the point at which something begins to happen or change • *We are on the threshold of a great discovery.*
[from Old English]

thrice *ADVERB* (*old use*) three times.
[from Old English]

thrift *NOUN* **1** careful spending or management of money or resources. **2** a plant with pink flowers.
▷ **thrifty** *adjective* **thriftily** *adverb*
[Old Norse, = thriving]

thrill *NOUN* **thrills** a feeling of excitement.

thrill *VERB* **thrills, thrilling, thrilled** have or give a feeling of excitement.
▷ **thrilling** *adjective*
[from Old English]

thriller *NOUN* **thrillers** an exciting story, play, or film, usually about crime.

thrive *VERB* **thrives, thriving, throve, thrived** or **thriven** grow strongly; prosper or be successful.
[from Old Norse]

throat *NOUN* **throats 1** the tube in the neck that takes food and drink down into the body. **2** the front of the neck.
[from Old English]

throaty *ADJECTIVE* **1** produced deep in the throat • *a throaty chuckle.* **2** hoarse.
▷ **throatily** *adverb*

throb *VERB* **throbs, throbbing, throbbed** beat or vibrate with a strong rhythm • *My heart throbbed.*
▷ **throb** *noun*
[imitating the sound]

throes *PLURAL NOUN* severe pangs of pain.
- **in the throes of** struggling with • *We are in the throes of exams.*
[origin unknown]

thrombosis *NOUN* the formation of a clot of blood in the body.
[from Greek *thrombos* = lump]

throne *NOUN* **thrones 1** a special chair for a king, queen, or bishop at ceremonies. **2** the position of being king or queen • *the heir to the throne.*
[from Greek *thronos* = high seat]

throng *NOUN* **throngs** a crowd of people.

throng *VERB* **throngs, thronging, thronged** crowd • *People thronged the streets.*
[from Old English]

throstle *NOUN* **throstles** (*poetical use*) a thrush.
[from Old English]

throttle *NOUN* **throttles** a device that controls the flow of fuel to an engine; an accelerator.

throttle *VERB* **throttles, throttling, throttled** strangle.
- **throttle back** or **down** reduce the speed of an engine by partially closing the throttle.
[from *throat*]

through *PREPOSITION* **1** from one end or side to the other end or side of • *Climb through the window.* **2** by means of; because of • *We lost it through carelessness.* **3** at the end of; having finished successfully • *He is through his exam.*

through *ADVERB* **1** through something • *We squeezed through.* **2** with a telephone connection made • *I'll put you through to the president.* **3** finished • *Wait till I'm through with these papers.*

through *ADJECTIVE* **1** going through something • *No through road.* **2** going all the way to a destination • *a through train.*
[from Old English]

throughout *PREPOSITION* & *ADVERB* all the way through; from beginning to end.

A B C D E F G H I J K L M N O P Q R S T U V W X Y Z

throve *past tense* of **thrive**.

throw *VERB* **throws, throwing, threw, thrown** **1** send a person or thing through the air. **2** put something in a place carelessly or hastily. **3** move part of your body quickly • *He threw his head back and laughed.* **4** put someone in a certain condition etc. • *It threw us into confusion.* **5** confuse or upset • *Your question threw me.* **6** move a switch or lever in order to operate it. **7** shape a pot on a potter's wheel. **8** hold a party.
▷ **throw** *noun* **thrower** *noun*
- **throw away** **1** get rid of something because it is useless or unwanted. **2** waste • *You threw away an opportunity.*
- **throw up** (*informal*) vomit.
- **throw yourself into** start doing something with energy or enthusiasm.
[from Old English]

thrum *VERB* **thrums, thrumming, thrummed** sound monotonously; strum.
▷ **thrum** *noun*
[imitating the sound]

thrush[1] *NOUN* **thrushes** a songbird with a speckled breast.
[from Old English]

thrush[2] *NOUN* an infection causing tiny white patches in the mouth and throat.
[origin unknown]

thrust *VERB* **thrusts, thrusting, thrust** push hard.
▷ **thrust** *noun*
[from Old Norse]

thud *VERB* **thuds, thudding, thudded** make the dull sound of a heavy knock or fall.
▷ **thud** *noun*
[originally Scots; probably from Old English]

thug *NOUN* **thugs** a rough and violent person.
▷ **thuggery** *noun*
[from Hindi: the *Thugs* were robbers and murderers in India in the 17th-19th centuries]

thumb *NOUN* **thumbs** the short thick finger set apart from the other four.
- **be under a person's thumb** be completely under his or her influence.

thumb *VERB* **thumbs, thumbing, thumbed** turn the pages of a book etc. quickly with your thumb.
- **thumb a lift** hitch-hike.
[from Old English]

thumbnail *ADJECTIVE* brief, giving only the main facts • *a thumbnail sketch.*

thumbscrew *NOUN* **thumbscrews** a former instrument of torture for squeezing the thumb.

thump *VERB* **thumps, thumping, thumped** **1** hit or knock something heavily. **2** punch. **3** thud. **4** throb or beat strongly • *My heart was thumping.*
▷ **thump** *noun*
[imitating the sound]

thumbtack *NOUN* **thumbtacks** (*American*) a drawing pin.

thunder *NOUN* **1** the loud noise that is heard with lightning. **2** a similar noise • *a thunder of applause.*
▷ **thundery** *adjective*

thunder *VERB* **thunders, thundering, thundered** **1** sound with thunder. **2** make a noise like thunder; speak loudly.
[from Old English]

thunderbolt *NOUN* **thunderbolts** a lightning flash thought of as a destructive missile.

thunderous *ADJECTIVE* extremely loud • *thunderous applause.*

thunderstorm *NOUN* **thunderstorms** a storm with thunder and lightning.

thunderstruck *ADJECTIVE* amazed.

Thursday *NOUN* the day of the week following Wednesday.
[from Old English *thuresdaeg* = day of thunder, named after Thor, the Norse god of thunder]

thus *ADVERB* **1** in this way • *Hold the wheel thus.* **2** therefore.
[from Old English]

thwart *VERB* **thwarts, thwarting, thwarted** frustrate; prevent someone from achieving something.
[from Old Norse]

thy *ADJECTIVE* (*old use*) your (referring to one person).
[from *thine*]

thyme (*say as* time) *NOUN* a herb with fragrant leaves.
[from Greek]

thyroid gland *NOUN* **thyroid glands** a large gland at the front of the neck.
[from Greek *thyreos* = a shield (because of the shape of the gland)]

thyself *PRONOUN* (*old use*) yourself. (COMPARE **herself**)

tiara (*say* tee-ar-a) *NOUN* **tiaras** a woman's jewelled crescent-shaped ornament worn like a crown.
[from Greek]

tic *NOUN* **tics** an unintentional twitch of a muscle, especially of the face.
[via French from Italian]

tick[1] *NOUN* **ticks 1** a mark (✔) put by something to show that it is correct or has been checked. **2** a regular clicking sound, especially that made by a clock or watch. **3** (*informal*) a moment • *I won't be a tick.*

tick *VERB* **ticks, ticking, ticked 1** put a tick by something. **2** make the sound of a tick.
- **tick off** (*informal*) reprimand someone.
[probably from old German or old Dutch]

tick[2] *NOUN* **ticks** a bloodsucking insect.
[from Old English]

ticket *NOUN* **tickets 1** a printed piece of paper or card that allows a person to travel on a bus or train, see a show, etc. **2** a label showing a thing's price.
[via French from old Dutch]

tickle *VERB* **tickles, tickling, tickled 1** touch a person's skin lightly in order to produce a slight tingling feeling and laughter. **2** (said about a part of the body) have a slight tingling or itching feeling. **3** amuse or please somebody.
[origin unknown]

ticklish *ADJECTIVE* **1** likely to laugh or wriggle when tickled. **2** awkward or difficult • *a ticklish situation.*

tidal *ADJECTIVE* to do with or affected by tides.

tidal wave *NOUN* **tidal waves** a huge sea wave.

tiddler *NOUN* **tiddlers** (*informal*) a very small fish.
[origin unknown]

tiddlywink *NOUN* **tiddlywinks** a small counter flicked into a cup by pressing with another counter in the game of **tiddlywinks**.
[origin unknown]

tide *NOUN* **tides 1** the regular rise and fall in the level of the sea, which usually happens twice a day. **2** (*old use*) a time or season • *Christmas-tide.*

tide *VERB* **tides, tiding, tided**
- **tide a person over** provide him or her with what is needed, for a short time.
[from Old English]

tidings *PLURAL NOUN* (*formal*) news.
[probably from Old Norse]

tidy *ADJECTIVE* **tidier, tidiest 1** with everything in its right place; neat and orderly. **2** (*informal*) fairly large • *It costs a tidy sum.*
▷ **tidily** *adverb* **tidiness** *noun*

tidy *VERB* **tidies, tidying, tidied** make a place tidy.
▷ **tidy** *noun*
[originally = at the right time or season: from *tide*]

tie *VERB* **ties, tying, tied 1** fasten something with string, ribbon, etc. **2** arrange something into a knot or bow. **3** make the same score as another competitor.
- **be tied up** be busy.

tie *NOUN* **ties 1** a strip of material worn passing under the collar of a shirt and knotted in front. **2** a result when two or more competitors have equal scores. **3** one of the matches in a competition. **4** a close connection or bond • *the ties of friendship.*
[from Old English]

tie-break or **tie-breaker** *NOUN* **tie-breaks** or **tie-breakers** a way to decide the winner when competitors have tied, especially an additional question in a quiz or an additional game at the end of a set in tennis.

tier (*say* teer) *NOUN* **tiers** each of a series of rows or levels etc. placed one above the other.
▷ **tiered** *adjective*
[from French *tire* = *rank*[1]]

tiff *NOUN* **tiffs** a slight quarrel.
[origin unknown]

A B C D E F G H I J K L M N O P Q R S T U V W X Y Z

tiger *NOUN* **tigers** a large wild animal of the cat family, with yellow and black stripes.
[from Greek]

tight *ADJECTIVE* **1** fitting very closely. **2** firmly fastened. **3** fully stretched; tense. **4** in short supply • *Money is tight at the moment.*
5 stingy • *He is very tight with his money.*
6 severe or strict • *tight security.* **7** (*informal*) drunk.
▷ **tightly** *adverb* **tightness** *noun*

tight *ADVERB* tightly or firmly • *Please hold tight.*
[probably from Old English]

tighten *VERB* **tightens**, **tightening**, **tightened** make or become tighter.

tightrope *NOUN* **tightropes** a tightly stretched rope high above the ground, on which acrobats perform.

tights *PLURAL NOUN* a piece of clothing that fits tightly over the feet, legs, and lower part of the body.

tigress *NOUN* **tigresses** a female tiger.

tile *NOUN* **tiles** a thin square piece of baked clay or other hard material, used in rows for covering roofs, walls, or floors.
▷ **tiled** *adjective*
[via Old English from Latin]

till[1] *PREPOSITION & CONJUNCTION* until.
[from Old English *til* = to]
USAGE It is better to use *until* rather than *till* when the word stands first in a sentence (e.g. *Until last year we had never been abroad*) or when you are speaking or writing formally.

till[2] *NOUN* **tills** a drawer or box for money in a shop; a cash register.
[origin unknown]

till[3] *VERB* **tills**, **tilling**, **tilled** plough land to prepare it for cultivating.
[from Old English *tilian* = try]

tiller *NOUN* **tillers** a handle used to turn a boat's rudder.
[from old French]

tilt *VERB* **tilts**, **tilting**, **tilted** move into a sloping position.

tilt *NOUN* a sloping position.
- **at full tilt** at full speed or force.
[origin unknown]

timber *NOUN* **timbers 1** wood for building or making things. **2** a wooden beam.
[from Old English]

timbered *ADJECTIVE* made of wood or with a wooden framework • *timbered houses.*

timbre (*say* tambr) *NOUN* **timbres** the quality of a voice or musical sound.
[French; related to *timpani*]

time *NOUN* **times 1** all the years of the past, present, and future; the continuous existence of the universe. **2** a particular point or portion of time. **3** an occasion • *the first time I saw him.* **4** a period suitable or available for something • *Is there time for a cup of tea?* **5** a system of measuring time • *Greenwich Mean Time.* **6** (*in music*) rhythm depending on the number and stress of beats in the bar.
- **at times** or
- **from time to time** sometimes; occasionally.
- **in time 1** not late. **2** eventually.
- **on time** punctual.

time *VERB* **times**, **timing**, **timed 1** measure how long something takes. **2** arrange when something is to happen.
[from Old English]

timeless *ADJECTIVE* not affected by the passage of time; eternal.

time limit *NOUN* **time limits** a fixed amount of time within which something must be done.

timely *ADJECTIVE* happening at a suitable or useful time • *a timely warning.*

timer *NOUN* **timers** a device for timing things.

times *PLURAL NOUN* (*in mathematics*) multiplied by • *Five times three is 15* (5 x 3 = 15).

time scale *NOUN* **time scales** the length of time that something takes or that you need in order to do something.

timetable *NOUN* **timetables** a list showing the times when things will happen, e.g. when buses or trains will arrive and depart, or when school lessons will take place.

timid *ADJECTIVE* easily frightened.
▷ **timidly** *adverb* **timidity** *noun*
[from Latin *timidus* = nervous]

timing *NOUN* **1** the choice of time to do something. **2** the time when something happens.

timorous *ADJECTIVE* timid.
[from Latin *timor* = fear]

timpani *PLURAL NOUN* kettledrums.
[Italian]

tin *NOUN* **tins 1** a silvery-white metal. **2** a metal container for food.

tin *VERB* **tins, tinning, tinned** seal food in a tin to preserve it.
[from Old English]

tincture *NOUN* **tinctures 1** a solution of medicine in alcohol. **2** a slight trace of something.
[from Latin *tinctura* = dyeing]

tinder *NOUN* any dry substance that catches fire easily.
[from Old English]

tine *NOUN* **tines** a point or prong of a fork, comb, or antler.
[from Old English]

tinge *VERB* **tinges, tingeing, tinged**
1 colour something slightly. **2** add a slight amount of another feeling • *Our relief was tinged with sadness.*
▷ **tinge** *noun*
[same origin as *tint*]

tingle *VERB* **tingles, tingling, tingled** have a slight pricking or stinging feeling.
▷ **tingle** *noun*
[probably from *tinkle*]

tinker *NOUN* **tinkers** (*old use*) a person travelling about to mend pots and pans etc.

tinker *VERB* **tinkers, tinkering, tinkered** work at something casually, trying to improve or mend it.
[origin unknown]

tinkle *VERB* **tinkles, tinkling, tinkled** make a gentle ringing sound.
▷ **tinkle** *noun*
[imitating the sound]

tinny *ADJECTIVE* **1** like tin. **2** (said about a sound) unpleasantly thin and high-pitched.

tinsel *NOUN* strips of glittering material used for decoration.
[from old French; related to *scintillate*]

tint *NOUN* **tints** a shade of colour, especially a pale one.

tint *VERB* **tints, tinting, tinted** colour something slightly.
[from Latin *tingere* = to dye or stain]

tiny *ADJECTIVE* **tinier, tiniest** very small.
[origin unknown]

-tion *SUFFIX*, SEE **-ion**.

tip[1] *NOUN* **tips** the part right at the top or end of something.

tip *VERB* **tips, tipping, tipped** put a tip on something.
[from Old Norse]

tip[2] *NOUN* **tips 1** a small present of money given to someone who has helped you. **2** a small but useful piece of advice; a hint. **3** a slight push.

tip *VERB* **tips, tipping, tipped 1** give a person a tip. **2** name someone as a likely winner • *Which team would you tip to win the championship?*
▷ **tipper** *noun*
- **tip off** give a warning or special information about something. **tip-off** *noun*
[probably from *tip*[1]]

tip[3] *VERB* **tips, tipping, tipped 1** tilt or topple. **2** empty rubbish somewhere.

tip *NOUN* **tips 1** the action of tipping something. **2** a place where rubbish etc. is tipped.
[probably from a Scandinavian language]

tipple *VERB* **tipples, tippling, tippled** drink alcohol.
▷ **tipple** *noun* **tippler** *noun*
[origin unknown]

tipsy *ADJECTIVE* slightly drunk.
[from *tip*[3]]

tiptoe *VERB* **tiptoes, tiptoeing, tiptoed** walk on your toes very quietly or carefully.
- **on tiptoe** walking or standing on your toes.

tiptop *ADJECTIVE* (*informal*) excellent; very best • *in tiptop condition.*
[from *tip*[1] + *top*[1]]

tirade (*say* ty-rayd) *NOUN* **tirades** a long angry or violent speech.
[via French from Italian]

tire *VERB* **tires, tiring, tired** make or become tired.
▷ **tiring** *adjective*
[from Old English]

A B C D E F G H I J K L M N O P Q R S T U V W X Y Z

tired *ADJECTIVE* feeling that you need to sleep or rest.
- **be tired of** have had enough of something • *I'm tired of waiting.*

tireless *ADJECTIVE* having a lot of energy; not tiring easily.

tiresome *ADJECTIVE* annoying.

tiro *NOUN* **tiros** a beginner.
[Latin, = recruit]

tissue *NOUN* **tissues 1** tissue paper. **2** a paper handkerchief. **3** the substance forming any part of the body of an animal or plant • *bone tissue.*
[from old French; related to *textiles*]

tissue paper *NOUN* very thin soft paper used for wrapping and packing things.

tit[1] *NOUN* **tits** a kind of small bird.
[probably from a Scandinavian language]

tit[2] *NOUN*
- **tit for tat** something equal given in return; retaliation.
[originally 'tip for tap': from *tip*[2] + *tap*[2]]

titanic (*say* ty-**tan**-ik) *ADJECTIVE* huge.
[from the *Titans*, gigantic gods and goddesses in Greek legend]

titanium *NOUN* a strong silver-grey metal used to make light alloys that do not corrode easily.

titbit *NOUN* **titbits** a nice little piece of something, e.g. of food, gossip, or information.
[from a dialect word *tid* = tender, + *bit*[1]]

tithe *NOUN* **tithes** one-tenth of a year's output from a farm etc., formerly paid as tax to support the clergy and church.
[from Old English *teotha* = tenth]

titillate *VERB* **titillates, titillating, titillated** stimulate or excite you pleasantly.
▷ **titillation** *noun*
[from Latin *titillare* = to tickle]

titivate *VERB* **titivates, titivating, titivated** put the finishing touches to something; smarten up.
▷ **titivation** *noun*
[origin unknown]

title *NOUN* **titles 1** the name of a book, film, song, etc. **2** a word used to show a person's rank or position, e.g. *Dr, Lord, Mrs.* **3** a championship in sport • *the world heavyweight title.* **4** a legal right to something.
[from Latin]

titled *ADJECTIVE* having a title as a noble.

titter *VERB* **titters, tittering, tittered** giggle.
▷ **titter** *noun*
[imitating the sound]

tittle-tattle *NOUN* gossip.
[from *tattle*]

TNT *ABBREVIATION* trinitrotoluene; a powerful explosive.

to *PREPOSITION* This word is used to show **1** direction or arrival at a position (*We walked to school. He rose to power*), **2** limit (*from noon to two o'clock*), **3** comparison (*We won by six goals to three*), **4** receiving or being affected by something (*Give it to me. Be kind to animals*).
Also used before a verb to form an infinitive (*I want to see him*) or to show purpose etc. (*He does that to annoy us*), or alone when the verb is understood (*We meant to go but forgot to*).

to *ADVERB* **1** to or in the proper or closed position or condition • *Push the door to.* **2** into a state of activity • *We set to and cleaned the kitchen.*
- **to and fro** backwards and forwards.
[from Old English]

toad *NOUN* **toads** a frog-like animal that lives mainly on land.
[from Old English]

toad-in-the-hole *NOUN* sausages baked in batter.

toadstool *NOUN* **toadstools** a fungus (usually poisonous) with a round top on a stalk.

toady *VERB* **toadies, toadying, toadied** flatter someone to make them want to help you.
▷ **toady** *noun*
[short for *toad-eater*]

toast *VERB* **toasts, toasting, toasted 1** heat bread etc. to make it brown and crisp. **2** warm something in front of a fire etc. **3** drink in honour of someone.

toast *NOUN* **toasts 1** toasted bread. **2** the call to drink in honour of someone; the person honoured in this way.
[from Latin *tostum* = dried up]

toaster *NOUN* **toasters** an electrical device for toasting bread.

tobacco *NOUN* the dried leaves of certain plants prepared for smoking in cigarettes, cigars, or pipes or for making snuff.
[via Spanish from a Central American language]

tobacconist *NOUN* **tobacconists** a shopkeeper who sells cigarettes, cigars, etc.

toboggan *NOUN* **toboggans** a small sledge used for sliding downhill.
▷ **tobogganing** *noun*
[via Canadian French from a Native American language]

tocsin *NOUN* **tocsins** (*old use*) a bell rung as an alarm signal.
[from old French]

today *NOUN* this present day • *Today is Monday.*

today *ADVERB* on this day • *Have you seen him today?*
[from *to* (preposition) + *day*]

toddler *NOUN* **toddlers** a young child who has only recently learnt to walk.
▷ **toddle** *verb*
[origin unknown]

toddy *NOUN* **toddies** a sweetened drink made with spirits and hot water.
[from Sanskrit *tadi*, a tree whose sugary sap was made into an alcoholic drink]

to-do *NOUN* **to-dos** a fuss or commotion.

toe *NOUN* **toes 1** any of the separate parts (five in humans) at the end of each foot. **2** the part of a shoe or sock etc. that covers the toes.
- **on your toes** alert.
[from Old English]

toffee *NOUN* **toffees** a sticky sweet made from heated butter and sugar.
[origin unknown]

toga (*say* toh-ga) *NOUN* **togas** a long loose piece of clothing worn by men in ancient Rome.
[Latin, from *tegere* = to cover]

together *ADVERB* with another person or thing; with each other • *They went to the party together.*
[from Old English]

toggle *NOUN* **toggles** a short piece of wood or metal etc. used like a button.
[originally a sailors' word; origin unknown]

toil *VERB* **toils, toiling, toiled 1** work hard. **2** move slowly and with difficulty.
▷ **toiler** *noun*

toil *NOUN* hard work.
[from old French]

toilet *NOUN* **toilets 1** a bowl-like object, connected by pipes to a drain, which you use to get rid of urine and faeces. **2** a room containing a toilet. **3** the process of washing, dressing, and tidying yourself.
[from French]

toilet paper *NOUN* paper for use in a toilet.

token *NOUN* **tokens 1** a piece of metal or plastic that can be used instead of money. **2** a voucher or coupon that can be exchanged for goods. **3** a sign or signal of something • *a token of our friendship.*
[from Old English]

tolerable *ADJECTIVE* able to be tolerated.
▷ **tolerably** *adverb*

tolerant *ADJECTIVE* willing to accept or tolerate other people's behaviour and opinions even if you do not agree with them.
▷ **tolerantly** *adverb* **tolerance** *noun*

tolerate *VERB* **tolerates, tolerating, tolerated 1** allow something even if you do not approve of it. **2** bear or put up with something unpleasant.
▷ **toleration** *noun*
[from Latin *tolerare* = endure]

toll[1] (*rhymes with* **hole**) *NOUN* **tolls 1** a charge made for using a road, bridge, etc. **2** loss or damage caused • *The death toll in the earthquake is rising.*
[via Old English and Latin from Greek *telos* = a tax]

toll[2] (*rhymes with* **hole**) *VERB* **tolls, tolling, tolled** ring a bell slowly.
▷ **toll** *noun*
[probably from Old English]

tom *NOUN* **toms** a male cat.
▷ **tomcat** *noun*
[short for *Thomas*]

tomahawk *NOUN* **tomahawks** a small axe used by Native Americans.
[from Algonquin, a Native American language]

tomato *NOUN* **tomatoes** a soft round red or yellow fruit eaten as a vegetable.
[via French, Spanish, or Portuguese from Nahuatl (a Central American language)]

tomb (*say* toom) *NOUN* **tombs** a place where someone is buried; a monument built over this.
[from Greek]

tombola *NOUN* a kind of lottery.
[from Italian *tombolare* = tumble (because often the tickets are drawn from a revolving drum)]

tomboy *NOUN* **tomboys** a girl who enjoys rough noisy games etc.
[from *tom* (short for *Thomas*) + *boy*]

tombstone *NOUN* **tombstones** a memorial stone set up over a grave.

tome *NOUN* **tomes** a large heavy book.
[from Greek *tomos* = roll of papyrus]

tommy gun *NOUN* **tommy guns** a small machine gun.
[from the name of its American inventor, J. T. *Thompson* (died 1940)]

tomorrow *NOUN* & *ADVERB* the day after today.
[from *to* (preposition) + *morrow*]

tom-tom *NOUN* **tom-toms** a drum beaten with the hands.
[from Hindi *tam tam*, imitating the sound]

ton *NOUN* **tons 1** a unit of weight equal to 2,240 pounds or about 1,016 kilograms. **2** a large amount • *There's tons of room.* **3** (*slang*) a speed of 100 miles per hour.
[a different spelling of *tun*]

tone *NOUN* **tones 1** a sound in music or of the voice. **2** each of the five larger intervals between notes in a musical scale (the smaller intervals are *semitones*). **3** a shade of a colour. **4** the quality or character of something • *a cheerful tone.*
▷ **tonal** *adjective* **tonally** *adverb*

tone *VERB* **tones, toning, toned 1** give a particular tone or quality to something. **2** be harmonious in colour.
- **tone down** make a thing quieter or less bright or less harsh.
[from Greek *tonos* = tension]

tone-deaf *ADJECTIVE* not able to tell the difference between different musical notes.

tongs *PLURAL NOUN* a tool with two arms joined at one end, used to pick up or hold things.
[from Old English]

tongue *NOUN* **tongues 1** the long soft muscular part that moves about inside the mouth. **2** a language. **3** the leather flap on a shoe or boot underneath the laces. **4** a pointed flame.
[from Old English]

tongue-tied *ADJECTIVE* too shy to speak.

tongue-twister *NOUN* **tongue-twisters** something that is difficult to say quickly and correctly, e.g. 'She sells seashells'.

tonic *NOUN* **tonics 1** a medicine etc. that makes a person healthier or stronger. **2** anything that makes a person more energetic or cheerful. (also **tonic water**) **3** a fizzy mineral water with a bitter taste, often mixed with gin. **4** a keynote in music.
▷ **tonic** *adjective*
[same origin as *tone*]

tonight *NOUN* & *ADVERB* this evening or night.
[from *to* (preposition) + *night*]

tonnage *NOUN* the amount a ship or ships can carry, expressed in tons.

tonne *NOUN* **tonnes** a metric ton (1,000 kilograms).
[French]

tonsil *NOUN* **tonsils** either of two small masses of soft tissue at the sides of the throat.
[from Latin]

tonsillitis *NOUN* inflammation of the tonsils.

too *ADVERB* **1** also • *Take the others too.* **2** more than is wanted or allowed etc. • *That's too much sugar for me.*
[from Old English]

tool *NOUN* **tools 1** a device that helps you to do a particular job • *A saw is a tool for cutting wood or metal.* **2** a thing used for a particular purpose • *An encyclopedia is a useful study tool.*
[from Old English]

toot *NOUN* **toots** a short sound produced by a horn.
▷ **toot** *verb*
[imitating the sound]

tooth *NOUN* **teeth 1** one of the hard white bony parts that are rooted in the gums, used for biting and chewing things. **2** one of a row of sharp parts • *the teeth of a saw.*
▷ **toothache** *noun* **toothbrush** *noun* **toothed** *adjective*
- **fight tooth and nail** fight very fiercely.
[from Old English]

toothpaste *NOUN* **toothpastes** a paste for cleaning your teeth.

toothpick *NOUN* **toothpicks** a small pointed piece of wood etc. for removing bits of food from between your teeth.

toothy *ADJECTIVE* having large teeth.

top[1] *NOUN* **tops 1** the highest part of something. **2** the upper surface. **3** the covering or stopper of a bottle, jar, etc. **4** a piece of clothing for the upper part of the body.
- **on top of** in addition to something.

top *ADJECTIVE* highest • *at top speed.*

top *VERB* **tops, topping, topped 1** put a top on something. **2** be at the top of something • *She tops the list.* **3** remove the top of something.
- **top up** fill up something that is half empty.
[from Old English]

top[2] *NOUN* **tops** a toy that can be made to spin on its point.
[origin unknown]

topaz *NOUN* **topazes** a kind of gem, often yellow.
[from Greek]

top hat *NOUN* **top hats** a man's tall stiff black or grey hat worn with formal clothes.

top-heavy *ADJECTIVE* too heavy at the top and likely to overbalance.

topic *NOUN* **topics** a subject to write, learn, or talk about.
[from Greek *topos* = place]

topical *ADJECTIVE* connected with things that are happening now • *a topical film.*
▷ **topically** *adverb* **topicality** *noun*
[originally = covering a particular place or topic]

topless *ADJECTIVE* not wearing any clothes on the top half of the body.

topmost *ADJECTIVE* highest.

topography (*say* top-og-ra-fee) *NOUN* **topographies** the position of the rivers, mountains, roads, buildings, etc. in a place.
▷ **topographical** *adjective*
[from Greek *topos* = place, + *-graphy*]

topping *NOUN* **toppings** food that is put on the top of a cake, dessert, pizza, etc.

topple *VERB* **topples, toppling, toppled 1** fall over; totter and fall. **2** make something fall; overthrow.
[from *top*[1]]

top secret *ADJECTIVE* extremely secret • *top secret information.*

topsy-turvy *ADVERB & ADJECTIVE* upside down; muddled.
[probably from *top*[1] + Middle English *terve* = turn upside down]

Torah (*say* tor-uh) *NOUN* in Judaism, the law of God as given to Moses and recorded in the first five books of the Bible.
[from Hebrew]

torch *NOUN* **torches 1** a small electric lamp that you can carry in your hand. **2** a stick with burning material on the end, used as a light.
[from old French]

toreador (*say* torree-a-dor) *NOUN* **toreadors** a bullfighter.
[from Spanish *toro* = bull]

torment *VERB* **torments, tormenting, tormented 1** make someone suffer greatly. **2** tease; keep annoying someone.
▷ **tormentor** *noun*

torment *NOUN* **torments** great suffering.
[from old French; related to *torture*]

torn *past participle* of **tear**[2].

tornado (*say* tor-nay-doh) *NOUN* **tornadoes** a violent storm or whirlwind.
[from Spanish *tronada* = thunderstorm]

a b c d e f g h i j k l m n o p q r s t u v w x y z

torpedo *NOUN* **torpedoes** a long tube-shaped missile that can be fired under water to destroy ships.

torpedo *VERB* **torpedoes, torpedoing, torpedoed** attack or destroy a ship with a torpedo.
[Latin, = a large sea fish that can give an electric shock which causes numbness]

torpid *ADJECTIVE* slow-moving, not lively.
▷ **torpidly** *adverb* **torpidity** *noun* **torpor** *noun*
[from Latin *torpidus* = numb]

torrent *NOUN* **torrents 1** a rushing stream; a great flow. **2** a heavy downpour of rain.
[from Latin]

torrential *ADJECTIVE* (said about rain) pouring down violently.

torrid *ADJECTIVE* **1** very hot and dry. **2** passionate • *a torrid love affair.*
[from Latin *torridus* = parched]

torsion *NOUN* twisting, especially of one end of a thing while the other is held in a fixed position.
[French; related to *torture*]

torso *NOUN* **torsos** the trunk of the human body.
[Italian, = stump]

tortoise *NOUN* **tortoises** a slow-moving animal with a shell over its body.
[from Latin]

tortoiseshell (*say* tort-a-shell) *NOUN* **tortoiseshells 1** the mottled brown and yellow shell of certain turtles, used for making combs etc. **2** a cat or butterfly with mottled brown colouring.

tortuous *ADJECTIVE* **1** full of twists and turns • *a tortuous path.* **2** complicated and not easy to follow • *tortuous logic.*
▷ **tortuosity** *noun*
[from Latin *tortum* = twisted]
USAGE Do not confuse with **torturous**.

torture *VERB* **tortures, torturing, tortured** make a person feel great pain or worry.
▷ **torture** *noun* **torturer** *noun*
[same origin as *tortuous*]

torturous *ADJECTIVE* like torture • *a torturous wait for news of survivors.*
USAGE Do not confuse with **tortuous**.

Tory *NOUN* **Tories** a Conservative.
▷ **Tory** *adjective*
[from Irish *toraidhe* = an outlaw]

toss *VERB* **tosses, tossing, tossed 1** throw something, especially up into the air. **2** spin a coin to decide something according to which side of it is upwards after it falls. **3** move restlessly or unevenly from side to side.
▷ **toss** *noun*
[origin unknown]

toss-up *NOUN* **toss-ups 1** the tossing of a coin. **2** an even chance.

tot[1] *NOUN* **tots 1** a small child. **2** (*informal*) a small amount of spirits • *a tot of rum.*
[originally a dialect word]

tot[2] *VERB* **tots, totting, totted**
– **tot up** (*informal*) add up.
[from *total*]

total *ADJECTIVE* **1** including everything • *the total amount.* **2** complete • *total darkness.*
▷ **totally** *adverb*

total *NOUN* **totals** the amount you get by adding everything together.

total *VERB* **totals, totalling, totalled 1** add up the total. **2** amount to something • *The cost of the damage totalled £5,000.*
[from Latin *totum* = the whole]

totalitarian *ADJECTIVE* using a form of government where people are not allowed to form rival political parties.
[from *totality*]

totality *NOUN* the whole of something.

totem pole *NOUN* **totem poles** a pole carved or painted by Native Americans with the symbols (*totems*) of their tribes or families.
[from Ojibwa, a Native American language]

totter *VERB* **totters, tottering, tottered** walk unsteadily; wobble.
▷ **tottery** *adjective*
[from old Dutch]

toucan (*say* too-kan) *NOUN* **toucans** a tropical American bird with a huge beak.
[via French and Portuguese from Tupi (a South American language)]

touch *VERB* **touches, touching, touched** 1 put your hand or fingers on something lightly. 2 be or come together so that there is no space between. 3 come into contact with something or hit it gently. 4 move or meddle with something. 5 reach • *The thermometer touched 30° Celsius.* 6 affect someone's feelings, e.g. by making them feel sympathy • *The sad story touched our hearts.*
▷ **touchable** *adjective*
- **touch and go** uncertain or risky.
- **touch down** 1 (said about an aircraft or spacecraft) land. 2 (in rugby football) touch the ball on the ground behind the goal line.
- **touch on** discuss a subject briefly.
- **touch up** improve something by making small additions or changes.

touch *NOUN* **touches** 1 the action of touching. 2 the ability to feel things by touching them. 3 a small amount; a small thing done • *the finishing touches.* 4 a special skill or style of workmanship • *She hasn't lost her touch.* 5 communication with someone • *We have lost touch with him.* 6 the part of a football field outside the playing area.
[from old French]

touchdown *NOUN* **touchdowns** the action of touching down.

touché (*say* too-shay) *INTERJECTION* used to acknowledge a true or clever point made against you in an argument.
[French, = touched, originally referring to a hit in fencing]

touching *ADJECTIVE* causing you to have kindly feelings such as pity or sympathy.

touchline *NOUN* **touchlines** one of the lines that mark the side of a sports pitch.

touchstone *NOUN* **touchstones** a test by which the quality of something is judged.
[formerly, a kind of stone against which gold and silver were rubbed to test their purity]

touchy *ADJECTIVE* **touchier, touchiest** easily offended.
▷ **touchily** *adverb* **touchiness** *noun*
[origin unknown]

tough *ADJECTIVE* 1 strong; difficult to break or damage. 2 difficult to chew. 3 able to stand hardship; not easily hurt. 4 firm or severe. 5 difficult • *a tough decision.*
▷ **toughly** *adverb* **toughness** *noun*
[from Old English]

toughen *VERB* **toughens, toughening, toughened** make or become tough.

tour *NOUN* **tours** a journey visiting several places.

tour *VERB* **tours, touring, toured** make a tour.
[from old French; related to *turn*]

tourism *NOUN* the industry of providing services for people on holiday in a place.

tourist *NOUN* **tourists** a person who makes a tour or visits a place for pleasure.

tournament *NOUN* **tournaments** a series of games or contests.
[from old French; related to *turn*]

tourniquet (*say* toor-nik-ay) *NOUN* **tourniquets** a strip of material pulled tightly round an arm or leg to stop bleeding from an artery.
[from French]

tousle (*say* towz-el) *VERB* **tousles, tousling, tousled** ruffle someone's hair.
[probably from an Old English word meaning 'to pull or shake']

tout (*rhymes with* **scout**) *VERB* **touts, touting, touted** try to sell something or get business.

tout *NOUN* **touts** a person who sells tickets for a sports match, concert, etc. at more than the original price.
[from Old English]

tow[1] (*rhymes with* **go**) *VERB* **tows, towing, towed** pull something along behind you.

tow *NOUN* an act of towing.
- **on tow** being towed.
[from Old English *togian*]

tow[2] (*rhymes with* **go**) *NOUN* short light-coloured fibres of flax or hemp.
[from Old English *tow*]

toward *PREPOSITION* towards.

towards *PREPOSITION* **1** in the direction of • *She walked towards the sea.* **2** in relation to; regarding • *He behaved kindly towards his children.* **3** as a contribution to • *Put the money towards a new bicycle.* **4** near • *towards four o'clock.*
[from Old English]

towel *NOUN* **towels** a piece of absorbent cloth for drying things.
▷ **towelling** *noun*
[via old French from Germanic]

tower *NOUN* **towers** a tall narrow building.

tower *VERB* **towers, towering, towered** be very high; be taller than others • *Skyscrapers towered over the city.*
[from Greek]

town *NOUN* **towns** a place with many houses, shops, offices, and other buildings.
[from Old English *tun* = enclosure]

town hall *NOUN* **town halls** a building with offices for the local council and usually a hall for public events.

township *NOUN* **townships 1** a small town. **2** (*S. African*) an urban area occupied by black people, and formerly (under apartheid) set aside for them.

towpath *NOUN* **towpaths** a path beside a canal or river, originally for use when a horse was towing a barge etc.

toxic *ADJECTIVE* poisonous; caused by poison.
▷ **toxicity** *noun*
[from Greek]

toxicology *NOUN* the study of poisons.
▷ **toxicologist** *noun*
[from *toxic* + *-ology*]

toxin *NOUN* **toxins** a poisonous substance, especially one formed in the body by germs.
[from *toxic*]

toy *NOUN* **toys** a thing to play with.

toy *ADJECTIVE* **1** made as a toy. **2** (said about a dog) of a very small breed kept as a pet • *a toy poodle.*

toy *VERB* **toys, toying, toyed**
- **toy with** handle a thing or consider an idea casually.
[origin unknown]

toyshop *NOUN* **toyshops** a shop that sells toys.

trace[1] *NOUN* **traces 1** a mark left by a person or thing; a sign • *There was no trace of the thief.* **2** a very small amount.

trace *VERB* **traces, tracing, traced 1** copy a picture or map etc. by drawing over it on transparent paper. **2** find a person or thing after following tracks or other evidence • *The police have been trying to trace her.*
▷ **tracer** *noun*
[from old French; related to *tract*[1]]

trace[2] *NOUN* **traces** each of the two straps or ropes etc. by which a horse pulls a cart.
- **kick over the traces** become disobedient or reckless.
[from old French; related to *traction*]

traceable *ADJECTIVE* able to be traced.

tracery *NOUN* a decorative pattern of holes in stone, e.g. in a church window.
[from *trace*[1]]

track *NOUN* **tracks 1** a mark or marks left by a moving person or thing. **2** a rough path made by being used. **3** a road or area of ground specially prepared for racing. **4** a set of rails for trains or trams etc. **5** one of the songs or pieces of music on a CD, tape, etc. **6** a continuous band round the wheels of a tank or tractor etc.
- **keep** or **lose track of** keep or fail to keep yourself informed about where something is or what someone is doing.

track *VERB* **tracks, tracking, tracked** **1** follow the tracks left by a person or animal. **2** follow or observe something as it moves.
▷ **tracker** *noun*
- **track down** find a person or thing by searching.
[from old French]

track events *PLURAL NOUN* (in athletics) races on a running track, as opposed to field events.

track record *NOUN* **track records** a person's past achievements.

track suit *NOUN* **track suits** a warm loose suit of the kind worn by athletes etc. before and after contests or for jogging.

tract[1] *NOUN* **tracts 1** an area of land. **2** a series of connected parts along which something passes • *the digestive tract.*
[from Latin *tractus* = drawing, draught]

WORD FAMILY There are a number of English words that are related to *tract* because part of their original meaning comes from the Latin words *tractus* meaning 'drawing or draught' or *tractum* meaning 'pulled'. These include *attract, contract, detract, distract, extract, protract, retract, subtract, traction,* and *tractor.*

tract[2] *NOUN* **tracts** a pamphlet containing a short essay, especially about religion.
[via Old English from Latin]

traction *NOUN* **1** pulling a load. **2** the ability of a vehicle to grip the ground • *The wheels were losing traction in the snow.* **3** a medical treatment in which an injured arm, leg, etc. is pulled gently for a long time by means of weights and pulleys.
[from Latin *tractum* = pulled]

traction engine *NOUN* **traction engines** a steam or diesel engine for pulling a heavy load along a road or across a field etc.

tractor *NOUN* **tractors** a motor vehicle for pulling farm machinery or other heavy loads.
[same origin as *traction*]

trade *NOUN* **trades 1** buying, selling, or exchanging goods. **2** business of a particular kind; the people working in this. **3** an occupation, especially a skilled craft.

trade *VERB* **trades, trading, traded** buy, sell, or exchange things.
▷ **trader** *noun*
– **trade in** give a thing as part of the payment for something new • *He traded in his motorcycle for a car.*
[from old German]

trademark *NOUN* **trademarks** a firm's registered symbol or name used to distinguish its goods etc. from those of other firms.

tradesman *NOUN* **tradesmen** a person employed in trade, especially one who sells or delivers goods.

trade union *NOUN* **trade unions** a group of workers organized to help and protect workers in their own trade or industry.

tradition *NOUN* **traditions 1** the passing down of beliefs or customs etc. from one generation to another. **2** something passed on in this way.
▷ **traditional** *adjective* **traditionally** *adverb*
[from Latin *tradere* = to hand on, deliver, or betray]

traffic *NOUN* **1** vehicles, ships, or aircraft moving along a route. **2** trading, especially when it is illegal or wrong • *drug traffic.*

traffic *VERB* **traffics, trafficking, trafficked** deal in something, especially illegally.
▷ **trafficker** *noun*
[from French]

traffic lights *PLURAL NOUN* coloured lights used as a signal to traffic at road junctions etc.

traffic warden *NOUN* **traffic wardens** an official who assists police to control the movement and parking of vehicles.

tragedian (*say* tra-**jee**-dee-an) *NOUN* **tragedians 1** a person who writes tragedies. **2** an actor in tragedies.

tragedy *NOUN* **tragedies 1** a play with unhappy events or a sad ending. **2** a very sad or distressing event.
[from Greek]

tragic *ADJECTIVE* **1** very sad or distressing. **2** to do with tragedies • *a great tragic actor.*
▷ **tragically** *adverb*

trail *NOUN* **trails 1** a track, scent, or other sign left where something has passed. **2** a path or track made through the countryside or a forest.

trail *VERB* **trails, trailing, trailed 1** follow the trail of something; track. **2** drag or be dragged along behind. **3** follow someone more slowly or wearily. **4** hang down or float loosely. **5** become fainter • *Her voice trailed away.*
[from Latin *tragula* = net for dragging a river]

trailer *NOUN* **trailers 1** a truck or other container pulled along by a vehicle. **2** a short piece from a film or television programme, shown in advance to advertise it.
[from *trail*]

A B C D E F G H I J K L M N O P Q R S **T** U V W X Y Z

train *NOUN* **trains 1** a railway engine pulling a line of carriages or trucks that are linked together. **2** a number of people or animals moving in a line • *a camel train.* **3** a series of things • *a train of events.* **4** part of a long dress or robe that trails on the ground at the back.

train *VERB* **trains, training, trained 1** give a person instruction or practice so that he or she becomes skilled. **2** practise, especially for a sporting event • *She was training for the race.* **3** make something grow in a particular direction • *We'd like to train roses up the walls.* **4** aim a gun or camera etc. • *He trained his gun on the bridge.*
[from French; related to *traction*]

trainee *NOUN* **trainees** a person who is being trained.

trainer *NOUN* **trainers 1** a person who trains people or animals. **2** a soft rubber-soled shoe of the kind worn for running or by athletes etc. while exercising.

traipse *VERB* **traipses, traipsing, traipsed** walk wearily; trudge.
[origin unknown]

trait (*say as* tray *or* trayt) *NOUN* **traits** one of a person's characteristics.
[from French; related to *tract*]

traitor *NOUN* **traitors** a person who betrays his or her country or friends.
▷ **traitorous** *adjective*
[from old French; related to *tradition*]

trajectory *NOUN* **trajectories** the path taken by a moving object such as a bullet or rocket.
[from *trans-* + Latin *jactum* = thrown]

tram *NOUN* **trams** a public passenger vehicle running on rails in the road.
[from old German or old Dutch *trame* = plank, shaft of a cart]

tramlines *PLURAL NOUN* **1** rails for a tram. **2** the pair of parallel lines at the side of a tennis court.

tramp *NOUN* **tramps 1** a person without a home or job who walks from place to place. **2** a long walk. **3** the sound of heavy footsteps.

tramp *VERB* **tramps, tramping, tramped 1** walk with heavy footsteps. **2** walk for a long distance.
[probably from old Dutch]

trample *VERB* **tramples, trampling, trampled** tread heavily on something; crush something by treading on it.
[from *tramp*]

trampoline *NOUN* **trampolines** a large piece of canvas joined to a frame by springs, used by gymnasts for jumping on.
[from Italian]

trance *NOUN* **trances** a dreamy or unconscious state rather like sleep.
[from old French; related to *transient*]

tranquil *ADJECTIVE* calm and quiet.
▷ **tranquilly** *adverb* **tranquillity** *noun*
[from Latin]

tranquillizer *NOUN* **tranquillizers** a medicine used to make a person feel calm.

trans- *PREFIX* **1** across; through. **2** beyond.
[from Latin *trans* = across]

transact *VERB* **transacts, transacting, transacted** carry out business.
▷ **transaction** *noun*
[from *trans-* + Latin *agere* = do]

transatlantic *ADJECTIVE* across or on the other side of the Atlantic Ocean.

transcend *VERB* **transcends, transcending, transcended** go beyond something; surpass.
[from *trans-* + Latin *scandere* = climb]

transcribe *VERB* **transcribes, transcribing, transcribed** copy or write something out.
▷ **transcription** *noun*
[from *trans-* + Latin *scribere* = write]

transcript *NOUN* **transcripts** a written copy.
[from Latin *transcriptum* = written out]

transept *NOUN* **transepts** the part that is at right angles to the nave in a cross-shaped church.
[from *trans-* + Latin *septum* = partition]

transfer *VERB* **transfers, transferring, transferred 1** move a person or thing to another place. **2** hand over.
▷ **transferable** *adjective* **transference** *noun*

transfer *NOUN* **transfers 1** the transferring of a person or thing. **2** a picture or design that can be transferred onto another surface.
[from *trans-* + Latin *ferre* = carry]

transfigure *VERB* **transfigures, transfiguring, transfigured** change the appearance of something greatly.
▷ **transfiguration** *noun*
[from *trans-* + Latin *figura* = figure]

transfix *VERB* **transfixes, transfixing, transfixed 1** make a person or animal unable to move because of fear or surprise etc. **2** pierce and fix with something pointed.
[from *trans-* + Latin *fixum* = fixed]

transform *VERB* **transforms, transforming, transformed** change the form or appearance or character of a person or thing.
▷ **transformation** *noun*
[from *trans-* + Latin *formare* = to form]

transformer *NOUN* **transformers** a device used to change the voltage of an electric current.

transfusion *NOUN* **transfusions** putting blood taken from one person into another person's body.
▷ **transfuse** *verb*
[from *trans-* + Latin *fusum* = poured]

transgress *VERB* **transgresses, transgressing, transgressed** break a rule or law etc.
▷ **transgression** *noun*
[from *trans-* + Latin *gressus* = gone]

transient *ADJECTIVE* not lasting or staying for long.
▷ **transience** *noun*
[from *trans-* + Latin *iens* = going]

transistor *NOUN* **transistors 1** a tiny semiconductor device that controls a flow of electricity. (also **transistor radio**) **2** a portable radio that uses transistors.
▷ **transistorized** *adjective*
[from *transfer* + *resistor*]

transit *NOUN* the process of travelling from one place to another • *The goods were damaged in transit.*
[from *trans-* + Latin *itum* = gone]

transition *NOUN* **transitions** the process of changing from one condition or form etc. to another.
▷ **transitional** *adjective*
[same origin as *transit*]

transitive *ADJECTIVE* (said about a verb) used with a direct object after it, e.g. *change* in *change your shoes* (but not in *change into dry shoes*). (COMPARE **intransitive**)
▷ **transitively** *adverb*
[from Latin *transitivus* = passing over]

transitory *ADJECTIVE* existing for a time but not lasting.
[same origin as *transit*]

translate *VERB* **translates, translating, translated** put something into another language.
▷ **translatable** *adjective* **translation** *noun* **translator** *noun*
[from *trans-* + Latin *latum* = carried]

transliterate *VERB* **transliterates, transliterating, transliterated** write a word in the letters of a different alphabet or language.
▷ **transliteration** *noun*
[from *trans-* + Latin *littera* = letter]

translucent (*say* tranz-loo-sent) *ADJECTIVE* allowing light to shine through but not transparent.
[from *trans-* + Latin *lucens* = shining]

transmission *NOUN* **transmissions 1** transmitting something. **2** a broadcast. **3** the gears by which power is transmitted from the engine to the wheels of a vehicle.

transmit *VERB* **transmits, transmitting, transmitted 1** send or pass on from one person or place to another. **2** send out a signal or broadcast etc.
▷ **transmitter** *noun*
[from *trans-* + Latin *mittere* = send]

transmute *VERB* **transmutes, transmuting, transmuted** change something from one form or substance into another.
▷ **transmutation** *noun*
[from *trans-* + Latin *mutare* = to change]

transom *NOUN* **transoms 1** a horizontal bar of wood or stone dividing a window or separating a door from a window above it. **2** a small window above a door.
[from French; related to *transverse*]

transparency *NOUN* **transparencies** **1** being transparent. **2** a transparent photograph that can be projected onto a screen.

transparent *ADJECTIVE* able to be seen through.
[from *trans-* + Latin *parens* = appearing]

transpire *VERB* **transpires, transpiring, transpired** **1** (said about information) become known; turn out • *It transpired that she had known nothing at all about it.*
2 happen • *The police need to know what transpired on the yacht.* **3** (said about plants) give off watery vapour from leaves etc.
▷ **transpiration** *noun*
[from *trans-* + Latin *spirare* = breathe]

transplant *VERB* **transplants, transplanting, transplanted** **1** remove a plant and put it to grow somewhere else.
2 transfer a part of the body to another person or animal.
▷ **transplantation** *noun*

transplant *NOUN* **transplants** **1** the process of transplanting. **2** something transplanted.
[from *trans-* + Latin *plantare* = to plant]

transport *VERB* **transports, transporting, transported** take a person, animal, or thing from one place to another.
▷ **transportation** *noun* **transporter** *noun*

transport *NOUN* the process or means of transporting people, animals, or things
• *The city has a good system of public transport.*
[from *trans-* + Latin *portare* = carry]

transpose *VERB* **transposes, transposing, transposed** **1** change the position or order of something. **2** put a piece of music into a different key.
▷ **transposition** *noun*
[from *trans-* + Latin *positum* = placed]

transverse *ADJECTIVE* lying across something.
▷ **transversely** *adverb*
[from *trans-* + Latin *versum* = turned]

transvestite *NOUN* **transvestites** a person who likes wearing clothes intended for someone of the opposite sex.
[from *trans-* + Latin *vestire* = to dress]

trap *NOUN* **traps** **1** a device for catching and holding animals. **2** a plan or trick for capturing, detecting, or cheating someone.
3 a two-wheeled carriage pulled by a horse.
4 a bend in a pipe, filled with water to prevent gases from rising up from a drain.

trap *VERB* **traps, trapping, trapped** **1** catch or hold a person or animal in a trap.
2 prevent someone from escaping, or from avoiding an unpleasant situation • *The driver was trapped in the wreckage.*
[from Old English]

trapdoor *NOUN* **trapdoors** a door in a floor, ceiling, or roof.

trapeze *NOUN* **trapezes** a bar hanging from two ropes as a swing for acrobats.
[French; related to *trapezium*]

trapezium *NOUN* **trapeziums** or **trapezia** a quadrilateral in which two opposite sides are parallel and the other two are not.
[from Greek *trapeza* = table]

trapezoid *NOUN* **trapezoids** a quadrilateral in which no sides are parallel.
[same origin as *trapezium*]

trapper *NOUN* **trappers** someone who traps wild animals, especially for their fur.

trappings *PLURAL NOUN* **1** the clothes or possessions that show your rank or position.
2 an ornamental harness for a horse.
[from French *drap* = cloth]

trash *NOUN* rubbish or nonsense.
▷ **trashy** *adjective*
[origin unknown]

trash can *NOUN* **trash cans** (*American*) a dustbin.

trauma (*say* traw-ma) *NOUN* **traumas** a shock that produces a lasting effect on a person's mind.
▷ **traumatic** *adjective* **traumatize** *verb*
[Greek, = a wound]

travail *NOUN* (*old use*) hard or laborious work.
▷ **travail** *verb*
[French]

travel *VERB* **travels, travelling, travelled** move from place to place.
▷ **travel** *noun*
[from *travail*]

travel agent *NOUN* **travel agents** a person whose job is to arrange travel and holidays for people.

traveller *NOUN* **travellers 1** a person who is travelling or who often travels. **2** a gypsy, or a person who does not settle in one place.

traveller's cheque *NOUN* **traveller's cheques** a cheque for a fixed amount of money that is sold by banks and that can be exchanged for money in foreign countries.

traverse *VERB* **traverses, traversing, traversed** go across something.
▷ **traversal** *noun*
[same origin as *transverse*]

travesty *NOUN* **travesties** a bad or ridiculous form of something • *His story is a travesty of the truth.*
[from *trans-* + Italian *vestire* = to clothe]

trawl *VERB* **trawls, trawling, trawled** fish by dragging a large net along the seabed.
[from old Dutch; related to *trail*]

trawler *NOUN* **trawlers** a boat used in trawling.

tray *NOUN* **trays 1** a flat piece of wood, metal, or plastic, usually with raised edges, for carrying cups, plates, food, etc. **2** an open container for holding letters etc. in an office.
[from Old English]

treacherous *ADJECTIVE* **1** betraying someone; disloyal. **2** dangerous or unreliable • *It's snowing and the roads are treacherous.*
▷ **treacherously** *adverb* **treachery** *noun*
[from old French *trechier* = to trick or deceive]

treacle *NOUN* a thick sticky liquid produced when sugar is purified.
▷ **treacly** *adjective*
[originally = ointment for an animal bite; from Greek *therion* = wild or poisonous animal]

tread *VERB* **treads, treading, trod, trodden** walk or put your foot on something.

tread *NOUN* **treads 1** a sound or way of walking. **2** the top surface of a stair; the part you put your foot on. **3** the part of a tyre that touches the ground.
[from Old English]

treadle *NOUN* **treadles** a lever that you press with your foot to turn a wheel that works a machine.
[from *tread*]

treadmill *NOUN* **treadmills 1** a wide mill wheel turned by the weight of people or animals treading on steps fixed round its edge. **2** monotonous routine work.

treason *NOUN* betraying your country.
▷ **treasonable** *adjective* **treasonous** *adjective*
[from old French; related to *tradition*]

treasure *NOUN* **treasures 1** a store of precious metals or jewels. **2** a precious thing or person.

treasure *VERB* **treasures, treasuring, treasured** value greatly something that you have.
[same origin as *thesaurus*]

treasure hunt *NOUN* **treasure hunts** a game in which people try to find a hidden object.

treasurer *NOUN* **treasurers** a person in charge of the money of a club, society, etc.

treasure trove *NOUN* gold or silver etc. found hidden and with no known owner.

treasury *NOUN* **treasuries** a place where money and valuables are kept.
- **the Treasury** the government department in charge of a country's income.

treat *VERB* **treats, treating, treated**
1 behave in a certain way towards a person or thing. **2** deal with a subject. **3** give medical care in order to cure a person or animal. **4** put something through a chemical or other process • *The fabric has been treated to make it waterproof.* **5** pay for someone else's food, drink, or entertainment • *I'll treat you to an ice cream.*

treat *NOUN* **treats 1** something special that gives pleasure. **2** the process of treating someone to food, drink, or entertainment.
[from Latin *tractare* = to handle or manage]

treatise *NOUN* **treatises** a book or long essay on a subject.
[from old French; related to *treat*]

treatment *NOUN* **treatments 1** the process or manner of dealing with a person, animal, or thing. **2** medical care.

a b c d e f g h i j k l m n o p q r s t u v w x y z

treaty *NOUN* **treaties** a formal agreement between two or more countries.
[from French; related to *treat*]

treble *ADJECTIVE* three times as much or as many.

treble *NOUN* **trebles 1** a treble amount. **2** a person with a high-pitched or soprano voice.

treble *VERB* **trebles, trebling, trebled** make or become three times as much or as many.
[from old French; related to *triple*]

tree *NOUN* **trees** a tall plant with a single very thick hard stem or trunk that is usually without branches for some distance above the ground.
[from Old English]

trefoil *NOUN* a plant with three small leaves (e.g. clover).
[from Latin *tres* = three + *folium* = leaf]

trek *NOUN* **treks** a long walk or journey.

trek *VERB* **treks, trekking, trekked** go on a long walk or journey.
[from Dutch *trekken* = pull]

trellis *NOUN* **trellises** a framework with crossing bars of wood or metal etc. to support climbing plants.
[from old French]

tremble *VERB* **trembles, trembling, trembled** shake gently, especially with fear.
▷ **tremble** *noun*
[from French; related to *tremulous*]

tremendous *ADJECTIVE* **1** very large; huge. **2** excellent.
▷ **tremendously** *adverb*
[from Latin *tremendus* = making someone tremble]

tremor *NOUN* **tremors 1** a shaking or trembling movement. **2** a slight earthquake.
[Latin]

tremulous *ADJECTIVE* trembling from nervousness or weakness.
▷ **tremulously** *adverb*
[from Latin *tremere* = tremble]

trench *NOUN* **trenches** a long narrow hole cut in the ground.

trench *VERB* **trenches, trenching, trenched** dig a trench or trenches.
[from old French; related to *truncate*]

trenchant *ADJECTIVE* strong and effective
• *trenchant criticism.*
[old French, = cutting]

trend *NOUN* **trends** the general direction in which something is going.
[from Old English]

trendy *ADJECTIVE* (*informal*) fashionable; following the latest trends.
▷ **trendily** *adverb* **trendiness** *noun*

trepidation *NOUN* fear and anxiety; nervousness.
[from Latin *trepidare* = be afraid]

trespass *VERB* **trespasses, trespassing, trespassed 1** go on someone's land or property unlawfully. **2** (*old use*) do wrong; sin.
▷ **trespasser** *noun*

trespass *NOUN* **trespasses** (*old use*) wrongdoing; sin.
[from old French *trespasser* = go beyond]

tress *NOUN* **tresses** a lock of hair.
[from French]

trestle *NOUN* **trestles** each of a set of supports on which a board is rested to form a table.
▷ **trestle table** *noun*
[from old French, = small beam]

tri- *PREFIX* three (as in *triangle*).
[from Latin or Greek]

triad (*say* try-ad) *NOUN* **triads 1** a group or set of three things. **2** (*in music*) a chord of three notes, made up of a given note with the third and fifth above it. **3** a Chinese secret organization involved in crime.
[via French from Greek *trias* = group of three]

trial *NOUN* **trials 1** the process of examining the evidence in a lawcourt to decide whether a person is guilty of a crime. **2** testing a thing to see how good it is. **3** a test of qualities or ability. **4** an annoying person or thing; a hardship.
- **on trial 1** being tried in a lawcourt. **2** being tested.
- **trial and error** trying out different methods of doing something until you find one that works.
[from old French; related to *try*]

triangle *NOUN* **triangles 1** a flat shape with three sides and three angles. **2** a percussion instrument made from a metal rod bent into a triangle.
▷ **triangular** *adjective*
[from *tri-* + Latin *angulus* = angle]

tribe *NOUN* **tribes 1** a group of families living in one area as a community, ruled by a chief. **2** a set of people.
▷ **tribal** *adjective* **tribally** *adverb*
tribesman *noun* **tribeswoman** *noun*
[from Latin]

tribulation *NOUN* **tribulations** great trouble or hardship.
[from Latin *tribulare* = to press or oppress]

tribunal (*say* try-bew-nal) *NOUN* **tribunals** a committee appointed to hear evidence and give judgements when there is a dispute.
[from Latin *tribunale* = tribune's seat]

tribune *NOUN* **tribunes** an official chosen by the people in ancient Rome.
[from Latin]

tributary *NOUN* **tributaries** a river or stream that flows into a larger one or into a lake.
[same origin as *tribute*]

tribute *NOUN* **tributes 1** something said, done, or given to show respect or admiration. **2** payment that one country or ruler was formerly obliged to pay to a more powerful one.
[from Latin *tribuere* = assign, grant, share]

trice *NOUN* (*old use*)
- **in a trice** in a moment.
[from old Dutch *trisen* = pull quickly, tug]

triceps (*say* try-seps) *NOUN* **triceps** the large muscle at the back of the upper arm.
[Latin, = three-headed (because the muscle is attached at three points)]

trick *NOUN* **tricks 1** a crafty or deceitful action; a practical joke • *Let's play a trick on Jo.* **2** a skilful action, especially one done for entertainment • *magic tricks.* **3** the cards picked up by the winner after one round of a card game such as whist.

trick *VERB* **tricks, tricking, tricked**
1 deceive or cheat someone by a trick.
2 decorate • *The building was tricked out with little flags.*
[from old French]

trickery *NOUN* the use of tricks; deception.

trickle *VERB* **trickles, trickling, trickled** flow or move slowly.
▷ **trickle** *noun*
[imitating the sound]

trickster *NOUN* **tricksters** a person who tricks or cheats people.

tricky *ADJECTIVE* **trickier, trickiest**
1 difficult; needing skill • *a tricky job.*
2 cunning or deceitful.
▷ **trickiness** *noun*

tricolour (*say* trik-ol-er) *NOUN* **tricolours** a flag with three coloured stripes, e.g. the national flag of France or Ireland.

tricycle *NOUN* **tricycles** a vehicle like a bicycle but with three wheels.

trident *NOUN* **tridents** a three-pronged spear, carried by Neptune and Britannia as a symbol of their power over the sea.
[from *tri-* + Latin *dens* = tooth]

triennial (*say* try-en-ee-al) *ADJECTIVE* happening every third year.
[from *tri-* + Latin *annus* = year]

trier *NOUN* **triers** a person who tries hard.

trifle *NOUN* **trifles 1** a pudding made of sponge cake covered in custard, fruit, cream, etc. **2** a very small amount.
3 something that has very little importance or value.

trifle *VERB* **trifles, trifling, trifled** treat a person or thing without seriousness or respect • *She is not a woman to be trifled with.*
[from old French]

trifling *ADJECTIVE* small in value or importance.

trigger *NOUN* **triggers** a lever that is pulled to fire a gun.

trigger *VERB* **triggers, triggering, triggered**
- **trigger off** start something happening.
[from Dutch *trekker* = puller]

trigonometry (*say* trig-on-om-it-ree) *NOUN* the calculation of distances and angles by using triangles.
[from Greek *trigonon* = triangle + *metria* = measurement]

trilateral *ADJECTIVE* having three sides.
[from *tri-* + *lateral*]

trilby *NOUN* **trilbies** a man's soft felt hat.
[named after *Trilby* O'Ferrall, the heroine of a popular book and play, who wore a similar hat]

trill *VERB* **trills, trilling, trilled** make a quivering musical sound.
▷ **trill** *noun*
[from Italian]

trillion *NOUN* **trillions 1** a million million. **2** (*old use*) a million million million.
[from *tri-* + *million*]

trilogy *NOUN* **trilogies** a group of three stories, poems, or plays etc. about the same people or things.
[from *tri-* + Greek *-logia* = writings]

trim *ADJECTIVE* neat and orderly.
▷ **trimly** *adverb* **trimness** *noun*

trim *VERB* **trims, trimming, trimmed 1** cut the edges or unwanted parts off something. **2** decorate a hat or piece of clothing by adding lace, ribbons, etc. **3** arrange sails to suit the wind.

trim *NOUN* **trims 1** cutting or trimming • *Your beard needs a trim.* **2** lace, ribbons, etc. used to decorate something.
- **in good trim** in good condition; fit.
[from Old English]

Trinity *NOUN* God regarded as three persons (Father, Son, and Holy Spirit).
[from Latin]

trinket *NOUN* **trinkets** a small ornament or piece of jewellery.
[origin unknown]

trio *NOUN* **trios 1** a group of three people or things. **2** a group of three musicians or singers. **3** a piece of music for three musicians.
[Italian, from Latin *tres* = three]

trip *VERB* **trips, tripping, tripped 1** catch your foot on something and fall; make someone do this. **2** move with quick light steps. **3** operate a switch.
- **trip up 1** stumble. **2** make a mistake. **3** cause a person to stumble or make a mistake.

trip *NOUN* **trips 1** a journey or outing. **2** the action of tripping; a stumble. **3** (*informal*) hallucinations caused by taking a drug.
[from old French]

tripartite *ADJECTIVE* having three parts; involving three groups • *tripartite talks.*
[from *tri-* + Latin *partitus* = divided]

tripe *NOUN* **1** part of an ox's stomach used as food. **2** (*informal*) nonsense.
[French]

triple *ADJECTIVE* **1** consisting of three parts. **2** involving three people or groups • *a triple alliance.* **3** three times as much or as many.
▷ **triply** *adverb*

triple *VERB* **triples, tripling, tripled** make or become three times as much or as many.
[from Latin *triplus* = three times as much]

triple jump *NOUN* an athletic contest in which competitors try to jump as far as possible by doing a hop, step, and jump.

triplet *NOUN* **triplets** each of three children or animals born to the same mother at one time.
[from *triple*]

triplicate *NOUN*
- **in triplicate** as three identical copies.
[from *tri-* + Latin *plicare* = to fold]

tripod (*say* try-pod) *NOUN* **tripods** a stand with three legs, e.g. to support a camera.
[from *tri-* + Greek *podes* = feet]

tripper *NOUN* **trippers** a person who is making a pleasure trip.

trireme (*say* try-reem) *NOUN* **triremes** an ancient warship with three banks of oars.
[from *tri-* + Latin *remus* = oar]

trisect *VERB* **trisects, trisecting, trisected** divide something into three equal parts.
▷ **trisection** *noun*
[from *tri-* + Latin *sectum* = cut]

trite (*rhymes with* **kite**) *ADJECTIVE* worn out by constant repetition; hackneyed • *a few trite remarks.*
[from Latin *tritum* = worn by use]

triumph *NOUN* **triumphs 1** a great success or victory; a feeling of joy at this. **2** a celebration of a victory.
▷ **triumphal** *adjective* **triumphant** *adjective* **triumphantly** *adverb*

triumph *VERB* **triumphs, triumphing, triumphed 1** be successful or victorious. **2** rejoice in success or victory.
[from Latin]

triumvirate *NOUN* **triumvirates** a ruling group of three people.
[from Latin *trium virorum* = of three men]

trivet *NOUN* **trivets** an iron stand for a pot or kettle etc., placed over a fire.
[from *tri-* + Latin *pedes* = feet]

trivia *PLURAL NOUN* unimportant details or pieces of information.
[same origin as *trivial*]

trivial *ADJECTIVE* small in value or importance.
▷ **trivially** *adverb* **triviality** *noun*
[from Latin *trivialis* = commonplace]

troglodyte *NOUN* **troglodytes** a person living in a cave in ancient times.
[from Greek *trogle* = hole]

troll (*rhymes with* **hole**) *NOUN* **trolls** (in Scandinavian mythology) a supernatural being, either a giant or a friendly but mischievous dwarf.
[from Old Norse]

trolley *NOUN* **trolleys 1** a small table on wheels or castors. **2** a small cart or truck. **3** a basket on wheels, used in supermarkets.
[probably from dialect *troll* = to roll or flow]

trolleybus *NOUN* **trolleybuses** a bus powered by electricity from an overhead wire to which it is connected.
[from an old sense of *trolley* = a pulley that runs along a track or wire]

trombone *NOUN* **trombones** a large brass musical instrument with a sliding tube.
[from Italian *tromba* = trumpet]

troop *NOUN* **troops 1** an organized group of soldiers, Scouts, etc. **2** a number of people moving along together.
USAGE Do not confuse with **troupe**.

troop *VERB* **troops, trooping, trooped** move along as a group or in large numbers
• *They all trooped in.*
[from Latin *troppus* = herd]

trooper *NOUN* **troopers** a soldier in the cavalry or in an armoured unit.
[from *troop*]

troops *PLURAL NOUN* armed forces.

trophy *NOUN* **trophies 1** a cup etc. given as a prize for winning a competition.
2 something taken in war or hunting as a souvenir of success.
[from Greek]

tropic *NOUN* **tropics** a line of latitude about $23\frac{1}{2}$° north of the equator (**tropic of Cancer**) or $23\frac{1}{2}$° south of the equator (**tropic of Capricorn**).
- **the tropics** the hot regions between these two latitudes.
[from Greek *trope* = turning (because the sun seems to turn back when it reaches these points)]

tropical *ADJECTIVE* to do with the tropics
• *tropical fish.*

troposphere *NOUN* the layer of the atmosphere extending about 10 kilometres upwards from the earth's surface.
[from Greek *tropos* = turning, + *sphere*]

trot *VERB* **trots, trotting, trotted 1** (said about a horse) run, going faster than when walking but more slowly than when cantering. **2** run gently with short steps.
- **trot out** (*informal*) produce or repeat • *He trotted out the usual excuses.*

trot *NOUN* a trotting run.
- **on the trot** (*informal*) one after the other without a break • *She worked for ten days on the trot.*
[via old French from Germanic]

troth (*rhymes with* **both**) *NOUN* (*old use*) loyalty; a solemn promise.
[a different spelling of *truth*]

trotter *NOUN* **trotters** a pig's foot used for food.
[from *trot*]

troubadour (*say* troo-bad-oor) *NOUN* **troubadours** a poet and singer in southern France in the 11th-13th centuries.
[from old French *trover* = write in verse]

trouble *NOUN* **troubles 1** difficulty, inconvenience, or distress. **2** a cause of any of these.
- **take trouble** take great care in doing something.

trouble *VERB* **troubles, troubling, troubled 1** cause trouble to someone.
2 give yourself trouble or inconvenience etc.
• *Nobody troubled to ask if I needed help.*
[from old French]

troublesome *ADJECTIVE* causing trouble or annoyance.

trough (*say* trof) *NOUN* **troughs 1** a long narrow open container, especially one holding water or food for animals. **2** a channel for liquid. **3** the low part between two waves or ridges. **4** a long region of low air pressure.
[from Old English]

trounce *VERB* **trounces, trouncing, trounced** defeat someone heavily.
[origin unknown]

troupe (*say as* troop) *NOUN* **troupes** a company of actors or other performers.
[French, = troop]
USAGE Do not confuse with **troop**.

trousers *PLURAL NOUN* a piece of clothing worn over the lower half of the body, with a separate part for each leg.
[from Irish or Scottish Gaelic]

trousseau (*say* troo-soh) *NOUN* **trousseaus** or **trousseaux** a bride's collection of clothing etc. to begin married life.
[from French, = bundle]

trout *NOUN* **trout** a freshwater fish that is caught as a sport and for food.
[from Greek]

trowel *NOUN* **trowels 1** a small garden tool with a curved blade for lifting plants or scooping things. **2** a small tool with a flat blade for spreading mortar etc.
[from Latin *trulla* = scoop]

troy weight *NOUN* a system of weights used for precious metals and gems, in which 1 pound = 12 ounces.
[said to be from a weight used at *Troyes* in France]

truant *NOUN* **truants** a child who stays away from school without permission.
▷ **truancy** *noun*
- **play truant** be a truant.
[old French, = criminal, probably of Celtic origin]

truce *NOUN* **truces** an agreement to stop fighting for a while.
[from Old English]

truck[1] *NOUN* **trucks 1** a lorry. **2** an open container on wheels for transporting loads; an open railway wagon. **3** an axle with wheels attached, fitted under a skateboard.
[probably from *truckle* = a pulley or castor]

truck[2] *NOUN*
- **have no truck with** refuse to have dealings with • *I'll have no truck with fortune-tellers!*
[origin unknown]

truculent (*say* truk-yoo-lent) *ADJECTIVE* defiant and aggressive.
▷ **truculently** *adverb* **truculence** *noun*
[from Latin *truculentus* = wild, fierce]

trudge *VERB* **trudges, trudging, trudged** walk slowly and heavily.
[origin unknown]

true *ADJECTIVE* **truer, truest 1** representing what has really happened or exists • *a true story.* **2** genuine or proper; not false • *He was the true heir.* **3** accurate. **4** loyal or faithful • *Be true to your friends.*
▷ **trueness** *noun*
- **come true** actually happen as hoped or predicted.
[from Old English]

truffle *NOUN* **truffles 1** a soft sweet made with chocolate. **2** a fungus that grows underground and is valued as food because of its rich flavour.
[probably from Dutch]

truism *NOUN* **truisms** a statement that is obviously true, especially one that is hackneyed, e.g. 'Nothing lasts for ever'.

truly *ADVERB* **1** truthfully. **2** sincerely or genuinely • *We are truly grateful.* **3** accurately. **4** loyally or faithfully.
- **Yours truly** see *yours*.

trump[1] *NOUN* **trumps** a playing card of a suit that ranks above the others for one game.

trump *VERB* **trumps, trumping, trumped** beat a card by playing a trump.
- **trump up** invent an excuse or an accusation etc.
[from *triumph*]

trump[2] *NOUN* **trumps** (*old use*) a blast of a trumpet.
[from old French *trompe* = trumpet]

trumpet *NOUN* **trumpets 1** a metal wind instrument with a narrow tube that widens near the end. **2** something shaped like this.

trumpet *VERB* **trumpets, trumpeting, trumpeted** **1** blow a trumpet. **2** (said about an elephant) make a loud sound with its trunk. **3** shout or announce something loudly.
▷ **trumpeter** *noun*
[same origin as *trump*[2]]

truncate *VERB* **truncates, truncating, truncated** shorten something by cutting off its top or end.
▷ **truncation** *noun*
[from Latin *truncare* = maim]

truncheon *NOUN* **truncheons** a short thick stick carried as a weapon, especially by police.
[from old French; related to *trunk*]

trundle *VERB* **trundles, trundling, trundled** roll along heavily • *He was trundling a wheelbarrow. A bus trundled up.*
[related to Old English *trendel* = ball]

trunk *NOUN* **trunks** **1** the main stem of a tree. **2** an elephant's long flexible nose. **3** a large box with a hinged lid for transporting or storing clothes etc. **4** the human body except for the head, arms, and legs. **5** (*American*) the boot of a car.
[from Latin]

trunk call *NOUN* **trunk calls** (*old use*) a long-distance telephone call.

trunk road *NOUN* **trunk roads** an important main road.
[regarded as a 'trunk' from which smaller roads branch off]

trunks *PLURAL NOUN* shorts worn by men and boys for swimming, boxing, etc.

truss *NOUN* **trusses** **1** a framework of beams or bars supporting a roof or bridge etc. **2** a bundle of hay etc. **3** a type of padded belt worn to support a hernia.

truss *VERB* **trusses, trussing, trussed** **1** tie up a person or thing securely. **2** support a roof or bridge etc. with trusses.
[from old French]

trust *VERB* **trusts, trusting, trusted** **1** believe that a person or thing is good, truthful, or reliable. **2** let a person have or use something in the belief that he or she will behave responsibly • *Don't trust him with your CD player!* **3** hope • *I trust that you are well.*
- **trust to** rely on • *I'm just trusting to luck.*

trust *NOUN* **trusts** **1** the belief that a person or thing can be trusted. **2** responsibility; being trusted • *Being a prefect is a position of trust.* **3** a legal arrangement in which money is entrusted to a person with instructions about how to use it.
▷ **trustful** *adjective* **trustfully** *adverb*
[from Old Norse]

trustee *NOUN* **trustees** a person who looks after money entrusted to him or her.

trustworthy *ADJECTIVE* able to be trusted; reliable.

trusty *ADJECTIVE* trustworthy or reliable • *my trusty sword.*

truth *NOUN* **truths** **1** something that is true. **2** the quality of being true.
[from Old English]

truthful *ADJECTIVE* **1** telling the truth • *a truthful boy.* **2** true • *a truthful account of what happened.*
▷ **truthfully** *adverb* **truthfulness** *noun*

try *VERB* **tries, trying, tried** **1** make an effort to do something; attempt. **2** test something by using or doing it • *Try sleeping on your back.* **3** examine the evidence in a lawcourt to decide whether a person is guilty of a crime. **4** be a strain on • *Very small print tries your eyes.*
- **try on** put on clothes etc. to see if they fit.
- **try out** use something to see if it works.

try *NOUN* **tries** **1** an attempt. **2** (in rugby football) putting the ball down behind the opponents' goal line in order to score points.
[from old French]

trying *ADJECTIVE* putting a strain on someone's patience; annoying.

tsar (*say* zar) *NOUN* **tsars** the title of the former ruler of Russia.
[Russian, from Latin *Caesar*]

tsetse fly (*say* tet-see) *NOUN* **tsetse flies** a tropical African fly that can cause sleeping sickness in people whom it bites.
[from Setswana (a language spoken in southern Africa)]

T-shirt *NOUN* **T-shirts** a short-sleeved shirt shaped like a T.

tsunami *NOUN* **tsunamis** a huge sea wave caused by an underwater earthquake.
[Japanese, from *tsu* = harbour + *nami* = a wave]

tub *NOUN* **tubs** a round open container holding liquid, ice cream, soil for plants, etc.
[probably from old Dutch]

tuba (*say* tew-ba) *NOUN* **tubas** a large brass wind instrument with a deep tone.
[Italian from Latin, = war trumpet]

tubby *ADJECTIVE* **tubbier**, **tubbiest** short and fat.
▷ **tubbiness** *noun*
[from *tub*]

tube *NOUN* **tubes 1** a long hollow piece of metal, plastic, rubber, glass, etc., especially for liquids or air etc. to pass along. **2** a container made of flexible material with a screw cap • *a tube of toothpaste.* **3** the underground railway in London.
[from Latin]

tuber *NOUN* **tubers** a short thick rounded root (e.g. of a dahlia) or underground stem (e.g. of a potato) that produces buds from which new plants will grow.
[Latin, = a swelling]

tuberculosis *NOUN* a disease of people and animals, producing small swellings in the parts affected by it, especially in the lungs.
▷ **tubercular** *adjective*
[from Latin *tuberculum* = little swelling]

tubing *NOUN* tubes; a length of tube.

tubular *ADJECTIVE* shaped like a tube.

TUC *ABBREVIATION* Trades Union Congress.

tuck *VERB* **tucks**, **tucking**, **tucked 1** push a loose edge into something so that it is hidden or held in place. **2** put something away in a small space • *Tuck this in your pocket.*
- **tuck in** (*informal*) eat heartily.
- **tuck someone in** or **up** make someone comfortable in bed by folding the edges of the bedclothes tightly.

tuck *NOUN* **tucks 1** a flat fold stitched in a piece of clothing. **2** (*informal*) food, especially sweets and cakes etc. that children enjoy.
▷ **tuck shop** *noun*
[from Old English]

tucker *NOUN* (*informal*) (*Australian/NZ*) food.

-tude *SUFFIX* forms nouns meaning 'quality or condition' (e.g. *altitude*, *solitude*).
[from French]

Tuesday *NOUN* the day of the week following Monday.
[from Old English *Tiwesdaeg* = day of Tiw, a Norse god]

tuft *NOUN* **tufts** a bunch of threads, grass, hair, or feathers etc. growing close together.
▷ **tufted** *adjective*
[from old French]

tug *VERB* **tugs**, **tugging**, **tugged 1** pull something hard or suddenly. **2** tow a ship.

tug *NOUN* **tugs 1** a hard or sudden pull. **2** a small powerful boat used for towing others.
[Middle English; related to *tow*[1]]

tug of war *NOUN* a contest between two teams pulling a rope from opposite ends.

tuition *NOUN* teaching, especially when given to one person or a small group.
[from Latin *tuitio* = looking after something]

tulip *NOUN* **tulips** a large cup-shaped flower on a tall stem growing from a bulb.
[from Persian *dulband* = turban (because the flowers are this shape)]

tulle (*say* tewl) *NOUN* a very fine silky net material used for veils, wedding dresses, etc.
[named after *Tulle*, a town in France, where it was first made]

tumble *VERB* **tumbles**, **tumbling**, **tumbled 1** fall or roll over suddenly or clumsily. **2** move or push quickly and carelessly.
▷ **tumble** *noun*
- **tumble to** (*informal*) realize what something means.
[from old German]

tumbledown *ADJECTIVE* falling into ruins.

tumble-drier *NOUN* **tumble-driers** a machine that dries washing by turning it over many times in heated air.

tumbler *NOUN* **tumblers 1** a drinking glass with no stem or handle. **2** a part of a lock that is lifted when a key is turned to open it. **3** an acrobat.

tumbrel or **tumbril** *NOUN* **tumbrels** or **tumbrils** (*old use*) an open cart of the kind used to carry condemned people to the guillotine during the French Revolution.
[from old French]

tummy *NOUN* **tummies** (*informal*) the stomach.
[imitating a small child trying to say 'stomach']

tumour (*say* tew-mer) *NOUN* **tumours** an abnormal lump growing on or in the body.
[from Latin *tumere* = to swell]

tumult (*say* tew-mult) *NOUN* an uproar; a state of noisy confusion and agitation.
[from Latin]

tumultuous (*say* tew-mul-tew-us) *ADJECTIVE* noisy and excited • *a tumultuous welcome.*

tucker *NOUN* (*Australian/NZ*)(*informal*) food.

tun *NOUN* **tuns** a large cask or barrel.
[from Old English]

tuna (*say* tew-na) *NOUN* **tuna** a large edible sea fish with pink flesh.
[American Spanish; related to *tunny*]

tundra *NOUN* the vast level Arctic regions of Europe, Asia, and America where there are no trees and the subsoil is always frozen.
[from Lappish (the language spoken in Lapland)]

tune *NOUN* **tunes** a short piece of music; a pleasant series of musical notes.
▷ **tuneful** *adjective* **tunefully** *adverb*
- **in tune** at the correct musical pitch.

tune *VERB* **tunes, tuning, tuned 1** put a musical instrument in tune. **2** adjust a radio or television set to receive a certain channel. **3** adjust an engine so that it runs smoothly.
▷ **tuner** *noun*
- **tune up** (said about an orchestra) bring the instruments to the correct pitch.
[a different spelling of *tone*]

tungsten *NOUN* a grey metal used to make a kind of steel.
[from Swedish *tung* = heavy + *sten* = stone]

tunic *NOUN* **tunics 1** a jacket worn as part of a uniform. **2** a piece of clothing reaching from the shoulders to the hips or knees.
[from Latin]

tunnel *NOUN* **tunnels** an underground passage.

tunnel *VERB* **tunnels, tunnelling, tunnelled** make a tunnel.
[from old French *tonel* = barrel]

tunny *NOUN* **tunnies** a tuna.
[from Latin]

turban *NOUN* **turbans** a covering for the head made by wrapping a strip of cloth round a cap.
[from Persian]

turbid *ADJECTIVE* (said about water) muddy, not clear.
▷ **turbidly** *adverb* **turbidity** *noun*
[from Latin *turba* = crowd, disturbance]

turbine *NOUN* **turbines** a machine or motor driven by a flow of water, steam, or gas.
[from Latin *turbo* = whirlwind, spinning top]

turbojet *NOUN* **turbojets** a jet engine or aircraft with turbines.
[from *turbine* + *jet*[1]]

turbot *NOUN* **turbot** a large flat edible sea fish.
[via old French from old Swedish]

turbulence *NOUN* violent and uneven movement of air or water • *We experienced turbulence during the flight.*

turbulent *ADJECTIVE* **1** moving violently and unevenly • *turbulent seas.* **2** involving much change and disagreement and sometimes violence • *a turbulent period of history.*
▷ **turbulently** *adverb*
[same origin as *turbid*]

tureen *NOUN* **tureens** a deep dish with a lid, from which soup is served at the table.
[from French *terrine* = earthenware pot]

turf *NOUN* **turfs** or **turves 1** short grass and the earth round its roots. **2** a piece of this cut from the ground.
- **the turf** horse racing.

turf *VERB* **turfs, turfing, turfed** cover ground with turf.
- **turf out** (*informal*) throw out.
[from Old English]

turgid (*say* ter-jid) *ADJECTIVE* **1** swollen and thick. **2** pompous and boring • *a turgid speech.*
[from Latin *turgere* = to swell]

turkey *NOUN* **turkeys** a large bird kept for its meat.
[originally the name of a different bird which was imported from Turkey]

turmoil *NOUN* wild confusion or agitation • *Her mind was in turmoil.*
[origin unknown]

turn *VERB* **turns, turning, turned 1** move round; move to a new direction. **2** change in appearance etc.; become • *He turned pale.* **3** make something change • *You can turn milk into butter.* **4** move a switch or tap etc. to control something • *Turn that radio off.* **5** pass a certain time • *It has turned midnight.* **6** shape something on a lathe.
- **turn down 1** fold down. **2** reduce the flow or sound of something. **3** reject • *We offered her a job but she turned it down.*
- **turn out 1** send out. **2** empty something, especially to search or clean it. **3** happen. **4** prove to be • *The visitor turned out to be my uncle.*
- **turn up 1** appear or arrive. **2** increase the flow or sound of something.

turn *NOUN* **turns 1** the action of turning; a turning movement. **2** a change; the point where something turns. **3** an opportunity or duty etc. that comes to each person in succession • *It's your turn to wash up.* **4** a short performance in an entertainment. **5** (*informal*) an attack of illness; a nervous shock • *It gave me a nasty turn.*
- **a good turn** a helpful action.
- **in turn** in succession; one after another.
[from Greek *tornos* = lathe]

turncoat *NOUN* **turncoats** a person who changes his or her principles or beliefs.

turning *NOUN* **turnings** a place where one road meets another, forming a corner.

turning point *NOUN* **turning points** a point where an important change takes place.

turnip *NOUN* **turnips** a plant with a large round white root used as a vegetable.
[from Latin]

turnout *NOUN* **turnouts** the number of people who attend a meeting, vote at an election, etc. • *Despite the rain, there was a pretty good turnout.*

turnover *NOUN* **turnovers 1** the amount of money received by a firm selling things. **2** the rate at which goods are sold or workers leave and are replaced. **3** a small pie made by folding pastry over fruit, jam, etc.

turnpike *NOUN* **turnpikes** (*old use*) a toll gate; a road with toll gates.
[originally = a barricade: from *turn* + *pike*]

turnstile *NOUN* **turnstiles** a revolving gate that lets one person in at a time.

turntable *NOUN* **turntables** a circular revolving platform or support, e.g. for the record in a record player.

turpentine *NOUN* a kind of oil used for thinning paint, cleaning paintbrushes, etc.
[from Latin]

turpitude *NOUN* (*formal*) wickedness.
[from Latin *turpis* = shameful]

turps *NOUN* (*informal*) turpentine.

turquoise *NOUN* **turquoises 1** a sky-blue or greenish-blue colour. **2** a blue jewel.
[from French *pierre turquoise* = Turkish stone]

turret *NOUN* **turrets 1** a small tower on a castle or other building. **2** a revolving structure containing a gun.
▷ **turreted** *adjective*
[from old French *tourete* = small tower]

turtle *NOUN* **turtles** a sea animal that looks like a tortoise.
- **turn turtle** capsize.
[probably from French *tortue* = tortoise]

turtle-dove *NOUN* **turtle-doves** a wild dove.
[from Old English]

tusk *NOUN* **tusks** a long pointed tooth that sticks out from the mouth of an elephant, walrus, etc.
[from Old English]

tussle *NOUN* **tussles** a struggle or conflict over something.

tussle *VERB* **tussles, tussling, tussled** take part in a tussle.
[originally Scots; origin unknown]

tussock *NOUN* **tussocks** a tuft or clump of grass.
[origin unknown]

tutor *NOUN* **tutors 1** a private teacher, especially of one pupil or a small group. **2** a teacher of students in a college or university.
[Latin, = guardian]

tutorial *NOUN* **tutorials** a meeting in which students discuss a subject with their tutor.

tutu (*say* too-too) *NOUN* **tutus** a ballet dancer's short stiff frilled skirt.
[French]

TV *ABBREVIATION* television.

twaddle *NOUN* nonsense.
[possibly from *tattle*]

twain *NOUN* & *ADJECTIVE* (*old use*) two.
[from Old English *twegen* = two]

twang *NOUN* **twangs 1** a sharp sound like that of a wire when plucked. **2** a nasal tone in a person's voice.

twang *VERB* **twangs, twanging, twanged 1** make a sharp sound like that of a wire when plucked. **2** play a guitar etc. by plucking its strings.
[imitating the sound]

tweak *VERB* **tweaks, tweaking, tweaked** pinch and twist or pull something sharply.
▷ **tweak** *noun*
[from Old English]

tweed *NOUN* thick woollen twill, often woven of mixed colours.
[originally a mistake; the Scottish word *tweel* (= twill) was wrongly read as *tweed* by being confused with the River Tweed]

tweeds *PLURAL NOUN* clothes made of tweed.

tweet *NOUN* **tweets** the chirping sound made by a small bird.
▷ **tweet** *verb*
[imitating the sound]

tweezers *PLURAL NOUN* small pincers for picking up or pulling very small things.
[from French *étui* = prison, in English = a case of surgical instruments, including tweezers]

twelve *NOUN* & *ADJECTIVE* the number 12.
▷ **twelfth** *adjective* & *noun*
[from Old English]

twenty *NOUN* **twenties** *ADJECTIVE* the number 20.
▷ **twentieth** *adjective* & *noun*
[from Old English]

twice *ADVERB* **1** two times; on two occasions. **2** double the amount.
[from Old English]

twiddle *VERB* **twiddles, twiddling, twiddled** turn something round or over and over in an idle way • *He tried twiddling the knob on the radio.*
▷ **twiddle** *noun* **twiddly** *adjective*
- **twiddle your thumbs** have nothing to do.
[origin unknown]

twig[1] *NOUN* **twigs** a small shoot on a branch or stem of a tree or shrub.
[from Old English]

twig[2] *VERB* **twigs, twigging, twigged** (*informal*) realize what something means.
[origin unknown]

twilight *NOUN* dim light from the sky just after sunset or just before sunrise.
[from Old English *twi-* = twice, double, + *light*]

twill *NOUN* material woven so that there is a pattern of diagonal lines.
[from Old English *twi-* = double, + Latin *licium* = thread]

twin *NOUN* **twins 1** either of two children or animals born to the same mother at one time. **2** either of two things that are exactly alike.

twin *VERB* **twins, twinning, twinned 1** put things together as a pair. **2** if a town is twinned with a town in a different country, the two towns exchange visits and organize cultural events together.
[from Old English]

twine *NOUN* strong thin string.

twine *VERB* **twines, twining, twined** twist or wind together or round something.
[from Old English]

twinge *NOUN* **twinges** a sudden pain or unpleasant feeling.
[from Old English]

twinkle *VERB* **twinkles, twinkling, twinkled** shine with tiny flashes of light; sparkle.
▷ **twinkle** *noun*
[from Old English]

twirl *VERB* **twirls, twirling, twirled** twist quickly.
▷ **twirl** *noun*
[origin unknown]

twist *VERB* **twists, twisting, twisted** **1** turn the ends of something in opposite directions. **2** turn round or from side to side • *The road twisted through the hills.* **3** bend something out of its proper shape • *a heap of twisted metal.* **4** pass threads or strands round something or round each other. **5** distort the meaning of something • *You're twisting my words.* **6** (*informal*) swindle somebody.
▷ **twister** *noun*

twist *NOUN* **twists 1** a twisting movement or action. **2** a strange or unexpected development in a story or series of events.
▷ **twisty** *adjective*
[from Old English]

twister *NOUN* **twisters** (*American*) a tornado or whirlwind.

twit *NOUN* **twits** (*slang*) a silly or foolish person.
[from *at* + Old English *witan* = to blame]

twitch *VERB* **twitches, twitching, twitched** move or pull with a slight jerk.
▷ **twitch** *noun*
[probably from old German]

twitter *VERB* **twitters, twittering, twittered** make quick chirping sounds.
▷ **twitter** *noun*
[imitating the sound]

two *NOUN* **twos** *ADJECTIVE* the number 2.
- **be in two minds** be undecided about something.
[from Old English]

two-bit *ADJECTIVE* (*American*)(*informal*) cheap or of very low quality.

two-faced *ADJECTIVE* insincere or deceitful.

tycoon *NOUN* **tycoons** a rich and influential business person.
[from Japanese *taikun* = great prince]

tying *present participle* of **tie**.

type *NOUN* **types 1** a kind or sort. **2** letters or figures etc. designed for use in printing.

type *VERB* **types, typing, typed** write something by using a typewriter.
[from Greek *typos* = impression]

typecast *VERB* **typecasts, typecasting, typecast** always give an actor the same kind of role to play • *She doesn't want to be typecast as a dumb blonde.*

typescript *NOUN* **typescripts** a typewritten document.

typewriter *NOUN* **typewriters** a machine with keys that are pressed to print letters or figures etc. on a piece of paper.
▷ **typewritten** *adjective*
[the word *typewriter* at first meant the person using the machine, as well as the machine itself]

typhoid fever *NOUN* a serious infectious disease with fever, caused by harmful bacteria in food or water etc.
[from *typhus*]

typhoon *NOUN* **typhoons** a violent hurricane in the western Pacific or East Asian seas.
[from Chinese *tai fung* = great wind]

typhus *NOUN* an infectious disease causing fever, weakness, and a rash.
[from Greek *typhos* = vapour]

typical *ADJECTIVE* **1** having the usual characteristics or qualities of a particular type of person or thing • *a typical school playground.* **2** usual in a particular person or thing • *He worked with typical carefulness.*
▷ **typically** *adverb*
[same origin as *type*]

typify (*say* tip-if-I) *VERB* **typifies, typifying, typified** be a typical example of something • *He typifies the popular image of a football manager.*

typist *NOUN* **typists** a person who types.

typography (*say* ty-pog-ra-fee) *NOUN* the style or appearance of the letters and figures etc. in printed material.
[from *type* + *-graphy*]

tyrannize (*say* tirran-I'z) *VERB* **tyrannizes, tyrannizing, tyrannized** behave like a tyrant to people.

tyrannosaurus *NOUN* **tyrannosauruses** a huge flesh-eating dinosaur that walked upright on its large hind legs.
[from Greek *tyrannos* = ruler + *sauros* = lizard]

tyranny (*say* tirran-ee) *NOUN* **tyrannies** **1** government by a tyrant. **2** the way a tyrant behaves towards people.
▷ **tyrannical** *adjective* **tyrannous** *adjective*

tyrant (*say* ty-rant) *NOUN* **tyrants** a person who rules cruelly and unjustly; someone who insists on being obeyed.
[from Greek *tyrannos* = ruler with full power]

tyre *NOUN* **tyres** a covering of rubber fitted round a wheel to make it grip the road and run more smoothly.
[from *attire*]

Uu

ubiquitous (*say* yoo-**bik**-wit-us) *ADJECTIVE* found everywhere • *Mobile phones are ubiquitous these days.*
▷ **ubiquity** *noun*
[from Latin *ubique* = everywhere]

-uble *PREFIX*, SEE **-able**.

U-boat *NOUN* **U-boats** a German submarine of the kind used in the Second World War.
[short for German *Unterseeboot* = undersea boat]

udder *NOUN* **udders** the bag-like part of a cow, ewe, female goat, etc. from which milk is taken.
[from Old English]

UFO *ABBREVIATION* unidentified flying object.

ugly *ADJECTIVE* **uglier**, **ugliest** **1** unpleasant to look at; not beautiful. **2** hostile and threatening • *The crowd was in an ugly mood.*
▷ **ugliness** *noun*
[from Old Norse *uggligr* = frightening]

UHF *ABBREVIATION* ultra-high frequency (between 300 and 3000 megahertz).

UHT *ABBREVIATION* ultra heat-treated; used to describe milk that has been treated at a very high temperature so that it will keep for a long time.

UK *ABBREVIATION* United Kingdom.

ukulele (*say* yoo-kul-ay-lee) *NOUN* **ukuleles** a small guitar with four strings.
[Hawaiian, literally = jumping flea]

ulcer *NOUN* **ulcers** a sore on the inside or outside of the body.
▷ **ulcerated** *adjective* **ulceration** *noun*
[from Latin]

ulterior *ADJECTIVE* beyond what is obvious or stated • *an ulterior motive.*
[Latin, = further]

ultimate *ADJECTIVE* furthest in a series of things; final • *Our ultimate destination is London.*
▷ **ultimately** *adverb*
[from Latin *ultimus* = last]

ultimatum (*say* ul-tim-**ay**-tum) *NOUN* **ultimatums** a final demand or statement that unless something is done by a certain time action will be taken or war will be declared.
[same origin as *ultimate*]

ultra- *PREFIX* **1** beyond (as in *ultraviolet*). **2** extremely; excessively (as in *ultramodern*).
[from Latin *ultra* = beyond]

ultramarine *NOUN* a deep bright blue.
[from *ultra-* + Latin *mare* = sea (because it was originally imported 'across the sea' from the East)]

ultrasonic *ADJECTIVE* (said about sound) beyond the range of human hearing.

ultrasound *NOUN* sound with an ultrasonic frequency, used in medical examinations.

ultraviolet *ADJECTIVE* (said about light rays) beyond the violet end of the spectrum and so not visible to the human eye.

umber *NOUN* a kind of brown pigment.
[from Italian *terra di Ombra* = earth of Umbria (a region in central Italy)]

umbilical (*say* um-**bil**-ik-al) *ADJECTIVE* to do with the navel.
[from Latin]

umbilical cord *NOUN* **umbilical cords** the tube through which a baby receives nourishment before it is born, connecting its body with the mother's womb.

umbrage *NOUN*
- **take umbrage** take offence.
[originally = shadow or shade: from Latin *umbra* = shadow]

umbrella *NOUN* **umbrellas** **1** a circular piece of material stretched over a folding frame with a central stick used as a handle,

or a central pole, which you open to protect yourself from rain or sun. **2** a general protection.
[from Italian *ombrella* = a little shade]

umlaut *NOUN* **umlauts** a mark (¨) placed over a vowel in German to indicate a change in its pronunciation.
[German, from *um* = about + *Laut* = a sound]

umpire *NOUN* **umpires** a referee in cricket, tennis, and some other games.

umpire *VERB* **umpires, umpiring, umpired** act as an umpire.
[from French *non* = not + *per* = an equal, *peer*²]

UN *ABBREVIATION* United Nations.

un- *PREFIX* **1** not (as in *uncertain*). **2** (before a verb) reversing the action (as in *unlock* = release from being locked).
[from Old English]
USAGE Many words beginning with this prefix are not listed here if their meaning is obvious.

unable *ADJECTIVE* not able to do something.

unaccountable *ADJECTIVE* **1** unable to be explained • *For some unaccountable reason I completely forgot your birthday.* **2** not accountable for what you do.
▷ **unaccountably** *adverb*

unadulterated *ADJECTIVE* pure; not mixed with things that are less good.
[from *un-* + *adulterate*]

unaided *ADJECTIVE* without help.

unanimous (*say* yoo-**nan**-im-us) *ADJECTIVE* with everyone agreeing • *a unanimous decision.*
▷ **unanimously** *adverb* **unanimity** (*say* yoo-nan-**im**-it-ee) *noun*
[from Latin *unus* = one + *animus* = mind]

unassuming *ADJECTIVE* modest; not arrogant or pretentious.
[from *un-* + *assume*]

unavoidable *ADJECTIVE* not able to be avoided.

unaware *ADJECTIVE* not aware.

unawares *ADVERB* unexpectedly; without warning • *His question caught me unawares.*

unbalanced *ADJECTIVE* **1** not balanced. **2** slightly mad or mentally ill.

unbearable *ADJECTIVE* not able to be endured.
▷ **unbearably** *adverb*

unbeatable *ADJECTIVE* unable to be defeated or surpassed.

unbeaten *ADJECTIVE* not defeated or surpassed.

unbecoming *ADJECTIVE* **1** not making a person look attractive. **2** not suitable or fitting.
[from *un-* + *become* (sense 2)]

unbeknown *ADJECTIVE* without someone knowing about it • *Unbeknown to us, they had planned a surprise party.*
[from *un-* + *be-* + *know*]

unbelievable *ADJECTIVE* not able to be believed; incredible.
▷ **unbelievably** *adverb*

unbend *VERB* **unbends, unbending, unbent** **1** change from a bent position; straighten up. **2** relax and become friendly.

unbiased *ADJECTIVE* not biased.

unbidden *ADJECTIVE* not commanded or invited.
[from *un-* + *bid*²]

unblock *VERB* **unblocks, unblocking, unblocked** remove an obstruction from something.

unborn *ADJECTIVE* not yet born.

unbridled *ADJECTIVE* not controlled or restrained • *unbridled rage.*

unbroken *ADJECTIVE* not broken or interrupted.

unburden *VERB* **unburdens, unburdening, unburdened** remove a burden from the person carrying it.
- **unburden yourself** tell someone your secrets or problems so that you feel better.

uncalled for *ADJECTIVE* not justified or necessary • *Such rudeness was quite uncalled for.*

uncanny *ADJECTIVE* **uncannier, uncanniest** strange or mysterious • *an uncanny coincidence.*
▷ **uncannily** *adverb* **uncanniness** *noun*
[from *un-* + an old sense of *canny* = knowing, able to be known]

unceremonious *ADJECTIVE* **1** without formality or ceremony. **2** offhand or abrupt

uncertain *ADJECTIVE* **1** not known certainly. **2** not sure about something. **3** not reliable
• *His aim is rather uncertain.*
▷ **uncertainly** *adverb* **uncertainty** *noun*
- **in no uncertain terms** clearly and forcefully.

uncharitable *ADJECTIVE* making unkind judgements of people or actions.
▷ **uncharitably** *adverb*

uncle *NOUN* **uncles** the brother of your father or mother; your aunt's husband.
[from Latin *avunculus* = uncle]

unclothed *ADJECTIVE* naked.

uncomfortable *ADJECTIVE* not comfortable.
▷ **uncomfortably** *adverb*

uncommon *ADJECTIVE* not common; unusual.

uncompromising (*say* un-komp-rom-I-zing) *ADJECTIVE* not allowing a compromise; inflexible.

unconcerned *ADJECTIVE* not caring about something; not worried.

unconditional *ADJECTIVE* without any conditions; absolute • *unconditional surrender.*
▷ **unconditionally** *adverb*

unconscious *ADJECTIVE* **1** not conscious. **2** not aware of things.
▷ **unconsciously** *adverb* **unconsciousness** *noun*

uncontrollable *ADJECTIVE* unable to be controlled or stopped.
▷ **uncontrollably** *adverb*

uncooperative *ADJECTIVE* not cooperative.

uncouple *VERB* **uncouples, uncoupling, uncoupled** disconnect.

uncouth (*say* un-kooth) *ADJECTIVE* rude and rough in manner.
[from *un-* + Old English *cuth* = known]

uncover *VERB* **uncovers, uncovering, uncovered** **1** remove the covering from something. **2** reveal or expose • *They uncovered a plot to kill the king.*

unction *NOUN* **1** anointing with oil, especially in a religious ceremony. **2** unctuousness.
[from Latin *unguere* = to oil or smear]

unctuous (*say* unk-tew-us) *ADJECTIVE* having an oily manner; polite in an exaggerated way.
▷ **unctuously** *adverb* **unctuousness** *noun*
[same origin as *unction*]

undecided *ADJECTIVE* **1** not yet settled; not certain. **2** not having made up your mind yet.

undeniable *ADJECTIVE* impossible to deny; undoubtedly true.
▷ **undeniably** *adverb*

under *PREPOSITION* **1** below or beneath • *Hide it under the desk.* **2** less than • *under 5 years old.* **3** governed or controlled by • *The country prospered under his rule.* **4** in the process of; undergoing • *The road is under repair.* **5** using • *He writes under the name of 'Lewis Carroll'.* **6** according to the rules of • *This is permitted under our agreement.*
- **under way** in motion or in progress.

under *ADVERB* in or to a lower place or level or condition • *Slowly the diver went under.*
[from Old English]

under- *PREFIX* **1** below or beneath (as in *underwear*). **2** lower; subordinate (as in *undermanager*). **3** not enough; incompletely (as in *undercooked*).

underarm *ADJECTIVE* & *ADVERB* **1** moving the hand and arm forward and upwards. **2** in or for the armpit.

undercarriage *NOUN* **undercarriages** an aircraft's landing wheels and their supports.

underclothes *PLURAL NOUN* underwear.
▷ **underclothing** *noun*

undercover *ADJECTIVE* done or doing things secretly • *an undercover agent.*

undercurrent *NOUN* **undercurrents** **1** a current that is below the surface or below another current. **2** an underlying feeling or influence • *an undercurrent of fear.*

undercut *VERB* **undercuts, undercutting, undercut** sell something for a lower price than someone else sells it.

underdeveloped *ADJECTIVE* **1** not fully developed or grown. **2** (said about a country) poor and lacking modern industrial development.

underdog *NOUN* **underdogs** a person or team that is expected to lose a contest or struggle.

A B C D E F G H I J K L M N O P Q R S T U V W X Y Z

underdone *ADJECTIVE* not thoroughly done; undercooked.

underestimate *VERB* **underestimates, underestimating, underestimated** make too low an estimate of a person or thing.

underfoot *ADVERB* on the ground; under your feet.

undergarment *NOUN* **undergarments** a piece of underwear.

undergo *VERB* **undergoes, undergoing, underwent, undergone** experience or endure something; be subjected to • *The new aircraft underwent intensive tests.*

undergraduate *NOUN* **undergraduates** a student at a university who has not yet taken a degree.

underground *ADJECTIVE* & *ADVERB* **1** under the ground. **2** done or working in secret.

underground *NOUN* a railway that runs through tunnels under the ground.

undergrowth *NOUN* bushes and other plants growing closely, especially under trees.

underhand *ADJECTIVE* done or doing things in a sly or secret way.

underlie *VERB* **underlies, underlying, underlay, underlain** **1** be the basis or explanation of something. **2** be or lie under something.

underline *VERB* **underlines, underlining, underlined** **1** draw a line under a word etc. **2** emphasize something.

underling *NOUN* **underlings** a person working under someone's authority or control; a subordinate.

underlying *ADJECTIVE* **1** forming the basis or explanation of something • *the underlying causes of the trouble.* **2** lying under something • *the underlying rocks.*

undermine *VERB* **undermines, undermining, undermined** weaken something gradually.

underneath *PREPOSITION* & *ADVERB* below or beneath.
[from *under-* + Old English *neothan* = beneath]

underpants *PLURAL NOUN* a piece of men's underwear covering the lower part of the body, worn under trousers.

underpass *NOUN* **underpasses** a road that goes underneath another.

underpay *VERB* **underpays, underpaying, underpaid** pay someone too little.

underprivileged *ADJECTIVE* having less than the normal standard of living or rights in a community.

underrate *VERB* **underrates, underrating, underrated** have too low an opinion of a person or thing.

undersell *VERB* **undersells, underselling, undersold** sell something at a lower price than another person.

undersigned *ADJECTIVE* who has or have signed at the bottom of this document • *We, the undersigned, wish to protest.*

undersized *ADJECTIVE* of less than the normal size.

understand *VERB* **understands, understanding, understood** **1** know what something means or how it works or why it exists. **2** know and tolerate a person's ways. **3** have been told • *I understand that you would like to speak to me.* **4** take something for granted • *Your expenses will be paid, that's understood.*
[from Old English]

understandable *ADJECTIVE* **1** able to be understood. **2** reasonable or natural • *She replied with understandable anger.*
▷ **understandably** *adverb*

understanding *NOUN* **1** the power to understand or think; intelligence. **2** sympathy or tolerance. **3** agreement in opinion or feeling • *a better understanding between nations.*

understanding *ADJECTIVE* sympathetic and helpful • *Thanks for being so understanding.*

understatement *NOUN* **understatements** an incomplete or very restrained statement of facts or truth • *To say they disagreed is an understatement; they had a violent quarrel.*

understudy *NOUN* **understudies** an actor who learns a part in order to be able to play it if the usual performer is ill or absent.

understudy *VERB* **understudies, understudying, understudied** be an understudy for an actor or part.

undertake *VERB* **undertakes, undertaking, undertook, undertaken** **1** agree or promise to do something. **2** take on a task or responsibility.

undertaker *NOUN* **undertakers** a person whose job is to arrange funerals and burials or cremations.

undertaking *NOUN* **undertakings** **1** a job or task that is being undertaken. **2** a promise or guarantee. **3** the business of an undertaker.

undertone *NOUN* **undertones** **1** a low or quiet tone • *They spoke in undertones.* **2** an underlying quality or feeling etc. • *His letter has a threatening undertone.*

undertow *NOUN* a current below that of the surface of the sea and moving in the opposite direction.

underwater *ADJECTIVE* & *ADVERB* placed, used, or done beneath the surface of water.

underwear *NOUN* clothes worn next to the skin, under indoor clothing.

underweight *ADJECTIVE* not heavy enough.

underwent *past tense* of **undergo**.

underworld *NOUN* **1** the people who are regularly involved in crime. **2** (in myths and legends) the place for the spirits of the dead, under the earth.

underwrite *VERB* **underwrites, underwriting, underwrote, underwritten** guarantee to finance something, or to pay for any loss or damage etc.

▷ **underwriter** *noun*

[because the underwriter used to sign his or her name underneath the names of the other people in the agreement]

undesirable *ADJECTIVE* not desirable; objectionable.

▷ **undesirably** *adverb*

undeveloped *ADJECTIVE* not yet developed.

undignified *ADJECTIVE* not dignified.

undo *VERB* **undoes, undoing, undid, undone** **1** unfasten or unwrap. **2** cancel the effect of something • *He has undone all our careful work.*

undoing *NOUN*

- **be someone's undoing** be the cause of their ruin or failure.

undoubted *ADJECTIVE* certain; not regarded as doubtful • *She has undoubted talent.*

▷ **undoubtedly** *adverb*

undress *VERB* **undresses, undressing, undressed** take your clothes off.

undue *ADJECTIVE* excessive; too great.

undulate *VERB* **undulates, undulating, undulated** move like a wave or waves; have a wavy appearance.

▷ **undulation** *noun*

[from Latin *unda* = a wave]

unduly *ADVERB* excessively; more than is reasonable.

undying *ADJECTIVE* lasting forever.

unearth *VERB* **unearths, unearthing, unearthed** **1** dig something up; uncover something by digging. **2** find something by searching.

unearthly *ADJECTIVE* **1** unnatural; strange and frightening. **2** (*informal*) very early or inconvenient • *We had to get up at an unearthly hour.*

uneasy *ADJECTIVE* **1** worried or anxious. **2** uncomfortable.

▷ **uneasily** *adverb* **uneasiness** *noun*

uneatable *ADJECTIVE* not fit to be eaten.

uneconomic *ADJECTIVE* not profitable.

unemployed *ADJECTIVE* without a job.

▷ **unemployment** *noun*

unending *ADJECTIVE* not coming to an end.

unequal *ADJECTIVE* **1** not equal in amount, size, or value. **2** not giving the same opportunities to everyone • *an unequal society.*

▷ **unequalled** *adjective* **unequally** *adverb*

unequivocal *ADJECTIVE* not at all ambiguous; completely clear • *an unequivocal reply.*

unerring (*say* un-er-ing) *ADJECTIVE* making no mistake • *unerring accuracy.*

[from *un-* + *err*]

uneven *ADJECTIVE* **1** not level or regular. **2** not equally balanced • *an uneven contest.*
▷ **unevenly** *adverb* **unevenness** *noun*

unexceptionable *ADJECTIVE* not in any way objectionable.
[from *un-* + *exception* as in 'take exception']
USAGE Do not confuse with **unexceptional**.

unexceptional *ADJECTIVE* not exceptional; quite ordinary.
USAGE Do not confuse with **unexceptionable**.

unexpected *ADJECTIVE* not expected.
▷ **unexpectedly** *adverb* **unexpectedness** *noun*

unfair *ADJECTIVE* not fair; unjust.
▷ **unfairly** *adverb* **unfairness** *noun*

unfaithful *ADJECTIVE* **1** not faithful or loyal. **2** not sexually loyal to one partner.

unfamiliar *ADJECTIVE* not familiar.
▷ **unfamiliarity** *noun*

unfasten *VERB* **unfastens, unfastening, unfastened** open the fastenings of something.

unfavourable *ADJECTIVE* not favourable.
▷ **unfavourably** *adverb*

unfeeling *ADJECTIVE* not caring about other people's feelings; unsympathetic.

unfit *ADJECTIVE* **1** not suitable. **2** not in perfect health because you do not take enough exercise.

unfold *VERB* **unfolds, unfolding, unfolded** **1** open; spread out. **2** make or become known slowly • *as the story unfolds.*

unforeseen *ADJECTIVE* not foreseen; unexpected.

unforgettable *ADJECTIVE* not able to be forgotten.

unforgivable *ADJECTIVE* not able to be forgiven.

unfortunate *ADJECTIVE* **1** unlucky. **2** unsuitable or regrettable • *an unfortunate remark.*
▷ **unfortunately** *adverb*

unfounded *ADJECTIVE* not based on facts.
[from *un-* + *found*^{2}]

unfreeze *VERB* **unfreezes, unfreezing, unfroze, unfrozen** thaw; cause something to thaw.

unfriendly *ADJECTIVE* not friendly.
▷ **unfriendliness** *noun*

unfrock *VERB* **unfrocks, unfrocking, unfrocked** dismiss a person from being a priest.
[from *un-* + an old sense of *frock* = a priest's robe]

unfurl *VERB* **unfurls, unfurling, unfurled** unroll; spread out • *They unfurled a large flag.*

unfurnished *ADJECTIVE* without furniture • *an unfurnished flat.*

ungainly *ADJECTIVE* awkward-looking or clumsy.
▷ **ungainliness** *noun*
[from *un-* + Middle English *gainly* = graceful]

ungodly *ADJECTIVE* **1** not giving reverence to God; not religious. **2** (*informal*) outrageous; very inconvenient • *She woke me at an ungodly hour.*
▷ **ungodliness** *noun*

ungovernable *ADJECTIVE* impossible to control.

ungracious *ADJECTIVE* not kindly or courteous.
▷ **ungraciously** *adverb*

ungrateful *ADJECTIVE* not grateful.
▷ **ungratefully** *adverb*

unguarded *ADJECTIVE* **1** not guarded. **2** without thought or caution; indiscreet • *He said this in an unguarded moment.*

unguent (*say* ung-went) *NOUN* **unguents** an ointment or lubricant.
[same origin as *unction*]

unhappy *ADJECTIVE* **1** not happy; sad. **2** unfortunate or unsuitable • *an unhappy coincidence.*
▷ **unhappily** *adverb* **unhappiness** *noun*

unhealthy *ADJECTIVE* not healthy.
▷ **unhealthiness** *noun*

unheard-of *ADJECTIVE* never known or done before; extraordinary.

unhinge *VERB* **unhinges, unhinging, unhinged** cause a person's mind to become unbalanced.

uni- *PREFIX* one; single (as in *unicorn*).
[from Latin *unus* = one]

unicorn *NOUN* **unicorns** (in legends) an animal that is like a horse with one long straight horn growing from its forehead.
[from *uni-* + Latin *cornu* = horn]

uniform *NOUN* **uniforms** special clothes showing that the wearer is a member of a certain organization, school, etc.

uniform *ADJECTIVE* always the same; not varying • *The desks are of uniform size.*
▷ **uniformly** *adverb* **uniformity** *noun*
[from *uni-* + Latin *forma* = form]

uniformed *ADJECTIVE* wearing a uniform.

unify *VERB* **unifies, unifying, unified** make a number of things into one thing; unite.
▷ **unification** *noun*
[same origin as *unit*]

unilateral *ADJECTIVE* done by one person or group or country etc. • *a unilateral decision.*
[from *uni-* + *lateral*]

unilateral disarmament *NOUN* getting rid of nuclear weapons without waiting for other countries to agree to do the same.

unimpeachable *ADJECTIVE* completely trustworthy • *unimpeachable honesty.*
[from *un-* + *impeach* + *-able*]

uninhabitable *ADJECTIVE* unfit to live in.

uninhabited *ADJECTIVE* with nobody living there.

uninhibited *ADJECTIVE* having no inhibitions.

uninterested *ADJECTIVE* not interested; showing or feeling no concern.
USAGE See the note at **disinterested**.

union *NOUN* **unions 1** the joining of things together; a united thing. **2** a trade union.
[from Latin *unio* = unity]

unionist *NOUN* **unionists 1** a member of a trade union. **2** a person who wishes to unite one country with another.

Union Jack *NOUN* **Union Jacks** the flag of the United Kingdom.

unique (*say* yoo-**neek**) *ADJECTIVE* being the only one of its kind • *This jewel is unique.*
▷ **uniquely** *adverb*
[French, from Latin *unicus* = one and only]
USAGE *Unique* does not mean 'unusual' or 'remarkable', so avoid saying things like *very unique* or *most unique*.

unisex *ADJECTIVE* designed to be suitable for both sexes • *a unisex hairdresser's.*

unison *NOUN*
- **in unison 1** with all sounding or singing the same tune etc. together, or speaking in chorus. **2** in agreement.
[from *uni-* + Latin *sonus* = sound]

unit *NOUN* **units 1** an amount used as a standard in measuring or counting things • *Centimetres are units of length.* **2** a group, device, piece of furniture, etc. regarded as a single thing but forming part of a larger group or whole • *an army unit; a sink unit.* **3** (*in mathematics*) any whole number less than 10.
[from Latin *unus* = one]

unite *VERB* **unites, uniting, united** join together; make or become one thing.
[same origin as *unit*]

United Kingdom *NOUN* Great Britain and Northern Ireland.
USAGE See note at **Britain**.

unity *NOUN* **1** being united; being in agreement. **2** something whole that is made up of parts. **3** (*in mathematics*) the number one.

universal *ADJECTIVE* to do with or including or done by everyone or everything.
▷ **universally** *adverb*

universe *NOUN* everything that exists, including the earth and living things and all the stars and planets.
[from Latin *universus* = combined into one]

university *NOUN* **universities** a place where people go to study at an advanced level after leaving school.
[from Latin *universitas*, literally = the universe, later = a community or group of people (i.e. the teachers and students)]

unjust *ADJECTIVE* not fair or just.

unkempt *ADJECTIVE* looking untidy or neglected.
[from *un-* + an old word *kempt* = combed]

a b c d e f g h i j k l m n o p q r s t **u** v w x y z

unkind *ADJECTIVE* not kind.
▷ **unkindly** *adverb* **unkindness** *noun*

unknown *ADJECTIVE* not known.

unlawful *ADJECTIVE* not legal.

unleaded *ADJECTIVE* (said about petrol) without added lead.

unleash *VERB* **unleashes, unleashing, unleashed** **1** set a dog free from a leash. **2** let a strong feeling or force be released.

unleavened (*say* un-lev-end) *ADJECTIVE* (said about bread) made without yeast or other substances that would make it rise.

unless *CONJUNCTION* except when; if ... not • *We cannot go unless we are invited.*

unlike *PREPOSITION* not like • *Unlike me, she enjoys cricket.*

unlike *ADJECTIVE* not alike; different • *The two children are very unlike.*

unlikely *ADJECTIVE* **unlikelier, unlikeliest** not likely to happen or be true.

unlimited *ADJECTIVE* not limited; very great or very many.

unload *VERB* **unloads, unloading, unloaded** remove the load of things carried by a ship, aircraft, vehicle, etc.

unlock *VERB* **unlocks, unlocking, unlocked** open something by undoing a lock.

unlucky *ADJECTIVE* not lucky; having or bringing bad luck.
▷ **unluckily** *adverb*

unmanageable *ADJECTIVE* unable to be managed.

unmarried *ADJECTIVE* not married.

unmask *VERB* **unmasks, unmasking, unmasked** **1** remove a person's mask. **2** reveal what a person or thing really is.

unmentionable *ADJECTIVE* too bad or embarrassing to be spoken of.

unmistakable *ADJECTIVE* not able to be mistaken for another person or thing.
▷ **unmistakably** *adverb*

unmitigated *ADJECTIVE* absolute • *an unmitigated disaster.*
[from *un-* + *mitigate*]

unnatural *ADJECTIVE* not natural or normal.
▷ **unnaturally** *adverb*

unnecessary *ADJECTIVE* not necessary; more than is necessary.

unnerve *VERB* **unnerves, unnerving, unnerved** make someone lose courage or determination.

unoccupied *ADJECTIVE* not occupied.

unofficial *ADJECTIVE* not official.
▷ **unofficially** *adverb*

unorthodox *ADJECTIVE* not generally accepted • *an unorthodox method.*

unpack *VERB* **unpacks, unpacking, unpacked** take things out of a suitcase, bag, box, etc.

unpaid *ADJECTIVE* **1** not yet paid • *an unpaid bill.* **2** not receiving payment for work you do.

unparalleled *ADJECTIVE* having no parallel or equal.

unparliamentary *ADJECTIVE* impolite or abusive.
USAGE It is a rule of debates in Parliament that speakers must be polite to each other. Impolite language is 'unparliamentary'.

unpick *VERB* **unpicks, unpicking, unpicked** undo the stitching of something.

unpleasant *ADJECTIVE* not pleasant.
▷ **unpleasantly** *adverb* **unpleasantness** *noun*

unpopular *ADJECTIVE* not popular.

unprecedented (*say* un-press-id-en-tid) *ADJECTIVE* that has never happened before.
[from *un-* + *precedent*]

unprejudiced *ADJECTIVE* without prejudice; impartial.

unprepared *ADJECTIVE* not prepared beforehand; not ready or equipped.

unprepossessing *ADJECTIVE* not attractive.

unprincipled *ADJECTIVE* without good moral principles; unscrupulous.

unprintable *ADJECTIVE* too rude or indecent to be printed.

unprofessional *ADJECTIVE* not professional; not worthy of a member of a profession.

unprofitable *ADJECTIVE* not producing a profit or advantage.
▷ **unprofitably** *adverb*

unqualified *ADJECTIVE* **1** not officially qualified to do something. **2** not limited • *We gave it our unqualified approval.*

unravel *VERB* **unravels, unravelling, unravelled 1** disentangle. **2** undo something that is knitted. **3** investigate and solve a mystery etc.
[from *un-* + an old word *ravel* = tangle]

unready *ADJECTIVE* not ready; hesitating.
USAGE In the title of the English king *Ethelred the Unready* the word means 'lacking good advice or wisdom'.

unreal *ADJECTIVE* not real; existing in the imagination only.
▷ **unreality** *noun*

unreasonable *ADJECTIVE* **1** not reasonable. **2** excessive or unjust.
▷ **unreasonably** *adverb*

unreel *VERB* **unreels, unreeling, unreeled** unwind from a reel.

unrelieved *ADJECTIVE* without anything to vary it • *unrelieved gloom.*

unremitting *ADJECTIVE* never stopping or relaxing; persistent.
[from *un-* + *remit*]

unrequited (*say* un-ri-kwy-tid) *ADJECTIVE* (said about love) not returned or rewarded.
[from *un-* + *requite* = reward or pay back]

unreserved *ADJECTIVE* **1** not reserved. **2** without restriction; complete • *unreserved loyalty.*
▷ **unreservedly** *adverb*

unrest *NOUN* trouble or rioting caused because people are dissatisfied.

unripe *ADJECTIVE* not yet ripe.

unrivalled *ADJECTIVE* having no equal; better than all others.

unroll *VERB* **unrolls, unrolling, unrolled** open something that has been rolled up.

unruly *ADJECTIVE* difficult to control; disorderly.
▷ **unruliness** *noun*
[from *un-* + *rule*]

unsavoury *ADJECTIVE* unpleasant or disgusting.

unscathed *ADJECTIVE* uninjured.
[from *un-* + Middle English *scathe* = harm or injure]

unscrew *VERB* **unscrews, unscrewing, unscrewed** undo something that has been screwed up.

unscrupulous *ADJECTIVE* having no scruples about wrongdoing.

unseat *VERB* **unseats, unseating, unseated** throw a person from horseback or from a seat on a bicycle etc.

unseemly *ADJECTIVE* not proper or suitable; indecent.

unseen *ADJECTIVE* not seen; invisible.

unseen *NOUN* **unseens** a passage for translation without previous preparation.

unselfish *ADJECTIVE* not selfish.

unsettle *VERB* **unsettles, unsettling, unsettled** make someone feel uneasy or anxious.
▷ **unsettling** *adjective*

unsettled *ADJECTIVE* **1** not settled or calm. **2** (said about weather) likely to change.

unshakeable *ADJECTIVE* not able to be shaken; firm • *an unshakeable belief.*

unshaven *ADJECTIVE* (said about a man) not recently shaved.

unsightly *ADJECTIVE* not pleasant to look at; ugly.
▷ **unsightliness** *noun*

unskilled *ADJECTIVE* not having or not needing special skill or training.

unsociable *ADJECTIVE* not sociable.

unsocial *ADJECTIVE* not social.
- **unsocial hours** time spent working when most people are free.

unsolicited *ADJECTIVE* not asked for • *unsolicited advice.*
[from *un-* + *solicit*]

unsound *ADJECTIVE* **1** not reliable; not based on sound evidence or reasoning • *unsound advice.* **2** not firm or strong. **3** not healthy • *of unsound mind.*
[from *un-*+ *sound*[3]]

unspeakable *ADJECTIVE* too bad to be described; very objectionable.

unstable *ADJECTIVE* not stable; likely to change or become unbalanced.

unsteady *ADJECTIVE* not steady.

unstinting *ADJECTIVE* giving generously.
[from *un-* + *stint*]

A B C D E F G H I J K L M N O P Q R S T U V W X Y Z

unstuck *ADJECTIVE*
- **come unstuck** **1** cease to stick. **2** (*informal*) fail or go wrong.

unsuccessful *ADJECTIVE* not successful.

unsuitable *ADJECTIVE* not suitable.

unsung *ADJECTIVE* (*formal*) not famous or praised but deserving to be • *the unsung heroes of the campaign.*

unsure *ADJECTIVE* not confident or certain.

untenable *ADJECTIVE* not able to be justified or defended.

unthinkable *ADJECTIVE* too bad or too unlikely to be worth considering.

unthinking *ADJECTIVE* thoughtless.

untidy *ADJECTIVE* **untidier**, **untidiest** not tidy.
▷ **untidily** *adverb* **untidiness** *noun*

untie *VERB* **unties**, **untying**, **untied** undo something that has been tied.

until *PREPOSITION* & *CONJUNCTION* up to a particular time or event.
[from Old Norse]
USAGE See the note on **till**[1].

untimely *ADJECTIVE* happening too soon or at an unsuitable time.

unto *PREPOSITION* (*old use*) to.
[from *until* + *to* (preposition)]

untold *ADJECTIVE* **1** not told. **2** too much or too many to be counted • *untold wealth* or *wealth untold.*

untoward *ADJECTIVE* inconvenient or unfortunate • *if nothing untoward happens.*
[from *un-* + *toward* = fortunate, promising]

untraceable *ADJECTIVE* unable to be traced.

untrue *ADJECTIVE* not true.

untruth *NOUN* **untruths** an untrue statement; a lie.
▷ **untruthful** *adjective* **untruthfully** *adverb*

unused *ADJECTIVE* **1** (*say* un-**yoozd**) not yet used • *an unused stamp.* **2** (*say* un-**yoost**) not accustomed • *He is unused to eating meat.*

unusual *ADJECTIVE* not usual; strange or exceptional.
▷ **unusually** *adverb*

unutterable *ADJECTIVE* too great to be described • *unutterable joy.*
[from *un-* + *utter* + *-able*]

unvarnished *ADJECTIVE* **1** not varnished. **2** plain and straightforward • *the unvarnished truth.*

unveil *VERB* **unveils**, **unveiling**, **unveiled** **1** remove a veil or covering from something. **2** reveal.

unwanted *ADJECTIVE* not wanted.

unwarranted *ADJECTIVE* not justified; uncalled for.
[from *un-* + *warrant*]

unwary *ADJECTIVE* not cautious or careful about danger.
▷ **unwarily** *adverb* **unwariness** *noun*

unwell *ADJECTIVE* not in good health.

unwholesome *ADJECTIVE* not wholesome.

unwieldy *ADJECTIVE* awkward to move or control because of its size, shape, or weight.
▷ **unwieldiness** *noun*
[from *un-* + *wield*]

unwilling *ADJECTIVE* not willing.
▷ **unwillingly** *adverb*

unwind *VERB* **unwinds**, **unwinding**, **unwound** **1** unroll. **2** (*informal*) relax after a time of work or strain.

unwise *ADJECTIVE* not wise; foolish.
▷ **unwisely** *adverb*

unwitting *ADJECTIVE* **1** unintentional. **2** unaware.
▷ **unwittingly** *adverb*

unwonted (*say* un-**wohn**-tid) *ADJECTIVE* not customary or usual • *She spoke with unwonted rudeness.*
▷ **unwontedly** *adverb*
[from *un-* + *wont*]

unworn *ADJECTIVE* not yet worn.

unworthy *ADJECTIVE* not worthy or deserving.

unwrap *VERB* **unwraps**, **unwrapping**, **unwrapped** open something that is wrapped.

up *ADVERB* **1** to or in a higher place or position or level • *Prices went up.* **2** so as to be upright • *Stand up.* **3** out of bed • *It's time to get up.* **4** completely • *Eat up your carrots.* **5** finished • *Your time is up.* **6** (*informal*) happening • *Something is up.*
- **up against** **1** close to. **2** (*informal*) faced with difficulties, dangers, etc.
- **ups and downs** alternate good and bad luck.
- **up to** **1** until. **2** busy with or doing something • *What are you up to?* **3** capable of • *I don't think I'm up to it.* **4** needed from • *It's up to us to help her.*
- **up to date** **1** modern or fashionable. **2** giving recent information etc.

USAGE Use hyphens when this is used as an adjective before a noun, e.g. *up-to-date information* (but *The information is up to date*).

up *PREPOSITION* upwards through or along or into • *Water came up the pipes.*
[from Old English]

up-and-coming *ADJECTIVE* (*informal*) likely to become successful.

upbraid *VERB* **upbraids, upbraiding, upbraided** (*formal*) scold or reproach someone.
[from Old English]

upbringing *NOUN* the way someone is trained during childhood.

update *VERB* **updates, updating, updated** bring a thing up to date.
▷ **update** *noun*

upgrade *VERB* **upgrades, upgrading, upgraded** **1** improve a machine by installing new parts in it. **2** raise a person or their job to a higher rank.
▷ **upgrade** *noun*

upheaval *NOUN* **upheavals** a sudden violent change or disturbance.
[from *up-* + *heave*]

uphill *ADVERB* up a slope.

uphill *ADJECTIVE* **1** going up a slope. **2** difficult • *It was an uphill struggle.*

uphold *VERB* **upholds, upholding, upheld** support or maintain a decision or belief etc.

upholster *VERB* **upholsters, upholstering, upholstered** put a soft padded covering on furniture.
▷ **upholstery** *noun*
[from *uphold* = maintain and repair]

upkeep *NOUN* keeping something in good condition; the cost of this.

uplands *PLURAL NOUN* the higher parts of a country or region.
▷ **upland** *adjective*

uplifting *ADJECTIVE* making you feel more cheerful.

upload *VERB* **uploads, uploading, uploaded** (*in computing*) move data from a personal computer to a computer network so that it can be read by other users.

upon *PREPOSITION* on.
[from *up* (adverb) + *on* (preposition)]

upper *ADJECTIVE* higher in place or rank etc.

upper case *NOUN* capital letters.

upper class *NOUN* **upper classes** the highest class in society, especially the aristocracy.
▷ **upper-class** *adjective*

uppermost *ADJECTIVE* highest.

uppermost *ADVERB* on or to the top or the highest place • *Keep the painted side uppermost.*
[from *upper* + *most*]

upright *ADJECTIVE* **1** vertical or erect. **2** strictly honest or honourable.

upright *NOUN* **uprights** a post or rod etc. placed upright, especially as a support.

uprising *NOUN* **uprisings** a rebellion or revolt.

uproar *NOUN* an outburst of noise or excitement or anger.

uproarious *ADJECTIVE* very noisy.

uproot *VERB* **uproots, uprooting, uprooted** **1** remove a plant and its roots from the ground. **2** make someone leave the place where he or she has lived for a long time.

upset *VERB* **upsets, upsetting, upset** **1** overturn; knock something over. **2** make a person unhappy or distressed. **3** disturb the normal working of something; disrupt • *This has really upset my plans.*

upset *ADJECTIVE* **1** unhappy or distressed. **2** slightly ill • *an upset stomach.*

A B C D E F G H I J K L M N O P Q R S T U V W X Y Z

upset *NOUN* **upsets 1** a slight illness • *a stomach upset.* **2** an unexpected result or setback • *There has been a major upset in the quarter-finals.*

upshot *NOUN* **upshots** the eventual outcome.
[originally = the final shot in an archery contest]

upside down *ADVERB & ADJECTIVE* **1** with the upper part underneath instead of on top. **2** in great disorder; very untidy • *Everything had been turned upside down.*

upstairs *ADVERB & ADJECTIVE* to or on a higher floor.

upstart *NOUN* **upstarts** a person who has risen suddenly to a high position, especially one who then behaves arrogantly.
[from an old verb *upstart* = to spring up suddenly]

upstream *ADJECTIVE & ADVERB* in the direction from which a stream flows.

uptake *NOUN*
- **quick on the uptake** quick to understand.
- **slow on the uptake** slow to understand.

uptight *ADJECTIVE* (*informal*) tense and nervous or annoyed.

upward *ADJECTIVE & ADVERB* going towards what is higher.
▷ **upwards** *adverb*
[from *up* + *-ward*]

uranium *NOUN* a heavy radioactive grey metal used as a source of nuclear energy.
[named after the planet *Uranus*]

urban *ADJECTIVE* to do with a town or city.
[from Latin *urbis* = of a city]

urbane *ADJECTIVE* having smoothly polite manners.
▷ **urbanely** *adverb* **urbanity** *noun*
[same origin as *urban*]

urbanize *VERB* **urbanizes, urbanizing, urbanized** change a place into a town-like area.
▷ **urbanization** *noun*

urchin *NOUN* **urchins 1** a poorly dressed or mischievous boy. **2** a sea urchin.
[from Latin *ericius* = hedgehog]

Urdu (*say* oor-doo) *NOUN* a language related to Hindi, spoken in northern India and Pakistan.

urge *VERB* **urges, urging, urged 1** try to persuade a person to do something. **2** drive people or animals onward. **3** recommend or advise.

urge *NOUN* **urges** a strong desire or wish.
[from Latin]

urgent *ADJECTIVE* needing to be done or dealt with immediately.
▷ **urgently** *adverb* **urgency** *noun*
[from Latin *urgens* = urging]

urinal (*say* yoor-rye-nal) *NOUN* **urinals** a bowl or trough fixed to the wall in a men's public toilet, for men to urinate into.
[from Latin *urinalis* = urinary]

urinate (*say* yoor-in-ayt) *VERB* **urinates, urinating, urinated** pass urine out of your body.
▷ **urination** *noun*

urine (*say* yoor-in) *NOUN* waste liquid that collects in the bladder and is passed out of the body.
▷ **urinary** *adjective*
[from Latin]

urn *NOUN* **urns 1** a large metal container with a tap, in which water is heated. **2** a container shaped like a vase, usually with a foot, especially a container for holding the ashes of a cremated person.
[from Latin]

US *ABBREVIATION* United States (of America).

us *PRONOUN* the form of *we* used when it is the object of a verb or after a preposition.
[from Old English]

USA *ABBREVIATION* United States of America.

usable *ADJECTIVE* able to be used.

usage *NOUN* **usages 1** use; the way something is used. **2** the way words are used in a language • *English usage often differs from American usage.*

use (*say* yooz) *VERB* **uses, using, used** perform an action or job with something • *Use soap for washing.*
- **used to 1** was or were in the habit of doing • *We used to go by train.* **2** accustomed to or familiar with • *I'm used to his strange behaviour.*
- **use up** use all of something.

use (*say* yooss) *NOUN* **uses 1** the action of using something; being used • *the use of computers in schools.* **2** the purpose for which something is used • *Can you find a use for this crate?* **3** the quality of being useful • *These scissors are no use at all.*
[from Latin]

used *ADJECTIVE* not new; second-hand • *used cars.*

useful *ADJECTIVE* able to be used a lot or to do something that needs doing.
▷ **usefully** *adverb* **usefulness** *noun*

useless *ADJECTIVE* not useful; producing no effect • *Their efforts were useless.*
▷ **uselessly** *adverb* **uselessness** *noun*

user *NOUN* **users** a person who uses something.

user-friendly *ADJECTIVE* designed to be easy to use.

usher *NOUN* **ushers** a person who shows people to their seats in a cinema, theatre, or church.

usher *VERB* **ushers, ushering, ushered** lead someone in or out; escort someone as an usher.
[from Latin *ostiarius* = doorkeeper]

usherette *NOUN* **usherettes** a woman who shows people to their seats in a cinema or theatre.

USSR *ABBREVIATION* (*old use*) Union of Soviet Socialist Republics.

usual *ADJECTIVE* such as happens or is done or used etc. always or most of the time.
▷ **usually** *adverb*
[from Latin *usum* = used]

usurp (*say* yoo-zerp) *VERB* **usurps, usurping, usurped** take power or a position or right etc. from someone wrongfully or by force.
▷ **usurpation** *noun* **usurper** *noun*
[from Latin *usurpare* = seize in order to use]

usury (*say* yoo-zher-ee) *NOUN* the lending of money at an excessively high rate of interest.
▷ **usurer** *noun*
[from Latin]

utensil (*say* yoo-ten-sil) *NOUN* **utensils** a tool, device, or container, especially one for use in the house • *cooking utensils.*
[from Latin *utensilis* = fit for use]

uterus (*say* yoo-ter-us) *NOUN* **uteruses** the womb.
[Latin]

utilitarian *ADJECTIVE* designed to be useful rather than decorative or luxurious; practical.
[from *utility*]

utility *NOUN* **utilities 1** usefulness. **2** an organization that supplies water, gas, electricity, etc. to the community.
[from Latin *utilis* = useful]

utilize *VERB* **utilizes, utilizing, utilized** use; find a use for something.
▷ **utilization** *noun*
[from French]

utmost *ADJECTIVE* extreme or greatest • *Look after it with the utmost care.*
▷ **utmost** *noun*
- **do your utmost** do the most that you are able to.
[from Old English *utemest* = furthest out]

Utopia (*say* yoo-toh-pee-a) *NOUN* **Utopias** an imaginary place or state of things where everything is perfect.
▷ **Utopian** *adjective*
[Latin, = nowhere; used in 1516 as the title of a book by Sir Thomas More, in which he describes an ideal society]

utter[1] *VERB* **utters, uttering, uttered** say or speak; make a sound with your mouth.
▷ **utterance** *noun*
[from old Dutch]

utter[2] *ADJECTIVE* complete or absolute • *utter misery.*
▷ **utterly** *adverb*
[from Old English *uttra* = outer]

uttermost *ADJECTIVE* & *NOUN* utmost.

U-turn *NOUN* **U-turns 1** a U-shaped turn made in a vehicle so that it then travels in the opposite direction. **2** a complete change of policy.

Vv

vacancy *NOUN* **vacancies 1** a position or job that has not been filled • *We have a vacancy for a typist.* **2** an available room in a hotel, guest house, etc. • *We have no vacancies.*

vacant *ADJECTIVE* **1** empty; not filled or occupied • *a vacant seat; a vacant post.* **2** without expression; blank • *a vacant stare.*
▷ **vacantly** *adverb*
[from Latin *vacans* = being empty]
WORD FAMILY There are a number of English words that are related to *vacant* because part of their original meaning comes from the Latin words *vacare* meaning 'to be empty or free from work' or *vacuus* meaning 'empty'. These include *evacuate, vacate, vacation, vacuous,* and *vacuum.*

vacate *VERB* **vacates, vacating, vacated** leave or give up a place or position.
[from Latin *vacare* = be empty or free from work]

vacation (*say* vak-ay-shon) *NOUN* **vacations 1** a holiday, especially between the terms at a university. **2** vacating a place etc.
[same origin as *vacate*]

vaccinate (*say* vak-sin-ayt) *VERB* **vaccinates, vaccinating, vaccinated** inoculate someone with a vaccine.
▷ **vaccination** *noun*

vaccine (*say* vak-seen) *NOUN* **vaccines** a substance used to give someone immunity against a disease.
[from Latin *vacca* = cow (because serum from cows was used to protect people from the disease smallpox)]

vacillate (*say* vass-il-ayt) *VERB* **vacillates, vacillating, vacillated** keep changing your mind; waver.
▷ **vacillation** *noun*
[from Latin *vacillare* = sway]

vacuous (*say* vak-yoo-us) *ADJECTIVE* **1** empty-headed; unintelligent. **2** without expression • *a vacuous stare.*
▷ **vacuously** *adverb* **vacuousness** *noun* **vacuity** *noun*
[same origin as *vacuum*]

vacuum *NOUN* **vacuums 1** a completely empty space; a space without any air in it. **2** (*informal*) a vacuum cleaner.
▷ **vacuum** *verb*
[from Latin *vacuus* = empty]

vacuum cleaner *NOUN* **vacuum cleaners** an electrical device that sucks up dust and dirt etc.

vacuum flask *NOUN* **vacuum flasks** a container with double walls that have a vacuum between them, used for keeping liquids hot or cold.

vagabond *NOUN* **vagabonds** a person with no settled home or regular work; a vagrant.
[same origin as *vagary*]

vagary (*say* vay-ger-ee) *NOUN* **vagaries** an impulsive change or whim • *the vagaries of fashion.*
[from Latin *vagari* = wander]

vagina (*say* va-jy-na) *NOUN* **vaginas** the passage that leads from the vulva to the womb.
[Latin, = sheath]

vagrant (*say* vay-grant) *NOUN* **vagrants** a person with no settled home or regular work; a tramp.
▷ **vagrancy** *noun*
[from old French; related to *vagary*]

vague *ADJECTIVE* **1** not definite or clear. **2** not thinking clearly or precisely.
▷ **vaguely** *adverb* **vagueness** *noun*
[from Latin *vagus* = wandering]

vain *ADJECTIVE* **1** conceited, especially about your appearance. **2** useless • *They made vain attempts to save her.*
▷ **vainly** *adverb*
- **in vain** with no result; uselessly.
[from Latin *vanus* = empty]
USAGE Do not confuse with **vane** or **vein**.

valance *NOUN* **valances** a short curtain round the frame of a bed or above a window.
[from old French *avaler* = to hang down]

vale *NOUN* **vales** a valley.
[from old French; related to *valley*]

valediction (*say* val-id-ik-shon) *NOUN* **valedictions** saying farewell.
▷ **valedictory** *adjective*
[from Latin *vale* = farewell + *dicere* = to say]

valency *NOUN* **valencies** (*in science*) the power of an atom to combine with other atoms, measured by the number of hydrogen atoms it is capable of combining with.
[from Latin *valentia* = power]

valentine *NOUN* **valentines 1** a card sent on St Valentine's day (14 February) to the person you love. **2** the person you send this card to.

valet (*say* val-ay or val-it) *NOUN* **valets** a man's servant who takes care of his clothes and appearance.
[French; related to *vassal*]

valetudinarian *NOUN* **valetudinarians** a person who is excessively concerned about keeping healthy.
[from Latin *valetudo* = health]

valiant *ADJECTIVE* brave or courageous.
▷ **valiantly** *adverb*
[from old French; related to *value*]

valid *ADJECTIVE* **1** legally able to be used or accepted • *a valid passport.* **2** (said about reasoning) sound and logical.
▷ **validity** *noun*
[from Latin *validus* = strong]

valley *NOUN* **valleys 1** a long low area between hills. **2** an area through which a river flows • *the Nile valley.*
[from Latin]

valour *NOUN* bravery, especially in battle.
▷ **valorous** *adjective*
[from Latin *valor* = strength]

valuable *ADJECTIVE* worth a lot of money; of great value.
▷ **valuably** *adverb*

valuables *PLURAL NOUN* valuable things.

value *NOUN* **values 1** the amount of money etc. that is considered to be the equivalent of something, or for which it can be exchanged. **2** how useful or important something is • *They learnt the value of regular exercise.* **3** (*in mathematics*) the number or quantity represented by a figure etc. • *What is the value of x?*

value *VERB* **values, valuing, valued 1** think that something is valuable. **2** estimate the value of a thing.
▷ **valuation** *noun* **valuer** *noun*
[from Latin *valere* = be strong]

valueless *ADJECTIVE* having no value.

valve *NOUN* **valves 1** a device for controlling the flow of gas or liquid through a pipe or tube. **2** a structure in the heart or in a blood vessel allowing blood to flow in one direction only. **3** a device that controls the flow of electricity in old televisions, radios, etc. **4** each piece of the shell of oysters etc.
[from Latin *valva* = a panel of a folding door]

vamp *NOUN* **vamps** (*informal*) an attractive woman who deliberately sets out to lead men astray.
[from *vampire*]

vampire *NOUN* **vampires** a dead creature that is supposed to leave its grave at night and suck blood from living people.
[from Hungarian)]

van[1] *NOUN* **vans 1** a covered vehicle for carrying goods. **2** a railway carriage for luggage or goods, or for the use of the guard.
[short for *caravan*]

van[2] *NOUN* the vanguard or forefront.

vandal *NOUN* **vandals** a person who deliberately breaks or damages things, especially public property.
▷ **vandalism** *noun*
[named after the *Vandals*, a Germanic tribe who invaded the Roman Empire in the 5th century, destroying many books and works of art]

vandalize *VERB* **vandalizes, vandalizing, vandalized** damage things as a vandal.

vane *NOUN* **vanes 1** a weathervane. **2** the blade of a propeller, sail of a windmill, or other device that acts on or is moved by wind or water.
[from Old English]
USAGE Do not confuse with **vain** or **vein**.

vanguard *NOUN* **1** the leading part of an army or fleet. **2** the first people to adopt a fashion or idea etc.
[from French *avant* = before + *garde* = guard]

vanilla *NOUN* a flavouring obtained from the pods of a tropical plant.
[from Spanish *vainilla* = little pod]

vanish *VERB* **vanishes, vanishing, vanished** disappear completely.
[from Latin]

vanity *NOUN* conceit; being vain.

vanquish *VERB* **vanquishes, vanquishing, vanquished** defeat thoroughly.
[from Latin *vincere* = conquer]

vantage point *NOUN* **vantage points** a place from which you have a good view of something.
[from Middle English *vantage* = advantage]

vapid *ADJECTIVE* not lively or interesting; dull.
[from Latin *vapidus* = without flavour, insipid]

vaporize *VERB* **vaporizes, vaporizing, vaporized** change or be changed into vapour.
▷ **vaporization** *noun* **vaporizer** *noun*

vapour *NOUN* **vapours** a visible gas to which some substances can be converted by heat; steam or mist.
[from Latin *vapor* = steam]

variable *ADJECTIVE* likely to vary; changeable.
▷ **variably** *adverb* **variability** *noun*

variable *NOUN* **variables** something that varies or can vary; a variable quantity.

variance *NOUN* the amount by which things differ.
- **at variance** differing or conflicting.
[from Latin *variare* = vary]

variant *ADJECTIVE* differing from something • *'Gipsy' is a variant spelling of 'gypsy'.*
▷ **variant** *noun*
[same origin as *variance*]

variation *NOUN* **variations 1** varying; the amount by which something varies. **2** a different form of something.

varicose *ADJECTIVE* (said about veins) permanently swollen.
[from Latin]

varied *ADJECTIVE* of different sorts; full of variety.

variegated (*say* vair-ig-ay-tid) *ADJECTIVE* with patches of different colours.
▷ **variegation** *noun*
[same origin as *various*]

variety *ADJECTIVE* **varieties 1** a quantity of different kinds of things. **2** the quality of not always being the same; variation. **3** a particular kind of something • *There are several varieties of spaniel.* **4** an entertainment that includes short performances of various kinds.
[same origin as *various*]

various *ADJECTIVE* **1** of several kinds; unlike one another • *for various reasons.* **2** several • *We met various people.*
▷ **variously** *adverb*
[from Latin *varius* = changing]

varnish *NOUN* **varnishes** a liquid that dries to form a hard shiny usually transparent coating.

varnish *VERB* **varnishes, varnishing, varnished** coat something with varnish.
[from French]

vary *VERB* **varies, varying, varied 1** make or become different; change. **2** be different.
[same origin as *various*]

vascular *ADJECTIVE* consisting of tubes or similar vessels for circulating blood, sap, or water in animals or plants • *the vascular system.*
[from Latin *vasculum* = little vessel]

vase *NOUN* **vases** an open usually tall container used for holding cut flowers or as an ornament.
[from Latin *vas* = vessel]

Vaseline *NOUN* (*trademark*) petroleum jelly for use as an ointment.
[from German *Wasser* = water, + Greek *elaion* = oil]

vassal *NOUN* **vassals** a humble servant or subordinate.
[from Latin *vassallus* = manservant]

vast *ADJECTIVE* very great, especially in area • *a vast expanse of water.*
▷ **vastly** *adverb* **vastness** *noun*
[from Latin *vastus* = unoccupied, desert]

VAT *ABBREVIATION* value added tax; a tax on goods and services.

vat *NOUN* **vats** a very large container for holding liquid.
[from Old English]

vaudeville (*say* vawd-vil) *NOUN* a kind of variety entertainment.
[French]

vault *VERB* **vaults, vaulting, vaulted** jump over something, especially while supporting yourself on your hands or with the help of a pole.

vault *NOUN* **vaults 1** a vaulting jump. **2** an arched roof. **3** an underground room used to store things. **4** a room for storing money or valuables. **5** a burial chamber.
[from Latin *volvere* = to roll]

vaulted *ADJECTIVE* having an arched roof.

vaulting horse *NOUN* **vaulting horses** a padded wooden block for vaulting over in gymnastics.

vaunt *VERB* **vaunts, vaunting, vaunted** boast.
▷ **vaunt** *noun*
[from Latin *vanus* = vain]

VCR *ABBREVIATION* video cassette recorder.

VDU *ABBREVIATION* visual display unit.

veal *NOUN* calf's flesh used as food.
[from Latin *vitulus* = calf]

vector *NOUN* **vectors** (*in mathematics*) a quantity that has size and direction, such as velocity (which is speed in a certain direction).
▷ **vectorial** *adjective*
[Latin, = carrier, traveller]

Veda (*say* vay-da or vee-da) *NOUN* the most ancient and sacred literature of the Hindus.
▷ **Vedic** *adjective*
[Sanskrit, = sacred knowledge]

veer *VERB* **veers, veering, veered** change direction; swerve.
[from old French]

vegan *NOUN* **vegans** a person who does not eat or use any animal products.
[from *veg* (short for *vegetable*) + *-an* = belonging to]

vegetable *NOUN* **vegetables** a plant that can be used as food.
[from Latin *vegetare* = enliven, animate]

vegetarian *NOUN* **vegetarians** a person who does not eat meat.
▷ **vegetarianism** *noun*
[from *vegetable* + *-arian*]

vegetate *VERB* **vegetates, vegetating, vegetated** live a dull or inactive life.
[originally = grow like a vegetable: same origin as *vegetable*]

vegetation *NOUN* **1** plants that are growing. **2** vegetating.
[from Latin *vegetatio* = the power to grow]

vehement (*say* vee-im-ent) *ADJECTIVE* showing strong feeling • *a vehement refusal.*
▷ **vehemently** *adverb* **vehemence** *noun*
[from Latin]

vehicle *NOUN* **vehicles** a means of transporting people or goods, especially on land.
[from Latin *vehere* = carry]

veil *NOUN* **veils** a piece of thin material worn to cover the face or head.
- **draw a veil over** avoid discussing something.
- **take the veil** become a nun.

veil *VERB* **veils, veiling, veiled 1** cover something with a veil. **2** partially conceal something • *veiled threats.*
[from Latin]

vein *NOUN* **veins 1** any of the tubes that carry blood from all parts of the body to the heart. (COMPARE **artery**) **2** a line or streak on a leaf, rock, insect's wing, etc. **3** a long deposit of mineral or ore in the middle of a rock. **4** a mood or manner • *She spoke in a serious vein.*
[from Latin]
USAGE Do not confuse with **vain** or **vane**.

veld (*say* velt) *NOUN* **veld** (*S. African*) an area of open grassland in southern Africa.
[from an Afrikaans word, from Dutch word *veld* = field]

vellum *NOUN* smooth parchment or writing paper.
[from old French *veel* = veal (because parchment was made from animals' skins)]

velocity *NOUN* **velocities** speed in a given direction.
[from Latin *velox* = swift]

velour (*say* vil-oor) *NOUN* a thick velvety material.
[from French *velours* = velvet]

velvet *NOUN* a woven material with very short soft furry fibres on one side.
▷ **velvety** *adjective*
[from Latin *villus* = soft fur]

venal (*say* veen-al) *ADJECTIVE* able to be bribed.
▷ **venality** *noun*
[from Latin *venalis* = for sale]

vend *VERB* **vends, vending, vended** offer something for sale.
[from Latin *vendere* = sell]

vendetta *NOUN* **vendettas** a long-lasting bitter quarrel; a feud.
[Italian, from Latin *vindicta* = vengeance]

vending machine *NOUN* **vending machines** a slot machine from which you can obtain drinks, chocolate, cigarettes, etc.

vendor *NOUN* **vendors** a seller.
[from *vend*]

veneer *NOUN* **veneers 1** a thin layer of good wood covering the surface of a cheaper wood in furniture etc. **2** an outward show of some good quality • *a veneer of politeness.*
[via German from French *fournir* = furnish]

venerable *ADJECTIVE* worthy of respect or honour, especially because of great age.

venerate *VERB* **venerates, venerating, venerated** honour with great respect or reverence.
▷ **veneration** *noun*
[from Latin *venerari* = revere]

venereal (*say* vin-eer-ee-al) *ADJECTIVE* to do with sexual intercourse.
[from *Venus*, the Roman goddess of love]

venereal disease *NOUN* **venereal diseases** a disease passed on by sexual intercourse.

venetian blind *NOUN* **venetian blinds** a window blind consisting of horizontal strips that can be adjusted to let light in or shut it out.
[from Latin *Venetia* = Venice]

vengeance *NOUN* revenge.
- **with a vengeance** with great intensity.
[from old French; related to *vindictive*]

vengeful *ADJECTIVE* seeking vengeance.
▷ **vengefully** *adverb* **vengefulness** *noun*

venial (*say* veen-ee-al) *ADJECTIVE* (said about sins or faults) pardonable, not serious.
[from Latin *venia* = forgiveness]

venison *NOUN* deer's flesh as food.
[old French, from Latin *venatio* = hunting]

Venn diagram *NOUN* **Venn diagrams** (*in mathematics*) a diagram in which circles are used to show the relationships between different sets of things.
[named after an English mathematician, John *Venn*]

venom *NOUN* **1** the poisonous fluid produced by snakes, scorpions, etc. **2** strong bitterness or spitefulness.
▷ **venomous** *adjective*
[from Latin *venenum* = poison]

vent *NOUN* **vents** an opening in something, especially to let out smoke or gas etc.
- **give vent to** express your feelings openly.

vent *VERB* **vents, venting, vented 1** make a vent in something. **2** give vent to feelings.
[from Latin *ventus* = wind]

ventilate *VERB* **ventilates, ventilating, ventilated** let air move freely in and out of a room etc.
▷ **ventilation** *noun* **ventilator** *noun*
[same origin as *vent*]

ventral *ADJECTIVE* on or to do with the abdomen • *This fish has a ventral fin.*
[from Latin *venter* = abdomen]

ventriloquist *NOUN* **ventriloquists** an entertainer who makes his or her voice sound as if it comes from another source.
▷ **ventriloquism** *noun*
[from Latin *venter* = abdomen + *loqui* = speak]

venture *NOUN* **ventures** something you decide to do that is risky.

venture *VERB* **ventures, venturing, ventured** dare or be bold enough to do or say something or to go somewhere • *We ventured out into the snow.*
[from *adventure*]

venturesome *ADJECTIVE* ready to take risks; daring.

venue (*say* ven-yoo) *NOUN* **venues** the place where a meeting, sports match, etc. is held.
[from French *venir* = come]

veracity (*say* ver-as-it-ee) *NOUN* truth.
▷ **veracious** (*say* ver-ay-shus) *adjective*
[from Latin *verus* = true]

veranda *NOUN* **verandas** a terrace with a roof along the side of a house.
[via Hindi from Portuguese *varanda* = railing, balcony]

verb *NOUN* **verbs** a word that shows what a person or thing is doing, e.g. *bring, came, sing, were.*
[from Latin *verbum* = word]
WORD FAMILY There are a number of English words that are related to *verb* because part of their original meaning comes from the Latin word *verbum* meaning 'word'. These include *adverb, proverb, verbal, verbatim,* and *verbose.*

verbal *ADJECTIVE* **1** to do with or in words; spoken, not written • *a verbal statement.* **2** to do with verbs.
▷ **verbally** *adverb*
[same origin as *verb*]

verbatim (*say* ver-**bay**-tim) *ADVERB* & *ADJECTIVE* in exactly the same words • *He copied down the whole paragraph verbatim.*
[same origin as *verb*]

verbose *ADJECTIVE* using more words than are needed.
▷ **verbosely** *adverb*
verbosity (*say* ver-**boss**-it-ee) *noun*
[same origin as *verb*]

verdant *ADJECTIVE* (said about grass or fields) green.
[from old French]

verdict *NOUN* **verdicts** a judgement or decision made after considering something, especially that made by a jury.
[from Latin *verus* = true + *dictum* = said]

verdigris (*say* **verd**-i-grees) *NOUN* green rust on copper or brass.
[from French *vert-de-gris*, literally = green of Greece]

verdure *NOUN* green vegetation; its greenness.
[from old French *verd* = green]

verge *NOUN* **verges 1** a strip of grass along the edge of a road or path. **2** the extreme edge or brink of something • *I was on the verge of tears.*

verge *VERB* **verges, verging, verged**
- **verge on** border on something; be close to something • *This puzzle verges on the impossible.*
[from old French; related to *verger*]

verger *NOUN* **vergers** a person who is caretaker and attendant in a church.
[originally = someone who carried a bishop's staff of office: from Latin *virga* = rod]

verify *VERB* **verifies, verifying, verified** check or show that something is true or correct.
▷ **verifiable** *adjective* **verification** *noun*
[same origin as *veracity*]

verisimilitude *NOUN* an appearance of being true or lifelike.
[from Latin *verus* = true + *similis* = like]

veritable *ADJECTIVE* real; rightly named • *a veritable villain.*
▷ **veritably** *adverb*
[French; related to *verity*]

verity *NOUN* **verities** truth.
[from Latin *veritas* = truth]

vermicelli (*say* verm-i-**sel**-ee) *NOUN* pasta made in long thin threads.
[Italian, = little worms]

vermilion *NOUN* & *ADJECTIVE* bright red.
[from Latin *vermiculus* = little worm]

vermin *PLURAL NOUN* animals or insects that damage crops or food or carry disease, such as rats and fleas.
▷ **verminous** *adjective*
[from Latin *vermis* = worm]

vernacular (*say* ver-**nak**-yoo-ler) *NOUN* **vernaculars** the language of a country or district, as distinct from an official or formal language.
[from Latin *vernaculus* = domestic]

vernal *ADJECTIVE* to do with the season of spring.
[from Latin *ver* = spring]

verruca (*say* ver-**oo**-ka) *NOUN* **verrucas** a kind of wart on the sole of the foot.
[Latin, = wart]

versatile *ADJECTIVE* able to do or be used for many different things.
▷ **versatility** *noun*
[from Latin *versare* = to turn]

a b c d e f g h i j k l m n o p q r s t u v w x y z

A B C D E F G H I J K L M N O P Q R S T U V W X Y Z

verse *NOUN* **verses 1** writing arranged in short lines, usually with a particular rhythm and often with rhymes; poetry. **2** a group of lines forming a unit in a poem or song. **3** each of the short numbered sections of a chapter in the Bible.
[via Old English from Latin *versus* = a line of writing]

versed *ADJECTIVE*
- **versed in** experienced or skilled in something.
[from Latin *versatus* = engaged in something]

version *NOUN* **versions 1** a particular person's account of something that happened. **2** a translation • *modern versions of the Bible.* **3** a special or different form of something • *the latest version of this car.*
[from Latin *versum* = turned, transformed]
WORD FAMILY There are a number of English words that are related to *version* because part of their original meaning comes from the Latin words *vertere* meaning 'to turn' or *versum* meaning 'turned or transformed'. These include *adverse, averse, avert, controversy, convert, divert, invert, introvert, perverse, pervert, reverse, revert, subvert, vertebra*, and *vertigo*.

versus *PREPOSITION* against; competing with • *The final was France versus Brazil.*
[Latin, = against]

vertebra *NOUN* **vertebrae** each of the bones that form the backbone.
[Latin, from *vertere* = turn]

vertebrate *NOUN* **vertebrates** an animal that has a backbone. (The opposite is **invertebrate**)
[from *vertebra*]

vertex *NOUN* **vertices**, (*say* ver-tis-eez) the highest point of a cone or triangle, or of a hill etc.
[Latin, = top of the head]

vertical *ADJECTIVE* at right angles to something horizontal; upright.
▷ **vertically** *adverb*
[same origin as *vertex*]

vertigo *NOUN* a feeling of dizziness and loss of balance, especially when you are very high up.
[Latin, = whirling around, from *vertere* = turn]

verve (*say* verv) *NOUN* enthusiasm and liveliness.
[French, = vigour]

very *ADVERB* **1** to a great amount or intensity; extremely • *It was very cold.* **2** (used to emphasize something) • *on the very next day; the very last drop.*

very *ADJECTIVE* **1** exact or actual • *It's the very thing we need.* **2** extreme • *at the very end.*
[from old French *verai* = true]

vespers *PLURAL NOUN* a church service held in the evening.
[from Latin *vesper* = evening]

vessel *NOUN* **vessels 1** a ship or boat. **2** a container, especially for liquid. **3** a tube carrying blood or other liquid in the body of an animal or plant.
[from old French; related to *vase*]

vest *NOUN* **vests** a piece of underwear covering the trunk of the body.

vest *VERB* **vests, vesting, vested 1** give something as a right • *The power to make laws is vested in Parliament.* **2** (*old use*) clothe.
[from Latin *vestis* = a piece of clothing]

vested interest *NOUN* **vested interests** a strong reason for wanting something to happen, usually because you will benefit from it.

vestibule *NOUN* **vestibules 1** an entrance hall or lobby. **2** a church porch.
[from Latin]

vestige *NOUN* **vestiges** a trace; a very small amount, especially of something that formerly existed.
▷ **vestigial** *adjective*
[from Latin *vestigium* = footprint]

vestment *NOUN* **vestments** a ceremonial garment, especially one worn by clergy or choir at a service.
[same origin as *vest*]

vestry *NOUN* **vestries** a room in a church where vestments are kept and where clergy and choir put these on.
[from Latin *vestiarium* = wardrobe]

vet *NOUN* **vets** a person trained to give medical and surgical treatment to animals.

vet *VERB* **vets, vetting, vetted** make a careful check of a person or thing, especially of someone's background before employing them.
[short for *veterinary surgeon*]

vetch *NOUN* a plant of the pea family.
[from Latin]

veteran *NOUN* **veterans** a person who has long experience, especially in the armed forces.
[from Latin *vetus* = old]

veteran car *NOUN* **veteran cars** a car made before 1916.

veterinary (*say* vet-rin-ree) *ADJECTIVE* to do with the medical and surgical treatment of animals • *a veterinary surgeon.*
[from Latin *veterinae* = cattle]

veto (*say* vee-toh) *NOUN* **vetoes 1** a refusal to let something happen. **2** the right to prohibit something.

veto *VERB* **vetoes, vetoing, vetoed** refuse or prohibit something.
[Latin, = I forbid]

vex *VERB* **vexes, vexing, vexed** annoy; cause somebody worry.
▷ **vexation** *noun* **vexatious** *adjective*
[from Latin *vexare* = to shake]

vexed question *NOUN* **vexed questions** a problem that is difficult or much discussed.

VHF *ABBREVIATION* very high frequency.

via (*say* vy-a) *PREPOSITION* **1** through; by way of • *The train goes from London to Exeter via Bristol.* **2** by means of.
[Latin, = by way of]

viable *ADJECTIVE* able to work or exist successfully • *a viable plan.*
▷ **viability** *noun*
[French, from *vie* = life]

viaduct *NOUN* **viaducts** a long bridge, usually with many arches, carrying a road or railway over a valley or low ground.
[from Latin *via* = road + *ducere* = to lead]

vial *NOUN* **vials** a small glass bottle.
[a different spelling of *phial*]

viands (*say* vy-andz) *PLURAL NOUN* (*old use*) food.
[from French]

vibrant *ADJECTIVE* full of energy; lively.
[same origin as *vibrate*]

vibraphone *NOUN* **vibraphones** a musical instrument like a xylophone with metal bars under which there are tiny electric fans making a vibrating effect.
[from *vibrate* + Greek *phone* = voice]

vibrate *VERB* **vibrates, vibrating, vibrated 1** shake very quickly to and fro. **2** make a throbbing sound.
▷ **vibration** *noun*
[from Latin *vibrare* = shake]

vicar *NOUN* **vicars** a member of the Church of England clergy who is in charge of a parish.
[same origin as *vicarious* (because originally a vicar looked after a parish for another clergyman, or for a monastery)]

vicarage *NOUN* **vicarages** the house of a vicar.

vicarious (*say* vik-air-ee-us) *ADJECTIVE* not experienced yourself but felt by imagining you share someone else's experience • *I got a vicarious pleasure from reading about his adventures.*
[from Latin *vicarius* = substitute]

vice[1] *NOUN* **vices 1** evil or wickedness. **2** an evil or bad habit; a bad fault.
[from Latin *vitium* = fault]

vice[2] *NOUN* **vices** a device for gripping something and holding it firmly while you work on it.
[from Latin *vitis* = vine]

vice- *PREFIX* **1** authorized to act as a deputy or substitute (as in *vice-captain*, *vice-president*). **2** next in rank to someone (as in *vice-admiral*).
[Latin, = in place of, by a change]

vice versa *ADVERB* the other way round • *Which do you prefer-blue spots on a yellow background or vice versa?*
[Latin, = the position being reversed]

vicinity *NOUN* the area near or round a place • *Is there a newsagent in the vicinity?*
[from Latin *vicinus* = neighbouring, a neighbour]

vicious *ADJECTIVE* **1** cruel and aggressive. **2** severe or violent.
▷ **viciously** *adverb* **viciousness** *noun*
[same origin as *vice*[1]]

vicious circle *NOUN* **vicious circles** a situation in which a problem produces an effect which in turn makes the problem worse.

vicissitude (*say* viss-iss-i-tewd) *NOUN* **vicissitudes** a change of circumstances or fortune.
[from Latin *vicissim* = in turn]

victim *NOUN* **victims** someone who is injured, killed, robbed, etc.
[from Latin *victima* = a person or animal sacrificed to a god]

victimize *VERB* **victimizes, victimizing, victimized** single someone out for cruel or unfair treatment.
▷ **victimization** *noun*

victor *NOUN* **victors** the winner.
[same origin as *victory*]

Victorian *ADJECTIVE* belong to the time of Queen Victoria (1837-1901).
▷ **Victorian** *noun*

victory *NOUN* **victories** success won against an opponent in a battle, contest, or game.
▷ **victorious** *adjective*
[from Latin *victum* = conquered]

victualler (*say* vit-ler) *NOUN* **victuallers** a person who supplies victuals.
- **licensed victualler** a person who is licensed to sell alcoholic drinks.

victuals (*say* vit-alz) *PLURAL NOUN* (*old use*) food and drink.
[from Latin *victus* = food]

video *NOUN* **videos 1** the recording on tape of pictures and sound. **2** a video recorder or cassette. **3** a television programme or a film recorded on a video cassette.

video *VERB* **videos, videoing, videoed** record something on videotape.
[Latin, = I see]
WORD FAMILY There are a number of English words that are related to *video* because part of their original meaning comes from the Latin words *videre* meaning 'to see' or *visum* meaning 'seen'. These include *advice, advise, provide, supervise, survey, televise, view, visa, visage, visible, vision,* and *visual.*

video game *NOUN* **video games** a game in which you press electronic controls to move images on a screen.

video recorder or **video cassette recorder** *NOUN* **video recorders** or **video cassette recorders** a device for recording television programmes on videotape and for playing video cassettes.

videotape *NOUN* **videotapes** magnetic tape suitable for recording television programmes.

vie *VERB* **vies, vying, vied** compete; carry on a rivalry • *vying with each other.*
[probably from *envy*]

view *NOUN* **views 1** what can be seen from one place, e.g. beautiful scenery. **2** sight; range of vision • *The ship sailed into view.* **3** an opinion • *She has strong views about politics.*
- **in view of** because of.
- **on view** displayed for inspection.
- **with a view to** with the hope or intention of.

view *VERB* **views, viewing, viewed 1** look at something. **2** consider or regard • *He viewed us with suspicion.*
[from Latin *videre* = to see]

viewer *NOUN* **viewers** someone who views something, especially a television programme.

viewpoint *NOUN* **viewpoints 1** an opinion or point of view. **2** a place giving a good view.

vigil (*say* vij-il) *NOUN* **vigils** staying awake to keep watch or to pray • *a long vigil.*
[from Latin]

vigilant (*say* vij-il-ant) *ADJECTIVE* watchful.
▷ **vigilantly** *adverb* **vigilance** *noun*
[from Latin *vigilans* = keeping watch]

vigilante (*say* vij-il-an-tee) *NOUN* **vigilantes** a member of a group who organize themselves, without authority, to try to prevent crime and disorder in their community.
[Spanish, = vigilant]

vigorous *ADJECTIVE* full of strength and energy.
▷ **vigorously** *adverb*

vigour *NOUN* strength and energy.
[from Latin]

Viking *NOUN* **Vikings** a Scandinavian trader and pirate in the 8th-10th centuries.
[from Old Norse]

vile *ADJECTIVE* **1** extremely disgusting. **2** very bad or wicked.
▷ **vilely** *adverb* **vileness** *noun*
[from Latin *vilis* = cheap, unworthy]

vilify (*say* vil-if-I) *VERB* **vilifies, vilifying, vilified** say unpleasant things about a person or thing.
▷ **vilification** *noun*
[same origin as *vile*]

villa *NOUN* **villas** a house, especially a holiday home abroad.
[Latin, = country house]

village *NOUN* **villages** a group of houses and other buildings in a country district, smaller than a town and usually having a church.
▷ **villager** *noun*
[old French; related to *villa*]

villain *NOUN* **villains** a wicked person or a criminal.
▷ **villainous** *adjective* **villainy** *noun*
[from Latin *villanus* = villager]

villein (*say* vil-an or vil-ayn) *NOUN* **villeins** a tenant in feudal times.
[a different spelling of *villain*]

vim *NOUN* (*informal*) vigour or energy.
[originally American; probably from Latin]

vindicate *VERB* **vindicates, vindicating, vindicated** **1** clear a person of blame or suspicion. **2** prove something to be true or worthwhile.
▷ **vindication** *noun*
[from Latin *vindicare* = set free]

vindictive *ADJECTIVE* showing a desire for revenge; spiteful.
▷ **vindictively** *adverb* **vindictiveness** *noun*
[from Latin *vindicta* = vengeance]

vine *NOUN* **vines** a climbing or trailing plant whose fruit is the grape.
[from Latin *vinum* = wine]

vinegar *NOUN* a sour liquid used to flavour food or in pickling.
[from Latin *vinum* = wine + *acer* = sour]

vineyard (*say* vin-yard) *NOUN* **vineyards** a plantation of vines producing grapes for making wine.

vintage *NOUN* **vintages 1** the harvest of a season's grapes; the wine made from this. **2** the period from which something comes.
[from French; related to *vine*]

vintage car *NOUN* **vintage cars** a car made between 1917 and 1930.

vinyl *NOUN* a kind of plastic.
[from Latin]

viola[1] (*say* vee-oh-la) *NOUN* **violas** a musical instrument like a violin but slightly larger and with a lower pitch.
[Spanish or Italian]

viola[2] (*say* vy-ol-a) *NOUN* **violas** a plant of the kind that includes violets and pansies.
[Latin, = violet]

violate *VERB* **violates, violating, violated** **1** break a promise, law, or treaty etc. **2** treat a person or place with disrespect and violence.
▷ **violation** *noun* **violator** *noun*
[from Latin *violare* = treat violently]

violence *NOUN* **1** physical force that does harm or damage. **2** strength or intensity • *the violence of the storm.*
[from Latin]

violent *ADJECTIVE* **1** using or involving violence. **2** strong or intense • *a violent dislike.*
▷ **violently** *adverb*

violet *NOUN* **violets 1** a small plant that often has purple flowers. **2** purple.
[related to *viola*[2]]

violin *NOUN* **violins** a musical instrument with four strings, played with a bow.
▷ **violinist** *noun*
[from Italian *violino* = small *viola*[1]]

VIP *ABBREVIATION* very important person.

viper *NOUN* **vipers** a small poisonous snake.
[from Latin *vipera* = snake]

virago (*say* vir-ah-goh) *NOUN* **viragos** a fierce or bullying woman.
[Latin, = female soldier]

virgin *NOUN* **virgins** a person, especially a girl or woman, who has never had sexual intercourse.
▷ **virginal** *adjective* **virginity** *noun*

virgin *ADJECTIVE* not yet touched or used • *virgin snow.*
[from Latin]

virginals *PLURAL NOUN* an instrument rather like a harpsichord, used in the 16th-17th centuries.
[from Latin *virginalis* = to do with virgins (because it was often played by young women)]

virile (*say* vir-I'l) *ADJECTIVE* having masculine strength or vigour, especially sexually.
▷ **virility** *noun*
[from Latin *vir* = man]

virology *NOUN* the study of viruses.
▷ **virological** *adjective* **virologist** *noun*
[from *virus* + *-ology*]

virtual *ADJECTIVE* being something in effect though not strictly in fact • *His silence was a virtual admission of guilt.*
[same origin as *virtue*]

virtually *ADVERB* nearly or almost.

virtual reality *NOUN* an image or environment produced by a computer that is so realistic that it seems to be part of the real world.

virtue *NOUN* **virtues 1** moral goodness; a particular form of this • *Honesty is a virtue.* **2** a good quality or advantage • *Jamie's plan has the virtue of simplicity.*
▷ **virtuous** *adjective* **virtuously** *adverb*
- **by virtue of** because of.
[from Latin *virtus* = worth]

virtuoso (*say* ver-tew-oh-soh) *NOUN* **virtuosos** or **virtuosi** a person with outstanding skill, especially in singing or playing music.
▷ **virtuosity** *noun*
[Italian, = skilful]

virulent (*say* vir-oo-lent) *ADJECTIVE* **1** strongly poisonous or harmful • *a virulent disease.* **2** bitterly hostile • *virulent criticism.*
▷ **virulence** *noun*
[same origin as *virus*]

virus *NOUN* **viruses 1** a very tiny living thing, smaller than a bacterium, that can cause disease. **2** a disease caused by a virus. **3** a hidden set of instructions in a computer program that is designed to destroy data.
[Latin, = poison]

visa (*say* vee-za) *NOUN* **visas** an official mark put on someone's passport by officials of a foreign country to show that the holder has permission to enter that country.
[Latin, = things seen]

visage (*say* viz-ij) *NOUN* **visages** a person's face.
[from Latin *visus* = sight, appearance]

vis-à-vis (*say* veez-ah-vee) *ADVERB* & *PREPOSITION* **1** in a position facing one another; opposite to. **2** as compared with.
[French, = face to face]

viscera (*say* vis-er-a) *PLURAL NOUN* the intestines and other internal organs of the body.
[Latin, = soft parts]

viscid (*say* vis-id) *ADJECTIVE* thick and gluey.
▷ **viscidity** *noun*
[same origin as *viscous*]

viscose (*say* vis-kohs) *NOUN* fabric made from viscous cellulose.

viscount (*say* vy-kownt) *NOUN* **viscounts** a nobleman ranking below an earl and above a baron.
▷ **viscountess** *noun*
[from old French *visconte* = vice- count]

viscous (*say* visk-us) *ADJECTIVE* thick and gluey, not pouring easily.
▷ **viscosity** *noun*
[from Latin *viscus* = a sticky substance spread on branches to catch birds]

visibility *NOUN* the distance you can see clearly • *Visibility is down to 20 metres.*

visible *ADJECTIVE* able to be seen or noticed • *The ship was visible on the horizon.*
▷ **visibly** *adverb*
[from Latin]
USAGE Do not confuse with **visual**.

vision *NOUN* **visions 1** the ability to see; sight. **2** something seen in a person's imagination or in a dream. **3** foresight and wisdom in planning things. **4** a person or thing that is beautiful to see.
[from old French; related to *visible* and *visual*]

visionary *ADJECTIVE* extremely imaginative or fanciful.

visionary *NOUN* **visionaries** a person with extremely imaginative ideas and plans.

visit *VERB* **visits, visiting, visited 1** go to see a person or place. **2** stay somewhere for a while.
▷ **visitor** *noun*

visit *NOUN* **visits 1** going to see a person or place. **2** a short stay somewhere.
[from Latin *visitare* = go to see]

visitant *NOUN* **visitants 1** a visitor, especially a supernatural one. **2** a bird that is a visitor to an area while migrating.

visitation *NOUN* **visitations** an official visit, especially to inspect something.

visor (*say* vy-zer) *NOUN* **visors 1** the part of a helmet that covers the face. **2** a shield to protect the eyes from bright light or sunshine.
[from old French; related to *visage*]

vista *NOUN* **vistas** a long view.
[Italian, = view]

visual *ADJECTIVE* to do with or used in seeing; to do with sight.
▷ **visually** *adverb*
[from Latin *visus* = sight]
USAGE Do not confuse with **visible**.

visual aid *NOUN* **visual aids** a picture, slide, film, etc. used as an aid in teaching.

visual display unit *NOUN* **visual display units** a device that looks like a television screen and displays data being received from a computer or fed into it.

visualize *VERB* **visualizes, visualizing, visualized** form a mental picture of something.
▷ **visualization** *noun*

vital *ADJECTIVE* **1** connected with life; necessary for life to continue • *vital functions such as breathing.* **2** essential; very important.
▷ **vitally** *adverb*
[from Latin *vita* = life]

vitality *NOUN* liveliness or energy.

vitamin (*say* vit-a-min or vy-ta-min) *NOUN* **vitamins** any of a number of substances that are present in various foods and are essential to keep people and animals healthy.
[from Latin *vita* = life + *amine*, a kind of chemical related to amino acids, which vitamins were once thought to contain]

vitiate (*say* vish-ee-ayt) *VERB* **vitiates, vitiating, vitiated** (*formal*) spoil or damage something and make it less effective.
▷ **vitiation** *noun*
[same origin as *vice*[1]]

vitreous (*say* vit-ree-us) *ADJECTIVE* like glass in being hard, transparent, or brittle • *vitreous enamel.*
[from Latin *vitrum* = glass]

vitriol (*say* vit-ree-ol) *NOUN* **1** sulphuric acid or one of its compounds. **2** savage criticism.
▷ **vitriolic** *adjective*
[from Latin]

vituperation *NOUN* abusive words.
[from Latin *vituperare* = to blame or find fault]

viva (*say* vy-va) *NOUN* **vivas** a spoken examination, usually for an academic qualification.
[short for *viva voce*]

vivacious (*say* viv-ay-shus) *ADJECTIVE* happy and lively.
▷ **vivaciously** *adverb* **vivacity** *noun*
[from Latin *vivus* = alive]
WORD FAMILY There are a number of English words that are related to *vivacious* because part of their original meaning comes from the Latin words *vivere* meaning 'to live' or *vivus* meaning 'alive'. These include *revive*, *survive*, *vivid*, and *vivisection*.

viva voce (*say* vy-va voh-chee) *ADJECTIVE* & *ADVERB* (said about an examination) spoken rather than written.
▷ **viva voce** *noun*
[Latin, = with the living voice]

vivid *ADJECTIVE* **1** bright and strong or clear • *vivid colours; a vivid description.* **2** active and lively • *a vivid imagination.*
▷ **vividly** *adverb* **vividness** *noun*
[from Latin *vividus* = full of life]

vivisection *NOUN* doing surgical experiments on live animals.
[from Latin *vivus* = alive + *sectio* = cutting]

vixen *NOUN* **vixens** a female fox.
[from Old English]

vizier (*say* viz-eer) *NOUN* **viziers** (*historical*) an important Muslim official.
[from Arabic *wazir* = chief counsellor]

vocabulary *NOUN* **vocabularies 1** all the words used in a particular subject or language. **2** the words known to an individual person • *She has a good vocabulary.* **3** a list of words with their meanings.
[from Latin *vocabulum* = name]

vocal *ADJECTIVE* to do with or using the voice.
▷ **vocally** *adverb*
[from Latin *vocis* = of the voice]
WORD FAMILY There are a number of English words that are related to *vocal* because part of their original meaning comes from the Latin words *vocare* meaning 'to call, speak, or summon' or *vocis* meaning 'of the voice'. These include *advocate*, *convoke*, *evoke*, *invoke*, *provoke*, *revoke*, *vocabulary*, *vocation*, and *vociferous*.

vocal cords *PLURAL NOUN* two strap-like membranes in the throat that can be made to vibrate and produce sounds.

vocalist *NOUN* **vocalists** a singer, especially in a pop group.

vocation *NOUN* **vocations 1** a person's job or occupation. **2** a strong desire to do a particular kind of work, or a feeling of being called by God to do something.
[from Latin *vocare* = to call]

vocational *ADJECTIVE* teaching you the skills you need for a particular job or profession • *vocational training.*

vociferous (*say* vo-sif-er-us) *ADJECTIVE* noisily and forcefully expressing your views.
[from Latin *vocis* = of the voice + *ferre* = carry]

vodka *NOUN* **vodkas** a strong alcoholic drink very popular in Russia.
[from Russian *voda* = water]

vogue *NOUN* **vogues** the current fashion • *Very short hair for women seems to be the vogue.*
- **in vogue** in fashion • *Stripy dresses are definitely in vogue.*
[via French from Italian]

voice *NOUN* **voices 1** sounds formed by the vocal cords and uttered by the mouth, especially in speaking, singing, etc. **2** the ability to speak or sing • *She has lost her voice.* **3** someone expressing a particular opinion about something • *Emma's the only dissenting voice.* **4** the right to express an opinion or desire • *I have no voice in this matter.*

voice *VERB* **voices, voicing, voiced** say something • *We voiced our opinions.*
[from Latin]

void *ADJECTIVE* **1** empty. **2** having no legal validity.

void *NOUN* **voids** an empty space or hole.
[from old French; related to *vacant*]

voile (*say* voil) *NOUN* a very thin almost transparent material.
[French, = veil]

volatile (*say* vol-a-tyl) *ADJECTIVE*
1 evaporating quickly • *a volatile liquid.*
2 changing quickly from one mood or interest to another.
▷ **volatility** *noun*
[from Latin *volatilis* = flying]

volcano *NOUN* **volcanoes** a mountain with an opening at the top from which lava, ashes, and hot gases from below the earth's crust are or have been thrown out.
▷ **volcanic** *adjective*
[Italian, from *Vulcan*, the ancient Roman god of fire]

vole *NOUN* **voles** a small animal rather like a rat.
[from Old Norse]

volition *NOUN* using your own will in choosing to do something • *She left of her own volition.*
[from Latin *volo* = I wish]

volley *NOUN* **volleys 1** a number of bullets or shells etc. fired at the same time. **2** hitting back the ball in tennis etc. before it touches the ground.

volley *VERB* **volleys, volleying, volleyed** send or hit something in a volley or volleys.
[from Latin *volare* = to fly]

volleyball *NOUN* a game in which two teams hit a large ball to and fro over a net with their hands.

volt *NOUN* **volts** a unit for measuring electric force.
[named after an Italian scientist, A. *Volta*, who discovered how to produce electricity by a chemical reaction]

voltage *NOUN* **voltages** electric force measured in volts.

volte-face (*say* volt-**fahs**) *NOUN* a complete change in your attitude towards something. [French]

voluble *ADJECTIVE* talking very much.
▷ **volubly** *adverb* **volubility** *noun*
[from Latin *volubilis* = rolling]

volume *NOUN* **volumes 1** the amount of space filled by something. **2** an amount or quantity • *The volume of work has increased.* **3** the strength or power of sound. **4** a book, especially one of a set.
[from Latin *volumen* = a roll (because ancient books were made in a rolled form)]

voluminous (*say* vol-yoo-min-us) *ADJECTIVE* **1** bulky; large and full • *a voluminous skirt.* **2** able to hold a lot • *a voluminous bag.*
[from Latin *voluminosus* = having many turns or coils]

voluntary *ADJECTIVE* **1** done or doing something willingly, not because you are forced to do it. **2** unpaid • *voluntary work.*
▷ **voluntarily** *adverb*

voluntary *NOUN* **voluntaries** an organ solo, often improvised, played before or after a church service.
[from Latin *voluntas* = the will]

volunteer *VERB* **volunteers, volunteering, volunteered 1** offer to do something of your own accord, without being asked or forced to. **2** provide something willingly or freely • *Several people volunteered their time.*

volunteer *NOUN* **volunteers** a person who volunteers to do something, e.g. to serve in the armed forces.
[from French; related to *voluntary*]

voluptuous *ADJECTIVE* **1** giving a luxurious feeling • *voluptuous furnishings.* **2** (said about a woman) having an attractively curved figure.
[from Latin *voluptas* = pleasure]

vomit *VERB* **vomits, vomiting, vomited** bring up food etc. from the stomach and out through the mouth; be sick.
▷ **vomit** *noun*
[from Latin]

voodoo *NOUN* a form of witchcraft and magical rites, especially in the West Indies.
[via American French from a West African language]

voracious (*say* vor-ay-shus) *ADJECTIVE* greedy; devouring things eagerly.
▷ **voraciously** *adverb* **voracity** *noun*
[from Latin *vorare* = devour]

-vore *SUFFIX* forms nouns meaning 'eating or feeding on something' (e.g. *carnivore*).
[same origin as *voracious*]

-vorous *SUFFIX* forms adjectives corresponding to nouns in **-vore** (e.g. *carnivorous*).

vortex *NOUN* **vortices** a whirlpool or whirlwind.
[Latin]

vote *VERB* **votes, voting, voted** show which person or thing you prefer by putting up your hand, making a mark on a paper, etc.
▷ **voter** *noun*

vote *NOUN* **votes 1** the action of voting. **2** the right to vote.
[from Latin *votum* = a wish or vow]

votive *ADJECTIVE* given in fulfilment of a vow • *votive offerings at the shrine.*
[same origin as *vote*]

vouch *VERB* **vouches, vouching, vouched**
- **vouch for** guarantee that something is true or certain • *I will vouch for his honesty.*
[from old French; related to *vocation*]

voucher *NOUN* **vouchers** a piece of paper that can be exchanged for certain goods or services; a receipt.
[from *vouch*]

a b c d e f g h i j k l m n o p q r s t u **v** w x y z

vouchsafe *VERB* **vouchsafes, vouchsafing, vouchsafed** grant something in a gracious or condescending way • *She did not vouchsafe a reply.*
[from *vouch* + *safe*]

vow *NOUN* **vows** a solemn promise, especially to God or a saint.

vow *VERB* **vows, vowing, vowed** make a vow.
[from old French; related to *vote*]

vowel *NOUN* **vowels** any of the letters a, e, i, o, u, and sometimes y, which represent sounds in which breath comes out freely. (COMPARE **consonant**)
[from Latin *vocalis littera* = vocal letter]

voyage *NOUN* **voyages** a long journey on water or in space.

voyage *VERB* **voyages, voyaging, voyaged** make a voyage.
▷ **voyager** *noun*
[from old French]

vulcanize *VERB* **vulcanizes, vulcanizing, vulcanized** treat rubber with sulphur to strengthen it.
▷ **vulcanization** *noun*
[from *Vulcan*, the ancient Roman god of fire (because the rubber has to be made very hot)]

vulgar *ADJECTIVE* rude; without good manners.
▷ **vulgarly** *adverb* **vulgarity** *noun*
[from Latin *vulgus* = the common or ordinary people]

vulgar fraction *NOUN* **vulgar fractions** a fraction shown by numbers above and below a line (e.g. $\frac{2}{3}$, $\frac{5}{8}$), not a decimal fraction.

vulnerable *ADJECTIVE* able to be hurt or harmed or attacked.
▷ **vulnerability** *noun*
[from Latin *vulnus* = wound]

vulture *NOUN* **vultures** a large bird that feeds on dead animals.
[from Latin]

vulva *NOUN* **vulvas** the outer parts of the female genitals.
[Latin]

vying *present participle* of **vie**.

Ww

wacky *ADJECTIVE* **wackier, wackiest** crazy or silly.
[from *whack* + *-y*]

wad (*say* wod) *NOUN* **wads** a pad or bundle of soft material or banknotes, papers, etc.

wad *VERB* **wads, wadding, wadded** pad something with soft material.
[from Dutch]

waddle *VERB* **waddles, waddling, waddled** walk with short steps, swaying from side to side, as a duck does.
▷ **waddle** *noun*
[probably from *wade*]

wade *VERB* **wades, wading, waded 1** walk through water or mud etc. **2** read through something with effort because it is dull, difficult, or long.
▷ **wader** *noun*
[from Old English]

wafer *NOUN* **wafers** a kind of thin biscuit.
[from old French; related to *waffle*[1]]

wafer-thin *ADJECTIVE* very thin.

waffle[1] (*say* wof-el) *NOUN* **waffles** a small cake made of batter and eaten hot.
[from Dutch]

waffle[2] (*say* wof-el) *NOUN* (*informal*) vague wordy talk or writing.
▷ **waffle** *verb*
[from an old word *waff* = to bark or yelp]

waft (*say* woft) *VERB* **wafts, wafting, wafted** carry or float gently through the air or over water.
[from old German or Dutch]

wag[1] *VERB* **wags, wagging, wagged** move quickly to and fro • *a dog wagging its tail.*
▷ **wag** *noun*
[from Old English]

wag[2] *NOUN* **wags** a person who makes jokes.
[from an old word *waghalter* = someone likely to be hanged]

wage *NOUN* or **wages** *PLURAL NOUN* a regular payment to someone in return for his or her work.

wage *VERB* **wages, waging, waged** carry on a war or campaign.
[via old French from Germanic]

wager (*say* way-jer) *NOUN* **wagers** a bet.
▷ **wager** *verb*
[from old French; related to *wage*]

waggle *VERB* **waggles, waggling, waggled** move quickly to and fro.
▷ **waggle** *noun*
[from *wag*]

wagon *NOUN* **wagons 1** a cart with four wheels, pulled by a horse or an ox. **2** an open railway truck, e.g. for coal.
[from Dutch]

wagoner *NOUN* **wagoners** the driver of a horse-drawn wagon.

wagtail *NOUN* **wagtails** a small bird with a long tail that it moves up and down.

waif *NOUN* **waifs** a homeless and helpless person, especially a child.
[from old French]

wail *VERB* **wails, wailing, wailed** make a long sad cry.
▷ **wail** *noun*
[from Old Norse]

wain *NOUN* **wains** (*old use*) a farm wagon.
[from Old English]

wainscot or **wainscoting** *NOUN* wooden panelling on the wall of a room.
[from old German]

waist *NOUN* **waists** the narrow part in the middle of your body.
[probably from Old English]
USAGE Do not confuse with **waste**.

waistcoat *NOUN* **waistcoats** a short close-fitting jacket without sleeves, worn over a shirt and under a jacket.

waistline *NOUN* **waistlines** the amount you measure around your waist, which indicates how fat or thin you are.

wait *VERB* **waits, waiting, waited 1** stay somewhere or postpone an action until something happens; pause. **2** be left to be dealt with later • *This question will have to wait until our next meeting.* **3** wait on people.
- **wait on 1** hand food and drink to people at a meal. **2** be an attendant to someone.

wait *NOUN* an act or time of waiting • *We had a long wait for the train.*
[from old French; related to *wake*[1]]

waiter *NOUN* **waiters** a man who serves people with food and drink in a restaurant.

waiting list *NOUN* **waiting lists** a list of people waiting for something to become available.

waiting room *NOUN* **waiting rooms** a room provided for people who are waiting for something.

waitress *NOUN* **waitresses** a woman who serves people with food and drink in a restaurant.

waive *VERB* **waives, waiving, waived** not insist on having something • *She waived her right to travel first class.*
[from old French]
USAGE Do not confuse with **wave**.

wake[1] *VERB* **wakes, waking, woke, woken 1** stop sleeping • *Wake up!* • *I woke when I heard the bell.* **2** make someone stop sleeping • *You have woken the baby.*

wake *NOUN* **wakes** (in Ireland) a party held after a funeral.
[from Old English]

wake[2] *NOUN* **wakes 1** the track left on the water by a moving ship. **2** currents of air left behind a moving aircraft.
- **in the wake of** following or coming after.
[probably from Old Norse]

wakeful *ADJECTIVE* unable to sleep.

waken *VERB* **wakens, wakening, wakened** wake.

walk *VERB* **walks, walking, walked** move along on your feet at an ordinary speed.
▷ **walker** *noun*

walk *NOUN* **walks 1** a journey on foot. **2** the manner of walking. **3** a path or route for walking.
[from Old English]

walkabout *NOUN* **walkabouts 1** an informal stroll among a crowd by an important visitor. **2** (*Australian*) a journey through a remote area taken by an Australian Aboriginal wishing to experience a traditional way of life.

walkie-talkie *NOUN* **walkie-talkies** (*informal*) a small portable radio transmitter and receiver.

walking stick *NOUN* **walking sticks** a stick used as a support while walking.

Walkman *NOUN* **Walkmans** (*trademark*) a personal stereo.

walk of life *NOUN* **walks of life** a person's occupation or social position.

walkover *NOUN* **walkovers** an easy victory.

wall *NOUN* **walls 1** a continuous upright structure, usually made of brick or stone, forming one of the sides of a building or room or supporting something or enclosing an area. **2** the outside part of something • *the stomach wall.*

wall *VERB* **walls, walling, walled** enclose or block something with a wall • *a walled garden.*
[from Old English]

wallaby *NOUN* **wallabies** a kind of small kangaroo.
[from an Australian Aboriginal language]

wallet *NOUN* **wallets** a small flat folding case for holding banknotes, credit cards, documents, etc.
[via old French from Germanic]

wallflower *NOUN* **wallflowers** a garden plant with fragrant flowers, blooming in spring.
[because it is often found growing on old walls]

wallop *VERB* **wallops, walloping, walloped** (*informal*) hit ot beat someone.
▷ **wallop** *noun*
[from old French; related to *gallop*]

wallow *VERB* **wallows, wallowing, wallowed 1** roll about in water, mud, etc. **2** get great pleasure by being surrounded by something • *a weekend wallowing in luxury.*
▷ **wallow** *noun*
[from Old English]

wallpaper *NOUN* **wallpapers** paper used to cover the inside walls of rooms.

walnut *NOUN* **walnuts 1** an edible nut with a wrinkled surface. **2** the wood from the tree that bears this nut, used for making furniture.
[from Old English]

walrus *NOUN* **walruses** a large Arctic sea animal with two long tusks.
[probably from Dutch]

waltz *NOUN* **waltzes** a dance with three beats to a bar.

waltz *VERB* **waltzes, waltzing, waltzed** dance a waltz.
[from German *walzen* = revolve]

wan (*say* wonn) *ADJECTIVE* pale from being ill or tired.
▷ **wanly** *adverb* **wanness** *noun*
[from Old English]

wand *NOUN* **wands** a thin rod, especially one used by a magician.
[from Old Norse]

wander *VERB* **wanders, wandering, wandered 1** go about without trying to reach a particular place. **2** leave the right path or direction; stray. **3** be distracted or digress • *He let his attention wander.*
▷ **wanderer** *noun*

wander *NOUN* a wandering journey.
[from Old English]

wanderlust *NOUN* a strong desire to travel.

wane *VERB* **wanes, waning, waned 1** (said about the moon) show a bright area that becomes gradually smaller after being full. (The opposite is **wax**) **2** become less, smaller, or weaker • *His popularity waned.*

wane *NOUN*
- **on the wane** becoming less or weaker.
[from Old English]

wangle *VERB* **wangles, wangling, wangled** (*informal*) get or arrange something by trickery or clever planning • *He's managed to wangle himself a trip to Paris.*
▷ **wangle** *noun*
[origin unknown]

want *VERB* **wants, wanting, wanted 1** wish to have something. **2** need • *Your hair wants cutting.* **3** be without something; lack.

want *NOUN* **wants 1** a wish to have something. **2** lack or need of something.
[from Old Norse]

wanted *ADJECTIVE* (said about a suspected criminal) that the police wish to find or arrest.

wanting *ADJECTIVE* lacking in what is needed or usual; deficient.

wanton (*say* wonn-ton) *ADJECTIVE* irresponsible; without a motive • *wanton damage.*
[from Old English]

war *NOUN* **wars 1** fighting between nations or groups, especially using armed forces. **2** a serious struggle or effort against crime, disease, poverty, etc.
- **at war** taking part in a war.
[via old French from Germanic]

warble *VERB* **warbles, warbling, warbled** sing with a trilling sound, as some birds do.
▷ **warble** *noun*
[via old French from Germanic]

warbler *NOUN* **warblers** a kind of small songbird.

war crime *NOUN* **war crimes** a crime committed during a war that breaks international rules of war.
▷ **war criminal** *noun*

ward *NOUN* **wards 1** a room with beds for patients in a hospital. **2** a child looked after by a guardian. **3** an area electing a councillor to represent it.

ward *VERB* **wards, warding, warded**
- **ward off** keep something away.
[from Old English]

-ward *SUFFIX* forms adjectives and adverbs showing direction (e.g. *backward, forward, homeward*).
[from Old English]

warden *NOUN* **wardens** an official who is in charge of a hostel, college, etc., or who supervises something.
[from old French; related to *guardian*]

warder *NOUN* **warders** (*old use*) an official in charge of prisoners in a prison.
[from old French; related to *guard*]

wardrobe *NOUN* **wardrobes 1** a cupboard to hang clothes in. **2** a stock of clothes or costumes.
[from old French *warder* = to guard, + *robe*]

-wards *SUFFIX* forms adverbs showing direction (e.g. *backwards, forwards*).
[from Old English *-weardes* = *-ward*]

ware *NOUN* **wares** manufactured goods of a certain kind • *hardware; silverware.*
- **wares** goods offered for sale.
[from Old English]

warehouse *NOUN* **warehouses** a large building where goods are stored.

warfare *NOUN* fighting a war.

warhead *NOUN* **warheads** the head of a missile or torpedo etc., containing explosives.

warlike *ADJECTIVE* **1** fond of making war. **2** threatening war.

warm *ADJECTIVE* **1** fairly hot; not cold or cool. **2** keeping the body warm • *a warm jumper.* **3** friendly or enthusiastic • *a warm welcome.* **4** close to the right answer, or to something hidden • *You're getting warm now.*
▷ **warmly** *adverb* **warmness** *noun* **warmth** *noun*

warm *VERB* **warms, warming, warmed** make or become warm.
[from Old English]

warm-blooded *ADJECTIVE* having blood that remains warm permanently.

warn *VERB* **warns, warning, warned** tell someone about a danger or difficulty that may affect them, or about what they should do • *I warned you to take your wellingtons.*
▷ **warning** *noun*
- **warn off** tell someone to keep away or to avoid a thing.
[from Old English]

warp (*say* worp) *VERB* **warps, warping, warped 1** bend or twist out of shape, e.g. by dampness. **2** distort a person's ideas, judgement, etc. • *Jealousy warped his mind.*

warp *NOUN* **1** a warped condition. **2** the lengthwise threads in weaving, crossed by the weft.
[from Old English]

warpath *NOUN*
- **on the warpath** angry and getting ready for a fight or argument.

warrant *NOUN* **warrants** a document that authorizes a person to do something (e.g. to search a place) or to receive something.

warrant *VERB* **warrants, warranting, warranted 1** justify • *Nothing can warrant such rudeness.* **2** guarantee.
[from old French; related to *guarantee*]

warranty *NOUN* **warranties** a guarantee.
[from old French; related to *guarantee*]

warren *NOUN* **warrens 1** a piece of ground where there are many burrows in which rabbits live and breed. **2** a building or place with many winding passages.
[from old French]

a b c d e f g h i j k l m n o p q r s t u v **w** x y z

warring *ADJECTIVE* involved in war.

warrior *NOUN* **warriors** a person who fights in battle; a soldier.
[from old French]

warship *NOUN* **warships** a ship used in war.

wart *NOUN* **warts** a small hard lump on the skin, caused by a virus.
[from Old English]

wartime *NOUN* a time of war.

wary (*say* wair-ee) *ADJECTIVE* cautious; looking carefully for possible danger or difficulty.
▷ **warily** *adverb* **wariness** *noun*
[from Old English]

wash *VERB* **washes, washing, washed**
1 clean something with water or other liquid. **2** be washable • *Cotton washes easily.* **3** flow against or over something • *Waves washed over the deck.* **4** carry along by a moving liquid • *A wave washed him overboard.* **5** (*informal*) be accepted or believed • *That excuse won't wash.*
- **be washed out** (*informal*) (said about an event) be abandoned because of rain.
- **wash up** wash the dishes and cutlery etc. after a meal.

wash *NOUN* **washes 1** the action of washing. **2** clothes etc. being washed. **3** the disturbed water behind a moving ship. **4** a thin coating of colour.
[from Old English]

washable *ADJECTIVE* able to be washed without becoming damaged.

washbasin *NOUN* **washbasins** a small sink for washing your hands etc.

washer *NOUN* **washers 1** a small ring of rubber or metal etc. placed between two surfaces (e.g. under a bolt or screw) to fit them tightly together. **2** a washing machine.

washing *NOUN* clothes etc. being washed.

washing machine *NOUN* **washing machines** a machine for washing clothes etc.

washing soda *NOUN* sodium carbonate.

washing-up *NOUN* washing the dishes and cutlery etc. after a meal.

wash-out *NOUN* **wash-outs** (*slang*) a complete failure.

wasn't (*mainly spoken*) was not.

wasp *NOUN* **wasps** a stinging insect with black and yellow stripes round its body.
[from Old English]

wassail (*say* woss-al) *VERB* **wassails, wassailing, wassailed** (*old use*) make merry with much drinking of alcohol.
▷ **wassailing** *noun*
[from Norse *ves heill* = be in good health]

wastage *NOUN* loss of something by waste.

waste *VERB* **wastes, wasting, wasted**
1 use something in an extravagant way or without getting enough results. **2** fail to use something • *You are wasting a good opportunity.* **3** become gradually weaker or thinner • *She was wasting away for lack of food.*

waste *ADJECTIVE* **1** left over or thrown away because it is not wanted. **2** not used or usable • *waste land.*
- **lay waste** destroy the crops and buildings etc. of an area.

waste *NOUN* **wastes 1** wasting a thing, not using it well • *a waste of time.* **2** things that are not wanted or not used. **3** an area of waste land • *the wastes of the Sahara Desert.*
▷ **wasteful** *adjective* **wastefully** *noun* **wastefulness** *noun*
[from Latin *vastus* = empty]
USAGE Do not confuse with **waist**.

wasteland *NOUN* **wastelands** a barren or empty area of land.

wastrel (*say* way-strel) *NOUN* **wastrels** a person who wastes his or her life and does nothing useful.
[from *waste*]

watch *VERB* **watches, watching, watched**
1 look at a person or thing for some time.
2 be on guard or ready for something to happen • *Watch for the traffic lights to turn green.* **3** pay careful attention to something • *Watch where you put your feet.* **4** take care of something • *His job is to watch the sheep.*
▷ **watcher** *noun*

watch *NOUN* **watches 1** a device like a small clock, usually worn on the wrist. **2** the action of watching. **3** a turn of being on duty in a ship.
[from Old English]

watchdog *NOUN* **watchdogs 1** a dog kept to guard property. **2** a person or committee whose job is to make sure that companies do not do anything harmful or illegal.

watchful *ADJECTIVE* watching closely; alert.
▷ **watchfully** *adverb* **watchfulness** *noun*

watchman *NOUN* **watchmen** a person employed to look after an empty building etc., especially at night.

watchword *NOUN* **watchwords** a word or phrase that sums up a group's policy; a slogan • *Our watchword is 'safety first'.*

water *NOUN* **waters 1** a colourless odourless tasteless liquid that is a compound of hydrogen and oxygen. **2** a lake or sea. **3** the tide • *at high water.*
- **pass water** urinate.

water *VERB* **waters, watering, watered 1** sprinkle or supply something with water. **2** produce tears or saliva • *It makes my mouth water.*
- **water down** dilute.
[from Old English]

water closet *NOUN* **water closets** a toilet with a pan that is flushed by water.

watercolour *NOUN* **watercolours 1** paint made with pigment and water (not oil). **2** a painting done with this kind of paint.

watercress *NOUN* a kind of cress that grows in water.

waterfall *NOUN* **waterfalls** a place where a river or stream flows over the edge of a cliff or large rock.

watering can *NOUN* **watering cans** a container with a long spout, for watering plants.

water lily *NOUN* **water lilies** a plant that grows in water, with broad floating leaves and large flowers.

waterlogged *ADJECTIVE* completely soaked or swamped in water.
[from *water* + *log*[1] (because water was said to 'lie like a log' in the hold of a waterlogged ship)]

watermark *NOUN* **watermarks 1** a mark showing how high a river or tide rises or how low it falls. **2** a design that can be seen in some kinds of paper when they are held up to the light.

watermelon *NOUN* **watermelons** a melon with a smooth green skin, red pulp, and watery juice.

watermill *NOUN* **watermills** a mill worked by a waterwheel.

water polo *NOUN* a game played by teams of swimmers with a ball like a football.

waterproof *ADJECTIVE* that keeps out water • *a waterproof jacket.*
▷ **waterproof** *verb*

watershed *NOUN* **watersheds 1** a turning point in the course of events. **2** a line of high land from which streams flow down on each side.
[from *water* + Old English *scead* = division, a parting]

water-skiing *NOUN* the sport of skimming over the surface of water on a pair of flat boards (**water-skis**) while being towed by a motor boat.

waterspout *NOUN* **waterspouts** a column of water formed when a whirlwind draws up a whirling mass of water from the sea.

water table *NOUN* **water tables** the level below which the ground is saturated with water.

watertight *ADJECTIVE* **1** made or fastened so that water cannot get in or out. **2** so carefully put together that it cannot be changed or set aside or proved to be untrue • *a watertight excuse.*

waterway *NOUN* **waterways** a river or canal that ships can travel on.

waterwheel *NOUN* **waterwheels** a large wheel turned by a flow of water, used to work machinery.

waterworks *PLURAL NOUN* a place with pumping machinery etc. for supplying water to a district.

watery *ADJECTIVE* **1** like water. **2** full of water. **3** containing too much water.

watt *NOUN* **watts** a unit of electric power.
[named after James *Watt*, a Scottish engineer, who studied energy]

wattage *NOUN* **wattages** electric power measured in watts.

wattle[1] *NOUN* **wattles 1** sticks and twigs woven together to make fences, walls, etc. **2** an Australian tree with golden flowers. [from Old English]

wattle[2] *NOUN* **wattles** a red fold of skin hanging from the throat of turkeys and some other birds. [origin unknown]

wave *NOUN* **waves 1** a ridge moving along the surface of the sea etc. or breaking on the shore. **2** a curling piece of hair. **3** (*in science*) the wave-like movement by which heat, light, sound, or electricity etc. travels. **4** a sudden build-up of something • *a wave of anger.* **5** the action of waving.

wave *VERB* **waves, waving, waved 1** move your hand to and fro as a greeting or signal etc. **2** move loosely to and fro or up and down. **3** make a thing wavy. **4** be wavy. [from Old English]
USAGE Do not confuse with **waive**.

waveband *NOUN* **wavebands** the wavelengths between certain limits.

wavelength *NOUN* **wavelengths 1** the distance between corresponding points on a sound wave or electromagnetic wave. **2** the size of a radio wave that a particular radio station uses to broadcast its programmes.

wavelet *NOUN* **wavelets** a small wave.

waver *VERB* **wavers, wavering, wavered 1** be unsteady; move unsteadily. **2** hesitate; be uncertain. [from Old Norse]

wavy *ADJECTIVE* full of waves or curves.
▷ **wavily** *adverb* **waviness** *noun*

wax[1] *NOUN* **waxes 1** a soft substance that melts easily, used to make candles, crayons, and polish. **2** beeswax.
▷ **waxy** *adjective*

wax *VERB* **waxes, waxing, waxed** coat or polish something with wax. [from Old English *waex*]

wax[2] *VERB* **waxes, waxing, waxed 1** (said about the moon) show a bright area that becomes gradually larger. (The opposite is **wane**) **2** become stronger or more important. **3** speak or write in a particular way • *He waxed lyrical about his childhood.* [from Old English *weaxan*]

waxen *ADJECTIVE* **1** made of wax. **2** like wax.

waxwork *NOUN* **waxworks** a model of a person etc. made in wax.

way *NOUN* **ways 1** how something is done; a method or style. **2** a manner • *She spoke in a kindly way.* **3** a line of communication between places, e.g. a path or road. **4** a route or direction. **5** a distance to be travelled. **6** a respect • *It's a good idea in some ways.* **7** a condition or state • *Things were in a bad way.*
- **get** or **have your own way** make people let you do what you want.
- **give way 1** collapse. **2** let somebody else move first. **3** yield.
- **in the way** forming an obstacle or hindrance.
- **no way** (*informal*) that is impossible!
- **under way** see *under*.

way *ADVERB* (*informal*) far • *That is way beyond what we can afford.* [from Old English]

wayfarer *NOUN* **wayfarers** a traveller, especially someone who is walking.

waylay *VERB* **waylays, waylaying, waylaid** lie in wait for a person or people, especially in order to talk to them or rob them.

-ways *SUFFIX* forms adverbs showing direction or manner (e.g. *sideways*). [from *way*]

wayside *NOUN*
- **fall by the wayside** fail to continue doing something.

wayward *ADJECTIVE* disobedient; wilfully doing what you want. [from *away* + *-ward*]

WC *ABBREVIATION* water closet.

we *PRONOUN* a word used by a person to refer to himself or herself and another or others. [from Old English]

weak *ADJECTIVE* **1** having little power, energy, or effect. **2** easy to break, damage, or defeat. **3** not great in intensity.
▷ **weakness** *noun*
[from Old English]

weaken *VERB* **weakens, weakening, weakened** make or become weaker.

weakling *NOUN* **weaklings** a weak person or animal.

A B C D E F G H I J K L M N O P Q R S T U V W X Y Z

weakly *ADVERB* in a weak manner.

weakly *ADJECTIVE* sickly; not strong.

weal *NOUN* **weals** a ridge raised on the flesh by a cane or whip etc.
[from Old English *walu* = ridge]

wealth *NOUN* **1** a lot of money or property; riches. **2** a large quantity • *The book has a wealth of illustrations.*
[from Old English]

wealthy *ADJECTIVE* **wealthier**, **wealthiest** having wealth; rich.
▷ **wealthiness** *noun*

wean *VERB* **weans**, **weaning**, **weaned** make a baby take food other than its mother's milk.
- **wean off** make someone give up a habit etc. gradually.
[from Old English]

weapon *NOUN* **weapons** something used to harm or kill people in a battle or fight.
▷ **weaponry** *noun*
[from Old English]

wear *VERB* **wears**, **wearing**, **wore**, **worn** **1** have clothes, jewellery, etc. on your body. **2** have a certain look on your face • *She wore a frown.* **3** damage something by rubbing or using it often; become damaged in this way • *The carpet has worn thin.* **4** last while in use • *It has worn well.*
▷ **wearable** *adjective* **wearer** *noun*
- **wear off** **1** be removed by wear or use. **2** become less intense.
- **wear on** pass gradually • *The night wore on.*
- **wear out** **1** use or be used until it becomes weak or useless. **2** exhaust.

wear *NOUN* **1** what you wear; clothes • *evening wear.* (also **wear and tear**) **2** gradual damage done by rubbing or using something.
[from Old English]

wearisome *ADJECTIVE* causing weariness.

weary *ADJECTIVE* **wearier**, **weariest** **1** tired. **2** tiring • *It's weary work.*
▷ **wearily** *adverb* **weariness** *noun*

weary *VERB* **wearies**, **wearying**, **wearied** **1** make weary. **2** grow tired of something.
[from Old English]

weasel *NOUN* **weasels** a small fierce animal with a slender body and reddish-brown fur.
[from Old English]

weather *NOUN* the rain, snow, wind, sunshine etc. at a particular time or place.
- **under the weather** feeling ill or depressed.

weather *VERB* **weathers**, **weathering**, **weathered** **1** expose something to the effects of the weather. **2** come through something successfully • *The ship weathered the storm.*
[from Old English]

weathercock or **weathervane** *NOUN* **weathercocks** or **weathervanes** a pointer, often shaped like a cockerel, that turns in the wind and shows from which direction it is blowing.

weave *VERB* **weaves**, **weaving**, **wove**, **woven** **1** make material or baskets etc. by crossing threads or strips under and over each other. **2** put a story together • *She wove a thrilling tale.* (*past tense* & **weaved**) **3** twist and turn • *He weaved through the traffic.*
▷ **weaver** *noun*

weave *NOUN* **weaves** a style of weaving • *a loose weave.*
[from Old English]

web *NOUN* **webs** **1** a cobweb. **2** something complicated • *a web of lies.*
- **the Web** the World Wide Web.
[from Old English *webb* = a piece of woven cloth]

webbed or **web-footed** *ADJECTIVE* having toes joined by pieces of skin, as ducks and frogs do.
[from *web*]

weblog *NOUN* **weblogs** a diary or journal on display on the Internet.

webpage *NOUN* **webpages** a hypertext document which can be read on the Internet.

website *NOUN* **websites** a place on the Internet where you can get information about a subject, company, etc.

wed *VERB* **weds**, **wedding**, **wedded** **1** marry. **2** unite two different things.
[from Old English]

wedding *NOUN* **weddings** the ceremony when a man and woman get married.

wedge *NOUN* **wedges** **1** a piece of wood or metal etc. that is thick at one end and thin at the other. It is pushed between things to force them apart or prevent something from moving. **2** a wedge-shaped thing.

wedge *VERB* **wedges, wedging, wedged** **1** keep something in place with a wedge. **2** pack tightly together • *Ten of us were wedged in the lift.*
[from Old English]

wedlock *NOUN* being married; matrimony.
[from Old English *wedlac* = marriage vow]

Wednesday *NOUN* the day of the week following Tuesday.
[from Old English *Wodnesdaeg* = day of Woden or Odin, the chief Norse god]

wee *ADJECTIVE* (*Scottish*) little.
[from Old English]

weed *NOUN* **weeds** a wild plant that grows where it is not wanted.

weed *VERB* **weeds, weeding, weeded** remove weeds from the ground.
[from Old English *weod*]

weedy *ADJECTIVE* **weedier, weediest** **1** full of weeds. **2** thin and weak.

week *NOUN* **weeks** a period of seven days, especially from Sunday to the following Saturday.
[from Old English]

weekday *NOUN* **weekdays** a day other than Saturday or Sunday.

weekend *NOUN* **weekends** Saturday and Sunday.

weekly *ADJECTIVE* & *ADVERB* happening or done once a week.

weeny *ADJECTIVE* (*informal*) tiny.
[from *wee* + *tiny*]

weep *VERB* **weeps, weeping, wept** **1** shed tears; cry. **2** ooze moisture in drops.
▷ **weep** *noun* **weepy** *adjective*
[from Old English]

weeping *ADJECTIVE* (said about a tree) having drooping branches • *a weeping willow.*

weevil *NOUN* **weevils** a kind of small beetle.
[from Old English]

weft *NOUN* the threads on a loom that are woven across the warp.
[from Old English]

weigh *VERB* **weighs, weighing, weighed** **1** measure the weight of something. **2** have a certain weight • *What do you weigh?* **3** be important or have influence • *Her evidence weighed with the jury.*
- **weigh anchor** raise the anchor and start a voyage.
- **weigh down** **1** keep something down by its weight. **2** depress or trouble somebody.
- **weigh out** take a certain weight of a substance from a larger quantity.
- **weigh up** estimate or assess something.
[from Old English]

weight *NOUN* **weights** **1** how heavy something is; the amount that something weighs. **2** a piece of metal of known weight, especially one used on scales to weigh things. **3** a heavy object. **4** importance or influence.
▷ **weighty** *adjective* **weightless** *adjective* **weightlessness** *noun*

weight *VERB* **weights, weighting, weighted** put a weight on something.
[from Old English]

weightlifting *NOUN* the sport of lifting a heavy weight.
▷ **weightlifter** *noun*

weir (*say* weer) *NOUN* **weirs** a small dam across a river or canal to control the flow of water.
[from Old English]

weird *ADJECTIVE* very strange; uncanny.
▷ **weirdly** *adverb* **weirdness** *noun*
[from Old English]
USAGE When spelling this word, note that the 'e' comes before the 'i', not the other way round.

welcome *NOUN* **welcomes** a greeting or reception, especially a kindly one.

welcome *ADJECTIVE* **1** that you are glad to receive or see • *a welcome gift.* **2** allowed or invited to do or take something • *You are welcome to come.*

welcome *VERB* **welcomes, welcoming, welcomed** **1** show that you are pleased when a person or thing arrives. **2** be glad to receive or hear of something • *We welcome this decision.*
[from *well*[2] + *come*]

weld *VERB* **welds, welding, welded 1** join pieces of metal or plastic by heating and pressing or hammering them together. **2** unite people or things into a whole.
[from Old English]

welfare *NOUN* people's health, happiness, and comfort.
[from *well*[2] + *fare*]

welfare state *NOUN* a system in which a country's government provides money to pay for health care, social services, benefits, etc.

well[1] *NOUN* **wells 1** a deep hole dug to bring up water or oil from underground. **2** a deep space, e.g. containing a staircase.

well *VERB* **wells, welling, welled** rise or flow up • *Tears welled up in our eyes.*
[from Old English *wella* = spring of water]

well[2] *ADVERB* **better, best 1** in a good or suitable way • *She swims well.* **2** thoroughly • *Polish it well.* **3** probably or reasonably • *This may well be our last chance.*
- **well off 1** fairly rich. **2** in a good situation.

well *ADJECTIVE* **1** in good health • *He is not well.* **2** satisfactory • *All is well.*
[from Old English *wel* = prosperously]

well-being *NOUN* good health, happiness, and comfort.

wellies *PLURAL NOUN* (*informal*) wellingtons.

wellingtons *PLURAL NOUN* rubber or plastic waterproof boots.
[named after the first Duke of *Wellington*, who wore long leather boots]

well-known *ADJECTIVE* **1** known to many people. **2** known thoroughly.

well-mannered *ADJECTIVE* having good manners.

well-meaning *ADJECTIVE* having good intentions.

wellnigh *ADVERB* almost.

well-read *ADJECTIVE* having read a lot of good books.

well-to-do *ADJECTIVE* fairly rich.

welsh *VERB* **welshes, welshing, welshed** cheat someone by avoiding paying what you owe them or by breaking an agreement.
▷ **welsher** *noun*
[origin unknown]

welt *NOUN* **welts 1** a strip or border. **2** a weal.
[origin unknown]

welter *VERB* **welters, weltering, weltered** (said about a ship) be tossed to and fro by waves.

welter *NOUN* a confused mixture; a jumble • *a welter of information.*
[from old German or old Dutch]

wen *NOUN* **wens** a large but harmless tumour on the head or neck.
[from Old English]

wench *NOUN* **wenches** (*old use*) a girl or young woman.
[from Old English]

wend *VERB* **wends, wending, wended**
- **wend your way** go.
[from Old English]

weren't (*mainly spoken*) were not.

werewolf *NOUN* **werewolves** (in legends and stories) a person who sometimes changes into a wolf.
[from Old English *wer* = man, + *wolf*]

west *NOUN* **1** the direction where the sun sets, opposite east. **2** the western part of a country, city, etc.

west *ADJECTIVE* **1** situated in the west • *the west coast.* **2** coming from the west • *a west wind.*

west *ADVERB* towards the west • *We sailed west.*
[from Old English]

westerly *ADJECTIVE* to or from the west.

western *ADJECTIVE* of or in the west.

western *NOUN* **westerns** a film or story about cowboys or American Indians in western North America during the 19th and early 20th centuries.

westward *ADJECTIVE* & *ADVERB* towards the west.
▷ **westwards** *adverb*

wet *ADJECTIVE* **wetter, wettest 1** soaked or covered in water or other liquid. **2** not yet dry • *wet paint.* **3** rainy • *wet weather.*
▷ **wetly** *adverb* **wetness** *noun*

wet *VERB* **wets, wetting, wet** or **wetted** make a thing wet.
[from Old English]

a b c d e f g h i j k l m n o p q r s t u v **w** x y z

wet suit *NOUN* **wet suits** a close-fitting rubber suit, worn by skin divers and windsurfers to keep them warm and dry.

whack *VERB* **whacks, whacking, whacked** (*informal*) hit someone or something hard.
▷ **whack** *noun*
[imitating the sound]

whale *NOUN* **whales** a very large sea mammal.
- **a whale of a** (*informal*) very good or great • *We had a whale of a time.*
[from Old English]

whaler *NOUN* **whalers** a person or ship that hunts whales.

whaling *NOUN* hunting whales.

wharf (*say* worf) *NOUN* **wharves** or **wharfs** a quay where ships are loaded and unloaded.
[from Old English]

what *ADJECTIVE* used to ask the amount or kind of something (*What kind of bike have you got?*) or to say how strange or great a person or thing is (*What a fool you are!*).

what *PRONOUN* **1** what thing or things • *What did you say?* **2** the thing that • *This is what you must do.*
- **what's what** (*informal*) which things are important or useful.
[from Old English]

whatever *PRONOUN* **1** anything or everything • *Do whatever you like.* **2** no matter what • *Keep calm, whatever happens.*

whatever *ADJECTIVE* of any kind or amount • *Take whatever books you need. There is no doubt whatever.*

whatsoever *ADJECTIVE* at all.

wheat *NOUN* a cereal plant from which flour is made.
▷ **wheaten** *adjective*
[from Old English]

wheedle *VERB* **wheedles, wheedling, wheedled** persuade by coaxing or flattering.
[probably from German]

wheel *NOUN* **wheels 1** a round device that turns on a shaft that passes through its centre. **2** a steering wheel. **3** a horizontal revolving disc on which clay is made into a pot.

wheel *VERB* **wheels, wheeling, wheeled** **1** push a bicycle or trolley etc. along on its wheels. **2** move in a curve or circle; change direction and face another way • *He wheeled round in astonishment.*
[from Old English]

wheelbarrow *NOUN* **wheelbarrows** a small cart with one wheel at the front and legs at the back, pushed by handles.

wheelchair *NOUN* **wheelchairs** a chair on wheels for a person who cannot walk.

wheel clamp *NOUN* **wheel clamps** a device that can be locked around a vehicle's wheel to stop it from moving, used especially on cars that have been parked illegally.

wheelie bin *NOUN* **wheelie bins** a large dustbin on wheels.

wheeze *VERB* **wheezes, wheezing, wheezed** make a hoarse whistling sound as you breathe.
▷ **wheeze** *noun* **wheezy** *adjective*
[probably from Old Norse]

whelk *NOUN* **whelks** a shellfish that looks like a snail.
[from Old English]

whelp *NOUN* **whelps** a young dog; a pup.
[from Old English]

when *ADVERB* at what time; at which time • *When can you come to tea?*

when *CONJUNCTION* **1** at the time that • *The bird flew away when I moved.* **2** although; considering that • *Why do you smoke when you know it's dangerous?*
[from Old English]

whence *ADVERB & CONJUNCTION* from where; from which.
[from Old English]

whenever *CONJUNCTION* at whatever time; every time • *Whenever I see it, I smile.*

where *ADVERB & CONJUNCTION* in or to what place or that place • *Where did you put it? Leave it where it is.*

where *PRONOUN* what place • *Where does she come from?*
[from Old English]

whereabouts *ADVERB* in or near what place • *Whereabouts are you going?*

whereabouts *PLURAL NOUN* the place where something is • *Do you know the whereabouts of my radio?*

whereas *CONJUNCTION* but in contrast • *Some people enjoy sport, whereas others hate it.*

whereby *ADVERB* by which.

wherefore *ADVERB* (*old use*) why.
[from *where* + *for* (preposition)]

whereupon *CONJUNCTION* after which; and then.

wherever *ADVERB* in or to whatever place.

whet *VERB* **whets, whetting, whetted**
- **whet your appetite** stimulate it.
[from Old English *hwettan* = sharpen]
USAGE Do not confuse with **wet**.

whether *CONJUNCTION* as one possibility; if • *I don't know whether to believe her or not.*
[from Old English]

whetstone *NOUN* **whetstones** a shaped stone for sharpening tools.
[from *whet* = sharpen, + *stone*]

whey (*say as* way) *NOUN* the watery liquid left when milk forms curds.
[from Old English]

which *ADJECTIVE* what particular • *Which way did he go?*

which *PRONOUN* **1** what person or thing • *Which is your desk?* **2** the person or thing referred to • *The film, which is a western, will be shown on Saturday.*
[from Old English]

whichever *PRONOUN* & *ADJECTIVE* no matter which; any which • *Take whichever you like.*

whiff *NOUN* **whiffs** a puff or slight smell of smoke, gas, etc.
[imitating the sound of a puff]

Whig *NOUN* **Whigs** a member of a political party in the 17th-19th centuries, opposed to the Tories.
[from *whiggamer*, a Scottish Presbyterian rebel in 1648]

while *CONJUNCTION* **1** during the time that; as long as • *Whistle while you work.*
2 although; but • *She is dark, while her sister is fair.*

while *NOUN* a period of time • *a long while.*

while *VERB* **whiles, whiling, whiled**
- **while away** pass time • *We whiled away the afternoon on the river.*
[from Old English]

whilst *CONJUNCTION* while.

whim *NOUN* **whims** a sudden wish to do or have something.
[origin unknown]

whimper *VERB* **whimpers, whimpering, whimpered** cry or whine softly.
▷ **whimper** *noun*
[imitating the sound]

whimsical *ADJECTIVE* quaint and playful.
▷ **whimsically** *adverb* **whimsicality** *noun*
[from *whim*]

whine *VERB* **whines, whining, whined**
1 make a long high miserable cry or a shrill sound. **2** complain in a petty or feeble way.
▷ **whine** *noun*
[from Old English]

whinge *VERB* **whinges, whinging** or **whingeing, whinged** grumble persistently.
▷ **whinge** *noun*
[from Old English]

whinny *VERB* **whinnies, whinnying, whinnied** neigh gently or happily.
▷ **whinny** *noun*
[imitating the sound]

whip *NOUN* **whips 1** a cord or strip of leather fixed to a handle and used for hitting people or animals. **2** an official of a political party in Parliament. **3** a pudding made of whipped cream and fruit or flavouring.

whip *VERB* **whips, whipping, whipped**
1 hit a person or animal with a whip. **2** beat cream until it becomes thick. **3** move or take something suddenly • *He whipped out a gun.* **4** (*informal*) steal something.
- **whip up** stir up people's feelings etc. • *She whipped up support for her plans.*
[from old German or old Dutch]

whippet *NOUN* **whippets** a small dog rather like a greyhound, used for racing.
[from *whip*]

whirl *VERB* **whirls, whirling, whirled** turn or spin very quickly.
▷ **whirl** *noun*
[from Old Norse]

whirlpool *NOUN* **whirlpools** a whirling current of water, often drawing floating objects towards its centre.

whirlwind *NOUN* **whirlwinds** a strong wind that whirls round a central point.

whirr *VERB* **whirrs, whirring, whirred** make a continuous buzzing sound.
▷ **whirr** *noun*
[imitating the sound]

whisk *VERB* **whisks, whisking, whisked** **1** move or brush something away quickly and lightly • *A waiter whisked away our plates.* **2** beat eggs etc. until they are frothy.

whisk *NOUN* **whisks 1** a kitchen tool used for whisking things. **2** a whisking movement.
[from Old Norse]

whisker *NOUN* **whiskers 1** a hair of those growing on a man's face, forming a beard or moustache if not shaved off. **2** a long bristle growing near the mouth of a cat etc.
▷ **whiskery** *adjective*
[from *whisk*]

whisky *NOUN* **whiskies** a strong alcoholic drink.
[from Scottish Gaelic *uisge beatha* = water of life]

whisper *VERB* **whispers, whispering, whispered 1** speak very softly. **2** talk secretly.
▷ **whisper** *noun*
[from Old English]

whist *NOUN* a card game usually for four people.
[origin unknown]

whistle *VERB* **whistles, whistling, whistled** make a shrill or musical sound, especially by blowing through your lips.
▷ **whistler** *noun*

whistle *NOUN* **whistles 1** a whistling sound. **2** a device that makes a shrill sound when air or steam is blown through it.
[from Old English]

Whit *ADJECTIVE* to do with Whitsun.

whit *NOUN* the least possible amount • *not a whit better.*
[from Old English]

white *NOUN* **whites 1** the very lightest colour, like snow or salt. **2** the transparent substance (*albumen*) round the yolk of an egg, which turns white when it is cooked. **3** a person with light-coloured skin.

white *ADJECTIVE* **1** of the colour white. **2** having light-coloured skin. **3** very pale from the effects of illness or fear etc. **4** (said about coffee) with milk.
▷ **whiteness** *noun*
[from Old English]

whitebait *NOUN* **whitebait** a small silvery-white fish.
[from *white* + *bait* (because it was used as bait to catch larger fish)]

white elephant *NOUN* **white elephants** a useless possession, especially one that is expensive to keep.

white-hot *ADJECTIVE* extremely hot; so hot that heated metal looks white.

white lie *NOUN* **white lies** a harmless or trivial lie that you tell in order to avoid hurting someone's feelings.

white meat *NOUN* poultry, veal, rabbit, and pork.

whiten *VERB* **whitens, whitening, whitened** make or become whiter.

whitewash *NOUN* **1** a white liquid containing lime or powdered chalk, used for painting walls and ceilings etc. **2** concealing mistakes or other unpleasant facts so that someone will not be punished.
▷ **whitewash** *verb*

whither *ADVERB & CONJUNCTION* (*old use*) to what place.
[from Old English]
USAGE Do not confuse with **wither**.

whiting *NOUN* **whiting** a small edible sea fish with white flesh.
[from Dutch *wijt* = white]

Whitsun *NOUN* Whit Sunday and the days close to it.
[from *Whit Sunday*]

Whit Sunday the seventh Sunday after Easter.
[from Old English *hwit* = white, because people used to be baptized on that day and wore white clothes]

whittle *VERB* **whittles, whittling, whittled 1** shape wood by trimming thin slices off the surface. **2** reduce something by removing various things from it • *We need to whittle down the cost.*
[from Old English]

whizz or **whiz** *VERB* **whizzes, whizzing, whizzed 1** move very quickly. **2** sound like something rushing through the air.
[imitating the sound]

who *PRONOUN* which person or people; the particular person or people • *This is the boy who stole the apples.*
[from Old English]

whoa *INTERJECTION* a command to a horse to stop or stand still.
[origin unknown]

whoever *PRONOUN* **1** any or every person who. **2** no matter who.

whole *ADJECTIVE* **1** complete. **2** not injured or broken.

whole *NOUN* **1** the full amount. **2** a complete thing.
- **as a whole** in general.
- **on the whole** considering everything; mainly.
[from Old English]

wholefood *NOUN* **wholefoods** food that has been processed as little as possible.

wholehearted *ADJECTIVE* without doubts or reservations • *You have my wholehearted support.*

wholemeal *ADJECTIVE* made from the whole grain of wheat.
[from *whole* + *meal*[2]]

whole number *NOUN* **whole numbers** a number without fractions.

wholesale *NOUN* selling goods in large quantities to be resold by others. (COMPARE *retail*)
▷ **wholesaler** *noun*

wholesale *ADJECTIVE* & *ADVERB* **1** on a large scale; including everybody or everything • *wholesale destruction.* **2** in the wholesale trade.

wholesome *ADJECTIVE* good for health; healthy • *wholesome food.*
▷ **wholesomeness** *noun*
[from an old sense of *whole* = healthy, + *-some*]

wholly *ADVERB* completely or entirely.

whom *PRONOUN* the form of *who* used when it is the object of a verb or comes after a preposition, as in *the boy whom I saw* or *to whom we spoke.*

whoop (*say* woop) *NOUN* **whoops** a loud cry of excitement.
▷ **whoop** *verb*
[imitating the sound]

whoopee *INTERJECTION* a cry of joy.

whooping cough (*say* **hoop**-ing) *NOUN* an infectious disease that causes spasms of coughing and gasping for breath.
[because of the sound the person makes gasping for breath]

whopper *NOUN* **whoppers** (*slang*) something very large.
[from Middle English *whop* = to strike or beat]

whopping *ADJECTIVE* (*slang*) very large or remarkable • *a whopping lie.*
[from *whopper*]

whorl *NOUN* **whorls 1** a coil or curved shape. **2** a ring of leaves or petals.
[a different spelling of *whirl*]

who's (*mainly spoken*) who is; who has.
USAGE Do not confuse with **whose**.

whose *PRONOUN* belonging to what person or persons; of whom; of which • *Whose house is that?*
[from Old English]
USAGE Do not confuse with **who's**.

why *ADVERB* for what reason or purpose; the particular reason on account of which • *This is why I came.*
[from Old English]

wick *NOUN* **wicks 1** the string that goes through the middle of a candle and is lit. **2** the strip of material that you light in a lamp or heater etc. that uses oil.
[from Old English]

wicked *ADJECTIVE* **1** morally bad or cruel. **2** mischievous • *a wicked smile.* **3** (*informal*) excellent.
▷ **wickedly** *adverb* **wickedness** *noun*
[from Old English *wicca* = witch]

a b c d e f g h i j k l m n o p q r s t u v w x y z

A B C D E F G H I J K L M N O P Q R S T U V W X Y Z

wicker *NOUN* thin canes or osiers woven together to make baskets or furniture etc.
▷ **wickerwork** *noun*
[from a Scandinavian language]

wicket *NOUN* **wickets 1** a set of three stumps and two bails used in cricket. **2** the strip of ground between the wickets.
[via old French from Germanic]

wicket-gate *NOUN* **wicket-gates** a small gate used to save opening a much larger one.
[from an old sense of *wicket* = small gate]

wicketkeeper *NOUN* **wicketkeepers** the fielder in cricket who stands behind the batsman's wicket.

wide *ADJECTIVE* **1** measuring a lot from side to side; not narrow. **2** measuring from side to side • *The cloth is one metre wide.* **3** covering a great range • *a wide knowledge of birds.* **4** fully open • *staring with wide eyes.* **5** missing the target • *The shot was wide of the mark.*
▷ **wideness** *noun*

wide *ADVERB* **1** to the full extent; far apart • *Open wide.* **2** missing the target • *The shot went wide.* **3** over a large area • *She travelled far and wide.*
- **wide awake** fully awake.
[from Old English]

widely *ADVERB* commonly; among many people • *They are widely admired.*

widen *VERB* **widens, widening, widened** make or become wider.

widespread *ADJECTIVE* existing in many places or over a wide area • *a widespread belief.*

widow *NOUN* **widows** a woman whose husband has died.
[from Old English]

widowed *ADJECTIVE* made a widow or widower.

widower *NOUN* **widowers** a man whose wife has died.
[from *widow*]

width *NOUN* **widths** how wide something is; wideness.
[from *wide*]

wield *VERB* **wields, wielding, wielded** **1** hold and use a weapon or tool • *a knight wielding a sword.* **2** have and use power or influence.
[from Old English]

wife *NOUN* **wives** the woman to whom a man is married.
[from Old English *wif* = woman]

wig *NOUN* **wigs** a covering made of real or artificial hair, worn on the head.
[short for *periwig*, from old French *perruque*]

wigeon *NOUN* **wigeon** a kind of wild duck.
[origin unknown]

wiggle *VERB* **wiggles, wiggling, wiggled** move from side to side.
▷ **wiggle** *noun* **wiggly** *adjective*
[from old German or old Dutch]

wigwam *NOUN* **wigwams** a tent formerly used by Native Americans, made by fastening skins or mats over poles.
[a Native American word]

wild *ADJECTIVE* **1** living or growing in its natural state, not looked after by people. **2** not cultivated • *a wild landscape.* **3** not civilized • *the Wild West.* **4** not controlled; very violent or excited. **5** very foolish or unreasonable • *You do have wild ideas.*
▷ **wildly** *adverb* **wildness** *noun*
[from Old English]

wildebeest *NOUN* **wildebeest** or **wildebeests** a gnu.
[from an Afrikaans word meaning 'wild beast']

wilderness *NOUN* **wildernesses** a wild uncultivated area; a desert.
[from Old English *wild deor* = wild deer, + *-ness*]

wildfire *NOUN*
- **spread like wildfire** (said about rumours etc.) spread very fast.

wildlife *NOUN* wild animals in their natural setting.

wile *NOUN* **wiles** a piece of trickery.
[origin unknown]

wilful *ADJECTIVE* **1** obstinately determined to do what you want • *a wilful child.* **2** deliberate • *wilful murder.*
▷ **wilfully** *adverb* **wilfulness** *noun*
[from *will*^{2} + *-ful*]

will[1] *AUXILIARY VERB* used to express the future tense, questions, or promises • *They will arrive soon; Will you shut the door? I will get my revenge.*
[from Old English *wyllan*]

will[2] *NOUN* **wills 1** the mental power to decide and control what you do. **2** a desire; a chosen decision • *I wrote the letter against my will.* **3** determination to do something • *They set to work with a will.* **4** a written statement of how a person's possessions are to be disposed of after his or her death.
- **at will** whenever you like • *You can come and go at will.*

will *VERB* **wills, willing, willed** use your will power; influence something by doing this • *I was willing you to win!*
[from Old English *willa*]

willing *ADJECTIVE* ready and happy to do what is wanted.
▷ **willingly** *adverb* **willingness** *noun*
[from *will*[2]]

will-o'-the-wisp *NOUN* **will-o'-the-wisps 1** a flickering spot of light seen on marshy ground. **2** an elusive person or hope.
[from *William* + *of* + *the* + an old sense of *wisp* = small bundle of straw burned as a torch]

willow *NOUN* **willows** a tree or shrub with flexible branches, usually growing near water.
[from Old English]

will power *NOUN* strength of mind to control what you do.

willy-nilly *ADVERB* whether you want to or not.
[from *will I, nill I* (= will I, will I not)]

wilt *VERB* **wilts, wilting, wilted 1** lose freshness and droop. **2** lose your strength or energy.
[originally dialect; probably from old Dutch]

wily (*say* wy-lee) *ADJECTIVE* cunning or crafty.
▷ **wiliness** *noun*
[from *wile*]

wimp *NOUN* **wimps** (*informal*) a weak or timid person.
[perhaps from *whimper*]

wimple *NOUN* **wimples** a piece of cloth folded round the head and neck, worn by women in the Middle Ages.
[from Old English]

win *VERB* **wins, winning, won 1** defeat your opponents in a battle, game, or contest. **2** get or achieve something by a victory or by using effort or skill • *She won the prize.* **3** gain someone's favour or support • *By the end he had won over the audience.*

win *NOUN* **wins** a victory.
[from Old English]

wince *VERB* **winces, wincing, winced** make a slight movement because of pain or embarrassment etc.
[from old French]

winch *NOUN* **winches** a device for lifting or pulling things, using a rope or cable etc. that winds on to a revolving drum or wheel.

winch *VERB* **winches, winching, winched** lift or pull something with a winch.
[from Old English]

wind[1] (*rhymes with* **tinned**) *NOUN* **winds 1** a current of air. **2** gas in the stomach or intestines that makes you feel uncomfortable. **3** breath used for a purpose, e.g. for running or speaking. **4** the wind instruments of an orchestra.
- **get** or **have the wind up** (*slang*) feel frightened.
- **get wind of** hear a rumour of something.

wind *VERB* **winds, winding, winded** put a person out of breath • *The climb had winded us.*
[from Old English *wind*]

wind[2] (*rhymes with* **find**) *VERB* **winds, winding, wound 1** go or turn something in twists, curves, or circles. (also **wind up**) **2** make a clock or watch work by tightening its spring. **3** wrap round • *She wound a bandage round her finger.*
▷ **winder** *noun*
- **wind up 1** close a business. **2** (*informal*) end up in a place or condition • *He wound up in jail.*
[from Old English *windan*]

windbag *NOUN* **windbags** (*informal*) a person who talks too much.

windfall *NOUN* **windfalls 1** a piece of unexpected good luck, especially a sum of money. **2** a fruit blown off a tree by the wind.

wind instrument *NOUN* **wind instruments** a musical instrument played by blowing, e.g. a trumpet.

windlass *NOUN* **windlasses** a machine for pulling or lifting things (e.g. a bucket from a well), with a rope or cable that is wound round an axle by turning a handle.
[via old French from Old Norse *vindass* = winding- pole]

windmill *NOUN* **windmills** a mill worked by the wind turning its sails.

window *NOUN* **windows 1** an opening in a wall or roof etc. to let in light and often air, usually filled with glass. **2** the glass in this opening. **3** (*in computing*) a framed area on a computer screen used for a particular purpose.
[from Old Norse *vind* = wind, air + *auga* = eye]

window-shopping *NOUN* looking at things in shop windows but not buying anything.

windpipe *NOUN* **windpipes** the tube by which air passes from the throat to the lungs.

windscreen *NOUN* **windscreens** the window at the front of a motor vehicle.

windshield *NOUN* **windshields** (*American*) a windscreen.

windsurfing *NOUN* surfing on a board that has a sail fixed to it.
▹ **windsurfer** *noun*

windward *ADJECTIVE* facing the wind • *the windward side of the ship.*

windy *ADJECTIVE* with much wind • *It's windy outside.*

wine *NOUN* **wines 1** an alcoholic drink made from grapes or other plants. **2** a dark red colour.
[same origin as *vine*]

wing *NOUN* **wings 1** one of the pair of parts of a bird, bat, or insect, that it uses for flying. **2** one of the pair of long flat parts that stick out from the side of an aircraft and support it while it flies. **3** a part of a large building that extends from the main part. **4** the part of a motor vehicle's body above a wheel. **5** a player whose place is at one of the far ends of the forward line in football or hockey etc. **6** a section of a political party, with more extreme opinions than the others.
- **on the wing** flying.
- **take wing** fly away.
- **under your wing** under your protection.
- **the wings** the sides of a theatre stage out of sight of the audience.

wing *VERB* **wings, winging, winged 1** fly; travel by means of wings • *The bird winged its way home.* **2** wound a bird in the wing or a person in the arm.
[from Old Norse]

winged *ADJECTIVE* having wings.

wingless *ADJECTIVE* without wings.

wink *VERB* **winks, winking, winked 1** close and open your eye quickly, especially as a signal to someone. **2** (said about a light) flicker or twinkle.

wink *NOUN* **winks 1** the action of winking. **2** a very short period of sleep • *I didn't sleep a wink.*
[from Old English]

winkle *NOUN* **winkles** a kind of edible shellfish.

winkle *VERB* **winkles, winkling, winkled**
- **winkle out** extract or obtain something with difficulty • *I managed to winkle out some information.*
[short for *periwinkle*[2]]

winner *NOUN* **winners 1** a person or animal etc. that wins. **2** something very successful • *Her latest book is a winner.*

winnings *PLURAL NOUN* money won.

winnow *VERB* **winnows, winnowing, winnowed** toss or fan grain etc. so that the loose dry outer part is blown away.
[from Old English]

winsome *ADJECTIVE* charming and attractive.
[from Old English *wynn* = a pleasure, + *-some*]

winter *NOUN* **winters** the coldest season of the year, between autumn and spring.
▷ **wintry** *adjective*

winter *VERB* **winters, wintering, wintered** spend the winter somewhere.
[from Old English]

wipe *VERB* **wipes, wiping, wiped** dry or clean something by rubbing it.
▷ **wipe** *noun*
- **wipe out 1** cancel • *He's wiped out the debt.* **2** destroy something completely.
[from Old English]

wiper *NOUN* **wipers** a device for wiping something, especially on a vehicle's windscreen.

wire *NOUN* **wires 1** a strand or thin flexible rod of metal. **2** a piece of wire used to carry electric current. **3** a fence etc. made from wire. **4** a telegram.

wire *VERB* **wires, wiring, wired 1** fasten or strengthen something with wire. **2** fit or connect something with wires to carry electric current.
[from Old English]

wireless *NOUN* **wirelesses** (*old use*) a radio.
[because it does not need wires to conduct sound]

wiring *NOUN* the system of wires carrying electricity in a building or in a device.

wiry *ADJECTIVE* **1** like wire. **2** lean and strong.

wisdom *NOUN* **1** being wise. **2** wise sayings or writings.
[from Old English *wis* = wise, + *-dom*]

wisdom tooth *NOUN* **wisdom teeth** a molar tooth that may grow at the back of the jaw of a person aged about 20 or more.

wise *ADJECTIVE* **1** judging well and showing good sense. **2** knowing or understanding many things.
▷ **wisely** *adverb*
[from Old English *wis*]

-wise *SUFFIX* forms adverbs meaning 'in this manner or direction' (e.g. *otherwise*, *clockwise*).
[from Old English *wise* = way or manner]

wish *VERB* **wishes, wishing, wished 1** feel or say that you would like to have or do something or would like something to happen. **2** say that you hope someone will get something • *Wish me luck!*

wish *NOUN* **wishes 1** something you wish for; a desire. **2** the action of wishing • *Make a wish when you blow out the candles.*
[from Old English]

wishbone *NOUN* **wishbones** a forked bone between the neck and breast of a chicken or other bird.

wishful *ADJECTIVE* desiring something.

wishful thinking *NOUN* believing something because you wish it were true rather than on the facts.

wisp *NOUN* **wisps 1** a few strands of hair or bits of straw etc. **2** a small streak of smoke or cloud etc.
▷ **wispy** *adjective*
[origin unknown]

wistaria (*say* wist-**air**-ee-a) *NOUN* a climbing plant with hanging blue, purple, or white flowers.
[named after an American professor, C. *Wistar*]

wistful *ADJECTIVE* sadly longing for something.
▷ **wistfully** *adverb* **wistfulness** *noun*
[from Middle English *whist* = quiet, + *-ful*]

wit *NOUN* **wits 1** intelligence or cleverness • *Use your wits.* **2** a clever kind of humour. **3** a witty person.
- **at your wits' end** not knowing what to do.
- **keep your wits about you** stay alert.
[from Old English]

witch *NOUN* **witches** a person, especially a woman, who uses magic to do things.
[from Old English]

witchcraft *NOUN* the use of magic, especially for evil purposes.

witch doctor *NOUN* **witch doctors** a magician who belongs to a tribe and is believed to use magic to heal people.

A B C D E F G H I J K L M N O P Q R S T U V W X Y Z

witch-hunt *NOUN* **witch-hunts** a campaign to find and punish people who hold views that are considered to be unacceptable or dangerous.

with *PREPOSITION* used to indicate **1** being in the company or care etc. of (*Come with me*), **2** having (*a man with a beard*), **3** using (*Hit it with a hammer*), **4** because of (*shaking with laughter*), **5** feeling or showing (*We heard it with pleasure*), **6** towards or concerning (*I was angry with him*), **7** in opposition to; against (*Don't argue with your father*), **8** being separated from (*We had to part with it*). [from Old English]

withdraw *VERB* **withdraws, withdrawing, withdrew, withdrawn** **1** take back or away; remove • *She withdrew her hand from his.* **2** go away from a place or people • *The troops withdrew from the frontier.* [from Old English *with-* = away, back, + *draw*]

withdrawal *NOUN* **withdrawals** **1** withdrawing. **2** an amount of money taken out of an account. **3** the process of stopping taking drugs to which you are addicted, often with unpleasant reactions • *withdrawal symptoms.*

withdrawn *ADJECTIVE* very shy or reserved.

wither *VERB* **withers, withering, withered** **1** shrivel or wilt. **2** make something shrivel or wilt. [a different spelling of *weather*]
USAGE Do not confuse with **whither**.

withering *ADJECTIVE* scornful or sarcastic • *a withering remark.*

withers *PLURAL NOUN* the ridge between a horse's shoulder blades. [origin unknown]

withhold *VERB* **withholds, withholding, withheld** refuse to give or allow something such as information or permission. [from Old English *with-* = away, back, + *hold*]

within *PREPOSITION* & *ADVERB* inside; not beyond something. [from Old English]

without *PREPOSITION* **1** not having • *without food.* **2** free from • *without fear.* **3** (*old use*) outside • *without the city wall.*

without *ADVERB* (*old use*) outside • *We looked at the house from within and without.* [from Old English]

withstand *VERB* **withstands, withstanding, withstood** endure something successfully; resist. [from Old English *with-* = against, + *stand*]

withy *NOUN* **withies** a thin flexible branch for tying bundles etc. [from Old English]

witness *NOUN* **witnesses** **1** a person who sees or hears something happen • *There were no witnesses to the accident.* **2** a person who gives evidence in a lawcourt.

witness *VERB* **witnesses, witnessing, witnessed** **1** be a witness of something • *Did anyone witness the accident?* **2** sign a document to confirm that it is genuine. [from *wit*]

witted *ADJECTIVE* having wits of a certain kind • *quick-witted.*

witticism *NOUN* **witticisms** a witty remark.

wittingly *ADVERB* intentionally. [from *wit*]

witty *ADJECTIVE* **wittier, wittiest** clever and amusing; full of wit.
▷ **wittily** *adverb* **wittiness** *noun*

wizard *NOUN* **wizards** **1** a male witch; a magician. **2** a person with amazing abilities.
▷ **wizardry** *noun*
[from an old sense of *wise* = a wise person]

wizened (*say* wiz-end) *ADJECTIVE* full of wrinkles • *a wizened face.* [from Old English]

woad *NOUN* a kind of blue dye formerly made from a plant. [from Old English]

wobble *VERB* **wobbles, wobbling, wobbled** move unsteadily from side to side; shake slightly.
▷ **wobble** *noun* **wobbly** *adjective*
[origin unknown]

woe *NOUN* **woes** **1** sorrow. **2** misfortune.
▷ **woeful** *adjective* **woefully** *adverb*
[from Old English]

woebegone *ADJECTIVE* looking unhappy.
[from *woe* + an old word *bego* = attack, surround]

wok *NOUN* **woks** a Chinese cooking pan shaped like a large bowl.
[from Chinese]

wold *NOUN* **wolds** an area of low hills.
[from Old English]

wolf *NOUN* **wolves** a fierce wild animal of the dog family, often hunting in packs.

wolf *VERB* **wolfs, wolfing, wolfed** eat something greedily.
[from Old English]

woman *NOUN* **women** a grown-up female human being.
▷ **womanhood** *noun*
[from Old English]

womanizer *NOUN* **womanizers** a man who has sexual affairs with many women.

womanly *ADJECTIVE* having qualities that are thought to be typical of women.

womb (*say* woom) *NOUN* **wombs** the hollow organ in a female's body where babies develop before they are born; the uterus.
[from Old English]

wombat *NOUN* **wombats** an Australian animal rather like a small bear.
[an Aboriginal word]

wonder *NOUN* **wonders 1** a feeling of surprise and admiration or curiosity. **2** something that causes this feeling; a marvel.
- **no wonder** it is not surprising.

wonder *VERB* **wonders, wondering, wondered 1** feel that you want to know; try to decide • *We are still wondering what to do next.* **2** feel wonder.
[from Old English]

wonderful *ADJECTIVE* marvellous or excellent.
▷ **wonderfully** *adverb*

wonderment *NOUN* a feeling of wonder.

wondrous *ADJECTIVE* (*old use*) wonderful.

wont (*say* wohnt) *ADJECTIVE* (*old use*) accustomed • *He was wont to dress in rags.*

wont *NOUN* a habit or custom • *He was dressed in rags, as was his wont.*
[from Old English]

won't (*mainly spoken*) will not.

woo *VERB* **woos, wooing, wooed** (*old use*) **1** court a woman. **2** seek someone's favour or support.
▷ **wooer** *noun*
[from Old English]

wood *NOUN* **woods 1** the substance of which trees are made. **2** many trees growing close together.
[from Old English]

woodcock *NOUN* **woodcock** a bird with a long bill, often shot for sport.

woodcut *NOUN* **woodcuts** an engraving made on wood; a print made from this.

wooded *ADJECTIVE* covered with growing trees.

wooden *ADJECTIVE* **1** made of wood. **2** stiff and showing no expression or liveliness.
▷ **woodenly** *adverb*

woodland *NOUN* **woodlands** wooded country.

woodlouse *NOUN* **woodlice** a small crawling creature with seven pairs of legs, living in rotten wood or damp soil etc.

woodpecker *NOUN* **woodpeckers** a bird that taps tree trunks with its beak to find insects.

woodwind *NOUN* wind instruments that are usually made of wood, e.g. the clarinet and oboe.

woodwork *NOUN* **1** making things out of wood. **2** things made out of wood.

woodworm *NOUN* **woodworms** the larva of a kind of beetle that bores into wooden furniture etc.; the damage done to wood by this.

woody *ADJECTIVE* **1** like wood; consisting of wood. **2** full of trees.

woof *NOUN* **woofs** the gruff bark of a dog.
[imitating the sound]

wool *NOUN* **wools 1** the thick soft hair of sheep and goats etc. **2** thread or cloth made from this.
[from Old English]

A B C D E F G H I J K L M N O P Q R S T U V W X Y Z

woollen *ADJECTIVE* made of wool.

woollens *PLURAL NOUN* woollen clothes.

woolly *ADJECTIVE* **1** covered with wool or wool-like hair. **2** like wool; woollen. **3** not thinking clearly; vague or confused • *woolly ideas.*
▷ **woolliness** *noun*

word *NOUN* **words 1** a set of sounds or letters that has a meaning, and when written or printed has no spaces between the letters. **2** a brief conversation • *Can I have a word with you?* **3** a promise • *He kept his word.* **4** a command or spoken signal • *Run when I give the word.* **5** a message; information • *We sent word of our safe arrival.*
- **have words** quarrel.
- **word for word** in exactly the same words.

word *VERB* **words, wording, worded** express something in words • *Word the question carefully.*
[from Old English]

wording *NOUN* the way something is worded.

word of honour *NOUN* a solemn promise.

word-perfect *ADJECTIVE* having memorized every word perfectly • *He was word-perfect at the rehearsal.*

word processor *NOUN* **word processors** a type of computer or program used for editing and printing letters and documents.

wordy *ADJECTIVE* using too many words; not concise.

wore *past tense of* **wear**.

work *NOUN* **works 1** something you have to do that needs effort or energy • *Digging is hard work.* **2** a job; employment. **3** something produced by work • *The teacher marked our work.* **4** (*in science*) the result of applying a force to move an object. **5** a piece of writing, painting, music, etc. • *the works of William Shakespeare.*
- **at work** working.
- **out of work** having no work; unable to find paid employment.

work *VERB* **works, working, worked 1** do work. **2** have a job; be employed • *She works in a bank.* **3** act or operate correctly or successfully • *Is the lift working?* **4** make something act; operate • *Can you work the lift?* **5** shape or press etc. • *Work the mixture into a paste.* **6** gradually move into a particular position • *The screw had worked loose.*
- **work out 1** find an answer by thinking or calculating. **2** have a particular result.
- **work up** make people become excited; arouse.
- **work up to** gradually progress to something more difficult or advanced.
[from Old English]

workable *ADJECTIVE* that can be used or will work.

worker *NOUN* **workers 1** a person who works. **2** a member of the working class. **3** a bee or ant that does the work in a hive or colony but does not produce eggs.

workforce *NOUN* **workforces** the number of people who work in a particular factory, industry, country, etc.

working class *NOUN* **working classes** people who work for wages, especially in manual or industrial work.

workman *NOUN* **workmen** a man employed to do manual labour; a worker.

workmanship *NOUN* a person's skill in working; the result of this.

work of art *NOUN* **works of art** a fine picture, building, etc.

workout *NOUN* **workouts** a session of physical exercise or training.

works *PLURAL NOUN* **1** the moving parts of a machine. **2** a factory or industrial site.

worksheet *NOUN* **worksheets** a sheet of paper with a set of questions about a subject for students, often used with a textbook.

workshop *NOUN* **workshops** a place where things are made or mended.

work-shy *ADJECTIVE* avoiding work; lazy.

world *NOUN* **worlds 1** the earth with all its countries and peoples. **2** all the people on the earth; everyone • *He felt that the world was against him.* **3** a planet • *creatures from another world.* **4** everything to do with a certain subject or activity • *the world of sport.* **5** a very great amount • *It will do him a world of good.*
[from Old English]

worldly *ADJECTIVE* **1** to do with life on earth, not spiritual. **2** interested only in money, pleasure, etc. **3** experienced about people and life.
▷ **worldliness** *noun*

worldwide *ADJECTIVE & ADVERB* over the whole world.

World Wide Web *NOUN* (*in computing*) a vast extensive information system that connects related sites and documents which can be accessed using the Internet.

worm *NOUN* **worms 1** an animal with a long small soft rounded or flat body and no backbone or limbs. **2** an unimportant or unpleasant person.
▷ **wormy** *adjective*

worm *VERB* **worms, worming, wormed** move along by wriggling or crawling.
- **worm out** gradually get someone to tell you something by constantly and cleverly questioning them • *We eventually managed to worm the truth out of them.*
[from Old English]

wormwood *NOUN* a woody plant with a bitter taste.
[from Old English]

worn *past participle* of **wear**.

worn-out *ADJECTIVE* **1** exhausted. **2** damaged by too much use.

worried *ADJECTIVE* feeling or showing worry.

worry *VERB* **worries, worrying, worried** **1** be troublesome to someone; make a person feel slightly afraid. **2** feel anxious. **3** hold something in the teeth and shake it • *The dog was worrying a rat.*
▷ **worrier** *noun*

worry *NOUN* **worries 1** the condition of worrying; being uneasy. **2** something that makes a person worry.
[from Old English]

worse *ADJECTIVE & ADVERB* more bad or more badly; less good or less well.
- **worse off** less fortunate or well off.
[from Old English; related to *war*]

worsen *VERB* **worsens, worsening, worsened** make or become worse.

worship *VERB* **worships, worshipping, worshipped 1** give praise or respect to God or a god. **2** love or respect a person or thing greatly.
▷ **worshipper** *noun*

worship *NOUN* **worships 1** worshipping; religious ceremonies. **2** a title of respect for a mayor or certain magistrates • *his worship the mayor.*
[from Old English *weorth* = worth, + *-ship*]

worshipful *ADJECTIVE* (in titles) respected • *the Worshipful Company of Goldsmiths.*

worst *ADJECTIVE & ADVERB* most bad or most badly; least good or least well.
[from Old English]

worsted *NOUN* a kind of woollen material.
[named after Worstead, a place in Norfolk, where it was made]

worth *ADJECTIVE* **1** having a certain value • *This stamp is worth £100.* **2** deserving something; good or important enough for something • *That book is worth reading.*

worth *NOUN* **1** value or usefulness. **2** the amount that a certain sum will buy • *a pound's worth of stamps.*
[from Old English]

worthless *ADJECTIVE* having no value; useless.
▷ **worthlessness** *noun*

worthwhile *ADJECTIVE* important or good enough to deserve the time or effort needed • *a worthwhile job.*
[from *worth the while* = worth the time]

worthy *ADJECTIVE* having great merit; deserving respect or support • *a worthy cause.*
▷ **worthiness** *noun*
- **worthy of** deserving • *This charity is worthy of your support.*
[from *worth*]

A B C D E F G H I J K L M N O P Q R S T U V W X Y Z

would *AUXILIARY VERB* used **1** as the past tense of *will*[1] (*We said we would do it*), in questions (*Would you like to come?*), and in polite requests (*Would you come in, please?*). **2** with *I* and *we* and the verbs *like*, *prefer*, *be glad*, etc. (e.g. *I would like to come, we would be glad to help*), where the strictly correct use is *should*. **3** of something to be expected • *That's just what he would do!*

USAGE For sense 2, see the note on **should 4**.

would-be *ADJECTIVE* wanting or pretending to be • *a would-be comedian.*

wouldn't (*mainly spoken*) would not.

wound[1] (*say* woond) *NOUN* **wounds 1** an injury done by a cut, stab, or hit. **2** a hurt to a person's feelings.

wound *VERB* **wounds, wounding, wounded 1** cause a wound to a person or animal. **2** hurt a person's feelings • *She was wounded by these remarks.*
[from Old English]

wound[2] (*say* wownd) *past tense* of **wind**[2].

wraith *NOUN* **wraiths** a ghost.
[originally Scots: origin unknown]

wrangle *VERB* **wrangles, wrangling, wrangled** have a noisy argument or quarrel.
▷ **wrangle** *noun* **wrangler** *noun*
[probably from old Dutch]

wrap *VERB* **wraps, wrapping, wrapped** put paper or cloth etc. round something as a covering.
- **wrap up** put on warm clothes .

wrap *NOUN* **wraps** a shawl, coat, or cloak etc. worn for warmth.
[origin unknown]

wrapped *ADJECTIVE* (*Australian*)(*informal*) extremely pleased.
[blend of *wrapped up* = engrossed, + *rapt*]

wrapper *NOUN* **wrappers** a piece of paper etc. wrapped round something.

wrapping *NOUN* material used to wrap something.

wrath (*rhymes with* **cloth**) *NOUN* anger.
▷ **wrathful** *adjective* **wrathfully** *adverb*
[from Old English]

wreak (*say as* reek) *VERB* **wreaks, wreaking, wreaked** inflict or cause • *Fog wreaked havoc with the flow of traffic.*
[from Old English]

USAGE Note that the past form of *wreak* is *wreaked* not *wrought*. The adjective *wrought* is used to describe metal that has been shaped by hammering or rolling.

wreath (*say* reeth) *NOUN* **wreaths 1** flowers or leaves etc. fastened into a circle • *wreaths of holly.* **2** a curving line of mist or smoke.
[from Old English *writhan* = writhe]

wreathe (*say* reeth) *VERB* **wreathes, wreathing, wreathed 1** surround or decorate something with a wreath. **2** cover • *Their faces were wreathed in smiles.* **3** move in a curve • *Smoke wreathed upwards.*
[from *wreath* and *writhe*]

wreck *VERB* **wrecks, wrecking, wrecked** damage or ruin something so badly that it cannot be used again.

wreck *NOUN* **wrecks 1** a wrecked ship or building or car etc. **2** a person who is left very weak • *a nervous wreck.* **3** the wrecking of something.
[via old French from Old Norse]

wreckage *NOUN* the pieces of a wreck.

wren *NOUN* **wrens** a very small brown bird.
[from Old English]

wrench *VERB* **wrenches, wrenching, wrenched** twist or pull something violently.

wrench *NOUN* **wrenches 1** a wrenching movement. **2** pain caused by parting • *Leaving home was a great wrench.* **3** an adjustable tool rather like a spanner, used for gripping and turning bolts, nuts, etc.
[from Old English]

wrest *VERB* **wrests, wresting, wrested** take something away using force or effort • *We wrested his sword from him.*
[from Old English]

wrestle *VERB* **wrestles, wrestling, wrestled 1** fight by grasping your opponent and trying to throw him or her to the ground. **2** struggle with a problem or difficulty.
▷ **wrestle** *noun* **wrestler** *noun*
[from Old English]

wretch *NOUN* **wretches 1** a person who is very unhappy or who you pity. **2** a person who is disliked.
[from Old English]
USAGE Do not confuse with **retch**.

wretched *ADJECTIVE* **1** miserable or unhappy. **2** of bad quality. **3** not satisfactory; causing a nuisance • *This wretched car won't start.*
▷ **wretchedly** *adverb* **wretchedness** *noun*
[from *wretch*]

wriggle *VERB* **wriggles, wriggling, wriggled** move with short twisting movements.
▷ **wriggle** *noun* **wriggly** *adjective*
- **wriggle out of** avoid work or blame etc. cunningly.
[from old German]

wring *VERB* **wrings, wringing, wrung** **1** twist and squeeze a wet thing to get water etc. out of it. **2** squeeze something firmly or forcibly. **3** get something by a great effort • *We wrung a promise out of him.*
▷ **wring** *noun*
- **wringing wet** so wet that water can be squeezed out of it.
[from Old English]

wringer *NOUN* **wringers** a device with a pair of rollers for squeezing water out of washed clothes etc.

wrinkle *NOUN* **wrinkles 1** a small furrow or ridge in the skin. **2** a small crease in something.

wrinkle *VERB* **wrinkles, wrinkling, wrinkled** make wrinkles in something; form wrinkles.
[origin unknown]

wrist *NOUN* **wrists** the joint that connects the hand and arm.
[from Old English]

wristwatch *NOUN* **wristwatches** a watch for wearing on the wrist.

writ (*say* rit) *NOUN* **writs** a formal written command issued by a lawcourt etc.
- **Holy Writ** the Bible.
[from Old English]

write *VERB* **writes, writing, wrote, written** **1** put letters or words etc. on paper or another surface. **2** be the author or composer of something. **3** send a letter to somebody. **4** enter data into a computer memory.
▷ **writer** *noun*
- **write off** think something is lost or useless.
- **write up** write an account of something.
[from Old English]

writhe *VERB* **writhes, writhing, writhed** **1** twist your body because of pain. **2** wriggle. **3** suffer because of great shame.
[from Old English]

writing *NOUN* **writings** something you write; the way you write.

wrong *ADJECTIVE* **1** incorrect; not true • *the wrong answer.* **2** not fair or morally right • *It is wrong to cheat.* **3** not working properly • *There's something wrong with the engine.*
▷ **wrongly** *adverb* **wrongness** *noun*

wrong *ADVERB* wrongly • *You guessed wrong.*

wrong *NOUN* **wrongs** something morally wrong; an injustice.
- **in the wrong** having done or said something wrong.

wrong *VERB* **wrongs, wronging, wronged** do wrong to someone; treat a person unfairly.
[probably from Old Norse]

wrongdoer *NOUN* **wrongdoers** a person who does wrong.
▷ **wrongdoing** *noun*

wrongful *ADJECTIVE* unfair or unjust; illegal • *wrongful arrest.*
▷ **wrongfully** *adverb*

wrought *ADJECTIVE* (said about metal) worked by being beaten out or shaped by hammering or rolling etc. • *wrought iron.*
[the old past participle of *work*]
USAGE See note at **wreak**.

wry *ADJECTIVE* **wryer, wryest** **1** slightly mocking or sarcastic • *a wry smile.* **2** twisted or bent out of shape.
▷ **wryly** *adverb* **wryness** *noun*
[from Old English]

Xx

xenophobia (*say* zen-o-**foh**-bee-a) NOUN strong dislike of foreigners.
[from Greek *xenos* = foreigner, + *phobia*]

Xerox (*say* zeer-oks) NOUN **Xeroxes** (*trademark*) a photocopy made by a special process.
▷ **xerox** *verb*
[from Greek *xeros* = dry (because the process does not use liquid chemicals, as earlier photocopiers did)]

-xion SUFFIX, SEE **-ion**.

Xmas NOUN (*informal*) Christmas.
[the X represents the Greek letter called chi, the first letter of *Christos* = Christ]

X-ray NOUN **X-rays** a photograph or examination of the inside of something, especially a part of the body, made by a kind of radiation (called **X-rays**) that can penetrate solid things.

X-ray VERB **X-rays, X-raying, X-rayed** make an X-ray of something.

xylophone (*say* zy-lo-fohn) NOUN **xylophones** a musical instrument made of wooden bars of different lengths that you hit with small hammers.
[from Greek *xylon* = wood + *phone* = sound]

Yy

-y[1] or **-ie** SUFFIXES form names showing fondness, or diminutives (e.g. *daddy*, *pussy*).
[origin unknown]

-y[2] SUFFIX forms adjectives meaning 'to do with' or 'like' (e.g. *angry*, *horsy*, *messy*, *sticky*).
[from Old English]

yacht (*say* yot) NOUN **yachts 1** a sailing boat used for racing or cruising. **2** a private ship.
▷ **yachting** *noun* **yachtsman** *noun* **yachtswoman** *noun*
[from Dutch *jaghtschip* = fast pirate ship]

yak NOUN **yaks** an ox with long hair, found in central Asia.
[from Tibetan]

yam NOUN **yams** the edible starchy tuber of a tropical plant, also known as a sweet potato.
[from Portuguese or Spanish, probably from a West Indian word]

Yank NOUN **Yanks** (*informal*) a Yankee.

yank VERB **yanks, yanking, yanked** (*informal*) pull something strongly and suddenly.
▷ **yank** *noun*
[origin unknown]

Yankee NOUN **Yankees** an American, especially of the northern USA.
[probably from Dutch *Janke* = Johnny]

yap VERB **yaps, yapping, yapped** bark shrilly.
▷ **yap** *noun*
[imitating the sound]

yard[1] NOUN **yards 1** a measure of length, 36 inches or about 91 centimetres. **2** a long pole stretched out from a mast to support a sail.
[from Old English *gerd*]

yard[2] NOUN **yards** an enclosed area beside a building or used for a certain kind of work
• *a timber yard.*
[from Old English *geard*]

yardstick NOUN **yardsticks** a standard by which something is measured.
[from *yard*[1]]

yarn NOUN **yarns 1** thread spun by twisting fibres together, used in knitting etc.
2 (*informal*) a tale or story.
[from Old English]

yarrow NOUN a wild plant with strong-smelling flowers.
[from Old English]

yashmak NOUN **yashmaks** a veil worn in public by Muslim women in some countries.
[from Turkish *yamak* = hide yourself]

yawl NOUN **yawls** a kind of sailing boat or fishing boat.
[from old German or Dutch]

yawn *VERB* **yawns, yawning, yawned**
1 open the mouth wide and breathe in deeply when feeling sleepy or bored.
2 form a wide opening • *A pit yawned in front of us.*
▷ **yawn** *noun*
[from Old English]

ye *PRONOUN* (*old use*) you (referring to two or more people).
[from Old English]

yea (*say* yay) *ADVERB* (*old use*) yes.
[from Old English]

year *NOUN* **years 1** the time the earth takes to go right round the sun, about $365\frac{1}{4}$ days. **2** the time from 1 January to 31 December; any period of twelve months. **3** a group of students of roughly the same age.
▷ **yearly** *adjective & adverb*
[from Old English]

yearling *NOUN* **yearlings** an animal between one and two years old.

yearn *VERB* **yearns, yearning, yearned**
long for something.
[from Old English]

yeast *NOUN* a substance that causes alcohol and carbon dioxide to form as it develops, used in making beer and wine and in baking bread etc.
[from Old English]

yell *VERB* **yells, yelling, yelled** give a loud cry; shout.
▷ **yell** *noun*
[from Old English]

yellow *NOUN* **yellows** the colour of buttercups and ripe lemons.

yellow *ADJECTIVE* **1** of yellow colour.
2 (*informal*) cowardly.
▷ **yellowness** *noun*
[from Old English]

yelp *VERB* **yelps, yelping, yelped** give a shrill bark or cry.
▷ **yelp** *noun*
[from Old English *gielpan* = to boast]

yen[1] *NOUN* **yen** a unit of money in Japan.
[from Japanese *en* = round]

yen[2] *NOUN* **yens** a longing for something.
[from Chinese]

yeoman (*say* yoh-man) *NOUN* **yeomen** (*old use*) a man who owns and runs a small farm.
▷ **yeomanry** *noun*
[probably from *young man*]

Yeoman of the Guard *NOUN* **Yeomen of the Guard** a member of the British sovereign's bodyguard, wearing Tudor dress as uniform.

yes *ADVERB* used to agree to or accept something or as an answer meaning 'I am here'.
[from Old English]

yesterday *NOUN & ADVERB* the day before today.
[from Old English]

yet *ADVERB* **1** up to this time; by this time • *The post hasn't come yet.* **2** eventually • *I'll get even with him yet!* **3** in addition; even • *She became yet more excited.*

yet *CONJUNCTION* nevertheless • *It is strange, yet it is true.*
[from Old English]

yeti *NOUN* **yetis** a very large animal thought to live in the Himalayas, sometimes called the 'Abominable Snowman'.
[from Tibetan]

yew *NOUN* **yews** an evergreen tree with dark green needle-like leaves and red berries.
[from Old English]

yield *VERB* **yields, yielding, yielded 1** give in or surrender. **2** agree to do what is asked or ordered; give way • *He yielded to persuasion.* **3** produce as a crop or as profit etc.

yield *NOUN* **yields** the amount yielded or produced • *What is the yield of wheat per acre?*
[from Old English]

yodel *VERB* **yodels, yodelling, yodelled**
sing or shout with the voice continually going from a low note to a high note and back again.
▷ **yodeller** *noun*
[from German]

yoga (*say* yoh-ga) *NOUN* a Hindu system of meditation and self-control; a system of physical exercises based on this.
[Sanskrit, literally = union]

yoghurt or **yogurt** (*say* yog-ert) *NOUN* milk thickened by the action of certain bacteria, giving it a sharp taste.
[from Turkish]

yoke *NOUN* **yokes 1** a curved piece of wood put across the necks of animals pulling a cart or plough etc. **2** a shaped piece of wood fitted across a person's shoulders, with a pail or load hung at each end. **3** a close-fitting upper part of a piece of clothing, from which the rest hangs.

yoke *VERB* **yokes**, **yoking**, **yoked** harness or join things by means of a yoke.
[from Old English]
USAGE Do not confuse with **yolk**.

yokel (*say* yoh-kel) *NOUN* **yokels** a simple country fellow.
[origin unknown]

yolk (*rhymes with* **coke**) *NOUN* **yolks** the round yellow part inside an egg.
[from Old English *geolu* = yellow]
USAGE Do not confuse with **yoke**.

Yom Kippur (*say* yom kip-**oor**) *NOUN* the Day of Atonement, a solemn Jewish religious festival, a day of fasting and repentance.
[Hebrew]

yon *ADJECTIVE* & *ADVERB* (*dialect*) yonder.
[from Old English]

yonder *ADJECTIVE* & *ADVERB* (*old use*) over there.
[Middle English; related to *yon*]

yore *NOUN*
- **of yore** of long ago • *in days of yore.*
[from Old English]

Yorkshire pudding *NOUN* **Yorkshire puddings** baked batter, usually eaten with roast beef.
[from *Yorkshire*, a former county in northern England, where it was first made]

you *PRONOUN* **1** the person or people being spoken to • *Who are you?* **2** anyone or everyone; one • *You can't tell what will happen next.*
[from Old English]

young *ADJECTIVE* having lived or existed for only a short time; not old.

young *PLURAL NOUN* children or young animals or birds • *The robin was feeding its young.*
[from Old English]

youngster *NOUN* **youngsters** a young person; a child.

your *ADJECTIVE* belonging to you.
[from Old English]
USAGE Do not confuse with **you're**.

you're (*mainly spoken*) you are.
USAGE Do not confuse with **your**.

yours *POSSESSIVE PRONOUN* belonging to you.
- **Yours faithfully, Yours sincerely, Yours truly** ways of ending a letter before you sign it. (*Yours faithfully* and *Yours truly* are more formal than *Yours sincerely*.)
USAGE It is incorrect to write *your's*.

yourself *PRONOUN* **yourselves** you and nobody else. (COMPARE **herself**)

youth *NOUN* **youths 1** being young; the time when you are young. **2** a young man. **3** young people.
▷ **youthful** *adjective* **youthfulness** *noun*
[from Old English]

youth club *NOUN* **youth clubs** a club providing leisure activities for young people.

youth hostel *NOUN* **youth hostels** a place where young people can stay cheaply when they are hiking or on holiday.

yowl *VERB* **yowls**, **yowling**, **yowled** wail or howl.
▷ **yowl** *noun*
[imitating the sound]

yo-yo *NOUN* **yo-yos** a round wooden or plastic toy that moves up and down on a string that you hold.
[probably from a language spoken in the Philippines]

Yule *NOUN* (*old use*) the Christmas festival, also called **Yuletide**.
[from Old English]

yuppie *NOUN* **yuppies** (*informal*) a young middle-class person with a professional job, who earns a lot of money and spends it on expensive things.
[from the initial letters of *young urban professional*, + -*ie*]

Zz

zany *ADJECTIVE* **zanier, zaniest** crazily funny. [from Italian *zanni* = a type of clown]

zap *VERB* **zaps, zapping, zapped** (*slang*) **1** attack or destroy something forcefully, especially in electronic games. **2** use a remote control to change television channels quickly.
▷ **zapper** *noun*
[imitating the sound of a blow or shot]

zeal *NOUN* enthusiasm or keenness.
▷ **zealous** (*say* zel-us) *adjective*
zealously *adverb*
[from Greek]

zealot (*say* zel-ot) *NOUN* **zealots** a zealous person; a fanatic.

zebra (*say* zeb-ra) *NOUN* **zebras** an African animal of the horse family, with black and white stripes all over its body.
[Italian, Spanish, or Portuguese]

zebra crossing *NOUN* **zebra crossings** a place for pedestrians to cross a road safely, marked with broad white stripes.

zebu (*say* zee-bew) *NOUN* **zebus** an ox with a humped back, found in India, East Asia, and Africa.
[from French]

zenith *NOUN* **1** the part of the sky directly above you. **2** the highest point • *His power was at its zenith.*
[from Arabic]

zephyr (*say* zef-er) *NOUN* **zephyrs** a soft gentle wind.
[from Greek *Zephyros* = god of the west wind]

zero *NOUN* **zeros 1** nought; the figure 0. **2** the point marked 0 on a thermometer etc.
[from Arabic *sifr* = cipher]

zero hour *NOUN* the time when something is planned to start.

zest *NOUN* **1** great enjoyment or interest. **2** the coloured part of orange or lemon peel.
▷ **zestful** *adjective* **zestfully** *adverb*
[from French]

zigzag *NOUN* **zigzags** a line or route that turns sharply from side to side.

zigzag *VERB* **zigzags, zigzagging, zigzagged** move in a zigzag.
[via French from German]

zinc *NOUN* a white metal.
[from German]

zip *NOUN* **zips 1** a zip fastener. **2** a sharp sound like a bullet going through the air. **3** liveliness or vigour. **4** (*in computing*) compress a computer file in order to email it at a higher speed or for long-term storage.
▷ **zippy** *adjective*

zip *VERB* **zips, zipping, zipped 1** fasten something with a zip fastener. **2** move quickly with a sharp sound.
[imitating the sound]

zip fastener or **zipper** *NOUN* **zip fasteners** or **zippers** a fastener consisting of two strips of material, each with rows of small teeth that interlock when a sliding tab brings them together.

zither *NOUN* **zithers** a musical instrument with many strings stretched over a shallow box-like body.
[from Greek]

zodiac (*say* zoh-dee-ak) *NOUN* a strip of sky where the sun, moon, and main planets are found, divided into twelve equal parts (called **signs of the zodiac**), each named after a constellation.
[from Greek *zoidion* = image of an animal]

zombie *NOUN* **zombies 1** (*informal*) a person who seems to be doing things without thinking, usually because he or she is very tired. **2** (in voodoo) a corpse that has been brought back to life by witchcraft.
[from a Bantu language]

zone *NOUN* **zones** an area of a special kind or for a particular purpose • *a war zone*; *a no-parking zone*.
[Greek, = girdle]

zoo *NOUN* **zoos** a place where wild animals are kept so that people can look at them or study them.
[short for *zoological gardens*]

zoology (*say* zoh-ol-o-jee) *NOUN* the scientific study of animals.
▷ **zoological** *adjective* **zoologist** *noun*
[from Greek *zoion* = animal, + *-logy*]

zoom *VERB* **zooms, zooming, zoomed**
1 move very quickly, especially with a buzzing sound. **2** rise quickly • *Prices had zoomed.* **3** (in photography) use a zoom lens to change from a distant view to a close-up.
▷ **zoom** *noun*
[imitating the sound]

zoom lens *NOUN* **zoom lenses** a camera lens that can be adjusted continuously to focus on things that are close up or far away.

zucchini (*say* zoo-keen-ee) *NOUN* **zucchini** (*say* zoo-keen-ee) or **zucchinis** (*American*) a courgette.
[from Italian]

Zulu *NOUN* **Zulus** a member of a South African people.

Appendices

APPENDIX 1

Some foreign words and phrases used in English

ad hoc done or arranged only when necessary and not planned in advance.
[Latin, = for this]

ad infinitum (*say* in- fin- I- tum) without limit; for ever.
[Latin, = to infinity]

ad nauseam (*say* **naw**- see- am) until people are sick of it.
[Latin, = to sickness]

aide-de-camp (*say* ayd- der- **kahm**) a military officer who is the assistant to a senior officer.
[French, = camp- helper]

à la carte ordered and paid for as separate items from a menu. (Compare *table d'hôte*)
[French, = from the menu]

alfresco in the open air •*an alfresco meal.*
[from Italian *al fresco* = in the fresh air]

alter ego another, very different, side of someone's personality.
[Latin, = other self]

au fait (*say* oh **fay**) knowing a subject or procedure etc. well.
[French, = to the point]

au gratin (*say* oh **grat**- an) cooked with a crisp topping of breadcrumbs or grated cheese.
[French]

au revoir (*say* oh rev- **wahr**) goodbye for the moment.
[French, = to be seeing again]

avant-garde (*say* av- ahn- **gard**) people who use a very modern style in art or literature etc.
[French, = vanguard]

bête noire (*say* bayt **nwahr**) a person or thing you greatly dislike.
[French, = black beast]

bona fide (*say* **boh**- na **fy**- dee) genuine; without fraud •*Are they bona fide tourists or spies?*
[Latin, = in good faith]

bona fides (*say* **boh**- na **fy**- deez) honest intention; sincerity •*We do not doubt his bona fides.*
[Latin, = good faith]

bon voyage (*say* bawn vwah- **yah***zh*) pleasant journey!
[French]

carte blanche (*say* kart **blahnsh**) freedom to act as you think best.
[French, = blank paper]

c'est la vie (*say* sel la **vee**) life is like that.
[French, = that is life]

chef-d'oeuvre (*say* shay **dervr**) a masterpiece.
[French, = chief work]

compos mentis in your right mind; sane. (The opposite is non compos mentis.)
[Latin, = having control of the mind]

cordon bleu (*say* kor- dawn **bler**) (of cooks and cookery) first-class.
[French, = blue ribbon]

corps de ballet (*say* kor der **bal**- ay) the whole group of dancers (not the soloists) in a ballet.
[French]

corps diplomatique (*say* kor dip- lom- at- **eek**) the diplomatic service.
[French]

coup de grâce (*say* koo der **grahs**) a stroke or blow that puts an end to something.
[French, = mercy- blow]

coup d'état (*say* koo day- **tah**) the sudden overthrow of a government.
[French, = blow of State]

crème de la crème (*say* krem der la **krem**) the very best of something.
[French, = cream of the cream]

curriculum vitae (*say* **veet**- I) a brief account of a person's education, career, etc.
[Latin, = course of life]

déjà vu (*say* day- *zha* **vew**) a feeling that you have already experienced what is happening now.
[French, = already seen]

de rigueur (*say* der rig- **er**) proper; required by custom or etiquette.
[French, = of strictness]

de trop (*say* der **troh**) not wanted; unwelcome.
[French, = too much]

doppelgänger (*say* **dop**- el- geng- er) the ghost of a living person.
[German, = double- goer]

dramatis personae
(*say* **dram**- a- tis per- **sohn**- I) the characters in a play.
[Latin, = persons of the drama]

en bloc (*say* ahn **blok**) all at the same time; in a block.
[French]

en masse (*say* ahn **mass**) all together.
[French, = in a mass]

en passant (*say* ahn **pas**- ahn) by the way.
[French, = in passing]

en route (*say* ahn **root**) on the way.
[French]

entente (*say* ahn- **tahnt** or on- **tont**) a friendly understanding between nations.
[French]

esprit de corps (*say* es- pree der **kor**) loyalty to your group.
[French, = spirit of the body]

eureka (*say* yoor- **eek**- a) I have found it!
[Greek]

exeunt (*say* **eks**- ee- unt) they leave the stage.
[Latin, = they go out]

ex gratia (*say* eks **gray**- sha) given without being legally obliged to be given • *an ex gratia payment.*
[Latin, = from favour]

faux pas (*say* foh **pah**) an embarrassing blunder.
[French, = false step]

hara-kiri a form of suicide formerly used by Japanese officers when in disgrace.
[from Japanese *hara* = belly, *kiri* = cutting]

hoi polloi the ordinary people; the masses.
[Greek, = the many]

Homo sapiens human beings regarded as a species of animal.
[Latin, = wise man]

hors-d'oeuvre (*say* or- **dervr**) food served as an appetizer at the start of a meal.
[French, = outside the work]

in camera in a judge's private room, not in public.
[Latin, = in the room]

in extremis (*say* eks- **treem**- iss) at the point of death; in very great difficulties.
[Latin, = in the greatest danger]

in memoriam in memory (of).
[Latin]

in situ (*say* **sit**- yoo) in its original place.
[Latin]

joie de vivre (*say* *zh*wah der **veevr**) a feeling of great enjoyment of life.
[French, = joy of life]

laissez-faire (*say* lay- say- **fair**) a government's policy of not interfering.
[French, = let (them) act]

maître d'hôtel (*say* metr doh- **tel**) a head waiter.
[French, = master of house]

milieu (*say* **meel**- yer) environment; surroundings.
[French, from *mi* = mid + *lieu* = place]

modus operandi (*say* moh- dus op- er- **and**- ee)
1 a person's way of working. **2** the way a thing works. [Latin, = way of working]

nem. con. unanimously.
[short for Latin *nemine contradicente* = with nobody disagreeing]

nom de plume a writer's pseudonym.
[French, = pen- name (this phrase is not used in France)]

non sequitur (*say* non **sek**- wit- er) a conclusion that does not follow from the evidence given.
[Latin, = it does not follow]

nota bene (*say* noh- ta **ben**- ee) (usually shortened to NB) note carefully.
[Latin, = note well]

nouveau riche (*say* noo- voh **reesh**) a person who has only recently become rich.
[French, = new rich]

objet d'art (*say* ob- *zh*ay **dar**) a small artistic object.
[French, = object of art]

par excellence (*say* par eks- el- **ahns**) more than all the others; to the greatest degree.
[French, = because of special excellence]

pas de deux (*say* pah der **der**) a dance (e.g. in a ballet) for two persons.
[French, = step of two]

pâté de foie gras (*say* pat- ay der fwah **grah**) a paste or pie of goose-liver.
[French, = paste of fat liver]

per annum for each year; yearly.
[Latin]

per capita (*say* **kap**- it- a) for each person.
[Latin, = for heads]

persona grata (*say* per- soh- na **grah**- ta) a person who is acceptable to someone, especially a diplomat acceptable to a foreign government. (The opposite is persona non grata.)
[Latin, = pleasing person]

pièce de résistance (*say* pee- ess der ray- zees- **tahns**) the most important item.
[French]

placebo (*say* plas- **ee**- boh) **placebos**
a harmless substance given as if it were medicine, usually to reassure a patient.
[Latin, = I shall be pleasing]

poste restante (*say* rest- **ahnt**) a part of a post office where letters etc. are kept until called for.
[French, = letters remaining]

prima facie (*say* pry- ma **fay**- shee) at first sight; judging by the first impression.
[Latin, = on first appearance]

quid pro quo (*say* kwoh) something given or done in return for something.
[Latin, = something for something]

raison d'être (*say* ray- zawn **detr**) the purpose of a thing's existence.
[French, = reason for being]

rigor mortis (*say* ry- ger **mor**- tis) stiffening of the body after death.
[Latin, = stiffness of death]

RIP may he or she (or they) rest in peace.
[short for Latin *requiescat* (or *requiescant*) *in pace*]

sang-froid (*say* sahn- **frwah**) calmness in danger or difficulty.
[French, = cold blood]

savoir faire (*say* sav- wahr **fair**) knowledge of how to behave socially.
[French, = knowing how to do]

sotto voce (*say* sot- oh **voh**- chee) in a very quiet voice.
[Italian, = under the voice]

status quo (*say* stay- tus **kwoh**) the state of affairs as it was before a change.
[Latin, = the state in which]

sub judice (*say* **joo**- dis- ee) being decided by a judge or lawcourt.
[Latin, = under a judge]

table d'hôte (*say* tahbl **doht**) a restaurant meal served at a fixed inclusive price. (Compare à la carte)
[French, = host's table]

terra firma dry land; the ground.
[Latin, = firm land]

tête-à-tête (*say* tayt- ah- **tayt**) a private conversation, especially between two people.
[French, = head to head]

vis-à-vis (*say* veez- ah- **vee**)
in a position facing one another; opposite to.
as compared with.
[French, = face to face]

viva voce (*say* vy- va **voh**- chee) in a spoken test or examination.
[Latin, = with the living voice]

volte-face (*say* volt- **fahs**) a complete change in your attitude towards something.
[French]

APPENDIX 2

Countries of the world

Country	People
Afghanistan	Afghans
Albania	Albanians
Algeria	Algerians
Andorra	Andorrans
Angola	Angolans
Antigua and Barbuda	Antiguans, Barbudans
Argentina	Argentinians
Armenia	Armenians
Australia	Australians
Austria	Austrians
Azerbaijan	Azerbaijanis or Azeris
Bahamas	Bahamians
Bahrain	Bahrainis
Bangladesh	Bangladeshis
Barbados	Barbadians
Belarus	Belorussians
Belgium	Belgians
Belize	Belizians
Benin	Beninese
Bermuda	Bermudans
Bhutan	Bhutanese
Bolivia	Bolivians
Bosnia-Herzegovina	Bosnians
Botswana	Batswana or Citizens of Botswana
Brazil	Brazilians
Brunei Darussalam	People of Brunei
Bulgaria	Bulgarians
Burkina Faso	Burkinans
Burundi	People of Burundi
Cambodia	Cambodians
Cameroon	Cameroonians
Canada	Canadians
Cape Verde	Cape Verdeans
Central African Republic	People of the Central African Republic
Chad	Chadians
Chile	Chileans
China, People's Republic of	Chinese
Colombia	Colombians
Comoros	Comorans
Congo, Democratic Republic of the	Congolese
Congo, Republic of the	Congolese
Costa Rica	Costa Ricans
Côte d'Ivoire	People of the Côte d'Ivoire
Croatia	Croats
Cuba	Cubans
Cyprus	Cypriots
Czech Republic	Czechs
Denmark	Danes
Djibouti	Djiboutians
Dominica	Dominicans
Dominican Republic	Dominicans
East Timor	East Timorese
Ecuador	Ecuadoreans
Egypt	Egyptians
El Salvador	Salvadoreans
Equatorial Guinea	Equatorial Guineans
Eritrea	Eritreans
Estonia	Estonians
Ethiopia	Ethiopians
Fiji	Fijians
Finland	Finns
France	French
Gabon	Gabonese
Gambia, The	Gambians
Georgia	Georgians
Germany	Germans
Ghana	Ghanaians

Country	People
Greece	Greeks
Grenada	Grenadians
Guatemala	Guatemalans
Guinea	Guineans
Guinea-Bissau	People of Guinea-Bissau
Guyana	Guyanese
Haiti	Haitians
Honduras	Hondurans
Hungary	Hungarians
Iceland	Icelanders
India	Indians
Indonesia	Indonesians
Iran	Iranians
Iraq	Iraqis
Ireland, Republic of	Irish
Israel	Israelis
Italy	Italians
Jamaica	Jamaicans
Japan	Japanese
Jordan	Jordanians
Kazakhstan	Kazakhs
Kenya	Kenyans
Kiribati	Kiribatians
Kuwait	Kuwaitis
Kyrgyzstan	Kyrgyz
Laos	Laotians
Latvia	Latvians
Lebanon	Lebanese
Lesotho	Basotho
Liberia	Liberians
Libya	Libyans
Liechtenstein	Liechtensteiners
Lithuania	Lithuanians
Luxembourg	Luxembourgers
Macedonia (Former Yugoslav Republic of Macedonia)	Macedonians

Country	People
Madagascar	Malagasies
Malawi	Malawians
Malaysia	Malaysians
Maldives	Maldivians
Mali	Malians
Malta	Maltese
Marshall Islands	Marshall Islanders
Mauritania	Mauritanians
Mauritius	Mauritians
Mexico	Mexicans
Micronesia	Micronesians
Moldova	Moldovans
Monaco	Monégasques
Mongolia	Mongolians
Morocco	Moroccans
Mozambique	Mozambicans
Myanmar (Burma)	Burmese
Namibia	Namibians
Nauru	Nauruans
Nepal	Nepalese
Netherlands	Dutch
New Zealand	New Zealanders
Nicaragua	Nicaraguans
Niger	Nigeriens
Nigeria	Nigerians
North Korea (People's Democratic Republic of Korea)	North Koreans
Norway	Norwegians
Oman	Omanis
Pakistan	Pakistanis
Palau	Palauans
Panama	Panamanians
Papua New Guinea	Papua New Guineans
Paraguay	Paraguayans
Peru	Peruvians
Philippines	Filipinos
Poland	Poles
Portugal	Portuguese

Country	People
Qatar	Qataris
Romania	Romanians
Russia (Russian Federation)	Russians
Rwanda	Rwandans
St Kitts and Nevis	People of St Kitts and Nevis
St Lucia	St Lucians
St Vincent and the Grenadines	St Vincentians
Samoa	Samoans
San Marino	People of San Marino
São Tomé and Principe	People of São Tomé and Principe
Saudi Arabia	Saudi Arabians
Senegal	Senegalese
Seychelles	Seychellois
Sierra Leone	Sierra Leoneans
Singapore	Singaporeans
Slovakia	Slovaks
Slovenia	Slovenes
Solomon Islands	Solomon Islanders
Somalia	Somalis
South Africa	South Africans
South Korea (Republic of Korea)	South Koreans
Spain	Spaniards
Sri Lanka	Sri Lankans
Sudan	Sudanese
Suriname	Surinamers
Swaziland	Swazis
Sweden	Swedes
Switzerland	Swiss
Syria	Syrians

Country	People
Taiwan	Taiwanese
Tajikistan	Tajiks
Tanzania	Tanzanians
Thailand	Thais
Togo	Togolese
Tonga	Tongans
Trinidad and Tobago	Trinidadians and Tobagans or Tobagonians
Tunisia	Tunisians
Turkey	Turks
Turkmenistan	Turkmens
Tuvalu	Tuvaluans
Uganda	Ugandans
Ukraine	Ukrainians
United Arab Emirates	People of the United Arab Emirates
United Kingdom	British
United States of America	Americans
Uruguay	Uruguayans
Uzbekistan	Uzbeks
Vanuatu	People of Vanuatu
Vatican City	Vatican citizens
Venezuela	Venezuelans
Vietnam	Vietnamese
Yemen	Yemenis
Yugoslavia (Montenegro and Serbia)	Yugoslavians (Montenegrins and Serbians)
Zambia	Zambians
Zimbabwe	Zimbabweans

APPENDIX 3

Weights and measures

Note The conversion factors are not exact unless so marked. They are given only to the accuracy likely to be needed in everyday calculations.

1. METRIC, WITH BRITISH EQUIVALENTS

Linear Measure

1 millimetre	= 0.039 inch
1 centimetre = 10 mm	= 0.394 inch
1 decimetre = 10 cm	= 3.94 inches
1 metre = 10 dm	= 1.094 yards
1 decametre = 10 m	= 10.94 yards
1 hectometre = 100 m	= 109.4 yards
1 kilometre = 1,000 m	= 0.6214 mile

Square Measure

1 square centimetre	= 0.155 sq. inch
1 square metre = 10,000 sq. cm	= 1.196 sq. yards
1 are = 100 sq. metres	= 119.6 sq. yards
1 hectare = 100 ares	= 2.471 acres
1 square kilometre = 100 hectares	= 0.386 sq. mile

Cubic Measure

1 cubic centimetre	= 0.061 cu. inch
1 cubic metre = 1,000,000 cu. cm	= 1.308 cu. yards

Capacity Measure

1 millilitre	= 0.002 pint (British)
1 centilitre = 10 ml	= 0.018 pint
1 decilitre = 10 cl	= 0.176 pint
1 litre = 10 dl	= 1.76 pints
1 decalitre = 10 l	= 2.20 gallons
1 hectolitre = 100 l	= 2.75 bushels
1 kilolitre = 1,000 l	= 3.44 quarters

Weight

1 milligram	= 0.015 grain
1 centigram = 10 mg	= 0.154 grain
1 decigram = 10 cg	= 1.543 grains
1 gram = 10 dg	= 15.43 grains
1 decagram = 10 g	= 5.63 drams
1 hectogram = 100 g	= 3.527 ounces
1 kilogram = 1,000 g	= 2.205 pounds
1 tonne (metric ton) = 1,000 kg	= 0.984 (long) ton

2. BRITISH AND AMERICAN, WITH METRIC EQUIVALENTS

Linear Measure

1 inch	= 25.4 mm (exactly)
1 foot = 12 inches	= 0.3048 metre
1 yard = 3 feet	= 0.9144 metre (exactly)
1 (statute) mile = 1,760 yards	= 1.609 km

Square Measure

1 square inch	= 6.45 sq. cm
1 square foot = 144 sq. in.	= 9.29 sq. dm
1 square yard = 9 sq. ft.	= 0.836 sq. metre
1 acre = 4,840 sq. yd.	= 0.405 hectare
1 square mile = 640 acres	= 259 hectares

Cubic Measure

1 cubic inch	= 16.4 cu. cm
1 cubic foot = 1,728 cu. in.	= 0.0283 cu. metre
1 cubic yard = 27 cu. ft.	= 0.765 cu. metre

Capacity Measure

British

1 pint = 34.68 cu. in	= 20 fluid oz = 0.568 litre
1 quart = 2 pints	= 1.136 litres
1 gallon = 4 quarts	= 4.546 litres
1 peck = 2 gallons	= 9.092 litres
1 bushel = 4 pecks	= 36.4 litre
1 quarter = 8 bushels	= 2.91 hectolitres

American dry

1 pint = 33.60 cu. in.	= 0.550 litre
1 quart = 2 pints	= 1.101 litres
1 peck = 8 quarts	= 8.81 litres
1 bushel = 4 pecks	= 35.3 litres

American liquid

1 pint = 16 fluid oz. = 28.88 cu. in	= 0.473 litre
1 quart = 2 pints	= 0.946 litre
1 gallon = 4 quarts	= 3.785 litres

Avoirdupois Weight

1 grain	= 0.065 gram
1 dram	= 1.772 grams
1 ounce = 16 drams	= 28.35 grams
1 pound = 16 ounces = 7,000 grains	= 0.4536 kilogram (0.45359237 exactly)
1 stone = 14 pounds	= 6.35 kilograms
1 quarter = 2 stones	= 12.70 kilograms
1 hundredweight = 4 quarters	= 50.80 kilograms
1 (long) ton = 20 hundredweight	= 1.016 tonnes
1 short ton = 2,000 pounds	= 0.907 tonne

3. POWER NOTATION

This expresses concisely any power of ten (any number that is composed of factors 10), and is sometimes used in the dictionary. 10^2 or ten squared = 10 x 10 = 100; 10^3 or ten cubed = 10 x 10 x 10 = 1,000. Similarly, 10^4 = 10,000 and 10^{10} = 1 followed by ten noughts = 10,000,000,000. Proceeding in the opposite direction, dividing by ten and subtracting one from the index, we have $10^2 = 100$, $10^1 = 10$, $10^0 = 1$, $10^{-1} = \frac{1}{10}$, $10^{-2} = \frac{1}{100}$, and so on; $10^{-10} = 1/10^{10}$ = 1/ 10,000,000,000.

4. TEMPERATURE

Fahrenheit: Water boils (under standard condition) at 212° and freezes at 32°.
Celsius or Centigrade: Water boils at 100° and freezes at 0°.
Kelvin: Water boils at 373.15 K and freezes at 273.15 K.

Celsius	*Fahrenheit*	*Celsius*	*Fahrenheit*
−17.8°	0°	50°	122°
−10°	14°	60°	140°
0°	32°	70°	158°
10°	50°	80°	176°
20°	68°	90°	194°
30°	86°	100°	212°
40°	104°		

To convert Celsius into Fahrenheit: multiply by 9, divide by 5, and add 32.
To convert Fahrenheit into Celsius: subtract 32, multiply by 5, and divide by 9.

5. METRIC PREFIXES

	Abbreviation or symbol	*Factor*		*Abbreviation or symbol*	Factor
deca-	da	10	deci-	d	10^{-1}
hecto-	h	10^2	centi-	c	10^{-2}
kilo-	k	10^3	milli-	m	10^{-3}
mega-	M	10^6	micro-	m	10^{-6}
giga-	G	10^9	nano-	n	10^{-9}
tera-	T	10^{12}	pico-	p	10^{-12}
peta-	P	10^{15}	femto-	f	10^{-15}
exa-	E	10^{18}	atto-	a	10^{-18}

These prefixes may be applied to any units of the metric system: hectogram (abbreviated hg) = 100 grams; kilowatt (abbreviated kW) = 1,000 watts.

6. SI UNITS

Basic SI units

Quantity	Unit	Symbol
Length	Metre	m
Mass	Kilogram	kg
Time	Second	s
Electric current	Ampere	A
Temperature	Kelvin	K
Light intensity	Candela	cd
Amount of substance	Mole	mol

Derived SI units

Quantity	Unit	Symbol
Area	Square metre	m2
Volume	Cubic metre	m3
Frequency	Hertz	Hz
Force	Newton	N
Pressure	Pascal	Pa
Energy	Joule	J
Power	Watt	W
Electrical potential	Volt	V
Electrical resistance	Ohm	Ω
Electrical charge	Coulomb	C
Radioactivity	Becquerel	Bq

Basic SI units and derived SI units

The seven basic SI units have scientific standards that define the size of the units with great precision. All derived units are related to the basic SI units. Each unit has its own entry in the dictionary.

Note: SI stands for Système International, the international system of units of measurement.

Oxford Children's Dictionaries
Age 8+
Oxford Primary Dictionary
9780199115334 HB
Oxford Primary Thesaurus
9780199115167 HB
Oxford Primary French Dictionary
9780199114931 HB
9780199113088 PB
Oxford Primary Spanish Dictionary
9780199115242 PB
Age 10+
Oxford School Dictionary
9780199115341 HB
Oxford School Thesaurus
9780199115358 HB
Oxford School Dictionary & Thesaurus
9780199115365 HB
9780199115372 PB
Oxford Pocket School Dictionary
9780199115389 PB
Oxford Pocket School Thesaurus
9780199115396 PB
Oxford Mini School Dictionary
9780199115174 PB
Oxford Mini School Thesaurus
9780199115181 PB
Oxford Mini School Dictionary & Thesaurus
9780199113736 PB
Oxford School French Dictionary
9780199115280 PB
Oxford School Spanish Dictionary
9780199115237 PB
Oxford School German Dictionary
9780199115303 PB
Oxford Mini School French Dictionary
9780199115273 PB
Oxford Mini School Spanish Dictionary
9780199115259 PB
Oxford Mini School German Dictionary
9780199115266 PB
Age 14+
Oxford Student's Dictionary
9780199115327 HB
9780199115310 PB
Oxford Student's Thesaurus
9780199116522 PB
Think Dictionaries.
Think Oxford.
www.oup.com